HONG KONG TAXATION

HONG KONG TAXATION
Law and Practice

2007–08 Edition

by

David G. Smith

and

Ayesha Macpherson

The Chinese University Press

ISBN 978–962–996–334–7

First edition	1981
Revised edition	1982
1983–84 edition	1983
1984–85 edition	1984
1986–87 edition	1986
1987–88 edition	1987
1988–89 edition	1988
1989–90 edition	1989
1990–91 edition	1990
1991–92 edition	1991
1992–93 edition	1992
1993–94 edition	1993
1994–95 edition	1994
1995–96 edition	1995
1996–97 edition	1996
1997–98 edition	1997
1998–99 edition	1998
1999–2000 edition	1999
2000–01 edition	2000
Second printing	2001
2001–02 edition	2001
2002–03 edition	2002
2003–04 edition	2003
2004–05 edition	2004
2005–06 edition	2005
2006–07 edition	2006
2007–08 edition	2007

The Chinese University Press
The Chinese University of Hong Kong
Sha Tin, N.T., Hong Kong
Fax: +852 2603 6692
+852 2603 7355
E-mail: cup@cuhk.edu.hk
Web-site: www.chineseupress.com

Printed in Hong Kong

Table of Contents

Acknowledgement

This book is based on the book originally authored by David Flux, a former Senior Tax Partner of KPMG, in 1981 and updated by him annually until 1992. Although the book has undergone substantial revision and expansion over the years since he retired and relinquished responsibility for its updating, the present authors gratefully acknowledge the thought and effort which David Flux put into its original creation without which the book would not exist.

Preface to 2007–08 Edition

There have been a number of significant developments in both the Hong Kong tax environment and this book in the twelve months since the last edition was published.

With regard to the book, the chapter covering Estate Duty has been deleted as a consequence of the abolition of that charge in respect of persons dying after 10 February 2006. In its place, a chapter has been added which briefly examines some basic international tax issues as well as looking more specifically at some of the main tax issues of relevance to investment into, and out of, Hong Kong. I hope that by including this material, which considers the interaction of the Hong Kong tax system with those of other jurisdictions, readers will find the book even more comprehensive and useful.

On the policy front, during the year the Hong Kong Government decided, in the face of public opposition, to shelve plans for the implementation of a Goods and Services Tax (GST). Readers will be aware that for a number of years the Government had been considering a GST and in fact a little over a year ago issued a consultation document outlining its proposals for such a tax. Although plans for a GST have been shelved, the problem of Hong Kong's narrow tax base remains and the Government has advised that other measures to address this issue will be considered. In this regard, the Government has identified a number of possible measures and has commented on the appropriateness of these against various objectives, but has to date taken no decisions on which, if any to adopt.

Hong Kong's policy of entering into double taxation agreements continued during the year with a comprehensive agreement with the Mainland of China being finalised and becoming operative. This agreement effectively replaces the limited scope agreement which the parties entered into in 1998. In addition to that agreement, it is understood that negotiations with seven other jurisdictions have commenced.

There were a number of significant court decisions during the year. The issue of source of profits continues to present difficulties. Of the three ongoing disputes involving stockbrokers, two were heard by the Court of Final Appeal during the year although the judgement in one of the cases had not been issued at the time of writing. In the other case, the hearings to date have concerned the question of whether the Board of Review should state a case and no hearing on the substantive issue has yet taken place. These cases are significant for a number of reasons. First, although the three cases involve broadly similar facts, differing approaches have been adopted by the various Boards of Review and courts to date making the judgements difficult to reconcile. One particular aspect where the courts have appeared to adopt varying views is the extent to which activities of agents should be considered relevant in the determination of the source of a taxpayer's profits. Hopefully as the cases are finally resolved, this issue as well as other aspects of the broader question of the source of profits will be addressed and some clearer and more consistent rules will emerge.

Another major decision during the year was the Court of Final Appeal's decision in the *Zeta Estates Limited* case where the taxpayer was successful in its claim to deduct interest expenses in relation to the financing of a dividend payment. This judgement contains some useful guidance on the interpretation of Sec. 16 IRO, particularly with regard to the degree of nexus required between an expense and the derivation of assessable profits for that expense to qualify for deduction. Finally, there were two important decisions of the courts in relation to the general anti-avoidance provision of Sec. 61A IRO. All of these cases are, of course, discussed in the appropriate section of the book.

Finally, I would once again express my thanks to Ayesha Macpherson for her valuable assistance in updating this book, although I continue to accept sole responsibility for any errors or omissions.

David G. Smith
August 2007, Queensland, Australia
David@taxhk.com

Abbreviations

The following abbreviations have been used in the text:—

AC	Appeal Cases (UK)
AITR	Australian Income Tax Reports
All E.R.	All England Law Reports
ATC	Australian Tax Cases (CCH)
ATD	Australian Tax Decisions
CACV	Hong Kong Court of Appeal — Civil Appeal
CH	Court of Chancery
Chief Executive	Chief Executive of the Hong Kong SAR
CIR	Commissioner of Inland Revenue
CLR	Commonwealth Law Reports
Collector	Collector of Stamp Revenue
Commissioner	Commissioner of Inland Revenue (except in Chapter 12, where it refers to the Commissioner of Estate Duty)
DTA	Double taxation agreement
EDO	Estate Duty Ordinance
FACV	Hong Kong Court of Final Appeal — Civil Appeal
FCA	Federal Court of Australia
FC of T	Federal Commissioner of Taxation (Australia)
Gazette	The Government of the Special Administrative Region Gazette and any supplements thereto
HCA	High Court of Australia
HKICPA	Hong Kong Institute of Certified Public Accountants
HKLR	Hong Kong Law Reports
HKLRD	Hong Kong Law Reports Digest
HKRC	Hong Kong Revenue Cases (CCH)
HKTC	Hong Kong Tax Cases
IRD	Inland Revenue Department
IRO	Inland Revenue Ordinance
IRR	Inland Revenue Rules

KB	King's Bench Division (UK)
MPF scheme	A mandatory provident fund scheme registered under the *Mandatory Provident Fund Schemes Ordinance*
MSTC	Malaysian and Singapore Tax Cases
NZ	New Zealand
PRC	People's Republic of China
QBD	Queen's Bench Division (UK)
SAR	Hong Kong Special Administrative Region of the People's Republic of China
SATC	South African Tax Cases
Sec(s).	Section(s) of the IRO unless otherwise specified, except in Chapter 11, where reference is to the SDO, and Chapter 12, where reference is to the EDO
SDO	Stamp Duty Ordinance
STC	Simon's Tax Cases (UK)
TC	UK Tax Cases
UKHL	UK House of Lords
WDV	Written Down Value
WLR	Weekly Law Reports (UK)
y/e	Year Ended

Latin Words and Phrases

ab initio	from the beginning
ad valorem	according to the value
bona fide	genuine
de novo	over again, anew
ex gratia	voluntary
in specie	in kind
inter alia	among other things
inter vivos	between living persons
obiter dictum (pl. dicta)	in relation to judicial decisions, refers to observations on legal points which are not critical to the decision
pari passu	on the same footing
prima facie	at first sight (i.e. on the face of it)
quid pro quo	one thing in return for another (i.e. consideration)
supra	above
ultra vires	beyond the powers (i.e. unauthorised)

Table of Cases

The following cases are referred to in the text:

McGuckian; CIR v [1997] (STC 908), 629, 915
McMillan v Guest (24 TC 190), 72, 863
Mehta, *see* C of I.T.
Memorex Pty. Ltd. v FC of T (87 ATC 5034), 199
Metal Manufacturers Limited; FCT v (2001 ATC 4152), 646
Mok Tsze Fung v CIR (1 HKTC 166), 573
Montana Lands Ltd.; CIR v (1 HKTC 334), 203, 253, 766, 767
Mount Morgan Gold Mining Co. Ltd. v C of I. T. (33 CLR 76), 206
Mudd v Collins (9 TC 297), 93
Mui, Y. F.; CIR v (HKTC 632), 544
Munby v Furlong (50 TC 491), 471
Mutual Investment Co. Ltd.; CIR v (1 HKTC 185), 246, 288
Myer Emporium Ltd.; FC of T v (85 ATC 87 ATC 4363), 285, 623

Nam Tai Trading Company Limited v CIR [2005] (1 HKRC 90-155), 609
Nash, *see* Mann
Nathan v FC of T (25 CLR 183), 240
National Employers' Mutual, *see* Faulconbridge
National Mutual Centre (HK) Ltd. v CIR [1997] (1 HKRC 90-086), 295, 324, 330
National Mutual Centre (HK) Ltd; CIR v [1998] (1 HKRC 90-094), 324
Ng Shun-loi, *see* Director of Immigration
Nina T. H. Wang, *see* Wang, Nina T. H.
Nolder v Walters (15 TC 380), 123

Orion Caribbean Ltd. v CIR [1996] (1 HKRC 90-077), 188, 238, 413; CIR v [1997] (1 HKRC 90-089), 188, 236, 703, 951, 952, 953
Ostime, *see* Duple Motor Bodies
Overseas Textiles Ltd. v CIR (3 HKTC 29), 201, 294
Owen v Southern Railway of Peru (36 TC 602), 299

Page, Peter Leslie; CIR v [2003] (1 HKRC 90-123), 95

Patrick v Broadstone Mills (35 TC 44), 350, 758
Pearce v Woodall-Duckham Ltd. (51 TC 271), 758, 764
Pearse v Woodall-Duckhall Ltd. [1978] (51 TC 271), 1007
Peabody v FCT (94 ATC 4663), 632, 633, 635, 644, 648, 908
Pemsel; Special Commissioners of Income Tax v (3 TC 53), 616
Pepper v Hart [1992] (65 TC 421), 3
Perry, *see* Laidler
Petrotim Securities Ltd. v Ayres (41 TC 389), 353, 354
Philbin, *see* Abbott
Philips Gloeilampenfabrieken, N.V.; CIR (NZ) v (10 ATD 435), 235
Phillip Frame Will Trust, Trustees of v CIR (53 SATC 166), 184
Powlson v Ben Odeco (52 TC 459), 472
Prendergast, *see* Cameron
Pritchard v Arundale (47 TC 680), 91
Privy Council case of Auckland Gas Co. Ltd v CIR [2000] (STC 527), 808
Procter, *see* Leeds
Pyne, *see* Burdge

Queen, The, *see* under name of taxpayer in alphabetical listing.
Quitsubdue Limited; CIR v [1999] (1 HKRC 90-099), 198, 351, 352, 353

Radofin Electronics (Far East) Ltd. and Another; The Queen v (HKTC 1252), 564
Rael-Brook [1967] (2 QB 65), 772
Ramsay, W. T. Ltd. v IRC [1982] (AC 300), 626, 627, 628, 629, 631, 742, 743, 915
Real Estate Investments (N. T.) Limited v CIR [2005] (1 HKRC 90-154), 193
Reed v Young (59 TC 196), 369
Regent Oil Co. v Strick (43 TC 1), 302
Reid v Seymour (11 TC 625), 83
Re Little Olympian Each Ways Ltd. [1995] (1 WLR 560], 858
Richardson v Delaney [2001] (STC 1328), 85, 86

Board of Review Decisions

The following Board of Review decisions are referred to in the text on the
indicated pages:

BR 27/69, 110
BR 13/70, 294
BR 19/71, 595
BR 3/73, 148
BR 18/73, 211, 283, 285
BR 19/73, 844
BR 13/74, 148
BR 19/74, 73, 74
BR 20/75, 239
BR 17/76, 148
BR 20/76, 99, 122
BR 21/76, 351
BR 80/76, 551
BR 89/77, 113
BR 116/77, 85
BR 9/78, 843

D 19/78, 125
D 20/78, 193
D 1/79, 418
D 3/79, 563, 662
D 5/79, 451
D 7/79, 551
D 5/80, 379
D 1/81, 73
D 2/81, 563
D 1/82, 551
D 2/82, 592
D 7/82, 69
D 8/82, 94

D 12/82, 117
D 1/83, 551
D 2/83, 551
D 4/83, 294
D 14/83, 601
D 15/83, 551
D 16/83, 94
D 20/83, 522
D 7/84, 412, 414
D 11/84, 64
D 23/84, 99
D 24/84, 551
D 26/84, 351
D 30/84, 196
D 5/85, 239
D 7/85, 43
D 13/85, 551
D 24/85, 551
D 28/85, 566
D 31/85, 66, 122, 168
D 35/85, 147, 148
D 2/86, 84
D 3/86, 201
D 12/86, 472
D 41/86, 94
D 52/86, 628, 652
D 58/86, 84, 355
D 3/87, 452, 773
D 4/87, 452, 773
D 7/87, 302

IRO, SDO and EDO

Reference to the relevant Sections of the IRO, IRR, SDO and EDO are as follows:

Chapter 1 ■

General Scheme of Taxation in Hong Kong

1.1 Law, Interpretation and Policy

The law governing the imposition of income based taxation in Hong Kong is contained in the *Inland Revenue Ordinance* (IRO) and its subsidiary legislation, the *Inland Revenue Rules* (IRR), and in various orders made by the Chief Executive in Council. The IRO, which was enacted in 1947 to impose income taxes in Hong Kong, is based on a legislative package developed by the UK for its colonies. The same package was the basis of the taxation system in many Commonwealth countries, although those countries have generally modified their legislation to such an extent that its original form is barely recognisable.

Nonetheless, the IRO contains similar, and in some cases, identical wording to taxation legislation currently in use in the UK, Australia, South Africa and various other Commonwealth countries, which is why interpretation of the IRO is influenced by legal decisions in those countries. The IRO has in fact been changed relatively little from its original form and the reasons for this can be easily understood by considering the policies of successive Government administrations as regards taxation of income in Hong Kong. The following terms of reference given to the Third Inland Revenue Ordinance Review Committee in 1976 speak for themselves and the sentiments have been reiterated in various Government speeches up to the present time:—

> "Having regard to the economic circumstances of Hong Kong which dictate:—
>
> (a) a comparatively low level of direct taxation;
> (b) that the system at given tax rates should be as productive of revenue as possible; and
> (c) that the relevant legislation should be simple and inexpensive to administer;
>
> To consider the present system of taxation of profits and other forms of income contained in the Inland Revenue Ordinance ..."

The law governing Stamp Duty is found in the *Stamp Duty Ordinance* (SDO) which is based on past UK legislation, as is equivalent legislation in a number of Commonwealth countries, and accordingly decisions of the courts in those jurisdictions provide useful guidance in interpreting the Hong Kong provisions. Additionally, the *Estate Duty Ordinance* (EDO) under which duty is imposed on assets passing on death still exists but has no application in respect of persons dying after 10 February 2006. As such, this book no longer contains an analysis of Estate Duty.

All laws, including amendments to the SDO, EDO, IRO and IRR are enacted by the Legislative Council. As such, any amendments are first tabled (and published in the *Gazette*) as a Bill. It is common for professional bodies and other interested parties to make comments and representations to the

Government on Bills once tabled. Indeed, in some cases, the Bills are circulated to professional bodies for comment prior to them being tabled. The Government will generally take into account legitimate and reasoned views when formulating the final versions of, or amendments to, a Bill. It is important to appreciate that, despite their collective title, the *Inland Revenue Rules* are not unilateral rules formulated by the Inland Revenue Department (IRD) but are effectively additional sections to the IRO which are subject to exactly the same legislative process as the IRO itself. Nevertheless, the IRD has a number of extra-statutory practices and concessions both published and unpublished and these are discussed in this book in the appropriate places.

As with all legislation, Hong Kong tax legislation is subject to the normal rules of statutory interpretation and, as discussed below, disputes may be resolved in the courts or, in the case of disputes over matters dealt with under the IRO, the Board of Review. In addition to the normal rules of statutory interpretation, some additional rules have been developed by the courts in the UK to deal with taxing statutes, which are, by their nature, somewhat unique in that they are a means of extracting money from the public. A good summary of the traditional view of the courts can be found in the Privy Council's decision in *Mangin v IRC* [1971] (AC 739). In that case, Lord Donovan noted that in interpreting tax statutes:

> "First, the words are to be given their ordinary meaning. They are not to be given some other meaning simply because their object is to frustrate legitimate tax avoidance devices. As *Turner* J. says in his (albeit dissenting) judgement in *Marx v. CIR (NZ)* [1970] NZLR at p. 208, moral precepts are not applicable to the interpretation of Revenue Statutes.
>
> Secondly, one has to look merely at what is clearly said. There is no room for any intendment. There is no equity about a tax. There is no presumption as to tax. Nothing is to be read in, nothing is to be implied. One can only look fairly at the language used [per *Rowlatt* J. in *Cape Brandy Syndicate v IRC* [1921] 12 TC 358].
>
> Thirdly, the object of the construction of a statute being to ascertain the will of the legislature it may be presumed that neither injustice nor absurdity was intended. If therefore a literal interpretation would produce such a result, and the language admits of an interpretation which would avoid it, then such an interpretation may be adopted."

The principle that one is only to look at the actual words of the legislation in interpreting the intent of the legislation was, however, to some degree eroded in the House of Lords case of *Pepper v Hart* [1992] (65 TC 421). In that decision, the court held that it was permissible to refer to parliamentary materials in order to assist in understanding the intention of the legislation where that legislation was unclear, ambiguous or obscure and the parliamentary materials were statements by the promoter of the legislation and made the intention of that legislation quite clear. Accordingly, if any aspects of the SDO, EDO or IRO are not clear, it is not wise to assume a favourable literal interpretation will be applied; rather, it may be necessary to go back to review the proceedings of the Legislative Council at the time of the introduction of the relevant Bill to see whether any guidance is available as to the intent of that legislation.

Care should also be taken in relying on the traditional approach to interpretation of tax statutes due to the emergence in more recent years of a trend for the courts to adopt a "purposive" approach in interpretation. In other words, the courts have tended to look to the underlying purpose of the statute in deciding how the provision should be applied to a particular transaction. This question has predominantly arisen in cases where a revenue authority has sought to deny the benefits of a statute to a transaction the revenue authority considered to be artificial, circular, contrived or to have no commercial purpose. This principle is discussed further in section 10.4.3, from which it will also be appreciated that the manner and degree to which the courts are prepared to allow a purposive approach to interpretation is likely to continue to evolve over time as more cases concerning the principle are decided. Section 10.4.3 also considers the interaction of a purposive approach to interpretation with the general anti-avoidance provisions of the IRO.

The IRD also from time to time issue documents explaining their views on statutory provisions. Such documents, when dealing with matters under the IRO are known as Departmental Interpretation & Practice Notes (DIPNs) and when dealing with matters under the SDO are known as Stamp Office Interpretation & Practice Notes (SOPNs). A list of current DIPNs and SOPNs is contained in Table 1.1. Many of these documents are reproduced as appendices to this book. Those which are not so reproduced can be found on the IRD's web site (see www.ird.gov.hk).

DIPNs and SOPNs purport to have no binding force in law (although see discussion below) and are issued only for the information and guidance of taxpayers. They are generally issued as means of explaining the IRD's approach in practice to certain situations or to outline the IRD's view as to how a statutory provision should be interpreted. With regard to the latter, it must be emphasised that the documents express only one view of the law, and that such view is not necessarily correct. Indeed, in at least one court decision, a view of the IRD as contained in a DIPN has been held to be incorrect. Where a DIPN is found by the courts to be incorrect, the IRD may amend or re-issue it. However, this does not permit taxpayers to reopen prior

Table 1.1 Practice Notes issued by IRD

A.	Departmental Interpretation & Practice Notes
No.	Topic
1	Valuation of stock-in-trade and work-in-progress and ascertainment of profits and the valuation of work-in-progress in building and engineering contracts, property development and property investment businesses.
2	Profits Tax — Industrial building allowances and commercial buildings allowances
3	Profits Tax — Apportionment of expenses
4	Lease premiums / Non-returnable deposits / Key or tea money / Construction fees, etc.
5	Profits Tax — Deductions for scientific research, technical education and patent rights, building refurbishment and prescribed fixed assets
6	Objections to the Commissioner, appeals to the Board of Review, appeals to the courts
7	Machinery and plant — depreciation allowances
8	Profits Tax — losses
9	Major deductible items under Salaries Tax
10	The charge to Salaries Tax
11	Elements of tax investigation
11A	Elements of field audit
12	Commissions, rebates and discounts
13	Profits Tax — Taxation of interest received
13A	Profits Tax — Deductibility of interest expense
14	Property Tax
15	Limitations on loss relief; Leasing arrangements; General anti-avoidance provisions; Loss companies; Ramsay principle; Penalty on tax avoidance cases; Guidelines on lease financing; Advance rulings
16	Salaries Tax — Taxation of fringe benefits
17	The taxation of persons chargeable to Profits Tax on behalf of non-residents
18	Assessment of individuals under Salaries Tax and Personal Assessment
19	The agreement between the United States of America and Hong Kong in respect of the taxation of shipping profits
20	Unit trusts, mutual fund corporations and similar collective investment schemes
21	Locality of profits
22	Computation of assessable profits from cinematograph films, patents, trademarks, etc.
23	Recognized occupational retirement schemes
24	Service company "Type II" arrangements — Profits Tax
25	Service company "Type I" arrangements — Salaries Tax
26	Specified securities for the purposes of Section 15E of the Inland Revenue Ordinance
27	Stock borrowing and lending
28	Profits Tax — Deductibility of foreign taxes
29	Tax relations between the Hong Kong Special Administrative Region and the People's Republic of China
30	Profits Tax — Section 20AA — Persons not treated as agents

Table 1.1 Cont'd

31	Advance rulings
32	Arrangement between the Mainland of China and the Hong Kong Special Administrative Region for the avoidance of double taxation on income
33	Insurance agents
34	Exemption from Profits Tax (Interest Income) Order 1998
35	Concessionary deductions — Sections 26E and 26F — Home loan interest
36	Concessionary deductions — Section 26D — Elderly residential care expenses
37	Concessionary deductions — Section 26C — Approved charitable donations
38	Employee share option benefits
39	Profits Tax — Treatment of electronic commerce
40	Profits Tax — Prepaid or deferred revenue expenses
41	Salaries Tax — Taxation of holiday journey benefits
42	Profits Tax — Taxation of financial instruments; taxation of foreign exchange differences
43	Profits Tax — Profits tax exemption for offshore funds
44	Arrangement between the Mainland of China and the Hong Kong Special Administrative Region for the avoidance of double taxation and the prevention of fiscal evasion with respect to taxes on income.
B.	**Stamp Office Interpretation & Practice Notes**
No.	**Topic**
1	Stamping of agreements for the sale and purchase of residential property
2	Relief for stock borrowing and lending transactions — commercial stock loans
3	Deemed consideration under Section 24 of the Stamp Duty Ordinance
4	Deemed sale and purchase under Section 19(1E) of the Stamp Duty Ordinance

years' assessments, other than in cases where the relevant assessments are still in dispute and open. This is because an assessment made under a prevailing practice cannot be re-opened by virtue of the fact that it is subsequently found that such practice is incorrect (Sec. 70A IRO, proviso).

Although DIPNs and SOPNs purport to have no binding force of law, in the UK case of *R v Inland Revenue Commissioners, ex parte MFK Underwriting Agencies Limited and related applications* (62 TC 607), it was suggested that if a revenue authority makes a statement of practice which taxpayers could legitimately expect would be followed, the revenue authority is bound by such statement of practice. Moreover, the case suggested that this will be the position even if it results in the authority foregoing tax which would otherwise be arguably payable on a correct interpretation of the relevant statutory provision. On the other hand, a taxpayer always has the usual rights of objection or appeal where, although the IRD has acted in accordance with a view contained in such a note, the taxpayer considers that such view is not consistent with the law. Nonetheless, irrespective of the extent to which DIPNs or SOPNs have force of law, if any, a taxpayer can normally expect the IRD to act in accordance with the spirit thereof although, as one would expect, cases do arise where differences in the interpretation occur.

The IRO has from time to time been subjected to review by committees, specifically appointed for the purpose whose brief was to report on various specific and general aspects of the IRO and to recommend appropriate changes. This has not been a standing committee but was separately constituted on each occasion. The first such committee, the Inland Revenue Ordinance Committee reported in 1954, the Second Inland Revenue Ordinance Review Committee reported in 1967 and also in 1968 and the Third Inland Revenue Ordinance Review Committee reported in 1976. The Committees solicited comments and representations from the public and, in particular, the professional bodies, major companies and trade associations. In addition, representations were invited from individuals. The Committees' reports and recommendations are published and the recommendations considered by a Government committee for rejection or ultimate incorporation of such into the IRO. Most of the Third Inland Revenue Ordinance Review Committee's recommendations were rejected, although some were ultimately adopted.

It has now been many years since the last such comprehensive review of the IRO. From time to time there have been calls from professional bodies and other observers for a fourth review and the matter has been raised in the Legislative Council. The current view of the IRD, however, is that no comprehensive review is appropriate as the Department continually conducts internal policy reviews. Additionally, the IRD considers that the Joint Liaison Committee on Taxation (a body of professionals including representatives of the IRD) provides a forum for discussion of relevant matters which did not exist at the time of the earlier reviews.

In 1997 the Government did issue a consultative document on the Profits Tax system which invited submissions from interested parties as to how to make the tax system and business environment of Hong Kong more competitive. This document followed an initiative announced by the Financial Secretary in his 1997/98 Budget Speech and the submissions received were considered for inclusion in the 1998/99 Budget proposals. Although the Government is to be applauded for this initiative, which resulted in a number of concessions being introduced in 1998, the scope of the consultation process was quite narrow and for that reason was quite different from the comprehensive reviews previously undertaken by the former Inland Revenue Ordinance Review Committees.

In the 2000/01 Budget, however, the Financial Secretary announced that two reviews were to be undertaken. The results of these reviews may herald significant changes to the tax system in Hong Kong. In particular, the Financial Secretary, noting that Budget deficits were forecast for the three succeeding years, announced that a task force headed by the Secretary for the Treasury would be formed to determine whether the expected deficits are a consequence of a short-term cyclical problem, or a result of a more fundamental shift in the revenue base. This initiative by the Financial Secretary reflected an apparent concern by the Government that the current tax system may be overly reliant on revenue from particular industries or sectors which may not be growing as fast as the general economy, thereby leading to an erosion of the growth rate of revenue collections. The Government's general concerns as to the sustainability of the present system proved founded as the task force concluded that the fiscal problems were persistent and that the budget deficits would continue to worsen even after an improvement in the general economy. As a consequence, the task force concluded that decisive action was required and that although the initial priority of the Government should be controlling the growth of Government expenditure, consideration should be given to new expenditure and/or revenue measures over the coming years as permitted by the economic situation.

The Financial Secretary also announced that at the same time as the Secretary for the Treasury's task force was examining the reasons for the forecast deficits, an independent committee of tax experts, professionals and academics would be formed to look into the suitability of introducing new types of broadly based taxes, including consumption-based taxes (e.g. value added tax or goods and services tax) and decide what form any such taxes should take and what would be the practical implications of their introduction. This Committee was subsequently formed and submitted its report to the Financial Secretary in February 2002. That report concluded that the most appropriate revenue measure to generate additional revenue for the Government would be a broadly based, multi-level, consumption tax, of the type more commonly referred to as a Goods and Services Tax (GST). Additionally, however, the committee recommended that, particularly as an interim measure, consideration should be given to increasing property rates, reducing personal allowances, and introducing a land and sea departure tax.

Clearly, the above reports together potentially paved the way for the most significant reform of the Hong Kong tax system for many decades. Indeed, in the 2003/04 Budget Speech the Financial Secretary advised that the Government was, in conjunction with other measures aimed at addressing the budget deficit, working towards the implementation of a GST. Further, in the 2006/07 Budget Speech the Financial Secretary gave a very strong indication that a GST would be introduced and outlined some of the features of the proposed system and the types of measures being considered to relieve the financial hardship which inevitably would accompany such a tax. Nonetheless, in the face of public opposition, the Financial Secretary subsequently announced in December 2006 that the Government was no longer advocating a GST at this time but would instead consider other measures to address the narrow tax base. Accordingly, the reviews undertaken in the early part of the decade may still result in a degree of tax reform, although the nature of any such reform is yet to be determined.

In addition to the IRO and SDO, there are a number of other ordinances under which taxes and duties are levied but which are not considered in this book. Such taxes include Betting Duty, Hotel Accommodation Tax, motor vehicle First Registration Tax and duties on a range of commodities including fuel, tobacco and methyl alcohol.

1.2 The Taxes in General

Brief summaries of the taxes discussed in this book are outlined later in this chapter. It is, however, worthwhile taking a moment to look at the broad scheme of taxation in Hong Kong and making some general observations about the taxes.

Stamp Duty is the oldest tax administered by the IRD in Hong Kong, having its origins in legislation enacted in 1866. The operative provisions of the legislation under which it is imposed, the SDO, are similar in many ways to past and present UK stamp duty legislation. Accordingly, decisions of the UK courts provide valuable guidance as to its interpretation, as do the decisions of courts of various Commonwealth countries which have enacted similar legislation. Essentially, Stamp Duty is a tax on documents evidencing certain transactions, and is technically not a tax on the transactions themselves. Notwithstanding the significant revenue yield which Stamp Duty provides to the Government, the range of transactions to which it applies is quite limited. Most Stamp Duty is generated from documents evidencing the sale of shares in Hong Kong companies, the sale of Hong Kong real property and the leasing of Hong Kong real property, although a number of other types of documents attract the duty.

Estate Duty is the second oldest tax administered by the IRD in Hong Kong, being first imposed in 1915, although it has now been abolished in respect of persons dying after 10 February 2006. As such, Estate Duty applies only to a small number of deceased estates which have not been finalised.

With its effective abolition, Hong Kong no longer has any direct taxes on capital.

Although the Stamp Duty system is not dissimilar to systems in other jurisdictions, the basis of taxing income in Hong Kong is in many ways unusual and unique. In particular, there is no total income tax in Hong Kong. Rather, there are three separate and distinct taxes on income, namely Profits Tax, Salaries Tax and Property Tax.

The IRO and IRR cover the whole of the law for each of the income based taxes. The IRO has separate parts for each of the taxes and parts common to all of the taxes, such as the law relating to assessment, collection and administration.

Certain fundamental principles are common to all of the taxes and an understanding of these assists greatly in understanding the taxes, their context and relationship with each other. These are:—

(1) There is no total income concept; each of the taxes is assessed without regard to what the taxpayer's income may be under other headings. There are, however, exceptions to this rule; for example, an individual may elect for Personal Assessment (see Chapter 6) which has the effect of bringing all of his sources of income into a single assessment. Similarly, in the case of a company, there is an effective merging of most sources of income into a single Profits Tax assessment.

Up to and including the 1992/93 year of assessment, unless an individual elected for Personal Assessment, he did not make a single return of all of his sources of assessable income; rather, he made separate returns in respect of any of the three taxes for which he was liable. The individual's total sources of assessable income were not, therefore, immediately brought to the attention of any single officer of the IRD. This resulted in the IRD having great practical difficulties in checking returns, particularly where enquiry into the adequacy and accuracy of returns was required by the Investigation Unit.

From the 1993/94 year of assessment, however, a system of Composite Tax Returns (CTRS) was introduced which generally requires all sources of income which are chargeable to any of the three taxes to be disclosed on the one return form. Notwithstanding this combined return form, the schedular system of tax remains and a separate assessment for each of the taxes is still issued, unless the individual elects for Personal Assessment. An exception to the CTRS applies in the case of jointly owned property, where the income from that property is subject to Property Tax; in these cases, a separate Property Tax return continues to be required.

The existence of separate rates of tax and deductions for each of the taxes gives rise to some interesting anomalies, particularly in respect of individuals in receipt of income subject to Salaries Tax, where there is an automatic right to personal allowances and progressive rates of tax, as well as income subject to either Property Tax or Profits Tax where no such automatic right exists.

These anomalies are illustrated in the examples below.

■ Example 1.1

Year of assessment 2007/08		Taxpayer A	Taxpayer B
(1) Salary from employment		$ 200,000	
(2) Profits from business		4,800,000	$5,000,000
		$5,000,000	$5,000,000
Profits Tax (A)	$4,800,000 @ 16% =	$ 768,000	
Profits Tax (B)	$5,000,000 @ 16% =		$ 800,000
Salaries Tax (A)	$200,000		
Less: Allowances	($200,000) =	Nil	
Total tax liability		$ 768,000	$ 800,000

Notes:—
(a) Despite having the same total income, B pays 4.2% more tax than A. If B elects for Personal Assessment (see Chapter 6) in order to enjoy the personal allowances, the rates of progressive tax are such that his liability would be $805,500 (assuming married allowances only) and the election would, therefore, not apply.
(b) The anomaly arises because income subject to Salaries Tax attracts personal allowances whatever the individual's other sources of income. For B to obtain those allowances, however, he must elect for Personal Assessment, but his income is too large to benefit therefrom.
(c) Assumes the only personal allowance available is the married person's allowance. For rates of tax and allowances, see relevant chapters.

■ Example 1.2

Year of assessment 2007/08	Taxpayer A	Taxpayer B
(1) Salary from employment	$370,000	
(2) Property Income (net of allowable deductions)	30,000	$ 30,000
(3) Profits from business		370,000
	$400,000	$400,000

Salaries Tax (A)	$370,000		
Less: Allowances (married)	$200,000		
Tax on	$170,000	$18,400	
Property Tax (A) and (B)	30,000 @ 16% =	4,800	$ 4,800
Profits Tax (B)	$370,000 @ 16% =		59,200
		$23,200	$64,000

If B elects Personal Assessment:—

Total income	$400,000	
Less: Allowances (married)	$200,000	
	$200,000	Tax = $23,500

Notes:—
(a) Although B can reduce his liability by electing Personal Assessment, he still pays
    more tax than A on the same total income.
(b) The reason for the anomaly is that B must elect Personal Assessment to obtain the
    personal allowance which A obtains automatically in his Salaries Tax Assessment,
    and by so doing, he subjects his property income to the progressive rate of 17%,
    whereas A remains liable to Property Tax at 16%.
(c) For rates of tax and allowances see relevant chapters.

For these and other reasons, the Third Inland Revenue Ordinance
Review Committee recommended that total income tax returns
should be introduced for all taxpayers and total income assessments
made mandatory. This would, of course, involve radical changes to
the present system. It should be emphasised that the move to the
CTRS does not represent a move to a total income system, although
clearly it facilitates the introduction of such a system should the
Government consider this desirable.

(2)   Except in the limited circumstances already illustrated, i.e. Salaries
      Tax and Personal Assessment, tax is levied at a fixed standard rate
      and is not progressive.

(3)   The extent of exposure to tax is not governed by residence status,
      either of individuals or companies, which is a familiar fundamental
      principle of many other tax jurisdictions. Residence status is of
      relevance only in limited and specific circumstances which are
      mentioned in their context. Otherwise, the extent of liability under
      each of the taxes is limited to income which "arises in or is derived
      from" Hong Kong (or, in the case of Property Tax, income from
      land or buildings in Hong Kong) and certain other sources which
      are deemed by the IRO to arise in Hong Kong. Such income is
      chargeable to tax in respect of residents and non-residents alike.
      Accordingly, determination of source of income is probably the single
      most important factor in determining liability to tax in Hong Kong.

(4)   There is no provision in the IRO which brings into tax all items of income not specifically charged elsewhere in the IRO. The logical feature of the schedular tax system is that any item of income which does not fall within any one of the charging heads is not subject to tax. Furthermore, certain other sources of income are specifically exempted from tax in circumstances where they would otherwise fall under one of the heads. One example is the exemption from Profits Tax of dividends received from companies which are subject to Profits Tax (Sec. 26(a)).

(5)   There is no tax on capital gains. Profits Tax may, however, be charged on the profits of speculative transactions if they can be shown to constitute an adventure in the nature of trade (see Chapter 4).

(6)   Because of the necessity to satisfy the requirement of simplicity in administration, there was historically very little strict anti-avoidance legislation in the IRO. Nonetheless, Sec. 61 was included from the very beginning and is a simple form of general anti-avoidance provision (that is aimed at avoidance in general as opposed to any specific technique). It provides that transactions which can be regarded as artificial or fictitious are to be disregarded for tax purposes. The apparently wide nature of this provision has, however, been limited by legal interpretation as a result of which the growth of more sophisticated tax planning arrangements in the 1980s led to some specific anti-avoidance provisions in the areas of leasing, loss companies, acquisition and licensing of intellectual property, sale of income streams, deductibility of interest expense, limited partnership losses and a more complicated general anti-avoidance provision in Sec. 61A (see Chapter 10).

(7)   Husbands and wives are treated as independent persons for Profits Tax, Property Tax and Salaries Tax except that, in certain circumstances for Salaries Tax where a combined assessment would result in less tax payable, an election may be made for combined assessment (see section 3.6.2). In the case of Personal Assessment, the income of a wife who is not living apart from her husband is aggregated with that of her husband.

(8)   There are no true withholding taxes, either on dividends or on any other source of income, whether paid to residents or non-residents. There are instances, however, where an assessment on a non-resident may be made on or through an agent or payer in Hong Kong who is required to retain the tax out of payments due to the non-resident (see Chapter 4).

Brief summaries of the taxes covered in this book follow.

1.3 Estate Duty (EDO)

Estate Duty has been abolished in respect of persons dying after 10 February 2006, and only a nominal amount of $100 is chargeable in respect of dutiable estates of persons dying between 15 July 2005 and 10 February 2006. Nonetheless, the *Estate Duty Ordinance* continues to apply and impose *ad valorem* rates of duty in respect of persons who died before 15 July 2005. As the importance of Estate Duty is now significantly diminished, a discussion of the charge is no longer contained in this book.

1.4 Stamp Duty (SDO)

Stamp Duty is a tax on instruments, with the instruments to which it applies being specified in the four Heads of the First Schedule to the SDO. The four Heads cover certain instruments dealing with:

- the transfer or lease of immovable property in Hong Kong;
- the transfer of Hong Kong stock;
- the issue of Hong Kong bearer instruments; and
- duplicates and counterparts of instruments themselves dutiable.

The most common types of Stamp Duty payable in practice are as follows:

(1) Stamp Duty at *ad valorem* rates up to a maximum of 3.75% of the consideration is payable on conveyances on sale (essentially the legal assignment) of immovable property in Hong Kong. In addition to actual conveyances on sale, certain other transactions are deemed to be conveyances on sale at market value, most notably certain gifts of immovable property or sales of such property at less than full value.

(2) In respect of residential property, Stamp Duty at *ad valorem* rates up to a maximum of 3.75% of the consideration is payable on agreements for the sale and purchase, and not merely on the legal assignment. For the purpose of this provision, notes or memoranda evidencing an unwritten agreement for sale and purchase of residential property are themselves deemed to be dutiable agreements for sale. A legal assignment in pursuance of a properly stamped sale and purchase agreement of residential property is, however, only subject to Stamp Duty at a flat rate of $100. Again, a

deed of gift or an agreement for the purchase and sale of residential property at less than market value is deemed to be an agreement for sale and purchase at market value. The imposition of Stamp Duty on agreements for the sale and purchase of residential property was introduced as measure to dampen speculation on residential property. Although the Government considers such measures are now no longer required, the provisions still exist but have been relaxed by extending the time for stamping of the dutiable agreements.

(3)   A lease of immovable property in Hong Kong is subject to Stamp Duty at *ad valorem* rates of up to 1% of the average annual rent. If the lease provides for payment of a lump sum premium, such amount is generally dutiable at the rates applicable to a conveyance on sale (i.e. at *ad valorem* rates of up to 3.75%).

(4)   A sale and purchase of Hong Kong stock is subject to Stamp Duty at *ad valorem* rates of 0.2% of the consideration paid, or the market value of the stock where the sale is at less than market value. Gifts of Hong Kong stock are generally deemed to be sales at market value and, therefore, also attract Stamp Duty at the above rate. An exemption applies, however, to certain transfers in connection with a stock borrowing and lending arrangement. Additionally, special rules apply to units in unit trusts which are within the definition of Hong Kong stock.

As noted above, Stamp Duty is a tax on instruments and is normally denoted on the face of the instrument, although provisions have been introduced to permit the electronic stamping of documents by way of the issue of a stamp certificate. Accordingly, there is generally no need to issue a notice of assessment to Stamp Duty. Sometimes, however, the consideration upon which the duty is to be calculated cannot be ascertained at the time of submission of the instrument for stamping and in such circumstances an assessment to Stamp Duty is subsequently issued.

Where Stamp Duty is not paid within the period required by statute, late stamping penalties apply. The amount of such penalty depends upon how late the relevant instrument is stamped, but is ten times the original duty where the document is stamped more than two months late. The Collector has, however, a discretion to waive any late stamping penalties in whole or in part.

The SDO contains procedures by which an appeal can be lodged against an assessment to Stamp Duty. Such appeal is to the District Court in the first instance and must be made within one month of the date of the assessment. Additionally, in order for the appeal to be valid, the Stamp Duty in dispute must generally be paid before the appeal is lodged.

1.5 Income Taxes

The main features of the IRO, under which income taxes are levied, are outlined below. A summary chart of the income taxes can be found in Table 1.3.

1.5.1 Year of assessment (Sec. 2 IRO)

Every assessment issued under the IRO is related to a year of assessment. The year of assessment is the year to 31st March, e.g. the year ended 31st March 2007 is known as the year of assessment 2006/07. Each tax has its own rules as to what income and deductions form the basis of the assessment for a given year of assessment.

1.5.2 Property Tax (Part II IRO)

Property Tax is levied at the standard rate on the owner of land and/or buildings on the net assessable value of land and/or buildings situated in Hong Kong. The net assessable value is based on rental income.

The charge is levied for a year of assessment on the rental income earned in the year of assessment and the only deductions permitted therefrom are property rates paid by the owner and a standard deduction of 20% of the rental income to cover repairs and outgoings. There are, however, relieving provisions for uncollectible rents. The charging of Property Tax incorporates a system of prepaid tax known as Provisional Property Tax. The provisional assessment is an estimate, normally based on the previous year's agreed assessment.

■ Example 1.3

Mr. B. Wong owns a block of 6 flats from which he receives total annual rents of $540,000. During 2007/08 he incurred expenses on repairs of $125,000, paid insurance of $15,000 and agency commission of $25,000.

(1) Total rental receipts	=	$540,000
Less: 20%		108,000
(2) Net Assessable Value		$432,000
Property Tax ($432,000 @ 16%)		$ 69,120

Note:—

He receives the standard deduction of 20% whether his actual outgoings are greater or less.

Exemptions apply to companies owning and letting the property as, in such cases, any rental income is included in the companies' Profits Tax returns instead (see Chapter 4).

1.5.3 Salaries Tax (Part III IRO)

Salaries Tax is imposed on income arising in or derived from Hong Kong from any office, employment of profit or pension. Income arises in or is derived from Hong Kong if the employment itself is in Hong Kong, in which case it is taxable irrespective of where the services are rendered. If, however, the employment is outside Hong Kong, the income therefrom is taxable only to the extent that the services are rendered in Hong Kong. Irrespective of the location of the employment, however, income is exempt, *inter alia*, if all services under the employment are rendered outside Hong Kong (except in the case of Government employees, seafarers and aircrew, to which special rules apply). In determining whether all services are rendered abroad, it is permissable to ignore services rendered during visits to Hong Kong not exceeding sixty days in any year of assessment.

Income from any office or employment includes any wages, salary, leave pay, fee, commission, bonus, gratuity, perquisite and allowance whether derived from the employer or others. Certain types of remuneration and cash benefits are exempt from the charge while certain other benefits are specifically taxable. In general, however, benefits in kind are not taxable unless they are convertible into cash or represent an employee's personal liability assumed by the employer.

Tax is levied for a year of assessment on income accrued and payable in the year although it cannot be assessed until it is actually received. The earnings accruing to a person less expenses wholly, exclusively and necessarily incurred in the production of assessable income, depreciation allowances on plant and machinery used for the production of assessable income and concessionary deductions (allowable charitable donations, home loan interest and elderly residential care expenses) are charged to tax. The tax charged is the lower of net assessable income less concessionary deductions charged at the standard rate or net chargeable income charged at progressive rates (see Table 1.3). Net chargeable income is net assessable income less personal allowances and concessionary deductions.

Husbands and wives are treated as separately chargeable persons except in certain limited circumstances where they may elect to be jointly assessed.

There are no provisions for deduction at source (except for a voluntary system whereby deductions are credited to a Tax Reserve Certificate account) and tax is required to be paid direct by the taxpayer to the IRD on or before the due date specified on the notice of assessment. The charging of Salaries Tax incorporates a system of prepaid tax known as Provisional Salaries Tax. The provisional assessment is an estimate, normally based on the previous year's agreed assessment and is generally payable in two instalments, one of 75% in the final quarter of the year of assessment and the remaining 25% three months later, just after the end of the year of assessment. When the actual income of the year of assessment is known, an assessment is issued based on the actual income and crediting the Provisional Salaries Tax already paid. At the same time, Provisional Salaries Tax is levied for the following year of assessment. Any excess/deficit of Provisional Salaries Tax over the actual finally determined liability is offset against/added to the Provisional Salaries Tax payable for the following year of assessment. There are provisions to enable collection of Salaries Tax and Provisional Salaries Tax to be held over in appropriate circumstances (see Chapter 3).

1.5.4 Profits Tax (Part IV IRO)

Profits tax is chargeable at the standard rate on every person who is carrying on a trade, profession or business in Hong Kong in respect of his assessable profits arising in or derived from Hong Kong from such trade, profession or business. There is no distinction between resident and non-resident persons; it is merely necessary to determine whether a person, which includes a company, a partnership or a body of persons, is carrying on a trade, profession or business in Hong Kong and, if so, whether they have a Hong Kong source of profits in connection therewith. In addition, certain sources of income are deemed to be from a business carried on in Hong Kong and are, therefore, subject to Profits Tax even if it is the recipient's only source of income in Hong Kong and the recipient has no business presence in Hong Kong.

Other than the deemed Hong Kong sources of income, the IRO gives no guidance in ascertaining the source of income or profits. It is, of course, not necessarily important to ascertain exactly where the geographical source is but merely to determine whether or not it is in Hong Kong. The determination of source requires a consideration of various factors and the applicable case law precedents. There are some important decisions of the Hong Kong Courts which are dealt with in Chapter 4 and, where relevant, legal decisions in other countries also provide guidance. Subject to the qualification that each case must be considered on its own merits, a good general rule for determining the source of profits is to ascertain "where in substance the operations which gave rise to the profits took place" after having isolated each step in the series of transactions involved in the particular trade or business.

Assessable profits are generally profits arrived at in accordance with normal accounting principles as adjusted to comply with the requirements of the IRO and case law principles. For example, adjustments are required in respect of differences between depreciation for accounting purposes and statutory rates of depreciation allowances for taxation purposes, the exclusion of non-Hong Kong source profits and capital profits, and adjustments where accounting principles and taxation principles conflict as to what constitutes capital and revenue expenditure. Where a part of a person's profit is taxable and part is not, it is of course necessary to disallow an appropriate proportion of expenditure and the IRR provide the various rules governing such apportionment. Similarly, the IRR provide rules for determining assessable branch profits of companies which have their head office elsewhere.

Profits Tax assessments are raised for a year of assessment and the IRO provides the rules for determining the basis period for a year of assessment with special rules for commencement, cessation and change of accounting date. The standard rate for the 2007/08 year of assessment is 16% for individuals and 17.5% for corporations. Partnerships are assessed as a single unit and the applicable tax rate is 16% to the extent that the profits are shared by individuals, and 17.5% in respect of that part of the profits attributable to corporate partners.

The charging of Profits Tax incorporates a system of tax paid on account during the year of assessment known as Provisional Profits Tax. An estimate is made of assessable profits for the year of assessment and Provisional Profits Tax is levied on this estimate. In the case of a continuing business, the estimate is based on the actual assessable profits for the preceding year of assessment. When the actual assessable profits for the year of assessment are ascertained, a final assessment is issued and credit is given for the Provisional Profits Tax paid. Any excess/deficit of Provisional Profits Tax paid over the final liability is offset against/added to the Provisional Profits Tax payable for the following year of assessment. In the event that there is any remaining balance of Provisional Profits Tax, it is refunded to the taxpayer. There are provisions to enable collection of Profits Tax and Provisional Profits Tax to be held over in appropriate circumstances. Furthermore, where the cessation of business has been reported in the current year's tax return, it is the IRD's practice not to demand payment of Provisional Profits Tax.

Because of the relative simplicity of the legislation, it is not necessarily adequate to cope with the taxation of special types of business and the IRO therefore includes specific provisions relating to the following types of business:—

- Life Insurance
- Other Insurance
- Shipping and Aircraft
- Clubs/Trade Associations

These are discussed fully in Chapter 4.

1.5.5 Depreciation allowances (Part VI IRO)

The IRO lays down statutory depreciation allowances in respect of specified categories of expenditure on capital assets. These are granted for the purposes of Profits Tax and, in limited circumstances for Salaries Tax, where capital assets are used wholly or partly to produce assessable profits or income. Allowances are granted for industrial buildings, commercial buildings, and plant & machinery.

The general scheme of depreciation allowances is to grant an initial allowance in the year in which the expenditure is incurred and annual allowances thereafter. Upon disposal of the asset or upon other specified occasions, a balancing allowance or charge may be made although as a general rule, no such charge or allowance arises in the case of plant & machinery. In the case of commercial buildings, however, only a fixed annual allowance is given.

The rates of initial allowance are fixed at 20% for industrial buildings and 60% for plant & machinery. The annual allowance is 4% for industrial and commercial buildings (or varying rates in respect of inherited expenditure) and 10%, 20% or 30% for plant & machinery, depending upon the exact nature of the asset (see Chapter 5).

By statutory concession, some types of capital expenditure may be written off over shorter periods than otherwise allowed under the depreciation provisions. For example, an outright deduction is permitted for certain plant and machinery used in manufacturing and computer hardware, software and systems. Also, expenditure on the renovation or refurbishment of most buildings and structures may be written off over five years. Where these concessions apply, however, the relevant expenditure is precluded from also qualifying for the depreciation allowances which would otherwise be available.

1.5.6 Rates of Tax (Schedule 2 IRO)

The Second Schedule to the IRO sets out the progressive rates of tax which are applicable, after deducting personal allowances, for Salaries Tax and, where an election has been made for a total income assessment, under Personal Assessment. The Second Schedule gives all of the rates since 1947/48, and the rates applicable for 2007/08 are:—

Upon the first	$35,000	2%
Upon the next	$35,000	7%
Upon the next	$35,000	12%
Upon the remainder		17%

In the case of Salaries Tax, the total tax payable is not to exceed tax at the standard rate (being 16% for 2007/08) on net assessable income before personal allowances. Accordingly, there is a break-even point, depending upon personal circumstances, above which the standard rate applies (see Chapter 3).

In the case of Personal Assessment, the tax payable is also not to exceed tax at the standard rate on total income less allowable deductions and losses, but not personal allowances (see Chapter 6).

■ Example 1.4

This example illustrates the relationship between the standard rate and the progressive rates for Salaries Tax, for the year of assessment 2007/08.

Salary, bonus and taxable benefits		$214,000
Less: Expenses and Depreciation Allowances	$3,000	
Less: Charitable Donations	250	3,250
Net Assessable Income		$210,750
Less: Personal Allowance (single person)		100,000
Net Chargeable Income		$110,750

$35,000 @ 2%	=	$ 700
35,000 @ 7%		2,450
35,000 @ 12%		4,200
5,750 @ 17%		977
		$8,327 .... (1)

16% on Net Assessable Income = 16% × $210,750
                                                = $33,720 .... (2)

Accordingly, since (2) is greater than (1), the progressive rates are applicable in this case. (Note that tax payable is rounded down to the nearest dollar.)

1.5.7 Personal allowances (Schedule 4 IRO)

Personal allowances are deductible for Salaries Tax, below the break-even point (see Chapter 3) and for Personal Assessment (see Chapter 6). The allowances for the 2006/07 and 2007/08 years of assessment are summarized in Table 1.2 below.

For further details of personal allowances, see Chapter 6.

Table 1.2 Personal Allowances

Types of Allowances	2006/07	2007/08
Basic Allowance	$100,000	$100,000
Married Person's Allowance	$200,000	$200,000
Child Allowance –		
1st to 9th children (each)	$ 40,000	$ 50,000
additional amount – year of birth	–	$ 50,000
Maximum aggregate Child Allowances	$360,000	$450,000
Dependent Parent (aged 60 years or above) –		
not resident with claimant	$ 30,000	$ 30,000
resident with claimant	$ 60,000	$ 60,000
Dependent Parent (aged 55 to 59 years)		
not resident with claimant	$ 15,000	$ 15,000
resident with claimant	$ 30,000	$ 30,000
Dependent Grandparent (aged 60 years or above)		
not resident with claimant	$ 30,000	$ 30,000
resident with claimant	$ 60,000	$ 60,000
Dependent Grandparent (aged 55 to 59 years)		
not resident with claimant	$ 15,000	$ 15,000
resident with claimant	$ 30,000	$ 30,000
Single Parent Allowance	$100,000	$100,000
Dependent Brother/Sister Allowance	$ 30,000	$ 30,000
Disabled Dependent Allowance	$ 60,000	$ 60,000

1.5.8 Personal assessment (Part VII IRO)

Although there is no total income concept in Hong Kong taxation, the IRO recognises the situation that a total income assessment could, in certain circumstances, result in a smaller total tax liability to an individual than the sum of his liabilities under the separate income taxes so long as the personal allowances and progressive tax rates, that only apply automatically to Salaries Tax, are extended to his total income.

The IRO therefore provides for an individual to elect for Personal Assessment of his total income which means that against his aggregate income assessable under the various heads, and subject to the various rules contained in Part VII of the IRO, he can deduct the personal allowances and have the net chargeable income taxed at progressive rates.

The ability to elect is only open to an individual who is ordinarily resident in Hong Kong or who falls within the definition of temporary resident.

An individual will elect, for example, in the following circumstances:—

(1)   he has losses for Profits Tax purposes and chargeable income under one or more of the other heads;

(2)   he has sources of income which do not automatically attract the personal allowances and progressive tax rates and his total income is below the "break-even" point (see Chapter 3 for break-even point);

(3)   his marginal rate of Salaries Tax is lower than the standard rate and he has another source of taxable income; or

(4)   he has incurred interest expenses in connection with the financing of a property which generates rental income subject to Property Tax.

Special rules apply to elections by married couples; essentially, however, both must elect and Personal Assessment will also result in joint assessment. These issues are discussed fully in Chapter 6.

■ Example 1.5

An illustration of (1) above.

Mr. X had an adjusted loss in his business of $20,500 for 2007/08 and his wife had earnings from employment for the same year of $800,000 on which she has been assessed to Salaries Tax of $91,500. He claims no allowance except for himself and his wife.

(1) Salary	$800,000
(2) Less: Losses	20,500
	$779,500
(3) Married Person's Allowance (Aggregate)	(200,000)
Net Chargeable Income	$579,500

$ 35,000 @ 2%	=	$	700
35,000 @ 7%			2,450
35,000 @ 12%			4,200
474,500 @ 17%			80,665
			$88,015 (see Note)

Personal Assessment	$88,015
Tax paid	$91,500
Refund	$ 3,485

Note:—

The alternative calculation is $779,500 @ 16% = $124,720 which is greater than $84,615 and therefore does not apply.

Where the Personal Assessment liability is limited to tax at the standard rate on total income less losses, the refund would be effectively the loss at standard rate. The refund could never be less than this and is greater where, as in the above example, the total income less losses is below the "break-even" point (see Chapter 3).

The IRO specifically provides that under Personal Assessment, the tax payable is limited to tax at the standard rate (being 16% for the 2007/08 year of assessment) on the total assessable income of the individual. That is, the top marginal progressive rate cannot apply to increase the total average tax rate above 16% for the 2007/08 year of assessment. Accordingly, the tax payable can never be greater under Personal Assessment than would have been the case if an election for Personal Assessment had not been made, except in limited circumstances where a loss is sustained in a business; an example of such a situation is as follows:

■ Example 1.6

Mr. Y is married and has the following income and losses for 2007/08.

(1) A loss from his business of $5,000.
(2) Income from a flat which he owns of $150,000, upon which Property Tax of $19,200 has been paid.
(3) His wife has employment income of $320,000 upon which Salaries Tax of $9,900 has been paid.

The Personal Assessment calculation is as follows:

(1) Business loss	$ (5,000)
(2) Rental income ($150,000 less 20% deduction)	120,000
(3) Wife's employment income	320,000
Total income	$435,000
(4) Allowances (Married)	(200,000)
Net Chargeable Income	$235,000
Tax thereon at progressive rates	$ 29,450

Accordingly, by electing for Personal Assessment, Mr. Y's total tax liability is $29,450, whereas if no election had been made, his total liability (or the combined liability of him and his wife had an election for joint assessment not been made) would have been only $29,100. In these circumstances, the IRD would probably invite Mr. Y to withdraw any election which he made.

1.5.9 Returns and information (Part IX IRO)

The IRO gives the IRD wide powers to obtain not only standard returns of income from taxpayers but also all kinds of information from a wide variety of persons including information which does not touch upon their own tax liability. In cases of fraud and wilful default, the IRD's powers are even wider including, in appropriate circumstances, the power of entry and search.

The Board of Inland Revenue has the power to specify any forms which are necessary for the administration of the IRO and is charged with the obligation of laying down the form and content of any return. Any return not made in the specified form is treated as invalid and, therefore, as not having been filed. Although traditionally returns have been in the nature of paper forms, provisions now exist for the filing of returns in electronic form or through the telephone filing (telefiling) system; however, this is only permitted in circumstances prescribed by the Commissioner.

There are extensive penalty provisions for failure to make returns or provide information statutorily requested within the statutory time limits, although there are provisions whereby the time limits can be extended at the Commissioner's discretion which, in practice, is delegated to officers of the IRD. The penalties can be either imposed by a court pursuant to a prosecution action brought by the Commissioner or, if he chooses not to so prosecute, by way of an amount of additional tax determined by the Commissioner but subject to statutory limits. If the Commissioner decides not to prosecute, but to impose additional tax, there is a statutory procedure which must be followed and which requires, *inter alia*, the Commissioner to seek representations from the taxpayer as to the reasons the return was late and take into account those representations when determining the amount of additional tax. The power to impose additional tax must be exercised by the Commissioner or a deputy commissioner personally.

Where returns are submitted late, it is usual that penalties are more commonly imposed by way of additional tax and at modest levels compared to the maximum possible amount. Nonetheless, the Commissioner does initiate prosecution action where he considers that circumstances dictate it appropriate, as is discussed further in Chapter 7.

1.5.10 Assessments and payment of Tax (Part X, XA, XB, XC, and XII IRO)

The Assessor is empowered to raise assessments and provisional tax assessments and has wide powers to raise estimated assessments in specified circumstances. Normally he will raise an assessment on an agreed figure and, at the same time, a provisional assessment for the following year in the same amount. In the absence of a valid return or where he cannot accept the amount shown in the return, he may estimate the assessable income or profits of the taxpayer. Similarly, where accounts of a business have not been kept in a satisfactory form, he may make an assessment based on the usual rate of profit applied to the actual turnover and the Board of Inland Revenue is

Table 1.3 Income Taxes (2007/08 Year of Assessment)

The Taxes	Property Tax	Salaries Tax	Profits Tax
Year of Assessment		— Year to 31st March —	
Nature of Income Charged	Property rental	Employment, office or pension	Business profits
Basis Period	Period of ownership in year of assessment	Year of assessment	Accounting period ending in year of assessment
Assessable Income	Rental income from property situated in Hong Kong	Earnings and assessable benefits from a Hong Kong employment or from services rendered in Hong Kong	Hong Kong source profits from business carried on in Hong Kong and certain deemed taxable sources
Deductible Expenses	Statutory deduction of 20% of assessable value and rates where paid by owner	Necessary expenses, depreciation, certain charitable contributions and other concessionary deductions	As in business accounts with statutory adjustments
Rate of Charge	Standard rate	Lesser of progressive rates (after allowances) or standard rate	17.5% for corporations; standard rate for others
How Collected	Assessment	Assessment	Assessment
Current Rate	16%	16% (maximum)	Corporations 17.5%; Others 16%
Progressive Rates		— 2% on the first $35,000 — — 7% on the next $35,000 — — 12% on the next 35,000 and — — 17% on the remainder —	
Personal Allowances		— See section 1.5.7 and Chapter 6 —	
Personal Assessment		— See Chapter 6 —	

empowered to prescribe the usual rates of profit, although it is believed that this power has never been exercised.

The time limit for making additional assessments is generally within 6 years after the end of the year of assessment, although in the case of fraud or wilful evasion, the time limit is extended to 10 years. An assessment becomes final and conclusive when either there has been no valid objection or, where an objection has been lodged, the objection has been determined by the Commissioner and no appeal lodged or the assessment has been adjusted as agreed between the taxpayer and the Assessor. Where an appeal has been lodged, the assessment becomes final and conclusive when determined by the Board of Review or a court. There are only limited circumstances in which a final assessment can be re-opened, the main ones being where the IRO specifically permits it in election cases or in the case of an "error or omission" claim, which is discussed in Section 8.7.1.

Upon raising an assessment, the dates of payment of the tax are fixed by the Commissioner and are then specified in the notice. The provisional tax may be payable in two instalments; indeed, this is always the case for Provisional Salaries Tax but only the case for Provisional Profits Tax where the first instalment normally falls due within the currency of the accounting period which forms the basis period for the year of assessment to which the Provisional Profits Tax assessment applies.

Even where a valid notice of objection or appeal has been submitted, there is no statutory entitlement of the taxpayer to a holdover of the tax payable; this is entirely at the Commissioner's discretion and there is no appeal against his decision. In the case of Provisional Profits Tax and Provisional Salaries Tax there are specific circumstances in which applications can be made for a holdover but the decision is again at the discretion of the Commissioner.

Where tax is not paid on or before the due date, the Commissioner can, and normally does, impose a 5% surcharge. Where tax is in default for 6 months or more, a further 10% surcharge can, and normally is, added.

The IRD has wide powers to enforce collection including provisions which aim to prevent defaulters from leaving Hong Kong (see Chapter 8).

1.5.11 Objections and appeals (Part XI IRO)

Any person in receipt of an assessment may, within the appropriate time limit, submit an objection subject to the rules as to the form of an objection. An objection is settled by agreement, or failing agreement, determined unilaterally by the Commissioner.

Where a taxpayer is dissatisfied with the Commissioner's determination, again within the allowed time limit and subject to the correct form, an appeal can be lodged. In the first instance the appeal is to the Board of Review which is an informal hearing by an independent panel drawn from a panel of laymen, although the chairman is always a person of legal experience and qualification and members of the panel may include persons with legal qualifications. Either the taxpayer or the Commissioner may appeal on a point of law from the Board of Review's decision to the Court of First Instance or, with leave, to the Court of Appeal. A decision of the Court of First Instance may be appealed, with leave, to the Court of Appeal. Similarly, a decision of the Court of Appeal may be appealed to the Court of Final Appeal. There are provisions whereby, with the agreement of both parties, an appeal from the Commissioner's determination may proceed directly to the Court of First Instance.

Because of the informality and nominal or nil costs involved, numerous cases proceed to the Board of Review, sometimes with the taxpayer conducting his own case, but the material cost and formality of taking a case to the Court of First Instance means that considerably fewer cases are heard at that level.

A more comprehensive discussion of the objection and appeal provisions can be found in Chapter 9.

1.5.12 Board of Inland Revenue (Sec. 3 IRO)

The Board of Inland Revenue has a limited although important administrative function. It comprises the Financial Secretary and four other members appointed by the Chief Executive, presently the Commissioner, a practising accountant, a practising solicitor and a banker. The secretary is a deputy commissioner of the IRD. They hold office until they resign or are removed by the Chief Executive. There must not be more than one Government employee among the members, apart from the Financial Secretary.

The Board's function is primarily to specify IRD forms, or the form of any such forms (including the content of returns to be filed electronically or through the telefiling system), as is required by Sec. 86 of the IRO. Another important function, however, is to specify the system and templates for electronic filing of returns and the particulars required to be provided by taxpayers taking advantage of the electronic filing or telefiling systems. The Board is empowered to, and normally does, transact business by circulating papers and voting upon resolutions without a formal meeting. It is also empowered to prescribe any matter or procedure where the IRO so requires and particularly to make the Inland Revenue Rules, although these are subject to the approval of the Legislative Council.

For a further discussion of the Board of Inland Revenue, see section 10.6.1.

1.6 Inland Revenue Department

The Commissioner is charged with the responsibility of administering the IRO, SDO and EDO and for this purpose heads the IRD which is divided into six operating divisions or "Units". The division of these functions is shown in Figure 1.1.

The Commissioner is assisted by two deputy commissioners, five assistant commissioners and numerous assessors and other officers of varying grades with a total complement of clerical and non-clerical staff of almost 2,900 persons. Where the legislation permits, various statutory functions are delegated by the Commissioner to other officers (e.g. Sec. 3A IRO) but there are circumstances where the Commissioner is required to act personally. For example, assessments to additional tax under Sec. 82A IRO consequent upon late or incorrect returns made without reasonable excuse can only be made by the Commissioner or a deputy commissioner personally. Consequently, all such cases are seen and judged personally by the Commissioner or a deputy commissioner. Similarly, before a statement of assets and liabilities can be requested from a person under Sec. 51A IRO, the Commissioner or a deputy commissioner must be personally of the opinion that the person has made an incorrect return or supplied false information without reasonable excuse.

Although the Commissioner is charged with the responsibility of administering the IRO, SDO and EDO as enacted, in practice the IRD adopts a number of extra-statutory practices and concessions where it is considered that equity or expedience dictates such a course. Some of these practices and concessions are published and some are not. It is also inevitable that many parts of the legislation are capable of alternative interpretations and the Commissioner sometimes attempts to clarify these through the issue of Departmental Interpretation & Practice Notes or Stamp Office Interpretation & Practice Notes, which are discussed in 1.1 above.

The Department also publishes a number of other explanatory pamphlets for the guidance of taxpayers. The Commissioner issues an annual Departmental Report containing useful information and a summary of the Department's work in the past year including its work in respect of the taxes it administers.

All employees of the Department have an obligation of secrecy under Sec. 4 IRO with limited official exceptions. The penalty for breach of secrecy

Figure 1.1   Organisation of Inland Revenue Department

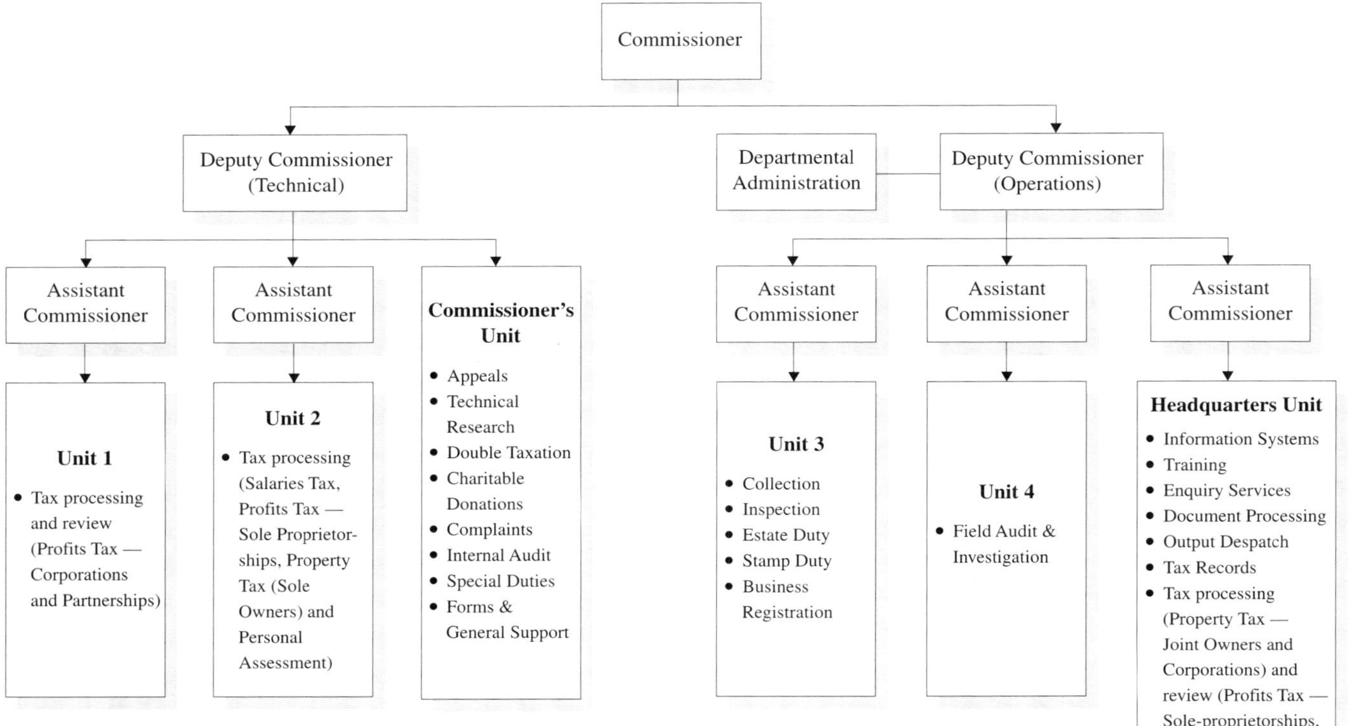

Source: Inland Revenue Department website

is a fine at level 5. (Penalty levels are explained in Chapter 7; a level 5 penalty, however, at the time of writing was $50,000).

1.7 Taxation System from 1st July 1997

1.7.1 The Basic Law

The Hong Kong taxation system after the reversion of sovereignty over Hong Kong to the Government of the People's Republic of China (PRC) on 1st July 1997 is dealt with in the document *The Basic Law of the Hong Kong Special Administrative Region of the People's Republic of China*, which is commonly referred to as the *Basic Law*. This document is essentially the constitution of the Hong Kong Special Administrative Region (the SAR).

Pursuant to Article 2 of the *Basic Law*, the National People's Congress of the PRC authorised the SAR to exercise a high degree of autonomy and to enjoy, amongst other things, independent judicial power, including that of final adjudication. Article 8 provides that all laws in force in Hong Kong as at 30th June 1997, including common law, rules of equity, ordinances and subordinate legislation are maintained, except where they otherwise contravene the *Basic Law*, and subject to any amendments passed by the legislature of the SAR. Other articles of the *Basic Law* which deal specifically with taxation issues are as follows:—

- Article 106 provides that the SAR shall have independent finances, that its revenues will not be handed over to the Central People's Government of the PRC and that the Central People's Government shall not levy taxes in the SAR.
- Article 107 requires the SAR to strive to maintain a balanced budget, avoid budget deficits and keep the budget commensurate with economic growth.
- Article 108 requires the SAR to maintain an independent tax system and to use its historically low tax rate system as a reference when formulating taxation laws and policy.

The combined effect of the above provisions is that the SDO, the EDO, the IRO, the IRR and case law as at 30th June 1997 remained applicable in Hong Kong on 1st July 1997 and the basic approach to taxation policy remained unaltered. Nonetheless, the SAR legislature has, and will undoubtedly continue to make amendments to the statutory provisions from time to time, just as the legislature did under British colonial rule, to update tax and personal allowance rates, to introduce or withdraw concessions, to introduce specific anti-avoidance provisions where considered appropriate and to clarify interpretation. For a further discussion of the *Basic Law* as it applies to taxation in Hong Kong, see *Departmental Interpretation & Practice Notes No. 29.*

Other changes to the tax system may arise from the change in the tax appeal process. In particular, appeals on tax issues (and other legal matters) to the Privy Council are no longer possible; rather, the final arbiter is the Court of Final Appeal which was established pursuant to the *Basic Law.* A consequence of this is that decisions of the Privy Council after 30th June 1997 in relation to other jurisdictions will no longer be binding authority on the Hong Kong courts, although they may well be considered persuasive in appropriate circumstances. Accordingly, it is possible that, over time, case law in Hong Kong will begin to diverge from that of the UK and other jurisdictions.

Because the taxation systems of the Hong Kong SAR and the Mainland of China are entirely separate but there is extensive investment and trade between the two jurisdictions, the issue of possible double taxation arises. In an effort to minimise such problems, a Memorandum concerning double taxation was entered into between the jurisdictions in 1998 and this was subsequently replaced with a comprehensive double taxation agreement. This issue of double taxation and double tax agreements is considered in chapter 11 and further information on the double taxation agreement with the Mainland of China can be found in *Departmental Interpretation & Practice Notes No. 44.*

1.7.2 The Hong Kong Reunification Ordinance

The Provisional Legislature of the Hong Kong SAR passed, on 1st July 1997, the *Hong Kong Reunification Ordinance.* The purpose of this ordinance was, *inter alia*, to give effect to the *Basic Law* provision that all laws are to continue in force in Hong Kong following the reversion of sovereignty; it provides, however, that such laws are to be interpreted in a manner so as not to be inconsistent with the *Basic Law* and to reflect Hong Kong's status as a Special Administrative Region of the People's Republic of China. A prime example of the operation of this ordinance is that it deems that all references in Hong Kong legislation to the "Governor of Hong Kong" are to be construed as references to the "Chief Executive of the Hong Kong SAR."

Similarly, the ordinance deems that references to the High Court and the Privy Council shall be construed as references to the Court of First Instance and the Court of Final Appeal respectively. This reflects the new structure of the courts which is provided for in the *Basic Law*. Other terms of colonial origin which are deemed to be construed in a more appropriate manner include "Her Majesty," "the Crown" and "Royal."

The ordinance also operates to remove concessions or exemptions provided for the United Kingdom or other Commonwealth countries, other than where such exemptions are necessary to give effect to any reciprocal arrangements. The application of this provision is explained in the relevant sections of this book.

Of course, the effect of the *Hong Kong Reunification Ordinance* could have been achieved by amending each individual ordinance. Indeed, subsequently there have been a number of ordinances passed which together have amended the IRO, SDO and EDO to more formally effect most of the changes dealt with by the *Hong Kong Reunification Ordinance*. Accordingly, although the *Hong Kong Reunification Ordinance* was a simple way of quickly achieving its purpose of removing uncertainties in legal interpretation which would otherwise arise as a consequence of the reversion of sovereignty, its practical effect is diminishing, and will continue to diminish, with the passage of time.

Throughout this book, wherever possible the terminology as provided for in the *Hong Kong Reunification Ordinance* has been adopted in dealing with legislative provisions containing old terms, but which are still in force. In a few cases, it has been considered appropriate for reasons of clarity or to highlight the origin of the provision, to use the previous terminology; in these cases, however, the effect of the *Hong Kong Reunification Ordinance* has been explained. In referring to provisions which were repealed prior to 1st July 1997, or considering a Board of Review or court decision handed down prior to that date, the previous wording of the provisions is generally used. Similarly, references to the new court structure are generally used where the context permits; however, the terms "High Court" and "Privy Council" still appear in reference to pre-1st July 1997 decisions.

Chapter 2 ■
Property Tax

2.1 Legislation

The relevant law concerning the charging of Property Tax is in Part II of the
IRO, Secs. 5 to 7C. The provisions regarding returns which are contained in
Part IX, and assessment and collection of tax contained in Parts X and XII
are also applicable to Property Tax, while Part XC deals with Provisional
Property Tax. The provisions of Part XI relating to objections and appeals
are applicable as are various other administrative provisions contained
elsewhere in the IRO.

2.2 Scope of the Tax

Property Tax is charged for each year of assessment on the owner of land or
buildings situated in Hong Kong at the standard rate (currently 16%) on the
net assessable value of such land or buildings (Sec. 5(1)). Land, together
with any buildings thereon, are assessed as a single unit where both the land
and the buildings have the same owner; otherwise, they are assessed
separately (Sec. 5(1) proviso (b)). Since, as a matter of property law, the
owner of the land (or more correctly the holder of the Government lease) is
the ultimate owner of any buildings on that land, this proviso seems incapable
of application in practice; this is discussed further in section 2.4.

Not all land and buildings in Hong Kong have always been within the
scope of Property Tax as certain areas in the New Territories were outside
of the charge until such time as the Governor by proclamation in the *Gazette*
declared them to be chargeable (Sec. 5(1) former proviso (e)). This was a
matter of Government policy and these areas were progressively brought
into Property Tax by proclamation; however, the last proclamation pursuant
to this proviso brought all remaining areas into the charge, and the proviso
(e) to Sec. 5(1) was accordingly repealed in 1993.

The term "land or buildings" includes piers, wharves and any other
structures which might not otherwise come within the normal understanding
of what constitutes a building and, furthermore, building includes a part of
a building. In practice, all parts of buildings which are separately rated
under the *Rating Ordinance* are separately assessed to Property Tax and,
accordingly, the single owner of a block of flats receives a number of
assessments on individual units which makes the tax administratively
cumbersome.

There are a number of provisions under which an exemption from Property
Tax is available, although the most notable is where the income from the
relevant property is earned by a corporation which is subject to Profits Tax
on that income. Details of the exemptions are contained in section 2.5.

A husband and wife are automatically separate persons for the purposes of Property Tax and receive separate assessments where they each own separately rated properties. Where, however, property is owned jointly or in common by two or more persons, a single assessment will be raised on each rateable unit, although the allocation of the tax between them may be relevant if an exemption from Property Tax is applicable.

There is a system of Provisional Property Tax assessment which is based upon the actual net assessable value for the immediately preceding year and is normally combined with the assessment for that preceding year of assessment.

A discussion of Property Tax and Provisional Property Tax is also contained in *Departmental Interpretation & Practice Notes No. 14* which is reproduced as Appendix 9.

2.3 The Charge

The charge to Property Tax is at the standard rate on the net assessable value. As explained in Chapter 1, the standard rate is 16% for the 2007/08 year of assessment.

Although "net assessable value" is based on actual rental income, the charge does not represent a true charge on the actual net income from property because only a fixed deduction is given in lieu of actual repairs, etc. It is, however, open to a qualifying individual to elect Personal Assessment to enable him to deduct mortgage interest (see Chapter 6).

2.3.1 Net assessable value

Net assessable value is the assessable value (see section 2.3.2) less certain deductions. The statutory deductions are:—

(i)   the rates where it is agreed that these are to be paid by the owner (Sec. 5(1A)(b)(i)). Where a property is available for letting but is in fact not let (i.e. it is vacant), it appears that the rates are not deductible as they are not paid by the owner under an agreement (see *D 71/02*) The term "rates" is not defined for the purpose of this provision, but is generally accepted as meaning the quarterly charge on an owner or occupier of a building levied under the *Rating Ordinance*. In *Departmental Interpretation & Practice Notes No. 14*, the IRD express the view that the Government rent payable (pursuant to the *Government Rent (Assessment and Collection) Ordinance*) after 1 July 1997 in respect of certain properties is not deductible; and

(ii)   an allowance for repairs and outgoings equal to 20% of the assessable value, after deducting any rates qualifying under (i) above (Sec. 5 (1A)(b)(ii)). This fixed percentage may be amended at any time by a resolution of the Legislative Council (Sec. 5(1B)).

These provisions for deductions are straightforward and interpreted literally. See, for example, *D 17/02* where a property owner was denied an additional deduction for management fees she was required to pay under the terms of a lease. Also, see *D 71/02* where a deduction for interest expenses was denied, although such a deduction is available to a taxpayer who elects for Personal Assessment (see Chapter 6). In the same decision, the Board of Review refused to allow a deduction for repairs in excess of the 20% statutory deduction.

■ Example 2.1

Gross rents receivable by flat owner	$240,000
Outgoings paid by owner — Rates	24,000
— Repairs	40,000

Property Tax assessment	
Assessable Value = rents due	$240,000
Less: Rates	24,000
	$216,000
Less: Statutory Deduction 20%	43,200
Net Assessable Value	$172,800
Property Tax =	$172,800 @ standard rate

2.3.2 Assessable value

Sec. 5B provides the rules for ascertaining the assessable value of land or buildings or land and buildings, for the 1983/84 and subsequent years of assessment; Sec. 5A, which has now been repealed, covered earlier years of assessment but is not discussed here.

The assessable value is the consideration payable in the year of assessment in money or money's worth in respect of the right to use the land or buildings or land and buildings (Sec. 5B(2)). The provision makes it clear that the consideration need not be paid directly to the owner to be assessable, as amounts paid to the order of, or the benefit of, the owner are also included in assessable value. See, however, *D 55/01* where an owner of a property allowed his mother to rent it out and keep the rents received for her maintenance. The Board of Review held that the taxpayer, as owner, was taxable on the rental income, although in reaching that decision the Board did not, unfortunately, explain why such rental should be considered to have been payable to, to the order of, or for the benefit of the taxpayer.

There is no exclusion from the charge to Property Tax of a capital sum; therefore, a premium or key money will be included in assessable value. Assessable value also includes any consideration payable in respect of the provision of any services or benefits in connection with the use of the property (Sec. 5B(6)). Typically included in this would be payment to cover management services and use of furniture. An amount payable which relates to a period of use covering more than one year of assessment is deemed to be payable in equal monthly instalments over the period of use or over a period of three years from the commencement of the period of use, whichever is the shorter (Sec. 5B(4)).

■ Example 2.2

Andy Munney let his flat for 4 years from 1st July 2007 for a premium of $500,000 and a monthly rent exclusive of rates of $15,000. His Property Tax liabilities are:—

2007/08

Rent — 9 months at $15,000	$135,000
Deemed rent — 9/36 × $500,000	125,000
Assessable Value	$260,000
Statutory Deduction 20%	52,000
Net Assessable Value	$208,000
Property Tax @ 16% =	$33,280

2008/09

Rent — 12 months at $15,000	$180,000
Deemed rent — 12/36 × $500,000	166,666
Assessable Value	$346,666
Statutory Deduction 20%	69,333
Net Assessable Value	$277,333
Property Tax @ 16% =	$44,373

For 2009/10 and 2010/11 he would have $166,666 and $41,668 respectively, of the premium included in the assessments.

Note:—
The premium relates to a 4-year period of use and is therefore deemed to arise over the shorter period of three years from 1st July 2007.

There are also important provisions to permit the deduction from assessable value of bad debts. Sec. 7C(1) permits deduction of any sum already included as assessable consideration which is proved to the satisfaction of the assessor to have become irrecoverable during the year of assessment (Sec. 7C(1)). Because, of course, consideration relating to more than one year may become irrecoverable in one year, Sec. 7C(3) provides that if the bad debt deduction exceeds the assessable value in the year in which it became irrecoverable, the excess can be deducted from the assessable value of the most recent previous year in which there was a positive assessable value. If the amount is subsequently recovered, it is treated as assessable consideration arising in the year of assessment in which it is recovered (Sec. 7C(2)).

■ Example 2.3

Bill Hy has been entitled to a rent of $15,000 per month for a number of years and has been so assessed for Property Tax for all years even though the tenant deferred further payments with effect from 1st October 2006 due to financial difficulties. In March 2008 the tenant was declared bankrupt with no assets available to pay Bill's rent.

Assessments would be adjusted as follows:—

2007/08

Rent payable	$180,000
Bad debt	(270,000)
Net Assessable Value	Nil

2006/07

Rent payable	$180,000
Bad debt unrelieved	(90,000)
Assessable Value	$90,000
Statutory Deduction 20%	18,000
Net Assessable Value	$72,000
Property Tax @ 16% =	$11,520

Notes:—
(a) Property Tax for 2006/07 would already have been paid because Bill would not have been able to show at the time that the debt was irrecoverable. He would therefore obtain a refund.
(b) If for some reason Bill was able to recover the $270,000 later, in say 2008/09, the assessable value would be $270,000 plus whatever rent was due in that year, less allowable deductions. It is not clear what the position would be if he did not own the property in the year in which the recovery was made.

2.4 Ownership

As the ownership of land or buildings or land and buildings is fundamental to the charge to Property Tax, it is essential to be able to determine who is the owner and the date on which ownership commences and ceases. The

IRO does not attempt to fully define ownership; rather, it contains an inclusive definition of owner in Sec. 2 which is fully reproduced as follows:—

"Owner in respect of land or buildings or land and buildings, includes a person holding directly from the Government, a beneficial owner, a tenant for life, a mortgagor, a mortgagee in possession, a person with adverse title to land receiving rent from buildings or other structures erected on that land, a person who is making payments to a co-operative society registered under the Co-operative Societies Ordinance for the purpose of the purchase thereof, and a person who holds land or buildings or land and buildings subject to a ground rent or other annual charge; and includes an executor of the estate of an owner."

It is necessary to understand two points of law before proceeding to consider the question of ownership further. First, land is subject to a Government rent where it is leased on condition that certain buildings be erected on it or that other improvements be made. Apart from some minor exceptions, all land in Hong Kong is owned by the Central People's Government and is let under Government leases for various terms. In the urban areas, some leases have been issued for 999 years, although the majority are for 75 years with a right of renewal for a further 75 years. Crown leases which expired on or before 30th June 1997, which were mainly over land in the New Territories and some non-renewable 75 year leases in the urban areas, were usually extended until 2047. Fundamentally, therefore, the Central People's Government is the true owner of virtually all land in Hong Kong but the holder of the lease from the Government falls within the definition of owner in Sec. 2 both because the definition specifically includes a person holding directly from the Government as well as a person who holds land and/or buildings subject to a ground rent. There are also persons who are permitted to occupy Government land and erect buildings thereon without the formality of a lease from the Government. These persons also fall within the definition of owner.

Second, it is a basic concept of the law of property relating to land and buildings that the owner of land also has title to all buildings erected thereon and any other person can only have an interest in the buildings as a lessee. Having regard to this, the provision for Property Tax purposes in Sec. 5(1) proviso (b) that the owner of land and the owner of buildings thereon, if different persons, are to be assessed separately seems incapable of application. In practice, however, this provision is likely intended to ensure that the individual owners of units in a multi-story building can be assessed separately from each other and from the registered owner of the land.

It is, of course, the case that the holder of the lease from the Government who, as we have seen, is the owner for Property Tax purposes, may assign all or part of his interest in the Government lease and accordingly subsequent assignees acquire ownership of the land and buildings or part thereof as appropriate. Any other person who merely takes an interest in land and buildings without taking an assignment of an interest in the Government lease is not an owner but a lessee.

Where property is purported to be held on trust for other persons it is important to establish who has interests therein and the nature of their interests in view of the inclusion of "tenant for life" and "beneficial owner" in the definition of owner in Sec. 2 of IRO. It is, therefore, always desirable to have proper documentation of the terms of a trust.

Although they may not be the registered Government lessee or the legal assignee of such a lessee, a person may nonetheless have a legal interest in land for a certain period; this can happen, for example, in the case of a squatter. Where such a person derives rental income from buildings or structures on that land, he is brought within the meaning of "owner" for Property Tax purposes through the inclusion in the statutory definition of persons with adverse title to land who derive such rental.

For a case where the incorporated owners of a building were held to be subject to Property Tax on income received from the renting out of car parking spaces, see *D 27/98*. In reaching its decision in that case, the Board of Review, relying on the terms of the *Buildings Management Ordinance*, noted that it was only the incorporated owners which had the right to let out commonly owned car parks and, therefore, they should be considered the owner. The Board also noted that although the position of the incorporated owners of a building was not specifically dealt with in the definition of "owner", that definition was inclusive only and, therefore, did not preclude such an interpretation. Nonetheless, the Board went on to note that even if the individual owners of the building were to be regarded as the owners for Property Tax purposes, as the *Buildings Management Ordinance* provides that the liabilities of owners in respect of common areas are enforceable against the incorporated owners to the exclusion of the individual owners, the Property Tax liability could still only be levied against the incorporated owners.

In view of the fact that a property can have more than one owner during a year of assessment, and that not only is the tax divisible between those owners but certain classes of owner can claim exemption from Property Tax (see section 2.5), it is essential to be able to identify the date of change of ownership. This is largely a question of fact to be determined in the circumstances from available documents. The ownership of a property can pass for this purpose even where the purchase price is paid by extended instalments and assignment is deferred until the final instalment is paid. The Sec. 2 definition of "owner" makes this clear where a person is making instalment payments to a co-operative society for the purpose of purchasing a property, by deeming that person to be the owner of the property. The position of a purchase by instalments from a property developer is, perhaps, less clear, although will ultimately depend on the precise terms of the relevant agreement. Generally, however, the date of acquisition of ownership is normally the date on which the purchase and sale agreement is concluded or when it becomes unconditional, if later.

Taxpayers may be required to produce evidence of title and change of ownership and documentation is therefore important because, although ownership is not contingent upon registration at the Land Registry, instruments in connection with the sale of land must be so registered and failure to do so can give rise to legal problems. This is particularly important in cases of "beneficial ownership" where there has been no formal conveyance of title. It would be usual, therefore, lacking any other evidence, to produce documents amounting to a purchase and sale agreement although these must be duly stamped under the *Stamp Duty Ordinance* before they can be valid as an instrument of sale (Sec. 15 *Stamp Duty Ordinance*). Note the decision in *D 7/85* where the facts were obscure as to whether a company or its director was the owner. It was held that acts undertaken by the director in respect of the property were as agent for the owner.

2.5 Exemptions and Reliefs

Various forms of exemption and relief from the charge are provided in the IRO and elsewhere and these are discussed in the following sections.

2.5.1 Governments

As a matter of practice, Property Tax is not levied where the owner of property is the Hong Kong Government. Furthermore, under the *Consular Relations Ordinance* prescribed foreign powers owning property are also exempt from the charge, but this is only applicable to property actually used for consular purposes, or as the residence of a consular employee. In practice, however, this exemption has no effect since such premises do not generate rental income and, therefore, since 1983/84 would have no assessable value.

2.5.2 Corporations and other persons carrying on business

A corporation which is carrying on a trade, profession or business in Hong Kong is normally liable to Profits Tax on its profits (see Chapter 4) and if it owns land or buildings which satisfy certain conditions, it can apply for exemption from Property Tax (Sec. 5(2)(a)). Such an application must, however, be in writing and will only be granted where the Commissioner is satisfied as to the facts of the case. Following the decision in *Harley Development Inc. & Anor. v CIR* [1993] (1 HKRC 90-069), [1994] (1 HKRC 90-071) and [1996] (1 HKRC 90-079), it is clear that it should not be assumed that an exemption has been granted unless written notification of such exemption has been received. In particular, a taxpayer should not assume an exemption has been granted simply because an application for exemption has been made, or because Profits Tax returns have been filed. Note, however, the unusual facts of that case.

A corporation is defined by Sec. 2 IRO as:—

"Any company which is either incorporated or registered under any enactment or charter in force in Hong Kong or elsewhere but does not include a co-operative society or a trade union."

The conditions for exemption under this provision are set out in proviso (a) to Sec. 25 and are that either:—

(1) the profits from the property are part of the profits of the trade, profession or business carried on by the corporation; or

(2) the corporation occupies the property for the purposes of producing profits subject to Profits Tax.

The exemption applies only whilst the relevant conditions continue to be fulfilled. In most cases, this means that the exemption will be lost if the profits from the property cease to be assessed to Profits Tax, although this would be rare in practice. It is interesting to note that in the *Harley Development* case (supra), the Commissioner argued that for the exemption to apply, the profits from the property had to be included in the owner's *assessable* profits, rather than just the *profits* of the owner's trade, profession or business as suggested by the statutory provision. Moreover, the Commissioner argued that the exemption applied only if there was actually Profits Tax payable in the year of assessment for which the exemption was sought and, therefore, would not apply if there was a loss sustained for tax purposes. These points were not, however, ruled upon by the courts as the case concerned an application for judicial review, which was rejected, and it was held that the Board of Review was the only appropriate venue to hear the substantive issue of the availability of the exemption from Property Tax.

Because of the statutory definition in Sec. 2 of the term "business" (see Chapter 4), it appears that every corporation with rental income is in a position to claim exemption from Property Tax in respect of the property from which it gains such rental income; similarly, a corporation which holds property for use in a trade or business from which assessable profits are generated can claim exemption from Property Tax. At first glance, therefore, it might be concluded that a corporation would always qualify for exemption from Property Tax. There are, however, situations where the exemption may not be available, although these arise only infrequently in practice. For example, it is well established that it is possible for a corporation to carry on a business in Hong Kong but derive only "offshore" non-taxable profits therefrom; if such a corporation owned property in Hong Kong which it used in the course of its business, it would appear not to qualify for the exemption, although there would be no assessable value in such a case. Additionally, it is possible, albeit somewhat exceptional, that a corporation may derive only capital sums from a property by, for example, granting rights to use for long periods in exchange for a lump sum. Since, unlike Profits Tax, there is no exclusion from Property Tax of capital receipts, such sums would appear to fall outside the conditions for exemption from Property Tax (assuming they were exempt from Profits Tax). For a further discussion on this point, see the *Harley Development* case referred to above.

Although the letting of property by a person other than a corporation is not deemed by Sec. 2 to be a business (unless the person is sub-letting property), such an activity may nonetheless amount to a business depending on the circumstances of a particular case. This is ultimately a question of fact to be determined by considering all of the surrounding facts and circumstances, although particularly relevant factors would include the number of properties let, whether staff are engaged to deal with the letting activities, the nature of the properties and whether additional services are rendered, and whether the activities are incidental to another business. For a discussion of cases on the question, see *Louis Kwan-nang Kwong, Carlos Kwok-nang Kwong v CIR* (2 HKTC 541), which is also discussed in section 4.3.4. Where a person other than corporation lets property in a manner which amounts to a business they will be subject to Profits Tax on the net profits. Nonetheless, such a person cannot claim an exemption from Property Tax in the same manner as a corporation because the exemption in Sec. 5(2)(a) specifically applies only to corporations. A set-off of any Property Tax paid against the person's Profits Tax liability is, however, available pursuant to Sec. 25, as is discussed below.

Although proviso (a) to Sec. 25 contains the conditions for exemption of a corporation from Property Tax, it should be noted that the main purpose of Sec. 25 is to allow Property Tax paid by a person to be set off against any Profits Tax payable by that person. It is important to note that the set-off is not merely against Profits Tax payable by the person on the profits from the property, but against any Profits Tax payable. Further, where the Property Tax paid exceeds the person's Profits Tax payable, Sec. 25 proviso (b) permits the repayment of the excess Property Tax. Although a corporation would, in practice, normally claim exemption from Property Tax, the set off procedure contained in Sec. 25 is still relevant where a corporation has not claimed the exemption or is not entitled to claim the exemption because it is only a co-owner or joint owner of property. Sec. 25 is also relevant in the case of a person other than a corporation whose property letting activities amount to a business and are, therefore, subject to Profits Tax.

■ Example 2.4

Ona Property Ltd. carries on a trade but also owns a flat which is rented out to give a net profit of $58,000 in its accounting period ended 31st December 2007. The net assessable value of the property is $60,000 on which it has paid Property Tax for 2007/08 of $9,600.

So long as it brings the rental profit of $58,000 into its Profits Tax computation it can claim exemption and this will be effective for all years for which it owns the flat and brings the rental income into its Profits Tax computation.

For 2007/08 it can either claim a refund of $9,600 under Sec. 79(1) (assuming an exemption is granted) or a set-off against its Profits Tax liability under Sec. 25.

This position is in fact unlikely to arise because a Property Tax assessment is based upon a return of rental income annually and a corporation liable to Profits Tax would normally claim exemption from Property Tax upon receipt of such a return.

Note:—

It would in fact have no option but to bring the rental income into its Profits Tax computation because this income is within the definition of business profits (see Chapter 4).

2.5.3 Clubs and trade associations

Clubs and trade associations are mutual trading bodies and are only deemed to be carrying on business and thereby subject to Profits Tax in certain specified circumstances (see Chapter 4). When subject to Profits Tax they can claim exemption from Property Tax (see section 2.5.2 above). Where, however, a club or trade association is not subject to Profits Tax, it will be, *prima facie*, subject to Property Tax although no actual charge will arise, of course, where the property is occupied by the club or trade association as its premises. This point was challenged by a club in *D 84/04* on the basis that Secs. 24 and 25 are to be read together and where Sec. 24 (see section 4.7.8) operates to render a club or trade association not chargeable to Profits Tax, an exemption from Property Tax under Sec. 25 should also be granted. In rejecting this argument, the Board of Review noted that once Sec. 24 deemed a club not to be carrying on a business (and therefore not chargeable to Profits Tax), the conditions for the exemption in Sec. 25 to apply (in particular those contained in proviso (a)) could no longer be fulfilled.

2.6 Assessment and Payment of Property Tax

The assessable value is based upon a return of actual income (see section 2.3.2). The method of assessment conforms with the system of assessing Salaries Tax and Profits Tax in that the assessment of Property Tax incorporates a system of Provisional Property Tax (Sec. 63L).

Generally, all wholly owned properties are included in an individual's composite tax return and only one assessment is issued covering all those properties. A separate Property Tax return is, however, required for each jointly owned property and each property owned by a corporation (unless an exemption has been granted).

Where there are one or more joint owners or owners in common of a property, Sec. 56A(1) renders each person whose name appears on the deed, or any other document registered in the Land Registry under the *Land Registration Ordinance,* answerable for doing anything which would be required to be done under the IRO by a sole owner. For a case concerning this provision, see *D 80/02* which involved the rental income from car parking spaces in the common areas of a housing estate where an assessment against one co-owner on behalf of all co-owners was challenged, *inter alia*, on the grounds that there was no document registered in the Land Registry which named all of the owners. This argument was rejected by the Board of Review, however, on the grounds that the Assignments under which individual owners acquired their legal interests together with the housing estate's Deed of Mutual Covenant were documents registered with the Land Registry and those documents together identified all of the co-owners. In that decision, the Board of Review also upheld the validity of assessing one co-owner on behalf of all other co-owners, and in doing so rejected the assessed owner's argument that such an assessment was too vague in that it did not identify all the individual owners (of which there were more than 1,400). An additional argument advanced that this course of action resulted in undue financial hardship to the taxpayer also failed on the basis that provided the assessment was correct in law, any financial hardship suffered by the taxpayer was not a relevant consideration.

Note that when the *Land Titles Ordinance (2004)* comes into force, Sec. 56A(1) will be extended to cover any person whose name is on the Title Register kept under the *Land Titles Ordinance*.

Where a person is assessed to and pays Property Tax in respect of a property in which he has only a part share (or, in fact, no share at all), Sec. 56A(3) gives that person a right to recover that tax (or an appropriate portion thereof) from the true owner, or each of the part owners, as the case may be.

The Provisional Property Tax assessment is made in an estimated amount and is followed, after a return has been made, by a final Property Tax assessment on the true figure in which the Provisional Property Tax already paid for the year of assessment is credited. The system is similar to Salaries Tax and Profits Tax in that a two-part assessment notice is issued comprising the final Property Tax assessment for a year of assessment and also the Provisional Property Tax assessment for the immediately succeeding year of assessment. This arrangement is specifically authorised by Sec. 63N(b) but a single Provisional Property Tax assessment is quite valid on its own (Sec. 63N(a)).

Upon acquiring a property which is let or upon commencing to let a property not previously let, the Provisional Property Tax assessment for the first year of assessment in which a liability to Property Tax arises is estimated (Sec. 63M(3)). Whilst a person becoming liable to Property Tax is obliged to bring such liability to the attention of the Commissioner it seems likely that in many, if not most, cases, due to delays in such notification and the administrative system, the first assessment will be a final assessment in true figures for the first part year and an estimated Provisional Property Tax assessment for the following year (Sec. 63M(2)). The estimate for the second year is normally, in accordance with usual practice, a precisely grossed-up equivalent of the actual part year figure for the first year. In subsequent years, the Provisional Property Tax assessment is always in the same figure as the immediately preceding final assessment (Sec. 63M(1)).

As a Provisional Property Tax assessment has to be made during the currency of the year of assessment and as it is common for tax rates and personal allowances to be fixed retrospectively, it can happen that those rates and allowances are changed after a Provisional Property Tax assessment has been issued. Sec. 63M(7) therefore provides that the assessment is not to be disturbed in this respect.

The assessor has further powers pursuant to Secs. 63M(4) & (5) to make an estimate for Provisional Property Tax purposes where:—

(a)   the taxpayer has failed to file a return by the due date;

(b)   the taxpayer is about to leave Hong Kong; or

(c)   for any other reason it is expedient to do so.

This latter provision merely mirrors the identical provision for Salaries Tax and Profits Tax but seems less relevant than the circumstances which arise in those cases.

Once assessed, the Commissioner is empowered to issue a notice of assessment and fix the due date for payment (Sec. 63M(6)). The due date for payment of the final Property Tax for a year of assessment and the Provisional Property Tax for the succeeding year of assessment is normally in November and as this is only two-thirds of the way through the financial year upon which the Provisional tax is based, there is an element of payment in advance which does not exist with Profits Tax and Salaries Tax where two instalments are used to obviate the inequity. When the final assessment for a year is raised, the Provisional Property Tax already paid for that year is credited against the final liability (Sec. 63P(a)). Any balance of final liability is added to and payable on the same date as the Provisional Property Tax for the following year. Where there is an overpayment of Provisional Property Tax, the excess is not refunded but is deducted from the Provisional Property Tax for the following year (Sec. 63P(b)). If there still remains a balance of overpayment, this is refunded. Where an excess of Provisional Property Tax over the final liability is applied against the Provisional Property Tax for the next year and an opportunity arises to hold over all or part of the Provisional Property Tax (see following paragraphs) which is frustrated by the fact that it is already paid by the overpayment set-off, it is the IRD's practice to refund the amount that would otherwise have been held over.

Because of the estimated nature of Provisional Property Tax, there are provisions to enable collection of the tax to be wholly or partly held over in appropriate circumstances. Given the appropriate grounds, the taxpayer must apply in writing not later than 28 days before the due date for payment, or not later than 14 days after the date of the notice for payment, whichever is later (Sec. 63O(1)).

The appropriate grounds in Sec. 63O(2) are:—

(1)   where the assessable value for the current year is, or is likely to be,

less than 90% of the assessable value of the immediately preceding year (upon which the Provisional Property Tax assessment will normally have been based) or of the estimated assessable value upon which the Provisional Property Tax assessment has been based. Note that this test is based on the assessable value, not on the amount of the assessment which is of course on the net assessable value. This difference is significant if rates are deductible in arriving at net assessable value;

(2) where the person assessed has ceased, or will cease before the end of the current year of assessment, to own the property as a result of which the assessable value for the current year of assessment is, or is likely to be, less than the assessable value upon which the Provisional Property Tax assessment has been based. Again, as in (1), note that the test is based on assessable value and not net assessable value;

(3) where the person assessed has elected for Personal Assessment (see Chapter 6) and this is likely to reduce his liability for the year of assessment; or

(4) where the final assessment for the preceding year (upon which the Provisional Property Tax assessment is of course based) is under objection (see Chapter 9). This is, of course, an opportunity to hold over an equivalent amount of tax on the final assessment as well.

Any holdover is entirely at the discretion of the Commissioner (Sec. 63O (3)) but, in practice, where the rules for application have been complied with and the grounds satisfied, the holdover will be given in all but exceptional cases. The holdover does not automatically apply to the whole of the Provisional Property Tax, only to the part which is shown to be affected by the grounds cited. The Commissioner must in all cases notify his decision in writing (Sec. 63O(4)) which he does on a standard form.

Where the holdover is granted, it will be effective until the final liability for the year of assessment is ascertained and due for payment but in the case of ground (4) above, if the objection against the previous year's assessment is determined or settled earlier, the earlier date will apply (Sec. 63O(1)).

For an illustration of the above, see Examples 3.20 and 4.51, where similar principles apply.

2.7 Time Limits and Objections

When an assessment is made, unless a valid objection is submitted within the appropriate time limit, it becomes final and conclusive in accordance with the rules applicable to all assessments under the IRO and such assessments can only be re-opened in prescribed circumstances (see Chapters 8 and 9).

Chapter 3 ■
Salaries Tax

> **NOTE**
>
> In the 2007/08 Budget, the Financial Secretary proposed a one-off measure under which there would be a waiver of 50% of the Salaries Tax assessed or tax assessed under Personal Assessment for each taxpayer for the 2006/07 year of assessment, subject to a ceiling of $15,000. Legislation giving effect to this waiver has been enacted. Although this edition of the book is concerned primarily with the 2007/08 year of assessment, some of the illustrative examples also refer to tax assessed for the 2006/07 year of assessment. In the interests of simplicity, however, these examples have ignored the effect of the above waiver of tax.

3.1 Legislation

The law governing Salaries Tax is primarily contained in Part III of the IRO, Secs. 8 to 13. Also relevant is the Second Schedule to the IRO which covers the progressive rates of tax, Part IVA and Schedules 3A, 3C and 3D which deal with certain concessionary deductions, Part V and Schedule 4 which set out personal allowances, Part VI concerning depreciation allowances and Part XA which covers Provisional Salaries Tax. Additionally, the general provisions covering double taxation relief in Part VIII, returns in Part IX, assessments in Part X, objections and appeals in Part XI and payment and recovery of tax in Part XII are applicable to Salaries Tax.

3.2 Scope of the Tax

Salaries Tax is imposed upon income which arises in or is derived from Hong Kong from any office or employment of profit and from pensions (Sec. 8(1)).

Ascertainment of the source of employment income depends upon a number of factors and the IRO gives no guidance other than providing that earnings from services rendered in Hong Kong are to be included (Sec. 8 (1A)(a)) and certain other sums are to be excluded.

An examination of what is included in assessable remuneration involves a study of relevant case law, which is discussed in section 3.4.2. Additionally, however, the IRO contains various specific provisions which deem certain amounts to either be included in, or excluded from, assessable income and these are discussed in sections 3.4.1 and 3.4.6 respectively.

The IRO substantially codifies what is a taxable "perquisite", embodying in the law the principles which were generally understood to apply from UK case law prior to a controversial decision of the Privy Council in *CIR v David Hardy Glynn* (3 HKTC 245). Nevertheless, reference to case law is still necessary for deciding what constitutes assessable remuneration. This is further discussed under section 3.4.2 and section 3.4.5.

Tax is levied for a year of assessment on the actual income accruing and payable in that year of assessment, although it cannot be assessed until it is actually received (Secs. 11B and 11D).

A husband and wife are treated for Salaries Tax purposes as separate single individuals, although there are provisions for an election for joint assessment in specified circumstances.

Secs. 12B and 13 provide that Salaries Tax payable is based upon the lesser of two basic alternatives. In particular, unlike Profits Tax and Property Tax which are automatically charged at the standard rate with personal allowances only being available to those who elect for Personal Assessment, the Salaries Tax charging provisions automatically include deductions for personal allowances where this is beneficial.

The tax chargeable is therefore the lesser of:—

(1) assessable income less various deductions under Secs. 12, 12A, 26C, 26D, 26E and 26G and personal allowances (see Chapter 6), charged at progressive rates of tax; and

(2) the same net income, but before deducting personal allowances, charged at the standard rate.

Alternative (1) applies at lower income levels and is automatically applied by the IRD where beneficial.

Salaries Tax is collected by direct assessment based on a return made at the end of the year of assessment and there is a system of Provisional Salaries Tax for the current year of assessment which is normally based on the previous year's agreed assessment and is combined with the final assessment for the immediately preceding year of assessment. Provisional Salaries Tax is normally payable in two instalments.

3.3 Source of the Income

3.3.1 General

Salaries Tax is generally chargeable on employment, office or pension income which arises in or is derived from Hong Kong (Sec. 8(1)). The IRO defines certain circumstances where income is to be treated as arising in Hong Kong and also circumstances where it is not to be so treated. It is, however, usually necessary to first establish whether the location of an employment is or is not in Hong Kong and the IRO gives no guidance in this regard. The source of directors' fees and pensions involve different principles from the source of employment income and are dealt with separately in sections 3.3.3 and 3.3.4 respectively. The tests for seafarers and aircrew are separately prescribed by the IRO and are dealt with in section 3.3.5.

Although this chapter predominantly examines the terms of the IRO, it is important to remember that these provisions may be over-ridden by the terms of a comprehensive double tax agreement, or a more limited shipping or air services agreement. Accordingly, such an agreement may provide an exemption where a liability to Salaries Tax would otherwise arise, as is discussed further in section 3.8.4.

A flowchart providing a diagrammatic analysis of liability to Salaries Tax is contained in Figure 3.1 below.

3.3.2 Employment Income

The question of source of employment income was particularly contentious for many years and during that time there were numerous Board of Review decisions on the subject. These produced, in total, a somewhat confusing collection of principles, in many cases conflicting with or adding to earlier decisions, but all pointing to the review of an increasing series of factors; this approach became known as the "totality of facts" test. All of these tests, however, ignored the place where work was performed. The IRD attempted to codify the totality of facts tests into six basic tests but further Board of Review decisions and the IRD's own stated position in some cases varied from the six tests. This, coupled with the fact that the six tests were invariably difficult to balance where all tests were not satisfied, led to considerable disputes which culminated in the case of *CIR v George Andrew Goepfert* (2 HKTC 210) from which some rules emerged.

The above confusion arose partly from how far the decisions of courts in other Commonwealth countries in relation to source of employment income should apply and whether the determination of source should focus on work done to earn the income (the Australian tests) or on where the employment itself is to be found (the UK tests). The *Goepfert* case came down on the side of the UK tests and specifically ruled that the place where the services were rendered was not a relevant consideration in determining the source of employment income. Accordingly, whilst the source of business or trading income subject to Profits Tax is determined according to the source of the

Figure 3.1 Determining chargeability of income to Salaries Tax

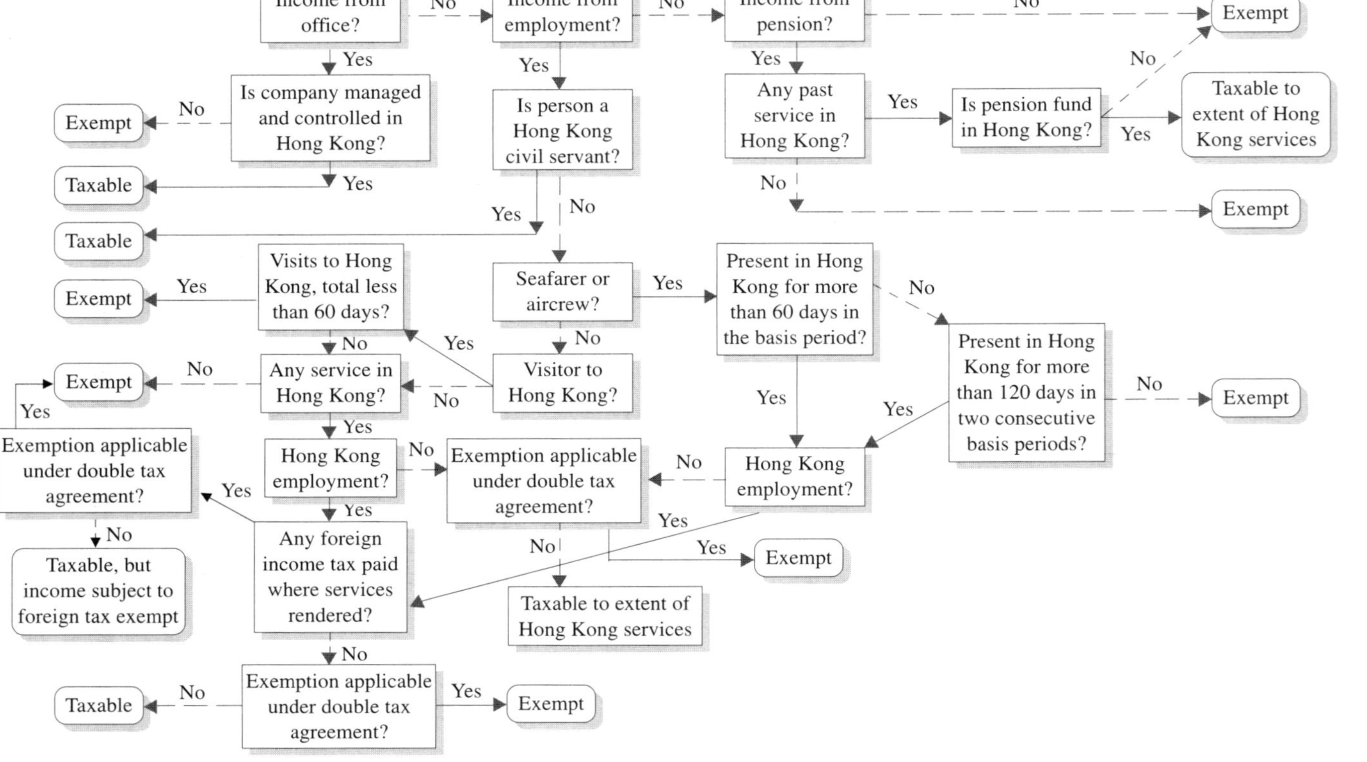

Note: This is intended to be a diagrammatic guide only and must be considered in conjunction with the text.

income rather than the location of the trade or business (case law and statute clearly pointing to the fact that they are quite separate questions), this is not so in relation to Salaries Tax where the *Goepfert* case has decided that it is the location of the employment which is relevant in the first instance in determining the source of the income therefrom; however, as discussed more fully below, income from a non-Hong Kong employment is deemed to have a Hong Kong source in certain circumstances.

The *Goepfert* case was, as noted above, decided on the basis of UK cases and recognised that in the first instance it was the contract of employment which must be examined to determine the location of an employment, although the court did not specifically state which elements of the contract were determinative. The court did, however, recognise that the contract itself might not always reflect the substance of an arrangement and endorsed the adoption of a "totality of facts" test to ascertain the location of an employment. That is, the court held that all relevant facts and circumstances should be examined because although the contract is generally the most important factor, a superficial examination of it may not always correctly point to the real location of the employment.

Following the decision in the *Goepfert* case, the IRD revised *Departmental Interpretation & Practice Notes No. 10* to state that generally there are three prime tests to determine the location of an employment, namely:–

(1)   the place where the contract of employment was negotiated and entered into and is enforceable;

(2)   the place of residence of the employer; and

(3)   the place of payment of the remuneration.

It was implied in that document that the *Goepfert* decision was authority for these three basic tests. The correctness of this, however, was doubtful as was pointed out by the Board of Review on at least two occasions (see *D 40/90* and *D 59/03*). Rather, the court in *Goepfert* appeared to merely endorse a broad "totality of facts" test (although the place where the services were rendered was held to be one factor which was to be ignored). The three tests adopted by the IRD appear to be derived from a quote from the earlier UK decision of *Bray v Colenbrander* (34 TC 73) which was reproduced in the *Goepfert* judgement; however, to suggest that these were the tests upon which *Goepfert* was decided would seem to involve taking that quote out of appropriate context.

Possibly as a result of the questionable technical basis adopted, the IRD revised *Departmental Interpretation & Practice Notes No. 10* in June 2007 and this is reproduced as Appendix 7. In the revised version of the document, the IRD appears to accept that a broader approach is required in determining the location of an employment. Nonetheless, the IRD have retained the view that particular emphasis is to be placed on the three tests identified above, although the revised document contains much more guidance on the IRD's views as to the determination of where a contract was negotiated and concluded and where an employer is resident. Controversially, however, the IRD also indicate that in determining the true identity of an individual's employer, they will look at representations made by a company to obtain entry of the individual to Hong Kong. In other words, if a company sponsors an individual for the purpose of obtaining a work permit, the IRD has advised of its intention to examine the relationship between that company and the individual to see whether this is evidence of an employer-employee relationship notwithstanding the existence of a contract of employment with a different group entity. Whilst it is undoubtedly appropriate for the IRD to examine all factors to determine the true nature of an employee-employer relationship, singling out one factor such as the person's sponsor for immigration purposes is of concern because it implies a greater degree of relevance to the question than is accorded to it by legislation or case law. (Note that although this factor has been considered relevant, but not on its own determinative, in at least one Board of Review decision (see *D 35/05*), this does not suggest that as a matter of law undue weight should be given to the factor.) Moreover, because such a factor is easily identified, there is a risk that in practice it will be looked to more frequently than it should be in deciding cases which otherwise would be decided by a proper examination of subjective factors and this is of particular concern because a sponsor for immigration purposes is inevitably a company carrying on business in Hong Kong, but may not be the true employer; indeed, this point is recognised by the IRD in Example 1 in the Appendix to the current version of *Departmental Interpretation & Practice Notes No. 10*.

Notwithstanding the questionable authority for placing greatest emphasis on the three prime tests identified above, the IRD's approach does serve to provide some practical guidance and a degree of certainty to taxpayers faced with the often difficult question of source of employment income. As noted, however, the IRD does recognise the appropriateness of looking to other factors in certain circumstances, particularly where the external or superficial features of an employment contract do not reveal the true nature of the employment relationship. Again, this is justified by the "totality of facts" approach adopted in the *Goepfert* case. In *Departmental Interpretation & Practice Notes No. 10* the IRD states that they will be particularly concerned with situations where an individual ceases to be employed by a Hong Kong resident and commences to be employed by a related non-resident, or where a locally engaged person claims to have a contract with an employer resident abroad. Undoubtedly, however, there will continue to be many other situations where the IRD will seek to look to broader factors, with one example being where a person claims to have an offshore employment but has a material attachment (i.e. a key role within) a Hong Kong resident company. For a Board of Review decision which looked to such broader factors to conclude that an employment was with a Hong Kong company notwithstanding the contract of employment was concluded with an offshore company, see *D 35/05*. In that decision, the Board of Review looked to the employee's registration with the Securities and Futures Commission, his representations to the Immigration Department and his title as shown on his business card to conclude that he was in substance employed by a Hong Kong company.

The application of the tests for determining the location of an employment are illustrated by the examples in the Appendix to *Departmental Interpretation & Practice Notes No. 10,* and also in the following examples.

■ Example 3.1

Wong Man is to be employed as General Manager of a Hong Kong company and this will involve some travelling on behalf of the company outside Hong Kong. However, it is arranged that his employment contract is with the US parent company and his contract of employment is concluded in and subject to the laws of the USA. He is also to be paid in US dollars into a bank account in New York. The US parent will recover the cost within the management charge which it makes to the Hong Kong subsidiary. Whilst Wong Man satisfies all three of the tests because his legal employer is the US company, clearly the reality of the situation is that his employment is with the Hong Kong company and his remuneration would, therefore, be considered to have a Hong Kong source.

Looking to a broader range of factors than the three prime tests as occurred in Example 3.1 is, however, something requiring care and common sense as is illustrated in Example 3.2 where circumstances are deliberately similar to those in the previous example.

■ Example 3.2

Hiram Offen is recruited in the USA by a US company to represent their interests in South East Asia for which he will be required to locate to Hong Kong and work in the offices of the Hong Kong subsidiary. He will be paid in US dollars by the company in the USA and his duties will require him to represent the interests of the US company in all the South East Asian countries where it has subsidiaries, reporting to the US company in respect of his visits to each country. While in Hong Kong he will act as General Manager of the Hong Kong subsidiary. The US company will recover the cost by management charges to the subsidiaries upon which he reports.

In this case, the foreign contact is clearly genuine and the fact that, amongst his duties, Hiram is General Manager of the Hong Kong subsidiary should not be enough to justify the IRD looking beyond the three prime tests.

There will, of course, be circumstances where not all of the three prime tests adopted by the IRD will point to an employment outside Hong Kong. Of the three tests, the place of payment of the remuneration will undoubtedly carry the least weight. Indeed, in *Departmental Interpretation & Practice Notes No. 10* the IRD confirms that the payment of remuneration outside Hong Kong will not by itself be a determinative factor in ascertaining the location of an employment; logically, the converse should also hold true with the payment of remuneration in Hong Kong not being, by itself, determinative of a Hong Kong employment. The other two factors will carry more weight, but where they point to different conclusions further examination of them may be appropriate to determine the substance of the arrangement. For example, there may be exceptional circumstances where it is clear that in substance an employment is with a non-resident company but because of special circumstances the contract was concluded with a Hong Kong resident company. Similarly, there may be cases where in substance a contract was negotiated abroad but was, as a matter of convenience ultimately signed in Hong Kong and made subject to Hong Kong law. Clearly, in view of the fact that ultimately a totality of facts approach is required, the substance rather than the form of the arrangement should be determinative. The appropriateness of this has effectively been confirmed in some of the cases discussed below.

Where there is an unclear distinction between a Hong Kong appointment and responsibilities to an overseas employer, separate contracts of employment covering the Hong Kong employment (the income from which would have a Hong Kong source) and the foreign employment (the income from which would have a non-Hong Kong source and, therefore, would be non-taxable to the extent that the services were rendered outside Hong Kong) may be desirable for clarification. In other words, the duties would be performed under two distinct employments, one being a Hong Kong employment and the other being an offshore employment. Although such arrangements may be quite legitimate, the IRD will often examine them to determine whether in fact there is a single employment (either in Hong Kong or elsewhere), but with the remuneration paid under two contracts. For two employments to exist, there would generally need to be two distinct sets of duties or responsibilities which were dealt with under the two contracts. For a case where it was held that two contracts were in respect of a single Hong Kong employment, see *D 67/01*. This decision highlights the potential pitfalls of dual contract arrangements, and emphasises that the tax effectiveness of any such arrangement will depend on the substance, rather than the form, of the arrangement. In particular, the decision makes it clear that establishing an offshore company predominantly for the purpose of implementing such an arrangement is unlikely to be effective in establishing that two separate employments exist.

Conversely, however, see *D 146/98* where an employment was held to be offshore notwithstanding that a contract was entered into with a Hong Kong company, that such contract was at least partly negotiated in Hong Kong and that the employee was mainly paid by the Hong Kong company in Hong Kong. This conclusion was reached on the basis that the individual had a single employment with a joint venture in the Mainland of China (with which he had a separate employment contract), but had entered into the contract with the Hong Kong company merely to permit him to have a paymaster outside the Mainland. The Board of Review accepted that the employee performed no separate duties for the Hong Kong company and, because he had a single non-Hong Kong employment, was taxable only in respect of services rendered in Hong Kong (see section 3.3.2.1 below). The same conclusion was reached in the later case of *D 76/00* despite the fact that both contracts were negotiated and concluded in Hong Kong, one being with a Hong Kong company, and the payments in respect of the contract with the Hong Kong company were paid into a bank account in Hong Kong.

The above cases should, however, be contrasted with *D 146/01* where an individual claimed that he had entered into an employment contract with a Hong Kong company only for immigration purposes (i.e. to facilitate the obtaining of a Hong Kong work permit). The taxpayer argued that notwithstanding the contract with the Hong Kong company, he should be considered to have a non-Hong Kong employment on the basis that he had regional responsibilities, he had not severed his links with an overseas company in the group, that he reported to management in London and that his costs were charged back to regional subsidiaries. In rejecting his claim, the Board of Review appeared to look no further than the fact that the individual had entered into a contract with the Hong Kong company, in respect of a post based in Hong Kong and that he was paid by that company in Hong Kong. This conclusion was essentially based strictly on the three prime tests adopted by the IRD and can probably be distinguished from the foregoing cases on the basis of the much closer connection of the individual to the employer group's Hong Kong business.

Having ascertained the location of an employment it is then possible to review the manner and the extent to which income therefrom is within the scope of Salaries Tax. The two alternative situations are considered below.

3.3.2.1 Non-Hong Kong employment

Where the employment is outside Hong Kong, only remuneration for services rendered in Hong Kong, including leave pay attributable to such services, is within the scope of Salaries Tax (Sec. 8(1A)(a)).

If, however, an individual only renders services in Hong Kong during visits which in aggregate amount to no more than sixty days in a year of assessment (other than where the individual is a Government employee, or a seafarer or aircrew to which the special rules which are discussed in section 3.3.5 apply), Sec. 8(1B) provides that such services are to be ignored for Salaries Tax purposes with the individual being treated as having rendered all services abroad and, therefore, exempt from Salaries Tax under Sec. 8 (1A)(b). To qualify for this exemption, which is commonly referred to as the "sixty-day" rule, it has traditionally been considered (see, for example, *D 11/84* and *D 29/89*) that the employee must be a visitor to Hong Kong; that is, he must not have some form of permanent base in Hong Kong and merely spend most of his time travelling abroad. In *D 54/97*, however, the Board of Review suggested that this interpretation of the word "visit" was perhaps too narrow, implying that a person could possibly be a visitor to Hong Kong even if that person's normal place of residence was Hong Kong. Nonetheless, although raising the issue, the Board chose not to rule on it on the basis that it was not crucial to their findings in the particular case.

It is visits for any purpose which are aggregated in applying the sixty-day rule, not merely days in Hong Kong on which duties are performed. For example, if an individual visits Hong Kong for a total of seventy days in a year of assessment but performs duties on only forty of those days, the exemption will not be available (see *CIR v So Chak Kwong, Jack* (2 HKTC 174)).

In calculating the aggregate number of days of visits to Hong Kong, the Board of Review held in *D 29/89* and *D 12/94* that both the day of arrival and the day of departure are to be counted. The logic of this approach was effectively questioned in *D 47/97* where the Board of Review noted that such practice could lead "... *to the absurd result in some cases of more than 365 days in a year*". Sympathy with those sentiments was again expressed in the later case of *D 37/01*. The correctness of the practice was also raised in *D 54/97* where, referring to Sec. 71(1) of the *Interpretation and General Clauses Ordinance*, the Board of Review noted that it is arguable that the day of arrival should be ignored when counting days for the purpose of the rule. Nonetheless, as the issue was not critical to the outcome of the case before it, the Board again chose not to rule on this point. In *D 20/00*, however, the Board of Review rejected this view and confirmed that any day during which at any time the taxpayer was in Hong Kong is to be counted as a day for the purposes of Sec. 8(1B). In reaching this conclusion, the Board of Review rejected the suggestion, based on UK authority, that a "day" should be considered to be a period of twenty four hours with the result that the taxpayer's total hours in Hong Kong should be aggregated and divided by twenty four to determine the number of days he was in Hong Kong. Nonetheless, despite this clear guidance, the Board of Review in *D 76/04* again questioned the correctness of this traditional interpretation and, in particular, queried whether when a person transits through Hong Kong for a few hours this should be considered a "visit" for the purpose of Sec. 8(1B). Although the Board of Review's comments were only *obiter dicta*, they do indicate a possible willingness to apply a less strict interpretation of the provision than is generally adopted by the IRD.

In *D 31/03* the Board of Review had cause to consider the situation where an individual's employment existed for only a part of a year of assessment and, in particular, whether when applying the "sixty-day" rule to such an employment it was relevant to count all days on which the individual was present in Hong Kong during the year of assessment or only the days he was present in Hong Kong during the period of employment. The Board of Review noted that the history of the provision did not provide a clear answer to this question, but considered that the better view was that it was days during the whole of the year of assessment which should be counted.

As noted above, where an individual has a non-Hong Kong employment but is either based in Hong Kong or visits Hong Kong for more than sixty days in a year of assessment, he is subject to Salaries Tax on remuneration for duties rendered in Hong Kong. The quantum of such income is, in practice, usually determined on a simple time apportionment basis having regard to the number of days in the year of assessment spent in Hong Kong plus leave days attributable to such Hong Kong service; this apportionment method is commonly referred to as the "time in time out" basis. It was, however, suggested in *D 106/89* that this basis is only appropriate where the apportionment cannot be carried out with reference to where the duties were actually rendered. Indeed, an example of this can be found in *D 146/98* where the Board of Review accepted that an individual rendered services in Hong Kong on only one day, notwithstanding the fact that he was present in Hong Kong for more than sixty days during the period of the employment in the relevant year of assessment. As such, it was held that the individual was taxable only on the income attributable to that one day's service.

Similarly, in *D 53/96* it was suggested, somewhat interestingly, that the application of the "time in time out" basis may be precluded by the relevant employment contract. Presumably what the Board of Review had in mind in making this comment was the possibility that the employment contract itself may apportion the total remuneration between services rendered in Hong Kong and services rendered abroad.

Although the "time in time out" basis of determining the amount of income attributable to services rendered in Hong Kong may be appropriate only in the absence of a more definitive basis, it is nonetheless adopted in the majority of cases and a taxpayer would generally need to adduce strong and convincing evidence in support of another basis. In this regard, see *D 28/04* where an apparently arbitrary proposal by a taxpayer was rejected in favour of the "time in time out" basis.

Although income will generally be apportioned on a "time in time out" basis, an exception may apply in the case of income in the form of a reimbursement by the employer of the employee's personal tax liability. In particular, in *D 31/85* and *D 106/89*, the reimbursement of an employee's Salaries Tax liability was held to be fully taxable, notwithstanding that the remainder of the employee's income was apportioned on a "time in time out" basis, on the grounds that such tax reimbursement related to duties in Hong Kong as it was such duties which gave rise to the reimbursed liability. Although there are no reported decisions on the point, it would appear that the principle would also apply in reverse; that is, that no part of a reimbursement of a foreign tax liability should be taxable where that tax liability arose from duties rendered abroad and the income from those duties was exempt from Salaries Tax through the application of "time in time out" apportionment. The principle would not, however, extend to a reimbursement of foreign tax on income earned for services rendered in Hong Kong, which is a situation which may arise where a person is a resident of another country and, as such, is taxed on his world-wide income. In this regard, see *D 1/90* where the reimbursement of an employee's US tax liability was held to be taxable.

Where income is apportioned under the "time in time out" basis, only one of the day of arrival and day of departure are, as a matter of practice, counted as days in Hong Kong. This is to be contrasted with the position under the "sixty-day" rule where both days are counted. Where a person departs from, and arrives in, Hong Kong on the same day, it appears to be the practice of the IRD to treat the person as having rendered services in Hong Kong for half of that day for the purpose of the apportionment. This was, however, criticised by the Board of Review in *D 6/06* where they remitted the matter back to the IRD to reconsider whether this was fair when a taxpayer had spent the entire business day in the Mainland of China. In the same case, the Board questioned the attribution of half a day's service to Hong Kong on days when the taxpayer departed from or arrived back in Hong Kong in connection with a more extended business trip.

The above principles are illustrated in the following examples.

■ Example 3.3

Tanya Hide was recruited in the USA by a US company and has been located in the company's South East Asian regional office in Hong Kong and paid in US dollars into her New York bank account. The Assessor has accepted that the location of her employment is therefore outside Hong Kong.

During the year of assessment she spent 84 days outside Hong Kong of which 21 days were holiday (being her entire holiday entitlement). The Hong Kong dollar equivalent of her emoluments for the year was $425,000.

Only the remuneration applicable to duties performed in Hong Kong is subject to Salaries Tax (Sec. 8(1A)(a)).

There is no statutory method of calculating this portion but, in practice, a simple time apportionment is adopted as follows:—

No. of Days in the year		365	
No. of Days outside HK on leave		21	
No. of Days outside HK on business		63	(84 − 21)
No. of Days inside HK		281	(365 − 84)
No. of Business Days in the year		344	(365 − 21)
Days attributable to HK duties		=	281
Leave days attributable to HK duties	$\dfrac{281}{344} \times 21$	=	17
Total days attributable to HK duties			298
Remuneration liable to Salaries Tax	$\dfrac{298}{365} \times \$425,000$	=	$346,986

Notes:—
(a) Weekends falling during the period of leave are treated as leave days and other weekends are treated as business days.
(b) There is no statutory method of calculation but this formula is accepted by the IRD.

(c) Where employment subject to time apportionment commences or finishes during the year, the number of days in the year, number of days in HK and number of business days in the year are reduced accordingly.

■ Example 3.4

Herr Kutt is a German national living in Germany and employed and paid in Euros by a German company. The assessor is satisfied that the location of his employment is outside Hong Kong. He is required, however, to make regular business trips to Hong Kong to confer with his Company's suppliers. During year of assessment 1, he was present in Hong Kong for a total of 53 days and performed duties on every day and during year 2 he made four trips to, and was present in, Hong Kong for an aggregate of 70 days of which 50 were for performing duties. His annual earnings from the employment are E88,000. His Salaries Tax position is:—

Year 1

He is exempt under the rule treating visits of not more than 60 days as if they represented services performed outside Hong Kong (Sec. 8(1B)). See Note (a) below.

Year 2

He is liable on remuneration for services performed in Hong Kong (Sec. 8(1A)(a)) and this is normally ascertained on a time basis.

Income for Salaries Tax purposes $\dfrac{66}{365} \times$ E88,000 = $\underline{\underline{\text{E15,912}}}$ (Note (c))

This is then converted to HK\$ at average rate of exchange for the year.

Notes:—
(a) If he established Hong Kong as his base and made his home there, he may not be classed as a visitor in which case he would be taxable on the relevant portion of his earnings even though he was present in Hong Kong for less than 60 days.
(b) Note that whilst his actual business days in year 2 are less than in year 1, it is the total visits, for whatever purpose, that are taken into account.
(c) Even though all visits are taken into account for purposes of the application of the sixty-day rule, it is probably more correct, in making the apportionment, to divide non-business days between duties in Hong Kong and duties outside Hong Kong as in Example 3.3. Also, note that in the numerator of the apportionment formula, 66, rather than 70, days has been used. This is because, unlike when counting days for the purpose of the sixty-day rule, only one of the day of arrival and day of departure in respect of each trip are counted for the purpose of apportionment. Accordingly, as he made four trips, only 66 days will be counted for apportionment purposes.

3.3.2.2 Hong Kong employment

Where an employment is located in Hong Kong, all remuneration for services under that employment, wherever rendered, is within the scope of Salaries Tax. One consequence of this is that if an individual who has a Hong Kong employment moves between Hong Kong and another country during a year of assessment without commencing a new employment, all of his remuneration for the year of assessment in which the move takes place will (subject to Sec. 8(1A)(c) which is discussed below) be chargeable to Salaries Tax. This is because the individual has a single Hong Kong employment under which part of the duties for the year of assessment were performed in Hong Kong, and apportionment on a time basis as discussed in section 3.3.2.1 above is not available (see *D 7/82, D 50/89* and *D 67/89*). See also *D 43/94, D 29/95* and *D 40/97* where the Board of Review decided that the taxpayer had only a single Hong Kong employment even though he had entered into a new employment contract with that employer when he was required to move to another country. See particularly *D 29/95* where the Board of Review reiterated that Salaries Tax is charged on income arising in or derived from Hong Kong from an employment, not a "contract of employment". Further, see *D 40/95* where income earned during study leave granted by a Hong Kong employer but taken overseas was taxable because it was attributable to services rendered in Hong Kong under a Hong Kong employment.

Where a person is seconded to work for another organisation, the employment would generally still be regarded as being with the original employer (see *Lee Hung Kwong v CIR* [2005] (1 HKRC 90-151)), although the question will presumably depend on the exact terms of the secondment in each particular case.

Even where income is derived from a Hong Kong employment, there are a number of provisions under which relief or exemption from Salaries Tax is granted and these are discussed below.

Sec. 8(1A)(b) provides that (notwithstanding the existence of a Hong Kong employment) remuneration is exempt from Salaries Tax where all services are rendered outside Hong Kong, other than in the case of Government employees, seafarers and aircrew where special rules apply (see section 3.3.5). In determining whether all services are rendered outside Hong Kong, the sixty-day rule discussed in section 3.3.2.1 above applies; that is, services rendered during visits of up to sixty days will be ignored for the purpose of the test. In practice, however, the exemption under the sixty-day rule is less likely to be available in the case of a Hong Kong employment than in the case of a non-Hong Kong employment; this is because, in the former case, an employee is more likely to have a base in Hong Kong, even if he spends most of his working days outside Hong Kong, which has traditionally precluded a claim for exemption under the rule (although the correctness of this was questioned in *D 54/97*).

Where the sixty-day rule does not apply, it is still possible to claim exemption from Salaries Tax under Sec. 8(1A)(b) if all services are rendered abroad. This test is, however, interpreted strictly in practice and it is usually not sufficient merely to demonstrate that the most important aspects of the employment are rendered abroad or that only incidental or minor duties are undertaken in Hong Kong. Rather, it seems that if any duties at all are rendered in Hong Kong in the relevant year of assessment, the exemption will be lost. In this regard, see *D 79/96, D 11/97, D 130/99, D 35/02* and *D 2/06*. A particularly strict interpretation was also applied in *D 54/97* where communicating by telephone from Hong Kong with the overseas factory in which the taxpayer was employed was considered to amount to the rendering of services in Hong Kong. Nonetheless, compare that decision with *D 129/ 98* where the Board of Review found that the bringing by the taxpayer of cheques and clothes samples from the factory in the Mainland of China where he worked, to his employer's office in Hong Kong, were purely gratuitous and could be ignored when considering the application of Sec. 8(1A)(b). See also *D 27/03* where the occasional purchase of spare parts by an employee while in Hong Kong was considered outside the scope of work of the employee and done for convenience only and, therefore, could be disregarded when considering whether all services were rendered abroad. Like all cases, however, these were decided on their particular facts and it would be dangerous to attempt to rely on them to draw broader inferences as to the scope of services in Hong Kong which can be disregarded; this is illustrated by the decision in *D 25/02* where a taxpayer's argument that services of an administrative nature should be disregarded was rejected with the Board of Review noting that administrative duties should not be considered any differently to any other duties for the purpose of Sec. 8(1A)(b).

Although no proportionate exemption on a time basis is available for remuneration for services rendered outside Hong Kong under a Hong Kong employment (as is available where the employment is outside Hong Kong), an exemption is granted in respect of such remuneration where it has been subject to tax of a substantially similar nature to Salaries Tax in the territory where the relevant services were rendered (Sec. 8(1A)(c)). The rules for this exemption are, however, strict and it is necessary not only that the income in question be subject to tax in the other territory but also that the tax has actually been paid. More specifically, it seems that a liability in the other territory is insufficient to qualify the individual for the exemption if that liability is covered by reliefs which result in no net tax actually being payable; see, however, *D 56/91* where the exemption was held to be available in respect of a "hardship" allowance for working in the People's Republic of

China (PRC) even though not all of the allowance had been subject to PRC tax.

As noted, the exemption under Sec. 8(1A)(c) applies only in respect of remuneration for services rendered in the other territory and subject to tax in that territory. Accordingly, the fact that income is taxed in the other territory is not, by itself, sufficient to qualify for the exemption if the income is for services rendered elsewhere. In this regard, see *D 17/04* where an exemption was held not to be available in respect of all of the income subject to tax in the Mainland of China as it was held that some of the income taxed in the Mainland was in respect of services rendered in Hong Kong; accordingly, the exemption was limited to that portion of the income taxed in the Mainland which was attributable to services rendered in the Mainland.

■ Example 3.5

Will Travill is a United States citizen employed by a Hong Kong company and his duties regularly take him to the Mainland of China. During the year of assessment he earned remuneration of $460,000 but due to the amount of time spent in the Mainland he had to report $100,000 to the Mainland tax authorities as earnings related to the time spent working there and he paid tax of $15,000 thereon. Will also spent one month working in the USA and, as a US citizen, reported $40,000 as US source earnings in his US Federal tax return. He did not however pay any US Federal tax because of exemptions and tax shelters.

When reporting income for Salaries Tax he reports $360,000 and seeks exemption for the $100,000 on which he paid tax in the Mainland. He would have to produce the assessment and receipt for the Mainland tax paid. He cannot claim exemption in respect of the $40,000 for duties performed in the USA because he did not actually pay any US tax thereon.

Where there is a delay in assessment and payment of the overseas tax, the Commissioner will assess the full earnings but will permit a holdover of the tax relating to the part earned overseas until such time as the overseas tax has been paid and a receipt can be produced, at which time the relevant portion of the Salaries Tax liability will be cancelled (see paragraph 17 et seq. of *Departmental Interpretation & Practice Notes No. 10*, which is reproduced as Appendix 7).

■ Example 3.6

Larry Lam was recruited in Hong Kong by a Hong Kong company and therefore accepts that the location of his employment is in Hong Kong. He is, however, now the company's representative in London where he has made his home. He visits Head Office in Hong Kong at regular intervals to report and participate in management meetings. During year of assessment 1 he visited Hong Kong for a total of 53 days and during year 2 his visits totalled 70 days. His annual earnings from the employment are £52,000. His Salaries Tax position is:—

Year 1

As a bona fide visitor he is exempt under the rule treating visits of not more than 60 days as if they represented services performed outside Hong Kong (Sec. 8(1B)). See Note (a) below.

Year 2

Because the location of his employment is in Hong Kong, there is no question of limiting his liability to services performed in Hong Kong as in Example 3.4 above. He has a full Salaries Tax liability on £52,000 converted at the average rate of exchange for the year. Nonetheless, assuming his income is subject to UK tax, a partial exemption from Hong Kong Salaries Tax may apply pursuant to Sec. 8(1A)(c) (see above).

Note:—

If, despite his absence abroad, he maintained his base and home in Hong Kong, he may not be classed as a visitor in year 1 in which case he would be fully liable on £52,000 unless an exemption under Sec. 8(1A)(c) was available.

3.3.3 Holder of an office

It may not be readily apparent that there is a distinction, in fact a substantial one, in the treatment for Salaries Tax purposes between income from an office and income from an employment. The distinction lies in the ascertainment of source and the statutory distinction in Sec. 8. An "office" is a position which is independent from the individual holding it and which continues to exist even though unfilled. The source of income from an office is the place where the office legally exists; in the obvious example of a directorship, it has been suggested that the office of director is located at the place where the central management and control of the company is located and that the director's services are deemed to be rendered at that place (*McMillan v Guest* (24 TC 190)). This view appears to have been accepted by the IRD in para. 15 of *Departmental Interpretation & Practice Notes No. 10*, which is reproduced as Appendix 7.

Such a view was also accepted by the Board of Review in *D 123/02*, although they rejected the suggestion that this was necessarily the place where board meetings were held. Rather, the Board of Review found in that case that the central management and control was embodied in one particular director and then looked at where that director rendered his services. On the basis that the relevant director performed substantial activities in Hong Kong, it was concluded that the company's management and control was in Hong Kong.

Notwithstanding the statements in paragraph 15 of *Departmental Interpretation & Practice Notes No. 10*, the IRD has been known on occasions to suggest that the source of directors' fees is the country under whose laws the company in question was incorporated, although there appears to be no sound authority for such a proposition.

Sec. 8(1A)(b)(ii), which grants exemption from Salaries Tax where all the services are performed outside Hong Kong or which, with Sec. 8(1B), grants the same exemption where services are performed in Hong Kong only during visits not amounting to more than sixty days, in fact only applies to an employment. A director of a company centrally managed and controlled in Hong Kong seems, therefore, liable to Salaries Tax on his director's remuneration, even if he never visits Hong Kong. It is, however, important to recognise that although an individual may be a director of a company he may in fact draw remuneration from the company in a dual capacity; that is, as an employee in addition to his directorship. This is particularly likely to be the position in the case of private companies. The duties of a director are statutory as laid down by the legislation under which the company is formed or by the company's articles, whereas the duties of an employee are as laid down from day to day by his employer. The division of his remuneration between the office of director and the employment is, therefore, important because the source of each is to be separately determined and, in any event, the remuneration from the employment may be exempt under Sec. 8(1A)(b)(ii). This important principle of duality, even where there is no formal division, was established in *BR 19/74* following the authority of *Lee v Lee's Air Farming Ltd.* (3 All E. R. 420). See also *D 1/81*.

The IRD will regard any individual who has obligations under the *Companies Ordinance* or similar obligations under the laws of another country, as the holder of an office, although as noted above it is important to ascertain whether any remuneration is earned from the holding of that office or as an employee. Note that although some Hong Kong Government employees may in fact be office holders, there is not usually any necessity to consider this position because Sec. 8(1A)(b)(i) denies Hong Kong Government employees the benefit of exemption in respect of services performed wholly outside Hong Kong.

For a further discussion of the above matters, see *Departmental Interpretation & Practice Notes No. 10*, which is reproduced as Appendix 7.

■ Example 3.7

Ivan Orfiz is a director of a company which has its registered office in and holds its directors' meetings in Hong Kong. He draws fees of $250,000 per annum but during the year under review he only visited Hong Kong for a total of 20 days during which he attended Board meetings, signed accounts and attended to various statutory duties.

Notes:—
(a) He will be liable to Salaries Tax on $250,000 because the source of his earnings is the place where the company is managed and controlled, i.e. Hong Kong.
(b) As the holder of an office and drawing remuneration therefrom, he is denied the exemption granted by Secs. 8(1A)(b)(ii) and 8(1B) to employees.

■ Example 3.8

Herr Lein is the owner and chief executive of a trading company in Europe. That company has a Hong Kong subsidiary, the business of which is to make local purchases of goods for the European company. The Hong Kong company has local directors and Herr Lein is also a director. Herr Lein visits Hong Kong for about 30 days each year during which he seeks out and interviews new suppliers and negotiates terms for the ensuing year and also checks on existing suppliers and re-negotiates their terms. He leaves the legal and administrative duties to his local directors. He draws remuneration of $150,000 per annum from the Hong Kong company.

Notes:—
(a) He is in fact the brains behind the Hong Kong business and his position as director is purely nominal. On the authority of *BR 19/74* he should be able to claim exemption from Salaries Tax in accordance with Secs. 8(1A)(b)(ii) and 8(1B) as his income is from an employment separate from his directorship.
(b) Even if he is allocated a nominal director's fee of say $10,000, this should be covered by personal allowances and, therefore, he would still pay no Salaries Tax.

3.3.4 Pensions

The liability to Salaries Tax of income in the form of a pension is also limited to such income which arises in or is derived from Hong Kong. Again the IRO gives no guidance as to the source of pension income, although it may be implied from the fact that there is a provision whereby, except for Hong Kong Government pensions, the part of a pension which is attributable to services outside Hong Kong is to be exempt (Sec. 8(2)(ca)), that the place where services were rendered is not a criterion in determining source because, if it were, the exemption clause would not be necessary.

The IRD adopts the view that the dominant factor in determining the source is the location of the fund from which payments are made. This can of course be the location of the employer's business if it funds the pension itself, or the location of an independent fund.

When it is necessary to divide a pension between service in Hong Kong and service elsewhere, this is normally done by simple time apportionment but it may be appropriate, where possible, to make the division on some other factual basis.

3.3.5 Seafarers and aircrew

The IRO lays down special rules for seafarers and aircrew because of their special position as regards performance of duties outside Hong Kong. Sec. 8(1A)(b)(i) denies them the exemption granted by Sec. 8(1A)(b)(ii) for services performed wholly outside Hong Kong, as extended by Sec. 8(1B), where duties are performed in Hong Kong during visits of not more than 60 days. Instead, they are granted exemption under Sec. 8(2)(j) where the rules in fact extend to a test of physical presence in Hong Kong over two years of assessment.

The tests for exemption for a crew member of a ship or aircraft are that he must not have been present in Hong Kong for more than:—

(1)   a total of 60 days in the year of assessment (Sec. 8(2)(j)(i)); and
(2)   a total of 120 days over 2 consecutive years of assessment, one of which is the year under review (Sec. 8(2)(j)(ii)).

The test is one of physical presence, irrespective of whether duties are performed, as is the case for the sixty-day rule applicable to other employees under Sec. 8(1B). In reviewing the position of a year of assessment under test (2) above, there are in fact two tests to be applied; first, physical presence during the year of assessment and the immediately preceding year must be aggregated and, second, a similar calculation must be undertaken for the year of assessment and the immediately succeeding year. Although it could be interpreted that it is necessary to satisfy the 120-day test in respect of both possible pairs of years, the IRD interpretation is that satisfying one pair of years is sufficient for exemption to be granted. These rules apply whether or not the employment is in Hong Kong but if the employment is outside Hong Kong and the individual fails the exemption tests, his liability cannot exceed tax on the remuneration which relates to services performed in Hong Kong. If the employment is in Hong Kong, failure to satisfy the exemption tests will mean the whole of the earnings are subject to tax except to the extent that foreign tax has been paid in the country where the services were rendered.

Notwithstanding the above, income of a crew member of a ship or an aircraft operated in international traffic may be exempt from Salaries Tax, irrespective of the individual's physical presence in Hong Kong, pursuant to an international agreement. For example, the income of a crew member of a ship operated by a resident of the Netherlands is exempt from Salaries Tax irrespective of the individual's physical presence in Hong Kong, provided that tax has been paid in respect of the income in the Netherlands. Similar provisions exist in the agreements covering shipping and air transport concluded with Singapore and Sri Lanka, although under those agreements the exemption is not dependent on tax being paid in the other jurisdiction. In the case of the agreement with Singapore, however, a Hong Kong resident employed on board a ship or aircraft operated by a Singaporean enterprise may still be subject to Salaries Tax in addition to Singaporean tax.

Additionally, Hong Kong's comprehensive double tax agreements provide that the remuneration of a person employed on board a ship or aircraft operated by an enterprise of a contracting state is taxable only in that state. In other words, the remuneration of a person employed on board an aircraft operated by, for example, a Thai airline, will be taxable only in Thailand irrespective of the extent of the person's physical presence in Hong Kong. Reciprocal provisions exist in respect of individuals employed on board Hong Kong ships or aircraft. It is important to remember, however, that this does not render such persons automatically liable to Hong Kong tax as they may still qualify for the exemption discussed above; the provision does, however, prevent such persons from being taxed in the treaty partner country.

■ Example 3.9

Eva Stone is a cabin crew member employed by a Hong Kong company which operates an airline. All factors are consistent with her employment having a location in Hong Kong. During the consecutive years of assessment 1, 2 and 3 her physical presence in Hong Kong was 75, 50 and 55 days respectively. Her earnings for each year were $275,000. Her Salaries Tax position for the three years is:—

Year 1
   She fails the sixty-day test in Sec. 8(2)(j)(i) and therefore whatever her presence in adjacent years, she will be fully liable on $275,000 (except to the extent that the income has been subject to foreign tax in a country where services were rendered).

Year 2
   She satisfies the sixty-day test in Sec. 8(2)(j)(i) but fails the 120-day test in Sec. 8(2)(j)(ii) in respect of the aggregate of years 1 and 2.
   However, she satisfies the 120-day test in respect of years 2 and 3 and the IRD will allow her exemption for year 2, cancelling any existing final assessment if necessary.

Year 3

She satisfies the sixty-day test in Sec. 8(2)(j)(i) and also the 120-day test in Sec. 8(2)(j) (ii) in respect of the aggregate of years 2 and 3.

The IRD will therefore grant exemption for year 3 whatever the amount of her presence in year 4.

3.4 Determination of Assessable Income

Having determined the source of income from an employment, office or pension, the next step is to ascertain what remuneration is assessable and what is not; this is essentially a question as to what constitutes *income* from an office or employment. For example, not all payments coming from an employer to an employee represent income and therefore, assessable remuneration, and some receipts by an employee from sources other than his employer do constitute income and, therefore, must be included as assessable. Furthermore, there are numerous rules governing the assessability of cash benefits and benefits-in-kind.

The best way to consider the whole question, therefore, is to consider it in compartments of what the IRO specifically includes and excludes, how this is modified by case law and, separately, the position of certain benefits-in-kind, cash benefits and pensions.

3.4.1 Inclusions in assessable income

Sec. 9 of the IRO deals with the definition of income from employment for the purposes of Salaries Tax but, significantly, it begins with the words *"Income from any office or employment includes —"*. It is not, therefore, exhaustive and, accordingly, it is necessary to revert to case law for a full understanding of what remuneration can be assessed.

The general definition in Sec. 9(1)(a) includes *"any wages, salary, leave pay, fee, commission, bonus, gratuity, perquisite or allowance"*. Furthermore, it is specifically provided that such income is to be included whether it comes from the employer or from some other person. This obviates reference to case law on the particular point but it must not be assumed that all such payments received by an employee are therefore subject to Salaries Tax; there are other important tests which are considered in section 3.4.2.

Most of the headings included under Sec. 9(1)(a) are easily understood and ascertainable but the one which gives rise to the most difficulty is "perquisite". It was previously necessary to refer to UK case law for an understanding of this, but legislative changes now effectively incorporate those case law principles into the IRO.

In addition to the general provision of Sec. 9(1)(a), the IRO contains various provisions which specifically deem certain amounts to be income from employment and, therefore, taxable if the other conditions for chargeability are satisfied. These are discussed in the following paragraphs.

(1) **Receipts from non-recognized retirement schemes:** Sec. 9(1)(aa) deems any sum received from a pension or provident fund scheme (other than a pension which is taxable under Sec. 8(1)(b)) to be income from employment so far as it is attributable to the employer's contributions to that scheme, unless the scheme is a recognized occupational retirement scheme (see definition in section 10.3.1) or a MPF scheme. Such a sum is taxable irrespective of whether it is received during or after the period of employment and whether or not it is a commutation of an annuity entitlement. Sums received after employment ceases are treated as having been received on the last day of employment and taxed accordingly, although it is possible to spread back certain lump sum payments where this proves beneficial (see section 3.6.1). Of course, if an annuity is drawn, it is taxable in full as a pension (subject to the normal source rules), irrespective of whether or not it is paid from a recognized occupational retirement scheme.

Because this provision effectively only applies to payments from retirement schemes other than recognized occupational retirement schemes and MPF schemes, and the contribution to or operation of such schemes is, pursuant to the *Occupational Retirement Schemes Ordinance*, permitted only in rare circumstances, the provision has very limited application in practice;

(2) **Certain receipts from recognized occupational retirement schemes:** Sec. 9(1)(ab) deems any amount (other than a pension which is taxable under Sec. 8(1)(b)) received by an employee, whether by way of commutation or otherwise, from a recognized occupational retirement scheme to be income from employment in so far as it is attributable to:—

(i) the employer's contributions, in a case where the payment was made other than because of termination of service, death, incapacity or retirement (Sec. 9(1)(ab)(i)). For a case where this provision was applied, see *D 60/01*; or

(ii) the employer's contributions in excess of the "proportionate benefit" calculated in accordance with Sec. 8(5), in cases where the payment is made upon termination of service other than on

retirement (as defined), death or incapacity (Sec. 9(1)(ab)(ii));
for a discussion as to the meaning of "proportionate benefit",
see point (6) in section 3.4.6. Sec. 9(1)(ab)(i) is complementary
to Secs. 8(2)(c) and 8(2)(cc)(i), which are discussed in section
3.4.6, in that Sec. 9(1)(ab)(i) brings into the charge to tax
amounts (other than a pension) received from a recognized
occupational retirement scheme which do not qualify for the
exemptions provided by Sec. 8(2)(c) or 8(2)(cc)(i) because they
are received other than on termination of service, death,
incapacity or retirement. Payments in connection with death,
incapacity or retirement do not usually give rise to
interpretational difficulties; however, it sometimes unclear
whether an amount was paid on termination of service,
particularly where service was terminated but the employee
was re-employed shortly afterwards. The question of whether
there was a termination of employment in such circumstances
has been considered in a number of Board of Review decisions.
See, for example, *D 83/04* where the Board of Review held
that there had been a termination of employment even though
the individual was re-employed with effect from the following
day to carry out the same duties. In reaching its conclusion, the
Board looked to whether the original employment contract had
been rescinded and a new one entered into or the original
contract had merely been amended. On the facts before them,
the Board concluded that a new contract had been brought into
existence, and in doing so distinguished an earlier contrary
decision, *D 101/89* on the basis that the intention of the parties
in that case was to vary an existing contract.

(3) **Certain receipts from a retirement scheme pursuant to a court
order:** Sec. 9(1)(ac) deems as income from employment, any
payment received by an employee pursuant to a court order under
Sec. 57(3)(b) of the *Occupational Retirement Schemes Ordinance*
to the extent it is attributable to the employer's contributions. Such
court orders can be made where an occupational retirement scheme
is wound up following the cancellation of its registration and there
is a shortfall in the funding of the employee's vested benefits under
the scheme; the Court may, in these circumstances, require the
employer to make up the shortfall by payment directly to the
employee or former employee. Although taxing such a payment
accords with the treatment generally applicable to receipts by an

employee of an employer's contributions other than upon termination of service, death, incapacity or retirement, it is arguably somewhat unfair in that it leads to the benefit being taxed as a result of the scheme being wound up (for reasons which would normally be expected to be beyond the employee's control) whereas the benefit would be wholly or partly exempt if the scheme had continued to be recognised until the employee terminated his service, retired, died or became incapacitated. Moreover, the provision seems particularly unfair in the situation where an employee had actually terminated his service, retired, died or become incapacitated but had not received his full entitlement from the scheme before it was de-registered and wound up. In these circumstances, if there was a shortfall in the funding of the scheme, a court order may be obtained requiring the employer to pay the balance outstanding to the former employee; however, this would be deemed taxable to the extent it represented the employer's contributions, notwithstanding that it would have been fully or partly exempt had it been paid directly by the scheme prior to de-registration;

(4) **Certain receipts from a MPF scheme:** Any benefits received from a MPF scheme which are attributable to the recipient's employer's contributions are deemed to be income from employment pursuant to Sec. 9(1)(ad) where not received on retirement, death, incapacity or termination of service.

Additionally, Sec. 9(1)(ae) deems any benefits received, or deemed to have been received, under any circumstances from an MPF scheme as are attributable to voluntary contributions by the employee's employer to be taxable to the extent that they exceed the "proportionate benefit". For a discussion as to the meaning of proportionate benefit, see point (6) in section 3.4.6. It is important to note that Sec. 9(1)(ae) technically applies irrespective of the circumstances under which the payment from the MPF scheme is made. However, it would seem that where an amount attributable to an employer's voluntary contributions was received other than on retirement, death, incapacity or termination of service, it would be taxable under Sec. 9(1)(ad) and the exemption for that part of the sum not exceeding the proportionate benefit would not be available. This is consistent with what appears to be the complementary provision of Sec. 8(2)(cc)(ii) which, as discussed in point (7) of section 3.4.6, operates to exempt amounts received from a MPF scheme which are attributable to an employer's voluntary contributions, but only up to the amount of the proportionate benefit and when payable on retirement, death, incapacity or termination of service;

(5) **Housing accommodation benefits:** The personal benefit derived from occupying a subsidised or rent-free place of residence provided by the employer or an associated corporation is deemed to be income from employment by Secs. 9(1)(b) and (c). This particular inclusion and the quantum of benefit is discussed in further detail in section 3.4.3;

(6) **Share option benefits:** Any gain realised upon the exercise or disposal of an option to acquire shares granted to an employee by virtue of his employment, is deemed employment income by Sec. 9(1)(d). This is discussed further in section 3.4.4;

(7) **Benefits convertible to cash:** Any benefit derived from an employer which is capable of being converted to cash by the employee is deemed income from the relevant employment due to the operation of Sec. 9(2A)(a). This effectively incorporates one of the case law definitions of "perquisite" into the IRO. Although this provision deems the relevant amounts to be employment income, it achieves this by providing that Sec. 9(1)(a)(iv), which generally applies to deem only perquisites which represent the assumption by the employer of an employee's personal liability as employment income, does not operate to exclude the amounts;

(8) **Child education expenses:** Any amount paid by an employer in connection with the education of an employee's child is deemed to be employment income by Sec. 9(2A)(b). As with cash convertible benefits, this provision operates by overriding the general provision in Sec. 9(1)(a)(iv) that perquisites which do not represent the assumption by the employer of an employee's personal obligation are not employment income. The provision is intended to give statutory effect to the decision in *CIR v David Hardy Glynn* (3 HKTC 245), the effect of which has otherwise been reversed by changes to the IRO. For this particular purpose, an employee's child includes a child of a spouse or ex-spouse and an illegitimate, adopted or step child (Sec. 9(6)(a));

(9) **Holiday travel benefits:** Sec. 9(2A)(c) provides that any amount paid by an employer in connection with a holiday journey is treated as employment income, even where the benefit is not convertible to cash. Again, this is achieved by overriding the general provision in Sec. 9(1)(a)(iv) that perquisites which do not represent the

assumption by the employer of an employee's personal liability are not employment income. A "holiday journey" is defined in Sec. 9(6) as, not surprisingly, a journey taken for holiday purposes but also includes an appropriate portion of a journey taken partly for holiday purposes and partly for some other purposes. In *Departmental Interpretation & Practice Notes No. 41*, the IRD explain in detail their views on determining whether a journey is for holiday purposes or whether any part of a business journey should be treated as a holiday journey. These views are illustrated with numerous practical examples;

(10) **Certain amounts paid to a service company or a trust:** Sec. 9A deems certain amounts paid to a service company or trust to be income of an individual, where that individual controls the company or is a beneficiary of the trust. These provisions are quite complex and are separately discussed in section 3.8.1 below.

The only specific inclusion as regards pensions is the provision in Sec. 9(3) that a pension is to include an ex-gratia pension or one that is capable of being unilaterally discontinued because, without this provision, a series of voluntary payments would not constitute a pension.

3.4.2 Case law discussion

Whilst the IRO describes the general charging heads for Salaries Tax and also provides specific exemptions and includes specific benefits as chargeable, it is nevertheless essential to look to case law for a full understanding of the scope and limitations of what constitutes assessable remuneration. The major issues to emerge from case law are discussed below.

3.4.2.1 Is the income from employment?

The first issue to consider when ascertaining the assessability of an amount is whether it arises from a relationship of "employment" or whether it is from a contract for the provision of services by an individual in his or her capacity as an independent contractor. This is important because, if it is the latter, the income will be subject to Profits Tax rather than Salaries Tax. Put another way, the question becomes one of whether an arrangement is a contract of service (i.e. an employment) or a contract for services (i.e. an independent contractor arrangement). This is largely a question of fact and, although the courts have sought to develop various tests over the years, the present view seems to be that one must look at all relevant factors and weigh them up in the light of the circumstances of each case. A good summary of the factors to be considered can be found in the UK case of *Market Investigations v Minister for Social Security* [1969] (2 QBD 173), although this was not a tax case. One such important factor is the degree of control exercised by the payer over the individual providing the services, although in modern authorities this is perhaps not given as much weight as in the past where it was used as the basis of the so-called "control test", upon which many cases were decided. Other important factors include whether the person providing the services provides his own tools and equipment or hires his own assistants, the degree of financial risk he bears and opportunities he faces, and the extent to which he forms an integral part of the organisation for which he renders services. See also the later decision of *Hall v Lorimer* (63 TC 349), in which the court endorsed the approach taken in the *Market Investigations* case (supra) but also took the opportunity to underscore the fact that the answer to the question was not to be found by carrying out a mechanical exercise of considering all factors; rather, the court noted that what was required was *"... to paint a picture from the accumulation of detail ..."* or, in other words, to consider the factors in light of the overall circumstances of the particular case. For some examples of Hong Kong cases on the issue, see *D 54/90, D 22/92, D 24/93, D 65/93, D 59/95, D 70/ 95, D 15/96, D 103/96* and *D 16/03* although there are numerous other cases.

The question of whether a relationship is one of employment is also important in determining the nature of spare-time work carried out by an otherwise full time employee. It may be that the spare-time activities are so closely related to the individual's full time work that they are to be regarded as casual employment falling within the scope of Salaries Tax; alternatively, the activities may properly be regarded as constituting a separate business which is chargeable to Profits Tax (see the discussion in *Fuge v McClelland* (36 TC 571))

3.4.2.2 Is the income for services rendered?

It is a well established principle under UK law that for income from employment to be taxable, the payments to be brought into account must arise as a reward for the services rendered, either in the past or present, or to be rendered in the future, and not for some other consideration (*Reid v Seymour* (11 TC 625)). In this regard, see also *Hochstrasser v Mayes* (38 TC 673) and *Mairs v Haughey* [1993] (3 WLR 393). In *D 24/97*, however, the Board of Review cautioned against relying on UK case law where the statutory provisions were not identical to those in Hong Kong. In particular, the Board noted that, unlike the UK legislation upon which *Mairs v Haughey* (supra) was decided, there was no specific statutory provision in the IRO which limited the charge to Salaries Tax to amounts received for services rendered, although they noted that this was arguably implied. Further, the Board in a clear case of prevarication noted that in previous decisions, for example *D 13/89*, there had been a reluctance to interpret Sec. 8(1) narrowly so as to imply such a limitation, although suggested that adopting such a narrow interpretation was still arguably permitted by the *Hochstrasser* and *Mairs* cases. In the end, however, the Board did not decide whether the broad or narrow interpretation of Sec. 8(1) was appropriate as they concluded that the amount in question was taxable under either interpretation. The issue of whether an amount is paid for the rendering of services usually arises in connection with payments on termination of employment and this is discussed more extensively in section 3.4.2.3 below. As will be seen from that discussion, some uncertainty has arisen as a result of various Board of Review decisions over the years that have accepted arguments on behalf of the IRD that because income is defined to include perquisites, all amounts received from an employer are taxable even if not a reward for the rendering of services. Nonetheless, the current trend of the courts appears to be to reaffirm the principle established in the UK that amounts not paid in return for the rendering of services are not taxable.

Note also *D 2/86*, where medical expenses reimbursed to an employee by his employer were held not to be a reward for services, although this is surprising in the light of the facts and should not be regarded as a precedent. Indeed, this can be contrasted with *D 56/86* where such a reimbursement was regarded as money's worth and a taxable benefit.

An example of a non-taxable receipt would be a wedding gift by an employer to an employee so long as the motive is solely to present a personal gift and not a reward for services. The employer's motive will generally be to foster and maintain goodwill among the employees in general but that should not prejudice the non-taxable nature in the employee's hands. This should not be confused with an ex-gratia payment made to an employee for services rendered which, although non-contractual and of a windfall nature, is still taxable because it comes as a reward for services (see *Cooper v Blakiston* (5 TC 347) and *D 12/92*).

Nonetheless, the dividing line between what is for services rendered (or to be rendered) and what is for other consideration is sometimes narrow, a point which is illustrated by the decision in *Ball v Johnson* (47 TC 155) where a bank employee took and passed the Institute of Bankers professional examinations for which his employer awarded him a sum of money which was held not to be taxable. See, however, the discussion above regarding

D 36/92 which would suggest that the *Ball v Johnson* decision may not be followed in Hong Kong.

3.4.2.3 **Payments on termination of employment**

One consequence of the principle that only payments attributable to the rendering of services are subject to Salaries Tax is that certain payments received on termination of employment may be exempt from tax. Many payments on termination of employment are contractual or *ex-gratia* in recognition of past services and there are many Board of Review decisions in Hong Kong confirming that these are taxable, although for a good summary of the principles involved, see *D 80/00*. Nonetheless, if the payment is not for services rendered, it is generally accepted that it is not taxable, although see the discussion below. Examples of payments made in connection with the termination of employment which are typically not taxable include:

(1)   an *ex-gratia* gift as a token of personal esteem on the occasion of retirement (see principles discussed in section 3.4.2.2 above);

(2)   compensation for loss of office, cancellation of service agreement, salary in lieu of notice etc. There are numerous legal decisions in the UK on these points of principle but for typical examples see *Hose v Warwick* (27 TC 459), *Duff v Barlow* (23 TC 633) and *Mairs v Haughey* [1993] (3 WLR 393). For Hong Kong decisions, see *BR 116/77*, *D 3/97* and *D 24/97*. The decisions of the Board of Review in Hong Kong on this point, however, need to be treated with a degree of caution since, as discussed below, the Board has not always accepted the principle that amounts received other than as remuneration for services rendered are not taxable.

The Board of Review in *D 17/05*, relying on the UK decision of *Richardson v Delaney* [2001] (STC 1328) noted that for an amount to be non-taxable compensation it must be for an identifiable breach of a contract. In that case, the Board went on to find that there was no evidence that the employer was in breach of the contract of employment and concluded that the sum in question was actually paid for the rendering of services. On such a finding of fact, the decision was clearly correct, as was the suggestion that for an amount to be compensation for breach of contract, the breach must be real and identifiable. Nonetheless, it would appear wrong to assume that only such compensation payments are non-taxable. In particular, previous decisions of the Board of Review (see, for example, *D 55/*

93, D 16/95 and *D 70/01*) have found that a payment to induce an employee to resign or accept a retirement or redundancy package may be non-taxable, even where it does not represent compensation for breach of a contractual or statutory right, and there appears to be nothing in the reasoning of *Richardson v Delaney* (supra) which suggests that logic adopted by the Board of Review in those cases is wrong. The difficulty, of course, is ascertaining whether a payment is such an inducement or is merely a gratuity in recognition of past services.

Great care also needs to be exercised in reaching a conclusion on payments representing some form of compensation because the following types have been held to be taxable:—

(i)   A terminal payment which has been pre-arranged as part of the terms of employment is in reality deferred remuneration (*Henry v Foster* (16 TC 605)) even if it is referred to in the service agreement as compensation for termination; see, for example, *Dale v De Soissons* (32 TC 118) and *D 90/96*. These cases should, however, be contrasted with the decision in *Yung Tse Kwong v CIR* [2004] (1 HKRC 90-136) where although a termination payment was provided for in the employment contract and was held to be partly an inducement to enter into that contract, the court also considered that it was partly paid for entering into a termination agreement and agreeing to certain restrictive covenants therein; as such, the court held that an apportionment of the amount was appropriate and only that portion which represented an inducement to enter into the employment agreement was taxable;

(ii) A payment for agreeing not to resign, which is in reality a payment for future services (*Cameron v Prendergast* (23 TC 122)) or for agreeing to serve for a smaller salary, which is in reality an advance payment of salary (*Tilley v Wales* (25 TC 136)); and

(3)   a payment for agreeing to enter into a covenant restricting an ex-employee's activities, for example for not competing in the same field of activity or business. For a case concerning such a sum, see the Court of First Instance decision in *CIR v Yung Tse Kwong* which is discussed above.

In *D 43/92*, however, which was concerned with leave pay, it was essentially argued by the IRD that all payments to employees should be considered as perquisites and caught by Sec. 9(1)(a), irrespective of why they were paid. The Board of Review, although still finding for the IRD, indicated that this interpretation of Sec. 9(1)(a) was too broad and, relying on the Privy Council's decision in *David Hardy Glynn v CIR* (3 HKTC 245), noted that for the payment to be caught by that provision, it must be paid in the course of executing the employment; this would suggest a reiteration of the principle that a payment must essentially be for services rendered if it is to be subject to Salaries Tax. See also *D 44/93*, *D 16/95* and *D 87/01* which further reaffirm this principle and, more specifically, the non-assessability of payments of compensation for loss of office. In *D 55/93*, this latter principle was upheld even though compensation was paid as a monthly sum, equivalent to the taxpayer's former salary, for a twelve-month period.

The decision in *D 104/99* is also interesting for the reason that the Board of Review did not try to reconcile all the previous authorities on the issue of assessability of payments on termination, but correctly noted in fact that two alternative lines of reasoning had been adopted by previous Boards of Review. In particular, the Board observed that sometimes a wider approach of simply looking to whether the payment in question was sourced from the employment, irrespective of whether or not it was for services rendered, had been adopted. On the other hand, they observed an alternative line of authorities under which payments other than for services rendered (e.g. compensation payments) had been held to be non-assessable. Interestingly, however, in reaching their conclusion that the amount was not taxable in the case before them, the Board of Review applied the wider interpretation but still found the sum was not sourced from the taxpayer's employment, as it was not made as a result of the contract of employment but on the advice of the Labour Department.

Although this decision highlights the disparity in views of various Boards of Review on the question of whether the charge to Salaries Tax is limited to amounts received for the rendering of services, it seems that the preponderance of cases do accept that the charge is limited in this manner. Nonetheless, cases continue to be decided on both bases. For examples of this, see *D 88/00* where the Board of Review, in quoting from an earlier decision, stated that *"… there is nothing in sections 8 or 9 of the Inland Revenue Ordinance which limit taxable payments to remuneration for services rendered or to be rendered …"*, and compare this to the decision in *D 87/01* where the Board stated *"… the test for salaries tax liability is … whether the sum arose from the employment for services past, present or future …"*.

Nonetheless, some clarity has been brought to the question by the decision of the Court of First Instance in *CIR v Yung Tse Kwong* [2004] (1 HKRC 90-136) which favoured the view that amounts not paid for the rendering of services are not taxable. See also the decision of the Court of Appeal in *CIR v Elliott, Stewart William George* [2006] (1 HKRC 90-173). Although the facts of that case were quite complex and demonstrate the importance of understanding the precise nature of a payment in order to ascertain its assessability, the reasoning of the decision reaffirmed the principle that amounts paid not for the rendering of services but as compensation for the loss or abrogation of rights, are not taxable even if those amounts were intended to replace sums which would have been taxable.

As is evident from the above discussion, it is often difficult to decide whether a lump sum paid on termination of employment is assessable, as it depends very much on the precise facts of each case and what line of authorities are applied. Additionally, it is often incorrectly assumed by taxpayers that any termination or severance payments are exempt from tax. This belief is sometimes justified on the basis that because the amounts are paid only on termination, they cannot be for services rendered. The fallacy of this was explained succinctly in *D 87/01* where the Board of Review noted that the relevant test for chargeability was not a *"... but for ..."* test (i.e. whether the amount would not have been paid but for the termination of employment), but a question of whether or not the amount was paid as a reward for services rendered or to be rendered. Nonetheless, by way of an apparent extra-statutory concession, the Commissioner accepts long service leave or severance payments made pursuant to the *Employment Ordinance* as exempt from Salaries Tax. For a discussion of this concession, see section 3.4.2.8 below.

Notwithstanding the inconsistent approach in determining what payments are taxable, the Board of Review traditionally found a payment in dispute to be of a single nature and either taxable or non-taxable. In more recent years, however, there have been a number of cases where a single sum has been apportioned into taxable and non-taxable components. See, for example, *D 3/97* where the Board recognised that the payment in question had hallmarks of both a gratuity for past services and compensation for loss of office. Rather than finding the whole sum to be either of one nature or the other, however, the Board arbitrarily apportioned the amount and treated 75% of it as attributable to compensation for loss of office and non-taxable, and the remaining 25% of it as a gratuity for past service and taxable. See also *D 76/98* where the Board of Review upheld an apportionment by the Commissioner of a single lump sum paid pursuant to an out of court settlement. That settlement was an undivided lump sum intended to cover claims for various items, only some of which would have been taxable if received separately. The Board of Review accepted that the nature of the lump sum was to be determined by looking at the items it effectively replaced and that a sensible apportionment of the amount taking into account the quantum of the original taxable and non-taxable items was appropriate. Apportionment of a single sum was also undertaken by the Court of First Instance in *CIR v Yung Tse Kwong* [2004] (1 HKRC 90-136), where the sum was found to be partly a taxable inducement for entering into an employment agreement and partly non-taxable consideration for entering into a restrictive covenant. See also *D 73/04* and *D 37/05* where the Board of Review apportioned an amount into four elements and held that two of those elements were taxable.

It is sometimes the case that where an individual's employment is terminated, the employer may continue to pay salary and benefits for the duration of the relevant notice period but not require the individual to attend the place of employment or perform any duties. It was held in *D 88/00* that payments under such an agreement were taxable. This decision was, however, reached on the basis that all amounts received in connection with employment are taxable, even if they are not related to services rendered. As discussed above, although such a view has been expressed in a number of cases, it seems to be more generally accepted that an amount must be for services rendered to be taxable. Nonetheless, it should not be readily assumed that a Board of Review adopting this more common view would have found the amounts in question not taxable, as the issue could only be decided after ascertaining the factual nature of the payments.

Indeed, in *D 80/03* such a payment was found by the Board of Review not to be a payment in lieu of notice and was held to be taxable. Note, however, that in their decision the Board of Review did not explicitly state that if the payment had been in lieu of notice that it would not have been taxable, although as discussed earlier this has been established in other cases and is generally accepted by the IRD. Nor did the published decision of the Board of Review analyse their decision in terms of whether or not the payment related to services rendered; rather, the Board simply examined the veracity of the taxpayer's claim that the amount was a payment in lieu of notice and, having found that it was not, concluded that it arose from the employment and dismissed the appeal.

Payments in the form of compensation for loss of office or cancellation of a service contract would, because of their nature, generally only be made upon involuntary termination of employment by an employer. Where a person voluntarily resigns from an employment, such payments would not generally be made and for this reason it would be unusual for any termination payments to be found to be other than in respect of the rendering of services. For commercial reasons, however, it is sometimes the case that an employee whose employment is to be terminated will be permitted to resign. Such a case was considered in *D 70/01*, where the Board of Review rejected the IRD's contention that because the employee formally resigned all termination payments should be taxable; rather, the Board of Review accepted that the resignation was in reality involuntary and that certain payments were in the nature of compensation for the employee's resulting loss and, therefore, not subject to Salaries Tax.

3.4.2.4 Payments on change of terms of employment

There have also been a number of Board of Review decisions concerning the assessability of payments made to an employee upon the change of the terms of employment. See, for example, *D 13/94* and *D 43/98* where amounts paid by an employer to obtain release from certain obligations which had accrued during a number of years of service by the employee were held to be non-taxable even though the employment continued (albeit on different terms). Similarly, in cases *D 58/98* and *D 59/98* amounts paid by an employer to compensate employees for the termination of a retirement scheme which, although set up voluntarily by the employer was regarded as a contractual entitlement under the terms of the individuals' employment, were held to be non-taxable. In these cases, the reasoning adopted by the Board of Review was that the amounts were compensation for the breach by the employer of the terms of the individual's employment.

Care needs to be taken in interpreting these decisions, however, since (as with all cases) they were determined on the particular evidence and facts found. Moreover, they need to be contrasted with the decisions in *D 26/94* and *D 27/94* where amounts paid on a change of terms of employment, and which were calculated on the same basis as a long service leave payment would have been calculated if the employee had been dismissed at the time, were found as a matter of fact to have been either a payment for past services or an inducement to continue in employment and, consequently, taxable. The decisions in those cases can, however, be reconciled to the decisions in *D 58/98* and *D 59/98*, which were discussed above. In particular, the Board of Review in *D 58/98* and *D 59/98* explicitly declined to follow the reasoning in *D 26/94* on the basis that in that earlier case the payment in question had been triggered by the employee seeking to terminate his employment in order to obtain the payment, whereas in the latter case the payment was made as a consequence of the employer taking a decision to amend the terms of the individual's employment in a disadvantageous manner. See also the similar cases of *D 25/98* and *D 104/98*, although in those cases the Board of Review seemed to concentrate more on the fact that there was no termination of employment and, therefore, the payments could not have been long service payments in accordance with the *Employment Ordinance*. Consequently, the Board held that the payments did not qualify for the concessionary treatment afforded to such long service payments.

Nonetheless, these decisions need to be compared with *D 104/99* where on closure of his employer's factory in Hong Kong, the taxpayer's employment was terminated but he was re-employed by the same employer with effect from the following day to work in China. The Board of Review held that a severance payment made on the advice of the Labour Department was compensation for loss of employment and not subject to Salaries Tax, notwithstanding the re-employment of the taxpayer. The Board of Review appears to have been swayed in its conclusion in this case by the fact that all of the employer company's factory workers in Hong Kong were paid severance payments and that the re-employment, although effective from the day after the termination, was actually not finalised until a few weeks after the termination; accordingly, the Board of Review considered that there had been a genuine termination of employment with no guarantee of re-employment at that time.

3.4.2.5 Payments on commencement of employment

As with certain payments on termination of employment, some payments made at the commencement of employment may also be outside the scope of Salaries Tax. For example, in *Pritchard v Arundale* (47 TC 680) a payment made to an individual, not as a reward for future services but as an incentive to encourage him to leave an existing gainful occupation and commence service with a new employer, was held not to be taxable. This decision is in line with the principle discussed above that if a payment is made for past, present or future services it is taxable, whereas if it represents consideration for something else it is not taxable. It is, therefore, surprising to find that in two decisions (*D 19/92* and *D 36/92*) the Board of Review has reached the opposite conclusion on facts which they have found, in substance, were the same as in the *Pritchard v Arundale* case. In the latter of these two cases, the IRD again argued that notwithstanding the *Pritchard v Arundale* decision, as a matter of law, the charge to Salaries Tax was not restricted to payments for services rendered or to be rendered; unfortunately, the Board of Review did not fully address this argument directly, but found for the IRD on the ground that the amount was a perquisite of the employment which was taxable under Sec. 9(1)(a). See, however, the discussion in previous paragraphs for examples of later decisions where the argument that "perquisite" includes all or most sums paid by an employer has been rejected.

See also *D 124/02*, where an employee was liable to pay his former employer an amount in lieu of three months' notice when he terminated his employment to take up a new position. The employee's new employer agreed to make (the majority of) the payment to the former employer on the employee's behalf and this amount was held to be taxable on the basis that it was a perquisite of the employee's new employment and that it was paid at least partly in discharge of the employee's personal liability.

3.4.2.6 Payments other than from the recipient's employer

It is not only payments which come to an employee from his employer which are within the scope of Salaries Tax; the principle of "reward for services" extends to a reward coming from any person so long as it is in return for the services which the employee is required by his employer to perform. The obvious example is "tips" which a customer may give to a taxi driver or waitress in return for good service. This is in any event covered by the inclusion in Sec. 9(1)(a) of the words "... *whether derived from the employer or others ...*" but apart from that, the principle was established in *Calvert v Wainwright* (27 TC 475).

3.4.2.7 Perquisites

Before the enactment of Secs. 9(1)(a)(iv) and 9(2A) it was necessary to make substantial reference to UK law case for an understanding of when and how "benefits-in-kind" were to be subject to tax. Nevertheless, there are still some areas of case law relevant to the meaning of "perquisite" in Sec. 9(1)(a) and this is dealt with in section 3.4.5. See also *Departmental Interpretation & Practice Notes No. 16* which is reproduced as Appendix 11.

A particular type of perquisite which sometimes arises is a loan waiver. For example, an employer may make a loan to an employee on the understanding that the repayment of the amount will be waived if, for example, the individual remains in employment for a minimum specified period. Such a waiver is probably deemed assessable by the specific provisions in Sec. 9(1)(a) (which is discussed in section 3.4.5). The matter has, however, also been dealt with by the UK courts in *Clayton v Gothorp* (47 TC 168), which held the amount to be taxable, and it was on the basis of this authority that a loan waiver was held by the Board of Review to be taxable in *D 83/00* and *D 119/02*.

3.4.2.8 Other issues

Although not provided for by either statute or case law, as an extra-statutory concession the Commissioner treats long service or severance payments under the *Employment Ordinance* as exempt from Salaries Tax. For a discussion of this concession, and how the Board of Review considered it should be applied in practice in the interests of consistency, see *D 38/94*.

Nonetheless, it appears from the decisions in *D 51/01* and *D 81/01* that this extra statutory concession is to be interpreted narrowly. In particular, these decisions involved employees who would have been entitled to payments under the *Employment Ordinance* but for the fact that they also received a contractual gratuity, which reduced their entitlement under the *Employment Ordinance* to nil. The Board of Review, by majority only in both cases, rejected the proposition that such part of the gratuity as did not exceed the amount which would otherwise have been payable under the *Employment Ordinance* should be exempt from Salaries Tax. The grounds for the Board's majority decisions were essentially that the Commissioner's extra-statutory concession only relates to amounts actually paid pursuant to the *Employment Ordinance*, whereas in the cases before them the taxpayers had no entitlements under that ordinance as the amounts arose from employment contracts.

Finally, although perhaps obvious in view of the preceding discussions, it has been established in *Mudd v Collins* (9 TC 297) that where an employee performs some special service outside of his or her normal line of duties, any amount paid to the employee by the employer in respect of that service is taxable. In other words, it is beyond doubt that a special gratuity for performing activities outside the defined scope of an individual's normal employment is taxable.

3.4.3 Housing accommodation benefit

One of the benefits specifically provided as taxable by the IRO is that derived by an employee from the occupation of rent free or subsidized accommodation at the expense of his employer. The taxable benefit is defined as:—

(1)   the "rental value" of any place of residence provided rent free by the employer or an associated corporation (Sec. 9(1)(b)); or

(2)   where some rent is paid by the employee, the excess of the "rental value" over the rent paid (Sec. 9(1)(c)).

With regard to (2), where an employee made a fixed contribution to his employer in respect of hotel rooms paid for by the employer and also paid part of the hotel service charge (levied as a percentage of room charge) directly to the hotel, only the contribution to his employer was regarded as rent paid for this purpose (*CIR v H. J. Walton Masters* (2 HKTC 22)). Contrast this, however, with the facts in *D 41/86* where an employee was required to pay his employer a sum equal to a fixed percentage of his salary plus a fixed monthly amount to cover utility services at the premises. The total contribution to the employer was held to be rent because it all arose out of arrangements strictly between employer and employee. The principle that emerges is, therefore, that an agreement between an employer and employee whereby the employee pays the employer consideration, in whatever form, for the use of the property will amount to rent whereas if the employee pays sums direct to the landlord which exceed the amount borne by his employer, it will be a question of fact whether or not this comprises rent.

In order to cover the equivalent circumstances where the employee rents the property himself and looks to his employer for full or partial reimbursement, the reimbursement or payment on his behalf is exempted from tax (Sec. 9(1A)(a)) and a full reimbursement or payment is treated as giving rise to a rental value as in (1) above (Sec. 9(1A)(b)) and a partial reimbursement or payment as giving rise to a reduced rental value as in (2) above (Sec. 9(1A)(c)). There is, however, a substantial difference in the tax treatment of a rent allowance, which may be disbursed at the discretion of the employee, and a rent reimbursement or payment which is nothing more than a replacement of a specific expense already incurred. The latter is specifically not taxable, and is replaced by the "rental value", but the former falls within the meaning of allowance as used in Sec. 9(1)(a) and is fully taxable as income; for Board of Review decisions in this regard, see *D 8/82*, *D 16/83* and *D 62/92*.

Nonetheless, it is not always clear whether an amount is a rent allowance or a reimbursement and a good case which illustrates this is *D 92/95*. In that case, an amount was considered a rent reimbursement, even though the relevant employment contract, although noting that total remuneration included a contribution to housing, was silent as to how that contribution was to be quantified. In finding for the taxpayer, the Board held that the term "refund" was to be given its ordinary meaning and, provided that the intention of the employer to refund the employee's rent was clear, the amount should attract the concessional treatment. The Board also rejected the suggestion by the IRD that the claim should fail because the amount would have been paid irrespective of the amount of rent actually paid by the taxpayer. Indeed, the IRD's argument was in essence that the amount was an allowance and it is interesting to note that in rejecting it, the Board noted that even if it was an allowance, that did not preclude the amount from attracting the concessional treatment afforded by Sec. 9(2); this is to be contrasted with the decisions mentioned in the previous paragraph.

A similar reasoning was applied by the majority of the Board of Review in *D 144/01* where an amount was treated as a rent reimbursement, again largely on the basis of the intention of the parties, notwithstanding that evidence was adduced that the employer treated the amount in question as a cash allowance, did not require the employee to be accountable for it and did not require the employee to provide receipts or copies of tenancy agreements. As with all cases, however, this was decided on the basis of its own particular facts and, in a relatively unusual move, one member dissented. The majority decision was, however, overturned on appeal to the Court of First Instance (see *CIR v Peter Leslie Page* [2003] (1 HKRC 90-123)). The court's reasoning was that although they accepted that the original intention of the parties under the employment contract was that the amount was a reimbursement of rent, by not requiring the production of a tenancy agreement and paying the amount irrespective of the rent expense actually incurred by the taxpayer, the parties by their conduct had effectively varied the obligations under that contract and the amount had become a cash allowance. In reaching this conclusion, however, the court was careful to reject the suggestion contained in an earlier Board of Review decision (*D 33/97*) that unless the employer exercises a significant degree of control over the payments an amount can never be considered to be a refund of rent, although noted that such control would generally be of great assistance to taxpayers seeking to have an amount afforded the concessional treatment.

Another decision which concerned the determination of whether an amount was a cash allowance or a refund of rent is *D 53/04*. The Board found against the taxpayer, predominantly on the basis of inconsistencies in evidence, but the decision was overturned by the Court of First Instance (see *Yau Wah Yau v CIR* [2005] (1 HKRC 90-160)) in a judgment which contains an interesting discussion of the test of burden of proof which is applicable in such cases. On appeal, however, the Court of Appeal (see *Yau Wah Yau v CIR* [2005] (1 HKRC 90-168)) considered that the lower court had applied the wrong test and that the Board of Review's decision was one which was open to them and, therefore, should be allowed to stand.

See also *D 140/00* where a taxpayer's claim for concessional treatment on amounts claimed to be refunds of rent was denied on the basis that the arrangement was implemented retrospectively after the end of each year. Given the decisions discussed above, where the Board of Review has either required the intention of the parties to be clear as to the reimbursement of rent, or the exercise by the employer of some degree of control over the rent refunds, it is perhaps not surprising that the taxpayer was unsuccessful in this case.

The wording of Sec. 9(1A) makes it clear that the concessionary treatment applies only where the employer has refunded rent. In *D 23/05*, the taxpayer's claim for amounts to be treated as refunds of rent failed on the basis that the intention of the employer in making the payments was to finance the acquisition of the employee's residence. In particular, the case involved a taxpayer who lived on a yacht which was owned by a company controlled by the taxpayer. Although the employer refunded rent in certain circumstances, this was not available in respect of a residence (including a boat) which was owned directly or indirectly by the employee. Rather, in such circumstances the employer would subsidise the mortgage payments in respect of the residence (or boat) owned and occupied by the employee. Accordingly, the Board of Review held that, irrespective of the description given to the amounts, the payments to the taxpayer were intended by the employer to assist with the mortgage payments in respect of the yacht which served as the taxpayer's residence and, as such, were fully taxable.

The same conclusion was reached in a substantially identical subsequent case, *D 3/06*, which was further upheld on appeal (see *Roger Jesse Robertshaw v CIR* [2006] (1 HKRC 90-184). The decision in the *Robertshaw* case further confirmed that the correct test to be applied in determining whether an amount was to be treated as a refund of rent was the intention of the parties at the time of making the payment; applying this test to the case before it, the court concluded that it was clear that the intention of the employer was not to provide rental assistance in respect of a property in which the employee had a direct or indirect interest.

Notwithstanding the above decision, situations arise where a taxpayer enters into a tenancy agreement in respect of a property owned by his or her spouse, or a company owned or controlled by the taxpayer or a relative of the taxpayer, and then arranges for the rent paid to be refunded by his or her employer. Indeed, there are even situations where an employer enters into a tenancy agreement over a property owned by an employee and then makes the property available for the employee's use. The IRD has indicated that such arrangements are acceptable and may qualify for the concessionary treatment afforded refunds of rent provided the terms of the tenancy agreement are commercial and the agreements are properly documented and the relevant stamp duty paid, the employer is not controlled by the employee and the rental income is reported in the employee's tax return (see the minutes of the meeting between the Commissioner and the Taxation

Committee of the Hong Kong Society of Accountants, which were published by the Hong Kong Society of Accountants on 16 April 1997). The acceptability in principle of such arrangements was further confirmed by the Commissioner's representative in *D 140/00*. Nonetheless, the requirement that the tenancy agreements be commercially realistic, properly documented and that the parties act in an arm's length manner appears to be strictly enforced. See, for example, *D 56/00*, *D 85/00*, *D 105/00* and *D 93/01* for examples of cases where the IRD has successfully challenged such arrangements where they have not been satisfied that the arrangements were genuinely entered into with the intention of creating binding legal obligations.

In summary, therefore, provided that any payment by an employer to an employee can be shown to be a reimbursement of rent, there is no difference in the tax treatment between a residence owned or rented directly by the employer and one rented in the first instance by the employee himself.

In the case of *CIR v Chow Hung-Kong* [1978] (HKLR 475) the employee successfully claimed that accommodation occupied as part of the duties of the employment, i.e. "representative occupation" is not a residence for purposes of the Salaries Tax charge. This has now been negated by the inclusion of a definition of "place of residence" in Sec. 9(6) to include such accommodation and the effectiveness of this amendment was confirmed in *D 30/92*. See, however, *D 46/87* where an employee was held not to be taxable in respect of a residence provided by his employer because the employee maintained a separate residence for the use of himself and his family. In finding for the taxpayer in that case, the Board of Review noted that a residence meant a place where a person is supposed to usually sleep and, therefore, did not extend to a place where an employee could rest and relax whilst on duty. See also *D 36/95* where a hotel room was not considered a place of residence because of various restrictions on its use by the taxpayer.

The "rental value" upon which tax is charged is defined in Sec. 9(2) and is a fixed percentage of the assessable income from employment for the period during which a place of residence was provided or the employee received a refund of rent paid, reduced by:

- any share option benefit (see section 3.4.4);
- certain amounts received from a retirement scheme which are assessable only as a consequence of the operation of Secs. 9(1)(aa), 9(1)(ab), 9(1)(ac), 9(1)(ad) and 9(1)(ae) (see section 3.4.1);
- outgoings, expenses and depreciation allowances (including balancing

allowances) as provided for in Secs. 12(1)(a) and 12(1)(b), to the extent to which they were incurred in the period during which the place of residence was provided or the employee received a refund of rent paid (refer to sections 3.5.1 and 3.5.2). It is interesting to note that although a balancing allowance will reduce the amount upon which the rental value is calculated, a balancing charge will not increase such amount. This is because, although deemed assessable for Salaries Tax purposes by Sec. 12(5), a balancing charge is not income from employment under normal concepts and, as such, is not included in the gross income amount which is the starting point for determining rental value; and

- any lump sum or gratuity paid or granted upon the retirement or termination of the employee. It is important to note that this applies only to gratuities paid on termination or retirement; in this regard, see *D 115/97* where the whole amount of a contractual gratuity (which was payable on completion of a period of service rather than on termination of service) was included in the calculation of the amount upon which the rental value was calculated, even though the gratuity related partly to service in earlier years of assessment. Refer also to *D 60/02* where a contractual gratuity was included on the basis that it was not paid in connection with a termination of employment and *D 16/90* where a taxpayer unsuccessfully argued that an education allowance should be excluded from this calculation.

Once the basis upon which the rental value is to be calculated has been ascertained in accordance with the above, it remains only to apply the appropriate percentage. The relevant percentages are:

- 4%   where the accommodation consists of not more than one room in a hotel, hostel or boarding house.
- 8%   where the accommodation consists of not more than two rooms in a hotel, hostel or boarding house.
- 10%   in all other cases except that the rateable value, as ascertained under the rating ordinance, may be substituted if smaller (Sec. 9(2)).

In *D 91/04*, the Board of Review had to consider the meaning of "*hotel, hostel or boarding house*" and, in particular, whether a serviced apartment fell within this term. Although the decision contains a comprehensive and useful discussion as to the meaning of "hotel", it was ultimately decided on the basis that the taxpayer had failed to discharge the burden of proving that a serviced apartment fell within such meaning and, therefore, the assessment based on 10% of the taxpayer's assessable income was upheld.

Where two or more employees share the same accommodation, there is no pro-rating of the assessable value. That is, if two employees share the same flat, each will be assessed on the basis of 10% of their assessable income, less any rent paid by them individually (see *D 78/90*).

Note that, in the context of a hotel, hostel or boarding-house, the Board of Review in *D 23/84* has held that a "room" is not to be narrowly defined as the space within four walls but is a single room if it is a suite of rooms containing one bedroom and ancillary rooms such as bathroom and sitting room.

If the individual's employment is outside Hong Kong (see section 3.3) and he performs part of his duties outside Hong Kong with the result that only a part of his income is liable to Salaries Tax, the rental value is computed not on the total earnings, but only on the proportion liable to Salaries Tax (*BR 20/76*). Any rent contribution by the employee or portion of rent suffered is not to be similarly pro-rated but is deducted in full per *CIR v R. P. Williamson* (HKTC 1215).

Note also that the housing accommodation benefit provisions apply even where the employee is based abroad and only visits Hong Kong for a limited period (see *D 54/94*).

See illustration in Example 3.10.

■ Example 3.10

Benny Fitt received a salary of $360,000 during the year of assessment and also received reimbursement from his employer of $15,000 per month of the $15,500 which he pays to his landlord for his flat. He also pays rates and management charges of $600 per month. The rateable value of the flat under the rating ordinance is $150,000. He retired in the following year and elected to relate back $60,000 of the terminal gratuity to this year of assessment (see section 3.6.1).

His income assessable to Salaries Tax is as follows.—

(1)	Salary		$360,000
(2)	Rental Value 10% × $360,000	= $36,000	
	Less: Rent paid (Note (b))	13,200	
	Net Rental Value	$22,800	22,800
(3)	Terminal gratuity related back		60,000
	Total Income Assessable to Salaries Tax		$442,800

Notes:—

(a) Although the benefit costs the employer and benefits Benny by $180,000, the assessable benefit is only $22,800.

(b) Although not strictly rent, the rates and management charges are treated as such in practice.

(c) The rateable value is larger than the rental value of $36,000 and therefore the election does not apply. In practice, the election is rarely appropriate except where assessable earnings are very large.

(d) The terminal gratuity of $60,000 related to this year is ignored in computing rental value (Sec. 9(2)).

(e) Note that it would have been marginally advantageous for Benny to have had a full reimbursement of $16,100 per month and his salary fixed at $1,100 per month lower. The cost to the employer would have been the same but Benny's total income assessable to Salaries Tax would be:—

Salary	$346,800
Rental Value (10%)	34,680
Gratuity	60,000
	$441,480

It is always more advantageous from a tax point of view to have a smaller salary than to contribute to rental cost.

The rental value is ascertained according to the period during which the benefit is enjoyed based on the actual assessable income and allowable outgoings for that period. There may be different residences attracting different rates of rental value during one year of assessment and although it is correct to apply the percentages to actual income and outgoings for the relevant periods, in practice this is often done by simple time apportionment, where there is only a single employer.

Where, during a year of assessment, an individual has more than one employer which provides a place of residence or refunds rent paid by the employee, the rental value for each employment is to be calculated separately. Moreover, if the rental value under one employment is a negative value (because, for example, the amount of rent paid but not refunded by the employer exceeds the appropriate percentage of the adjusted assessable income from that employment), this does not serve to reduce the overall rental value to be assessed to the employee; rather, as is normally the case, the negative rental value is treated as being nil for that employment (see *D 115/97*).

■ Example 3.11

Ernie Nuff came to Hong Kong for employment on 1st April 2007 at a salary of $24,000 per month for the first six months and $30,000 per month thereafter. He also received a bonus of $75,000 in March for the year ended 31st March 2008. During the first three months, his employer paid $54,000 for him to live in a single hotel room and also gave him a meal allowance of $1,800 per month. He then moved into a flat for which he paid rent, rates and management charges of $19,000 per month and the employer agreed to reimburse a maximum of $18,000 per month. His allowable expenses and outgoings for the year were $10,000. The rateable value of the flat is $180,000.

His income assessable to Salaries Tax for 2007/08 is as follows:—

		First 3 months	Last 9 months
(1) Salary	$24,000 × 3	$72,000	
	$24,000 × 3		$ 72,000
	$30,000 × 6		180,000
(2) Bonus (Time apportioned)		18,750	56,250
(3) Meal Allowance ($1,800 × 3)		5,400	—
Total Employment Income		$96,150	$308,250
(4) Allowable Expenses (Time apportioned)		2,500	7,500
		$93,650	$300,750
(5) Rental Value:			
4% × $93,650		3,746	
10% × $300,750	$30,075		
Less: Rent paid	9,000		
	$21,075		21,075
		$97,396	$321,825
Total Income Assessable to Salaries Tax			$419,221

Notes:—
(a) Although the benefit costs the employer and benefits Ernie by $216,000, the assessable benefit is only $24,821.
(b) The meal allowance is taxable as an allowance under Sec. 9(1)(a).
(c) Although not strictly rent, the rates and management charges are treated as such in practice.
(d) The rateable value of $135,000 (9 months) is larger than the rental value of $30,075, therefore the election does not apply.

It would be easy to avoid or minimise the benefit assessable by arranging for an employee to have a separate employment with an associated company which provided the residence and also a minimal or nil salary. This opportunity has been prevented by the inclusion in the charging sections of the wording "*by an employer or an associated corporation*". This has the effect of aggregating his earnings from all associated corporations for the purposes of applying the percentage to arrive at rental value. For this purpose an associated corporation is defined in Sec. 9(6) as:—

(1)   a corporation over which the employer has control; or
(2)   if the employer is itself a corporation, a corporation which has control over the employer or which is under the control of the same person as controls the employer corporation.

In this context, control is widely defined as the ability to conduct the affairs of a corporation in accordance with one's wishes whether by the holding of shares, by direct or indirect voting power or by virtue of any power conferred by the articles of association or any other document which confers similar powers directly or indirectly (Sec. 9(6)). It is important to note here that the employer could be an individual and the residence could be provided by a company associated with that individual. For the anti-avoidance provision to apply, it is certainly not necessary that both parties be companies. However, the provision does not apply where the employer is a company but the residence is provided by an associated individual (e.g. a shareholder or director).

■ Example 3.12

Mr. U. B. Court is employed by a Hong Kong company (1) which pays him a salary of $360,000 per annum. He is also employed as a consultant to a subsidiary company (2) which pays him an annual fee of $15,000 and provides rent-free accommodation.
His Salaries Tax position is:—

Salary (1)	$360,000	
Rental Value 10%	36,000	(Note a)
Salary (2)	15,000	
Rental Value 10%	1,500	(Note b)
Total Assessable to Salaries Tax	$412,500	

Notes:—
(a) As the residence is provided by an associated company of company (1), the rental value is computed on the salary from company (1).
(b) The residence is provided by the employer in this case and therefore the rental value is also calculated on the income from that employer.
(c) If Mr. Court's consultancy had instead been with the controlling shareholder of company (1), on the assumption that such shareholder is an individual, the residence is not provided by an associated *company* but an associated individual. His rental value would therefore be limited to $1,500.

3.4.4 Share option benefit

The IRO contains specific provisions to deal with the position where a person is granted, in connection with his employment, an option to acquire shares in a company. These provisions operate to override the decision in *Abbott v Philbin* (39 TC 82) which held that because any gain from the sale of shares obtained through the exercise of such an option flowed more directly from the option itself than from the grantee's employment, any such gain could not be considered a perquisite of that employment and, consequently, was not taxable.

As a consequence of the above decision, Sec. 9(1)(d) was introduced into the IRO. This provision deems any gain realised on the exercise, release or assignment of an option to acquire shares in a corporation which was obtained by an individual as the holder of an office or an employee of that or any other corporation, to be income of that individual from such employment or office. The provision applies irrespective of whether or not the individual is still employed, at the time the deemed gain arises, by the employer who granted the option. This point was confirmed by the Court of First Instance in *CIR v Sawhney, Subhash Chander* [2005] (1 HKRC 90-166) where the court overturned a decision of the Board of Review (see *D 34/05*) that no deemed gain could be assessed if the exercise of the options took place after the relevant employment had ceased. Because the provision does not require the shares which are the subject of the option to be in the same corporation of which the individual is an employee or office-holder, the provisions cannot be frustrated by an employer granting options in an associated, or indeed a non-associated, company. On the other hand, if the grantee can demonstrate that the options were acquired not as a consequence of the holding of an office or employment, but as a normal investment opportunity, the provisions cannot, of course, apply to tax any gain.

As noted above, the liability is triggered by the exercise, release or assignment of the option and the computation of the gain takes place at that time. In the case of a release or assignment, Sec. 9(4)(b) deems the gain to be simply the amount of any consideration received less the amount, if any, paid for the option. In the case of an exercise of an option, however, there is no consideration received and no actual gain will arise until such time as the acquired shares are sold. Nevertheless, Sec. 9(4)(a) deems there to be a gain on exercise equal to the amount that a person might reasonably expect to obtain from a sale in the open market at the time the shares are acquired less the consideration paid, if any, for the option and the amount paid for the shares. For the avoidance of doubt, the proviso to Sec. 9(4) states that in determining the amount "paid" for an option, no value can be attributed to services rendered. The amount which a person could expect to obtain from a sale of the relevant shares in the open market would generally be the open market value at the time less brokerage commission and other transaction costs which would normally be incurred on a sale. In determining the open market value of the shares, *D 66/94* and *D 46/95* provide authority for having regard to any effect on the price which may be brought about by placing all the shares on the market at once. The latter of these decisions provides some practical guidance as to how to estimate such effect on the price. The principle of a downward adjustment to quoted prices to reflect the "slump effect" of placing a large number of shares on the market at one time is now accepted by the IRD, as noted in paragraph 22 of *Departmental Interpretation & Practice Notes No. 38*, which is reproduced as Appendix 14. See also paragraphs 24 to 26 of that document, which explain the IRD's practice regarding the valuation of unquoted shares.

Paragraph 21 of *Departmental Interpretation & Practice Notes No. 38* suggests that where the shares acquired on exercise of an option have restrictions on their sale, this is to be taken into consideration when calculating the deemed gain. This view, which was not always accepted, stems directly from the decision of the Board of Review in *D 120/02* which chose to follow UK administrative guidelines for valuing shares which carried restrictions on their resale. Note, however, that this case involved a share purchase arrangement rather than an employee share option arrangement, although the Board of Review still analysed the tax consequences with regard to Sec. 9(1)(d).

As noted above, the amount of any deemed gain on exercise of an option is to be calculated, pursuant to Sec. 9(4)(a), as the difference between the amount which the person could reasonably expect to obtain from a sale of the shares on the open market at the time of exercise and the amount paid for the grant or exercise of the option. There have been a number of decisions which have considered exactly when the shares are to be valued for the purpose of this provision. In particular, given that the starting point is the amount which the person could "reasonably expect to obtain" from the sale of the shares, there has been debate as to whether the relevant time of calculating the value should be the date of exercise of the option, or the date when the person was first in a position to actually trade the shares, if this was later. In one of the earlier decisions, *D 14/90*, the taxpayer was assessed on a notional gain calculated with reference to the market value on the date of exercise, notwithstanding that he was unable to trade the shares until a month later, at which time he sustained a loss. Contrast this, however, with the later case of *D 43/99* where a different reasoning was adopted and it was held that the gain should be calculated as at the date the shares could first be traded; in that case, this was considered to be the first date on which the share certificates were available for collection, which was approximately two weeks after the taxpayer served notice on his employer exercising the option. Interestingly, in this case part of the reasoning of the Board of Review stemmed from differences in interpretation of the English and Chinese versions of the statutory provisions. The English version of the provision tends to suggest that the time for making the valuation is the time of exercise of the option, whilst the Chinese version implies the relevant time is the time the shares were actually acquired. On the basis that the *Interpretation and General Clauses Ordinance* requires the adoption of the version "... *which best reconciles the two texts, having regard to the objects and purposes of the Ordinance ...*", the Board of Review decided that the Chinese interpretation was more appropriate. Note, however, that in the later decision of *D 120/02* it was held that the non-availability of share certificates did not prevent a deemed gain arising under Sec. 9(1)(d), although the gain could only arise at the time the shares could be said to have been acquired which, although not necessarily the time of exercising the option, was not dependent on the receipt of share certificates. That decision was quoted with approval in *D 84/03*. In paragraph 17 of *Departmental Interpretation & Practice Notes No. 38* (which is reproduced as Appendix 14), the IRD state that following the decisions in *D 43/99* and *D 120/02*, if a taxpayer can establish that because of circumstances beyond his control he did not acquire the relevant shares until a date after the exercise of the options, that later date will be adopted for the purpose of calculating the gain from the exercise. The IRD suggest, however, that shares are considered to be acquired when the holder's name is entered in the share register and the holder becomes entitled to vote at meetings and receive dividends, irrespective of when any share certificates are received. Such a view is, of course, in accordance with *D 120/02*.

It will be noted that Sec. 9(1)(d) deals only with gains on the exercise, release or assignment of an option; it does not deal with the tax consequences of the original grant of the option. Under general rules and following the decision in *Abbott v Philbin* (supra), a taxable benefit may arise at the time an option is granted if the value of the option at the time of the grant exceeds the amount paid for it. However, if such a benefit was assessed and the option was subsequently exercised, released or assigned, the operation of Sec. 9(1)(d) would result in double taxation as the computation of the gain under that provision allows only the amount paid for the option, not its value at the time of grant, to be deducted. In order to overcome this potential inequity, Sec. 9(5) provides that where the grant of an option may ultimately result in the application of Sec. 9(1)(d), Salaries Tax will not be imposed under any other provision of the IRO in respect of that grant.

It is also important to remember that Sec. 9(1)(d) only deems the relevant amounts to be income from the employment of the person to whom the option was granted; the amount then falls into the charge to Salaries Tax by virtue of Sec. 8(1), the general Salaries Tax charging provision. As such, it is still necessary to determine the source of the deemed gain, as if it can be established that the deemed gain arises or is derived from outside Hong Kong, the amount will not be taxable. Unfortunately, the IRO and case law provide no guidance on the determination of the source of such gains. Clearly, the underlying employment is fundamental in determining the source of any deemed gain. Accordingly, where the option was granted as a consequence of a Hong Kong employment or office (see sections 3.3.2.2 and 3.3.3 above), any deemed gain will be taxable unless all services under the employment are rendered abroad (or are rendered in Hong Kong only during visits totalling less than sixty days in each year of assessment). Similarly, where the deemed gain arises from an option granted in connection with a non-Hong Kong employment but under which all services were rendered in Hong Kong, there appears to be little scope for arguing that the deemed gain has an offshore source. The real difficulty arises, however, where an option is granted in connection with a non-Hong Kong employment and the services have been rendered in a number of different jurisdictions.

Consider, for example, the position of an individual who is employed by a US corporation and worked in the US for five years, after which he is granted an option to acquire shares in the corporation. Assume the individual continued to work in the US for another five years and is then transferred to the Hong Kong branch of the corporation; one year after moving to Hong Kong, he exercises his options. The question arises as to whether the source of the gain on the option is the service up to the grant of the option, the individual's place of employment at the time of grant of the option, the place where the services were rendered between the time the option was granted and the time it was exercised, the place of employment at the time of exercise, or, indeed, some other factor. Although the IRO provides no specific guidance, it is submitted that as the wording of Sec. 9(1)(d) requires the establishment of a nexus between the employment and the **grant** of the option, rather than between the employment and the **exercise** of the option, it is generally more logical to look to the service at and before the grant of the option as the most important factor in determining the source of any deemed gain resulting from the exercise, release or assignment of that option. In the above example, this would lead to the conclusion that the deemed gain on exercise would have a non-Hong Kong source and, hence, would not be subject to Salaries Tax. Conversely, however, on the basis of this view, an individual with a non-Hong Kong employment who was granted options while in Hong Kong and as a consequence of Hong Kong service, but who exercised those options after leaving Hong Kong would be liable to Salaries Tax on the deemed gain.

The uncertainty surrounding the determination of the source of deemed gains relating to employee share options has been partly addressed by the issue of *Departmental Interpretation & Practice Notes No. 38*. In that document, the IRD has accepted the view that the source of a deemed gain will be determined by the circumstances of the individual's employment at the time of the grant of the option, but only if the grant was unconditional (i.e. was not subject to a vesting period, being a period after the grant during which certain conditions need to be satisfied for the benefit of the options to unconditionally pass to the grantee). In other words, the deemed gain from the exercise of an unconditional option will generally be taxable in the same manner as the individual's other income from the relevant employment was taxed in the year of assessment of the grant of the option. (An exception to this applies where the grant was made in a year in which the individual had an offshore employment but rendered services in Hong Kong; in particular, if the grant was made before any services were rendered in Hong Kong in that year of assessment, any deemed gain from a subsequent exercise, assignment of release will be accepted as non-taxable.)

Where, however, the grant of the option was subject to a vesting period, the IRD considers it appropriate to look to the period between the grant of the option and the expiration of the vesting period in determining the source of the deemed gain on exercise, assignment or release. Accordingly, where the grant was in connection with a non-Hong Kong employment, the deemed gain on exercise, assignment or release will be apportioned and taxed on the basis of the number of days of the vesting period on which services were rendered by the individual in Hong Kong together with leave days attributable to such Hong Kong service. However, if in a year of assessment during the vesting period the individual was not subject to Salaries Tax at all on the basis that he rendered services in Hong Kong during visits totaling less than sixty days, all of the days of that year of assessment can be excluded in calculating the apportionment ratio. On the other hand, where a grant subject to a vesting period is in connection with a Hong Kong employment, the IRD takes the view that there is no apportionment to be applied. That is, the IRD will accept that no liability arises under Sec. 9(1)(d) if in **each** year of assessment in the vesting period the taxpayer renders no services in Hong Kong (or renders services only during visits totalling less than sixty days), but will treat the whole of the deemed gain as taxable if in **any** year of assessment during the vesting period the taxpayer renders services in Hong Kong (other than only during visits totalling less than sixty days).

A further apportionment may be required where during a vesting period the holder of share options changes his employment from a Hong Kong to a non-Hong Kong employment, or *vice versa*. Such scenarios are discussed in paragraphs 56 and 57 of *Departmental Interpretation & Practice Notes No. 38*. Additionally, such a scenario was considered by the Board of Review in *D 32/04*, which upheld the need to apportion the total gain between the two employments when ascertaining the overall taxable gain.

The above is only a brief summary of the IRD's stated practice with regard to the determination of the source of a deemed gain from the exercise of an option to acquire shares. For a more comprehensive explanation, together with many practical examples of how the practice is applied by the IRD, see paragraphs 36 to 57 of *Departmental Interpretation & Practice Notes No. 38*, which is reproduced as Appendix 14.

The IRD's views on the source of a deemed gain from the exercise of employee share options should, however, be contrasted with the decision in *D 4/02*. In that case, the taxpayer left Hong Kong on 25 March 1997 to take up employment in the UK. On 3 April 1997, the taxpayer exercised options which had been granted to him in earlier years in connection with his Hong Kong employment. The taxpayer sought to argue that the deemed gain on exercise of the options was non-taxable under Sec. 8(1A)(b)(ii) (see section 3.3.2.2) as all services in the year in which the exercise took place (i.e. the 1997/98 year) were rendered outside Hong Kong. The IRD, on the other hand, argued that the entire gain was taxable; this may have been in accordance with the IRD's practice as described above although, unfortunately, the published decision contained no information on vesting periods and whether all of the taxpayer's income had been subject to Salaries Tax in the earlier years of assessment. Nonetheless, in rejecting the taxpayer's argument, the Board of Review held that Sec. 8(1A)(b)(ii) only applied to exempt income where, *inter alia*, the income was derived from services rendered and that the share option gain was not income derived from services rendered and, therefore, it could not be exempt pursuant to that provision. This analysis, therefore, calls into doubt the correctness of the IRD's practice of apportioning deemed share option gains where a part of the employee's income during the vesting period has been granted exemption pursuant to Sec. 8(1A)(b)(ii).

Nonetheless, applying the IRD's views regarding the determination of the source of a deemed gain from the exercise, assignment or release of a stock option, it is clear that there will be cases where a taxable gain arises after the individual has permanently left Hong Kong. In such circumstances, it is likely to be often difficult in practice for the IRD to collect the tax due from the individual. Presumably in recognition of this, the IRD, in paragraph 58 of *Departmental Interpretation & Practice Notes No. 38*, states that it will allow individuals who are permanently departing Hong Kong to finalise their tax liabilities by electing to treat the unexercised options as having been exercised on a day within seven days before the person's final tax return in respect of the year of assessment in which they departed Hong Kong is submitted. The IRD will also permit such an election to be made within three months after the date of permanent departure, in which case the notional exercise is to be treated as having been made on the date of such departure. Moreover, the IRD states that if upon a subsequent actual exercise of the options the deemed gain is a smaller amount than was assessed on departure from Hong Kong, they will favourably consider an application for amendment or re-assessment. Whilst this approach may assist the IRD in collecting tax (or a portion thereof) which may otherwise be uncollectable, it has no basis in law and cannot be insisted upon by the IRD.

■ Example 3.13

Percy Vere is a director of Stocks Ltd., a Hong Kong company, and in consideration of his services, he is given a special opportunity to invest in the parent company, Shares Ltd. He pays $50 for an option to acquire 2,000 shares in Shares Ltd. at $10 each. At the time of taking up the option the shares have an open market value of $20 each. Unfortunately the value drops and a month later Percy exercises his option when the value is $15.

The "profit" assessable to Salaries Tax is:

Open Market Value at date of exercise	2,000 @ $15 =	$30,000
Consideration given for Shares	2,000 @ $10 = $20,000	
Consideration given for Option	50	20,050
Subject to Salaries Tax		$ 9,950

Notes:—
(a) On the principle of *Abbott v Philbin*, there is a taxable profit at the time of granting the option because the market value of the shares at that time exceeds what he has to pay for them. Such amount is not however assessed because Sec. 9(5) exempts it.
(b) If it had not been clear that the option had been granted to him because of his directorship, this question would have to be considered on the facts.
(c) It is assumed that Percy was in a position to dispose of the shares immediately upon exercise. If he had not, *D 43/99* and paragraph 17 of *Departmental Interpretation & Practice Notes No. 38* (see text) may provide authority for calculating the market value of the shares at a later date.

■ Example 3.14

Mr. Lee King was employed as a vice president of Village Bank in New York in 1998. On 1 April 2000 he was granted options to acquire 10,000 shares in Village Bank for US$5 each. Of these options, 5,000 could be exercised at any time after 31 March 2002, whilst the other 5,000 could only be exercised after 31 March 2004. Any unexercised options would lapse if Mr. King ceased to be employed by Village Bank or its subsidiaries. On 1 April 2003, Mr. King was transferred to work in the Hong Kong branch of Village Bank and on 30 June 2006 he exercised all of his options, at a time when the share price was US$12. The IRD accepts that Mr. King has a non-Hong Kong employment.

Because the vesting period in respect of 5,000 options had already passed when Mr. King moved to Hong Kong, no deemed gain will be considered to arise in respect of the exercise of those options, even though the exercise took place while he was in Hong Kong. (Refer to paragraph 43 of *Departmental Interpretation & Practice Notes No. 38*.)

In respect of the other 5,000 options, the vesting period was four years, of which during one year Mr. King was working in Hong Kong. Accordingly, the IRD will accept that only 25% of the otherwise deemed gain will be taxable. (Refer to paragraph 55 of *Departmental Interpretation & Practice Notes No. 38*.)

The deemed taxable gain derived by Mr. King on exercise of the options is, therefore:

$$5,000 \times (12 - 5) \times 0.25 = US\$8,750 @ 7.8 = HK\$68,250$$

Note that for simplicity it is assumed that from 1 April 2003 Mr. King rendered all his services in Hong Kong (i.e. he did not travel abroad on business). If he did render services outside Hong Kong during this period, however, his deemed taxable gain would likely be reduced. This is because it is likely that Mr. King would be considered to have a non-Hong Kong employment (even from 1 April 2003) and, therefore, any remuneration attributable to services rendered abroad would be exempt from Salaries Tax. This is effectively incorporated into the formula used by the IRD in paragraph 35(vii) of *Departmental Interpretation & Practice Notes No. 38* as the numerator of that formula is days spent rendering services in Hong Kong during the vesting period and not the number of days during which the employee was based in Hong Kong.

Finally, it must be remembered that *Departmental Interpretation & Practice Notes No. 38* only contains the IRD's view and it is open to a taxpayer to argue that a different basis of determining the deemed taxable gain in circumstances such as in this example is applicable.

The situation of the granting of options to acquire shares is sometimes considered as different from the position where a person is allowed to immediately subscribe for shares at a price below the market value at the time. Certainly, the IRD in paragraph 11 of *Departmental Interpretation & Practice Notes No. 38* appears to draw such a distinction on the basis that an invitation to subscribe for shares is not a legally enforceable right and, therefore, may be withdrawn at any time. The position of a share subscription at a discount was, nonetheless, considered and held to give rise to an immediate taxable benefit, in the UK case of *Weight v Salmon* (19 TC 174). This decision was followed in *BR 27/69*, although it should be noted that this was decided before Sec. 9(1)(d) was enacted. Arguably, however, the position of an employee being allowed to subscribe for shares at a discount is the same as the position of the granting of an option to acquire shares except that there is no vesting period between the granting of the option and the time the option can be exercised. This view appears to have been implicitly adopted in *D 102/02* where the Board of Review analysed the position of a share purchase at a discount by applying Sec. 9(1)(d).

On the other hand, see *D 198/03* for a case where an employee accepted shares in settlement of amounts of salary and other employment and director's remuneration which were owing to him. In that case, the Board of Review rejected the taxpayer's claim that the shares received were not assessable on the grounds that they represented a settlement of claims against the employing company. More interestingly, however, because the case involved the issue of shares directly without first granting an option, the Board of Review held that the provisions of Sec. 9(1)(d) did not apply. One consequence of this was that the assessable amount was not related to the market value of the shares received, but was determined as the original amount owing to the taxpayer, the liability for payment of which had been discharged by the issue of shares.

3.4.5 Other perquisites

As will have been seen in section 3.4.1, the general definition in Sec. 9(1)(a) of what comprises assessable income includes one item which has always given rise to difficulty, namely "perquisites". The general commercial understanding of what comprises a perquisite is relatively wide, meaning any emolument or reward of value to an employee in addition to salary and wages. When the definition had to be judicially considered for tax purposes in the UK many years ago, however, the meaning of perquisite was substantially limited. It was, in effect, limited to those emoluments that could be turned into cash or which represented "cash equivalents". The reasoning for this was that taxation is a cash imposition and, therefore, should only be imposed upon cash which an individual has or could have.

This legal understanding of what comprises a perquisite for tax purposes was adopted for Salaries Tax purposes in Hong Kong for many years in respect of those types of perquisites not specifically dealt with in the IRO. Housing accommodation and share option benefits are both perquisites but subject to specific rules as already described in sections 3.4.3 and 3.4.4 respectively and not, therefore, subject to the case law principles as were all other perquisites.

This was the case until the decision in *CIR v David Hardy Glynn* (3 HKTC 245) which went against the UK principles and effectively took the commercial understanding of the meaning of perquisite and applied it for Salaries Tax purposes. As this considerable broadening of the basis of Salaries Tax was contrary to Government policy it was necessary to change the law to substantially return to the old principles that had been understood from UK case law. Accordingly, the IRO was changed to include as taxable only those perquisites which would have been taxable under the old principles plus education benefits in whatever form provided (see (7) and (8) in section 3.4.1). To complete the exercise, it was necessary to exclude from the IRO those types of perquisite that had been brought into charge by the *Glynn* case but which were not taxable under the previously understood principles (see (20) in section 3.4.6).

Students of Hong Kong taxation can be forgiven for being confused by these developments and as to why the *Glynn* case was ever brought by the Commissioner in the first instance and, furthermore, as to why education benefits should be singled out from other perquisites for special adverse treatment. In general, it is no longer necessary to know the old case law principles although certain types of perquisites which were caught by these principles have not been effectively excluded from the IRO and could, therefore, still be taxed. These comprise the "cash equivalents" which may be taxable at face value if they enable an employee to make independent purchases (even if they can only be spent at one store), because they represent money's worth. The classic example is gift vouchers or luncheon vouchers (see *Laidler v Perry* (42 TC 351)).

It must be remembered that even if a cash payment or a cash convertible benefit is derived by an individual from their employer, it will, in essence, only be taxable if it is a reward for services rendered or to be rendered. For a further discussion of this principle and examples of cases where the Board of Review has rejected arguments by the Commissioner that all amounts received from an employer are perquisites and, therefore, taxable pursuant to Sec. 9(1)(a), see section 3.4.2.

See also Example 3.15 and *Departmental Interpretation & Practice Notes No. 16*, which is reproduced as Appendix A13.

3.4.6 Exclusions from assessable income

The IRO contains a number of specific provisions which deem certain receipts, which would otherwise fall within the scope of Salaries Tax, to be exempt from Salaries Tax. These are:—

(1) **Certain consular staff emoluments:** Sec. 8(2)(b) exempts the emoluments of consuls, vice-consuls and persons on the staff of any consulate provided that they are subjects or citizens of the country which they represent. The meaning of "represent" in this context was considered in *D 81/98,* where it was held that this was a reference to consular relations and only individuals recognised by the Hong Kong Government as consular representatives of the

foreign government in whose consulate they were employed, qualified for the exemption. See also (8) and (13) below;

(2) **Emoluments of certain staff of International Organisations:** In addition to the exclusion granted in (1) above, the Chief Executive is empowered, under the *International Organisations and Diplomatic Privileges Ordinance*, by notice in the *Gazette* to exempt all or certain classes of staff of an international organisation, as may be specified in that notice. An international organisation for this purpose is defined as one of which one or more sovereign powers are members and of which either the Government of Hong Kong or the Government of the PRC is a member or associate member. Additionally, pursuant to Sec. 87, the Chief Executive in Council has issued an order exempting from Salaries Tax the remuneration of all Chinese nationals and Hong Kong permanent residents from employment with the International Finance Corporation;

(3) **Lump sums from commutation of a pension:** Sec. 8(2)(c) exempts any lump sum received by way of commutation of a pension under a recognised occupational retirement scheme (see definition in section 10.3.1) upon termination of service, death, incapacity or retirement, or under the *Pensions Ordinance*, the *Pension Benefits Ordinance* or the *Pension Benefits (Judicial Officers) Ordinance*. This provision appears to apply only to a commutation of a presently existing pension entitlement and not to a lump sum which affects a person's rights to, or terms of, a future pension (see *BR 89/77* and *D 28/91*).

   A further restriction on the exemption provided by Sec. 8(2)(c) is contained in Sec. 8(4). This restriction applies upon termination of service other than upon retirement, death or incapacity, and provides that any portion of such a payment as represents the employer's contributions can only be excluded to the extent that it does not exceed the "proportionate benefit". The term "proportionate benefit", which is defined in Sec. 8(5), is discussed in point (6) below;

(4) **Pensions attributable to non-Hong Kong services:** Sec. 8(2)(ca) exempts pension benefits as far as they are attributable to services rendered outside Hong Kong, other than services of Hong Kong Government servants. See section 3.3.4 for a further discussion of this;

(5) **Amounts attributable to mandatory contributions withdrawn from a MPF scheme:** Any accrued benefits received on retirement from employment, death, incapacity or permanent departure from

Hong Kong from a MPF scheme are exempt to the extent they are attributable to mandatory contributions (Sec. 8(2)(cb));

(6) **Amounts withdrawn from a recognized occupational retirement scheme:** Sec. 8(2)(cc)(i) exempts any amount, other than a pension, withdrawn from a recognized occupational retirement scheme (see definition in section 10.3.1) upon termination of service, death, incapacity or retirement. This exemption is, however, subject to two restrictions. Firstly, Sec. 8(4) provides that in respect of a termination of service the exempt amount cannot exceed the "proportionate benefit", which is defined in Sec. 8(5) as:

$$PB = CMS/120 \times AB$$

where: **PB** is the proportionate benefit;
           CMS is the number of completed months service with the employer; and
           AB is the amount of the person's "accrued benefit" from the recognized occupational retirement scheme.

"Accrued benefit" is defined in Sec. 8(6) as the maximum amount that the person would have been entitled to receive on the basis of his completed service had he retired at the date on which his employment terminated. Of course, the individual's employment may have actually terminated due to retirement in which case the accrued benefit would presumably be the amount actually received; however, where the termination was for reasons other than retirement it is possible that the scheme rules provide for less than the amount payable on retirement. Retirement for this purpose is defined in Sec. 8(3) and means retirement from the service of the employer at a specified age not less than 45 years, retirement after a specified period of service with the employer of not less than ten years, or the attainment of the age of sixty or some other specified retirement age, whichever is later. The last alternative appears to permit a person to be treated as having retired for the purpose of obtaining the exemption from tax on payments from a recognized occupational retirement scheme, notwithstanding that they actually continue in employment with the same employer.

The effect of the proportionate benefit rule is that the exemption under Sec. 8(2)(cc)(i) (and various other provisions discussed elsewhere in this chapter), is pro-rated on the basis of months of service with the full exemption only being available after ten years service.

Secondly, Sec. 8(7) provides that the exempt amount is to be further limited where the relevant employer is not subject to Profits Tax. The calculation of this further limitation is contained in Sec. 8(8) and is essentially:

$$A = EI \times 15\% \times YCS$$

where: **A** is the amount to which the exemption is limited;

EI is the amount of the employee's income from the employer for the 12 months preceding the date on which the relevant benefit is received or taken to be received; and

YCS is the employee's completed years of service with the employer.

In other words, the exemption is limited to an amount equal to 15% of the employee's last year's earnings, multiplied by the number of years completed service.

(7)   **Amounts attributable to voluntary contributions withdrawn from a MPF scheme:** Any accrued benefits received on retirement, death, incapacity, termination of service, from a MPF scheme are exempt to the extent they are attributable to voluntary contributions (which are defined in Sec. 2 as contributions pursuant to Sec. 11 of the *Mandatory Provident Fund Schemes Ordinance*) made by the recipient's employer (Sec. 8(2)(cc)(ii)). This exemption is, however, limited to the proportionate benefit calculated in accordance with Sec. 8(5), which is discussed in point (6) above. Note, however, that in calculating the proportionate benefit, the term "accrued benefit" has a slightly different meaning in relation to a MPF scheme from that described above in relation to recognized occupational retirement schemes. In particular, when dealing with an MPF scheme, the term is defined simply to mean the employee's accrued benefits in relation to voluntary contributions paid to the scheme. For the purpose of this provision, Sec. 8(9) deems a person whose service with an employer has been terminated to have received any amounts attributable to the employer's voluntary contributions which have been left in the MPF scheme or have been transferred to another MPF scheme. This is, of course, important as although Sec. 8(2)(cc)(ii) is an exempting provision, it effectively means that amounts received, or deemed to have been received, in excess of the

proportionate benefit are taxable (as such amounts are income from employment which do not attract any exemptions). Nonetheless, any benefits so retained or transferred are effectively exempt from Salaries Tax when subsequently received, pursuant to Sec. 8(10).

As with Sec. 8(2)(cc)(i), the exemption under Sec. 8(2)(cc)(ii) is further restricted, pursuant to Secs. 8(7) and 8(8), where the employer is not subject to Profits Tax. The formula for this restriction is the same as discussed in point (6) above with the exception that the limit is further reduced by the amount of the accrued benefit received by the person as is attributable to the mandatory contributions paid to the MPF scheme by the person's employer;

(8) **Emoluments of Commonwealth civil servants:** Sec. 8(2)(d) provides an exemption for emoluments paid by Commonwealth Governments to members of Her Majesty's (i.e. British Government) forces and permanent civil servants in the employ of those Governments. The interpretation of this provision has been altered by the amendments to the *Interpretation and General Clauses Ordinance* which were introduced by the *Hong Kong Reunification Ordinance*. In particular, provisions relating to British Government forces stationed in Hong Kong are now to be interpreted, subject to the Basic Law and the Garrison Law of the Hong Kong SAR, as applying to military forces of the People's Republic of China who are stationed in Hong Kong. Nonetheless, the exemption still only applies to remuneration paid to members of those forces by Commonwealth Governments and, therefore, it would appear the exemption will have little practical application. The continuing application of Sec. 8(2)(d) to Commonwealth civil servants is less clear. Amendments introduced by the *Hong Kong Reunification Ordinance* operate to render ineffective any statutory provisions which confer privileges on the UK or other Commonwealth countries except where such provisions give effect to reciprocal arrangements. However, it is not clear whether this is intended to extend to revoking privileges conferred upon employees of the Governments of such countries. See also (13) below;

(9) **Wound and disability pensions:** Sec. 8(2)(e) exempts wound and disability pensions granted to members of Her Majesty's (i.e. British Government) forces. Following the amendments introduced by the *Hong Kong Reunification Ordinance*, it appears that the reference in this provision to Her Majesty's forces is to be read as a reference to the forces of the Government of Hong Kong, although as Hong

Kong does not have its own forces it seems that the provision will have no application;

(10) **War service gratuities:** Sec. 8(2)(f) exempts war service gratuities granted to members of Her Majesty's (i.e. British Government) forces. Again, as a result of the amendments introduced by the *Hong Kong Reunification Ordinance* it appears that the reference to Her Majesty's forces is to be read as a reference to forces of the Government of Hong Kong and, therefore, this exemption appears to have only limited, if any, application;

(11) **War Memorial Pensions:** An exemption is contained in Sec. 8(2)(fa) for the Hong Kong War Memorial Pensions and additional benefits paid under the *Hong Kong War Memorial Pensions Ordinance*;

(12) **Education endowments:** Sec. 8(2)(g) exempts any amounts arising from a scholarship, exhibition, bursary, or similar educational endowment held by a person receiving full time education at a recognised educational establishment. This only applies to the education of the employee himself and not any other person (e.g. a child of the person);

(13) **Emoluments of certain PRC Government servants:** Emoluments payable by the Central People's Government to temporary servants who in the Commissioner's opinion satisfy specified criteria are exempt under Sec. 8(2)(h). The criteria are that the individuals:—

(i)   are serving in Hong Kong on Mainland of China based terms because they normally serve in the Mainland of China but are liable for overseas tours of duty; or

(ii) are recruited in the Mainland of China specially for service in Hong Kong.

For a review of the principles involved, see *D 12/82*, although note that this decision related to the pre-1997 position where the provision applied to UK Government servants;

(14) **Alimony or maintenance payments:** Alimony or maintenance payments received by a person from his or her spouse or ex-spouse are exempt pursuant to Sec. 8(2)(i);

(15) **Seafarers and aircrew:** Sec. 8(2)(j) exempts seafarers and aircrew from Salaries Tax where they satisfy the physical presence rules. For a further discussion, see section 3.3.5;

(16) **Non-deductible salary and other remuneration:** Sec. 8(2)(k) exempts from tax any salary or other remuneration received by a person from a business carried on by that person's spouse, or from a

partnership in which the person or the person's spouse is a partner, where the salary or other remuneration is deemed non-deductible for Profits Tax purposes by Sec. 17(2) (see section 4.5.10). This exemption is, therefore, essentially a corollary to Sec. 17(2) in that it avoids double taxation by exempting from Salaries Tax certain amounts which are rendered non-deductible by Sec. 17(2). This exemption, together with Sec. 17(2), is generally straightforward, although problems can sometimes occur in relation to remuneration from a partnership. This is due to the fact that sometimes individuals are referred to as partners, but are remunerated in a manner similar to that of employees and do not directly share in losses of the partnership; such individuals are often referred to as "salaried partners". In such cases, it is necessary to decide whether the individual is a partner or an employee and although each case must be decided on its own facts, a good summary of the principles involved can be found in *D 68/03*;

(17) **Certain pension benefits:** The Governor-in-Council (i.e. the predecessor to the Chief Executive in Council), pursuant to the powers contained under Sec. 87 (see Chapter 10), exempted all pensions granted under regulation 31 of the Pension Regulations, Sec. 15(1) of either the *Pension Benefits Ordinance* or the *Pension Benefits (Judicial Officers) Ordinance* or Sec. 3(1) of the *Auxilliary Forces Pay and Allowances (Pensions) Regulation*. Additionally, a limited exemption has been granted, from the 1993/94 year of assessment, in respect of benefits granted to officers of the Hong Kong Monetary Authority who were appointed under Sec. 5A(1) or 5A(3) of the *Exchange Fund Ordinance* from any retirement scheme to which the Hong Kong Monetary Authority is a party. The exemption applies to afford such benefits the same tax treatment as they would receive if the retirement schemes in question were recognized occupational retirement schemes (see (3) and (6) above), provided all the requirements under the IRO which would normally need to be met for a payment to receive such exemption are fulfilled in granting the benefit. Put another way, the provision merely deems certain retirement schemes operated by the Hong Kong Monetary Authority, which would not otherwise qualify, to be recognised occupational retirement schemes for Salaries Tax purposes when considering the assessability of benefits received therefrom by the specified class of members;

(18) **Holiday warrants or passage allowance:** Up until, and including,

the 2002/03 year of assessment Secs. 9(1)(a)(i) and (ii) exempted the value of any holiday warrant or passage granted to an employee or any allowance for the purchase of such provided that it was expended for that purpose. There was no limit to the amount or frequency of such tax free benefits; the only qualification was that it was actually expended for the given purpose. Indeed, it seemed that it was not even necessary for the allowance to have been *only* available to be used for holiday travel; rather, in *D 21/00* it was held that the only requirement was that it be expended for that purpose if the exemption from Salaries Tax was to apply and that the exemption could apply even if the whole amount of the allowance was not expended for the intended purpose (although, of course, the exemption applied only to the amount actually so expended). In that decision, the Board of Review rejected the submission of the Commissioner's representative that an allowance which could be expended at the discretion of the taxpayer could not qualify for the exemption. Interestingly, the Board of Review also rejected the Commissioner's representative's submission that the amount of the allowance should be treated as taxable salary on the grounds that the terms of the relevant employment had changed to effectively convert a portion of what had previously been the taxpayer's assessable salary into a holiday allowance.

An exemption was also granted in respect of any allowance for the transportation of personal effects in connection with journeys as discussed above, although again only to the extent that the allowance is expended for such purpose (Sec. 9(1)(a)(iii)).

As Secs. 9(1)(a)(i), (ii) and (iii) were repealed with effect from the 2003/04 year of assessment, the above exclusions from assessable income no longer apply. Moreover, provisions have been introduced to render holiday travel benefits taxable even where under the general rules dealing with perquisites the amounts would not otherwise be taxable (see point (9) in section 3.4.1);

(19) **Housing benefit:** Sec. 9(1A)(a) exempts refunds of rent to an employee in respect of his residence or rent paid direct to a landlord on behalf of an employee. A taxable benefit may arise in these cases under a separate formula; see section 3.4.3 above;

(20) **Payments to third parties:** Sec. 9(1)(a)(iv) exempts amounts paid by an employer to a third party in discharge of a contractual obligation incurred by the employer (provided that no person has given a surety in respect of that obligation) even though the payment

gives rise to a benefit (not convertible to cash) for an employee of the person making the payment. This is to counteract the effect of the decision in *CIR v David Hardy Glynn* (3 HKTC 245) which would otherwise have included such a benefit to an employee within the definition of "perquisite". The reason for the qualification relating to those cases where the liability is guaranteed by the employee or any other person is unclear, although it is to be noted that such a surety was, in fact, given by the taxpayer in the *Glynn* case;

(21) **Income taxed in other countries:** Income earned in another country is exempt under Sec. 8(1A)(c) where that income is subject to tax in the country where the services are performed and the Commissioner is satisfied that the tax has been paid in that other country. For a more detailed discussion on this provision, see section 3.3.2.2; and

(22) **Salary paid by certain service companies:** Sec. 9A(5)(b) exempts salary paid to an individual by a service company or trust where the amounts earned by that company or trust for the provision of the individual's services are deemed under Sec. 9A(1) to be income of the individual. See further section 3.8.1 below.

Although not specifically provided for under the IRO, by way of an extra-statutory concession the Commissioner accepts long service or severance payments under the *Employment Ordinance* as exempt from Salaries Tax. For a discussion of this concession, see section 3.4.2.8.

The following example brings together many of the issues discussed in section 3.4.

■ Example 3.15

Ian Mee has the following remuneration package for a year of assessment. He is employed by a non-Hong Kong company under a contract concluded outside Hong Kong and is paid in foreign currency so that the assessor is satisfied that he has a non-Hong Kong employment. He is able to show that, during the year of assessment 30% of his services were performed outside Hong Kong.

(1)   Salary $360,000
(2)   Bonus $90,000
(3)   Allowance for high cost of living $45,000
(4)   The company rents a car at a cost of $45,000 for the year and allows him to use it wholly for private purposes. They also pay the licence and insurance costing $17,500 and have reimbursed his garage bills of $15,000 during the year. He pays for his own fuel.
(5)   Two years ago he was granted, at a cost of $100, an option to subscribe for 1,000 shares in his employer company at $20 each. This year their market value rose to

$25 each and he exercised his option. He still has the shares which also paid a dividend to him of $1,500.

(6)   He rents his own flat at a cost of $24,000 per month including rates and service charge and his employer reimburses this in full but deducts 3% from his salary as a rent contribution.

(7)   His domestic servant is employed by the company at a cost of $45,000 for the year and the employer also refunds his electricity bill of $12,500 for the year. In addition, his employer has entered into a contract with a pest control company and paid them $20,000 during the year. Ian had to guarantee this contract.

(8) $75,000 holiday travel allowance for himself and family which he wholly spent for that purpose in the year.

(9)   Under a tax equalization agreement, his employer paid his US Tax bill of $15,000 and Salaries Tax bill of $90,000 during the year.

(10) His employer has a contractual arrangement with a school in Hong Kong at which Ian's son receives education and the employer paid the school fees of $90,000 under that contractual arrangement.

His assessable income for Salaries Tax is:—

(1)	Salary		$360,000	
(2)	Bonus		90,000	
(3)	Cost of living allowance		45,000	
(4)	Use of car		15,000	(Note (a))
(5)	Share option — Market value	$25,000		
	Cost, including option	20,100	4,900	(Note (b))
(7)	Household benefits		32,500	(Note (c))
(9)	US Tax paid by employer		15,000	(Note (d))
(10)	School fees		90,000	(Note (e))
(11)	Holiday travel allowance		75,000	(Note (h))
			$727,400	
	Exclusion of services outside Hong Kong (30%)		218,220	(Note (f))
			$509,180	
(9)	Salaries Tax paid by employer		90,000	(Note (d))
	Net Assessable Income before Housing Accommodation benefit		$599,180	
(6)	Housing Accommodation benefit (10% × ($599,180 – 70% of $4,900))	$59,575		
	Less: Rent contribution (3% × $360,000)	10,800	48,775	(Note (g))
	Assessable to Salaries Tax		$647,955	

Notes:—

(a)   There is no chargeable benefit in respect of the use of the car or the licence and insurance because these items cannot be converted into cash (Sec. 9(2A)(a)). However, he incurs his own bills at the garage and reimbursements thereof are therefore taxable. Even if he presented the bills to the employer for direct payment after receiving them personally, this would be a taxable perquisite. It would be tax free if the employer contracted with the garage and was therefore billed direct, provided that Ian did not guarantee the arrangement (Sec. 9(1)(a)(iv)).

(b)   The taxable benefit is triggered by the exercise of the option (Sec. 9(1)(d)) irrespective of the fact that he has not yet realised the gain. The dividend is not taxable.

(c)   The same principles as discussed in Note (a) apply. As the liability for the electricity bill was incurred by Ian, the reimbursement is taxable and, as he guaranteed the contractual arrangements with the pest control company, this is also taxable.

(d) The US Tax bill paid by the employer is part of the remuneration for all services and is therefore apportioned between Hong Kong and non-Hong Kong duties. The Salaries Tax is however, per *D 31/85* and *D 106/89*, attributable only to Hong Kong duties and is therefore not apportioned (see section 3.3.2.1).

(e) Even though the school fees are paid by the employer under contractual arrangements made between the employer and the school and Ian has not guaranteed those arrangements, the benefit is nevertheless specifically taxable (Sec. 9(2A)(b)).

(f) See section 3.3.2.1.

(g) The rental value is calculated on assessable income after excluding the share option benefit net of the proportion which is exempt because it relates to offshore duties (*BR 20/76*). The rent contribution is not, however, pro-rated per the decision in *CIR v R. P. Williamson* (HKTC 1215). See section 3.4.3 above.

(h) The holiday travel allowance was previously exempt pursuant to Sec. 9(1)(a)(ii). However, such amount is, from the 2003/04 year of assessment fully taxable following the repeal of Sec. 9(1)(a)(ii) (see point (18) in section 3.4.6) and the enactment of Sec. 9(2A)(c) (see point (9) in section 3.4.1).

3.5 Deductions from Assessable Income

As will be seen in section 3.6, in order to arrive at net chargeable income, deductions may be claimed for certain expenses, depreciation allowances, charitable contributions, home loan interest, elderly residential care expenses, contributions to recognized retirement schemes and losses. These are dealt with under separate headings below.

3.5.1 Expenses

A deduction may be claimed for all outgoings and expenses, other than expenses of a domestic, private or capital nature, which have been wholly, exclusively and necessarily incurred in the production of assessable income (Sec. 12(1)(a)).

Admissable expenses under this heading are relatively few because of the stringent requirements for their deductibility. The provision is very similar to an equivalent provision in UK tax law and therefore the numerous UK Court decisions which relate to the UK equivalent are looked to for guidance. Although the law is sufficiently similar for the UK decisions to be authoritative, it is questionable whether reliance should be placed upon them where the decision turned upon whether or not, for UK purposes, the expenditure had been incurred "in the performance of the duties"; this is because in Hong Kong the relevant wording is "in the production of the assessable income" which is different from the UK provision, although in the Hong Kong case of *CIR v Humphrey* (HKTC 451) this distinction was not considered important. This view that the differences in the wording of the legislation is of no consequence was more recently endorsed by the Court of First Instance in *CIR v Tong Sui Lun* [2006] (1 HKRC 90-180).

The preclusion from deduction of domestic and private expenditure seems hardly necessary as any such expenditure is unlikely to be able to be considered as wholly, exclusively and necessarily incurred in the production of assessable income. In practice, however, the provision operates to deny deduction of expenses which could be argued to have an indirect nexus to the earning of assessable income but where that nexus is so remote as to make the expenditure essentially private in nature. One of the most common examples of this is expenses incurred in travelling to and from work. While the earning of income would clearly not be possible without incurring such expenses, it is a fundamental principle that those expenses are not incurred in the course of earning the income, but merely put the employee in a position to earn the income; accordingly, the expenses essentially retain a private or domestic nature. There are numerous UK and Australian cases which support this proposition although direct authority in Hong Kong can be found in *CIR v Humphrey* (supra). This principle applies even where the employer reimburses the costs of travelling to and from work; in this regard, see *D 47/03* where the reimbursement of taxi fares to and from work was held to be assessable income against which no deduction was allowed. Note, however, that where an employee has more than one place of business, the costs of travelling between them is a deductible expense (see *C v C of T* (28 SATC 127)).

In determining whether expenditure is private or domestic, it is necessary to look not only at the nature of the expenditure itself but also the circumstances in which it is incurred. For example, food and drink would normally be considered essentially private in nature but may nonetheless be deductible when it is incurred as part of genuine business entertainment by an employee and satisfies all the other tests for deductibility. Moreover, it is well established that where an employee is required to travel in the execution of his duties, expenditure on food and drink while away from home on duty is deductible (see *Nolder v Walters* (15 TC 380)).

There is little direct case law in Hong Kong on what constitutes disallowable capital expenditure for Salaries Tax purposes. It is clear that purchases of equipment which would otherwise meet the tests for deductibility would nonetheless be precluded from deduction as capital; generally, however, such expenditure would qualify for depreciation allowances (see section 3.5.2 below). Additionally, however, case law in other jurisdictions suggests that various other items of expenditure by an employee may, in some circumstances at least, be capital in nature; examples include certain legal expenses in connection with employment matters and education costs in acquiring a new or additional qualification although, in some cases, this has been held to depend upon how closely the new qualification relates to an existing employment. Note, however, that the deductibility of self education costs is now dealt with by Sec. 12(1)(e), which is discussed in section 3.5.3 below.

The three tests of wholly, exclusively and necessarily, when taken together, are extremely narrow. In practice the wholly and exclusively tests have, historically, not been strictly applied; for example, if it was demonstrated that an employee must use his car for business purposes, his total expenses on repairs, fuel, insurance, etc. would have been apportioned between business and private and the business proportion would be allowed, although, as noted above, expenditure incurred on travelling between home and office was never deductible. Indeed, in paragraph 6 of *Departmental Interpretation & Practice Notes No. 9*, which is reproduced as Appendix 6, the Commissioner explicitly states that the provision is not to be interpreted too narrowly. In *D 18/94*, however, the Board of Review adopted a much stricter approach and denied a taxpayer's motor vehicle expense claim on the basis that it was not wholly and exclusively incurred in the production of assessable income, even though the Board accepted that the use of the motor vehicle was necessary for the taxpayer's employment.

Although the IRD may, in practice, still relax the wholly and exclusively test on occasions, this is not extended to every case where there is a duality of purpose; for example, an executive or hotel manager claiming the cost of a suit because of the necessity to appear in business suitably dressed will not be successful because clothing, unless very peculiar to an employee's job, is inherently of a domestic nature.

The test of necessity is probably the most stringent as the IRD will always want to be satisfied as to why, under a master/servant relationship, if the employer requires the expense to be met he does not pay for it himself or reimburse it. The fact that the employee incurs the expense because it assists him in his employment or is convenient for him is insufficient to qualify it for deduction; it must be required by the employer to be incurred by the employee if it is to be deductible. In this regard, see the case of *Ricketts v Colquhoun* [1926] (AC 1) where Lord Blanesburgh held that for an expense to be "necessarily" incurred it must be one *"… which each and every occupant of the particular office is necessarily obliged to incur in the performance of its duties …"*. His Lordship went on further to note that deductibility does not extend to those expenses *"… which the (office) holder has to incur mainly, or it may be, only because of circumstances in relation to his office which are personal to himself or are the result of his own volition".*

An expense is more likely to be considered "necessary" where an employee earns commission by special and relatively independent effort (for example, a salesman), and is required to bear all expenses of earning that commission, such as entertainment. In *D 19/78*, for example, a stock-broker's runner who was paid on a commission basis was allowed to deduct the cost of paying assistants. In *D 25/87*, however, the claimant failed to obtain a deduction for the costs of running his own car partly for business to earn commission because he was unable to demonstrate that his employer actually required him to use his own car. Similarly, in *D 89/89*, a university lecturer was denied a deduction for costs of attending an overseas conference, even though those costs were subsidised by his employer, as the decision to attend the conference was the lecturer's alone and it could not be said that every person in his position would have found it necessary to attend.

Another interesting case regarding the necessity test is *D 4/93*. In that case, a payment by an employee to a substitute who performed the relevant duties whilst the taxpayer travelled to China was disallowed as a deduction on the grounds that it was not incurred in the course of employment but was to enable the taxpayer to take time off. One member of the Board of Review, however, dissented and, in finding for the taxpayer, avoided considering the application of the necessity test; instead, he considered that the taxpayer was not, in fact, claiming a deduction for the amount but was seeking to exclude the amount from assessable income as not being a reward for his services, but for the services of another person. This case should be contrasted with *D 19/78*, which was discussed above. For a recent case which highlights how strictly the tests of "necessity" and "wholly and exclusively" can be interpreted, see *D 51/99*. In that case, a part time lecturer was denied a deduction for expenses which, although clearly related to his employment, and undoubtedly permitted him to perform his duties more efficiently, were not considered absolutely essential.

The importance of the phrase *"in the production of the assessable income"* is illustrated by *CIR v Robert P. Burns* (HKTC 1181) which involved the payment of legal expenses by a racehorse trainer employed by the Royal Hong Kong Jockey Club for the purpose of regaining his training license. It was held that the expenses were incurred for the purpose of seeing that he was not precluded from earning his assessable income; they were not incurred in the production of that income. Put another way, the court held that the expenditure put the taxpayer in a position to earn income, but was not incurred in actually earning income, which is, of course, the same basis upon which the costs of travelling to work are considered non-deductible. This case was applied in *D 91/03* to deny a solicitor a deduction for professional indemnity insurance premiums which she was required to pay under the terms of her employment, again on the basis that the payment of the amount enabled the taxpayer to earn income but the amount was not incurred in the actual earning of income.

A similarly strict approach was adopted in *D 35/04*. In that case, an employee earned commission income for business introduced, but was required to reimburse his employer for any losses suffered by way of bad debts or dealing errors as a result of a breach by the employee of the employer's credit control policies. The Board of Review denied a deduction for such reimbursement amounts deducted by the employer on the basis that they were not incurred in the performance of the employee's duties, but were payable as a result of a breach of the terms of those duties.

Interestingly, in a slightly later case involving similar facts, *D 57/05*, the Board of Review reached the opposite conclusion and allowed the deduction of amounts of bad debts reimbursed to the employer by the employee which arose in relation to customers handled or referred by the employee. That decision was, however, overturned by the Court of First Instance in *CIR v Tong Sui Lun* [2006] (1 HKRC 90-180). In doing so the court accepted the submission by counsel for the Commissioner that the expenses in question were contingent liabilities in the nature of personal obligations of the employee arising out of the employment contract and were not referable to the performance of the employee's duties. In other words, although it was accepted that the expenses related to the employment contract, this was not, by itself, sufficient for the expenses to be considered *"incurred in the production of the assessable income"*. The court, in reaching this conclusion, reasoned that although the expenses were incurred **for** the production of income, they were not incurred **in** the production of income. This judgment appears to have applied an even narrower interpretation to the test for deductibility than that adopted in *CIR v Robert P. Burns* (supra) by denying a deduction not only for expenses incurred in order to permit an employee to earn income or to continue to earn income, but also for certain expenses accepted as being incurred in connection with the earning of income but not directly in the course of actually performing the duties of the employment. Nonetheless, at the time of writing the decision in the *Tong Sui Lun* case was under appeal.

Another area which illustrates the stringency of the *"in the production of assessable income"* test is professional subscriptions incurred by an individual exercising his profession as an employee. These are not strictly deductible because although they may be very much in connection with, and relevant to, his employment and also assist him in his work in that he receives regular updating of technical information, the expenditure is not incurred in producing his earnings. The fact that the employer may have chosen him because of his professional qualification is also not sufficient. The case of *Simpson v Tate* (9 TC 314) is considered as authority for this. However, in practice, the IRD will usually allow the deduction of one such subscription as an extra-statutory concession where:—

(1)   the holding of a full professional qualification is a prerequisite of employment. Note that anything less than a full qualification is not acceptable (see *D 24/87*); and

(2)   retention of membership is of regular use and benefit to him in his employment.

A number of cases concerning the deductibility of professional subscriptions have come before the Board of Review and the Board has consistently emphasised the extra-statutory nature of the IRD's practice regarding this item and refused to extend it (see, for example, *D 23/90, D 72/90, D 5/91* and *D 16/92*). Moreover, the Board has consistently refused to extend the concession on a number of occasions where it has been demonstrated that the obtaining of the professional qualification was a necessary prerequisite to a promotion which had been obtained (see *D 34/90, D 17/91* and *D 22/91*). Further, in *D 11/01*, the Board of Review refused to allow a taxpayer to deduct a fee in respect of a professional membership where, although the membership was not a prerequisite for holding the position, attaining it entitled the taxpayer to be considered for a salary increment. Although there appeared to be at least an indirect nexus between the membership fee and the salary increment, the Board concluded that the membership fee could not be considered incurred in the production of that salary increment.

Although an employee may have a binding obligation to pay his employer a sum of money in lieu of notice if he wants to secure a new employment quickly, that payment does not, nevertheless, constitute an expense incurred in the production of the income from the new employment (*CIR v Sin Chun Wah* (2 HKTC 364)).

Where a claim for deduction is allowable in principle, it is still necessary for the taxpayer to be able to document the quantum of the expense with reasonable precision. This point has been reinforced in a number of Board of Review cases where the taxpayer's claim failed because the quantum of the claim was no more than a rough estimate. See, for example, cases *D 25/87*, *D 37/92* and *D 59/93*.

It is, however, quite common for an employer to pay an employee a regular "allowance" to cover business expenditure, for example, an entertaining allowance. An allowance is strictly taxable under Sec. 9(1)(a) and it is up to the employee to then make a claim under Sec. 12(1)(a). In practice, however, if it is shown that the allowance in fact is normally fully expended by the employee in a manner which qualifies for deduction, the allowance is not assessed and no annual claim is called for.

For a further examination of the IRD's practice in relation to the deductibility of expenses, see *Departmental Interpretation & Practice Notes No. 9* which is reproduced as Appendix 6. This document contains, amongst other things, an analysis of the IRD's attitude to claims to deduct expenditure on clothing, commission payments, entertainment, payments to assistants, professional subscriptions, travelling expenses and capital expenditure.

3.5.2 Depreciation allowances

Also deductible are depreciation allowances in respect of plant and machinery which is essential to the production of assessable profits (Sec. 12(1)(b)). Rules governing the computation of such allowances are contained in Part VI of the IRO (see Chapter 5). Whilst this is an extension of the expense allowance provision, it does not contain the "wholly and exclusively" tests; in fact, the IRO specifically recognises the dual purpose asset by providing that the allowances are to be apportioned in a manner which the assessor considers to be fair and reasonable (Sec. 12(2)). Nonetheless, in *D 18/94* the IRD argued that the word "essential" in Sec. 12(1)(b) was to be interpreted as "necessarily" and, although not specifically commenting on this argument, the Board of Review found that depreciation allowances were not available in respect of the taxpayer's motor vehicle as, although its use was accepted as necessary for the taxpayer's employment, the vehicle was purchased predominantly for private purposes. See also *D 7/04* where, after considering previous authorities, the Board of Review again confirmed that the test of objective necessity in Sec. 12(1)(a) was imported into the test for granting of depreciation allowances under Sec. 12(1)(b). Nonetheless, on the facts of that particular case, the Board of Review allowed a concertmaster depreciation allowances in respect of an expensive antique violin.

Where a disposal of such plant or machinery gives rise to a balancing charge, the charge is treated as income chargeable to Salaries Tax (Sec. 12(5)).

3.5.3 Self-education expenses

From the 1996/97 year of assessment onwards, a deduction is available for qualifying self-education expenses up to a specified limit (Sec. 12(1)(e) and Sec. 12(6)(a)). The maximum deduction is prescribed by Schedule 3A and, for the 2007/08 year of assessment, is $60,000. The deduction is available in respect of amounts actually paid in the year of assessment, irrespective of the period to which it relates. For cases where a deduction was denied in respect of amounts paid in an earlier year but which related to a course undertaken in the year of assessment in which the deduction was claimed, see *D 88/99* and *D 99/00*.

Self-education expenses for this purpose are defined in Sec. 12(6)(b) as expenses paid by an individual on fees (including tuition and examination fees) in connection with a prescribed course of education undertaken by that person. The definition excludes, however, any expenses for which a deduction is allowable, or has been allowed, to the individual for any year of assessment under any provision of the IRO; this effectively simply prevents the double deduction of an expense, although it is unlikely that self-education expenses of an individual would very often qualify for deduction under any other provision. Also excluded from deduction are otherwise qualifying expenses to the extent that they have been reimbursed, or are reimbursable, to the taxpayer by his employer or any other person, unless such reimbursement is or will be included in the assessable income of the taxpayer.

A "prescribed course of education" is defined in Sec. 12(6)(c) as a course undertaken to obtain or maintain a qualification for use in any employment, being

- a course is provided by an "education provider" (see below);
- a training or development course provided by a trade, professional or business association. These terms are not defined in the IRO and therefore, take their ordinary meanings; or
- a training or development course accredited or recognized by an institution specified in Schedule 13. Schedule 13 is a list of professional bodies established under an ordinance in Hong Kong, and can be amended at any time by order of the Secretary for Financial Services and the Treasury (Sec. 12(6)(f)).

An "education provider" for the purpose of Sec. 12(6)(c) is in turn defined in Sec. 12(6)(d) as:

- a university, university college or technical college;

- a place of education to which the *Education Ordinance* does not apply by virtue of Sec. 2 of that ordinance (Sec. 12(6)(d)(ii)). Such places of education are listed in Table 3.1 below;
- any school registered under Sec. 13(a) of the *Education Ordinance*;
- any school exempted from registration under Sec. 9(1) of the *Education Ordinance*. This essentially covers schools operated by the Hong Kong Government, schools providing only religious education and schools which have been granted exemption, by notification in the *Gazette* from legislation which was superseded by the *Education Ordinance*, provided such exemption has not been withdrawn;
- any institution approved by the Commissioner for the purpose of Sec. 16C (which is concerned with approval of educational institutions for the purpose of obtaining deductions for Profits Tax purposes for technical education expenses);
- any other institution approved by the Commissioner for the purpose of this provision. The power of the Commissioner to approve an institution for this purpose is contained in Sec. 12(6)(e); there are no apparent limitations on this power and it is specifically provided that the approval operates from the date specified in the approval and may be withdrawn by the Commissioner at any time.

For a case where a police constable was denied a deduction for the fees paid to undertake a Chinese opera course which the taxpayer claimed would both benefit his present employment and permit him to obtain further employment after retirement from the police force, see *D 139/00*. In this case, the principal reason for finding against the taxpayer was the

Table 3.1 Educational institutions referred to in Sec. 12(6)(d)(ii)

- The Chinese University of Hong Kong
- The City University of Hong Kong
- The Hong Kong Academy for Performing Arts
- The Hong Kong Baptist University
- The Hong Kong Institute of Education
- The Hong Kong Polytechnic University
- The Hong Kong University of Science and Technology
- Lingnan University
- The Open University of Hong Kong
- The University of Hong Kong
- Any technical college, technical institute, industrial training centre or skills centre as defined in Sec. 2 of the *Vocational Training Council Ordinance*
- Any post secondary college registered under the *Post Secondary Colleges Ordinance*

fact that the course was not provided by an institution qualifying under Sec. 12(6). However, even if the institution had so qualified, the Board of Review indicated that the taxpayer would still have needed to establish that the course led to a qualification which was relevant to his present or future employment.

3.5.4 Charitable contributions

If a taxpayer, or his or her spouse who is living with the taxpayer, has made contributions to approved charities and such total contributions amount to at least $100 in the year of assessment, these may be deducted pursuant to Sec. 26C(1). This deduction does not need, in any way, to be related to employment income. The deduction is, however, subject to the following rules:—

(1)   the claim must be in the specified form and contain such particulars and be supported by such proof as the Commissioner may require (Sec. 26B(2)). There is no particular form specified, other than the normal tax return forms as specified by the Board of Inland Revenue, although the second part of this requirement allows the IRD to reject any claims not supported by appropriate receipts or other documentary evidence;

(2)   a deduction is not allowed if the amount is also an allowable deduction for Profits Tax purposes (Secs. 26C(2)(a)(i) and 26C(2)(b) (i)). This restriction is necessary to prevent double deduction of a qualifying amount, as a similar deduction provision applies for Profits Tax purposes (Sec. 16D). Accordingly, if an individual derives profit subject to Profits Tax as well as income subject to Salaries Tax, a qualifying charitable donation would, apart from this restriction, qualify for deduction under both provisions. It is interesting to note that the Profits Tax provision also contains a restriction denying a deduction for a charitable donation which is allowable as a deduction under Sec. 26C, but there is no indication in the IRO as to which deduction provision takes priority. Although the restriction was probably drafted specifically with the Profits Tax provision regarding charitable donations in mind, it actually also operates in the (somewhat unusual) situation where the amount is deductible for Profits Tax purposes under any other provision (e.g. the general deduction provision);

(3)   the claim is limited to a maximum percentage, as specified in Sec. 26C(2A), of the assessable income of the claimant reduced by

expenses allowable under Sec. 12(1)(a) and depreciation allowances deductible under Sec. 12(1)(b) (see sections 3.5.1 and 3.5.2 above). Sec. 26C(2A) specifies the relevant percentage to be 10% for years of assessment up to and including 2002/03, and 25% for the 2003/04 and subsequent years of assessment. The assessable income of the claimant for this purpose is not merely that person's own income chargeable to Salaries Tax (Sec. 26C(2)(a)(ii)(A)), but includes the aggregate of the assessable incomes of himself and his spouse where an election under Sec. 10(2) has been made (Sec. 26C(2)(a)(ii)(B)), and his assessable income and profits from other sources (after adding back any allowable self education expenses) where he has elected for Personal Assessment (Sec. 26C(2)(b)(iii)). In circumstances where an individual has elected for Personal Assessment, however, the relevant percentage limit is reduced by any charitable donation deduction allowed under the Profits Tax provisions (Sec. 26C(2)(b)(iii)). For a further discussion of Personal Assessment, see Chapter 6.

Also, because the deduction is available in respect of donations made by a person or their spouse (other than a spouse living apart from the person), there is potential for more than one person to claim a deduction for the same amount. To prevent double deductions, however, Sec. 26C(3)(a) provides that the same amount shall not be allowable to more than one person. Further, Sec. 26C(3)(b) provides that where the same donation is claimed or allowed to more than one person, Secs. 33(2) to (4) shall apply to govern such deductions in the same manner as those provisions apply to dependent parent, dependent grandparent, dependent brother, dependent sister, child and disabled dependent allowances. Essentially, this means that where the Commissioner is of the view that more than one person is entitled to make a claim in respect of a particular donation, he is not permitted to consider any claim until he is satisfied that the potential claimants have agreed amongst themselves as to who is entitled to make the claim (Sec. 33(2)).

Similarly, where a deduction has been allowed to more than one person in respect of the same donation, or has been allowed to one person and within six months of such deduction being granted another person appears also eligible to make a claim in respect of the same donation, the Commissioner is required to invite the claimant and potential claimant to decide amongst themselves as to who is to make the claim. If, however, the claimant and potential claimant cannot so agree within a reasonable time, the Commissioner is empowered to act as he considers just and in doing so is required to take into account only such information as is in his possession at the time (Secs. 33(3) and (4)).

For the purpose of the deduction, an approved charitable donation is defined in Sec. 2 as a donation of money to the Government for charitable purposes or to any charitable institution or trust of a public character which has been granted exemption from tax under Sec. 88. Such approved charitable institutions are listed in Special Supplements to the *Gazette* and are also available on the IRD's website. It has been held in *CIR v Sanford Yung-Tao Yung* (HKTC 959) that an inflated price paid to a charity for tickets to a social event does not constitute a donation.

For a further discussion and more practical examples of approved charitable contribution deductions, see *Departmental Interpretation & Practice Notes No. 37.*

3.5.5 Home loan interest

A deduction is available for home loan interest expenses in certain circumstances and subject to specified limits. In particular, Sec. 26E(1) provides that where a person pays during the year of assessment any home loan interest on a home loan obtained in respect of a dwelling (including a car parking space) used at any time during that year of assessment exclusively or partly as the person's place of residence, a deduction in respect of such interest shall be allowable subject to the other provisions of Sec. 26E.

Most of the terms used in Sec. 26E(1) are defined in Sec. 26E(9). Some of the more important of these terms and their meanings are as follows:—

* **"home loan"** — a loan of money which is applied wholly or partly for the acquisition of a dwelling, and which is secured by a mortgage over that dwelling or any other property in Hong Kong, being a dwelling in which the claimant had an interest at a time during the year of assessment as sole owner, joint tenant or tenant in common and which was used during that time by the claimant exclusively or partly as his place of residence. This ownership requirement is made clear by the legislation, although was nonetheless the subject of dispute in *D 84/02*. In that decision, the Board of Review upheld the Commissioner's refusal to allow a deduction for interest paid by a taxpayer who made the payments on behalf of his deceased sister until such time as the relevant property was sold. A similar reasoning was applied, and conclusion reached, in *D 70/05*.

    In *D 106/00* the Board of Review confirmed that "home loan" extended to a new loan taken out to refinance a loan which was originally taken out to finance the acquisition of a qualifying property. Moreover, where a loan was taken out to partly refinance an existing qualifying home loan as well as for other purposes, the interest could still qualify for deduction to the extent that the new loan was used to refinance the existing loan. For decisions where such an apportionment was held to be required, see *D 22/01*, *D 18/02* and *D 33/04*. In those cases, the Board of Review upheld the Commissioner's decision to apportion the otherwise deductible interest on the basis of the proportion of the new loan proceeds which were applied to pay off the original loan balance.

See, however, *D 123/01* where the Board of Review commented that the acquisition of a dwelling was complete as soon as the purchaser completes the purchase from the vendor and pays the purchase price, notwithstanding that part of the purchase price is financed by a borrowing secured by a mortgage over the property. As such, the Board indicated that where a new borrowing is taken out to replace the original loan, the Commissioner is not strictly required to grant a home loan interest deduction in respect of the new loan, although it is policy and practice to do so.

As noted, in order to qualify as a "home loan", the loan proceeds must be applied wholly or partly for the *acquisition* of a qualifying dwelling. The meaning of "acquisition" was considered by the Board of Review in *D 2/01*. In that case, the taxpayer purchased a flat from the Hong Kong Housing Society. The purchase price was below market value, but the taxpayer was not entitled to sell or otherwise alienate the property without, *inter alia*, paying a premium to the Hong Kong Housing Society. The taxpayer applied to have the restriction on alienation of the property lifted and took out a loan to finance the payment of the required premium. The Board of Review held that the interest on the loan did not qualify for deduction under Sec. 26E as the original purchase price gave the taxpayer the ownership and right to occupy the dwelling and this was effectively the acquisition of the dwelling. The Board accordingly rejected the taxpayer's claim that the premium was effectively deferred purchase consideration on the basis that it simply removed a restriction on sale that existed on a flat which was already owned and occupied by the taxpayer.

- **"home loan interest"** — interest paid by the claimant on a home loan to the Government, a financial institution (as defined in Sec. 2), a credit union registered under the *Credit Unions Ordinance*, a money lender licensed under the *Money Lenders Ordinance*, the Hong Kong Housing Society, an employer of the claimant, or an organization or association recognised for the purpose by the Commissioner, who is given the power to recognise such organizations or associations by Sec. 26E(7). It is important to note that the deduction is only available in respect of interest actually paid; it is not sufficient that the interest has merely been incurred. Accordingly, interest incurred for, say, the period 1 January, 2007 to 31 March, 2007, but not paid until 15 April, 2007, will only be deductible in the 2007/08 year of assessment. Also, because a home loan is defined to include a loan, the proceeds of which were only partly applied towards the purchase of the claimant's residence (see above), home loan interest may comprise only part of the interest on a loan. Logically, the necessary apportionment would be carried out by multiplying the total interest by the proportion of the loan proceeds used for the purchase of the residence. In paragraph 26 of *Departmental Interpretation & Practice Notes No. 35*, the Commissioner endorses such an apportionment as being the general rule but, interestingly, admits the possibility of accepting another basis if the claimant can demonstrate that the general apportionment method is inequitable or inappropriate.

- **"place of residence"** — this is not fully defined except to deem it to mean a person's principal place of residence if they have more than one place of residence. The reference to a person having more than one place of residence appears to mean more than one residence at the same time, as the provisions of Sec. 26E implicitly recognise that a person can have interests during a year in more than one dwelling, each of which can be a place of residence at different times during that year.

  In *D 8/04* the Board of Review held, on the basis of earlier decisions governing different provisions, that a "place of residence" meant a place where a person normally lives and sleeps and that for the purpose of Sec. 26E the term implies that the person at least has or shares a sleeping apartment in the dwelling. This means that a deduction will not be available in respect of interest relating to a property which, although owned and used, for some purpose, by the taxpayer, is not the place where the taxpayer normally sleeps.

In the situation where a person borrows the money for the purchase of a qualifying dwelling, but has no income or profits subject to tax, Sec. 26F(1) allows that person to nominate their spouse to claim the deduction, provided that the spouse is not living apart from the person. Where a person makes such a nomination, he immediately becomes disentitled to a deduction for the interest, and the person nominated becomes entitled to such deduction (Sec. 26F(2)(a)). In order to avoid any confusion, where a nomination under Sec. 26F(1) is made by a person and the deduction for home loan interest allowed to the person's spouse, the Commissioner is required by Sec. 26F (3) to give written notification thereof to the person making the nomination. Within six months after the issue of such notification by the Commissioner, the person making the nomination can revoke it by notice in writing to the Commissioner (Sec. 26F(4)(a)). Where such notice of revocation is given, the original nomination is deemed by Sec. 26F(4)(b) to not have been made.

The amount of the deduction available for home loan interest is set out in Sec. 26E(2)(a) as the lesser of:—

- the amount specified in Sch. 3D as applicable to the relevant year of assessment. For 2007/08, this amount is set at $100,000;
- where the dwelling is used by the person exclusively as his place of residence during the whole of the year, the amount of the interest paid; and
- where the dwelling was not used by the person exclusively as his place of residence during the whole of the year, such amount as is reasonable in the circumstances. In paragraph 15 of *Departmental Interpretation & Practice Notes No. 35*, the Commissioner states that maximum allowable deduction will generally not be subject to time apportionment. Moreover, from the examples provided in that paragraph, it seems that the IRD will treat as qualifying for deduction (subject to the statutory limit) the whole of any interest paid on a qualifying loan in respect of a period where the relevant dwelling was used exclusively as the claimant's residence. Nonetheless, an apportionment of the interest paid will be required where, for any part of the relevant period, the dwelling was used only partly as the claimant's residence and partly for some other purpose. For example, if the claimant lets out half of the residence, an apportionment of the interest will be appropriate, although it appears that the qualifying portion will still be deductible up to the amount of the statutory limit. An illustration of this situation is Example 8 in paragraph 14 of *Departmental Interpretation & Practice Notes No. 35.*

Where, however, the dwelling is not wholly owned by the claimant, the amount of interest incurred is the claimant's proportionate share of the total interest on the loan and the maximum specified in Sch. 3D is proportionately reduced to ensure that the maximum claim in respect of the dwelling in question is limited to the amount specified in that Schedule. More specifically, Sec. 26E(2)(b)(i) provides that where a dwelling is held by two or more persons as joint tenants, each owner is treated as having paid a share of the total interest determined by dividing the total by the number of joint tenants. Similarly, Sec. 26E(2)(c)(i) provides that the maximum amount of deduction for each joint tenant is ascertained by dividing the maximum amount in Schedule 3D (currently $100,000) by the number of joint tenants. That is, if there are two joint tenants, each is deemed to have paid half of the total interest on the loan and the maximum amount of each joint tenant's deduction is half of the amount specified in Schedule 3D.

In *D 20/01*, two individuals held a property as joint tenants but the taxpayer claimed that she had a beneficial interest in 90% of the property and, therefore, that she should be entitled to 90% of the maximum allowable interest. The Board or Review rejected this claim, however, on the basis that the wording of Sec. 26E(2)(b)(i) is unambiguous. Similarly, in *D 108/02* the Board of Review refused to treat a beneficial owner of a property as the sole owner for the purpose of the provision. In that case the claimant was the legal owner of 20% of the property in question, but the owner of the other 80% had executed a declaration of trust in favour of the claimant; nonetheless, the Board of Review held that "owner" for the purpose of the provision should be interpreted narrowly as meaning legal ownership. In reaching this conclusion, the Board appeared swayed by the fact that the specific provisions concerning joint ownership were concerned with joint tenants and tenants in common, both of which relate to legal rather than beneficial ownership.

See also *D 94/01* where a taxpayer's claim that she did not jointly own the property was rejected. In that case, the taxpayer had owned the property as joint tenant with her spouse. The couple, were, however, divorced in 1997 and a condition of the decree nisi being made absolute was that the husband transfer his share of the property to the taxpayer. Notwithstanding that the decree nisi became absolute in July 1997, the transfer of the husband's share of the property was not effected until January 2001. As the husband remained the legal owner of a half share until that time, the Board of Review rejected the taxpayer's claim that she was the sole owner for the 1998/99 and 1999/2000 years of assessment.

In yet another decision on the point, *D 5/02,* one of the two joint tenants in a property unsuccessfully sought a deduction for the maximum amount specified in Schedule 3D on the basis that the other joint tenant did not contribute to the payment of the interest and had no financial means to do so.

Where two or more persons own the property as tenants in common, Sec. 26E(2)(b)(ii) provides the proportion of the total interest deemed to have been paid by each is determined on the basis of their respective shares in the property. Similarly, the maximum amount of the claim specified in Sch. 3D is reduced on the basis of each tenant's proportionate share in the property (Sec. 26E(2)(c)(ii)).

The amount of interest paid on a loan can also be reduced, for the purposes of the provision, by an amount considered reasonable in the circumstances where the proceeds of the relevant loan were not applied wholly for the acquisition of the dwelling which is the claimant's place of residence (Sec. 26E(3)(a)). Similarly, where a claimant has paid interest on two or more home loans during the year of assessment, each of which is in respect of a dwelling which at some time during that year was the claimant's place of residence, a deduction for interest shall be allowable in respect of each home loan in an aggregate amount as is reasonable in the circumstances, although the legislation envisages that this may be the full aggregate amount of the interest on the loans in appropriate circumstances (Sec. 26E(3)(b)). Indeed, the examples contained in paragraph 15 of *Departmental Interpretation & Practice Notes No. 35* indicate that the IRD will accept the full aggregate of the interest on both loans as qualifying for the deduction (subject to the statutory limit), to the extent that the interest was attributable to a period when the dwelling was the claimant's place of residence.

Sec. 26E(4) specifies that a home loan interest deduction is not allowed where:—

- the amount is allowable as a deduction under any other provision of the IRO;
- any other home loan interest paid has been allowed as a deduction to the claimant in the same year of assessment, except as permitted by Sec. 26E(3)(b), which is discussed above; or
- a deduction for home loan interest has been allowed to the claimant under Sec. 26E(1) (whether in respect of the same or a different dwelling) for ten years of assessment, whether or not those years of assessment are continuous. Prior to the 2005/06 year of assessment the deduction was available for only seven years, and prior to 2003/04 year of assessment it was available for only five years of assessment. The extension of the provision to ten years applies, however, to all loans and not just to acquisitions or loans taken out after the amendment to the provision.

This last restriction gives effect to the intention that this concessionary deduction is only to be allowed to a taxpayer for ten years of assessment. In interpreting this provision, Sec. 26E(5) provides that a person is to be taken as having been allowed a deduction under Sec. 26E(1) if in a year of assessment his net chargeable income for Salaries Tax purposes was reduced by an amount of home loan interest, he had elected to be jointly assessed with his spouse (see section 3.8.3) and their aggregate net chargeable income was reduced by such an amount, or he had elected for Personal Assessment (see Chapter 6) and the resulting assessment was reduced by such an amount. Where a person has nominated his or her spouse to claim an amount of interest pursuant to Sec. 26F(1), that person, but not the spouse who actually claimed the deduction, shall be treated as having been allowed the deduction for that year (Sec. 26F(2)(b)).

Sec. 26E(6)(a) provides that a person may revoke a claim for home loan interest deduction by notice in writing to the Commissioner within six months after the date on which the claim is allowed to him. This presumably is to be interpreted as six months after the issue of the notice of assessment incorporating the deduction. For the avoidance of doubt, Sec. 26E(6)(b) provides that where a claim is so revoked, the deduction shall be deemed not to have been made. This provision allows taxpayers some flexibility as to the years in respect of which the claim is to be made. A taxpayer can, therefore, choose to claim the amount in years when interest payments are high, or their marginal tax rate is high, thereby maximising the value of the concession. Sec. 26E(6) also makes it clear that notwithstanding the fact that Sec. 26E(1) states that where the relevant conditions are met a deduction *"... shall be allowable ..."*, the deduction is in fact voluntary rather than mandatory.

For a further discussion of the practical application of the home loan interest deduction provisions, see *Departmental Interpretation & Practice Notes No. 35.*

3.5.6 Elderly residential care expenses

Sec. 26D(1) grants a deduction to a person in specified circumstances for any residential care expenses paid by that person or his or her spouse (not being a spouse living apart from the person), in respect of a parent or grandparent of the person. Sec. 26D(5) defines parent and grandparent for the purpose of the provision as extending to a parent or grandparent of the person's spouse; further, Sec. 2 contains comprehensive definitions of the terms "parent or parent of his or her spouse" and "grandparent or grandparent of his or her spouse" and these are discussed in sections 6.6.4 and 6.6.5

respectively of Chapter 6. To qualify for the deduction, the parent or grandparent of the person or his or her spouse must be aged 60 years or more or, if under 60 years, must be eligible to claim an allowance under the Government's Disability Allowance Scheme. For a discussion of the meaning of "eligible to claim an allowance under the Government's Disability Allowance Scheme", see section 6.6.6 which considers the same term in relation to disabled dependent allowance.

"Residential care expenses" is defined in Sec. 26D(5) as expenses payable in respect of residential care received at a "residential care home", which is itself defined in the same provision as meaning any premises:—

- which are currently licensed under the *Residential Care Homes (Elderly Persons) Ordinance*;
- in respect of which a current certificate of exemption has been issued under that ordinance;
- to which that ordinance does not apply by virtue of Sec. 3 of that ordinance. Essentially, this operates to include in the definition residential care homes operated by the Government or the Housing Society, residential care homes intended solely for persons requiring medical treatment and other premises excluded from registration under the ordinance by order of the Director of Social Welfare; or
- which is a nursing home in respect of which any person has been registered under Sec. 3 of the *Hospitals, Nursing Homes and Maternity Homes Registration Ordinance.*

The amount of the available deduction in any year of assessment is limited to the amount specified in Sch. 3C which, since the 1998/99 year of assessment has been set at $60,000.

In order to limit the deduction available in respect of an individual, Sec. 26D(4)(a) provides that a deduction shall not be available to more than one person for any year of assessment in respect of the same parent or grandparent. Nonetheless, it may be the case that two or more persons are, in fact, eligible to claim the deduction in respect of the same individual where, for example, they share the residential care expenses. In such circumstances, Sec. 26D(4)(b) provides that Secs. 33(2) to (4) shall apply to govern such deductions in the same manner as those provisions apply to dependent parent, dependent grandparent, dependent brother, dependent sister, child and disabled dependent allowances. Essentially, this means that where the Commissioner is of the view that more than one person is entitled to a claim in respect of a particular parent or grandparent, he is not permitted to consider any claim until he is satisfied that the potential claimants have agreed amongst themselves as to who is entitled to make the claim (Sec. 33(2)).

Similarly, where a deduction has been allowed to two or more persons in respect of the same parent or grandparent, or has been allowed to one person and within six months of such deduction being granted another person appears to the Commissioner to also be eligible to claim the deduction in respect of the same individual, the Commissioner is required to invite the claimants or potential claimants to decide amongst themselves as to who is to make the claim. If, however, the claimants and potential claimants cannot so agree within a reasonable time, the Commissioner is empowered to act as he considers just and in doing so is required to take into account only such information as is in his possession at the time (Secs. 33(3) and (4)).

Because an individual may be a parent of one person and a grandparent of another, Secs. 33(3A), (3B) and (3C) make it clear that the above procedures for dealing with more than one claimant or potential claimant are to be applied to ensure there is only one claim in respect of an individual even though the relationship of the individuals to the claimants is different.

Secs. 30(5) and 30A(5) provide that a dependent parent or dependent grandparent allowance (see Chapter 5) cannot be granted in respect of an aged person in respect of whom a deduction for elderly residential care expenses has been allowed. In other words, either a personal allowance is available in respect of a person, or a deduction for that person's elderly residential care expenses (if any) is available. However, the drafting of the law makes it clear that it is the latter (i.e. the deduction) which takes precedence over the former (i.e. the personal allowance).

For a further discussion of the practical application of the elderly residential care expense deduction, see *Departmental Interpretation & Practice Notes No. 36.*

3.5.7 Retirement scheme contributions

Sec. 26G provides for deductions for certain contributions to retirement schemes. In particular, a deduction is available for a contribution paid by the claimant to a recognized retirement scheme during the relevant year of assessment. For this purpose, a "recognized retirement scheme" is defined in Sec. 2 as a recognized occupational retirement scheme (see definition in section 10.3.1) or a MPF scheme. A MPF scheme is defined in Sec. 2 as a provident fund scheme registered under the *Mandatory Provident Fund Schemes Ordinance.*

The determination of the amount of the deduction available under this provision depends partly on whether the contribution is to a recognized occupational retirement scheme or a MPF scheme. In the case of a recognized occupational retirement scheme, the starting point for determining the allowable deduction is the amount of contributions paid, but this is limited to the mandatory contributions which the person would have had to pay had he or she been a member of a MPF scheme instead. Where the person is actually a member of a MPF scheme, the starting point is the mandatory contributions made to that scheme. In either case, however, the amount of the deduction is further limited by Sec. 26G(2)(b) to the amount specified in Sch. 3B, which is currently $12,000. This amount is the maximum amount of annual mandatory contributions to a MPF scheme which a person could be required to make under the current terms of the *Mandatory Provident Fund Schemes Ordinance*. Accordingly, despite the complex drafting of the provision, Sec. 26G effectively simply grants a deduction for payments made up to the amount of mandatory contributions the person would be required to make under the *Mandatory Provident Fund Schemes Ordinance*.

Notwithstanding the above, a deduction is nonetheless denied for any amount which qualifies for deduction for Profits Tax purposes (Sec. 26G(2)(a)). For example, an individual may have both income subject to Profits Tax (derived as a sole proprietor of a business) and employment income subject to Salaries Tax and may elect for Personal Assessment. The contributions to the recognized retirement scheme may relate to MPF contributions the claimant is required to make as the sole proprietor of the business and, as such, would (subject to certain limits) be deductible under Sec. 16AA (see Chapter 4). Sec. 26G(2)(a), therefore, precludes the same amount being also deductible pursuant to Sec. 26G against the individual's income subject to Salaries Tax or Personal Assessment.

3.5.8 Losses

Although in practice a very rare event, it is possible for losses to arise under Salaries Tax rules. This happens where allowable expenses and depreciation allowances exceed the assessable income. Charitable contributions cannot augment the loss because relief is restricted to a specified percentage, currently 25%, of the income after expenses and depreciation allowances which in these circumstances is, of course, 25% of nil. Similarly, otherwise allowable deductions for home loan interest, elderly residential care expenses, self education expenses and retirement scheme contributions cannot be taken into account in computing losses to be carried forward (Sec. 12A(1)).

The general rule for relief is that the loss may be carried forward and deducted from assessable income in subsequent years (Sec. 12A(1)). This must be carried out in strict chronological order beginning with the year of assessment immediately after the one in respect of which the loss occurred (Sec. 12A(3)). This is, however, subject, in the case of husband and wife, to the following:—

(1) in the case of a husband and wife who have elected under Sec. 10(2) to be jointly assessed (see section 3.8.3), where the deductions for expenses, depreciation allowances and losses brought forward in respect of one spouse, exceed that spouse's assessable income, the excess is to be deducted from the other spouse's assessable income (Sec. 12(3));

(2) where, in the case of a husband and wife, who have elected under Sec. 10(2) to be jointly assessed (see section 3.8.3) for a year of assessment, an excess is brought forward to that year, the order of set-off is:—

   (a) first, against the assessable income of the spouse whose deductions created the loss and then against the assessable income of the other spouse (Sec. 12A(4)(a)); and

   (b) next, in the following year, in the same order of priority as (a) above if an election under Sec. 10(2) has been made for that year (Sec. 12A(4)(b)(ii)) and, where no such election has been made, is allocated as in (1) above (Sec. 12A(4)(b)(i)),

   and so on until fully utilized.

The following example illustrates a number of the issues discussed in section 3.5.

◼ Example 3.10

Mr. Cheung is a salesman and has a base salary of $650,000 for a year of assessment and also earned commission of $120,000. In earning his income, Mr. Cheung's employer requires him to bear whatever expenses are necessary and he has incurred entertainment expenditure of $15,000. He also used his own car 60% for business and submits details of total motoring expenditure of $35,000. Total depreciation allowances on the car for the year total $26,000. Mr. Cheung made contributions to approved charitable institutions of $40,500 and his wife, who has no earnings subject to Salaries Tax, made contributions of $4,000. He also paid interest totalling $125,000 to a bank in respect of a loan taken out in the previous year to finance the purchase of his flat, $40,000 to a nursing home licensed under the *Residential Care Homes (Elderly Persons) Ordinance* in which his mother lived, and $12,000 to a Mandatory Provident Fund scheme.

Mr. Cheung's Salaries Tax position is:

(1) Salary		$350,000
Commission		120,000
Assessable Income		$470,000
(2) Expenses (Sec. 12(1)(a))		
– Entertainment	$15,000	
– Car (60% of $35,000)	21,000	(Note (a))
(3) Depreciation Allowances (Sec. 12(1)(b))		
– 60% of $26,000	15,600	51,600 (Note (b))
Net Assessable Income		$418,400
(4) Concessional Deductions		
– Home Loan Interest (Sec. 26E)	100,000	(Note (c))
– Elderly Residential Care Expenses (Sec. 26D)	40,000	
– Charitable Contributions (Sec. 26C)	44,500	(Note (d))
– MPF Contributions (Sec. 26G)	12,000	196,500
Net Chargeable Income before deduction of Personal Allowances		$221,900

Notes:

(a) Although there is no statutory right to apportion expenses incurred for a dual purposes, in practice this is commonly done with car expenses (although see discussion of *D 18/94* in text).

(b) Depreciation allowances can, however, be statutorily apportioned (Sec. 12(2)), although see discussion in text.

(c) Home Loan Interest deduction claim is limited to the statutory maximum of $100,000.

(d) The total contributions are $44,500, which is less than the statutory maximum of 25% of assessable income of the claimant as prescribed by Sec. 26C(2A). Note, however, that prior to the 2003/04 year of assessment, the limit was 10% of assessable income and, therefore, Mr. Cheung's claim would have been restricted to $41,840. Note also that Mr. Cheung's wife's contributions can be aggregated with Mr. Cheung's and the total deducted. If his wife had income subject to Salaries tax, they would have to agree between them as to who would claim the deduction (Sec. 26C(3)(b)).

3.6 Basis of Assessment

Having ascertained what income is chargeable to Salaries Tax, the method of assessment is relatively straightforward. It is first necessary to isolate the assessable income for the basis period and then consider what deductions may be made from that assessable income. Sec. 12B provides that the net chargeable income is to be arrived at by deducting allowable charitable donations, home loan interest, elderly residential care expenses and recognized retirement scheme contributions, together with personal allowances, from net assessable income. Net assessable income is defined by Sec. 12 as assessable income (i.e. taxable remuneration accruing in the year of assessment) less adjustments for expenses, depreciation allowances, self education expenses and losses. In the case of a husband and wife, they are treated as two separate and single individuals, each with their own net chargeable income other than where they have elected for joint assessment, in which case they have a single net chargeable income comprised of their aggregated net assessable incomes less allowable charitable donations, home loan interest, elderly residential care expenses, retirement scheme contributions and appropriate personal allowances (Sec. 12B(2)). In other words, net chargeable income is ascertained as follows:—

Assessable income accruing in year of assessment (Sec. 11B)

Less
(i)   expenses incurred in producing the income (Sec. 12(1)(a));
(ii) qualifying depreciation allowances (Secs. 12(1)(b) and 12(2));
(iii) excess of deductions (i) and (ii) of a previous year of assessment over assessable income of that year (Sec. 12(1)(c));
(iv) excess of deductions (i), (ii) and (iii) of spouse over assessable income of spouse for current year of assessment where an election for joint assessment has been made (Sec. 12(1)(d));
(v)   qualifying self-education expenses to the statutory maximum, which is presently $60,000 (Sec. 12(1)(e))

Plus   Balancing charge in respect of depreciation allowances granted (Sec. 12(5))

Equals   **Net assessable income** (Sec. 12(1))

Less
(i)   allowable charitable donations (Secs. 12B(1)(a) and 26C(1));
(ii) qualifying elderly residential care expenses to a statutory maximum, which is presently $60,000 (Secs. 12B(1)(a) and 26D(1));
(iii) qualifying home loan interest expenses to a statutory maximum, which is presently $100,000 (Secs. 12B(1)(a) and 26E(1));
(iv) contributions to a recognized retirement scheme subject to specified conditions and the statutory maximum, which is currently $12,000 (Secs. 12B(1)(a) and 26G and Sch. 3B); and
(v)   personal allowances (Sec. 12B(1)(b)) (see Chapter 6);

Equals   **Net chargeable income** (Sec. 12B(1))

The size of the net chargeable income determines whether it is charged to tax under Sec. 13(1) at progressive rates, or alternatively under Sec. 13 (2) at the standard rate on the net assessable income after deducting allowable charitable donations, home loan interest, elderly residential care expenses and retirement scheme contributions, but not personal allowances. The point at which the method changes from the former to the latter is discussed in section 3.6.3 below.

The method of assessment and payment of Salaries Tax involves a system of Provisional Salaries Tax which is explained in section 3.7.3.

3.6.1 Basis period and income falling therein

The IRO simply states that liability to Salaries Tax for a year of assessment is on the aggregate remuneration from all sources within the scope of Salaries Tax which accrue in that year of assessment (Sec. 11B). For the purpose of Sec. 11B, it is provided in Sec. 11C that a person is deemed to commence or cease, as the case may be, to derive income from a source whenever and as often as he commences or ceases to hold an office or employment of profit or becomes entitled to a pension. The meaning of this provision was considered in *CIR v Sawhney, Subhash Chander* [2005] (1 HKRC 90-166) where the court overturned the decision of the Board of Review (see *D 34/ 05*) which had interpreted the provision to mean that an amount received after cessation of employment was not taxable. The Board of Review recognised that generally post-employment receipts would be taxable by virtue of Sec. 11D (see below), but that this could not apply to employee share option gains, which was the issue in dispute, because these did not represent a payment from the employer. Rather, the court held that although the original purpose of Sec. 11C had become obscured by various legislative changes to the IRO, it was to simply make it clear that provisions regarding commencement and cessation of employment were to apply to every commencement or cessation of an employment (i.e. even where one employment ceased and another immediately commenced) and not just where a person commenced employment for the first time or permanently ceased all employment.

As the basis is income which "accrues" within a year of assessment, it is important to know precisely what this term means. Income accrues to a person when he is entitled to receive it, whether he actually receives it or not (Sec. 11D(b)). Accordingly, the day or date on which salary or wages is payable is the governing factor and in regard to other sources, such as a bonus, it is a question of fact when a person becomes entitled to claim payment. It would be usual to look to a service agreement for evidence of entitlement but in the absence of a written agreement, oral evidence or evidence of an existing code of practice might be relevant.

If a bonus contractually relates to the employer's profits and has no discretionary element, it accrues during the accounting period to which it relates, even though the amount may not be finally quantified and paid until some time after the end of that accounting period. This was confirmed (albeit as *obiter dicta*) in *D 46/98* where the bonus related to the year to 31 March and was calculated according to a formula contained in the employer's articles of association, but was not finally determined and paid until early July. The Board of Review held that as all the conditions for entitlement had been fulfilled at 31 March, the amount should be seen as having accrued at that date notwithstanding that it could not be finally quantified at that time. The Board, in reaching its decision, distinguished *D 35/85*, where the opposite conclusion was reached, on the grounds that in that case the bonus had a discretionary element.

Where a bonus is wholly at the employer's discretion, it will not accrue until it is made known to the employee that it will be paid and, in the absence of a stated date of payment, will accrue when actually paid. Apart from this, it is specifically provided by Sec. 11D(a) that income is deemed to have been received by a person when it has either been made available to him or has been dealt with in accordance with his instructions. In other words, if it is credited to a current account upon which he can draw or he has been told that it is available when he comes to call at the office, it is deemed to be paid notwithstanding that he may choose not to draw upon it or collect it. Similarly an amount is deemed to be paid if the employee asks the employer to invest it for him or pay it to a creditor. See, for example, *D 65/94* where it was held that amounts had been received by the taxpayer even though the employer deducted the sums from the employee's salary and paid them to a retirement scheme.

Leave pay occasionally gives rise to difficulties as to the period or periods in which it accrues. The rule is that if there is some specific reference in a person's service agreement to entitlement of leave pay in one lump sum at a particular time, then the period into which it falls is governed by that due date. However, as is often the case, the arrangements may be informal in which case the following general rules are applicable:—

   (1)   a payment in lieu of leave not taken accrues when actually paid;

   (2)   a single payment for terminal leave accrues when paid or in the year of assessment in which cessation of employment occurred if paid after cessation; and

(3) a lump sum payment made at the beginning of a period of leave that is in fact made as an advance for the employee's convenience, is treated as accruing when the usual salary payments would have been made but for the advance.

Notwithstanding the above discussion, although Sec. 11B fixes the year of assessment for which a payment accrues, a person cannot be assessed upon the amount until he actually receives it, although when he does ultimately receive it, the assessment is for the year in which he was due to receive it (Sec. 11D(a)). The Board of Review have on a number of occasions considered the date on which income accrues for Salaries Tax purposes. See for example *BR 3/73, BR 13/74, BR 17/76, D 35/85, D 78/88* and *D 31/89.*

■ Example 3.17

An individual commences employment in Hong Kong on 1st November 2006 and his service agreement includes the following:

(1) Salary of $21,000 per month payable in arrears on the 5th of the following month.
(2) Annual bonus in respect of the company's year to 31st December, payable on 31st March each year. In 2007 he is entitled to $30,000 for the part year and due to the fact that the accounts were not prepared in time, it was not ascertained nor paid until 5th July 2007 after both he and the employer had submitted their Salaries Tax returns for 2006/07.
(3) A high cost of living allowance of $15,000 for a full year payable in advance on the commencement of employment and each anniversary thereafter.

His income for Salaries Tax purposes for 2006/07 is:—

(1) Salary 4 × $21,000	$ 84,000	(Note (a))
(2) Bonus	30,000	(Note (b))
(3) Allowance	15,000	(Note (c))
	$129,000	

Notes:—
(a) Although he has earned 5 months salary he is only due to be paid 4 payments.
(b) Strictly the bonus relates to 2006/07 because that was when it was due. If an assessment had already been raised for 2006/07 on the basis of returns which excluded it, an additional assessment should be raised after 5th July 2007 (Sec. 11D(a)). In practice, however, it would probably be assessed in 2007/08 on a receipts basis, although if because of personal circumstances, his marginal tax rate for 2006/07 was lower than for 2007/08 it would pay him to seek the statutory treatment.
(c) Although a substantial part of the allowance relates to 2007/08, it was due in 2006/07 and therefore is assessable in that year.

There are two other rules which concern post-cessation receipts and lump sum receipts. If a sum which would otherwise be within the scope of Salaries Tax is paid by an employer to an employee after he has ceased that employment, it is deemed to have accrued to the employee on the last day of that employment (Sec. 11D(b) proviso (ii)). For examples of the practical application of this provision, see *D 28/95* and *D 75/04*. Note, however, that this provision does not apply to a deemed gain on exercise of an option to acquire shares granted to an employee (see section 3.4.4) as this is not a payment by an employer to the employee; this point is accepted by the IRD in paragraph 38 of *Departmental Interpretation & Practice Notes No. 38*, which is reproduced as Appendix 15.

In *D 45/89*, the Board of Review considered whether this provision applied where a person ceased to be an employee of a company and became a director thereof; in finding that the provision did apply, the Board of Review observed that the office of director was entirely new and distinguishable from the previous employment. See also *D 51/94* where the Board of Review confirmed that the provision applies to an amount received under a Labour Tribunal award.

As regards lump sums, there is a provision by which these can be related back (Sec. 11D(b) proviso (i)):

(1)   over the period of service for which the payment is made; or, if less

(2)   over the period of three years up to the date of accrual of the payment or the date of cessation of employment, whichever is earlier.

This rule is applicable only to two types of payment, namely:—

(1)   a lump sum payment or gratuity paid upon the termination of an office or employment; or

(2)   a lump sum payment of deferred pay or arrears of pay

In *D 19/94* the Board of Review considered whether this provision applied to allow the relating back of a performance gratuity which was calculated with regard to the earnings and performance of an employee over a three-year period. In finding that the amount could not be related back, the Board of Review held that the term "lump sum payment of deferred pay or arrears of pay", as used in the second limb of the test, specifically excluded a gratuity. Accordingly, it seems that only gratuities paid on termination of employment can be related back.

Where the relating back provisions apply, the payment is treated as having accrued evenly over the period in (1) or (2) above, although, of course, there is only a benefit in claiming the application of this rule if the marginal rate of tax in the earlier years is lower than that for the year in which the lump sum would otherwise fall. This may arise, for example, because the income was smaller in the earlier years, there were other reliefs available by Personal Assessment (see Chapter 6) or because of a change in tax rates. Even where an assessment is otherwise final and conclusive, it can be disturbed to admit a claim made in writing within two years of the end of the year of assessment in which the payment is made. In technical terms, an application within this time limit is treated as a valid objection against the assessment affected and, therefore, if the IRD fails to admit the claim, the dispute can be processed under the objection and appeal procedures (see Chapter 9).

Note that a lump sum or gratuity paid on retirement or cessation of employment is excluded from the calculation of rental value (see section 3.4.3) whether the sum is spread back or not.

■ Example 3.18

Ivan A. Ward has worked for his employer for 5 years and on 1st October 2007 receives a lump sum of $120,000 in respect of arrears of pay relating to his whole period of service.

If he elects by 31st March 2010 for the benefit of Sec. 11D(b) proviso (i), the lump sum will be treated as arising evenly over the three year period to 1st October 2007 as follows:—

2007/08	$20,000
2006/07	40,000
2005/06	40,000
2004/05	20,000
	$120,000

If his employment had commenced on 1st April 2005, the spread would have been:—

2007/08	$ 24,000
2006/07	48,000
2005/06	48,000
	$120,000

3.6.2 Calculation of tax

Having ascertained the net assessable income and net chargeable income, the tax payable is calculated in one of two ways, whichever turns out to give the smallest liability. The two methods are:—

(1) net chargeable income, before deduction of personal allowances, charged at the standard rate (Sec. 13(2)); and

(2) net chargeable income charged at the progressive rates provided in the Second Schedule to the IRO (Sec. 13(1)).

In the case of husbands and wives, net chargeable incomes may be aggregated by election in certain circumstances (see section 3.8.3).

The personal allowances and progressive rates are listed in Table 1.1 and the necessary rules for claiming personal allowances are detailed in Chapter 6. Note that if (2) above applies, the entitlement to deduct personal allowances is automatic for Salaries Tax purposes, regardless of the individual's residence status. Salaries Tax is the only one of the three Hong Kong income taxes where there is an automatic entitlement to the personal allowances. If they are required to be claimed against income which is subject to one of the other two taxes, a Personal Assessment election is necessary for which there is a residential qualification (see Chapter 6).

■ Example 3.19

Mr. I. Q. Upp has the following personal circumstances:—

(1)	Salary and bonus for the year of assessment 2007/08	$460,000
(2)	Rent-free accommodation for full year (contribution to rent $12,000)	
(3)	Agreed allowable expenses	$ 6,000
(4)	Agreed allowable Depreciation Allowances for car	$ 5,000
(5)	Approved Charitable Donations by wife	$ 4,000
(6)	Qualifying elderly residential care expenses in respect of his mother	$120,000
(7)	MPF scheme contributions	$ 12,000
(8)	Personal Allowances due for wife and 1 child.	

His wife has no income liable to Salaries Tax.

His Salaries Tax is computed as follows:—

(1)	Salary and Bonus		$460,000
(2)	Rental Value (10% of $449,000) less $12,000 (Note (a))		32,900
	Assessable Income		$492,900
(3)	Expenses allowable	$6,000	
(4)	Depreciation Allowances	5,000	(11,000)
	Net Assessable Income		$481,900
(5)	Charitable Donations		(4,000)
(6)	Elderly residential care expenses (Note (b))		(60,000)
(7)	MPF scheme contributions (Note (c))		(12,000)
			$405,900
(8)	Personal Allowances — Married	$200,000	
	Child	50,000	

	$250,000		(250,000)
Net Chargeable Income			$155,900
(i) Salaries Tax per Sec. 13(1)	$35,000	@ 2% =	$700
	35,000	@ 7% =	2,450
	35,000	@12% =	4,200
	50,900	@17% =	8,653
	$155,900		$16,003
(ii) Salaries Tax per Sec. 13(2)	$405,900	@16% =	$64,944

The Salaries Tax liability is the smaller of the two alternatives and is therefore $16,003.

Notes:—
(a) The rental value is 10% of taxable earnings after deducting allowable expenses and depreciation allowances, i.e. 10% of ($460,000 – $11,000) and the rental contribution is deducted therefrom (see section 3.4.3).
(b) Claim limited in accordance with Sch. 3C.
(c) MPF contributions are deductible pursuant to Sec. 26G.
(d) It will be noted that the marginal rate under alternative (i) is 17% as compared to the flat rate of 16% under alternative (ii). As his income increases, the gap between the alternatives narrows until a break-even point is reached beyond which alternative (ii) is always advantageous (see section 3.6.3 "Break-even point" below).
(e) If his wife had income liable to Salaries Tax, different rules would apply (see section 3.8.3).

3.6.3 Break-even point

There is a point at which tax charged at progressive rates on net chargeable income is exactly equal to tax at standard rate on net assessable income less charitable donations and beyond which the tax at standard rate will always be less. This is illustrated as follows in respect of tax and personal allowance rates applicable for 2007/08, in respect of an individual whose spouse does not have income liable to Salaries Tax.

Net Assessable Income	$4,450,000			
Personal Allowance				
— Married	200,000			
Net Chargeable Income	$4,250,000			
	$35,000	@ 2% =	$	700
	35,000	@ 7% =		2,450
	35,000	@ 12% =		4,200
	4,145,000	@ 17% =		704,650
	$4,250,000			$712,000
Alternative	$4,450,000	@ 16% =		$712,000

Any increase in net assessable income above $4,450,000 would be charged at 17% on the progressive rate basis or 16% on the standard rate basis and, therefore, the standard rate basis will always be applicable and no deduction will be given for personal allowances. Break-even points will, of course, depend upon personal circumstances but the following are correct for the stated circumstances (assuming none of the children in respect of whom allowances are claimed were born in the year of assessment).

	Net Assessable Income Break-Even Point
Personal Allowances for:	**2007/08**
Single	$2,750,000
Married	$4,450,000
Married + 1 Child	$5,300,000
Married + 2 Children	$6,150,000
Married + 3 Children	$7,000,000
Married + 4 Children	$7,850,000

Note, however, that if both husband and wife have income liable to Salaries Tax, they are normally treated as single persons (see section 3.8.3).

3.7 Assessment and Payment of Tax

The assessment system for Salaries Tax consists of a Provisional Salaries Tax assessment in an estimated amount followed, after a return has been made, by a final Salaries Tax assessment on the true figure in which the Provisional Salaries Tax already paid for the year of assessment is credited.

3.7.1 Filing requirements

Section 51(1) of the IRO empowers an assessor to give notice to any person requiring him to complete and submit a return within a reasonable time, as stated on the return. The return can be submitted as an appropriately completed paper form or, in circumstances prescribed by the Commissioner, either electronically or via the telephone filing (telefiling) system. It is necessary for the Commissioner to be able to prescribe the circumstances in which electronic filing or telefiling is permitted as those systems contain limitations as to the types of taxpayer claims they can handle. Currently, electronic filing is available in a broader range of circumstances than telefiling and, in particular, is available to all individuals provided they are not claiming exemption from Salaries Tax in respect of any part of their employment income, they do not operate a sole proprietorship business with gross income for the year greater than $500,000, they do not have deemed assessable profits under Sec. 20AE and they have not obtained an advance ruling on any tax matter. As noted, telefiling is available only in more limited circumstances and, *inter alia*, is not available to taxpayers claiming deductions for general outgoings or expenses, home loan interest, elderly residential care expenses, dependent parent allowance, dependent brother or sister allowance or disabled dependent allowance, or to married persons who wish to elect for Personal Assessment.

Irrespective of the method chosen, however, the return is generally required to be submitted within one month from the date the return was issued. Further, Section 51(2) imposes a duty on each person who is chargeable to tax for any year of assessment to notify the IRD in writing, within four months of the end of the year of assessment, that he is so chargeable if he has not already received a return form from the assessor. For a more detailed discussion of filing requirements, see Chapter 7.

3.7.2 Objections and appeals

Section 64(1) grants any person aggrieved by an assessment one month, from the date of the assessment, to lodge a valid objection with the Commissioner. Upon receipt of a valid objection, the assessor and the taxpayer will usually attempt to negotiate the objection. If the assessor and the taxpayer fail to reach an agreement, the Commissioner will determine the objection. If the taxpayer does not accept the Commissioner's determination, he may appeal to the Board of Review and possibly proceed through the Court of First Instance and the Court of Appeal to the Court of Final Appeal. For a more detailed discussion of objections and appeals, see Chapter 9.

3.7.3 Provisional Salaries Tax

A Salaries Tax assessment notice usually comprises a final Salaries Tax assessment for a year of assessment and also a Provisional Salaries Tax assessment for the immediately succeeding year of assessment (Sec. 63D(1)(b)). A single Provisional Salaries Tax assessment is, however, quite valid on its own (Sec. 63D(1)(a)).

The charge to Provisional Salaries Tax is authorised by Sec. 63B and, at the commencement of employment in Hong Kong, the Provisional Salaries Tax assessment for the first year of assessment may be estimated (Sec. 63C(2)), although in practice such estimates are usually made on the basis of figures supplied by the taxpayer in a Provisional Salaries Tax return.

Often, however, the administrative machinery does not catch up with new employees soon enough and the first assessment becomes a final assessment of the actual assessable income for the first part year and an estimated Provisional Salaries Tax assessment for the following year. The estimate for the second year is usually based on a precisely grossed-up equivalent of the actual part year figure for the first year. In subsequent years, the Provisional Salaries Tax assessment is always in the same figure as the immediately preceding final assessment except that any losses under Sec. 12A set off in that preceding year must be added (Sec. 63C(1)). Just as in the calculation of final tax (see section 3.6.2), the Provisional Salaries Tax is to be the lesser of net chargeable income at progressive rates or net assessable income less charitable donations and qualifying elderly residential care and home loan interest expenses, at the standard rate (Sec. 63C(1) proviso).

As a Provisional Salaries Tax assessment is usually made during the currency of the year of assessment but tax rates and personal allowances can be fixed retrospectively, it can happen that these are changed after a Provisional Salaries Tax assessment has been issued. Sec. 63C(6A) provides that in these circumstances, the assessment is not to be disturbed.

The assessor has further powers to estimate a Provisional Salaries Tax assessment, in the case of cessation of employment (Sec. 63C(3)), where the employee is about to leave Hong Kong or it is otherwise expedient to quickly raise an assessment (Sec. 63C(5)) or in the absence of a return (Sec. 63C(1)). In practice, by the time the assessor is aware that an employee is ceasing employment or about to leave Hong Kong, a current Provisional Salaries Tax assessment is already in existence and this is usually quickly adjusted to a final assessment on actual figures.

Once assessed, the Commissioner is empowered to issue a notice of assessment and fix the due dates for payment (Sec. 63C(6)). It is usual for the Provisional Salaries Tax to be payable in two instalments with 75% being fixed for payment in January or February in the year of assessment and the remaining 25% three months later. However, it is now a matter of policy that if the first instalment is in default, the second instalment becomes immediately due. This enables the Commissioner to impose a surcharge on both instalments and enforce collection of both. There is, therefore, apart from the policy in the case of defaulters, no question of payment in advance; in fact, in the usual case of an increasing income, tax is payable in arrears. When the final assessment for a year is raised, the Provisional Salaries Tax already paid for that year is credited against the final liability (Sec. 63F(1)(a)). Any balance of liability is added to and payable on the same date as the first instalment of Provisional Salaries Tax for the following year. Where, exceptionally, there is an overpayment of Provisional Salaries Tax, the excess is not refunded but is deducted first from the first instalment of Provisional Salaries Tax for the following year and then from the second instalment (Sec. 63F(1)(b)). If there still remains a balance of overpayment, this is refunded. Where an excess of Provisional Salaries Tax over the final liability is applied against the Provisional Salaries Tax for the next year and an opportunity arises to hold over all or part of the Provisional Salaries Tax (see following paragraphs) but this is frustrated by the fact that it is already paid by the overpayment set-off, it is IRD practice to refund the amount that would otherwise have been held over.

Because of the estimated nature of Provisional Salaries Tax, there are provisions to enable collection of the tax to be wholly or partly held over in appropriate circumstances. Such applications must be in writing and lodged with the IRD not later than 28 days before the due date of payment for the holdover to be made, or not later than 14 days after the date of the notice for payment, whichever is later (Sec. 63E(1)). If the opportunity is missed in respect of the first instalment, all or part of the second instalment may still be held over. An application for holdover of Provisional Salaries Tax can only be made on certain grounds. These grounds are specified in Sec. 63E(2) and are:

(1) the taxpayer has become entitled during the year of assessment to a personal allowance which was not taken into account in determining his net chargeable income for the prior year or in estimating his Provisional Salaries Tax liability. This ground will normally not apply in the case of taxpayers who pay Salaries Tax at the standard rate on their net assessable income less charitable donations, elderly residential care and home loan interest expenses;

(2) where the net chargeable income of the current year is, or is likely to be, less than 90% of the sum which has been assessed to Provisional Salaries Tax;

(3) where during the year of assessment the taxpayer has ceased or will cease before the following 31 March to derive a source of income chargeable to Salaries Tax; or

(4) where the final assessment for the preceding year (upon which the Provisional Salaries Tax assessment is, of course, based) is under objection (see Chapter 9). As will be seen, this is also an occasion for a holdover claim in respect of the final assessment as well.

Any holdover is entirely at the discretion of the IRD (Sec. 63E(3)) but in practice, where the rules for application have been complied with and the grounds satisfied, the holdover will be given in all but exceptional cases. The holdover does not automatically apply to the whole of the Provisional Salaries Tax, only to the part which is shown to be affected by the grounds cited. The IRD must in all cases notify their decision in writing (Sec. 63E(4)).

Where the holdover is granted, it will be effective until the final liability for the year of assessment is ascertained and due for payment except in the case of ground (4) above where, if the objection against the previous year's assessment is determined or settled earlier, the earlier date will apply (Sec. 63E(1)).

■ Example 3.20

N. E. Oldiron has received the following composite assessment based on his Salaries Tax return for the year ended 31st March 2007:—

2006/07 Final Salaries Tax

Net Assessable Income	$495,000
Personal Allowances (Self & Wife)	200,000
Net Chargeable Income	$295,000
Tax Thereon	$ 45,550
Provisional Salaries Tax Paid	39,719
Balance Due	$ 5,831

2007/08 Provisional Salaries Tax

Net Assessable Income	$495,000
Personal Allowances (Self & Wife)	200,000
	$295,000
Tax Thereon	$ 39,650
Total Tax Payable	$ 45,481
Due on:— 8th February 2008	$ 35,568*
8th May 2008	9,913

*(75% × $39,650 plus $5,831)

He has a child born in August 2007 and can therefore apply for a holdover as follows:—

Additional allowances for child	$100,000
Reduced Provisional Tax by	$100,000 @ 17% = $17,000

Holdover notice issued by IRD:—

Tax Due	8.2.2008	8.5.2008
2006/07 Final	$ 5,831	
2007/08 Provisional	29,737	$9,913
	$35,568	$9,913
Less: Holdover (75%/25%)	12,750	4,250
Due and Payable	$22,818	$5,663

Notes:—
(a) If the baby had been born after 11th January 2008 or he had otherwise missed the

> 28-day deadline (assuming the notice of assessment had been issued prior to 29th December 2007), the $17,000 would be wholly held over against the second instalment.
> (b) No further tax is payable until the final liability for 2007/08 is established when Provisional Salaries Tax paid of $22,650 (Tax payable of $39,650 less Provisional Salaries Tax of $17,000 on amount heldover) will be credited and any balance due will be payable in early 2009.

3.8 Other Issues

3.8.1 Treatment of payments to service companies and trusts

Sec. 9A is a legislative provision which was first foreshadowed by the former Financial Secretary in his 1994 Budget Speech and is aimed at overcoming Salaries Tax planning arrangements involving individuals providing their services through a company which they (or their associates) control, a trust of which they (or an associate) are a beneficiary or a company controlled by such a trust. Such companies and trusts are commonly referred to as service companies and trusts and, prior to the introduction of this legislation, potentially allowed many individuals to obtain tax benefits through being able to structure employment contracts in a more tax efficient manner than was offered by their employer.

Sec. 9A is applied mechanically to all service company arrangements, irrespective of whether they were established principally to derive tax benefits. Interestingly, however, it is arguably not necessary to strike down those more blatantly tax motivated arrangements, which it is clear were the category of arrangements which the former Financial Secretary found offensive and the reason for the introduction of the provision. In this regard, see *Cheung Wah Keung v CIR* [2002] (1 HKRC 90-116) and [2003] (1 HKRC 900-124) which concerned a service company arrangement in years of assessment before the introduction of Sec. 9A. In that case, the Court of First Instance upheld the decision of the Board of Review that the general anti-avoidance provisions of both Sec. 61 and Sec. 61A (see Chapter 10) could apply to deem the fees received by a service company to be salary income of the individual who controlled the service company and rendered all the services on behalf of the service company. On appeal, the decision of the Court of First Instance was upheld by the Court of Appeal.

Essentially, Sec. 9A seeks to "look through" such arrangements by deeming the amounts paid to the service company or trust to be income of the individual providing the services from employment with the person making the payments; where the provision operates, all the provisions of the IRO, including the reporting requirements contained in Sec. 52 and the associated offence provisions, are deemed to apply.

More specifically, Sec. 9A(1) applies where a person (known as the "relevant person") who is carrying on, or is deemed to be carrying on, a trade, profession or business or an activity prescribed by the Commissioner under Sec. 9A(6), has entered into an agreement for the provision of services by an individual (known as the "relevant individual") under which remuneration is paid or credited to either:

(a)   a company controlled by the relevant individual and/or one or more associates of the relevant individual;

(b)   a trustee of a trust estate under which the relevant individual and/ or one or more associates of the relevant individual are beneficiaries; or

(c)   a company controlled by such a trustee.

For the purpose of the above tests, "associate" of a relevant individual is widely defined in Sec. 9A(8) as:—

(i)   a relative of the individual;

(ii)   a partner of the individual and any relative of such a partner;

(iii) a partnership in which the relevant individual is a partner;

(iv)   a company controlled by either the relevant individual, a partner of the relevant individual, or a partnership in which the relevant individual is a partner;

(v)   a director or principal officer (as also defined in Sec. 9A(8)) of a company referred to in (iv) above; or

(vi)   another relevant individual under the same agreement with the relevant person to provide services.

"Control" is clearly a critical element in deciding whether the provisions of Sec. 9A apply as if the relevant individual does not control the company (or if the individual is not a beneficiary, as defined, of the trust), the provisions cannot apply. In relation to a company, "control" is also defined in Sec. 9A(8) and means the power of a person to secure that the affairs of the company are conducted in accordance with the wishes of that person either through the holding of shares or voting power over that or any other company, or by virtue of the articles of association or any other document regulating the operation of that or any other company. Clearly, therefore, where a temporary worker (e.g. a nurse or secretary) is employed by an agency company and sent to work at different locations for short periods, the provisions would not normally operate to deem the worker to be in employment with all the different organisations for which he worked. Rather, he would continue to be treated as in employment only with the agency company since, amongst other reasons which are discussed below, he would not generally be in control of the agency company.

A "beneficiary" under a trust is also defined extremely broadly in Sec. 9A(8) as not only an existing beneficiary of the trust but also any person who is capable of benefiting under the trust, either directly or through any interposed person, or who is able or might reasonably be expected to be able, whether directly or indirectly, to control the activities of the trust or the application of the income or capital of the trust. This definition appears so broad ranging as to potentially apply to any discretionary trust other than one which has a carefully specified range of excluded beneficiaries.

Although for Sec. 9A(1) to apply there must be an "agreement" in existence, there is clearly no requirement for the agreement to be reduced to writing; accordingly, the provisions are not frustrated by having a verbal agreement. It is also important to note that there is no requirement for the agreement to specify that the activities are to be carried out by a particular person; in other words, the provisions will potentially apply not only to an agreement whereby a company or trust undertakes to procure the services of one or more particular individuals, but also to an agreement for the provision of services with no specification as to who will render those services.

Where the tests laid down in Sec. 9A(1) are met then, unless an exemption is granted under either Sec. 9A(3), Sec. 9A(4), or Sec. 9A(7)(b), the following will apply:

(a) the relevant individual is deemed to have commenced an employment with the relevant person on the date the agreement was entered into or 18th August 1995, whichever is later, except in the case where the relevant person is undertaking a prescribed activity, in which case he is deemed to have commenced employment with the relevant person on the date specified in the notice in the *Gazette* prescribing that activity. Such employment is deemed to continue until the agreement terminates without the relevant individual continuing to provide services as an employee of the relevant person;

(b) whilst the agreement is in force, the relevant individual is deemed to be an employee of the relevant person. This seems to be for the avoidance of doubt as it adds little to (a) above;

(c) the remuneration paid under the agreement is deemed to be income from an employment of profit (in other words salary or wage income) receivcd by and accrued to the relevant individual at the time it is paid or credited to the company or trust in question; and

(d)   all the provisions of the IRO apply accordingly, including the reporting and withholding provisions relating to employments which are contained in Sec. 52 as well as the associated penalty provisions.

One of the effects of (d) above is that where a person carrying on business makes a payment to a company or trust for the provision of the services of an individual and none of the specific exemptions apply, that person needs to ascertain whether the individual controls that company (or is a beneficiary under the trust) and, if so, must report the commencement of an employment and file an annual return of the remuneration paid under the arrangement. Failure to comply with these requirements without reasonable cause constitutes an offence. Often, however, it is very difficult for the person making the payments to determine whether the individual controls the company (or is a beneficiary under the trust), or is exempt from the provisions pursuant to either Sec. 9A(3) or Sec. 9A(4) (see below), and the provisions deal with this by providing as a statutory defence, the right to rely, in certain circumstances, on written representations by the individual. This is discussed in more detail in section 7.4.1.

For the avoidance of doubt, Sec. 9A(7) provides that where there is more than one relevant individual under an agreement (i.e. the service company or trust is used to provide the services of more than one person), the provisions of Sec. 9A(1) are to be applied to each person individually rather than collectively. Where the agreement permits a breakdown of the payments between services attributable to each of the relevant individuals, this provision will ensure that each individual is taxed only on an appropriate portion of the service company or trust's income, rather than having each relevant individual taxed on the total amount earned by the service company or trust under the agreement.

However, Sec. 9A(2) provides that where the remuneration attributable to a relevant individual is not specified in the agreement, all amounts derived by the service company or trust are deemed to be remuneration for the individual's services unless the Commissioner is satisfied otherwise. This provision appears aimed at the situation where a company or trust receives an undissected sum for both services of a relevant individual and some other purpose (e.g. the supply of goods). Nonetheless, in practice, where there is one agreement which covers more than one relevant individual but the remuneration is not broken down between the services of those individuals, the Commissioner may interpret this provision so as to assess each relevant individual on the whole of the payments made to the service company or trust until such time as he is satisfied as to the breakdown of the total payment. In this regard, see paragraph 19 of *Departmental Interpretation & Practice Notes No. 25*.

Even where the tests laid down in Sec. 9A(1) are met, exemption from the provisions of that Section may be granted in a number of circumstances. The first of these is contained in Sec. 9A(3) and involves satisfying six tests which are commonly used to decide whether a contract is one of employment or one of an independent contractor. In particular, for this exemption to apply, the following conditions must be met:

(a)   neither the agreement in question nor any related undertaking provides for remuneration to include annual leave, passage allowance, sick leave, pension entitlements, medical payments, accommodation or any similar benefit, or any benefit (including money) in lieu thereof;

(b)   if the agreement, or a related undertaking, requires any of the services to be carried out personally by the relevant individual, the relevant individual carries out similar services for persons other than the relevant person during the term of the agreement;

(c)   the performance of any of the services by the relevant individual is not subject to any control or supervision commonly exercised by an employer over his employee's duties by any person (including, and presumably particularly, the relevant person) other than the company or trust in question;

(d)   the remuneration is not paid or credited periodically in a manner similar to that of remuneration under a contract of employment;

(e)   the relevant person does not have the right to order the cessation of the services in a manner or for reasons which are commonly provided for in a contract of employment; and

(f)   the relevant individual is not held out to the public to be an officer or employee of the relevant person.

The Commissioner's view on the interpretation of these provisions can be found in paragraphs 20 to 31 of *Departmental Interpretation & Practice Notes No. 25*. See also *D 13/06* where the Board of Review extensively analysed the provisions of Sec. 9A(3) when considering whether it applied to the case before them.

As noted, the tests set out in Sec. 9A(3) are commonly used as a means of determining whether under a contract an individual is an employee or independent contractor. Nonetheless, where not all of the tests in Sec. 9A

(3) are satisfied, an exemption from the provisions of Sec. 9A(1) is still available, under Sec. 9A(4), where the relevant individual satisfies the Commissioner that at all relevant times the carrying out of the services did not, in substance, amount to the holding of an office or employment of profit by the relevant individual with the relevant person. It is important to note that this exemption requires the Commissioner to form an opinion as to its applicability, although as a matter of administrative law the Commissioner is required to act reasonably in doing so. Nonetheless, it appears that the exemption will not apply until such time as the matter has been considered and decided upon by the IRD, or the Board of Review or court in the event that the IRD holds that the provision does not apply and the taxpayer appeals against that decision. Accordingly, it is not permissible for a person to reach their own conclusion on Sec. 9A(4) and on that basis not apply the provisions of Sec. 9A(1). Instead, unless an exemption is available under one of the other specific provisions, the relevant person should comply with all of the reporting requirements until such time as the Commissioner, the Board of Review or a court rules that an exemption under Sec. 9A(4) is available. Similarly, a relevant individual should disclose the arrangement and then clearly claim an exemption pursuant to Sec. 9A(4) if they consider the facts support such a claim.

For a case where the Board of Review considered whether Sec. 9A(4) should apply, see *D 108/01*. It is not clear from that decision whether the taxpayer's grounds of appeal specifically covered Sec. 9A(4), although the Board did analyse the provision in deciding whether Sec. 9A(1) applied. In doing so, they rejected the application of Sec. 9A(4) for a number of reasons including the fact that the interposed company's role was only to provide the services of the relevant individual and that it provided no equipment or other support nor assumed any financial risk, and that the individual was subject to the strict control of the person making the payments to the interposed company. This decision was followed in the similar case of *D 62/03*, although note that Sec. 9A(4) was a specific ground of appeal in that case. A similar reasoning and conclusion was reached in *D 13/06* on the basis of Australian and UK case law concerning the question of whether or not an individual was an employee.

The information required by the Commissioner in order to consider a request for exemption under Sec. 9A(4), together with a discussion as to the factors he considers relevant when ruling on such requests, can be found in paragraphs 32 to 40 of *Departmental Interpretation & Practice Notes No. 25*.

Exemptions are also contained in Sec. 9A(7)(b). In particular, Sec. 9A

(7)(b)(i) provides an exemption where the relevant person is also the relevant individual; this would occur where, for example, a sole trader or practitioner used a company to provide services to his business or practice and was an employee or office holder of that company. Similarly, Sec. 9A(7)(b)(ii) provides an exemption where the relevant person is a partnership and the relevant individual is a partner in that partnership. This would typically apply where a professional partnership had an agreement with a company to provide services to the partnership and the partners were directors or employees of that company. It is interesting to note that the use of service companies by professional practitioners and partnerships (i.e. the situations covered by Sec. 9A(7)(b)) was originally described by the former Financial Secretary in his 1994 Budget Speech as amounting to abuse and he indicated that such arrangements would be covered by the proposed legislation. It appears, however, that the Government's view of these arrangements subsequently changed and it is now policy that such arrangements will be tolerated within the guidelines explained in *Departmental Interpretation & Practice Notes No. 24*, which is discussed in section 4.5.10. As a consequence of this policy, it was necessary to ensure that Sec. 9A did not operate to counter such arrangements.

To ensure that the provision does not result in double taxation, where it operates to deem the relevant individual to be taxable on the income paid to the company or trust, Sec. 9A(5) deems the company or trust to be exempt from tax on those amounts. Moreover, if the company or trust pays or credits any amounts to the relevant individual as remuneration under an employment with the company or trust, such remuneration is exempt from tax in the hands of the individual to the extent it is attributable to amounts derived by the company or trust which are deemed to be income of the individual. Put another way, any salary paid by the service company or trust is exempt from Salaries Tax where Sec. 9A(1) applies.

■ Example 3.21

Andrew Derek provides his services to Trimble Limited through a company which he beneficially owns and controls called Mossman Limited. The terms of the agreement between Trimble and Mossman provide for remuneration to be paid on a monthly basis and for Andrew to take four weeks annual leave. The agreement also provides that Andrew is to be personally under the supervision of the managing director of Trimble, Mr. Keenan. The agreement between Mossman and Andrew provides for a monthly salary plus various non-taxable fringe benefits.

Because Andrew controls Mossman, Sec. 9A(1) operates to deem the amounts paid by Trimble to Mossman to be employment income of Andrew with the entire amount being subject to tax with no relief available to reflect the fact that Andrew ultimately receives some of the remuneration from Mossman in the form of non-taxable fringe benefits. An exemption under Sec. 9A(3) would not be available because of the control exercised over Andrew by Mr. Keenan and the fact that the agreement with Trimble provides for Andrew to take annual leave. However, as a consequence of the operation of Sec. 9A(1), Mossman will be exempt from Profits Tax on the amounts received from Trimble and Andrew will be exempt from Salaries Tax on the amounts received from Mossman.

■ Example 3.22

The situation is as in Example 3.21 except for the fact that Mossman is owned and controlled by an unrelated company, Bilgola Limited, over which neither Andrew nor his associates exercise any control.

In the absence of control by Andrew (or his associates) of Mossman and/or Bilgola, Sec. 9A(1) cannot apply to the arrangement. Accordingly, subject to the normal rules, Mossman will be liable to Profits Tax on amounts derived from Trimble, but will obtain a deduction for salary and benefits paid to Andrew. Andrew will, again subject to the usual rules, be liable to Salaries Tax on the amounts derived from Mossman.

■ Example 3.23

Andy Kam is a freelance photographer who owns and controls a company called Flasher Limited. Flasher contracts and receives fees to make Andy available to undertake short assignments and also sells photographs taken by Andy to newspapers and magazines.

Flasher is hired by a local newspaper, the *South China Standard Express*, to photograph visitors to a trade fair which lasts five days.

Notwithstanding the fact that Andy controls Flasher, it is likely that all six tests in Sec. 9A(3) would be met and, as a consequence, an exemption from the provisions of Sec. 9A (1) would be available. Accordingly, Flasher would be liable to Profits Tax on the fee from the *South China Standard Express* and Andy would be liable to Salaries Tax only on any remuneration derived from Flasher (subject to the normal rules).

■ Example 3.24

The same facts as in Example 3.23 except that Flasher enters into an agreement whereby Andy will work exclusively for the *South China Standard Express*, under the direction of the chief photographer, for four months for a fee of HK$50,000 per month.

Because Andy is working exclusively for, and under the direct supervision of, the *South China Standard Express* and is being paid a monthly flat fee, it is likely that the tests in Secs. 9A(3)(b), 9A(3)(c) and 9A(3)(d) would not be met. Accordingly, Sec. 9A(1) would, *prima facie*, apply. Nonetheless, given the established freelance business of Flasher and the temporary nature of the assignment with the *South China Standard Express*, it is possible that the Commissioner would accept that Andy was not, in substance, holding an employment of profit with the *South China Standard Express* and exercise his discretion under Sec. 9A(4) to exempt the arrangement from the provisions of Sec. 9A(1).

■ Example 3.25

Dr. K. A. Vity is a self-employed dentist. He owns and controls a company, Amalgam Limited, which provides his surgery and equipment and employs his nurse and receptionist, in return for a management fee from Dr. Vity. Dr. Vity is employed by Amalgam to provide administrative services to the dental practice in return for which he is paid an annual salary of HK$200,000 plus tax-free fringe benefits.

Prima facie, Sec. 9A(1) would apply to the arrangement and would deem a portion of the management fee paid to Amalgam to be income of Dr. Vity (although it is not clear how the quantum of that amount would be determined). However, Sec. 9A(7)(b)(i) would provide an exemption from the provision on the grounds that Dr. Vity was both the relevant person and the relevant individual. (See, however, section 4.5.10.)

3.8.2 Tax on tax

Where an employer pays an employee's tax for him, this constitutes additional remuneration of the year in which the tax is paid. Because the tax is, of course, payable partly within the year of assessment, by virtue of the incidence of Provisional Salaries Tax, and partly within the following year and also because, normally, no tax at all is paid in the first year, the taxable income year by year is inconsistent even if the salary remains the same. Furthermore, there has to be a grossing-up in the final year in order to "catch up".

■ Example 3.26

Bill Dupp is employed from 1st April for 5 years at $1,800,000 p.a. and his employer agrees to pay the tax. He leaves Hong Kong at the end of his employment. It is assumed, as is usual, that no tax is payable in his first year and that, in subsequent years, Provisional Salaries Tax is payable as to 75% in the year of assessment and the balance in the following year. Assuming Bill is single and has no dependents and is not entitled to any deductions, tax payable would be as follows:

Year	Salary	Tax paid in year by employer	Taxable income	Tax thereon
1	$1,800,000	—	$1,800,000	$ 270,000
2	$1,800,000	$ 472,500	2,272,500	340,875
3	$1,800,000	394,031	2,194,031	329,104
4	$1,800,000	320,276	2,120,276	318,041
5	$1,800,000	$1,401,426	$2,201,426	$1,330,213
Total		$1,588,233		$1,588,233

Tax paid in year by employer is as follows (Note (c)):—

	Year 2	Year 3	Year 4	Year 5
Year 1 Final	$270,000			
Year 2 Provisional (75%)	202,500			
Year 2 Provisional (balance)		$ 67,500		
Year 2 Final		70,875		
Year 3 Provisional (75%)		255,656		
Year 3 Provisional (balance)			$ 85,219	
Year 3 Final			(11,771)	
Year 4 Provisional (75%)			246,828	
Year 4 Provisional (balance)				$ 82,276
Year 4 Final				(11,063)
Year 5 Provisional (75%)				238,531
Year 5 Final				91,682
Total	$472,500	$394,031	$320,270	$401,420

Notes:—
(a) Calculation of final year 5 involves a "gross-up" because otherwise the computation would be infinite. The calculation is as follows:

Salary	$1,800,000
Taxes paid to date by employer	
($82,276 + $238,531 – $11,063) =	309,744
Taxable to date	$2,109,744
Tax @ 15% (Note (c))	$ 316,461 (Year 5)
Provisional Tax paid	238,531
Net tax payable	$ 77,930

$$77,930 \times \frac{100}{85} = 91,682$$

(b) For an explanation of Provisional Salaries Tax, see section 3.7.3.
(c) These calculations assume for the purposes of simplicity that the applicable tax rate is 15% throughout and that there is no "rental value."

There is, therefore, an uneven level of tax liability each year despite the fixed salary. This problem can be obviated in the case of medium or long term employment by fixing the salary at a given net-of-tax figure and reporting the notional gross equivalent for tax purposes. However, the fact that the earnings have been computed in this manner should be disclosed to the IRD otherwise the Department could charge that the full facts have not been reported, although the Department does not lose because, over the life of an employment, the total tax is the same by either method.

■ Example 3.27

The employee in Example 3.26 is to receive annually $1,800,000 net of tax. The amount reported for tax is $\frac{100}{85} \times \$1,800,000 = \$2,117,647$

Taxable income reported $2,117,647
Tax thereon @ 15%   317,647 Paid by employer
                                $1,800,000 Received by employee

The total tax for the 5 years is therefore 5 × $317,647 = $1,588,235 which is the same as in Example 3.26 (apart from a minor rounding difference).

Note that, again for simplicity, a 15% tax rate has been assumed to apply throughout the relevant period.

The calculation of the notional gross equivalent is more complicated in a case where personal allowances are deductible, tax is payable at progressive rates and rental values are involved, in which case an algebraic calculation is necessary. However, the principle holds good and it will be seen from the above examples that the latter method has the merit of consistency although it must be said that the IRD favours the method in Example 3.26, which is, therefore, the method normally adopted.

Where the employee has a non-Hong Kong employment such that he is only subject to Salaries Tax on the proportion of his earnings which relate to duties performed in Hong Kong (see section 3.3.2.1) and his employer also pays his Salaries Tax, his salary etc. is apportioned on a time basis but not the benefit from the payment of his Salaries Tax liability as the Board of Review in *D 31/85* held that this benefit was receivable only by virtue of services rendered in Hong Kong. See also *D 106/89* and Example 3.15.

The payment by an employer of an employee's foreign tax liability may also be assessable and give rise to the difficulties identified above; see, for example, *D 1/90*.

3.8.3 Taxation of married couples

Husbands and wives are generally treated as separate persons for tax purposes, with each responsible for filing their own tax return and paying their own tax liabilities (Sec. 10(1)). Married couples can, however, elect pursuant to Sec. 10(2) to be jointly assessed in which case the individuals' net chargeable incomes are aggregated and a single assessment raised. For the meaning of the terms "husband", "wife" and "spouse", see section 3.8.3.3.

The objective of the election is to provide for those situations where individual Salaries Tax liabilities would amount to more tax in total than on a single combined assessment with married persons' allowances. The opportunity for an election arises in two specific situations, namely:—

(1) where the personal allowances to which one of the spouses is entitled exceeds that spouse's net assessable income after deducting allowable charitable contributions, elderly residential care expenses and home loan interest expenses and recognized retirement scheme contributions (Sec. 10(2)(a)). In other words where one spouse's net chargeable income is a negative amount (see Example 3.28); and

(2) where the tax under an assessment on aggregated net chargeable incomes with married persons' allowance would be less than tax on individual net chargeable incomes (Sec. 10(2)(b)). This only occurs where a higher deduction is available for charitable donations against combined incomes than the aggregate of the deductions against the single incomes (see Example 3.29).

The effect of an election is that a single assessment is made upon the couple's aggregate net chargeable income and, in arriving at such net chargeable income, allowable charitable donations (Sec. 26C), elderly residential care expenses (Sec. 26D), home loan interest expenses (Sec. 26E), retirement scheme contributions (Sec. 26G) and personal allowances (see Chapter 6) are deductible (Sec. 12B(2)). The personal allowance deductible is the married person's allowance; each spouse would otherwise only be entitled to single person's allowance where each had a net chargeable income. Personal allowances are described in detail in Chapter 6.

Where the election is made because one spouse has negative net chargeable income, the combined assessment is raised upon the other spouse because he or she is the only one who would have paid any tax under separate taxation (Sec. 10(3)(a)). Where the election is made simply because a combined assessment would give a smaller tax liability, it is up to the spouses to nominate which of them is to be assessed (Sec. 10(3)(b)).

■ Example 3.28

A husband and wife have the following earnings liable to Salaries Tax and outgoings for 2007/08.

	Husband	Wife
Salary etc.	$143,000	$87,000
Expenses	(5,000)	—
Net Assessable Incomes	$138,000	$ 87,000
Charitable Donations	(3,000)	(4,000) (note)
	$135,000	$ 83,000

Personal Allowance	(100,000)	(100,000)
Net Chargeable Income	$ 35,000	$ (17,000)
Tax Thereon	$ 700	—

Under Sec. 10(1) they would each be subject to their own Salaries Tax after sending in their own Salaries Tax return and would have to pay tax as indicated.

However, because the wife cannot use all of her allowances, they can elect for joint assessment in accordance with Sec. 10(2)(a) and a joint assessment as follows would be made upon the husband in accordance with Sec. 10(3)(a):—

Salary etc	$230,000
Expenses	(5,000)
Net Assessable Income	$225,000
Charitable Donations	(7,000)
	$218,000
Married Person's Allowance (aggregate)	(200,000)
Net Chargeable Income	$ 18,000
Tax Thereon	$ 360

They would therefore save $340 by making the election, or rather, the husband would save $340 because he gets the benefit of his wife's excess allowances.

Note:
Where separately assessed, the husband could actually claim the $4,000 charitable donation made by his wife in which case his tax would be reduced to $620.

■ Example 3.29

A husband and wife have the following earnings liable to Salaries Tax and outgoings for 2007/08. The husband has made a charitable donation of $83,000.

	Husband	Wife
Salary etc	$260,000	$105,000
Expenses	(5,000)	—
Net Assessable Incomes	$255,000	$105,000
Charitable Donations (max. allowable)	(63,750)	—
	$191,250	$105,000
Personal Allowances	(100,000)	(100,000)
Net Chargeable Incomes	$ 91,250	($ 5,000)
Tax Thereon	$ 5,700	$ 100
Total Tax Paid		$ 5,800

If they were to elect under Sec. 10(2)(b) for joint assessment, the tax would be calculated as follows and would be assessed upon whichever of themselves they chose to nominate per Sec. 10(3)(b):—

Salary etc	$365,000
Expenses	(5,000)
Net Assessable Income	$360,000
Charitable Donations	(83,000)
	$277,000

Aggregate Married Person's Allowance	(200,000)
Net Chargeable Income	$ 77,000
Tax Thereon	$ 3,990

They would therefore save $1,810 by making the election. It seems that the election under Sec.10(2)(b) would apply only in minor cases such as this and arises because a greater deduction for charitable contributions is available where the incomes are combined, than when the husband and wife are separately assessed in which case the husband's deduction is limited to 25% of his net assessable income. This advantage is lost where higher incomes are involved because the combined income more quickly progresses to the higher rate bands.

Where the husband or wife dies before the election can be made, their executor is empowered to sign the election (Sec. 10(4)).

In the year of marriage, for the purposes of calculating the tax on combined income following an election under Sec. 10(2), a couple are deemed to have been married on 1st April at the commencement of the year (Sec. 10(5)). Accordingly, they must both bring their pre-marital earnings into the calculation of tax on joint income and this will reduce the chances of an election being beneficial as illustrated in Example 3.30.

It is particularly important to note that the higher personal allowance is only available for Salaries Tax either where a valid election for joint assessment is made under Sec. 10(2) or where only one of the spouses has income liable to Salaries Tax in the year of assessment (Sec. 29(1)(a)). Therefore, where marriage takes place during the year of assessment and the wife immediately ceases working, the husband cannot claim the married personal allowance because the wife had earnings during the year of assessment, albeit prior to marriage. Such allowance would, however, be available if they elected for joint assessment but, as already mentioned, this may not be beneficial because of the requirement to bring pre-marital earnings into the calculation (see Example 3.30).

■ Example 3.30

Jack and Jill were married on 1st October 2007 and their respective earnings from employment for the year ended 31st March 2008 were as follows:—

Jack, 1st April 2007 to 31st March 2008	$220,000
Jill, 1st April 2007 to 30th September 2007	110,000

Although Jill has no post-marriage earnings, Jack cannot claim the higher personal allowance because Jill had earnings during 2007/08, albeit as a single person. Accordingly, they are assessed as follows:—

	Jack	Jill
Salary	$220,000	$110,000
Allowances	(100,000)	(100,000)
Net Chargeable Incomes	$120,000	$ 10,000
Tax Thereon	$ 9,900	$ 200
Total		$10,100

They could not elect for joint assessment under Sec. 10(2) because it would not be advantageous. Jack would be obliged to bring into the calculation Jill's pre-marriage earnings and the combined assessment would be:—

Salary	$330,000
Allowances	(200,000)
Net Chargeable Income	$130,000
Tax Thereon	$ 11,600

Particular aspects of the separate taxation provisions are considered under various headings below.

3.8.3.1 The election

There are, of course, provisions which specify how and when an election is to be made. It must be in a form specified by the Board of Inland Revenue which means that a letter is not sufficient; rather, there is a place on the individual tax return form where the election can be made. If an election is to be made after the relevant returns have been filed, there is a printed form available for the purpose, which is available from the IRD on request. The election is to be made jointly by husband and wife and can be withdrawn by them by joint notice (Sec. 11(1)). A withdrawn election is treated as if it had never been made; therefore, any assessments based upon the election would be adjusted to take account of the withdrawal (Sec. 11(3)). Once withdrawn however, the couple cannot remake the election for the same year if they happen to change their mind (Sec. 11(4)).

Timing is, of course, important and an election or withdrawal in relation to a given year of assessment must be made:—

(1) within that year of assessment or the immediately following year of assessment; or

(2) before a period of one month after the date upon which the assessment for that year of assessment becomes final and conclusive (see section 8.7), if later than (1).

The Commissioner does, however, have the power to extend the time limit for election or withdrawal to such date as he considers reasonable in the circumstances (Sec. 11(2)).

3.8.3.2 Provisional Salaries Tax

Normally, of course, a husband and wife, separately taxed as individuals, will be liable for their own Provisional Salaries Tax. However, in the situation where, for a year of assessment, a married couple has elected to be assessed jointly and therefore the assessment is upon only one of the spouses, the question arises as to how the Provisional Salaries Tax for the immediately succeeding year of assessment is to be charged having regard to the fact that both assessments are normally on the same form and joint assessment may not apply in the succeeding year of assessment. It is therefore provided in Sec. 63B(2) that the individual who is named as chargeable on the joint election assessment is to be solely responsible for paying the Provisional Salaries Tax for the immediately succeeding year. Clearly, where there is no joint election in the succeeding year of assessment, it is likely that the spouse who paid the Provisional Salaries Tax will have overpaid it and the other spouse will, of course, have paid none (see Example 3.31).

■ Example 3.31

A couple were jointly assessed for 2006/07 and the husband was nominated to be the one to be assessed. Their respective incomes in 2007/08, however, are such that a joint election is not appropriate and Salaries Tax payable for 2007/08 by husband and wife is $250 and $100 respectively, the position on Provisional Salaries Tax will be as follows:—

2006/07 Salaries Tax	Income	$241,000	
	Expenses	(5,000)	
	Charitable Donations	(5,000)	
	Allowances (married)	(200,000)	
	Net Chargeable Income	$31,000	
	Tax Payable		$670
2007/08 Provisional Salaries Tax	Net Chargeable Income	$31,000	
	Tax Payable		620
Total Payable by Husband			$1,290

When they each individually receive their 2007/08 Salaries Tax assessments, the amounts demanded will be:—

	Husband	Wife
Salaries Tax 2007/08	$250	$100
Provisional Salaries Tax Paid	620	—
Refund due to Husband	$370	
Due and Payable by Wife		$100

The amount overpaid by the husband would be treated as a part payment of his Provisional Salaries Tax for 2008/09.

3.8.3.3 Definitions

When applying the provisions applicable to married couples, it is important to understand the terms used, the more important of which are defined as follows:—

Spouse, although a statement of the obvious, can mean either a husband or a wife (Sec. 2(1)), each of which has its own statutory definition as discussed below.

Husband means a married man whose marriage is recognised by the laws of Hong Kong or was entered into outside Hong Kong and recognised by law in the place where the marriage took place. In the case of polygamous marriages, which are possible but not under the laws of Hong Kong, only the marriage between the husband and the principal wife is recognised for tax purposes. There is, however, no statutory definition of what constitutes a principal wife (Sec. 2(1)).

Wife means a married woman whose marriage is recognised in the same way as a husband's as discussed in the previous paragraph (Sec. 2(1)).

Living Apart is defined in Sec. 2(3) and refers to a husband and wife living apart:—

(1) Under a Court order or decree made in Hong Kong or elsewhere.
(2) Under a deed of separation or similar instrument.
(3) In circumstances which, in the Commissioner's opinion, is likely to be permanent. This is a question of intent of the parties rather than purely geographical circumstances. For a case where the Board of Review considered whether a couple should be treated as living apart for the purpose of this limb of the definition, see *D 42/01*.

These definitions apply, not only for Salaries Tax, but for all purposes of the IRO and are particularly important for Personal Assessment (see Chapter 6).

3.8.4 Double Taxation Agreements

This chapter has primarily been concerned with examining the provisions of the IRO and the manner in which those provisions have been interpreted by the courts and Board of Review. As is more fully discussed in chapter 12, however, the provisions of the IRO may be over-ridden by the terms of an international agreement concerning taxation. Such an agreement may be a comprehensive double taxation agreement, the Memorandum with the Mainland of China concerning double taxation, or the shipping or air services agreements containing provisions concerning taxation which have been concluded with numerous jurisdictions.

It is important to remember that international agreements concerning taxation do not impose a liability to Hong Kong tax where one does not otherwise exist; however, they can operate to provide an exemption from a liability which would otherwise arise under the IRO.

The terms of double taxation agreements, as well as shipping and air services agreements, are individually negotiated between the parties and are not necessarily consistent from one agreement to another. Accordingly, it is always essential to refer to the appropriate agreement before concluding whether it offers exemptions in any particular case. Nonetheless, as a generalisation, under a comprehensive double taxation agreement a resident of one jurisdiction may enjoy an exemption from tax on employment income derived from the other jurisdiction where his physical presence in that other jurisdiction is limited, although other conditions may also need to be satisfied. For example, under the double taxation agreement concluded with Belgium, a Belgian resident is exempt from Salaries Tax if he is present in Hong Kong for less than 183 days in any twelve month period commencing or ending in the relevant year of assessment and the remuneration is not paid by a Hong Kong resident employer, is not borne by a permanent establishment in Hong Kong and is subject to tax in Belgium. A reciprocal exemption from Belgian tax is available to a Hong Kong resident. Essentially identical provisions are contained in the double taxation agreement concluded with Thailand and the Arrangement with the Mainland of China concerning double taxation.

The shipping and air services agreements may also contain exemptions in relation to Salaries Tax, although this tends to be the exception rather than the rule. For example, the shipping agreement between Hong Kong and the Netherlands contains a clause which provides reciprocal exemptions from tax on remuneration from employment aboard a ship operated by an enterprise of one of the jurisdictions provided that such income is taxed in that jurisdiction. In other words, income derived by an individual employed on board a ship operated by a resident of the Netherlands is exempt from Salaries Tax, irrespective of the individual's physical presence in Hong Kong, provided that such income is taxable in the Netherlands. Similar provisions are contained in the agreements concerning shipping and air services concluded with Singapore and Sri Lanka.

Chapter 4 ■
Profits Tax

4.1 Legislation

Profits Tax has the greatest amount of legislation of the three income taxes, the main provisions being in Secs. 14 to 26A under Part IV of the IRO. Also directly relevant are Rules 2A to 2D of the IRR governing apportionment of allowable deductions, Rules 3 and 5 of the IRR governing the ascertainment of branch assessable profits and Part XB governing Provisional Profits Tax. The provisions governing depreciation allowances in Part VI are also primarily concerned with Profits Tax and are dealt with separately in Chapter 5.

The general provisions governing returns in Part IX, assessments in Part X, objections and appeals in Part XI, payment and recovery of tax in Part XII, double tax relief in Part VIII and penalties in Part XIV are also applicable to Profits Tax.

4.2 Scope of the Tax

Profits Tax is, in general, levied on the Hong Kong sourced profits derived by a person (as defined) from the carrying on of a trade, profession or business in Hong Kong. The source of profits is largely ascertained in accordance with case law principles. Additionally, however, the IRO contains a series of provisions which deem certain profits to have a Hong Kong source and, in some cases, as arising from a business carried on in Hong Kong, thereby rendering the amounts taxable where they would not otherwise be taxable under general principles.

Historically there was no distinction in the scope of the charge between residents and non-residents, but certain rules are laid down concerning dealings between residents and non-residents and the ascertainment of the assessable profits of a non-resident. In 2006, however, legislation was introduced (some aspects of which have retrospective application) which grants non-residents exemption from tax in specified circumstances on a range of transactions. This legislation was originally conceived to give exemptions in relation to the fund management industry in Hong Kong, but the final provisions have broader application. These provisions are examined in section 4.5.3.

There is a distinction between the rate of taxation of corporations and of other persons; for the 2007/08 year of assessment corporations are charged at 17.5% and others at 16%. Apart from this, however, there are few distinctions between the taxation of corporations and other persons.

In general, assessable profits are profits arrived at under generally accepted accounting principles, as adjusted to comply with the specific requirements of the IRO, e.g. a difference in depreciation rates for accounting and tax purposes, the exclusion of net profits from a source outside Hong Kong and adjustments to exclude capital expenditure and profits. In addition to the specified profits of non-residents referred to above, dividends and certain categories of interest and profits from qualifying debt instruments are specifically excluded from the charge to Profits Tax, as are certain profits of mutual fund corporations and unit trusts and other similar collective investment vehicles where specified requirements are met. Certain other types of profits, being profits arising on other specified categories of debt instruments and qualifying offshore reinsurance profits of insurance companies, are taxed at concessional rates.

Profits Tax is assessed on the basis of years of assessment ending on 31 March and assessable profits are ascertained on the basis of the accounting period ending in the year of assessment. There are provisions governing the basis of assessment which are applicable in the commencement and cessation years and also where there is a change of a previously established accounting date.

Losses are computed in the same way as profits and can be carried forward indefinitely against any source of profits liable to Profits Tax in the case of companies; in the case of individuals and partnerships, however, there are restrictions on the income or profits against which losses can be offset.

Partnerships are assessed as a single entity with no separate assessments on the individual partners. Normally, the manner in which partners share profits and losses is not of importance except where:

(1)   a company is a partner, in which case the corporate rate of Profits Tax will apply to its share of profits. Similarly, a company's share of losses can only be set off against profits only;

(2)   a partner wishes to claim Personal Assessment; and/or

(3)   there are changes in the partners and losses are carried forward.

There are also provisions which allow for the basis of assessment to remain undisturbed notwithstanding the withdrawal or addition of a partner in a partnership.

Depreciation allowances are separately computed for tax purposes and are governed by the detailed rules in Part VI of the IRO.

In addition to the general rules for the ascertainment of assessable profits, the IRO recognises that certain types of business need special rules for determining the source of profits and computing assessable profits and, in particular, contains specific provisions to deal with:

(1) life insurance business;
(2) other insurance business;
(3) shipping and aircraft businesses; and
(4) financial institutions.

Profits Tax is payable by direct assessment and incorporates a system of Provisional Profits Tax under which a provisional assessment is raised based on the assessable profits of the immediately preceding year of assessment. Where the date of payment falls due within the accounting period which will form the basis for the final assessment, the Provisional Profits Tax is payable in two instalments in order to reduce any element of payment in advance; the first such instalment is 75% of the liability and the second, which is payable about three months later, is the remaining 25%.

When the actual assessable profits for the year of assessment are agreed, a final assessment is issued and credit is given for the Provisional Profits Tax paid. Any excess of final liability over Provisional Profits Tax paid or vice versa is added to or subtracted from the first instalment of Provisional Profits Tax for the following year. Provisions exist for an application to be made for the Provisional Profits Tax or part thereof to be held over in a number of situations and, although it is at the discretion of the Commissioner whether the holdover is granted, it is exceptional for a holdover to be refused.

4.3 Liability to Profits Tax

Sec. 14 is the general charging section for Profits Tax and, under this provision, three conditions must be satisfied before a person can be liable for the tax. These are that the person:—

(1) carries on a trade, profession or business in Hong Kong;
(2) derives profits from that trade, profession or business, other than profits arising from the sale of capital assets; and
(3) those profits arise in or are derived from Hong Kong (i.e. the profits have a Hong Kong source).

In addition to this provision, there are specific sections which deem the conditions for chargeability to be met in respect of certain items where those conditions would not otherwise be met. If a liability arises, tax is charged on the profit as adjusted for tax purposes, at the rate (for the 2007/08 year of assessment) of 17.5% in the case of corporations and any share of a partnership's profits attributable to a corporation, and at the rate of 16% in respect of other persons.

Therefore, determining whether or not a liability to Profits Tax arises depends upon a consideration of a number of basic principles. The questions to be considered in any particular case are whether the "person" is chargeable to tax, whether he is carrying on a trade, profession or business in Hong Kong, whether profits arise from that trade, profession or business and, if so, what is the source of those profits. If, after dealing with these questions, it is found that a liability to Profits Tax does not exist, consideration must be given to the specific deeming sections of the IRO to determine if, not-withstanding that no liability exists under the general charging provision, a liability is created by such specific provisions. Similarly, if a liability is found to exist under general principles, consideration needs to be given to whether any specific statutory exemption applies. Finally, if a liability is found to exist, various provisions of the IRO must be examined to determine the quantum of the assessable profits. All of these matters are discussed in detail in the following sections of this chapter.

Although a number of factors need to be considered in determining chargeability to Profits Tax, it is important to note that unlike the position in most other jurisdictions, the place of residence or domicile of the person (and the place of incorporation in the case of a company) generally play no part in determining whether a liability exists and the quantum of any such liability although a specific exemption for certain profits of non-residents exists (see point (17) in section 4.5.3). Except where those provisions apply, non-residents are generally subject to Profits Tax in exactly the same way as residents and non-Hong Kong companies are taxed in the same manner as Hong Kong companies. Nonetheless, there are some provisions which deal with the quantification of the assessable profits of non-residents to overcome practical difficulties which may otherwise exist, and these are discussed in appropriate places in this chapter.

4.3.1 Persons chargeable

Sec. 14 imposes Profits Tax on a "person", which is defined very widely in Sec. 2 as including a corporation, partnership, trustee, whether incorporated or unincorporated, or a body of persons. Further, a "corporation" is defined as any company which is either incorporated or registered under any enactment or charter in force in Hong Kong or elsewhere but does not include a co-operative society or a trade union. Furthermore a "body of persons" is defined to mean any body public, corporate or collegiate and any company, fraternity, fellowship and society of persons whether corporate or not corporate.

A "partnership" is not defined in the IRO but is generally assumed to have the meaning given to the term by the *Partnership Ordinance* which is *"the relation which subsists between persons carrying on a business in common with a view to profit"*.

The term "trustee" is defined widely in Sec. 2 to include a guardian, curator, manager or other person having the direction, control or management of any property on behalf of any person, but does not extend to an executor. The effect of the inclusion of the word "trustee" in the definition of person in 1981 is somewhat uncertain; in particular, there is doubt as to whether the inclusion is sufficient to impose a charge to Profits Tax on a trustee in respect of trust income to which, of course, the trustee has no beneficial entitlement but merely receives in a fiduciary capacity. This doubt is reinforced by the wording of Sec. 14 which only imposes Profits Tax on a person in respect of "his" profits which, again, would arguably not extend to profits earned on behalf of another person.

The position of a trustee was considered in the South African case of *Trustees of the Phillip Frame Will Trust v CIR* (53 SATC 166). This case held that a trust is not a person (as it is nothing more than a fiduciary relationship) and, furthermore, that a representative person (e.g. a trustee) cannot be assessed unless:—

(a)   the law specifically provides for such assessability; and

(b)   the party to whom the income accrues is itself a person.

Applying this decision to the position in Hong Kong, it would seem that as the IRO does not specifically authorise assessments upon trustees in respect of trust income, and as a trust is not a person, it is arguable that a Profits Tax assessment cannot be made in respect of a trust's profits.

The matter was, however, considered by the Board of Review in *D 37/93* where the Board held that the words *"his profit"* in Sec. 14 were critical and meant that the trustee could only be assessed where the profits were his. The Board of Review went on to hold that where the nature of the trust was nothing more than a nominee arrangement, the trustee could not be assessed as the profits were those of another person who would be subject to Profits Tax on them if the other conditions for chargeability were met. Somewhat confusingly, however, the Board of Review then proceeded to conclude that where a trustee actively manages and carries on a business as part of a trust, the profits belong to the trustee and no beneficiary can lay claim directly to those profits; accordingly, the Board concluded, the trustee could be assessed to Profits Tax on those profits in such circumstances.

Although the Board of Review's approach in the above case to the question of assessability of trustees was undoubtedly an attempt to find a practical solution to an uncertain area of the law, it is difficult to reconcile the two alternate situations identified by the Board of Review as in neither case does the trustee have beneficial entitlement to the profits concerned; moreover, there is nothing in the IRO which suggests that the nature of the profits earned by a trustee, or the ability of the beneficiaries to lay claim to the trust income, are of any relevance in determining the assessability of the trustee.

The decision of the Board of Review in *D 37/93* that a nominee arrangement should be "looked through" should be contrasted with the decision of the High Court in *Hong Wah Investment Co. Ltd. v CIR* [1990] (1 HKRC 90-041). In the latter case, the court refused to look further than the legal owner of a property in determining to whom the rental income should be assessed; in doing so, the court found the legal owner, a corporation, to be assessable on the income notwithstanding that a director provided all funds for the construction of the building, arranged all lettings and retained all profits from those lettings. The court further upheld the conclusion of the Board of Review in the case that it was unnecessary to make a finding as to the beneficial ownership of the property and, therefore, the issue of the existence of a trust or agency was not properly considered.

It will be appreciated from the preceding paragraphs that the question of assessability of trustees to some extent still remains unclear. The matter may eventually be clarified by further litigation; alternatively, the matter would be put beyond doubt if the definition of person included a trust, rather than a trustee, and the IRO then provided for assessments on trustees as agents for the trust. The clarification of this area of law is important for amongst other reasons, the position of unit trusts, which are an important industry in Hong Kong; nonetheless, even if a unit trust is a "person" for tax purposes, many unit trusts would, in fact, be exempt from Profits Tax (see points (9) and (17) in section 4.5.3).

Husbands and wives are treated independently for Profits Tax purposes with each receiving an assessment in respect of their own profits subject to Profits Tax (if any). The exception to this rule is in the case of an election for Personal Assessment where the incomes of a husband and wife are aggregated, although the total liability is apportioned between them.

4.3.2 Carrying on a trade, profession or business

The next question of importance is whether a trade, profession or business is being carried on by the person in Hong Kong and this is largely a question of fact. It does not, of course, follow that because a person is deriving a source of income from Hong Kong that he is necessarily carrying on business there, although, as will be seen later, in certain circumstances a business will be deemed to be carried on (see section 4.5.4). It is, therefore, important to distinguish between carrying on business *with* Hong Kong and carrying on business *in* Hong Kong. For example, a manufacturer in the United States may sell his products in Hong Kong and visiting salesmen may spend a considerable amount of time in Hong Kong tracing and negotiating outlets. Nevertheless, the manufacturer is likely to be considered as only doing business with Hong Kong, rather than carrying on a business in Hong Kong, and probably cannot be subjected to Profits Tax on his profits. If, however, he opens a warehouse in Hong Kong and has salesmen resident there, it is more likely that he would be considered to be carrying on a business in Hong Kong; accordingly, it would become necessary to determine whether the activities in Hong Kong gave rise to a Hong Kong source of profits.

Rule 5 of the IRR, which deals with the ascertainment and determination of the profits of a branch in Hong Kong of a person whose head office is elsewhere, introduces the concept of a "permanent establishment." Permanent establishment is defined in Rule 5 of the IRR as:—

"a branch, management or other place of business, but does not include an agency unless the agent has, and habitually exercises, a general authority to negotiate and conclude contracts on behalf of his principal or has a stock of merchandise from which he regularly fills orders on his behalf" (Rule 5(1)).

In other words, IRR 5 suggests that the existence of an agent in Hong Kong is important in determining whether a liability will arise, although it must be remembered that this rule is actually concerned with the quantification of assessable profits, rather than imposing a charge to tax, and does not specifically cover the situation where no permanent establishment exists; that is, the rule deals with the determination of the amount of assessable profits where a permanent establishment exists, but does not specifically state that in the absence of a permanent establishment no liability will arise. Nonetheless, the rule arguably implies that a permanent establishment or agent is generally a prerequisite for a liability to Profits Tax to arise and, in determining whether a permanent establishment exists, it is irrelevant whether the agent is an employee of the principal or an independent third party. Rather, the fundamental question is the extent of the agent's authority to contract on behalf of his principal. An isolated and specific authority to conclude a contract on behalf of the principal is not enough to constitute a permanent establishment under the above rule; it must be a general authority to negotiate *and* conclude and one which is regularly exercised. In these circumstances, not only does the principal come within the scope of Profits Tax, but assessments can be made upon the agent (see section 4.8.3).

The relevance of the existence of an agent with authority has also been considered in a number of UK cases, in particular see *Adams v Cape Industries Plc*. [1990] (1 Ch 433) and *Jabbour v Custodian of Israeli Absentee Property* [1954] (1 WLR 139). These cases were actually concerned with the question of "residence" or "presence" under UK law but contain some interesting observations as to what constitutes the carrying on of business in a jurisdiction and on the nature of the presence required by a person in a jurisdiction before that jurisdiction can exercise a power to tax that person. For example, in the *Adams* case, Scott J., noted that, under UK law, for a person to be within the jurisdiction of the revenue authorities it was not merely sufficient for that person to be trading in a country, but that the trading "*... must be reinforced by some residential feature such as a branch office or a resident agent with a power to contract"*. Similarly, in the *Adams* case, the court quoted with approval an extract from the *Jabbour* case where it was noted that "*... in the case of an agency, the principal test to be applied in determining whether the corporation is carrying on business at the agency is to ascertain whether the agent has the authority to enter into contracts on behalf of the corporation without submitting them to the corporation for approval ...*"

Accordingly, there is considerable support for the proposition that a person can only be considered to be carrying on a business in Hong Kong if they have a fixed presence in Hong Kong or have an agent in Hong Kong with authority (and, arguably, it must be a regularly exercised general authority) to enter into contracts on behalf of the person. In *D 27/92*, however, this analysis was expressly rejected in favour of an approach adopted in earlier UK cases concerned with the question of where a trade was exercised and which looked at where the activities which in substance gave rise to the profits were undertaken, without placing much emphasis on whether an agent with authority was involved. Nonetheless, as explained below, the Board of Review still found as a fact that authority was regularly exercised in Hong Kong on behalf of the company and, although this does not appear to have been fundamental to the Board's conclusion, it is possible that such conclusion would have been different had the authority in Hong Kong not existed.

The facts in *D 21/92* were quite complex, but involved a company incorporated outside Hong Kong which borrowed money from associated financial institutions and on-lent it to unrelated borrowers. With respect to the lending business, it appeared that all business decisions were taken, and all authority exercised, outside Hong Kong; the company had an agreement, however, with its Hong Kong parent under which the parent undertook significant activities on the company's behalf in Hong Kong, although the terms of that agreement stipulated that the parent did not have the power to enter into contracts on behalf of the company and did not otherwise constitute an agent of the company. Nonetheless, the Board of Review found that this agreement was breached as the Hong Kong parent regularly exercised full authority on behalf of the company in arranging the borrowings for the company although, as noted, there is little to suggest that this was fundamental to the Board's conclusion. Rather the Board, in applying the test discussed in the previous paragraph, found on balance that the operations giving rise to the profits in question took place in Hong Kong and, therefore, that the company's business was carried on in Hong Kong. Note that this case was the subject of an appeal to the Court of Appeal (*Orion Caribbean Limited v CIR* [1996] (1 HKRC 90-077)), and then the Privy Council (*CIR v Orion Caribbean Limited* [1997] (1 HKRC 90-089)). Those appeals, however, concerned the questions of source of interest income generally and whether the offshore company was a "financial institution" within the meaning of the definition found in Sec. 2; the issue of whether the company's business was carried on in Hong Kong, being a finding of fact by the Board of Review, was not considered again by the courts.

If an office is opened by a non-resident person it is also important to establish its purpose to see whether it is in fact for carrying on a business from which profits may directly arise. For example, numerous non-resident banks have a representative office in Hong Kong and these offices are only for the purposes of liaising with customers and introducing them to branches elsewhere with whom they do business. It is arguable, but by no means clear, that these representative offices do not constitute the carrying on of a business in Hong Kong since they are not themselves entering into business contracts; in any event, it is usually clear that even if the activities could be construed as amounting to a business, no Hong Kong sourced profits arise from that business. Similarly a "buying" office set up in Hong Kong to supervise purchases for shipment elsewhere arguably does not amount to the carrying on of a business (see *Sully v Attorney-General* (2 TC 149)), although that case actually concerned the question of where a "trade", rather than a business, was carried on; in practice, however, this is not an issue as the IRD accepts that "buying" offices do not give rise to Hong Kong sourced profits (see section 4.4.5 and *Departmental Interpretation & Practice Notes No. 21*, which is reproduced as Appendix 13).

The fact that little is done in Hong Kong does not necessarily mean that a business is not carried on in Hong Kong. This is likely to be particularly true where the person's business itself does not involve substantial activities. In this regard, see *D 45/03* which involved a non-Hong Kong company which owned and licensed trademarks to related companies. In that case, the Board of Review rejected the suggestion that because only limited activities were undertaken in Hong Kong the taxpayer should not be considered to be carrying on business in Hong Kong. Rather, the Board noted that the taxpayer had an office address in Hong Kong, that directors' meetings were held in Hong Kong, that directors in Hong Kong resolved to acquire and license the trademarks, that instructions were given to solicitors in Hong Kong and that payments were approved in Hong Kong and concluded that these activities amounted to the carrying on of business by the taxpayer in Hong Kong. This finding was upheld by the Court of First Instance in *Lam Soon Trademark Limited v CIR* [2004] (1 HKRC 90-137).

Another often difficult area as to whether a business is carried on in Hong Kong is the situation where a company does nothing in Hong Kong other than maintain a bank account which is actually controlled and operated from abroad. This is actually a combination of two questions; the first being whether the operating of the bank account is itself a business (which is further discussed in section 4.3.4 below) and the second is, if so, where that business is carried on. Although in any particular case this will be a question of fact, the Board of Review has considered two somewhat similar cases and, not only did they reach different conclusions, but appeared to do so by adopting different bases of reasoning. In particular, see *D 5/97* where the Board of Review looked to, amongst other things, the location of the assets of the business in determining where that business was carried on. Additionally, the Board considered it relevant that the bank account was maintained in Hong Kong, that all receipts and payments went through that bank account and instructions were given to the bank in Hong Kong. In *D 27/93*, however, the Board of Review appeared to ignore these factors and suggested that the business was carried on where the negotiations took place and all the decisions were made. On appeal to the High Court, however, this decision was overturned (see *CIR v Bartica Investment Limited* [1996] (1 HKRC 90-080)). In reaching this decision, the court firmly rejected the view that a company's business was carried on where the business decisions were taken; instead, the court concentrated on the fact the company's directors were based in Hong Kong (notwithstanding that those directors merely acted in a nominee capacity on instructions from persons abroad) and held board meetings in Hong Kong, that the company's accounting and other records were maintained by an accounting firm in Hong Kong, and that the Hong Kong based nominee directors were the official signatories for the bank accounts even though the bank actually acted on the instructions of persons abroad.

The advent of electronic commerce and trading over the internet has raised the issue of where a business which is largely undertaken by a computer server is carried on and, in particular, what importance the location of the server may be in determining that issue. This matter is considered in *Departmental Interpretation & Practice Notes No. 39* in which the IRD has indicated that it will look beyond the computer server and examine the extent of the other operations in Hong Kong in deciding where such a business is carried on. More specifically, the IRD considers that if a company only has a computer server in Hong Kong (even one capable of concluding contracts, processing payments or delivering digital goods) without the involvement of human activities in Hong Kong, it will generally take the view that the company is not carrying on business in Hong Kong and thus, the income derived therefrom will not be chargeable to Hong Kong Profits Tax. The IRD's conclusion applies irrespective of whether the server is owned, leased or provided by an internet service provider.

There is generally no necessity to distinguish between a trade, profession and business, although each has entirely different meanings. It is, however, important to establish the date of commencement of the trade, profession or business, which is largely a question of fact, because this affects the determination of the first basis period (see section 4.6.2) and the treatment of expenditure incurred before commencement (see section 4.5.13).

The circumstances constituting a trade are, in general, fairly easy to identify, and also, as a question of fact and by applying the principles already mentioned, it can usually be easily determined whether it is carried on in Hong Kong. The more difficult question of what constitutes a trade in isolated cases is considered in section 4.3.3 below.

In the case of an individual carrying on a profession outside Hong Kong who visits Hong Kong on business, there is more difficulty in deciding what amounts to the carrying on of a profession *in* Hong Kong. The IRD takes the view in practice that the performance in Hong Kong of any professional service gives rise to a liability to Profits Tax on the fee earned. This is extremely doubtful except in the cases where, for example, an entertainer may perform for a whole season in Hong Kong. For a discussion of the principles involved see *Davies v Braithwaite* (18 TC 198) where an actress was held to be carrying on a single profession in her home country notwithstanding various performances were given in other countries. As to the meaning of "profession", this is not statutorily defined but is discussed in *IRC v Maxse* (12 TC 41). It is yet another question as to what constitutes a "business", and this is discussed in section 4.3.4.

4.3.3 What constitutes trading

It is often difficult to determine whether an isolated transaction or a series of transactions constitutes a trade giving rise to a profit subject to Profits Tax. Sec. 2 defines trade as including *"every trade and manufacture and every adventure and concern in the nature of trade"*. A taxpayer may claim that the purchase and sale of a property or of shares was an investment giving rise to a capital profit, whereas the IRD may claim that it was an adventure in the nature of trade giving rise to a revenue profit. The matter has to be judged on the facts and, as the UK definition of trade is similar, there is a considerable amount of UK case law to which the reader is referred. So far as general rules are applicable, the question to be answered is essentially that of the intention of the taxpayer at the time of acquisition of the asset and whether that intention ever subsequently changed; this can only be objectively judged from oral evidence and documents prepared at the time the transactions in question were undertaken and where these are inconclusive, regard will generally be had to all other surrounding circumstances in making a subjective judgement as to that intention. For a UK decision containing a good summary of these principles, see the House of Lords judgement in *Simmons (as liquidator of Lionel Simmons Properties Ltd.) v CIR* (53 TC 461), from this judgement comes the following often quoted phrase.

> *"Trading requires an intention to trade. Normally the question to be asked is whether this intention existed at the time of the acquisition of the asset. Was it acquired with the intention of disposing of it at a profit or was it acquired as a permanent investment? ... intentions may be changed. What was first an investment may be put into trading stock — and I suppose vice versa...."*

As noted above, however, establishing a taxpayer's intention is a factual matter which is not to be ascertained solely on the basis of the taxpayer's representations. In this regard, see the judgement of Mortimer J in *All Best Wishes Limited v CIR* [1992] (1 HKRC 90-067) where he stated:—

> *"In particular, the stated intention of the taxpayer cannot be decisive and the actual intention can only be determined upon the whole of the evidence. Indeed, decisions upon a person's intention are commonplace in the law. It is trite to say that intention can only be judged by considering the whole of the surrounding circumstances, including things said and done. Things said at the time, before and after, and things done at the time, before and after. Often it is rightly said that actions speak louder than words."*

The numerous legal decisions on the matter were considered by the Royal Commission on the Taxation of Profits and Income which reported in 1955 in the United Kingdom and the main relevant factors to be examined were conveniently summarized under what the Committee referred to as the six "badges of trade". Their verbatim description of these is as follows:—

> *"(1)   The subject matter of the realisation. While almost any form of property can be acquired to be dealt in, those forms of property, such as commodities or manufactured articles, which are normally the subject of trading, are only very exceptionally the subject of investment. Again property which does not yield to its owner an income or personal enjoyment merely by virtue of its ownership is more likely to have been acquired with the object of a deal than property that does.*
>
> *(2)   The length of the period of ownership. Generally speaking, property meant to be dealt in is realised within a short time after acquisition. But there are many exceptions from this as a universal rule.*
>
> *(3)   The frequency or number of similar transactions by the same person. If realisations of the same sort of property occur in succession over a period of years or there are several such realisations at about the same date a presumption arises that there has been dealing in respect of each.*
>
> *(4)   Supplementary work on or in connection with the property realised. If the property is worked up in any way during the ownership so as to bring it into a more marketable condition; or if any special exertions are made to find or attract purchasers, such as the opening of an office or large-scale advertising, there is some evidence of dealing. For when there is an organised effort to obtain profit there is a source of taxable income. But if nothing at all is done, the suggestion tends the other way.*
>
> *(5)   The circumstances that were responsible for the realisation. There may be some explanation, such as a sudden emergency or opportunity calling for ready money, that negatives the idea that any plan of dealing prompted the original purchase.*
>
> *(6)   Motive. There are cases in which the purpose of the transaction of purchase*

and sale is clearly discernible. Motive is never irrelevant in any of these cases. What is desirable is that it should be realised clearly that it can be inferred from surrounding circumstances in the absence of correct evidence of the seller's intentions and even, if necessary, in the face of his own evidence."

It is sometimes suggested that the approach in the *Simmons* case (supra) is different to an analysis based on the badges of trade. This is not, however, the case as an examination of the badges of trade is merely an exercise aimed at ascertaining the taxpayer's intention. This was confirmed by the Board of Review in *D 65/87*, which was quoted with approval by the Court of First Instance in *Real Estate Investments (N.T.) Limited v CIR* [2005] (1 HKRC 90-154), where they stated:

We see no inconsistency between Lord Wilberforce's statement in <u>Simmons</u> and the badges of trade approach. For there to be an adventure in the nature of trade, an intention to trade is required. In deciding whether there was such an intention, one must look at all the circumstances and examine whether the transactions bore any of the badges of trade. If the transaction bore the badges of trade, it would mean that an intention to trade was present notwithstanding protestations by the Taxpayer to the contrary.

The decision of the Court of First Instance was upheld by the Court of Appeal (see *Real Estate Investments (NT) Limited v CIR* [2006] (1 HKRC 90-175)).

The question has come before the Courts in Hong Kong on numerous occasions. See, for example, *CIR v Jebsen & Co.* (HKTC 1), *Wing On Cheong Investment Co. Ltd. v CIR* (3 HKTC 1), *Richfield International Land and Investment Co. Ltd. v CIR* (3 HKTC 167), *Beautiland Co. Ltd. v CIR* (1 HKRC 90-053), *All Best Wishes Ltd. v CIR* [1992] (1 HKRC 90-067) and *Chanway Investment Co. Ltd. v CIR* [1997] (HKRC 90-084). For two recent cases on the topic which contain particularly interesting discussions on how various factual and evidentiary matters are considered in determining whether a trading intention existed, see *Hostal Hengan Limited and Harvest International Limited v CIR* [2002] (1 HKRC 90-115) and *Stanwell Investments Limited v CIR* [2004] (1 HKRC 90-130).

For a discussion on the special circumstances of an insurance company which owns real property, see *CIR v Sincere Insurance & Investment Co. Ltd.* (HKTC 602). Insurance companies are, in general, regarded as holding real estate or shares on revenue account if those assets are held as part of their insurance reserves. This is also true of banks and other financial institutions, although the contrary can be proved in appropriate circumstances (see *D 20/78*). See also the Privy Council decision in the case of *CIR v*

Waylee Investments Ltd. (3 HKTC 410) where the question turned upon whether banking motives can be attributed to a non-banking subsidiary of a bank. The Privy Council's decision was to the effect that not only can the banking motive not be automatically assumed to be applied within a bank's subsidiary company, but that it is quite open for a bank itself to hold investments as long-term capital investments and whether it does so or not in given circumstances is a question of fact to be judged on the evidence.

There are also numerous Board of Review decisions where the principle of whether or not a transaction is an adventure in the nature of a trade has been discussed. Many of these cases involve individuals who have bought and sold a number of real properties at a profit, and in the majority of those cases the individuals have been found to be trading and, therefore, assessable on their profits. It must be remembered, however, that not all trading results in a profit and if a transaction which amounts to an adventure in the nature of a trade results in a loss, that loss would generally be deductible. The IRD are, however, often reluctant to allow a deduction for such losses and can be expected to critically examine any such claims in order to determine their validity. Nonetheless, it was interesting in *D 25/04* that the IRD attempted to deny a deduction for losses to an individual who had an established history of property trading and who had been previously assessed on his profits; quite correctly, however, the Board of Review found for the taxpayer and allowed the losses. See also *D 117/01* where a deduction was allowed for a loss arising out of a forfeited deposit and estate agent commissions where a taxpayer failed to complete a contract for the purchase of a property.

Other Board of Review cases of particular interest are *D 60/87* where the necessity to sell newly developed properties to repay development finance was not regarded as necessarily importing a trading intent, and *D 61/87* which determined that the holding of Letter B entitlements is not necessarily trading.

Another decision of note is *D 142/00*. In that case, a company was held to be trading in shares of an offshore incorporated subsidiary and, therefore, taxable on the profit derived from the disposal thereof. What is of particular interest about this decision was that the situation was not a typical trading scenario. Rather, the transaction was one structured so as to avoid a Hong Kong Stamp Duty liability arising on the disposal of the taxpayer's 50% interest in a Hong Kong company which owned real property. More specifically, the taxpayer owned Company H, which in turn owned one of two issued shares in the Hong Kong company (Company G). In order to effect the disposal of its interest in Company G, the taxpayer acquired the sole share in the offshore company (Company J) for US$1. Company G then issued 9,998 new shares at their par value of US$1 each; of these, 4,999 were issued to Company J, with the remainder being issued to the party which held the other 50% interest in company G. Company H then sold its single share in Company G, which due to the above share issue represented only 0.01% of the issued capital of Company G, to Company J. The taxpayer then sold its share (representing the entire interest) in Company J for a substantial sum.

The Board of Review, in finding for the Commissioner, rejected the taxpayer's argument that it had no intention to trade in the shares of Company J. Rather, the Board of Review noted that the share in Company J was acquired with the express intention of being resold at a profit and that there was never a change in that intention. As such, the Board held that the acquisition and disposal of the Company J share was a trading transaction. Although the Board of Review recognised that the transaction was in substance a means of disposing of its interest in the property held by Company G, it refused to decide the case by looking beyond the transaction in Company J shares. Moreover, the Board held that in computing the assessable profit derived from the disposal of the Company J share, it was not possible to deduct the value of the shares in Company G which were effectively gifted to Company J. As a result, the taxpayer was assessable on the consideration received for selling the Company J share, less the US$1 it had paid for the share. This gave rise to a Profits Tax liability of more than HK$23.3 million, which far outweighed the Stamp Duty saving achieved of approximately HK$848,000.

In the case of whether or not a sale of land or buildings comprises a trade of dealing in land, the onus of proof by the taxpayer that it does not comprise such a trade is much more onerous where the taxpayer is an acknowledged land trader or where his audited accounts indicate that the land or buildings had been held as current assets (see *Central Enterprises Ltd. v CIR* (2 HKTC 240) and also *Chinachem Investment Co. Ltd. v CIR* (2 HKTC 261)). Merely stating properties in the financial accounts to be fixed assets however is not conclusive of that fact unless there is other evidence to support it. Furthermore, acceptance of a Profits Tax assessment on any profit on sale, no matter how small or insignificant the transaction may have been, may imply that the properties remaining may also be regarded by the owners as current assets and this may be the case even where it can be proved that they were originally acquired as fixed assets (see *Richfield International Land and Investment Co. Ltd. v CIR* (3 HKTC 167)).

Ultimately, however, this is still a question of fact to be decided in each particular case and for an example of where a contrary conclusion was reached to that of the *Richfield International Land and Investment Co. Ltd.* case (supra), see *D 104/01*. In that case, the taxpayer had developed a building and sold the majority of the units in the 1970s; when one of the unsold units was subsequently sold in 1996, the IRD attempted to assess the gain relying, *inter alia*, on the fact that the taxpayer had accepted the assessments on the profit earned from the sales in the 1970s. In finding for the taxpayer, however, the Board of Review decided on the basis of the evidence that the taxpayer had never held an intention to trade in the units which were not sold in the 1970s.

Notwithstanding the necessity to produce positive evidence of intention, it is nevertheless not open to the Board of Review to speculate upon a taxpayer's intentions; in particular, the Board cannot decide that a company appropriated property from fixed to current assets just because it sold the property (see *Wing On Cheong Investment Co. Ltd. v CIR* (3 HKTC 1)).

In the case of profits from the purchase and sale of shares, it is difficult to lay down general rules as to whether these arise from a share trading activity. See, however, *CIR v Dr. Chang Liang-Jen* (HKTC 975), *D 30/84*, *D 111/97*, *D 74/00* and the Court of First Instance decision of *Lee Yee Shing, Jacky and Yeung Yuk Ching v CIR* [2005] (1 HKRC 90-163), which was upheld by the Court of Appeal (CACV 180/2006), for discussions of the principles involved. Apart from the first, all of these cases concerned individuals who sought to deduct losses from share transactions but which the IRD denied on the basis that no share trading business existed. It appears from those decisions that the IRD and the Board of Review generally consider that speculative transactions in shares by an individual do not amount to a trade, although it is recognised that each case needs to be considered on its own merits.

For example, in *D 74/00* the Board of Review stated that where an individual was engaged in speculative dealings, there was a *prima facie* assumption that he was not carrying on a business. Similarly, in *D 61/04* the Board again noted that it was a question of fact whether a person is carrying on a trade or business, but went on to conclude that pure speculation is a factor which weighs against such a finding. In that case, the Board of Review held that the taxpayer's activities did not amount to a trade or business, and this decision was ultimately upheld by both the Court of First Instance and the Court of Appeal in the *Lee Yee Shing, Jacky & Anor.* case (supra). The Court of Appeal judgment is interesting, *inter alia*, because counsel for the taxpayer sought to argue that the test applied by the Board of Review was wrong because they treated speculation as the antithesis of trading, whereas this was not consistent with earlier UK case law, and that once the Board found that the taxpayers were speculators it concluded that they could not have been trading. Counsel for the taxpayer's argument in this regard was based on the fact that the statutory definition of "*trade*" includes an "*adventure and concern in the nature of a trade*" and that the effect of this was to enlarge the meaning of trade to include speculation. Although it seems that, as in previous decisions, the Board of Review in *D 61/04* was inclined to consider speculation and trading as opposites, the Court of Appeal reiterated that the Board was in fact only noting that the presence of speculation was a factor which weighed against a finding that a trade or business was being carried on where there was no systematic conduct of a trade or business, but that the question was ultimately to be decided by considering all relevant factors. While this decision clearly established that trading and speculation are not to be considered as mutually exclusive alternatives, unfortunately it did not explain why the argument on behalf of the taxpayers that speculation must in fact be trading was not accepted.

Aside from the question of the relationship between speculation and trading, *D 61/04* and the subsequent appeals (the *Lee Yee Shing, Jacky* cases) are also notable for highlighting the difficulty an individual faces in establishing that his share transactions amount to a trade or business. In that case, the IRD and the Board of Review found that the appellant was not carrying on a trade despite the existence of evidence that, *inter alia*, during the relevant period he entered into hundreds of transactions each year, his average holding period for the shares was relatively short (between 42 and 93 days), he had direct telephone lines to the dealing rooms of two securities firms and he was a majority owner of a securities broking firm for a part of the relevant period.

The reluctance of the IRD to accept speculative share transactions as trading is interesting considering that they actively pursue taxpayers in respect of speculative property trading transactions, as is evidenced by the large number of Board of Review cases each year concerning such activities. In particular, the factors looked to in order to ascertain whether a share trading business exists (e.g. systematic approach, number of transactions, extent of research, quality of business records, etc.) would appear to be equally relevant, but often even less evident, in the case of speculative property transactions than with share transactions. One possible reason for this practice is that the IRD find it easier to collate comprehensive information on property transactions because of the title registration system, than in the case of share transactions, although it is not clear why this should be a relevant consideration in determining whether a trade is being carried on.

Where a business of share dealing is established, the case of *CIR v Ting*

Kwan-Che (HKTC 901) provides authority as to the treatment of bonus shares.

Where an established property trading group of companies sells shares in subsidiaries holding trading property, it does not follow that the trading motive should be assumed to be imported into the share transactions as well; it is not normally the case that a group trades in its subsidiaries and the activities within the subsidiaries are arguably not relevant to the question. In this connection see *Beautiland Co. Ltd. v CIR* (3 HKTC 184 & 322, 1 HKRC 90-053) and also *D 65/87*.

Similarly, the intention of the shareholders with regard to the holding of their shares should not be imported into the intention of the company with regard to its assets. See, for example, *CIR v Quitsubdue Limited* [1999] (1 HKRC 90-099) where the issue was whether a property being redeveloped by the taxpayer had been acquired as a capital or trading asset and whether that intention had subsequently changed when the company's shareholders changed. In overturning the decision of the Board of Review (see *D 75/96*) and finding that the asset had always been a capital asset of the company, the Court of First Instance remarked that the Board of Review had incorrectly equated the company's intention with that of the shareholders. That is, the fact that the shareholders may have intended to dispose of their indirect interest in the property by means of a sale of the shares, was not relevant in deciding the intention of the company itself with regard to the property.

It has been held that gambling does not necessarily constitute the carrying on of a trade (*Graham v Green* (9 TC 309)), but where the gambling is related to a trading activity in which the person has some knowledge or expertise, the profits may be taxable (*Burdge v Pyne* (45 TC 320)). See, however, the *Dr. Chang Liang-Jen* and *Lee Yee Shing, Jacky* cases discussed above which demonstrate the reluctance of the IRD and the Board of Review to find that share transactions by an individual constitute a trade or business even where the individuals have particular knowledge or expertise in the investment industry. Where a gambling activity is not linked in any way to the person's existing trade or expertise, it is much more difficult to establish that such activity amounts to a trade or business and for the IRD to assess the profits, or for the taxpayer to deduct the losses.

An interesting question which sometimes arises concerns whether assets acquired and held as part of a leasing business, but which may be sold at the end of a lease or at some other time, should be seen as capital assets or trading stock. As with all capital versus revenue questions, this is largely a question of fact heavily dependent upon the intention of the taxpayer. Nonetheless, in other jurisdictions there has been a tendency to categorize such assets as trading stock (see, for example, *Gloucester Railway Carriage and Wagon Co. Ltd. v IRC* (12 TC 720), *FC of T v Cyclone Scaffolding Pty. Ltd.* (87 ATC 5083) and *Memorex Pty. Ltd. v FC of T* (87 ATC 5034); in the only reported Hong Kong decision on the question, *D 31/92*, this view was followed.

Note that the fact that the activity giving rise to a profit may be illegal does not disqualify it from being taxable. See, for example, *Mann v Nash* (16 TC 523) concerning profits made from the illegal operation of gaming machines.

4.3.4 Meaning of business

The scope of Profits Tax extends to the carrying on of "business" which is a term vastly wider than trade or profession. It is defined in Sec. 2 as including:—

> *"agricultural undertaking, poultry and pig rearing and the letting or sub-letting by any corporation to any person of any premises or portion thereof, and the sub-letting by any other person of any premises or portion of any premises held by him under a lease or tenancy other than from the Government."*

Note, therefore, that a corporation which lets any property is immediately regarded as carrying on business whereas any other person is normally not so regarded unless he sub-lets property; in other words, letting by a Crown leaseholder (who is regarded as the "owner" under the IRO — see Chapter 2) who is not a corporation is not necessarily regarded as carrying on business. However, care should be exercised in applying the definition in Sec. 2 because it is only stated to "include" the things which it mentions and, therefore, its scope can be much wider. Although the decision in *Lam Woo Shang v CIR* (HKTC 123) is now superseded by a change in the definition of business in Sec. 2 it nevertheless contains a good summary of the principles involved in defining business. As already mentioned, an individual letting a property is not normally regarded as carrying on a business but will be subject to Property Tax. In *Louis Kwun-nung Kwing, Charles Kwok-nung Kwong v CIR* (2 HKTC 541), however, two individuals letting out a cinema as a going concern were held to be carrying on a business subject to Profits Tax.

■ Example 4.1

Mr. O. Nurr owns a flat which he lets to Mr. Smarty at $75,000 per annum who immediately sub-lets it to Mr. A. Sucker for $100,000 per annum. Rates of $5,000 per annum and repairs are paid by Nurr.

O. Nurr is not carrying on business and therefore pays Property Tax on $56,000 (i.e. ($75,000 – $5,000) × 80%).
Smarty is carrying on business and pays Profits Tax on $25,000 profit.

Whereas trade and profession are normally associated with some active function, the wider term business includes those circumstances where there is a purely passive receipt of income. For example, a holding company whose function is solely to hold shares in other companies, even subsidiaries, is carrying on a business whether or not there is any active management participation in the companies in which it has interests. For an examination of the principles in borderline cases see *IRC v Korean Syndicate* (12 TC 181). Because of the wide definition of business, it is possible for a corporation to commence business before it commences trading.

The ascertainment of whether or not a corporation is carrying on business is most significant in the cases where it is in receipt of Hong Kong source interest when, if it is carrying on business, it is liable to Profits Tax on net profit after deducting relevant expenses and, if it is not carrying on business, is not so liable. This leads into the question of whether the mere depositing of money can constitute a business. There have been a number of cases on this question in other jurisdictions and it is clear that it is a question that can only be answered on the facts of each particular case. It is much more difficult for a company to establish that its depositing activities do not constitute a business than in the case of an individual as there is a presumption (which can possibly be rebutted) that anything a company does amounts to a business (see *American Leaf Blending Co. Sdn Bhd v Director General of Inland Revenue* [1979] (AC 676)). In *Departmental Interpretation & Practice Notes No. 13*, however, the IRD states that the mere depositing of money by a corporation will not amount to the carrying on of a business, but that actions beyond "mere passive acquiescence" may constitute the carrying on of a business. Additionally, the IRD suggests that a period of inactivity does not rebut the fact that a company is still carrying on business; accordingly, a company which ceases to trade but continues to passively deposit money is likely to be considered by the IRD to be carrying on a business. For cases where the Board of Review in Hong Kong has considered this question, see *D 15/87, D 33/91* and *D 27/93*.

Although under the mutuality principle bodies such as clubs, trade associations and mutual insurance corporations are not regarded as carrying on business to the extent that they trade only with members, Sec. 24 deems clubs and trade associations as carrying on business for Profits Tax purposes in certain circumstances (see section 4.7.8). Further, Sec. 23AA deems mutual insurance corporations to be subject to Profits Tax.

4.3.5 Commencement of business

The date of commencement is largely a question of fact; for example, a retail shop would generally be considered to commence business when it first acquires trading stock or opens its doors to the public. In the case of a manufacturing business, it was held in *Birmingham & District Cattle By-Products Co., Ltd v IRC* (12 TC 92) that acts such as research, the construction of buildings, the acquisition of plant and machinery and the entering into of agreements with suppliers were of a preparatory nature only and the "trade or business" did not commence until the company commenced to acquire raw materials for processing into their product. This approach of disregarding preparatory acts in determining when business commenced was followed by the Board of Review in *D 3/86*.

The mistake should not be made of looking for the first sale or receipt of income because this may be a long time after commencement of the business leading up to it. In this regard, there is a useful discussion of the date of commencement of a property trading business where the facts were quite complex in *D 3/86*. In that particular case, land had originally been acquired for non-trading purposes, but was subsequently redeveloped for sale and the Board of Review held that the property development business commenced when an architect was employed to draw up redevelopment plans. The position of a person developing property for letting is, however, likely to be viewed differently and, on the basis of the reasoning in the *Birmingham & District Cattle By-Products* case (supra), such business would probably be viewed as commencing when the property first becomes available for letting.

It should also be noted that evidence of intention at a given date does not necessarily denote commencement at that date, it merely indicates commencement not later than that date. This is of great significance where a property previously held as a fixed asset in a business is redeveloped and then sold (see *Overseas Textiles Ltd. v CIR* (3 HKTC 29)).

Although the foregoing paragraphs consider when particular types of business commence, it must be remembered that the investment of money can also constitute a business (see section 4.3.2). Accordingly, if a company is set up which actively invests its share capital and / or shareholder loans, it may be considered to be carrying on a business of investment, even before the principal business which the company was established to operate has commenced. This is important because the carrying on of an investment business will generally render any Hong Kong source interest income subject to Profits Tax (although an exemption from payment of that tax in respect of bank interest may be available), even though only preparatory activities in connection with the principal business are being undertaken.

See section 4.5.13 below for a discussion as to the treatment of pre-commencement expenditure.

■ Example 4.2

Impex Ltd. is incorporated on 1 June 2006 for the purpose of carrying on an import and export business. Due to delay in finding suitable office premises the directors actively engage in investing the Company's funds in interest-earning deposits with banks in Hong Kong. On 1 January 2007 office premises are found and staff are employed to establish office routines and set up book-keeping procedures. On 1 March 2007 the first import transaction is entered into and the first profit derived on 15 April.

The trade commences on 1 March 2007 and, in practice the rent and wages for the period 1 January 2007 to 1 March 2007 will be treated as if they were incurred on 1 March 2007 (see section 4.5.13 below).

Also, the Company was carrying on an investment business in the period before it commenced the import/export trade and, therefore, would be subject to Profits Tax on any Hong Kong source interest earned in that period (although payment of the actual tax is not currently required because of an order of the Chief Executive in Council, as discussed in point (16) of section 4.5.3).

4.3.6 Cessation of business

It is also important to be able to establish the date of cessation of business because upon this depends the final basis period (see section 4.6.1). Additionally, it is important because of the special treatment afforded to post-cessation payments and receipts and the treatment of trading stock upon cessation (see section 4.5.14).

Again, the date of cessation is largely a question of fact and it is important to distinguish between the temporary suspension of a trade and its final cessation. This is particularly difficult in the case of property development when the completion of a development does not of itself signify cessation of trade because there could be a considerable period of inactivity while further suitable property is sought for development. Furthermore, the appointment of a liquidator does not of itself signify cessation of trade; this must be judged on the facts because a liquidator may continue the trade for a period of time in order to protect the assets. However, if the liquidator is merely realising assets, including trading stock, in order to wind up a company this is unlikely to constitute trading (see *Tai Shun Investment Co. v CIR* (HKTC 370)). The circumstances could also exist, for example, in the case of a property developer who sells his last property on an instalment basis and, although he does not seek to acquire or develop any more property, continues to collect the instalments. As it may be appropriate to bring in the profit on sale only in relation to each instalment received (*CIR v Montana Lands Ltd.* (HKTC 334)) it is quite likely that the business can be said to continue until the final instalment is received although this should be contrasted with the facts in the *Tai Shun Investment Co.* case where only a few instalments remained to be collected and the liquidator was held to be merely tidying up.

The circumstances in Example 4.2 could equally apply in reverse so that a company could cease trading yet still be in business.

4.4 Source of Profits

As with Salaries Tax, the determination of the source of income for Profits Tax purposes is fundamental in ascertaining whether a liability to the tax exists. This territoriality principle is, of course, also embodied in the Property Tax provisions, although in the case of that tax the issue is less complex as it is manifested by levying the tax only on property situated in Hong Kong.

As was noted in section 4.3, under Sec. 14, the general Profits Tax charging provision, a liability to Profits Tax exists only where all of the following conditions are fulfilled:

(i)   the taxpayer carries on a trade, profession or business in Hong Kong;
(ii) the taxpayer derives profits from that trade, profession or business; and
(iii) those profits arise in or are derived from Hong Kong.

The first of these tests was discussed in section 4.3, while the second is usually (but by no means always) a relatively straightforward question of fact. The final test, the determination of the source of profits, is undoubtedly the test which consistently gives rise to the greatest practical difficulties and is the subject of this section. To fully understand what determines the source of profits it is necessary to carefully analyse the statutory provisions and the relevant case law and this is done below. Also discussed below is the Commissioner's Departmental Interpretation & Practice Note on the matter which provides a practical insight into how the IRD approaches the question of source of profits.

4.4.1 Statutory provisions

Unfortunately, the IRO provides no comprehensive guidance as to how the source of profits is to be determined. Sec. 14, the general charging provision, merely uses the phrase *"profits arising in or derived from Hong Kong"*, although Sec. 2 further defines the phrase for Profits Tax purposes to *"... without in any way limiting the meaning of the term, include all profits from business transacted in Hong Kong, whether directly or through an agent"*.

The terms *"arising in"* and *"derived from"* have been held to have identical meanings (see *C of T (NSW) v Kirk* [1900] (AC 588), which was quoted with approval in *CIR v The Hong Kong and Whampoa Dock Co. Ltd.* (1 HKTC 85)). Although the Court of Appeal in *CIR v Hang Seng Bank Ltd.* (2 HKTC 614) suggested that *"derived from"* was a broader term than *"arising in"*, this was subsequently rejected by the Privy Council in that case (3 HKTC 351).

The effect of the Sec. 2 definition of the phrase *"profits arising in or derived from Hong Kong"* has been considered in a number of Hong Kong decisions, although the Courts have, usually by implication rather than directly, generally been reluctant to read the term as significantly expanding the phrase as used in Sec. 14; for a case where the Court specifically stated that the definition did not widen the term, however, see the Court of Appeal judgement in the *Hang Seng Bank* case (supra).

It cannot be emphasised too much that the very structure of Sec. 14 presupposes that the questions of where a business is carried on and the source of the profits of that business are to be determined independently of each other and are not to be confused; similarly, it is clear that the section envisages that a business carried on in Hong Kong may earn profits which, as a matter of law, arise elsewhere, even though that business does not have a branch elsewhere.

This issue was discussed at some length in the report of the Third Inland Revenue Ordinance Review Committee and that committee ultimately recommended that the law be changed to exclude from Profits Tax only those profits the generation of which was substantially brought about by the activities of a branch of the taxpayer outside Hong Kong. These recommendations were, however, never implemented (except in respect of certain types of income earned by financial institutions); accordingly, it must be assumed that the Government is satisfied with the scope of the charge imposed by Sec. 14 as currently structured.

Nonetheless, despite the fundamental nature of the distinction between the place where a business is carried on and the place where the profits of a business arise, the two appear to have been confused at times by the courts and Board of Review.

4.4.2 Case law — general principles

A term which is frequently encountered when dealing with the ascertainment of the source of profits is the "operations test". Unfortunately, although the origins of this test are clear, it has been applied in different ways in various cases and, as a result, the term has come to mean slightly different things to different people; consequently, care needs to be taken when using the term and its use has been limited in this book.

The "operations test" stems from the words of Lord Atkin in *F. L. Smidth & Co. v Greenwood* (8 TC 193) where he said *"… the question is, where do the operations take place from which the profits in substance arise?"* Whilst this may well be an appropriate general test for determining the source of profits, it is somewhat ironic that the *Smidth v Greenwood* case involved the interpretation of UK legislation and, in particular, the question of where the taxpayer's trade was exercised; this issue was relevant because under the UK legislation at the time, a person's profits were taxable in the UK if they arose from a trade exercised in the UK, irrespective of the legal source of those profits. In other words, the case was not about source of profits at all; if it had any direct relevance to the IRO, it is arguably more likely to be with regard to the question of where a person's trade, profession or business is carried on. In this regard, although, as we shall see, the questions of where a business is carried on and the source of profits have been confused at times, it is worth emphasising again that the structure of Sec. 14 makes it clear that the two questions are to be considered independently.

Notwithstanding the fact that the statutory test being considered in the *Smidth v Greenwood* case (supra) was not one of source of profits, the "operations test" as formulated by Lord Atkin is not necessarily inappropriate as a test for source of profits. Indeed, in *CIR v Lever Brothers & Unilever Ltd.* (14 SATC 1), which was a source case, Watermeyer CJ introduced the somewhat similar, although perhaps slightly broader, concept of "originating cause". This concept is explained in the following passage from the judgement:

> *"The word source has several possible meanings. In this section it is used figuratively and when so used in relation to the receipt of money one possible meaning is the originating cause of the receipt of the money, another possible meaning is the quarter from which it is received … the inference which I think*

should be drawn ... is that the source of receipts, received as income, is not the quarter whence they come, but the originating cause of them being received as income and that this originating cause is the work which the taxpayer does to earn them, the quid pro quo which he gives in return for which he receives them. The work which he does may be a business which he carries on, or an enterprise which he undertakes, or an activity in which he engages and it may take the form of personal exertion, mental or physical or it may take the form of employment of capital either by using it to earn income or by letting its use to someone else. Often the work is some combination of these."

The test formulated by Atkin LJ in the *Smidth v Greenwood* case (supra) has, despite its origins, been heartily embraced as a source test by the courts in a number of Hong Kong cases including the *Hong Kong and Whampoa Dock* case (supra) and the Privy Council decisions in *CIR v Hang Seng Bank Limited* (3 HKTC 351) and *CIR v HK-TVB International Limited* [1992] (1 HKRC 90-064). In the *Hong Kong and Whampoa Dock* case, the Court accepted Atkin LJ's test as valid for determining source but still clearly noted that the question of source was not to be answered by determining where the business was carried on; in particular, the Court quoted with approval, certain dicta of Higgins J in *Mount Morgan Gold Mining Co. Ltd. v Commissioner of Income Tax* (33 CLR 76) wherein he succinctly made this point as long ago as 1923.

Atkin LJ's test was also adopted by the Hong Kong courts in *CIR v International Wood Products Ltd.* (HKTC 551). That case concerned the question of source of commission income and the Court held that this was the place where the services were rendered to earn the commission. The court went on to note that the source of commission was offshore where agents overseas undertook the services for which the commission was in substance paid, even though those agents were paid by the taxpayer for their services and the taxpayer undertook certain ancillary services in Hong Kong. Once again, the Court rejected the argument that the commission had a Hong Kong source because the taxpayer's principal place of business was in Hong Kong. The reasoning in this case of looking to the overseas agents to see what was done to earn the relevant income was endorsed by the Board of Review in *D 14/96*. In the slightly later case of *D 71/97*, however, the Board was less willing to accept such a view. The taxpayer in that case was a securities broker who charged customers a commission for executing securities transactions abroad, and then engaged a broker in the relevant overseas jurisdiction to actually carry out the transaction. Because of a reduced rate of commission charged by, or a rebate received from, the overseas broker, the taxpayer in Hong Kong derived a profit and it was the source of that profit which was in dispute in the case. The taxpayer's representative pointed out that the overseas broker was the agent of the taxpayer for the purposes of executing the transaction, and this was, at least partly, accepted by the Board. Somewhat confusingly in view of earlier authorities and without any clear explanation, however, the Board of Review concluded that the activities of the overseas broker had to be looked at separately from the activities of the taxpayer and, therefore, that the activities of the overseas broker could not be viewed as those of the taxpayer.

The question of the relevance of activities undertaken by agents of the taxpayer has been considered in a number of subsequent cases, although on the basis of the *Baring Securities (Hong Kong) Limited* and *Indosuez WI Carr Securities Limited* cases (which are discussed below) it seems that current judicial views are that such activities are to be treated as activities of the taxpayer for the purpose of ascertaining the source of profits. Nonetheless, although not rejecting the point, the Court of Final Appeal in *Kim Eng Securities (Hong Kong) Limited v CIR* (FACV 11/2006) suggested that it may not always be appropriate to consider the acts of an agent to be those of the principal when determining the source of profits.

Following the decision in the *International Wood Products* case, the Commissioner issued a circular, dated 25 August 1971, of Departmental practice which illustrated a number of typical situations where commission would be regarded as arising outside of Hong Kong. This circular has now been superseded by *Departmental Interpretation & Practice Notes No. 21* (see Appendix 13), although much of the content has been incorporated, unchanged, into that Practice Note.

The decision in the *International Wood Products* case should be contrasted with the earlier decision in *CIR v Karsten Larssen & Co. (H.K.) Ltd.* (HKTC 11) where, somewhat similarly, commission was earned by a ship broker for finding charterers and concluding charter agreements. Where the work was carried out abroad by an agent appointed by the taxpayer, the profit retained by the taxpayer was found to have a Hong Kong source. The difference between the two cases, however, is that in the *Karsten Larssen* case the agreement for the payment of the commission to the taxpayer separately named the overseas agent and identified the portion of the total income which was to be paid to that agent; in other words, the agreement was, in reality, for the payment of two amounts of commission and the amount earned by the taxpayer was considered only possibly attributable to services rendered in Hong Kong.

The distinction between the place where a business is carried on and the source of the profits from that business became blurred due to a number of court and Board of Review decisions during the 1980s. These decisions tended to flow from that of Hunter J in *CIR v Sinolink Overseas Ltd.* (2 HKTC 127) as this was the first case to throw doubt on some aspects of what may be considered relevant operations to be taken into account when determining source of profits. In particular, Hunter J adopted an "operations test" but, rather than focusing on the operations which in substance gave rise to the profits (i.e. the test from the *Smidth v Greenwood* case), divided the whole of the company's activities in relation to the profits in question into four broad categories and then looked at where each of the categories was undertaken. Inevitably, this approach meant that the central place of a company's business became an important factor in determining the source of that company's profits yet, as we have seen, this is clearly not the intention of the legislation. Hunter J was, however, insistent that the case should not be seen as a test case and was strongly critical as to the lack of evidence on material issues (the Board of Review having been bypassed and no evidence beyond the limited facts in the Commissioner's determination was adduced); accordingly, little of significance to other cases should have been able to be deduced from it. Nonetheless, the case was discussed and applied in a number of subsequent decisions which served to further confuse the issue. Although the correctness, at the time, of the decision in the *Sinolink* case is arguable, it seems to have been subsequently over-ruled by the decision of the Privy Council in the *Hang Seng Bank* case which is discussed below.

The decision in *Exxon Chemical International Supply S. A. v CIR* (3 HKTC 57), which came after the *Sinolink* case but before the Privy Council's decision in the *Hang Seng Bank* case, seems to have been based on the type of operations test developed in *Smidth v Greenwood*, rather than the broader test adopted in the *Sinolink* case, although this is not entirely clear. This case, like the *Sinolink* case, concerned trading profits although the profits in dispute arose from what was largely a reinvoicing operation; in other words, the company did little to earn those profits other than process paperwork. The court recognised this latter point but found that what the company did do, it did in Hong Kong and, therefore, that the profits had a Hong Kong source. As noted, however, the reasoning in the case is not entirely clear, with the consequence that it is difficult to draw meaningful conclusions from the decision. A possible criticism of the decision, however, is that the court concentrated only on what the taxpayer itself did to earn the profits and ignored the activities of the overseas associates in arranging the contracts for the purchase and sale of goods and organising the delivery of those goods; those associates were, in effect, agents for the company and, as we shall see later, it has been accepted by the Privy Council and the Court of Final Appeal that it is permissible to look to what agents do on behalf of a taxpayer when determining the source of the taxpayer's profits.

In the 1988 decision of *Bank of India v CIR* (2 HKTC 503) an operations test similar to that found in the *Smidth v Greenwood* case was again adopted in the case of a bank deriving profits from the purchase of overseas bills at a discount and presenting them through agents outside Hong Kong. Given that the business in question was carried out predominantly in Hong Kong, and in view of the previous cases, the decision is perhaps not surprising. The case is, however, of interest because of the fact that counsel for the taxpayer urged the court to reject the *Smidth v Greenwood* type of operations test as the correct determinant of source and instead to adopt as the appropriate test the question of "... *where do those acts/operations take place which are more immediately/ proximately/directly responsible for the receipt by the appellant of the particular income ...?*" This question stems from a test developed by Dixon J in the case of *Commissioner of Taxation (New South Wales) v Hillsdon Watts Limited* (4 ATD 199), slightly qualified as a result of dicta in two other Australian cases. The High Court, however, rejected this approach in favour of a test based on the operations of the bank; in particular, the court considered that to adopt the test argued by counsel for the taxpayer would mean that it was appropriate to look only to the presentation of the bill to the overseas bank in determining the source of the profit from the transaction and that this was unrealistic. The court did not, however, appear to reject outright the test developed in the *Hillsdon Watts* case; they really only questioned the interpretation of the test advanced by counsel for the taxpayer and then decided that the *Smidth v Greenwood* principle was more appropriate to the facts of the case.

Many of the uncertainties which had crept into the determination of the question of source of profits during the 1980s were addressed and clarified in the 1991 decision of the Privy Council in *CIR v Hang Seng Bank Limited* (3 HKTC 351). This case involved the trading by a bank based in Hong Kong, of certificates of deposit through agents in London and Singapore. The principal argument for the Commissioner in this case was that because all of the bank's operations were carried out in Hong Kong, the source of the bank's profits must have been in Hong Kong; this argument, once again, confused the two quite separate and distinct tests of where a business is carried on and the source of the profits from that business. The Privy Council rejected this argument, however, and confirmed that the structure of Sec. 14 presupposes that the profits of a business carried on in Hong Kong can accrue from different sources, some in Hong Kong (which are taxable) and others outside Hong Kong (which are not taxable). The rejection of the Commissioner's submissions in this case is also an effective rejection of the reasoning of the High Court in the *Sinolink* case. The Privy Council went on to explain that although Sec. 14 seeks to tax only net profits (i.e. gross profits less an appropriate portion of administrative overhead expenses), when determining the source of profits it was appropriate to look at gross profits; that is, the fact that a portion of general administrative overhead expenses incurred in Hong Kong is taken into account in ascertaining the net profit from a transaction cannot influence the determination of the source of the profit from that transaction.

The Privy Council's decision in the *Hang Seng Bank* case is also noteworthy for their Lordships' general observations as to the source of profits. In particular, they observed that the "*... broad guiding principle, attested by many authorities, is that one looks to see what the taxpayer has done to earn the profit ...*". Their Lordships went on to consider particular types of profit and lay down general rules for the determination of the source thereof. These can be summarized as follows:—

(a)   the source of profits from the rendering of services is the place where those services are rendered;

(b)   the source of profits from engaging in an activity such as the manufacture of goods is the place where that activity or manufacturing is carried out;

(c)   profit from the letting of property has its source where the property is located;

(d)   profit from the lending of money arises at the place where the money is lent;

(e)   profit from dealing in commodities or securities has its source where the contracts of purchase and sale are effected;

The type of profit in dispute in the *Hang Seng Bank* case was that described in (e) above and, on the basis of the facts of the case, it was considered to arise outside Hong Kong. That is, the Privy Council decided that what the bank did to earn the profits was to effect contracts of purchase and sale of certificates of deposit and that this was done outside Hong Kong; clearly, the fact that the effecting of those contracts was carried out by the bank's overseas agents rather than staff of the bank was not considered relevant by the Privy Council. Similarly, the fact that all the decisions as to the buying and selling of the certificates of deposit were taken in Hong Kong on the basis of research and analysis undertaken in Hong Kong, was not considered relevant. The decision in this case followed directly from the 1938 decision of the Privy Council in the Indian case of *Commissioner of Income Tax Bombay Presidency and Aden v Chunilal B Mehta* [1938] (1 ITR 521). A similar decision was reached in the Board of Review case *BR 18/73*.

It is submitted that the decision in the *Hang Seng Bank* case provides clear authority for the proposition that where all of the trading activities take place abroad, but certain administrative matters are dealt with in Hong Kong, the source of the resulting profits is offshore. Accordingly, it follows that the profits of a traditional reinvoicing company, where staff or agents in Hong Kong play no part in the negotiation of terms or the conclusion of contracts, are not subject to Profits Tax; this view is accepted by the IRD in their Practice Note, which is discussed in section 4.4.5 below. In view of this, the decision in *D 47/93* appears somewhat surprising; in particular, in that case the profits of what appear to be a typical reinvoicing company were held to be assessable on the grounds that what the company really did was to earn a fee for the preparation of documentation and the trading profits it earned were in reality compensation for this service.

Although the structure of Sec. 14 was cogently analysed by the Privy Council in the *Hang Seng Bank* case, the decision of the Privy Council in *CIR v HK-TVB International Limited* [1992] (1 HKRC 90-064) reintroduced some of the previous confusion between the tests of where a business is carried on and the source of its profits. That case concerned a Hong Kong based company which acquired the non-Hong Kong rights to films from its parent company which produced the films and then sub-licensed those rights to unrelated television stations and film distributors outside Hong Kong. The taxpayer usually negotiated the deals with the overseas parties by sending a representative abroad; the representative sometimes actually concluded the contract abroad. The Privy Council rejected the example given in their decision in the *Hang Seng Bank* case, that the source of profit from the exploitation of property was the location of that property, as the correct determinant of the taxpayer's profits in the *HK-TVBI* case; instead, they adopted the more general and broad statement that the source of profit is a function of what a person does to earn the profit. Their Lordships then proceeded to observe that the *"... relevant business of (HK-TVBI) was the exploitation of film rights exercisable overseas and it was a business carried on in Hong Kong"*.

In other words, notwithstanding the clear and unambiguous analysis of the *Hang Seng Bank* decision, the Privy Council still looked to where HK-TVBI carried on its business when ascertaining the source of its profits;

moreover, their decision seems to have ignored the fact that some contracts were both negotiated and concluded abroad which is potentially indicative of a non-Hong Kong source of the resulting profits, particularly given the passive nature of those profits. Perhaps even more surprising is the fact that their Lordships considered it irrelevant that the rights which were exploited were only exercisable outside Hong Kong, although there is a hint in the judgement that their conclusion may have been different had HK-TVBI had a continuing financial interest in the exercise of the rights by the sub-licensee, rather than simply granting the rights in exchange for a lump sum. This latter point casts some doubt on the applicability of the decision to a more traditional sub-licensing situation where the royalties payable are linked to the income or profits of the sub-licensee in relation to the rights. Nonetheless, in *D 45/03* which concerned royalties under a trademark licensing agreement which were calculated with reference to gross revenue of the licensee, the source was still determined on the basis of the place where the licensor undertook most of its business activities, with no consideration given to where the trademarks were used. This decision was upheld by the Court of First Instance (see *Lam Soon Trademark Limited v CIR* [2004] (1 HKRC 90-137)).

The next decision of the Hong Kong courts concerning source of profits under Sec. 14 was the Court of Appeal judgement in *Wardley Investment Services (Hong Kong) Limited v CIR* [1993] (1 HKRC 90-068); this decision was an appeal from the High Court which was in turn an appeal from the Board of Review (case *D 30/90*). The taxpayer was a Hong Kong incorporated investment adviser and fund manager which carried on its business only in Hong Kong. In the course of its business, it arranged for transactions in overseas securities to be undertaken on behalf of its customers; as a consequence of these activities, certain overseas stockbrokers rebated a portion of their commission income on the transactions to the taxpayer. The Board of Review, in considering the source of the commission rebates adopted Lord Atkin's "operations" test (as developed in *Smidth v Greenwood*) of "… *where do the operations take place from which the profits in substance arise?*" The Board did not, however, seek to limit the interpretation of this test to the operations of the taxpayer; rather, they identified the rebates as being a share of the overseas brokers' commission which, they concluded, arose where those brokers' operations were carried on (i.e. outside Hong Kong). Accordingly, the Board found that the rebates derived by the taxpayer arose outside Hong Kong.

The Board's decision was, however, overturned by the High Court in a confusing judgement which, as noted, was the subject of a further appeal to the Court of Appeal. The Court of Appeal, in a two to one majority decision, found in favour of the Commissioner. Each of the judges gave a separate written opinion and the reasoning between the two judges in the majority varied significantly. In particular, Fuad V-P applied the test of looking at what *the taxpayer* had done to earn the profits (rather than the Board's test of identifying the operations from which the profits arose) and concluded that because the taxpayer itself did nothing outside Hong Kong to earn the profits, the source of those profits must be in Hong Kong. This reasoning, in ignoring the activities of the taxpayer's agents, conflicts with the clear authority of the Privy Council in the *Hang Seng Bank* case (supra) as well as that in the Hong Kong case of *International Wood Products* (supra). The other judge in the majority, Penlington JA, whilst endorsing the comments of Fuad V-P, seemed to place a great deal of reliance on the fact that the rebates arose from the commission paid by the taxpayer's customer in Hong Kong, a portion of which was refunded by the overseas brokers to the taxpayer; whilst such reasoning has certain logical appeal, it does not have the support of very much case law. Sir Derek Cons V-P, in a dissenting judgement, reasoned that since the rebates arose from securities transactions carried out overseas and were paid by the overseas brokers rather than the Hong Kong customers, the source of those rebates must be abroad. This reasoning, which looks to the operations of the overseas brokers rather than the taxpayer, is, of course, reminiscent of that of the Board of Review

The decision in *CIR v Euro Tech (Far East) Limited* [1995] (1 HKRC 90-074), which was an appeal by the Commissioner from a decision of the Board of Review concerning the source of trading profits, has attracted much commentary and the taxpayer has often been described as a "reinvoicing" company, which is a form of business operation the profits from which are generally accepted by the IRD as not subject to Profits Tax in accordance with *Departmental Interpretation & Practice Notes No. 21* (see section 4.4). Unfortunately, it appears, however, that the facts of the case, which were clearly the crux of the dispute, were unclear as evidenced by the fact that the Board of Review and the High Court essentially found different facts; this confusion appears to stem, at least partly, from the fact that the taxpayer was represented at both hearings by only its finance director and, with respect to the individual concerned, it appears that the evidence as to the facts of the case was incomplete. This, combined with the fact that that Board of Review originally found for the taxpayer on different grounds to those argued by the taxpayer, cast significant doubt on the value of the case as a precedent.

More specifically, the Board of Review found as a fact that the taxpayer did nothing more than process paperwork and collect payments, with it taking no part in the effecting of sale or purchase contracts. The High Court, on the other hand, found that the taxpayer must have performed activities in Hong Kong in connection with the sale and purchase contracts and, indeed, indicated that there was no evidence that such activities took place anywhere else. On the basis of this finding, the High Court overturned the decision of the Board of Review and held the profits to have a Hong Kong source. Again, however, it is important to note that the differences in the judgements of the Board of Review and the High Court revolved almost entirely around the facts; in both cases the reasoning applied to the facts, once found, was in essence the same with both bodies largely following the decision of the Privy Council in the *Hang Seng Bank* case (supra). Nonetheless, it is perhaps unclear whether the High Court was looking to the operations of the taxpayer, or the place where the purchase and sale contracts were effected, in applying that case. It is submitted that this is another reason for being cautious in seeking to treat this decision as a particularly important precedent as to the legal source of profits. Nonetheless, there are some interesting aspects of the decision and the more notable of these are:

(i)   that it reiterated that the burden of proof is on the taxpayer and that positive evidence of the taxpayer's contentions is required;

(ii) that it established clearly that the level of a taxpayer's activity in Hong Kong was not, by itself, a relevant factor in determining the source of profits. The proper test was to determine what was done to earn the profits and where that was done. Even if little was done to earn the profits, it was still appropriate to look to where that was done to determine the source of the profits; and

(iii) that it adopted and further expanded on the quote of Lord Jauncey in the *HK-TVBI* case that *"it can only be in rare cases that a taxpayer with a principal place of business in Hong Kong can earn profits which are not chargeable to profits tax under Section 14 ..."* The court went on to note that this was a common sense statement that where a taxpayer's principal place of business was in Hong Kong, it is likely that the profits of that business will have a Hong Kong source and that it will be difficult to show otherwise. This appears to be yet another example of the courts confusing the tests of where a business is carried on with the source of the profits of that business and is somewhat surprising considering the decision of the Privy Council in the *Hang Seng Bank* case. (Although this issue is an important point, it was probably not critical to the High Court's decision.)

The question of the source of trading profits was subsequently considered in depth by the Court of Appeal in *CIR v Magna Industrial Company Limited* [1997] (1 HKRC 90-082). This decision contains some useful discussions of IRD practice and also considers clearly the relevance to the issue of activities undertaken on behalf of a taxpayer by its agents.

The facts of the case, as far as they were pertinent to the decision, are that the taxpayer (Magna) was a Hong Kong incorporated company which had no overseas branches. It derived profit from the buying and selling of goods. The sales were made through independent agents abroad, whilst the purchases were made on an automatic back-to-back basis from an associated company (Company A) at a cost-plus price. The goods were purchased by Company A, on its own account, from independent suppliers. Company A warehoused the goods and arranged the shipping of the goods to Magna's customers for which Magna paid it a fee. As a consequence of the structure of the operations of the group, Magna had few staff (in addition to its sales agents abroad), whilst Company A's operations were more substantial.

The decision of the High Court ([1996] (1 HKRC 90-078)) concerned an appeal by the Commissioner from a decision of the Board of Review (see *D 10/95*). The Board had found for Magna on the grounds that it was the selling activities of the sales agents abroad which gave rise to the profits in question, rather than the limited activities involved in ordering the goods. The High Court, however, overturned this judgement in a decision which was surprising in two respects. Firstly, the High Court, quoting the *Sinolink* case (supra), decided that it was necessary to carry out a weighting of all the activities undertaken to earn the profits, not just the effecting of the purchase and sale contracts as suggested by the Privy Council in the *Hang Seng Bank* case (supra) and as adopted by the Commissioner in *Departmental Interpretation & Practice Notes No. 21* (see section 4.4.5 below). In applying this principle, the High Court, again what surprisingly and with no clear authority, held that the selling activities of the overseas sales agents should be given little weight because they were agents of Magna and had a degree of independence in their activities.

Secondly, the High Court, again with no clear authority and, indeed, in remarkable contrast to previous Hong Kong decisions, took the view that Company A was a mere "puppet" or extension of Magna, even though there appears to be no evidence that Company A was actually an agent of Magna; in reaching this conclusion, and effectively lifting the corporate veil, the court described Company A as *"in truth an agent [of Magna]"*, considered that the corporate distinction between the parties was *"… a wholly artificial creation ...*" and described the sales between Company A and Magna as "*... wholly unreal ...*" notwithstanding that those sales were clearly documented. On this basis, the court concluded that it was entitled to look at the activities of Company A in deciding what Magna did to earn its profits and went on to conclude that it was those activities (i.e. the making of the purchases (which it must be remembered Company A did for its own account) and the processing of sales contracts after they had been made) which were of most importance in earning Magna's profits; as those activities were carried out in Hong Kong, the High Court found that the source of the relevant profits was in Hong Kong.

The decision of the High Court was, however, overturned by the Court of Appeal (see [1997] (1 HKRC 90-082)). Specifically, the Court of Appeal rejected the High Court's finding that the activities of the overseas sales agents should be given little weight and, indeed, noted that it was those activities which underpinned the Board of Review's original conclusion that the source of profits was offshore. The Court of Appeal also rejected the High Court's finding that Company A was a mere "puppet" of the taxpayer, although it did so not on the grounds that this was necessarily wrong, but because it was not part of the Commissioner's case before the Board of Review. Nonetheless, the decision is an important case as the Court of Appeal clearly separated the issues of carrying on business and source of profits and reiterated that it is appropriate to look to the activities of agents abroad in determining what was done to earn the profits in question. It is also a notable decision in that it appeared to depart from the *obiter dicta* of the Privy Council in the *Hang Seng Bank* case (supra) which suggested that the source of trading profits should be determined solely by where the contracts for sale and purchase were effected; in particular, the Court of Appeal suggested that although these factors were undoubtedly important, other matters including how the goods were procured and stored, the sales solicited, the orders processed, the goods shipped, the financing arranged and the payments made were all relevant activities to be considered and weighed up when determining the source of trading profits.

Notwithstanding the guidance provided by the courts in recent cases concerning the source of trading profits, readers should have regard to the decision in *D 2/96* where, notwithstanding that the case was argued as a source of trading profits case by both the IRD and the taxpayer, the Board of Review found otherwise. In particular, although the taxpayer company made its profits by buying garments and on-selling them at a higher price, the Board held that the company was not trading, but rather earned its "mark-up" for providing administrative services; the Board was helped with this finding by the fact that the company's profit was earned at the rate of one US dollar per garment. On this basis, the Board found the place where the sales and purchase contracts were effected was irrelevant and, given that the company's activities were largely undertaken in Hong Kong, held that the source of the "administrative services" was Hong Kong. Whilst this is a novel approach by the Board of Review to a case which the parties to the dispute agreed was a trading profits case, it is submitted that it revolved around its own facts and is unlikely to become an important precedent.

Another decision concerning the source of trading profits which highlights the fact that every case will be considered on the basis of its own facts and circumstances is *D 3/05*. In that case, the Board of Review accepted that the taxpayer derived its profits from the buying and selling of petroleum products and that the selling activities took place through unrelated companies in the Mainland of China, which negotiated and concluded sales and remitted the proceeds net of certain charges to the taxpayer in Hong Kong but were not responsible for losses as a result of the default of a customer. Nonetheless, the Board of Review held that the unrelated entities were not the agents of the taxpayer (because, *inter alia*, the agreements signed between the taxpayer and the unrelated companies had a duration of only one year) and, therefore, the activities of those parties were not relevant in determining the source of the taxpayer's profits. Further, the Board rejected the taxpayer's suggestion that the purchasing activities in Hong Kong were only ancillary or incidental in nature; however, the main basis upon which the Board appeared to conclude that the profits had a Hong Kong source was that the placing of orders and the settling of the purchases the issue of letters of credit were important activities in the profit generating process and these took place in Hong Kong.

A Board of Review decision subsequent to the *Magna* case which clearly analysed and brought together many of the principles emerging from modern case law in *D 14/06*. This case concerned a travel agency which earned profits by organising package tours abroad. The principal issue in dispute was the source of the profits from the organisation and operation of such tours. The Board of Review began its analysis by applying the test formulated by the Privy Council in the *Hang Seng Bank* case (supra) and confirmed in the *HK-TVB International* case (supra) of looking to what activity produced the profit and where that activity took place. The Board then went on to find that the relevant activities were the marketing and selling of the tours through the taxpayer's retail outlets in Hong Kong, the purchase of airline tickets on behalf of the customers and the provision of tour services to the customers (notwithstanding that such services were undertaken by agents of the taxpayer). Of these activities, the Board held that the first two took place in Hong Kong while the third took place largely outside Hong Kong. On this basis the Board considered that an apportionment of the relevant profits may be appropriate; however as apportionment had not been argued by either party, and the profits were an inseparable whole, the Board felt itself bound to follow the test which originated from the *Hillsdon Watts* case (supra) and was followed in the *Hong Kong & Whampoa Dock* case (supra) of looking to the acts which are *"… more immediately responsible for the receipt of the profit …"*. These activities, the Board held, were the marketing and sale of the tours in Hong Kong and, therefore, the source of the profits was in Hong Kong.

A similar approach was taken in the later case of *D 8/00* which was concerned with the source of, *inter alia*, commissions earned by a stockbroker in respect of trades executed on overseas stock markets. In that case, the Board of Review held that the activities most directly relevant to the determination of the source of the commissions were the establishing and maintaining the relationship with the client, providing quality research and advice to clients, providing a reliable and efficient service in executing transactions and managing the clients' accounts, and projecting an image of repute and reliability. Where the transactions were executed on behalf of clients outside Hong Kong, the Board of Review concluded that the source of the commissions was substantially outside of Hong Kong. It is notable that this conclusion was reached not on the basis that the transactions were executed on the overseas stock exchange by the foreign broker acting as agent of the taxpayer; indeed, the Board of Review found that it could not conclude that those brokers were the taxpayer's agents and, therefore, could not conclude that the acts of the brokers could be regarded as the acts of the taxpayer for the purpose of ascertaining the source of the profits. Rather, the Board of Review's conclusion as to the source of the relevant profit was reached on the basis that the overseas affiliates of the taxpayer who liased with the clients, processed and managed the orders and provided research to the clients were the agents of the taxpayer and, therefore, their acts could be considered the acts of the taxpayer.

Where, on the other hand, the transaction was executed on behalf of a client in Hong Kong, the Board of Review took the view that the source was 60% in Hong Kong and 40% outside of Hong Kong; again, however, in reaching this conclusion the Board of Review did not accept that the overseas brokers were the agents of the taxpayer and, therefore, the acts of those agents were not attributed to the taxpayer in determining the source of the profits. Notwithstanding that the source of these profits was found to be

40% offshore, the Board reluctantly concluded that notwithstanding *obiter dicta* of the Privy Council in *CIR v Hang Seng Bank Limited* (3 HKTC 351) which they considered authorised apportionment, they felt barred from so apportioning on the basis that they were bound by the decision of the Hong Kong Court of Appeal in that case which ruled that apportionment was not possible. Accordingly, as in *D 14/96*, the Board of Review considered it appropriate to follow the tests adopted in the *Hillsdon Watts* and *Hong Kong & Whampoa Dock* cases (supra) and concluded that the entire profit had its source in Hong Kong.

The above decision was, however, appealed to the Court of First Instance (see *CIR v Indosuez W I Carr Securities Limited*; *Indosuez W I Carr Securities Limited v CIR* [2002] (1 HKTC 90-117)). In addition to the critical question of apportionment of profits, much of the decision in the appeal focussed on whether the overseas affiliates and brokers were the taxpayer's agents as it was accepted by the parties that in determining the source of a profit it was necessary to look to what the taxpayer has done to earn the profits and not what some other person has done. It is also implicit that the parties agreed that the acts of an agent of a taxpayer are to be considered the acts of the taxpayer itself for the purpose of determining the source of the taxpayer's profits.

The Court of First Instance reached a number of conclusions in relation to the agency issues, although ultimately remitted the matters back to the Board of Review to make the final findings of fact. Firstly, the court held that the Board of Review had erred in concluding in the absence of direct evidence that the overseas affiliates were the agents of the taxpayer. The court noted, however, that the Board's conclusion could well have been reached on the basis of other evidence, including the fact that the client agreements were signed with the taxpayer, the taxpayer accepted liability for losses from wrongful trading and that transaction documentation suggested the client was the client of the taxpayer.

Secondly, the court concluded that the overseas brokers were the agents of the taxpayer, at least as far as Hong Kong clients were concerned. In relation to overseas clients, the issue of whether the overseas brokers were the taxpayer's agents depended, in the court's view, on whether the clients were clients of the taxpayer or the overseas affiliate and that was a matter on which the court directed the Board of Review to conclude.

Finally, the court held that apportionment of profits which arose in two or more jurisdictions was, as a matter of law, permissible and remitted the matter back to the Board of Review to apportion the relevant profits as they considered appropriate. In reaching this conclusion, the court held that as a result of the *dicta* of the Privy Council in *CIR v Hang Seng Bank Limited*, it was open to them depart from the decision in *CIR v The Hong Kong and Whampoa Dock Company Limited* case that apportionment was not permissible.

Interestingly, the court's wording on this point referred only to profits derived from acting for clients in Hong Kong, which the Board of Review had previously held were 40% offshore but which it had declined to apportion. Subsequently, however, counsel for the Commissioner successfully sought an order to have the issue of apportionment of profits from overseas clients (which the Board of Review had held were entirely offshore) also remitted to the Board of Review for consideration.

As noted, the Court of First Instance, although reaching certain conclusions as to matters of law, remitted most matters back to the Board of Review in order that the Board could make the relevant findings of fact and apply those facts to the law as decided. The Board of Review reviewed the case and handed down its decision (see *D 79/03*). In that decision, the Board started by noting that the relevant test to determine the source of the profits in question was to look to what the taxpayer *or its agent* had done to earn the profit and where it had done it. Applying this test, the Board upheld its previous conclusion that the source of the profits derived in respect of overseas customers was entirely outside Hong Kong and, therefore, not taxable. In reaching this conclusion, the Board noted that some of the activities of the overseas affiliates were carried out as agents of the taxpayer, but found that others (in particular, the building up and maintaining of client relationships and the provision of quality research) were not undertaken as agent of the taxpayer and, therefore, should be ignored in determining the source of the profits. The Board also accepted (as directed by the Court of First Instance) that the overseas brokers were the agents of the taxpayer. Nonetheless, the Board recognised that some activities were undertaken by the taxpayer in Hong Kong but considered these to be minor and indirect and held that they should be ignored in determining the source of the profits.

With regard to Hong Kong customers, the Board of Review in *D 79/03* considered that the execution of the trades by the overseas brokers was important as were the efforts of the sales team in Hong Kong and the taxpayer's presence in Hong Kong. On this basis, the Board considered the profits should be apportioned as arising 50% from a Hong Kong source and 50% from a non-Hong Kong source. Originally, the Board had held the profits to be 40% offshore, with the increase in the offshore percentage being largely attributable to the recognition of the fact that the overseas brokers were the agents of the taxpayer, but disregarding the provision of research by overseas associates on the grounds that this was not undertaken as agent of the taxpayer.

Following the decision of the Board of Review in *D 79/03*, the Commissioner requested the Board of Review to state a case for the opinion of the court. The Board of Review refused on the grounds that the case predominantly concerned matters of fact and the questions which the Commissioner wished to have addressed were not proper questions of law. The Commissioner sought to have the Board's refusal to state a case overturned pursuant to judicial review proceedings. The taxpayer was also a party to those proceedings and in addition to the Board's argument that the Commissioner's questions in the stated case were not proper questions of law, the taxpayer argued that the Commissioner's application was an abuse of process as it sought to have issues considered which could have been, but were not, raised at earlier hearings.

The Court of First Instance allowed the Commissioner's application for judicial review (see *CIR v Board of Review and Indosuez W I Carr Securities Limited* [2005] (1 HKRC 90157)) and that decision was subsequently upheld by the Court of Appeal (see CACV 57/2006). Nonetheless, it is important to understand that although the Board of Review is now required to state a case, this does not mean that the substantive issues will be decided in the Commissioner's favour. What is particularly interesting about the judicial review proceedings, however, is the questions which the Commissioner is seeking to have considered. In particular, the Commissioner has raised thirteen questions and amongst these are questions suggesting that the Commissioner wishes to challenge the correctness of looking to the activities of a taxpayer's agent in determining the source of the taxpayer's profits and that even if activities are undertaken by agents that the precise commercial arrangements between the taxpayer and the agent must be examined in determining whether the agent's activities are relevant to the determination of the source of the taxpayer's profits. What the Commissioner appears to be suggesting in relation to the last point is that where an agent (i.e. the overseas brokers in the present case) is paid a commercial fee or commission for the work they undertake, their activities should be ignored in determining the source of the taxpayer's profits. Interestingly, this is an argument which the IRD have advanced from time to time, but it appears never to have been part of the Commissioner's case in earlier hearings in the *Indosuez WI Carr Securities Limited* case.

Although the *Indosuez WI Carr Securities Limited* case is likely to become a landmark case on the question of apportionment of profit, it is interesting to compare it to the later Court of First Instance decision in *Baring Securities*

(Hong Kong) Limited v CIR [2005] (1 HKRC 90-144) which concerned very similar facts. That decision involved an appeal from the decision of the Board of Reivew (see *D 152/01*) which had found for the Commissioner on the basis that the taxpayer had not proved their contentions and, therefore had not discharged the burden of proof. Nonetheless, the court found that the operation which in substance gave rise to the brokerage commission earned from transactions in overseas securities was the execution of those transactions through the overseas affiliated brokers and, as such, the source of the profit was outside Hong Kong irrespective of the location of the client. In particular, the court considered that the research and sales activities were not critical to the derivation of the profit and should, therefore, be ignored in determining the source of that profit, although there is evidence that this conclusion was reached having regard to the nature of the clients of the taxpayer. Although the conclusions of the courts in these two cases appear different, it must be remembered that the courts were considering questions of law raised in the cases stated by the Board of Review. It is differences in those cases stated that are partly responsible for the different approaches of the courts. In particular, although both decisions reviewed some findings of fact by the Board of Review, in the *Indosuez WI Carr Securities Limited* case the question of apportionment of profits was raised, while this was not an issue in the *Baring Securities (Hong Kong) Limited* case. Nonetheless, it does appear that in the latter case the court looked to a slightly narrower range of activities when deciding the operations from which the relevant profits in substance arose. Note, however, that the Court of First Instance's decision in the *Baring Securities* case was overturned by the Court of Appeal (see *Baring Securities (Hong Kong) Limited v CIR* [2005] (1 HKRC 90-169)). Nonetheless, this was not on the basis that the reasoning of the Court of First Instance as to what governed the source of the relevant profits was necessarily wrong; rather the Court of Appeal considered that lower court had rejected certain findings of fact by the Board of Review and had substituted its own findings and, as such had incorrectly assumed the Board's fact finding role and, therefore, the judgement was flawed. The decision of the Court of Appeal was further appealed to the Court of Final Appeal and although at the time of writing the case had been heard, the judgement had not been issued.

Although, as discussed above, the decisions in the *Indosuez WI Carr Securities Limited* and *Baring Securities (Hong Kong) Limited* cases can possibly be reconciled, there is a third case concerning similar facts which appears to have been decided on a completely different basis. In particular, see *Kim Eng Securities (Hong Kong) Limited v CIR* [2005] (1 HKRC 90-

164) which was a direct appeal to the Court of Appeal from the Board of Review (see *D 72/03*). As with the *Indosuez WI Carr Securities Limited* and *Baring Securities (Hong Kong) Limited* cases, this case involved a Hong Kong company which took orders from customers for the execution of stock transactions on an overseas stock exchange. One difference, although of questionable relevance to the determination of the source of the profits, was that in the *Kim Eng Securities* case all of the customers were outside Hong Kong. Another difference, again of questionable relevance, was that the taxpayer in *Kim Eng Securities* was established to circumvent minimum commission rules of the Singapore Stock Exchange, to allow the provision of margin facilities to customers in respect of securities where margin facilities were not permitted in the foreign jurisdiction and to allow the aggregation of orders of a customer dealing for a number of sub-accounts. The Board of Review held that the source of the profits of the taxpayer was Hong Kong. It reached this conclusion on the basis that the reason for the taxpayer being brought into existence was to circumvent the rules in other jurisdictions by bringing together the complementary needs of the various parties, and this activity was carried out in Hong Kong. In particular, the Board of Review specifically identified the activities undertaken in Hong Kong as the source of the profits, notwithstanding that those activities were largely clerical and administrative in nature, such as the opening of trading accounts, noting settlement instructions, booking trades as advised by overseas parties, matching confirmations, generating contract notes, etc.

On appeal to the Court of Appeal, Cheung JA found that the Board of Review's conclusion was one which was open to it. Rogers JA, however, provided a more extensive reasoning and considered that the source of the profits was the contractual arrangements between the taxpayer and its customers and that these were contracts in Hong Kong. He went on to note that the profit arose from the various charges raised in the bought/sold notes and that these were created in and sent from Hong Kong, thereby giving the profits a Hong Kong source. In reaching this conclusion, Rogers JA (contrary to the decisions in the *Indosuez WI Carr Securities Limited* and *Baring Securities (Hong Kong) Limited* cases) specifically rejected the argument that it was the execution of the trades on the overseas stock exchange which generated the profit by noting that the bill presented to the customer came from the taxpayer in Hong Kong. Interestingly, he went on to suggest that if the Singapore broker had executed the transaction directly for the client and then forwarded a share of the brokerage commission to the taxpayer in Hong Kong, that the source of the taxpayer's profit may have been considered to be outside Hong Kong; however, that was the arrangement in the *Wardley*

Investment Services (Hong Kong) Limited case where, of course, the Court of Appeal held that the source of the profit was in Hong Kong.

Finally, when considering the issue of apportionment, Rogers JA agreed with the Board of Review that apportionment was not appropriate. In doing so, he held that the overseas elements in the transaction (i.e. the execution of the transactions on the Singapore Stock Exchange) had *"… already been catered for by reason of the commission received by [the Singapore broker] …"*. In other words, the court sought to play down the relevance of the activities undertaken by the overseas brokers in determining the source of the taxpayer's profits on the basis that they were paid for their services; as discussed above, this is a point that the Commissioner is seeking to have addressed in the *Indosuez WI Carr Securities Limited* case.

This decision was upheld on appeal to the Court of Final Appeal (see FACV 11/2006). Bokhary PJ, with whom three other judges agreed, essentially held that the Board of Review's decision contained no errors of law or perverse findings of fact and, therefore, must be allowed to stand. Indeed, he endorsed a finding of fact by the Board that (in his own words) in each case the order on the overseas stock exchange was executed before the paperwork which made the customer a customer of the taxpayer in relation to that trade had been prepared and agreed that this meant that what was done by the taxpayer to earn the profit was done in Hong Kong. Additionally, Bokhary PJ made some comments concerning treating the acts of an agent as the acts of the taxpayer when determining the source of profits; however, the comments were somewhat vague and did not suggest this was wrong, but rather implied that a degree of caution should be exercised in doing so. Finally, Bokhary PJ held that the apportionment question did not need to be considered because the Board's finding of fact that what the taxpayer did to earn the profit was done in Hong Kong was not perverse and did not leave any room for ascribing any foreign element to the source of the profits. Lord Scott NPJ agreed with Bokhary PJ but added his own comments and observations. He was concerned with the question of whether the overseas broker was acting for the taxpayer or the taxpayer's customer when executing a transaction. He analysed the position under either scenario and concluded that in each case the taxpayer's profit stemmed from a contractual arrangement between the taxpayer and the customer, rather than with the overseas broker and that the source of such arrangements was in Hong Kong. Nonetheless, he summed up by concluding that the taxpayer's customers were in reality the customers of the overseas broker and the taxpayer's role was no more than a "book-entry role in Hong Kong". As such, it appears that Lord Scott NPJ was of the view that as that role existed in Hong Kong, the profits from that role must have a Hong Kong source.

As noted above, it is difficult to reconcile the decision in *Kim Eng Securities Limited* to those in the *Indosuez WI Carr Securities Limited* and *Baring Securities (Hong Kong) Limited* cases and there are a number of reasons for this. For example, there were some findings of fact in the *Kim Eng Securities Limited* case, in particular the finding that the customers were not customers of the taxpayer in relation to the trades at the time of execution, which clearly had an impact on the analysis applied by the courts. Also, in the *Kim Eng Securities Limited* case the court appeared swayed by the argument urged upon them by the Commissioner that the arrangement was not one of the taxpayer contracting with the customer to arrange execution of trades abroad, but rather that it was a fee sharing arrangement between the taxpayer and the overseas broker. Perhaps the greatest reason for the difficulty in reconciling the cases, however, is the fundamentally different approach in the *Kim Eng Securities Limited* case where the courts looked more to the reasons for the establishment of the taxpayer and concluded that the activities undertaken in Hong Kong were critical to those reasons and, therefore, were the source of the profits. On the other hand, in the other two cases the analysis was the more traditional approach of looking solely to the activities which gave rise to the profits and where they were undertaken without analysing the rationale for the taxpayer's existence.

Another way of looking at the two approaches is to consider that one, such as adopted by the Board of Review in the *Indosuez WI Carr Securities Limited* case and the Court of First Instance in the *Baring Securities (Hong Kong) Limited* case, is that it is appropriate to look to the execution of the transactions as being the source of the profit, and the other is to look to the operations of the taxpayer which permit it to derive a profit. This is a subtle distinction which has not generally been considered in depth by the courts. Nonetheless, the Court of Appeal in the *Baring Securities (Hong Kong) Limited* case touched on the point when they criticised the lower court judge for "... *adopting the approach which had been advocated by [counsel for the taxpayer] and which he had professed to reject, namely focussing on the transactions which produced the profits to the taxpayer rather than the acts and operation of the taxpayer itself which generated the profits.*" In other words, the court appeared to be advocating a move away from the traditional analysis (such as that adopted by the Privy Council decision in the *Hang Seng Bank* case) of looking to the actual transactions which immediately generated the profits in order to determine the source of those profits, to looking more broadly to the operations of the taxpayer from which the profits arose. This latter approach is reminiscent of some earlier cases which appeared to confuse the tests of where a business was carried on with the source of the profits from that business. Nonetheless, the above comments from the *Baring Securities (Hong Kong) Limited* case were possibly *obiter dicta* only as ultimately the Court of Appeal allowed the original decision of the Board of Review to stand on the grounds that the Court of First Instance, in overturning that decision, had assumed the fact finding role of the Board and that it was not permitted to do so in the absence of a finding that the Board's findings of fact were perverse.

It is trite to say that before analysing what activities give rise to a profit, it is necessary to understand the nature of the profit. Nonetheless, there have been at least two cases where, particularly in the early stages, there was dispute over the nature of the appellant's business and profits. In *D 172/01*, part of the dispute revolved around whether the taxpayer was in the business of manufacturing or trading. Because the manufacturing of the goods in which the taxpayer dealt was undertaken outside Hong Kong, it aided the taxpayer's case that its profits arose outside Hong Kong if it could treat itself as undertaking the manufacturing of those goods. On the basis that the manufacturing was actually carried out by a subcontractor, however, the Board of Review rejected the proposition that the taxpayer was a manufacturer and instead treated it as a trader. The consequence of this is that the source of the taxpayer's profit was determined largely with respect to where the contracts for sale of finished products, and for the purchase of raw materials, were carried out. This case proceeded to the Court of First Instance (see *Consco Trading Company Limited v CIR* [2004] (1 HKRC 90-132)), which upheld the decision of the Board of Review.

Another case where the nature of the appellant's business was, at least initially, unclear culminated in the Court of Final Appeal's decision of *Kwong Mile Services Limited (in members' voluntary winding up) v CIR* [2004] (1 HKRC 90-135). This case originated in the Board of Review (see *D 38/01*) and was then appealed by the Commissioner to the Court of First Instance (see *CIR v Kwong Mile Services Limited (in members' voluntary winding up)* [2002] (1 HKRC 90-122). The taxpayer then appealed against the decision of the Court of First Instance to the Court of Appeal (see *Kwong Mile Services Limited (in members' voluntary winding up) v CIR* [2003] (1 HKRC 90-127) and, finally, the Court of Final Appeal. The case involved a company which entered into an underwriting agreement with a property developer ("the Developer") in respect of properties located in the Mainland of China. The terms of the underwriting were such that the taxpayer derived a profit if the properties were sold for more than a specified sum, and was required to indemnify the Developer if the sale price was below that value. As such, it was in the taxpayer's interest to ensure that properties were sold for as high a price as possible and, to achieve this, the taxpayer, through an associated company, undertook marketing of the properties in Hong Kong, although all transactions were concluded between the Developer and the end purchasers. In other words, the taxpayer's business in some ways resembled the buying and selling of property, although the formal agreement indicated the arrangement was one of underwriting. Indeed, the taxpayer argued that they were in substance a property trader but in form an underwriter. In these circumstances, the first issue for the Board of Review to decide was the nature of the transaction, which they decided in substance was one of underwriting. This finding was not the subject of the appeal to the Court of First Instance.

Having decided the nature of the transaction, the second issue for the Board of Review to consider was the source of the resulting profit. On this point, the majority of the Board of Review (one member dissented) concluded that the source of the profit from the underwriting was the assumption of risk and that such risk was outside Hong Kong. This, together with the fact that the underwriting agreement was signed outside Hong Kong, led the Board of Review to conclude that the profit in question had a non-Hong Kong source. Interestingly, the majority of the Board went on to consider the implications should the assumption of risk not be the essence of the underwriting and concluded that, contrary to the argument advanced by the IRD's representative, the sales and marketing in Hong Kong would not be the only factor to look to in determining the source of the profit, but the place where the underwriting agreement was negotiated and signed, the location of the underwritten properties and the place where the agreements for the purchase of the properties were entered into would also be relevant considerations. Moreover, the majority considered the position should it be held that the nature of the business was held to be property trading, in which case they concluded that the profit would have been treated as offshore on the basis that the properties in question were located outside Hong Kong.

On appeal, however, the decision of the Board of Review was overturned by the Court of First Instance. In particular, the court held that because a profit was derived by the taxpayer only when the properties were marketed and sold, the marketing activities undertaken by the taxpayer through its associate were the activities from which the underwriting profit arose. The court considered that the fact that the associate was the agent of the Developer did not detract from this conclusion. Moreover, contrary to the comments by the Board of Review, the court appeared to consider that the marketing activities were the only activities or factors to look to in determining the location of the underwriting profits. On this basis, the court held that those profits had a Hong Kong source. The conclusions of the Court of First Instance were effectively upheld by both the Court of Appeal and the Court of Final Appeal. The Court of Final Appeal, however, succinctly summarised their reasoning by noting that what the taxpayer did in the Mainland of China was to assume an underwriting risk, but it was not that assumption of risk which generated the profits as it only provided an opportunity to make a profit. The court then noted that the undertaking of marketing activities in Hong Kong (albeit through its agent) was the activity by which the taxpayer exploited the opportunity provided by the underwriting agreement and allowed it to make a profit. As that activity was undertaken in Hong Kong, the source of the profit was in Hong Kong.

In summary, the question of the determination of the source of profit continues to give rise to disputes as a consequence of uncertainties. This is, of course, less than ideal given the fundamental nature of the issue to ascertaining Profits Tax liabilities. In particular, despite the clear analysis provided by the Privy Council in the *Hang Seng Bank* case, some cases continue to confuse the question of where a business is carried with the question of the source of the profits from that business. Accordingly, notwithstanding the useful guidance provided by recent cases, it must be expected that the issue will continue to give rise to disputes and further litigation.

4.4.3 Case law — other issues

Apart from the general source principles emerging from case law which are discussed above, a number of other noteworthy source related issues have from time to time been considered by the courts. Some of the more important of these are considered below.

(a) **Apportionment of Profits:** Under any of the tests commonly adopted at present or in the past for determining the source of profits, the problem arises from time to time of how to deal with profits which arise in two or more jurisdictions. In the *Whampoa Dock* case (supra), one of the earliest Hong Kong cases on source, the court rejected the suggestion that as the final part of the salvage operation was undertaken in Hong Kong waters, a portion of the profits should be considered to have a Hong Kong source. In reaching this conclusion, the Court followed the decision in the *Hillsdon Watts* case (supra) which found that in the absence of a specific provision for apportionment, the source of an inseparable item of profit must fall into one jurisdiction or another, with the guiding principle involving a consideration of the acts more immediately responsible for the receipt of the profit. It was, however, recognised in the *Hillsdon Watts* decision that if it can be ascertained how much of an item of profit was earned at successive stages of the operations (albeit in an unrealised form), then it was permissible to apportion the total profit between the places where the various stages of the operations took place.

This principle remained largely intact right through the 1980s and, indeed, was reaffirmed by the Court of Appeal in the *Hang Seng Bank case* (*supra*). The Privy Council in that case, however, noted, as *obiter dicta*, that the absence of a specific apportionment provision did not prevent apportionment of profits between two or more jurisdictions in appropriate cases (although the case under review was not considered a case for apportionment); the Privy Council did not, unfortunately, go on to consider the practical problems associated with carrying out such an apportionment. Nonetheless, following that decision, the possibility of apportionment of profits was accepted by the Commissioner and incorporated into his *Departmental Interpretation & Practice Notes No. 21* on the source of profits (see section 4.4.5 below), although, in practice, the IRD generally appear reluctant to apportion profits other than in the case of financial institutions and manufacturing companies. See, however, case *D 77/94* where the Board of Review considered apportionment of profits appropriate and remitted the case back to the parties to agree on a basis of such apportionment, and *D 14/96* where the Board of Review suggested it would have apportioned the profits in dispute had either party argued for it.

More recently, however, in *D 8/00* the Board of Review, although finding that the profits in question arose in two jurisdictions, declined to apportion them on the grounds that there was no binding decision of the courts where an apportionment was actually made. In reaching this conclusion, the Board of Review indicated that in many respects they were convinced by the comments of the Privy Council in the *Hang Seng Bank* case but emphasised that they were *obiter dicta* and, therefore, not binding. They considered with some reluctance, however, that the comments of the Court of Appeal in that case rejecting apportionment were binding upon them and accordingly did not allow apportionment but decided the case on the basis of where the acts more immediately responsible for the receipt of the profits were undertaken.

On appeal, however, the Court of First Instance (see *CIR v Indosuez W I Carr Securities Limited*; *Indosuez W I Carr Securities Limited v CIR* [2002] (1 HKRC 90-117)) held that the *dicta* of the Privy Council in *CIR v Hang Seng Bank Limited* provided authority to ignore the earlier authorities which prohibited apportionment. Accordingly, it now appears that apportionment is to be permitted in respect of any profits arising in two or more jurisdictions.

(b) **Offshore Profits — Is an Overseas Branch Necessary?:** As has been noted in several places above, the structure of Sec. 14 makes it clear that the source of a person's profits is a matter quite independent of the place where that person's business is carried on and that a business carried on in Hong Kong is quite capable of deriving profits from a source outside Hong Kong. These principles are clearly illustrated in a number of court decisions. It should, therefore, be quite clear that in order to derive "offshore" profits, it is not necessary that a person carry on business abroad through a branch or other place of business outside Hong Kong. Nonetheless, there have been some statements in recent cases which have introduced confusion to this fundamental issue. The first of such statements was made by Godfrey J in the High Court judgement in the *HK-TVBI* case (supra) where he said, "*... The time has come to make it clear that it is only where a taxpayer has established the existence of a profit-generating operation carried on by him outside Hong Kong that he can hope to escape the charge to Profits Tax imposed by Sec. 14*". This statement was made prior to the Privy Council's decision in the *Hang Seng Bank* case and so one can only speculate as to whether Godfrey J's view would have been different had he had the benefit of the guidance of that judgement, which clearly advocates an opposite conclusion.

Of potentially more concern is the statement of Lord Jauncey, on behalf of the Privy Council, in the *HK-TVBI* case that "*... it can only be in rare cases that a taxpayer with a principal place of business in Hong Kong can earn profits which are not chargeable to Profits Tax ...*". Lord Jauncey did, however, go on to note that the *Mehta, Whampoa Dock* and *Hang Seng Bank* cases (supra) were examples of exceptions to his general rule and, given the potentially wide number of cases which could fall within the principles established by those cases, care should obviously be exercised when interpreting his use of the word "rare".

Nonetheless, this dictum of Lord Jauncey was picked up and further explained in the *Euro Tech* case where the court said that the statement was no more than common sense and that it meant that where *"... a taxpayer has a principal place of business in Hong Kong, it is likely that it is Hong Kong where he earns his profits. It will be difficult for such a taxpayer to demonstrate that the profits were earned outside Hong Kong ..."*.

However, the principle that an overseas branch is not a pre-requisite for a successful "offshore" profits claim was reiterated in *D 64/93*. In that decision, the Board of Review allowed the taxpayer's claim that certain trading profits arose offshore on the basis that the operations which gave rise to the profits in question were undertaken during visits abroad by a director of the taxpayer.

D 64/93 should, however, be contrasted with the decision in *D 66/93* which also involved employees travelling abroad, in this case to conclude sales contracts. In finding that the profits were sourced in Hong Kong, the Board of Review, after deciding that the taxpayer was a manufacturer, held that the operation giving rise to the profit was not the manufacture of the goods, nor the entering into of sale contracts for those goods, but the *"... decision reached in Hong Kong to explore the possibility of securing purchasers overseas"*. Although the Board of Review cited the *HK-TVB* case as broad authority for this decision, it is submitted that the Board in fact went beyond the reasoning of that case, as well as most other relevant case law, in ignoring the manufacture and sale of the goods in determining the activities which gave rise to the profits. As a consequence, caution should be applied in interpreting the decision and seeking to apply it, particularly in cases where the relevant facts are not identical.

Clearly, an element of confusion still surrounds this issue. Perhaps the best conclusion which can be reached at this stage is that "offshore" profit claims can succeed where no overseas place of business is maintained, although it will usually be necessary to clearly demonstrate that the profits are attributable to the exploitation of property overseas, the activities of an overseas agent or the carrying out of at least some activities abroad. See also paragraph 12 of *Departmental Interpretation & Practice Notes No. 21* which is reproduced as Appendix 13, with regard to this point. In that paragraph, the IRD implies that it accepts that a non-Hong Kong source profit (in particular a trading profit) may arise where contracts of purchase and/or sale are concluded by fully accredited agents abroad or by employees travelling abroad. Whilst this seems totally in accordance with case law, it appears inconsistent with their approach, discussed in section 4.4.2, in relation to the ongoing litigation in the *Indosuez WI Carr Securities Limited* case. As discussed, in that case the IRD appear to be seeking to argue that activities undertaken by an agent should be ignored for the purpose of determining the source of the principal's profits where the agent is appropriately remunerated for the activities undertaken.

(c) **Relevance of Place of Conclusion of Contract:** It is often suggested that the place of conclusion of a contract is relevant in determining the source of the profit from that contract. In support of this proposition a number of UK cases are often quoted, including *F. L. Smidth & Co. v Greenwood* (8 TC 193), *Grainger & Son v Gough* (3 TC 462) and *Maclaine v Eccott* (10 TC 572). These cases were not, however, concerned with the source of profits but with where the taxpayer's trade was carried on. Nonetheless, the place of conclusion of sale contracts was, prior to the decision in the *Sinolink* case (supra), generally considered relevant in determining the source of profits from the simple buying and selling of goods, although apart from the above cases, the authority for this is not particularly clear. The confusion introduced by the *Sinolink* decision was clarified by the Privy Council decision in the *Hang Seng Bank* case (supra), which altered the traditional thinking in this regard in two ways. Firstly, that case suggested that the source of trading profits was to be determined by looking to the contract of purchase as well as the contract of sale; secondly, it was suggested that it was the place where those contracts were *effected*, rather than concluded, that was the relevant consideration. The term "effected" was not explained by the Privy Council, although it is generally thought to encompass the negotiation and the steps leading up to, and including, the conclusion of the contract; it could also, arguably, include some aspects of the performance of the contract. As noted in section 4.4.2, however, the Court of Appeal in *CIR v Magna Industrial Company Limited* appeared to consider the place where the contracts for purchase and sale were effected as only one factor, albeit an important factor, to be considered when determining the source of trading profits. In this regard, also see *Departmental Interpretation*

& Practice Notes No. 21, which is discussed in section 4.4.5 below.

Although the foregoing concentrates on the relevance of the conclusion of contracts in a trading situation, it has also been argued as relevant in other situations. For example, in the *Whampoa Dock* case (supra), the place where the salvage contract was concluded was argued by Counsel for the Commissioner as relevant to the determination of the source of the salvage profits; this argument was, however, rejected by the Court. In *D 102/89*, on the other hand, the source of sub-underwriting commission, earned by a trustee of a unit trust, and for which virtually no active services were rendered, was held to have its source where the relevant contracts were concluded and this was determined in accordance with the legal rules concerning the offer and acceptance of contracts. At first glance a contrary conclusion was reached in the case of *Kwong Mile Services Limited (in members' voluntary winding up) v CIR* [2004] (1 HKRC 90-135) where the Court of Final Appeal considered that the execution of an underwriting agreement only gave the underwriter the opportunity to make a profit and was not the activity from which the profit arose; rather, the court concluded that it was the subsequent marketing activities which generated the profit and which were to be looked to in determining the source of the profit. However, it was these active services of marketing which potentially allow this decision to be reconciled to the decision in *D 102/89* where no significant active services were undertaken to earn the profit.

The current position, therefore, appears to be that the place of conclusion of contracts is of very limited relevance generally in determining the source of profits. The possible exception to this rule is in situations where the profits are of a passive nature; that is, where little other than the conclusion of a contract is required to be done to earn the profit.

4.4.4 Source of interest income

As with the question of source of profits generally, there are no statutory provisions which provide meaningful guidance in determining the source of interest income. This is perhaps surprising given that the question is important not only in relation to the general charging provision, Sec. 14, but also various deeming provisions contained in Sec. 15(1) which deal specifically with interest. Furthermore, there were, until the 1990s, no Hong

Kong court cases on the issue of source of interest and, although there were a few Board of Review cases on the question, these concerned fairly narrow factual situations and none of the decisions contain a particularly extensive analysis of the law.

One of the reasons for the lack of litigation of the issue in Hong Kong is undoubtedly the fact that the IRD has adopted tests based on decisions of the courts in other jurisdictions and published their views in connection therewith in *Departmental Interpretation & Practice Notes No. 13* as long ago as 1973, although the document has been revised a number of times since. While the correctness of these tests in terms of the case law from which they are purportedly derived could possibly be questioned, the tests themselves are sufficiently clear cut as to allow taxpayers to relatively easily arrange loan transactions so as to give the resulting interest an offshore or onshore source as may be desirable in the particular circumstances. Unfortunately, however, the tests are not adopted consistently by the IRD and it is difficult to reconcile, and not always easy to predict, the situations in which the IRD will depart from those tests. These issues are discussed in more detail below.

As a starting point in analysing case law on the source of interest, it is worthwhile summarizing the various factors which the courts have from time to time considered relevant to the question. Case law in South Africa, Australia and New Zealand is particularly fruitful in this respect and all of the following factors have, at some time or other, been regarded as relevant in determining the source of interest:—

- the place at which the credit is provided;
- the place where the loan agreement is concluded;
- the country under the laws of which the agreement is enforceable;
- the place where the interest is paid;
- the currency of the transaction;
- the place where the borrower is resident or has his operations; and
- the place where the loan funds are used.

In Australia, for example, no single factor has, historically, been regarded as necessarily persuasive but a totality of the foregoing factors have been considered. In Hong Kong, however, guidance has been drawn from the judgement in *CIR v Lever Brothers & Unilever Ltd.* (14 SATC 1). A general principle which emerged from that case is that in determining the source of a given receipt of income, one must look to what the party receiving the income had to do in order to qualify for that receipt; in other words, what consideration did he have to give under the contract? A further discussion on the origins of this principle, which is known as the "originating cause" of income, is contained in section 4.4.2 above.

Further, on the basis of the *Lever Brothers* case (supra) and also the cases of *Commissioner of Inland Revenue (NZ) v N.V. Philips Gloeilampen-fabrieken* (10 ATD 435) and *Commissioner-General of Income Tax v Esso Standard Eastern Inc.* [1969] (Court of Appeal for East Africa, unreported), the IRD has adopted the view that in the majority of cases, the originating cause in respect of interest is the provision of the credit to the borrower; in other words, it is considered that it is the making available of the loan funds that causes interest to be paid for the use of the money. The source of interest under this test, which has become known as the "provision of credit" test, is, therefore, the place where the credit is made available to the borrower. This, of course, in turn depends upon the manner in which the loan or deposit funds have been moved around. The practical application of the "provision of credit" test is illustrated by the following examples.

■ Example 4.3

A loan is made in cash handed over personally to the borrower in Hong Kong.
   The credit is clearly provided in Hong Kong and, therefore, the interest on the loan has a Hong Kong source.

■ Example 4.4

A lender resident in Hong Kong has funds available in US dollars in a bank account outside Hong Kong and makes a loan to a Hong Kong company by transferring these funds to the bank account in New York maintained by that company. The credit is, therefore, made available to the company outside Hong Kong, and the interest on the loan has a non-Hong Kong source.

■ Example 4.5

A lender resident in New York wishes to make a loan in US dollars to a Hong Kong company and he remits a bank draft or other negotiable instrument to that company through the post.
   The receipt of a negotiable instrument physically in Hong Kong by a borrower of funds which that instrument represents amounts to the provision of credit in Hong Kong because the borrower has the ability to exercise dominion over the instrument by endorsement. The source of the interest on those funds is therefore in Hong Kong.

■ Example 4.6

A Hong Kong resident borrows US dollars from a finance company in New York and that company credits a current account opened in his name with a bank in New York.

The borrower has received credit in New York because he has funds there under his control which he can draw upon by signing a cheque. Even if he draws a cheque and brings the funds to Hong Kong, the source of the interest which he pays has its origin in the funds made available to him in New York and is therefore outside Hong Kong.

The IRD endorses the "provision of credit" test as the general test for determining the source of interest in paragraph 2 of *Departmental Interpretation & Practice Notes No. 13*. The IRD does, however, note in that Practice Note that there are instances where the test is not appropriate and cites the position of a mortgage, where the source is the mortgage itself, and the situation where the interest is part of a trading transaction, in which case the source of the interest follows that of the trading profit.

The IRD also notes in paragraph 4 of *Departmental Interpretation & Practice Notes No. 13* that the "provision of credit" test is inappropriate where the loan is not a simple loan of money, but is part of a money lending business. In such circumstances, and on the authority of the Privy Council in *CIR v Orion Caribbean Limited* [1997] (1 HKRC 90-089), which is discussed further below, the IRD points out that an operations test should be adopted; that is, the source of interest in such circumstances should be determined by looking to what the recipient of the interest has done to earn the sum and where he has done it.

In practice, however, the IRD seems to consider that there are many more types of situations where the "provision of credit" test should not be applied. For example, in the case of bank deposits, the IRD takes the view that the source of the interest is the location of the branch with which the account is maintained, irrespective of where that account is physically operated or how and where the deposit funds are made available to the bank. In other words, the IRD practice is to view the interest on an account with the Hong Kong branch of a bank as having a Hong Kong source even though the account is always operated outside Hong Kong and all funds are physically deposited through an overseas branch of that bank. Conversely, interest on an account maintained with an overseas branch of a bank will be considered to have a non-Hong Kong source even if all deposits and withdrawals are made through a Hong Kong branch of the same bank. Whilst such a view may have certain practical appeal, it is difficult to consider it a logical application of the "provision of credit" test.

The adoption of the provision of credit by the IRD was reiterated in an article by the IRD published in *The Hong Kong Accountant*, the journal of the Hong Kong Society of Accountants, in January 1998. The article noted that the source of interest on a bank deposit is "*… the place where the funds are deposited with the bank …*", although it did not try to explain the practical application of this statement. Interestingly, the article also confirmed that the provision of credit test was to be applied to interest on bonds (and presumably other tradeable debt instruments) by looking to where the initial funds are received by the issuer and that subsequent transactions in those bonds, wherever they may take place, will not alter the source of the interest as determined by the initial subscription.

The reader is entitled to be confused by apparently conflicting tests and practices currently adopted. The position was considered but, arguably, further confused in *D 33/90* where the Board stated that when considering source issues, it was inappropriate to create and apply non-statutory tests such as the "provision of credit" test. Instead, the Board took the view that all factors must be considered and, in that particular case, decided that, notwithstanding the fact that the loans were denominated in US dollars and created by the handing over of cheques representing funds in US bank accounts, the source of interest was in Hong Kong because the transaction was a "Hong Kong transaction", a conclusion apparently reached on the basis that both parties were in Hong Kong and entered into the transaction in Hong Kong. That case should, however, be contrasted with the Singapore court case of *C H Pte Limited v Commissioner of Income Taxes* [1987] (1 MSTC 7022) which involved similar facts but a different conclusion was reached on the basis that the interest arose where the money was lent, and although the loan agreement was concluded in Malaysia and the proceeds were made available by the handing over of a cheque in Malaysia, that cheque was drawn on a Singapore bank account and, therefore, the loan was in reality made available in Singapore.

Subsequently, the question of the source of interest has been touched upon in other Hong Kong court decisions. In particular, the Privy Council in *CIR v Hang Seng Bank Limited* (3 HKTC 351), after observing that a broad guiding principle in determining source of profits is to look to what the taxpayer has done to earn those profits, noted that the source of interest from the lending of money was the place where "*… the money was lent …*". Although it is sometimes suggested that this is an endorsement of the "provision of credit" test, this cannot be logically inferred from the words used by the Privy Council. In any event, the Privy Council's comments were only intended as a very broad observation and were not relevant to the issue under consideration in that case. The matter was, however, considered somewhat more closely in *Orion Caribbean Limited v CIR* (1 HKRC 90-077) where, in upholding the view of the Board of Review (see *D 21/92*), the Court of Appeal agreed that the source of interest from loans was the place where the money was lent which, in turn, was determined by examining the location of the bank accounts through which the lender made the funds available. As, in that case, the lender's bank accounts were all maintained outside Hong Kong, the Court concluded that the interest had an offshore source under general principles.

This decision was, however, overturned on appeal by the Commissioner to the Privy Council (*CIR v Orion Caribbean Limited* [1997] (1 HKRC 90-089)). In doing so, the Privy Council made a number of interesting observations with regard to the question of the source of interest income, and most of these revolve around the interpretation of the words of the Lord Bridge in the *Hang Seng Bank* case (supra). Firstly, it was noted that Lord Bridge was referring to the "exploitation of property assets" when giving his examples of the source of different types of profit. The Privy Council thought that this may have been a reference to the exploitation of assets owned by the taxpayer rather than, as was the case in hand, the lending of money which had been borrowed by the taxpayer. Accordingly, the Privy Council thought it appropriate to also consider the borrowing activities, and the place where they took place, in determining the source of the interest in question.

Secondly, the Privy Council noted that even Lord Bridge had accepted that the source of profit was ultimately a question of fact to be decided in each individual case and that no simple, single, legal test can be employed to decide the question.

Finally, the Privy Council, somewhat confusingly, tried to ascertain what the company did to earn its profit and, rather than finding that it borrowed and lent money, found that it *"... allowed itself to be interposed between (the Hong Kong parent company) and the ultimate borrowers."* The Privy Council then, applying an operations type test, concluded that everything of significance in connection with the transaction was done in Hong Kong and, therefore, the profits had a Hong Kong source.

In summary, the Privy Council's decision in the *Orion Caribbean* case (supra) has cast considerable doubt on the validity of the "provision of credit" test as a broad test for determining source of interest income. Nonetheless, the decision provides only very general guidance as to how such source should be determined. Indeed, probably the most which could be said is that an operations test should be employed; in other words, that the source is the place where the operations from which the interest flow in substance take place. This is, of course, far more subjective than the relatively straight-forward "provision of credit" test; nonetheless, although following this decision the IRD amended *Departmental Interpretation & Practice Notes No. 13* and accepted that an operations test should be applied to determine the source of interest of a money lending business, they continue to consider the "provision of credit test" to be the normal determinant of the source of interest income in most other circumstances.

In an Australian case on the matter, the court, as in *D 33/90*, indicated that many factors could be relevant but seemed to place particular emphasis on the location where the loan contract is made and the place where the money is lent (see *Spotless Services Ltd. v FCT* (93 ATC 4397)). It is sub-mitted that although such a test is more subjective than the "provision of credit" test, it may be more appropriate as it is better able to deal with the myriad of differences which exist between various types of loans.

In cases where there is no advancement of money at the time of giving the credit, the question of the source of interest is more difficult, particularly if the "provision of credit" test is considered the most appropriate determinant. If, for example, X is due to pay a sum of money to Y on 30 June (such debt not being in respect of cash advanced to X) but does not pay it until 30 September, Y may charge him interest for the overdue debt. In this case it is probably appropriate to look to the nature of the debt that was payable in the first instance to determine the source of that interest as there is clearly no provision of credit in the normal sense. In *BR 20/75* such circumstances occurred where a debt arose as the result of sales by Y to X and interest was chargeable as a result of extended credit granted to X. Although the interest was charged separately by means of a bill of exchange accepted outside Hong Kong, the Board of Review held that the "interest" was inextricably bound up with, and therefore became part of, the trading transaction. Accordingly it was held that the source of the "interest" followed that of the trading profit. Somewhat similarly, in the case of interest on a debt created on the sale of shares in a company outside Hong Kong, it was held that the credit was provided outside Hong Kong, where the title to the shares changed hands, regardless of the place where the agreement was concluded (*D 5/85*).

In summary, the question of the source of interest income remains uncertain as a matter of law, and potentially in practice. The tests developed by the courts in different jurisdictions at different times vary considerably. However, presumably in an effort to add some certainty to the matter, the IRD profess to adopt the "provision of credit" test in dealing with the issue. Nonetheless, whilst the attempt to add certainty is, of course, desirable, the failure of the IRD to consistently apply this test, together with the fact that recent Hong Kong case law on the matter casts doubt upon the appropriateness of the test, means that the present situation remains far from satisfactory.

4.4.5 IRD's practice

Following the Privy Council's decisions in *CIR v Hang Seng Bank Limited* [1990] (1 HKRC 90-044) and *CIR v HK-TVB International Limited* [1992] (1 HKRC 90-064), the IRD issued, in November 1992, *Departmental Interpretation & Practice Notes No. 21 — Locality of Profits* ("DIPN 21"). This was updated and re-issued in April 1996 to reflect changes in the Commissioner's views on the issue following the decision in *CIR v Euro Tech (Far East) Ltd.* [1995] (1 HKRC 90-074) and again in March 1998 to address the decision in *CIR v Magna Industrial Company Limited* [1997] (1 HKRC 90-082). The current version of DIPN 21 is reproduced as Appendix 13 to this book. This document purports to express the IRD's views on the source of profits based on their interpretation of the legislation and case law. It must, however, be remembered that DIPN 21 is only the IRD's view of the law; it has no legally binding effect and can be challenged, if necessary, by a taxpayer in any litigation.

Paragraph 5 of DIPN 21 sets out the basic tenets from which the conclusions in the Practice Note are drawn. These are as follows:—

(i)   The question of the source of profits is a hard, practical matter of fact: These words actually came from the judgement of Isaacs J. in the 1918 case of *Nathan v FC of T* (25 CLR 183) and were preceded by the observation that the legislature intended the word source to mean what a practical man would regard as the real source. Given the very large number of cases which have been had on the issue of source of income since the *Nathan* case, it is doubtful whether the practical man's view has as much relevance as it did eighty years ago. At the very least, it is submitted, the question is now a mixture of fact and law.

(ii) The broad guiding principle is that one looks to see what the taxpayer has done to earn the profits in question and where he has done it: These words come from the Privy Council's judgement in the *Hang Seng Bank* case and are considered by the IRD to be an endorsement of an "operations" test. Care should, however, be exercised in interpreting this statement as the Privy Council further qualified it by specifically commenting on the source of different types of profits and not all of these were determined by the taxpayer's activities. Also, the statement is lacking in that it fails to consider whether the activities of overseas agents of the taxpayer can be looked to in determining the source of profits, although in the particular decision, the Privy Council clearly found that this was acceptable.

(iii)　The distinction between onshore and offshore profits is to be made by reference to gross, rather than net, profits.

(iv)　Where an item of gross profit arises in two or more places, an apportionment of that profit is possible in appropriate circumstances.

(v)　The place where investment decisions are taken is not generally relevant in determining the source of profits.

(vi)　The absence of an overseas permanent establishment does not, by itself, mean that all the profits of a Hong Kong business arise in Hong Kong. This comment is, however, qualified by the inclusion of the quote from the *HK-TVB International Limited* case where Lord Jauncy noted that *"… it can only be in rare cases that a taxpayer with a principal place of business in Hong Kong can earn profits which are not chargeable to profits tax …"*.

The last four of these tenets came directly from the Privy Council's decision in the *Hang Seng Bank* case and, apart from (iv), were all well established in case law prior to that decision.

On the basis of the above six tenets, the IRD have drawn conclusions as to the source of various types of income. Of these, perhaps the most controversial is the IRD's view on the source of trading profits. In earlier versions of DIPN 21, the IRD adopted the comments in the Privy Council's decision in the *Hang Seng Bank* case (supra) that the source of trading profits is the place where the contracts of purchase and sale are effected; DIPN 21 then went on to state that the IRD considered "effected" to mean the "… *actual steps leading to the existence of the contracts including the negotiation and in substance, conclusion of the contracts*". DIPN 21, however, ignored the Privy Council's comments on apportionment and concluded that where *either* the contract of purchase or the contract of sale are effected in Hong Kong, the whole of the profit from the transaction would be considered to arise in Hong Kong and, therefore, taxable. Many observers considered this interpretation to be too sweeping and unsupported by case law; also, it was in direct contradiction to paragraph 10 of DIPN 21 (paragraph 11 in the earlier version) which states that where an overseas company sets up a branch in Hong Kong to act as a buying office which is not involved in the sale of the goods, no liability to Profits Tax was considered to arise. Indeed, the correctness of this view was one of the points of law for consideration by the High Court in *CIR v Magna Industrial Company Limited* [1996] (1 HKRC 90-078). Although the point was ultimately not critical to the decision on the substantive issue in that case, the High Court noted firmly that the Commissioner's view, as expressed in DIPN 21, had no basis in law.

Following the Court of Appeal's decision in the *Magna* case (supra), the IRD amended DIPN 21, including the paragraph referred to above. Their view appears now to be that although the source of trading profits is generally to be determined by the place where the contracts of purchase and sale are effected, the totality of facts must be considered when determining what a taxpayer did to earn the profits in question. In particular, the IRD in paragraph 6 of DIPN 21 now refer to a number of factors other than the effecting of the purchase and sale contracts which they consider may be relevant in determining the source of trading profits. These factors were specifically mentioned by the Court of Appeal in the *Magna* case (supra) although the IRD in DIPN 21 quotes them in support of a proposition of the High Court in that case, which is interesting given that the decision of the High Court was overturned on appeal. The quoting of the Court of Appeal's comments, and the identification of the various factors to be examined is, however, presumably intended to support the suggestion by the Court of Appeal that the taking of a totality of factors approach in determining the source of trading profits is appropriate. In this regard, whilst comments by the Court of Appeal do appear to support such an approach, it must be noted that that court simply upheld the finding of the Board of Review which, in determining that the source of the profits was outside Hong Kong, held that all activities other than the sale and purchase (including invoicing, shipping and collection of payment) were ancillary in nature and not the source of the profit; in other words, although not ruling out a totality of factors approach, the Court of Appeal did not disturb the finding of the Board of Review that, at least in the case before them, it was only the purchasing and selling which were relevant in the determination of the source of the taxpayer's trading profit.

Nonetheless, DIPN 21 now further states that where *either* the purchase or sale contract is effected in Hong Kong, the IRD will initially presume that the profits are fully taxable, although the factors mentioned in paragraph 6 of DIPN 21 will be examined to finally determine the issue. In other words, the IRD have slightly modified their previous controversial view that where either the purchase or sale contract is effected in Hong Kong the resultant profit will always have a Hong Kong source, to one where it is presumed that such a profit will have a Hong Kong source but which needs to be finally determined by an examination of other factors. Given how soundly the IRD's original view was rejected by the courts in the *Magna* decisions, however, it seems unlikely that the slight modification has really gone far enough in bringing the IRD's views into line with those of the courts. Moreover, the view currently expressed in DIPN 21 is arguably of little help in resolving the issue as although it provides some guidance as to what factors may be considered relevant in determining the source of profits, it provides no guidance as to how those activities are to be weighted in arriving at the source. It must, however, be recognised that this issue has also not been properly addressed by the courts.

DIPN 21 goes on, in paragraph 9, to state that where the activities of a trading company in Hong Kong are limited to all, or any, of the following, the IRD will consider that no liability to Profits Tax arises:—

(1)   Issuing or accepting an invoice (but not an order) to or from a customer or supplier outside Hong Kong on the basis of a contract already concluded by an offshore associate.

(2)   Arranging letters of credit.

(3)   Operating a bank account and receiving and making payments.

(4)   Maintaining accounting records.

The intention of this is to continue to exempt from Profits Tax the profits of a traditional reinvoicing company (i.e. a company which enters into trading transactions with overseas group companies in order to shift profits from another jurisdiction, but which carries on no real trading activities in Hong Kong). However, the requirement that such companies not issue or accept orders in Hong Kong in order to enjoy the exemption seems overly restrictive and, if strictly enforced will undoubtedly render many true reinvoicing companies taxable.

DIPN 21 also considers, in some depth, the source of profits from manufacturing. In particular, it expresses the view that manufacturing profits arise in the place or places that the manufacturing is carried out; by implication, this suggests that the place the goods are sold is not a relevant consideration. DIPN 21 specifically recognises that the manufacturing of a product can be carried out partly in Hong Kong and partly abroad; in such circumstances, the profit can, according to DIPN 21, be apportioned to reflect the onshore and offshore elements but such an apportionment is usually to be made on a 50:50 basis, regardless of the facts of the case. This treatment is not, however, extended to situations where manufacturing is sub-contracted to a party abroad as this is not considered manufacturing abroad by the Hong Kong business. Apart from the question of apportionment, deciding whether a person's activities amount to manufacturing or trading is important also because the determination of the source of the profits from the business would be analysed differently; in this regard, see for example, *D 172/01* where the Board of Review effectively agreed with the IRD's view that where a company subcontracts out its manufacturing activities it is not to be treated as a manufacturer, and therefore the actual manufacturing activities are to be ignored, when determining the source of its profits. This decision was effectively upheld on appeal by the Court of First Instance (see *Consco Trading Company Limited v CIR* [2004] (1 HKRC 90-132)).

For a more detailed discussion of the circumstances where the IRD considers apportionment of manufacturing profits is appropriate, see paragraphs 15 and 16 of DIPN 21; see also *D 132/99* and *D 55/00* for cases where the IRD's apportionment on this basis has been upheld. Further, see *D 163/01* for a case concerning such apportionment where the taxpayer claimed that they undertook manufacturing in the Mainland of China through another company which acted as its nominee. The IRD sought to deny the benefit of apportionment on the basis that they were not convinced the taxpayer operated through the nominee. Nonetheless, once the Board of Review found, as a matter of fact, that the taxpayer did operate through the nominee, the IRD accepted the apportionment of the profits.

The source of various other types of profits are also considered in DIPN 21. These include profits from the rental and sale of real property, the sale of listed and unlisted investments, service fee income, sale or purchase commissions and certain income of financial institutions; none of the interpretations on these issues are particularly controversial, although the reader is encouraged to study this aspect of DIPN 21 in order to obtain a more practical appreciation of the IRD's view of the source of these types of profits.

More controversial perhaps are the views expressed on source of royalties (other than those taxable under Sec. 15(1)(a), (b) or (ba)) and the source of cross-border land transportation income. In the former of these, DIPN 21 suggests that the source is to be determined on the same basis as trading profits. This view is quite difficult to understand as the nature of trading profits is quite different to that of royalties, and the activities undertaken to derive the two types of income are also quite different. Nonetheless, on the basis of the decisions in the *HK-TVB International Limited* and *Lam Soon Trademark Limited* cases (supra) it seems that the source of royalties is to be determined on the basis of where the operations in respect of the business from which the royalties arise are in substance undertaken. Whether or not this is the same basic approach used to determine the source of trading profits is, therefore, largely academic.

On the question of source of cross border land transportation income, DIPN 21 states that the place of uplift of the relevant passengers or goods is the determinant, but then goes on to state that apportionment will not be permitted where the contract of carriage does not distinguish between outward and inward transportation. This seems quite unfair since on the one hand it is apparently accepted that where goods are brought into Hong Kong from abroad (i.e. Mainland China) the source of the profit is outside Hong Kong, but on the other hand an offshore claim will be denied entirely merely because the relevant contracts do not specify whether the carriage is into or out of Hong Kong, even though it may be obvious that there is uplift of goods and passengers outside Hong Kong.

In addition to manufacturing profits, DIPN 21 recognises that other types of profits can be apportioned in certain circumstances (see paragraphs 21 and 22 of DIPN 21). Again, the IRD expresses the view that such apportionment should be done on a 50:50 basis unless compelling circumstances dictate otherwise. Whilst it is appreciated that this general rule is suggested in an effort to bring simplicity and a degree of certainty to the issue, it does, of course, entirely ignore the economic reality of many situations.

The more specific issue of source of profits from electronic commerce, or trading over the internet, is considered in *Departmental Interpretation and Practice Notes No. 39*. In that document, the IRD reiterates that the general principles governing the determination of the source of profits as discussed in DIPN 21 are equally applicable to the source of profits from electronic commerce. Nonetheless, the IRD goes on to note that the place where automated server-based activities are performed (such as the provision of information about products and services, processing of on-line purchase orders, delivery of digitized products or services electronically or the processing of payments) does not, of itself, determine the source of profits. Rather, the IRD considers that such factors have to be weighed against the core business operations required to conduct electronic commerce transactions and that these are usually carried out within a physical office. Such activities would include operations in connection with the automation, management and control the functions which are undertaken electronically. The IRD is also of the view that, irrespective of the e-commerce model adopted, human control remains important in carrying on the overall business operations and, therefore, it is the location of the physical business operations, rather than the location of the server alone, which would generally determine the locality of the profits. In other words, the IRD considers that the focus in determining the source of profits from electronic commerce should be more on the physical operations rather than those operations carried out electronically.

4.5 Ascertainment of Assessable Profits

Profits Tax is levied on a person's "profits", which is not defined but is essentially an accounting concept; accordingly, the usual starting point in practice for the ascertainment of the assessable profits of a business is the profits revealed by the commercial accounts, provided that these are prepared in accordance with generally accepted accounting principles. The profit or loss disclosed by the accounts is then adjusted as required by the terms of the IRO.

The correctness of taking the commercial accounting profit and adjusting it as required by the taxing statutes was confirmed in *Usher's Wiltshire Brewery v Bruce* (6 TC 399). In *CIR v Mutual Investment Co. Ltd.* (1 HKTC 185), however, the importance of accounting principles was played down by the Privy Council which suggested instead that "profit" was to be taken as the surplus of "total receipts" over allowable expenditure. It is submitted, however, that this decision did not serve to significantly clarify the issue of how to correctly determine assessable profits as the meaning of "total receipts" was not examined other than to note it excluded amounts which are statutorily exempt from tax; moreover, the case did not discuss how, or why, the approach adopted was expected to give a different result from the adoption of the accounting profit or loss and then adjusting that figure in line with specific legislative provisions. Certainly, the *Mutual Investment* case did not provide authority for determining profit by taking "income" and then deducting allowable expenses, an approach which would have provided a clear basis for excluding from Profits Tax all capital receipts (which, on the basis of case law in other jurisdictions, are not "income"). In summary, it seems that the approach taken in the *Usher's Wiltshire Brewery* case will only give a different result from the approach adopted in the *Mutual Investment* case where an amount is a receipt of a business but is not reflected in the recipient's profit and loss account under generally accepted accounting principles and this is likely to happen only in unusual circumstances.

More recent authorities in the UK have continued to emphasise the relevance of accounting principles in determining assessable profit, but subject to overriding statutory provisions or judge made rules; see, for example, *Gallagher v Jones* (66 TC 77) and *Herbert Smith v Honour* [1999] (STC 173). The correctness of this approach has also been confirmed in Hong Kong in the *Secan* case which is discussed below. The exception from the general principle for judge made rules, while still recognised, seems to have less application currently than in the past as there appears to be a trend by the UK courts to be less inclined to depart from the general principle that assessable profits are to be ascertained on the basis of normal commercial accounting principles. The main area where disputes arise in relation to the relevance of normal commercial accounting principles is in the timing of the recognition of profits, particularly unrealised profits, and this is discussed further in section 4.5.1 below.

Although the relevance of commercial accounting principles in ascertaining assessable profits seems well established, it is interesting to note that in a recent case a dispute was decided without reference to normal accounting rules. In this regard, see *Lo Tim Fat v CIR* [2005] (1 HKRC 90-165) which involved an insurance agent who was subject to Profits Tax, but who did not prepare accounts in accordance with normal accounting principles. In a dispute over the timing of the recognition of certain payments made to him, which were conditional on continuing service for a specified period, the court decided the matter (in the IRD's favour) without any discussion of the correct accounting treatment. Even though the taxpayer did not prepare accounts in accordance with normal accounting principles (and was not required to do so), this does not appear to be a valid reason to depart from the general principle that profits should be prepared in accordance with such principles. Interestingly, if normal commercial accounting principles were looked to in order to decide the case, it is likely that the taxpayer would have been successful as HKAS 18 is unlikely to have permitted full recognition of the amount in dispute in the relevant accounting period.

As discussed, profits ascertained in accordance with normal accounting principles are subject to statutory adjustments. In this regard, the IRO deals little with the receipts side of the account except to exclude profits from the sale of capital assets, income derived from a non-Hong Kong source (see section 4.4 above) and certain other limited items, and to include certain receipts as deemed business receipts; these points are discussed in the following sections. Whether or not the sale of an asset is an adventure in the nature of trade, giving rise to a revenue profit or loss or whether it is the disposal of a capital asset, giving rise to a capital profit or loss, is a contentious area on which there is a considerable amount of UK case law and this is discussed in section 4.3.3 above.

On the expenditure side, the IRO contains various provisions which deem amounts to be deductible or non-deductible, as the case may be, and these are dealt with in detail under various headings below. There are also a number of general principles on which there is a considerable amount of law and practice and these are also covered under appropriate headings.

Accordingly, after ascertaining the profit or loss shown by commercial accounts, the next step in ascertaining the assessable profits is to add back expenses deducted in arriving at the profit or loss which are not deductible for tax purposes, and receipts which are not included in the profit and loss account but which are deemed to be taxable. Adjustments are also required to deduct any profits included in the profit and loss account but which are exempt from tax (e.g. dividends, certain capital profits or profits which have a source outside Hong Kong). Where such profits are excluded, however, it will also be necessary to treat as non-deductible any related expenditure and this may involve adopting an apportionment method, which is provided for in the IRR.

Traditionally, it was widely considered appropriate to subtract revenue expenses which had been incurred but which had not been included in the profit and loss account. In *D 58/96*, however, where the Board of Review effectively held that notwithstanding specific provisions governing deductibility of an item, the timing of that deduction could still be governed by the accounting treatment adopted. Specifically, the case concerned the deductibility of interest which had been capitalised for accounting purposes but for which a deduction was sought for tax purposes in the year in which it was incurred. The Board of Review, in denying the deduction, held that in capitalising the interest it had already been deducted, notwithstanding that a portion of that deduction was subsequently written back against unsold stock and work in progress at year end. In other words, the Board rejected the suggestion that the provisions of Secs. 16(1) and 16(1)(a) permit an interest expense to reduce assessable profits in the period in which it is incurred (assuming that the other conditions for deductibility are satisfied) irrespective of the accounting treatment, and considered that a deduction had been allowed for the amount in question notwithstanding that it had been capitalised and, therefore, only reduced the assessable profits of a future period. This decision was firmly overturned by both the Court of First Instance and the Court of Appeal in *Secan Limited v CIR*; *Ranon Limited v CIR* [1999] (1 HKRC 90-097) and *CIR v Secan Limited*; *CIR v Ranon Limited* [2000] (1 HKRC 90-103) in judgments which reaffirmed the principle that deduction of expenses is governed by the relevant specific statutory provisions of, *inter alia*, Sec. 16 and not by the accounting treatment afforded to the expense item in question. Those decisions were, however, themselves overturned by the Court of Final Appeal in *CIR v Secan Limited & Anor* [2001] (1 HKRC 90-107).

In particular, the Court of Final Appeal adopted somewhat similar logic to that of the Board of Review in that it considered that the interest in question had been "deducted" notwithstanding that it had been added back in the accounts to the value of trading stock. As with the decision of the Board of

Review, however, it is not entirely clear how this reasoning was reconciled to the wording of the relevant statutory provision which does not appear to be concerned with the accounting treatment of an expense, but rather provides for a deduction in *"… ascertaining the profits in respect of which a person is chargeable to tax …"*. That is, the statutory provision seems concerned only with deducting amounts in a computation of assessable profits and, therefore, it is difficult to see how an amount could be treated as having been "deducted" if it never reduced the taxpayer's assessable profits. Nonetheless, an explanation of the court's reasoning is possibly found in the following passage of the judgment (which was delivered by Lord Millett):

> *"But the profits of a business cannot be ascertained without deducting the expenses and outgoings incurred in making them, and … (Section 16(1)) is not needed to authorise them to be deducted. Sections 16 and 17 (which disallow certain deductions) are enacted for the protection of the revenue, not the taxpayer, and in my opinion Section 16 is to be read in a negative sense. It permits outgoings to be deducted only to the extent to which they are incurred in the relevant year."*

Put simply, the court appears to be suggesting that Sec. 16 does not authorise the deduction of expenses; rather, the deductibility of expenses flows from the expensing of them in the profit and loss account and Sec. 16 exists solely to deny a deduction for amounts so expensed but which do not meet the other requirements of that provision. Nonetheless, for this approach to deny a deduction for an expense already borne by a taxpayer requires the term "incurred" as used in Sec. 16(1) to be interpreted as meaning expensed in the profit and loss account. This, however, conflicts with the traditional case law view that an expense is incurred when it becomes due and payable or when the taxpayer has rendered themselves liable for the amount. For a further discussion of the implications of this decision, see sections 4.5.5, 4.5.6 and 4.5.8.

Following the Court of Final Appeal's decision in the *Secan* case (supra), the IRD issued *Departmental Interpretation & Practice Notes No. 40*. This document is concerned predominantly with the issue of prepaid expenses (i.e. expenses paid but which, because the benefits of the expenditure are expected to be realised partially in future years, are amortised for accounting purposes). On this substantive matter, the IRD states that the tax deduction must follow the treatment of the amount in the accounts, assuming that the accounts are prepared in accordance with normal commercial principles; nonetheless, it also makes it clear that the IRD views the *Secan* decision as providing authority for the general principle that no deduction of a revenue expense will be allowed if that expenses is not reflected in the claimant's accounts for that year.

Apart from Sec. 16, with which the *Secan* decision was concerned, there are a number of other provisions which grant a deduction for amounts which would not otherwise qualify for deduction (see section 4.5.8 below) and these must also be deducted from the accounting profit in determining assessable profit. It appears that the IRD's view that no deduction can be allowed in respect of an amount not expensed in ascertaining the profit under commercial accounting principles is not adopted where an amount is deemed deductible under a provision other than Sec. 16.

The net result of the above adjustments is an "adjusted profit" for Profits Tax purposes to which the relevant tax rate is applied. Note, however, that certain limited types of profits are taxed at concessionary rates and where such concessions apply, the adjusted profit may need to be further apportioned in order to ascertain the total tax payable.

In the case of non-residents carrying on business in Hong Kong or having a source of assessable income in Hong Kong and the profits therefrom are not readily ascertainable by the usual methods, there are provisions in the IRO and IRR for ascertaining the measure of assessable profits. Likewise, in the case of certain special types of business there are specific rules for the ascertainment of assessable profits (see section 4.7).

4.5.1 When income and profit arises

It is important to ascertain the time at which an item of income or profit arises for tax purposes as this may not always coincide with the accounting treatment adopted and an adjustment may, therefore, be required.

Because Sec. 14 imposes tax on profit which is essentially an accounting concept, in most cases the recognition of an amount of profit or income for accounting purposes will determine the timing of the amount's derivation for tax purposes. Nonetheless, disputes and uncertainties do occasionally arise over recognition of timing of derivation for tax purposes, although these usually concern amounts which are unrealised, but which have been recognised for accounting purposes.

One reason for the uncertainty as to the treatment of unrealised profits can be traced to the decision in *BSC Footwear v Ridgway* (47 TC 495) where it was suggested by the House of Lords that although assessable profits are generally to be determined by applying the principles of commercial accounting, this is subject to the well established but non-statutory rule that neither profit nor loss may be anticipated. Care must, however, be exercised when interpreting this principle to distinguish anticipation of a profit or loss from the situation where a profit or loss has crystallised but only payment is deferred.

Nonetheless, the principle derived from the *BSC Footwear* case seems to have found less favour in more recent decisions. See for example, *Gallagher v Jones* (66 TC 77) and *Herbert Smith v Honour* ([1999] STC 173) where the court took the view that profit determined in accordance with ordinary accounting principles was the correct basis for determining profit for tax purposes and should not be considered to involve an anticipation of profit or loss. Caution is required in applying these recent UK cases to Hong Kong, however, because of differences in the statutory provisions. In particular, although those cases are probably relevant for the purpose of determining gross profits for Hong Kong purposes, the existence of Sec. 16 could be interpreted as suggesting that the deductibility of expenses is to be determined solely in accordance with that provision, rather than by the accounting treatment adopted. Nonetheless, the Court of Final Appeal in *CIR v Secan Limited & Anor.* [2001] (1 HKRC 90-107) suggested that Sec. 16 shouldn't be seen as authorising the deduction of an amount not expensed for accounting purposes. For a further discussion of that decision, see section 4.5.6.

From time to time, disputes arise as to the assessability of unrealised foreign exchange gains (and deductibility of unrealised foreign exchange losses). See, for example, *D 36/86* where it was held that such unrealised gains were not assessable, although contrast this with the decision in *D 35/86* where the opposite conclusion was reached. Although the decision in *D 36/86* was arguably correct at the time on the basis of the authority of earlier cases, including the *BSC Footwear* case and *Willingale v International Commercial Bank Ltd* (52 TC 242) which is discussed below, the later authorities of *Gallagher v Jones* and *Herbert Smith v Honour* would perhaps suggest that *D 35/86* was, in fact, the correctly decided of the two cases.

Willingale v International Commercial Bank Ltd. (52 TC 242) was concerned with anticipated discounts on bills of exchange which matured after the balance sheet date and the Court decided that such amounts, although recognised in the taxpayer's accounts for accounting purposes, could be excluded for tax purposes and brought into the tax computation for the following period. This decision is, interestingly, not necessarily in conflict with the later decisions of *Gallagher v Jones* and *Herbert Smith v Honour* as it was accepted that although recognition of the amounts for accounting purposes was permissible under generally accepted accounting principles, so would have been the exclusion of such amounts. In other words, there was no accounting standard which explicitly dictated whether such amounts should be recognised or not for accounting purposes; accordingly, it was held to be permissible to adopt one treatment for accounting purposes and another for tax purposes.

Another type of unrealised profits which can give rise to disputes is gains from the increase in value of securities. This has become more of an issue in recent years following the introduction in 1999 of the Statement of Standard Accounting Practice 24 issued by the Hong Kong Society of Accountants. In particular, under the benchmark treatment prescribed by that accounting standard, a broad range of securities are reflected in a company's accounts at fair value, with any increases in fair value over the reporting period being reflected as profit in the company's profit and loss account. Because the increases in value are recorded as profit, notwithstanding that such profit is unrealised, it appears that the amounts are, *prima facie*, assessable to Profits Tax unless the source of the unrealised gains is outside Hong Kong or the relevant securities are capital assets. Whilst it would appear possible to argue that such unrealised gains should not, on the basis of the decisions in the *BSC Footwear* case and *Willingale v International Commercial Bank Limited*, be assessable, for the reasons discussed above it seems likely that those authorities would be rejected in favour of the approach taken in the later cases of *Gallagher v Jones* and *Herbert Smith v Honour*. Certainly, the IRD has a stated policy that where unrealised profits are recognised pursuant to this accounting standard, there is no basis for excluding them for tax purposes (see the Tax Bulletin issued on 31 October 2000 by the Hong Kong Society of Accountants in relation to the meeting held on 3 March 2000 between the Society and the Inland Revenue Department).

For completeness, it should be noted that the benchmark treatment described above under Statement of Standard Accounting Practice 24 was not mandatory, and under the alternative treatment any unrealised gains were reflected directly in the balance sheet rather than passing through the profit and loss account; as such, the issue of taxation of unrealised gains was avoided. Nonetheless, Statement of Standard Accounting Practice 24 has now largely been superseded by Hong Kong Accounting Standard 32 and Hong Kong Accounting Standard 39. Together, these two new standards require a large range of financial assets and liabilities to be reflected in an enterprise's accounts at fair value, with movements in such value often being required to be reflected in the profit and loss account. In response to the promulgation of these new standards, the IRD issued *Departmental Interpretation & Practice Notes No. 42*, which is reproduced as Appendix 15. In that document, the IRD reaffirm their view that the accounting treatment of an item is to be followed in ascertaining the person's assessable profits, unless that treatment is overridden by a specific statutory exemption. As a result, the changes in profit recognition brought about by the new accounting standards will result in a change in the way profits from the types of transactions dealt with in those standards are assessed. Nonetheless, profits which have a non-Hong Kong source or are capital in nature will still generally be exempt from tax.

The timing of the derivation of interest is also somewhat uncertain. Although interest is usually calculated on the basis of the number of days or months for which the principal balance is outstanding, the relevant agreements normally provide that the interest is actually to become payable on specified dates. On the basis of the *BSC Footwear* and *Willingale v International Commercial Bank Limited* cases, which suggested that only realised profits are taxable, it would seem that interest should be taxable only in the year of assessment when it becomes due and payable. In *D 73/91*, however, it was held that interest accrued for Profits Tax purposes on a day by day basis; In coming to this conclusion, the Board of Review paid particular attention to the wording of Sec. 15(1)(f), where the relevant phrase is "... *received by or accrued to* ...", rather than the normal *"arising"* or *"derived"* as used in Sec. 14. It is unclear whether the Board would have reached a different conclusion if the terms used in Sec. 14 had been the relevant test, although this is perhaps unlikely as the terms *"arising," "derived"* and *"accruing"* have been held to be synonymous in *C of T (NSW) v Kirk* [1900] (AC 588), which has been quoted with approval in a number of Board of Review decisions.

In a case concerning property sales by instalments (*CIR v Montana Lands Limited* (HKTC 334)), the profit was regarded as arising in pro-rata amounts as the instalments were received, although this decision seems to have been influenced by the fact that the profit was accounted for in that manner. Accordingly, it seems likely that where all of the profit is accounted for in the basis period in which the sale is made, the whole of that profit would also be taxable in the same period. Indeed, such a case came before the Board of Review in *D 103/99* where the Board upheld the authority of the *Montana Lands* case but nonetheless found the whole of the profits from the properties sold by instalments as taxable in the basis period in which the sale took place. The Board of Review reasoned that as the profits had been paid to the taxpayer's parent company as an interim dividend in the basis period in which the sale took place, it was not possible to consider those profits as unrealised. This reasoning appears based on a presumption that taxable profits are to follow profits as disclosed in a company's statutory accounts and, although there is certainly recent judicial authority which supports such a presumption (see, for example, *Herbert Smith v Honour* ([1999] STC 173)), it is interesting to note that earlier in the judgment the Board of Review had specifically accepted that, as a matter of law, a profit only becomes taxable when it is due and payable.

The timing of the recognition of profit from property development in Hong Kong is dealt with in *Departmental Interpretation & Practice Notes No. 1*, which is reproduced as Appendix 1. In particular, the IRD accepts that profit is treated as arising when the sale and purchase agreement is capable of completion by performance and the purchaser can be given possession. In the case of a completed property, this would generally be the time of execution of the sale and purchase agreement. It is, however, common for sale and purchase agreements to be entered into during the construction of a property and in such circumstances the IRD accepts that the profit will only be considered to arise when the Occupation Permit is respect of the property is issued by the Building Authority.

In the case of the sale of goods it is a question of fact and of law when the sale takes place and it is irrelevant that payment may be received much later. Furthermore, where it is subsequently agreed to make an additional payment, that payment relates back to the original date of sale per *Frodingham Ironstone Mines v Stewart* (16 TC 728). Nonetheless, as noted elsewhere, more modern authorities would suggest that the timing of the assessability of such profits is to be determined simply by the correct accounting treatment.

Where payment is received in advance of the rendering of the related services and it is accounted for as unearned income (i.e. as a balance sheet item), it is possible to defer recognition for tax purposes until the income is reflected in the profit and loss account; specific authority for this is found in *Arthur Murray (NSW) Pty. Ltd. v CIR* (14 ATD 98), although it arguably follows from the basic principle of Sec. 14 which only seeks to tax "profits" and, therefore, any amount not considered profit under generally accepted accounting principles (which the amount should not be if excluded from the profit and loss account) should not be taxable unless caught by one of the deeming provisions. Note that this was essentially the position in *Lo Tim Fat v CIR* [2005] (1 HKRC 90-165); however, the taxpayer, as an individual, did not prepare accounts in accordance with normal accounting principles. In deciding that the amounts received but which were refundable if the taxpayer's service did not continue for a specified period were nonetheless assessable in full, the court did not consider the correct accounting treatment of the amount (which would likely be not to recognise them fully), but decided the matter solely on the basis of an old UK authority. Given the increasing reliance on normal accounting principles to ascertain assessable profits, the failure of the court to consider accounting principles is noteworthy.

Although there is no statutory foundation for the practice, accounts for some professions are prepared and accepted for Profits Tax purposes on a cash, rather than an accruals, basis.

4.5.2 Treatment of capital profits

In many tax jurisdictions, capital receipts or profits are excluded from the charge to income tax, although they may be subject to a separate capital gains tax regime. Under the IRO, however, Sec. 14 excludes only profits from the sale of capital assets and, therefore, in the circumstances where a receipt is of a capital nature but is not from the sale of an asset it seems there is no authority to exclude it if it arises from the trade, profession or business. This point has been considered by the Privy Council in the case of *CIR v Far East Stock Exchange* (HKTC 1036) and although that case was decided on another point, the Privy Council appeared to suggest that the exclusion in Sec. 14 was not to be read any wider than its literal meaning.

In practice, however, the IRD appears to accept the exclusion of a wide range of capital receipts, although whether this is a concessional extension of the specific exclusion in Sec. 14 or stems from a view that capital receipts do not arise from the carrying on of a person's trade or business (i.e. by their nature they arise outside the ordinary course of such business) is not clear. If, however, the practice stems from the latter view, it is arguable that the exclusion in Sec. 14 would not be necessary, other than for the avoidance of doubt, as the sale of a capital asset is not a transaction in the normal course of a person's trade or business.

If the exclusion from Profits Tax contained in Sec. 14 is to be read literally as applying only to profits from the "sale" of capital assets, it could not be relied upon to exempt a compensation payment which was of a capital nature, such as an amount received for the destruction or impairment of a capital asset or a contract which formed the essence of a business; again, however, it is open to argument whether such an amount is a receipt or profit from a trade or business or a receipt from the loss or diminution in a trade or business. In this regard, see, for example, *D 12/90* where a lump sum compensation payment for giving up a part of the taxpayer's business was held to be of a revenue nature and taxable. Compare this, however, with the decision in *D 64/98* where the opposite conclusion was reached. These two contrasting decisions merely serve to emphasise that, like many other tax issues, the issue of the nature of a compensation receipt will depend largely on the facts of the particular case. See also *D 33/95* for a case where a payment received under a rental guarantee granted in connection with the purchase of a property was considered revenue in nature and taxable. For a case regarding the assessability of compensation received by a property investment company on the early termination of a lease, see *D 170/98*. In that case, the Board of Review rejected the assertion that the amount was paid for the impairment of a capital asset, being the lease over the property, on the grounds that the taxpayer's capital asset was the property itself rather than the lease and there was no evidence of impairment of that asset.

Examples of other types of receipts which could be capital in nature, but which may not be from the sale of a capital asset, include restrictive covenant payments, profits on disposal of certain futures contracts and exchange gains; for a discussion as to the nature of the latter of these, see section 4.5.7 below.

4.5.3 Other excluded profits

In addition to profits from the sale of capital assets (and, possibly, other capital items), excluded in arriving at adjusted profits are:

(1) **Profits not arising in or derived from Hong Kong:** The words of Sec. 14 specifically provide that only profits arising in or derived from Hong Kong are chargeable to profits tax.

(2) **Dividends from corporations which are chargeable to Profits Tax:** These amounts are excluded by Sec. 26(a), the wording of which seems to imply that a dividend from a company which is itself not subject to Profits Tax (i.e. because it does not carry on business in Hong Kong or derives only "offshore" or otherwise non-taxable profits), may fall outside of this exemption. In practice, however, the IRD treats all dividends as non-taxable; this may be because a company which carries on business in Hong Kong but derives only exempt profits is nonetheless "chargeable" to Profits Tax but just has no assessable profits, and a dividend from a company not carrying on a business in Hong Kong has a non-Hong Kong source and, therefore, falls into the exclusion in (1) above.

(3) **Profit already charged to Profits Tax in the name of another person:** Such amounts are excluded by Sec. 26(b) which might apply, for example where a company is a member of a partnership. The partnership is independently assessed on its profits (see section 4.7.9) and the company will, of course, bring its share of profits into its accounts. It would, however, be unfair to also subject the company to Profits Tax on those profits and Sec. 26(b) operates to avoid this inequity. Although this provision effectively only allows profits to be taken into account once, in cases of disputes as to who actually derived certain profits it is not unusual for the IRD to raise alternative assessments in respect of the same amounts on different taxpayers; this practice was held to be acceptable in *Nina T. H. Wang v CIR* [1992] (1 HKRC 90-059) and [1994] (1 HKRC 90-072) and, therefore, would appear not to be

precluded by this provision, at least not until one of the alternative assessments becomes final and conclusive.

(4) **Interest earned on Tax Reserve Certificates:** Interest on Tax Reserve Certificates is specifically excluded by Sec. 26A(1)(a). Tax Reserve Certificates are discussed in more depth in section 10.6.2.

(5) **Interest arising on certain Government bonds:** Interest arising on any bonds issued by the Government under the *Loans Ordinance* or the *Loans (Government Bonds) Ordinance* is specifically excluded from the calculation of assessable profits by Sec. 26A(1)(b).

(6) **Gains on the sale of certain Government bonds:** Any profit on the sale, disposal or redemption on maturity or presentment of any bonds of the type described in (5) is excluded from adjusted profits by Sec. 26A(1)(c).

(7) **Interest or profit on Exchange Fund debt instruments:** Any interest which is paid or payable, and any profit on the sale, disposal, or redemption on maturity of an Exchange Fund debt instrument is excluded by Secs. 26A(1)(d) and (e) respectively.

An Exchange Fund debt instrument is an instrument issued under the *Exchange Fund Ordinance* which evidences a deposit in Hong Kong dollars into the Exchange Fund, being an instrument recognising an obligation to pay a stated sum with or without interest and which is transferable in a manner as laid down by the Monetary Authority. An instrument is widely defined as not only the usual document but also entries in books of account or information stored in a computer (Sec. 26A(2)).

(8) **Interest or profit on certain debt agency instruments:** Interest paid or payable on a Hong Kong dollar denominated multi-lateral debt agency instrument is specifically excluded by Sec. 26A(1)(f). Similarly, any profit on the sale, disposal or redemption on maturity of such an instrument is excluded by Sec. 26A(1)(g). Multilateral agency debt instrument means an instrument issued by one of the institutions listed in Schedule 6, Part II, which are currently the following:—

- The Asian Development Bank
- The International Bank for Reconstruction and Development
- The International Finance Corporation
- The European Investment Bank
- The European Bank for Reconstruction and Development
- The Inter-American Development Bank
- The Nordic Investment Bank

- The European Company for the Financing of Railroad Rolling Stock
- The Council of Europe Social Development Fund
- The African Development Bank

An instrument for this purpose is defined in Schedule 6, Part I, as:—

(a)   a bill of exchange as defined in Section 3 of the *Bills of Exchange Ordinance*;

(b)   a promissory note as defined in Section 89 of the *Bills of Exchange Ordinance*;

(c)   any other instrument (which has the same meaning as used in (7) above) which evidences a debt, whether bearer or to order, with or without interest and which can be transferred by delivery with or without endorsement.

(9)   **Certain income and profits received by or accrued to qualifying collective investment vehicles:** Sec. 26A(1A) specifically excludes sums derived by particular classes of persons in respect of a "specified investment scheme".

The classes of persons to whom this exemption applies are:—

(a)   mutual fund corporations and unit trusts which are authorized under Sec. 15 of the *Securities Ordinance*. Sec. 26A(2) gives the terms "mutual fund corporation" and "unit trust" the meaning as defined in the *Securities Ordinance*;

(b)   mutual fund corporations and unit trusts established outside Hong Kong which the Commissioner considers are *bona fide*, widely held and comply with the requirements of a supervisory authority within an acceptable regulatory regime; and

(c)   persons chargeable to Profits Tax in respect of any other similar collective investment scheme which the Commissioner considers is *bona fide*, widely held and complies with the requirements of a supervisory authority within an acceptable regulatory regime.

A "specified investment scheme" is defined in Sec. 26A(1A)(b) as essentially any investment made in accordance with the constitutive documents of the relevant mutual fund corporations, unit trust or similar collective investment scheme which were approved:—

(i)   in the case of a person within the definition of (a) above, by the Hong Kong Securities and Futures Commission; or

(ii)   in the case of a person within the definition of (b) or (c) above, by the supervisory authority within the acceptable regulatory regime.

The terms *"bona fide,"* "widely held" and "supervisory authority within an acceptable regulatory regime" are not defined in the legislation for the purpose of this provision. Nonetheless, the Commissioner has provided his view of the interpretation of these terms in *Departmental Interpretation & Practice Notes No. 20*. In particular, the Commissioner states that a scheme may be presumed to be *"bona fide* widely held" if at no time during the relevant year of assessment were all the units or shares held by fewer than 50 persons *and* at no time during that year did fewer than 21 persons hold units or shares that entitled those holders, directly or indirectly, to 75% or more of the income or property of the scheme. However, a scheme may still be considered as bona fide widely held, even if it does not meet those benchmarks, if it is clear from its constitutive documents and other relevant material that it was established with a view to wide public participation and genuine efforts are being made to achieve that objective.

In determining whether a scheme complies with the requirements of a "supervisory authority within an acceptable regulatory regime," the Commissioner will consider whether the regulatory regime lays down standards comparable to those contained in the Hong Kong Securities and Futures Commission's Code on Unit Trusts and Mutual Funds ("the Code") and actively promotes compliance with those standards. Nonetheless, in the absence of evidence to the contrary, the Commissioner will consider that a scheme is adequately regulated if it is of a kind listed in Appendix A1 to the Code and has received recognition of such status from the supervisory authority corresponding to the Hong Kong Securities and Futures Commission in the jurisdiction concerned.

For schemes which do not meet the Commissioner's benchmark criteria as widely held and adequately supervised, an application can still be made to the Commissioner, on a case by case basis, for an advance ruling that the scheme be treated as qualifying for the exemption. Details of what evidence is required to support such applications is listed in paragraphs 23, 24 and 26 of *Departmental Interpretation & Practice Notes No. 20*.

Apart from this specific exemption, there is also the question of whether a unit trust can be charged to Profits Tax at all (see section 4.3.1).

Despite the concessions granted by Sec. 26A(1A), it is clear that not all mutual funds, unit trusts and similar collective investment vehicles qualify for the exemptions. This has caused uncertainties within the managed fund industry and, as a result of this, the Financial Secretary announced in his 2003–04 Budget Speech that the IRO was to be amended to exempt offshore funds from Profits Tax, in order to bring Hong Kong into line with other major find management centres. This initiative, after consultation with the fund management industry, resulted in the introduction of Secs. 20AB, 20AC, 20AD and 20AE which together provide exemptions for all non-residents (i.e. not just managed funds) in respect of profits from a specified range of transaction provided certain conditions are met. A discussion of these exemptions can be found under point (17) below.

(10) **Certain distributions received by a lender under a stock borrowing and lending arrangement:** Where a stock lender receives a payment, in accordance with a stock borrowing and lending agreement, which is in respect of an amount which would have been received by, but not subject to Profits Tax in the hands of, the lender if the stock had not been lent, Sec. 15E(3) operates to exclude those receipts from the charge to Profits Tax. In other words, the provision accords the same treatment to amounts received by the borrower of stock which are passed to the lender, as would have applied had the stock not been lent. The types of distributions to which these provisions apply are interest, dividends, bonus shares, payments by the trustee of a unit trust (other than in respect of a redemption, realisation or liquidation) and units in a unit trust; the provision does not require the exact distribution received by the borrower to be passed to the lender and the provision will equally apply where identical property is distributed. A stock borrowing and lending arrangement is extensively defined for the purpose of this provision in Secs. 15E(1), (8) and (9) and Sec. 19(16) of the *Stamp Duty Ordinance*. The first point to note about the provisions are that they apply only in respect of stock traded on the Stock Exchange of Hong Kong or stock which, although not so traded, has been notified by the Commissioner pursuant to Sec. 15E(8) as being included within the term "specified securities" the purpose of the provisions. The power of the Commissioner to effectively establish a category of "specified securities" for the purposes of the provisions is designed to allow the development of a market in borrowing and lending overseas securities without adverse tax implications. The provisions are of particular relevance in respect

of overseas stocks as most gains and profits from such stocks would have an offshore source and, therefore, be non-taxable; however, in the absence of these provisions, it is by no means certain that compensatory payments received in connection with a borrowing and lending of overseas securities would also qualify for exemption.

The Commissioner exercised his power under Sec. 15E(8) in August 1996, to define as "specified securities" for the purpose of the provision, a wide range of securities where associated parties are not involved (see discussion below). The Commissioner's order in this regard is contained in *Departmental Interpretation & Practice Notes No. 10*. The securities so specified are:—

(a)   any debt or equity security listed on any stock exchange or over-the-counter market recognised by the Commissioner for the purpose of the provision;

(b)   any unlisted debt securities issued or guaranteed to third parties by a listed company or a 50% or more owned affiliate of such a company;

(c)   any unlisted sovereign debt (including government agency or multilateral agency debt or debt guaranteed by a multilateral agency or sovereign government); and

(d)   any unlisted debt or equity securities issued pursuant to a private placement authorised by the Hong Kong Securities and Futures Commission or a similar body in another jurisdiction.

The above covers most non-Hong Kong securities which are marketable anywhere in the world. As noted, however, such securities are not "specified securities" where associated parties are involved. The Commissioner considers associated parties are involved if, under what would otherwise be a stock borrowing and lending agreement, the lender is an associate of the borrower or it is intended by any of the parties to the transaction that all or any of the securities will be on lent to an associate of the lender. Furthermore, if the lender, borrower or a subsequent borrower is a trustee of a trust, or a corporation controlled by such a trustee, such lender or borrower will, for the purpose of determining whether associates are involved, be considered each of the trustee, the corporation and the beneficiary under the trust. For the purpose of the provision, "associate" is given the meaning as defined in Sec. 21A.

The Commissioner goes on to say, however, that parties which are associated will nonetheless be deemed not to be associated where the parties are securities dealing and underwriting firms (and their at least 50% owned affiliates) which are regulated by the Hong Kong Securities and Futures Commission or a similar supervisory body in another jurisdiction.

Finally, the Commissioner in *Departmental Interpretation & Practice Notes No. 26* states that he will consider, on a case by case basis, applications to have securities treated as "specified securities" where associates are involved. Such applications will, however, only be granted where the Commissioner is satisfied that the transaction is *bona fide*, entered into on an arm's-length basis and undertaken for a purpose other than the obtaining of a tax benefit.

See also *Departmental Interpretation & Practice Notes No. 27* which also deals with this provision.

(11) **Certain compensatory payments made pursuant to a stock borrowing and lending arrangement:** Pursuant to Sec. 15E(4), certain compensatory payments made by a stock borrower to a stock lender in respect of a distribution made or the grant of a right or option, which would otherwise have been distributed or granted to the lender had the stock not been lent, are excluded from the charge to Profits Tax in the hands of the lender. In particular, such amounts are deemed not taxable where, had the recipient received the underlying distribution, right or option himself and immediately disposed of it for an amount equal to the compensatory payment, no liability to Profits Tax would have arisen. Where, however, an amount subject to Profits Tax would have arisen under the conditions specified in the previous sentence, an equivalent amount is deemed taxable. For these purposes, "distribution" and "stock borrowing and lending arrangement" have the same meaning as in the previous paragraph and "option" means an option respectively to acquire shares or units in a unit trust and "right" means a right to acquire shares, units in a unit trust or an option over such shares or units. See also *Departmental Interpretation & Practice Notes No. 27*.

(12) **Any profit derived (or loss sustained) under a stock borrowing or lending arrangement:** Profits or losses, other than fees, derived by either a borrower or a lender are excluded from the calculation of assessable profits. This is achieved, in the case of a lender, by deeming the transaction to have never taken place (Sec. 15E(2)) and, in the case of a borrower, by deeming the borrowing and return to have taken place at the market value of the stock at the time of the borrowing (Sec. 15E(5)). For this purpose, a stock borrowing

and lending arrangement has the same meaning as in the two previous paragraphs. This provision has only limited application as under a stock borrowing and lending arrangement of the type concerned, it would not be usual for either the borrower or the lender to account for an acquisition or disposal of stock as there would be no intention to change the beneficial ownership of the stock and, therefore, no profit would be reflected in the accounts; accordingly, there would be no profit to be excluded by the provision. In other words, as there are no legislative provisions which deem a disposal to have taken place when the legal ownership of stock changes, the mere lending of stock to enable the borrower to settle a stock exchange transaction, with an intention that equivalent stock be returned, would not be expected to result in the derivation of any profit (other than a fee) to which this exclusion provision could apply. See also *Departmental Interpretation & Practice Notes No. 27*.

(13) **Amounts paid or credited to a service company or trust:** Where a service company or trust has derived an amount in respect of services of an individual and that individual is deemed under Sec. 9A(1) to have derived those amounts personally, Sec. 9A(5)(a) specifically exempts those amounts from the charge to profits tax in the hands of the service company or trust. This provision ensures that where Sec. 9A(1) operates to look through a service company or trust and tax the underlying individual on the amounts in question, there is no double taxation through also assessing the service company or trust on those amounts. For a more detailed discussion of this provision, see section 3.8.1.

(14) **Interest and gains on qualifying medium term debt instruments:** Although not strictly an exemption, Sec. 14A(1) effectively operates to exempt one half of any profits derived by way of interest on, or gain or profit on the sale, other disposal or redemption on maturity or presentment of, a qualifying medium term debt instrument; the provision achieves this by halving the effective rate of Profits Tax on these amounts. A debt instrument for this purpose is an instrument within the terms of Schedule 6, Part I of the IRO and which meets the additional requirements specified in Sec. 14A(4).
Schedule 6, Part I covers:—
- a bill of exchange as defined in Sec. 3 of the *Bills of Exchange Ordinance*;
- a promissory note as defined in Sec. 89 of the *Bills of Exchange Ordinance*; and

- any other instrument which evidences an obligation to pay a stated or determinable amount to bearer or to order, on or before a fixed time, with or without interest, being an instrument by the delivery of which, with or without endorsement, the right to receive that stated or determinable amount, with or without interest, is transferable.

Sec. 14A(4) requires that the debt instrument:—

(a) is in respect of a debt issue, the entirety of which has been lodged with and cleared by the Central Moneymarket Unit of the Hong Kong Monetary Authority;

(b) has at all relevant times a credit rating acceptable to the Hong Kong Monetary Authority from a rating agency recognized by the Hong Kong Monetary Authority. Under Sec. 14A(5)(a), however, the Financial Secretary may order that this requirement not apply to debt instruments issued by such person as specified in the order. The Hong Kong Monetary Authority has advised that the following ratings are acceptable for the purposes of this provision: BBB– from Fitch IBCA, BBB+ from Rating and Investment Information, Inc., Baa3 from Moody's, BBB– from Standard & Poor's, BBB– from Duff & Phelps Credit Rating Co. or BBB+ from Thomson Bank Watch;

(c) has a minimum denomination of HK$500,000 (or its equivalent in foreign currency) if issued before 1 April 1999, or HK$50,000 (or its equivalent in foreign currency) if issued on or after 1 April 1999. Again, however, the Financial Secretary may order a different minimum denomination in respect of debt instruments issued by such person as is specified in the order. The Financial Secretary has, in fact, issued an order pursuant to this power. Under the order, the minimum denomination requirement is reduced to HK$50,000 (or its equivalent in foreign currency) in respect of instruments issued before 1 April 1999 by the MTR Corporation Limited, the Airport Authority, the Kowloon-Canton Railway Corporation or The Hong Kong Mortgage Corporation Limited. Of course, because of the reduced minimum denomination requirements which generally apply from 1 April, 1999, there is no need for the Financial Secretary's order to apply to instruments issued after that date;

(d) is issued to the public in Hong Kong. The meaning of this provision is not defined and no guidance as to its interpretation has been given by the IRD. Nonetheless, it is expected that the IRD will be more concerned with ensuring that the issue is not closely held, rather than the extent to which the issue is marketed in Hong Kong;

(e)   if issued in scripless form would nonetheless qualify under Sec. 14A if, in fact, it had been issued in physical form; and

(f)   is issued on or after 24 May 1996.

A medium term debt instrument is defined in Sec. 14A(4) as a debt instrument which is either:

(1)   issued before 5 March 2003 with an original maturity of not less than five years or is undated, and which cannot be redeemed within five years of its issue; or

(2)   issued on or after 5 March 2003, has an original maturity of between three and seven years or is undated, and which can be redeemed only between three and seven years after issue.

This definition has its origins in changes to the provisions first announced by the Financial Secretary in his 2003/04 Budget Speech. Prior to that date, the provision applied only to instruments which, *inter alia*, met the conditions in paragraph (1) of the above definition. In the 2003/04 Budget Speech, however, the Financial Secretary announced that with effect from that day (5 March 2003), a distinction would be made between long term debt instruments (essentially those with maturities of greater than seven years) the interest and profits on maturity or redemption of which would be completely exempt from tax, and medium term debt instruments (generally those with maturities of between three and seven years) which would continue to enjoy the existing exemption of one half of the normal Profits Tax rate. Subsequently, the above definition was introduced along with Secs. 26A(1)(h) and 26A(1)(i) which together grant the full exemption for long term debt instruments (see below).

(15) **Interest and gains on qualifying long term debt instruments.** With effect from the 2003/04 year of assessment, Sec. 26A(1)(h) was introduced to provide an exemption for interest on long term debt instruments. Concurrently, Sec. 26A(1)(i) was enacted to provide an exemption for any gain on the sale, other disposal, redemption on maturity or presentment of a long term debt instrument. These provisions were in effect an extension and enhancement of the concessions contained in Sec. 14A (see paragraph 14 above) for longer term debt instruments and were first foreshadowed in the Financial

Secretary's 2003/04 Budget Speech. Indeed, Sec. 26(2) defines a long term debt instrument as a debt instrument as defined in Sec. 14A that is issued on or after 5 March 2003 with an original maturity of at least seven years or is undated, and cannot be redeemed within seven years from the date of issue. Because the term "debt instrument" takes the meaning given to the term by Sec. 14A(4), in order to enjoy the exemption an instrument must meet all of the conditions specified in Sec. 14A in relation to, *inter alia*, credit ratings and minimum denominations which are discussed under point (14) above.

(16) **Interest on bank deposits:** interest (denominated in any currency) which accrued on or after 22 June 1998 on deposits with, or on certificates of deposit issued by, authorized institutions is effectively exempt from Profits Tax. Authorized institution for this purpose is as defined in the *Banking Ordinance* and means a bank or restricted license bank licensed under that ordinance, or a deposit-taking company registered under that ordinance. This exemption technically only applies to amounts derived by corporations carrying on a trade, profession or business in Hong Kong (other than financial institutions, the meaning of which is discussed in section 4.7.7) and persons other than corporations who carry on a trade, profession or business in Hong Kong where the interest is in respect of the funds of that trade, profession or business. Except for amounts derived by a financial institution, however, it is only in such circumstances that interest income is ever subject to Profits Tax.

This exemption flows from an order made by the Chief Executive in Council under Sec. 87. Technically, the order does not exempt the income from Profits Tax, but exempts any person who derives such amounts from the payment of tax in respect thereof. In other words, the amounts remain chargeable to tax, but an exemption is granted from payment of that tax. One consequence of the amounts remaining technically assessable to Profits Tax is that without further provisions, any expenses incurred in connection with the derivation of the amounts would remain deductible as they would be incurred in earning assessable profits and, therefore, would continue to meet the requirements of Sec. 16(1) (see section 4.5.5). To deal with this, however, the Chief Executive's order provides that it is only the amount of tax on interest net of attributable expenses which is exempt from payment. Another consequence of the amounts remaining technically chargeable to tax is that where a deposit is used to secure a borrowing by the person making the deposit (or an associate of that person) the interest expense on such borrowing would, contrary to the intention of Secs. 16(2)(c), (d) and (e) (see section 4.5.9.3), continue to be deductible, assuming all other conditions for deductibility were met. Again, however, the Chief Executive's order addresses this by denying the exemption to interest on a deposit which is used to secure or guarantee a loan, the interest on which qualifies as deductible by meeting the conditions of either Sec. 16 (2)(c), (d) or (e) and the restriction on deductibility in Sec. 16 (2A) does not apply.

As noted, the Chief Executive's order grants an exemption from payment of tax on qualifying interest income, but technically does not provide that interest has assessable to Profits Tax. This is because the order was made pursuant to Sec. 87 which allows the Chief Executive to exempt any person from the payment of tax, rather than by enacting a specific statutory exemption. The exemption was presumably granted in this manner to permit it to take effect quickly by bypassing the legislative process, and also to allow it to be withdrawn quickly if desired. Nonetheless, for practical purposes any interest income within the terms of the order is treated as exempt profits by the IRD in that it is excluded from the calculation of assessable profit. Practical examples of how the IRD treat the amounts, as well as a discussion of other aspects of the Chief Executive's order, can be found in *Departmental Interpretation & Practice Notes No. 34.*

(17) **Specified profits of non-residents:** In 2006, the *Revenue (Profits Tax Exemption for Offshore Funds) Ordinance 2006* was enacted to amend the IRO to exempt non-residents from Profits Tax on profits from specified types of transactions. The exemptions provided by this legislation (but not the anti avoidance provisions discussed below) have retrospective effect from the 1996/97 year of assessment and specific provisions are included to allow the reopening of previous assessments to give effect to the new provisions and to allow a refund of tax paid.

In particular, the legislation introduced Secs. 20AB, 20AC, 20AD, 20AE, 70AB and Schedules 15 and 16 into the IRO. The name of the amending Ordinance suggests that it deals with offshore funds and although it was concern by the managed fund industry over the position of offshore funds which led the Government to introduce these changes, they actually apply equally to all non-residents of Hong Kong. A non-resident for this purpose is defined in Sec. 20AB.

An individual will be considered a resident if they ordinarily reside in Hong Kong or they are physically present in Hong Kong for more than 180 days in the relevant year of assessment or for more than 300 days in two consecutive years of assessment, one of which is the year under consideration. A company, partnership or trustee of a trust will be deemed a resident where the central management and control of the company, partnership or trust is exercised in Hong Kong in the relevant year of assessment. Although the term "central management and control" is not defined for this purpose, it has been the subject of consideration in a number of court decisions in other jurisdictions. Although those decisions inevitably revolve around their own facts, it is generally accepted that the phrase refers to the overall stewardship of the entity, which in the case of the company is usually equated with the functions of the board of directors, and this needs to be distinguished from the day to day business activities of that entity. Accordingly, it is possible that an offshore fund may retain its central management and control outside Hong Kong and, therefore, remain a non-resident of Hong Kong, even though the day to day business of investing its assets is undertaken by personnel in Hong Kong.

The profits deemed exempt are set out in Sec. 20AC and Schedule 16 and, subject to the conditions discussed below, are profits from transactions in securities, futures contracts, foreign exchange contracts, foreign currencies or exchange traded commodities, or the making of a deposit other than by way of a money-lending business. The terms "securities", "futures contract", "foreign exchange contract", "deposit" and "exchange traded commodity" are all extensively defined in Schedule 16 and the reader is referred to that schedule for a more complete understanding of the terms. Nonetheless, it is worth noting that the definition of securities excludes shares in a Hong Kong private company. Also, the definition of exchange traded commodity is narrowly defined to comprise only gold or silver traded on a commodity exchange in Hong Kong; nonetheless, although a much broader range of commodities are traded on overseas exchanges, it was presumably not considered necessary to extend the exemption to those as profits from trading such commodities would have a non-Hong Kong source and already be exempt from Profits Tax.

The above profits are, however, exempt only where the relevant transactions are carried out through a "specified person" which is defined in Sec. 20AC(6). In relation to a transaction carried out prior to 1 April 2003, a specified person is a bank (as defined in the *Banking Ordinance*), a registered dealer or commodity trading adviser under the now repealed *Commodities Trading Ordinance*, a registered dealer, investment adviser or securities margin financier under the now repealed *Securities Ordinance* or a licensed leveraged foreign exchange trader under the now repealed *Foreign Exchange Trading Ordinance*. From 1 April 2003, a specified person is defined as a corporation licensed under the *Securities and Futures Ordinance*, or an authorized financial institution registered under that ordinance, to carry on any regulated activity within the meaning of Part 1 of Schedule 5 of that ordinance.

Additionally, profits from transactions incidental to the foregoing will also be exempt provided the total receipts from such incidental transactions do not exceed 5% of the total receipts from the other exempt transactions (Secs. 20AC(1)(b) and 20AC(4)).

One further important condition which must be fulfilled for the exemption to apply is that the non-resident does not at any time during the relevant year of assessment carry on any trade, profession or business in Hong Kong involving any transactions other than those which attract the exemption (Sec. 20AC(3)). This appears to suggest that if any business is undertaken in Hong Kong by the non-resident which gives rise to non-exempt income, the exemption will not be available in respect of any otherwise assessable income of the non-resident.

For the avoidance of any doubt, Sec. 20AD provides that any loss sustained from transactions qualifying for the exemption cannot be carried forward to subsequent years when the taxpayer may have assessable profits (because, for example, a business deriving non-exempt profits is commenced in Hong Kong).

Clearly, the above provisions are intended to grant tax exemptions only to non-residents. Accordingly, in order to prevent residents taking advantage of the exemptions by investing through non-resident entities, the legislation contains extensive anti-avoidance provisions in Sec. 20AE. These provisions essentially apply where a resident, together with associates, holds directly or indirectly more than a 30% interest in a non-resident which benefits from the exemptions, or where a resident holds any interest in such an associated non-resident (Secs. 20AE(1), 20AE(2) and 20AE(3)). In these circumstances, the exempt profits of the non-resident which are attributable to the interest of the resident person are taxable in the hands of that resident. These provisions apply irrespective of whether or not the resident has received or will receive any money or other property representing the profits of the non-resident (Sec. 20AE(4)) The resident's share of the non-resident's profits is determined according to a formula contained in Schedule 15, which also contains further rules for ascertaining the extent of a person's beneficial interest in the non-resident. An exemption from these anti-avoidance provisions will, however, apply where the Commissioner is satisfied that the interests in the non-resident held by residents are *bona fide* widely held, which reflects the Government's intention to provide broad exemptions in relation to genuine offshore funds. Although the exemptions contained in Sec. 20AC are generally retrospective to the 1996/97 year of assessment, it should be noted that the anti-avoidance provisions contained in Sec. 20AE apply only from the 2006/07 year of assessment.

Because the above exemptions were only enacted in 2006, but are retrospective to the 1996/97 year, provisions needed to be inserted to allow assessments which were otherwise final and conclusive to be reopened to permit taxpayers to obtain the benefit of the exemptions. Such provisions are contained in Sec. 70AB, which allows taxpayers twelve months from the date of effect of the new provisions (which was 10 March 2006), or six years after the end of the relevant year of assessment, whichever is later, to apply to have an assessment reopened to take advantage of the new provisions and to obtain a refund of tax paid.

Although the above provisions are quite complex, in summary they are intended to make it clear that a non-resident who does not otherwise carry on business in Hong Kong, but who deposits money in Hong Kong or enters into transactions in securities or certain other financial assets through a bank or broker in Hong Kong, will not be subject to Profits Tax. Prior to the introduction of these provisions, this position was not clear because of the possibility that the non-resident may be considered to be carrying on business in Hong Kong through the bank or broker in Hong Kong, and deriving Hong Kong source profits from that business. This uncertainty was an issue not only for the non-residents, but also for the Hong Kong banks or brokers who, if the non-residents were taxable, had an obligation to collect and pay the tax on their behalf.

For a further discussion of these provisions, including examples of the types of arrangements which the IRD considers benefit from the concessions, see *Departmental Interpretation & Practice Notes No. 43.*

4.5.4 Amounts deemed taxable

In addition to profits assessable under the general rules, there are a number of types of amounts which, if not otherwise subject to Profits Tax, are deemed to be Hong Kong source receipts of a business carried on in Hong Kong. Accordingly, persons in receipt of such sources of income are, even if they have no presence in Hong Kong at all, assessed on those receipts as if they were carrying on business in Hong Kong. In addition there are deemed business receipts applicable to persons who are actually carrying on business in Hong Kong but who would not otherwise be obliged to bring them into their Profits Tax computation. Some amounts which would be within these deeming provisions are, in fact, already liable to Profits Tax under the general charging rule; in these cases, the amounts concerned should probably be treated as assessable only under the general rule, although in practice it would rarely make any difference and so the point is largely academic.

The types of amounts deemed to be Hong Kong source receipts of a business carried on in Hong Kong are considered separately in the following paragraphs.

(1) **Film royalties:** Payments not taxable under the general charging provision, for the use in Hong Kong of any cinema or television film or any tape or sound recording or any advertising material connected with any of these things are covered by Sec. 15(1)(a). This is a straightforward factual provision and is most commonly applicable to payments made by cinemas and television companies to non-resident film distributors. The assessable profit is, further, normally deemed by Sec. 21A to be 30% of the payment if the amount was received by or accrued to the recipient on or after 1 April 2003, or 10% in the case of an amount received or accrued prior to that date. If, however, the sum is derived by an associate of the payer and the Commissioner is not satisfied that that no person carrying on a trade, profession or business in Hong Kong has, at any time, wholly or partly owned the property in respect of which the sum is paid, the assessable profit is deemed to be 100% of the payment. The recipient's liability in respect of the 2006/07 year of assessment is, therefore, effectively either 5.25% or 17.5% of the

payment if a company, or 4.8% or 16% otherwise, depending on the particular circumstances of the case.

For these purposes, "associate" is defined, very broadly, in Sec. 21A(3); the definition is similar to that in Sec. 39E(5) which is discussed in section 5.10.2. Furthermore, in *Departmental Interpretation & Practice Notes No. 22*, the Commissioner notes that "owned" refers to direct ownership and that the IRD will not look through a company to its shareholders for the purpose of ascertaining ownership; it should, however, be noted that the definition of "associate" in Sec. 21A(3) allows the IRD to look through a company to a person who controls that company, although such a person may or may not be a shareholder. In cases of doubt, however, an advance ruling can be sought (see section 10.5) and paragraph 21 of *Departmental Interpretation & Practice Notes No. 22* outlines some specific requirements of the IRD when considering such a request.

See also the discussion in (2) below regarding *Departmental Interpretation & Practice Notes No. 39* as it applies to payments for pre-packed or shrink wrapped products which grant the acquirer a right to use, but not to commercially exploit, the product.

(2)   **Other royalties:** Payments not taxable under the general charging provision, for the use of, or right to use, in Hong Kong a patent, design, trademark, copyright material, secret process or formula or any other similar property or for imparting know-how in connection with the use of any of those things are within Sec. 15(1)(b). This provision applies to various types of payments by companies for the use of another's intellectual property. Note that it is applicable to the "right to use" even when there is no actual use. In those cases, however, where there is no actual use but Hong Kong is merely not excluded from the worldwide right to use, the *Emerson Rado Corporation* case, which is discussed below, has confirmed that it is not correct to assess the entire payment; rather, it appears that only payments for the actual use or right to use in Hong Kong will be assessable.

It is important to remember that this provision can apply only where the amounts in question are not otherwise taxable. Accordingly, where amounts are derived by a person who is chargeable to tax on such amounts pursuant to Sec. 14, Sec. 15(1)(b) cannot apply. In this regard, see *Lam Soon Trademark Limited v CIR* [2004] (HKRC 90-137) where the taxpayer sought, albeit unsuccessfully, to argue that because certain amounts had been assessed under Sec. 15(1)(b), the Commissioner could not subsequently assess them under Sec. 14. The ground for the taxpayer's argument was that in applying Sec. 15(1)(b), the Commissioner had concluded that the amounts were not otherwise assessable under Sec. 14 or any other provision. This argument was, however, rejected by the Court of First Instance [2004] (1 HKRC 90-137), the Court of Appeal [2005] (1 HKRC 90-149) and the Court of Final Appeal [2005] (1 HKRC 90-171), all of which upheld the Commissioner's power to take a different view of the facts to that originally adopted and issue an additional assessment where appropriate.

With effect from 25 June 2004, Sec. 15(1)(ba) was enacted which effectively extends the scope of Sec. 15(1)(b) by bringing amounts for the use of, or the right to use, the relevant types of property outside Hong Kong into the charge where those amounts are deductible for Hong Kong Profits Tax purposes. The Government decided that this extension of the charge was appropriate after losing in the Court of Final Appeal in the case of *CIR v Emerson Radio Corporation; Emerson Radio Corporation v CIR* [2000] (1 **HKRC** 90-102). That case concerned the question of where intellectual property was used and although the effect of the ultimate decision has largely been over-ridden by legislation, it is still interesting to study this decision for an insight into how the courts analysed and interpreted the provisions. Also, the decision is potentially still relevant in determining whether Sec. 15(1)(b) applies to an amount for which a deduction is not claimed in Hong Kong. For example, there may be cases where a Hong Kong business makes a payment to an overseas party for the use of, or right to use, intellectual property but does not claim a deduction for the amount because it arises in connection with the derivation of profits which arise substantially outside Hong Kong; although no deduction is claimed, the decision in the *Emerson Radio Corporation* case (supra) may still be relevant to determining whether the intellectual property in question is used in Hong Kong, in which case Sec. 15(1)(b) would still apply.

The taxpayer in the *Emerson Radio Corporation* case (supra) was a US company which had a wholly owned Hong Kong subsidiary. The subsidiary arranged for goods to be manufactured by third parties, such goods carrying trademarks for which the subsidiary paid a royalty to the taxpayer. The subsidiary purchased the goods and sold them to customers in the United States in a manner whereby all of its profits were subject to Profits Tax. The Court of First

Instance, in overturning the decision of the Board of Review (see *D 23/96*), held that the trademarks in question were used where they were affixed to the relevant goods as part of the manufacturing process. The court also found that because some of the goods in question were manufactured in Hong Kong and some abroad, the total royalties needed to be apportioned and only that part attributable to goods manufactured in Hong Kong was assessable under Sec. 15 (1)(b). In reaching its decision, the court rejected, amongst other things, the suggestion that because the Hong Kong subsidiary was granted a right to use in Hong Kong (the royalty agreement containing no geographical restriction on the use of the trademark), the whole payment was taxable on a strict reading of the provisions of Sec. 15(1)(b). Also rejected was the propostion adopted by the Board of Review that the use of a trademark took place where the licensee carried on its business.

The decision and reasoning of the Court of First Instance was largely upheld by the Court of Appeal, except that one judge adopted a different reasoning on the question of the place of use of the property. In particular, although two of the judges adopted the reasoning of the lower court that the use of the trademark was where the mark was affixed to the goods during the manufacturing process, the other judge focused solely on the sale of the goods and held that the use was outside of Hong Kong in the location where the goods were sold.

Both the Commissioner and the taxpayer appealed the decision of the Court of Appeal to the Court of Final Appeal. As was the case in the lower courts, the Court of Final Appeal rejected the Commissioner's contention that all the royalties received were for use of the trademarks in Hong Kong. In doing so, it focussed on the fact that the trademarks being exploited were those registered in the country of use. Accordingly, if the Hong Kong subsidiary authorised a manufacturer in, say, Thailand to affix the mark to goods, it was the trademark registered in Thailand which was being used and that trademark, as a matter of law, could only be used in Thailand. Moreover, the court rejected the argument that by licensing its subsidiary in Hong Kong to use the trademark in Hong Kong and elsewhere, the taxpayer was actually using that trademark in Hong Kong. This conclusion was reached on the basis that "use" for the purpose of Sec. 15(1)(b) was meant to be a reference to use by the licensee (i.e. the Hong Kong subsidiary) and not the licensor (i.e.

the taxpayer). Finally, the court once again rejected the argument advanced by the Commissioner that because Sec. 15(1)(b) extends to the right to use and not merely actual use, and it was clear that the licensee had a right to use in Hong Kong, all the royalties derived should be taxable. The grounds for the rejection of this argument were simply that the royalties were calculated on the basis of, and paid for, actual use and not the right to use; accordingly, it was not necessary to look further than the actual use.

A more complete insight into the Court of Final Appeal's analysis of this issue can, however, be found in its decision on the cross appeal (i.e. the appeal by the taxpayer that even royalties paid in respect of goods manufactured in Hong Kong should not be taxable). In dealing with this issue the court began by analysing the licensing agreement to decide for what the royalties were payable. In this regard, the licensing agreement referred to the licensor holding the rights to the trademark for goods sold in the United States (US) and required the payment of royalties in respect of sales to US customers. The court implied that this meant that royalties were payable in respect of the US trademark and should, therefore, be considered to be for use only in the US. However, counsel for the taxpayer had argued that the license contained an implied term for the use of the trademark in Hong Kong and other countries, that is, that if the Hong Kong subsidiary was authorised to sell the products in the US, it must effectively have also been granted a right to affix the trademark to those goods in the country of manufacture. As counsel for the taxpayer insisted that the case be decided on such a basis, the court felt compelled to do so. In doing so, however, the court held that once it was accepted that a right to affix the trademark to goods during the manufacturing process had been granted, it was necessary to decide on the consideration payable for that right and this could only be the royalty itself. As such, the court upheld the finding of the lower courts that to the extent that royalties were payable in respect of goods manufactured in Hong Kong, the trademark had been used in Hong Kong. Interestingly, the court still found that the royalties payable in respect of goods manufactured in Hong Kong were partly in respect of the manufacture and partly in respect of the sale to customers in the US; however, an apportionment was not possible and, as the relevant royalties were partly for the use in Hong Kong, they were assessable pursuant to Sec. 15(1)(b).

Apart from the question of where a right is used, difficulties have also arisen in more recent times concerning the nature of rights over computer software. In particular, it is now common to purchase an item of standard software (often referred to as "shrink wrapped" software) either from a retailer in Hong Kong, by mail order or by downloading from the internet. Although such a transaction in many ways looks like a purchase of a good, invariably the legal form of the transaction is the granting of a right to use, by way of a license, of intellectual property. Moreover, it is inevitably necessary to agree to the terms of the license (which normally prohibit the sub-licensing, modification or sale of the intellectual property and make it clear that the licensee has no rights in that intellectual property other than the right to use) before the software can be installed on the licensee's computer.

The possible confusion over whether or not payments for the purchase of shrink wrapped software can possibly fall within Sec. 15(1)(b) has, however, been considered and clarified by the IRD in *Departmental Interpretation & Practice Notes No. 39*. In particular, the IRD have stated that a payment to a non-resident for shrink-wrapped software or for digital software downloadable from the internet will not fall within Sec. 15(1)(b) provided the contract only grants the customer a license to use the software to a limited extent (i.e. to use software either on a single computer or on a specified number of the customer's computers or network servers). This exemption will also only apply where the customer is not granted the right to reproduce, modify or adapt the software program or otherwise exploit the copyright in the software.

Similarly the IRD has confirmed that payments to non-residents for the following will not fall within Sec. 15(1)(b) (or, where applicable, Sec. 15(1)(a)):

(a)   the downloading of a digital product (e.g. software, images, sounds or text) to a Hong Kong customer's computer for the customer's own use provided the customer is not allowed to modify, adapt or copy the product;

(b)   the hosting of software (e.g. business, accounting or financial management software applications) on a server maintained by the non-resident outside Hong Kong (i.e. application hosting arrangements);

(c)   the use of a software application owned by or licensed by a non-resident and maintained on the non-resident's server outside Hong Kong which automates a back-office business function of the Hong Kong customer (e.g. inventory control). The Hong Kong customer's right to use the software must be restricted to the running of the software on the application service provider's server; or

(d)   the creation of new online content by a non-resident pursuant to an agreement under which the Hong Kong customer (e.g. a Hong Kong server operator) becomes the copyright owner of the online content.

Departmental Interpretation & Practice Notes No. 39 was issued before the enactment of Sec. 15(1)(ba) and has not been updated for that provision; nonetheless, the logic adopted by the IRD in exempting the above payments from Sec. 15(1)(a) and (b) would appear to equally apply to exempt the payments from the application of Sec. 15(1)(ba).

The IRD indicates in *Departmental Interpretation & Practice Notes No. 39*, however, that payments to non-residents for the following will be chargeable and generate a withholding tax obligation:

(a)   the downloading of a digital product (e.g. software, images, sounds or text) where the Hong Kong customer obtains the right to commercially exploit the copyright material; or

(b)   the displaying on a Hong Kong customer's website of online content owned by the non-resident for the purpose of attracting users to the Hong Kong customer's website.

As with liabilities under Sec. 15(1)(a), Sec. 21A fixes the assessable profit in respect of amounts deemed assessable by Sec. 15(1)(b) or (ba) to be 30% or 100% of the payment, depending upon the particular circumstances (see (1) above).

■ Example 4.7

Electronigames Ltd. is a Hong Kong company and manufactures toys including one particular design under license from a German company. It pays the German company a royalty of 3% on sales which, in the basis period, for the 2007/08 year of assessment amounted to a payment of $60,000. The German company has no other interests in Hong Kong.

The German company is deemed to be carrying on business in Hong Kong and to have profits arising in Hong Kong from that business of 30% of $60,000, that is, $18,000 (Secs. 15(1)(b) and 21A). This would be assessed upon Electronigames Ltd. under Sec. 20B (see section 4.8.4).

If, however, Electronigames Ltd. and the German company were associates within the meaning of Sec. 21A(3) and the design for which Electronigames Ltd. pays the royalty had previously been owned, wholly or partly, by a person carrying on business in Hong Kong, the German company's assessable profits from any royalties would be deemed to be 100% of the amount (i.e. $60,000).

■ Example 4.8

The 2007/08 year of assessment was the first year of the arrangement and Electronigames Ltd. paid the German company $100,000 for initial advice on meeting specifications in manufacturing the toy. This amount is still be caught by Sec. 15(1)(b), notwithstanding that this is a once and for all payment, and the measure of the assessable profit in that year is $30,000 plus 30% of any royalty also paid (assuming, again, that no associate in Hong Kong had previously owned the property in question).

■ Example 4.9

Electronigames Ltd. enters into an agreement with Business Solutions Inc. (BSI), an application service provider in the United States which does not carry on business in Hong Kong, to use BSI's software and server to maintain Electronigames Ltd.'s accounting records and produce its financial accounts. In exchange for this service, Electronigames Ltd. pays BSI a monthly fee. Although the fee payable by Electronigames Ltd. is, at least partly, a payment for the right to use BSI's intellectual property, the IRD will accept that BSI does not have a liability to Profits Tax under Sec. 15(1)(b) provided that Electronigames Ltd. does not have the right to reproduce, modify or adapt BSI's software or otherwise have the right to commercially exploit the copyright in that software (see *Departmental Interpretation & Practice Notes No. 39*).

(3) **Grants, subsidies, etc.:** Payments by way of grant, subsidy or similar financial assistance in connection with a trade, profession or business carried on in Hong Kong but excluding any such payment which is connected with capital expenditure, are deemed assessable by Sec. 15(1)(c). In other words, any form of grant or aid from a public body or otherwise that is trade related must be brought in as part of the trading income except where the grant is related to capital expenditure; if, however, that expenditure attracts depreciation allowances (see Chapter 5), the cost for that purpose will be reduced by the grant, etc. This obviously only applies to a person who is already carrying on business in Hong Kong and would generally only operate to bring into the charge to Profits Tax any such amounts not reflected in the recipient's profit and loss account. Nonetheless, the provision also effectively precludes any arguments that such an

amount is non-taxable because it is a capital receipt (unless it relates to capital expenditure to be made).

(4) **Lease payments:** Payments for the use of, or right to use, movable property in Hong Kong are deemed assessable by Sec. 15(1)(d). Again, this is a plain factual provision and may be considered an extension to (2) above; under this provision, however, Sec. 21A does not apply in fixing the assessable profit. The assessable profit is, therefore, the gross amount of the payment, less allowable expenses and depreciation allowances. Even where there is no actual use of the asset in Hong Kong, the payment may be caught where there is a "right to use", and consideration must be given to how much of the payment is applicable to the right to use in Hong Kong having regard to where else the asset may also be used in consideration for the payment. Cases can arise where, for a single payment, an asset is used partly in Hong Kong and partly elsewhere in which case apportionment on some practical basis is necessary.

■ Example 4.10

Diganole Ltd. is a Hong Kong building contractor and it hires some heavy machinery from a French company for which it pays an annual rental of $200,000. The French company has no other interests in Hong Kong.

The French company is deemed to be carrying on business in Hong Kong and to have profits arising in Hong Kong from that business. The measure of its assessable profits is determined by the receipt of $200,000 per annum less direct expenses and depreciation allowances. It may also be able to justify an allocation of overhead expenses.

■ Example 4.11

A Hong Kong exporting company hires containers from a Swiss company which it loads in Hong Kong and sends to various parts of the world. The Swiss company has no other interests in Hong Kong.

Strictly the Swiss company is deemed to be carrying on business in Hong Kong to the extent that the containers are used there. As the containers are used both in Hong Kong and on shipments outside Hong Kong, if the liability is pursued there will have to be a practical apportionment of the rental payment and associated expenses and depreciation allowances.

---

(5) **Interest derived by non-financial institution corporations:** Interest derived from a Hong Kong source which is received by or accrued to a corporation carrying on a trade, profession or business

in Hong Kong is caught by Sec. 15(1)(f), other than where the recipient is a financial institution where more onerous rules apply (see (8) below). Therefore, all companies carrying on business in Hong Kong are subject to Profits Tax on their interest income where such interest has a source in Hong Kong, even if that interest income does not arise from the business carried on in Hong Kong. Accordingly, a company which carries on business in Hong Kong as well as, say, Singapore, would be subject to Profits Tax under this provision in respect of all its Hong Kong source interest income, even where it was attributable to its Singapore operations. The source of interest for this purpose is generally determined in accordance with the "provision of credit" rule (see section 4.4.4 above).

In *D 73/91* it was held that the terms "received by" and "accrued to" were not intended to be synonymous and that interest accrued day by day, not when it became payable or was actually paid.

Notwithstanding this deemed inclusion in assessable profits, the Chief Executive has, pursuant to Sec. 87, granted an exemption *from the payment* of Profits Tax on interest which accrued on or after 22 June 1998 on deposits with an authorized institution (except where derived by a financial institution, the meaning of which is discussed in section 4.7.7). See further, the discussion in point (16) in section 4.5.3, and Example 4.12 below.

(6) **Interest derived by non-corporations:** Interest derived from a Hong Kong source which is received by or accrued to a person other than a corporation and is in respect of the funds of the person's trade, profession or business is deemed assessable by Sec. 15(1)(g).

This provision brings into the charge interest which is in effect really a part of the business profits, because it derives from investment of the business funds. In the case of firms of solicitors, who regularly retain interest income derived from the depositing of funds held on behalf of clients, it was held in *CIR v Messrs. Lau, Wong & Chan, Solicitors* (2 HKTC 470) that although the funds on deposit may not at the material time belong to the firm of solicitors, any interest retained by them is in consideration for their services and is, therefore, "derived from their profession"; accordingly, such amounts are subject to Profits Tax under the general charging provision.

Notwithstanding this deemed inclusion in assessable profits, the Chief Executive has, pursuant to Sec. 87, granted an exemption *from the payment* of Profits Tax on interest which accrued on or after 22

June 1998 on deposits with an authorized institution (except where derived by a financial institution, the meaning of which is discussed in section 4.7.7). See further, the discussion in point (16) in section 4.5.3, and Example 4.13 below.

■ Example 4.12

Lotsaloot Ltd. carries on a retail trade in Hong Kong on which it has an adjusted profit for 2007/08 of $120,000. It also has surplus funds which it has placed on deposit with two banks, one being in Hong Kong and the other in Singapore, receiving interest of $15,000 on each deposit.

The Hong Kong source interest is included in the total Profits Tax assessment of the taxpayer. However, as a result of the order of the Chief Executive, there is generally an exemption from the payment of the Profits Tax on bank deposit interest to the extent that it accrued on or after 22 June 1998. The offshore interest is not liable to tax in Hong Kong at all as it does not arise in Hong Kong.

■ Example 4.13

A partnership of architects has some funds temporarily available before being required again in the business and invests these in a Hong Kong bank account for one month.

Because the interest arises out of the funds of the business it is technically to be included in the partnership Profits Tax assessment. However, as a result of the order of the Chief Executive, there is generally an exemption from the payment of the tax to the extent the interest accrued after 22 June 1998.

---

(7)   **Retirement scheme refunds:** Refunds of contributions paid as an employer to a recognized occupational retirement scheme (see definition in section 10.3.1), and refunds of amounts paid as an employer representing voluntary contributions to a MPF scheme are deemed assessable by Sec. 15(1)(h) to the extent that the recipient obtained a deduction for Profits Tax purposes for those contributions.

This provision may apply where an employer has contributed to a recognized occupational retirement scheme but the relevant employee resigns or retires prematurely with the result that he or she is not entitled to the full balance in their account with the scheme. A similar result can occur in respect of voluntary contributions to an MPF scheme, which are not subject to preservation under the MPF legislation, and therefore may not become payable to the employee in certain circumstances. In such circumstances, the balance may be refunded to the employer in which case the provision deems the refund assessable to the extent that a deduction had been allowed. In other words, the provision operates to reverse the tax benefit previously granted in respect of an expense which is refunded.

Interestingly, the provision does not apply only where the refund is to the employer who was originally granted the deduction. This means that the provision will not be frustrated where the refund is made to a person who has acquired the business which originally made the contribution which is then refunded, or to an associate of the contributing employer.

(8) **Interest derived by financial institutions:** Interest income that would otherwise be regarded as having a non-Hong Kong source which arises through or from the carrying on of business in Hong Kong by a financial institution is within the scope of Sec. 15(1)(i). This is a complex matter and is dealt with separately in section 4.7.7.

(9) **Profits of a non-financial institution from certificates of deposit, bills of exchange, etc.:** Profits arising in or derived from Hong Kong by a corporation carrying on a trade or business in Hong Kong from the disposal of, or on the redemption on maturity or presentment of, a certificate of deposit or bill of exchange are covered by Sec. 15(1)(j), other than in the case of a financial institution where more onerous rules apply (see (11) below). For this purpose, certificate of deposit is defined in Sec. 2 but bill of exchange is not defined and is generally assumed to take the meaning as defined in the *Bills of Exchange Ordinance*. Where the profit on maturity is in fact interest, as it would be on a certificate of deposit, it is Sec. 15(1)(f) that applies (see (5) above) and not Sec. 15(1)(j). Where the certificate of deposit is sold before maturity, the profit is not interest and, therefore, Sec. 15(1)(j) applies. These points are illustrated in Example 4.14.

■ Example 4.14

Kash-my-chek Ltd. is a real estate investment company in Hong Kong which has temporary surplus cash. If it has, say, $100 to invest it may:—

(a) Place $100 on deposit and receive a CD which it holds to maturity and receives $110.
   The profit of $10 is interest on which it pays Profits Tax of $1.75 (Sec. 15(1)(f)).

(b) Buy in the secondary market for $100 a CD with a nominal value of $90 which it holds to maturity and receives $110.
   Its profit is $10 but the $110 includes interest of $20 which Kash-my-chek must report

for Profits Tax, paying $3.50 tax (Sec. 15(1)(f)). It should, however, be able to claim a deduction for the loss sustained through paying $100 for the CD which had a face value of only $90, thereby reducing its tax liability by $1.75.

(c) As for (b) but it sells again in the secondary market one day before maturity for $109.90.

Its profit is $9.90 and it pays Profits Tax on this of $1.73 (Sec. 15(1)(j)).

(d) Buy in the secondary market for $100 a CD with a nominal value of $100 but which had been first issued at a discount of $90, which it holds to maturity and receives $110.

Its profit is $10 which represents interest and it pays Profits Tax on this of $1.75 (Sec. 15(1)(f)).

(e) Deposit the $100 with a financial institution and pay no Hong Kong tax at all on the interest earned (as the interest would have a non-Hong Kong source if the financial institution was offshore, or would be effectively exempt if the financial institution was in Hong Kong due to the operation of the *Exemption from Profits Tax (Interest Income) Order*).

Note that despite the above analyses, any amounts of interest in respect of a CD issued by an authorized institution in Hong Kong would effectively be generally exempt pursuant to the exemption from Profits Tax (Interest Income) Order (see point (16) in section 4.5.3).

This provision refers only to profits which arise in or derive from Hong Kong, i.e. which have a Hong Kong source. It is likely that such an amount would only have a non-Hong Kong source if the sale was effected outside Hong Kong by an agent outside Hong Kong along the lines of the decisions in *BR 18/73* and *CIR v Hang Seng Bank* (3 HKTC 351). It would not have an offshore source merely because it was in a non-Hong Kong currency nor would it necessarily be so if it was sold directly to an offshore counterparty.

(10) **Profits of a non-corporation from certificates of deposit or bills of exchange:** Sec. 15(1)(k) deals with profits arising in or derived from Hong Kong which are identical to those dealt with in (9) above but where the investor is any person other than a corporation but who is carrying on a trade, profession or business in Hong Kong and where the profits from the disposals of the certificates of deposit or bills of exchange are in respect of the funds of the business.

This provision mirrors the subjection of Hong Kong source interest to Profits Tax in the same circumstances (see (6) above). Accordingly, it only applies where the profit in question is not interest, i.e. disposal of a bill of exchange at any time and disposal of a certificate of deposit before maturity. Note, however, that if the funds used are not funds of the business, the Profits Tax charge does not apply. Therefore, where an individual is carrying on a business it is important to determine whether the funds used have been permanently extracted from the business for investment or whether they have been temporarily invested prior to further business requirements. The determination of the source of gains of this nature is as discussed in (9) above.

■ Example 4.15

The partnership in Example 4.13 has invested business funds partly in a HK$ certificate of deposit and partly in a deposit with a bank.

The CD is sold before maturity at a profit of $10,000. The interest on the deposit is $11,000.

The profit of $10,000 is subject to Profits Tax at 16% (Sec. 15(1)(k)). The interest of $11,000 is, *prima facie*, subject to Profits Tax, but no tax is likely to be payable because of the *Exemption from Profits Tax (Interest Income) Order* (see point (16) in section 4.5.3).

---

(11) **Profits of a financial institution from certificates of deposit or bills of exchange:** Profits arising from the carrying on in Hong Kong of business by a financial institution (see definition in section 4.7.7) in respect of the disposal of or on redemption on maturity or presentment of a certificate of deposit or bill of exchange are deemed assessable by Sec. 15(1)(l). For this purpose, certificate of deposit is as defined in Sec. 2 but bill of exchange is not defined and, therefore, is generally assumed to take the meaning as defined in the *Bills of Exchange Ordinance*. Where the profit on maturity is in fact interest, as it would normally be on a certificate of deposit, it is Sec. 15(1)(i) that applies (see (8) above) and not Sec. 15(1)(l). However, where a certificate has been purchased at a discount to face value and is held to maturity, the profit on maturity would comprise both final interest, which would be assessable under Sec. 15(1)(i), and profit representing excess of face value over purchase price, which would be assessable under Sec. 15(1)(l). Where the certificate of deposit is sold before maturity, the profit cannot be interest and, therefore, Sec. 15(1)(l) applies. The difference, however, is probably academic because the tests are substantially the same. Nonetheless, both tests are to an extent unclear as they rely upon the uncertain test of what arises from the carrying on of business in Hong Kong; this has given rise to particular difficulty in connection with the taxability of interest pursuant to Sec. 15(1)(i) (see the discussion of this in section 4.7.7).

The provision specifically overrides the tests that would otherwise determine the source of the profits, namely the place of conclusion of the transaction, either by the taxpayer or their agent, as established in *BR 18/73* and *CIR v Hang Seng Bank* (3 HKTC 351). It also denies any reference to the funds for the acquisition being made available outside Hong Kong (i.e. the "provision of credit" rule) in determining the source of such profits but this does not seem relevant because it is the source of interest which is determined by this rule and Sec. 15(1)(l) does not apply to interest.

(12) **Receipts from the assignment of an income stream:** Certain consideration which has been received or is receivable for the transfer of a right to receive profits, rent, interest or royalties which would otherwise be liable to Profits Tax are deemed assessable by Secs. 15(1)(m) and 15A(1).

The intention of the provisions is to counteract the possibility that a person could sell the right to taxable income to another person for a lump sum in circumstances where the lump sum would be treated as a receipt for the sale of a capital asset, and so avoid Profits Tax, whilst still retaining the ownership of the underlying asset which gives rise to the income. Such an arrangement was the subject of a case in Australia (*FC of T v Myer Emporium Ltd*. (85 ATC 411)) in which the Court held that the receipt was indeed of a capital nature. After Sec. 15A was enacted, however, that decision was reversed in Australia by a higher court which found that the sum was a trading receipt which, of course, is what Secs. 15A and 15(1)(m) deem it to be; the provision, nevertheless, remains for the avoidance of doubt.

Any person in receipt of such a sum is deemed to receive it as a trading receipt arising in Hong Kong from a business carried on in Hong Kong. If, therefore, he is already carrying on business in Hong Kong it just becomes an additional trading receipt, if it is not already included in the person's assessable profits. A liability under this provision cannot, however, arise unless the person is already liable to Profits Tax, because the definition of income transferred only applies to income which is already liable to Profits Tax (Sec. 15A(4)). There could, of course, be a position where a non-resident person is in receipt of royalties from a copyright used in Hong Kong as a result of which he is deemed to be carrying on business in Hong Kong and who then sells the right to receive the royalties for a lump sum without disposing of the underlying copyright. In that case the lump sum would still be regarded as a trading receipt from a business carried on in Hong Kong.

It is important to note that if the underlying property is sold at the same time and to the same person to whom the right to receive the income was transferred, the provisions do not apply (Sec. 15A(3)). In other words, the provisions would not apply if the non-resident referred to in the previous paragraph sold the copyright itself together with the right to receive the income therefrom.

Consideration received other than in cash must be valued at its money value (Sec. 15A(2)), which would normally mean its market value.

(13) **Debt releases:** Where a deduction has been allowed for a debt incurred in the course of a trade, profession or business and that debt is subsequently wholly or partly released, the part released is deemed to be a receipt of the trade, profession or business in the basis period in which the release is effected (Sec. 15(2)). This provision applies only to the release of a debt which implies some act of forgiveness on the part of the creditor. For example, in a bankruptcy where only a percentage of the debt is paid, the balance is not released but in effect remains uncollectable. The provision is included to nullify the decision in *British Mexican Petroleum Co. Ltd. v Jackson* (16 TC 570).

(14) **Stock borrowing and lending — distributions:** An amount received by a lender under a stock borrowing and lending arrangement where the payment is in respect of an amount which would have been received by, and subject to Profits Tax in the hands of, the lender if the stock had not been lent are taxable under Sec. 15E (3). This is the converse to the situation where an amount received is exempt where it would not have been taxable had the lender not lent the stock; this is discussed in more depth in point (10) of section 4.5.3 above.

(15) **Stock borrowing and lending — compensatory payments:** Amounts paid made pursuant to a stock borrowing and lending arrangement, by a stock borrower to a stock lender in respect of a distribution made or the grant of a right or option are taxable under Sec. 15E(4) to the extent that such distribution or grant of right or option would have been taxable if received by the lender directly. Again, this is the converse of the situation where certain such payments are exempt where the underlying distribution or grant of right or option would not have been taxable if received directly, which is discussed in point (11) of section 4.5.3 above.

Of the above fifteen deeming provisions, all except (1), (2) and (4) in fact only apply to persons already carrying on or deemed to be carrying on business in Hong Kong and merely increase the assessable profits in circumstances where the receipt in question would otherwise not be within the scope of Profits Tax. On the other hand, headings (1), (2), and in some circumstances (4), actually deem a business to be carried on where no such business would exist under the normal rules, as well as deeming a Hong Kong source of profits. Because of the difficulties of collection from persons not actually carrying on business in Hong Kong, extensive powers are provided for assessing upon, and collecting from, agents or payers in Hong Kong. These provisions are dealt with in sections 4.8.3 and 4.8.4 below.

Under headings (1) and (2) the ascertainment of the amount of the assessable profit is clearly prescribed by Sec. 21A but it would be open to a non-resident to show that he was in fact carrying on a business in Hong Kong and that his actual assessable profits were less than as prescribed by that provision. This is because if he is carrying on business in Hong Kong, Sec. 14 is applicable and Secs. 15(1)(a), 15(1)(b) and 15(1)(ba) would generally not be applicable. Under heading (4), however, there is no deemed assessable profit; the assessable profit must, therefore, be ascertained as a question of fact. Failing an ascertainment of the true profit arising in Hong Kong, Sec. 21 provides that it may be computed on a fair percentage of the receipt in question.

The identification by the IRD of sources of income arising under headings (1), (2) and (4) to persons not carrying on a business in Hong Kong is usually from an examination of the tax returns of the payer who is obliged to report the existence of any such payments in accordance with specific questions on his return form.

4.5.5 Expenditure — general deductibility rules

The general rule for deductibility of expenditure is contained in Sec. 16(1) which provides that a deduction is allowable for all outgoings and expenses to the extent to which they are incurred during the basis period for the year of assessment in the production of profits chargeable to Profits Tax. The question of when expenses are incurred is dealt with in section 4.5.6. As will be seen from that section, the interpretation as to when an expense is "incurred" was apparently changed by the decision of the Court of Final Appeal in *CIR v Secan Limited & Anor.* [2001] (1 HKRC 90-107). Nonetheless, the question of when an expense is incurred is still critical as it is only in that period which a deduction is allowed by Sec. 16, and not the period in which the assessable profit to which the expense relates is derived.

This latter point is made quite clear by the wording of Sec. 16 which specifically provides that the expense can be related to the derivation of assessable profits of "any period" and was further confirmed by the Privy Council in *CIR v Mutual Investment Co. Ltd.* (1 HKTC 185).

The question of whether or not expenditure is related to the production of assessable profits is largely a question of fact. Occasionally, an amount may be paid which is not considered related to the derivation of the payer's profits, but is for some other purposes. See, for example, *D 17/99* where a management fee was held by the Board of Review to effectively be a gift made with the intention of securing a deduction for the payer, but which would have been sheltered from assessability by the tax losses of the recipient, which was a related company. As the amount was not considered to be attributable to the derivation of the payer's assessable profits, it was not deductible.

Another situation where expenses may be argued as non-deductible is where they are incurred in connection with the payment of a dividend by a company. Because the payment of a dividend is essentially a distribution of profits, it is not part of the process of deriving those profits. As such, any expenses incurred in connection with the payment of a dividend may be argued as being non-deductible. The issue was, however, considered by the courts in the context of interest expenses incurred in funding a dividend payment and was ultimately allowed by the Court of Final Appeal in *Zeta Estates Limited v CIR* (FACV 15/2006). That case began in the Board of Review (see *D 34/04*) and involved a company which declared a dividend, which the three shareholders immediately agreed to loan back to the company at interest. This had the effect of converting retained profits of the company into interest bearing shareholder loans, and clearly established a direct nexus between the interest and the payment of the dividend. The Board of Review held that the interest was non-deductible on the basis that it was not incurred in the earning of the company's profits. This decision was upheld by the Court of First Instance [2005] (1 HKRC 90-143) and the Court of Appeal [2005] (1 HKRC 90-161).

Although the outcome was the same, the Court of Appeal's reasoning was different to that of the Board of Review and the Court of First Instance as although all three decisions proceeded on the basis that there was no need for the additional borrowings, the Board and the Court of First Instance held that the conditions for deductibility in Sec. 16(1) (i.e. the requirement of a nexus to the derivation of assessable profits) was not met. The Court of Appeal, however, held that the interest would have met the conditions for deductibility had it been established that there was a need for the additional borrowings. Interestingly, it appears that the Court of Appeal misunderstood the nature of the company's accounts or the accounting evidence adduced as once a dividend had been declared, additional sources of funds were required to continue to finance the company's assets.

This apparent misunderstanding was corrected by the Court of Final Appeal which confirmed that the borrowings were required and that the conditions for deductibility were met, therefore rendering the interest in question deductible. In addition, the Court of Final Appeal held that the lower courts had read Sec. 16(1) too narrowly (as is discussed further below) and had appeared to incorrectly impose a requirement that expenses must be wholly and exclusively incurred in the production of profits to be deductible. With regard to the last point, the Court of Final Appeal observed that an expense may be incurred for various purposes and the fact that one purpose was to finance a dividend would not necessarily preclude the amount from being deductible; this comment appears to suggest that the court considered that an amount solely related to the payment of a dividend may be non-deductible but if there were various purposes in incurring the expenditure, one or more of which had a nexus to the production of assessable profits, the amount would be deductible. As noted, in the case before them the Court of Final Appeal held that although one purpose of incurring the interest was to finance the dividend, at the same time it was also necessary to provide continuing finance for the company's assets and, therefore, the amount was deductible.

The Court of Final Appeal also suggested that the lower courts had been influenced by the question of whether it was prudent for the company to declare a dividend when it did not have the cash to pay it, but noted that that decision was one for the company to make and played no part in determining the deductibility of interest on any borrowings rendered necessary by such decision.

Notwithstanding the above cases, it is well established that expenditure can be incurred partly for the purpose of generating assessable profits and partly for generating non-assessable profits. In this regard, the use of the words "*to the extent that*" is sufficient to require disallowance of expenditure not related to, or only partly related to, the generation of assessable profits, but the specific apportionment provisions in the IRR put the matter beyond doubt (see section 4.5.14 below). For a decision of the Board of Review concerning apportionment of expenses, see *D 71/97*. That case concerned a securities dealer which borrowed funds from its parent company (which was a bank) on a subordinated basis and immediately placed the funds back on deposit with its parent in a manner whereby the interest income earned was not assessable. Because the borrowing and lending back was undertaken to ensure that the taxpayer met the liquidity margin requirements imposed on it under the *Securities Ordinance*, which was required in order that the taxpayer could carry on its business, the Board of Review accepted that the relevant interest expense was incurred partly for the purpose of producing assessable profits, even though all of the interest income derived from depositing the loan funds were non-assessable. As a result, a deduction for a portion of the interest expense, being the amount in excess of the interest income earned, was allowed as a deduction.

Another situation where only part of an amount may be deductible is where an expense is considered to be commercially excessive. Again, it has been held that the words *"to the extent that"* permit the limiting of the deduction to a commercially reasonable level; in this regard see *So Kai Tong Stanley trading as Stanley So & Co v CIR* [2004] (1 HKRC 90-131) and *D 51/05*. Note, however, that this principle should not be seen as giving the Commissioner a broad power to determine the amount that a business should have paid for goods and services, but is probably limited to extreme situations such as where the payment is made to a related party and is significantly in excess of what would be expected in an arm's-length situation.

The term *"... in the production of profits ..."* is, in practice, interpreted fairly broadly and it is not usually necessary to show a direct nexus to assessable profits in order to obtain a deduction; for example, demonstrating that an expense was incurred in the ordinary course of carrying on a business from which assessable profits are derived is usually sufficient to ensure a deduction, although if non-assessable profits are also produced an apportionment will probably be required. Authority for the proposition that only an indirect nexus to assessable profits is needed for a deduction to be allowable can be found in *CIR v Swire Pacific Limited* (HKTC 1145) where the court allowed a deduction for payments to avert a strike which would have seriously damaged the company's business, even though no profits were generated as a direct result of the payment.

Nonetheless, the IRD, the Board of Review and courts have still grappled with this point on occasions. Part of the reason for this is that often Australian case law is looked to in interpreting Sec. 16(1) because of the similar statutory provisions. Nonetheless, the Australian provision is worded differently and has two "limbs" under which an expense may qualify for deduction. The first of these limbs is almost identical to Sec. 16(1) and requires that the expense be incurred in producing assessable income. The second limb allows a deduction for an expense necessarily incurred in carrying on a business for the purpose of producing assessable income. The second of these limbs appears to specifically authorise a deduction for amounts which are necessary business expenses but which themselves do not directly generate assessable income. Nonetheless, the courts in Australia have consistently been of the view that the second limb adds little to the first limb; that is, they have been of the view that any expense only indirectly related to the production of assessable income will still qualify for deduction under the first limb, making the second limb largely superfluous (see, for example, *Ronpibon Tin NL v FCT* [1949] (78 CLR 47)). Despite this, the IRD have on occasions argued that because the second limb does not appear in Sec. 16(1), the Hong Kong provision is more restrictive than the Australian provision, thereby seeking to reject Australian authorities. Indeed, the Board of Review appeared to reach this conclusion in *D 34/04*, with such view being upheld on appeal to the Court of First Instance in *Zeta Estates Limited v CIR* [2005] (1 HKRC 90-143). On appeal to the Court of Appeal (see *Zeta Estates Limited v CIR* [2005] (1 HKRC 90-161)), however, this view was rejected with Tang JA, quoting with approval the *Swire Pacific Limited* case, noting that "… *in my opinion, the words "incurred … in the production of profits in section 16(1) (a) covers both limbs of [the Australian provision] …"*. On further appeal, the Court of Final Appeal (see FACV 15/2006) endorsed the reasoning of the Court of Appeal. Accordingly, it currently appears well established that only an indirect nexus between an expense and the derivation of assessable profits is required for the amount to be deductible and that there is no basis for interpreting Sec. 16(1) more restrictively than the corresponding provisions in the Australian legislation.

Another interesting decision on the question of the nexus of an item of expenditure to the derivation of assessable profits is *D 128/01*. That case concerned a securities dealer business in which an employee committed serious fraud, as a result of which the taxpayer was required to engage a consultancy firm to prepare a report for the Stock Exchange of Hong Kong. Additionally, the taxpayer made significant accounting provisions in respect of clients' securities and funds which had been misappropriated, although these losses were recoverable under an insurance policy. The issue of the deductibility of both the consultancy fees and the provision for losses were considered by the Board of Review.

In finding that the consultancy fee was deductible, the Board of Review rejected the Commissioner's argument that because the fee was incurred for the purpose of protecting the company's asset (being its membership of the Stock Exchange of Hong Kong), that it could not be considered incurred for the purpose of producing assessable profits and therefore was not deductible. This (unsuccessful) argument of the Commissioner was based, *inter alia*, on the 1906 decision in *Strong v Woodifield* (5 TC 215) which concerned a brewing company which owned licensed premises in which it carried on the business of innkeepers. The company incurred damages in respect of injuries suffered by a patron when a chimney collapsed. A deduction for the amount was denied on the basis that it was not *"... connected with or arising out of ..."* the company's business as a brewer, being the relevant test under the UK law of the time. The Board of Review correctly noted, however, that the statutory test in Sec. 16 is quite different from the former UK provisions and, as such, the principle established in *Strong v Woodifield* was not useful when ascertaining deductibility of amounts in Hong Kong. Accepting the Commissioner's argument would have significantly eroded the normal practice discussed above and meant that a much more direct nexus between an item of expenditure and the derivation of assessable profits would have been required in order for an amount to satisfy the statutory conditions for deductibility.

On the question of deductibility for the provisions for losses due to employee misappropriation, the Board of Review in *D 128/01* accepted that any liability existing at the end of the relevant year of assessment would be deductible, but rejected the taxpayer's claim on the basis that, in the particular circumstances of the case, no accrued liability actually existed at the relevant accounting date, or if it did it was not adequately measured. Moreover, because the taxpayer was indemnified for any losses under an insurance contract, the Board of Review held that a deduction for any otherwise deductible amount would be denied by Sec. 17(1)(e) (see section 4.5.9).

Notwithstanding the clear authority of, *inter alia*, the Court of Appeal and Court of Final Appeal in the *Zeta Estates* case and the Board of Review in D 128/01 that only an indirect nexus is required to the earning of assessable profits for an amount to be deductible, some cases still appear to be decided on a contrary basis. See, for example, *CIR v Chu Fung Chee* [2005] (1 HKRC 90-167) where a more restrictive view was adopted, largely on the basis of the *Strong v Woodifield* case discussed above. That case concerned a barrister who faced disciplinary proceedings before the Bar Council. The outcome of those proceedings was, *inter alia*, that the barrister was required to make substantial payments to the Bar Council and the Bar Disciplinary Tribunal by way of their cost of the proceedings. The Board of Review (see *D 19/05*) accepted that there was a direct nexus between the expenses and the taxpayer's practice as a barrister and that the expenditure was not of a capital nature, thereby concluding that it was deductible. In reaching this conclusion, the Board of Review did not, at least in their written judgement, consider the *Strong v Woodifield* case.

On appeal, the Commissioner specifically argued that Sec. 16(1) requires expenses to be incurred in the production of profits to be deductible and that this was to be interpreted as being incurred in the course of conducting profit making activities. The Court of First Instance accepted this argument and in doing so quoted extensively from *Strong v Woodifield* (despite the different legislative provisions) and held that:

> *"Thus the degree of connection between expenses and the profit-earning process of the trade, profession or business is important ... and must satisfy the tests of being "really incidental to the trade itself" or having been incurred "for the purpose of earning the profits" ".*

Although this quote could be interpreted in various ways or to differing degrees, it must be remembered that it was used to justify disallowing an amount which the Board of Review had found as a fact was related to the taxpayer's trade, although the Court of First Instance did hold that such finding was perverse and lacking an evidential basis.

Although the court's conclusion as to the degree of nexus required between an expense and the earning of profits relied heavily on *Strong v Woodifield*, they also considered authority existed for the proposition in more modern Hong Kong decisions. For example, they noted that the Court of Appeal in *CIR v Cosmotron Manufacturing Company Limited* |1996| (1 HKRC 90-081) had stated that the words *"in the production of profits"* had a narrower ambit than the words *"for the purpose of the trade"* as used in UK legislation, although given that the taxpayer was still successful in that case and the comments in question were made in a dissenting judgement, how authoritative those comments are is questionable. The court also quoted from the decision of the Court of First Instance in *Tai Hing Cotton Mill (Development) Limited* [2005] (1 HKRC 90-150) where it was stated:

> *"It is necessary to ... attend to the true nature of the expenditure and to ask oneself the question....is it expenditure laid out as part of the process of profit earning?"*

Again, the strength of this authority is debatable as the comments were made in the context of criticising the Board of Review for focusing on the quantum of the expense and, in any event, the decision of the Court of First Instance was overturned on appeal. Moreover, the above quote has its origins in a 1937 case concerning a provision in the Indian income tax legislation of the time which was more restrictive than the present Sec. 16(1).

In summary, the approach to the question of the extent of the nexus required between an expense and the earning of assessable profits which was adopted in the *Chu Fung Chee* case appears based on questionable authority and, in any event, is difficult to reconcile to the subsequent decision of the Court of Final Appeal in the *Zeta Estates* case. Accordingly, as noted above, the better view on the basis of current authority appears to be that only an indirect nexus to assessable profits is required for an amount to be deductible.

A relatively common example of types of payments which are generally not incurred in the production of assessable profits are those made with a view to going out of business and, accordingly, these are not deductible (see *James Snook & Co. v Blasdale* (33 TC 244), *Overseas Textiles Ltd. v CIR* (3 HKTC 29) and *BR 13/70*). As noted above, however, in *CIR v Swire Pacific Ltd.* (HKTC 1145) a company which was about to merge its business with that of another company and paid out large sums of money to avert a strike which would have damaged its business prior to transfer, was granted a deduction for the amounts because they were for the purpose of enabling the business to continue, notwithstanding that the paying company could not make a profit. See also *CIR v Cosmotron Manufacturing Company Limited* [1995] (1 HKRC 90-075) where severance payments made under the *Employment Ordinance* on cessation of business were held to be deductible. The reasoning of the High Court in that case was that the payments represented a discharge of statutory obligations incurred in the running of the business prior to its closure; more specifically, the payments accrued as a cost of employing staff and the fact that the liability only crystallised on cessation of the business did not render the payments non-deductible. This decision was upheld, by majority, on appeal to the Court of Appeal [1996] (1 HKRC 90-081) and by the Privy Council [1997] (1 HKRC 90-091) on further appeal.

Also, where the nature of business changes but does not amount to a cessation of business, as in *D 4/83* where a company ceased to be a taxi operator but, instead, rented out taxis to individual operators, the problem does not arise.

A particular type of expenditure which often gives rise to questions as to deductibility is fines imposed for breaches of the law. Although there is a great deal of case law on this point in other jurisdictions, it was not until the decision in *D 99/01* that the matter was considered in Hong Kong. That decision, which contains a useful summary of the law in the UK, Australia, New Zealand and Canada, ultimately held that fines were not deductible. Interestingly, this conclusion was not, as may have been expected, reached on the basis that the expenditure was not incurred in the production of assessable profits; rather, it was reached on the basis of UK, Australian and New Zealand case law which suggested the existence of a presumption that the legislature would not normally sanction the deduction of fines as to do so would undermine the intention of the statutory provisions under which the fines were imposed. In other words, the courts suggested that to allow deduction of the fines would encourage businesses to see them as business expenses rather than as what they are (i.e. as punishment for not adhering to the law).

Because the decision in *D 99/01* was decided on the basis of this presumption as to public policy, it was not strictly necessary for the Board of Review to consider whether the fines were incurred in the production of assessable profits. Nonetheless, the Board commented that if the fines could be regarded as business expenses, they would hold that they were incurred in the production of assessable profits.

Other types of payments which may not be considered to be for the purpose of producing assessable profits are those made (particularly voluntarily) with a view to obtaining a tax advantage even though they may still give rise to assessable profits; in this regard see *FCT v Ilbery* (81 ATC 4661), *Fletcher v FCT* (92 ATC 4950) and *D 44/92*.

Apart from this general rule as to deductibility, various provisions of the IRO deem certain items of expenditure to be specifically deductible or non-deductible and these are discussed in sections 4.5.8 and 4.5.9 below.

4.6.6 When expenditure is incurred

As with the timing of the derivation of income, it is important to be able to ascertain when an expense is incurred as this will generally determine when the expense becomes deductible.

There is a great deal of case law concerning the interpretation of the deduction provision in the Australian tax legislation, which is very similar in wording to Sec. 16 and, in particular, grants a deduction for expenses "incurred" in the earning of assessable income. Much of the Australian case law considers the meaning of "incurred" and under the general rules which have emerged, an expense is considered incurred when it becomes due and payable, or when the taxpayer becomes definitively committed to the expense even though payment may not be due until later or indeed may never become payable because it is defeased or the liability removed as a result of subsequent events. The principle that an expense can be incurred in a period notwithstanding that it will not actually be payable until a later period was also confirmed by the High Court in *National Mutual Centre (HK) Limited v CIR* [1997] (1 HKRC 90-086) and by the Court of Appeal in the subsequent appeal (see *CIR v National Mutual Centre (HK) Limited* [1998] (1 HKRC 90-094)).

A basic tenet of accounting, however, is that expenses should be matched with income; accordingly, in many cases, expenses will be reflected in the commercial accounts not when incurred, but in the period in which the income with which they are most closely connected arises. A typical example of this situation would be where a prepaid expense is amortised for accounting purposes over a number of periods; for tax purposes, however, the Australian cases make it clear that there is no requirement to match the income with the expenses and that the full amount, if deductible at all, will be deductible in the period in which it was incurred. See, for example, *A.G.C. (Advances) Limited v FCT* (75 ATC 4057). The correctness of ignoring the accounting treatment in determining when an amount is incurred for tax purposes was also made clear in *FCT v James Flood Pty. Ltd.* (1953) (88 CLR 492) where the court noted:

> *"Commercial and accountancy practice may assist in ascertaining the true nature and incidence of the item as a step towards determining whether it answers the test laid down by … (the deduction provision) … but it cannot be substituted for the test."*

Accordingly, on the basis of the Australian cases, in circumstances where the accounting treatment results in an expense being reflected in the profit and loss account in a period other than that in which it was incurred, adjustments are required for tax purposes to deduct the amount in the period incurred and add it back as non-deductible in the period or periods it is expensed in the profit and loss account.

The above interpretation of the term "incurred" was historically generally accepted as applying in Hong Kong. For example, the IRD traditionally accepted as deductible in the year in which they were incurred, prepaid expenses reflected in the taxpayer's profit and loss account in the periods to which they relate rather than when legally incurred. The correctness of this position was, however, called into doubt by the decision of the Court of Final Appeal in *CIR v Secan Limited & Anor.* [2001] (I HKRC 90-107). That case concerned two companies which developed property for sale. The property developments of the taxpayers were financed by way of bank borrowings and, in accordance with normal accountancy principles, the interest incurred on those borrowings was capitalised to the trading stock under construction. In determining their assessable profits, however, that taxpayers sought to deduct the interest incurred both in relation to properties sold and in relation to properties unsold at year end. Essentially, the taxpayers argued that Sec. 16(1) (and more particularly Sec. 16(1)(a)) authorised a deduction for all interest expenses when incurred, even though those expenses related to assessable profit to be derived in a future period (when the relevant property was sold).

Both the Court of First Instance (see *Secan Limited v CIR*; *Ranon Limited v CIR* [1999] (1 HKRC 90-097)) and the Court of Appeal (see *CIR v Secan Limited*; *CIR v Ranon Limited* [2000] (1 HKRC 90-103)) effectively held that the interest was deductible when it was due and payable even though it was capitalised for accounting purposes and related to the derivation of future assessable profits. In doing so, those courts accepted that the deductibility of an expense was to be determined solely by reference to Sec. 16 and that this provision authorised the deduction of an amount incurred even if not reflected in the taxpayer's profit and loss account.

On appeal, however, the Court of Final Appeal reached the opposite conclusion. In that judgment (delivered by Lord Millett), the court took the view that assessable profits were to be determined by looking to profits determined in accordance with ordinary accounting principles and that such profits could only be determined by deducting the expenses incurred in earning those profits. As such, the court held that Sec. 16 was not necessary to authorise the deduction of such expenses, but was enacted to protect the Revenue and was to be read "... *in a negative sense* ..." as denying a deduction for expenses which were not incurred in the relevant period. It seems, therefore, that the court was suggesting that the accounting treatment of an expense determines whether it can be admitted as a deduction for tax purposes and if the expense is not debited to the taxpayer's profit and loss account in the particular year, a deduction is not permitted. If this interpretation is correct, it effectively means that the meaning of "incurred" as developed by the Australian courts no longer applies in Hong Kong but has been replaced by the interpretation that an amount is "incurred" when expensed in the taxpayer's profit and loss account.

At this stage, however, it is not clear how broadly the Court of Final Appeal's judgment in the *Secan* case (supra) may be interpreted in subsequent decisions and, more specifically, whether its application will be restricted to expenses in connection with trading stock, or whether it will be applied to all expenses for which a deduction is sought. In particular, the case concerned the deductibility of expenses incurred in the creation of trading stock which are generally accepted as not being deductible until such stock is sold. The rationale for this treatment of trading stock is arguably that trading stock is taken into account in calculating gross profit and, in the absence of any broad statutory provision governing the recognition of profit for tax purposes, this should follow the accounting treatment. On the other hand, however, in deducting expenses for the purpose of determining net profit, it is necessary to meet the conditions set out in Sec. 16. Accordingly, it is possible that the court had in mind that their judgment would apply only in respect of expenses related to the creation of trading stock. Certainly, the Court of Final Appeal paid particular attention to the accounting for the interest expenses in question and noted that it had been debited to the taxpayer's profit and loss account but then credited back to that account and debited to the value of trading stock. Moreover, they noted that the first step in determining a taxpayer's profit or loss was to determine the trading profit or loss (i.e. the gross profit or loss). These factors together could be taken as suggesting that the Court of Final Appeal was approaching the issue as one of gross profit recognition rather than one of deduction of expenses to arrive at net profit; under such circumstances it would then arguably be correct to ignore Sec. 16. On the other hand, however, the court specifically analysed Sec. 16 and did not conclude it was irrelevant, but rather, as discussed above, held that it was to be read only as denying a deduction for expenses included in the taxpayer's profit and loss account but which were not incurred in the relevant period.

Subsequent to the Court of Final Appeal's decision, the IRD issued *Departmental Interpretation & Practice Notes No. 40*. That document is concerned specifically with prepaid expenses, although it is clearly implied by the IRD's analysis that they believe the decision in *Secan* is to be interpreted very broadly, and not limited to expenses in connection with trading stock. On the question of prepaid expenses, *Departmental Interpretation & Practice Notes No. 40* concludes that on the basis of the *Secan* decision, these are to be deducted for tax purposes not when they are paid, but when they are amortised in the claimant's profit and loss account. Interestingly, the document goes on to note that allowing the deduction of an amortised portion of an amount in a year subsequent to that in which it was paid is not inconsistent with Sec. 16 on the grounds that it is only in that year that the amount is incurred; this conclusion, although based on the Court of Appeal's judgement, still stands in stark contrast to decades of established case law both in Hong Kong and elsewhere.

The prudence concept of accounting will often necessitate a provision for an anticipated expense or loss and this may need to be adjusted for tax purposes if it cannot be said to have been incurred (*Edward Collins and Sons v CIR* (12 TC 773)). Even where a liability has arisen in a year, however, it is not necessarily the case that it can be quantified accurately; for example, where a customer has notified a claim for damages which is admitted but not yet agreed in amount, a provision will usually be made for accounting purposes and that provision will be deductible if:—

(1)   it is a specific provision for a liability that has accrued in the basis period; and

(2)   it is ascertained with substantial accuracy.

For a discussion on the principles and a summary of earlier authorities see *Owen v Southern Railway of Peru* (36 TC 602) and the Hong Kong case of *CIR v Lo & Lo* (2 HKTC 34). Where, however, the liability is contingent upon some future event, it cannot be said to have been incurred and is not, therefore, deductible until the contingency crystallizes.

■ Example 4.16

Payool Ltd. has an accounting date of 01 December and each year makes a provision in respect of bonuses to employees. The employees fall into two groups.

The office staff have contracts of employment which entitle them to an annual bonus, subject to good conduct, based on the company's results. If they have not worked for the company's full year they are paid a pro-rata amount. The bonuses are paid at the Chinese New Year.

The factory staff are paid an additional month's salary at the Chinese New Year provided they are in employment at that date.

The provisions are calculated as accurately as possible at 31 December and the figure is rounded off.

The provision in respect of office staff will be allowed because a liability is incurred day by day throughout the year and it is ascertained with substantial accuracy.

The provision in respect of factory staff will not be allowed because the liability is not incurred until Chinese New Year, being contingent upon being in service at that date. It will be allowed when paid in the following period.

4.5.7 Expenditure — capital v revenue

There are a number of provisions in the IRO which deem certain expenses, which are otherwise incurred in the production of assessable profits, to be non deductible; most of these provisions are discussed in section 4.5.8 below. Sec. 17(1)(c), however, is one such provision which, because of its significance, is more appropriately considered separately. In particular, this provision disallows as a deduction any expenditure of a capital nature or any loss or withdrawal of capital.

The following is a general discussion of the basic principles which govern the identification of capital expenditure; the reader is, however, referred to the substantial body of case law in the UK and elsewhere, for a more in-depth analysis and for examples of how specific items have been considered by the courts.

One of the earliest tests to identify capital expenditure was put forward by Lord Dunedin in *Vallambrosa Rubber Co. v Farmer* (5 TC 529) when he suggested that capital expenditure is that which is made "once and for all" whereas revenue expenditure will "recur year by year". Unfortunately this test is really much too simple and has so many exceptions that it cannot be regarded as a general rule standing on its own. A little later the test was expanded and qualified into what is now regarded as the classic and most often quoted rule, that of Viscount Cave in *British Insulated and Helsby Cables v Atherton* (10 TC 155) when he stated:—

> *"But when an expenditure is made, not only once and for all but with a view to bringing into existence an asset or an advantage for the enduring benefit of a trade, I think that there is very good reason (in the absence of special circumstances leading to an opposite conclusion) for treating such an expenditure as properly attributable, not to revenue, but to capital."*

Most decisions flow from and can be reconciled to this rule; nevertheless, it must be treated with caution lest its wording be given too wide a meaning. It is perhaps relatively simple to identify the cases in which an asset is brought into existence, whether it be a tangible or intangible asset. As regards the creation of an enduring advantage, it is too simplistic to refer to the *Atherton* case and conclude that because an expenditure in question gives rise to an advantage it is of a capital nature. What must be remembered is that all expenditure gives rise to an advantage or it would not have been incurred. What is important is whether the advantage is enduring in nature and this implies something which is not necessarily permanent but of which the span is appreciably longer than that created by normal revenue expenditure. In other words, an annual bonus to employees certainly creates the advantage of willing service for a full year but if it is not paid next time, the advantage quickly fades; accordingly, such payments are of a revenue nature. On the other hand, a payment to a departing employee in order to secure his covenant not to compete after he has left is a long lasting advantage and, therefore, of a capital nature (*Associated Portland Cement Manufacturers v IRC* (27 TC 103)).

Similarly, regular contributions to maintain an employee pension scheme are of a revenue nature but the initial contribution to create the nucleus of the fund is of a capital nature (the *Atherton* case and also *Rowntree & Co. v Curtis* (8 TC 678)), although a deduction may be available over five years for such amounts pursuant to Sec. 16A (see point (9) in section 4.5.8).

It is not always clear, however, whether an advantage should be considered as enduring or not. In the case of *FCT v Citylink Melbourne Limited* ([2006] (HCA 35)) the Australian High Court considered the position of a series of semi-annual payments made in exchange for the grant of a right by a government to the company to design, build, commission and operate a toll road over a period of 38 years. The Australian tax authorities had sought to treat the expenditure as capital in nature on the grounds that the payments were incurred to acquire a bundle of rights which established the profit-yielding structure of the taxpayer. This argument was rejected, however, on the basis that the payments were in the nature of periodic license fees in respect of the use of assets that ultimately were to be surrendered back to the government; as such, there was no enduring benefit obtained as a result of the payments and the payments were deductible.

That decision should, however, be contrasted with the decisions in *D 21/ 06* and *D 28/06* where lump sum payments to obtain a franchise right for seven years were held to be capital in nature and not deductible. The payments in question resulted in the grant of rights to carry on the business and to use the franchisor's trade name and certain other business assets but, as in the *Citylink Melbourne Limited* case, there was no permanent acquisition of those assets. Although these cases were decided without reference to the *Citylink Melbourne Limited* case, it is clear that the difference in the structuring of the payment for the rights (i.e. as a lump sum payment rather than a periodic license fee) was a critical factor which weighed against the taxpayers' arguments that the amounts were deductible.

For another case which considered the nature of an advantage, see *D 62/87* where payments to an extortionist to prevent disruption of a business were held not to create an enduring advantage and did not, therefore, constitute capital expenditure.

The fact that the intended advantage does not materialize or that the intended asset is not acquired and, therefore, expenditure laid out in anticipation thereof is abortive is not a ground for regarding it as revenue expenditure (*Southwell v Savill Bros.* (4 TC 430)).

There are a number of cases which establish the principle that depreciation of capital assets, whether tangible or intangible, is a capital item. This is, however, replaced by the statutory depreciation allowances (see Chapter 6).

There are also principles which emerge from case law regarding expenditure on getting rid of some undesirable factor that is a hindrance to business. More specifically, the cost of removing an undesirable capital asset has been held to be of a capital nature (*Mallett v Staveley Coal and Iron Co.* (13 TC 772)) because this creates an advantage as enduring as the asset itself, whereas the cost of commuting a future onerous revenue charge in fact does nothing more than replace that revenue expenditure and, therefore, is itself of a revenue nature (*Hancock v General Revisionary and Investment

Co. (7 TC 358)). See also *D 95/89* where a forfeited rental deposit in respect of a tenancy agreement which was not proceeded with when the taxpayer decided that the proposed business venture was not viable, was held, by a majority, to be non-deductible on the grounds that it related to a capital asset, albeit an onerous one. Similarly, in *D 58/02* a rental deposit which was written off following the insolvency of the landlord was held to be non-deductible because, *inter alia*, it was of a capital nature. A payment to terminate an onerous trading agreement, however, has been held to be of a revenue nature (*Anglo-Persian Oil Co. Ltd. v Dale* (16 TC 253)).

Although the cost of bringing into existence or improving or adding to an asset, together with all related incidental expenditure such as legal fees, is of a capital nature, once in existence the cost of protecting that asset is of a revenue nature (*Southern v Borax Consolidated* (23 TC 597)).

The question of whether a payment under a guarantee is of a capital or revenue nature, will depend upon the precise facts of the case, although *D 7/87* is a useful summary of a number of decisions on this issue.

Where a payment is in the nature of compensation or damages, it is necessary to consider to what it relates as it normally follows the treatment of the transaction upon which the liability arose. In other words, if it is damages arising out of a trading contract, say for the supply of faulty goods, it is of a revenue nature but if it is in respect of a capital asset, it would normally be of a capital nature. It is, however, important not to confuse the basis of calculation of the compensation with the reason for its payment. For example, compensation may be paid for the destruction of all or part of a business, but may be calculated on the basis of lost profits; although the profits would have been taxable, the compensation should still be considered of a capital nature and non-taxable.

Notwithstanding a wealth of legal decisions on the issue, many cases revolve very much around their own facts; accordingly, the cases should be treated as no more than guidelines unless an exact parallel of facts exists. For example, some decisions may appear to be exactly contrary to the rules quoted above and, whilst this does sometimes happen, a close examination of the facts and the judgement will usually indicate why. For a review of many of the more important decisions see the case of *Regent Oil Co. v Strick* (43 TC 1).

The rules established by case law are modified, in certain circumstances, by specific provisions in the IRO, which will be identified in their context, and by concession and practice. For example, the Second Inland Revenue Ordinance Review Committee considered the case of the cost of removal of a business to a new location, which is probably of a capital nature but often allowed as a deduction in practice; in particular, they reported the IRD practice as follows:—

"In considering any claim for removal expenses it is necessary to look into the circumstances and the nature of the expenditure incurred. The cost of removal of trading stock is normally admitted as a revenue expense. Where the removal has been undertaken wholly or mainly as part of a scheme for improvement and expansion or in the interests of the business, and the removal has been made voluntarily, the removal expenses should normally be regarded as of a capital nature. In such circumstances, the part of the expenditure which relates to the dismantling, transport and re-erection of machinery, etc. would be treated as qualifying for initial and annual allowances. Where, however, the removal is not voluntary but is primarily forced upon the trader by circumstances such as the refusal of a landlord to renew a lease or the redevelopment of the site, the cost of removal is normally allowed as a revenue charge. In such cases, the cost may include not merely the actual transport between the old and new premises, but also the cost of dismantling and reinstalling plant, machinery, fittings, etc."

An area which regularly gives rise to disputes in Hong Kong is that of the treatment of foreign exchange gains and losses. It follows that where a business of dealing in foreign currencies is carried on, the profits there-from must be of a revenue nature. In this regard, see the decision in *D 5/96*, which was confirmed on appeal to the Court of First Instance (see *CIR v General Garment Manufactory (Hong Kong) Limited* [1997] (1 HKRC 90 090)). That decision confirms the revenue nature of gains or losses arising from currency speculation and provides some guidance as to the determination of whether such a business is, as a matter of fact, carried on. The decision also makes it clear that a business of speculating in foreign currency can be carried on even if the principal business of the taxpayer is something else.

The more difficult questions concern foreign exchange gains and losses which arise out of keeping accounts in foreign currencies and/or incurring liabilities in, and earning income in, foreign currencies in the course of carrying on some trade or business. In such cases, the principal determinant of whether the gains or losses are assessable or deductible is whether they are of a capital or revenue nature. If the gains or losses are of a revenue nature they will be assessable or deductible, as the case may be. If, on the other hand, the gains or losses are of a capital nature, they will, as with other capital sums, not be assessable or deductible.

Whether exchange gains and losses are realised or unrealised has traditionally sometimes also been relevant in determining the timing of the assessability or deductibility (see sections 4.5.1 and 4.5.6 above). In particular, it had long been accepted by the IRD that taxpayers other than financial institutions could choose to exclude unrealised exchange gains and losses from their computation of assessable profits, provided that the practice was consistently applied and that appropriate adjustments were made to the assessable profits computations when the gains or losses are realised. As discussed in section 4.5.1, however, there is now a clear trend by the courts to look to the accounting treatment of an amount to determine its assessability or deductibility, irrespective of whether or not the amount is realised; accordingly, the correctness of the IRD's traditional practice, given the current state of case law, became questionable. Accordingly, it was not surprising that when the IRD issued *Departmental Interpretation & Practice Notes No. 42,* which generally deals with the taxation of financial instruments, that they took the opportunity to advise that from the 2005/06 year of assessment, the IRD would not accept any claims for the exclusion from assessable profits of any foreign exchange gains and losses on the basis that they are unrealised.

A full discussion of the principles governing whether or not exchange gains or losses are of a capital or revenue nature is highly complicated and outside the scope of this book. There are, however, some general guidelines by which these problems can be solved. The most important rule in dealing with an exchange gain or loss which is not derived from a transaction undertaken for speculative purpose is that it always arises out of some other transaction and is, therefore, tied to it such that the gain or loss has the same character as the transaction to which it is related.

For example, a profit on sale of goods is, of course, a revenue transaction. If, however, a trader who keeps his accounts in Hong Kong dollars bills a foreign customer, and receives payment, in euros and during the period between the time of the transaction and the receipt of the euros the movement in exchange rates creates a profit on exchange, that profit is merely an addition to the profit on sale of goods. Nonetheless, if upon receipt of the euros the trader places them on deposit, any further exchange gain or loss may be of a capital nature (and not assessable or deductible) on the basis of the decision in *CIR v Li & Fung Limited* (see below).

As another example, if a euro loan is taken out to finance the fixed assets of a business and between the date of taking up the loan and repaying it some years later there is an upward movement of euros against Hong Kong dollars, the loss on exchange is in effect a loss of fixed capital and non-deductible. Alternatively, if the loan had been a temporary overdraft to finance working capital, the loss would likely have been a loss of working or circulating capital and of a revenue nature and, therefore, deductible.

The following legal decisions illustrate these principles further:—

(1)   *Golden Horseshoe (New) Ltd. v Thurgood* (18 TC 280) — This case contains a good discussion of the distinction between, and the relevance of, fixed capital and circulating capital.

(2)   *Beauchamp v F. W. Woolworth Plc.* (61 TC 542) — If a loan adds to the capital structure of a business, any exchange differences on repayment will be on capital account, irrespective of the use to which the borrowed funds are put. An exchange difference on a loan will be of a revenue nature where the loan is a temporary and fluctuating facility and is incidental to the day to day carrying on of the business. Where, however, a loan is of a long term fixed nature it will be viewed as an addition to the capital structure of the business and any exchange differences thereon will be capital in nature. This decision was followed in *D 14/92* where an exchange loss was disallowed on the grounds that the underlying loan was an addition to the company's capital structure notwithstanding that it was used to finance a property which the Board of Review had concluded was a trading asset.

(3)   *FC of T v Hunter Douglas Ltd.* (83 ATC 4562) — Although exchange differences on the repayment of loans will generally be on capital account, there are exceptions to this rule and these are identified by looking to the purpose for which the borrowing was made. A borrowing by a finance company for on lending to customers or a borrowing by a trader for the financing of the purchase of his trading stock are examples of such exceptions and exchange differences on such transactions would be on revenue account. Contrast this with (2) above.

(4)   *Theiss Toyota Pty. Ltd. v FC of T* (78 ATC 4463) — An exchange difference on financing trading stock is of a revenue nature, but only where the financing transaction is closely linked to the trading transaction.

(5)   *CIR v Chinachem Finance Co. Ltd.* (3 HKTC 529) — Exchange losses on loans, of varying terms of up to 9.5 years but which were repayable on demand, taken out by a group finance company were held to be revenue in nature. The loans were considered to be an integral and ordinary part of the taxpayer's business operations and did not add to the capital structure of that business. The case was distinguished from (2) above on the basis of the nature of the business.

(6)   *Texas Co. (Australasia) Ltd. v FC of T* (5 ATD 298) — Exchange differences on the settlement of debts in relation to the purchase of trading stock (as opposed to the financing of trading stock) were held to be on revenue account.

(7)   *Davies v Shell Co. of China* (32 TC 133) — Deposits made with a

principal by a selling agent to cover future liabilities to account for sales proceeds were regarded as fixed capital and, therefore, exchange losses on those deposits were capital losses.

(8) *Landes Bros. v Simpson* (19 TC 62) — Advances made to a principal against sales made on behalf of the principal were regarded as incidental to the sales and, therefore, of a revenue nature. Contrast this with (7) above.

(9) *CIR v Li & Fung Ltd.* (HKTC 1193) — Receipts in a foreign currency from trade debtors were placed on deposit on 7-day call after which they were either used to meet debts in that currency or remitted to Hong Kong. The funds were regarded as having changed their character from trading receipts to capital investments at the time they were placed on deposit. Therefore, foreign exchange losses on the deposits were of a capital nature.

(10) *CIR v Hang Seng Bank Ltd.* [1972] (HKTC 583) — Exchange differences on a bank's assets were held to be generally of a revenue nature as money is the trading stock of a financial institution. Accordingly, an exchange loss incurred by a Hong Kong business on deposits in overseas accounts was held to be deductible, notwithstanding that the interest on those deposits had a non-Hong Kong source.

4.5.8 Expenditure deemed deductible

The IRO also contains a number of provisions which specifically deal with the deductibility certain expenditure and these are discussed below; in some cases, these provisions appear to exist solely for the avoidance of doubt, whilst in other cases the provisions deem as deductible expenditure which would otherwise fail the general tests for deductibility and yet others impose restrictions on what would otherwise be deductible. With regard to the latter, following the decision of the Court of Final Appeal in the *Secan* case (see discussion in section 4.5.6), it seems likely that at least those provisions discussed below which are contained in Sec. 16(1) would operate only to restrict deductibility and, in particular, would not authorise a deduction for amounts not expensed in the claimant's accounts. For a more detailed discussion of the reasoning for this, see the discussion under point (1) below.

It is important to remember, however, that it is not only expenditure that meets the following rules which is deductible; any expenditure which satisfies the general rules for deductibility will be allowable unless precluded by these rules or by the rules discussed in section 4.5.7 above or section 4.5.10 below.

The specific items to which the deeming provisions apply are separately considered in the following paragraphs.

(1) **Loan interest and related expenditure:** Sec. 16(1)(a), Sec. 16(2) and Secs. 16(2A) to (2H), together impose extensive and complex restrictions on the deductibility of interest and related expenditure. Moreover, these rules have undergone extensive changes recently. Due to their complexity, these rules are considered separately in section 4.5.9 below.

(2) **Rent:** Rent paid in respect of land or buildings occupied for the purpose of producing assessable profits is specifically made deductible by Sec. 16(1)(b). This is, perhaps, obvious and it is not really necessary to have a specific provision for deductibility. It is, however, provided that where the rent is paid to the spouse of the tenant or is paid by a partnership to one or more of the partners, or the spouse of a partner, the deduction is limited to rent equal to the assessable value of the land or buildings for Property Tax purposes (see section 2.3.2). This really dates back to the circumstances which applied many years ago because, since 1983/84, the assessable value has been based on actual rent; therefore, there is little room for avoidance between such related parties and the limitation is unnecessary.

(3) **Foreign taxes:** Sec. 16(1)(c) provides that a deduction is available for foreign taxes paid by corporations, or by persons other than corporations who are carrying on a trade, profession or business in Hong Kong, on interest income or profits from the disposal or redemption of certificates of deposit or bills of exchange assessable to Profits Tax under Sec. 15(1)(f), Sec. 15(1)(g), Sec. 15(1)(i), Sec. 15(1)(j), Sec. 15(1)(k) or Sec. 15(1)(l) (see section 4.5.4 above). A further condition for deductibility is that the tax is of substantially the same nature as tax imposed under the IRO, which presumably means that it must be an income tax, although it can be assessed either directly or by withholding. This does not amount to full double taxation relief because the foreign tax is only deductible, rather than creditable against the Hong Kong liability. The deduction is, however, denied if the corporation or other person qualifies for double tax relief under Part VIII of the IRO in respect of such profits. Double tax relief is discussed in Chapter 10, although it need only be noted at this point that only limited relief is currently available under Part VIII and, therefore, this limitation on deduction is likely to have little application in practice.

The various qualifications for the deduction are, therefore, that:

(i)   the underlying income must be subject to Profits Tax under Sec. 15(1)(f), Sec. 15(1)(g), Sec. 15(1)(i), Sec. 15(1)(j), Sec. 15(1)(k) or Sec. 15(1)(l);

(ii) the foreign tax must be an income tax; and

(iii) the claimant must not qualify for any other form of double tax relief (see Chapter 10).

Prior to the 1997/98 year of assessment, there was a further condition contained in the provision which restricted its application, in the case of a corporation, to those managed and controlled in Hong Kong. The deletion of this extra condition can be traced to case *D 43/91*, a decision which considerably widened the scope for deductibility of foreign taxes. In particular, in that case, which involved a shipping company, it was held that foreign taxes which were imposed on gross income (rather than profits) and the payment of which were necessary for the taxpayer to continue to derive income in the overseas territory were expenses incurred in the production of assessable profits and, therefore, qualified for deduction under Sec. 16(1). Although not discussed in the judgement, it seems that the Board of Review did not consider that Sec. 16(1) (c) should be interpreted as imposing limitations on the general deductibility of foreign taxes; that is, they considered that a foreign tax which was deductible under the general provision of Sec. 16(1) did not need to also qualify under Sec. 16(1)(c). This should be contrasted to the decision in *CIR v County Shipping* (3 HKTC 267) concerning the interpretation of Sec. 16(1)(a).

Although for a number of years following the handing down of the judgement in *D 43/91* the IRD continued to argue that the case had only limited application, it appears that they ultimately realised that such an argument was not sustainable. Accordingly, in his 1997 Budget Speech, the Financial Secretary announced that IRD practice was to give broad application to the decision in *D 43/91* and that the IRO would be amended to give effect to that practice. It is interesting to note that, as discussed above, the decision in *D 43/91* suggested that only taxes levied on turnover or gross income qualified for deduction; however, the 1997 amendments to Sec. 16(1)(c), by still granting a deduction for taxes of substantially the same nature as those imposed under the IRO, clearly also allow a deduction for taxes levied on a net profit basis.

Following the amendments to Sec. 16(1)(c), the Commissioner

issued *Departmental Interpretation & Practice Notes No. 28*. In this document it is noted that Sec. 16(1)(c) applies only to taxes imposed on sums which are assessable to Profits Tax only pursuant to the specified deeming provisions. It goes on to observe, however, that where an amount of foreign tax does not qualify for deduction under Sec. 16(1)(c), it may still be deductible pursuant to the general provision of Sec. 16(1), but only where the tax is an expense which must be borne regardless of whether or not a profit is derived and is not an appropriation of profit.

(4)   **Bad and doubtful debts:** Sec. 16(1)(d) provides a deduction for bad debts as well as doubtful debts that have become bad during the basis period notwithstanding that the debts may have been due and payable in an earlier period. Because it is often a subjective matter whether a debt has become bad, the provision requires the assessor to be satisfied that the debts have become bad before a deduction is allowed. In this regard, it is usually necessary to show that positive action has been taken to enforce collection and that this has proved fruitless; the fact that the debt is doubtful is insufficient; it must have become bad and clearly, therefore, if a provision has been made, it must be a specific provision.

However, if an accounting provision has not been made, it is unlikely that the assessor will be satisfied that the debt has become bad. Quite often, in respect of a particular accounting period an accounting provision will not have been made but events subsequent to the accounting date will make it clear that the debt was, in fact, irrecoverable. In these circumstances, as a matter of practice, the IRD will not entertain a claim that the debt was deductible in the earlier period. For cases where taxpayers were unsuccessful in reopening earlier year's assessments in such circumstances, see *D 39/91* and *D 52/99*.

Furthermore, in practice for a deduction that the debt in question must have been originally brought in as a trading receipt; in other words, a loan to a customer for example, even if it was in default and irrecoverable, would not be deductible because it would not represent a trading receipt. The exception to this rule, of course, is a loan in the ordinary course of a money-lending business because, although there is no equivalent credit to the profit and loss account, money is nonetheless the trading stock of such a business and it would be unfair to deny tax relief for such a loss of trading stock (Sec. 16(1)(d) proviso (i)).

It is clear that whether a person is engaged in the *"... ordinary course of a moneylending business ..."* is a question to be determined on the particular facts of each case and that the phrase does not necessarily apply only to what is perhaps the layman's view of moneylenders as financial institutions and mainstream finance companies. A good summary of the principles involved can be found in *Shun Lee Investment Co. Ltd. v CIR* (HKTC 322). For cases where the investment of surplus funds with financial institutions has been considered to amount to a moneylending business see *FCT v Marshall and Brougham* (87 ATC 4522) and *D 104/89*. Contrast these cases, however, with *D 55/95* where an engineering company was unsuccessful in claiming a deduction for a bank deposit which was lost when the bank concerned went into bankruptcy. This case was interesting in that although Sec. 16(1)(d) was considered, the taxpayer's case was primarily that the loss qualified for deduction under the general provision of Sec. 16(1) on the grounds that it was an expense incurred in the production of assessable profits. In rejecting this argument, the Board of Review noted that what was suffered was a loss, and that a loss was quite different from an "expense" or "outgoing," which are what are permitted to be deducted under Sec. 16(1). Moreover, the Board went on to note that even if a loss was within the ambit of Sec. 16(1), it was not possible to demonstrate a nexus between the incurring of the loss in question and the derivation of assessable profits; that is, the Board could not accept that the depositing of the funds in a bank was critical to the earning of the company's trading profits.

For a case where a company which acted as a finance company only for other group companies was considered to be in the business of lending money see *CIR v Chinachem Finance Co. Ltd.* (3 HKTC 529), although this was a case concerning the deductibility of exchange losses rather than the application of Sec. 16(1)(d). A similar conclusion was reached in *D 153/98*, although this case should be contrasted with *D 38/89* and *D 67/91* where the opposite conclusion was reached on the particular facts and evidence. The latter of these cases contains an interesting summary of the factors which the Board of Review considered were relevant in determining whether a business of moneylending was being carried on.

If any bad debt which has previously been allowed as a deduction is ultimately recovered, it is treated as a trading receipt of the period in which it is recovered (Sec. 16(1)(d) proviso (ii)).

See (iii) of section 4.7.7 for a specific discussion of the position of a financial institution with regard to bad debt deductions.

(5) **Repairs:** Sec. 16(1)(e) grants a deduction for costs of repairs to premises, plant, machinery, implements, utensils or articles which are employed in the production of assessable profits. The terms implement, utensil or article are defined by IRR2(1) as including the following:—

- Belting
- Crockery and cutlery
- Kitchen utensils
- Linen
- Loose tools
- Soft furnishings (including curtains and carpets)
- Surgical and dental instruments
- Tubes for X-ray and infra-red machines

As will be seen in Chapter 5, these items do not qualify for depreciation allowances on their initial purchase.

(6) **Replacements:** The cost of replacing any implement, utensil or article as defined in IRR2(1) (see (5) above) is deductible under Sec. 16(1)(f) so long as no depreciation allowance is claimed, although such a claim is specifically prohibited by IRR2(1). Without this provision, the expenditure would constitute disallowable capital expenditure and the relationship between this provision and the disallowance of depreciation allowances is merely a means of granting relief on a replacement basis for a limited class of capital expenditure.

(7) **Registration of trade marks, patents and designs:** Normally, expenditure on these items would be disqualified as capital expenditure but for Sec. 16(1)(g) which permits a deduction where the trade mark, patent or design is used for the purposes of earning assessable profits. Note that it is only expenses "for the registration" of a trademark or design which are allowable under Sec. 16(1)(g), although the provision allows a deduction for either the registration or grant of a patent. See, however, Sec. 16E which is discussed in (8) below and which grants a deduction for sums expended in connection with the acquisition of certain patent rights and know-how.

(8) **Purchase cost of patent rights etc.:** These items would also be capital expenditure and, therefore, disallowable but for Sec. 16E. In particular, this provision allows a deduction in the basis period in which the expenditure is incurred for the cost of purchasing patent rights or rights to any know-how, provided that the rights are to be used in Hong Kong in producing profits chargeable to Profits Tax (Sec. 16E(1)). "Patent rights" are defined in Sec. 16E(4) as the right

to do or authorise the doing of anything which would, but for that right, be an infringement of a patent.

Sec. 16E(2A), however, denies the deduction where the rights are purchased from an associate. For these purposes, an "associate" is widely defined in Sec. 16E(4). The definition is substantially the same as for some other purposes in the IRO and is discussed in detail in section 5.10.2. Further provisions in Sec. 16E(2B) are designed to prevent avoidance of this restriction by the use of trust arrangements.

Where the rights are to be used partly in Hong Kong and partly elsewhere, only that part of the cost which is attributable to the use in Hong Kong is to be deductible (Sec. 16E(2)). There is no guidance in the law as to how any necessary apportionment is to be made, only that the method should be "reasonable and appropriate". Any practical and realistic method, such as one based on turnover or units produced, should be acceptable.

Expenditure incurred on only a share or interest in any qualifying rights is deductible in the same way as the cost of the whole rights would be (Sec. 16E(5)).

If the rights are subsequently sold, the proceeds of sale are to be brought in as a trading receipt and, therefore, charged to Profits Tax for the basis period in which the sale falls or the final basis period if it is a post cessation receipt. If only a proportion of the original cost had been deductible, because the rights were only partly for use in Hong Kong, only a relevant proportion of the sale proceeds are to be brought in as a trading receipt (Sec. 16E(3)). It is not clear how the sale proceeds are to be apportioned, particularly where the extent of use in Hong Kong has varied over the period of ownership. Logically, however, the apportionment of sales proceeds should be identical to the apportionment of the original cost. It should also be noted that the taxable amount is not limited to original cost so there is potentially taxation of a capital gain.

It should be noted that where a right is sold which had been acquired before the basis period for 1982/83, the sales proceeds are not to be taxed because the original cost would not have been deductible as Sec. 16E did not apply before that time. However, proceeds of sale of any trade mark or design for which a deduction had been obtained under the law as it existed between the date of commencement of the law and 18 April 1991, when the provision was amended to be more restrictive, continue to be taxable (Sec. 16E(6)).

(9) **Contributions to retirement schemes:** Regular contributions to a retirement scheme in respect of employees would generally be considered of a revenue nature and, therefore, deductible to the extent that they satisfy the other normal rules for deductibility. The deductibility of such payment would not generally be dependent upon whether or not the retirement scheme is recognized under the *Occupational Retirement Schemes Ordinance* (see Chapter 10), although it should be noted that it is an offence under that ordinance to make a contribution to a scheme which is not registered under, or been granted exemption from, that ordinance, unless the scheme is established under another Hong Kong ordinance. Moreover, as is discussed in section 4.5.10 below, Sec. 17(1)(l) specifically denies a deduction for contributions to a retirement scheme other than a recognized occupational retirement scheme. Additionally, there are other provisions which restrict the deductibility of payments to retirement schemes generally and these are also dealt with in section 4.5.10 below.

Although ordinary contributions to retirement schemes in respect of employees would generally be deductible pursuant to the general deductibility rules, the same cannot be said in respect of contributions by a sole proprietor in respect of himself, or by a partnership in respect of a partner. This is because remuneration of a sole proprietor or a partner is not considered incurred in earning the assessable profits of the sole proprietor or partnership. Nonetheless, the Government has decided that because sole proprietors and partnerships are required to make contributions to a MPF scheme, in respect of the sole proprietor and partners respectively, such contributions should be deductible. Accordingly, Sec. 16AA grants a deduction for such contributions by deeming them to be have been incurred wholly and exclusively in the production of the profits of the sole proprietor or partnership. Of course, if a portion of the profits of the sole proprietor or partnership are not assessable to Profits Tax (for example, because they have a non Hong Kong source), the deduction will need to be apportioned.

The deduction is limited to the mandatory contributions required to be made (i.e. voluntary contributions in excess of the minimum required contributions will not be deductible) and cannot exceed the amount to be specified in Sch. 3B. The amount specified by Sch. 3B is currently $12,000 per year of assessment, which is the maximum mandatory contributions which can be required to be made in respect of a person under the current terms of the *Mandatory Provident Fund Schemes Ordinance*.

Finally, the deduction is further limited by any amount which can be deducted under Sec. 26G (see section 3.5.7). This restriction could possibly apply where a sole proprietor also derived income subject to Salaries Tax and made mandatory contributions to an MPF scheme in relation to that employment. In such circumstances, those contributions would be deductible under Sec. 26G and this would reduce or eliminate the deduction available under Sec. 16AA.

Payments to retirement schemes other than ordinary annual contributions may, however, be of a capital nature, as was held to be the position of an initial contribution in the case of *Atherton v British Insulated and Helsby Cables Ltd.* (10 TC 155). Nonetheless, Sec. 16A provides for the deduction of such payments, subject to certain limitations including the denial of a deduction for all payments for which a provision had previously been made and a deduction granted. In particular, where a contribution is made, other than an ordinary annual contribution, or an insurance premium payment is made, other than an ordinary annual insurance premium, in respect of a recognized occupational retirement scheme, such payments are deductible in five equal instalments over five years of assessment beginning with the basis period in which the payment was made (Sec. 16A(2)). This provision also extends to any contribution, other than a regular contribution, to a MPF scheme. For this purpose, regular contributions are defined by Sec. 16A(3) to be contributions made at regular intervals which are either similar, or substantially similar, or are of amounts calculated by reference to a scale or a fixed percentage of a person's salary or other remuneration.

Sec. 16A applies only to "payments"; therefore, where there is no independent fund but annual provisions are set aside, the deductibility would normally be governed by the general rules regarding provisions which are discussed in section 4.5.6 above. It is important to note that where there is a binding obligation to pay an amount in due course, the provisions are not contingent (as it is only a question of when, rather than if, the amounts become payable) and, therefore, such provisions would generally be deductible provided that they are computed with substantial accuracy, and this principle extends to a mandatory provision for back years service (*IRC v Titaghur Jute Factory* (53 TC 675) and *CIR v Lo & Lo* (2 HKTC 34)). Following the decision in the *Lo & Lo* case, however, the IRO was amended by inserting Sec. 17(1)(j) which renders provisions in respect of retirement schemes deductible only where they are in respect of ordinary annual contributions to a recognized occupational retirement schemes (see definition in section 10.3.1) or regular contributions to a MPF scheme. Deductions for such provisions are also limited to 15% of the relevant employee's emoluments, less any actual contributions deducted in the relevant year of assessment. Accordingly, a provision for a special payment is rendered non-deductible by Sec. 17(1)(j), notwithstanding that the actual payment of the amount would qualify for tax relief under Sec. 16A. For a more complete discussion of Sec. 17(1)(j), see points (9) and (10) in section 4.5.10.

(10) **Research and development expenditure:** Specific provisions, contained in Sec. 16B, exist to grant deductions for research and development expenditure, whether capital or revenue in nature, in prescribed circumstances where it is appropriately related to the trade, profession or business of the person incurring that expenditure. These provisions formerly referred to "scientific research" but were amended with effect from the 2004/05 year of assessment to refer to "research and development" which is given a wider definition than the previous terminology. Because of the change in terms and definitions, however, certain transitional provisions were introduced to deal with assets for which a deduction in respect of the acquisition cost was granted under the former provisions.

In particular, relief is granted for:

(i)   payments to an approved research institute for research and development which may be specific to the requirements of the trade, profession or business or which may be merely within that class of trade, profession or business. The point is that it must have some relevance to the trade, profession or business carried on: in other words, a contribution for cancer research would not be deductible to a textile manufacturer but would be to the operator of a sanatorium (See. 16B(1)(a)); and

(ii) expenditure by the taxpayer on research and development, including capital expenditure, other than expenditure on the acquisition of land or buildings or on alterations, additions or extensions to buildings. Expenditure on plant and machinery, for example, would attract the full deduction instead of the depreciation allowances normally granted. Upon disposal of the plant and machinery, however, the sale proceeds or other disposal receipts are, to the extent they are not otherwise subject to Profits Tax, to be brought in as a trading receipt, either in the basis period in which the disposal takes place or as a post-cessation receipt (Sec. 16B(3)). The amount of proceeds to be brought into the charge to tax is, however, limited to the amount of deduction previously granted in respect of the acquisition of that plant and machinery. For this purpose, plant and machinery the cost of which was deducted under the former provisions of Sec. 16B(1) (i.e. as "scientific research") is deemed by Sec. 16B(3)(d) to have been deducted under the present provisions and the amount of deduction granted is deemed to be the aggregate of amounts granted under either the former or the present provisions. Again the expenditure must be related to the trade, profession or business (Sec. 16B (1)(b)). Capital expenditure incurred before the commencement of trading is treated as incurred on the day of commencement and therefore deductible in the first basis period (Sec. 16B(6) (b)).

Research and development is defined in Sec. 16B(4)(a) as:

(1)   any activities in the fields of natural or applied science for the extension of knowledge;
(2)   any systematic, investigative or experimental activities carried on for the purposes of any feasibility study or in relation to any market, business or management research;
(3)   any original and planned investigations undertaken with the prospect of gaining new scientific or technical knowledge or understanding; or
(4)   the application of any research findings or other knowledge to a plan or design for the production or introduction of new or substantially improved materials, devices, products, processes, systems or services prior to the commencement of their commercial production or use.

An approved research institute is also defined in Sec. 16B(4)(a) as a university, college, institute, association or organisation approved by the Commissioner as undertaking research and development which is or may prove to be of value to Hong Kong. Such approval may operate from a date before or after the approval is granted and may be withdrawn at any time (Sec. 16B(4)(b)). Whether any given research or development is appropriately related to a trade or business is largely a question of fact but Sec. 16B(5)(b) specifies some circumstances which are to be specifically regarded as so related and these are:—

(i)   research which may lead to or facilitate an improvement or extension in the technical efficiency of that trade or business; for example, research carried out by an approved university into the processing of multifibres would benefit all textile manufacturers; and

(ii) medical research which is of special benefit to the welfare of workers in a particular industry; for example, research into the harmful effects of and alleviation of excessive noise would be of special benefit to a company employing persons in an enclosed area with noisy machinery. It is not sufficient to say that all medical research is in the interests of the welfare of all employees, as in the case of the cancer research mentioned earlier.

Expenditure is not allowed where it is for the purpose of acquiring rights in, or arising out of, scientific research but only for the original research (Sec. 16B(5)(a)). Also, where the taxpayer receives some form of direct or indirect grant, subsidy or other reimbursement for the expenditure from the Government, a local authority or any other person, only the net expenditure incurred will qualify for the deduction (Sec. 16B(6)(a)).

Where the expenditure is made or incurred outside Hong Kong and the business is carried on partly in Hong Kong and partly else where, it will be necessary to apportion the expenditure on some reasonable basis (Sec. 16B(2)). However, if the expenditure is made or incurred in Hong Kong, there is no requirement to apportion, even if part of the profits arises outside Hong Kong and is not subject to Profits Tax. This is because the deduction criteria are related to trades and businesses not to profits, presumably to encourage local research.

If any rights arising out of research and development for which a deduction under this provision has been allowed in the 1998/99 or a subsequent year of assessment are sold, the sale proceeds are, unless otherwise subject to Profits Tax, deemed by Sec. 16B(3A) to be an assessable trading receipt. Where the original expenditure was apportioned in accordance with Sec. 16B(2), however, the sales proceeds are apportioned on the same basis for the purpose of determining the assessable amount. Further, any amount assessed under this provision is limited to the amount of the original deduction in respect of the expenditure which gave rise to the rights sold. When determining the proceeds of sale, it is necessary to exclude any amount attributable to the disposal of plant or machinery (Sec. 16B (3A)(b)(i)), although any amount so excluded is nonetheless likely to be assessable, in whole or in part, pursuant to Sec. 16B(3). Where an amount of proceeds of the sale of rights is assessable under this provision, it is assessed in the year in which such sale is completed, unless the sale takes place after the permanent discontinuation of the relevant trade, profession or business, in which case it is deemed assessable in the period immediately prior to such discontinuance.

Again, as a transitional provision, Sec. 16B(3A)(c) provides that where a deduction has been allowed under the earlier form of Sec. 16B provisions (i.e. for scientific research) and any rights arising out of the relevant expenditure are sold, those rights are deemed as having arisen out of expenditure deducted under the existing (i.e. research and development) provisions; further, the amount of the deduction granted for the purpose of the provision is deemed to be the aggregate of amounts for which a deduction was claimed under either the former or the current provisions.

See also *Departmental Interpretation & Practice Notes No. 5*, which is reproduced as Appendix 4, for the IRD's views as to the interpretation of these provisions, although this document has yet to be updated for the changes made from the 2004/05 year.

(11) **Technical education:** Expenditure on technical education is likely to often fail to meet the general rules for deductibility or may specifically fall within the disallowance provisions (see section 4.5.9 below). However, presumably as an incentive for business to contribute to technical education, it is provided by Sec. 16C that, in the specified circumstances, relief is to be given. The circumstances are simply that the payment must be to any university, university college, technical college or other educational institution which has been approved in writing by the Commissioner and must be related to the trade, profession or business against which the payment is to be deducted (Sec. 16C(1)).

There is no requirement that the educational institution be in Hong Kong and the relationship between the nature of the business and the type of education is, of course, a question of fact although it is specifically stated that it must be education of a kind which is specially requisite for persons employed in the class of business in which the business operates (Sec. 16C(2)).

The approval of the Commissioner can be given with retrospective effect, if necessary, but is also revocable by the Commissioner at any time (Sec. 16C(3)). See also *Departmental Interpretation & Practice Notes No. 5* which is reproduced as Appendix 4.

(12) **Building refurbishment expenditure:** For the 1998/99 and subsequent years of assessment, a deduction is available, in equal instalments over five years of assessment, in respect of certain expenditure incurred on the refurbishment or renovation of a building or structure, other than a domestic building or structure (Sec. 16F (1)).

"Building or structure" is not defined for the purpose of this provision, other than to provide that it includes any part of a building or structure (Sec. 16F(5)), and therefore takes its normal broad meaning. "Domestic building or structure" is, however, defined in Sec. 16F(5) as any building or structure used for habitation, other than a hotel or guesthouse or any part of a building used as a hotel or guesthouse. The terms "hotel" and "guesthouse" take the meanings as defined in the *Hotel and Guesthouse Accommodation Ordinance*.

To qualify for the deduction, the relevant expenditure must be capital expenditure, although revenue expenditure would normally qualify for an outright deduction. Additionally, Sec. 16F(4) provides that capital expenditure will not qualify for the deduction where it is incurred:—

- for a building intended to be used as a domestic building or structure. This is little more than a reiteration of the provisions of Sec. 16F(1), although it does serve to make it clear that expenditure on a building currently used for non-domestic purposes, but which is intended to be used in the future for domestic purposes, will not qualify for deduction;

- by a person to enable a building or structure to be first used substantially for the production of assessable profits of that person. The effect of this is to prevent a deduction of initial fit out costs. However, because the provision does not apply only to expenditure incurred by the owner of the building or structure, it prevents a deduction being available under Sec. 16F(1) for any part of the original construction costs of the building or structure as well as any costs incurred by a new tenant, in either a new or existing building or structure, in respect of expenditure on the initial fitting out by them of the leased premises; or

- by a person to enable a building to be used for a purpose different from that for which it was used immediately before the incurring of that expenditure. This means that where a person used a building as, for example, a restaurant and then refurbished it for use as a retail store, the relevant refurbishment expenditure would not qualify for deduction under Sec. 16F(1).

Where a deduction is allowed under this provision, the relevant expenditure is deemed by Sec. 16F(3) to be ineligible for any depreciation allowances under Part IV of the IRO (see Chapter 5). This merely ensures that tax relief for the expenditure is given only once.

(13) **Charitable contributions:** These amounts would, in general, not be deductible because they are normally unlikely to be incurred for the purposes of earning assessable profits as required by Sec. 16. Sec. 16D, therefore, introduces specific provisions to enable deductions to be made, subject to limitations.

To qualify for deduction, the payment must be a donation of money to a charitable institution or trust of a public character which is exempt from tax under Sec. 88 of the IRO, or to the Government, for charitable purposes (Sec. 2). The payment must be a pure donation and not confer any benefit at all upon the donor. For this purpose, an inflated payment for a ticket for a social function has been held not to be a donation for this purpose (*CIR v Sanford Yung-Tao Yung* (HKTC 959)). The limitations are that:

(i)   the aggregate of allowable donations must be not less than $100 (Sec. 16D(1));

(ii)   the deduction is limited to 25% of assessable profits (or 10% in respect of years of assessment prior to 2003/04) after depreciation allowances but before charitable donations. Therefore, where there are adjusted losses for a year of assessment (ignoring losses brought forward from earlier years), there can be no deduction for charitable donations at all (Sec. 16D(2)(b));

(iii) the sum must not qualify for deduction under any other Profits Tax provision (specifically Secs. 16, 16B or 16C, all of which are discussed above) (Sec. 16D(2)(a)); and

(iv)   the sum must not qualify for deduction under Part IVA (Sec. 16D(2)(aa)). Part IVA deals with concessionary deductions for the purposes of Salaries Tax and Personal Assessment, such concessionary deductions comprising charitable donations, elderly residential care expenses and home loan interest expenses (see Chapter 3), although it is likely to be only the first of these which is relevant in the current context.

It must not be assumed that all donations have to be considered for deduction only under Sec. 16D. It is possible that a donation which is not deductible under Sec. 16D may qualify under Sec. 16 if the circumstances and motive fulfil the argument that it is business motivated. Accordingly a payment which would be limited under the 25% rule might qualify in full under Sec. 16, although this would be exceptional.

■ Example 4.17

Andouts Ltd. is a textile manufacturer with an adjusted profit for the year of assessment of $65,000 and it has made an approved charitable donation of $20,000 to the Textile Workers Orphans Fund which has not been added back in arriving at the adjusted profit. It also has depreciation allowances of $12,000 and a balancing charge of $4,500 to be taken into account.

The assessable profit is as follows:—

Adjusted Profit		$65,000
Add back donation		20,000
		85,000
Less: Depreciation Allowances	$12,000	
Add: Balancing Charge	4,500	(7,500)
		77,500
Less: Charitable Donation (25%)		(19,375)
Assessable Profit		$58,125

Note:—
Andouts may have a case for saying that the donation is for the purpose of fostering and maintaining employee goodwill being directly related to its business and is therefore deductible under Sec. 16(1) instead of Sec. 16D. In this case, the assessable profit would be:—

Adjusted Profit	$85,000
Net Depreciation Allowances	7,500
	92,500

(14) **Prescribed fixed assets:** Notwithstanding the general prohibition on deduction of capital expenditure contained in Sec. 17(1)(c), Sec. 16G(1) grants a deduction for capital expenditure incurred on the provision of a "prescribed fixed asset", other than capital expenditure which is deductible under another provision (for example Sec. 16B) and expenditure under a hire purchase agreement (see section

5.10.1). The deduction is, however, available only to the extent to which the relevant asset is used in the production of profits chargeable to Profits Tax and accordingly an apportionment is required where the asset is used both for producing assessable profits and for some other non-assessable income producing purpose (Sec. 16G(2)). A "prescribed fixed asset" is defined in Sec. 16G(6) as:

(a)   an item of plant and machinery specified in items 16, 20, 24, 26, 28, 29, 31, 33 or 35 of the First Part of the Table annexed to Rule 2 of the IRR, and which is used specifically and directly in any manufacturing process;

(b)   computer hardware, other than hardware which is an integral part of any machinery or plant; or

(c)   computer software and computer systems,

but does not include any asset in which any person holds rights as lessee; in other words, the definition does not extend to an asset which is leased to any person. An interesting question arises as to whether plant and machinery provided by a Hong Kong taxpayer to a Mainland enterprise under a typical contract processing arrangement would still qualify as prescribed fixed assets. A lease in relation to any plant or machinery is defined in Sec. 2 and the fact that a plant or machinery is provided free of charge under a contract processing arrangement does not appear to exclude it from the statutory definition of a lease.

Where a prescribed fixed asset in respect of which a deduction for the acquisition expenditure has been allowed under Sec. 16G(1) is sold, the sale proceeds are, unless otherwise subject to Profits Tax, deemed by Sec. 16G(3)(a) to be an assessable trading receipt. Where the original expenditure was apportioned in accordance with Sec. 16G(2), however, the sales proceeds are apportioned on the same basis for the purpose of determining the assessable amount. Further, any amount assessed under this provision is limited to the amount of the original deduction granted in respect of the acquisition of the asset. To counter tax avoidance opportunities which would otherwise be possible by arranging to sell the asset to an associate at an artificially low price, Sec. 16G(3)(c) provides that the Commissioner may substitute the true market value for the actual sales proceeds for the purpose of this provision in certain situations where the buyer and seller are related. In particular, the Commissioner has these powers where the buyer has control over the seller or vice versa, both the buyer and seller are under the control of a third person or the sale is between a husband and wife (other than where the wife is living apart from the husband). In the situation where a prescribed fixed asset is destroyed, the asset is deemed by Sec. 16G(3)(b) to have been sold immediately before such destruction and any insurance moneys or other compensation received in respect thereof are treated as sale proceeds.

Where an amount of sale proceeds or deemed sale proceeds is assessable under Sec. 16G(3), it is assessed in the year in which such sale is completed or possession of the asset is given, whichever is earlier, unless the sale takes place after the permanent discontinuation of the relevant trade, profession or business, in which case it is deemed assessable in the period immediately prior to such discontinuance (Secs. 16G (3)(a) and (d)).

4.5.9 Deductibility of interest and related expenses

The deductibility of interest, together with related expenditure such as loan fees, legal fees, procuration fees and stamp duties, is the subject of specific provisions in the IRO. In particular, Sec. 16(1)(a) provides that interest on money borrowed for the purpose of producing assessable profits, together with other expenditure related to such borrowings, is deductible provided the conditions specified in Sec. 16(2) are met, although whether the Sec. 16(2) conditions are met is also subject to Secs. 16(2A), (2B) and (2C).

Because interest would normally meet the general conditions for deductibility in Sec. 16(1), there has been uncertainty at times as to the effect of Sec. 16(1)(a) and, more specifically, whether it is intended to broaden or narrow the scope of the general deduction provision of Sec. 16(1). This point, together with other aspects of the interpretation of Sec. 16(1)(a), is discussed in section 4.5.9.1 below.

The additional conditions for deductibility imposed by Sec. 16(2) underwent significant changes during 2004. Although Sec. 16(2) has imposed additional restrictions on the deductibility of loan interest and related expenditure since 1986, a great deal of tax planning had been undertaken over the intervening years aimed at circumventing those restrictions. Although much of that planning was potentially open to challenge by the IRD pursuant to Sec. 61A (see section 10.4.5), because this requires a judgement to be made as to the taxpayer's motive in each case the Government considered strengthening the provisions to eliminate the planning opportunities was a preferable option for preserving their intended effect. Accordingly, after much debate, Sec. 16(2) was amended with effect from 25 June 2004.

It is, however, still necessary to have an understanding of both the position prior to the amendments as well as the new provisions. This is because for the 2004/05 year of assessment, both provisions will apply as interest and related expenditure incurred prior to 25 June 2004 are dealt with under the former provisions, and amounts incurred after that date generally fall within the amended provisions. Moreover, Sec. 16(5A) provides that where interest is incurred pursuant to a transaction in respect of which the IRD has issued an advance clearance or advance ruling prior to 25 June 2004 stating that the transaction would not fall within the provisions of Sec. 61A, the amendments to Sec. 16(2) which would otherwise apply from 25 June 2004 are to have no application to such interest. Accordingly, the position prior to the 2004 amendments is discussed in section 4.5.9.2, and the position after the amendments is discussed in section 4.5.9.3.

4.5.9.1 Interpretation of Sec. 16(1)(a)

The wording of Secs. 16(1) and 16(1)(a) suggest that a deduction is intended to be available in calculating assessable profits for the year of assessment in which a qualifying interest expense is incurred, irrespective of the accounting treatment of that interest. However, in *CIR v Secan Limited & Anor.* [2001] (1 HKRC 90-107), the Court of Final Appeal held that interest expenses incurred in the construction of trading stock and capitalised to the cost of trading stock for accounting purposes were deductible only in the period in which the relevant trading stock was sold and the interest expensed for accounting purposes. As discussed in section 4.5.6, it is unclear at this stage whether this decision should be interpreted as denying a deduction for all interest expenses (or indeed any other types of expenses) which are incurred but are not expensed for accounting purposes in the period in which the deduction is claimed, although this situation would only arise in exceptional circumstances.

In *D 30/93* it was held that whilst there was a requirement that the sums be "payable" in order to be deductible under this provision, they did not have to be due for payment in the period in which they were incurred, which is, of course, the period in which any deduction would be available. The decision in that case was upheld by both the High Court (see *National Mutual Centre (HK) Limited v CIR* [1997] (1 HKRC 90-086)) and the Court of Appeal (see *CIR v National Mutual Centre* [1998] (1 HKRC 90-094)). Interestingly, in contrast to the decision in the *Secan* case discussed above, these cases were decided solely on the basis of an examination of whether the taxpayer was committed to the payment of the expense and the accounting treatment adopted was not discussed in the judgments.

In the case of *CIR v County Shipping* (3 HKTC 267) it was claimed, with certain technical merit, that the limitations imposed by this provision are ineffective because to override the general rule of deductibility in Sec. 16 (1) the limitation should be in Sec. 17. However, the Court of Appeal rejected this approach and supported the apparent intention behind the drafting. This approach is also consistent with the judgement of the Court of Final Appeal in the *Secan* case (supra) which suggested that Sec. 16(1) was *"… to be read in a negative sense …"*; that is, as restricting deductibility rather than granting it

Whether interest and associated expenses are incurred for the purpose of producing assessable profits is usually judged by how the loan proceeds are applied. For example, if the proceeds are applied to acquire an asset which does not generate assessable profits, for example real estate outside Hong Kong, the interest and related expenses will not be deductible. Another example is interest on money borrowed to purchase shares which were not held as trading assets. As dividends, together with any gains on disposal of shares which are not trading assets are not subject to tax, no assessable profits would be derived from those assets; nonetheless, the disallowance of such interest expenses is also specifically provided for in Inland Revenue Rule 2B (see section 4.5.15) which also authorises apportionment of interest on money used both for the purchase of such shares and some other purpose. See also the case of *Zeta Estates Limited v CIR*, which is discussed in section 4.4, where both the Court of First Instance and the Court of Appeal denied a deduction for interest related to the financing of a dividend on the grounds that it was not incurred in the production of assessable profits. These decisions were, however, overturned by the Court of Final Appeal (see FACV 15/2006) and it now seems that such interest will not normally be precluded from deduction even though it relates more directly to the distribution of profits than the derivation of assessable profits.

Where the proceeds of a loan cannot be traced to a particular asset or expense but the person has both assessable and non-assessable income producing assets, a general apportionment of interest expenses on the basis of assets is usually sought by the IRD. See, however, *D 71/97* where an investment advisory company borrowed funds from its parent bank on a subordinated basis to satisfy capital requirements and maintain liquidity margins imposed by the *Securities Ordinance*. The borrowed funds were then placed back on deposit with the parent bank outside Hong Kong, such that the interest derived therefrom was not subject to Profits Tax. The Board of Review had to consider whether the purpose of the borrowing was to maintain the required liquidity margin or to derive non-assessable interest income. Although the Board was satisfied that the loan assisted the taxpayer to maintain the required liquidity margin, they also noted that it directly generated non-assessable interest income. Despite this, the Board was not sure that it could be said that part of the interest was incurred for one purpose and another part of the interest was incurred for a different purpose, thereby allowing apportionment in accordance with IRR 2A. Nonetheless, they implicitly recognised a duality of purpose because their decision was to allow the interest expense as a deduction to the extent that it exceeded the interest income earned.

A difficulty previously sometimes arose in respect of interest incurred to finance the acquisition of land for use in the development of an investment property and, indeed, in the financing of the construction of such a building. Whilst it is IRD practice to allow such expenses when incurred after the occupation permit is issued and the building commences to generate rental income, the treatment of such expenses during the construction period was sometimes disputed. In particular, the IRD took the view that such expenses were of a capital nature, being incurred in the creation of a capital asset, and the case of *CIR v Tai On Machinery Works Ltd.* (HKTC 411) provided some support for this view. This decision should, however, be compared with the later Papua New Guinea case of *Travelodge Papua New Guinea Ltd. v Chief Collector of Taxes* (85 ATC 4432) where such expenses were held to be of a revenue nature. Given that the wording of Sec. 16(1) suggests that an expense is deductible in the basis period in which it is incurred provided it is incurred in the generation of profits of some period, and that Sec. 16(1)(a) specifically renders interest deductible subject to the meeting of specified conditions, it is difficult to reconcile disallowing interest as being capital in nature during the construction period, but allowing it as a deduction once the property is generating assessable income.

Moreover, it is difficult to see how interest, which is by its very nature recurring, could ever be considered to be capital expenditure when one of the earliest tests developed to distinguish capital from revenue expenditure looked at whether the expenditure was "once and for all" or "recur(ing) year by year" (see the *Vallambrosa Rubber Co.* case, which is discussed in section 4.5.7 above).

It is sometimes argued that because interest on financing the construction of a building is included in the definition of capital expenditure for the purpose of calculating Industrial Buildings Allowance and Rebuilding

Allowance (see Chapter 5), a deduction should not be allowed under Sec. 16(1)(a); however, the definition for depreciation allowance purposes specifically excludes interest which is deductible under the Profits Tax provisions and, accordingly, should not operate to preclude a deduction being granted under Sec. 16(1)(a). If, however, such interest failed to qualify under Sec. 16(2), then it would clearly fall within the definition of capital expenditure for depreciation allowance purposes. In any event, the definition for depreciation allowance purposes does not ever apply to interest incurred in financing the acquisition of land, which the IRD equally consider to be of a capital nature when incurred during the construction period.

Many of the above issues were considered in the case of *Wharf Properties Limited v CIR* [1994] (1 HKRC 90-073), [1996] (1 HKRC 90-076 and [1997] 1 HKRC 90-085). The High Court found that whilst interest expenses incurred on financing the acquisition of land for redevelopment for the purpose of deriving future rental income qualified for deduction under Sec. 16(1)(a), and that the interest was not capital expenditure, the interest expenditure in question was, when all the relevant surrounding circumstances were examined, of a "capital nature" and, therefore, precluded from deduction by Sec. 17(1)(c).

The Court of Appeal upheld the decision of the High Court, although the judges took a slightly different approach in reaching that conclusion. Litton, V-P agreed with the decision of the High Court that "expenditure of a capital nature" meant more than capital expenditure and that whether interest expense was of a capital nature depended upon the purpose of the borrowing: in the case in question, as the interest was incurred to acquire land for the construction of a capital asset, he considered that the interest was itself of a capital nature. It is interesting, however, to note that Litton, V-P agreed with the Commissioner's position that any interest incurred after the asset financed by the loan became income producing would be deductible. His conclusion in this regard was reasoned by reading down the words "... *in any period* ..." as they appear in Sec. 16(1); in particular, he considered that, especially as the relevant loans were all for short terms, the interest incurred in any year was incurred predominantly for the purpose of obtaining the use of the borrowed funds for that year only and that any nexus to future assessable profits was too remote to qualify the interest for deduction under Sec. 16 (1). In other words, notwithstanding the words of Sec. 16(1), the use of the loan proceeds was to be considered on a year-by-year basis when determining whether the interest was of a capital nature.

Ching, J.A., on the other hand, while agreeing with Litton, V-P (and Godfrey, J.A.) that the interest was not deductible in the years in dispute, considered that the interest on the loans would not change its nature when the asset financed by the loans became income producing; rather, he considered that the purpose of a loan determined whether the interest thereon was of a capital nature and that if it was concluded that the interest started out as capital, this should not change just because the underlying asset became income producing. The logical conclusion of such a view would seem to be that interest on loans taken out to finance the construction of a capital asset will never be deductible, irrespective of the amount of assessable profit generated by that asset.

On further appeal, the Privy Council upheld the Court of Appeal's judgement. The Privy Council summarised the matter by reaffirming that the interest was, *prima facie*, deductible under Sec. 16(1) as it was incurred in earning future assessable profits, but ruled that an amount otherwise deductible under that provision can still be rendered non-deductible by Sec. 17. With regard to the latter point, the Privy Council ruled that the interest was of a capital nature and, therefore, precluded from deduction by Sec. 17 (1)(c). Moreover, their Lordships, in rejecting the appellant's arguments, held that the only way to determine whether interest was of a capital or revenue nature was to look at the purpose for which the money was borrowed and, where the money was borrowed to put in place the structure from which profits were to be derived, the interest was of a capital nature. Their lordships did, however, reject the reasoning of Ching, J. A. in the Court of Appeal and held that as soon as the asset was generating assessable profits, the interest ceased to be of a capital nature and became deductible.

Although the Privy Council's decision in this case must be accepted as settling the issue in Hong Kong, it is interesting to note that the High Court of Australia had to subsequently consider substantially the same issue. The decision of the Privy Council in the *Wharf Properties* case (supra) was considered at some length and, interestingly, the majority of the High Court of Australia chose not to follow it and the case was, as a consequence decided differently notwithstanding the essentially identical statutory provisions (see *Steele v Deputy Commissioner of Taxation* [1999] HCA 7).

4.5.9.2 Provisions of Sec. 16(2) — Prior to 25 June 2004

As noted, the restrictions in Sec. 16(2) were originally introduced in 1986 although minor amendments had been made over subsequent years. The terms of those restrictions as applied immediately before 25 June 2004 are discussed in this section.

To understand the nature of these restrictions it is necessary to appreciate that they were introduced to counter tax planning arrangements which relied upon the fact that an interest payment could be deductible to a taxpayer but the corresponding receipt of interest, which could be derived by an associate of the taxpayer (including a member of the same corporate group) may be non-assessable because it had an offshore source. In an effort to counter the leakage of tax revenue from such arrangements, the Government moved to allow a deduction for interest expense only where the receipt was chargeable to Hong Kong tax. Nonetheless, because there were numerous situations where the mismatch between deductibility and assessability of an interest payment was not as a result of tax planning but was a normal incident of a genuine commercial arrangement, it was necessary to introduce diverse exceptions to the general principle which the Government sought. The mechanism adopted in drafting the provisions was to precisely prescribe the circumstances in which interest was to be deductible, thereby disallowing a deduction for any interest which fell outside those prescribed circumstances. The circumstances in which interest and related expenditure were deductible can be broadly divided into four classes according to:–

(a)   the status of the borrower;
(b)   the status of the lender;
(c)   the application of loan funds; and
(d)   the nature of the loan.

The restrictions imposed by Sec. 16(2) in respect of amount incurred prior to 25 June 2004 are as follows:

(a)(i)   There is no limitation upon interest paid by a financial institution, as defined (see section 4.7.7) (Sec. 16(2)(a)).

(ii)   There is also no limitation upon interest paid by the public utility companies listed in the Third Schedule of the IRO (presently the Hong Kong Electric Company, Ltd., China Light and Power Company, Ltd. and The Hong Kong and China Gas Company, Ltd.) provided that the rate of interest paid does not exceed a rate prescribed from time to time by the Financial Secretary and published in the Gazette (see 16(2)(b)). Historically, an actual interest rate was prescribed by the Financial Secretary. From 1 December 2002, however, the relevant rate is prescribed as being the highest interest rate on Hong Kong dollar savings account as quoted from time to time by the banks set out in the Schedule to the *Legal Tender Notes Issue Ordinance.*

(b)(i)   Where the funds have been borrowed other than from a financial institution as defined (see section 4.7.7), or an overseas financial institution, the interest is deductible if the lender is liable to tax thereon under the IRO (Sec. 16(2)(c)). This essentially means that the lender must be subject to Profits Tax on the interest. For the purpose of this provision, an overseas financial institution is defined as a person (which includes a company) engaged in the business of banking or deposit-taking outside Hong Kong other than a person which the Commissioner, in accordance with the powers vested in him by Sec. 16(4), determines shall not be recognised as an overseas financial institution (Sec. 16(3)(c)); Sec. 16(4) provides that the Commissioner may determine that a person shall not be recognised as an overseas financial institution where their banking or deposit-taking business is, in his opinion, not adequately supervised by a supervisory authority. This proviso is to thwart the formation of a group finance company in a tax haven which may be argued as being a financial institution.

It was held in *D 30/93* that for the purpose of this provision, the amounts did not have to be taxable in the hands of the lender in the same period as that in which the deduction was granted. In particular, in that case the amounts were incurred but not actually payable until certain other loans taken out by the borrower had been repaid; in finding that the amounts were deductible, the Board held that the amounts were still "payable" and were chargeable to the former Interest Tax, notwithstanding that such liability would not arise until the amounts were actually paid or credited (and, in fact, never arose because of the abolition of Interest Tax). This decision was upheld by both the High Court and the Court of Appeal in *CIR v National Mutual Centre (HK) Limited* [1997] (1 HKRC 90-086) and [1998] (1 HKRC 90-094).

(ii) Where the funds have been borrowed from a financial institution as defined (see section 4.7.7) or an overseas financial institution (see (i) above), the interest is deductible provided that the repayment of neither the principal nor the interest is secured or guaranteed, in whole or in part, directly or indirectly, by or on behalf of the borrower or an associate of the borrower against a deposit with any financial institution or overseas financial institution where the interest on that deposit is not chargeable to Profits Tax (Sec. 16(2)(d)).

Following the granting of an order under Sec. 87 by the Chief Executive in Council to abolish payment of Profits Tax on bank interest accrued after 22 June 1998 (see point (16) in section 4.5.3), the effect of this provision could have been diminished.

This is because bank interest technically remained chargeable to Profits Tax where it had a Hong Kong source notwithstanding that an exemption from the payment of such tax had been granted. To avoid this result, however, the Chief Executive's order contains a clause which denies the exemption where the relevant deposit secures or guarantees a loan, the interest on which is deductible.

For the purposes of this provision, "associate" of a person is extensively defined in Sec. 16(3) as follows:

(a) Where the person is a natural person:
   (i)   a relative of that person. The term "relative" is also extensively defined;
   (ii)   a partner of the person or any relative of that partner;
   (iii) a partnership in which the person is a partner;
   (iv)   any corporation controlled by the person, by a partner of that person or by a partnership in which the person is a partner; or
   (v)   any director or principal officer (the term "principal officer" is separately and extensively defined) of any such corporation as is referred to in (iv) above.

(b) Where the person is a corporation:
   (i)   an associated corporation, which is defined as a corporation over which the person has control, a corporation which has control over the person, or a corporation under the control of the same person as controls the first mentioned person. "Control" is also widely defined as the power to arrange for the affairs of a corporation to be conducted in accordance with the wishes of a person through the holding by that person of shares, the possession of voting power in relation to that or another corporation or by virtue of any powers conferred by the articles of association or other document regulating that or any other corporation;
   (ii)   any person who controls the corporation and any partner of such person, and where any such person is a natural person, any relative of that person;
   (iii) any director or principal officer of that or any associated corporation and any relative thereof; or
   (iv)   any partner of the corporation and, where such partner is a natural person, any relative of such partner.

(c) Where the person is a partnership:

(i)　a partner and, where the partner is itself a partnership, any partner of that partnership;

(ii)　a partner with the person in any other partnership and, where such a partner is itself a partnership, any partner of that partnership;

(iii)　where any of the partners included in the above provisions is a natural person, any relative of that partner;

(iv)　a corporation controlled by the person or by any partner or relative of a partner or any director or principal officer of such corporation; or

(v)　a corporation of which a partner is a director or principal officer.

Note that if a loan is only partly secured by a deposit in the circumstances described, the whole of the interest is disallowed; there is no apportionment in such circumstances, which seems unreasonable. Note, however, that a loan secured by any asset other than a deposit is not affected by this restriction.

(c)　A deduction is permitted (by Sec. 16(2)(e)) if the funds are borrowed, subject to certain limitations as to the lender, for the purpose of wholly and exclusively financing:—

(i)　capital expenditure incurred on providing plant and machinery which qualifies for depreciation allowances; or

(ii)　the purchase of trading stock used for the purposes of producing profits chargeable to Profits Tax.

The limitations relating to the lender are that the lender must not be:

(i)　an associate of the borrower. For a discussion as to what constitutes an associate for this purpose, see (b) above; or

(ii)　where the money is borrowed from, or the interest is payable to, a trustee of a trust or a corporation controlled by such a trustee, neither the trustee, the corporation nor a beneficiary under that trust are associates of the borrower. "Beneficiary" for this purpose is widely defined to include not only a named beneficiary but also a person who is capable by any means of benefiting under the trust, either directly or through an interposed person, or who may reasonably be expected to be able, either directly or indirectly, to control the activities of the trust or the application of its corpus or income.

Again it appears that to qualify, the loan must be wholly applied in the manner specified and that the question of apportionment does not, therefore, arise.

(d)(i) A corporation can deduct interest paid on debentures listed on the Hong Kong Stock Exchange or any other stock exchange recognised by the Commissioner for the purpose (Sec. 16(2)(f)(i)). A corporation can also deduct interest on moneys borrowed from an associated corporation (see above) where that associated corporation raised the funds originally by way of an issue of debentures listed as above. The interest paid by the claimant corporation cannot, however, exceed the interest payable on the debentures by the associated corporation (Sec. 16(2)(f)(iii)).

(ii) A corporation can also deduct interest payable to the holder of an instrument (for example a bond or promissory note) which is marketable in Hong Kong or in a financial centre outside Hong Kong approved by the Commissioner for this purpose, or which has been issued pursuant to an agreement or scheme of arrangement authorised by the Securities and Futures Commission under the *Protection of Investors Ordinance* (Sec. 16(2)(f)(ii)). A corporation can also deduct interest on moneys borrowed from an associated corporation (see (b)(ii) above) where that associated corporation raised the funds originally by way of an issue of such an instrument provided that the interest paid by the claimant corporation does not exceed the interest payable on the instrument by the associated corporation (Sec. 16(2)(f)(iii)).

4.5.9.3 Provisions of Sec. 16(2) — From 25 June 2004

As noted earlier, the original provisions of Sec. 16(2) were the subject of much tax planning involving transactions which permitted taxpayers to adopt the position that the conditions for deductibility were technically fulfilled, even though it was questionable whether the spirit of the provisions had been met. Although many such arrangements could potentially be struck down through the application of Sec. 61A (see section 10.4.5), this required the IRD to identify the existence of the transactions and then go through a time consuming process in each case to determine the taxpayer's motive and, where appropriate raise assessments to counter the tax benefit. As an alternative means of dealing with the loss of revenue from such arrangements, the Government decided to further tighten the restrictions in Sec. 16(2).

As a consequence, Sec. 16(2) was amended with effect from 25 June 2004 (the 2004 amendments) to impose additional requirements in order for interest and related expenses to be deductible. The 2004 amendments generally apply to interest and related expenses incurred on or after 25 June

2004; nonetheless, amounts incurred after that date but which relate to a transaction upon which the IRD had issued an advance ruling or advance clearance prior to that date in which it was confirmed that Sec. 61A would not apply to the transaction, need only fulfil the provisions as they applied immediately before the 2004 amendments in order to be deductible (Sec. 16 (5A)).

In broad terms, the 2004 amendments left the basic existing framework of Sec. 16(2) in place, but added new legislative provisions which imposed additional requirements and restrictions. Accordingly, in considering the new rules, it is useful to examine how the original provisions have been effected by the 2004 amendments rather than considering the new rules as a whole new regime. For this reason, the paragraphs below build on the discussion of the former provisions as contained in section 4.5.9.2 above. It must, however, be emphasised that the additional restrictions imposed by the 2004 amendments are quite complex and the following is only a high level summary of their effect. It is strongly recommended that the actual provisions be read carefully and fully understood before attempting to conclude as to the application of the provisions in any particular case.

The provisions granting deductibility on the basis of the status of the borrower were unchanged by the 2004 amendments. These provisions are contained in Secs. 16(2)(a) and 16(2)(b), and are discussed as scenarios a(i) and a(ii) in section 4.5.9.2. Not only are Secs. 16(2)(a) and 16(2)(b) unchanged, but none of the additional restrictions introduced by the 2004 amendments apply to interest or related expenses which qualify for deduction pursuant to those provisions.

The provisions granting deductibility on the basis of the status of the lender, however, were significantly tightened by the 2004 amendments. These provisions are contained in Sec. 16(2)(c) and 16(2)(d), and the original form of them is discussed as scenarios b(i) and b(ii) in section 4.5.9.2. The wording of Sec.16(2)(c), which grants a deduction on interest where the money was borrowed from a person other than a financial institution or overseas financial institution and the interest is subject to Hong Kong tax in the hands of the lender, is unchanged. It is, however, now subject to additional restrictions as contained in Secs. 16(2A) and 16(2B).

Sec. 16(2A) is similar to, but more extensive than, the restrictions which formerly applied in relation to bank borrowings secured by a deposit (i.e. Sec. 16(2)(d)). More specifically, Sec. 16(2A) provides that where any part of the principal or interest on the borrowing in question is secured or guaranteed, either directly or indirectly, in whole or in part, by a deposit or loan made by the borrower or an associate of the borrower with or to:

    (a)   the lender or an associate of the lender;
    (b)   a financial institution or an associate of a financial institution; or
    (c)   an overseas financial institution or an associate of such an institution,

and the interest payable on that loan or deposit is not subject to Hong Kong tax, then the amount of the interest deduction is to be reduced, having regard to the amount of interest payable on the deposit or loan, by an amount which is considered reasonable in the circumstances. One of the main additional restrictions imposed by this test compared to the restrictions contained in the original Sec. 16(2)(d) are that it applies to loans and deposits (i.e. not just deposits as was previously the case). Moreover, the application of the new provisions is no longer restricted only to loans or deposits with a financial institution or an overseas financial institution, but extends to any loan or deposit with the lender or an associate of the lender whether or not the lender is a financial institution or overseas financial institution. Also, the new provision does not require an instrument to be executed or an undertaking given for an arrangement to be brought within the provision.

For the purpose of this provision, where a deposit or loan is made by the trustee of a trust estate, or a corporation controlled by such a trustee, the deposit or loan is deemed to have been made by each of the trustee, the corporation and the beneficiary under the trust (Sec. 16(2D)).

There is no statutory guidance provided as to how the amount of the reduction in the otherwise available interest deduction is to be calculated. Nonetheless, it is likely that the intention of the legislature was to generally reduce the deduction by the amount of related non-taxable interest income earned during the relevant period on the deposit or loan as the provision specifically provides that regard must be such amount when ascertaining the amount of the reduction. This principle appears to be accepted by the IRD as is evidenced by the examples in paragraph 24 of *Departmental Interpretation & Practice Notes No. 13A* which is reproduced in Appendix 8.

In those examples, the IRD essentially suggests that where the amount of the deposit or loan is less than the borrowing, and secures only borrowings where the interest would otherwise be deductible, the interest deduction will be reduced by the amount of the non-taxable interest income. Where the amount of the deposit or loan exceeds the borrowing, the IRD's examples suggest that only the non-taxable interest on the relevant portion of the deposit or loan which actually secures the borrowing will be considered as reducing the interest deduction. This principle is extended where additional security (i.e. security other than in the form of a deposit or loan) is provided in that the IRD will take the amount of the borrowing divided by the value of the total security given as the portion of the loan or deposit which secures the borrowing. The IRD's examples also recognise that where a deposit or loan secures both a borrowing which gives rise to taxable income and a borrowing used in the production of non-taxable income, an apportionment of the interest on the securing loan or deposit is appropriate before then considering how much of the non-taxable interest earned on the portion of the deposit or loan which relates to the borrowing for taxable income producing purposes is to be taken as reducing the otherwise allowable interest deduction.

Accordingly, although Sec. 16(2A) is generally more restrictive than the restriction previously contained in Sec. 16(2)(d), it is fairer in that the interest deduction is only reduced by the amount on the non-taxable interest on the deposit or loan which secures the borrowing; under the original Sec. 16(2)(d), if there was any deposit which gave rise to non-taxable interest which secured even only a part the borrowing, the entire amount of the interest on that borrowing was rendered non-deductible. Additionally, the IRD has clarified in paragraph 22 of *Departmental Interpretation & Practice Notes No. 13A* that Sec. 16(2A) will not be applied where a bank has a right of set off of a deposit giving rise to non-taxable interest income, against a borrowing provided that there are no restrictions on the borrower's right to withdraw the deposit while the loan is not in default. Under the previous Sec. 16(2)(d), there was a concern that technically such a right of set off would result in the interest on the loan being wholly non-deductible (assuming that the interest on the deposit was not taxable).

Sec. 16(2)(c) is also subject to Sec. 16(2B) which is concerned with potential arrangements between any parties whereby any interest payable on money borrowed which would otherwise be deductible is payable, either directly or through an interposed person, to the borrower or a person connected with the borrower. This is aimed squarely at the types of arrangements which sought to circumvent the original provisions by arranging a borrowing from a person and in a manner whereby the interest qualified for deduction under a strict interpretation of the provisions, but with the loan funds ultimately being provided by, and the interest payable to, an associate of the borrower who was not taxable on the interest received. Sec. 16(2B)(b) stipulates that where such an arrangement exists, the amount of the otherwise deductible interest is to be reduced by apportioning the interest on the loan, or that part of the loan, which is the subject of the arrangement on the basis of that proportion of the basis period (or the part of the basis period for which the loan was outstanding) during which the arrangements existed.

Sec. 16(2B) appears to be concerned with situations where a person ("the borrower") borrows from, and pays interest to, an unrelated party ("the lender"), but the lender has an arrangement with an associate of the borrower ("the associate") whereby the associate funds the loan and effectively derives the interest paid by the borrower. If, however, instead of the lender having the arrangement with the associate, a party related to the lender ("the lender's associate") entered into the arrangement with the associate and there was no lending between the lender and the lender's associate, it might be difficult for the IRD to establish that the interest paid by the borrower was payable to the associate. This would be the case even if the loan from the associate secured the loan to the borrower, or the payment of interest to the associate was conditional on the payment of interest by the borrower. To prevent this from allowing circumvention of the rules, Sec. 16(2E) contains further anti avoidance provisions which deem that for the purpose of Sec. 16(2B), interest shall be considered payable to the borrower or an associate of the borrower if a loan has been made between any persons whereby the payment of interest on that loan is secured by, or is conditional upon, the payment of principal or interest on the loan by the borrower.

Sec. 16(2E)(c), however, also contains a definition of "excepted person" which is relevant in that the provisions of Sec. 16(2B) do not apply where the borrower or the person connected with the borrower, (and being the person to whom the interest on the money borrowed is directly or indirectly payable) is an "excepted person". Essentially, an excepted person is a person who is:

- subject to Profits Tax on the interest derived;
- acting as trustee of a trust and is not beneficially entitled to the interest;
- a beneficiary of a unit trust to which Sec. 26A(1A)(a)(i) applies (see point (9) in section 4.5.3);
- a member of a recognized retirement scheme or an acceptable retirement scheme established outside Hong Kong;
- a public body;
- a body corporate of which the Government owns more than half of the issued share capital; or
- a financial institution or an overseas financial institution.

For information on how the IRD intends to apply Sec. 16(2B) in practice, see the examples in paragraphs 28 and 29 of *Departmental Interpretation & Practice Notes No. 13A*.

The drafting of Sec. 16(2)(d), which deals with interest payable to a financial institution and was discussed as scenario (b)(ii) in section 4.5.9.2, was simplified by the 2004 amendments, although the conditions under which a deduction for interest pursuant to that provision have in fact been further restricted. This is because the restrictions on deductibility previously contained in Sec. 16(1)(d) have now been incorporated into Sec. 16(2A). As with Sec. 16(2)(c), Sec. 16(2)(d) is subject to the additional requirements of Secs. 16(2A) and 16(2B), both of which are discussed above.

The wording of Sec. 16(2)(e), which grants an interest deduction on the basis of the use to which the borrowed funds were put and was discussed as scenario (c) in section 4.5.9.2 is in essence unchanged by the 2004 amendments, notwithstanding some slight tidying up of the drafting. Again, however, this provision has been made subject to Secs. 16(2A) and 16(2B) which are discussed above, and which impose significant additional restrictions on the circumstances under which a deduction pursuant to this provision is available.

Similarly, only minor changes were made by the 2004 amendments to the wording of the provision which grants a deduction where specified conditions are met for interest payable on debentures or other marketable instruments (Sec. 16(2)(f)), which is discussed as scenarios (d)(i) and (ii) in section 4.5.9.2. One change, however, is that the requirement under Sec. 16 (2)(f)(ii)(A) that the instruments were **marketable** in Hong Kong or a major financial centre outside Hong Kong recognized by the Commissioner, has been replaced with the requirement that the instruments be actually **marketed** in such a manner. Paragraph 17 of *Departmental Interpretation & Practice Notes No. 13A* states that whether or not an instrument has been marketed is a question of fact, but outlines the factors which the IRD considers provide evidence of the marketing of the instruments. Such factors include the holding of road-shows or meetings with potential investors, the issue of research papers by major market participants, the rating of the issue by a major rating agency, the clearing of the instruments through a recognised clearing system, the quoting of bid prices by one or more market participants and the quoting of the instrument on major financial information networks.

A more significant change to Sec. 16(2)(f) is that it has been made subject to a new provision, Sec. 16(2C). The effect of Sec. 16(2C) is substantially identical to that of Sec. 16(2B), which is discussed above, in that it is concerned with arrangements whereby the interest on the debentures or other instruments, (or a part thereof), for which a deduction is sought is payable directly or through an interposed person to the borrower or a person connected with the borrower. Again, this is aimed directly at the types of arrangements which were previously commonly adopted in an attempt to circumvent the provisions involving a group company issuing marketable securities which were then subscribed for by another group company; the subscriber company argued that it did not carry on business in Hong Kong and, therefore, was not subject to tax on the interest income derived. Where such an arrangement exists, Sec. 16(2C) now provides that the otherwise deductible interest shall be apportioned on a time basis with respect to the portion of the basis period, or that part of the basis period for which the debentures or other instruments were in issue, during which the arrangements were in place. Sec. 16(2F) contains further anti-avoidance provisions, essentially in the same form as Sec. 16(2E) which is discussed above, regarding the interpretation of Sec. 16(2C).

Note, however, that the further restrictions imposed by Sec. 16(2C) do not apply where the borrower, or the person connected with the borrower to whom the interest on the debentures or instruments is payable, is an "excepted person". An "excepted person" for this purpose is defined in Sec. 16(2E)(a) in the same terms as used in Sec. 16(2E) which was discussed above.

Additionally, Sec. 16(2G) provides an exemption from Sec. 16(2C) where the instruments are held by a market maker acting in the ordinary course of his business for the purpose of providing liquidity in the market for the instruments. A "market maker" for this purpose is defined in Sec. 16(2H) and essentially means a securities dealer licensed in Hong Kong or another jurisdiction recognized by the Commissioner, who in the ordinary course of his business holds himself out as willing to buy and sell on a regular basis for his own account the instruments in respect of which the interest deduction is being sought, and which is also actively involved in market making activities for other securities issued by a wide range of unrelated institutions.

For examples of how the IRD intend to apply Sec. 16(2C) in practice, see paragraph 33 of *Departmental Interpretation & Practice Notes No. 13A*.

In summary, therefore, despite the complexity of the 2004 amendments the basic framework of Sec. 16(2) has been left unchanged, but interest and related expenses which would otherwise meet the conditions for qualification in Sec. 16(2)(a), (d), (e) or (f) have become subject to additional restrictions. The additional restrictions are in essence two fold. First, interest which would otherwise qualify for deduction under Sec. 16(2)(c) or (e) is now subject to a more stringent form of the restrictions regarding security arrangements which previously only applied to interest which qualified for deduction under Sec. 16(2)(d). Second, a deduction for interest pursuant to either Sec. 16(2)(c), (d), (e) or (f) will be denied to the extent there are arrangements in place whereby the borrower, or a person connected with the borrower, is effectively the ultimate recipient of the interest; in other words, where there is an arrangement in place where a lender is interposed in loan which is ultimately effectively between connected parties. Moreover, this restriction is deemed to extend to arrangements where although the interest cannot be said to flow from the borrower back to that borrower or an associate thereof, other loans are in place which are secured by or are conditional upon the original borrower meeting their obligations under the original loan.

For further information regarding interest deductibility, see *Departmental Interpretation & Practice Notes No. 13A*.

4.5.10 Expenditure deemed non-deductible

The IRO contains, in Sec. 17, a series of provisions which deem certain types of expenses and outgoings which may otherwise be deductible, to be non-deductible for Profits Tax purposes. These items must, therefore, be added back in arriving at adjusted profits. The provisions deny deductions for the following amounts:—

(1) **Domestic or private expenses:** Private expenditure including the cost of travelling by a person between his residence and place of business are deemed non-deductible by Sec. 17(1)(a)(i). In the case of a corporation, it would appear that an expense could only be disallowed under this provision in exceptional circumstances. In the case of individuals, however, the provision has potentially much wider application. For a case where a court relied on this provision to reject a claim that medical expenses of a sole proprietor were deductible on the grounds that they were necessary for the taxpayer to carry on his business, see *Fahy v CIR* [1992] (1 HKRC 90-062); in that case, the court appeared to accept that the expenditure had a dual purpose, being partly a business expense and partly a private expense (with the latter being disallowable under Sec. 17(1)(a)), but in the absence of a sensible basis of apportionment, it was appropriate to disallow the whole of the expense. This decision should, however, be contrasted with that of *D 46/02* which concerned, *inter alia*, the deductibility of gymnasium expenses incurred by a professional jockey. In that decision, the Board of Review held that the expenses were incurred predominantly for business purposes, but recognised that a personal element also existed; in these circumstances, the Board considered apportionment appropriate and allowed a deduction for 80% of the relevant amount;

(2) **Contributions to MPF schemes:** Sec. 17(1)(a)(ii) deems as non-deductible contributions made by a person to a MPF scheme in the

person's capacity as a member of that scheme. This provision is, however, subject to Sec. 16AA which, in specified circumstances, authorises a deduction for such contributions (see paragraph (9) in section 4.5.8);

(3) **Disbursements or expenses which are not for the purpose of producing assessable profits:** Sec. 17(1)(b) mirrors Sec. 16(1) by denying a deduction for expenditure not incurred in producing assessable profits. Nonetheless, the fact that this provision and Sec. 16(1) operate to disallow a portion of business expenditure incurred in earning profits exempt from Profits Tax by specific statutory provisions (e.g. Secs. 26(a) and 26(A)) is often overlooked;

(4) **Capital expenditure:** Capital expenditure, including capital losses and withdrawals of capital which otherwise do not fall within the meaning of "expenditure", are deemed non-deductible under Sec. 17(1)(c). This provision has been extensively considered in section 4.5.7 above;

(5) **Improvements:** Although the cost of improvements are, in any event, probably capital expenditure and already disallowed under (3) above, a deduction for any expenditure incurred in connection therewith is specifically denied under Sec. 17(1)(d); some of this type of expenditure will, however, qualify for depreciation allowances or a deduction under Sec. 16F (see paragraph (12) of section 4.5.8);

(6) **Insurance recoveries:** A deduction for expenses and losses which may otherwise be deductible, but which are recoverable under an insurance or indemnity policy, is denied by Sec. 17(1)(e). This adjustment should not normally be necessary because the commercial accounts should already contain a credit where an expense or loss incurred is recoverable. In any case, even if it was deductible, it would only be a matter of timing difference because the insurance receipt would be taxable (*Green v J. Gliksten & Son Ltd.* (14 TC 364)). For a case where an amount was denied deduction under this provision, see D 128/01;

(7) **Rent and expenses for premises which are not used for producing assessable profits:** Although this is hardly surprising as it would fail the basic test in Sec. 16(1), Sec. 17(1)(f) specifically denies any deduction for rent and other expenses in connection with premises not used in the business;

(8) **Taxes payable under the IRO:** Any taxes imposed by the IRO, other than Salaries Tax paid on behalf of an employee, which is, of

course, nothing more than additional salary, are deemed by Sec. 17(1)(g) to be not deductible;

(9) **Contributions to a retirement scheme in excess of 15% of emoluments:** An ordinary annual contribution or an insurance premium in respect of a retirement scheme established for employees and which is a recognized occupational retirement scheme (see section 10.3.1), or a regular contribution to a MPF scheme, in so far as the total of such payments exceeds 15% of the employee's total emoluments for the period in respect of which the payment or payments are made, is denied deductibility under Sec. 17(1)(h). This limitation is computed separately in respect of each employee and not in aggregate in respect of total employees' remuneration. The limitation is, however, in respect of total emoluments and not merely taxable emoluments; therefore it should be appropriate to include rent reimbursements, and other exempt or concessionally taxed remuneration in the calculation.

For the purpose of applying the provision to MPF scheme contributions, regular contributions are defined in Sec. 16A(3) as contributions made at regular intervals which are either similar, or substantially similar, or are of amounts calculated by reference to a scale or a fixed percentage of a person's salary or other remuneration.

As this restriction in fact only refers to actual contributions to approved retirement schemes, an anomaly would exist if the contribution was not actually paid but, instead, a provision was made in the accounts for the known liability. On the assumption that the provision satisfied the case law principles governing deductibility of provisions for known liabilities (see section 4.5.6 above) it would be deductible without the 15% limitation. Therefore, Sec. 17(1)(i) extends the 15% limitation to such provisions or the aggregate of any such provision and any actual contribution in a basis period.

It is important to appreciate that the 15% limitation does not apply to an actual contribution to a scheme which is not a recognized occupational retirement scheme; this would normally be governed by the general deduction test in Sec. 16(1). Sec. 17(1)(l), however, denies a deduction for any contribution to a scheme which is not a recognized occupational retirement scheme; it should, however, be noted that under the *Occupational Retirement Schemes Ordinance* it is an offence to contribute to a scheme which is not registered under, or exempt from, that ordinance or established under another

Hong Kong ordinance. For the position regarding a provision (as opposed to a contribution) in respect of a scheme, see (10) below.

It should further be noted that a special contribution other than an ordinary annual contribution would generally not be deductible under the general rules on the grounds that it was capital expenditure; in the case of a recognized occupational retirement scheme or an MPF scheme, however, a deduction may be available under Sec. 16A (see section 4.5.8 above);

(10) **Provisions for contributions to retirement schemes:** A provision (as opposed to an actual contribution) for a payment in respect of an occupational retirement scheme other than for the payment of any sum referred to in Sec. 17(1)(h), which is discussed in (9) above, is deemed non-deductible under Sec. 17(1)(j). As discussed in (9) above, however, even a provision for the payment of a sum referred to in Sec. 17(1)(h) is subject to a further limit based on 15% of the relevant employee's emoluments. Schedule 9 provides that this provision applies to a retirement scheme as was defined in Sec. 2 prior to the repeal of that definition as of 19 November 1993. This is largely a transitional provision consequent upon the introduction of the *Occupational Retirement Schemes Ordinance* in 1993 and, as it is an offence to contribute to a retirement scheme other than a recognized occupational retirement scheme or a MPF scheme, this provision now has little, if any, practical effect;

(11) **Retirement scheme contributions relating to previously deducted provisions.** Any sum paid in respect of a contribution to, or a premium in respect of an insurance policy under, a recognized occupational retirement scheme, or a contribution to a MPF scheme, is deemed non-deductible by Sec. 17(1)(k) to the extent that a provision for the amount has been made and deducted in a prior year. This provision is simply intended to ensure that a taxpayer does not receive a double deduction for the same sum (i.e. when a provision is made, for which a deduction may not be denied under Sec. 17(1)(i), and again when actual payment is made, when the deduction may not be denied by Sec. 17(1)(h));

(12) **Payments to unrecognised retirement schemes:** Contributions made as an employer in respect of a retirement scheme other than a recognised occupational retirement scheme (see definition in section 10.3.1), are rendered non-deductible by Sec. 17(1)(l). This provision has little, if any, practical application, however, as it is illegal for a Hong Kong employer to contribute to a retirement scheme which is

not registered under, or been granted exemption from, the *Occupational Retirement Schemes Ordinance*, unless the scheme is established under another Hong Kong ordinance, including the *Mandatory Provident Fund Schemes Ordinance*; and

(13) **Salary, interest and MPF contributions for a sole proprietor, partner or spouse:** In the case of a sole proprietorship, any salary or other remuneration of, and any interest on capital or loans provided by, the proprietor's spouse is deemed non-deductible by Sec. 17(2). This restriction also extends, in the case of a partnership, to any salary or other remuneration, and any interest on capital or loans, paid to a partner or the spouse of a partner. It can sometimes be unclear whether a person is a partner in, or an employee of, a partnership for the purpose of this provision. Such confusion arises because it is common in partnerships for certain individuals to be "salaried partners"; that is, the individual bears the title of partner but is remunerated in a manner akin to a salaried employee and does not bear the risk of losses of the partnership. Although the applicability of Sec. 17(2) in such cases must be decided on the basis of the facts of each case, a good summary of the principles involved can be found in *D 68/03*. Where, however, an amount of salary or other remuneration is denied under this provision, that amount is exempt from Salaries Tax (see section 3.4.6). This provision extends to MPF scheme contributions made in respect of a sole proprietor's spouse, or in respect of a partner, or the spouse of a partner, in a partnership. Nonetheless, as discussed in paragraph (9) of section 4.5.8, a deduction for mandatory contributions made to a MPF scheme by a sole proprietor, or by a partnership in respect of a partner, is granted by Sec. 16AA subject to a limit prescribed by Sch. 3B (currently $12,000 per year of assessment), with such limit being reduced by any deduction allowed under Sec. 26G (see section 3.5.7). It is, however, important to note that although this provision overrides Sec. 17(2) to a degree, a deduction is still denied in respect of contributions to a MPF scheme in respect of the spouse of a sole proprietor or a spouse of a partner in a partnership.

In addition to items statutorily disallowed, the case of *Banque Nationale de Paris Hong Kong Branch v CIR* (2 HKTC 139) highlighted an apparent weakness in the IRO. In that case, interest charged by the bank's head office to the Hong Kong branch was disallowed on the basis that the head office and branch are part of the same legal entity and as a person cannot lend moncy to himself, the sums in question were neither "incurred", as required by Sec. 16(1), nor "sums payable by way of interest", as dealt with by Sec. 16(1)(a). This was not the basis upon which the Commissioner had sought to disallow the sums in the first instance and, indeed, his practice both before and after the case has been to accept inter-branch expenses and assess inter-branch income as if the Hong Kong branch was a separate entity. It seems, however, that although the strict wording of the IRO does not support this obviously common sense approach, the IRD have not changed their practice as a result of the case and, therefore, the case is largely of academic interest only.

4.5.11 Payments to "service companies"

In the 1994/95 Budget Speech, the Financial Secretary foreshadowed the introduction of specific anti-avoidance legislation to counter a perceived loss of revenue through the abuse of "service companies". Two types of situations were identified by the Financial Secretary. The first, referred to as Type I arrangements, involved individuals providing their services to an employer through a company or trust which they controlled in an attempt to disguise an employment relationship; legislation (Sec. 9A) was ultimately introduced to deal with these arrangements and this is considered in depth in section 3.8.1.

The second type of arrangement identified by the Financial Secretary, Type II arrangements, involve the use of service companies by unincorporated sole traders or partnerships; these service companies typically provide the unincorporated business with premises and administrative services in exchange for a management fee. The management fee would generally be deductible, and the proprietors or partners in the unincorporated business, who would be employees or directors of the service company, would receive remuneration from the service company; however, as employees or directors, such remuneration could be structured to take advantage of the generally favourable tax treatment of non-cash remuneration applicable under the Salaries Tax provisions which would not otherwise be available to the individuals as sole traders or partners in a partnership. After much lobbying, the Government decided that such arrangements would be tolerated, within limits; in particular, it was considered that the benefits available under such arrangements should be commensurate with the scope of the service company's activities. As such, it was decided that legislation was not necessary but that it was more appropriate to deal with the matter through the issue of a Practice Note.

Accordingly, in August 1995 the Commissioner issued *Departmental Interpretation & Practice Notes No. 24* ("DIPN 24") which outlines the terms under which such arrangements will be accepted and warns that arrangements outside those guidelines may be challenged under either general principles or the general anti-avoidance provisions of the IRO. It must, however, be remembered that DIPN 24, like all other Practice Notes, has no force of law and is not binding on either the Commissioner or taxpayers; accordingly, arrangements outside the guidelines can still be argued on their technical and factual merits. In this regard, the IRD's powers to partially disallow a properly documented management fee simply because they consider it excessive are probably, as a matter of law, limited; however, there are a number of cases where the Board of Review has upheld the IRD's attempts to do so (see, for example, *D 61/91*).

Moreover, the validity of the IRD's view that a deduction for any fees paid to service companies which are outside the guidelines of DIPN 24 can be challenged under the general anti-avoidance provisions is also doubtful. In particular, in order to apply the main general anti-avoidance provision, Sec. 61A (which is discussed in Chapter 10), it must be concluded that the sole or dominant purpose of the transaction is to obtain a tax benefit. Given that the type of transactions in question involve an unincorporated business being provided with premises, support staff, etc., it is questionable (assuming all aspects are properly documented) whether it could be concluded that the sole or dominant purpose of the transaction was to obtain a tax benefit; that is, if those services are genuinely provided under the transaction, it is arguable that the provision of those services is the sole or dominant purpose of the transaction and that, as a consequence, Sec. 61A should not strike down that transaction simply because the consideration paid by the unincorporated business is considered by the IRD to be excessive. Similarly, because each transaction must be looked at separately when considering the anti-avoidance provisions, the IRD's suggestion that any transaction outside their arbitrarily determined guidelines was undertaken for the sole or dominant purpose of obtaining a tax benefit would seem highly questionable. Nonetheless, in practical terms, taxpayers must be aware that the claiming of deductions for payments to service companies outside the DIPN 24 guidelines is inviting dispute with the IRD.

For an arrangement to be acceptable under DIPN 24, it must first be established as being entered into on an arm's-length basis. In order to demonstrate this, the IRD will normally expect the arrangement to be properly documented. This means that the relevant agreement must be reduced to writing, be properly executed and deal with all relevant details of the arrangement, for example, the services to be rendered, the calculation of the fee and the period for which the services are to be rendered. Also, there should exist minutes of meetings at which the arrangement was approved, invoices and receipts for payments, bank records and employment contracts in respect of persons employed.

Secondly, DIPN 24 sets out a formula to determine the maximum allowable management fee payable by the unincorporated business to the service company. This formula essentially limits the deductible management fee to 112.5% of the costs to the service company of providing "qualifying services" plus the costs of providing certain non-qualifying services. For this purpose, "qualifying services" means non-professional services which provide the infrastructure in which the unincorporated business operates. Examples of such services are the provision of premises, administration staff, plant and equipment and office supplies. Excluded from "qualifying services", however, are any services rendered by the proprietors or partners of the unincorporated business, or any professional (i.e. fee earning) employees of that business, who may be partly involved in the provision of such services. However, although not costs of providing "qualifying services", the costs of any fee earning professional staff (other than the proprietors or partners) incurred in the service company can be passed onto the unincorporated business by way of a management fee but without a mark-up. Accordingly, no salary or benefits paid by the service company to employees or directors who are also proprietors or partners of the unincorporated business can be included when determining the amount of the deductible management fee. Similarly, the costs of running the service company (e.g. audit and secretarial fees) are excluded from such calculation.

The effect of the formula set out in DIPN 24 for calculating the deductible management fee is to effectively limit the gross profit of the service company to 12.5% of the costs of providing the infrastructure of the unincorporated business. This, in turn, limits the amount of tax efficient benefits which can be derived by the proprietors or partners of the unincorporated business through also being employees or directors of the service company. Of course, a management fee in excess of the guidelines can still be legally paid, although if the Commissioner applies the guidelines and seeks to deny a full deduction for it, the service company will bear an extra liability for which there will be no corresponding relief; this is because, notwithstanding the partial denial of a deduction, the service company will still be fully taxable on the management fee. This point is discussed further below.

There are number of Board of Review decisions concerning the application of DIPN 24. See, for example, *D 19/99*. In this decision the

Commissioner restricted a taxpayer's deduction for management fees paid to a service company in accordance with DIPN 24. The Board of Review held that the service company was an artificial device and the payment of the management fee an artificial transaction and, therefore could be ignored pursuant to Sec. 61 (see Chapter 10), notwithstanding that some of the expenses of the service company were expenses which genuinely related to the provision of the infrastructure of the taxpayer's practice as a barrister. Despite the finding that the transactions were artificial, however, the Board did not deny a deduction for the whole of the management fees, but allowed a deduction for the amount determined by the Commissioner to be acceptable (per the guidelines in DIPN 24). In particular, the Board of Review chose not to disturb the practice of the Commissioner, which had been accepted in previous Board of Review decisions, of dissecting the expenses of the service company and allowing, with a mark-up, those relevant to the barrister's business. It is, however, important to note that the Board of Review considered that such action was appropriate only after having decided that the interposition of the service company was artificial and, therefore, open to be ignored pursuant to Sec. 61. This case suggested that if in future a Board of Review was to find that a service company arrangement was not artificial, the Commissioner may have difficulty in persuading the Board to reduce the quantum of the deductible management fee in accordance with DIPN 24.

However, in a subsequent case (*D 94/99*), where the Commissioner did not seek to apply Sec. 61 or otherwise argue that the service company arrangement was artificial, the Board of Review still upheld the application of DIPN 24. In reaching this conclusion, the Board of Review questioned why the Commissioner had not sought to apply Sec. 61 but, given that the issue had not been raised, did not enter a finding that the arrangement was artificial. Rather, the Board simply found that the taxpayer had not discharged the burden of proof of demonstrating that the expenses had been incurred in earning assessable profits and then chose to allow the deduction to the extent that IRD was willing to do so (i.e. in accordance with DIPN 24).

See also *D 53/00* where, although the IRD argued that the taxpayer's service company arrangement was artificial and fictitious, the Board of Review entered no finding on this point. Nonetheless, the Board once again found for the IRD on the basis that the taxpayer had not discharged the burden of proof of showing that the assessments were excessive. In reaching its conclusion, the Board reasoned that the taxpayer's principal ground of objection was the retrospective application of DIPN 24 and that he adduced no evidence as to the lack of artificiality of the arrangement. As such, it was not possible for the taxpayer to discharge the burden of proof in showing that the IRD's disallowance of the management fees and the substitution of an amount calculated in accordance with DIPN 24 resulted in excessive assessments.

Finally, it must be reiterated that DIPN 24 is concerned only with determining the amount of management fees which are deductible to the unincorporated business and has no application to the taxation of the service company itself. Accordingly, in the event that the unincorporated business is denied a deduction for a portion of the fee paid to the service company through the application of DIPN 24, there is no basis for the service company to claim exemption from Profits Tax on the portion so disallowed. This was confirmed by the Board of Review in *D 62/01*.

■ Example 4.18

Young and Jackson is a firm of lawyers. It owns a service company, Chloe Services Limited ("Chloe") which employs all the support staff and solicitors, leases office premises which it makes available to Young and Jackson, provides office equipment, supplies, stationery and the professional library. The partners of Young and Jackson are all directors of Chloe, from which they receive a small director's fee, plus rent-free accommodation and a motor vehicle.

The following expenses are incurred by Chloe:—

(1) Salaries and benefits for support staff	$6,500,000
(2) Office rental, rates and management fees	7,500,000
(3) Updating professional library	10,000
(4) Office equipment lease	350,000
(5) Office supplies	658,000
(6) Salaries and benefits of solicitors	12,000,000
(7) Fees and benefits of directors	8,500,000
Total	$35,518,000

Young and Jackson paid Chloe a management fee, calculated as 105% of Chloe's expenses, of $37,293,900.

Young and Jackson's profit and loss account was as follows:

Fees		$57,500,000
Management fee	$37,293,900	
Other revenue expenses	7,500,000	
		(44,793,900)
Profit		$12,706,100

Under the guidelines in DIPN 24, the maximum deductible management fee to Young and Jackson is 112.5% of the aggregate of items (1) to (5) above, plus item (6), i.e. $15,018,000 × 112.5% + $12,000,000 = $28,895,250

Accordingly, Young and Jackson would lose a deduction of $8,398,650 of the management fee paid to Chloe, but Chloe would still be taxable on its profit of $1,775,900. The favourable tax treatment afforded the benefits provided by Chloe to the directors would be retained. In other words, as a result of the application of DIPN 24, the group's combined tax liability would increase by $1,343,784 (i.e. 16% of $8,398,650).

In these circumstances, the group could slightly improve overall tax efficiency by amending the terms of the management agreement to calculate the fee in accordance with DIPN 24 and restricting the fees and benefits paid to partners to the amount of Chloe's profit before such amounts; in other words, by having Young and Jackson pay a management fee of only $28,895,250 and Chloe pay aggregate fees and benefits to directors of $1,877,250. This would give Chloe no net profit and would save it tax of $310,782 (i.e. 17.5% of $1,775,900). Assuming that the fees and benefits to directors were structured so as to give no liability to Salaries Tax under any alternative, Chloe's tax saving will represent the net benefit to the group as the liabilities of Young and Jackson and the directors will remain unchanged as compared to the application of DIPN 24 to the original arrangement. Of course, both the profits of Chloe and the directors' remuneration from Chloe would be reduced under such an arrangement (the aggregate reduction being $8,087,868), but this would be more than compensated by increased after-tax profits of the partnership of $8,398,650, the difference of $310,782 being the benefit flowing from Chloe's tax saving.

4.5.12 Trading stock and work-in-progress

Because the inclusion of trading stock and work-in-progress (subsequently referred to as stock) in commercial accounts on a valuation basis can be materially influential upon the results shown by the accounts, the amount at which such stock is brought into the accounts is a very sensitive area from a taxation point of view. As a result there are challenges from time to time as to whether a given basis of valuation is valid for tax purposes. There are a number of relevant legal decisions and, as regards the practice in general in Hong Kong in relation to the stock, the *Departmental Interpretation & Practice Notes No. 1* is essential reading (see Appendix 1).

Generally, the treatment for tax purposes follows the accounting treatment but, nevertheless, there are cases where the method of valuation adopted is not acceptable for tax purposes. For example, the LIFO method of valuation was held to be unacceptable in *Minister of National Revenue v Anaconda American Brass* (34 TC 330) as was the base stock method in *Patrick v Broadstone Mills* (35 TC 44) and the replacement value method in *Freeman, Hardy & Willis v Ridgeway* (47 TC 519).

See also *D 8/01* where the Board of Review upheld the Commissioner's assessment which denied a deduction for a provision for diminution in the value of that trading stock, thereby effectively ignoring the valuation of trading stock in the accounts. The reasoning of the Board in reaching this conclusion revolved around the taxpayer not being able to establish the true value of trading stock as at balance sheet date, as a formal valuation was carried out only at a date a number of months after balance date. In other words, the Board concluded that the accounts were incorrectly prepared and essentially re-wrote them for the purpose of ascertaining the taxpayer's assessable profits.

For a discussion on the necessity or otherwise to include overheads in a stock valuation for tax purposes see *Duple Motor Bodies v Ostime* (39 TC 537), although this has been largely overtaken by the standard accounting requirements now laid down by the accountancy bodies. In general, the IRD accepts the principles laid down in the accounting standards issued by the Hong Kong Institute of Certified Practicing Accountants and the few reservations which the IRD has are dealt with in its *Departmental Interpretation & Practice Notes No. 1*.

A number of special points arise out of case law in connection with trading stock. For example, the decision in the UK case of *Sharkey v Wernher* (36 TC 275) suggests that where trading stock is appropriated to some other use, perhaps for personal consumption or for use in the business as a fixed asset, it is to be treated as a sale at open market value. The applicability of this principle in Hong Kong was confirmed in *BR 21/76* and *D 26/84*, although in the latter of these cases the Board of Review urged caution in applying the principle and, in particular, cautioned against extending it.

In *D 75/96*, however, the Board of Review refused to apply the *Sharkey v Wernher* (supra) principle in a case where there was no actual disposal of property. That case concerned a company which it was found had held a number of properties as trading stock but had subsequently changed the intention to one of holding them for rental income. Although the Commissioner argued that the change of intention gave rise to an assessable profit pursuant to the *Sharkey v Wernher* decision (supra), this was rejected on the basis that in that case there had been an actual disposal of trading stock by the relevant business and the only issue for consideration was the amount of income to be brought in as a consequence of that disposal; in the case before the Board, however, there had been no disposal of trading stock as the properties in question continued to be held, albeit as capital assets. Accordingly, although the Board held that the principle in *Sharkey v Wernher* (supra) was generally applicable in Hong Kong, they remarked that even though the company in question may have had an intention to trade, it could not be taxed until it actually traded.

On appeal, the Court of First Instance (see *CIR v Quitsubdue Limited* [1999] (1 HKRC 90-099)) disagreed with the Board of Review and held that the *Sharkey v Wernher* principle was not generally applicable in Hong Kong. This observation was, however, technically *obiter dicta* as the court had found as a matter of fact that the properties in question had been acquired as, and had always remained, capital assets; as such, there was no question of *Sharkey v Wernher* being applicable in that case.

For another similar case, see the decision of the Court of First Instance in *Wah Hing Fat Realty Company Limited v CIR* [2003] (1 HKRC 90-125). In that case, which was an appeal from the Board of Review, the taxpayer had sought to argue that certain properties had been acquired as trading stock but that the intention in holding them had changed to one of holding as a capital assets. Ultimately the taxpayer's case failed on the grounds that it had not established that a change of intention had taken place and the decision provides a useful insight into the level of evidence that a court will require to establish such a change. Unfortunately, however, the court was silent on what the tax consequences would have been if a change of intention had been found and, in particular, whether any unrealised gain up until the change of intention should have been taxable and, if so, whether it would have been taxable at the time of the change or upon the subsequent disposal.

The situation may also arise, particularly in connection with real property, where an asset was originally acquired as an investment but is subsequently appropriated as a trading asset and then sold. For the purposes of arriving at the taxable profit on sale, the acquisition cost has generally been accepted as not the historical cost but the open market value at the time of appropriation. The difficulty is, of course, in establishing the date when the intention with respect to the property changed. Whilst the IRD is understood to still accept this principle, *D 47/91* arguably calls the correctness of it into doubt by suggesting that assessable profit must be determined by taking into account actual, rather than notional, cost. Nonetheless, in a later Board of Review decision (*D 49/92*), the Board had no hesitation, when calculating the assessable profit upon disposal of property, in using as the cost the market value at the date the taxpayer changed its intention in holding the property from that of a fixed asset to a trading asset. See also *D 21/02* in which the Board of Review refused to extend the comments regarding *Sharkey v Wernher* in the *Quitsubdue* case to the situation where a capital asset had become trading stock through a change of intention and was subsequently sold. The Board of Review in that decision reasoned that the court in the *Quitsubdue* case (and, indeed, the *Sharkey v Wernher* case) was concerned with notional profits, while the case before the Board involved real profits and the issue was merely whether they were of a capital or revenue nature. Note, however, that the quantification of assessable profits in that case was not discussed as the amount in dispute had been agreed between the parties. Accordingly, it would seem that the decision in the *Quitsubdue* case does not affect the long standing practice, as endorsed in *D 49/92*, in relation to cases where a capital asset becomes a trading asset and is then sold.

The *Sharkey v Wernher* principle was extended in *Petrotim Securities Ltd. v Ayres* (41 TC 389) to allow the substitution of market value to transactions outside the ordinary course of business. In that case, valuable investments held as trading stock were sold to an associate at a nominal price to produce a loss. It was held that this could not constitute a trading transaction and, therefore, on the basis of the *Sharkey v Wernher* decision the open market value must be substituted. The Commissioner, in two Board of Review cases (see *D 41/91* and *D 47/91*), attempted to rely on this decision to justify substituting, in computing a taxpayer's Profits Tax liability, market value for the actual consideration in the transactions where the parties to the transaction were related. The Board of Review, however, rejected the Commissioner's assertions in both cases. In doing so, the Board of Review expressed the opinion that the existence of Sec. 61 in the IRO (see section 10.4.4) meant that it was inappropriate for the Commissioner to exercise the common law principle established in the *Petrotim Securities* case. Some caution is, however, required in interpreting these judgements as the Board distinguished both cases from the *Petrotim Securities* case on the grounds that the latter involved transactions the terms of which were grossly uncommercial and intended to result in a substantial loss and, therefore, the company was to be considered as no longer acting in the course of its trade; in cases before them, however, the Board noted that the sales may have been at undervalue but seemed to suggest that this was not to anywhere near the same extent. Nonetheless, it is by no means clear that this distinction was relevant to the Board's decision, indeed, the Board went on to note that any attempt by the IRD to categorise the transaction (or, presumably, any other similar transaction) as a sham would be flawed on the basis that the consideration was real. Moreover, the fact that this principle stemmed from the *Sharkey v Wernher* case which, it has been suggested, has no application in Hong Kong (see *CIR v Quitsubdue Limited* [1999] (1 HKRC 90-099) casts further doubt as to its applicability in Hong Kong.

The converse of the position in the *Petrotim Securities* case is, of course, the position of the purchaser of an asset at under- or over-value. *Ridge Securities v CIR* (44 TC 373) suggests that an equivalent adjustment can be made by the purchaser to raise the purchase cost from the nominal figure to open market value for the purpose of calculating their assessable profit on a subsequent disposal. This is supported in the Hong Kong case of *Wing Tai Development Co. Ltd. v CIR* (HKTC 1115) where shares were acquired by reference to their nominal value but the taxable profit on subsequent sale had to be measured on the basis of acquisition at their true value. The correctness of this decision is called into doubt by *D 47/91* (see above) which suggests that "notional" values have no relevance in determining assessable profits. Additionally, given the increasing reliance on accounting principles in determining assessable profits, there seems less scope for the application of such principles.

The IRO also provides for special treatment with regard to trading stock on the cessation of a trade or business. This treatment, which applies only to trading stock and not to work-in-progress, is as follows:—

(1)   where the stock is sold to a person who will use the stock in a business carried on in Hong Kong and will be claiming the purchase cost as a deductible expense, the actual sale proceeds are not disturbed, whether they be at open market value or otherwise (Sec. 15C(a)); or

(2)   in any other situation, the disposal is to be brought in at open market value (Sec. 15C(b)). In other words the *Sharkey v Wernher* (supra) principle is statutorily applied on a cessation, whereas otherwise it might not apply.

■ Example 4.19

Sharedealers Ltd. holds a number of securities as trading stock with a historical cost of $250,000 and a current market value of $600,000. It is decided to cease the share dealing business and liquidate the company and in doing this the shares are sold to Shareinvest Ltd. for $250,000 and Shareinvest holds these as a fixed assets for income.

If Sharedealers had instead decided to hold the securities as fixed assets for income purposes and had therefore appropriated them to fixed assets, the principle in *Sharkey v Wernher* would suggest that an immediate taxable profit of $350,000 would have arisen although there would be great practical difficulty in demonstrating that a cessation of sharedealing had actually taken place. The decision in *D 75/96*, however, suggests that the *Sharkey v Wernher* principle would not be applied in Hong Kong in such circumstances. In any event, it would escape this principle by merely selling them into a separate investment company at cost but for Sec. 15C(b) which ensures that the notional profit of $350,000 is taxable on cessation. If, however, Shareinvest had been a dealing company, Sec. 15C(a) would have applied and Sharedealers would have had no taxable profit but Shareinvest company would have an acquisition price of $250,000.

If Sharedealers had not been ceasing business Sec. 15C would not apply but the sale to Shareinvest at $250,000 might be attacked under the principles established in the *Petrotim Securities v Ayres* case, although see the text for a discussion on the applicability of this principle in Hong Kong.

Note that it has been held by the Court of First Instance in *Southtime Limited v CIR* [2002] (1 HKRC 90-119) that the reference in Sec. 15C to the cessation of a trade or business does not mean the cessation of all of the person's business activities; rather, the court held that the provision could apply when one trade ceased, but other business activities continued. The facts in that case were essentially that a company was established to undertake the purchase, sale and rental of units in a building. Some of the units were sold to third parties and some were retained as capital assets to generate rental income. Some of the units held for resale could not be sold due to market conditions and, as a result, it was decided that these would be sold to the company's shareholders at less than market value, after which the company no longer held any trading stock. (It is implicit in the court's decision, although not explicitly stated, that the units sold to the shareholders and directors were not trading stock in the hands of the purchasers.) The court, in applying Sec.15C held that the business of trading (i.e. the trade) had ceased, even though the business of letting continued. As such, Sec. 15C operated to effectively deem the units on hand at the time of cessation to have been sold at market value. Again, the decision of the court implicitly held that the cessation took place (presumably immediately) prior to the sale of the remaining units held as trading stock to the company's shareholders and directors; that is, the court apparently, but for reasons not explained in the judgement, did not consider the sale to the shareholders and directors to be a transaction in the course of the trading business, in which case Sec. 15C would have had no effect as there would not have been any trading stock on hand at the time of cessation. Nonetheless, the fact that the sales to the shareholders and directors were at less than market value may have been considered indicative of them not being undertaken in the ordinary course of the trading business.

It should be noted that trading stock does not have to be owned by the trader, it having been established in *D 58/86* that gold which had been borrowed by a gold trader from his relatives and which had been held out for sale was nevertheless trading stock.

4.5.13 Pre-commencement expenditure

The strict legal position of expenditure incurred before the commencement of a trade, profession or business is that it is not deductible: in particular, being related to the establishment of a trade, profession or business, such expenditure comes too early in the profit producing process to be considered to be incurred directly in the production of profits. In practice, however, the IRD will allow pre-commencement expenditure of a revenue nature, which would be allowable if incurred after commencement, to be deducted in the first basis period. This practice was succinctly described in the report of the Third Inland Revenue Ordinance Review Committee, as follows:—

"The owner of a business may thus incur outlay on wages or on rent for some time before the technical date of commencement. We understand, however, that the Inland Revenue Department does not adopt a rigid attitude in this matter. In general, we are informed, expenditure of the type that would normally qualify as revenue outlay may be deducted as an expense of the first accounting period. In particular, the wages of office staff engaged before trading begins and of operatives taken on in readiness for the start of production would qualify for this treatment. An exception occurs when maintenance engineers are set to work on the installation of machinery; but in this case their remuneration will be effectively allowed in the long run by adding it to the capital cost of the machinery so that the capital allowances are based on the cost as so increased."

Notwithstanding the significant passage of time since the above report was prepared, the IRD's practice with regard to this matter appears to remain unchanged.

4.5.14 Post-cessation receipts and payments

Because Profits Tax is only imposed on persons carrying on business in Hong Kong, the question arises as to the correct treatment of income and expenses earned or incurred after the cessation of business. This question has been resolved by the inclusion of Sec. 15D.

In particular, Sec. 15D(1) provides that sums received after cessation which, had they been received before, would have been within the scope of Profits Tax, are to be included in the Profits Tax computation for the year of assessment in which the cessation occurred provided, of course, that they have not already been included. If necessary, an additional assessment is raised. Where accounts are prepared on a proper accruals basis, however, such post-cessation receipts should be relatively rare.

Similarly, if expenditure is incurred after cessation which would have been deductible if incurred before, it is treated as if it had been incurred in the year of assessment in which the cessation took place (Sec. 15D(2)). If necessary, a final assessment is re-opened to admit the deduction. The treatment of trading stock upon cessation is subject to special provisions (see section 4.5.11 above).

■ **Example 4.20**

Snarlup Ltd. is a road construction company which ceased business on 31 December 2006 and had an assessable profit of $625,000 for 2006/07. On 15 March 2007 it received $15,000 compensation from a concrete supplier for faulty goods supplied in 2006. On 14

June 2007 Snarlup paid out damages of $25,000 to a motorist as compensation for an accident caused by faulty road construction.

When the receipt of $15,000 is reported, if the 2006/07 assessment on $625,000 had already been finalised, an additional assessment for 2006/07 on $15,000 would be raised. Likewise, the payment of $25,000 can be claimed as a deduction in 2006/07 and, although Sec. 15D(2) does not specifically provide that the 2006/07 final assessment may be re-opened, this is in fact done in practice and repayment would be made of $25,000 @ 17.5% (the rate applicable in that year).

4.5.15 Apportionment of expenses

Because various items of profit are not taxable in Hong Kong, particularly profits which do not arise in or derive from Hong Kong and dividends wherever they arise, it will be apparent that it would not be correct to exclude such items from the Profits Tax computation without making some appropriate adjustment in respect of related expenditure. Whilst authority for disallowing a proportion of expenditure can be inferred from the general deduction test in Sec. 16(1), and its complement in Sec. 17(1)(b) whereby only expenditure incurred in the production of assessable profits is allowable, there are nevertheless some specific apportionment provisions contained in the IRR.

In addition to these specific provisions, the Board of Review, in *D 96/89* and *D 61/91*, has shown a certain willingness to allow deductions for expenses only to the extent to which they are considered commercially reasonable. Those cases involved professionals paying fees to "service" companies which they controlled and the Board of Review allowed a portion of the expenses having regard to the underlying expenses of the service companies. In the similar, but later, case of *D 32/94*, however, the Board of Review held that the fee paid to the professional's service company was an indivisible fee which was either deductible in full or not at all; in other words, the Board held that the fee was not apportionable at all. This seems somewhat harsh in that the meaning of S.6A, it appears to presuppose that an expense can be apportioned; accordingly, even if it is found as a fact that the motive for the payment was partly to earn assessable profits and partly some other (possibly tax motivated) purpose, the legislation still seems to allow scope for apportionment along the lines of the decisions in *D 96/89* and *D 61/91*.

The specific rules regarding apportionment of expenses are as follows:

(1)   **IRR 2A:** The general rule in IRR 2A provides for the situation where profits are derived partly from a source within Hong Kong and partly from a source outside Hong Kong and stipulates that

outgoings and expenses are to be apportioned "on such basis as is most appropriate to the trade, profession or business".

Where a portion of the profits is not taxable for some reason other than that it has a source outside Hong Kong, or there is some other reason why it is necessary to apportion expenses and out-goings, it is provided that this is to be on a *"basis as is most reasonable and appropriate in the circumstances"*.

In neither case, therefore, is the method of apportionment rigidly laid down; it is left to fact and common sense, although there is a subtle difference in the case of onshore/offshore profits where the circumstances of the business must be considered and in other cases where any reasonable basis is appropriate.

■ Example 4.21

Eerzacase Ltd. earns its profits from the sale of textile products both from an office in Hong Kong and an office in Taiwan. The following facts are relevant for the year of assessment:—

(1) Total adjusted gross profits: $450,000 (Turnover $1,400,000)
(2) Adjusted gross profits (Taiwan): $90,000 (Turnover $200,000)
(3) Offshore interest income from deposit of surplus funds in Singapore: $40,000
(4) Overhead expenditure: $280,000
(5) Taiwan office has two sales staff and Hong Kong office has six. Each office is autonomous but the directors are in Hong Kong.
(6) There is an interest charge of $35,000 in the profit and loss account which relates wholly to bills of exchange.

First of all, no adjustment to overhead expenditure should be necessary in respect of the offshore interest income because a deposit will incur no material management time or other expenditure. Also the interest outgoing is not related to it and should not require adjustment.

There are a number of methods of possible apportionment in respect of onshore/offshore trading profits:—

Method A based on turnover			
Total gross profit			$450,000
Less offshore profit			(90,000)
Onshore gross profit			$360,000
Allowable overheads	12/14 × 280,000	=	240,000
Assessable profit			$120,000

Method B based on profit			
Onshore gross profit			$360,000
Allowable overheads	36/45 × 280,000	=	224,000
Assessable profit			$136,000

Method C based on staff			
Onshore gross profit			$360,000

Allowable overheads	6/8 × 280,000	=	210,000
Assessable profit			$150,000

Method D more detailed

Onshore gross profit			$360,000
Interest outgoing (by turnover)	12/14 × 35,000	=	(30,000)
Other overheads (by staff)	6/8 × 24,5000	=	(183,750)
Assessable profit			$146,250

Equally it can be seen that there are other methods involving a combination of Method D and the other methods, each of which will give a different answer. None of these methods is necessarily the "right" one. They all have their merits and demerits and in the end it is a question of judgement and negotiation.

(?)   **Interest on money used to buy shares:** This issue is dealt with in IRR2B. Clearly the purchase of shares yields no taxable income, unless the business consists of share dealing, because dividends are not taxable. Therefore, if shares are purchased with borrowed money, it is obvious that the interest incurred thereon is not for the purpose of earning assessable profits and should therefore be disallowed under the general deduction test in Sec. 16(1). It also seems logical that where money is borrowed and is used partly to buy shares and partly for purposes which will yield an assessable profit, that the relevant proportion of interest be disallowed. Although again this may be inferred from Sec. 16(1), the point is specifically covered by IRR2B(1) which provides that the proportion used to buy shares is not deductible and is to be ascertained on "*such basis as is most reasonable and appropriate in the circumstances*".

As in the case of apportionments under IRR2A, there is no "right" method of doing it, although it is easier to be more positive under IRR2B because an apportionment is only required where money is borrowed and actually used to buy shares. If existing cash resources are used to buy shares and a new loan is taken up to loosely to provide working capital, IRR2B does not apply but of course, it would have to be proved that the funds were used in that manner.

No adjustment is called for in respect of the purchase of shares by a share dealing business (IRR2B(2)).

■ Example 4.22

Bishops Investments Ltd. is carrying on a trading business in Hong Kong as well as a share investment business. During the year it took up a fixed loan from its bankers, to acquire shares in an associated company (loan 1) and a further loan of $100,000 (loan 2) of which $60,000 was used to pay off pressing trade creditors and the balance to purchase a portfolio of share investments. During the year Bishops Investments paid interest of $9,000 on loan 1, interest of $12,000 on loan 2 and further interest of $6,500 on its overdraft which has been used for general trading purposes.

Notes:—
(a) The interest of $9,000 on loan 1 is disallowable, not under IRR2B but under the general deduction test in Sec. 16(1) because the whole of the loan was used to buy shares.
(b) Of the interest of $12,000 paid on loan 2, 40% or $4,800 is disallowable under IRR2B being the proportion related to purchase of shares.
(c) If any shares had been purchased out of the main bank account on which the overdraft arises there can be great practical problems in applying IRR2B. If, as is often the case, the account is in overdraft from year to year, it would not be proper to make a disallowance every year based on the current overdraft interest rate and the amount originally withdrawn to buy shares. It must be recognised that an overdraft is constantly changing in character and that withdrawals are ultimately repaid by credits notwithstanding that new withdrawals keep the account in overdraft. A practical solution is to ascertain the amount of the debit balance immediately before buying the shares, e.g.:—

Debit balance at 15.6.06	$165,000
Shares purchased 15.6.06	40,000
	$205,000

and then to ascertain the date by which aggregate credits have amounted to $205,000 which is on the assumption that repayment is on a first-in-first-out basis. The average rate of interest for the period ascertained could be applied to $40,000 for that period to give the disallowance. Even this does not allow for the fact that there will have been a period during which the outstanding principal of $40,000 will have been gradually reduced and more complicated research and computation would be required to allow for this.

---

(3) **Overhead cost of investment portfolios:** This matter is covered by IRR2C. The logic of this provision is that where a business which is otherwise earning assessable profits also has a material investment portfolio which does not, of course, yield assessable income, some of the overhead expenditure charged against business profits must relate to the cost of supervision and management of the portfolio and should, therefore, be disallowed. An investment portfolio, in the context of IRR2C, would generally include securities and other similar investments but would not include an independently managed subsidiary. Nevertheless, other adjustment methods may still be adopted to disallow overhead expenditure relating to the investment in a subsidiary where the facts are sufficient to warrant such a disallowance.

The provision is only applicable if, in the opinion of the assessor, the portfolio is sufficiently substantial (IRR2C(2)) and this must, of course, be judged in relation to the business as a whole. Where it is decided that an adjustment is required, this is to proceed on the basis of a fixed percentage of the total cost of the investments unless a more practical and suitable basis is available in the circumstances. As a fixed percentage is completely arbitrary, it is often possible to adopt a more practical method, usually related to actual costs. For example a portfolio which undergoes few changes would attract a nominal or nil adjustment because no staff time or other costs are involved in its maintenance.

If the percentage method is adopted the rate is to be such as is most reasonable and appropriate in the circumstances but not exceeding:

(i) $\frac{1}{8}\%$ where the business is share dealing. This is merely to cover the cost of collection of non-taxable dividends.

(ii) $\frac{1}{2}\%$ in other cases.

Where the cost of the portfolio is continually changing it is common to apply the percentage to the average cost for the year ascertained by taking the mean of the opening and closing figures for the basis period.

Because the IRR are in fact no more than an extension to the IRO, any dispute as to their application is subject to the same right of objection and appeal as other provisions (IRR2D). See also *Departmental Interpretation & Practice Notes No. 3.*

4.5.16 Losses

In most respects, losses are computed in the same way as profits and by reference to the same basis periods (Sec. 19D). In the same way that depreciation allowances and balancing charges decrease or increase assessable profits respectively, so do they increase and decrease allowable losses (Sec. 19E(1)). If a balancing charge exceeds adjusted losses, an assessable profit arises (Sec. 19E(2)). Similarly, where depreciation allowances exceed the adjusted profit, an allowable loss results (Sec. 18F(2)). It must, however, be remembered that approved charitable donations cannot add to an allowable loss because any deduction for such amounts is limited to 25% of the assessable profits before such deduction; accordingly, where there are no assessable profits there can be no deduction (see (13) in section 4.5.8).

Because some types of profits are taxed at concessional rates, provisions are required to prevent any losses from such business from operating to shelter profits from businesses which are taxed at the full rate. These provisions are quite complex and are discussed in section 4.5.15.1 below. Additionally, although losses are calculated in the same manner for all taxpayers, the treatment or utilisation of losses depends to some extent on the nature of the taxpayer incurring the losses and the positions of various types of taxpayer are discussed in sections below.

An interesting question arises as to the calculation of losses where a taxpayer maintains his accounts in a foreign currency. Where such a taxpayer derives profits, the assessable profits are determined in the foreign currency amount and then converted into Hong Kong dollars. Where, however, a loss is sustained, the question arises as to whether the losses should be converted to Hong Kong dollars each year or, alternatively, they should be carried forward in the foreign currency and offset against subsequent profits in the foreign currency with only the net assessable amount being converted to Hong Kong dollars. The legislation provides no guidance on this question, but it was held by the High Court in *CIR v Malaysian Airline System Berhad* [1994] (1 HKRC 90-070), in overturning the Board of Review, that the former treatment (i.e. converting the loss each year to Hong Kong dollars) was more correct. This case specifically concerned Sec. 19C(4), as the taxpayer was a company, although the principle would presumably be followed for other types of taxpayers.

Unlike many other jurisdictions, there are no provisions for the transfer of losses between companies in the same corporate group. Nonetheless, calls are mounting for some form of such relief, generally known as group relief, to be introduced in Hong Kong. The reasoning for such calls is that currently enterprises that are formed as corporate groups with more than one operating company (for example due to regulatory or legal requirements) are denied the same tax loss relief enjoyed by an enterprise organised as a single operating company, even though in substance both structures are single economic entity groups. Some observers believe that the current approach is inequitable and results in relative inefficiencies between taxpayers in similar industries and carrying on similar businesses but with different legal structures. Nonetheless, in his 2006/07 Budget Speech, the Financial Secretary again rejected calls for reform in this area. The reasoning for the rejection included the fear of the loss of billions of dollars in revenue from the abuse of such a system; whilst it goes without saying that the legislation must be capable of stopping evasion through abuse, this does not appear to be a significant issue in other jurisdictions and this, together with Hong Kong's broad general anti-avoidance provisions (see chapter 10), suggest that revenue loss through abuse of a group relief system should not be a significant problem if the relevant legislation is appropriately drafted.

See also *Departmental Interpretation & Practice Notes No. 8* which further considers issues regarding losses.

4.5.16.1 Losses involving taxpayers deriving concessionary trading receipts

Secs. 19CA and 19CB deal with the position where losses are incurred by a taxpayer who derives both income taxed at normal rates and income which attracts concessional rates of tax. Because profits from these different types of receipts are taxed at different rates, it is necessary to have provisions which deal with the situation where there are losses from one type of business and profits from another, or there are losses to be carried forward from one type of business but which may ultimately fall to be set off against profits from the other type of business.

As is discussed more fully below, Sec. 19C generally provides that a loss can be carried forward and set off against profits derived in a subsequent year of assessment. This is, however, subject to Sec. 19CB, the intention of which, in simple terms, is to double the amount of losses from normal business where they arc set off against profits from concessionary trading receipts and to halve the amount of losses from concessionary trading receipts when set off against profits from normal business. For this purpose, concessionary trading receipts are amounts taxable under Sec. 14A (see (14) in section 4.5.3) or offshore reinsurance business profits taxable under Sec. 14B (see section 4.7.2). Profits or losses attributable to concessionary trading receipts taxable under Sec. 14A are arrived at after deducting outgoings and expenses incurred in the relevant basis period in the production of those receipts, together with depreciation allowances on assets used in the production of such receipts, and adding back any related balancing charges. No such adjustments are, however, required in respect of amounts taxable under Sec. 14B as any such amounts are calculated pursuant to Sec. 23A(2) and are already net of related expenses.

More specifically, Sec. 19CB(2) deals with the position where there is a loss from concessionary trading receipts and a profit from normal business and provides that where the loss is not greater than the assessable profits multiplied by the adjustment factor, the assessable profits are to be reduced by the loss *divided* by the adjustment factor and that loss will be deemed fully set off for all purposes of the IRO (Sec. 19CB(2)(a)). The term "adjustment factor" is defined in Sec. 19CA and means the normal tax rate applicable to the taxpayer divided by the rate specified in either Sec. 14A or 14B (whichever is appropriate) as applicable to the taxpayer. Since the rates in

Secs. 14A and 14B are specified as being one half of the rate otherwise applicable, the adjustment factor is, in fact, always 2. Where, however, the loss is greater than twice the assessable profits, the person is deemed to have no assessable profits for the year and the loss is reduced by what would otherwise have been the assessable profits from the normal business *multiplied* by the adjustment factor (Sec. 19CB(2)(b)).

Sec. 19CB(3), on the other hand, deals with the position where there is a loss from normal business but a profit from concessionary trading receipts and provides that where the loss is not greater than the profit *divided* by the adjustment factor (i.e. 2), the assessable profits are reduced by the loss *multiplied* by the adjustment factor (i.e. 2) (Sec. 19CB(3)(a)). In cases where the loss is greater than the profit *divided* by the adjustment factor, the loss to be carried forward is reduced by an amount equal to the assessable profits from the concessionary trading receipts *divided* by the adjustment factor and the person is deemed to have no assessable profits for the year (Sec. 19CB(3)(b)).

If a person derives only profits from normal business (or, somewhat exceptionally, only profits from concessionary trading receipts), Sec. 19CB will have no application.

The situation where a loss is carried forward to a subsequent year of assessment is dealt with by Sec. 19CA. This provision largely mirrors Sec. 19CB and provides that where there is a loss brought forward which is attributable to concessionary trading receipts and the person in the current year has a profit from normal business, if the loss is not greater than the profit *multiplied* by the adjustment factor, the assessable profits are to be reduced by the loss *divided* by the adjustment factor (i.e. 2) (Sec. 19CA(2)(a)). Conversely, where the loss is greater than the assessable profits *multiplied* by the adjustment factor, the person is deemed to have no assessable profits for the year and the loss is reduced by what would otherwise have been the assessable profits from the normal business *multiplied* by the adjustment factor (Sec. 19CA(2)(b)).

Similarly, Sec. 19CA(3) deals with the position where a person has a loss brought forward which is attributable to normal business but a profit in the current year from concessionary trading receipts and provides that where the loss is not greater than the profit *divided* by the adjustment factor (i.e. 2), the assessable profits are reduced by the loss *multiplied* by the adjustment factor (i.e. 2) (Sec. 19CA(3)(a)). In cases where the loss is greater than the profit *divided* by the adjustment factor, the loss to be carried forward is reduced by an amount equal to the assessable profits from concessionary trading receipts *divided* by the adjustment factor and the person is deemed to have no assessable profits for the year (Sec. 19CB(3)(b)).

Where a loss brought forward arises from normal business and is to be set off only against profits from normal business (or is from concessionary trading receipts and is to be set off only against profits from such receipts), Sec. 19CA will have no application.

Some of the above rules are illustrated by the following examples.

■ Example 4.23

Risky Ltd. is an insurance company and has an agreed assessable profit for the year from normal business of $3,000,000 and an agreed loss from qualifying offshore reinsurance business which it has elected to have taxed in accordance with Sec. 14B of $600,000. Its assessable profits for the year are, therefore, in accordance with Sec. 19CB(2)(a):

Normal business profits	$3,000,000
Less: concessionary loss divided by 2	(300,000)
Assessable profits	$2,700,000

The above result would also arise if the concessionary trading loss had been carried forward from the prior year (Sec. 19CA(2)(a)).

Note that if Risky Ltd.'s loss under Sec. 14B had instead been $7,000,000, it would have been reduced to the extent of the profits from the normal business multiplied by 2 (i.e. $3,000,000 × 2 = $6,000,000). Accordingly, there would be a loss from concessionary trading of $1,000,000 to be carried forward and there would be no assessable profits for the year (Sec. 19CB(2)(b))

■ Example 4.24

Shaky Ltd. is a construction company which invests some of its surplus cash in debt instruments, the interest and profits from which attract a concessionary rate of tax under Sec. 14A. Its construction activities resulted in a loss for the year of $2,500,000, but it derived a profit (net of expenses) of $250,000 from its investment in the qualifying debt instruments.

Shaky's loss for the year is calculated as follows pursuant to Sec. 19CB(3)(b):

Normal business loss	($2,500,000)
Less: profit from concessionary trading receipts divided by 2	125,000
Loss to be carried forward	($2,375,000)

The above result would also arise if the loss from the construction activities had, in fact, been carried forward from the prior year (Sec. 19CA(3)(b)).

If Shaky's loss from its construction business had been only $100,000, the provisions of Sec. 19CB(3)(a) would apply and the assessable profits from the concessionary trading receipts (i.e $250,000) would be deemed to be reduced by twice the loss from the construction activities (i.e. $100,000 × 2 = $200,000) and the balance of $50,000 would be taxable at the rate specified in Sec. 14A (currently 8.75%). Further, the losses from the construction activities would be deemed to be nil.

4.5.16.2 Individuals

An individual who incurs a loss in a trade, profession or business may either elect for Personal Assessment and thereby have the loss allowed against his other sources of income assessable under the IRO for the same year of assessment as that in which the loss was incurred (see Chapter 6) or he may have the loss carried forward indefinitely and set off against future profits from the same trade, profession or business in which the loss was incurred (Sec. 19C(1)). If the individual does not elect for Personal Assessment, any unutilised loss is lost if the individual ceases to carry on the same trade or business. This is to be contrasted with the position where an election is made for Personal Assessment in which case the loss remains available until fully utilised (Secs. 19C(3) and 42(5)). This fact, together with the cash flow advantages of immediately utilising losses against any other source of assessable income rather than carrying them forward, means that it will usually be to a taxpayer's benefit to elect for Personal Assessment where he has more than one source of income.

Similar rules apply in the case of an individual who is a member of a partnership in that he can take his share of any partnership loss and claim Personal Assessment, in which case the loss can be set off against his other sources of assessable income and any excess carried forward, or he can carry it forward in the partnership for set off against his share of the future assessable profits of the partnership.

Sec. 19C(7) defines a "partnership" as not including a partnership of more than 20 partners (other than a partnership referred to in Sec. 345(2) of the *Companies Ordinance*, which are broadly partnerships of solicitors, accountants and certain other professions). A consequence of this is that losses incurred by a partnership of more than 20 partners (other than a partnership referred to in Sec. 345 of the *Companies Ordinance*) are carried forward by the partnership and set off against future assessable profits of that partnership. Note, however, that when Part 2 of Schedule 4 of the *Companies (Amendment) Ordinance 2004* becomes effective (by publication of a notice in the *Gazette*), Sec. 19C(7) will be repealed and all partnerships will then be treated the same way with regard to losses. To deal with the position of partnerships of more than 20 partners which had carried forward losses at the time of the repeal of Sec. 19C(7), transitional provisions will be introduced as Sec. 22C which will permit those losses to continue to be carried forward by the partnership and set off against future assessable profits. Moreover, Sec. 22C will stipulate that the set off of losses against assessable profits shall be undertaken before apportioning the profits between partners for the purpose of Sec. 22A(1) (see section 4.7.9). This transitional provision will, therefore, have the effect of over-riding the general rule in Sec. 22A(2) that a partnership cannot carry forward tax losses (see section 4.5.16.4). Nonetheless, this will be necessary because following the repeal of Sec. 19C(7) any current losses of such a partnership will be dealt with at the partner level, but any carried forward losses from earlier years will not be able to be dealt with in the same manner; accordingly, to ensure that the benefit of such losses will not be lost, the losses will be deemed available to be carried forward by the partnership.

If an individual who has not elected for Personal Assessment withdraws from a partnership while he still has an unutilized loss from that partnership, his share of those losses will not be available for him to offset against future assessable profits as such a loss can only ever be set off against assessable profits from the same partnership (Sec. 19C(2)). If, however, the individual elects for Personal Assessment, any part of the loss not set off against current year income from other sources may be carried forward and set off against future income aggregated in a Personal Assessment calculation even if the individual has in the interim withdrawn from the partnership (Secs. 19C(3) and 42(5)). Note, however, the additional restrictions which apply to any losses of a limited partner pursuant to Sec. 22B, which is discussed in section 4.5.16.5 below.

A husband and wife who are partners in a partnership are treated independently for the purpose of the allocation of losses.

4.5.16.3 Corporations and other persons

More advantageous rules for relief of losses apply in the case of corporations and persons other than individuals and partnerships. Pursuant to Sec. 19C(7), these rules apply to partnerships of more than 20 partners (other than partnerships referred to in Sec. 345 of the *Companies Ordinance*, which are broadly partnerships of solicitors, accountants and certain other professions). Sec. 19C(7) will, however, be repealed when Part 2 of Schedule 1 of the *Companies (Amendment) Ordinance 2004* becomes operative upon publication of notice in the *Gazette* and the effect of the repeal and the transitional provisions to be introduced as a result are discussed in section 4.5.16.2 above.

Any loss sustained by a person in this category is automatically set against any other source of profit liable to Profits Tax for the year of assessment in which the loss was incurred and, so far as not fully relieved, can be carried forward indefinitely and set off against any profits subject to Profits Tax in subsequent years (Sec. 19C(4)). In particular, any such losses can be set off against the person's share of profits of a partnership in which they are a partner. The IRD were previously of the view that losses could only be set off against the share of profits of a partnership in which the person was a partner at the time they incurred the losses. However, such an interpretation was expressly rejected by the Board of Review in *D 65/02*.

Where an estimated assessment for a year of assessment has become final and conclusive, even though it may be possible to show that there was in fact an actual loss as computed under Profits Tax rules, it is not available for relief under Sec. 19C(4) because there is deemed to be no loss for that year in view of the final assessment; in this regard, see *Corpora Enterprises Ltd. v CIR* (2 HKTC 656).

Where a corporation or person other than an individual or a partnership is a member of a partnership, its share of losses which are not set off against current profits are carried forward indefinitely and set off against profits of any type subject to Profits Tax but they must be set off in priority against its share of profits from the partnership. The losses do not, however, cease to be available if it withdraws from the partnership (Sec. 19C(5)). Note, however, the restrictive provisions of Sec. 22B which apply to limited partners (see section 4.5.16.5 below). For a further discussion on the treatment of partnerships, see section 4.7.9 below.

4.5.16.4 Partnerships — general

Although assessed to Profits Tax as a person, a partnership has its losses dealt with in accordance with the capacities of its individual partners. Therefore, they are dealt with as described in 4.5.16.2 above. Limited partners are subject to the restrictions in Sec. 22B in their ability to set partnership losses against their own income, which is discussed below.

4.5.16.5 Partnerships — loss limitation

It would normally be the case that a corporate partner in a partnership which incurs an allowable loss for Profits Tax purposes would be able to set its share of such loss against its own profits subject to Profits Tax. The widespread use of limited partnerships to transact leverage leases to take advantage of that tax benefit whilst limiting the exposure of partners to commercial liability has attracted the attention of tax authorities in the countries where such arrangements have been used. In the UK, the tax authorities attempted to limit the allowable share of loss of a limited partner to the amount of capital contributed by the partner. This attempt was, however, unsuccessful (see *Reed v Young* (59 TC 196)) and the law was changed to achieve the same result.

Statutory amendments were subsequently made in Hong Kong on very similar terms and these are embodied in Sec. 22B.

The effect of the provisions is to limit the amount of the share of a partnership loss by a limited partner to the smaller of:—

(a)   the limited partner's share of the loss; or

(b)   an amount referred to as the "relevant sum" (Sec. 22B(3)).

For this purpose, "limited partner" and "relevant sum" are defined in Secs. 22B(1) and 22B(2).

"Limited Partner" means any of the following:

(i)   a limited partner in a limited partnership which is registered under the *Limited Partnerships Ordinance*;

(ii)   a general partner but who is, in reality, a limited partner by virtue of the fact that either he has no right to participate in partnership management or in fact has the right but does not actually participate and, furthermore, has the right to have his liabilities, or liabilities up to a given ceiling, for debts or obligations of the partnership to be discharged or reimbursed by some other person. This would seem to apply where a general partner insures his liabilities but it is thought that it would not be so applied where such insurance is a normal commercial procedure, e.g. professional indemnity insurance; or

(iii) is effectively a limited partner under the laws of another country whereby, under those laws he has no right to take part in partnership management or factually does not do so and is not liable beyond a certain limit for partnership debts or obligations.

"Relevant Sum" is defined to mean the amount of a partner's contribution to the partnership as at the last day of the year of assessment in which the loss was incurred. Where a partner has ceased to be a partner before that date, the relevant date is the date on which he so ceased. To limit any dispute as to the amount of a partner's contribution, this is further defined as:—

(a)   The amount of his contributed capital

       Less (i)   any capital directly or indirectly withdrawn or paid back; and

       Less (ii) anything that he may be entitled to receive or be reimbursed by another person while the partnership is in business even if his entitlement is not enforceable.

Plus

(b)   His undistributed profit entitlement.

The effect of these provisions is to negate, in practice, the expected tax benefits in a leverage lease and, if the benefits are to be obtained, there is no choice but to accept exposure to commercial liability and participate as a general partner.

See also paragraphs 2 to 7 of *Departmental Interpretation & Practice Notes No. 15*, which is reproduced as Appendix 10.

■ Example 4.25

Cablecom Ltd. is a limited partner in the Muchloss Leasing Partnership which is managed and controlled in Hong Kong and each have an accounting period ending on 15 April. Cablecom is entitled to an interest in 90% of the profits of the partnership. The Muchloss Partnership has acquired a Boeing 747–400 and began leasing it to the local Dragon Pacific Airlines on 16 May 2006. Cablecom's capital contribution to Muchloss stood at $30 million as at 31 March 2008 and has the benefit of an informal arrangement whereby the parent company of the general partner will pay Cablecom a sum equal to 10% of its capital half way through the lease.

The IRD has agreed that Muchloss has an allowable loss of $120 million for 2007/08. (i.e. for the year to 15 April, 2007). Cablecom has assessable profits of $150 million for 2007/08.

Because Cablecom is a limited partner, the provisions of Sec. 22B apply.

Basis Period 12 months to 15 April 2007		Loss ($120 million)
Amount attributable to Cablecom 90%		= ($108 million)

Effect of Sec. 22B on Cablecom

Allowable loss = Lesser of ($108 million) or relevant sum		(Sec. 22B(3))
Relevant Sum = Contribution at 31/3/2008	$30 million	
Less refundable	(3 million)	(Secs. 22B(1) and
	$27 million	22B(2)(a)(ii))
Allowable loss is therefore		($27 million)

This is claimable by Cablecom against its own profits for 2007/08.
Balance of ($81 million) is carried forward in the partnership.
To avoid this loss limitation, Cablecom would have to be a genuine general partner.

4.5.16.6 Trustees

Although a trustee is within the definition of a "person" for Profits Tax purposes, his liability to tax generally remains confused. This issue is discussed further in section 4.3.1 above. With respect to losses, however, the matter is perhaps a little clearer due to the inclusion in the IRO of Sec. 19C(6)(e). In particular, this provision makes it clear that any losses sustained in a trade, profession or business carried on for the benefit of a trust by a person in their capacity as a trustee can be offset only against future assessable profits of the trust from that trade, profession or business. This would seem to suggest that in the case of a trust, any Profits Tax liability is to be assessed against the trustee, although that assessment is to be separate from any assessment in respect of profits derived by the trustee in their own right or, indeed, in respect of another trust. Although such a suggestion is undoubtedly reasonable and practical, as discussed in section 4.3.1 above, the Board of Review has not consistently adopted this practice in situations where profits are derived.

■ Example 4.26

Percy Vere is a married man with no children whose wife has no separate income. He carries on a motor repair business and has made an adjusted loss of $80,000 for the year of assessment 2006/07. He is entitled to depreciation allowances of $3,000 for 2006/07. He owns a property on which he pays Property Tax on a net assessable value of $19,200 for each of the years 2006/07, 2007/08 and 2008/09. For 2007/08 he has an adjusted profit of $15,000 and depreciation allowances of $3,500. For 2008/09 he has an adjusted profit of $300,000 and depreciation allowances of $2,000. Losses would be utilised as follows:—

(1) If Percy elects for personal assessment for 2006/07 he will obtain repayment of the Property Tax paid and the balance of loss will be:—

Adjusted loss	($80,000)	
Depreciation allowances	(3,000)	
Allowable loss	($83,000)	
Net assessable property value	19,200	(Recovery $3,072)
Loss carried forward	($63,800)	

Because the loss can only be offset against total income, Percy will, in order to obtain the benefit of the losses, elect in 2007/08 for personal assessment (see Chapter 6) and he will again obtain repayment of the Property Tax paid and the balance of loss will be:—

Adjusted profit	$15,000	
Depreciation allowances	(3,500)	
Assessable profit	$11,500	
Loss brought forward	(63,800)	
	($52,300)	
Net assessable property value	19,200	(Recovery $3,072)
Loss carried forward	($33,100)	

For 2008/09 he will again need to elect for personal assessment in order to obtain the benefit of the losses (see Chapter 6) and he will pay tax on total income:—

Adjusted profit	$300,000
Depreciation allowances	(2,000)

Assessable profit	$298,000	
Net assessable property value	19,200	
Total income	$317,200	
Loss brought forward	(33,100)	
Taxable income	$284,100	Tax = $4,842

(2) If Percy does not elect for personal assessment in 2006/07, the loss will only be available for set-off against profits from the same business in subsequent years and the position would be as follows:—

2006/07 Allowable loss	$ 83,000	
less 2007/08 assessable profit	(11,500)	
Carried forward	$ 71,500	
2008/09 Assessable profit	298,000	
Net assessable profit 2008/09	$226,500	Tax = $530
Property Tax (for 3 years)	$ 9,216	

Under method (1) his total tax for the three years is $4,842. Under method (2) his total tax for the three years is $9,746 (three years Property Tax plus 2008/09 Profits Tax). It would therefore pay him to elect for personal assessment but this would not always be the case.

There is a third alternative which is to elect for personal assessment in 2008/09 only, but the total tax payable would still be greater than method (1).

■ Example 4.27

Mr. Hop, Mr. Skip and Jump Ltd. are in a general partnership as engineers and they share profits and losses equally. Recent results of the partnership are as follows:—

2005/06	Allowable loss	($150,000)
2006/07	Assessable profit	12,000
2007/08	Assessable profit	120,000

Mr. Hop withdrew from the partnership at the end of 2006/07 and therefore does not share in 2007/08. Hop and Skip have no other sources of income but Jump Ltd. has other income subject to Profits Tax of $20,000 per annum.

The partnership tax position is as follows:—

		Hop	Skip	Jump Ltd.	Partnership
2005/06	Loss	($50,000)	($50,000)	($50,000)	
	Other Income	—	—	20,000	
	Loss C/F	($50,000)	($50,000)	($30,000)	($130,000)
2006/07	Profit	$ 4,000	$ 4,000	$ 4,000	
	Loss B/F	(50,000)	(50,000)	(30,000)	
		($46,000)	($46,000)	($26,000)	
	Other Income	—	—	20,000	
	Loss C/F	($46,000)	($46,000)	($ 6,000)	($ 98,000)
2007/08	Profit		$60,000	$60,000	
	Loss B/F		($46,000)	(6,000)	
	Assessable Profit		$14,000	$54,000	$ 68,000

Notes:—

(a) Hop's share of losses ceases to be available either to him or the partnership upon his withdrawal.

(b) If the individual partners had other income, the position would be the same as above if they did not elect for personal assessment.

(c) Skip would on the above figures elect for Personal Assessment for 2007/08 because he would then obtain personal allowances against his share of net profits after losses and no liability would arise.

(d) Jump Ltd. must bring in its remaining share of partnership losses against the 2007/08 share of profits in priority to all other income.

(e) Assuming Skip's election for Personal Assessment for 2007/08, the assessment on the partnership would be $54,000 @ 17.5% and Jump Ltd. would be assessed separately on its own profits, i.e. at 17.5% on $20,000 (The rate applicable to 2007/08).

(f) For Personal Assessment rules see Chapter 6.

(g) Had this been a limited partnership, the limited partners would have been subject to the restrictive effect of Sec. 22D upon their ability to set partnership losses against other income.

4.6 Basis of Assessment

Because commercial and accounting requirements normally dictate that accounts of business profits and losses are made up for periods which do not necessarily coincide with years of assessment, it is necessary to have rules for allocating profits and losses of accounting periods to years of assessment. Also, because accounting periods are open to manipulation, some of the rules are necessarily complicated in order to counter avoidance, although the position was greatly simplified from 1 April 1974 when an "actual" basis was adopted, superseding the "previous year" basis which applied before that date. The old basis and the transitional provisions to the new basis are not dealt with in this book except in so far as it is necessary to refer to them in clarification of certain of the new provisions.

4.6.1 Normal basis

The assessable profits for a year of assessment are to be computed on the basis of the profits arising during the year of assessment (Sec. 18B(1)). This is of course straightforward where the accounting year is co-terminous with the year of assessment, i.e. to 31 March, but where, as is common, the accounts are made up to some other date, the basis is the amount of the profits arising in the year which ends with the accounting date which falls within the year of assessment (Sec. 18B(2)). For example:—

A/Cs year to 1.4.2007   = year of assessment 2007/08
A/Cs year to 31.12.2007 = year of assessment 2007/08

A/Cs year to 28.2.2008   = year of assessment 2007/08

This basis is, technically, not automatic as the section provides only that the Commissioner is empowered to direct that this shall be the basis. In fact, however, this basis is in practice consistently adopted from year to year where the accounting date is consistent. Where, however, the accounting date is changed, there are other considerations as there are in commencement and cessation years.

4.6.2 Commencement

If the commercial accounts are made up to 31 March each year the determination of the assessable profits in the first year is straightforward and will simply be the profits arising from the date of commencement to the following 31 March; the second assessment will be for the year to the succeeding 31 March, and so on.

Where, however, the accounting date is other than 31 March, special rules apply. The following rules apply on commencement of a trade, profession or business:—

(1) Where the first accounts are for a period of a year or less and:—
   (i)   they are made up to a date within the same year of assessment as the date of commencement of business, the first assessment is based on the profits of that period (Sec. 18C(1)(a)). Subsequent assessments are on the normal basis; or
   (ii) they are made up to a date within the year of assessment following the year of assessment in which the date of commencement falls, there is deemed to be no assessable profits for the year of assessment in which the business commenced (Sec. 18C(2)) but the first assessment is for the year of assessment in which the first accounting date falls and is based on the profits of that first accounting period.
(2) Where the first accounts are for a period in excess of a year, obviously the accounts embrace at least two years of assessment and, in some cases, more. In these circumstances, the assessment for the year in which the commencement occurred is at the entire discretion of the Commissioner (Sec. 18C(1)(b)). The section gives the Commissioner no discretion over the following year of assessment which is therefore subject to the rules in Sec. 18B described in section 4.6.1 above. It is, however, the normal intention of the IRD to allocate profits to years of assessment in such a way that ensures that total

assessments equal total profits earned during the life of a business with no overlap and no falling out of account. Accordingly, they will normally allocate the profits of periods in excess of 12 months by reference to the expected future accounting date (see Example 4.30).

■ Example 4.28

A business commenced on 1 June 2007 and future accounts will be prepared to 31 December each year. Adjusted profits are:—

7 months to 31 December 2007	$50,000
Year ended 31 December 2008	$180,000

The first assessments will be:—

2007/08 Basis period 1.6.07 to 31.12.2007	$50,000	(Sec. 18C(1)(a))
2008/09 Basis period Yr/Ended 31.12.2007	$180,000	(Sec. 18B(2))

■ Example 4.29

A business commenced on 1 June 2005 and future accounts will be prepared to 30th April each year. Adjusted profits are:

11 months to 30 April 2006	$350,000
Year ended 30 April 2007	$520,000

The first assessments will be:—

2005/06	No assessment (Sec. 18C(2))		
2006/07	Basis period 1.6.2005 to 30.4.2006	$350,000	(Sec. 18C(2))
2007/08	Basis period 12/Ended 30.4.2007	$520,000	(Sec. 18B(2))

■ Example 4.30

A business commenced on 1 March 2005 and future accounts will be prepared to 30 April 2006 (year average) so that the first accounts are prepared up to 30 April 2006. Adjusted profits are:

14 months to 30 April 2006	$420,000
Year ended 30 April 2007	$500,000

The year of commencement (2004/05) is at the discretion of the Commissioner (Sec. 18C(1)(b)) but he will normally allocate profits by reference to the expected regular accounting date (30 April) and the first assessments would therefore normally be:—

2004/05	Nil		
2005/06	Basis period 1.3.2005 to 30.4.2005 (2/14)	$60,000	(Sec. 18B(2))
2006/07	Basis period 12 months to 30.4.2006 (12/14)	$360,000	(Sec. 18B(2))

2007/08   Basis period year to 30.4.2007 $500,000 (Sec. 18B(2))

For a discussion of what constitutes commencement of business, see section 4.3.5.

4.6.3 Cessation

In the case of a cessation, the rules are different depending upon whether or not the business commenced before 1 April 1974. This is because those businesses which commenced before 1 April 1974 will have been subject to the old system wherein, at the commencement, they may have been assessed more than once on the same profits and, therefore, on cessation, are able to redress the balance by allowing some profits to drop out of account.

(a) **Business commenced after 1 April 1974:** Where a trade, profession or business ceases and was commenced after 1 April 1974, the assessable profits for the year in which the cessation takes place are based on the period which begins immediately after the end of the basis period for the preceding year of assessment and ends on the date of cessation (Sec. 18D(1)). In other words there is complete continuity with no double assessment or drop out of profits.

Where, exceptionally, a business commences in a year of assessment and then ceases in the immediately following year of assessment, special rules apply if there was no assessment for the year of commencement by virtue of Sec. 18C(2). In these circumstances the assessment for the year in which the cessation takes place is based on the whole of the profits from commencement to cessation (Sec. 18D(5)).

■ Example 4.31

A business which has been carried on since 1977 and for which accounts have annually been made up to 31 December, ceased on 16 June 2007. Adjusted profits are:—

Year ended 31 December 2006	$75,000
Period 1 January 2007 to 16 June 2007	$15,500

The final assessments will be:—

2006/07	Basis period Yr/Ended 31.12.2006	$75,000	(Sec. 18B(2))
2007/08	Basis period 1.1.2007 to 16.6.2007	$15,500	(Sec. 18D(1))

■ Example 4.32

A business commenced on 15 July 2006 and made up its first accounts to 30 June 2007. The business ceased on 12 December 2007. Adjusted profits are:—

Period to 30.6.2007	$84,000
Period 1.7.2007 to 12.12.2007	$25,000

The assessments will be:—

2006/07   Nil per Sec. 18C(2) (see Example 4.29)
2007/08 $109,000 (Sec. 18D(5))

(b) **Business commenced before 1 April 1974:** Where a trade, profession or business, which commenced before 1 April 1974 ceases, the assessable profits for the year of assessment in which the cessation takes place are based on the profits for the period from 1st April in the year of assessment to the date of cessation (Sec. 18D(2)) plus the profits for the period from the day after the end of the previous basis period to 31 March in the year of assessment less a calculated sum called the "transitional amount" (Sec. 18D(2A)). If, of course, the basis period for the preceding year of assessment ended on 31 March, the basis period for the year of assessment is quite simply the amount under Sec. 18D(2) i.e. the whole of the profits since the end of the last basis period.

These provisions do not apply to all businesses which commenced before 1 April 1974. In particular, where a person ceases business but that business is wholly or partly transferred to or carried on by another person, the basis period for the year in which cessation takes place is the same as for a business which commenced after 1 April 1974, i.e. the whole of the profits since the last basis period are brought to account. This proviso will not, however, apply if the cessation is the result of the death of an individual who was carrying on the trade, profession or business as the sole proprietor (Sec. 18D(2) proviso).

The reason for the complexity of the cessation provisions is that, as compensation for the doubling-up of commencement assessments that applied before 1974, the final year of assessment was limited to the amount of profits from 1 April in the final year of assessment as provided in Sec. 18D(2) and, therefore, the profits from the end of the previous basis period up to 31 March fell out of account. This "drop-out" was therefore open to manipulation.

The effect of the law as it now stands, therefore, except where the proviso to Sec. 18D(2) applies (see above), is that the basis period for the year of assessment in which the cessation takes place is the period from the end of the basis period for the previous year of assessment up to the date of cessation (i.e. the same as for a business which commenced after 1 April 1974) less a "transitional amount". The "transitional amount" is the broad equivalent of the drop-out which would have occurred under the old rules, but is based on a proportion of the assessable profits for the 1974/75 year of assessment and is, therefore, already fixed in respect of cessations which have not yet taken place although, as will be seen, even this is the maximum amount because there are limitations to the transitional amount depending upon what profits arise in the cessation period.

Sec. 18D(2A) contains a number of special phrases which are now briefly explained before their application is examined:—

> "Relevant trade, profession or business" means one commenced before 1 April 1974 and to which Secs. 18D(2) and 18D(2A) apply (i.e. excluding those where someone else carries on the business and the cessation was not the result of the death of a sole proprietor) and where the basis period for the penultimate year of assessment ended on a date other than 31 March.
>
> "Excepted trade, profession or business" means a relevant trade, profession or business for which the basis period for the year of assessment 1974/75 ended on a date other than 31 March and was either the accounting period ended in 1974/75 per Sec. 18(2) or the accounting period ended in the previous year per Sec. 18A(2).
>
> "Relevant period" is the period which otherwise drops out of account under Sec. 18D(2), i.e. from the day following the end of the basis period for the penultimate year of assessment to the following 31 March.
>
> "Relevant profits" are the profits of the relevant period which would be assessable but for Sec. 18D(2) and notwithstanding the deductibility of depreciation allowances.
>
> "Transitional amount" is the equivalent of the previous drop-out but is instead calculated as a proportion of the 1974/75 assessable profits.

Where a person ceases to carry on a relevant trade, profession or business the assessable profits for the year of assessment in which the cessation took place are computed as follows:—

> (A) Assessable profits to the date of cessation from the immediately preceding 1 April (i.e. as per Sec. 18D(2))
>   *plus*
> (B) Assessable profits of the relevant period (i.e. relevant profits)
>   *less*
> (C) The transitional amount

If (C) is greater than (B) it is limited to (B). In other words, the drop-out cannot be greater than would have been the case if the law had not changed.

The calculation of the transitional amount proceeds as follows:—

(1)   If the basis period for the 1974/75 year of assessment was the profits of the accounting period ended in the preceding year of assessment (i.e. as per Sec. 18(2)) the amount is the assessable profits from the corresponding date in the year ended 31 March 1975 (not necessarily the accounting date falling in that year, although it usually will be) up to 31 March 1975.

(2)   If the basis period for the 1974/75 year of assessment was the profits of the accounting period ended in the year of assessment (i.e. as per Sec. 18A(2)) the amount is the assessable profits from that date up to 31 March 1975.

(3)   In the case of any relevant trade, profession or business which is not an "excepted trade, profession or business", in other words where the basis period for 1974/75 was anything other than (1) or (2), the transitional amount is nil.

Furthermore, where the calculation in (1) or (2) results in a loss, the transitional amount is regarded as nil. In order to make the necessary apportionments to arrive at the transitional amount, it is necessary to look to the authority of Sec. 18E for the method of apportionment. Sec. 18E(4) provides that, specifically for the purposes of Sec. 18D(2A), the Commissioner may make divisions, apportionments or aggregations on whatever basis he considers appropriate in the circumstances. Usually this will be done on a time basis but any reasonable option is open to the Commissioner. Before the introduction of Sec. 18D(2A), and thereby Sec. 18E(4), the method of allocation of profits to a specific period was strictly by time apportionment, it was not open to the Commissioner to indicate that the profits arose on a particular date and should therefore be wholly allocated to the period in which that date falls (see *D 5/80*). Presumably he can now do so under Sec. 18E(4).

■ **Example 4.44**

The assessable profits of a business which commenced in 1961 for all relevant periods up to 30 June 2006 when it ceased business have been as follows:—

Year ended 31 December 1974	$224,000
Year ended 31 December 1975	$180,000
Year ended 31 December 1976	$196,000
Year ended 31 December 2005	$120,000
Period to 30 June 2006	$100,000

(1) The year of cessation is 2006/07.

(2) This is a "relevant trade, profession or business" because it commenced before

1 April 1975 and the basis period for 2005/06 (y/e 31.12.2005) ended on a date other than 31 March and Secs. 18D(2) and 18D(2A) would apply (the business has not been transferred to another person).

(3) The 1975/76 assessment was, under Sec. 18A(2), based on the previous year's profits (i.e. $224,000 for the y/e 31.12.74) and therefore this is an "excepted trade, profession or business."

(4) The "transitional amount" is as follows:—
> End of basis period for 1975/76 is 31.12.74
>
> Equivalent date in 1975/76 is 31.12.75 (which happens to coincide with the next accounting date as it usually will).
>
> It is necessary therefore to ascertain assessable profits for the period 1.1.76 to 31.3.76, i.e.:—
>
> 1/4 × $196,000 = $49,000

(Note that the Commissioner is not obliged to make the apportionment on a time basis.)

(5) The assessment for 2006/07 will be as follows:—

Assessable profits 1.4.2006 to 30.6.2006 (3/6 × $100,000)	=	$50,000	(a)
Plus: Relevant profits (1.1.2006 to 31.3.2006) (3/6 × $100,000)	=	$50,000	(b)
		$100,000	
Less: Transitional amount (not limited because			
Relevant profits (b) are greater)		(49,000)	(c)
Assessable profits 2006/07		$51,000	

Notes:—

(a) If in fact the results for the years ended 31 December 1974 and 1975 had been transposed, the basis period for 1975/76 would have been the year ended 31 December 1975 under Sec. 18(2). The transitional amount would therefore have been the same.

(b) If the results for the year ended 31 December 1976 had been a loss, the transitional amount would have been nil.

(c) If the business had been transferred to another person, the 2006/07 assessment would have been $100,000 (Sec. 18D(2) proviso).

4.6.4 Change of accounting date

Because the normal basis of assessment limits the basis period to one of 12 months up to the accounting date, it would be easy to arrange for large profits to fall out of account by judicially changing the accounting date. This is frustrated by the provisions in Sec. 18E which give the IRD considerable discretionary powers in the situation where the assessable profits of a trade, profession or business have been computed by reference to accounts made up to a particular day in a year of assessment and then either of two possible events occurs, namely:—

(1) accounts are not made up to the corresponding day in the following year of assessment; or

(2) accounts are made up to more than one day in the following year of assessment.

The year of assessment in which (1) or (2) takes place is the "year of change" and the Commissioner is empowered to compute the assessable profits for the year of change and the immediately preceding year on whatever basis he considers fit (Sec. 18E(1)). Where the business commenced after 1 April 1974, the Commissioner is entitled to adopt a basis period for the affected years which may be longer than the normal 12 months (Sec. 18E(2)(b)); this is because the intent behind the rules governing basis periods for businesses commencing after 1 April 1974 is that not less than the total profits made over the life of the business are to be assessed.

The fact that Sec. 18E(2)(b) specifically authorises the adoption of a basis period longer than 12 months in the case of a business which commenced after 1 April, 1974 could be interpreted as implying that the adoption of such a basis period for business which commenced prior to that date is not permitted. This interpretation was confirmed by the Board of Review in both *D 71/90* and *D 44/97*; on appeal, however, the Court of First Instance overturned the decision in the latter of these cases, thereby deciding that Sec. 18E(2)(b) did not in any way operate to limit the Commissioner's discretion under Sec. 18E (see *CIR v Yick Fung Estates Limited; Yick Fung Estates Limited v CIR* [1999] (1 HKRC 90 096)). Unfortunately, that case did not convincingly explain the purpose of Sec. 18E(2)(b), other than to suggest it was intended to make it clear that the Commissioner was permitted, or possibly even required, to consider using a basis period in excess of twelve months for businesses which commenced on or after 1 April, 1974. The view of the Court of First Instance was, however, overturned by the Court of Appeal (see *Yick Fung Estates Limited v CIR* [2001] (1 HKRC 90-112). Interestingly, this conclusion was reached in two different ways. In particular, one judge reached the conclusion by analysing the historical evolution of the statutory provision and concluding that the intention had always been that a twelve-month basis period be used for pre 1 April, 1974 businesses. However, he also agreed with the other judges that because of the specific provision in Sec. 18E(2)(b) permitting longer basis periods for businesses which commenced on or after 1 April, 1974, it was clear that it was never intended that extended basis periods be permitted for other companies.

The decision in *D 44/97* was also notable because, after finding that the Commissioner was not entitled to use a basis period of more than twelve months (a decision upheld by the Court of Appeal), the Board went on to find that the change of accounting date was made for the sole or dominant purpose of obtaining a tax benefit through the expected "drop out" of a portion of its profits as a result of a long accounting period being reduced to twelve months for tax purposes. As such, the Board held that the benefit which would otherwise have been obtained could be countered by the application of Sec. 61A. This provision, and the decision of the Board of Review (which was upheld on appeal), are discussed further in Chapter 10.

Because it is normal for a basis period to comprise a period of 12 months, there will be a duplication of profits assessed if a change of accounting date results in an accounting period of less than 12 months. In the case of a business which commenced after 1 April 1974, however, the IRD is normally prepared to limit the basis period to the period of less than 12 months, by concession, if the change of accounting date is for "compelling reasons"; in other words if there was no tax motive. For example, a company joining a group and having to change its accounting date to conform with that of the group would be a compelling reason (see Example 4.33). In the case of businesses which commenced prior to 1 April 1974, however, the IRD will always insist on a 12-month basis period for the year of change and, therefore, some profits will be double assessed if the accounting date is brought forward; conversely, some profits will always "drop-out" if the accounting date is put back, provided that this does not result in a year of assessment in which there is no accounting date. As noted above, however, the benefit of such a "drop-out' may be countered by the application of Sec. 61A. The reasonableness of the Commissioner exercising his discretion in a manner whereby some profits are, in effect, assessed twice was considered in *D 71/ 90* and was held to not necessarily be unreasonable. The Commissioner and the Board of Review in that case found support for the practice in the UK case of *CIR v Helical Bar Ltd.* (48 TC 221), notwithstanding that the relevant UK legislation was substantially different in that it gave the Commissioner the power to adopt *any 12-month basis period* he thinks fit rather than *any basis* he thinks fit as is the case in Hong Kong.

It is not possible to guarantee how the Commissioner will select a basis period but in fixing the period for the year of change it is usual to take a period of 12 months up to the new accounting date, or longer than 12 months if the business commenced after 1 April 1974 and the accounting date has been put back. The basis period for the preceding year will be adjusted to the equivalent 12 months only if this would result in an additional assessment but in the case of businesses which commenced after 1 April 1974 an adjustment to the preceding year will not normally be required because no profits will have fallen out of account (see Example 4.35).

■ Example 4.34

A business which commenced prior to 1 April 1974 has been making its accounts up to
30 June. In 2006 the accounting date is changed to 31 December and adjusted profits
are as follows:—

12 months to 30.6.2005	$220,000
12 months to 30.6.2006	$350,000
6 months to 31.12.2006	$250,000
12 months to 31.12.2007	$300,000

The "year of change" is 2006/07 because it has two accounting dates in that year and
therefore the affected years are 2006/07 and 2005/06. It is likely that the assessments
would be as follows:—

2006/07 —	Year to 31.12.2006: 1/2 × 350,000	=	$175,000
	plus		250,000
			$425,000
2005/06 — Year to 31.12.2005:	1/2 × $220,000	=	$110,000
	1/2 × $350,000	=	175,000
			$285,000
Previously assessed (year ended 30.6.2005)			($220,000)
Additional Assessment			$ 65,000

Notes:—

(a)   Had the profits for the year ended 01.10.2006 been less than those already assessed
      for the year ended 30.6.2006 it is unlikely that the assessment for 2005/06 would be
      disturbed.

(b)   The effect of the change in basis period upon the depreciation allowances is ignored
      in this illustration for the purposes of simplicity. In fact, the apportionments would be
      made in respect of adjusted profits before depreciation allowances and then the
      depreciation allowances would be recomputed in accordance with the new basis
      periods for the relevant years of assessment (see Example 5.19).

(c)   It is noted that six months worth of profits "drop out" of assessment in this example
      (i.e. the profits for the period 1 July 2004 to 31 December 2004). This has traditionally
      been accepted by the IRD, although it is apparent from the *Yick Fung Estates* case
      (see text) that the IRD is now reluctant to permit this, particularly where they believe
      the accounting date was changed predominantly to enjoy the tax benefit which such
      a drop out may confer. Nonetheless, their traditional practice of limiting basic periods
      to twelve months (for pre 1 April, 1974 businesses) has been found by the Court of
      Appeal to be correct and, therefore, the only means at the disposal of the IRD to
      counter any tax benefit therefrom is Sec. 61A (see Chapter 10).

■ Example 4.35

A business which commenced after 1 April 1974 has made up accounts to 30 April until
2007 when it brought forward its accounting date to 31 January. Adjusted profits are as
follows:—

12 months to 30.4.2004	$250,000

12 months to 30.4.2005	$275,000
12 months to 30.4.2006	$300,000
9 months to 31.1.2007	$210,000
12 months to 31.1.2008	$400,000

The "year of change" is 2006/07 because it has two accounting dates in that year and therefore the affected years are 2005/06 and 2006/07. It is likely that the assessments would be as follows:—

2006/07 — Existing assessment: Year to 30.4.2006	$300,000
Additional assessment: 9 months to 31.1.2007	210,000
	$510,000

This is to bring it up to the new accounting date and is for a 21-month period to ensure that no profits fall out of account. This is allowed by Sec. 18E(2)(b).

| 2005/06 — Year to 30.4.2005 | $275,000 |

Note:—

The effect of the change in basis period upon the depreciation allowances is ignored in this illustration for the purposes of simplicity. In fact, the apportionments would be made in respect of adjusted profits before depreciation allowances and then the depreciation allowances would be recomputed in accordance with the new basis periods for the relevant years of assessment (see Example 5.19).

■ Example 4.36

A business which commenced after 1 April 1974 has made up accounts to 30 September each year until 2007 when the accounting date was brought forward to 30 June. Adjusted profits are as follows:—

12 months to 30.9.2005	$250,000
12 months to 30.9.2006	$280,000
9 months to 30.6.2007	$175,000
12 months to 30.6.2008	$300,000

The "year of change" is 2007/08 because an account was not made up to the corresponding date of 30.9.2007. The affected years are therefore 2006/07 and 2007/08. It is likely that the assessments would be as follows:—

2007/08 — 9 months to 30.6.2007	$175,000
3 months to 30.9.2006 (3/12)	70,000
	$245,000

The IRD could, theoretically, re-open the 2006/07 year, but are unlikely to do so in practice, other than in exceptional circumstances.

As a general rule, the IRO considers that the basis period must be of twelve months; therefore there is a duplication of three months because the basis period for the 2006/07 assessment is likely to remain the year ended 30 September 2006 as this gives a higher assessable profits than if a basis period of the year to 30 June 2006 was adopted. Even if the basis period for the 2006/07 year was so changed, however, there would still be a duplication of profits, but for an earlier-three-month period.

2006/07 — Year ended 30.9.2006 $280,000

However, if the change of accounting date was for compelling reasons (see section 4.6.4), the IRD may be prepared to limit the 2007/08 assessment to the 9 months to 30.6.2007, i.e. $175,000.

Note:—
The effect of the change in basis period upon the depreciation allowances is ignored in this illustration for the purposes of simplicity. In fact, the apportionments would be made in respect of adjusted profits before depreciation allowances and then the depreciation allowances would be recomputed in accordance with the new basis periods for the relevant years of assessment (see Example 5.19).

Occasionally accounts are made up to the end of the Lunar Year and therefore will have a different balance date each year. In these circumstances it will not be treated as a change of accounting date (Sec. 18E(2)(a)).

4.6.5 Apportionment

As will have been seen, there are a number of cases where it is necessary to adopt as a basis period, only a portion of the adjusted profits of a longer accounting period or to aggregate such a portion with a portion of the adjusted profits of another accounting period. Sec. 18E(3) validates these apportionments and provides that such apportionment may be made on the basis of days or months in the respective periods or alternatively the Commissioner may direct that the apportionment is to be made on some other basis if special circumstances should so dictate. The alternative would only be adopted where, for example, a large proportion of profits clearly fell within a specific part of an accounting period and it would be inappropriate to effectively spread it by time apportionment. Note that depreciation allowances are not apportioned; they are, instead, re-calculated in accordance with the new basis period (see section 5.11.1).

4.7 Special Classes of Business

Although the general rules for ascertainment of assessable profits, basis periods, etc. are applicable to every type of business that falls within the scope of Profits Tax, certain types of business require specific legislation if they are to be adequately taxed and not to escape solely by virtue of the specialised nature of their business. The IRO therefore includes specific legislation in respect of a number of types of business and these are dealt with in the following paragraphs. Also included are partnerships, although these are not a special class of business there are nevertheless a number of special points which must be considered when dealing with a partnership.

4.7.1 Life insurance corporations

Sec. 23 deals with the ascertainment of the assessable profits of life insurance corporations and, for this purpose, life insurance business is specifically defined as the following types of business which are specified in more detail in the *Insurance Companies Ordinance* (Sec. 23(9)):

- Life and annuity
- Marriage and birth
- Linked long term
- Tontines

The provisions apply equally to mutual and to proprietary corporations (Sec. 23(1)). Without the specific inclusion of mutual corporations, the mutual profits would not be taxable on the general principle that a person cannot make a profit out of himself (*Faulconbridge v National Employers' Mutual* (33 TC 103)).

There are two ways of ascertaining the assessable profits of a life insurance corporation. One is a straightforward rule-of-thumb which gives a notional profit but is easy to ascertain and, therefore, may be acceptable for that reason; the other is a sophisticated computation involving actuarial valuations and is only applicable upon specific election. Where no election is made, the simple method automatically applies. The rules only apply to the assessable profits from life insurance (including annuity) business and therefore if a corporation is carrying on other business as well, the ascertainment of the assessable profits of that other business is not affected.

The assessable profits of life insurance business for a given year of assessment are therefore ascertained as follows:—

(1) 5% of the premiums from life insurance business in Hong Kong during the basis period for the year of assessment (Sec. 23(1)(a)); or

(2) if the corporation so elects, that part of the adjusted surplus, ascertained in accordance with specific rules laid down in Sec. 23, which is deemed to arise in the basis period less any dividends received from corporations which are themselves subject to Profits Tax (Sec. 23(1)(b)). The reason why it is necessary to deem adjusted profits to have arisen in a basis period is explained by the fact that the adjusted surplus will normally cover more than one basis period and has, therefore, to be allocated as described later.

Under alternative (1) the calculation is limited to premiums from life insurance business in Hong Kong, thereby retaining the Hong Kong source concept. For this purpose "premiums from life insurance business in Hong Kong" are specifically defined to include:—

(i)   all premiums received or receivable in Hong Kong whether from residents or non-residents; and

(ii)   all premiums, received or receivable elsewhere, from Hong Kong residents where the premiums are in respect of policies the proposals for which were received by the corporation in Hong Kong.

Returned premiums or re-insurance premiums relating to those received may be deducted before ascertaining the 5% (Sec. 23(9)).

The election for treatment under Sec. 23(1)(b) is irrevocable and once made is deemed to apply to all subsequent years of assessment (Sec. 23(1) proviso (i)). Furthermore, the election is only effective if certain documents are submitted to the IRD. There is no time limit for the election as such but there is a time limit on the submission of certain documents. In respect of companies which are subject to the requirements of Sec. 18 or Sec. 52(3) of the *Insurance Companies Ordinance*, the IRO requires an actuary's report and the election under Sec. 23(1)(b) is only valid if a certified true copy of that report is submitted to the IRD within two years of the date to which the report is made up (Secs. 23(2) and 23(3)).

The procedure is then to ascertain the "adjusted surplus" for the period of the actuarial report and to allocate it between the basis periods for years of assessment. An actuarial report is often for a period covering a number of years, although it may be only for one year, so a number of years of assessment are often affected. In order that collection of tax should not be delayed pending ascertainment of the adjusted surplus, assessments are raised annually on the 5% of premiums basis (Sec. 23(1) proviso (ii)). Although these assessments become final and conclusive it is specifically provided that they may be re-opened and adjusted upon the ascertainment of the adjusted surplus. Such an adjustment may, of course, involve an additional assessment or a reduction and repayment (Sec. 23(3)).

The adjusted surplus is obtained by making specified adjustments to the surplus, which is the amount by which the value of the life insurance fund (i.e. the accumulated investments representing invested premiums) exceeds the company's estimated liability on its policies which the fund represents (obtained from the actuary's report) at the end of the period in respect of which the actuarial report is made (Sec. 23(4)(a)).

The adjustments which are required to the surplus are as laid down in Sec. 23(4)(b) and are in effect only to adjust for the surplus or deficit shown by the immediately preceding actuarial report (obviously no such adjustment is required in respect of the first actuarial report covering the opening years of business) and to deduct from or add to the surplus certain other expenses and receipts in accordance with the general rules applicable to Profits Tax. In summary, the adjustments are as follows:—

Deduct from surplus:—
  (1) any surplus of a previous period retained in the life fund;
  (2) any transfer or appropriation to policy holders which has not been charged against the life fund in the actuarial report;
  (3) outgoings or expenses allowable under Sec. 16 which have not already been charged against the life fund;
  (4) capital receipts or transfers from reserve which have been credited to the life fund; and
  (5) depreciation allowances.

Add to surplus:—
  (6) any deficit of a previous period where such deficit is included in the report;
  (7) outgoings or expenses charged against the life fund which are not allowable under Sec. 16 or which are specifically disallowable under Sec. 17;
  (8) other sources of taxable income not already included in the life fund other than non-life-insurance business (because the profits from such a source are computed under the rules in Sec. 23A, which are dealt with in section 4.7.2);
  (9) any appropriations of profits or transfers to reserve which have been charged against the life fund, other than transfers to policy holders; and
  (10) any balancing charge.

The concept of limiting Profits Tax to those profits which arise in or derive from Hong Kong is effected by apportioning the adjusted surplus between life insurance business within Hong Kong and life insurance business elsewhere, with the latter proportion being exempt from Profits Tax (Sec. 23(5)).

The apportionment is made on the basis of the total premiums arising during the period of the actuarial report from life insurance business in Hong Kong to the total aggregate premiums for the period (Sec. 23(6)). The meaning of premiums from life insurance business in Hong Kong is discussed above.

Allocation to basis periods of the proportion of the adjusted surplus which is applicable to life insurance business in Hong Kong is done similarly on the basis of the proportion which the premiums from life insurance business in Hong Kong arising in each basis period bears to the total aggregate of such premiums arising during the period of the actuarial report (Sec. 23(7)).

The ascertainment of adjusted losses, their limitation to losses arising from life insurance business in Hong Kong and allocation over basis periods is carried out in precisely the same manner as adjusted profits (Sec. 23(8)).

■ Example 4.07

Livelong Life Insurance Ltd. is carrying on life insurance and accident insurance business in Hong Kong which it commenced on 1 January 2004. It makes up accounts to 31 December each year and has submitted an actuarial report for the period 1 January 2004 to 31 December 2007. The following facts are extracted from the actuarial report and accounts:—

Value of life fund at 31 December 2007	$2,875,000
Actuarial liability on policies comprising life fund at 31 December 2007	$1,850,000

Premiums received and receivable:

	Hong Kong Office	Macau Office
in year ended 31.12.2004	$175,000	$25,000
31.12.2005	$200,000	$40,000
31.12.2006	$275,000	$65,000
31.12.2007	$570,000	$185,000

Premiums arising to the Macau office derive from proposals made to that office.

The company has incurred management expenses over the four years of $1,000,000 and the proportion which relates to life insurance is $875,000 which has not been charged to the life fund.

The life fund includes credits of $8,700 for profits on disposal of fixed assets, $12,000 for profits on disposal of shares comprising part of the life fund and $15,000 for transfer from reserve for contingencies. There has also been debited to the life fund a transfer to contingency reserve of $75,000 and a general provision for doubtful debts of $35,000. A sum of $50,000 has been appropriated to policy holders from the life fund.

Depreciation allowances on assets of both branches applicable to life business have been computed as:—

2004/05	$80,000
2005/06	$45,000
2006/07	$40,000
2007/08	$35,000

Adjusted profits (losses) of the accident business, after taking into account the relevant proportion of management expenses and relevant depreciation allowances:

2004/05	($ 7,500)
2005/06	($ 1,500)

2006/07	$20,000
2007/08	$90,000

Assessment

The basis periods for four years of assessment are covered by the actuarial report as follows:—

year ended 31.12.2004	=	2004/05
year ended 31.12.2005	=	2005/06
year ended 31.12.2006	=	2006/07
year ended 31.12.2007	=	2007/08

An election under Sec. 23(1)(b) cannot be made until the actuarial report has been submitted and this must be done within two years of the date to which it is made up. If the election is made it will therefore be made some time between 31 December 2007 and 31 December 2009. This would only apply to the life business.

In the meantime assessments on the life business are raised on the basis of Sec. 23(1)(a) as follows:—

		Life	Accident	Assessment
2004/05	5% × $175,000	$ 8,750	($ 7,500)	$ 1,250
2005/06	5% × $230,000	$11,500	($ 1,500)	$ 10,000
2006/07	5% × $375,000	$18,750	$20,000	$ 38,750
2007/08	5% × $570,000	$28,500	$90,000	$118,500

Note that all other adjustments in respect of life business are ignored, including depreciation allowances because these are deemed to have been made in arriving at the notional profit under Sec. 23(1)(a).

If the election under Sec. 23(1)(b) is made, the first step is to ascertain the adjusted surplus which is:—

Life Fund at 31.12.2007		$2,875,000
Liability at 31.12.2007		1,850,000
Excess		$1,025,000
Less: Management expenses	$875,000	
Disposal of fixed assets	8,700	
Transfer from reserve	15,000	
Depreciation allowances	200,000	(1,098,700)
		($ 73,700)
Add: Transfer to reserve	$ 75,000	
Provision for doubtful debts	35,000	110,000
Adjusted surplus for period 1.1.2004 to 31.12.2007		$ 36,300

The next step is to divide the adjusted surplus between onshore and offshore business:—

Total onshore premiums for period	$1,350,000
Total offshore premiums for period	315,000
	$1,665,000

Onshore portion of adjusted surplus
$$\frac{1{,}350{,}000}{1{,}665{,}000} \times 36{,}300 = \$29{,}432$$

The next step is to allocate this portion of the adjusted surplus over the basis periods:—

Year ended 31.12.2004 $= \dfrac{175{,}000}{1{,}350{,}000} \times \$29{,}432 = \$3{,}815$ (2004/05)

$$31.12.2005 = \frac{230,000}{1,350,000} \times \$29,432 = \$5,014 \ (2005/06)$$

$$31.12.2006 = \frac{375,000}{1,350,000} \times \$29,432 = \$8,176 \ (2006/07)$$

$$31.12.2007 = \frac{570,000}{1,350,000} \times \$29,432 = \$12,427 \ (2007/08)$$

The final step is to merge these results with the accident business profits to form the total assessment on the company:—

	Life	Accident	Loss b/f	Total
2004/05	$ 3,815	($ 7,500)	Nil	Nil
2005/06	$ 5,014	($ 1,500)	$3,685	Nil
2006/07	$ 8,176	$20,000	$ 171	$ 28,005
2007/08	$12,427	$90,000	Nil	$102,427

Notes:—
(a) A surplus of losses is carried forward from 2004/05 and 2005/06 and used up in 2006/07.
(b) The assessment for each year is automatically reduced from the figure provisionally assessed under Sec. 23(1)(a) and a refund is made.
(c) For subsequent years the election must apply because it is irrevocable but until the next actuarial report is available, assessments are again provisionally made on the 5% basis under Sec. 23(1)(a).

4.7.2 Non-life Insurance corporations

The ascertainment of the assessable profits of insurance business other than life insurance is governed by Sec. 23A and is much less complicated than the life insurance provisions.

Nonetheless, there is sometimes confusion over the scope of Sec. 23A as although there is a statutory definition of "life insurance business", there is no definition in the IRO of insurance business. Generally, it has been accepted that any business authorised under the *Insurance Companies Ordinance* is to be considered insurance business for the purposes of the IRO and, if the business falls outside the definition of "life insurance business" it will be assessed in accordance with Sec. 23A. In 1993, however, when legislation governing retirement schemes was introduced, retirement scheme management business was included as Classes G and H under Long-term business in Part 2, Schedule 1 of the *Insurance Companies Ordinance*. Although retirement scheme management is often undertaken by insurance companies, it is more a fund management activity than the provision of insurance, or if some insurance is provided this is generally not the principal object of the business. In view of this, the IRD has advised that from the 2005/06 year of assessment, Class G or H business will be assessed pursuant to Sec. 14, rather than Sec. 23A.

The computation in most cases probably follows the financial accounts subject to any apportionment between onshore and offshore business and the usual statutory adjustments. However, it is specifically provided that the assessable profits are to be ascertained as follows:—

Gross premiums from non-life insurance business in Hong Kong
Less:— • Returned premiums
        • Corresponding re-insurance premiums
        • Any increase in the provision for unexpired risks as provided in the accounts
        • Actual losses less recoveries (note: provisions not deductible)
        • Agency expenses
        • Head office administration expenses so far as related to that business
        • Depreciation allowances less balancing charges so far as related to that business.
Plus:— • Any interest or other income arising in or derived from Hong Kong.

The effect of the inclusion of interest and other income arising in or derived from Hong Kong was considered in the case of *CIR v Carlingford Life and General Assurance Co. Ltd. and Carlingford Insurance Co. Ltd.* (3 HKTC 229). In that case it was held that the provision effectively only operates to include sums which would be caught by the general charging provision of Sec. 14 and does not extend to sums which would normally be taxable only because of the deeming provisions of Sec. 15. Also, it is important to note that the inclusion extends only to *income*, which is not the same as profits; accordingly, a capital receipt which was not a profit from the sale of a capital asset and which was, therefore, arguably not excluded from Profits Tax under Sec. 14 would, nonetheless, clearly not be caught by Sec. 23A. See, however, *CIR v Sincere Insurance & Investment Co. Ltd.* (HKTC 602) which established that profits on realisation of investments by an insurance company will normally be of a revenue, rather than capital, nature.

Where a corporation is carrying on life insurance business and non-life insurance business and, indeed, any other business, apportionments of expenses and depreciation allowances as appropriate are necessary to arrive at the foregoing computation.

In the case of a non-Hong Kong resident insurance company, if the Hong Kong business is of a limited extent and it would be unreasonable to attempt to extract the foregoing information relating to Hong Kong business, the assessable profits may be ascertained as the proportion of worldwide profits and income which its premiums from Hong Kong insurance business bears to total premiums. Alternatively, any other equitable basis may be applied. Both of these alternatives are at the Commissioner's discretion (Sec. 23A(1) proviso).

For all these purposes the meaning of *"premiums from insurance business in Hong Kong"* is defined by Sec. 23A(2) as:—

(1) premiums in respect of insurance contracts made in Hong Kong; and
(2) premiums on policies the proposals for which were made to the corporation in Hong Kong.

Note that this definition is narrower than the equivalent definition for life insurance business in Sec. 23 where receivability in Hong Kong is sufficient.

Although the assessable profits from non-life insurance business are ascertained in accordance with the above, from the 1998/99 year of assessment it may be necessary, if the corporation is authorised under Sec. 8 of the *Insurance Companies Ordinance* to carry on in Hong Kong reinsurance business only, to further apportion those assessable profits between profits attributable to any business of reinsurance of offshore risks and profits from reinsurance of onshore risks. This is because, pursuant to Sec. 14D(1), assessable profits attributable to any business of reinsurance of offshore risks are taxed at a concessional rate of one half of the normal Profits Tax rate applicable to corporations if the corporation so elects. If the corporation wishes to take advantage of this concession it is required to make the necessary election in writing and, once made, the election is irrevocable (Sec. 14B(1)).

Sec. 23A(2) defines the assessable profits from a business of reinsurance of offshore risks as equal to:—

$$(B/C) \times D$$

Where: **B** is the assessable profits of the corporation calculated in accordance with Sec. 23A(1) (i.e. the formula described above);

C is the total gross income earned by or accrued to the corporation during the basis period for the relevant year of assessment; and

D is total gross offshore reinsurance income earned by or accrued to the corporation during the basis period for the relevant year of assessment. "Offshore reinsurance income" is further defined in Sec. 23A(3) as sums attributable to, or in respect of:

(a) premiums from reinsurance of offshore risks. Offshore risks are defined in Sec. 23A(3) and are, in respect of facultative general reinsurance, risks where the reinsured is not a person who is resident in Hong Kong or does not have a permanent establishment in Hong Kong, and in respect of treaty general reinsurance, are risks where not less than 75% of the total risk in terms of gross premiums is outside Hong Kong or is in transit in Hong Kong. "Permanent establishment" is also defined for this purpose in Sec. 23A (3) and means a branch, management or other place of business, but does not include an agency unless the agent has, and habitually exercises, a general authority to negotiate and conclude contracts on behalf of his principal; and

(b) gains or profits from offshore reinsurance investments. Again, this is defined in Sec. 23A(3) and means gains or profits from the sale or other disposal or redemption on maturity or presentment of, or any interest on, investments made with premiums from reinsurance of offshore risks (see above) or investments representing the technical reserves referable to premiums from reinsurance of offshore risks. "Technical reserves" is defined for this purpose as reserves made in the corporation's accounts for additional amounts for unexpired risks, claims outstanding or unearned premiums or, where the relevant insurance business is accounted for on a fund accounting basis, the fund related to that business as defined in Third Schedule to the *Insurance Companies Ordinance*, but which in practical terms in the present context means the assets representing the actuarial liability of that business.

4.7.3 Shipping and aircraft businesses — general

The international nature of shipping and aircraft businesses would, in the absence of special provisions, give rise to particular problems under Hong Kong's territorial basis of taxation because of the difficulties in ascertaining how much of their profit arises in Hong Kong. That is, although it is clear that some part of the business of a shipping company or airline whose ships or aircraft visit Hong Kong is carried on in Hong Kong, and that some portion of the profits of such businesses arises in Hong Kong, objectively quantifying those assessable profits is difficult. This problem was highlighted in the case of *CIR v Hong Kong and Whampoa Dock Co. Limited* (1 HKTC 85), one of the earliest decisions in Hong Kong on the source of profits. As a result, specific provisions were introduced to deal with these types of businesses.

The provisions dealing with shipping and aircraft businesses have undergone changes over the years, but currently there are three main sections of the IRO which are relevant. These are:

- Sec. 23B, which deals with the taxation of ship owners, with no distinction being made between resident and non-resident owners;
- Sec. 23C, which deals with the taxation of resident aircraft owners, and
- Sec. 23D, which deals with the taxation of non-resident aircraft owners.

These provisions are considered in detail in the following sections.

4.7.4 Shipowning businesses

The provisions of Sec. 23B apply by deeming certain shipowning operations to amount to the carrying on of business in Hong Kong and then go on to define the ascertainment and extent of taxable profits and specific exemptions. In particular, the following are deemed to be carrying on business in Hong Kong.

(1)   a shipowning business which is normally controlled or managed in Hong Kong (Sec. 23B(1)(a));

(2)   a shipowner being a corporation incorporated in Hong Kong (Sec. 23B(1)(b)); and

(3)   any other shipowner whose ships call at any location in Hong Kong waters (Sec. 23B(2)). However, where the Commissioner, at his absolute discretion, considers that any call by a ship is a casual call and further calls by any ship of the same shipowner are unlikely, he will disregard such casual call (Sec. 23B(6)).

A shipowner also includes a person who charters a ship from another owner and so both the owner and the charterer may be regarded as carrying on business in Hong Kong under Sec. 23B. Carrying on a business of owning ships means both chartering out ships to other persons as well as operating ships for trade but it does not include dealing in ships or shipping agency business which would be considered on their own merits under Sec. 14.

Control or management for the purposes of (1) above is not defined but is assumed to mean the same principles as govern the residence of a company under UK case law, i.e. the place where the directors meet and exercise central management and control over the company. This is, however, far from clear because the UK law refers to the residence of the company whereas control or management in the context of Sec. 23B(1)(a) refers to the business.

Having established that a shipowner is deemed to be carrying on business in Hong Kong, it is then necessary to establish the amount of taxable profits and this is quite complicated with certain shipping income being specifically exempt, other shipping income being effectively exempt by not being specifically included (primarily certain charterhire income) and extensive definitions of special terms used.

In substance, the assessable profits for a given year of assessment are ascertained in the following manner:—

Assessable Profits = Total Shipping Profits × A/B   (Sec. 23B(3)).

And for this purpose:—
A = An amount referred to as "Relevant Sums"
B = Total Shipping Income

Where there are practical difficulties in applying this detailed formula to the income and profits of a shipowner it is provided that if the assessor is of the opinion that the formula cannot be satisfactorily applied, the assessable profits for that particular year of assessment may instead be computed on the basis of a fair percentage of the relevant sums accruing to the shipowner during the basis period (i.e. a percentage of A) (Sec. 23B(4)).

If an assessment has been made on the basis of this fair percentage method, it is open to the shipowner to elect at any time within two years after the end of the year of assessment to have the profits revised to those ascertained by the formula method and any assessment which is final and conclusive can be re-opened to admit the revision (Sec. 23B(5)).

It is important to be able to precisely understand the special terms used in the formula and these are defined in Sec. 23B(12). Some of the more important terms are as follows:

"**Total Shipping Income**" is the worldwide income, i.e. turnover, from the person's business as an owner of ships as shown in the person's commercial accounts. Note that it does not exclude the "exempt sums" which are referred to below but it will, of course, exclude investment income and any other income not specifically related to the shipping business. It would include certain Government grants (see *CIR v Zim Israel Navigation Co.* (HKTC 573)). This case was applicable to a previous provision but would be equally applicable to the existing Sec. 23B.

"**Total Shipping Profits**" is quite simply the profits derived from "total shipping income" as shown by the commercial accounts but must, of course, exclude any expenditure which relates to any income which has been excluded from "total shipping income". It is quite usual to adopt the commercial accounting profits without adjustment for requirements of the IRO and the definition of total shipping profits allows for this. However, where this is likely to differ materially from tax-adjusted profits, which is more likely in the area of capital income/expenditure and depreciation allowances, Sec. 23E provides for "total shipping profits" to be adjusted where necessary so as to make them correspond so far as possible to the requirements of the IRO. The more usual application of this provision is to exclude commercial depreciation and profits/losses on sale of ships and to compute instead the relevant depreciation allowances, balancing charges etc. (see Chapter 5). It may be that these adjustments are only made in respect of the ships, leaving commercial depreciation for other assets such as office furniture unadjusted. This is perfectly permissible.

Practical difficulties in relation to depreciation allowances will arise where a ship first comes on to the Hong Kong Shipping Register during a basis period for a year of assessment or, similarly ceases to be so registered during a basis period because this will generally mean that it begins or ceases to earn exempt income (see "Exempt Sums" below). It is perhaps a statement of the obvious but, nevertheless, Sec. 23B(7)(b)(i) provides that depreciation allowances are only available for that part of the period during which the ship is not registered (i.e. when it is not automatically exempt) and it is operated for the purpose of producing profits chargeable to Profits Tax. This may result in apportionment of the allowances as required by Secs. 18F and 19E (see section 5.10.2). Where apportionments are made and in some subsequent year a balancing allowance or charge falls to be made (see section 5.8.3), Sec. 23B(7)(b)(ii) provides that the total balancing charge or allowance that would otherwise arise is to be apportioned on the basis of:—

Total allowances granted (after apportionments)

Total allowances that would have been due without apportionment

Where a ship ceases to be on the Hong Kong register during a basis period for a year of assessment and depreciation allowances begin to be claimed, allowances are to be based on reduced cost after deducting any initial allowances actually granted and also any annual allowance that would have been granted since acquisition by a person treated as carrying on a shipowning business in Hong Kong by Sec. 23B(1) or Sec. 23B(2) if the ship had been operated in circumstances giving rise to taxable profits (Sec. 23B(8)). This is similar to the provisions applicable generally in the case of assets previously owned suddenly becoming eligible for depreciation allowances as dealt with by Sec. 37(2A) (see section 5.8.2).

"**Relevant Sums**" are effectively the income which forms the numerator A in the formula. It specifically excludes "exempt sums" which are described later and specifically includes the following:—

(i) Sums derived from the uplift of goods, livestock, mail or passengers in Hong Kong but excluding that applicable to goods etc. in transit or re-embarking passengers. Goods, livestock etc. are regarded as in transit if they are clearly specified in the bill of lading as emanating from and going to a foreign port and are brought to Hong Kong solely for the purpose of onward shipping to elsewhere and where the onward freight charges from Hong Kong are not payable in Hong Kong. Re-embarking passengers are those whose tickets indicate that neither their place of departure nor their destination, for that voyage, is Hong Kong. See the definition of "exempt sums" below for amounts which are not to be included.

(ii) Sums derived from towage operations in Hong Kong waters or beginning within Hong Kong waters. See the definition of "exempt sums" below for amounts which are not to be included.

(iii) Sums derived from dredging operations within Hong Kong waters.

(iv) Charterhire income, which is income accruing to a person who is either the owner or a charterer of a ship from a charter party in respect of use of the ship by another person and which is in respect of:—

   (a) the operation of the ship solely or mainly in Hong Kong waters. This allows for the ship to operate partly outside of Hong Kong waters without excluding any part of the charterhire income from taxable income; or

   (b) any charter party where one of the parties is a limited partnership which was registered before 3 December 1990 and the main asset of which is a ship or an interest in a ship which was acquired before that date. This is an anti-avoidance provision because such partnerships were previously used to obtain tax advantages and, therefore, the provision effectively ensures that the charterhire income continues to be taxable even though it does not fit within (a) above.

(v) One half of any charterhire income in respect of ship operations between Hong Kong waters and ports within the Pearl River Delta, i.e. Macau and the Mainland ports in the Pearl River Delta. This area of waters is referred to as the "river trade limits" and is precisely defined as in the *Merchant Shipping Ordinance* (Sec. 2(1)).

It should be noted that, for the purposes of the definition of relevant sums, any charterhire income that relates, somewhat exceptionally, to only part of a ship is not treated as charterhire income for consideration under (iv) or (v) above but is treated as included in (i) so far as attributable to a voyage beginning in Hong Kong waters (Sec. 23B(10)).

"**Exempt Sums**" are excluded from the numerator A of the formula and comprise any amount otherwise included under (i) or (ii) above to the extent the ship which uplifted the goods, livestock, mail or passengers in Hong Kong, or is engaged in towing operations, is proceeding to sea from Hong Kong (i.e. the operation of the ship is not simply between points in Hong Kong), and which are:–

(a)   attributable to a ship which is registered in Hong Kong under the *Merchant Shipping (Registration) Ordinance* (i.e. is on the Hong Kong Shipping Register). Proof of a ship's status as to the Hong Kong Shipping Register is provided by a suitably certified copy or extract from that register (Sec. 23B (11)); or

(b)   derived by a person who has "reciprocity status". A shipowner has "reciprocity status" if they are subject to Profits Tax by virtue of Sec. 23B(2) (i.e. solely because they own ships which call at Hong Kong) *and* they are resident in a territory outside Hong Kong which, the Commissioner is satisfied, grants exemption from income or profits tax to shipowners controlled, managed or incorporated in Hong Kong in respect of income derived from a business carried on in that territory (Sec. 23B(4A)). The IRD from time to time will be required to consider whether a particular foreign jurisdiction provides a reciprocal exemption for Hong Kong ship owning businesses. In this regard, the IRD have advised that shipowners from New Zealand and the Republic of Korea qualify for reciprocity status. Nonetheless, it is possible that other jurisdictions provide an appropriate exemption for Hong Kong shipowners, which would result in ship operators from that jurisdiction qualifying for exemption in Hong Kong. The onus is on the individual claimant, however, to satisfy the IRD as to the existence of the appropriate provisions in their home jurisdiction.

It will be noted that excluded from the definition of "exempt sums" is charterhire income attributable to international operations; nevertheless, there is effective exemption for such income by virtue of the fact that such charterhire income does not fall within (iv) or (v) of the definition of "relevant sums".

■ Example 4.38

Ankazawei Ltd. is a Hong Kong company which owns a number of ships engaged in both local and international shipping activities. Besides operating its own ships it runs agencies in a number of overseas ports but does not have an agency business in Hong Kong.

The profits shown by the profit and loss account for a basis period are as follows:—

Total Profits before tax	$4,750,000
Agency Profits included therein	$ 350,000

Total Turnover of $58,250,000 is analysed as follows:—

(1) Hong Kong Shipping Register	
(a) Goods & Passengers transported from Hong Kong to foreign ports	$ 9,500,000
(b) Goods & Passengers transported to Hong Kong from foreign ports	$ 6,250,000
(c) Passengers transported to Macau and Guangzhou from Hong Kong	$ 4,000,000
(d) Passengers brought to Hong Kong from Macau and Guangdong	$ 4,500,000
(e) Charterhire income from operations between Hong Kong and USA	$ 2,500,000
(f) Charterhire income from operations between Hong Kong and Zhuhai	$ 3,750,000
(g) Charterhire income from operations between Central and Cheung Chau	$ 2,500,000
(h) Towage fees for towage between Hong Kong and Taiwan	$ 1,800,000
(2) Panama Shipping Register	
(a) Goods & Passengers transported from Hong Kong to foreign ports	$11,500,000
(b) Goods & Passengers transported to Hong Kong from foreign ports	$ 5,800,000
(c) Charterhire income from operations between Hong Kong and USA	$ 4,250,000
(3) Agency Receipts	$ 1,500,000
(4) Interest on Investments — Hong Kong	$ 150,000
Interest on Investments — Elsewhere	$ 250,000
(overhead costs estimated at 5%)	
	$58,250,000

It is necessary to analyse the impact of Sec. 23B upon turnover and then to quantify the amounts of "Total Shipping Income," "Total Shipping Profits" and "Relevant Sums."

Analysis of Turnover:—	Relevant Sums	Total Shipping Income
(1) (a) An "exempt sum"	—	$ 9,500,000
(b) Not a relevant sum	—	6,250,000
(c) Not international	$ 4,000,000	4,000,000
(d) Not a relevant sum	—	4,500,000
(e) Not a relevant sum	—	2,500,000
(f) Relevant sum comprises 50%	1,875,000	3,750,000
(g) Relevant sum	2,500,000	2,500,000
(h) Exempt sum	—	1,800,000
(2) (a) Relevant sum	11,500,000	11,500,000
(b) Not a relevant sum	—	5,800,000
(c) Not a relevant sum	—	4,250,000
(3) Non-shipping income		—
(4) Not shipowning Firm		—
	$19,875,000	$56,250,000

Total Shipping Profits		
Total Profits before tax		$ 4,750,000
Less: Agency profits	$ 350,000	
Less: Interest less attributable expenses	380,000	730,000
Less: Total Shipping Profits		$ 4,020,000

$$\text{Assessable Profits per Sec. 23B} = \frac{\text{Relevant Sums}}{\text{Total Shipping Income}} \times \text{Total Shipping Profits}$$

$$= \frac{\$19,875,000}{56,250,000} \times \$4,020,000$$

$$= \$1,417,879$$

Add Hong Kong Source Interest	142,500
(Less Expenses)	
Profits Assessable to Profits Tax	$1,560,379

Notes:—
(a) Ships registered in Hong Kong give rise to exempt income in relation to international carriage of goods and passengers and towage.
(b) Charterhire income, wherever the ship is registered, is only taxable where the operations are mainly in Hong Kong waters and is taxable as to 50% in respect of operations within the "river trade limits", i.e. between Hong Kong and Pearl River Delta ports.
(c) Capital allowances is not affected by notional statutory depreciation allowances unless the difference is material.
(d) The agency business is not "shipowning business" under Sec. 23B and comprises offshore income so is not assessable under Sec. 14.
(e) Only Hong Kong source interest is assessable per Sec. 15(1)(f).

Notwithstanding the above, a shipowner who is resident or incorporated in the USA has the benefit of an agreement between Hong Kong and the USA concerning double taxation under which, in appropriate circumstances, it is exempt from Profits Tax under Sec. 23B in consideration of a reciprocal exemption for Hong Kong residents from US tax (see *Departmental*

Interpretation & Practice Notes No. 19). The further requirement under the agreement is that either:—

(a)   the corporation's shares are primarily and regularly traded on an established securities market in the USA, Hong Kong or other country that offers a similar tax exemption to Hong Kong residents; or

(b)   more than 50% by value of the corporation's shares are owned by individuals resident in the USA or in a country that offers a similar tax exemption to Hong Kong residents or are owned by a corporation which is incorporated in a country that offers a similar tax exemption to Hong Kong residents and whose shares are primarily and regularly traded on an established securities market in that country or another country that offers a similar tax exemption to Hong Kong residents.

Additionally, agreements have been entered into by the Hong Kong SAR with the United Kingdom, the Netherlands, Denmark, Germany, Norway, Singapore and Sri Lanka which deal with shipping income. Also, the comprehensive double taxation agreements entered into with Belgium, Thailand and the Mainland of China contain provisions dealing with shipping income. The form of these agreements is substantially different from the agreement with the USA but they nonetheless have the effect of exempting the profits of residents of those countries from Profits Tax in respect of the operation of ships in international traffic and gains on the disposal of ships operated in international traffic and associated movable property. (Exceptions apply in the case of the agreements with Thailand and Sri Lanka under which the tax otherwise payable is reduced by 50%.)

These agreements are reciprocal in that they provide for exemptions from tax in the relevant countries for ship owning or chartering enterprises which are managed and controlled in Hong Kong. The exemptions provided for under these agreements are granted under the double tax relief provisions of Sec. 49 (see chapter 11); interestingly, however, once the international agreements have been concluded and ratified, an exemption would also appear to be available under the "reciprocity status" provisions contained in Sec. 23B(4A) which are discussed above, although theoretically that exemption is not as broad as it does not extend to gains from the disposal of ships operated in international traffic.

As noted above under the agreements concluded with Thailand and Sri Lanka, there is no reciprocal exemption in respect of shipping profits; rather, the rate applicable is reduced by fifty percent when an enterprise of one jurisdiction is subject to tax in the other jurisdiction. Accordingly, unlike the other agreements discussed above, this would not result in "reciprocity status" under Sec. 23B(4A).

As discussed in section 3.3.5, some of the above international agreements also provide for reciprocal exemptions from salaries tax for crew members of ships operated in international traffic, subject to various conditions being met.

4.7.5 Resident aircraft-owning businesses

The taxation of aircraft-owning businesses is very similar in principle to that of shipping operations in that profits assessable to Profits Tax are ascertained as a proportion of worldwide profits based on a formula. There is, however, no exemption for Hong Kong registration as there is in the case of ships and the inclusion of charterhire income to which there is in the case of ships.

Although, in general, the residence concept familiar in other taxation jurisdictions is not applicable in Hong Kong, there are separate provisions for the ascertainment of the assessable profits of so-called resident aircraft owners and non-resident aircraft owners. Sec. 23C applies to resident aircraft owners although the Section itself, apart from the heading, does not use the term "resident". It is in fact applicable to:—

(1)   aircraft-owning businesses which are normally managed or controlled in Hong Kong (Sec. 23C(1)(a)); and

(2)   aircraft-owning businesses carried on by companies incorporated in Hong Kong (Sec. 23C(1)(b)).

An aircraft owner also includes a person who charters an aircraft from another person and so both the owner and the charterer may be regarded as carrying on business in Hong Kong under Sec. 23C. Aircraft include helicopters and carrying on a business of owning aircraft means both chartering out aircraft to other persons as well as operating aircraft for trade but it does not include dealing in aircraft or aircraft agency business which would be considered on their own merits under Sec. 14.

Management or control for the purposes of (1) above is not defined but is assumed to mean the same principles as govern the residence of a company under UK case law, i.e. the place where the directors meet and exercise central management and control over the company. This is, however, far from clear because the UK law refers to the residence of the **company** whereas management and control in the context of Sec. 23C(1)(a) refers to the **business**.

Having established that an aircraft owner is deemed to be carrying on business in Hong Kong, it is then necessary to establish the amount of taxable profits. In this regard, the assessable profits for a given year of assessment are ascertained in the following manner:—

Assessable Profits = Total Aircraft Profits × A/B (Sec. 23C(2))

And for this purpose:—

A = An amount referred to as "Relevant Sums"
B = Total Aircraft Income

It is, therefore, important to be able to precisely understand the special terms used in the formula and these are defined in Sec. 23C(5). Some of the more important terms are as follows:

"**Total Aircraft Income**" is the worldwide income, i.e. turnover, from the person's business as an owner of aircraft as shown in the person's commercial accounts. It will therefore exclude investment income and any other income not specifically related to the aircraft business.

"**Total Aircraft Profits**" is quite simply the profits derived from "total aircraft income" as shown by the commercial accounts but must of course exclude any expenditure which relates to any excluded non-aircraft income.

It is quite usual to adopt the commercial accounting profits without adjustment for requirements of the IRO and the definition of total aircraft profits allows for this. However, where this is likely to differ materially from tax-adjusted profits, which is more likely in the area of capital receipts and expenditure and depreciation allowances, Sec. 23E provides for "total aircraft profits" to be adjusted where necessary so as to make them correspond so far as possible to the requirements of the IRO. The more usual application of this provision is to exclude commercial depreciation and profits or losses on sale of aircraft and to compute instead the relevant depreciation allowances, balancing charges etc. (see Chapter 5). It may be that these adjustments are only made in respect of the aircraft, leaving commercial depreciation for other assets such as office furniture unadjusted. This is perfectly permissible.

"**Relevant Sums**" is effectively the income which forms the numerator A in the formula. The following types of aircraft income are included therein:—

(i) Sums derived from the uplift of goods (which is defined to include livestock and mail) or passengers in Hong Kong or in an "arrangement territory" (see definition below), but excluding sums attributable to goods or passengers in transit (also defined below);

(ii) Charterhire income (see definition below) which is not attributable to a permanent establishment outside Hong Kong or an arrangement territory, but excluding amounts separately dealt with in (iii) and (iv) below. "Permanent establishment" for this purpose is defined as a branch, management or other place of business including an agency if the agent has, and habitually exercises, a general authority to negotiate and conclude contracts on behalf of his principal. This meaning is almost the same as that in IRR5 and most double taxation agreements;

(iii) Charterhire income in respect of flights between points in Hong Kong or between points in an arrangement territory. (Note that this does not extend to charterhire income from flights between a point in Hong Kong and a point in an arrangement territory, although such income may be included in (ii) above); and

(iv) One half of any charterhire income in respect of flights between Hong Kong and Macau.

A flowchart illustrating the process of determining whether an amount is a "relevant sum" is contained in Figure 4.1.

"Arrangement territory" is defined in Sec. 23C(5) and, when read in conjunction with Sec. 23C(2D), effectively means a territory outside Hong Kong which:—

(i)   has entered into a double taxation agreement with Hong Kong pursuant to Sec. 49; and

(ii)   under which an aircraft owner to which Sec. 23C applies is exempt from tax in that territory on sums derived from the uplift of goods and passengers in that territory and charterhire income attributable to that territory.

At that time of writing, Hong Kong had entered into such agreements with more than twenty-five other countries, in addition to an agreement with the Mainland. The majority of these agreements are currently incorporated into the Air Services Agreements, which are agreements between the respective governments regulating commercial aviation traffic between those territories, and it is expected that similar clauses will continue to be included in future Air Services Agreements. Nonetheless, the Memorandum with the Mainland concerning double taxation and the comprehensive double taxation agreements with Belgium and Thailand (see chapter 10) all deal with airline profits, although in the first two cases there were earlier agreements incorporated into the Air Services Agreements. Additionally, agreements dealing with both airline and shipping profits have been entered into with Singapore and Sri Lanka.

"**Charterhire**" is a term with a specific meaning for the purposes of Sec. 23C. It refers to sums accruing to an owner or charterer of an aircraft under a charter party by demise. It does not, however, apply to the somewhat exceptional circumstances where the charter party does not extend to the whole of the aircraft.

Accordingly, any other type of charter income, i.e. the following, does not fall within the definition of "charterhire" income as used in the definition of "relevant sums" (see above):—

(a)   Where the charter party is not by demise;

(b)   Whether by demise or not, where the charter party does not extend to the whole of the aircraft.

In the case of charter income arising under (b) above, so far as it is attributable to flights commencing in Hong Kong it is to be included with income under (i) of "relevant sums" (see above) (Sec. 23C(3)).

In the case of charter income arising under (a) above, a proportion is to be included with income under (i) of "relevant sums" (see above). The proportion is as follows:—

(a)   In respect of a "flight charter", the amount attributable to any outward flight commencing in Hong Kong. (Sec. 23C(4)(a)).

(b)   In respect of a "time charter", the total income under the charter party is apportioned on the basis of:—

$$\frac{\text{Total flying hours on flights commencing in Hong Kong}}{\text{Total flying hours under the charter party}}$$

(Sec. 23C(4)(b)).

"**Goods in transit**" in relation to Hong Kong refers to goods clearly specified in an air waybill or post office delivery bill as emanating from, and going to, a country other than Hong Kong, and brought to Hong Kong by air solely for the purpose of onward carriage and any freight charges for the onward carriage are not payable in Hong Kong. Note, therefore, that goods may be in transit through Hong Kong to an arrangement territory yet the revenue earned in connection therewith may still not be a relevant sum. In relation to an arrangement territory, goods are considered as in transit if they are specified in an air waybill or post office delivery bill as emanating from, and going to, a country other than an arrangement territory, are brought to the relevant arrangement territory solely for the purpose of onward carriage and any freight charges for the onward carriage are not payable in an arrangement territory. It should be noted that the definition of goods in transit through an arrangement territory is

Figure 4.1   Determination of relevant sums in respect of resident aircraft owners

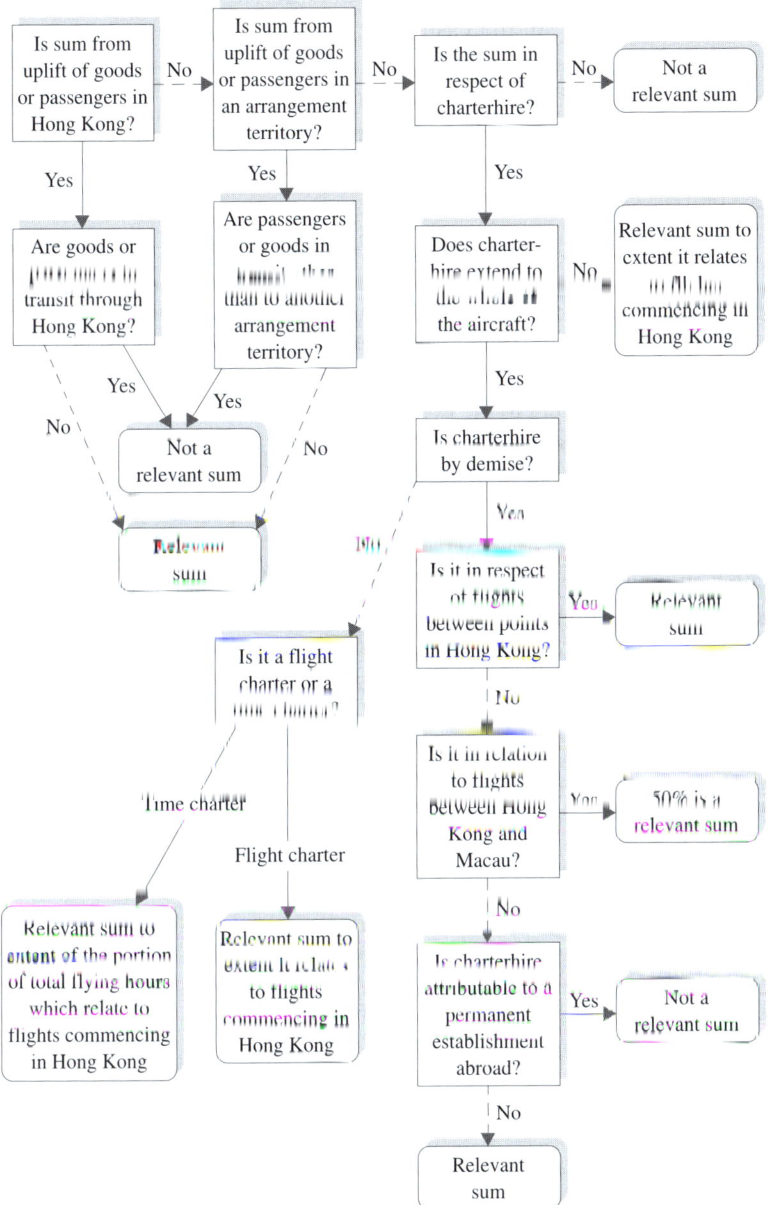

Note: This is intended to be a diagrammatic summary and must be considered in conjunction with the text.

more restrictive than in the case of goods in transit through Hong Kong. In particular, goods can be in transit through Hong Kong irrespective of their origin or destination or where, outside Hong Kong, the freight charges are payable; in the case of an arrangement territory, however, goods will not be regarded as in transit if they originated in, or were destined for, another arrangement territory or the onward freight charges were payable in another arrangement territory, although it should be emphasised that Hong Kong is not, of course, an arrangement territory for these purposes.

"Passenger in transit" in relation to Hong Kong is a passenger whose ticket for the flight specifies that neither their port of departure nor their destination for that flight is Hong Kong; alternatively, a passenger will be regarded as in transit in Hong Kong if they depart from Hong Kong on the same carrier (but not necessarily the same aircraft) within 24 hours of arrival to a destination different to the port from which they arrived. Note that this provision will operate to exclude sums attributable to passengers transiting Hong Kong to or from an arrangement territory. In relation to an arrangement territory, to be regarded as in transit a passenger's ticket for the flight must not specify any arrangement territory (which, of course, does not include Hong Kong) as either the port of departure or the destination. Alternatively, a passenger will be regarded as in transit through an arrangement territory if they depart from the arrangement territory on the same carrier (but not necessarily the same aircraft) within 24 hours of arrival to a destination different to the port from which they arrived.

■ Example 4.39

Dragon Pacific Airlines is incorporated in Hong Kong and leases all of its aircraft from leasing companies.

It operates and charters out a number of aircraft. The profit and loss account for the basis period are as follows:—

Total Profits before tax	$20,500,000
Hong Kong airline agency profits included therein	750,000

Total Turnover of $116,150,000 is analysed as follows:—

(1) Sales of Passenger tickets
    (a) Passengers transported from Hong Kong to other countries (see Note (a) — $25,500,000
    (b) Passengers transported to Hong Kong from other countries (other than "arrangement territories") — 18,750,000
(2) Freight Charges
    (a) Goods transported from Hong Kong to other countries (see Note (b)) — 19,850,000

	(b) Goods transported to Hong Kong from other countries (other than "arrangement territories")	15,450,000
	(c) Goods transported from Korea to Canada	4,000,000
(3)	Charterhire by demise	
	(a) Pleasure flights in Hong Kong	2,500,000
	(b) Flights between Hong Kong and Macau	3,600,000
	(c) Charterhire parties concluded by Manila branch (for flights entirely outside Hong Kong)	8,000,000
(4)	Charterhire not by demise	
	(a) Flight charters out of Hong Kong	6,000,000
	(b) Flight charters between Papua New Guinea and other countries (excluding Hong Kong)	4,000,000
	(c) Time charters (total flight hours 4,000 hrs.) (Flight hours from Hong Kong to other destinations 700 hrs.)	7,000,000
(5)	Agency Receipts	2,500,000
(6)	Dividend Income (attributable overheads estimated at $25,000)	5,000,000
		$122,150,000

Notes:—
(a) Included in (1)(a) is $3,500,000 in respect of passengers arriving on Dragon Pacific Airlines who continued their journey to other destinations within 24 hours.
(b) Included in (2)(a) is $3,000,000 in respect of goods brought to Hong Kong solely for onward carriage to other countries and freight charges were billed in and payable in Hong Kong. $2,000,000 is in respect of goods brought to Hong Kong solely for onward carriage to Korea; the freight charges were billed and payable outside Hong Kong.

It is necessary to analyse the impact of Sec. 23C upon turnover and then to quantify the amounts of "Total Aircraft Income", "Total Aircraft Profits" and "Relevant Sums".

Analysis of Turnover:—	Relevant Sums	Total aircraft income
(1) (a) Excludes passengers in transit (Note (a))	$22,000,000	$25,500,000
(b) Not a relevant sum	—	18,750,000
(2) (a) No goods in transit (Note (b))	17,850,000	19,850,000
(b) Not a relevant sum	—	15,450,000
(c) Relevant sum (Note (c))	4,000,000	4,000,000
(3) (a) Relevant sum	2,500,000	2,500,000
(b) 50% taxable	1,800,000	3,600,000
(c) Not a relevant sum	—	8,000,000
(4) (a) Deemed relevant sum	6,000,000	6,000,000
(b) Not a relevant sum	—	4,000,000
(c) Deemed relevant sum	1,225,000	7,000,000
(5) Not aircraft-owning income	—	—
(6) Not aircraft-owning income	—	—
	$55,375,000	$114,650,000

Total Aircraft Profits	
Total Profits before tax	$20,500,000

Less: Agency profits (Note (d)) $ 750,000
      Dividends less expenses   4,975,000   (5,725,000)
                                                                  $14,775,000

$$\text{Assessable Profits per Sec. 23C} = \frac{\text{Relevant Sums}}{\text{Total Aircraft Income}} \times \text{Total Aircraft Profits}$$

$$= \frac{\$55,375,000}{114,650,000} \times \$14,775,000$$

$$= \$7,136,203 \text{ (Sec. 23C)}$$

Add Hong Kong Agency Profits   750,000 (Sec. 14) (Note (e))
  (Less Expenses)
Profits Assessable to Profits Tax $7,886,203

Notes:—
(a) Passengers in transit are those who arrive and leave by the same carrier and do not stay longer than 24 hours. Their ticket sales are not relevant sums.
(b) Revenue from goods in transit does not qualify for exclusion from relevant sums if the freight charges are payable in Hong Kong. The goods to Korea are, however, considered in transit through Hong Kong as the freight charges are payable abroad.
(c) As Korea is an "arrangement territory", these amounts are relevant sums.
(d) The agency business is not an "aircraft-owning business" under Sec. 23C and not therefore subject to the formula. It is however a business under Sec. 14 and therefore the profits are still subject to Profits Tax.
(e) Depreciation is not adjusted for depreciation allowances unless the difference is material (Sec. 23E).

4.7.6 Non-resident aircraft-owning businesses

Sec. 23D covers the position of all aircraft owners and operators who are not covered by Sec. 23C. Once again, the terms "resident" and "non-resident" are not actually used in the wording of the section but, in effect, the provisions cover all aircraft owners not incorporated in Hong Kong where the business is not normally controlled or managed from within Hong Kong (otherwise it would be within the scope of Sec. 23C) but an aircraft lands at an airport in Hong Kong (Sec. 23D(1)). If the Commissioner can be satisfied that a landing is of a casual nature, it will be ignored and no liability will arise (Sec. 23D(5)).

The general impact of Sec. 23D is virtually the same as Sec. 23C in that the assessable profit is based on a proportion of worldwide profit and in fact there is very little difference in the calculation as the important words "total aircraft income" and "total aircraft profits" have the same meaning. Also, the only differences with respect to "relevant sums" is a difference in the treatment of charterhire income and the exclusion of sums from uplift of goods and passengers in an "arrangement territory". Under Sec. 23C, charterhire income is only excluded if it is concluded through a permanent establishment outside Hong Kong, whereas under Sec. 23D, it is only included if it is concluded through a permanent establishment in Hong Kong. Otherwise, all of the definitions, inclusions and exclusions which are applicable to Sec. 23C are also applicable to Sec. 23D and the computation proceeds exactly as in Example 4.39 when the relevant sums have been established.

The only additional provision is one enabling a simplified method of profit ascertainment which may be desirable where there are practical difficulties in carrying out the apportionment calculation. More specifically, Sec. 23D(3) provides that where in the assessor's opinion the apportionment formula cannot be satisfactorily applied the assessable profits may be computed on a fair percentage of the aggregate of the "relevant sums" which would otherwise form the numerator of the apportionment fraction.

If an assessment has been made on this alternative basis and has become final and conclusive it can, nevertheless, be re-opened and adjusted to the profit ascertained on the apportionment basis if a claim is made within two years of the end of the year of assessment (Sec. 23D(4)). As in the case of Sec. 23C, the provisions of Sec. 23E also allow for the worldwide profit on shipping as revealed in the financial accounts to remain unadjusted for the purposes of Sec. 23D unless there are material differences.

As noted in section 4.7.5 above, Hong Kong has entered into agreements with more than twenty other countries which provide for reciprocal exemptions from tax on profits from the operation of aircraft in international traffic. Additionally, the Memorandum on double taxation entered into with the Mainland of China and the comprehensive double taxation agreements concluded with Belgium and Thailand provide for similar reciprocal exemptions. Because these agreements override domestic law, they will generally provide for an exemption from the provisions of Sec. 23D in respect of an aircraft owner or operator resident in one of the jurisdictions with which an agreement has been concluded. Accordingly, many foreign airlines are now exempt from Profits Tax in Hong Kong.

4.7.7 Financial institutions

There are a number of aspects of the taxation of financial institutions which differ from other types of businesses and these are considered separately below.

(i) **Taxation of Interest Income:** This is undoubtedly the most contentious area of the taxation of financial institutions. The problems stem from the fact that there is a provision in the IRO which deems interest income derived by a financial institution (as defined) to be subject to Profits Tax in specified circumstances notwithstanding that under the source rules normally applicable to interest (see the discussion on the provision of credit test in section 4.4.4), the source would not be in Hong Kong. Unfortunately, the wording of the law is incapable of precise and consistent interpretation and, therefore, for a considerable number of years its application had been uncertain. Attempts at legal clarification were confused by a Board of Review decision (*D 7/84*) which called into question the appropriateness of the provision of credit test for interest income of financial institutions notwithstanding that this test, developed from case law, had been acceptable to the Commissioner and to taxpayers for over twenty years. However, financial institutions are now able to settle their affairs on the basis of a compromise set of rules agreed between professional advisers and the Commissioner and these rules are discussed further in the following paragraphs. Nevertheless, the matter remains less than satisfactory in that, whilst there is at least a basis for settlement which financial institutions can find acceptable, there is no clear support in law for the compromise rules. As such, the rules cannot be interpreted by the Board of Review or a court, and, therefore, financial institutions need to rely on the IRD consistently and fairly applying the rules. In the case of a dispute the Board of Review or court would need to decide the matter on the basis of the statutory wording rather than the compromise rules.

The statutory provisions are contained in Sec. 15(1)(i) and apply to financial institutions as defined in Sec. 2(1). Financial institution means:—

(1)   an authorized institution licensed or registered under the *Banking Ordinance*; or

(2)   an associated company of (1) which would be liable to be registered or licensed as a deposit-taking company or restricted licence bank under the *Banking Ordinance* but for the fact that it only takes deposits from licensed banks or registered or licensed deposit-taking companies.

The provision in (2) is an anti-avoidance provision but does not apply automatically to all associated companies, but only those that are carrying on a deposit-taking business, which would normally imply a systematic acceptance of deposits. A deposit for this purpose is very broadly defined in the *Banking Ordinance* and includes almost any loan of money, other than a loan by means of the issue of securities involving the registration of a prospectus under the *Companies Ordinance*, or a loan between a parent company and its subsidiary (or between companies which have a common parent company), although this exclusion does not apply where one of the companies is an authorised institution under the *Banking Ordinance*. Associated company is further defined by Sec. 2(2) to mean a company controlled by, controlling or under common control with the authorised institution. Control is also widely defined. For a case concerning the interpretation of this extended definition of "financial institution", see the Court of Appeal's judgement in *Orion Caribbean Limited (in voluntary liquidation) v CIR* [1996] (1 HKRC 90-077).

Sec. 15(1)(i) merely provides that, notwithstanding that credit may have been provided outside Hong Kong, interest income earned by a financial institution through or from the carrying on of its business in Hong Kong is deemed to have a Hong Kong source. Unfortunately there is no further statutory guidance as to what constitutes "through or from the carrying on of business in Hong Kong" and, therefore, the practical position is important. This is dealt with further below.

The position is recognised where a company may only fall within the definition of financial institution for part of a basis period and it is provided that the interest deeming provision applies only for the relevant part of the basis period during which it is caught by the definition (Sec. 15(3)). It may be acceptable to do this on the basis of time apportionment as authorised by Sec. 18E(3) but it would be more correct to identify the dates on which the interest income was derived and allocate it accordingly and then to make consequential allocations of the related outgoings on some suitable basis.

Because of these provisions interest income will often be subject to tax in its country of source as well as to Profits Tax in Hong Kong. Because of this and the fact that the double taxation relief provisions are currently limited (see Chapter 10), there is a provision to specifically grant a measure of double taxation relief by deducting the foreign tax as an expense (see (3) under section 4.5.8).

The practical considerations have proved to be of fundamental importance in determining the liability of financial institutions to Profits Tax on their interest income in the absence of any legal guidance as to the meaning of *"arising through or from the carrying on of business"*.

When Sec. 15(1)(i) was introduced in 1978 it replaced the situation where the normal source rules had applied to the interest income which was ascertained in accordance with the easy to understand (and easy to avoid) "provision of credit" test. It was promised both by the Financial Secretary at the time and by the Commissioner in *Departmental Interpretation & Practice Notes No. 13* (which has subsequently been amended) that multinational financial institutions should not be concerned about the new law where they were in receipt of interest on loans that had been merely "booked or garaged" in Hong Kong because such interest would not be charged to Profits Tax. Furthermore, it was promised, where a loan had involved the substantial intervention of a branch elsewhere then there would be an apportionment of the interest income on such loans so that only the relevant part would be subjected to Profits Tax.

A number of important developments then occurred. In particular:

(a)   The practice note indicated the Commissioner's view of the important steps in the loan-making process; and

(b)   Intervention of a group company was accepted as the same as intervention by a branch.

However, returns submitted with computations which identified the steps in the loan-making process and which based apportionments upon the place where those steps had been undertaken were not accepted by the Commissioner. There was also a failure to agree what was understood by "booked" or "garaged".

There followed a long period of dispute during which no real progress was made. During this period one case proceeded before the Board of Review (*D 7/84*) and this added further confusion to the issue by deciding that the provision of credit test was always inappropriate for determining the source of interest income of a financial institution and that the proper test is one involving a consideration of the totality of a range of factors similar to those which the Commissioner had identified as important to the loan-making process. This was, in effect saying that Sec. 15(1)(i) was irrelevant and that the basic charging provision, Sec. 14, is to be construed in similar terms to Sec. 15(1)(i) as far as financial institutions are concerned. The decision did not, therefore, give the hoped for clarification to enable the substantial number of disputes still outstanding to be settled quickly and consistently.

Wishing to abide, so far as possible, with original promises, the Commissioner came to agreement with professional advisers on a formula to be adopted in settling past disputes and for proceeding for the foreseeable future, notwithstanding that any financial institution was always entitled to not accept the compromise but to pursue its legal remedies so far as it saw fit.

In general terms the compromise adopts the following approach:—

(1)   Only two factors are considered relevant, namely the place where

the loan was initiated and the place where the loan funding was raised.

(2)   Where the initiation and funding were both outside Hong Kong the loan is treated as booked or garaged and the interest is not assessable.

(3)   Where either the initiation or the funding was outside Hong Kong, only 50% of the interest is assessable.

(4)   Where both the initiation and funding were in Hong Kong the whole of the interest is assessable.

(5)   In the absence of a more precise calculation, factually supported, the disallowance of overhead expenditure attributable to the non-assessable income should be based on the arithmetical ratio of assessable to non-assessable income. In fact, there should be no need to compromise on the matter of this allocation which is a factual matter and fully covered in an undisputed manner by IRR 2A. Furthermore, common sense dictates that where the interest is not assessable because of no material involvement in Hong Kong, an equal apportionment of overhead expenses across all income is quite inappropriate. It is therefore in the interests of financial institutions with material booked income to provide evidence for actual overhead to be disallowed

Some six years after the negotiation of this compromise formula, the IRD incorporated most aspects of it into their *Departmental Interpretation & Practice Notes No. 21* on the locality of profits. This is reproduced as Appendix 13 and should be studied for a more comprehensive analysis of the compromise formula.

In summary, the compromise formula provides a readily acceptable method of bringing past matters up to date but, notwithstanding its broad acceptance by the IRD and taxpayers, is unsatisfactory as a permanent method by which financial institutions should be taxed on their interest income and some better legal provision should be devised.

(ii)   **Profits on Sale, Maturity etc. of Certificates of Deposit and Bills of Exchange:**   The IRO contains another provision, Sec. 15(1)(l), which, like Sec. 15(1)(i) discussed above, seeks to subject to Profits Tax certain profits attributable to a financial institution's business in Hong Kong, notwithstanding that the source of those profits under ordinary rules would be outside Hong Kong. In particular, the provision applies to profits from the disposal of, or redemption on maturity or presentment of, a certificate of deposit or bill of exchange which is attributable to the financial institution's business in Hong Kong, notwithstanding that all factors consistent with an offshore source under general principles may be present. Unfortunately, this legislation suffers from the same shortcomings as Sec. 15(1)(i) in that it fails to explicitly recognise that in a modern multinational financial institution such profits can arise from the activities of two or more branches of the institution concerned and, as a consequence, fails to address the question of whether apportionment is appropriate and, if so, on what basis it should be carried out. Unlike Sec. 15(1)(i), however, this provision has not been the subject of any extra-statutory compromise agreements and its interpretation has not been addressed in any *Departmental Interpretation & Practice Note*.

A more complete discussion of this provision is contained in point (11) under section 4.5.4.

■ Example 4.40

Townbank Inc. has a Hong Kong branch which has made a loan to an Australian resident and in the year of assessment has received interest on the loan of $650,000 from which Australian withholding tax of $65,000 has been deducted. Branch officers negotiated and finalized the loan and used branch funds to advance to the customer in US$ through bank accounts in New York.

Notwithstanding that the source of the interest is outside Hong Kong under the provision of credit test, the interest is subject to Profits Tax under Sec. 15(1)(i) because it arises from the branch's business.

Relief for the Australian tax may be available under Sec. 16(1)(c) (refer to point (3) in section 4.5.8).

(iii) **Bad Debts:** These are deductible by financial institutions in the same way as other businesses and there are specific rules in Sec. 16(1)(d) for losses of money lent in the ordinary course of a money lending business in Hong Kong (see point (4) in section 4.5.8). Difficulties do, however, arise for financial institutions in two areas, namely losses on loans where the interest income has been agreed to be wholly or partially exempt from Profits Tax and potential losses on loans that represent sovereign risk or country debt.

In the case of loans where, under the compromise agreement, the interest income has been treated as wholly or partially exempt from Profits Tax, the Commissioner is only willing to admit a deduction for any loan loss to the extent that the interest has been taxed; in other words, where loan interest has been treated as 50% taxable, any qualifying loan loss would be treated by the Commissioner as only 50% deductible. Similarly, where the interest on a loan has been treated as non-taxable, the Commissioner will not permit any deduction for loan losses. The basis for this approach by the

Commissioner is that if the interest is agreed to be outside the provisions of Sec. 15(1)(i) which applies to interest earned *"through or from the carrying on of business in Hong Kong"* then the loan cannot be said to have been made *"in the ordinary course of the business of lending money in Hong Kong"* as required by the proviso to Sec. 16(1)(d). There is, however, doubt as to whether that argument is necessarily always correct as a strict matter of law having regard to the decision in *CIR v Hang Seng Bank* (HKTC 583), which is discussed in section 4.5.7. In particular, if a loan is made out of a pool of funds under the sole control of the financial institution in Hong Kong but the interest is only 50% taxable because of the assistance in the initiation of the loan given by an overseas branch, it would still appear to be upon to the financial institution in general, that any loan suffered was a loss of trading stock of the Hong Kong moneylending business, notwithstanding that the trading stock was temporarily employed in a manner which did not generate profits completely subject to Profits Tax. As a practical matter, however, there is likely to be a reluctance by taxpayers to pursue such an argument for fear that the Commissioner will seek to not apply the compromise agreement on interest income in their case, this is, of course, another unfortunate by-product of the poor drafting of Sec. 15(1)(i).

In the case of sovereign and country risk debt where loan repayments are in arrears and are doubtful because of a combination of political and economic factors peculiar to the country of the borrower, the strict legal position is that deductibility of any provision made against the debt depends upon being able to show that the debt has become bad rather than merely doubtful; traditionally, however, there has been a widely held view amongst revenue authorities that these debts were never bad, just in arrears, as a country could never default on its obligations. In the late 1980s, however, it became recognised that this view is not totally realistic and that even if debts are recovered in the distant future, some tax relief is still warranted. The problem was considered by the tax authorities of other countries and the Commissioner agreed, in practice, to adopt a similar position to that taken in the UK. In the UK the Bank of England has published guidelines for banks in determining provisions to be made by them in their accounts. These guidelines take the form of a complicated table of points to be allocated to individual countries and individual loans, based upon a range of economic factors which, when aggregated, arrive at a percentage of the loan to be provided against. This of course has to be re-assessed every year and may therefore result in subsequent write-backs or further write-offs. The Commissioner has agreed that, if banks adopt the Bank of England formula in making their provisions, these will be acceptable for the purpose of obtaining deductions under Sec. 16(1)(d), subject to proving, where considered necessary, that the formula has been correctly followed.

4.7.8 Clubs and trade associations

If there was no specific provision in the IRO, mutual clubs and trade associations would only be liable to Profits Tax on the income which they derived from non-members. This is because of the principle that a person cannot make a profit from himself (*Faulconbridge v National Employers' Mutual* (33 TC 103)) and, therefore, that profit which derives solely from sums paid in by members, and which belongs to the members on the mutuality principle, would not be taxable. Receipts from non-members are, however, outside of the mutuality principle and would be taxable (*Carlisle & Silloth Golf Club v Smith* (6 TC 48)).

However, Sec. 24 overrides this principle, somewhat artificially, by deeming the whole of the profits, including receipts that would otherwise not be taxable, of clubs and trade associations to be the profits of a business for Profits Tax purposes when given circumstances apply.

In the case of a club or similar institution the test is based on gross receipts on revenue account which by specific definition includes entrance fees and subscriptions, the former normally constituting capital receipts under ordinary principles. If less than half of such gross receipts are received from members, the whole of the profits from both members and others and including entrance fees and subscriptions is subject to Profits Tax as if it was derived from a business (Sec. 24(1)). For this purpose, a member is a person who is entitled to vote at a general meeting of the club or institution (Sec. 24(3)). The exclusion of certain capital profits from the general scheme of Profits Tax does not override the specific taxing provision in respect of entrance fees in Sec. 24(1) (*CIR v Far East Stock Exchange* (HKTC 1036)); this is a Privy Council decision which, in fact, related to a trade association but which nevertheless holds good for clubs as well. It is the test of entitlement to vote which is the artificial element although it was introduced to prevent avoidance of tax by, for example, night clubs which sign in customers as quasi members. A club is not defined and must therefore take its natural meaning but it is interesting that in *D 1/79* a credit union was held to be a club, although in *Kowloon Stock Exchange v CIR* (2 HKTC 99) a stock exchange was held not to be a club but a trade association.

In the case of a trade, professional or business association, the test relates to its subscription income. Where more than half of the receipts from subscriptions are from persons who either claim, or would be entitled to claim, that their subscriptions are allowable deductions against their own business profits (and this would normally be the case), the association is deemed to be carrying on business and is subject to Profits Tax on the whole of its profits including entrance fees and subscriptions (Sec. 24(2)).

In the *Kowloon Stock Exchange* (supra) case it was held that entrance fees and founders contributions, which were once and for all payments, were not to be treated as subscriptions.

■ Example 4.41

The Wanchai Missionaries Club owns a building, one-third of which is used by members for club activities and the other two-thirds of which is let out to local business. An analysis of the income and expenditure account for a basis period reveals the following:—

Subscriptions from members	$100,000
Catering and bar receipts	85,000
Rental receipts	245,000
	$430,000
General administration expenses	($250,000)
Property outgoings	(60,000)
	($310,000)
Net profit	$120,000

All members are permitted to attend annual meetings and only members can purchase food and drinks.

Entrance fees of $25,000 have been credited direct to the Accumulated Fund.

If it were not for Sec. 24(1) assessable profits would be limited to income from non-members, namely:

Rental income		$245,000
Outgoings (2/3)	$40,000	
Administration expenses,* say	10,000	(50,000)
		$195,000

* An arbitrary figure for this illustration. It would be subject to negotiation.

However, the test under Sec. 24(1) is as follows:—

	Members	Non-Members
Subscriptions	$100,000	
Catering etc.	85,000	
Rents		245,000
Entrance fees	25,000	
	$210,000	$245,000

As less than half derives from members, the whole of the profits are subject to Profits Tax and the assessment would be:—

Profits per income and expenditure account	$120,000
Add entrance fees	25,000
	$145,000

It works out favourably in this case because the rental profits are in fact subsidising club activities and the loss on club activities would not be allowable but for Sec. 24(1).

4.7.9 Partnerships

There is nothing different about the ascertainment of the assessable profits of a partnership or about the ascertainment of basis periods for years of assessment. There are, however, a number of additional rules which it is convenient to bring together under this paragraph. The position of losses of a partnership was discussed in sections 4.5.16.2 and 4.5.16.3. To recap, however, losses are allocated to each partner and where the partner is an individual he may elect for Personal Assessment and set off his share of the loss against other sources of assessable income, or he can carry the loss forward and set it off against his share of any future assessable profits of the partnership (Secs. 19C(2) and (3)). Note, however, that if the individual ceases to be a partner in the relevant partnership, he loses the benefit of the losses. Where a partner is a corporation, its share of the losses of a partnership can be set off against assessable profits from other sources and to the extent not so set off, can be carried forward and be set off first against the corporation's share of any future assessable profits of the partnership and then against any other future assessable profits of the corporation (Sec. 19C(5)).

In other words, losses incurred by a partnership are generally not carried forward by the partnership, but are dealt with by the individual partners. Note, however, that Sec. 19C(7) defines a partnership as excluding a partnership of more than 20 partners (other than a partnership referred to in Sec. 345 of the *Companies Ordinance*, which essentially refers to partnerships of solicitors, accountants and certain other professions). The effect of this is that a partnership which falls outside of the definition is treated as a corporation and carries any losses forward in the partnership (i.e. in the same way a company does). Nonetheless, Sec. 19C(7) is to be repealed when Part 2 of Schedule 4 of the *Companies (Amendment) Ordinance 2004* becomes operative by notice in the *Gazette*, at which time all partnerships will be treated the same with regard to losses. The repealing of Sec. 19C(7) will be accompanied by the introduction of transitional provisions, and these are discussed in section 4.5.16.2.

It is necessary to establish whether a partnership exists between two or more persons, whether they be individuals, companies or a mixture of both because a partnership is assessed to Profits Tax as a single legal entity regardless of the individual identity of the partners (Sec. 22(1)). Furthermore, even where a partnership has ceased or been dissolved, an assessment may be made upon it and the tax recovered from any of the former partners (Sec. 22(5)). Whether a number of persons acting together constitutes a partnership is a question of fact and of law. The law in connection with partnerships in Hong Kong is contained in the *Limited Partnerships Ordinance* and the *Partnership Ordinance*. The taxation rules applicable to partnerships apply equally to limited and unlimited partnerships in all respects except in the ability of a limited partner to use his share of partnership losses against his own income, which is a restriction which apply, for a full description of the restrictions see section 4.5.16.5). Also, an individual may be a partner whether he takes a full equity share in profits or whether his share is limited to a fixed amount which may be called a "salary". It is merely a question of law as to whether he has the obligations of a partner. No formal partnership agreement is required in Hong Kong law and, in the absence of a formal agreement, it is necessary to look to the actual course of business between the partners. Very broadly, a partnership is a relationship between persons carrying on business in common with a view to profit and potentially can include arrangements between two persons, usually companies, termed "joint ventures". It would not, however, include an arrangement such as an investment club where the purpose is merely to place funds into a common pool and take out profits rateably.

The precedent partner has the responsibility to submit returns of partnership profits and, normally, but if there is not a first partner in Hong Kong, it becomes the responsibility of the resident manager or agent (Sec. 22(2)). However, as regards recovery of unpaid tax, the IRD is entitled to collect from any partner (see *CIR v Tse Kai-Wan and Sian Wong* (HKTC 921)) or out of the partnership assets (Sec. 22(4)). Precedent partner is defined by Sec. 2 as the first named in the partnership agreement or, failing that, the first named in the usual partnership name or in any statutory statement of the names of the partners.

Although a partnership is assessed as a single legal entity, because of the various ways in which the partners may, or are mandatorily required to, use their individual shares of profits or losses, the final computation of assessable profits or losses of a partnership is of necessity a combination of computations for each individual partner. Of course, if all of the partners are individuals, have been in partnership together throughout the whole of the basis period for the year of assessment, do not elect for Personal Assessment and there is an assessable profit and no losses brought forward, there will be no necessity to compute individual shares for tax purposes and a single assessment is made at the standard rate applicable to individuals. It is a matter for the partners themselves as to how they allocate the tax payment between themselves. Even so, however, a partner in a partnership may have reason to elect for Personal Assessment (see Chapter 6) in which case it will be necessary to ascertain his share of the profit for inclusion in the personal assessment computation. The share of the assessable profit or adjusted loss is ascertained in accordance with the manner in which they actually shared accounting profits or losses during the basis period for the year of assessment (Sec. 22A(1)), not during the year of assessment itself. Where losses are brought forward from an earlier year, the whole loss is *not* automatically set against the whole profits (Sec. 22A(2)). This would be incorrect because it is necessary to allocate the loss in the same way as profits under Sec. 22A (1) and bring forward each partner's share against his subsequent share of profits. If there has been a change in profit sharing ratio or a partner has retired, the loss may be limited.

■ Example 4.42

A, B, C and D have been in a general partnership many years and recent results, as adjusted for Profits Tax purposes, have been as follows:—

Year ended 31.12.2006	Adjusted loss	($480,000)
Year ended 31.12.2007	Adjusted profit	$500,000

They had always shared profits equally until D retired on 31.12.2006 and C semi-retired. From 1.1.2007 therefore C took 1/5 of the profits and A and B shared the balance equally.

	A	B	C	D	Asst.
2006/07 (Note b)					
Basis period (year ended 31.12.2006)					
Loss ($480,000)	($120,000)	($120,000)	($120,000)	($120,000)	Nil
(Allocation per	C/F	C/F	C/F	Ceased	
Sec. 22A(1))					
2007/08 (Note b)					
Basis period (year ended 31.12.2007)					
Profit $500,000	$200,000	$200,000	$100,000		
(Allocation per					
Sec. 22A(1))					
Net	$ 80,000	$ 80,000	—		$160,000
Loss			($ 20,000)		
			C/F		

Notes:—
(a) D's loss can only be set against *his* share of profits (Sec. 19C(2)) and therefore it lapses on his retirement (see section 4.5.15.4). Equally C's loss is limited to his share of profit and the balance is carried forward.
(b) Notwithstanding the retirement of D, the business is treated as continuing, therefore the cessation rules do not apply (Sec. 22(3) — see discussion below).
(c) See also Example 4.27.

Difficulties can arise in the allocation of profits or losses among partners where some of the partners are entitled to a salary (which is nothing more than a fixed share of profits) with or without a share of any balance of profit. An initial allocation can result in some partners with a profit and others with a loss but this is not acceptable for tax purposes (see ¶ 22A (1)). Where the overall result is an assessable profit, any partner's share resulting in a loss must be sub-allocated among the partners with allocated shares of profits in the proportion in which they share profits. The treatment is vice versa where there is an overall allowable loss and a partner (usually a salaried partner) has an allocated profit. Example 4.43 illustrates all of these principles.

■ Example 4.43

A, B and C are in a general partnership and they share profits as to one-third each of the balance after A's entitlement to an annual salary of $100. The results, after deducting partner's salary for three years are as follows:—

Basis period 1	$600	profit
Basis period 2	$180	loss
Basis period 3	$ 00	loss

Allocation — year of assessment 1	Total	A	B	C
Profit after A's salary	$300	$100	$100	$100
Add A's salary	100	100		
Adjusted assessable profits	$400	$200	$100	$100

Allocation — year of assessment 2	Total	A	B	C
Loss after A's salary	($180)	($ 60)	($ 60)	($ 60)
Add A's salary	100	100	—	—
Adjusted profit/(allowable loss)	($ 80)	$ 40	($ 60)	($ 60)
Sub-allocation		($ 40)	20	20
	—		($ 40)	($ 40)

Allocation — year of assessment 3	Total	A	B	C
Loss after A's salary	($ 60)	($ 20)	($ 20)	($ 20)
Add A's salary	100	100		
Adjusted assessable profit/(allowable loss)	$ 40	$ 80	($ 20)	($ 20)

Sub-allocation	($ 40)	20	20
	$ 40	—	—

Note:—
B and C could either claim Personal Assessment for year 2 (if eligible) or carry forward their shares of losses against their shares of profits in year 4 or subsequent years.

Where a corporation is a partner in a partnership it is necessary to ascertain that corporation's share of profits and losses because its profits are assessed at the corporate rate of Profits Tax (not separately assessed but embodied in the assessment on the partnership) and its losses are treated differently to those of partners who are individuals. For an illustration of the principles see Example 4.27 and the more detailed discussion in section 4.5.16.

If there is a change in a partnership by virtue of one or more partners withdrawing or the dissolution of the partnership or of the admission of one or more new partners, this would normally constitute a cessation of one business and the commencement of a new business with the consequent adjustments to the basis periods for years of assessment affected by the change. However, Sec. 22(3) provides that, so long as at least one person who was a partner (or sole proprietor) before the change is a partner after the change, the business is to be treated as continuous throughout so that there is no adjustment to basis periods. However, losses applicable to withdrawing partners lapse because of the operation of Sec. 19C(2). See Example 4.42.

There are some particular provisions in relation to the ascertainment of the assessable profits of a partnership and these are summarised as follows:—

(1) Rent payable to one of the partners or the spouse of a partner in respect of property used for the business of the partnership is only deductible to the extent of an amount equal to the assessable value of the land or buildings for Property Tax purposes (see section 2.3) (Sec. 16(1)(b)). This restriction was introduced at a time when Property Tax was based on a fixed notional amount. Now that Property Tax is based on actual rent paid, there is no real purpose in the restriction.

(2) Nothing can be deducted in respect of salaries or other remuneration of partners or their spouses, for MPF contributions in respect of the spouse of the proprietor or a partner, or for interest on partners' or their spouses' capital or loan accounts (Sec. 17(2)). Where the salary is paid to a spouse of a partner, there is an equivalent exemption from Salaries Tax under Sec. 8(2)(k).

4.8 Non-residents

Generally, a person's residence status is irrelevant for tax purposes in Hong Kong. Certainly, the basic test for chargeability to Profits Tax is framed without reference to a person's residence, domicile or place of incorporation. That is, if a person carries on a trade, profession or business in Hong Kong from which they derive profit, and those profits have a Hong Kong source, a liability to Profits Tax will generally arise irrespective of the person's residence.

Nonetheless, there are a number of places in the IRO where residence is relevant. For example, for the purpose of being able to elect for Personal Assessment, in the transfer pricing provisions of Sec. 20 and, most notably, the range of statutory exemptions available to non-residents which are discussed in point (17) of section 4.5.3.

Additionally, the IRO deals with a number of special situations where the potential tax payer is not physically or legally in Hong Kong and, in some places, the IRO uses the word "resident" without defining it. Also, a number of provisions are aimed at non-residents by implication; for example the deeming provisions in Sec. 15(1) (see section 4.5.4), many of which are aimed at payments made to persons who are not actually carrying on business in Hong Kong. In practice, where the IRO uses the terms "resident" or "non-resident" it is usually possible to identify the parties affected with no problem but if the question is ever disputed it is possible that the UK case law principles would be applicable. A detailed consideration of these is beyond the scope of this book but very broadly, residence in the case of an individual is governed by whether or not he has a place of accommodation available to him as a place of abode or whether he makes visits of a habitual and substantial nature; in the case of a company it is governed by where its central management and control is exercised, i.e. where its directors meet and in the case of a partnership it is governed by where it is managed and controlled.

An analysis of some of the provisions aimed at non-residents or persons without a place of business in Hong Kong is contained below.

4.8.1 Non-residents carrying on business in Hong Kong

As noted at the beginning of this chapter (see section 4.3), the residence of a person currently plays no part in determining that person's basic liability to Profits Tax, although a non-resident may be entitled to exemption in respect of certain specified types of profit. Accordingly, a non-resident is generally taxed in the same manner as a resident. Nonetheless, where a business which is based outside Hong Kong carries on a part of its business in Hong Kong (for example, through a branch), the IRD may encounter practical difficulties in ascertaining the assessable profits, for Profits Tax purposes, of that business. Such difficulties may arise for numerous reasons, including, for example, because the accounts of the business may be kept in a manner different to that normally adopted in Hong Kong, or because information relating to transactions between the Hong Kong branch and the head office, or even transactions undertaken by the head office which impact the assessable profits of the branch, is not readily available.

Rule 5 of the IRR deals, in effect, with the ascertainment of the assessable profits of a non-resident carrying on business in Hong Kong, but in fact refers to the "... *profits of a person having a permanent establishment in Hong Kong whose head office is situated elsewhere ...*". As discussed below, this Rule applies to persons who have a permanent establishment in Hong Kong; however, because this Rule deals only with ascertainment of the quantum of assessable profits, care should be taken in interpreting it, as it is often incorrectly interpreted as meaning that the absence of a permanent establishment will mean no Profits Tax liability can exist. Rather, in the absence of a permanent establishment, a person's assessable profits cannot be ascertained in accordance with Rule 5; however, they may still have a liability to Profits Tax if all the conditions necessary for such a liability are present, although the quantification will need to be determined without reference to Rule 5.

For the purpose of Rule 5, the definition of person in Sec. 2 is unnecessarily repeated in Rule 5(1), i.e. that a person includes a company, partnership or body of persons. The definition of permanent establishment in Rule 5(1) is, however, important and is similar to definitions contained in double taxation agreements. The definition includes the obvious physical place of business, i.e. a branch, management or other place of business which is purely a factual matter and it also includes an agency. An agent becomes a permanent establishment if:—

(1)   he has, and habitually exercises, a general authority to negotiate and conclude contracts on behalf of his principal; or

(2)   he has a stock of merchandise from which he regularly fills orders on behalf of his principal.

Note that (1) is not satisfied by a one-off authority to negotiate and conclude a specific contract; it must be a general authority and be regularly exercised for the principal to be regarded as having a place of business in Hong Kong. However, the principle applies equally in the case of an independent agent as to one under the employment or control of the principal, unlike in many double taxation agreements where an independent agent acting in the normal course of his business is excluded from the definition of permanent establishment. Situation (2) covers goods held on consignment by an agent in Hong Kong. Apart from constituting a place of business of the principal, goods sold on consignment give rise to an effective withholding tax liability as discussed under section 4.8.2.

Interestingly, an agent who has the power to purchase goods on behalf of a principal for shipment outside Hong Kong would appear to constitute a permanent establishment under paragraph (1) of the definition. However, such an agent arguably does not amount to the carrying on of a business by the principal in Hong Kong (see *Sully v Attorney-General* (2 TC 149), although it should be noted that that decision was concerned with slightly different statutory provisions and the question of whether a trade (which is a narrower term than business) was carried on. In any event, the IRD accepts that no liability to Profits Tax arises in respect of a person, who otherwise has no presence or activities in Hong Kong, merely because they have an office or agent in Hong Kong which is involved in the buying of goods. Accordingly, even though in such a situation the non-resident person may have a permanent establishment in Hong Kong, Rule 5 would not operate to impose a Profits Tax liability on that person.

Once it is established that a non-resident has a permanent establishment in Hong Kong in accordance with Rule 5, the method of ascertainment of assessable profits is laid down by Rule 5(2) as follows:

(1)   If branch accounts are kept which show the true profits arising in Hong Kong, these are adopted and adjusted in accordance with all the rules of Profits Tax. It is quite possible that a large part or even all of the profits may have a non-Hong Kong source in which case no liability would arise on that part.

(2)   Failing the provision of accounts for the branch, or where the accounts do not show the true position for the Hong Kong branch, the assessable profits may be ascertained by adjusting the worldwide profits to conform to Profits Tax principles and apportioning them on the basis of Hong Kong turnover to worldwide turnover.

(3)   Failing either (1) or (2), which would be exceptional, the assessor is empowered to fix the assessable profits as a fair percentage of the Hong Kong turnover. Clearly this is an arbitrary method and a tax payer would normally strive to ensure that his assessable profits could be ascertained under (1) or (2).

Rule 5 is part of the IRO and therefore any assessment made under its authority is subject to the objection and appeal procedure in the same way as assessments made under the authority of Part IV of the IRO.

■ Example 4.44

Ahso Ltd. is a Japanese company which sells portable radios around the world. It has no branch or office in Hong Kong but has appointed an independent wholesale agent in Hong Kong to represent it and accept orders from retailers on its behalf. Ahso ships orders direct to the retailers. The results for a year of assessment indicate the following:—

Worldwide profit (as adjusted)	$1,470,000
Turnover — Sales to Hong Kong retailers	$ 840,000
Worldwide sales	$5,880,000

If no branch accounts are prepared, the assessable profit is:—

$$\frac{840}{5,880} \times \$1,470,000 = \underline{\underline{\$210,000}}$$

Notes:—
(a) The worldwide profit will have been adjusted in accordance with the rules of Profits Tax as required by Rule 5(2)(c).
(b) If, for example, sales were being made into Hong Kong at a lower price than elsewhere, perhaps to break into the market, it would pay Ahso to prepare branch accounts as the profit is likely to be smaller than $210,000.
(c) If the agent only solicited orders which he then submitted to Japan for formal acceptance, Rule 5 would not apply and there may be no Profits Tax liability.

Rule 3 of the IRR is in principle similar to Rule 5 except that it applies specifically to banks whose head office is elsewhere than in Hong Kong. There is no reference to "permanent establishment" in Rule 3, presumably because in the special nature of banking business it is quite clear whether or not a non-resident bank has a branch in Hong Kong. In any event, a license is required from the Banking Commissioner before a banking business can be carried on in Hong Kong.

The methods of ascertaining assessable profits of the Hong Kong branch of a non-resident bank are, apart from straightforward branch accounts, not quite the same as for other types of business under Rule 5. The methods laid down in Rules 3(2) and 3(3) are:—

(1) If branch accounts are kept which show the true profits arising in Hong Kong, these are adopted and adjusted in accordance with the rules of Profits Tax.

(2) Failing the provision of accounts for the branch, or where the accounts do not show the true position for the Hong Kong branch, the assessable profits may be ascertained by adjusting the worldwide profits to conform to Profits Tax principles and apportioning them on the basis of the total Hong Kong assets to worldwide assets.

Note that in the case of other types of business under Rule 5, the basis of apportionment is turnover.

(3) Failing either (1) or (2), which would be exceptional, the assessor is empowered to estimate the Hong Kong profits. This is even more arbitrary than the similar provision for the businesses under Rule 5 where at least a fair percentage is applied to Hong Kong turnover, but it would be unusual for a bank to be unable to satisfy (1) or (2).

Rule 3 is part of the IRO and therefore any assessment made under its authority is subject to the objection and appeal procedure in the same way as assessments made under the authority of Part IV of the IRO.

See section 4.7.7 "Financial Institutions" for details of the special provisions which to apply in ascertaining the assessable profits of banks.

4.8.2 Goods on consignment

Goods on consignment which are held in Hong Kong on behalf of a non-resident principal and which are sold on behalf of that principal give rise to an automatic tax liability, often loosely referred to as consignment tax, which is akin to a withholding tax (Sec. 20A(3)). It is important to note that the section is not a charging section; rather, it is concerned with the collection of tax. The IRD's view appears to be that the agent should comply with the provision irrespective of whether the non-resident principal is actually liable to Profits Tax under the general charging provision of Sec. 14.

Sec. 20A(3) requires an agent who makes such consignment sales to submit a quarterly return to the Commissioner showing gross proceeds of such sales and at the same time remitting a sum equal to 1% of the gross proceeds or such lesser sum as the Commissioner may agree. In practice, only $^1\!/_2$% of gross proceeds is demanded.

The quarterly return is required to be made on Form BIR 52B. Disclosure is required in respect of sales made on behalf of residents as well as non-resident principals, although there is no obligation to retain tax from the proceeds of sales made on behalf of residents. Where the agent is unclear about the ownership of the goods, a certificate of ownership should be obtained by the agent from the principal and submitted to the IRD on Form IR89. If satisfied that Sec. 20A(3) does not apply, the IRD will issue a certificate of authority (Form IR89A) to the agent to remit the proceeds to the principal without deduction of tax.

The act of selling goods on consignment constitutes a permanent establishment under Rule 5 (see section 4.8.1) whereby the non-resident principal is regarded as carrying on business in Hong Kong and his assessable profits are to be ascertained in accordance with Rule 5. Accordingly, his true assessable profits may be ascertained and assessed in which case the consignment tax already paid would be taken into account. In practice, the consignment tax is usually regarded as the final liability but it would always be open to a non-resident principal to produce financial statements to show that his liability was in fact less than $^1/_2$% of gross sales proceeds.

The Commissioner is given power by Sec. 20A(3) to exempt from the consignment tax any person on such conditions as he thinks fit. In practice, it is understood that the Commissioner will generally limit the exemption to cases where an undertaking has been provided by the non-resident principal to settle his tax liability directly with the IRD.

■ Example 4.45

Billy Kan is Hong Kong agent for Desca Ltd., a Japanese company manufacturing T.V. sets for worldwide sale. Billy holds a consignment of the sets in Hong Kong and regularly fills local orders from the stock. Sales for the year have been:—

1st Quarter	$125,000	Billy's Commission	$12,500
2nd Quarter	$60,000	Billy's Commission	$6,000
3rd Quarter	$110,000	Billy's Commission	$11,000
4th Quarter	$95,000	Billy's Commission	$9,500

Billy is required by Sec. 20A(3) to submit a return of these sales to the IRD each quarter and to pay over the following sums which represent Desca's tax liability:—

1st Quarter	1/2% × $125,000 =	$ 625
2nd Quarter	1/2% × $ 60,000 =	300
3rd Quarter	1/2% × $110,000 =	550
4th Quarter	1/2% × $ 95,000 =	475
Tax for the year		$1,950

Note that the commission is not taken into account.

In fact, Desca's profits would be taxable pursuant to Inland Revenue Rule 5 and if it could produce a financial statement to show that its true profit from these sales was less than $11,143 ($11,143 @ 17.5% = $1,950) that would be to its advantage. Otherwise it is likely that $1,950 will be Desca's final liability for the year and will be paid by Billy deducting it from his remittances.

4.8.3 Hong Kong agents

Sec. 20A(1) gives the IRD wide powers to collect tax due from non- residents in respect of profits from business undertaken through a Hong Kong agent. A non-resident may be assessed directly, or in the name of his agent and, with regard to the latter point, it is specifically provided that an assessment can be raised on an agent irrespective of whether or not the agent has receipt of the profits.

Collection of the tax due may be enforced out of the assets of the non-resident or directly from the agent. Moreover, under Sec. 20A(2), an agent is required to retain out of any assets of the non-resident coming into his possession or control sufficient sums to meet the non-resident's tax liability; the agent is statutorily indemnified against claims by the non-resident in respect of such withholding.

Where more than one agent is involved, those agents may be assessed jointly or severally in respect of the non-resident's profits and collection may be enforced jointly and severally.

For these purposes, an agent is widely defined by Sec. 2 as including:

(1)   an agent, attorney, factor, receiver, or manager in Hong Kong of a non-resident principal; and

(2)   any person in Hong Kong through whom a non-resident principal is in receipt of profits or income arising in Hong Kong.

It was originally thought that this definition included a payer of a royalty etc. to an overseas principal; however, in *CIR v Asia Television Ltd.* (2 HKTC 198) it was held that the principal does not receive his income *through* but rather *from* a payer and, therefore, a payer cannot be an agent unless, of course, he is an agent contractually or otherwise as indicated in the definition in Sec. 2. Assessments upon payers who are not within the definition of agent may, however, be made under Sec. 20B (see paragraphs below).

The provisions of Secs. 20A(1) and (2), when combined with the wide definition of agent contained in Sec. 2, are very broad and can effectively impose withholding obligations on a wide range of businesses in respect of dealings on behalf of overseas customers. Nonetheless, such withholding obligations will only arise where the non-resident has a liability to Profits Tax under general principles; this, however, will often not be apparent to the agent and, therefore, gives rise to practical difficulties in trying to determine whether the provisions apply. The Government, in the 1996/97 Budget, finally acknowledged these practical difficulties and foreshadowed legislation to exempt certain types of business from the provisions. This legislation was ultimately enacted as Sec. 20AA which, in specified circumstances (see discussion below), deems stock brokers and investment advisers not to be agents for the purposes of Sec. 20A.

The position of stock brokers and invesment advisers was considered worthy of this special treatment due to the fact that they commonly deal with funds of non-resident clients on a discretionary basis. This means that if the non-resident's investment activities amount to a business, that business may be considered carried on in Hong Kong through the stock broker or investment adviser. Under general Profits Tax principles, therefore, any Hong Kong source profits of the non-resident risk being subject to Profits Tax. Further, under Sec. 20A, the stock broker or investment adviser could be assessed as agent for the non-resident and, in any event, would strictly be required to withhold sufficient amounts to meet the non-resident's liability. The practical difficulties in applying this provision, however, stem from the fact that the stock broker or investment adviser will often be unable to determine whether the non-resident's investment activities amount to a business, or to determine the non-resident's actual tax liability in respect of those profits. (With regard to the latter point, although the stock broker or investment adviser may know the amount of gross profit derived from the business done on behalf of the non-resident, he is unlikely to have full details of the non-resident's deductible expenses, his carried forward tax losses, or whether other loss making transactions were undertaken during the same year through another agent.) It was in recognition of the above difficulties, and presumably the potential adverse effect of the provisions on the stock broking and investment advisory business in Hong Kong, that the Government introduced Sec. 20AA to limit the application of Sec. 20A in respect of stock brokers and investment advisers.

Secs. 20AA(1)(a) and (b) are the main operative provisions and state that where the appropriate conditions are met, a "broker" or an "approved investment adviser" will not be deemed for the purposes of Sec. 20A to be an agent of a non-resident person. For these purposes, a "broker" is defined in Sec. 20AA(6) as either a registered dealer under Part VI of the *Securities Ordinance*, or an exempt dealer under that legislation to the extent of its activities as a dealer. Similarly, Sec. 20AA(6) defines "approved investment adviser" as a person registered as an investment adviser under Part VI of the *Securities Ordinance* or a person who would be required to be so registered but for an exemption under that ordinance but, again, only to the extent of its activities as an investment adviser.

The conditions for the exemption to apply to a transaction carried out through a broker are contained in Sec. 20AA(2). These restrict the granting of the exemption from Sec. 20A to transactions where:—

- the broker was carrying on the business of a broker at the time of the transaction. The purpose behind this requirement is unclear but it would seem to operate to deny the benefit of the provision to a person within the definition of a "broker" but whose business at the time of the transaction was not that of a broker. For example, it might apply to a broker acting as a fund manager in the transaction, although it is not clear why the benefit of the provisions should be denied in such circumstances;

- the transaction was carried out by the broker for the non-resident in the ordinary course of the business. Again, the purpose of this requirement is unclear but is presumably intended as an anti-avoidance provision, although it is difficult to see how the provisions could be abused in the absence of this restriction;

- the remuneration received by the broker is not less than the customary rate for the class of business. This appears to be yet another requirement aimed at restricting the provision to transactions carried out in the ordinary course of business;

- after the application of Sec. 20AA, the non-resident has no assessable profits for the year of assessment in respect of which the broker would be treated as his agent. In other words, all transactions through the broker must meet the conditions set out in Sec. 20AA(2), and

- the broker was not an associate of the non-resident. The term "associate" is extensively defined in Sec. 20AA(6) and essentially follows the definition used elsewhere in the IRO. See, for example, the discussion of the term in relation to Sec. 39E which is contained in section 5.9.2.

Similarly, the conditions under which the exemption from Sec. 20A is granted to an approved investment adviser are outlined in Sec. 20AA(3). These provide that the exemption is only available in respect of transactions where:—

- at the time of the transaction, the approved investment adviser was carrying on the business of an approved investment adviser. As with the similar provision in Sec. 20AA(2), this appears to operate to preclude the application of the provision where, although the transaction was carried out through a person within the definition of an approved investment adviser, that person carried out the transaction otherwise than in the course of such a business;

- the transaction was carried out for the non-resident in the ordinary course of the approved investment adviser's business;

- the remuneration of the approved investment adviser in connection with the transaction was at a rate not less than the customary rate for that class of business. Again, this seems to be merely another requirement to ensure that the transaction was carried out in the ordinary course of business;

- after the application of Sec. 20AA, the non-resident has no assessable profits for the year of assessment in respect of which the approved investment adviser would be treated as his agent. In other words, the exemption will only be granted if all transactions through the approved investment adviser meet the conditions set out in Sec. 20AA(3);
- the approved investment adviser was not an associate of the non-resident during the relevant year of assessment. For a discussion as to the meaning of associate, see the analysis of Sec. 20AA(2) above; and
- the approved investment adviser acted for the non-resident in an independent capacity. The meaning of "independent" for this purpose is dealt with in Sec. 20AA(5), which provides that an approved investment adviser will not be regarded as acting in an independent capacity unless, having regard to the legal, financial and commercial characteristics of the relationship with the non-resident, it would be considered a relationship between persons carrying on independent businesses and dealing with each other at arm's length. In practice, this will mean that the exemption will not be available when the approved investment adviser acts only, or predominantly, for the non-resident.

A diagrammatic analysis of the liability of a Hong Kong person to tax on behalf of a non-resident is contained in Figure 4.2.

4.8.4 Payers other than agents

Because a Hong Kong resident who pays sums of money to a non-resident person who is subject to Profits Tax thereon may not be an agent of the non-resident person (see previous paragraph), the IRD would be obliged to raise an assessment directly upon the non-resident person and this may be difficult to enforce. Nonetheless, Sec. 20B provides that an assessment can be raised upon the Hong Kong resident who makes payments to a non-resident in certain specified circumstances. The circumstances cover, broadly, two types of income upon which a non-resident is chargeable to Profits Tax, namely:—

(1)   The deemed business receipts chargeable under Secs. 15(1)(a), 15 (1)(b) or 15(1)(ba) (see section 4.5.4). This covers copyright royalties and payments for the use of intellectual property in Hong Kong, or

Figure 4.2   Determination of liability of Hong Kong person to assessment on behalf of non-resident (Sec. 20A)

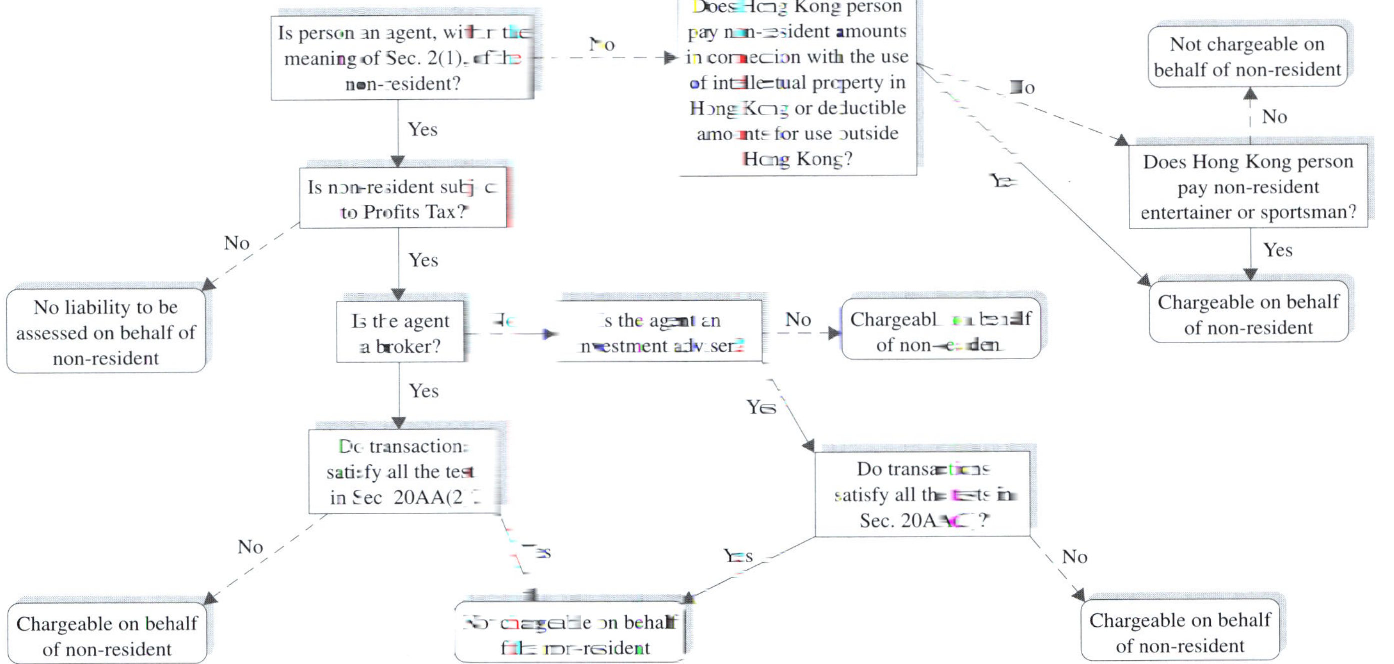

Note: This is intended to be a diagrammatic summary and must be considered in conjunction with the text.

      for use outside Hong Kong if those payments are deductible in Hong Kong (Sec. 20B(1)(a)).

(2) Payments in respect of appearances or performances in Hong Kong by entertainers or sportsmen (Sec. 20B(1)(b)).

Whilst liability under (1) is specifically deemed by the IRO, there are no specific provisions under which entertainers or sportsmen are deemed liable to Profits Tax. It may be the case that a professional entertainer or sportsman would be regarded as carrying on a business or profession in Hong Kong where a performance was given in Hong Kong, with a consequent liability arising under Sec. 14, but circumstances could be envisaged where this might not be so, e.g. a casual payment to an amateur.

It must be remembered that the provisions in Sec. 20B only provide for assessment and collection in circumstances where Profits Tax is already chargeable by provisions elsewhere in the IRO; Sec. 20B does not create chargeability. However, it seems that the provisions in Sec. 20B are only intended to apply in the case of entertainers or sportsmen in circumstances where Profits Tax liability is likely to already exist. In particular an entertainer or sportsman is defined by Sec. 20B(4) as someone who gives public performances, although it is not essential that the public must pay for admission. Furthermore, the performances have to be in connection with a commercial occasion or event which is defined in Sec. 20B(4) as comprising an occasion or event at which the performer might expect to be paid by virtue of his performance or which is intended to promote some sales or commercial activity by advertising, endorsement or sponsorship.

Where a non-resident person is chargeable to Profits Tax and his circumstances fall within (1) or (2) above, the assessment is raised upon any person in Hong Kong who has paid or credited the sums in question to the non-resident or, indeed, to any other non-resident person (Sec. 20B(2)). As an illustration of the fact that payments not made direct to the non-resident person who is taxable are still caught, payment might be made to the non-resident's agent outside Hong Kong. If, however, payment is made to his agent in Hong Kong, Sec. 20B(2) does not apply to the payer. In these circumstances the agent in Hong Kong would be assessable under Sec. 20A or alternatively upon that agent under Sec. 20B if he remits the funds to the non-resident.

Whether raised under Sec. 20A or Sec. 20B, the collection of tax is enforceable upon the payer in accordance with all the powers of enforcement and recovery provided in the IRO (Secs. 20A(1) and 20B(2)).

A payer in Hong Kong who is liable to receive an assessment under Sec.

20B in respect of a non-resident is required to retain out of his payments sufficient amounts to pay the tax and he is indemnified against the non-resident in respect of any such sum retained (Sec. 20B(3)). This poses a practical problem upon a payer who needs to know exactly how much the liability is going to be. In the case of liability under Sec. 15(1)(a), 15(1)(b) or 15(1)(ba) this is easy because Sec. 21A fixes the assessment at either 30% or 100% of the sum paid depending upon the particular circumstances (see section 4.5.4). However, in the case of entertainers or sportsmen there is no similar provision in the IRO and the extent of the assessment would depend upon the level of expenses claimable by the non-resident. Current practice, however, allows the payer to assume that allowable expenses amount to one-third of the payments and therefore to expect an assessment on the remaining two-thirds. The only other doubt that might arise is whether the person chargeable is an individual or a corporation. For example, it is quite common for entertainers to be employed by and perform on behalf of their own corporation and a payer might not be aware of this. If any doubt exists it is obviously wise to retain tax at the higher rate applicable to corporations.

Where an overpayment arises on an assessment under Sec. 20B, the repayment may be made to either, but of course not both, of the non resident or the payer (Sec. 79(3)).

See also *Departmental Interpretation & Practice Notes No. 17.*

■ Example 4.46

The Hongkong Hilama Hotel Ltd. organised a dinner theatre evening after which it had to remit $240,000 to an actor from the United Kingdom who had performed on the evening and $100,000 to a copyright-production company in the United States for music played on the evening. In addition a production adviser from the United Kingdom had advised upon and personally supervised the design and construction of sets, lighting and electronics and the hotel remitted $90,000 to him as well.

Assuming that the actor was appearing in his own right and not as an employee, he will be regarded as carrying on business in Hong Kong and be liable to Profits Tax under Sec. 14.

The musical copyright royalties are liable to Profits Tax under Sec. 15(1)(a).

Assuming that the production adviser is providing services in his own right and not as an employee, like the actor he would be liable to Profits Tax under Sec. 14.

The hotel company, being a person in Hong Kong, can expect to receive assessments under Sec. 20B(2) as follows:—

(1) $240,000 less expenses, say, $80,000 = $160,000 @ 16% = $25,600
(2) $100,000 × 30% = $30,000 @ 17.5% (Note)   = $ 5,250

The hotel company should retain the above sums when making payment and neither the actor nor the copyright production company could have any claim against the hotel company for the sums retained (Sec. 20B(3)).

It will not receive any assessment in respect of the sum paid to the production adviser because he is neither an entertainer nor a sportsman and the sum is not assessable under either Sec. 15(1)(a) or Sec. 15(1)(b). On the assumption that the hotel is not a contractual agent for this person, no assessment can be raised on the hotel company under Sec. 20A either and the IRD can resort only to direct assessment upon the production adviser.

Note:—

In the somewhat unlikely event that the hotel company was paying the musical copyright to an associate within the meaning of Sec. 21A(3) and the copyright had previously been owned, wholly or partly, by a person carrying on a trade, profession or business in Hong Kong, the hotel company's liability under Sec. 20B(2) would be $100,000 \times 100\% \times 17.5\% = \$17,500$.

■ Example 4.47

The facts are the same as in Example 4.46 except that all contractual arrangements in Hong Kong on behalf of all the parties were handled by a firm of Hong Kong solicitors, Messrs Monson, Jokes & Starter who also collected all funds from the hotel for ultimate remittance to their clients.

The hotel company has no liability to be assessed under Sec. 20B(2) because it has only made payments to another person in Hong Kong.

Monson, Jokes & Starter are agents of the non-residents by virtue of being contractual agents and/or being a person through whom the non-residents receive funds (see definition of agent in section 4.8.3).

They may therefore be assessed under Sec. 20B(2) in respect of payments to the actor and the copyright company in the amounts indicated in Example 4.46 and under Sec. 20A(1) in respect of the payment to the production adviser.

Alternatively, all three assessments could be raised under Sec. 20A(1).

4.8.5 Arm's length pricing

Arm's length pricing is not normally a problem to the IRD because it is more common for transactions between associated residents and non-residents to give rise to more profits to the resident in view of the usually higher tax rates which apply elsewhere.

However, there are provisions in Sec. 20 which are designed to counteract the diversion of profits from Hong Kong to a closely connected non-resident person. For this purpose a person is closely connected with another person if the Commissioner, in his complete discretion, considers that such persons are substantially identical or that the ultimate controlling interest of each is owned directly or indirectly by the same person or persons (Sec. 20(1)(a)). In the case of companies it is necessary to look at the ultimate controlling interests of each, if necessary looking through one company or series of companies that own shares in other companies. Also, nominee holdings must be ignored and the beneficial ownership ascertained (Sec. 20(1)(b)). Accordingly, the Commissioner has wide powers to identify persons as closely connected.

Where a resident person is found to be closely connected with a non-resident person under these rules (and resident is not defined but see section 10.1.1) and they carry on business together in such a manner that the profits which arise in Hong Kong to the resident are either nil or less than might be expected, the provisions of Sec. 20(2) are applicable. It is not as may be unexpected that the pricing in favour of the resident is adjusted to an arm's length price so that the resident's taxable profit is increased; the counteracting procedure is much more complicated in that the business done by the non-resident in pursuance of his connection with the resident is deemed to be carried on in Hong Kong and the profit derived by the non-resident therefrom is assessed in the name of the resident person as if he was the non-resident's agent.

A point to note is that it is not only underpriced sales proceeds or over-priced purchase costs which are caught but also the position where, because of special arrangements between the parties, the profits do not have a source in Hong Kong. The IRD of course has practical difficulties in identifying circumstances where the provisions apply and it is not commonly enforced other than in blatant avoidance cases.

■ Example 4.18

Dodger Ltd. is incorporated in Hong Kong and is owned equally by A, B, C and D. Ripoff S. A. is incorporated in Panama and is also owned equally by A, B, C and D. Dodger sells thingummybobs in Hong Kong at $20 each and, in respect of customers outside Hong Kong, sells to Ripoff at $10 each which in turn sells to the customers at $20 each.

(1) Dodger and Ripoff are sufficiently identical to be regarded as closely connected under Sec. 20(1) and it is therefore a question of whether Dodger is making less profit than might reasonably be expected.

(2) If Ripoff has a sales force which actively seeks out customers, bears shipping costs, deals with letters of credit, takes debt risks etc., the lower sale price may well be no lower than may be expected in the circumstances.

(3) However, if Ripoff does factually nothing other than reinvoice, the position will be challengeable under Sec. 20(2).

   In this event, the profit of $10 per unit earned by Ripoff, less any expenses properly attributable to that profit is deemed to be from a business carried on in Hong Kong and will be assessed in the name of Dodger Ltd. as agent.

(4) It is assumed that Ripoff concludes sales with customers independently of Dodger

because if in fact Dodger is concluding the sales and merely booking them in Ripoff, Ripoff would probably be regarded as carrying on business in Hong Kong regardless of Sec. 20(2).

4.9 Assessment and Payment of Tax

The assessing system for Profits Tax consists of a Provisional Profits Tax assessment in an estimated amount followed, after a return has been made, by a final Profits Tax assessment on the true figure in which the Provisional Profits Tax already paid for the year of assessment is credited. In practice the notice of assessment is a two part set containing the final Profits Tax assessment for a year of assessment and also the Provisional Profits Tax assessment for the immediately succeeding year of assessment (Sec. 63I(b)). A single Provisional Profits Tax assessment which is sometimes issued during the year of assessment in which a new business has commenced is, however, quite valid on its own (Sec. 63I(a)).

The charge to Provisional Tax is authorised by Sec. 63G and, when a new business has commenced, the Provisional assessment for the first year of assessment is estimated (Sec. 63H(4)) and the estimate is made from the details supplied by the tax payer in a Provisional Profits Tax return giving date of commencement, first accounting date and estimated profit or loss for the first six months of business in addition to other details of the business. The assessor is also empowered to estimate the Provisional assessment for the second year of assessment which he would do if the first year's true profit had not been ascertained by the time the assessment for the second year was due to be issued. He would base his estimate upon whatever information was available to him. In subsequent years the Provisional Profits Tax assessment is always in the same figure as the immediately preceding final assessment less any unrelieved losses carried forward from that final assessment (Sec. 63H(1)). However, any losses which have been deducted from that final assessment cannot, of course, be taken into account because they would not be available again (Sec. 63H(2)).

■ Example 4.49

Giddy Ltd. has an agreed assessable profit for 2006/07 as follows:—

Assessable profit	$165,000
Losses brought forward under Sec. 19C	($280,000)
Assessable profit	Nil
Losses carried forward under Sec. 19C	$115,000

The Provisional Profits Tax assessment for 2007/08 will be:—

Previous year's assessable profit	$165,000	
Losses brought forward under Sec. 19C	($115,000)	
Provisional assessment	$50,000	@ 17.5%

Where a final assessment is based on an accounting period of more or less than 12 months which could be the case in respect of a year of commencement or a year affected by a change of accounting date (see section 4.6.4) it would obviously be inappropriate to base the Provisional Profits Tax assessment for the succeeding year on the same figure and the assessor therefore is empowered to estimate the Provisional Profits Tax assessment in such circumstances (Sec. 63H(3)). What he in fact normally does is to pro-rate the figures to correspond to a twelve month period.

The assessor has further powers to estimate where the person is about to leave Hong Kong or it is otherwise expedient to quickly raise a Provisional Profits Tax assessment (Sec. 63H(6) or in the absence of a return Sec. 63H(5)).

Once assessed, the Commissioner is empowered to issue a notice of assessment and fix the due dates for payment (Sec. 63H(7)). As a Provisional Profits Tax assessment has to be made during the currency of the year of assessment and as it is common for tax rates and personal allowances to be fixed retrospectively, it can happen that these are changed after a Provisional Profits Tax assessment has been issued. Sec. 63H(7A) therefore provides that the assessment is not to be disturbed in this respect. The dates of payment are entirely at the discretion of the Commissioner but these are normally fixed in a consistent pattern which ensures that there is no element of payment in advance. The normal due date of payment is between November and January but, obviously, if an accounting date falls after the normal due date, to ask for full payment of the Provisional Profits Tax on the normal due date would call for a part payment in advance and, therefore, in those circumstances only 75% is demanded on the due date and the balance of 25% about three months later. However, as a matter of policy, if the first instalment is in default, the second instalment becomes immediately due. This enables the Commissioner to impose a surcharge on both instalments and enforce collection of both at the earlier date.

■ Example 4.50

If Giddy Ltd. had an agreed assessable profit of $165,000 for 2007/08 based on an accounting year ended 30th June 2007 its Provisional Profits Tax liability for 2008/09 would be:—

$165,000 @ 17.5% = $28,875 payable November 2008

If, however, its accounting date had been 31st March 2008, the payment dates would probably have been:—

$21,656   in January 2009
 7,219   after 31st March 2009
$28,875

If Giddy defaults on paying the January instalment, the total tax of $28,875 becomes immediately due together with a 5% surcharge.

When the final assessment for a year is raised, the Provisional Profits Tax already paid for that year is credited against the final liability (Sec. 63K(a)). Any balance of final liability is added to and payable on the same date as the first instalment of Provisional Profits Tax for the following year. Where the Provisional Profits Tax paid for a year of assessment exceeds the final liability for that year, the excess is not refunded but is deducted first from the first instalment of Provisional Profits Tax for the following year and then from the second instalment (Sec. 63K(b)). Any balance of overpayment still remaining is then repaid. Accordingly an overpayment for a year may not be recoverable until after the final liability for the following year has been ascertained and, therefore, a taxpayer should pay careful heed to the holdover provisions which are open to him. However, where an excess of Provisional Profits Tax over the final liability is applied against the Provisional Profits Tax for the next year and an opportunity arises to hold over all or part of the Provisional Profits Tax (see following paragraphs) which is frustrated by the fact that it is already paid by the overpayment set-off, it is departmental practice to refund the amount that would otherwise have been held over.

Because of the estimated nature of Provisional Profits Tax, there are provisions to enable collection of the tax to be wholly or partly held over in appropriate circumstances. Given the appropriate grounds, the taxpayer must apply in writing at least 28 days before the due date of payment for the holdover to be granted, or not later than 14 days after the date of the notice for payment, whichever is later (Sec. 63J(1)). If the opportunity is missed in respect of the first instalment, all or part of the second instalment may still be held over. The appropriate grounds in Sec. 63J(2) are:—

(1)   where the assessable profits for the year of assessment assessed to

Provisional Profits Tax are, or are likely to be, less than 90% of the amount assessed to Provisional Profits Tax. This is before taking into account losses brought forward. In the case of a claim under this heading it is normally necessary to submit documentary evidence such as management accounts although these need not be for the whole of the basis period; they can be for as long a period as is practicable in the circumstances and be grossed up to a 12-month period. It is normally not necessary to adjust the projected profit in accordance with Profits Tax principles except where differences are material;

(2) where a loss brought forward under Sec. 19C has not been taken into account or is incorrect;

(3) where the tax payer has ceased business or will cease before the end of the year of assessment and the assessable profits for the year of assessment assessed to Provisional Profits Tax are, or are likely to be, less than the amount assessed. Similar evidence will be required as in (1);

(4) where the tax payer has elected for Personal Assessment (see Chapter 6) and this is likely to reduce his liability for the year of assessment; or

(5) where the final assessment for the preceding year (upon which the Provisional Profits Tax assessment is of course based) is under objection (see Chapter 9). As will be seen, this is also an occasion for a holdover claim in respect of the final assessment as well.

Any holdover is entirely at the discretion of the IRD (Sec. 63J(3)) but in practice, where the rules for application have been complied with and the grounds satisfied, the holdover will be given in all but exceptional cases. The holdover does not automatically apply to the whole of the Provisional Profits Tax, only to the part which is shown to be affected by the grounds cited. The IRD must in all cases notify their decision in writing (Sec. 63J(4)).

Where the holdover is granted, it will be effective until the final liability for the year is ascertained and due for payment but in the case of ground (5) above, if the objection against the previous year's assessment is determined or settled earlier, the earlier date will apply (Sec. 63J(1)).

■ Example 4.51

Oldit Ltd. has received the following composite assessment after submitting its Profits Tax return based on its accounting year ended 28 February 2007:—

2006/07 Final

Assessable Profits		$275,000
Sec. 19C losses brought forward		(55,000)
Net chargeable		$220,000
Profits Tax @ 17.5%		$ 38,500
Less: Provisional Profits Tax assessed	$42,000	
Less heldover	12,000	(30,000)
Net due		$ 8,500

2007/08 Provisional

Assessable	$275,000	
Provisional tax @ 17.5%		48,125
		$ 56,625

Total tax payable as follows:—

	23.01.2008	23.04.2008
2006/07 Final	$ 8,500	
2007/08 Provisional	36,094	$12,031
	$44,594	$12,031

The management accounts for the period from 1 March 2007 to 30 November 2007 show a net profit of $161,000 including a capital profit of $20,000. Oldit's tax representatives therefore submit a holdover claim on 23 December 2007 under Sec. 63J(2)(a) showing the following expected profit for the year ended 28 February 2008:—

Profits for 9 months to 30.11.2007	$161,000
Less: Capital profit	(20,000)
	$141,000
Extended to 12-month period ($\times$ 4/3) =	$188,000

The tax to be held over is therefore ($275,000 – $188,000)

$$= \$87,000 @ 17.5\%$$
$$= \$15,225$$

75% is held over against the first instalment and 25% against the second instalment as follows:—

	23.01.2008	23.04.2008
Due — Final	$ 8,500	
Due — Provisional	36,094	$12,031
	$44,594	$12,031
Held over	(11,419)	(3,806)
Now payable	$33,175	$ 8,225

Notes:—

(a) If the claim had not been made by 27 December 2007 (assuming the notice for payment was issued prior to 13 December 2007), the whole of the first instalment of $44,594 would have been payable but the whole of the second instalment of $12,031 could have been held over.

(b) If there is default in paying the first instalment of $33,175, both instalments totalling $41,400 become immediately payable together with a 5% surcharge.

(c) No further tax is payable until the final liability for 2007/08 is established when Provisional Tax paid of $32,900 is credited and any balance due will be payable in early 2009.

Apart from the foregoing, the general provisions governing assessments, objections and appeals, payment of tax and double taxation relief as contained in Parts X, XI, XII and XIII of the IRO respectively, are applicable (see Chapters 8, 9 and 10).

Chapter 5 ■

Depreciation Allowances

5.1 Legislation

The law governing depreciation allowances is contained in Part VI of the IRO (Secs. 33A to 40). Subsidiary legislation covering, primarily, the rates of depreciation is contained in Rule 2 of the IRR.

5.2 Scope of the Reliefs

Depreciation allowances represent the statutory means of allowing tax relief for capital expenditure incurred on the acquisition of fixed assets and essentially replaces, for tax purposes, the depreciation charge in the financial accounts. In addition to providing the rates at which allowances are granted, the statutory rules also determine the type of expenditure which qualifies for the various types of allowances. A consequence of the limitations on the types of qualifying expenditure is that some capital expenditure will not qualify for depreciation allowances nor, due to the operation of Sec. 17(1) (c), for any other form of tax relief. On the other hand, some capital expenditure on fixed assets qualifies for an outright deduction under Secs. 16F and 16G, which are considered in detail in section 1.5.8.

Depreciation allowances are, in practice, predominantly granted in respect of Profits Tax, although it must not be overlooked that Sec. 12(1)(b) provides for depreciation allowances in respect of relevant capital expenditure to be deductible for Salaries Tax purposes.

There are broadly three areas of capital expenditure for which separate rules apply in computing depreciation allowances. These are—

- Industrial Buildings;
- Commercial Buildings; and
- Plant and Machinery.

In the case of industrial buildings and plant and machinery, both an initial allowance at the outset and an annual allowance are available. For commercial buildings, only an annual allowance is granted. When an industrial or commercial building is disposed of, or indeed in certain other specified circumstances, a balancing allowance or balancing charge may arise, which is a means of adjusting the total allowances to the actual net cost of the building over its period of use. Although this is the theoretical intention, it does not always prove to be the case because of statutory adjustments to the cost or to the disposal proceeds in certain circumstances. In the case of plant and machinery, however, the normal method of calculation of the allowances is designed to avoid, other than in certain circumstances, the necessity to calculate balancing allowances or charges.

There are special provisions to cover plant and machinery on hire purchase, basis periods, assets bought from or sold to associated persons at other than market value and assets replaced by similar assets.

In the case of certain plant and machinery subject to a lease, there are extensive anti-avoidance provisions which limit depreciation allowances thereon.

5.3 Industrial Buildings

Separate rules apply to expenditure incurred on the construction of an industrial building, the meaning of which is extensively defined. An industrial building must be distinguished from a commercial building which is also defined and for which the allowances are less generous. It is also important to isolate expenditure which, although for most purposes may be considered part of a building, may in fact separately qualify as plant and machinery and thereby attract more generous allowances; examples of such expenditure include air conditioning and lift machinery.

5.3.1 Qualifying expenditure

In order to qualify for relief a person must incur capital expenditure on the construction of a building or structure which is to be an industrial building occupied for the purposes of a trade (Sec. 34(1)). A number of important points emerge from this, including the following:—

(1)   It must be capital expenditure, although naturally one would expect revenue expenditure to be deductible in full against profits; in fact, the definition of capital expenditure for this purpose in Sec. 40(1) specifically provides that expenditure which is otherwise deductible must be excluded. Furthermore, that definition provides that grants, subsidies or similar financial assistance must be deducted from the otherwise qualifying expenditure. Sec. 40(1) does, however, specifically provide that capital expenditure includes interest and commitment fees which have been incurred on a loan made for the sole purpose of financing the provision of the asset, but only if not deductible under any other provision. Following the decision in *Wharf Properties Ltd. v CIR* [1997] (1 HKRC 90-085), interest incurred on loans used to finance the construction of an industrial building where the person incurring the expenditure is intending to hold the building as a capital asset, is not deductible during the construction period and therefore, such interest is included in the

definition of capital expenditure for the purpose of calculating depreciation allowances. Where, however, the person constructing the building is intending to sell the completed building (i.e. the building is constructed by a property developer), such interest will be deductible to the developer under Sec. 16(1)(a) providing it meets the other conditions for deductibility (which are discussed in section 4.5.8). Accordingly, such interest is generally not included in the definition of capital expenditure for the purpose of industrial building allowances. This does not, however, put a subsequent purchaser of the building at a disadvantage since, as discussed below, such a person's allowances are based on the net sale price of the building rather than the expenditure incurred by the developer of that building.

(2)   The expenditure need only be incurred by legal obligation in the basis period; there is no requirement that relief depends upon actual payment (see section 4.5.6 for a discussion of when a liability is incurred).

(3)   The expenditure must be on the construction of a building or structure and, therefore, expenditure not directly related to construction does not qualify. In particular, expenditure on the acquisition of, or of rights in or over land is excluded by Sec. 40(3). Similarly, expenditure on demolition of a previous building does not qualify but site investigation work does (D 5/79). However, capital expenditure on an existing industrial building or part of a building will qualify even though it does not physically give rise to any additional structure, i.e. improvements. As will be seen, there are provisions which grant annual allowances to the purchaser of a completed building. However, unless the purchase is of an unused building from a person whose business comprises property development and sale, the expenditure which qualifies is based upon the original cost of construction rather than the purchase price (unless the latter is lower).

(4)   It must be an industrial building or structure as defined in Sec. 40(1) which is used for the purpose of a trade, although it does not necessarily need to be used by the person who incurs the expenditure. In other words, a property investment company can lease a building to another person and still obtain the industrial building allowance so long as the building itself qualifies by virtue of the lessee's use of it. The most important criterion is the use to which the building is put because this largely governs whether it falls within the definition of industrial building.

The types of use which can qualify a building or structure as an industrial building or structure are laid down in Sec. 40(1) as follows:—

(1) Use in a trade carried on in a mill, factory or other similar premises. This is, of course, largely a question of fact but see *Ellerker v Union Cold Storage Co.* (22 TC 195) wherein it was held that premises used to manufacture and store ice fell within this definition.

(2) Use in a transport, tunnel, dock, water, gas or electricity undertaking or a public telephone or telegraph service. Thus, the mass transit railway tunnels and stations qualify as industrial buildings as do power stations, telephone exchanges, etc. This definition extends to all forms of transport businesses, for example buildings associated with airline activities and even with taxi businesses although, as will be seen, certain buildings or parts of buildings are specifically excluded even if connected with a qualifying trade.

(3) Use in a trade consisting of the manufacture of goods or materials or the subjection of any goods or materials to any process. A manufacturing trade is relatively easy to identify but whether or not goods have been subjected to a process is more difficult to determine. The processing must be the nature of the trade and not something which is incidental to a trade consisting primarily of some other activity, e.g. distributing (see *CIR v Tai On Machinery Works Ltd.* (HKTC 411)). UK law in this respect is identical and in *Kilmarnock Equitable Co-operative Society v CIR* (42 TC 675) it was held that screening and packaging coal was a process for this purpose. A motor repair workshop is regarded as within the definition although, for example, a workshop where motor cars are polished and tuned before being placed in a showroom may not be. In the case of *CIR v Aberdeen Restaurant Enterprises Ltd.* (2 HKTC 330) a kitchen was held not to be an industrial building because, although cooking of food is subjecting it to a process, the process is only incidental to the service business of running a restaurant. See also *D 3/87* and *D 4/87* where pest fumigation was held to be a process.

(4) Use in a trade which consists of the storage of:—
  (i)   goods or materials to be used in the manufacture of other goods or materials;
  (ii)   goods or materials which are to be subjected to a process;
  (iii) goods or materials on their arrival into Hong Kong.
  Note that the trade must be one of storage. Of course, if the building was to house goods awaiting manufacture or process by the store

owner, the building would qualify under (3) above but if the building was for storing goods on their arrival into Hong Kong and the store owner was a retailer or distributor, the building would not qualify because the trade is not one of storage nor is it within (1), (2) or (3) above.

(5) Use in a farming business.

(6) Use in research and development related to any type of trade, profession or business. Thus a laboratory attached to a trade, profession or business which did not otherwise qualify would attract the allowances. This should not be confused with the 100% relief given for capital expenditure on research and development under Sec. 16B because expenditure on buildings is specifically excluded. Otherwise, the definition of research and development in Sec. 16B (4)(a) probably applies (see (10) under section 4.5.8).

It must be remembered that the allowances are available not only in respect of building, but also "structures". The term "structure" is not defined for this purpose and, must, therefore, be given its usual meaning which clearly extends beyond what one normally understands as a building. The IRD in *Departmental Interpretation & Practice Notes No. 2* (see Appendix 2) accepts that "structure" includes:—

- Walls
- Bridges
- Dams
- Roads
- Boreholes and wells
- Sewers
- Water mains
- Tunnel linings
- Wharves (which are specifically excluded from the definition of plant and machinery by Rule 2(3) of the IRR)
- Railing sidings

It is not essential that the whole of a building or structure should qualify as an industrial building or structure. If a part qualifies, the relevant proportion of capital expenditure attracts the allowances. However if that part of a building or structure which does not qualify attracts not more than 10% of the capital expenditure on the whole, the whole is treated as qualifying expenditure.

However, proviso (ii) to the definition of "industrial building or structure" in Sec. 40 states that the following buildings, structures, or any part, thereof do not qualify, regardless of the fact that they may be associated with a qualifying trade:—

- Dwelling house (other than for housing manual workers)
- Retail shop
- Showroom
- Hotel
- Offices

These non-qualifying uses are subject to the 10% rule mentioned earlier if they represent part of a total building. However, it is also specifically provided that any building or part of a building which is provided for the welfare of workers in the employment of a person engaged in one of the qualifying trades (1) to (5) listed earlier, qualifies as an industrial building. This would apply, for example, to a canteen or sporting facilities for staff.

Not every person, however, constructs his own industrial building; in fact most persons either buy them from a property developer or buy a used building from another person. The IRO lays down what is to constitute the base for calculating the allowances in these cases but, as will be seen, the principle of "cost of construction" still remains unless the purchase is from a person whose business comprises property development and sale and who has not used the property.

If a taxpayer purchases a building which is to be used as an industrial building and capital expenditure was incurred on its construction by the vendor who was not in the business of developing buildings for sale and did not bring the building into use as an industrial building, the vendor is entitled to no allowances (Sec. 35B(a)). However, the purchaser is entitled to allowances and these will be based upon the lesser of his net purchase price and the costs to the vendor of the construction. For this purpose, the "net" price paid by the taxpayer is the gross price less that portion attributable to the acquisition of rights over the land upon which the building is constructed. Further, assuming the purchaser actually brings the building into use as an industrial building, this expenditure will be deemed to have been incurred on the date when the purchase price becomes payable (Sec. 35B(b)(ii)). If there is a string of sales before the building is brought into use, it is only the person who first brings it into use who qualifies for the allowances which, again, will be based upon the lower of the purchase price and the actual cost of construction (Sec. 35B(b) proviso (b)).

Where, on the other hand, a taxpayer purchases a building unused from a person whose business includes developing buildings for sale, he is (assuming he brings it into use as an industrial building) deemed to have incurred expenditure on the construction thereof equal to the net price paid by him (Sec. 35B(b)(i)). Where there is a string of sales before the building is brought into use, only the person who actually first brings the building into use can obtain the allowances. In such circumstances, the allowances are based on the lower of the net price paid by the first purchaser and the net price paid by the person who first brought the building into use (Sec. 35B(b) proviso (a)).

■ Example 5 1

Plastigames Ltd. was expanding rapidly and decided to purchase a new factory in Kwai Chung from the builder, Buildafac Ltd., and did so at a cost of $15 million which included $6 million for the associated land. The construction work cost Buildafac $7 million. The factory proved insufficient and Plastigames acquired an identical factory on adjacent land from a textile company which constructed the building but reductions in trade prevented it being used. It cost the textile company $7 million to build and Plastigames paid $15 million including $6 million for the land. Under Sec. 35B(b)(i) the allowable cost of the first factory to Plastigames is $9 million, i.e. what it paid but under Sec. 35B(b)(ii) the allowable cost of the second factory is $7 million, i.e. the textile company's cost of construction.

Where a taxpayer purchases a building or structure from a person who has previously used it, either as an industrial building or otherwise, his allowances are based on the residue of expenditure immediately after the purchase (Sec. 34(2)(b)). The term "residue of expenditure" for the purposes of industrial buildings allowance is defined in Sec. 40(1) and is effectively the amount by which tax relief given on the cost of the property is limited to the cost of construction, no matter how many taxpayers have claimed allowances in respect of such construction expenditure. A claimant can, in effect, only claim relief on the balance of any construction cost in respect of which allowances have not already been granted to another claimant; since, however, balancing allowances and charges are taken into account, it is often the case that, upon sale, a balancing charge equal to the whole of the allowances granted arises and, therefore, the purchaser can claim relief on the entire construction expenditure again. The residue of expenditure is quite simply:—

The historical cost of construction
Less: Initial, annual and balancing allowances given
Plus: Balancing charges made

Previously, when calculating the residue of expenditure for an industrial building it was necessary only to take into account initial and annual allowances and balancing charges and allowances arising under the industrial buildings provisions. Because a building may be a commercial building at some time and an industrial building at other times, however, Sec. 40(1) was amended from the 2004/05 year of assessment to provide that the original construction cost is to be also adjusted for any annual allowances or balancing charges and allowances under the commercial building provisions when calculating the residue of expenditure.

In computing this residue it is also necessary to take into account notional annual allowances at the rate of 2% for years of assessment up to 1964/65 and at 4% thereafter for any year of assessment for which a claim was not made. In other words, the write-off available for the construction costs operates on an availability basis rather than a usage basis, and therefore is reduced by notional allowances in respect of any years when allowances were not granted.

■ Example 5.2

Soldafac Ltd. has owned an industrial building since May 1994 for which the cost of construction was $9,000,000. It sold the building to Bortafac Ltd. in July 2007 for $20 million which includes the land value of $8 million.

Soldafac had received depreciation allowances of $6,120,000 but no claim had been made for 2000/2001 when the building had been temporarily out of use.

Upon sale, Soldafac has a balancing charge of $6,120,000 (see section 5.3.4) and, therefore, immediately after the sale, the residue of expenditure is as follows:—

Cost of Construction		$9,000,000
Less: Allowances given	$6,120,000	
Notional Allowance — 2000/2001 (4%)	360,000	6,480,000
		$2,520,000
Plus: Balancing Charge		6,120,000
Residue of Expenditure		$8,640,000

Bortafac's qualifying expenditure is $8,640,000.

When the purchase price is less than the cost of construction, the qualifying expenditure to the purchaser cannot, of course, exceed what he pays. This is illustrated as follows:—

■ Example 5.3

The same facts as Example 5.2 except that the sale price is $8 million for the building.

Soldafac's balancing charge is computed as follows (see section 5.3.4):—

Sale Proceeds		$8,000,000
Notional Residue		(2,520,000)
Balancing Charge		$5,480,000

The residue of expenditure immediately after the sale is:—

Cost of Construction		$9,000,000
Less: Allowances given	$6,120,000	
Notional Allowance 2000/2001 (4%)	360,000	6,480,000
		$2,520,000
Plus: Balancing Charge		5,480,000
		$8,000,000

Bortafac's qualifying expenditure is therefore equal to its cost of purchase, $8,000,000.

5.3.2 Initial allowance

A person who incurs capital expenditure on the construction of a building
or structure which is to qualify as an industrial building becomes entitled to
an initial allowance for the year of assessment which relates to the basis
period in which the expenditure was incurred (Sec. 34(1)). The allowance is
available even if the building or structure is not yet in use as an industrial
building. Furthermore, expenditure incurred before a trade is commenced is
treated as if it was incurred on the day on which trading commences (Sec.
40(2)). However, if, when the building or structure is first brought into use,
it does not qualify as an industrial building, any initial allowance already
given is withdrawn by additional assessment (Sec. 34(1) proviso (b)).

The initial allowance is 20% of the qualifying expenditure and is only
granted to the person who incurs the cost of construction. It is not given on
qualifying expenditure obtained by purchase except where under Sec. 35B
a purchaser is treated as having incurred the expenditure by virtue of the
fact that he purchases the building or structure unused.

5.3.3 Annual allowance

In order to qualify for an annual allowance, it is not necessary for a claimant
himself to incur expenditure on the cost of construction; he must, however,
have an interest in the building or structure at the end of the basis period for
the year of assessment and that interest must be the "relevant interest" in
relation to the capital expenditure incurred on the cost of construction.
"Relevant interest" is defined by Sec. 40(1) and merely means that the
claimant must hold the same legal interest in the property as the person who
incurred the original expenditure. In other words, expenditure by an owner
entitles the owner and subsequent owners to claim annual allowances in

relation to that expenditure and expenditure by a lessee entitles that lessee and his subsequent assignees to claim annual allowances in relation to that expenditure.

Furthermore the building or structure must be in qualifying use at the end of the basis period. The annual allowance in respect of cost of construction incurred by the claimant is 4% of the qualifying expenditure (Sec. 34(2)(a)). In the case of persons inheriting the residue of the expenditure, the amount of the annual allowance varies according to the formula discussed after Example 5.4.

■ Example 5.4

Constructafac Ltd. built a building in its accounting year ended 31st December 2005 at a cost of $6 million. It could not find a tenant until the year ended 31st December 2006 when it granted a lease to Yewsafac Ltd. In its year ended 31st May 2007 Yewsafac incurred additional qualifying expenditure of $800,000 before bringing the factory into use on 15th January 2007.

Initial allowance depends on the cost of construction; therefore both companies qualify for initial allowance as follows:—

   Constructafac   20% × $6 million = $1.2 million for 2005/06
   Yewsafac   20% × $800,000 = $160,000 for 2007/08

Annual allowance depends upon the "relevant interest" as follows:—

   Allowance based on $6 million (or the residue thereof) to the owner at the end of his basis period.
   Allowance based on $800,000 (or the residue thereof) to the lessee at the end of his basis period.

Accordingly the following allowances arise:—

   To Constructafac, 4% × $6 million for 2006/07 and each subsequent year of assessment at the end of the basis period for which it is still the owner and the building is in use for a qualifying purpose. Subsequent owners will receive annual allowances based on $6 million or the residue thereof (Note (a)).

   To Yewsafac, 4% × $800,000 for 2007/08 and each subsequent year of assessment at the end of the basis period for which it is still the lessee. Subsequent assignees of Yewsafac's lease will receive annual allowances based on $800,000 or the residue thereof (Note (b)).

Notes:—
(a) Constructafac receives no annual allowance for and 2005/06 because the factory was not in use at 31st December 2005.
(b) There can be any number of sub-tenants and each would have a separate "relevant interest". If Yewsafac granted a sub-lease it could continue to claim annual allowances based on $800,000. If Constructafac sold its interest as owner, this would not affect Yewsafac's continuing claim based on $800,000.

When the relevant interest changes hands, the purchaser inherits the residue of the expenditure related to that relevant interest as discussed in section 5.3.1. The rate of the purchaser's annual allowance depends upon a formula which takes into account when the building or structure was first used and an assumed depreciable life based on that first date of use. To understand why there are two different formulae dependent upon the date of first use, it only needs to be known that until 1964/65 the rate of annual allowance was 2% (i.e. a 50-year assumed life) and from 1965/66 it has been 4% (i.e. a 25-year assumed life).

The annual allowance for a building or structure purchased from a previous user is therefore as follows (Sec. 34(2)(b)):—

(1)   First used before the basis period for 1965/66

$$\text{Residue of Expenditure} \times \frac{2}{\text{No. of years of assessment from the year the purchaser acquired the building or structure to the 50th year after first use}}$$

(2)   First used during or after the basis period for 1965/66

$$\text{Residue of Expenditure} \times \frac{1}{\text{No. of years of assessment from the year the purchaser acquired the building or structure to the 25th year after first use.}}$$

Although these formulae and the fixed 4% annual allowance provide a fixed annual allowance year by year, the total allowances (including any initial allowance) must not exceed the total allowable expenditure; accordingly, the final annual allowance is often a balancing figure (Sec. 34(2)(c)). If the building is not in use for any year of assessment it is necessary to write off a notional allowance and the amount to be written off is 4% of original cost and not, for example, any recomputed allowance as above (see Examples 3 and 4 in *Departmental Interpretation & Practice Notes No. 2*, which is reproduced as Appendix 2).

As each new item of expenditure on an existing building constitutes, in effect, another "part" of the building, a purchaser will normally have to make separate computations under the foregoing formulae for each piece of expenditure because the period of depreciable life will run from the date of the expenditure and not the date of first use of the original building.

■ **Example 5.5**

Same facts as in Example 5.2 and assuming that the companies' accounting periods are to 31st December in each case.

The residue of expenditure available to Bortafac has been ascertained at $8,640,000. The year of assessment of first use was 1994/95. The 25th year thereafter is 2019/2020. The year of assessment in which Bortafac acquired the building is 2007/08.

Therefore the annual allowance to Bortafac for 2007/08 et seq. until the residue is used up is:—

$$\$8,640,000 \times \frac{1}{2006/07 \text{ to } 2018/19 \text{ inclusive}} = \$8,640,000 \times \frac{1}{13}$$

$$= \$664,615$$

Notes:—

(1) If Soldafac had incurred further expenditure since first use, there would have to be a separate computation, as in Example 5.2, of each residue of expenditure and consequently a separate computation as above of each amount of annual allowance in respect of each residue.

(2) If Bortafac did not use the building as an industrial building for any year of assessment, it would be necessary to write off a notional allowance of 4% of original cost of $9,000,000, i.e. $360,000, and not $664,615 (see Examples 3 and 4 in Appendix 2).

5.3.4 Balancing allowances and charges

In order to relate the total depreciation allowances to a claimant over his period of relevant interest in a building or structure to the exhaustion of his qualifying expenditure, balancing allowances are granted or balancing charges made on specified occasions which are related to the cessation of use by the claimant having the relevant interest in the building or structure. The specific occasions identified by Sec. 35(1) are as follows:—

(1) The relevant interest in the building or structure is sold;

(2) If the relevant interest is a leasehold, the lease comes to an end other than in circumstances where the leaseholder acquires the reversionary interest. However, notwithstanding the termination of a lease, this is not to apply as an event giving rise to a balancing allowance or charge if either:—

   (i) the lessee remains in possession without being granted a new lease in which case the lease is regarded as subsisting so long as he remains in possession (Sec. 35A(a)); or

   (ii) a new lease is granted either by re-grant or under the terms of an option in the first lease in which case the original lease is regarded as continuing throughout the life of the new lease (Sec. 35A(b)); or

(3)   The building or structure is destroyed or demolished or ceases altogether to be used. Demolition would, of course, normally result in a balancing allowance because there are no disposal proceeds. Sec. 35(b)(ii), however, denies a person a balancing allowance if the building or structure is demolished for purposes not connected with, or not in the ordinary course of, the trade, profession or business for which the building or structure was used before the demolition and which gave rise to the annual allowances under either the industrial buildings or commercial buildings provisions. In other words, the allowance can be given where a factory is demolished to build a better one for the same business but not where it is demolished for re-development for resale. If, however, the building is sold giving rise to a balancing allowance and the new owner demolishes it, the proviso cannot deny the allowance because it is only applicable where demolition is the reason for claiming a balancing allowance.

Moreover, Sec. 35(b)(i) provides that a balancing allowance is not available where the building or structure was not in use either as a commercial building or structure or an industrial building or structure immediately before it was sold, demolished or the leasehold interest came to an end. It is not immediately apparent why this restriction, which disadvantages a person who ceases to use a building or structure in their business but then leaves it vacant for a period before selling it, was inserted into the provisions. Granting a balancing allowance in such circumstances would not appear to be open to exploitation or be disadvantageous to the IRD when compared to selling the building or structure while it is being used as a commercial or industrial building or structure, particularly since the amount of the balancing allowance would effectively be reduced by any notional allowances for the period the building or structure was not being used.

A balancing allowance equal to the remaining unrelieved qualifying expenditure arises where there are no sale proceeds or insurance, salvage or compensation moneys; where there are any such receipts, the balancing allowance is the excess of the residue of expenditure over such receipts (Sec. 35(2)(a)). Where the receipts exceed the residue of expenditure, the excess is a balancing charge (Sec. 35(3)(a)). The balancing charge cannot, however, exceed the aggregate of initial and annual allowances already given to that person on the building or structure (Sec. 35(3)(b)); in other words the balancing charge procedure cannot amount to a capital gains tax. It follows, of course, that the disposal proceeds of a building or structure must be suitably apportioned where part or parts of the original expenditure did not qualify for relief.

As noted, a balancing charge or allowance is calculated by comparing the residue of expenditure to the sale, insurance, salvage or compensation "moneys". In *D 26/02*, a taxpayer sought to argue that "moneys" referred to cash only and did not extend to consideration in kind. As, in that case, an industrial building was exchanged for another property, the taxpayer sought to claim a balancing allowance for the whole of the residue of expenditure on the grounds that no "sale moneys" were received. The Board of Review, in rejecting the taxpayer's claim, justified the adoption of a broader interpretation of the term "sale moneys" than sought by the taxpayer on a number of different grounds. In particular, they considered that the narrower interpretation would give rise to an absurd result where a property was transferred to a creditor in settlement of a debt, and also that the use of a different term in the related provision of Sec. 38B indicated an intention to adopt a broader meaning. Further, the Board looked to provisions in the UK legislation upon which Sec. 35 was based and found that these made it clear that the legislature had intended a broader interpretation of the term.

■ Example 5.6

Onafac owned a piece of land on which are Factory A and Factory B which it used for its business and for which the residual value of unrelieved qualifying expenditure after 2006/07 allowances is $278,000 and $1,120,000 respectively. During the accounting year ended 31st December 2007 Factory A was demolished to allow Onafac to build a bigger one on the same site. When it was completed in the year ended 31st December 2008, Factory B and the piece of land on which it stands was sold for $5 million. The original cost of construction of Factory B was $2 million. The annual allowance for 2007/08 on Factory B is $80,000.

Onafac has a balancing allowance of $278,000 for 2007/08 on Factory A but it would not have been allowed if the objective had been to build something on the vacant site for resale.

For 2008/09 it has a balancing charge in respect of the disposal of Factory B, which is computed as follows:—

Qualifying Expenditure	$2,000,000
Allowances given up to 2007/08	960,000 .... (1)
Residual Value	$1,040,000
Sale Proceeds (Note (a))	2,500,000
Excess	$1,460,000 .... (2)

The balancing charge is the lesser of (1) or (2) and is therefore $960,000.

Notes:—

(a) It is necessary to divide the sale proceeds between the building, or part, which qualifies for industrial building allowances and the land plus any part of the building which does not qualify. For the purpose of this example 50% is taken as the relevant apportionment. In practice, the apportionment is generally agreed with the IRD and a lower proportion is often attributed to the building. It is, however, a question of fact, open to be established accurately through original records.

(b) The balancing charge is either deducted from depreciation allowances or added to assessable income; the effect is the same.

See also *Departmental Interpretation & Practice Notes No. 2*, which is reproduced as Appendix 2.

5.4 Commercial Buildings (For years of assessment prior to 1998/99)

Prior to the 1998/99 year of assessment, only a small annual allowance was available in respect of expenditure on commercial buildings. Although the position has now been improved, it is important to appreciate the previous provisions in order to properly understand the transition to the new, more generous system which now applies. Accordingly, the provisions applying prior to 1998/99 are explained below.

Again, it is important to remember that these provisions apply only to expenditure on buildings and structures and there may be elements included in the construction cost of a building or structure which in fact represent the provision of plant and machinery which qualifies for more generous allowances; examples of this would be expenditure on air conditioning and lift machinery.

5.4.1 Qualifying expenditure

In order to qualify for relief, a person must have had an interest in a commercial building or structure at the end of the basis period for the year of assessment and that interest must have been the relevant interest under which capital expenditure was incurred on the construction of the building or structure (Sec. 36). Some of these points are now examined in more detail:—

(1)   It must have been capital expenditure. The comments in relation to capital expenditure on industrial buildings in section 5.3 also apply to commercial buildings.

(2)   The claimant did not have to incur the capital expenditure himself; it was sufficient that he held the relevant interest in relation to which the expenditure was originally incurred. In other words, expenditure incurred by an owner was available for allowances to him and subsequent owners and expenditure incurred by a lessee was available

       for allowance to him and his assignees but a lessee could not inherit the owner's expenditure.

(3) Expenditure must have been on the construction of a building or structure and, therefore, expenditure not directly related to construction did not qualify. In particular, expenditure on the acquisition of, or of rights in or over, land was excluded by Sec. 40(3). Similarly, expenditure on demolition of a previous building did not qualify. However, capital expenditure on an existing commercial building or part of a building qualified even though it did not physically give rise to any additional structure; accordingly, expenditure on improvements may have qualified.

(4) A commercial building or structure is defined in Sec. 40(1) as any building or structure, or part of a building or structure, used by the person entitled to the relevant interest on which the expenditure was incurred in his trade, profession or business and which does not qualify as an industrial building or structure. Therefore, the comments as to what qualifies as a structure for industrial building allowance purposes in section 5.3.1 apply to commercial structures.

5.4.2 Allowances

There were no initial allowances or balancing allowances or charges. There was a single allowance for each year of assessment of 2% of the qualifying expenditure. In theory, therefore, it was possible for the aggregate allowances given to ultimately amount to more than the expenditure.

5.5 Commercial Buildings (For 1998/99 and subsequent years of assessment)

The system of depreciation allowances for commercial buildings was significantly enhanced with effect from the 1998/99 year of assessment. In particular, the rate of annual allowance was increased to 4% although, as a *quid pro quo*, balancing charges and allowances were introduced and a cap (equal to qualifying expenditure) was placed on the total allowances available.

Because of the changes regarding balancing charges and allowances and total available allowances, transitional provisions were required to ensure that expenditure dealt with under the former, less generous provisions, was not made subject to the more onerous aspects of the new rules. The new rules, including the transitional provisions affecting those rules, are discussed in the following sections.

5.5.1 Annual allowances

As noted above, an annual allowance of 4% of the relevant capital expenditure is granted to a person who, at the end of a basis period for a year of assessment, has an interest in a commercial building or structure which is the relevant interest in relation to the capital expenditure incurred on the construction of that building or structure (Sec. 33A(1)). The terms "commercial building or structure", "relevant interest" and "capital expenditure" have the same meanings as under the old provisions and are discussed in sections 5.3 and 5.4 above.

As a transitional measure, Sec. 33A(4)(a) provides that where a person had a relevant interest in the capital expenditure on a commercial building or structure at the end of the basis period for their 1997/98 year of assessment, such capital expenditure is deemed to be the original capital expenditure on the construction less the annual allowances which would have been available under Sec. 36 (i.e. the former provisions) had the person used the building or structure for the purpose of producing profits chargeable to Profits Tax at all times during their ownership. In other words, the expenditure is deemed to be the original expenditure less any allowances actually granted as well as notional allowances in respect of any year where allowances were not actually granted. Note that only allowances and notional allowances related to the period of ownership by the person who held the relevant interest at the end of the basis period for the 1997/98 year of assessment are deducted from the original cost, but not any allowances granted to (or notional allowances in respect of) a former owner.

Additionally, Sec. 33A(4)(b) provides that where a person has a relevant interest in a commercial building or structure at the end of the basis period for the 1997/98 year of assessment, 1998/99 is deemed to be the first year of assessment in which the building or structure is used. This is relevant in determining the calculation of annual allowances where the relevant interest in the building or structure is subsequently sold, as is discussed further below. For practical examples of the operation of the transitional provisions of Sec. 33A(4), see Examples 5 to 8 in the Appendix to *Departmental Interpretation & Practice Notes No. 2*, which is reproduced as Appendix 2 to this book.

As was the case under the old system, where an interest in a commercial building or structure is sold, the purchaser can claim the allowances in the year of acquisition and subsequent years whilst the relevant interest continues to be held. Unlike the old system, however, where the purchaser was merely entitled to 2% of the original expenditure, the new rules (Sec. 33A(2)) require the calculation of a "residue of expenditure" in much the same way as is done for industrial buildings allowance (see section 5.3.3). "Residue of expenditure" is defined in Sec. 40 as the capital expenditure (which means the original expenditure or the expenditure as defined in Sec. 33A(4)(a) where the asset was held by the seller at the end of the basis period for the 1997/98 year of assessment), less:–

(1) any initial or annual allowances granted from the 1998/99 year of assessment onwards under the industrial buildings provisions;

(2) any annual allowances granted under the commercial buildings provisions from the 1998/99 year of assessment onwards;

(3) any notional annual allowances for any year of assessment from 1998/99 onwards when the building or structure was not used as either a commercial building or an industrial building; and

(4) any balancing allowance granted under either the industrial or commercial building allowance provisions from the 1998/99 year of assessment onwards,

and increased by any balancing charge made under either the commercial or industrial building allowance provisions in the 1998/99 or a later year of assessment.

Once the residue of expenditure is obtained, it is divided by the number of years starting from the year in which the purchaser acquired the interest in the building and ending in the 25th year after the year of assessment in which the building or structure was first used or, in the case where the seller had the relevant interest in the expenditure at the end of the basis period for the 1997/98 year of assessment, the 2023/24 year of assessment.

The effect of the above in the case of a building or structure on hand at the beginning of the basis period for the 1998/99 year of assessment is to either increase or decrease the annual allowances available under the new system compared to those which would have been available had the old system been retained, depending upon the age of the building or structure.

The calculation of annual allowances is, however, subject to the over-riding proviso in Sec. 33A(3) that the amount of any such allowance is not to exceed the balance of the residue of expenditure which exists immediately prior to the calculation of any allowance. In other words, the aggregate of allowances granted to all persons who have held the relevant interest at any time in respect of a building or structure (plus notional allowances in respect of any year of assessment in which no allowance was available), cannot exceed the original capital expenditure on the building or structure.

5.5.2 Balancing allowances and charges

For the 1998/99 and subsequent years of assessment, if capital expenditure has been incurred on the construction of a commercial building or structure and, while that asset is still a commercial building or structure:

(1)   the relevant interest therein is sold;
(2)   the relevant interest is a leasehold interest and such interest comes to an end (other than in circumstances where the lessee acquires the reversionary interest in the property); or
(3)   the building or structure is demolished or destroyed or otherwise ceases to be used altogether,

an assessable balancing charge or a deductible balancing allowance is deemed to arise. Until the 2003/04 year of assessment, balancing charges and allowances in relation to commercial buildings or structures were dealt with in Sec. 33D. From the 2004/05 year, however, the provisions have effectively been merged with the provisions regarding industrial buildings and structures and are dealt with in the amended Sec. 35, which is discussed in section 5.3.4 above. Following this amendment, Sec. 33B was repealed. The merging of the balancing charge and allowance provisions for commercial buildings with those of industrial buildings reflects the fact that the provisions are similar, but also better provides for the situation where a building or structure changes at some time during its use by a person from a commercial building to an industrial building, or vice versa.

As discussed in section 5.3.4, a balancing allowance is deemed by Sec. 35(2) to arise where either there is no sale, insurance, salvage or compensation moneys in respect of the relevant event or such moneys are less than the residue of expenditure (see discussion in section 5.5.1 above) in respect of the asset immediately prior to the relevant event. The amount of the balancing allowance is the residue of expenditure where there is no sale, insurance, salvage or compensation moneys (Sec. 35(2)(a)(ii)(A)) or the excess of the residue of expenditure over such moneys in other cases (Sec. 35(2)(a)(ii)(B)). Nonetheless, a balancing allowance is denied by Sec. 35(b)(i) where the building did not qualify as a commercial or industrial building immediately before the occurrence of the relevant event, although as discussed in section 5.3.4 it is not clear why this restriction exists. Also, Sec. 35(b)(ii) precludes a balancing allowance where a building or structure is demolished for purposes not connected with, or not in the ordinary course of, the trade, profession or business for the purpose for which the building or structure had been used prior to being demolished and which qualified the building for annual allowances.

A balancing charge, on the other hand, arises pursuant to Sec. 35(3)(a) where the sale, insurance, salvage or compensation moneys received in connection with the sale, demolition or termination of leasehold interest exceed the amount of the residue of expenditure immediately prior to that event, and the amount of the balancing charge is equal to such excess. Where there was no residue of expenditure prior to the sale, demolition or termination of leasehold interest, the balancing charge is therefore equal to the sale, insurance, salvage or compensation moneys received. Sec. 35(3)(b), however, operates to ensure that any balancing charge does not exceed the amount of annual allowances made to the person pursuant to either Sec. 33A or Sec. 34(2) in respect of that asset; in other words, a balancing charge can only claw back any allowances granted to the person at any time under the industrial building allowance provisions, or since the 1998/99 year of assessment under the commercial building allowance provisions. This limitation ensures that the balancing charge does not operate as a tax on capital gains.

For further information on allowances available in respect of commercial buildings, see *Departmental Interpretation & Practice Notes No. 2*, which is reproduced as Appendix 2.

5.6 Expenditure Qualifying as Plant and Machinery

Plant and machinery attracts the most generous allowances of all assets qualifying for depreciation allowances. It is, therefore, important to be able to identify which assets fall within the definition as opposed to being classified as expenditure on buildings, and, as will be seen, the dividing line is often very narrow.

In order to qualify for relief, capital expenditure on the provision of machinery or plant must be incurred by a person carrying on a trade, profession or business for the purposes of producing profits chargeable to Profits Tax (Secs. 37(1) and 39B(1)) or by an employee on machinery or plant the use of which is essential to the production of income assessable to Salaries Tax (Sec. 12(1)(b)). There are, therefore, a number of essential ingredients to qualification for relief and these are:—

(1)   the expenditure must have been incurred by the person claiming the allowance. Although this seems, perhaps, obvious, it must be

remembered that annual allowances in respect of both commercial and industrial buildings are granted in respect of the original construction expenditure but are available to the person who has the relevant interest in the building even if they are not the person who incurred the expenditure. Although the identity of the person who incurred an item of expenditure is usually clear, see *D 49/97* where a taxpayer claimed allowances in respect of a portion of the plant and equipment installed in the common areas of a building in which the taxpayer owned several floors. The Board of Review rejected the claim, although only on the grounds of lack of evidence as to what, if anything, had been purchased and the purchase price paid. In particular, the Board rejected the submission by the IRD's representative that annual allowances can only be claimed by an exclusive owner of the property who has exclusive use of that property;

(2)   the expenditure must be capital expenditure and for further comments on this, see section 5.3.1 in connection with capital expenditure on industrial buildings. However, capital expenditure qualifying as scientific research expenditure under Sec. 16B or expenditure on the acquisition of prescribed fixed assets (see (14) in section 4.5.8) is specifically excluded because such expenditure qualifies for full deduction under Sec. 16B(1)(b) or Sec. 16G(1) respectively;

(3)   the expenditure need only be incurred by legal obligation in the basic period; there is no requirement that relief depends upon actual payment (see section 4.5.6 for a discussion of when a liability is incurred). There are, however, some special provisions affecting both the availability and timing of relief in respect of expenditure incurred under a hire purchase agreement; these are dealt with later in this chapter;

(4)   ignoring the position of an employee, the claimant must be carrying on a trade, profession or business which is subject to Profits Tax and the assets in question must be used to earn assessable profits; and

(5)   the assets must fall within the definition of plant and machinery and this is considered in detail below.

The IRO contains no definition of plant and machinery and it is therefore necessary to turn to case law of which there are numerous UK decisions which are generally accepted authorities in Hong Kong. The IRO does, however, state in Sec. 40(1) that capital expenditure on the provision of machinery or plant includes capital expenditure on alterations to an existing building incidental to the installation of plant or machinery. As will be seen, certain expenditure incurred on and during the construction of a building will qualify as expenditure on plant and machinery and the provision in Sec. 40(1), therefore, only seems to provide additional relief on the extra expenditure necessitated by having to make the installation in an existing building, such as demolition, making good etc.

As to the judicial interpretation of the meaning of plant and machinery, the earliest case of importance is the UK case of *Yarmouth v France* (19 QBD 647) which was not a tax case but which, nevertheless, identified a general rule which holds good to this day. It was held that plant includes *"whatever apparatus is used by a businessman for carrying on his business, not his stock-in-trade which he buys or makes for sale, but all goods and chattels, fixed or moveable, live or dead, which he keeps for permanent employment in his business"*. From this and subsequent cases, the general principle emerged that expenditure on plant and machinery may be identified and distinguished from expenditure on buildings in that the former relates to the "tools" *with which* the business is carried on, whereas the latter is the "environment" *in which* the business is carried on (see particularly *J. Lyons & Co. v AG* (1 All E.R. 477), although, again, this was not a tax case). This principle comes to the fore in dealing with expenditure on partitioning within a building. In *Jarrold v John Good & Sons* (40 TC 681), it was held that partitioning which was moveable and which was required to be regularly moved due to the changing nature of the business requirements, qualified as plant and machinery. However, merely being moveable or demountable is not, of itself, sufficient as demonstrated in *St. Johns School v Ward* (49 TC 524) wherein a portable laboratory and a gymnasium were held to be buildings.

It will be seen, therefore, that it is not only the obvious pieces of machinery that fall within the definition but everything which is used as a "tool" within the business, whether or not it is fixed to a building. It is difficult in many cases to distinguish those parts of a building which qualify although a certain amount of logic can be applied. Electric lighting, for example, is clearly part of the "environment" but special lighting installed in a photographic studio would qualify as equipment, even if wired into the building. Plumbing fixtures such as washbasins and toilets qualify and, as they cannot function without piping, the plumbing from the equipment to the main should also qualify. This can also extend to special trunking and wiring installed to service a computer. Other parts of a building which may so qualify include fire extinguishing equipment, air conditioning and lifts.

It is solely a question of fact and logic where the building ends and equipment begins. In the case of *IRC v Scottish & Newcastle Breweries Ltd.* (55 TC 252), pictures, murals and decor in a hotel were regarded as equipment necessary to provide atmosphere and therefore qualified as plant and machinery. Similarly, special decorative windows in the offices of a building society were held to be plant and machinery in *Leeds Permanent Building Society v Procter* (56 TC 293). The principle established in these cases was largely upheld in *Wimpy International Ltd. v Warland*; *Associated Restaurants Ltd. v Warland* (61 TC 51) although it was made clear that there is a limit as to how far that principle can be stretched. In particular, in the Chancery Division judgement of that case, Hoffmann J. introduced what he termed the "business use" test when he suggested that where an asset was neither premises nor trading stock but was used for the carrying on of a person's business, it will normally qualify as "plant". His Honour went on, however, to emphasise that even if the asset was used in the carrying on of the person's business, it still had to be established that it was not simply used as the premises for that business. Applying this principle, it was held that various items, whilst arguably fulfilling a function in attracting customers or providing an atmosphere, were nonetheless still part of the premises; in particular, the Court held that shopfronts, floor and wall tiles and other coverings, a trapdoor and ladder, certain suspended and decorative ceilings, mezzanine floors, raised flooring, balustrading and stairs, amongst other things, failed to qualify as plant for these reasons.

It has been held in *Cooke v Beach Station Caravans* (49 TC 514) that a swimming pool provided by a caravan site operator is a "tool" and therefore qualifies. Similarly, the functional nature of a dry dock for ship repairs qualified it as plant and machinery in *IRC v Barclay, Curle & Co.* (45 TC 221). At one time it was the position that the technical library of a solicitor, or indeed of any other professional person, was not plant and machinery but the earlier decision in *Daphne v Shaw* (11 TC 256) has been overruled by *Munby v Furlong* (50 TC 491). Although, ostensibly, a ship does constitute plant or machinery, in a case in which one was used as a restaurant, it was held that it constituted the environment for the business and was, therefore, not plant or machinery (*CIR v Aberdeen Restaurant Enterprises Ltd.* (2 HKTC 330)). See also the similar circumstances in *Benson v Yard Arm Club* (53 TC 67).

Relief is only available in respect of expenditure incurred on the provision of the plant or machinery; this, broadly, means expenditure incurred in purchasing or constructing the asset. Additionally, Sec. 40(1) specifically also allows the inclusion of incidental expenditure on altering a building. Accordingly, whether or not incidental expenditure such as legal fees, commissions and other similar expenses can be included will clearly depend on the strength of the nexus to the provision of the asset. Unfortunately, there is no case law guidance in Hong Kong on this matter and each case must ultimately be considered on its own facts; however, with many such expenses, a lack of nexus to the acquisition of a capital asset may, in fact, suggest that they are revenue expenses qualifying for deduction under Sec. 16(1). In *IRC v Barclay Curle & Co.* (supra), the cost of excavation was allowed as it was considered an essential element in the construction of the dock. On the other hand, in *Powlson v Ben Odeco* (52 TC 459) capitalised interest paid on a loan specifically taken out to finance the construction of an oil rig was not regarded as part of the cost of provision of the oil rig. However, Sec. 40 provides that qualifying capital expenditure includes interest and commitment fees which have been incurred on a loan made for the sole purpose of financing the provision of plant and machinery, but only if not deductible under any other provision. In this regard, interest incurred on loans taken out to finance the *purchase* of a capital asset would generally be deductible pursuant to Sec. 16(1)(a), although note restrictions on interest deductibility discussed in section 4.5.8. However, interest on loans taken out to *construct* a capital asset will, following the decision in *Wharf Properties Ltd. v CIR* [1997] (1 HKRC 90-085), generally not be deductible under that provision and will, therefore, be included in the definition of capital expenditure for the purpose of calculating depreciation allowances.

Having determined the judicial definition of plant and machinery, the IRR makes some amendments in Rule 2. Firstly in Rule 2(3), wharves are specifically excluded from the definition of plant and machinery and, accordingly, qualify only for industrial building allowances. Secondly, the following items are excluded from plant and machinery and are, instead, deemed to be "implements, utensils and articles":—

- Belting
- Crockery and cutlery
- Kitchen utensils
- Linen
- Loose tools
- Soft furnishings (including curtains and carpets)
- Surgical and dental instruments
- Tubes for X-ray and infra-red machines

Accordingly, initial expenditure on these items is disallowed as capital expenditure (see *D 12/86*) and no depreciation allowances are available but the cost of replacement of these items is wholly deductible (Sec. 16(1)(f)).

See also *Departmental Interpretation & Practice Notes No. 7*, which is reproduced as Appendix 5, and in particular Appendices B and C which give the IRD's views on expenditure falling within and outside of the definition respectively. Some of the items in Appendix C might be challenged on the basis of case law.

5.7 Plant and Machinery Allowances (General)

At one time the depreciation allowances applicable to plant and machinery were calculated individually in respect of each separate item, involving considerably cumbersome calculations where many items were involved. For the prime purpose of minimising the number of calculations of balancing allowances and charges, the method of computing annual allowances is now based on the "pooling" system (Sec. 36A(1)). The pooling system involves aggregating single items of expenditure into classes or "pools" which expand or contract with additions and disposals. However, there are specific circumstances where the pooling system will not apply and individual calculations are still necessary in respect of some or all of the items. The exceptions are:

(1)   in relation to any qualifying expenditure, the Commissioner can direct that the non-pooling provisions shall apply if the operation of the pooling provisions would seem to him to be impracticable or inequitable. He can also direct for what period his direction is to apply (Sec. 36A(2)):

(2)   plant and machinery acquired under a hire-purchase agreement is subject to the non-pooling method of computation (see section 5.9.1) until such time as title passes under the agreement to the purchaser, when the unrelieved expenditure is transferred to the pool (Secs. 39C(1)(a) and 39C(2)). Title passes when the option to purchase is exercised, usually at the end of the period of the agreement, and the transfer of the unrelieved expenditure to the pool takes place in the year of assessment following the year of assessment relating to the basis period for which the transfer of title takes place. See section 5.10.1 as to the meaning of a hire-purchase agreement; and

(3)   where, because not all of a person's profits or income are assessable, the depreciation allowances are apportioned and Sec. 39A applies to the computation of residual value (see section 5.11.2). It would complicate the calculations if such expenditure was included in the pool; accordingly, it is excluded from the pool and allowances continue to be calculated under the non-pooling method (Sec. 39C (3)). Where plant and machinery expenditure has been included in

the pool and, during a basis period, is thereafter not used wholly for the purpose of earning assessable profits, the allowances thereafter will require apportionment and so the expenditure must then be excluded from the pool. Similarly, if ownership of an asset is retained but it is not used at all in the business, it must, of course, henceforth be removed from the pool. Sec. 39C(3) requires that an amount equal to the estimated open market value of the relevant items of plant and machinery is to be deducted from the pool in the basis period in which the change of use takes place. If the asset is partly used in the business, allowances for that year of assessment commence to be computed under the non-pooling method.

5.8 Plant and Machinery Allowances (Pooling System)

The "pooling" system is designed largely to minimise the work and records required for computing balancing allowances and charges. The difference between this system and the non-pooling system described in section 5.9 primarily concerns the method of calculating the annual allowances and the substantial elimination of balancing allowances and charges except in certain specified circumstances.

5.8.1 Initial allowance

An initial allowance is given for the year of assessment relating to the basis period in which the expenditure is incurred (Secs. 39B(1) and 39B(1A)). This allowance is currently 60% of the qualifying expenditure. It is not necessary for the asset to be brought into use in the basis period; it is sufficient that the expenditure is incurred while a trade, profession or business is carried on. Furthermore, there is no requirement, as there is for annual allowance, for the claimant to own the asset; he can claim initial allowances on a contribution to the cost of an asset owned by another person, provided that the claimant has the use of the asset.

5.8.2 Annual allowance

Whereas under the non-pooling system, annual allowances are computed on an item by item basis and cease, with respect to any given asset, upon the disposal of that asset (with such disposal possibly resulting in a balancing allowance or charge), under the pooling system annual allowances are computed in a single amount for all assets within a class and there is normally no balancing allowance or charge upon disposal.

An asset qualifies for annual allowance if it is owned by the claimant and has been in use in a business giving rise to assessable income in any basis period. There is no requirement for it to be in use at the end of the basis period of claim, as is the case under the non-pooling system. This is to permit, following disposal of an asset, annual allowances to continue to be claimed on the residue of expenditure left in the pool. The difference is that the allowance is granted in respect of each "class" of plant or machinery (Sec. 39B(2)). A "class" exists for all assets of which the prescribed rate of depreciation is identical (Sec. 40(1)). Sec. 39B(3) specifies that the rates are as prescribed by the Board of Inland Revenue and are to be applied to the reducing value of each class of plant or machinery.

The rates specified by the Board of Inland Revenue as applying from the 1980/81 year of assessment are contained in the First Part of the Table in Inland Revenue Rule 2; these rates have also been included as Appendix A(i) of *Departmental Interpretation & Practice Notes No. 7* which is reproduced as Appendix 5 of this book. Therefore, there is a maximum of three possible classes to accommodate the rates 10%, 20% and 30%, however, there could be additional classes to accommodate any other rate which may apply by virtue of the Commissioner's discretionary power under Sec. 39B(11) to allow a higher rate than the three prescribed rates. Before exercising that discretion, however, the Commissioner would need to be satisfied that the higher rate was justified by exceptional circumstances leading to an unusually short life for the asset in question. In paragraph 48 of *Departmental Interpretation & Practice Notes No. 7* (which is reproduced as Appendix 5), however, the IRD state that in view of the current rates it is unlikely that any claim for a higher annual allowance rate could be justified. Nonetheless, in paragraph 47 of that document, the IRD set out the information which they would require in order to consider any such claim for increased allowance rates.

Having identified which assets fall into each class it is necessary to ascertain the reducing value of the class. Reducing value is calculated as follows (Sec. 39B(4)):—

(1)   Capital expenditure incurred on the provision of the plant and machinery

Less: (2)   Initial allowances given under either the pooling or earlier non-pooling systems.

(3)   Annual allowances given under either the pooling or earlier non-pooling systems.

(4)   Sale, insurance, salvage or compensation moneys received in

respect of any plant or machinery in the class. Such amounts must, if necessary, be limited to the original qualifying expenditure in respect of that plant or machinery which was brought into the class (Secs. 39D(6) and 39D(7)).

(5) The estimated open market value of assets which are to be excluded by virtue of not being wholly used for earning assessable profits but which were previously wholly used. See (3) in section 5.7.

(6) The written down value of any assets for which a balancing allowance or charge has been computed for 1979/80 or earlier (Sec. 39B(5)).

Item (6) was necessary during the transition to the pooling system in 1980/81 when the reducing value of each class for 1980/81 was created by classifying and aggregating written down values brought forward from 1979/80. This automatically took care of (1), (2), (3) and (6) above and of course items within (5) were not classified because the non-pooling system continues to apply to them. From then on additional qualifying expenditure, less initial allowances thereon, is added and sales proceeds (limited where necessary) deducted and, of course, item (6) is not encountered again. After such adjustments have been made for each year, the relevant percentage is applied to arrive at the annual allowance which is then deducted from the reducing value carried to the next year.

Where, however, an asset which has been owned for some time is suddenly brought into use for the purpose of earning assessable profits there will, of course, be no qualifying expenditure to bring into the reducing value. Instead, the original cost, less notional annual (but not initial) allowances from the outset computed as if the asset had been in use, is added (Sec. 39B(6)). Similarly, Sec. 23B(8) provides that where a ship ceases to be on the Hong Kong Register of Shipping and it commences to give rise to assessable income, depreciation allowances are to be calculated on the reducing value after deducting any initial allowance given and notional annual allowances (see section 4.7.4).

If a person acquires a trade, profession or business together with assets used therein from another person other than by way of purchase (for example, by way of gift or succession on death), the successor, of course, has no qualifying expenditure to add to the reducing value of the class. Sec. 39B(7), however, provides that he is to bring in the predecessor's reducing value, i.e. he stands in the predecessor's shoes. The successor is not, however, entitled to any initial allowance thereon (Sec. 39B(8)).

Although it is a statement of the obvious, if the various deductions from the reducing value have the effect of reducing this to nil or a negative figure, no annual allowance is given on that class for the year (Sec. 39B(9)). In fact, in this situation a balancing charge will arise (see section 5.8.3).

■ Example 5.7

Puh Ling Ltd. has carried on a manufacturing business for many years and the following are the written down values of its various pools of plant and machinery after 2004/05 depreciation allowances have been granted:—

	Motor Vehicles (30%)	Office Equipment, Fixtures, etc. (20%)	Air Conditioning and Lifts (10%)
	$160,667	$137,677	$170,366

During its accounting periods ending 31st December 2005 and 2006 it has the following transactions in its plant and machinery:—

31st December 2005
Air conditioning sold for $25,000 (cost $75,000)
Bought desks and chairs for $15,000
Transferred office equipment from Taiwan office (cost $104,688 in 2003)
Photocopier sold for $35,000 (cost $30,000)

31st December 2006
Transferred office equipment to Taiwan office
   (cost $100,000, market value $120,000)
Sold motor vehicle for $20,000 (cost $40,000)
Bought motor vehicle for $45,000

The depreciation allowances for 2005/06 et seq. proceed as follows:—

		30% Class	20% Class	10% Class	Allowances
Reducing Value brought forward		$160,667	$137,677	$170,366	
2005/06					
Additions:—					
Desk and Chairs	$15,000				
Initial Allowance					
60%	9,000				$ 9,000
	$ 6,000		6,000		
Equipment from Taiwan					
(Note (a))			67,000		
Disposals:—					
Air conditioning				(25,000)	
Photocopier (Note (b))			(30,000)		
		$160,667	$180,677	$145,366	
Annual Allowance		48,200	36,135	14,537	98,872
					$107,872
Reducing Value		$112,467	$144,542	$130,829	

2006/07

Additions:—

Motor Vehicle	$45,000			
Initial Allowance				
60%	27,000			
	$18,000	18,000		$ 27,000

Disposals:—

Motor Vehicle		(20,000)		
Equipment Transferred				
(Note (c))		(120,000)		
	$110,467	$24,542	$130,829	
Annual Allowance	33,140	4,908	13,083	51,131
				$ 78,131
Reducing Value	$ 77,327	$19,634	$117,746	

Notes:—

(a) The cost of the office equipment previously used in circumstances not giving rise to assessable profits must be written down by notional annual allowances since acquisition (Sec. 39B(6)).

Cost in 2003	$104,688
2003/04 notional annual allowance (@ 20%)	20,938
	$ 83,750
2004/05 notional annual allowance (@ 20%)	16,750
Reducing Value	$ 67,000

No notional initial allowance is to be deducted.

(b) Sale proceeds of photocopier must be limited to original cost (Sec. 39D(6)).

(c) Sec. 39C(3) requires the market value to be deducted from the pool with no restriction to cost as is the case in respect of sales. This is an anomaly.

5.8.3 Balancing allowance/charge

It can be seen from the procedure whereby sale, insurance, salvage or compensation proceeds are merely deducted from the reducing value (or pool) brought forward that balancing allowances and charges do not normally arise under the pooling system.

However, a balancing charge can arise in two situations and a balancing allowance in only one situation.

A balancing charge arises when, at the end of a basis period for a year of assessment, the reducing value of a class of plant and machinery is a negative figure because the deductions from the pool for that period have exceeded the reducing value brought forward plus additions. The negative amount then becomes a balancing charge for the year of assessment related to the basis period and the reducing value carried forward becomes nil (Sec. 39D (1)). This situation may arise, for example, where it is necessary to go over to the non-pooling system after a period of time on the pooling system (see Example 5.9). In this situation, a balancing allowance cannot arise.

A balancing charge and/or a balancing allowance may arise when a person ceases to carry on a trade, profession or business. At the end of the basis period in which the cessation takes place, the reducing value of each class of plant and machinery is reduced by the sale, insurance, salvage or compensation proceeds from the relevant assets and if there is a positive balance, this becomes a balancing allowance. If there is a negative balance, this becomes a balancing charge (Sec. 39D(2)). However, in arriving at a balancing charge, the amount of sale, etc. proceeds deducted must not exceed the original qualifying expenditure in respect of that plant or machinery which was brought into the class (Secs. 39D(6) and 39E (7)).

Where there are no sale, etc. proceeds as a result of another person succeeding to the business by way of gift or on death of the owner, there is no balancing allowance or charge (Sec. 39D(3)). The successor inherits the reducing value (see section 5.8.2).

Where, however, there are no sale, etc. proceeds and there is no succession to the business by another person, the Commissioner will estimate the open market value of the plant and machinery and deduct this from the relevant class as if it had been sale etc. proceeds received immediately prior to cessation. The balance of each class then becomes the subject of a balancing allowance or charge (Sec. 39D(4)). However, if there is an actual sale within 12 months of the date of cessation, the taxpayer can claim an adjustment to the balancing allowance or charge by substituting the sale price for the estimated open market value previously adopted and the assessment is adjusted, even if it had become final and conclusive (Sec. 39D(5)). This provision appears to suggest that if plant and machinery is scrapped on cessation of business and no proceeds received, for the purpose of calculating balancing charges and allowances there is a deemed sale at market value. However, if plant and machinery is scrapped in these circumstances it would usually be because the assets had no significant open market value; in other words, if the assets had an open market value, they would probably not have been scrapped. This is probably one reason why the provision appears to have only limited application in practice; another reason, however, is that because of the usual delay between the cessation of business and the filing of the return, the actual proceeds of any sale are known at the time of filing the return and, therefore, an estimation is not required.

■ Example 5.8

The facts are as in Example 5.7. In the year ended 31st December 2007, there are no purchases of fixed assets and a photocopier is sold for $20,000, having cost $25,000 some years ago. On 10th April 2008, all of the remaining assets except the lift were sold and the business ceased. Sales proceeds were:—

Motor Vehicles	$ 40,000
Air Conditioning	$100,000
Office Equipment etc.	$ 5,000

The lift which had an estimated open market value of $60,000 in April 2008 was sold in December 2008 for $50,000.

Depreciation Allowances are:—

	30% Class	20% Class	10% Class	Allowances
Reducing Value brought forward	$77,327	$19,634	$117,746	
2007/08				
Disposal		20,000		
		($ 366)		
Balancing Charge		366		($ 366)
		Nil		
Annual Allowance	23,198		11,775	34,973
				$34,607
Reducing Value	$54,129	Nil	$105,971	
2008/09 (Final)				
Sales	40,000	5,000	100,000	
	$14,129	($ 5,000)	$ 5,971	
Market Value of Lifts			60,000	
			($ 54,029)	
Balancing Charges		5,000	54,029	($59,029)
Balancing Allowance	14,129			14,129
				($44,900)

Notes:—

(a) The 2008/09 assessment being the cessation year is initially settled with a balancing charge of $44,900. When the lifts are sold in December 2008, Puh Ling Ltd. can claim to adjust the assessment, even if it is final and conclusive, by amending the balancing charge to $34,900 because of the substitution of sale proceeds of $50,000 for the estimated market value of $60,000.

(b) This example assumes that allowances remain the same up to 2008/09.

■ Example 5.9

The facts are the same as in Example 5.7 except that on 1st March 2007, the nature of the business changed so that the assets were only used 75% for earning assessable profits. The estimated market values of the plant and machinery at that date were:—

Motor Vehicles	$ 70,000

Office Equipment, etc.	$ 30,000
Air Conditioning and Lifts	$150,000

As the change takes place during the basis period for 2007/08, the annual allowances for that year are computed on the non-pooling method starting with the open market values as if they were the amounts of unrelieved expenditure brought forward.
The calculations would proceed as follows:—

2007/08	30% Class	20% Class	10% Class	Allowances
Reducing Value				
brought forward	$77,327	$19,634	$117,746	
Market Values	70,000	30,000	150,000	
Reducing Value	$ 7,327 (b)	($10,366)	($ 32,254)	
Balancing Charge		10,366	32,254	($42,620)

	Motors Vehicles 30%	Office Machinery 20%	Lifts and Air Conditioning 10%	
Expenditure per				
Sec. 39C(3)	$70,000	$30,000	$150,000	
Annual Allowance	21,000	6,000	15,000	$31,500
				(75%)
Written Down Value at				
1.1.2008	$49,000	$24,000	$135,000	($11,120)

Notes:—
(a) No initial allowance arises in respect of the transfer from the pools to the non-pooling system because no expenditure has been incurred in the basis period. Sec. 39C(3) only deems the reducing value of the expenditure to be equal to the market value figures.
(b) There is no provision for a balancing allowance in these circumstances. It is not clear whether annual allowances continue to be claimable on this amount of $7,327 and, if so, whether they have to be apportioned according to non-assessable use. If the latter is correct it would of course defeat the point of transferring the expenditure of $70,000 to a computation on the non-pooling system.

5.9 Plant and Machinery Allowances (Non-Pooling System)

The arithmetically cumbersome non-pooling system applied in all cases up to and including 1979/80; since 1980/81, however, it has only applied where the pooling system (see section 5.8) is specifically not to be applied. There are, therefore, specific circumstances (see section 5.7) where the non-pooling system may still apply in respect of one asset, a group of assets or, indeed, all assets of the business. The fundamental difference is that, whereas under the pooling system assets are grouped into classes or pools which expand or contract upon acquisitions and disposals without, in general, the necessity to calculate balancing allowances and charges, under the non-pooling system calculations have to be made for each individual asset with balancing adjustments on disposal in each case.

5.9.1 Initial allowance

An initial allowance is given for the year of assessment relating to the basis period in which the expenditure is incurred (Sec. 37(1)). The current rate of this allowance is 60% of the qualifying expenditure. It is not necessary for the asset to be brought into use in the basis period; it is sufficient that the expenditure is incurred while a trade, profession or business is carried on. Where a person succeeds to a trade, profession or business and the assets used for that business are acquired other than by way of purchase, he can, as will be seen, claim annual allowances notwithstanding having incurred no expenditure; he cannot, however, claim an initial allowance (Sec. 37(5)).

Where the plant or machinery is acquired under a hire-purchase agreement, the initial allowance is spread over the period during which instalments are paid. The relief is given on the instalments paid in each basis period and is only given on the capital element of the instalments (Secs. 37A(1) and 37A(1A)). The revenue element, being interest, would normally qualify as a deductible expense in the period in which it was incurred. This is illustrated in Example 5.10.

■ Example 5.10

Nevanevva Ltd. has entered into a hire-purchase agreement on 1st June 2005 to acquire some hydrofoils for its Hong Kong shipping business. The cash price of the hydrofoils was $24,000,000 and the Company agreed to pay $31,200,000 by 24 monthly instalments commencing 1st June 2005. The Company's accounting date is 31st December.

The instalments are $1,300,000 per month
The capital element is $1,000,000 per month

Initial Allowance — 2005/06	— Instalments to 31.12.2005	$ 7,000,000
	— Initial Allowance (60%)	$ 4,200,000
— 2006/07	— Instalments in year to 31.12.2006	$12,000,000
	— Initial Allowance (60%)	$ 7,200,000
— 2007/08	— Instalments in period to 31.12.2007	$ 5,000,000
	— Initial Allowance (60%)	$ 3,000,000

The interest element of $300,000 per month would be allowed as a revenue expense in the three years of assessment.

Notes:—
(a) The calculation is not included with other assets in calculations under the pooling

system because assets being acquired by hire purchase are specifically excluded from the pooling system because of the obvious necessity to make an individual calculation (Secs. 39C(1)(a) and 39C(2)). It is transferred to the pooling system when the option to purchase is exercised (see Example 5.12).
(b) The meaning of hire-purchase is defined in Sec. 40(1) which has adopted the common law definition (see section 5.10.1).

5.9.2 Annual allowance

An annual allowance is available where, at the end of a basis period for a year of assessment, a person owns and has in use machinery or plant for the purposes of producing profits assessable to Profits Tax (Sec. 37(2)). Note that the two important criteria of "ownership" and "in use" do not apply for initial allowance. Accordingly, initial allowance can be claimed on a capital contribution to an asset owned by another person, provided that the claimant has the use of the asset, but no further allowances are available. Also, where an asset is acquired but not brought into use for a period of time, the initial allowance is available at the outset but the annual allowances are deferred.

The annual allowances for each basis period are computed on the amount of the qualifying expenditure less:—

(1)   the initial allowance given on that expenditure; and
(2)   previous annual allowances given.

There are also two situations where notional annual allowances have to be deducted in arriving at the net expenditure upon which annual allowances are to be given. These are:

(1)   where an asset was used by the owner for other purposes prior to bringing it into use for the purpose of producing profits chargeable to Profits Tax, notional annual allowances must be deducted as if such allowances had been available since the owner's acquisition of the asset (Sec. 37(2A)); and

(2)   in the taxation of shipping operations where because a ship ceases to be on the Hong Kong Register of Shipping, it may commence to give rise to assessable income. In these circumstances, Sec. 23B(8) provides that depreciation allowances are to be calculated on the reducing value after deducting any initial allowance given and notional annual allowances (see section 4.7.3).

There is no single rate of annual allowance prescribed by the IRO. The rates are to be as prescribed by the Board of Inland Revenue (Sec. 37(2)).

The prescribed rates are laid down in Rule 2 of the IRR and the table is contained in *Departmental Interpretation & Practice Notes No. 7*, which is reproduced as Appendix 5. The Commissioner is empowered by Sec. 37(2) proviso (b) to allow a higher rate of annual allowance in appropriate circumstances. In paragraph 47 of *Departmental Interpretation & Practice Notes No. 7*, the IRD set out the information which they would require in order to consider any such claim for increased allowance rates. Nonetheless, in paragraph 48 of that document, the IRD go on to say that given the current rates of allowances, it is unlikely that any claim for increased rates could be justified.

■ Example 5.11

Ben Dover has an earth moving business in Hong Kong and in his accounting year ended 31st December 2005, he bought a new bulldozer for $2,800,000. The machine required special modifications, however, and he was unable to bring the machine into use until July 2007. He also brought into his Hong Kong business in December 2005 a grader which he had bought in 2003 for $2,000,000 and which had been in use in his Taiwan business. Of his Hong Kong profits, 10% is not assessable to Profits Tax.

Extracts from Ben's depreciation allowance schedules are as follows:—

	Bulldozer (30%)	Grader (30%)	Other Plant & Machinery (20%)	Total
Written Down Value at 1.1.2005			$630,000	
2005/06				
Acquisition in year	$2,800,000	$980,000 (b)		
Initial Allowance (60%)	1,680,000	—	—	$1,680,000
	$1,120,000			
Annual Allowance	—	294,000	126,000	420,000
				$2,100,000 (d)
Written Down Value at 1.1.2006	$1,120,000	$686,000	$504,000	
2006/07				
Annual Allowance	—	205,800	100,800	$ 306,600 (d)
Written Down Value at 1.1.2007	$1,120,000	$480,200	$403,200	
2007/08				
Annual Allowance	336,000	144,060	80,640	$ 560,700 (d)
Written Down Value at 1.1.2008	$ 784,000	$336,140	$322,560	

Notes:—

(a) Because not the whole of his profit is assessable, his depreciation allowances have to be apportioned under Sec. 39A, therefore the non-pooling system must apply.

(b) Because the grader has been previously used in circumstances not attracting depreciation allowances (used in trade outside Hong Kong) it must be notionally written down for earlier use as follows:—

Cost 2003	$2,000,000
Notional Allowance 2003/04	600,000
	$1,400,000
Notional Allowance 2004/05	420,000
Written Down Value at 1.1.2005	$ 980,000

No initial allowance is available because the expenditure was incurred at a time when the asset did not qualify.
There is no requirement to deduct a notional initial allowance.

(c) No annual allowance can be given for 2005/06 and 2006/07 because the machine was not in use at 31st December 2005 and 2006. There is no requirement in these circumstances to deduct notional allowances.

(d) 10% of the total allowances would be disallowed under Sec. 39A.

If a person acquires a trade, profession, or business other than by way of asset purchase or share purchase (for example, by way of gift or succession on death), neither the former proprietor nor the new proprietor can claim depreciation allowances; the former no longer carries on the business and the new proprietor would not have incurred qualifying expenditure for the purpose of annual allowances. However, Sec. 37(4) allows the new proprietor to assume his predecessor's position and claim annual allowances based on the written down values at the time of the succession.

There are also special provisions relating to annual allowances in respect of assets purchased under hire purchase agreements (Secs. 37A(2) and 37A (3)). As seen in Example 5.10, the initial allowance is apportioned over the life of the hire purchase agreement with reference to the capital portion of the payments. This is not, however, the case with annual allowances. If the asset is in use at the end of the basis period, the annual allowance is calculated with reference to the full cash cost (excluding interest) and is not subject to the apportionment procedures of the initial allowance (Secs. 37A(1) and 37A(1A)).

■ Example 5.12

The same facts as in Example 5.10.
   Nevanevva's full depreciation allowance schedule for the machine is as follows:—

Cash Price June 2005	$24,000,000	
2005/06		
Initial Allowance (Note (a))	4,200,000	$4,200,000
	$19,800,000	

Annual Allowance (20%)	3,960,000	3,960,000
Written Down Value at 1.1.2006	$15,840,000	$8,160,000
2006/07		
Initial Allowance (Note (a))	7,200,000	$7,200,000
	$ 8,640,000	
Annual Allowance (20%)	1,728,000	1,728,000
Written Down Value at 1.1.2007	$ 6,912,000	$8,928,000
2007/08		
Initial Allowance (Note (a))	3,000,000	$3,000,000
	$ 3,912,000	
Annual Allowance (20%)	782,400	782,400
Written Down Value at 1.1.2008	$ 3,129,600	$3,782,400

Notes:
(a) For the calculation of the initial allowance see Example 5.10.
(b) Although the pooling provisions described in section 5.8 in general apply to 1980/81 et seq., the pooling provisions do not apply to expenditure which is subject to a hire-purchase agreement (see section 5.10.1). However, if for example the title passed with the payment of the final instalment in May 2007 this would mean that, with effect from the basis period after the basis period in which this date falls, the pooling method would apply. Therefore, the written down value of $3,129,600 would be transferred to the 20% pool for 2008/09.

5.9.3 Balancing allowance/charge

In order that the total depreciation allowances given to a claimant over his period of ownership of an asset can be related to the exhaustion of his qualifying expenditure, balancing allowances or charges are computed upon certain specified events occurring where an initial or an annual allowance has been given on the asset (Sec. 38(1)). The events are:—

(1) where the machinery or plant is sold whether while still in use or not (Sec. 38(1)(a));
(2) where the machinery or plant is destroyed (Sec. 38(1)(b)); or
(3) where the machinery or plant is permanently put out of use (Sec. 38(1)(c)).

Where one of these events takes place while the person is carrying on a trade, profession or business or is coincident with his ceasing of that trade, profession or business, an allowance or charge is computed and is allowed or assessed for the year of assessment in the basis period for which the event occurs.

Where the sales proceeds or other receipts upon disposal such as insurance or salvage receipts are either nil or are less than the unrelieved qualifying expenditure, the result is a balancing allowance equal to the difference. Where the receipts exceed the unrelieved qualifying expenditure, the result is of course a balancing charge equal to the difference. In the case where the starting cost is ascertained under Sec. 37(2A) in respect of an asset being used for other purposes before being brought into use to produce profits assessable to Profits Tax, the ascertained starting cost rather than the actual original cost represents the qualifying expenditure for the purpose of the allowance or charge. Also, where annual allowances have been given to a successor to a business, other than by purchase, under Sec. 37(4), the inherited written down value is the qualifying expenditure for the purpose of the allowance or charge (Sec. 38(2)).

Where a person ceases to carry on a trade profession or business and a balancing allowance or charge arises as a result of machinery or plant being put out of use, the disposal receipts to be brought into account is the open market value which the Commissioner considers should be attached to the machinery or plant as at the date of cessation. If, however, the machinery or plant is sold within 12 months of the date of cessation, the taxpayer may claim to adjust the allowance or charge to the figure which would have been computed if the actual sale proceeds were substituted for the open market value. If the result necessitates a reduction to an assessment which has become final and conclusive, the assessor must make the reduction notwithstanding the provisions to the contrary in Sec. 70 (Sec. 38(4)).

A balancing charge must do no more than recover an initial allowance and annual allowances actually given; it is not a tax on a capital profit (Sec. 38(5)). In cases where the amount on which allowances were first calculated is lower than the original cost, the lower figure is treated as the original qualifying expenditure for balancing charge purposes.

■ Example 5.13

Artie Vee inherited a printing business from his deceased father's estate together with the printing machine which had cost his father in excess of $1 million. At the date of his father's death, the written down value of the machine was $250,000. Artie used the machine in the business for two years, receiving annual allowances as follows:—

Inherited Cost (Sec. 37(4))	$250,000	
Annual Allowance Year 1 (20%)	50,000	$50,000
	$200,000	
Annual Allowance Year 2 (20%)	40,000	40,000
Written Down Value	$160,000	$90,000

He then sold the machine for $300,000.

His balancing charge is:—

Sale proceeds	$300,000
Unrelieved qualifying expenditure	160,000
	$140,000
However, it is restricted to actual allowances granted	$90,000

No part of the allowances claimed by his father can be recovered by the balancing charge. Had his father lived and continued the business, his balancing charge would have been $140,000.

Where a balancing charge arises in respect of the disposal of plant or machinery and that plant or machinery is replaced, tax on the balancing charge can be deferred by making an election to reduce the qualifying expenditure on the replacement asset and thereby reduce future initial and annual allowances (Sec. 39). The election must be made in writing and although no time limit for the election is given, this would have to be before an assessment incorporating the balancing charge became final and conclusive because there is no specific authority to re-open an assessment to admit the election and it is unlikely that failure to make an election could be construed as an error or mistake within the provisions of Sec. 70A (see Chapter 8).

The election is effected as follows:—

(1) Where the balancing charge exceeds the qualifying expenditure on the replacement asset, the following consequences ensue:—
   (i) The balancing charge is restricted to the difference between the original balancing charge and the replacement expenditure.
   (ii) No initial or annual allowances can be given on the replacement expenditure because it effectively becomes nil.
   (iii) When a balancing charge comes to be made on a disposal of the replacement asset, the amount of such charge is the smaller of the sales proceeds or the amount of the replacement expenditure.

■ Example 5.14

Assume in the facts in Example 5.13 that Artie had been able to buy another printing machine for $50,000.

If he made the election under Sec. 39, the following consequences would ensue:—

(1) His balancing charge would be restricted to $90,000 – $50,000 = $40,000.
(2) He could claim no initial or annual allowances on the replacement machine.
(3) If in due course he disposes of the replacement machine for, say, $30,000, he

would have a balancing charge of $30,000. If he disposed of it for, say $60,000, he would have a balancing charge of $50,000. In either case he could, of course, again elect under Sec. 39 if he replaced the machine.

---

(2) Where the balancing charge is less than the qualifying expenditure on the replacement asset, the following consequences arise:—
 (i)   The balancing charge is completely eliminated;
 (ii) The initial allowance and annual allowances on the replacement asset are to be given on expenditure equal to the difference between the actual qualifying expenditure and the eliminated balancing charge; and
 (iii) In computing the balancing allowance or charge on disposal of the replacement asset, the initial allowance under (ii) is deemed to have been increased by the amount of the eliminated balancing charge.

■ Example 5.15

Assume in the facts in Example 5.13 that Artie had bought a replacement printing machine for $150,000.

If he made the election under Sec. 39, the consequences would be:—

(1) His balancing charge would be reduced to nil;

(2) Allowances on the replacement asset would proceed as follows:

Cost	$150,000
Less: Balancing Charge	90,000
	$ 60,000
Initial Allowance (60%)	36,000
	$ 24,000
Annual Allowance (20%)	4,800
Written Down Value	$ 19,200

(3) If the machine is then sold for, say $70,000, the balancing charge calculation proceeds as follows:—

Sale Proceeds	$70,000
Written Down Value	19,200
Balancing Charge	$50,800

Notes:—
(a) Ordinarily, the balancing charge would be limited to the allowances actually given, namely $40,800, but as the balancing charge of $90,000 which has been set off is deemed to be an initial allowance, the maximum balancing charge on disposal of the replacement is $130,800 and therefore the above calculation is correct.
(b) Artie could of course again elect under Sec. 39 if he replaced it again.

5.10 Leasing

In order to curb a perceived loss of revenue in connection with sale and leaseback of secondhand plant and machinery and certain leverage lease arrangements, some complicated provisions (Sec. 39E) were introduced to deny initial and annual allowances to a lessor of plant and machinery in certain of the following situations:—

(1) Plant and machinery is purchased from and leased back to the same person or an associate of that person ("sale and leaseback").
(2) Certain leverage leases involving ships or aircraft.
(3) Certain leverage leases involving other plant and machinery used wholly or principally outside Hong Kong, or financed wholly or predominantly by non-recourse debt.

The provisions affect only initial and annual allowances otherwise claimable by the lessor; there are no other tax effects although the provisions attempt to make clear what is a lease as distinct from a deferred purchase of an asset. The provisions do not, however, in any way address the issue of the assessability of lease rentals. It should, however, be noted that in paragraph 20 of *Departmental Interpretation & Practice Notes No. 21* (see Appendix 13), the Commissioner has stated that where Sec. 39E operates to deny a lessor depreciation allowances in respect of leased plant and machinery, the income from the leasing of the plant and machinery will generally be regarded as non-taxable. This appears to be quite a generous concession in practice since, as noted above and discussed in more detail later, Sec. 39E can operate to deny depreciation allowances in respect of plant and machinery in a number of situations and while the exemption of lease rentals derived in respect of assets used mainly outside Hong Kong is arguably within the source concept fundamental to Profits Tax, the exemption of sums derived from the leasing of assets financed wholly or predominantly by non-recourse debt or which have been the subject of a sale and leaseback between associates has no logical basis in law; further, the exemption of such sums undoubtedly leaves the way open for exploitation through creative tax planning.

The provisions affecting ships and aircraft apply to leases predominantly financed by way of non-recourse debt and also to cross border leases where the lessee in not a "Hong Kong operator" of ships or aircraft.

5.10.1 When is a lease not a lease?

It is important to be able to ascertain when an arrangement constitutes a lease and when it does not. This is because generally the entire periodic payments under a lease are rentals which are, subject to the usual profits tax provisions, fully assessable to the lessor and fully deductible to the lessee. Where, however, an arrangement is not a lease but some form of purchase arrangement, the periodic payments will normally be partly interest and partly capital.

In deciding whether an arrangement is to be considered a lease, it is appropriate in the first instance to consider the definition of "lease" in Sec. 2. This definition excludes from the meaning of a lease a hire-purchase agreement and a conditional sale agreement, unless the Commissioner is of the opinion that the right under such an agreement to purchase or obtain the property in the goods would reasonably be expected not to be exercised. The terms "hire-purchase agreement" and "conditional sale agreement" are themselves defined as follows:

(1) **Hire-Purchase Agreement:** This follows the common law definition in referring to an agreement for the bailment (hire) of goods under which the bailee (hirer) may buy the goods or under which the property in the goods will or may pass to the bailee (Sec. 2). Note that this seems to cover the situation where there is an opportunity to acquire the asset even at a full market value. The right or opportunity must, however, be under the agreement although a side letter with no separate consideration may well be part of the agreement.

The above definition does not extend to the situation where an associate of the hirer may purchase or otherwise obtain the goods. Nonetheless, in *Departmental Interpretation & Practice Notes No. 15*, the IRD express the view that such an arrangement is unacceptable, which presumably means that they consider that they can challenge an arrangement where a person seeks to avoid the definition of a hire-purchase agreement (and therefore potentially fall within the definition of a lease), by arranging for an associate to acquire the right to purchase or obtain title to the goods.

In addition to being relevant to the definition of a lease, the statutory definition of a hire-purchase agreement is also relevant for the purpose of Sec. 37A which sets out rules for claiming depreciation allowances in respect of goods acquired under a hire-purchase agreement, as was discussed in sections 5.9.1 and 5.9.2.

(2) **Conditional Sale Agreement:** This is defined in Sec. 2 and means a sale agreement where the consideration is payable by instalments but ownership remains with the seller until the conditions laid down in the agreement as to payment of instalments or otherwise, are satisfied.

It is also appropriate to note that the definition of a lease in Sec. 2 extends to arrangements that do not amount to a formal lease but under which the owner of plant and machinery grants a right to use that plant and machinery to another person. Successive grants to other persons are also so recognised as a lease.

Although the term "lease" is statutorily defined, the IRD in *Departmental Interpretation & Practice Notes 15* provide further factors which they consider need to be satisfied for an arrangement to be accepted as a lease. In particular, the IRD state that a lease or any related documentation cannot contain any provision under which the ownership of the goods may pass to the lessee. This requirement effectively already exists through the exclusion of hire-purchase and conditional sale agreements from the statutory definition of a lease. Additionally, however, the IRD state that an arrangement will not be considered a lease unless the residual value provided for in the lease is reasonable. This requirement has no statutory basis, however, and for the IRD to challenge an arrangement on this basis would presumably require the application of Sec. 61 or 61A (see chapter 10).

Notwithstanding the reasonably extensive definition of "lease" in Sec. 2, the application of that definition in other statutory provisions raises some uncertainties. This is because the term is not used to specify the normal treatment of lease rentals, but is relevant only for a limited number of specific provisions. For example, it is relevant for the purpose of Sec. 39E (an anti-avoidance provision discussed in sections 5.10.2 and 5.10.3), but because the statutory definition excludes hire-purchase and conditional sale agreements, the lessor or seller under such arrangements cannot be denied depreciation deductions pursuant to Sec. 39E. It is not clear whether this is because the legislature intended that the lessor or seller claim the depreciation allowances in such circumstances or the allowances are not considered available to that party anyway.

In the case of a hire purchase agreement, the lessee (buyer) can certainly claim allowances under Sec. 37A but there is nothing in the IRO which says that the lessor (seller) cannot also claim them on the grounds that he is still the owner and he may regard the instalments as lease rental income. Sec.

39E does nothing to change this because it does not apply to hire purchase arrangements. The lessee (buyer) cannot, of course, claim both the depreciation allowances and the instalments as lease rental payments, but does he have an option?

However, reference to case law may decide the issue; in particular, *Littlewoods Mail Order Stores Ltd. v McGregor* (45 TC 519) is of relevance. In that case, a company surrendered an 88-year lease on a building for a 22-year lease at a materially higher rent as part of a transaction in which a subsidiary of the company acquired the freehold. The additional rent paid was disallowed as capital expenditure in acquiring an asset, namely the freehold notwithstanding that the asset was acquired by a subsidiary. *Departmental Interpretation & Practice Notes No. 15* (see Appendix 10 paragraphs 65 to 66) indicate that this may be the IRD's view as applied to a hire-purchase agreement, thereby ensuring that the lessee (buyer) has no option but to claim depreciation allowances. The lessor (seller) would, in the same light and depending upon his circumstances, probably be treated as either a dealer in the goods which are the subject of the agreement or having, in effect, made a loan. Either way it would be unlikely to be treated as a lease.

There must, however, be a strong doubt as to whether the principle established in the *Littlewoods* case could apply where there is a lease at a normal market rent with an option to purchase at any time at the market value at that time. Such an agreement would fall into the definition of hire purchase agreement in Sec. 40(1) but the rental payments lack the hallmarks of a hidden purchase element. In those circumstances it would seem open to the lessee to claim the rentals as a deduction and for the lessor to claim depreciation allowances and yet not be subject to the restrictions in Sec. 39E.

In the case of a conditional sale agreement, there can never be any question of treating the instalments as rental payments either in the hands of the buyer or the seller because the agreement is quite simply a sale and not a hire arrangement. It is, therefore, not surprising that it is excluded from the application of Sec. 39E because, fundamentally, it can never be a lease. The buyer can claim initial allowances on the instalments as they become due but cannot claim the annual allowances until such time as the agreement becomes unconditional and he becomes the owner. There is, however, no good reason why a purchaser under a conditional sale agreement should not have the same entitlement to annual allowances from the outset as a purchaser under a hire-purchase agreement but Sec. 37A does not presently permit this.

5.10.2 Sale and leaseback

Initial and annual allowances are denied to a lessor of plant and machinery where, prior to acquisition by the lessor, the plant and machinery had been owned and used by the person who is now the lessee or part lessee with others or by any person associated with the lessee (Sec. 39E(1)(a)). Because this is an anti-avoidance provision, various terms used in this connection are widely defined in Sec. 39E(5). For example an "associate" is very widely defined to include all kinds of connected persons and companies under common control as follows:—

(a) Where the lessee is a natural person:
   - a relative.
   - a partner or any relative of a partner.
   - a partnership of which he is a partner.
   - a company controlled by the lessee or by his partner or a partnership of which he is a partner or a director or principal officer of any such company.
(b) Where the lessee is a company:
   - a company which it controls or is controlled by it or is under the same control directly or indirectly as the lessee company.
   - a person who controls the company and any partner or relative of such person.
   - a director or principal officer of the lessee company or of any company under common control with it as above and any relative of such director or officer.
   - a partner of the lessee company or any relative of such partner.
(c) Where the lessee is a partnership:
   - a partner and, where a partner is itself a partnership, any partner of that partnership.
   - a partner with the lessee partnership in any other partnership and, where such a partner is itself a partnership, any partner of that partnership.
   - where any of the partners included in the above provisions is a natural person, any relative of that partner.
   - a company controlled by the lessee partnership or by any partner or relative of a partner or any director or principal officer of such company.
   - a company of which a partner is director or principal officer.

"Control" is further defined widely to mean any power exercisable by the holding of shares or voting power or any other power contained in the articles of association or other document regulating the affairs of a company. Both "relative" and "principal officer" are also widely defined.

Once it has been identified that the lessor has purchased the relevant asset from the lessee or an associated person, it is necessary to see whether the lessee or associated person owned and used the plant and machinery in question. It is often the case that the lessee may have been initially contracted with a supplier for the equipment but, before delivery, sold the benefit of the purchase agreement to a financier who will become the lessor. If these arrangements are such that the lessor obtains title directly from the supplier, there is no question of denial of depreciation allowances to the lessor under Sec. 39E(1)(a). Even if title does pass from the supplier to the lessee and then to the lessor, there is still no question of the application of Sec. 39E(1)(a) unless the lessee actually used the equipment before selling to the lessor. Whether the equipment has been used is a question of fact but it is defined in Sec. 39E(5) to include equipment which is installed ready for use and held in reserve.

The law does, however, recognise the realistic position that, due to a temporary delay in financing arrangements, equipment may for a short period actually be in the ownership and use of the lessee. The lessor will still be entitled to the initial and annual allowances provided that:—

(a) the lessor's purchase price paid to the lessee or lessee's associate was not more than the price which the lessee or associate paid to the supplier. This relaxation is not available if the supplier or his associate was in fact an owner and user of the equipment. This prevents the use of an intermediate between the original supplier and the lessee to increase the cost which can be passed on to the lessor (Sec. 39E (2)(a)); and

(b) no initial or annual allowances have been granted to the lessee in respect of his initial acquisition of the equipment (Sec. 39E(2)(b)). Because mere acquisition by the lessee will result in at least initial allowances being available to him it is provided that, to enable the relaxation to be effective, he may disclaim any allowances by notice in writing to the Commissioner within 3 months of his initial acquisition of the equipment or such longer time as the Commissioner may permit (Sec. 39E(3)).

Throughout these provisions, when reference is made to an acquisition of plant and machinery, whether by the lessor or the lessee or any associate, this means not only where he becomes the legal owner but also includes holding under the benefit of a hire-purchase or conditional sale agreement (the meanings of which are discussed in section 5.10.1) because, otherwise, until the exercise of the option or the contingency under such agreements, the "hirer" is in legal terms not the owner (Sec. 39E(5)).

Also, to further tighten the provisions, plant and machinery either owned or leased by a trustee or by a company controlled by such trustee is treated as owned or leased, as appropriate, additionally by the beneficiary of the trust or the company or, in the case of a discretionary trust, by any such beneficiary as the Commissioner may, in his discretion, decide (Sec. 39E (4)). For this purpose, a beneficiary may include an indirect beneficiary through another person or who may be able, directly or indirectly to control the activities of the trust or the application of its income or capital (Sec. 39E (5)).

The provisions of Sec. 39E are also discussed in *Departmental Interpretation and Practice Notes No. 15*, which is reproduced as Appendix 10.

■ Example 5.16

Bremridge Ltd. has contracted with a Japanese shipbuilder for the supply of a passenger ferry at a cost of $20 million. When the ship was ready for delivery, Bremridge Ltd. found that, upon negotiating with financiers, there was a considerable reduction in the cost of financing if it sold the ship to the financier and leased it back over a period of 15 years. The negotiations took a little time, however, and Bremridge Ltd. has taken delivery of the ship and it had been on standby ready for immediate service, although it was not actually put into service, for one month before it was sold to the Hong Kong Taxsavers Leasing Partnership and leased back.

Two questions would arise on this:—

(1) Whether Bremridge Ltd., assuming that it was using the ship for the purposes of earning assessable profits in Hong Kong, could deduct the lease payments.
(2) Whether Taxsavers, also assuming that it was carrying on business in Hong Kong and the lease income represents Hong Kong source income, is entitled to initial and annual allowances on the ship.

Question (1): It would be necessary to check whether the payments constituted lease rentals. If Bremridge has any option or opportunity to purchase the ship at the end of the lease or at any earlier time this would amount to a hire-purchase agreement (see section 5.10.1) and Bremridge could therefore probably only claim the interest element of the payments, assuming that they qualify for relief under Sec. 16(2) (see section 4.5. 8). It would also be entitled to depreciation allowances as a hire purchaser. If, however, the purchase option was at a full market value, although this would still amount to a hire purchase agreement for depreciation allowance purposes, Bremridge may well be able to claim the instalments as lease rentals instead of depreciation allowances (see discussion in section 5.10.1).

Question (2): First of all if question (1) determined the lease to be a hire-purchase arrangement, Taxsavers could obtain no depreciation allowances because its expenditure on the initial purchase from Bremridge would probably not be regarded as capital expenditure in view of the immediate resale back to Bremridge. So far as Taxsavers is concerned it is therefore probably treated as a financing transaction with the income to Taxsavers being the interest element of the payments and no entitlement to depreciation allowances.

   If, however, the leaseback was accepted as constituting a lease, Sec. 39E(1)(a) would operate initially to deny initial and annual allowances to Taxsavers because Bremridge had owned and used the ship before selling it to Taxsavers. Keeping it on standby amounts to it being used for this purpose.

   Taxsavers is, however, protected by Sec. 39E(2) provided that —

(a) It pays Bremridge not more than $20 million for the ship; and

(b) Bremridge writes to the Commissioner within 3 months of the conclusion of its contract with the shipbuilder, disclaiming any depreciation allowances. If, as is often the case in the purchase of substantial assets such as ships, the purchase contract had been concluded long ago, the Commissioner may permit an extension to the period of disclaimer. If, however, Bremridge had claimed initial allowance on progress payments it is not clear whether these could be disclaimed and reversed.

Notes:—

(a) Even though Taxsavers may have eventually passed the tests under Secs. 39E(1) and 39E(2), it will also have to pass the leverage lease tests relating to ships (see next paragraphs) and, having passed those, the general anti-aviodance tests in Sec. 61A (see section 10.4.5) before it can be certain of obtaining the allowances.

(b) The assumptions have been simplified for the purpose of illustration. Even so, the complexity and inter-relationship of numerous taxation principles should demonstrate to the reader the severe complexity that anti-avoidance legislation injects into a commercial transaction.

(c) See also Appendix 10 for the IRD's view on these issues.

5.10.3 Leveraged leases — general

The type of leveraged lease which has attracted adverse attention is, in very broad terms, one whereby the lessor finances his acquisition of the plant and machinery substantially by way of loan finance where the lender has recourse only to the asset itself or the income arising from the leasing of the asset and, furthermore, where the lessee's use of the asset does not give significant economic benefit to Hong Kong. The reason why these factors have attracted attention is that a lease of a substantial piece of plant or machinery, such as an aircraft, could be structured whereby the lessor is a Hong Kong registered limited partnership carrying on business in Hong Kong and the lessee may use the equipment wholly outside Hong Kong.

The lease could be concluded so that the profit therefrom has a Hong Kong source and, therefore, substantial losses for Profits Tax purposes could arise in the early years due to depreciation allowances and the high interest charge. As a consequence, limited partners with taxable profits in Hong Kong could reduce those profits by their shares of the losses and yet not be at risk because the lender has no recourse to their assets.

The anti-avoidance provisions strike at these apparent benefits in two ways. Firstly, in Sec. 39E, by denying depreciation allowances to the lessor where identified tests are not met and secondly, in Sec. 22B, by preventing limited partners from using their shares of partnership losses against other income. It is important to appreciate, however, that even if the tests in Secs. 39E and 22B are satisfied, the arrangements may still be considered by the Commissioner in the light of the general anti-avoidance provisions in Sec. 61A (see section 10.4.5). The requirements of Sec. 39E are considered in appropriate circumstances in the following sections and those of Sec. 22B in section 4.5.15.5.

Finally, for the purposes of the provisions relating to leveraged leases as described in the following paragraphs, a lease is as discussed in section 5.10.1 and does not include hire-purchase or conditional sale agreements unless the Commissioner considers that the option to purchase is, in all the circumstances, unlikely to be exercised (Sec. 39E(5)).

5.10.4 Non-recourse debt

What constitutes a "non-recourse debt" in the case of a lease is very important in determining what is a leverage lease affected by Sec. 39E.

Sec. 39E(5) defines a non-recourse debt as one where the rights of the creditor in the event of any default in the repayment of the principal or payment of the interest are wholly or predominantly limited to no more than:—

(a)   rights against the equipment itself or its use;

(b)   rights against goods or services provided or produced by the use of the equipment;

(c)   rights in relation to any loss or disposal of the equipment in whole or in part, e.g. sale proceeds or insurance recovery;

(d)   rights against any money payable in connection with (a), (b) or (c) or any conjunction of rights under (a), (b) and (c);

(e)   rights in respect of any mortgage or security over the equipment; or

(f)   rights related to the financial obligations of the lessee towards the lessor in connection with the equipment, e.g. recourse against the lease rentals.

Even if the rights of the creditor are not specifically limited to all or any of the foregoing rights, the debt will be treated as a non-recourse debt if, in the Commissioner's opinion, the rights can be effectively so limited because the extent of the lessor's assets or the effect of any arrangements to which the lessor is a party, have the result that the creditor's rights are in effect no more than those listed. For example, where the lessor comprises a limited partnership whose only asset is the equipment in question and the general partners have no material assets, a lender to the partnership would effectively have no more rights than those listed and so any debt would be within the definition of non-recourse debt. Even where the lessor has assets other than the equipment in question, if those other assets are not available to discharge the whole of the debt, including outstanding interest, on the equipment in question, they are to be ignored for the foregoing purposes. Furthermore, if there are other assets but they are pledged as security for another debt, they are also to be ignored for the foregoing purpose. The definition cannot, therefore, be circumvented by having more than one asset in a partnership or company if each is secured against debt.

5.10.5 Leveraged leases — ships or aircraft

Initial and annual allowances are denied to a lessor of ships or aircraft or any part thereof, such as an engine, if:—

(a) the lessee is not an operator of a Hong Kong ship or aircraft; or

(b) the whole or a predominant part of the cost of acquisition or construction of the ship or aircraft was financed directly or indirectly by non-recourse debt (see section 5.10.4) (Sec. 39E(1)(c)).

The purpose of this provision is essentially to restrict Hong Kong leveraged leasing transactions to ships and aircraft of Hong Kong based businesses. Without such a restriction, it would be possible to structure leveraged lease transactions in a manner whereby the benefit of tax depreciation allowances on ships and aircraft which had only limited connection to Hong Kong could be enjoyed by Hong Kong taxpayers. Notwithstanding that this would also require the income from the leasing of such assets to be brought into the charge to Hong Kong Profits Tax, the generous nature of the depreciation allowances and the typical rental stream flows under such transactions could potentially result in significant revenue losses to the IRD in either absolute, or net present value, terms.

For the purpose of paragraph (b) in the above definition, the Commissioner, in *Departmental Interpretation & Practice Notes No. 15* (see Appendix 10) considers, quite logically, that finance will only be considered predominantly non-recourse where at least 51% of such finance is obtained on a non-recourse basis. This, coupled with the requirement that the lessee must be *"... an operator of a Hong Kong ship or aircraft ...,"* means that the ability of lessors to obtain depreciation allowances for ships and aircrafts is quite restricted.

An *"operator of a Hong Kong ship"* is defined as a person who:—

(a) carries on a business of operating ships and the business is managed and controlled in Hong Kong; *and*

(b) is responsible for paying all or a substantial part of the ship operating expenses and the ship operates mainly in Hong Kong waters or between Hong Kong waters and ports in the Pearl River Delta (Sec. 39E(5)).

It is also worth noting that, if the above conditions are not met, the lessor's charter hire income will not be subject to Profits Tax (see section 4.7.4), so the question of depreciation allowances would not arise in any event. Leveraged leasing of ships in international waters, therefore, cannot be undertaken to generate Hong Kong tax benefits.

An *"operator of a Hong Kong aircraft"* is defined as a person who:—

(a) carries on a business of operating aircraft and the business is managed and controlled in Hong Kong; *and*

(b) holds an air operators' certificate issued under the Air Navigation (Hong Kong) Order 1995 (Sec. 39E(5)).

Requirement (b) is highly limiting and, effectively, means that leverage leases of aircraft in order to generate Hong Kong tax benefits are only possible where the lessee operates Hong Kong registered aircraft under Hong Kong aviation law. Foreign airlines would not be able to satisfy this requirement.

See also the discussion on loss limitation for partnerships in section 4.5.15.5; this affects the availability of loss set-offs to limited partners.

■ Example 5.17

Dragon Pacific Airlines Ltd. is incorporated in Hong Kong and has just taken delivery of a new aircraft which it will operate between Tokyo and Vancouver. To finance its acquisition it has decided to lease the aircraft from a Hong Kong registered limited partnership which has two limited partners who are substantial corporate taxpayers in Hong Kong and a general partner which is a Hong Kong company with only nominal assets. The limited partners have advanced capital to the partnership amounting to 10% of the cost of the aircraft and the balance has been financed by an advance from a bank secured by a mortgage on the aircraft.

Ignoring Sec. 39E, the partnership would be in receipt of assessable lease rentals and could claim initial and annual allowances and could deduct the loan interest.

Sec. 39E(1)(c) has to be considered and one of the two necessary requirements is not met because the bank loan is clearly "non-recourse debt," because the bank only has rights against the aircraft, partnership income and nominal assets of the general partner. To satisfy this test, the bank would have to be given the right of recourse against the assets of the limited partners to the extent of at least 41% of the cost of the aircraft so that the non-recourse part of the loan amounted to only 49% of the cost. Alternatively, the partners might contribute a higher portion of capital. However, this is not the only test. It is also essential that Dragon Pacific Airlines be an "operator of Hong Kong aircraft". Incorporation in Hong Kong and management of its business in Hong Kong is insufficient if it is just a subsidiary of a foreign airline, operating its aircraft under the laws of another country. If however it meets the tests of a Hong Kong airline it can satisfy the requirements of Sec. 39E.

Notes:—

(a) Although Sec. 39E is not applicable, the Commissioner would consider the circumstances under Sec. 61A (see section 10.4.5) and he may decide to challenge the tax benefits accruing to the limited partners under those provisions. In the particular circumstances he would be unlikely to grant advance clearance if only because the capital contribution of 10% would be regarded as insufficient.

(b) Notwithstanding satisfying Secs. 39E and 61A, the ultimate hurdle that would destroy the tax benefits in the particular circumstances is the provisions of Sec. 22B (see section 4.5.15.5) which would limit the extent to which the limited partners could claim their share of partnership losses to be set against their own profits to the amount of their capital contribution. To overcome this, the partnership would have to be a general partnership which highlights the requirements that, to achieve tax benefits, the parties need to have substantial exposure to commercial liability.

(c) If Dragon Pacific Airlines had an option to purchase in the lease agreement, the agreement would then be a hire purchase agreement and not caught by Sec. 39E. Dragon Pacific Airlines could claim depreciation allowances under Sec. 37A but, for whether it could alternatively claim the rentals as a deduction and what the tax treatment of the partnership would be, see the discussion on what constitutes a lease in section 5.10.1.

5.10.6 Leveraged leases — machinery or plant other than ships or aircraft

Sec. 39E(1)(b) provides that initial and annual allowances are denied to a lessor of machinery or plant, other than ships or aircraft, if:

(a) the equipment is used wholly or principally outside Hong Kong by the lessee; or

(b) the whole or a predominant part of the cost of acquisition or construction of the equipment was financed directly or indirectly by non-recourse debt (see section 5.10.4).

It should be noted that that the effect of the word "or" after (a) is that falling within either or both of the above situations will result in the denial of the allowances. The Commissioner, in *Departmental Interpretation & Practice Notes No. 15* (see Appendix 10) considers, quite logically, that finance will only be considered predominantly non-recourse where at least 51% of such finance is obtained on a non-recourse basis.

Where plant and machinery has been provided by a Hong Kong taxpayer to a Mainland enterprise under a contract processing arrangement, it would appear that the arrangement is to be considered a lease even though no rental is charged. As the plant and machinery would be used by the Mainland enterprise outside Hong Kong, strictly Sec. 39E(1)(b) would operate to deny any depreciation allowances. In practice, however, the IRD does not apply the provision of Sec. 39E(1)(b) for contract processing arrangements falling within the 50:50 apportionment concession under *Departmental Interpretation & Practice Notes No. 21*. Nevertheless, the IRD is not prepared to extend this concession to other cases, such as import processing arrangements (see minutes of the 2004 Annual Meeting between the IRD and the Taxation Committee of the HKICPA).

See also the discussion concerning loss limitation of partnerships in section 4.5.15.5; this affects the availability of loss set-offs to limited partners.

■ Example 5.18

Bacon Construction Company Ltd. has just taken delivery of a new earth-moving vehicle and, in view of the fact that it will only be required for two projects, had decided to lease rather than buy. It will lease from a Hong Kong registered limited partnership which has three limited partners who are substantial corporate taxpayers in Hong Kong and a general partner which is a Hong Kong company with only nominal assets. The limited partners have advanced capital to the partnership amounting to 10% of the cost of the vehicle and the balance has been financed by an advance from a bank secured by a mortgage on the vehicle.

In year 1 Bacon used the vehicle exclusively in a construction project in Hong Kong and, in year 2, the vehicle was moved to a construction site on the Mainland where it was used except for a period of 3 months when it was brought back to Hong Kong for use in the Hong Kong project. The lease agreement was negotiated and concluded in Hong Kong.

Ignoring Sec. 39E, the partnership would be in receipt of assessable lease rentals and could claim initial and annual allowances and could deduct the loan interest.

Sec. 39E(1)(b) has to be considered and one of the two necessary requirements is not met because the bank loan is clearly "non-recourse debt" because the bank only has rights against the equipment, partnership income and nominal assets of the general partner. To satisfy this test, the bank would have to be given the right of recourse against the assets of the limited partners to the extent of at least 41% of the cost of the equipment so that the non-recourse part of the loan amounted to only 49% of the cost. Alternatively, the partners might contribute a higher portion of capital. As Bacon satisfies the second test by wholly using the equipment in Hong Kong in year 1, Sec. 39E(1)(b) would not be applicable and the allowances would not be denied under Sec. 39E so long as the financing structure was changed as indicated.

In year 2 it could not be said that the equipment is predominantly used in Hong Kong; therefore Sec. 39E(1)(b) would be applicable, even if the financing was restructured, and no annual allowance is available for year 2. Further, on the basis of *Departmental Interpretation & Practice Notes No. 21* (see section 5.10) the rentals in year 2 would generally be considered to be exempt from Profits Tax on the grounds that the equipment is used predominantly outside Hong Kong and, therefore, the interest would also cease to be deductible. This overall situation may not be satisfactory to the limited partners as they may have been expecting the partnership to sustain a loss after deduction of depreciation allowances and interest, with such loss being available to shelter some portion of their other profits. It is therefore apparent that the partnership is, in effect, at the mercy of Bacon in relation to obtaining allowances and it would have to dictate the place of use in the agreement if it was to avoid the problem.

Notes:

(a) Even if Sec. 39E is not applicable in year 1, the Commissioner would consider the circumstances under Sec. 61A (see section 10.4.5). In the particular circumstances, he would be unlikely to grant advance clearance if only because the capital contribution of 10% would be regarded as insufficient.

(b) Notwithstanding satisfying Secs. 39E and 61A, the ultimate hurdle that would destroy the tax benefits in the particular circumstances is the provisions of Sec. 22B (see section 4.5.15.5) which would limit the extent to which the limited partners could claim their share of partnership losses to be set against their own profits to the amount of their capital contribution. To overcome this, the partnership would have to be a general partnership which highlights the current requirements that, to achieve tax benefits, the parties need to have substantial exposure to commercial liability.

5.11 Miscellaneous Points Relating to Depreciation Allowances

There are some provisions which are not related just to one class of depreciation allowances but which cover the application of depreciation allowances in general. These are discussed below.

5.11.1 Basis periods

It is, of course, necessary to relate depreciation allowances to a year of assessment. This is achieved in the same way as profits or losses are related to a year of assessment in that events which govern the allowances (acquisition, disposal, use, etc.) give rise to adjustments for the year of assessment of which the period in which these events occur is the basis period.

However, this general rule cannot be applied where an event falls into a period which either falls out of account in computing profits or which forms the basis period or part of a basis period for more than one year of assessment. These situations can arise on commencement, cessation of business or change of accounting date (see sections 4.6.2 to 4.6.4). In these circumstances the rules in Sec. 40(1) are as follows:—

(1) where two basis periods overlap, the period which is common to both is deemed to fall into the first basis period only; or

(2) where there is an interval between the end of a basis period for one year of assessment and the beginning of a basis period for the next year of assessment, the interval is deemed to fall into the second basis period.

■ Example 5.19

Because of a change of accounting date from 31st December to 30th June, a company's Profits Tax assessments for 2006/07 and 2007/08 are based on the following basis periods:—

2006/07	Year ended 31st December 2006
2007/08	12 months to 30th June 2007

The company purchased a machine on 31st December 2006 and a lorry on 1st January 2007.

As the period 1st July 2006 to 31st December 2006 is common to both 2006/07 and 2007/08, this period is deemed to fall only into the basis period for 2006/07 for depreciation allowance purposes. Accordingly the machine purchased on 31st December 2006 qualifies for initial allowance for 2006/07 and for annual allowances for 2006/07 and 2007/08 but the lorry qualifies for initial and annual allowances only for 2007/08.

■ Example 5.20

A company whose normal accounting date was 31st December and which had been in business for 40 years, changed its accounting date to 31st March as a result of which Profits Tax assessments were based on the following basis periods:—

2006/07	Year ended 31st December 2006
2007/08	Year ended 31st March 2008

It sold one of its industrial buildings on 1st January 2007 on which a large balancing allowance arose.

As the period 1st January to 31st March 2007 does not fall into the basis period for either year of assessment, it is deemed to fall into the basis period for 2007/08 for depreciation allowance purposes. Accordingly the balancing allowance arising on the sale of the building will fall into 2007/08.

5.11.2 Apportionment

When only a part of the profits of a business are liable to Profits Tax, it is necessary to appropriately apportion the expenses and outgoings (see section 4.5.14). It is equally necessary to apportion depreciation allowances in the same circumstances and the authority for this is the use of the phrase "to the extent to which the relevant assets are used in the production of assessable profits" in Sec. 18F(1). Accordingly, the full depreciation allowances are computed and then apportioned to the amount allowable. It is specifically provided that the calculation is to be made in this way and not by computing a reduced initial and annual allowance before deducting it from the expenditure brought forward (Sec. 39A).

5.11.3 Commissioner's powers to determine cost or value of asset

There are certain situations where the cost of an asset can be manipulated to obtain a tax advantage or where it is not possible to accurately determine the cost of a single asset. The IRO deals with these circumstances by giving the Commissioner power to determine the position.

Where an asset is acquired together with other assets as a bargain at a single price and it is necessary to determine the individual price of any one or more of these assets for the purpose of computing depreciation allowances, the Commissioner is empowered to allocate a price to each individual asset, having regard to all the circumstances of the transaction (Sec. 38A).

Where an asset which qualifies for depreciation allowances is sold and the purchaser and seller are persons under common control, or are husband and wife, the Commissioner has the power to substitute his determination of the true market value if he considers that the sale price does not represent a true market value at the date of sale (Sec. 38B). Because it is generally difficult to ascertain the market value of depreciated assets, this power is, in practice, generally only exercised in blatant cases (e.g. where assets are transferred at a price which has the effect of shifting profits between related parties through the creation of balancing charges, balancing allowances and initial and annual allowances).

In each of these cases, as a matter of practice, the power is delegated to assessors in the normal course of their duties.

Chapter 6 ■
Personal Assessment

6.1 Legislation

The law governing Personal Assessment is contained in Part VII of the IRO Secs. 40B to 43. Personal allowances, also dealt with in this chapter, are contained in Part V of the IRO Secs. 27 to 33 and Schedule 4. Also relevant are the assessing provisions in Part X and provisions covering returns and information in Part IX.

6.2 The Purpose of Personal Assessment

The income based taxation system in Hong Kong, unlike most income tax systems, does not involve a computation of total income upon which tax is charged, but rather consists of three separate taxes, Property Tax, Salaries Tax and Profits Tax, each of which is separately assessed quite independently of the others. Furthermore, only Salaries Tax carries an entitlement to deduct personal allowances and to be charged at progressive rates of tax; the other taxes are charged at a fixed single rate of tax with no deductions for personal allowances.

There are a number of circumstances where assessment under a total income computation would, in fact, produce a smaller overall tax liability than the combined separate taxes. For this reason, the Personal Assessment provisions provide an opportunity for an individual to elect for total income assessment involving the personal allowances and progressive tax rates that otherwise apply only to Salaries Tax. In addition, Personal Assessment provides for some other deductions that would not otherwise be available for the purposes of Profits Tax or Property Tax and also allows business losses to be set off against other sources of income. It does not, however, cause any sources of income to be taxed that would not be taxed under the separate taxes.

The following occasions would give cause for an individual to elect for Personal Assessment:—

(1) having agreed losses for Profits Tax purposes and having a source or sources of income under Salaries Tax or Property Tax;

(2) having a source of income under Profits Tax or Property Tax where the total income does not reach the break-even point (for break-even point, see section 3.6.3);

(3) being liable to Salaries Tax at a marginal rate which is lower than the standard rate and having a source of income liable to Profits Tax or Property Tax;

(4) having incurred interest expenses in connection with the financing

of a property which generates rental income subject to Property Tax; and/or

(5)   where charitable donations statutory limit under Salaries Tax or Profits Tax but there is a source of income subject to Property Tax.

Under each of these circumstances, the individual's total tax payable can be reduced by bringing all assessable income together in a single assessment attracting personal allowances and progressive rates of tax. The Personal Assessment provisions and IRD practice, however, ensure that the tax cannot be greater than would be the case under the separate heads bearing in mind that for the 2007/08 year of assessment the progressive rates rise to 17% whereas the standard rate for individuals is only 16%.

6.3 Persons Who Qualify

An election for Personal Assessment applies, of course, only to individuals. Additionally, an election can only be made by an individual aged 18 years or more, or under that age if both his parents are dead, who is a permanent or temporary resident of Hong Kong.

In the case of married couples, either spouse can elect provided that they are 18 years of age or more (or under that age if both his or her parents are dead) and either they or their spouse are permanent or temporary residents of Hong Kong (Sec. 41(1)). In the case of married couples not living apart, however, both must enter into the election if they both have income to be included and both are eligible to elect. See, however, further comment on husbands and wives in section 6.4.

This is one of the few places in the IRO where residency status is significant. The terms permanent resident and temporary resident are defined in Sec. 41(4). "Permanent resident" is defined as an individual who ordinarily resides in Hong Kong. Although the term "ordinarily resident" is not defined, its meaning was considered in *D 57/02*. In that case, which concerned the meaning of the term for the purpose of dependent parent and dependent grandparent allowances, the Board of Review rejected the taxpayer's claim that certain dependents were ordinarily resident in Hong Kong on the basis that they owned property in Hong Kong and maintained bank accounts, credit cards and club memberships in Hong Kong, notwithstanding that they actually lived abroad. In reaching their decision, the Board of Review applied the definition given to the term in an immigration case (*Director of Immigration v Ng Shun-loi* [1987] (HKLR 798)). In that decision, Hunter J, quoting from *Levene v IRC* (13 TC 486), stated that the words "ordinarily resident" mean:

"... that the person must be habitually and normally resident here apart from temporary or occasional absences of long or short duration ...".

He also went on to quote from *R v Barnet London Borough Council, ex parte Nilish Shah* [1982] (1 QB 688) wherein it was stated that:

"A person is resident where he resides....When is he ordinarily resident ? I think that is when he resides there in an ordinary way. That must be the meaning of the adverb. The expression is therefore contemplating residence for the purposes of everyday life. It is residence in the place where a person lives and conducts his daily life in circumstances which lead to the conclusion that he is living there as an ordinary member of the community would live for all the purposes of his daily life".

In *D 57/02*, the dependents in question lived abroad and had been physically absent from Hong Kong for significant periods. In these circumstances, it was arguably a straightforward matter for the Board of Review to find that the individuals were not resident or ordinarily resident in Hong Kong. A similar conclusion was reached in *D 7/05* where an individual who, although born and raised in Hong Kong, lived abroad and made only occasional visits to Hong Kong. In these circumstances, the individual was held not to be ordinarily resident in Hong Kong and, therefore, ineligible to elect for Personal Assessment. Quite often, however, the facts will not be as clear cut and in such cases it may be appropriate to consider the tests developed by the courts in the UK as to the meaning of "ordinarily resident". In addition to the cases above, there are numerous other UK cases which consider the meaning of "resident" including *Cooper v Cadwalader* (5 TC 101) and *Lysaght v CIR* (13 TC 511). These decisions are generally concerned with the meaning of "resident", although "ordinarily resident" has usually been taken to mean residence with a degree of continuity apart from temporary absences, as opposed to residence for more limited or temporary periods. On the basis of these UK decisions, the Hong Kong IRD is understood as a matter of practice to generally adopt the following rules:

(1) Where a residence is maintained in Hong Kong which is available as a place of abode, an individual will be considered a permanent resident if he makes regular and substantial visits to Hong Kong from year to year, and this will apply even to an isolated intervening year in which he does not visit Hong Kong at all.

(2) In the absence of an available place of abode in Hong Kong, an individual will not be regarded as a permanent resident unless there are regular visits of more than 180 days in a year or 300 days in two consecutive years, although under these circumstances the individual would be deemed by Sec. 41(4) to be a "temporary

resident", as discussed further below. Nonetheless, if in an intervening year there was no visit, the individual would not be treated as a resident, unlike the position in (1) above.

(3)   A person with no available place of abode in Hong Kong and who does not visit Hong Kong in a year of assessment will not be considered a permanent resident, even if they were resident in a previous year. Note that this was effectively the position in *D 57/02*.

Under established UK Revenue practice, an individual is also generally treated as ordinarily resident if he or she visits the UK regularly and the visits average more than 90 days in a tax year. The period of ordinary residence will commence in the first year in which visits started if there is an intention to regularly visit can be established at that time; otherwise, the period of ordinary residence will generally commence in the fifth year. As noted, however, this is merely UK Revenue practice and, although it has its origins in case law, is essentially only an administrative guideline which is not binding on law. Accordingly, the test should not be automatically adopted in Hong Kong as a determinant of ordinary residence (and therefore permanent residence), and it does not appear to be Hong Kong IRD practice to adopt it. Nonetheless, the test may provide some guidance in appropriate circumstances.

■ Example 6.1

(1)   Barry Munday normally lives in Australia but he owns a flat in Hong Kong which he lets except for one room which is retained as a bed-sitting room for him to use on his visits to Hong Kong. He visits for about one month every year to attend to business matters.

On the basis that he maintains a place of abode in, and makes regular and substantial visits to, Hong Kong, the IRD may accept Barry as a permanent resident and, if so, he or his wife could elect for Personal Assessment.

(2)   Eileen Dover normally lives in the UK but made a number of visits to Hong Kong in the year ended 31st March 2004 totalling 190 days and returned again for a number of visits in the year ended 31st March 2008 totalling 185 days. She stayed in a hotel.

Because Eileen's visits are not regular, she is unlikely to be considered a permanent resident. Nonetheless, she will be a temporary resident under the statutory definition for the 2003/04 and 2007/08 years of assessment and could, therefore, elect for Personal Assessment in those years.

(3)   Justin Smith lived and worked in Hong Kong for many years and holds a permanent Hong Kong ID card. He sold his flat in Hong Kong and moved to Australia in February 2007. Although he retained bank accounts, credit cards and a club membership in Hong Kong, he did not have an available place of abode in Hong Kong, nor did he visit Hong Kong during the year ended 31 March 2008.

Justin is not treated as either a permanent resident or a temporary resident for the 2007/08 year even though he had been a permanent resident for many years prior to that.

(4) Horst Diel normally lives in Germany but visited Hong Kong in 2004/05, 2005/06, 2006/07 and 2007/08 for 112 days, 82 days, 92 days and 79 days respectively. He stayed in a hotel during his visits.

   Horst's visits over the four years total 365 days and therefore average over 91 days per year. Under UK practice, he would be regarded as resident and ordinarily resident from 2008/09 (unless it was clear from the outset that it was his intention to make regular visits). Accordingly, following the UK tests for ordinary residence he or his wife could elect for Personal Assessment in 2008/09. It is not, however, automatic that this UK test would be adopted in Hong Kong in determining whether Horst was ordinarily resident.

"Temporary resident" is defined in Sec. 41(4) as an individual who is present in Hong Kong for a period or periods during the year of assessment amounting to more than 180 days or for more than 300 days over two consecutive years one of which is the year for which an election is sought. This is a clear definition involving no necessity to refer to case law. Eileen Dover in Example 6.1 would clearly qualify as a temporary resident for 2003/04 and 2007/08.

Unlike Salaries Tax, there are no separate taxation provisions for Personal Assessment. Accordingly, an election by a married couple automatically brings with it joint assessment, although there are provisions for apportioning the tax between them.

Where an individual has died, his executor can make the election in respect of his income, assuming of course that the deceased's residence status so qualified (Sec. 41(2)).

There is a special provision in Sec. 41(2A) in respect of an individual (or his executor who has elected for Personal Assessment for the year of assessment in which the death occurred) and the individual was a partner in a partnership. If the individual had a share in the partnership profits or losses for a year of assessment following that in which the death occurred, the executor may claim to have his share of assessable profit or adjusted loss for that latter year brought back into the year of assessment in which the death occurred.

6.4 The Election

Sec. 41(3) provides that the election must be made in writing and must be received by the Inland Revenue Department not later than the latter of:—

(1) two years after the end of the year of assessment in respect of which the election is to be made; or

(2)   one month (or such further period as the Commissioner may allow) after any notice of assessment on any income which will fall into the total income election has become final and conclusive; in other words, within two months (or such further period as the Commissioner may allow) after the issue of an assessment against which no objection has been lodged or within one month after the settlement or withdrawal of any objection or appeal.

The election is, in fact, generally made on the composite tax return which contains a space for making the election and also either contains details of sources of income to be included in the Personal Assessment calculation or is cross-referenced to the appropriate Profits Tax or Property Tax returns (for cases where the taxpayer is a partner of a partnership or jointly owns property). Where, however, a person wishes to make the election after having filed one or more returns covering income which would be included in a Personal Assessment calculation, there is a separate form on which the election can be made.

There are no specific provisions for revoking an election once it has been made. However, as occasionally a taxpayer will make an election which is not favourable to him (see Example 6.2 for typical circumstances), the IRD practice is to permit him to withdraw his election within six years of the end of the relevant year of assessment.

As noted in section 6.3 above, in the case of a married couple not living apart from each other (see definition in section 3.8.3.3), an election for Personal Assessment must be made jointly if both have assessable income and are eligible to elect. Where, on the other hand, one spouse is not eligible to elect (for example, because he or she is under 18 years of age), the other spouse can elect by himself or herself. Irrespective of whether a joint election is made, however, the total income of both spouses (adjusted for allowable deductions) is aggregated into one assessment (Sec. 42A(1)). The total liability is then apportioned between the spouses on the basis of each individual's respective proportion of the total aggregated income (Secs. 43 (1) and 43(2B)). In other words, there is no separate taxation of married couples (other than couples living apart) as there is in the case of Salaries Tax, although the total liability is apportioned between them.

Because aggregation of the income of married couples is mandatory under Personal Assessment and because progressive rates of tax apply up to the break-even point, it is possible that more tax is payable under Personal Assessment in the case of a married couple than would have been paid in total if the two individuals were not married but had the same income and had both elected for Personal Assessment. This position was the subject of the dispute in *Wong Tai Wai, David & Lee Chi Man v CIR* [2004] (1 HKRC 90-128). In that case, the Court of First Instance upheld the decision of the Board of Review (see *D 64/02*) in rejecting the taxpayer's claim that this result was inequitable and contrary to Articles 8,11 and 25 of the Basic Law. The decision of the Court of First Instance was upheld on appeal to the Court of Appeal (see *Wong Tai Wai David v CIR* (2004) [1 HKRC 90-134]).

6.5 Computation of Total Income

The computation proceeds by aggregating assessable income from the various heads of charge, deducting from that aggregate certain interest payments which are not otherwise deductible and the net result is the statutory "total income". From this total income are deducted, subject to the normal rules, charitable donations, home loan interest, elderly residential care expenses, retirement scheme contributions and allowable losses under Profits Tax rules. This net amount then figures in the assessment before deduction of allowances (see section 6.6). Throughout these calculations, income of an individual which is included is only that income to which he is beneficially entitled (Sec. 40B). This provision is intended to ensure that an individual cannot bring in income which he has derived as a trustee, although such a specific provision seems hardly necessary as a matter of law.

In the case of a husband and wife who are living together and have jointly elected for Personal Assessment (or only one has elected where the other is ineligible to elect), the total income as computed here is an aggregation of each of their total incomes (Sec. 42A(1)). It is, however, necessary to individually calculate their total incomes before aggregating them (Sec. 42(10)). There is no entitlement, as there is with Salaries Tax for separate taxation, although the total liability is apportioned between them. Where a couple have married during the year of assessment and both have income, they are deemed to have married at the commencement of the year of assessment so that their pre-marital income comes into the Personal Assessment (Sec. 42A(2)).

More specifically, the total income is the aggregate of the following items:—

(1)   the person's share of the net assessable value of any income subject to Property Tax (see section 2.3.1) (Sec. 42(1)(a)(ii));

(2)   net assessable income (see section 3.6) for Salaries Tax purposes (Sec. 42(1)(b)); plus

(3)   profits assessable to Profits Tax, after deduction of losses brought

forward (Sec. 42(1)(c)). Where, however, such profits include amounts arising from concessionary trading receipts, only the amount of profits from concessionary trading receipts divided by the "adjustment factor" is to be included in the total income calculation. For this purpose, "concessionary trading receipts" is as defined in Sec. 19CA and means profits from certain debt instruments which are taxed in accordance with Sec. 14A (see point (14) in section 4.5.3) and profits from qualifying offshore reinsurance business taxed under Sec. 14B (see section 4.7.2). Sec. 14B, however, can only ever apply to a corporation and as only individuals can elect for Personal Assessment, it would not be possible for profits from qualifying offshore reinsurance business to be included in a total income calculation for Personal Assessment purposes. The term "adjustment factor" is also defined in Sec. 19CA and means the normal Profits Tax rate applicable to the person divided by the rate of tax applicable to profits from concessionary trading receipts. As Sec. 14A specifies that the rate of tax applicable to profits from certain debt instruments is one half of the normally applicable tax rate, the adjustment factor will always equal 2. The effect of applying the adjustment factor to profits from concessionary trading receipts is, therefore, to include only half of such amounts in the total income calculation, which in turn ensures that the intention of taxing such profits at the reduced rate is preserved.

The amount of profits included under this item may also be after deduction of charitable donations, although it must be borne in mind that the same donations cannot be deducted for both Salaries Tax and Profits Tax purposes. If there is a loss for Profits Tax purposes for the year of assessment, "nil" is brought into the total income calculation at this stage and the loss is deducted later (see (A) below).

From the aggregate so obtained, the following is then deducted:—

(4)   interest payable on money borrowed for the purpose of producing income included in head (1) above, provided that the interest has not already been deducted in calculating the person's assessable profits for Profits Tax purposes (Sec. 42(1) proviso). This would cover interest on any money borrowed to purchase, improve or repair let property, the income from which is subject to Property Tax. It is important to note that such amounts would not normally be deductible under the Property Tax provisions and, therefore, the availability of this deduction is an important encouragement for individuals to

elect for Personal Assessment where they own rent producing property.

A deduction for interest expense incurred in a particular year of assessment is only possible if incurred to finance a property from which rental income was derived in that year of assessment. It is not possible to claim a deduction on the basis that the property generated rental income in a past year, or is expected to generate income in a future year (see *D 86/99* and *D 96/01*). It also appears from the drafting of the provisions that the interest expense deductible under this provision is limited to the amount of income from property which has been included in the total income calculation under item (1) above; any excess interest appears not to be able to be offset against other income incorporated into the Personal Assessment calculation or carried forward. Such an interpretation has been upheld by the Board of Review in *D 4/01*. This case is also interesting in that the Commissioner's representative appears to have argued that the amount of deductible interest should be determined on a property by property basis, rather than by aggregating all property income and allowing a deduction for the aggregate of all interest expenses incurred in respect of those properties for the purpose of determining the limit on deduction. However, this point was not critical to the analysis of the case and the Board of Review, as in *D 2/91* where the point was previously raised, did not make a clear ruling on whether such an approach is correct. In *D 51/04*, however, the Board of Review specifically addressed the point and agreed with the IRD's view that a global deduction of interest expenses against the aggregate net assessable income from property was not allowed. In other words, the Board confirmed that the allowable interest deduction was to be calculated in respect of each property and was limited to the amount of the net assessable income from the property to which the interest related.

Although this provision does not extend to interest incurred in the production of income subject to Profits Tax, such interest would generally have been deducted in arriving at the amount to be included under item (3) above. For a case concerning the level of evidence required to support an interest deduction under the provision, see *D 103/89*. See also *D 50/96* where the Board of Review confirmed that the money borrowed must be used for the purpose of producing income chargeable to Property Tax and it was not sufficient merely that the loan in question was secured by mortgage over a property the income from which was chargeable to Property Tax if the borrowed funds were used for a non-income producing purpose. In that decision the Board of Review noted that the "purpose" for which the money was borrowed was determined on the basis of the person's design or intention. In that case, it was held that the purpose of the borrowing was to finance the purchase of a property as a family residence in order to improve the family's living conditions, notwithstanding that a consequence of acquiring that property was that the former family residence was let out to generate assessable rental income. The generation of that assessable rental income, it was concluded, could not be considered a "purpose" in the context of the deduction available for interest expenses under the proviso to Sec. 42(1). This line of reasoning was also followed in *D 39/01*.

From this total income, the following are deducted to arrive at a net total income:—

A   The amount of the individual's loss, or share of loss when he or she is a partner in a partnership, for the year of assessment as computed for Profits Tax purposes (Sec. 42(2)(b)). See section 4.5.15 for a discussion as to the computation of losses for Profits Tax purposes. If the amount of such loss exceeds the total income as computed under (1) to (3) above, as reduced by allowable interest expenses as described in (4) above, the excess can be carried forward and set off against the total income of the individual for future years of assessment (Sec. 42(5)). Where spouses are jointly assessed (which is required under Personal Assessment unless the spouses are living apart), any loss must first be set off against the income of the other spouse before the excess can be carried forward and set off against the total income of the person and their spouse (provided that the spouse is then not living apart from the person) for future years. Note, however, that in computing the loss to be carried forward, no deduction is permitted for otherwise allowable charitable donations, elderly residential care, home loan interest expenses or contributions to recognized retirement schemes as are discussed in (B) below (Sec. 42(5)(a)).

Where a spouse has an excess loss carried forward but has no income to be brought into the other spouse's Personal Assessment calculation for the year to which the loss is brought forward, the excess can nevertheless be brought into the total income calculation for that year (Sec. 42(6)).

B.   Approved charitable donations (see section 3.5.4) to the extent not deducted in computing the profits included under (3) above, qualifying elderly residential care expenses (see section 3.5.6), home loan interest expenses (see section 3.5.5) and contributions to recognized retirement schemes (see section 3.5.7); deduction of these amounts are authorised by Sec. 42(2)(a). Sec. 26C(2)(b) and Sec. 26C(2A) provide that the aggregate of approved charitable donations deductible under this heading and deductible in computing profits included under (3) above is limited to 25% of the total income before such deductions but after deduction of interest under (4) above and after adding back any self education expenses deducted in arriving at (2) above.

In computing the total income of an individual who is a member of a partnership it is appropriate to bring into the computation his share of profits under (3) above and his share of losses under A above. Nonetheless, Sec. 42 (8) provides that this does not extend to an individual who is a member of a partnership with more than 20 partners, unless it is a partnership referred to in Sec. 345(2) of the *Companies Ordinance* (which essentially deals with partnerships of solicitors, accountants and certain other professions). This does not prevent an individual who is a partner in a partnership of more than 20 partners from electing for Personal Assessment; it merely prevents the individual from bringing his share of the profits or losses of such a partnership into his total income calculation as such partnerships are effectively treated as corporations for Profits Tax purposes. Note, however, that when Part 2 of Schedule 4 of the *Companies (Amendment) Ordinance 2004* becomes operative by notice in the *Gazette*, Sec. 42(8) will be repealed and all interests in partnerships will be treated the same for Personal Assessment purposes. The repeal of Sec. 42(8) will be accompanied by transitional provisions dealing with losses in partnerships of more than 20 partners and these are discussed further in sections 4.5.16.2 and 4.7.9.

6.6 Personal Allowances

In computing the charge to tax, personal allowances are deductible from the total income as computed in section 6.5. The personal allowances prescribed in Part V and Schedule 4 of the IRO are applicable both in computing liability under Personal Assessment and, in appropriate circumstances, for Salaries Tax. The allowances are always to be claimed on prescribed forms and are given only after such proof of their validity as the Commissioner requires is provided (Sec. 27). The personal allowances currently available are discussed below.

6.6.1 Basic allowance (Sec. 28)

An allowance, of $100,000 for the 2007/08 year of assessment, is available to all individuals except where they, or their spouse, are entitled to the married person's allowance. There is no apportionment of the allowance in the year of either marriage or death.

6.6.2 Married person's allowance (Sec. 29)

This allowance, which is $200,000 for the 2007/08 year of assessment, is as its name suggests, only available if, *inter alia*, the individual is married (see definition in section 3.8.3.3). There are, however, further qualifications which must be met before the allowance is available because married couples who each have income liable to Salaries Tax are, in general, treated as individual single persons. The married person's allowance is, therefore, only available in the following situations.—

(1)   where the individual's spouse has no income liable to Salaries Tax. From this it will be noted that either a husband or a wife will be entitled to the married person's allowance if his or her spouse has no income liable to Salaries Tax;

(2)   where the couple have elected for joint assessment to Salaries Tax (see section 3.8.3.1) under Sec. 10(2); or

(3)   where an election has been made for Personal Assessment.

Where a husband and wife are living apart (see definition in section 3.8.3.3), neither can claim the married person's allowance unless the spouse claiming is maintaining or supporting the other, which is a question of fact depending upon their relative financial circumstances. Although the allowance can be claimed in these circumstances, it cannot be claimed where a couple is divorced, even though one spouse may maintain and support the other. This is because the couple cannot be considered husband and wife, as has been confirmed by both the Court of First Instance and the Court of Appeal in *Sit Kwok Keung v CIR* [2002] (1 HKRC 90-113) and [2002] (1 HKRC 90-121).

Where a claim is permitted in respect of a husband and wife living apart, the couple is not treated as living apart for the purposes of Personal Assessment and, accordingly, their income would be aggregated. Furthermore, any such claim may be revoked by the claimant at any time within the year of assessment of claim or within six years from the end of such year; in such a case, the other spouse's income would not then be aggregated with the claimant's under Personal Assessment.

6.6.3 Child allowance (Sec. 31)

Allowances are available to an individual who has an unmarried child who was living and was maintained by that individual at any time during the year of assessment, so long as the child was either under 18 years of age or, if over 18, but under 25, was receiving full-time education at a university, college, school or other similar educational establishment or is over 18 but unable to work because of physical or mental disability. The allowances for the 2007/08 year are $50,000 for each of the first to ninth children, plus an additional $50,000 for any child in respect of whom an allowance is available and who was born within the year of assessment.

Thus the maximum child allowances are $450,000 plus an extra $50,000 for each qualifying child who was born in the year of assessment. For the purposes of child allowances, "child" means:—

(1)   a child of the claimant;
(2)   a child of the claimant's spouse or former spouse;
(3)   an adopted child of the claimant or their spouse, recognised by the laws of Hong Kong as adopted; or
(4)   a step child of the claimant or their spouse.

Because a husband and wife who are living together and who both have income liable to Salaries Tax are normally assessed as single individuals for Salaries Tax purposes, problems would arise as to who should claim the child allowances. Sec. 31(3) therefore provides that only one spouse may claim the whole of the child allowances and the couple must nominate which of them is to be the claimant. A nomination for a year of assessment may not be revoked unless the Commissioner agrees. The Commissioner's decision is final and not subject to objection or appeal (Sec. 31(4)).

It is, of course, possible that two (or, indeed, more than two) individuals who are not married and living together, may be entitled to claim for the same child for the same year of assessment. This is most likely to happen in the case of a separated husband and wife. In these circumstances, the Commissioner has the power to divide the allowance between those persons on such basis as is considered appropriate, having regard to the contributions to the maintenance and education of the child made by each individual (Sec. 31(2)).

There can also be circumstances other than as covered in the preceding two paragraphs where more than one individual may be entitled to claim. In these circumstances, the Commissioner will not consider a claim until the individuals have agreed between themselves which of them will make the claim (Sec. 33(2)). Where an allowance has already been granted to more than one individual for the same year of assessment, or has been given to one individual and another individual claims or the Commissioner becomes aware that another individual appears to be eligible to claim in respect of the same child within six months of the allowance having been granted to the first individual, the Commissioner has certain powers; in particular, he must invite the individuals who have already been granted the allowance plus those others who appear entitled to claim, to agree amongst themselves who will claim, in which case the Commissioner is empowered to raise any additional assessments to correct the position, subject to the statutory six-year time limit in Sec. 60. If the individuals do not agree within a reasonable time, the Commissioner can raise additional assessments as he sees fit (Sec. 33(3)).

6.6.4 Dependent parent allowance (Sec. 30)

Allowances are available in prescribed circumstances to an individual, or his or her spouse who is not living apart from that person (see definition in section 3.8.3.3), who maintains a parent or a parent of his or her spouse. The amount of the allowance depends on the age of the parent, whether they are eligible for an allowance under the Government's Disability Allowance Scheme and whether they are resident with the claimant

In particular, for the 2007/08 year of assessment Sec. 30(1) grants an allowance of $30,000 in respect of any maintained parent who was 60 years of age or older at any time during the year of assessment, or who was less than 60 years but was eligible to claim an allowance under the Government's Disability Allowance Scheme. For a discussion as to the meaning of "Government's Disability Allowance Scheme" and "eligible to claim" under that scheme, see the discussion in section 6.6.6 below. Furthermore, if the parent resided with the claimant continuously throughout the year of assessment, other than for full valuable consideration, an additional allowance of $30,000 (for the 2007/08 year of assessment) will be granted.

Additionally, from the 2005/06 year of assessment, Sec. 30(1A) grants allowances in respect of any maintained parent aged between 55 and 59 years. More specifically, an allowance of $15,000 for the 2007/08 year of assessment is granted in respect of a parent who had reached the age of 55 years, but who had not turned 60, at any time during the year of assessment and throughout the year was not eligible to claim an allowance under the Government's Disability Allowance Scheme. Moreover, an additional allowance of $15,000 (for the 2007/08 year of assessment) is granted where the parent resided with the claimant continuously throughout the year of assessment otherwise than for full valuable consideration.

There are, however, a number of restrictions and qualifications which must be met before the above allowances are available. First, the parent must be ordinarily resident in Hong Kong at some time during the relevant year of assessment. Note that this does not require the parent to be ordinarily resident throughout the whole of the year of assessment, as was confirmed in *D 13/90* where the full allowance was granted in respect of a parent who was resident in Hong Kong during only part of the relevant year.

"Ordinarily resident" is not defined in the IRO. Interestingly, until 1989 the equivalent provision required that the parent be a "permanent resident" and although this term was not defined for the purpose of that provision, it was (and still is) defined in Sec. 41(4) for the purpose of the election for Personal Assessment as a person who is "ordinarily resident". Accordingly, notwithstanding the change in statutory wording, the test essentially remains the same. In a number of Board of Review decisions concerning the former provisions (see, for example, *D 20/83*, and *D 57/87*) it was held appropriate to adopt the definition in Sec. 41(4) for the purpose of the dependent parent allowance.

Although "ordinarily resident" is not defined, its meaning has been considered in numerous UK cases and by the Board of Review in *D 57/02* and *D 7/05*. For a discussion of these cases and IRD practice, see section 6.3 which considers the meaning of the term in the context of the eligibility to elect for Personal Assessment.

Second, the parent must be maintained and Sec. 30(4) provides that a parent can only be regarded as maintained if:—

(1)   the parent resides with the claimant and his or her spouse for at least a continuous period of six months in the year of assessment and not for full valuable consideration. This seems to require a husband and wife to live together before they can claim for a dependent relative; or

(2)   the claimant or his or her spouse contributes at least $12,000 in money towards the maintenance of the parent in the year of assessment.

A further restriction on the allowance is imposed by Sec. 30(5) which provides that no allowance shall be granted in respect of a parent of a person or his or her spouse where any person has been allowed a deduction for elderly residential care expenses under Sec. 26D (see section 3.5.6) in respect of the same parent.

For the purposes of this provision, a parent of a person or his or her spouse is defined in Sec. 2 and means:—

(1)   a parent of whose marriage (see definition in section 3.8.3.3) the claimant or his or her spouse is a child;

(2)   a parent by whom the claimant or his or her spouse was adopted in an adoption recognised by the law in Hong Kong;

(3)   a step-parent of the claimant or his or her spouse;

(4)   the natural father or mother of the claimant or his or her spouse; or

(5)   a parent of a deceased spouse of the claimant. Such parent can satisfy any one of the descriptions (1) to (4).

The above definition is, of course, very specific. In *D 45/99* the Board of Review, with obvious regret, denied a deduction for a claims by a taxpayer in respect of a couple who had looked after her since birth, at which time her natural mother had disappeared. However, the couple in respect of whom the claims were made had not formally adopted the taxpayer and, therefore, did not come within the terms of paragraph (2) (or any other paragraph) of the above definition.

The allowance can only be given to one person in respect of each parent (Sec. 33(1)) and so there are provisions to deal with the position where more than one individual is entitled to claim or indeed has claimed. There is no question of apportionment. However, an individual can claim for the allowance and the further allowance in respect of more than one parent.

Where more than one person is entitled to claim, the Commissioner will not consider a claim until the individuals concerned have agreed between themselves which of them will make the claim (Sec. 33(2)).

Where an allowance has already been granted to more than one individual for the same year of assessment or has been given to one individual and another individual claims or the Commissioner becomes aware that another individual appears to be eligible to claim in respect of the same parent within six months of the allowance having been granted to the first individual, the Commissioner has certain powers. In particular, the Commissioner must invite the individuals who have already been granted the allowance plus those others who appear entitled to claim, to agree amongst themselves who will claim in which case the Commissioner is empowered to raise any additional assessments to correct the position, subject to the statutory six-year time limit in Sec. 60. If the individuals do not agree within a reasonable time, the Commissioner can raise additional assessments as considered appropriate (Sec. 33(3)). It is, however, important to remember that the Commissioner only has these powers if he becomes aware of another person being entitled to claim the allowance within six months of the allowance being granted to the first person. For a case where the Commissioner's attempt to raise additional assessments to deny an allowance failed because the Commissioner only became aware of the second claimant outside the six month period, see *D 100/00*.

6.6.5 Dependent grandparent allowance (Sec. 30A)

Allowances are available in prescribed circumstances to an individual, or his or her spouse who is not living apart from that person (see definition in section 3.8.3.3), who maintains a grandparent or a grandparent of his or her spouse. A separate allowance is available in respect of each grandparent maintained. The amount of the allowance depends on the age of the grandparent, whether they are eligible for an allowance under the Government's Disability Allowance Scheme and whether they are resident with the claimant.

In particular, for the 2007/08 year of assessment Sec. 30A(1) grants an allowance of $30,000 in respect of any maintained grandparent who was 60 years of age or older at any time during the year of assessment, or who was less than 60 years but was eligible to claim an allowance under the Government's Disability Allowance Scheme. For a discussion as to the meaning of "Government's Disability Allowance Scheme" and "eligible to claim" under that scheme, see the discussion in section 6.6.6 below. Furthermore, if the grandparent resided with the claimant continuously throughout the year of assessment, other than for full valuable consideration, an additional allowance of $30,000 (for the 2007/08 year of assessment) will be granted.

Additionally, from the 2005/06 year of assessment, Sec. 30A(1A) grants allowances in respect of any maintained grandparent aged between 55 and 59 years. More specifically, an allowance of $15,000 for the 2007/08 year of assessment is granted in respect of a grandparent who had reached the age of 55 years, but who had not turned 60, at any time during the year of assessment and throughout the year was not eligible to claim an allowance under the Government's Disability Allowance Scheme. Moreover, an additional allowance of $15,000 (for the 2007/08 year of assessment) is granted where the grandparent resided with the claimant continuously throughout the year of assessment otherwise than for full valuable consideration.

To qualify for any allowance under these provisions, the grandparent must be ordinarily resident in Hong Kong at some time during the year of assessment. For a discussion as to the meaning of "ordinarily resident" for this purpose, see sections 6.3 and 6.6.4 above.

A grandparent is only considered to be maintained by the claimant or his or her spouse if either the grandparent resides, other than for full valuable consideration, with the claimant and his or her spouse for a continuous period of not less than six months in the year of assessment *or* the claimant or his or her spouse contributed money of at least $12,000 towards the maintenance of the grandparent in the year of assessment (Sec. 30A(4)).

A further restriction on the allowance is imposed by Sec. 30A(5) which provides that no allowance shall be granted in respect of a grandparent of a person or his or her spouse where a deduction for elderly residential care expenses under Sec. 26D has been allowed in respect of the same grandparent.

For the purposes of the provision, a grandparent of a person or his or her spouse is defined in Sec. 2 as:—

(1)   a natural grandparent of the person or his or her spouse;

(2)   an adoptive grandparent of the person or his or her spouse. This is further defined to include an adoptive parent of a natural parent, adoptive parent or step parent as well as a natural parent of an adoptive parent, in relation to both the person and his or her spouse;

(3)   a step grandparent of the person or his or her spouse. Again, this is further defined to include a step parent of a natural parent, or a natural parent of a step parent, in relation to both the person and his or her spouse, or

(4)   In the case of a deceased spouse, a person who would have been considered a grandparent under any of (1) to (3) above had the spouse not died.

As with dependent parent allowances and child allowances, Sec. 33(1) provides that not more than one person can claim a dependent grandparent allowance in respect of the same grandparent. Similarly, Sec. 33(2) provides a procedure for dealing with the situation where more than one person is eligible to make a claim in respect of the same grandparent and essentially prevents the Commissioner from considering any claims until the potential claimants have agreed between themselves who is to claim the allowance. Moreover, where the Commissioner has granted the allowance to more than one person, he is required to invite the persons to whom the allowances have been granted, as well as any other potential claimants, to decide amongst themselves as to who is to claim the allowance (apportionment of the allowance not being permitted) and, in consequence of such is empowered to raise appropriate additional assessments under Sec. 60; if the parties are unable to agree amongst themselves as to who is to claim the allowance, the Commissioner is empowered to make a decision on the basis of what he considers just taking into account only the information which he has in his possession at the time he makes that decision (Sec. 33(3)).

Additionally, because one individual may be a dependent parent of one person at the same time as they are a dependent grandparent of another person, Sec. 33(1A) provides that a dependent grandparent allowance and a dependent parent allowance cannot be granted in the same year of assessment in respect of the same individual. Likewise, where in respect of the same individual, the Commissioner has granted both a dependent parent allowance and a dependent grandparent allowance for the same year of assessment, or is of the opinion that there are one or more eligible claimants for each of those allowances in respect of the same individual, Secs. 33(3A), 33(3B) and 33(3C) provide mechanisms for ensuring that there are no dual claims, and for resolving disputes as to who can claim; these provisions operate on a similar basis as Secs. 33(2) and 33(3), which are discussed above, in that the Commissioner is to invite the claimants or potential claimants to decide amongst themselves as to who is to claim but failure to so agree results in the Commissioner being empowered to act as he sees just. In any case, the Commissioner is permitted to raise additional assessments, subject to the usual statutory limitations, to give effect to either the agreement of the parties or the exercise of his own powers.

An important restriction on the Commissioner's powers applies, however, where an allowance has been granted to one taxpayer in respect of an individual and the Commissioner subsequently becomes aware that there is another potential claimant in respect of that same individual. In particular, the Commissioner's powers to invite the claimants to agree amongst themselves as to who is entitled to the allowance, or to decide in the absence of such an agreement, can only be exercised if he becomes aware of the other potential claimant within six months of the allowance being granted to the first claimant (Secs. 33(3) and 33(3C)). For a case where the Commissioner's attempt to raise additional assessments to deny an allowance failed because the Commissioner only became aware of the second claimant outside the six month period, see *D 100/00*.

6.6.6 Disabled dependent allowance (Sec. 31A)

An allowance is available to an individual in respect of every dependent who is eligible to claim an allowance under the Government's Disability Allowance Scheme. The rate of this allowance for the 2007/08 year of assessment is $60,000. For the purpose of this allowance, "dependent" in relation to an individual is defined in Sec. 31A(4) as:—

(1)   a spouse in respect of whom the individual is entitled to be granted a married person's allowance;

(2)   a parent, or parent of the individual's spouse, in respect of whom the individual is entitled to be granted a dependent parent allowance or a deduction for otherwise qualifying elderly residential care expenses under Sec. 26D (see section 3.5.6);

(3)   a grandparent, or grandparent of the individual's spouse, in respect of whom the individual is entitled to be granted a dependent grandparent allowance or a deduction for otherwise qualifying elderly residential care expenses under Sec. 26D (see section 3.5.6);

(4)   a child in respect of whom the individual is entitled to be granted a child allowance; or

(5)   a brother or sister, or a brother or sister of the individual's spouse, in respect of whom the individual is entitled to a dependent brother or sister allowance.

The meaning of the requirement that the person in respect of whom the claim is made must be eligible to claim an allowance under the Government's Disability Allowance Scheme (the Scheme) was considered in *D 92/97*. That case involved a claim for the disabled dependent allowance in respect of the year of assessment prior to the relevant dependent actually being granted an allowance under the Scheme. It was held that to qualify for the disabled dependent allowance, it was not necessary that an allowance under the Scheme was actually claimed; rather, it was only necessary to demonstrate that all the conditions required to qualify for such an allowance were satisfied. On the basis that the person was granted an allowance under the Scheme after the end of the relevant year of assessment, and the Board of Review was satisfied on the evidence that the person was suffering from the disease in respect of which that allowance was granted at the end of the relevant year of assessment, the person was considered *eligible to claim* an allowance under the Scheme in the relevant year of assessment, notwithstanding that no allowance was actually received. Some caution is, however, required in applying this decision; in particular, it is unlikely that a claim for the disabled dependent allowance would succeed in respect of a person who has never been granted an allowance under the Scheme. This is because one requirement for qualifying for an allowance under the Scheme is that the person is certified by the Director of Health or the Chief Executive, Hospital Authority (or in special circumstances by a medical practitioner of a private hospital) as severely disabled within the meaning of the Scheme. Accordingly, a claim in respect of a person who has never been granted an allowance under the Scheme is unlikely to succeed as the person would presumably never have been so certified.

Notwithstanding the guidance provided in *D 92/97*, it is interesting to note that the term "allowance under the Government's Disability Allowance Scheme" is not defined in the IRO. In *D 137/01*, the Commissioner's representative suggested that the term meant the Disability Allowance Scheme operated by the Director of Social Welfare and did not extend to compensation received under the *Pneumoconiosis (Compensation) Ordinance*. Although not explicitly stated, this view appears to have been accepted by the Board of Review as they found against the taxpayer, principally on the basis of evidence from the Director of Social Welfare that the dependent in question would not have qualified for a disability allowance.

Where the disabled dependant is a child in respect of whom the child allowance is apportioned between two or more persons under Sec. 31(2) (see section 6.6.3 above), the disabled dependent allowance will be apportioned on the same basis. Similarly, where a husband and wife who are not living apart and who are separately assessed to Salaries Tax have decided amongst themselves, pursuant to Sec. 31(3), who is to claim any child allowances in respect of their children, any disabled dependant allowance in respect of those children will be granted only to the individual entitled to the child allowances.

As with dependent parent, dependent grandparent, dependent brother and sister and child allowances, Sec. 33(1) provides that an allowance cannot be claimed by more than one person in respect of the same disabled individual (other than in the case of a disabled dependent child in respect of whom the allowance is apportioned between two or more persons in accordance with Sec. 31A(2)). Similarly, Sec. 33(2) provides that where it appears that more than one person may be eligible to claim the allowance, the Commissioner shall not consider any claim until the persons concerned have agreed amongst themselves which of them shall claim the allowance for a particular year. Furthermore, where the allowance has been granted to more than one person in respect of the same individual, Sec. 33(3) requires the Commissioner to invite the persons to whom the allowance has been granted, as well as any other potential claimants, to decide amongst themselves as to who is to claim the allowance (apportionment not generally being permitted); as a consequence of such agreement being reached, the Commissioner is empowered to raise additional assessments in accordance with Sec. 60. Where the individuals cannot agree amongst themselves as to who is to claim the allowances, the Commissioner is empowered to make a decision on the basis of what he considers just taking into account only the information which he has in his possession at the time he makes the decision (Sec. 33(3)).

Again, however, an important restriction on the Commissioner's powers applies where an allowance has already been granted to one taxpayer in respect of an individual and the Commissioner subsequently becomes aware that there is another potential claimant in respect of that same individual. In particular, the Commissioner's powers to invite the claimants to agree amongst themselves as to who is entitled to the allowance, or to decide in the absence of such an agreement, can only be exercised if he becomes aware of the other potential claimant within six months of the allowance being granted to the first claimant (Secs. 33(3) and 33(3C)). For a case where the Commissioner's attempt to raise additional assessments to deny an allowance failed because the Commissioner only became aware of the second claimant outside the six month period, see *D 100/00*.

6.6.7 Dependent brother or dependent sister allowance (Sec. 30B)

An allowance is available for each dependent brother or sister of a taxpayer or of the spouse of the taxpayer (other than of a spouse living apart from the taxpayer). The rate of the allowance for the 2007/08 year of assessment is $30,000. Brother or sister of a person or their spouse is defined in Sec. 30B (3) and includes a natural, adopted or step brother or sister of the person, their spouse or of a deceased spouse. To qualify for the allowance, however, the brother or sister must be maintained by the taxpayer and be under the age of 18 years or, if over, be either under 25 years of age and receiving full time education at a university, college or similar institution or be incapacitated for work by reason of physical or mental incapacity.

For the purpose of this allowance, an individual is considered maintained by the taxpayer if, at any time during the year of assessment, the taxpayer or his spouse had sole or predominant care of the individual. As different taxpayers may have sole or predominant care of the same individual at different times during a single year of assessment, more than one taxpayer may, *prima facie*, be entitled to the allowance in respect of a particular individual. Sec. 33(1), however, provides that only one taxpayer can claim the allowance in respect of a single individual. Moreover, Sec. 33(1A)(b) provides that a dependent brother or sister allowance and a child allowance cannot be granted in respect of the same individual.

As with dependent parent, dependent grandparent, child and disabled dependent allowances, Sec. 33(2) provides that where more than one taxpayer is entitled to claim a dependent brother or sister allowance in respect of the same individual in the same year of assessment, the Commissioner shall not consider any claim until he is satisfied that all potential claimants have agreed amongst themselves who is entitled to the claim in that particular year. Similarly, Sec. 33(3A)(b) provides that where it appears to the Commissioner that there are taxpayers entitled to claim a dependent brother or sister allowance in respect of the same individual as whom other taxpayers may be entitled to claim a child allowance for the same year of assessment, he will not consider any claims until he is satisfied that all potential claimants have agreed amongst themselves who is entitled to the claim in that particular year.

In cases where:—

(a)   a dependent brother or sister allowance has already been granted to two or more taxpayers in respect of the same individual;

(b)   a dependent brother or sister allowance has been granted to a taxpayer in respect of the same individual as another taxpayer has been granted a child allowance;

(c)   a dependent brother or sister allowance has been granted to a taxpayer and within six months thereof it appears to the Commissioner that another person may be entitled to a brother or sister allowance for the same year of assessment in respect of the same individual; or

(d)   a dependent brother or sister allowance has been granted to a taxpayer and within six months thereof it appears to the Commissioner that another taxpayer is entitled to claim a child allowance for the same year of assessment in respect of the same individual, or vice versa;

the Commissioner is required to invite the person(s) to whom the allowances have been granted, as well as any other potential claimants, to decide amongst themselves as to whom is to claim the allowances. Any such agreement must be consistent with the statutory provisions and, in this regard, it will be noted that apportionment is not possible. Where agreement is reached, the Commissioner is empowered to raise any necessary additional assessments in accordance with Sec. 60. If, however, the relevant taxpayers cannot reach agreement, the Commissioner is empowered to make a decision as he considers just and raise additional assessments accordingly;

in reaching his decision, the Commissioner need take into account only information which he has in his possession at the time he takes his decision (Secs. 33(3), 33(3B)(b), 33(3C)(b) and 33(3D) in conjunction with Sec. 33 (4)).

6.6.8 Single parent allowance (Sec. 32)

An allowance of $100,000 (for the 2007/08 year of assessment) is available to an unmarried person having care and maintenance of a child or children. This allowance is granted in addition to any child allowances to which the person is entitled. The qualifications for the allowance are as follows:

(1)   the claimant must be unmarried or, if married, living apart from his or her spouse (see definition in section 3.8.3.3); and

(2)   the claimant must have sole or predominant care of a child for which he or she is entitled to a child allowance. This precludes a claim in respect of a child for whom a child allowance is obtained solely by virtue of contributions to the child's maintenance and education. For a case where a claim on such a basis was rejected, see *Sit Kwok Keung v CIR* [2002] (1 HKRC 90-113) and [2002] (1 HKRC 90-122).

Only one single parent allowance is available to any individual, no matter how many children there are in respect of which the claimant is entitled to child allowances.

In the circumstances where more than one person may be entitled to claim a single parent allowance in respect of the same child, the Commissioner may apportion the allowance between them taking into account the respective periods for which each claimant had the sole or predominant care of the child during the year of assessment or, if such method cannot be applied with certainty, on such basis as the Commissioner considers appropriate in the circumstances (Sec. 32(3)). For a case where the Board of Review apportioned a single parent allowance, see *D 140/01*. In that decision, the Board rejected the Commissioner's proposition that "sole or predominant care" should be equated with custodial responsibility. In particular, they noted that although each case needed to be decided on its own facts, "care" was not necessarily the same as "custody". Nonetheless, the Board went on in that case to find that although the child lived mainly with her mother, she spent a day or two each week with her father, who was claiming the single parent allowance, and that in the circumstances of the case the mother and father could be regarded as having joint custody, care and control of the child. In these circumstances, the Board held that the father should be regarded as having predominant care of the child for an aggregate period of 30% of the relevant year of assessment and that an apportionment on such basis should be made.

6.7 The Charge to Tax

The objective of the Personal Assessment election is to bring together all sources of income subject to Hong Kong taxes, to deduct certain permissible deductions and personal allowances and then charge the remainder at the progressive rates of tax with the ultimate objective of achieving a smaller overall liability than the combined standard rate tax on each source. The assessment proceeds as follows:—

(1)   Total income reduced in the manner discussed in section 6.5;
       less
(2)   The personal allowances as per section 6.6.

The result is then charged to tax at the progressive rates of tax which, for the 2007/08 year of assessment, are:—

The first	$35,000 @ 2%
The next	35,000 @ 7%
The next	35,000 @ 12%
The remainder	@ 17% (Sec. 43(1))

However, the tax so computed must not exceed the amount ascertained in (1) above charged at the standard rate, which for the 2007/08 year of assessment is 16% (Sec. 43(1A)). All tax already paid under the separate heads is credited against the tax charged under the total income assessment (Sec. 43(2)) and any excess is refunded (Sec. 43(3)).

In the case of a husband and wife who both have assessable income and who therefore both have to join in the election for Personal Assessment, the assessment is jointly determined and the tax payable is apportioned between them and charged upon each of them accordingly (Sec. 43(1)). The apportionment is to be made on the basis of their respective total incomes after deducting charitable donations, qualifying elderly residential care and home loan interest expenses, permitted contributions to recognized retirement schemes and allowable losses, although where an additional assessment is issued, the whole of the additional tax is to be charged to the individual assessed in respect of that income (Sec. 43(2B)); see Example 6.3 for a sample calculation.

It is not always advantageous to elect for Personal Assessment even if there are deductions available for certain interest, losses and additional charitable donations, as is seen in the next example.

■ Example 6.2

Dan Ger is married and a permanent resident of Hong Kong. He has paid the following tax for 2007/08:—

Property Tax on flat owned and wholly let	$120,000	@ 16% – $19,200
Salaries Tax on employment earnings	$400,000	Tax = $21,800
(after charitable donation deduction)		

He has an agreed loss in his business of $5,000 for 2007/08 and has made approved charitable donations of $10,000.

The Personal Assessment computation is as follows:—

Income — Property			$120,000
Salary			400,000
Total Income			$520,000
Less: Loss		$ 5,000	
Donation		10,000	(15,000)
Net Total Income			$505,000
Personal Allowances — Married Person		$200,000	
			(200,000)
Taxable			$305,000
Tax Chargeable	$ 35,000 @ 2%	=	$ 700
under Sec. 13(1)	35,000 @ 7%		2,450
	35,000 @ 12%		4,200
	200,000 @ 17%		34,000
			$41,350 .... (1)
under Sec. 43(1A)	$505,000 @ 16%		$80,800 .... (2)

Note:—
The tax chargeable under Personal Assessment is therefore $41,350 whereas, without election, he pays only $41,000; therefore Dan would not elect or, if he did, the Inland Revenue Department would not raise a total income assessment and would permit Dan to withdraw his election.

The reason for this situation is that the earnings subject to Salaries Tax already attract the full married person's allowance of $200,000 and a deduction for charitable donations of $10,000 and, under the Sec. 43(1) calculation, the property income is charged at progressive rates which exceed the standard rate, the effect being that the difference exceeds the tax savings on the loss available under the total income calculation.

Ironically, if the earnings subject to Salaries Tax had been, say, $2,500,000, they would not have attracted the personal allowances and tax chargeable under Sec. 43(1A) would have given a better result so that an election would be worthwhile.

■ Example 6.3

David Osborne has a number of sources of income liable to tax in Hong Kong for the 2007/08 year of assessment. He owned a flat of which 25% was used by him for storage purposes and the remaining 75% was fully let at a rental of $84,000 per annum giving a net assessable value subject to Property Tax of $67,200. He had a mortgage used to buy the flat on which interest paid during the year was $40,000.

His business in Hong Kong had resulted in an agreed loss of $26,000. His wife is in employment and earned $550,000. His wife also had a part time business on which the assessable profits for the year were $45,000.

David has one teenage son and his mother living with him. His son and mother were in a terrible accident last year and have been infirm since and qualify for an allowance under the Government's Disability Allowance Scheme. David also has a brother, Jim, who does not live with David and their mother, but who contributed $20,000 in cash to their mother's maintenance.

He received a director's fee of $40,000 during the year.

He made donations to the Community Chest during the year of $60,000.

His wife had made donations to the Maryknoll Convent of $10,000 of which $5,000 had been allowed in arriving at her assessable business profits.

The following taxes were paid in 2007/08:—

— Property Tax	$10,752
— Profits Tax	7,200
— Salaries Tax (Note (a))	6,150
	$24,102

As both David and his wife have assessable income they would both have to enter into the election (Sec. 41(1A)).

Personal Assessment 2007/08

Wife's Salary		$550,000
Director's Fee		40,000
Let Property		67,200
Wife's Business		45,000
Total income (Note (b))		$702,200
Less: Interest Paid (Note (c))		(30,000)
Total Income		$672,200
Less: Business Loss	$26,000	
Donations (Note (d))	65,000	(91,000)
Net Total Income		$581,200
Allowances — married		(200,000)
— disabled child		(110,000)
— diabled parent		(120,000)
		$151,200

Tax Chargeable	$35,000 @ 2% =	$ 700
under Sec. 43(1)	$35,000 @ 7% =	2,450
	$35,000 @ 12% =	4,200
	$46,200 @ 17% =	7,854
Tax Due (Note (e))		$ 15,204
Tax Paid		(24,102)
Refund due		$ 8,898

Notes:—

(a) The Salaries Tax paid is as follows because they would have elected for joint
assessment as, on an individual basis, the husband's allowances would exceed his
income liable to Salaries Tax:—

Salary	$550,000	
Director's Fee	40,000	$590,000
Donations (Note (d))		(65,000)
		$525,000
Allowances — married		($200,000)
— child and disabled child		(110,000)
— dependent parent and		(120,000)
disabled dependent parent		
Taxable		$ 95,000
Tax Thereon		$ 8,156

(payable by
wife per Sec.
10(3)(a))

(b) Wife's salary is aggregated with David's income. No charitable deduction is made at
this stage. No separate taxation as in Salaries Tax.

(c) As the loan was used to buy the property, the interest paid can be said to earn the
income so that it is deductible but only to the extent of the income included i.e. only
70% of it.

(d) The total donations were $70,000, but $5,000 had been deducted in arriving at David &
wife's assessable business profits.

(e) The maximum tax, which is not applicable in this case, is the net total income charged
at standard rate, i.e.:—

$581,200 @ 16% = $92,992

Because they both have assessable income, in strictness their total incomes should
be computed separately then aggregated. The tax is then apportioned on the basis
of their respective total incomes:—

	David	Wife	Joint
Salary		$550,000	$550,000
Director's Fee	$ 40,000		40,000
Property	$ 67,200		67,200
Business		45,000	45,000
	$107,200	$595,000	$702,200
Interest Paid	(30,000)		(30,000)
Total Income	$ 77,200	$595,000	$672,200
Business Loss	(26,000)		(26,000)
Charitable Donations (Note (f))	(19,300)	(45,700)	(65,000)
	$ 31,900	$549,300	$581,200

The liability under Personal Assessment is therefore:—

David $\dfrac{31,900}{581,200} \times \$15,204 = \$834$

Wife $\dfrac{549,300}{581,200} \times \$15,204 = \$14,370$

The assessments and refunds are therefore arranged as follows:—

David	Liability		$ 834
	Tax Paid — Property Tax		10,752
	Refund (Note (g))		$ 9,918
Wife	Liability		$14,370
	Profits Tax Paid	$7,200	
	Salaries Tax Paid	6,150	(13,350)
	Tax Due		$ 1,020

(f) It is not clear from the IRO that the allocation should be made in this way but this is the most logical and seems to be in accordance with Secs. 42(2) and 42(3) treating each spouse as an independent individual. Although David made donations of $60,000, in the absence of an election for Personal Assessment his deduction would be limited to 25% of his total income before deduction of his business loss, but the balance could be transferred to his wife. Accordingly, for the purpose of this calculation only 25% of $77,200 of the total deduction is allocated to David. The balance of the combined donations does not exceed 25% of David's wife's income, even after taking into account the $5,000 deducted in calculating her assessable business profits.

(g) The reason why the husband has a refund and the wife a liability is because in the joint Salaries Tax assessment on which she was subject to tax, she was allocated a relevant proportion of the personal allowances. It may be that the wife would not want to elect in this case and, as it must be a joint election (Sec. 41(1A)), she could prevent it.

(h) David is entitled to a total of five allowances. These are the married allowance plus a child and a dependent parent allowance. Additionally, since both the mother and the teenage son are infirm, David is also entitled to a disabled person allowance for each of them. Because David's brother, Jim, contributed more than $20,000 towards the maintenance of their mother, he would, *prima facie*, also be entitled to claim dependent parent and disabled dependent parent allowances in respect of her. However, David and Jim agreed amongst themselves (per Sec. 33(2)) that only David would claim the allowances for 2007/08.

7.1 Legislation

The law covering returns and information to be provided by taxpayers and others is contained in Part IX of the IRO, Secs. 51 to 58. Penalties in respect of returns, information and other matters are covered by Part XIV, Secs. 80 to 84.

7.2 Returns and Information

Most of the provisions in Part IX deal with returns and information in general in respect of all taxes covered by the IRO, but there are some provisions which deal specifically with only Salaries Tax or Profits Tax.

7.2.1 Returns — general

An assessor has the power to issue a return, in a form specified by the Board of Inland Revenue, to any person and to require him to complete and submit the return within a reasonable time as stated in the notice to him. This provision applies to returns in respect of each of the income taxes as well as composite tax returns covering all three taxes (Sec. 51(1)). The same powers apply in respect of returns required for Personal Assessment purposes (Sec. 51(2A)). Where a Personal Assessment return is issued to a married person, a notice is also required to be sent to that person's spouse and they are required to submit a return of their joint incomes (Sec. 51(2B)). However, since the introduction of composite tax returns from the 1993/94 year of assessment, there have been no separate Personal Assessment forms and, therefore, Secs. 51(2A) and (2B) have little practical application. Indeed, when composite tax returns were introduced, Sec. 51(2C) was added to the IRO which provides that compliance with a notice issued under Sec. 51(1) is to be deemed to be compliance with a notice issued under Sec. 51(2A) or Sec. 51(2B).

The form in which the return is to be made is laid down by the Board of Inland Revenue pursuant to Sec. 51AA and, if a statement purporting to be a return is submitted which does not conform in every material particular with the required form, it will be rejected and the taxpayer will be treated as if he had not made a return. In this regard, see *CIR v Mayland Woven Labels Factory* (HKTC 627).

Historically, returns were required to be made on printed paper forms. Nonetheless, provisions now exist for returns to be made in electronic form (Sec. 51AA(2)) or by telefiling (Sec. 51AA(3)). Because of the nature of these alternative methods of filing, there are (currently at least) limitations as to the matters they can deal with. As such, these filing methods can only be adopted in cases specified by the Commissioner. The Commissioner is empowered by Sec. 51AA(5) to specify classes or descriptions of persons or returns permitted to be filed electronically or through the telefiling system by publication of a notice in the *Gazette,* which in fact has been done. The Commissioner, pursuant to Secs. 51AA(6) and (7) is also empowered to specify matters relating to, *inter alia*, attachments, digital signatures and passwords in relation to electronic filing and telefiling; nonetheless, it remains the Board of Inland Revenue's responsibility to specify the system, templates and information required to be provided for electronic filing (Sec. 51AA(2)(a) to (c)). Interestingly, in the case of telefiling the Board of Inland Revenue's responsibility is limited to specifying the information required to be provided by taxpayers.

In practice, one month is normally allowed for the submission of returns of income and, if a return has not been submitted by the due date specified on the return it is in default, in which case penalties become exigible unless the assessor has granted an extension; any extension granted has the effect of deferring the statutory due date to the new date specified in the extension notice. In the case of Profits Tax returns, which are normally issued around 1st April each year, there is an automatic extension arrangement available to tax representatives provided they submit suitably detailed lists of affected clients when invited to do so. These arrangements recognize the fact that it is not possible for accountants to audit and present all of their clients' accounts by the end of April each year and, therefore, the period of extension varies with the proximity of the accounting date to the following April. The automatic extensions granted in respect of 2006/07 returns are as follows:—

(1)   for accounting periods ending in December, extensions are granted to 15th August 2007, and

(2)   for accounting periods ending between 1st January and 31st March, extensions are available on a proportionate basis to dates up to 15th November 2007 although for loss cases an extension until 31 January 2008 is available on application.

These extensions can, in some cases, themselves be further extended by individual application specifying good grounds, but such extensions are entirely at the discretion of the assessor and only granted exceptionally.

Tax returns for individuals (i.e. composite tax returns) may also have their one month time limit extended by individual application. In the case of individuals who have appointed a tax representative, an automatic extension in respect of 2006/07 returns is granted to 3 July 2007 in cases where there is no sole proprietor business involved, or to 3 October 2007 where the individual does carry on a sole proprietorship business.

If the assessor is not satisfied with the extent of information contained in the return, even if it is properly completed within the specification, he can give notice by letter requiring fuller or further information within a reasonable time limit specified in the notice (Sec. 51(3)). There are penalties for failure to comply with this notice (see section 7.4.1).

It is not sufficient excuse for failure to report taxable income that no return form was received from an assessor. Any person chargeable to tax for a year of assessment is obliged to inform the Commissioner in writing that he is so chargeable within four months after the end of the basis period for the relevant year of assessment unless he has already received a specified return form, in which case he must, of course, comply with the due date of that return (Sec. 51(2)).

Similarly, when a person ceases to carry on a trade, profession or business within the charge to Profits Tax or ceases to own a source of income chargeable to Salaries Tax, Profits Tax, Property Tax or Personal Assessment, he must so inform the Commissioner within one month (Sec. 51(6)). There is also a requirement to notify change of address within one month (Sec. 51(8)).

Any person who is chargeable to Salaries Tax, Profits Tax or Personal Assessment who is about to leave Hong Kong for a period which will exceed one month must inform the Commissioner in writing at least one month before departure of his expected date of departure and return. This does not, however, apply to an individual who must leave Hong Kong frequently in the course of his business or employment (Sec. 51(7)). The purpose of this is to enable the Commissioner to protect the Government from any loss of tax which could result from the departure of an individual.

7.2.2 Persons responsible

Where anything in the IRO requires a return, statement or form to be submitted by a person and it is in fact submitted in a manner whereby it purports to have been submitted or authorised by that person, it is deemed to have been so submitted or authorised unless the contrary is proved (Sec. 51(5)).

If, however, the person who is required to perform any act under the IRO is incapacitated or is a non-resident, the obligation falls upon the trustee of the incapacitated person or upon the Hong Kong agent of the non-resident person (Sec. 53). An agent for this purpose is defined by Sec. 2 as the agent attorney, factor, receiver or manager in Hong Kong or any person in Hong Kong through whom the non-resident receives any income or profits arising in Hong Kong. This, amongst other things, enables a duly appointed tax representative of a non-resident taxpayer to sign the non-resident's return on his behalf.

Similarly, Sec. 54 provides that the obligations of a deceased person fall upon his executor, who is also competent to be assessed to tax in respect of income accruing to the deceased before his death. In respect of a person who died before 11 February 2006, however, no proceedings or penalty imposed under Part XIV of the IRO, other than under Sec. 82A (see section 7.4.2), can be imposed upon the executor in respect of any act of the deceased. Furthermore, the ability to raise an assessment in respect of income accrued prior to the date of death is restricted to a period of one year from the date of death or one year from the date of filing the Estate Duty Affidavit, whichever is the later; however, this restriction does not apply to Sec. 82A additional tax assessments. In respect of a person who dies on or after 11 February 2006, no Estate Duty Affidavit is required (as Estate Duty was abolished from that date) and the time limit for raising an assessment (other than an assessment for additional tax under Sec. 82A) is three years after the end of the year of assessment in which the person died.

Where a partnership incurs an obligation under the IRO, the person answerable is the precedent partner and as to which partner this is, is a question of fact. Any person who has received any notice addressed to him as precedent partner cannot deny responsibility unless he can prove that he is either not a partner or that another person is the precedent partner (Sec. 56(1)). Where persons are not in partnership but act jointly, they are jointly and severally responsible for obligations under the IRO (Sec. 56(2)).

In the case of land and buildings which are owned by two or more persons jointly or in common, any one of those owners is responsible and answerable for all obligations under the IRO in the same way as if he was the sole owner (Sec. 56A(1)). This is, of course, just a provision in respect of tax matters and does not in any way limit the commercial obligations of joint owners as between themselves (Sec. 56A(2)). Furthermore, where any one person pays Property Tax and is either not liable for it or is entitled to contribution from other owners, he is given specific authority by Sec. 56A (3) to recover it, or the relevant proportion, from the proper party or parties.

Where a corporation incurs an obligation under the IRO, the person answerable can be the secretary, manager, director or liquidator of the corporation or, in the case of a body of persons, the principal officer. If there is no such person who is ordinarily resident in Hong Kong, the corporation or body of persons must inform the Commissioner of the name and address of an individual who is ordinarily resident in Hong Kong and who will be responsible for the obligations of the corporation or body of persons under the IRO (Sec. 57). If a corporation purports to submit a return which has been signed by an individual other than one authorised under Sec. 57, the return will be invalid.

7.2.3 Returns by employers

Employers have a number of obligations under the IRO to report information about the commencement and cessation of employees and of their remuneration in order to ensure effective processing and collection of Salaries Tax.

When an employee commences employment in Hong Kong and is likely to be liable to Salaries Tax, the employer is obliged by Sec. 52(4) to report such commencement within three months giving the name and address of the individual, the date of commencement and the terms of his employment. Accordingly, if an employer takes on an employee who will wholly work outside Hong Kong, he will not be liable to Salaries Tax and there will, therefore, be no obligation to report his commencement. Similarly there is an obligation to report the cessation of employment of an employee at least one month before the cessation (Sec. 52(5)). The Commissioner is, however, empowered to accept a shorter period of notice and this is to accommodate the position where the employer is not aware of the date of cessation at least one month before it occurs.

Furthermore, in addition to reporting the cessation of employment, the employer must report when an employee is about to leave Hong Kong for a period in excess of one month and he must report at least one month before the intended departure. This does not, however, apply to an employee who is required to travel outside Hong Kong frequently in the course of his employment (Sec. 52(6)). Where, as commonly occurs, the cessation of employment is also accompanied by the employee leaving Hong Kong, the employer can make a report on both events on a single form which the IRD supplies for the purpose.

There is also a further provision to protect Government revenue where an employee is about to leave Hong Kong and may owe some Salaries Tax. When an employer has reported the impending departure of an employee in accordance with Sec. 52(6) he must not pay to or on behalf of the employee any money or money's worth, without the Commissioner's written consent, within one month of having given the notice (Sec. 52(7)). This provision gives the employer a valid defence in any action brought by the employee against the employer for non-payment. There is, of course, nothing to prevent the employer making the payment on the day before giving the notice under Sec. 52(6) provided such notice is given within the required time limit.

Apart from these returns giving the movement of employees, an employer is obliged to make a return at the end of the tax year giving details of taxable remuneration paid to each employee plus other specified details (Sec. 52(2)). An employer will not usually be required to report details of employees earning less than a specified amount (being $100,000 per annum for the 2006/07 year of assessment, or a proportionately reduced amount where the employee was not employed for the whole year) unless they are in part time employment, because a single person is exempt from Salaries Tax up to the amount so specified.

For all of the above purposes, in order that there can be no doubt, Sec. 52(3) provides that a company director or individual engaged in the management of the company is to be regarded as an employee.

7.2.4 Information

The IRD has wide powers to obtain information and as will be seen is not restricted to obtaining it from the taxpayer himself.

The main provisions are contained in Sec. 51(4) which is drawn in extremely broad terms in that it provides for the obtaining of full information from *any* person:—

- in respect of *any* matter
- which may affect *any* liability or obligation
- of *any* persons

Where an assessor believes that any person is in possession of information that would be useful to the IRD, he can give him notice to report such information, within a reasonable time which must be stated in the notice; this provision extends not only to reporting of facts or figures but also the production of any relevant documents. A solicitor is not, however, required to produce the actual account which he has with a client; it is sufficient for him to produce a copy certified as correct by him (Sec. 51(4)(a)). This privilege does not extend to any other person, professional or otherwise.

Where the IRD requires a person to attend an interview at which such information will be sought, the notice giving the time and place must be sent by an assistant commissioner if it is to be valid (Sec. 51(4)(b)). At such an interview, the person under examination must answer all questions truthfully and there are penalties if he fails to comply (see section 7.4).

It is important to appreciate that the person receiving these notices may be the taxpayer where he has been slow in providing information; in these circumstances the provision provides a means of enforcing a reply within a specified period under threat of penalty. Alternatively, a notice under this provision could be issued to any other person who knows something which could affect a particular taxpayer's liabilities, responsibilities or obligations.

Sec. 51(4A) expands upon who can be called upon to provide information and also what information can be demanded from them. It also makes a further important point that the existence of privilege between the person under enquiry and the person from whom information about him is sought is not a valid defence, except in the case of a solicitor or counsel in possession of privileged information which has been communicated to him in that capacity. In other words, a solicitor can be forced to divulge information in his possession about a partner or a next door neighbour but not about a client. A bank cannot, for example, plead a bank secrecy agreement with customers when information is sought about a customer's bank account.

It should be noted that a fundamental feature of these provisions is that the person from whom the information is sought must be in possession of the information before he can be forced to make it available. This gives rise to considerable doubt and practical difficulties where, for example, information is sought from the Hong Kong branch of a bank with a head office elsewhere in respect of a customer's account with a branch outside Hong Kong. The Hong Kong branch manager is not personally in possession of the information but the bank, as a legal person, is in possession of the information; however, the bank staff who are actually in possession of the information concerning the account will probably plead secrecy regulations in their own country and that they are outside the jurisdiction of the IRO. For a discussion on what constitutes "possession" and the fact that it is not limited to physical possession, see *CIR v Mui, Y. F.* (HKTC 632).

The Commissioner can also call upon any Government employee or any employee of a public body to provide any information which is in his possession unless the person is under a statutory oath of secrecy with regard to that information (Sec. 52). There is no reciprocal obligation because Sec. 4 imposes a secrecy obligation upon employees of the IRD.

7.2.5 Statement of assets and liabilities

Where the IRD suspects that a person has filed an incorrect return which has omitted or understated taxable income, one of the methods of detecting and quantifying undisclosed sources of income is to prepare annual statements of assets and liabilities to determine whether, as should be the case, the increase in net assets over a given period equal the income for that period less outgoings. The taxpayer can then be called upon to explain any discrepancy and, in the absence of a suitable explanation, may be assumed to have been in receipt of undisclosed taxable income (see *Departmental Interpretation & Practice Notes No. 11 — Elements of a Tax Investigation*). This method of estimating undisclosed profits, although by its nature imprecise, has been held to be legitimate by the Board of Review on a number of occasions (see for example *D 28/88 and D 93/03*). The IRD is, therefore, given power by Sec. 51A to demand from a person, a statement of assets and liabilities but the following constraints upon the Department's ability to demand such a statement apply:

(1)   the Commissioner or a deputy commissioner must be personally of the opinion that the person has filed an incorrect return or other false information;

(2)   the Commissioner or a deputy commissioner must personally consider that the act was not the result of an innocent mistake and that the person does not have a reasonable excuse for it;

(3)   the Commissioner must have the consent of the Board of Review (see comment below);

(4)   the Commissioner must give written notice requiring the statement within the time stated in the notice which cannot be less than 30 days from the date of service of the notice; and

(5)   the notice cannot demand a statement in respect of any period earlier than seven years before the commencement of the year of assessment in which the notice is given (Sec. 51A(2)) (see comment below).

As regards point (3), there is a laid down procedure for application to the Board of Review for such consent. The application must be addressed by the Commissioner to the Clerk to the Board in writing and be accompanied by details of why the Commissioner wishes to exercise his power (Sec. 51A(3)). A board of three members including a Chairman or Deputy Chairman (it is also usually three members for a tax appeal, see Chapter 9) considers the application and the Commissioner, or his delegate, may attend but not the person under investigation or his representative (Secs. 51A(4) and 51A(5)). The person under investigation does not, of course, know that such an application has taken place and indeed the name of the person concerned is not disclosed to the Board (Sec. 51A(6)). The Board will merely consider whether, on the facts, the Commissioner is entitled to hold the views in (1) and (2) above and their decision will be final (Sec. 51A(8)). The person who receives the notice can request the Commissioner to produce a certificate from the Board of Review to the effect that the Board has given consent and in those circumstances it is, of course, necessary for the Commissioner to disclose the person's name to the Board (Sec. 51A(7)).

As regards point (5) it is perhaps surprising that only seven years' information can be requested in view of the extended time limit by which an assessment can be raised in cases of fraud or wilful evasion (see Chapter 8). If, for example, a notice is issued in December 2007, it can demand information back to 1st April 2000 which would be relevant for the 2000/01 year of assessment. It is interesting to note, however, that the IRD would generally be beyond the normal six-year time limit for raising an additional assessment for the 2000/01 year of assessment, although the information could be relevant to a previously raised but disputed assessment. In the case of fraud or wilful evasion, however, additional assessments for the 1997/98 and subsequent years of assessment could be raised but the statement would not, of course, reveal any information relevant to the 1997/98, 1998/99 or 1999/2000 years of assessment.

The statement of assets and liabilities must reveal the following information (Sec. 51A(1)):—

(1) all assets in the person's or spouse's possession in Hong Kong including the relevant proportion of those assets which are shared jointly or severally with some other person;

(2) all liabilities to which the person or his spouse was subject in Hong Kong including the relevant proportion of those liabilities which are shared jointly or severally with some other person;

(3) all expenditure and disbursements out of funds in Hong Kong by the person or his spouse. This will detect gifts made and funds transferred out of Hong Kong; and

(4) all sums whether by way of gift or remittance from overseas funds received in Hong Kong by the person or his spouse.

7.2.6 Search warrants

In the case of fraud or wilful evasion, a notice requiring a statement of assets and liabilities may not result in the obtaining of the desired information, particularly where there is a possibility that records will be removed, altered or even destroyed if the person under investigation becomes aware that an enquiry has commenced. For this, and whatever other reason may be appropriate, the IRO gives the IRD the power of entry and search and the ability to take away relevant documents (Sec. 51B).

The powers can only be granted by a magistrate and only then if he is satisfied by a statement on oath from the Commissioner or other officer authorised in writing by the Commissioner, who is a chief assessor or higher, that:—

(1)   there are reasonable grounds to suspect that the person has made an incorrect return or otherwise supplied false information so that his assessable income has been understated and that he does not have a reasonable excuse for his action and that it was not an innocent omission; or

(2)   the person has failed to comply with a Court order to complete a tax return or provide the further information requested by an assessor under Sec. 51(3).

It will be noticed that the cause outlined in (1) is the same as that which gives the Commissioner power to demand a statement of assets and liabilities. He therefore has, in effect, an option in these cases, the exercising of which would be governed by his judgement, as to whether the more usual course of demanding an assets statement would produce the desired result.

Once the warrant has been obtained, the Commissioner or his authorised officer may exercise the following powers:—

(1)   the power of entry to any premises where it is suspected that there may be any books, records or other information which would be helpful in assessing the liability to tax of the person under investigation and to search for and then examine those books, records, etc.; and

(2)   the power to take possession of and retain any books, records, etc. of the person under investigation or that person's spouse and to make copies of any parts of books, records, etc. of any other person, so long as any such information may assist in assessing the liability to tax of the person under investigation.

Where any records are retained for more than 14 days, the person may apply in writing to the Board of Review for an order for their return. Following a hearing at which the person and the Commissioner may be represented, the Board may make any order, with or without condition, as they see fit.

In carrying out these powers, the Commissioner or authorised officer may enlist the assistance of any other IRD officer (Sec. 51B(1A)) but must produce his warrant to search if required to do so (Sec. 51B(2)).

The person whose books have been retained may examine them and take extracts in accordance with whatever conditions the Commissioner may attach to such rights (Sec. 51B(3)).

Although the power of entry is not confined to premises of the person under investigation, it is important to note that the right to take and retain books, records, etc. relates only to those of the person under investigation. Only copies may be taken of other person's property. In this connection it is interesting to note the UK proceedings in *CIR v Rossminster Ltd. and Others* (52 TC 160) wherein during the course of an authorised search by tax officials in the UK the amount of documents was so considerable that all was taken and it was discovered that the property taken included a child's school report. Upon application to the Courts, the Court of Appeal held that the search had been invalidly carried out and the whole of the property was ordered to be returned. The House of Lords, however, ultimately reversed the decision of the Court of Appeal but, nevertheless, the proceedings are of interest in considering how these powers of search and entry may be carried out.

The Commissioner is not required to give notice of his intention to enter and, in fact, it would of course not be in his interests to do so.

7.2.7 Business records

There would, of course, be practical problems in enforcing most of the information and return provisions without some form of statutory obligation concerning the keeping of business records. This is contained in Sec. 51C and requires every person carrying on a trade, profession or business to keep sufficient records, either in the English or Chinese language, of his income and expenditure to enable his assessable profits to be readily ascertained. Furthermore, there is an obligation to retain such records for at least seven years after the transactions to which they relate, subject only to the following exceptions:—

(1) when a corporation has been dissolved, in which case all records may be destroyed; or
(2) where the Commissioner has specified that the records need not be preserved.

Sec. 51C also specifies in some detail the type of records to be kept and the nature of the transactions in respect of which records are required. "Records" is defined in Sec. 51C(3) as books of account, which may be in a legible or non-legible (i.e. electronic) form, recording receipts and payments, or income and expenditure together with vouchers, bank statements, invoices, receipts and other documents as are necessary to verify the entries in such books of account.

Further, Sec. 51C(4) provides that, without limiting the above general requirement to keep records, the following records must be kept:

(a)   a record of the assets and liabilities of the business;

(b)   a day to day record of all monies received and expended by the business and the matters in respect of which the receipts and payments took place;

(c)   where the business involves dealing in goods:

    (i)   a record of all goods purchased and sold, other than those sold for cash in a retailing business normally conducted in cash, showing sufficient detail to enable the IRD to readily identify the quantities and value of goods bought and sold together with the identities of the buyers and sellers, as well as the relevant invoices; and

    (ii)   statements showing the quantity and value of trading stock at the end of the basis period for the business together with details of stocktakings; and

(d)   where the business involves the provision of services, sufficient records of the services provided to allow the IRD to readily verify the entries referred to in (b) above.

Sec. 51D contains record keeping requirements in relation to rental income for Property Tax purposes which are effectively identical to Sec. 51C, but without the detailed definitions included in Secs. 51(3) and (4). That is, the provision imposes a general requirement to keep sufficient records, in either the English or Chinese language, of all income and expenditure so as to enable the assessable income to be readily ascertained, subject to the exceptions in respect of dissolved companies and records which the Commissioner has specified need not be preserved.

7.3 Service of Notices

In view of the fact that there are time limits within which returns and information must be provided and the fact that there are penalties for failure to comply, it is essential that the law be precise as to the form of notices and the manner of their delivery.

Every notice must bear the name of the Commissioner or other officer authorised by the IRO to deliver the notice, although it is sufficient that his name be merely printed or stamped on the notice (Sec. 58(1)). A notice can be served personally or be sent by post to the person's last-known address, whether a private or business address, or to any address at which he was, during the year to which the notice relates, employed or carrying on business; if the return or notice is in respect of Property Tax, it may be delivered to the land or buildings which are the subject of the tax (Sec. 58(2)). Where a notice is sent by post, regardless of when it is actually received, it is deemed to have been served on the day following the day when it would have been expected to be received in the ordinary course of the post, unless the contrary is shown (Sec. 58(3)). However, it is difficult to predict what day that might be in view of the inconsistencies in delivery of post in different parts of Hong Kong. In the case of *Charles C. Y. Cheng v CIR* (HKTC 1087), the taxpayer claimed that a penalty assessment sent to his last-known private address in Hong Kong should be invalid because he had told the assessor that he had intended to emigrate to the USA and had done so by the time the notices were delivered, although he had not advised his actual change of address to the Commissioner. The Court, however, held that the notices were valid.

If the IRD is called upon to prove that a notice was posted within the requirements of the IRO it is sufficient to bring evidence that the notice was duly addressed and posted; it is not necessary to prove that it was delivered because of the presumption of delivery in Sec. 58(3) (Sec. 58(4)). It is important to realise, however, that the time limit for objection against a notice of assessment (see Chapter 9) is measured in relation to the date of the assessment, not the date on which it is received or deemed to have been received.

Any time limit stated in a notice can be extended by the Commissioner or authorised officer at his discretion (Sec. 58(6)). This is normally done where a good reason is shown. This general power to extend, however, only applies to a time limit set by the IRD and stated in the notice. It does not apply to statutory time limits such as the time within which an objection against an assessment must be lodged.

7.4 Penalties

The sanctions for failure to observe obligations imposed by the IRO are primarily fiscal penalties but also involve Court orders to do things which a taxpayer has failed to do. The penalties for fraud are naturally more serious and can, and do, involve imprisonment. Where there is no question of fraud or wilful evasion, the IRO imposes penalties where some act has been done or, alternatively, has not been done and where there is no "reasonable excuse". There is not, and could not be, any statutory definition of "reasonable excuse" which must depend upon the circumstances of each case.

The Hong Kong Courts have not had occasion to consider the meaning of "reasonable excuse" but reference to legal decisions in other countries as to what constitutes a reasonable course of conduct for various purposes adduces the fact that the person would have to show that he had acted reasonably and in good faith in doing what he did and that a reasonable man would regard this as an excuse consistent with a reasonable standard of conduct. In *BR 80/76* an individual was held to have had a reasonable excuse for omitting a source of income from his return because he had been professionally advised that the income was not taxable and it was quite reasonable that he should rely on that advice notwithstanding that it subsequently proved to be taxable. A similar decision was reached in *D 18/91*, although the Board of Review emphasised that reliance on professional advice did not automatically constitute a reasonable excuse and every case was to be determined on its own merits. In *D 1/82* and *D 24/85*, however, a taxpayer's profits were substantially understated in returns prepared by a qualified tax representative but this was not regarded as a reasonable excuse because the taxpayer must have known that they were understated. See also *D 46/89* where negligence of a professional accountant was rejected as a reasonable excuse.

It was held in *D 7/79* and *D 15/83* that it was not a reasonable excuse for understating income chargeable to Salaries Tax that the amount in question had been correctly reported in the employer's return of employee remuneration. Conversely, however, in a number of cases (see, for example, *D 102/95*, *D 106/95* and *D 107/95*), it has been held that reliance upon an incorrect employer's return of employee remuneration is not a reasonable excuse for omitting income from a Salaries Tax return. Indeed, in those cases the Board stated that each salary earner should keep a careful record of their remuneration for the purpose of completing their Salaries Tax returns, and should only use the employer's return to check their own records. Further, *D 1/83*, *D 24/84* and *D 50/93* confirm the old adage that ignorance of the law is no excuse for breaking the law nor is, as was the case in *D 1/83* and *D 50/93*, an inability to speak or read English. See also *D 2/83* with respect to failure to report a spouse's income where there was held to be no reasonable excuse in the absence of strained relations.

Forgetfulness brought on by domestic pressures is also not a reasonable excuse for a substantial omission (see *D 15/83*). However, in *D 13/85* it was established that a taxpayer must not be assumed to live in a perfect world and cannot expect to be penalised for a genuine mistake such as a slip of the mind; similarly, in *D 44/89* the Board noted that it was appropriate to consider the nature of the mistake, rather than the quantum of tax involved, when assessing penalties. These decisions should, however, be contrasted with *D 32/05* where the Board of Review accepted that a mistake was entirely inadvertent and arose from simple carelessness, but still held that additional tax calculated as a percentage of the tax in question was appropriate. Of course, the Commissioner and Board of Review will make their own judgements as to the genuineness of mistakes.

The cases cited above represent only a small number of the cases heard by the Board of Review on the question of what constitutes a reasonable excuse. Moreover, although they may provide some insight into what may be considered a reasonable excuse, it must be noted that ultimately the existence or not of a reasonable excuse can, and will, only be determined in the light of all relevant aspects of a particular case. Accordingly, rarely can reliance be placed on one or two factors as constituting a reasonable excuse as those factors will be considered in the light of other circumstances of the particular case. In other words, what amounts to a reasonable excuse for one person, will not necessarily constitute a reasonable excuse in another person's case.

The penalties stipulated in the IRO were originally set as fixed dollar amounts plus, in some cases, a percentage of the tax involved. When inflation dictated an increase in the dollar amount of the penalties, numerous amendments were required to the IRO. In order to overcome this problem, in 1995 each dollar penalty amount was amended to a "level". There are six such levels and these are specified in Sec. 113C of the *Criminal Procedures Ordinance*; in future, if it is considered appropriate to update penalties, this can be achieved by simply amending the penalty levels under that provision. Details of the penalties appropriate to each level at the time of writing are contained in Table 7.1.

Table 7.1 Levels of penalties imposed by the IRO

Level	Fine applicable for an offence
1	$ 2,000
2	$ 5,000
3	$ 10,000
4	$ 25,000
5	$ 50,000
6	$100,000

Source: *The Criminal Procedure Ordinance.*

7.4.1 Omissions, failure to make returns, etc.

A person is guilty of an offence under Sec. 80(1) if, without reasonable excuse, he:—

(1)   fails to supply the further information requested by an assessor under Sec. 51(3);

(2)   fails to supply a statement of assets and liabilities under Sec. 51A;

(3)   fails to supply information under Sec. 52(1);

(4)   fails to supply an Employer's return of employees' remuneration under Sec. 52(2);

(5)   fails to supply information under Sec. 64(2) in connection with an objection against an assessment;

(6)   fails to attend following a summons under Sec. 64(2) to answer questions in connection with an objection against an assessment or attends but fails to answer questions;

(7)   fails to attend following a summons under Sec. 68(6) to provide evidence at a hearing of the Board of Review or attends but fails to answer questions;

(8)   is a corporation exempt from Property Tax and fails to notify change of ownership of property;

(9)   fails to notify under Sec. 51(6) cessation of business or cessation of a source of income chargeable to Salaries Tax, Profits Tax, Property Tax or Personal Assessment;

(10) is a person chargeable to Salaries Tax, Profits Tax, Property Tax or Personal Assessment and fails to notify departure from Hong Kong under Sec. 51(7) or change of address under Sec. 51(8);

(11) is an employer who fails to notify the commencement of an employee under Sec. 52(4), cessation of an employee under Sec. 52(5) or departure of an employee from Hong Kong under Sec. 52(6) or fails to retain monies owing to the employee in accordance with Sec. 52(7), or

(12) is a person receiving a notice under Sec. 76 to pay over to the Commissioner sums held to the credit of a tax defaulter and fails to notify inability to comply under Sec. 76(3).

Not all of these offences requires the person to have received a notice before he commits a default. Every person should, therefore, be aware of his obligations without prompting, and it is unlikely that ignorance of the obligation would ever be accepted as constituting a "reasonable excuse".

In the case of the foregoing offences, the fine is at level 3 but the Commissioner may, and commonly does, compound this penalty to a smaller figure (Sec. 80(5)). In addition to the fine, the Court may order the person to do the thing which he has failed to do and may specify a time within which he must do it. If he further fails to do the act within the specified time he may be subject to a further fine at level 4 (Sec. 80(2B)). A prosecution cannot, however, be brought without the sanction of the Commissioner (Sec. 84).

A discussion as to what might constitute a reasonable excuse for committing offences under the IRO appears in section 7.4 above. In respect of the offences listed under (11) above, however, Sec. 80(1AA) provides that where the failure of an employer to notify commencement, cessation or departure of an employee, or to withhold monies from an employee about to leave Hong Kong, is in respect of an individual who is only deemed to be an employee by virtue of Sec. 9A (see section 3.8.1), it is a reasonable excuse for such failure for the employer to have reasonably relied upon a written statement by the individual concerned, in the form specified by Sec. 80(1AC), in concluding that Sec. 9A did not apply in the circumstances. Sec. 80(1AC) gives the Commissioner the power to specify the form of an acceptable statement for these purposes; the Commissioner has exercised his power in this regard and the relevant forms are reproduced in Appendix C of *Departmental Interpretation & Practice Notes No. 25*. Sec. 80(1AB), however, provides that if a person knowingly or recklessly makes a false statement of the kind prescribed by Sec. 80(1AC), they shall be guilty of an offence punishable by a fine at level 3.

The position of a person who fails to supply information when requested to do so pursuant to Sec. 51(4)(a) or to attend after receiving a summons under Sec. 51(4)(b), or attends but fails to answer questions, is not dealt with in Sec. 80. However, these matters are covered by Sec. 51(4B) which provides that, in the absence of a reasonable excuse, such failures will attract a penalty up to level 3. The provision does, however, grant the Commissioner power to compound the penalty. If the matter is dealt with before a court, it is specifically provided that the court may give judgement in a lesser amount if it thinks fit; the court may also order the person to do what he has failed to do.

In addition to the foregoing offences, Sec. 80(1A) makes it an offence for a person, without reasonable excuse, to fail to comply with the record keeping requirements of Sec. 51C. The penalty for this offence is a fine at level 6. In addition to the fine, it is provided that the Court may order the person to do, within a specified time, what he failed to do. This seems somewhat strange as a failure to keep records could be difficult to rectify; that is, if a business kept absolutely no records to enable its income and expenditure to be ascertained for a given period, it seems nonsensical and futile for a Court to order that records be retrospectively prepared for that period. Nonetheless, Sec. 80(2C) provides that a further level 6 fine may be imposed for a failure to comply with such a court order.

All of the foregoing relate to the failure of a person to do some act although failure to submit a return of his income or notify liability to tax is not included. Sec. 80(2) deals with these and with the position where some incorrect statement has been made and the penalties in these cases are more serious. More specifically, where a person without reasonable excuse has committed certain acts, he is guilty of an offence under Sec. 80(2). The relevant acts are that the person has:

(1)   made an incorrect return by omitting or understating something;
(2)   made an incorrect statement when claiming a deduction or an allowance;
(3)   supplied incorrect information in respect of his own or any other person's tax liability;
(4)   failed to submit a return by the due date; or
(5)   failed to notify the Commissioner under Sec. 51(2) of chargeability to tax.

In these cases, the penalty is a fine at level 3 plus treble the amount of the tax that was either underpaid as a result of the omission, understatement or failure or which would have been underpaid had the information been taken as correct or the offence been undetected. However, like the penalties under Sec. 80(1), the Commissioner can, and commonly does, compound the penalty to a smaller sum.

The offences under (1) and (2) above cover most of the situations where a taxpayer has understated his income or overstated his deductible expenses and, as a result, adjustments have been made to his assessable profits. Assessable profits as included in a taxpayer's tax computation may, however, also be increased through the operation of Sec. 61A, which is discussed in section 10.4.5. This provision, very broadly, applies where the Commissioner concludes that a transaction was undertaken solely or predominantly to obtain the tax benefit which it conferred and, in these circumstances, the Commissioner is granted broad powers to assess the person in a manner which counters that tax benefit. It is, however, not possible for a taxpayer to be certain whether the Commissioner will conclude that a transaction was undertaken for a purpose which attracts the application of Sec. 61A or, if the Commissioner does so conclude, how the Commissioner will assess the taxpayer to counter the tax benefit. As such, a taxpayer has little option in practice but to treat a transaction in his tax return in accordance with the law but assuming that Sec. 61A will not apply. In such circumstances, it is difficult to conclude that treating the transactions in the person's tax return in accordance with their strict tax consequences would, by itself, amount to the omitting or understating anything, making an incorrect statement in claiming a deduction or supplying incorrect information; it is even more difficult to conclude that in the unlikely event that it did amount to such, that the person did not have a reasonable excuse for completing the return in such a manner. Nonetheless, the IRD suggest in *Departmental Interpretation & Practice Notes No. 15* that penalties can be applied in Sec. 61A (and Sec. 61) cases. It is not clear, however, whether this view relates to all cases where Sec. 61A has been applied or only those where a contravention of one of the penalty provisions can be established.

The authority of the court may be invoked to enforce the failure under (4) and the court may order the return to be submitted within whatever period may be specified (Sec. 80(2A)). Failure to comply with an order of the court to submit a return amounts to a further offence for which the penalty is a fine at level 4 (Sec. 80(2B)).

None of the foregoing penalties are limited to the person actually committing the offence. They equally apply to any other person who aids, abets or incites the person in committing the act and this can of course include professional advisers (Sec. 80(4)).

There is a time limit within which these penalties may be invoked and this is within six years after the end of the year of assessment for which the offence took place (Sec. 80(3)).

7.4.2 Penalty assessments (additional tax)

For the five offences under Sec. 80(2), there is an alternative penalty under Sec. 82A which involves an assessment to so-called additional tax which is not, however, additional tax as it is normally understood but is merely a fiscal penalty imposed in addition to the actual tax liability (Sec. 82A(2)). The provisions of Sec. 82A are only applicable if the penalty provisions under Sec. 80(2) itself have not been imposed and the person has not been prosecuted for fraud or wilful evasion (see section 7.4.3). Further, once an assessment has been made under Sec. 82A, the person cannot be further prosecuted under Sec. 80(2) or Sec. 82(1) for the same offence (Sec. 82A(7)).

The "additional tax" assessable is in essence a constituent of the penalty that would have been imposed under Sec. 80(2) in that it can be up to three times the amount of the tax that was either underpaid as a result of the omission, understatement or failure or would have been underpaid had the information been taken as correct or the offence been undetected (Sec. 82A (1)). There is no need for the Commissioner to have separate power to compound the penalty because the additional tax can be any figure which he chooses up to a maximum of three times the tax.

Before an assessment can be made, there is a specific procedure to be followed and this involves the sending of a notice by the Commissioner or a deputy commissioner personally to the person concerned. The notice must:—

(1) specify the offence in respect of which the additional tax is to be assessed;

(2) inform the person of his right to submit written representations; and

(3) specify a date by which the representations must be received. This date must not be sooner than 21 days from the service of the notice (Sec. 82A(4)(a)).

The form and manner in which a notice under Sec. 82A(4) is issued must conform to the same rules as apply to any notice of assessment (see section 7.3) (Sec. 82A(5)).

The notice can only be dispensed with in limited circumstances and this is where the person concerned is about to leave Hong Kong. As delay may result in an inability to collect the additional tax in such circumstances, the Commissioner or a deputy commissioner is empowered to issue an assessment immediately without inviting any representations (Sec. 82A(4A))

Where, however, the notice is issued, the Commissioner or a deputy commissioner will give due consideration to any representations made by the person, or on his behalf, before raising the assessment (Sec. 82A(4)(a)). Representations would normally give reasons why it was considered the person concerned had a reasonable excuse for the omission, understatement or failure or would otherwise admit culpability but request the Commissioner or a deputy commissioner's clemency. The views of the Commissioner or deputy commissioner on the representations made are reflected in the amount of the assessment that is finally issued.

Sec. 82A(3) provides that the assessment to additional tax must be issued by the Commissioner or a deputy commissioner personally. Moreover, it was held in *D 15/98* that such assessment must, in fact, be issued by the same taxing officer (i.e. the Commissioner or deputy commissioner) who issued the notice pursuant to Sec. 82A(4). In particular, in that case an assessment to additional tax was held to be invalid because it was issued by a deputy commissioner whereas the notice under Sec. 82A(4) was issued by the Commissioner. Interestingly, following that decision the Commissioner went back and personally considered the taxpayer's original representations made pursuant to Sec. 82A(4)(a) and issued a new assessment to additional tax. However, the Board of Review, in *D 154/98* held that such action was not permissible and that the decision in *D 15/98* was final. It seems, therefore, that if an assessment to additional tax is invalid on technical grounds, it is not open to the Commissioner to correct the technical deficiency and issue another additional tax assessment in respect of the same offence.

The decision in *D 15/98* was, however, not followed in a later case with virtually identical facts (*D 133/98*). In that decision, the Board of Review was persuaded that the taxpayer had not been prejudiced by the fact that the additional tax notice was issued by a different taxing officer to the one who invited representations and, in any event, that Sec. 63 provided that no notice was rendered invalid for want of form. In an even later case (*D 53/99*), however, the Board of Review, having had the opportunity to consider both *D 15/98* and *D 133/98*, held that the former of these was the better decision. Presumably in order to finally resolve the issue, the Commissioner appealed this decision to the Court of First Instance (see *CIR v Mr. Loganathan, Suresh Babu* [2000] (1 HKRC 90-104)). The Court overturned the decision of the Board of Review and held that notwithstanding the use of the word "personally" in Sec. 82A(3), provided all the steps set out in Sec. 82A(4) were undertaken by either a Commissioner or deputy commissioner, a notice of assessment to additional tax should be considered valid. Moreover, the court considered that Sec. 82A was concerned with substantial compliance and, as any irregularity in following the steps set out in Sec. 82A(4) in the particular case did not prejudice the taxpayer, it did not render the assessment to additional tax invalid.

An assessment to additional tax under Sec. 82A is still competent upon the executor of a deceased person (Sec. 82A(6)).

As noted, the amount of the additional tax is at the discretion of the Commissioner, but cannot exceed three time the tax undercharged as a result of the incorrect return or statement or the failure to comply with the relevant requirement, or the tax which would have been undercharged had the offence not been detected. The IRD has published guidelines as to how this discretion is exercised and these can be found on their website (www.info.gov.hk/ird).

The most complex part of these guidelines concerns additional tax in field audit and investigation cases. The additional tax in such cases is made up of two elements. First, a "normal loading" is applied to the tax undercharged; this is essentially the penalty for non-compliance with the law and is intended to reflect the culpability of the taxpayer. The IRD guidelines suggest that the amount of this element will range between 5% and 210% of the tax undercharged, depending on the nature of the offence and the degree of co-operation of the taxpayer in disclosing details of the offences. For example, a 5% normal loading is applied to cases where the taxpayer simply failed to exercise reasonable care, but made a full voluntary disclosure of the errors or omissions. On the other hand, a normal loading of 210% applies where the taxpayer has shown intentional disregard of the law by engaging in deliberate tactics to understate taxable profits and has consistently denied the offences. In recognition of the fact that each case is different, however, the IRD goes on to note that the normal loading suggested can be further increased or decreased by up to 25% with reference to relevant aggravating or mitigating factors. The IRD consider, for example, that the degree of sophistication of the taxpayer and the business, the attitude of the taxpayer, and the relative size of the understatements may all be aggravating or mitigating factors in appropriate circumstances.

Second, in addition to the normal loading, the IRD imposes commercial restitution. In essence, this is interest on the tax undercharged and is currently calculated at the best lending rate compounded on a monthly basis. However, the IRD guidelines indicate a maximum additional tax level inclusive of commercial restitution. For example, in a case where the normal loading is 5%, the maximum additional tax including commercial restitution would generally be 30% of the tax undercharged. At the other end of the spectrum, where the normal loading is 210%, the maximum total additional tax including commercial restitution would generally be 260%. Although the normal loading may be increased or decreased from the guidelines due to aggravating or mitigating factors, the commercial restitution appears not to be intended to be similarly adjusted.

The IRD guidelines also deal with additional tax in the case of late filing of Profits Tax, Salaries Tax, Property Tax or Personal Assessment returns. Generally, the level of additional tax is 10% for a first offence, 20% for a second offence within five years and 35% for a third or subsequent offence within five years. In the case of Profits Tax returns, however, if the relevant return is filed after two or more estimated assessments have been issued, the general level of additional tax is respectively 20%, 30% or 50% for a first, second or third and subsequent offence within five years. Again, all of these rates may be increased or decreased depending on aggravating or mitigating factors present in each individual case.

Although the quantum of any additional tax imposed under Sec. 82A is at the discretion of the Commissioner (although subject to review by the Board of Review or courts as discussed below), it is important to note that contractual agreements can be reached between the Commissioner and a taxpayer as to whether such additional tax will be imposed or the quantum thereof. For example, if adjustments are proposed by the Commissioner as a result of an investigation or field audit, the taxpayer may seek to tie the quantum of additional tax into any agreement reached with the Commissioner as to the amount of the adjustments in respect of the substantive issue;

although such a course of action is, in practice, generally resisted by IRD assessors, it is as a matter of law possible and, in fact, sometimes occurs. Indeed, in *D 36/99* the Board of Review held that the withdrawal of a taxpayer's objections in a dispute case was part and parcel of an agreement whereby the Commissioner undertook not to impose additional tax, even though such agreement was not documented and was denied by the relevant assessor.

A person assessed to additional tax under Sec. 82A may appeal to the Board of Review against such assessment. Sec. 82B(1) provides that such an appeal must be made in writing and be filed within one month after the notice of assessment is given to the person, or such further time as the Board of Review may allow. The Board of Review's power to extend the time for filing the notice of appeal is limited by Sec. 82B(1A) which only permits the time to be extended where the Board of Review is satisfied that the appellant was prevented by illness, absence from Hong Kong or other reasonable cause from filing the notice within one month. The Board of Review can also extend the time limit only in respect of a notice of assessment issued after 24 June, 2004, being the date on which Sec. 82B was amended to give the Board of Review this power. Prior to that date, there was no statutory provision for the one month time limit to be extended and this was strictly enforced. In this regard, see *Wong Wing Piu & Wong Wing Piu trading as Tai Yip Glass Co. v CIR* (2 HKTC 134) and *Chan Min-Ching trading as Chan Siu Wah Herbalist Clinic v CIR* [1999] (1 HKRC 90-100).

In order to be valid, a notice of appeal against an assessment under Sec. 82A must include the following:

(1)   a copy of the notice of assessment;
(2)   a statement of the grounds of appeal;
(3)   a copy of the notice of intention to assess, if any, issued under Sec. 82A(4); and
(4)   a copy of any written representations made in response to that notice.

The permitted grounds of appeal are set out in Sec. 82B(2) and are that:–

(1)   the person has a reasonable excuse and is not, therefore, liable for additional tax. A discussion of what may constitute a reasonable excuse is contained in section 7.4;
(2)   the additional tax exceeds the amount for which the person is chargeable. In other words it is more than three times the amount of tax affected by the omission, understatement or failure. In this connection see *CIR v Kwok Siu-Tong* (HKTC 1012); or

(3)   although the tax is validly chargeable, it is excessive having regard to the circumstances.

With regard to the last point, the Board of Review merely makes an independent judgement of whether the amount of the tax is reasonable and not clearly excessive in the circumstances. The Board of Review does not readily interfere with the amount of additional tax imposed by the Commissioner unless he has clearly exercised his judgement unreasonably in the circumstances. Nonetheless, it is not uncommon for the Board of Review to reduce penalties in circumstances which they consider appropriate. See, for example, *D 56/94* which concerned a penalty imposed on a company for the late filing of its Profits Tax return. The company had requested an extension of time for filing the return but this was rejected and, several days before the due date for filing the return, the company purchased Tax Reserve Certificates equal to its expected liability. The Board of Review held that the purchase of the Tax Reserve Certificates did not prevent the Commissioner from imposing a penalty, but considered it a strong mitigating factor and reduced the penalty significantly. Indeed, the Board noted that had the company not had a previous record of late filings, it would have had no hesitation in reducing the penalty to zero. See also *D 23/98* where penalties were substantially reduced by the Board of Review on the basis that the offence was considered only a technical breach of the law. That case concerned the filing of a return which, although correct, was incomplete because the auditor's certificate was unsigned and the accounts were not properly certified; an estimated assessment was raised on the basis of the incomplete return and, accordingly, there was no loss of revenue. These cases indicate that the actual or potential loss of revenue as a result of the offence may be considered a significant factor by the Board of Review when considering penalties, particularly where taxpayers have taken reasonable steps to mitigate the effect on revenue collection of the offence.

Sec. 82B(3) provides that, *inter alia*, the provisions of Sec. 68 apply to appeals against additional tax. This means that when hearing such an appeal the Board of Review has the power to increase, as well as to decrease, confirm or annul an additional tax assessment. It is not uncommon for the Board of Review to increase an additional tax assessment pursuant to this power and examples can be found in *D 110/01*, *D 47/05* and *D 50/05*.

There are, however, many other decisions of the Board of Review concerning penalties under Sec. 82A; indeed, a significant portion of all Board of Review cases concern this topic. Although the facts of these cases vary widely, as do the outcomes, the Board of Review has, on numerous occasions, stated that the appropriate starting point when imposing penalties under this provision is 100% of the underlying tax with increases or decreases depending upon any especially aggravating or mitigating factors present in the particular case before them. In this regard, see for example *D 53/88*. It is important to note that this benchmark of 100% as the starting point for imposition of additional tax was not applied only to understatement of income cases, but also to late filing cases; in the latter category of cases, however, the Board of Review has generally shown a willingness to reduce the level of additional tax significantly in the absence of a history of late filing by the taxpayer. Indeed, in a number of more recent cases (see for example *D 112/99* and *D 67/03*), it has been suggested that 10% of the tax is the appropriate starting point for late filing cases where there are no previous offences. The Board of Review also appears to accept that additional tax for a simple failure to disclose income subject to Salaries Tax should be imposed at lower levels than in Profits Tax cases. Indeed, in *D 113/99* it was suggested that the starting point for additional tax in such cases should also be 10%.

As noted earlier, the IRD have their own guidelines as to the amount of additional tax to be imposed in particular cases. For a case where these were discussed and apparently endorsed by the Board of Review, see *D 125/98*. Conversely, however, in *D 110/01* the Board of Review held that additional tax imposed, in accordance with the IRD's guidelines, at rates between 60% and 86% of tax undercharged as a result of non-disclosure of income subject to Salaries Tax were inadequate when considered against the benchmark of 100% consistently adopted by the Board of Review; as a result, the Board increased the amount of additional tax to 100% of the tax undercharged. See also the decisions in *D 166/01, D 171/01* and *D 22/02* where the Board of Review when refusing to reduce penalties pointed out that they were imposed below the benchmark rate of 100%.

Although there has been much inconsistency, and arguably confusion, between cases as to the applicability of a benchmark penalty rate of 100% and the validity of the IRD's own guidelines, the Board of Review in *D 118/ 02* attempted to reduce this by undertaking an excellent analysis of previous decisions and the IRD's practice. In that decision, the Board of Review chose to follow certain earlier authorities which indicated that a benchmark penalty level of 100% was not relevant in all cases, but only in cases where the taxpayer had totally disregarded his obligations and had not been particularly co-operative. They agreed that the 100% benchmark theoretically applied equally to both omission of income cases and late filing cases, but noted that late filing cases did not generally fall into the category of more serious cases which attracted that level of penalty. The decision also contains an excellent and useful analysis of the factors which various Boards of Review have considered relevant in deciding whether aggravating or mitigating factors exist. On the matter of the IRD's policy, the Board of Review in that decision did not reject the IRD's guidelines, although they did express concerns over certain aspects of them and, in reducing the penalty in the case before them noted that the IRD had over-estimated the gravity of the offence.

In the case of *Charles C. Y. Cheng v CIR* (HKTC 1087) the taxpayer appealed to the Board of Review on the ground that he had been prevented by duress from appealing against the original assessments on which the Sec. 82A assessments were based, the duress being that he was about to emigrate, had confided this to the assessor and did not want to delay his departure. The Sec. 82A assessments were reduced by the Board of Review but reinstated by the Court. Note also that where the assessment under Sec. 82A has been based upon an assets betterment statement following an investigation and the statement has been accepted by the taxpayer, it has been held that he cannot deny such acceptance in any appeal against penalties imposed under Sec. 82A (see *D 18/87*).

It is also important to note that the charge to additional tax can only be imposed upon a "person" which is specifically defined by Sec. 2 (see the definition of "person" in section 4.3.1). In *D 3/79*, a Sec. 82A assessment had been raised upon the personal representative of a deceased's estate in respect of incorrect returns relating to the estate submitted by the personal representative. The assessment was held to be invalid because an estate cannot be a person but, in passing, it was noted that an assessment on the personal representative in a personal capacity would have been competent.

Furthermore, an assessment to additional tax can only be made where tax has been undercharged as a result of the incorrect return or failure to file a return or to notify existence of liability to tax. If, for example, a loss has been overstated, no tax is payable; therefore no penalty assessment can be raised (see *D 2/81*). However, if the overstated loss had been carried forward and reduced tax payable in a subsequent year, then additional tax can be charged. The penalty provisions of Sec. 82A are also applicable where an official return form has not been issued and a person does not notify the Commissioner that a return should be made as required of him by Sec. 51(2), notwithstanding that a correct return may have been submitted later. In this regard, see *Dodge Knitting Co. Ltd., Dodge Trading Ltd., v CIR* (2 HKTC 597).

Sec. 82B(3) provides that various, but not all, of the provisions applicable to appeals against assessments contained in Part XI of the IRO are applicable to an appeal against additional tax under Sec. 82A. In particular, this ensures a taxpayer's right to take the appeal further to the Court of First Instance and beyond.

7.4.3 Fraud and wilful evasion

As would be expected, the most severe penalty provisions relate to offences of fraud and wilful evasion. The penalties for these offences include, in addition to the usual fines, possible imprisonment. The level of the fine and imprisonment which can be imposed depends upon the level at which the prosecution is brought. It must not be assumed that every detected case of fraud or wilful evasion brings imprisonment, because the Commissioner cannot impose a prison sentence and it is his decision whether or not to bring a case before the Courts; moreover, the IRO gives the Commissioner specific power to compound any offence and settle for a monetary penalty (Sec. 82(2)). Many such cases are settled in this way. Of course, where the Commissioner has a doubt as to whether he could prove fraud or wilful default, he would opt for penalties under Sec. 82A or Sec. 80 as described in sections 7.4.1 and 7.4.2. Nonetheless, the number of prosecutions under Sec. 82 appears to be increasing and prison sentences are commonly imposed where defendants are found guilty.

The serious provisions of Sec. 82 apply to any person who commits any of the specified acts with the deliberate objective of evading tax or assisting someone else to do so; again, therefore, it can apply to professional advisers. The specified acts are:

(1) omitting a sum from a return;
(2) making a false entry or statement in a return;
(3) making a false statement in connection with a claim for a deduction or allowance;
(4) signing a statement or return without reasonable grounds to believe that it is true;
(5) making a false reply to any question whether orally or in writing;
(6) preparing, maintaining or authorizing false books and records; or
(7) making use of or authorizing any fraud, art or contrivance. This should not apply to contrived tax avoidance schemes which use legal loopholes, although the wording of the relevant provision (Sec. 82(1)(g)) must leave some doubt. It is, however, essential for the Government to demonstrate criminal intent for a prosecution to succeed (see *The Queen v Radofin Electronics (Far East) Ltd. and Another* (HKTC 1252)).

Any person caught by any of those provisions is guilty of a misdemeanour with the following maximum penalties:

(a)   On summary conviction
- Fine at level 3;
- Additional fine of three times the tax which was or would have been underpaid; and
- Imprisonment for six months.

(b)   On indictment
- Fine at level 5;
- Additional fine of three times the tax which was or would have been underpaid; and
- Imprisonment for three years.

No prosecution can be brought without this being at the instance of or with the sanction of the Commissioner, although this is not intended to derogate from the powers of the Attorney-General in bringing criminal prosecutions (Sec. 84).

For a review of evidence and discussion of the legal aspects of successful prosecution and conviction under Sec. 82(1) see the case of *The Queen v Lee Shea Sze* (2 HKTC 164). In a further case, the Court of Appeal reviewed the norms for custodial sentences in the case of offences under Sec. 82(1) and indicated stronger action on subsequent convictions (*The Queen v (1) Ma Lai Wu, (2) Ma Yee Keung, (3) Homer Industrial Company Ltd.* (2 HKTC 190)). Subsequently, the principle of custodial sentencing in appropriate cases was affirmed in *The Queen v Ho Lui* (3 HKTC 289) and it is now relatively common for such sentences to be imposed.

An act of omission or understatement of a single item for one year would, of course, amount to more than one misdemeanour under Sec. 82 because the omission or understatement would amount to an offence under (1) or (2) above and signing the return with the false entry in it would amount to an offence under (4) above. Also if it was a Profits Tax return prepared from falsified records, even though the return was in agreement with the records, the result would be a further offence under (6) above. The result could, therefore, be multiple fines and this would certainly be so when more than one year was involved. However, it is usually the multiplicity of offences and the amount of tax involved that influences the Commissioner in his decision as to the level of prosecution or, if he decides to compound the offences, the extent of fine which he would impose.

The IRD often bases its investigations and back duty assessments upon assets betterment statements which necessarily involve estimates and assumptions, but such statements are fully enforceable as justification for assessments and penalties because the onus is upon the taxpayer to prove that they are incorrect. In this regard, see *D 28/85* and *D 18/87*.

See also *Departmental Interpretation & Practice Notes No. 11 — Elements of a Tax Investigation*, and *No. 11A — Elements of a Field Audit*.

7.4.4 Miscellaneous

All employees of the IRD, and, in fact, anybody who has to perform duties under the IRO, are subject to the secrecy provisions of Sec. 4 and must sign an oath of secrecy under Sec. 4(2). Any such person who acts in contravention of those secrecy provisions or who aids, abets or incites any other person to do so is subject to a penalty at level 5 under Sec. 81. This cannot be compounded to any smaller sum.

Although the IRO may impose severe penalty provisions, including imprisonment, for tax offences, the imposition and suffering of such a penalty does not absolve the person from being assessed in respect of the tax in question which he must still pay as well as suffering the penalty (Sec. 83).

Chapter 8 ■

Assessments and
Payment of Tax

8.1 Legislation

The provisions for the assessment and payment of tax affect all three income based taxes and are contained in various parts of the IRO. However, the legislation dealing with the matters specifically covered in this chapter is contained in Part X in respect of the powers to assess and the form and validity of notices, in Part XII in respect of the payment of tax and enforcement of collection and in Part XIII in respect of tax refunds. Provisional Salaries Tax, Provisional Profits Tax and Provisional Property Tax are covered in Parts XA and XB and XC respectively but a discussion of those Parts is dealt with in Chapters 2, 3 and 4 respectively.

8.2 The Power to Assess

The powers granted by the legislation to raise assessments must cover more than the obvious authority to issue demands for payment. They must also deal with matters such as the timing of assessments, authority to raise estimated assessments, procedures for dealing with persons who elect Personal Assessment, powers and time limits relating to additional assessments for prior years and means of correcting errors. All of these matters are dealt with in this chapter.

8.2.1 General

There is a general power for an assessor to raise an assessment upon any person who, in his opinion, is liable to tax under the IRO. An assessor, cannot, however, raise an assessment at any time; he is generally limited to raising an assessment only after the time limit for submitting a return for that year of assessment has expired. Additionally, as discussed further in section 8.2.4 below, the assessor can generally only raise an assessment within six years after the end of the relevant year of assessment.

Because of the general prohibition on raising assessments until the time for submitting the relevant return has expired, an assessor cannot normally raise an assessment until a month after the issue of a return for that year of assessment or after the date to which the time limit may have been extended (see Chapter 7). In order to protect the IRD's ability to collect tax, however, there is a power to assess at any time when a person is about to leave Hong Kong or when it is otherwise expedient to urgently raise an assessment, such as in the case of impending liquidation or bankruptcy (Sec. 59(1)).

From time to time the Commissioner may also raise assessments under Sec. 59(1) where a person has been, or is suspected of having been, engaged in illegal activities and an amount of money has been seized by the police; in these circumstances the Commissioner may raise an assessment and issue a notice to the Commissioner of Police under Sec. 76 (see section 8.5.2) ordering him to pay the money to the IRD, particularly where it seems likely that the money would otherwise be about to be returned to the person. The Commissioner's entitlement to so act was upheld by the High Court in an application for judicial review of such actions in the case of *Lee Sap Pat v CIR & Anor.* [1991] (1 HKRC 90-055). In doing so, the court effectively held that Secs. 59(1) and 59(3) (see discussion below) were to be interpreted broadly and, with regard to the former of these, rejected the taxpayer's contention that the particular circumstances required the Commissioner to wait for the expiration of the time for submitting the Profits Tax return form issued to the taxpayer before raising an assessment.

See, however, the later case of *Lee Ma Loi v CIR & Anor.* [1992] (1 HKRC 90-057) & (1 HKRC 90-063) where the Court of Appeal upheld the finding of the High Court that the Commissioner was acting in concert with the Commissioner of Police to seize the proceeds of an illegal activity and that this was an abuse of power; accordingly, the court quashed the assessments concerned and ordered the repayment of the money. In reaching the decision that the process was an abuse of the Commissioner's powers, the court relied upon UK authorities which state that a public official must exercise his powers only for the purpose for which they were granted and not for any collateral purpose. Although the court had no doubt that the Commissioner had abused his powers in the circumstances of the case, there was some discussion as to whether the quashing of the assessments was the only appropriate remedy available; although the Court of Appeal ultimately decided not to disturb the action of the High Court with regard to this point, it should not be assumed that in all cases a court would quash assessments in similar circumstances.

The power to raise estimated assessments must not be confused with the powers to raise Provisional Property Tax, Provisional Salaries Tax and Provisional Profits Tax assessments which must, of course, be raised long before a return for the relevant year of assessment is issued. The rules governing these Provisional assessments are dealt with in Chapters 2, 3 and 4 respectively.

Where a return is submitted and the assessor accepts the figure on the return, he merely raises an assessment accordingly (Sec. 59(2)(a)). Where he does not accept the figure reported, or the return is not submitted by the due date, he has additional powers which are dealt with below.

Occasionally there is dispute as to who derived certain profits and, accordingly, to whom an assessment should be issued in respect of those profits. In such circumstances, the IRD may raise assessments against a number of different persons in respect of those profits and allow the Board of Review or courts to ultimately determine which, if any, of the assessments is correct. This practice of raising alternative assessments has been held to be acceptable until one of the assessments becomes final and conclusive. In this connection, see *Dodd and Tranfield v Haddock* (42 TC 229) which was quoted with approval by the Court of Appeal in *Nina T. H. Wang v CIR* [1992] (1 HKRC 90-059).

8.2.2 Estimated assessments

There are three specific circumstances in which an assessor can raise an estimated assessment and, again, this should not be confused with Provisional Property Tax, Provisional Profits Tax or Provisional Salaries Tax assessments, which are necessarily estimates. The difference between Provisional assessments and estimated final assessments are that the former are always adjusted to the final figure for the year when known, whereas the latter can only be adjusted under the formal objection and appeal procedure (see Chapter 9).

The three specific circumstances under which the assessor may estimate the final assessment are:—

(1) where he does not accept the figure reported on the return (Sec. 59(2)(b)). This may only be because he disagrees with an amount claimed as a deduction or with an amount treated as not taxable. In these circumstances his estimate will probably be the return figure plus the amount in dispute. There is nothing, however, to prevent him raising an estimate which has no bearing upon the returned figure and this is done in cases of fundamental disagreement;

(2) where a return has not been submitted (Sec. 59(3)). Such an assessment is not valid if the return has been lodged with the IRD, even if it is overdue. This occasionally happens when an assessor raises an estimated assessment before he is aware that the return has been received by the Department. In these circumstances the assessment is generally cancelled and no formal objection is required; or

(3) where the accounts of a trade or business have not been kept in a satisfactory form with the result that the return is unreliable (Sec. 59(4)). In these cases, the estimate takes the form of the application of the usual rate of profit for that type of trade or business to the

turnover for the relevant period, and the Board of Inland Revenue is empowered to prescribe the usual rates of profit. It should be noted that this provision does not seem to apply to the profits of a profession. It is understood that, in practice, Sec. 59(4) is rarely invoked.

In each of these cases, the taxpayer is entitled to object against the assessments, but in the case of assessments under Sec. 59(3) he has more difficulty in validly objecting because not only must he object within the prescribed time limit, he must also submit a valid return within the prescribed period (see Chapter 9). When assessments are made under any of these three provisions, the actual provision of the IRO under which it is raised is stated on the assessment, otherwise the person assessed would not know what objection rights or obligations he had.

Except in the case of assessments under Sec. 59(2)(b), which are based on the return figure, the estimates are necessarily arbitrary and large assessments may be raised where, in reality, there is a much smaller profit or indeed there is a loss. Notwithstanding this fact, such an estimate becomes final and conclusive and the tax payable unless a valid objection is submitted.

8.2.3 Personal assessment

Because Property Tax and Profits Tax assessments are made at a fixed standard rate with no regard for personal allowances, an election for Personal Assessment may result in a total or partial refund. Accordingly, in order to limit the administration, the assessor is empowered to refrain from raising assessments in certain cases where an election for Personal Assessment would result in a total refund. If only a partial refund would be made then the full assessment is made and the refund procedure applied.

The specific cases identified are:—

(1)   all Property Tax assessments where a Personal Assessment election would result in a total refund (Sec. 59(1A));

(2)   where an individual eligible for Personal Assessment, or his or her spouse, has income from a trade, profession or business carried on by him or her as a sole proprietor of not more than the amount in the second column of item 1(c) in the Fourth Schedule and neither he or she nor his or her spouse have any other sources of income liable to tax under the IRO (Sec. 59(1B)). The amount in the second column of item 1(c) in the Fourth Schedule was until 1997/98 the basic allowance for a single person; from 1998/99, however, there

is no item 1(c) in the Fourth Schedule and, therefore, the provision can technically have no application. Nonetheless, under the intended application of the provision, there would, of course, be a total refund in such circumstances because the profits would be covered by the personal allowance. The ceiling could be even higher in view of the more generous allowances for married persons and further allowances for those with children, dependent parents, grand-parents and/or brothers or sisters, but these circumstances are covered by the next case; and

(3)   where an individual who is eligible for Personal Assessment, or his or her spouse, has income from a trade, profession or business either carried on solely or in partnership with others, neither the individual nor his or her spouse have any other source of income chargeable to tax under the IRO and the profits, or share of profits, from the business are less than the personal allowances available to the individual under Personal Assessment. Further, if the assessor has already raised an assessment on the individual or a partnership of which he is a partner, he is empowered to cancel the individual's assessment or reduce the partnership's assessment by the individual's share, notwithstanding that it may have become final and conclusive (Sec. 59(1C)).

8.2.4 Additional assessments

Sec. 60 grants certain powers to an assessor to raise additional assessments. Although Sec. 60 appears to be primarily concerned with additional assessments, it applies also to original assessments for a year in respect of which no assessment has previously been issued.

An assessor is empowered to raise an additional (or original) assessment for a year of assessment at any time within six years after the end of that year of assessment if he is of the opinion that a person has been under-assessed, or has not been assessed, for that year (Sec. 60(1)). In *D 27/91*, it was unsuccessfully argued that the notice of additional assessment had to be delivered to the taxpayer within the six-year time limit; in rejecting this argument, the Board of Review confirmed that the IRD merely had to raise the additional assessment within the stipulated time and noted that it was irrelevant when the taxpayer actually received the notice or even whether the notice was correctly addressed. In the case of fraud or wilful evasion the time limit for additional assessment is extended to ten years after the end of the year of assessment (Sec. 60(1) proviso (b)). There is no necessity for the additional assessment to be an accurate figure; it can, if necessary, be an estimate (*Mok Tsze Fung v CIR* (HKTC 166)). That decision also established that Sec. 60 stood on its own and was not dependent on the circumstances under which any previous assessment was raised. This point was further confirmed in *Lam Soon Trademark Limited v CIR* by the Court of First Instance [2004] (1 HKRC 90-137), the Court of Appeal [2005] (1 HKRC 90-149) and the Court of Final Appeal [2005] (1 HKRC 90-171), all of which agreed that the Commissioner was entitled to invoke Sec. 60 to raise an assessment pursuant to Sec. 14 in respect of amounts which had previously been assessed under Secs. 15(1)(b) and 21A.

It is sometimes suggested that if no tax is assessed because a loss is sustained, or the assessable profits are set off against losses carried forward, that there is no "assessment" and therefore the normal time limit for amending the calculation of a loss to be carried forward does not apply. Such a view was, however, rejected in *D 13/03* where the Board of Review held, *inter alia*, that the six year time limit was introduced to provide certainty in tax matters, and that to allow the calculation of a loss to be kept open indefinitely (or effectively until six years after it had been set off against assessable profits) would defeat this object. Accordingly, the Board of Review held that the IRD could not recalculate the amount of a loss to be carried forward outside the six year time limit even if subsequent information revealed that the original calculation was incorrect. Nonetheless, in *CIR v Yau Lai Man, Agnes trading as L.M. Yau & Company* [2005] (1 HKRC 90-146) which was an appeal by the Commissioner from another Board of Review decision, the Court of First Instance rejected this approach and held that a statement of loss did not constitute an "assessment". The court reached this decision on the basis of examining the use of the word "assessment" in the IRO and noted that such usage generally implied that an amount of tax was payable. This reasoning was followed in *CIR v Common Empire Limited* by both the Court of First Instance ([2005] (1 HKRC 90-158)) and the Court of Appeal ([2006] (1 HKRC 90-176)).

Where the taxpayer has died, the time limit for additional assessment (other than an assessment to additional tax under Sec. 82A) upon the executor in respect of periods up to the date of death is one year from the date of death or one year from the date of filing the Estate Duty Affidavit, whichever is the later (Sec. 54). Note, however, that if the *Revenue (Abolition of Estate Duty) Bill 2005*, which was before the Legislative Council at the time of writing, is passed in its present form, Sec. 54 will be amended. Under the proposed amendment, Sec. 54 will operate as at present in respect of a person who dies before the date of abolition of Estate Duty. In respect of a person who dies on or after the date of abolition of Estate Duty, no affidavit will, of course, be required for Estate Duty, and the time limit for raising an assessment (other than an assessment for additional tax under Sec. 82A) will be three years after the end of the year of assessment in which the person died.

Where a repayment of tax has been made and it appears to the assessor that the repayment was made as the result of a mistake in law or in fact, he may make an additional assessment within the six-year time limit to correct the mistake (Sec. 60(2)). This power is, however, not applicable where either:—

(1)   the repayment was made as a result of the determination of an assessment by objection or appeal (Sec. 60(2)); or

(2)   the repayment was made as a result of a practice generally prevailing at the time when the repayment was made (Sec. 60(3)). In other words, if a subsequent legal decision changes, in favour of the IRD, what was generally thought to be the position previously, and a repayment had been made in an earlier year on that previous understanding, an additional assessment cannot be made on the basis of the subsequent legal decision.

It must be emphasised that these two restrictions apply only to additional assessments in repayment cases. Similar restrictions do not apply to an assessor's powers to raise an additional assessment in any other circumstances.

The full rights of objection and appeal apply to all additional assessments (see Chapter 9).

8.3 Notices of Assessment

An assessment, of course, involves the sending of a notice to the person assessed and the form of such notice is laid down by the IRO. Every notice must separately state the amount assessed and the tax charged and must state the due date or dates of payment as fixed by the Commissioner (Sec. 62(1)).

If the law changes after an assessment has been validly made so as to affect the amount of tax charged in the assessment, the Commissioner can make the necessary amendments and send a notification to the person assessed in which case the notification is treated as a notice of assessment so far as the changed details are concerned (Sec. 62(3)). Therefore, an objection can be given against the details in the notification as if it was an assessment.

An assessment which contains mistakes or omissions in describing the person assessed, or in respect of other details, is not rendered invalid so long as the assessment is clearly in accordance with the intent and meaning under which it was issued (Sec. 63).

In *Hong Kong Flour Mills v CIR* [2002] (1 HKRC 90-118) the Court of First Instance, relying on this provision, refused to treat as invalid an assessment issued pursuant to Sec. 15(1)(b) wherein the word "Limited" was not added to the end of the taxpayer's name.

The regulations governing delivery of notices of assessment are dealt with in section 7.3.

8.4 Payment of Tax

Once the amount of tax has been fixed by an assessment, the Commissioner, in his complete discretion, decides upon the due date of payment. In the case of Provisional Salaries Tax and Provisional Profits Tax, the tax is fixed to be paid in two instalments in certain circumstances. Detailed comments on fixing of dates for payment under Provisional assessments are contained in Chapters 3 and 4.

When the due date has been fixed by the Commissioner and stated in the notice, the assessment is due for payment on or before that date, subject to any agreed holdover or instalment payment plan; if it is not so paid, it is deemed to be in default. The defaulter is the person named in the assessment, and, in the case of a partnership, each partner is a defaulter (Sec. 71(1)).

Where tax is in default, a surcharge is added to the tax and is recoverable in the same way as the tax. Although a 5% surcharge is generally added, in fact any amount up to but not exceeding 5% can be charged (Sec. 71(5)). Furthermore, if any part of the tax or earlier surcharge remains in default for six months or more, a further surcharge on the unpaid tax and surcharge is added. Whilst, again, it is usual to charge the maximum of 10%, the surcharge can in fact be any amount not exceeding 10% of the tax in default plus any surcharge imposed for earlier default (Sec. 71(5A)). Where tax is payable in two instalments and the first instalment is in default, it is the Commissioner's current practice to bring forward the due date of the second instalment and to add the 5% surcharge to both. If tax in dispute has not been held over, non payment still carries a surcharge, notwithstanding a valid objection; in this regard, see *Sam Kwong Weaving Factory v CIR* (2 HKTC 313).

Notwithstanding a due date stated on a notice of assessment, the Commissioner is empowered to accept payment by instalments (Sec. 71(6)).

Payment by instalments is not granted unless the taxpayer can show hardship or other good reason why he could not pay on the specified due date. Furthermore, upon agreeing to payment by instalments, it is usual for the surcharge to be added.

Sec. 71(2) provides that tax assessed must be paid notwithstanding that a valid objection or appeal against the assessment has been filed and is still outstanding. In *Tak Wing Investment Company Limited v CIR* [2001] (1 HKRC 90-110) where the taxpayer was seeking an order to stop the Commissioner taking enforcement action against an assessment in dispute, the taxpayer essentially sought to argue that this provision should not apply where the Commissioner had been slow in dealing with an objection. The taxpayer's submission was, however, rejected on the basis of the clear wording and intention of Sec. 71(2). Nonetheless, the court considered that the Commissioner's tardiness in dealing with the objection was a matter appropriately considered under judicial review and granted the taxpayer leave to apply for judicial review of the Commissioner's failure to determine the objections and for an order for *mandamus* compelling the Commissioner to determine the objections.

Notwithstanding the requirement to pay tax in dispute, there are provisions which enable tax in dispute in an assessment under objection or appeal to be held over pending determination of the objection or appeal. It is, however, entirely within the discretion of the Commissioner whether or not to hold over any of the tax; there is no automatic right of holdover with an objection or appeal.

If after considering an application the Commissioner decides to grant a holdover, he may do so in any one of the three following ways:—

(1)   by an unqualified holdover;
(2)   by a holdover on condition that a Tax Reserve Certificate (see section 10.5.3) is purchased to cover the amount of tax in dispute; or
(3)   by a holdover on condition that the taxpayer furnishes a bank guarantee to cover the tax in dispute plus any interest that may accrue (see below).

An unqualified holdover will, in practice, only be granted where it is immediately apparent to the Commissioner that the objection should be allowed (e.g. a mistake has been made by the assessor, new facts are presented or the assessment is estimated and a return has been supplied giving the correct assessment amount) or where a highly contentious point of law is involved. Where any tax so held over is ultimately found to be payable, it carries interest from the later of the original due date or the date of the holdover notice to the date that the appeal or objection is determined or withdrawn (Sec. 71(10)).

In most other objection cases, the Commissioner will normally order the purchase of a Tax Reserve Certificate as a condition of granting holdover. The certificate is specially marked (Sec. 71(7)(b)) to distinguish it from other tax reserve certificates because, although it carries the same rate of interest, interest is paid only if the tax is ultimately held not to be payable and the Certificate is surrendered for cash (Sec. 71(7)(d)). If it is used in payment of the tax ultimately held to be due, no interest is paid (Sec. 71(7)(c)). When the tax is ultimately held not to be due, the taxpayer has an option, if the Certificate is not more than three years old, to cash it in with interest or to have a normal Tax Reserve Certificate issued in its place carrying the same rate of interest and date of issue (Sec. 71(7)(d)). Where the purchase of a Tax Reserve Certificate is ordered by the Commissioner, it must be purchased within 14 days of the order or by the due date of payment of the tax if later. If it is not so purchased, the tax is regarded as in default and is payable in cash (Sec. 71(7)(n))

It is the Commissioner's present practice to accept a bank guarantee instead of the purchase of a Tax Reserve Certificate only where such purchase is claimed to cause financial hardship. This is somewhat surprising in that a person suffering financial hardship would be expected to have difficulty in obtaining a bank guarantee! However, where the obtaining of a bank guarantee is ordered, the guarantee must be in a form acceptable to the Commissioner, be irrevocable, and must cover the tax in dispute plus any interest chargeable from the original due date of payment to the date that the objection or appeal is determined or withdrawn. Further, the bank guarantee must be provided within 14 days of the order, or by the due date of payment of the tax, whichever is later. Failing any of these requirements, the tax becomes due and payable on the due date (Sec. 71(9)).

Interest chargeable in the case of a bank guarantee or where an unconditional holdover has been granted is charged at the rate fixed from time to time under Sec. 50 of the *District Court Ordinance* (Sec. 71(11)).

In any case where the Commissioner considers that an objection has little or no merit, he may choose to grant no holdover, although he would hardly lose by ordering the purchase of a Tax Reserve Certificate because the revenue is fully protected. Where no holdover is granted, but the objection is ultimately allowed, there is no provision for the payment of interest on the tax which then becomes refundable. This was confirmed by the Court of First Instance in *Weson Investment Limited v CIR* [2005] (1 HKRC 90-148) and upheld by the Court of Appeal [2006] (1 HKRC 90-183).

These arrangements do not apply to holdovers of Provisional Salaries, Profits or Property Tax which are governed by separate sections of the IRO.

The above policies are further explained in *Departmental Interpretation & Practice Notes No. 6.*

Where the Commissioner has granted a holdover and subsequently, before determination of the objection or appeal, discovers that the tax is likely to become irrecoverable or that the person assessed is unreasonably delaying settlement of his objection or appeal, the Commissioner can rescind the holdover and make such other order as he sees fit (Sec. 71(3)).

If the Commissioner rescinds a holdover order or, if tax previously held over becomes payable, either in the same, a lesser or a greater amount, the Commissioner must send a notice specifying a new date of payment and any tax not paid by that date is deemed to be in default (Sec. 71(4)).

8.5 Recovery of Tax

Apart from surcharges which may be added to tax which is in default there must, of course, be statutory provisions to enable collection of tax to be enforced. In all of the enforcement provisions discussed in the following sections, the tax collectible includes the surcharges and also any fines, penalties, fees or costs incurred in enforcement as well as any interest charged on tax held over and subsequently found to be payable (Sec. 72).

8.5.1 District Court procedure

The Commissioner can take action to recover tax in default through a civil debt action in the District Court (Sec. 75). Although there is normally a limit on the amounts which can be recovered in a District Court action, there is no such limit to an action by the Commissioner.

As evidence of the debt upon which the Court can give judgement, it is sufficient authority for the Commissioner to sign a certificate giving the address of the defaulter and particulars of the tax which he owes. The taxpayer cannot plead that the tax is excessive because there are sufficient options open to him under the IRO to dispute the assessment (i.e. the objection and appeal procedure) and the Court is only concerned with the enforcement of debts not the accuracy of them. For cases where the Commissioner has successfully sought to strike out defences filed by taxpayers on the basis that an assessment is excessive or incorrect, see *CIR v Choy Sau Kam and Chan Yun* (2 HKTC 10), *CIR v Lai Yin Ha formerly trading as China Skin Specialist Clinic* (2 HKTC 374) and *CIR v Ewig*

Industries Co. Limited [2006] (1 HKRC 90-179). However, in the case of a penalty under Sec. 51(4B)(a) which is referred to the Court, because it is the Court's function to determine the quantum of penalties as opposed to debts, the Court may give judgement in a smaller amount.

Where the Court has given judgement on tax in default, collection proceeds in accordance with those avenues of the law which apply to the enforcement of judgement debts.

8.5.2 Collection from debtor of taxpayer

Where tax is in default or the taxpayer has left Hong Kong or is likely to leave Hong Kong without paying his tax, there is a procedure for recovering tax from any third party who:—

(1)   owes or is about to pay money to the defaulter;
(2)   holds money for or on account of the defaulter;
(3)   holds money on account of some other person for payment to the defaulter; or
(4)   has authority from some other person to pay money to the defaulter.

The Commissioner may commence recovery by issuing a notice to the third party, with a copy to the defaulter, requiring him to pay over to the IRD either the sum which he owes, holds, etc. or the amount of the tax in question if it is less (Sec. 76(1)). The requirement relates to all such monies in his possession or due from him at the date of the notice or at any time within 30 days after its issue. In the case of a bank, this extends to the balance due to an account holder and even where there is a joint account and only one of the parties is the debtor, the bank must still hand over any sum up to the amount of the balance; in this regard, see *The Hongkong and Shanghai Banking Corporation v The Attorney-General* (HKTC 1243). See also *Wong Yu Cho Rolly trading as Marco Polo and China Overseas Technical Development v IRD* [2006] (1 HKRC 90-188) where the issue of Sec. 76 notices to two banks was considered both valid and appropriate.

Where a third party pays over such money to the IRD, he is indemnified by Sec. 76(2) in respect of any action brought by any person entitled to that money.

When a person receives such a notice he must either pay over the required sum or, if he is unable to comply with the notice because he is not holding or owing any money, he must notify the Commissioner of such inability in writing within 14 days after the expiry of the 30-day period from the date of the notice (Sec. 76(3)). If he fails to notify such inability there are penalty provisions under Sec. 80(1) (see Chapter 7). Alternatively, if he could have complied but failed to do so within 14 days after the 30-day period, he is personally liable for the tax which he should have paid and this may be recovered from him as if he was a tax defaulter (Sec. 76(4)).

These provisions most commonly apply to Salaries Tax when the notice is sent to the employer or ex-employer. This ties in with the information provision in Sec. 52(6) under which an employer must notify when an employee is about to leave Hong Kong and with Sec. 52(7) under which after giving such notice the employer must retain money due to an employee.

8.5.3 Detention of defaulters leaving Hong Kong

Whilst there is no formal tax clearance procedure in Hong Kong, Sec. 77 provides authority to prevent defaulters from leaving Hong Kong.

In particular, Sec. 77 permits, subject to the meeting of strict requirements, the issue of an order, known as a "departure prevention direction" (DPD), by a District Judge, but also contains provisions by which the person can apply to the Commissioner for a DPD to be varied and can appeal to the High Court to have a DPD set aside. For a DPD to be issued under this provision, the Commissioner or his authorised officer is required to satisfy a District Judge, by statement on oath, that the person has an outstanding tax debt and that there are reasonable grounds to believe that the person is about to depart, or has departed, Hong Kong to reside elsewhere. Where the District Judge is so satisfied and is also satisfied that it is in the public interest that the person does not leave Hong Kong, he is required to issue a DPD to the Director of Immigration and the Commissioner of Police requiring them to prevent the person leaving Hong Kong without first paying the tax or furnishing appropriate security (Sec. 77(1)). A copy of the DPD is also required to be served on the person owing the tax, if he can be found (Sec. 77(2)).

Where a DPD has been issued, the Commissioner may, upon the application of the person concerned or on his own initiative, authorise the person to depart from Hong Kong on one or more occasions as specified in the authorisation (Sec. 77(6)). Notwithstanding Sec. 77(6), once issued, a DPD remains in force until the tax is paid, appropriate security is furnished, or it is set aside by the Court of First Instance. With regard to this latter point, a person aggrieved by a DPD may appeal to the Court of First Instance which may either set aside or temporarily suspend the DPD, on such conditions as the Court considers necessary, or dismiss the appeal (Sec. 77(9)).

Where a person has been advised that a DPD has been issued, that DPD is still in force, and neither the Commissioner nor the Court of First Instance have varied the DPD or authorised the person to leave Hong Kong, the person who is the subject of the DPD commits an offence (punishable by a level 4 fine or imprisonment for six months) if he attempts to leave Hong Kong (Secs. 77(4) and 77(5)).

8.5.4 Impounding ships or aircraft

Apart from all of the other means of collection and enforcement, an owner or charterer of ships or aircraft who is in default of his Profits Tax liability in respect of the profits from the operating of such ships or aircraft is liable to have the ships or aircraft impounded by the Director of Marine or Director of Civil Aviation (Sec. 77A(1)). The Commissioner must obtain the approval of the Chief Secretary before he may issue the necessary certificates to the relevant authorities. The ships and aircraft remain impounded until the tax is paid or security for payment is furnished (Sec. 77A(2)). The fact that a ship or aircraft is detained against the owner's or charterer's will is not a valid defence against paying the liability in dispute thereon. Furthermore, no action can be brought against any of the authorities for carrying out their duties under these provisions (Sec. 77A(3)).

8.6 Repayment of Tax

There are specific provisions in Sec. 79 to enable repayments of tax to be made where payment has been made in excess of the amount for which a person is properly chargeable. It is perhaps surprising that statutory authority should be needed because it ought to follow that any sum paid beyond the legal liability of the payer should rightfully be returned to the payer without specific authority. The provision does not operate to re-open assessments which are final and conclusive and in no way extends the time limits for objection or appeal (proviso to Sec. 79(1)). Accordingly, repayments will arise in the case of:—

(1)   an excessive payment made in error;
(2)   a paid assessment becoming validly reduced or cancelled either by objection or appeal or by statutory options or Personal Assessment;
(3)   an assessment being found to be invalid;
(4)   an assessment being re-opened by the error or omission procedure under Sec. 70A (see section 8.7.1); or
(5)   Property Tax being applied against a person's Profits Tax liability (Sec. 25).

The claim to repayment must be made within six years after the end of the year of assessment affected or within six months after the notice of assessment was served, whichever is the later. In the case of a revised assessment issued following the settlement of an objection or appeal, the six-month time limit would apply to the date of the service of the revised notice, not of the original assessment.

The same rights to repayment arise to an executor, trustee or receiver for the benefit of an incapacitated, deceased or bankrupt person (Sec. 79(2)).

If an assessment in respect of a non-resident person has been raised upon, and paid by, a person in Hong Kong under Sec. 20A or Sec. 20B (see sections 4.8.3 and 4.8.4), either the non-resident or the Hong Kong person (but not both) may claim the repayment. Where the refund is made to the Hong Kong person, the IRD is effectively indemnified in respect of a claim by the non-resident (Sec. 79(3)).

8.7 Assessments Final and Conclusive

When considering the legal authorities for recovering tax assessed, it is essential to know when an assessment becomes final and conclusive and the tax thereby legally due, whether or not the assessment may be in accordance with the taxpayer's actual income. Sec. 70 determines when an assessment is final and conclusive and defines the circumstances as:—

(1)   where no valid objection or appeal has been lodged;
(2)   where an objection or appeal has been withdrawn or an appeal has been dismissed;
(3)   where an assessment under objection has been agreed; or
(4)   where an assessment is determined upon objection or appeal and no appeal or higher appeal is given.

The fact that an assessment is final and conclusive does not prevent an assessor from raising an additional assessment so long as it does not involve re-opening any question which has been determined on objection or appeal (proviso to Sec. 70).

A taxpayer cannot re-open a final and conclusive assessment except:—

(1)   where he has statutory options, e.g. the right to amend the basis of assessment of a life insurance company to the adjusted surplus basis; or
(2)   when he makes an error or omission claim.

8.7.1 Error or omission claim (Sec. 70A)

An assessment which is otherwise final and conclusive can be re-opened within six years after the end of the year of assessment or within six months after the service of the notice of assessment, whichever is the later, if it can be shown that the assessment is excessive by virtue of:—

(1) an error or omission in a return or statement submitted; or

(2) an arithmetical error or omission in the calculation of the net assessable value for Property Tax purposes, the net assessable income for Salaries Tax purposes, the assessable profit for Profits Tax purposes or the tax charged (Sec. 70A(1)).

The assessment cannot be re-opened for an error or omission in a return or statement where that return or statement was made on the basis of a prevailing practice (proviso to Sec. 70A(1)). It is, of course, a question of fact as to what is a prevailing practice but where a legal decision is made in favour of a taxpayer, it is not possible to apply that decision to re-open assessments which became final and conclusive prior to that decision because following the law as it was previously understood is a prevailing practice. See *D 39/91* for a useful discussion of the prevailing practice limitation on Sec. 70A claims.

The second area of claim mentioned above really provides for arithmetical errors or omissions by the assessor in transferring the figures from the return to the assessment which should, of course, be picked up in the time permitted for objection and settled by objection. The Sec. 70A procedure, however, allows for spotting assessor's mistakes, and correcting errors in a return, after the objection time limit has expired.

The typical errors which might be the subject of a claim under Sec. 70A are when:—

(1) a taxpayer (or his representative):—
    (a) fails to exclude income which is not assessable;
    (b) fails to deduct a relief which is available;
    (c) mistakenly adds back an item which is deductible;
    (d) submits a computation on an incorrect basis; or
    (e) makes an arithmetical error in a return, schedule or computation; or

(2) the assessor:—
    (a) makes an arithmetical error in adjusting the return or transmitting the figures to the assessment; or
    (b) mistakenly omits a deduction that has been claimed.

Apart from the proviso regarding prevailing practice, there are no limits on the type of errors which may be corrected under Sec. 70A. This point was confirmed in *D 6/91* where the Board of Review rejected a submission by the Commissioner's representative that where a taxpayer, subsequent to the expiration of the objection period, took a different view of known facts and concluded that as a matter of law an item should have been treated differently, Sec. 70A could not operate to re-open the assessment; in other words, the Board of Review rejected the proposition by the Commissioner's representative that Sec. 70A was intended only to correct errors of fact and not errors of law. The Board noted, however, that where the facts of a case supported two equally acceptable treatments of an item, a taxpayer could not rely on Sec. 70A to substitute one treatment for the other as there was no error in adopting one over the other in the first place.

In *D 137/02* the Board of Review (in choosing not to follow the reasoning of an earlier decision, *D 55/88*) rejected the proposition that Sec. 70A could have no application in circumstances where there had been a dispute over the assessable profits for a year of assessment and that dispute had been resolved pursuant to an agreement with the IRD. Nonetheless, the Board of Review reiterated that a taxpayer must still demonstrate the existence of an error or omission in a return required to be submitted by the IRO or in a statement in such a return. Accordingly, an error in a document which sets out the terms of a negotiated settlement with the IRD would not by itself entitle a person to make a claim under Sec. 70A.

Although it seems all types of errors are correctable under the provision, the meaning of "error" was somewhat limited by the Board of Review in *D 82/95*, a decision which was subsequently upheld by the High Court in *Extramoney Limited v CIR* [1997] (1 HKRC 90-083). In particular, that case established that an error was something which happened inadvertently and did not extend to a deliberate act. The facts of the case were quite complex but, essentially, involved the taxpayer company deliberately attributing to itself share trading profits which it did not derive. Although the accounts of the company were audited and an unqualified audit report given with respect to those profits, the auditors were subsequently successfully sued for negligence on this point. In the judgement of the negligence action, the High Court had found, as a fact, that the profits in question were never made.

The Board of Review, in finding for the IRD, noted that although it could consider the High Court's findings of fact, they were not binding on the Board. They went on to note that, on the evidence, all indications were that the inclusion of the disputed profits was deliberate and that, as such, it could not be considered an error. The Board also pointed out that in order to establish that an error had occurred, the former director responsible for the preparation of the accounts and tax returns should have been called to give evidence as to how the error had occurred. One can deduce from this that "error" for the purpose of Sec. 70A encompasses only inadvertent errors and will not extend to deliberate errors, for the Board appeared to accept that the tax returns were wrong, but still required evidence as to how they came to be wrong. As noted above, the Board of Review's decision was upheld by the High Court in *Extramoney Limited v CIR* [1997] (1 HKRC 90-083). The reasoning of the court was essentially the same as that of the Board of Review although the court noted that the Sec. 70A claim in the case was premised on the accounts being wrong and it considered that to allow the accounts to effectively be re-written would be "... *contrary to the spirit of the Ordinance that there should be finality in taxation matters.*" Nevertheless, the court appeared to leave open the possibility that accounts could contain an error which could be corrected pursuant to Sec. 70A. In particular, Chan J accepted that "... *in some cases where it can be proved that the profits stated in the accounts of a taxpayer had not in fact been made, this may be sufficient to show that there has been an error justifying a correction in the assessment.*" Given the final verdict, however, it is likely that the courts or Board of Review will be reluctant to find such errors exist in most cases. Indeed, in *D 52/99* the Board of Review, in rejecting the taxpayer's claims, followed the *ratio* in the *Extramoney* case (supra) and went on to note that Sec. 70A could not be used to change the accounting treatment adopted where a deliberate choice had been made to adopt that treatment.

One particular area where Sec. 70A is from time to time raised is in respect of bad debts, as often it is only after the accounts are drawn up that it is realised that a debt has become bad. Nonetheless, Sec. 70A would appear to be not generally available to reopen the assessments in such circumstances. See, for example, *D 39/91* where the Board of Review held that a Sec. 70A claim in respect of bad debts could not be allowed because the company's accounts for the relevant periods were drawn up in accordance with generally accepted accounting principles, which required a proper determination of the extent to which the company's debts were bad or doubtful. As those accounts did show the debts in question as bad, and there was no evidence that the accountants or auditors had made a mistake, the Board of Review concluded that the claims must fail on the grounds that that it was not possible to introduce evidence with the benefit of hindsight to attempt to show that the debts were bad at the time the accounts were prepared. This was decided before the High Court's decision in the *Extramoney* case (supra). As would be expected, however, the same conclusion was reached in a similar case, *D 142/01*, which was decided after the *Extramoney* case (supra).

See also *D 25/01* where a taxpayer had sought to treat certain profits as non-taxable on the grounds that they arose from a source outside Hong Kong. The IRD sought further information in connection with the claim, but this was not provided by the taxpayer and the IRD eventually disallowed the claim. The taxpayer did not file an objection against that disallowance, but sought to resurrect the claim pursuant to Sec. 70A some time later after similar claims had been allowed in respect of later years. In denying the Sec. 70A claim, the Board of Review held that there had been no error or omission as the course of action followed by the taxpayer was deliberate.

Where a claim has been made to reduce an assessment in accordance with Sec. 70A(1) and, for whatever reason, the assessor refuses to correct the assessment, he must send a written notice of refusal to the claimant who is then entitled to treat the notice as if it was a notice of assessment and accordingly the objection and appeal procedure is open to him (Sec. 70A(2)). For discussions of the objection and appeal procedures see Chapter 9.

Note that Sec. 70A(1) does not apply if the assessor treats as taxable something which is not shown as taxable in the return or changes the basis of assessment or, indeed, does anything which does not amount to an omission or an arithmetical error. Neither does it apply where an estimated assessment has been made in the absence of a valid return because it is not an error that an estimate does not coincide with an amount that would have been assessed had the assessor been in possession of the return; in this connection, see *Sun Yau Investment Co. Ltd. v CIR* (2 HKTC 17) and also *D 8/87, D 93/89* and *D 40/91*. In all of these circumstances, the dispute must be the subject of the objection procedure (see Chapter 9).

Where a husband and wife have jointly elected for Personal Assessment pursuant to Sec. 41(1A) and one of them makes an application for correction under Sec. 70A, both are deemed to have applied and, therefore, either or both of their assessments can be amended upon settlement of the application (Sec. 70B).

In addition to the above Sec. 70AA was introduced in 2004 as a transitional provision in relation to amendments to the home loan interest and self education deduction provisions (see Chapter 3) enacted by the *Inland Revenue (Amendment) Ordinance 2004*. Those amendments were deemed to take effect from earlier years of assessment and slightly broadened the circumstances in which the relevant deductions were available. Although the amendments were passed, in most cases the earlier year's assessments of potential claimants would be final and conclusive. Moreover, Sec. 70A would not permit those assessments to be reopened because there would not have been an error in the relevant returns (as they would generally have been prepared on the basis of the law at the time). Accordingly, Sec. 70AA permits a claim to reopen earlier year assessments to allow taxpayers to claim a home loan interest or self education expense deduction where that deduction was permitted only because of the 2004 legislative amendments.

Chapter 9 ■

Objections and Appeals

9.1 Legislation

The legislation covering objections and appeals is contained in Secs. 64 to 69A, which are in Part XI of the IRO.

9.2 Objections

An objection is the initial means by which a taxpayer may statutorily dispute an assessment made upon him. The IRO lays down strict rules as to the form and timing of an objection and failure to follow these rules may render the objection invalid. Furthermore, the IRO governs how an objection is to be dealt with by the IRD. There are circumstances under which an individual may object to an assessment raised upon his or her spouse or may be deemed to be included in an objection or appeal made by his or her spouse. These and other issues are discussed in detail below.

9.2.1 The form of an objection

To be valid, an objection against an assessment must satisfy the rules in Sec. 64(1) which are as follows:

(1) it must be in writing addressed to the Commissioner. In practice, notices addressed to the assessor are treated as satisfying this requirement;

(2) it must state precisely the grounds for the objection. It is insufficient merely to state that the assessment is disputed; the objection must clearly state exactly what is in dispute; and

(3) it must be received by the Commissioner within one month after the date of the notice of assessment. The Commissioner has discretionary power to extend the permitted period of one month in cases where he is satisfied that, because of absence from Hong Kong, sickness, or other reasonable cause, the person submitting the objection was prevented from giving the notice within one month. This discretion is exercised only sparingly and not where the taxpayer has been ignorant of his rights, busy etc. In the case of *Lam Ying Bor Investment Co. Ltd. v CIR* (HKTC 1098), it was claimed on behalf of the company that the Commissioner should have exercised his discretion and accepted a late notice on the grounds that, of the three directors of the company who were responsible, one was sick, one was too old and the other was too busy. It was held, however, that the Commissioner had not acted unreasonably. In the later case

of *Chun Yuet Bun trading as Chong Hing Electrical Co. v CIR* (2 HKTC 325), a similar decision was reached, although it is interesting to note that the judge in that case expressed the view that the reasoning in the *Lam Ying Bor Investment Co. Ltd.* case was no longer correct due to decisions of the House of Lords in relation to judicial review matters.

There is a further requirement in the case of an assessment made under Sec. 59(3) (i.e. estimated assessment made in the absence of a return). In such cases, it is not sufficient to just object in accordance with (1), (2) and (3) above that the estimate is incorrect and may prove to be excessive (which is a satisfactory ground for an estimated assessment). Rather, for the objection to be valid, the relevant return (including all the documents required to be submitted in connection therewith) must also be submitted within one month from the issue of the notice of assessment or such extended period as the Commissioner in his absolute discretion may allow (Sec. 64(1)(b)). It is not essential that the objection and the return be submitted together; it is usually desirable to submit the objection immediately and then to submit the return, if possible, within the required month or, if not possible, to seek a reasonable extension of time to submit the return. It is essential to realise that, failing the causes mentioned in (3) above it is not possible to extend the time for objection but, given a good reason, a reasonable extension for submission of the return will often be given. If, however, the return is not submitted within the time limit given, the objection is not valid and the estimated assessment becomes final and conclusive.

In respect of composite tax returns, the more onerous provisions of Sec. 64(1)(b) as discussed in the previous paragraph, apply where, although a return has been lodged, it failed to disclose details of a source of income, property or profits and the assessment is estimated by the IRD in respect of that source of income, property or profits (Sec. 64(1A)). In other words, if, for example, a taxpayer lodges a composite tax return which discloses his income chargeable to Profits Tax but omits details of his income chargeable to Property Tax, the IRD can issue an estimated Property Tax assessment and an objection will not be valid unless the details required on the return form are provided within one month of the issue of the notice of assessment or such further time as the Commissioner may, in his discretion, allow.

If the assessment comprises a re-assessment which either increases or reduces the person's liability to tax, and such a re-assessment would normally result from an objection against the original assessment, no new right of objection arises except in relation to any new or additional liability imposed by the re-assessment (Sec. 64(1) proviso (c)).

Where no tax is payable, i.e. where there is a loss, even after the disallowance of a disputed item, no objection can be made (see *D 2/82*). When, however, the disputed loss is applied against subsequent profits leaving a net assessment, an objection can be made against the net assessment.

Also, an objection against a total income assessment under the Personal Assessment procedure can only be against the composition of that assessment from agreed amounts of income under the income taxes. It cannot have the effect of re-opening any existing assessment under any of the income taxes which is already final and conclusive. The objection can, however, be effective in respect of the allocation to the individual of his share of the agreed profits of a partnership of which he is a partner (Sec. 64(7)). However, any objection by an individual involving the allocation of the profits of a partnership is treated as an objection by all of the partners so that they are all bound by its determination (Sec. 64(8)). An objection against a Personal Assessment upon a married person which includes income of the other spouse, is deemed to include an objection by that other spouse (see section 9.4).

In addition to all of the other requirements, a person must have a legal capacity to file an objection. In the case of a deceased person, the power to object is vested in the executor of the person by Sec. 54. Similarly, it appears that where a person is adjudged bankrupt, the power to object becomes vested in the person's trustee or, where no trustee has been appointed, the Official Receiver. In this regard, see *D 79/04,* although note that this actually dealt with the power to appeal.

9.2.2 Negotiation of objection

Upon receiving a valid objection, Sec. 64(2) provides that the Commissioner may confirm, reduce, increase or annul the assessment objected to. Other than where the Commissioner allows the objection in full, an assessment will usually only be increased, decreased or confirmed with the agreement of the taxpayer pursuant to Sec. 64(3), which is discussed further below, although the assessment may also be confirmed where the taxpayer withdraws the objection. This is because if there is no agreement (or withdrawal of the objection), the matter must proceed to a Commissioner's determination in accordance with Sec. 64(4), which is discussed in section 9.2.3. The duties of the Commissioner under Sec. 64(2) are, in practice, delegated to individual assessors.

In order to ensure progress of an objection, the Commissioner is empowered by Sec. 64(2) to give written notice of further information required including production of any relevant books or documents. He may also give notice to any person to attend and give oral evidence in connection with the objection. Where, however, the Commissioner intends to examine any person on oath, he is required to give written notice of his proposed action to the taxpayer who has lodged the objection in order that such taxpayer, or his authorized representative, may be present at the examination. An authorized representative may also, of course, act in supplying any information or documentation requested.

Sec. 64(2) also imposes upon the Commissioner a duty to act within a reasonable time to confirm, reduce, increase or annul the assessment against which the objection was lodged. In the case of *Nina T H Wang v CIR* [1991] (1 HKRC 90-072) the taxpayer sought a court order to quash certain objection determinations on the grounds that it had taken the Commissioner several years to issue them and that he had not, therefore, acted within a reasonable time. The Privy Council, in agreeing with the Court of Appeal and overturning the High Court, held that even if the Commissioner had not acted within a reasonable time, the legislation should not be interpreted as taking away a statutory power granted to the Commissioner simply because he was slow in exercising that power. Accordingly, the Privy Council held that it was not appropriate to quash determinations, or to prevent the Commissioner from issuing determinations, on the grounds that he had been slow in dealing with the objections in question.

In view of the above, it seems that in cases where the Commissioner is dilatory in dealing with an objection, the only action open to a taxpayer is to seek a court order to force the Commissioner to determine the matter, although it is likely that the taxpayer would need to show that he had suffered prejudice before such an order was granted. In this regard, see the decision of the Court of Appeal in *Tak Wing Investment Company Limited v CIR* [2001] (1 HKRC 90-110). In that case the taxpayer was seeking a stay of enforcement action in respect of an assessment to which it had objected, and in respect of which the Commissioner had been slow in determining that objection. The essence of the taxpayer's case was that the tax in dispute would become refundable if the objections were ultimately allowed, and therefore the taxpayer was possibly being prejudiced by the Commissioner's tardiness in dealing with the objection. Although refusing to stay the enforcement action, the court agreed to grant the taxpayer leave to apply for judicial review of the Commissioner's failure to determine the objection and for an order for *mandamus* compelling the Commissioner to determine the objection.

It is usual for the negotiation of an objection to proceed through correspondence and for a revised assessment to be based upon an agreement reached between the assessor (under power delegated from the

Commissioner) and the taxpayer. In the case of certain joint assessments on a husband and wife, the agreement of both husband and wife must be obtained (see section 9.4). Upon the assessment being adjusted in accordance with the agreement it becomes final and conclusive (Sec. 64(3)). Where a notice is issued requesting information under Sec. 64(2), such notice will contain a date by which the information is required and if that deadline is not met, a fine may result (see section 7.4).

If the assessor does not agree to make any adjustment or does not agree to make the adjustments sought by the taxpayer, he will submit the case to the Commissioner for determination.

For the purposes of negotiating an objection, the Commissioner is granted certain of the powers under the *Commissions of Inquiry Ordinance* (Sec. 64(5)).

9.2.3 Commissioner's determination

When the assessor cannot reach agreement with the taxpayer or his representative on the determination of an objection, the matter must be formally determined by the Commissioner. In practice, determinations are made by the Commissioner or a deputy commissioner or, in respect of Property Tax cases, by an assistant commissioner, Unit 2. The Commissioner can determine the assessment in any amount which he can justify but it will, of course, be an amount with which the taxpayer does not agree because otherwise the objection could be settled by agreement under Sec. 64(3). Once the Commissioner has made his determination he must, within one month, send a written notice of his determination to the person who lodged the objection and such notice must contain a statement of the facts upon which the determination is based and also the reasoning behind the determination (Sec. 64(4)).

In practice, the assessor will prepare the statement of facts beforehand and he usually sends them to the taxpayer who lodged the objection for his agreement or observations. Although the assessor has no statutory obligation to present the facts prior to agreement, it is obviously in the interests of all parties to do so in the event of the case proceeding to hearing before the Board of Review, because the statement is submitted to the Board of Review in an appeal. In practice, however, the Commissioner does not regard himself as bound by the statement of facts submitted to him; in particular, he may exclude facts which he may deem to be irrelevant to the point at issue and may include facts which have emerged from correspondence which he considers should be included.

If the person does not appeal against the Commissioner's determination, the assessment as determined becomes final and conclusive.

9.3 Appeals

An appeal is different from an objection in that it is presented to an independent arbitrator for determination. There are a number of levels of appeal beginning with a semi-formal hearing before the Board of Review and possibly proceeding through the Court of First Instance and Court of Appeal to the Court of Final Appeal.

9.3.1 Board of Review

If a person does not agree with the Commissioner's determination of his objection, he has the right of appeal to the Board of Review.

Sec. 66 lays down the following requirements which must be met for an appeal to be valid.

(1)   Notice must be given to the Clerk to the Board of Review in writing by the taxpayer or his authorised representative;

(2)   Such notice must be given within one month of the transmission to the taxpayer of the Commissioner's determination. In *D 2/04* it was held that the one month period runs from when the transmission of the Commissioner's determination to the taxpayer was completed (i.e. from when it was delivered to the taxpayer's address) and not from when it was despatched by the IRD. Moreover, in *D 41/05* it was held that the one month period is measured against the date the notice of appeal is received by the Board of Review rather than the date the notice was posted by the appellant. The Board of Review may extend the one month time limit to whatever period it considers fit in the event that the appellant was prevented by illness, absence from Hong Kong or other reasonable cause from giving the notice within one month (Secs. 66(1) and 66(1A)). The power of the Board to extend the time for lodging an appeal has been interpreted as applicable only in cases where a taxpayer has taken no steps whatsoever to appeal. In particular, the Board has held that the provision confers no power to extend the time for submitting the grounds of appeal or any other necessary documents once an actual notice of appeal has been lodged; in this connection, see *BR 19/71* and *D 18/92*. Furthermore, it is important to note that the power to extend the time for lodging an appeal is not a general one

but can be exercised only where the Board of Review is satisfied that the taxpayer was *prevented* from lodging the appeal. That is, it is not enough that the taxpayer was too busy or simply forgot. This point has been emphasised in the recent decisions of *D 96/99*, *D 105/99*, and *D 98/00*. Indeed, even absence from Hong Kong or illness are not guaranteed to result in the Board of Review exercising its power to extend the time for filing. See, for example, *D 19/01* where the Board reiterated that absence from Hong Kong does not confer an automatic right of extension for filing the notice of appeal. Another interesting case which emphasised the need to be able to demonstrate that the taxpayer was *prevented* from filing a notice of appeal in order for the time limit to be extended is *Chow Kwong Fai, Edward v CIR* [2005] (1 HKRC 90-140). The Court of First Instance in that case held that notwithstanding that the Clerk to the Board of Review had provided incorrect advice to the taxpayer, there was no evidence that such advice had prevented the taxpayer from filing a valid notice of appeal within the statutory time limit. That decision was upheld on appeal by the Court of Appeal (see *Chow Kwong Fai, Edward v CIR* [2005] (1 HKRC 90-153)). See, however, *D 22/92* and *D 62/98* for cases where the Board of Review has extended the time for lodging an appeal where the IRD sent the Commissioner's determination to the wrong address;

(3)   The notice must be accompanied by a copy of the Commissioner's determination, the statement of facts upon which the determination is based and a statement of the grounds of appeal (Sec. 66(1)); and

(4)   A copy of the notice of appeal including the grounds of appeal must be sent to the Commissioner (Sec. 66(2)).

In addition to the above requirements, it is also important to remember that a person must have a legal capacity to file an appeal. In the case of a deceased person, the power to object is vested in the executor of the person by Sec. 54. Similarly, where a person is adjudged bankrupt, the power to appeal becomes vested in the person's trustee or, where no trustee has been appointed, the Official Receiver. In this regard, see *D 79/04*. That decision is also interesting because after having found that a bankrupt had no power to appeal, the Board of Review concluded that the appeal was not validly constituted, but questioned whether it had power to dismiss the appeal in light of the fact that the IRO did not explicitly deal with the situation. After considering the question, the Board of Review concluded that common sense and the scheme of the IRO gave them the power to ignore the appeal.

Whilst the grounds of appeal do not have to agree with the grounds for the original objection, no grounds can be relied upon at the Board's hearing of the appeal other than those contained in the notice of appeal, except with the specific consent of the Board (Sec. 66(3)). This provision, however, does not apply to prevent the IRD from relying on arguments before the Board of Review which were not contained in the Commissioner's determination (see *D 27/91*).

The Board of Review is an independent body of persons appointed by the Chief Executive and the constitution and powers of its members are laid down by Sec. 65. At a hearing of an appeal there are usually three members constituting the panel of which the head (who is either the Chairman or a Deputy Chairman of the Board of Review) must have legal training and experience (Sec. 65(1)). The other members of the panel may or may not have legal experience but, if not, will otherwise be members of the community selected for the experience and knowledge which they can bring to the panel.

The hearing of the appeal is an informal matter or at least lacks the strict formality of a Court hearing. The hearing is in private but many cases are published for information purposes in a manner which does not reveal the identity of the appellant (Sec. 68(5)). Either the appellant in person or his authorised representative can, and commonly does, conduct his case although from time to time Counsel is briefed to conduct the hearing on behalf of the appellant. Also, from time to time, Counsel is briefed to conduct the Commissioner's case, although this is more usually done by an officer of the IRD.

Despite the lack of formality, Sec. 68 sets down a number of regulations concerning the hearing of appeals by the Board. First, the section provides that unless the appeal is transferred for direct hearing by the Court of First Instance pursuant to Sec. 67 (see section 9.3.4), or the Board endorses under Sec. 68(1B)(b) a settlement reached between the appellant and the Commissioner (see below), the Clerk to the Board is charged with the responsibility of fixing the time and place of the hearing as soon as possible and giving at least 14 days' notice to the appellant and the Commissioner. The hearing cannot be fixed, however, for a time before the expiry of the time limits within which the appeal can be set down for direct hearing by the Court of First Instance (Sec. 68(1)). In practice, the hearings are at the Board of Review offices, either during the day or in the evening, with the number of sessions set aside depending upon the complexity of the case. At any time prior to the scheduled hearing, the appellant can withdraw his appeal by giving notice in writing to the Clerk to the Board of Review (Sec. 68 (1A) (a)), in which case the hearing is, of course, cancelled. In such circumstances, the assessment will become final and conclusive, although Sec. 68(1D) allows an assessor to raise an additional assessment in accordance with the normal provisions (see section 8.2.4). Note that although Sec. 68(1A) allows an appellant to withdraw an appeal before the hearing of that appeal, there is no right of withdrawal once the hearing has commenced. This was confirmed in *D 44/02* where a hearing was adjourned to allow the appellant company additional time to prepare its case; following the adjournment, the appellant applied to withdraw the appeal but this was rejected by the Board of Review as not being permitted by Sec. 68(1A).

Prior to 13 June 1997, a hearing was still required to be held even if the appellant and the Commissioner agreed as to a basis for settlement of the dispute. In such circumstances, the hearing was usually a formality to endorse the settlement, although occasionally this was not so; see, for example, the decision in *D 37/95*. From that date, however, a statutory procedure was introduced by which a hearing can possibly be avoided in such circumstances. In particular, Sec. 68(1A)(b) and 68 (1B) provide that where a settlement of the appeal is reached between the parties at any time prior to the hearing, the terms of such settlement shall be reduced to writing in a form specified by the Board, signed by both parties and submitted to the Board for endorsement. The Board does not, however, have to endorse the settlement and, in such circumstances, the hearing shall proceed (Sec. 68(1E)), unless of course the appellant decides to withdraw the appeal. The Board may have a number of reasons for not endorsing a proposed settlement; for example, the Board may not consider that it is in accordance with the law or may wish to satisfy itself that the appellant has fully understood the terms of the settlement. In any event, there is nothing to prevent the Board from endorsing the settlement after holding a hearing.

If, however, the Board does endorse the settlement without a hearing, Sec. 68(1C) provides that any necessary adjustments shall be made to the relevant assessments and such assessment shall be final and conclusive for all purposes of the IRO as regards the amount of the relevant income, profits or net assessable value, save that Sec. 68(1D) permits an assessor to raise an additional assessment in accordance with the normal provisions (see section 8.2.4), provided it does not involve reopening any matter which has been endorsed by the Board.

Where a hearing is held, the appellant or his authorised representative must attend the hearing in person (Sec. 68(2)) but if either fails to appear at the appointed time the Board have the option, pursuant to Sec. 68(2B), of:

(1) postponing or adjourning the hearing if they are satisfied that the absence is due to sickness or other reasonable cause. In *D 58/93*,

the Board of Review held that the fact that the appellant was outside Hong Kong was not, by itself, a reasonable excuse for failing to appear at the hearing;

(2)   hearing the appeal; or

(3)   dismissing the appeal.

In *D 135/02*, the Board of Review had to consider whether they could exercise their powers under Sec. 68(2B) in a case where an appellant appeared not to have received the notices of the hearing, as they had been returned undelivered from an overseas address and the appellant had made no attempt to contact the Board of Review or the IRD for four years. The Board of Review held that they could exercise their powers in such circumstances on the basis that there was no explicit requirement in Sec. 68(2B) for the appellant to have actually received the notice of the hearing and that the failure of the appellant to make contact with the Board of Review for an extended period could be regarded as not attending any hearing properly fixed by the Clerk. See also *D 46/03* where the Board of Review considered that the fact that a warrant for the arrest of the taxpayer on criminal charges had been issued and the taxpayer did not want to return to Hong Kong for fear of arrest, did not amount to a reasonable excuse for not attending the hearing; as such, the Board exercised its power under Sec. 68(2B)(c) to dismiss the appeal.

If the appeal is dismissed, the appellant has the chance, within 30 days after the order, to request the Board of Review to reconsider their decision in the light of facts which he may bring to show that due to sickness or other reasonable cause an appearance was not possible. If satisfied they will amend their order and hear the appeal (Sec. 68(2C)).

If satisfied that the appellant is, or will be, outside Hong Kong on the date of the scheduled hearing and is unlikely to return to Hong Kong within a period which the Board considers reasonable, the Board may, upon application of the appellant, hear the appeal in the appellant's absence (Sec. 68(2D)). The appellant's application under this provision, however, must be in writing and be received by the Clerk to the Board of Review at least seven days prior to the scheduled hearing. In those circumstances the Board may consider the appellant's written submissions (Sec. 68(2E)). An officer of the IRD must attend the hearing as there is no provision for his absence (Sec. 68(3)).

At the hearing, the facts as contained in the Commissioner's statement of facts are normally accepted unless challenged by the appellant. Also any additional facts sought to be introduced will usually be accepted if such facts have been agreed between the Commissioner and the appellant but, if not so agreed, will have to be supported by appropriate oral or documentary evidence. Both the appellant and the Commissioner's representative are entitled to seek to adduce additional facts or evidence; in either case, however, when considering such evidence the Board of Review may accept or reject it as it sees fit and it is specifically provided that the provisions of the *Evidence Ordinance* (which sets out the rules as to admissibility of evidence in court hearings) is not to apply (Sec. 68(7)). See, however, the discussion in section 9.3.2 regarding further appeals on findings of fact and, in particular, the power of the courts to review perverse findings of fact by the Board of Review.

In hearing evidence, the Board of Review has power to summon witnesses as necessary and pay their reasonable expenses (Sec. 68(6)).

Under Sec. 85(2)(d), the Board of Inland Revenue has the power to prescribe procedures to be followed in relation to appeals to the Board of Review. At the time of writing, however, no such rules had been prescribed. Nonetheless, it is usual for the Board of Review to hear the appellant's case first, during which the Commissioner's representative is allowed to question any witnesses brought by the appellant, then to hear the Commissioner's case, allowing the appellant or his representative to question any witnesses, and finally to permit the appellant's final comments.

Following the hearing the members of the Board will meet and reach their decision which will be to confirm, reduce, increase or cancel the assessment or they may remit the assessment back to the Commissioner to make whatever adjustments are necessary consequent upon their decision (Sec. 68(8)). If the assessment is not cancelled or reduced, the Board is empowered to impose costs of not more than the amount specified in Part I of Schedule 5, which is currently $5,000 (Sec. 68(9)). It is generally accepted that the intention of this provision is to deter vexatious or trivial appeals but it is questionable whether or not it is an effective deterrent. Historically, it was only on rare occasions that the Board of Review would order costs be imposed. In recent years, however, it has become relatively common; see, for example, *D 102/97*, *D 54/98*, *D 88/98*, *D 42/99*, *D 109/00* and *D 131/00*.

Sec. 68(4) provides that at the hearing of an appeal, the onus of proof is on the appellant to prove that the assessment is excessive or incorrect. One of the earliest cases on this provision is *In re Herald International Limited* (1 HKTC 393) and an excellent summary of that decision as well as subsequent cases on the interpretation of the provision is contained in *CIR v Common Empire Limited* [2006] (1HKRC 90-174). Additionally, it should be noted that in *D 31/87*, the Board of Review rejected the Commissioner's representative's submission that the onus of proof was "a heavy one" and held that, in fact, Sec. 68(4) means no more than that the appellant must substantiate his case. It seems, therefore, that an appeal should be decided on the basis of the balance of probabilities, rather than placing upon the taxpayer a requirement to produce incontrovertible evidence to disprove the Commissioner's contentions. This view also appears to have been accepted by the Court of Appeal in *Chanway Investment Co. Limited v CIR* [1998] (1 HKRC 90-092). Nonetheless, it is quite common for the Board of Review to find for the IRD on the basis that the taxpayer has not discharged the burden of proof. This raises a question of how far the Board of Review should go in actually ruling on the arguments advanced by the parties. This point was considered in *China Map Limited & Others v CIR* [2006] (1 HKRC 90-172) where it was held that it is open to the Board of Review to simply dismiss a case on the basis that the burden of proof has not been discharged without going on to make a positive finding on the substantive issue; for example, without specifically ruling that an amount in dispute is taxable, non-deductible, etc. See, however, *D 25/90* where the Board of Review held that where the Commissioner is alleging the existence of a partnership, the burden of proof is reversed and falls upon the Commissioner.

In *Brand Dragon Limited and Harvest Island International Limited v CIR* [2002] (1 HKRC 90-115), an appeal from the Board of Review, the taxpayer unsuccessfully sought to argue that the burden of proof was reversed because the Board of Review rejected certain board minutes and other evidence adduced as being self serving. In particular, the taxpayer sought to argue that the Board of Review was effectively arguing that the relevant documents were shams and that, in such circumstances, the Commissioner should be required to prove his contention. The Court of First Instance rejected this argument on the basis that the Board of Review was required to assess and test all evidence placed before it and could accept or reject evidence as it considered appropriate; however, just because it chose to reject or place little weight on evidence did not necessarily mean that it was considered a sham.

Note that in the somewhat unusual circumstances where an appellant acts for a deceased person, the Board of Review has held (in *D 14/83*) that the onus of proof is no less than it would have been for the deceased, even though the appellant may be disadvantaged by not being able to bring evidence known only to the deceased.

Apart from the foregoing cases, the interpretation of Sec. 68(4) has been considered in a number of other court decisions in Hong Kong. For a summary of the principles arising from those cases, see *D 55/03*.

The decision of the Board of Review, together with the reasons therefor, is notified later to the appellant in writing, his authorised representative if there is one, and the Commissioner. The chairman usually prepares the written determination and, therefore, the delay between the hearing and the written determination depends upon the workload of the chairman.

Penalty assessments under Sec. 82A are also subject to the appeal procedure (see Chapter 7). As such assessments have to be made by the Commissioner or a deputy commissioner personally, disputes proceed direct to the Board of Review because the objection procedure would be a mere formality.

The unsuccessful party to a Board of Review hearing, whether it be the appellant or the Commissioner, is entitled, in certain circumstances, to appeal to the Court of First Instance or the Court of Appeal but, in the absence of such further appeal, the assessment becomes final and conclusive in accordance with the Board's decision.

9.3.2 Appeal against decision of Board of Review

If either the appellant or the Commissioner disagrees with a decision of the Board of Review he may apply in writing to the Clerk to the Board requiring the Board to state a case for the opinion of the Court of First Instance. Sec. 69(1) provides that the application must be made within one month of the Board's decision, although if that decision is notified to the appellant or the Commissioner in writing, the one month period runs from the date of the communication notifying the relevant party of the decision. In *D 30/06*, this was interpreted as meaning that the one month period commenced on the date on which the communication reached the address to which it was sent. The application must also be accompanied by the fee specified in Part I of Schedule 5, which is currently $770. The amount of this fee may be amended at any time by order of the Secretary for Financial Services and the Treasury.

Sec. 69(1) specifically provides that the opinion of the Court of First Instance can only be obtained on a point of law, as the Board of Review is intended to be the last arbiter on questions of fact. For cases where the courts have dismissed appeals on the grounds that they did not concern any points of law, see *CIR v Asia Securities International Limited* [1991] (1 HKRC 90-052) and *Aust-Key Company Limited v CIR* [2001] (1 HKRC 90-109). As to what constitutes a question of law, see the discussion in *CIR v Karsten Larssen & Co. (HK) Limited* (HKTC 11) and the more recent Board of Review decision of *D 26/05*. In this latter decision, the Board of Review, quoting from an unpublished decision (but which actually involved the

Indosuez WI Carr Securities Limited case, which is discussed in chapter 4), stated that it should not accede to a request to state a case unless the applicant could show that a proper question of law can be identified. The Board went on to note that a proper question of law was one which:

(a)   was a question of law;
(b)   related to the decision sought to be appealed against;
(c)   was arguable; and
(d)   would not amount to an abuse of process if submitted to the court for consideration.

Nonetheless, the Board of Review considered that the threshold for the appellant to satisfy was low and suggested that a case should be stated unless the point of law sought to be submitted to the court was plainly and obviously unarguable.

Although a case may not generally be stated in respect of findings of fact by the Board of Review, if those findings are clearly unreasonable in light of the evidence presented this becomes a question of law on which a case may be stated. For example, in *CIR v Karsten Larssen & Co. (HK) Limited* (supra), the court noted that "... it is always a question of law whether the primary facts include any material upon which the conclusion could reasonably be found." The more commonly quoted authority for the proposition, however, is the House of Lords judgement in *Edwards (Inspector of Taxes) v Bairstow & Anor.* (36 TC 207) in which Lord Radcliffe stated:

> "... it may be that the facts found are such that no person acting judicially and *properly instructed* as to the relevant law could have come to the determination under appeal. In those circumstances, too, the Court must intervene."

This principle has subsequently been widely adopted in Hong Kong. See, for example, the High Court decision in *CIR v Waylee Investments Limited* (2 HKTC 483) where Barnett J noted:

> "... the Court can set aside the decision of the Board only if it is clear that the Board have misunderstood the law and consequently misdirected themselves; or because their findings are perverse, that is to say, where the only true and reasonable conclusion contradicts the Board's findings."

In other words, the Board of Review has a duty imposed upon it to act reasonably in finding facts even though the IRO gives the Board extremely wide powers to accept or reject evidence and specifically provides that it is not bound by the legal rules of evidence (Sec. 68(7)).

If a party to an appeal wishes to dispute a finding of fact by the Board of

Review, he has to identify that fact which he wishes to challenge; it is not appropriate to ask the Court to review the whole of the evidence. Unless a specific challenge is made, the Board of Review may refuse to state a case; in this connection, see the High Court's decision in *CIR v Inland Revenue Board of Review, Aspiration Land Investment Ltd.* (2 HKTC 575). For a useful discussion of where the responsibilities in preparing a stated case lie, see the Court of Appeal's review of this decision, which is reported at 3 HKTC 223. In that case the Commissioner was unsuccessful in his application to have the stated case amended. What did, however, emerge from this decision was that although the Board of Review is free to consider drafts or comments prepared by either of the parties, the final responsibility for stating a case still rests with the Board of Review. The responsibility of the Board in this matter flows from the fact that the Board has the sole responsibility to find the facts.

Apart from the *Aspiration Land Investment Limited* case discussed above, there have been a number of other instances where the Board of Review has refused to state a case and the matter has been referred to the courts for a judicial review of the decision with a view to obtaining an order for the Board of Review to state the case. See, for example, *CIR v Board of Review & Lam Chi Kwong* [2004] (1 HKRC 90-138) and *Chow Kwong Fai, Edward v Inland Revenue Board of Review* [2004] (1 HKRC 90-133). In the former of these cases, the application was made by the Commissioner while in the latter the applicant was the taxpayer. In both cases, the court found for the applicant and ordered the Board of Review to state a case. See also the decision of the Court of First Instance in *CIR v Board of Review and Indosuez WI Carr Securities Limited* [2005] (1 HKRC 90-157) where the Commissioner's application for the court to direct the Board of Review to state a case was granted. That case is interesting because not only did the Board of Review argue that the questions on which the Commissioner sought to have a case stated were not questions of law, but the taxpayer involved argued against the Commissioner's application on the basis that it was an abuse of process and, although not successful, the judgement contains an interesting discussion of when such an argument may succeed. The decision to order the Board of Review to state a case was upheld on appeal (see CACV 57/2006), although the abuse of power question was not considered in that appeal.

The stated case must contain the facts upon which the Board of Review reached their decision and the decision and reasons therefor. For a discussion on incorporation by the Board of Review of the facts which it has found into its stated case and, in particular, a disapproval of the practice of merely attaching a copy of their written decision, see *Winfat Enterprise (HK) Ltd. v CIR* [1992] (1 HKRC 90-058). The person requiring the case must transmit it to the Court of First Instance within 14 days of receiving it (Sec. 69(2)). The 14-day requirement is not flexible and the Court has no power to extend the period (see *Li Kam Ming T/A Ming Kee Shipping Service Company v CIR* (3 HKTC 419)). Furthermore, the person must send a copy to the other party at or before the time of transmitting it to the Court of First Instance and must notify the other party that it was obtained upon his application (Sec. 69(3)).

Upon receipt by the Court of First Instance, any judge may return the stated case for amendment (Sec. 69(4)). Otherwise a judge of the Court of First Instance hears the case in accordance with the formalities applicable to court hearings. Although the statutory purpose of an appeal to the Court of First Instance is to consider a point of law as set out in the stated case prepared by the Board of Review, it has been held that it is open to either party to the appeal to seek the opinion of the court on questions additional to those framed in the stated case, provided they arise from the findings and decision of the Board (see *CIR v Rico Internationale Limited* (HKTC 229) and *Emerson Radio Corporation v CIR* [1999] (1 HKRC 90-095)). After the hearing, the Court hands down its decision on the matters before it, which may result in an increase or reduction or cancellation of the assessment.

Alternatively, the Court may remit the assessment back to the Board of Review to make whatever adjustments may be necessary consequent upon its opinion (Sec. 69(5)). It is important to note that the power to remit the case to the Board of Review is limited. Essentially, the intention is for the Board of Review to find facts and apply the law as opined upon by the court to those facts. In *CIR v Hang Seng Bank* [1989] (1 HKRC 90-016) the Court of Appeal observed that there was no power to remit a case for the Board of Review to reconsider their findings of fact, although as discussed above in certain circumstances the court may review the Board's finding of facts. Further, in *Yau Wah Yau v CIR* [2006] (1 HKRC 90-178) the Court of Appeal held that they had no power to remit a case to be heard *de novo* by a differently constituted Board of Review, even though the Board of Review had originally not found certain facts which were necessary for consideration of a point of law raised on appeal. The court in that case did, however, suggest that where a case was stated and one of the parties believed that the consideration of the relevant question of law required additional findings of fact, the appropriate procedure would be for an application to be made to the Court of First Instance to remit the case stated to the Board of Review to have the additional findings of fact incorporated into it. This was endorsed by the Court of Appeal in the later case of *Lee Yee Shing, Jacky and Yeung Yuk*

Ching v CIR (CACV 180/2006) where it was noted that it is permissible to remit a case stated to the Board of Review for additional findings of fact before the hearing of the substantive appeal, although such findings are strictly to be made by the Board. That is, the court cannot direct the Board of Review as to facts to be found or how those facts are to be presented and if the case stated is not remitted to the Board, there is no basis for additional findings of fact to be admitted even if consented to by the parties to the appeal.

Where a court remits a case to the Board of Review to revise an assessment in accordance with the court's opinion on a point of law but one party is dissatisfied with the way in which the Board revises the assessment, a question arises as to whether there is scope for another request for a case to be stated for the opinion of the court. The legislation does not specifically address this point but the Court of Appeal considered the matter in *CIR v Board of Review and Indosuez W I Carr Securities Limited* (CACV 57/2006) where they decided that a second case stated was possible. In reaching this conclusion, the Court noted that Sec. 69(1) permitted an application for a case to be stated when the Board of Review made a "decision", and a decision was made not only when the Board ruled on a substantive appeal, but also when they revised an assessment in accordance with Sec. 69(5).

The Court may also make any order which it sees fit in connection with the costs of the case and the $770 fee paid to the Clerk to the Board (Sec. 69 (6)). If the unsuccessful party disagrees with the decision he may appeal to the Court of Appeal and then to the Court of Final Appeal, subject to the *Supreme Court Ordinance*, the Rules of the Supreme Court and the Orders and Rules governing appeals to the the Court of Final Appeal (Sec. 69(7)).

The cost of a Court hearing is inevitably high because of the necessity to employ legal representatives and this, plus the thought that the Commissioner's costs may have to be borne by the taxpayer if he is unsuccessful, are a sufficient deterrent to many taxpayers from taking their case beyond the Board of Review.

9.3.3 Direct appeal to Court of Appeal

Where a case has been determined by the Board of Review, either the appellant or the Commissioner may appeal direct to the Court of Appeal, thereby bypassing the Court of First Instance, provided that the Court of Appeal grants leave for such an application (Sec. 69A(1)). The Court of Appeal may grant such leave where, in their opinion, it is desirable by virtue of the amount of tax involved, the public importance or complexity of the matter in dispute or for any other good reason (Sec. 69A(2)).

The procedure for submitting a case direct to the Court of Appeal is identical to that for a case submitted to the Court of First Instance except, of course, that where action is required by a judge, the reference is to a judge of the Court of Appeal (Sec. 69A(3)). Obviously, if the matter is of such importance that the unsuccessful party is likely to appeal from the Court of First Instance to the Court of Appeal, it makes sense from a cost and timing point of view to bypass the Court of First Instance.

9.3.4 Direct appeal to Court of First Instance

There are provisions whereby the Board of Review procedure can be bypassed and the Commissioner's determination of an objection submitted directly for the opinion of the Court of First Instance. This would not, of course, be a cost-saving measure but where a point of considerable importance is at issue it may be considered desirable to obtain a court opinion as soon as possible and the provisions of Sec. 67 provide this opportunity. Because the Board of Review is intended to be the primary tribunal for finding facts and has broad powers to do so, however, it is not generally appropriate to appeal directly to the Court of First Instance unless the matter in dispute is largely a point of law and there is no material disagreement between the parties as to the facts of the case. More to protect the taxpayer than the Commissioner, a case cannot be referred direct to the Court of First Instance by either party without the consent of the other party. This is because the case may not have proceeded further than the Board of Review and, therefore, reference directly to the court introduces a substantial cost element.

The procedure can only be commenced after a notice of appeal has been given to the Board of Review. Within 21 days after the date on which the notice of appeal is received by the Clerk to the Board of Review, or such further time as the Board may in any particular case permit upon application in writing by either party, the appellant or the Commissioner can give notice to the other party that he desires to transfer the appeal to the Court of First Instance. At the same time, the party giving such notice must send a copy to the Board of Review (Secs. 67(1) and 67(2)).

If the party who receives such notice agrees to the transfer of the case to the Court of First Instance, he must give his consent in writing to the Board, and serve a copy on the other party, within 21 days after the date on which the notice was given, or such further time as the Board of Review may in any particular case permit upon application in writing by the person.

Obviously, if the party receiving the notice does not reply, the consent is not given and the appeal is not, therefore, transmitted to the Court of First Instance. Upon receipt of a notice of consent, however, the Clerk to the Board to Review transmits the appeal to the Court of First Instance together with all documents submitted to the Board with the appeal (Sec. 67(3)). So far as the Court is concerned, the case is then heard and determined in the same way as an appeal from a determination of the Board of Review (Sec. 67(4)). The difference, however, is that the Court becomes the fact finding body as well as giving an opinion on points of law. The matter could, indeed, be entirely factual with no point of law involved at all, although as noted above, it may not be appropriate to by-pass the Board of Review in such circumstances.

Unlike an appeal to the Board of Review, once referred to the Court of First Instance, there is no automatic right of withdrawal of the appeal before the hearing; this can only be done with the specific consent of the court and subject to such costs as the court may determine (Sec. 67(6)).

The following further rules apply to the appeal (Sec. 67(5)):

(1)   The court must give at least 14 days' notice to the parties of the date of the hearing, and may adjourn the hearing;

(2)   The Commissioner is entitled to be heard at the hearing;

(3)   As in an appeal to the Board of Review, the appellant cannot rely upon any grounds of appeal other than those contained in the notice of appeal, except with the leave of, and subject to the conditions of, the court;

(4)   It is stated that the onus is upon the taxpayer to prove that the assessment is excessive or incorrect. However, there is authority in numerous UK cases, where there is a similar provision, for the view that the appeal is to be determined upon the balance of probability and that there is no automatic acceptance of the Commissioner's assessment until proved wrong; and

(5)   The court may summon and examine any relevant witnesses.

In determining the appeal the court can either increase, reduce or cancel the assessment or remit the case to the Commissioner to make appropriate adjustments. Also, the court can make whatever order as regards costs as it sees fit (Sec. 67(7)).

9.3.5 Judicial Review

Although the IRO contains a broad framework for objecting and appealing against an assessment, increasingly the legal process known as judicial review is being used by taxpayers who are dissatisfied with the actions of the Commissioner. Judicial review is a process by which a person can apply to a court for injunctive relief from the consequences of a decision of a public official. More commonly, judicial review cases involve reviewing the exercise of discretion by a public official, but can also extend to findings of fact by such an official which adversely impact upon the effect of a statutory provision on a person. As a matter of common law, a public official when exercising statutory discretion must act reasonably and properly take into account all relevant considerations and disregard irrelevant matters; failure to act in such a manner may give rise to a judicial review action.

A judicial review action can only be commenced with the leave of the court and over the last two decades, the courts in the UK have demonstrated an increased willingness to allow such actions in tax cases. In Hong Kong, judicial review cases involving tax matters have also become more common over that period, although it is not clear whether this reflects a greater willingness of the courts to allow such actions, or simply that taxpayers and their advisers have become more aware of the availability of this course of action. Although leave may be granted by a court to commence a judicial review action, this does not mean that the action will be successful; indeed, the majority of decisions of the Hong Kong courts on such actions are in favour of the Commissioner. One reason for this is that to be successful, the courts would generally need to be satisfied that the decision making process by the Commissioner was so flawed as to be clearly unreasonable and amount to an abuse of power of an act of bad faith, or that the reasoning (including the consideration of evidence) was not rational. In other words, generally the court will not just reconsider the decision on its merits, but will need to be satisfied that the decision making process in reaching the decision was fundamentally flawed if the application is to be allowed.

One interesting question concerning judicial review, however, is what is its role in tax matters given the extensive objection and appeal procedure provided for in the IRO. The answer to this is two-fold. First, some decisions (notably certain administrative decisions) are not subject to the objection and appeal procedures. Examples of such decisions include whether or not to grant an unconditional holdover of tax which is the subject of an objection (see *Interasia Bag Manufacturers Limited v CIR* [2004] (1 HKRC 90-139), *Chia Tai Conti-Hong Kong Limited* [2005] (1 HKRC 90-147) and *Nam Tai Trading Company Limited v CIR* [2005] (1 HKRC 90-155)), and the refusal of the Board of Review to state a case for the opinion of the Court of First Instance (see cases discussed in section 9.3.2). Also, the refusal of the

Commissioner to accept a late objection was the subject of (an unsuccessful) judicial review application in *Asia Master Limited v CIR* [2006] (1 HKRC 90-177). Interestingly, this case also involved a judicial review application of the Commissioner's decision to refuse to amend an assessment pursuant to Sec. 70A, although in line with the cases mentioned below, this was refused on the basis that the other avenues of appeal had not been exhausted.

Second, judicial review may be permitted in exceptional circumstances, most notably where there has been an abuse of power, notwithstanding the existence of an alternative mechanism for disputing an assessment. In other than these exceptional cases, however, the courts are generally reluctant to permit judicial review to be used as an alternative to the normal objection and appeal procedures (see, for example, *Lee Sap Pat v CIR* (2 HKTC 251) and *Harley Development Inc. & Anor. v CIR* [1996] (1 HKRC 90-079)). In the latter of these cases, Lord Jauncey, delivering the judgement of the Privy Council, said:

> *"Their Lordships consider that, where a statute lays down a comprehensive system of appeals procedures against administrative decisions, it will only be in exceptional circumstances, typically an abuse of power, that the courts will entertain an application for judicial review of a decision which has not been appealed."*

One Hong Kong case where the court held that there was an abuse of power which justified granting the judicial review application notwithstanding the existence of an alternative statutory objection and appeal procedure was *Lee Ma Loi v CIR* [1992] (1 HKRC 90-063) which is discussed in section 8.2.1.

In summary, therefore, judicial review, although having a limited role in tax matters, should not be seen as an alternative to the normal objection and appeal procedures other than in exceptional cases. Where such action is appropriate, however, it is unlikely to be successful unless the applicant can demonstrate not just that a decision was unreasonable, but that it was arrived at by a flawed process of reasoning or administration.

9.4 Provisions Regarding Married Couples

Whilst all of the foregoing provisions apply to a husband and wife there are additional provisions which are necessary to deal with certain special circumstances that apply where a husband and wife both have assessable income. This is because the IRO contains provisions under which their incomes may be assessed jointly and in the event of objection or appeal by one of them, that person's rights must be subject to some limitation but, also, the interests of the other may need protection.

Where a husband and wife who each have income liable to Salaries Tax, enter into an election for joint assessment because one of them has allowances which exceed his or her income, the joint assessment is made in the name of the other spouse (see Chapter 3). In these circumstances the spouse assessed would have the sole right of objection or appeal but for Sec. 64(9) which gives the other spouse a similar right of objection or appeal but such right is limited to those things to which he or she could have taken exception in the event that an assessment had been made on his or her income; in other words, it is limited to matters involving that spouse's income or allowances.

When the unassessed spouse objects in accordance with Sec. 64(9), the Commissioner has powers, in addition to his usual rights of confirming, reducing, increasing or cancelling the assessment, to cancel the assessment and raise one upon the person objecting (Sec. 64(10)(a)). It is, however, difficult to foresee circumstances in which this might happen. There is a protection for the spouse who was assessed, in the event of an objection by the unassessed spouse, in relation to the settlement of the objection. In particular, the Commissioner can only settle the assessment by agreement if he obtains the agreement of both spouses (Sec. 64(10)(b)(i)). If he fails to obtain this agreement he must issue a determination and either spouse, or both of them, may appeal to the Board of Review (Sec. 64(10)(b)(ii)).

It should be carefully noted that these special arrangements concerning objections only apply where a joint assessment is made by virtue of one of the spouses having unabsorbed allowances. A right of election for joint assessment also exists where this would give rise to less tax payable than the total of separate assessments on each spouse. The joint assessment is made upon the spouse nominated by both of them (see Chapter 3) and no rights of objection or appeal then accrue to the other spouse, presumably because their agreement as to who is to be assessed is an effective nomination of all rights to that person.

Of course, where individual assessments are made upon each spouse as if they were single persons, they each have their own rights and obligations in relation to their own assessment.

Otherwise, where an election is made for Personal Assessment and both spouses have income included in the assessment and either spouse objects or appeals against the joint assessment, the other spouse is deemed to be joined in the objection or appeal and a re-assessment can be made in respect of either spouse and amended assessments can be issued to both spouses (Sec. 70B).

For further information on objection and appeal procedures, see *Departmental Interpretation & Practice Notes No. 6.*

Chapter 10 ■
Miscellaneous Matters

10.1 Double Taxation Relief

This book is essentially concerned with the application of the taxation laws of Hong Kong to financial transactions. That is, it is concerned with examining the impact of Hong Kong taxation on such transactions. Many transactions, however, take place across national borders and one consequence of this is that the same profit may attract taxation in two or more jurisdictions. Typically, this occurs because the country of residence of the person deriving the profit or income seeks to tax the amount, as does the jurisdiction from which the profit or income is sourced. Most jurisdictions, however, recognise that such double taxation should be mitigated or eliminated and this essentially occurs through one jurisdiction giving up or modifying its rights to tax profits from specified transactions. This relief may be given on a unilateral basis under domestic taxation law, or on a bilateral basis through a double taxation agreement. International custom is that the jurisdiction in which an item of profit has its source is generally regarded as having the primary or most legitimate right to tax the profit or income and any other jurisdiction which seeks to tax the amount on the basis of the residence of the person deriving the sum should either exempt the amount from tax or allow a credit for the tax paid in the source jurisdiction.

Because of its territorial basis of taxation, Hong Kong traditionally was not particularly concerned about taking steps to eliminate double taxation. In other words, because Hong Kong generally only taxes income or profit from a Hong Kong source, there was generally little need under international custom for it to give up its right to tax any amounts or to give credits for tax suffered elsewhere on the same amount. Nonetheless, although having limited practical application, until 1998 statutory relief was available for tax incurred in certain Commonwealth countries in respect of income which was taxable in Hong Kong. Moreover, there remain various provisions under which some form of relief for foreign tax may be available. These provisions are discussed elsewhere in the book, but the main provisions are as follows:

(1)   With the introduction of certain Profits Tax provisions under which specified amounts which had a source outside Hong Kong were nonetheless deemed to be taxable, limited relief (by way of deduction) for foreign taxes suffered on such amounts was introduced by Sec. 16(1)(c). This provision is discussed in section 4.5.8.

(2)   The IRD has accepted that in certain circumstances a deduction for foreign taxes may be available under the general deduction provision of Sec. 16(1). Again, this is discussed in section 4.5.8.

(3) Reciprocal exemptions are provided to certain non-resident shipping companies and non-resident aircraft-owning businesses pursuant to agreements entered into between Hong Kong and other jurisdictions. These agreements are discussed in sections 4.7.4 and 4.7.6.

(4) More recently, Hong Kong has entered into a number of comprehensive double taxation agreements which provide for relief from double taxation and it is expected that more such agreements will be entered into in due course. The effect of such agreements is discussed in chapter 11.

For a more comprehensive discussion of the issue of double taxation in an international context and the means by which it is addressed generally, see chapter 11.

10.2 Exemptions

The IRO contains specific exemptions from each of the taxes in the relevant Parts, for example Sec. 5(2) contains an exemption from Property Tax, Sec. 8(2) the exemptions from Salaries Tax and Secs. 26, 26A and 20AC the exemptions from Profits Tax.

Apart from these, there are two other general exemption provisions in Part XV of the IRO.

Sec. 87 gives the Chief Executive in Council a general power to exempt any person, office or institution from all or any part of the taxes imposed under the IRO and this is done by making an order to that effect. Any person or body may, of course, petition the Chief Executive for exemption for some specific person or class of income or persons. For example, the following exemption orders have been issued under the powers in Sec. 87:—

(1) an exemption from payment of Salaries Tax in respect of pensions received under Sec. 31 of the Pensions Regulations, Sec. 15(1) of either the *Pension Benefits Ordinance* or the *Pension Benefits (Judicial Officers) Ordinance* or Sec. 3(1) of the *Auxillary Forces Pay and Allowances (Pensions) Regulation*; and

(2) an exemption from payment of Profits Tax on interest accrued after 22 June, 1998 on deposits with authorized institutions, other than where derived by a financial institution. This is discussed fully under point (15) in section 4.5.3.

In addition, many organisations which do not qualify for exemption under Sec. 88 (see below) have been granted full or partial exemption from taxes imposed under the IRO by this provision.

The second general exemption is granted under Sec. 88 to charitable institutions or trusts of a public character. It is, therefore, important to be able to identify that which qualifies as a charity. For this, it is necessary to refer to the case of *Special Commissioners of Income Tax v Pemsel* (3 TC 53) which laid down the basic tests of charitable purpose as:—

(1) the relief of poverty;
(2) the advancement of religion; or
(3) the furtherance of education.

When the charitable status has been proved to the satisfaction of the Commissioner, the body is exempt from all taxes under the IRO except that, in the case of profits from a trade or business carried on by the charitable body, there are additional qualifications to the exemption from the Profits Tax thereon. In particular, the exemption only applies to such Profits Tax if:—

(1) the profits are applied solely for charitable purposes; and
(2) they are not expended substantially outside Hong Kong;

and either:—

(1) the trade or business is exercised in the course of carrying out the objects of the charity as, for example, the operation of a school; or
(2) the work in connection with the trade or business is mainly performed by persons who are the beneficiaries of the charity as, for example, goods manufactured by disabled persons, the proceeds going to relief for the disabled.

Note that "applied" for charitable purposes includes being donated to another charitable trust or added to the reserve fund, per the decision in *CIR v Helen Slater Charitable Trust* (55 TC 230).

10.3 Retirement Schemes

Employers have traditionally often set up schemes to provide for their employees upon retirement, and from 1 December, 2000 this became mandatory. In Hong Kong, such schemes usually take the form of provident funds which pay out lump sums, although pension schemes are not unknown. The establishment of such a scheme has tax implications for both the employer and the relevant employees; additionally, the tax position of any income earned on any assets of the scheme needs to be considered.

The law regarding retirement schemes underwent substantial changes in 1993; in particular, the *Occupational Retirement Schemes Ordinance* (ORSO) came into effect on 15th October 1993 and brought in a whole new regulatory regime for retirement schemes. The ORSO introduced provisions regarding, amongst other things, procedures and requirements for registration, auditing of accounts, annual returns, trustees, investment of scheme assets, disclosure of information to members and the establishment of consultative committees. The ORSO did not, however, make the establishment of retirement schemes by employers compulsory.

Although the IRO had contained provisions concerning the tax implications of retirement schemes for many years, substantial changes were made as a result of the enactment of the ORSO and these have been dealt with in the appropriate context throughout the book. Both before and after the introduction of the ORSO, however, the tax treatment of contributions and provisions made by the employer, and benefits received by employees, has been dependent upon whether the scheme has obtained certain approval, although the consequences of having obtained such approval vary slightly before and after the introduction of the ORSO. The approval process also changed with the introduction of the ORSO as prior to that approval was granted by the Commissioner. After the introduction of the ORSO, however, approval for tax purposes was essentially automatic for a retirement scheme subject to regulation or exemption under the ORSO or another Hong Kong ordinance.

The situation regarding retirement schemes underwent further changes with the enactment of the *Mandatory Provident Funds Schemes Ordinance* (MPFO) which, from 1 December, 2000, made it mandatory for employers to establish retirement schemes for their employees. Moreover, the MPFO makes contributions to a MPF scheme effectively mandatory for both employers and employees. Additionally, the MPFO provides a statutory framework for the regulation of MPF schemes which is quite independent of the ORSO. Nonetheless, the MPFO does not override the ORSO; rather, the two ordinances co-exist and, indeed, interface, as a scheme established under the ORSO can continue to be operated either as a scheme to provide benefits additional to those provided by the employer's MPF scheme or, providing certain conditions are met, effectively as an alternative to a MPF scheme.

10.3.1 Taxation consequences of retirement schemes

There are a variety of tax issues which arise as a consequence of the operation of retirement schemes. These issues are discussed in detail in the relevant sections of this book, most of which are in chapters 3 and 4. Nonetheless, these matters are summarised together in this section.

The provisions of the IRO dealing with issues in connection with retirement schemes generally distinguish between retirement schemes which are "recognized" (a concept discussed below) and those which are not. This distinction is largely historic in that it has its origins in earlier legislation under which the Commissioner had the authority to approve retirement schemes for the purpose of granting the contributions thereto, and the benefits therefrom, concessional tax treatment. The distinction is, however, now largely irrelevant as the Commissioner no longer has the power to approve schemes for tax purposes. In particular, the regulation of retirement schemes has evolved significantly since the early 1990s with the introduction of the ORSO and, subsequently, the MPFO and it is now generally illegal to participate in an unregulated scheme unless the scheme has been granted an exemption from regulation. Since regulated schemes and schemes granted exemption from the regulations are generally "recognized" for tax purposes, it is in effect not possible to participate in a scheme which is unrecognized for tax purposes.

Nonetheless, throughout the IRO, when considering the deductibility of contributions to retirement schemes (and accounting provisions in respect thereof), and the assessability of benefits derived therefrom, the provisions generally refer to either a "recognized occupational retirement scheme" or a "recognized retirement scheme". It is, therefore, important to understand the meaning of these terms.

To understand the meaning of "recognized occupational retirement scheme" it is first necessary to consider the definition of an "occupational retirement scheme". For this purpose, an "occupational retirement scheme" is as defined in the ORSO and means any scheme, other than a contract of insurance under which benefits are payable only upon the death or disability of the insured, which is comprised of one or more instruments and provides for the payment of pensions, allowances, gratuities or other payments on termination of service, death or retirement to or in respect of persons employed under a contract of service. Because of the broad drafting, it could be argued that an employment contract which provides for a termination gratuity or other payment could fall within the definition. This would mean, amongst other things, that such an employment contract would need to be recognised under the legislation if payments under that contract were to be deductible. Nonetheless, the ORSO also provides that an employment contract will not be considered within the definition of an occupational retirement scheme solely by reason of a provision for a termination payment, if the period of employment does not exceed four years. As an anti-avoidance measure, however, this exemption does not apply in respect of successive contracts of employment for periods of less than four years if all or a substantial part of the end of contract gratuity is withheld by the employer or repaid by the employee upon being re-employed under the new contract.

A "recognized occupational retirement scheme" is defined in Sec. 2 with reference to the ORSO itself and, in effect, is an occupational retirement scheme which:—

(1)   was approved by the Commissioner under the former Sec. 87A and such approval has not subsequently been withdrawn,

(2)   is registered under Sec. 18 of the ORSO;

(3)   is exempt from registration pursuant to Sec. 7(1) of the ORSO. Essentially, this exemption applies to foreign schemes where only a small proportion of members are Hong Kong residents;

(4)   is operated by a foreign government or a non-profit agency or undertaking of a foreign government; or

(5)   is established by, or contained in, any other Hong Kong ordinance other than the *Mandatory Provident Fund Schemes Ordinance.*

Sec. 2(2A) further provides that where a scheme is a recognized occupational retirement scheme by virtue of either (2) or (3) above, it is deemed to have been so recognized from the date of the relevant application or the date on which the terms of the scheme came into effect, whichever is earlier.

A "recognized retirement scheme" is defined as a recognized occupational retirement scheme or a MPF scheme. This term, however, is used much less frequently in the IRO than the term "recognized occupational retirement scheme".

The implications of a scheme being a recognized occupational retirement scheme (which, it must be remembered, does not include a MPF scheme) are as set out below.

A. For the employer

(1)   A deduction is available, subject to certain limitations (see sections 4.5.8 and 4.5.10 and (2) below), for contributions or provisions, whereas no such deductions are available for any contributions or provisions in respect of unrecognized schemes.

(2)   The maximum deduction for ordinary annual contributions or provisions is 15% of the employee's total emoluments.

(3) Special contributions are deductible over five years (Sec. 16A —
     refer to section 4.5.8). Again, no deduction for such amounts is
     available in respect of an unrecognized scheme.

B. For the employee

(1) No Salaries Tax liability will arise on a lump sum attributable to the
     employer's contributions received on:
     (a) termination after at least ten years' service with the employer;
     (b) retirement from the service of the employer after a specified
          age of at least 45;
     (c) reaching the age of 60 or a later specified retirement age without
          retiring or terminating service; or
     (d) death or incapacity.
(2) If a lump sum attributable to the employer's contributions is received
     on termination of service before completion of ten years' service, a
     proportionate exemption from Salaries Tax is still available.
(3) No Salaries Tax liability will arise on a lump sum received on
     termination of service, death, incapacity or retirement, to the extent
     the sum is not attributable to the employer's contributions.
(4) Sec. 9(1)(aa), which renders payments from unrecognized retirement
     schemes subject to Salaries Tax to the extent they represent employer
     contributions, has no application.
(5) Subject to certain limits, a deduction for contributions is permitted
     by Sec. 26G (see section 3.5.7).

These points are covered in more detail in the relevant sections of this
book. See also *Departmental Interpretation & Practice Notes No. 23*.

Most of the above benefits for employers also essentially apply in respect
of MPF schemes. The consequences for employees are, however, slightly
different in respect of MPF schemes. In particular, because payments from
an MPF scheme are generally only made on death, incapacity, retirement
(at age 65, or some other age of at least 60 in certain circumstances) or
permanent departure from Hong Kong, points 1(b) and 1(c) in B above
have no application to MPF schemes. Also, it is only benefits attributable to
any voluntary contributions by the employer which possibly attract a Salaries
Tax liability under point (2) in B above in relation to MPF schemes. In other
words, benefits from an MPF scheme attributable to mandatory contributions
of the employer, both mandatory and voluntary contributions by the
employee, and investment income will generally be exempt from Salaries
Tax; the only exception to this is where a payment is made from a MPF

scheme otherwise than on retirement, death, incapacity or termination of service in which case all amounts attributable to mandatory or voluntary contributions by the employer will be taxable in full. This is likely to a relatively uncommon scenario but would appear to apply where an employee permanently leaves Hong Kong without terminating their service (e.g. they continue to work for the employer abroad), or where a payment is made outside of the scheme rules and MPF regulations. Amounts received by an employee from a MPF scheme attributable to voluntary contributions by an employer will also generally be exempt, except when received on termination of service in which case the proportionate benefit rules of Sec. 8(5) will apply and, as discussed above, when received other than on retirement, death, incapacity or termination of service, in which case they are assessable in full.

Note that in addition to granting a deduction for contributions to a recognized occupational retirement scheme by an employee, Sec. 26G also grants a deduction (subject to the same limitations) for contributions by an employee to an MPF scheme. These deductions are, however, allowed only for the purposes of Salaries Tax and Personal Assessment. For Profits Tax purposes, contributions in respect of a sole proprietor or a partner in a partnership are deductible only when they are to a MPF scheme (see Sec. 16AA). Nonetheless, although unlikely to be common in practice, it appears that a sole proprietor or partner in a partnership who contributed to a recognized occupational retirement scheme could obtain a deduction for those contributions, subject to the usual limitations, by electing for Personal Assessment (if the conditions for making such an election are satisfied) and claiming the deduction under Sec. 26G.

Another issue of interest in relation to retirement schemes concerns the assessability of the investment earnings of retirement schemes. The investment activities of the trustee or administrator of a retirement scheme may be sufficient to constitute a carrying on of business. Theoretically, therefore, any Hong Kong source profits derived from that business would be subject to Profits Tax. The IRO, however, does not address this issue. In *Departmental Interpretation & Practice Notes No. 23*, the Commissioner observes that:

> *"In holding and managing funds, the trustees of retirement schemes will from time to time, and perhaps occasionally with a degree of frequency, acquire and dispose of investments. That notwithstanding, as retirement schemes are operated for the common advantage of their constituent members (i.e. the employees), the trustees' fiduciary duties are to maintain the investment funds in a healthy financial state to meet long-term commitments. Taken overall, recognized retirement schemes and their trustees are not considered to be subject to profits tax on their investment income".*

Although the intention of the above statement is clear, it is difficult to reconcile it to the legislative provisions regarding Profits Tax as neither the fact that an entity operates for the benefit of its constituent members, nor has as its investment strategy the maintaining of funds in a state to meet long-term commitments, is conclusive that a business is not carried on; although not explicitly stated, it is presumably on the basis that no business is carried on that the IRD in the Practice Note conclude that retirement schemes are not subject to Profits Tax. Nonetheless, although trustees and administrators of retirement schemes (including MPF schemes) can draw comfort from the above statement that it is not the intention of the IRD to subject such schemes to Profits Tax, a degree of uncertainty will remain until such time as the issue is addressed by legislation rather than administrative guidelines.

10.4 Anti-avoidance Legislation

The policies and objectives which govern the construction of the Hong Kong tax system have been discussed in Chapter 1 and, arising out of the basic principle of simplicity is the fact that the IRO, from the outset, contained very little strict anti-avoidance legislation. This is presumably because such legislation is necessarily detailed, complicated and difficult to administer, which clearly conflicts with the policy of simplicity; however, due to the growth of sophisticated tax planning arrangements that have proved a threat to revenue collection, this position changed over the years.

Many sections of the IRO contain sub-sections aimed at countering possible loopholes, but these do not really amount to the broad anti-avoidance legislation which has become a common feature in countries with much more sophisticated legislation.

Genuine anti-avoidance provisions can be divided into two classes, specific anti-avoidance provisions, which aim at specifically identified classes of transactions, and general anti-avoidance provisions which are designed to frustrate any area of tax planning. The IRO contains both types of provisions, although perhaps less in the way of specific anti-avoidance than developed tax systems elsewhere. The provisions which, for example, extend the Profits Tax liability of shipowners and aircraft owners (Secs. 23B, 23C and 23D) and financial institutions (Sec. 15(1)(i)) are not really anti-avoidance provisions but are deeming provisions to extend the tax base. However, the provisions in Sec. 15A which are designed to bring into the charge to Profits Tax sums received for the sale of rights to receive income can only be described as specific anti-avoidance measures.

10.4.1 Specific anti-avoidance

There are a number of provisions in the IRO which amount to specific anti-avoidance provisions and some of these are discussed below.

There is a transfer pricing provision in Sec. 20, although the effectiveness of this is severely limited when compared to its sophisticated equivalents in other developed tax jurisdictions. This provision is discussed in detail in section 4.8.5.

Also, there are provisions, in Sec. 39E, designed to curb a perceived loss of revenue in connection with leveraged lease arrangements and the sale and leaseback of second-hand plant and machinery. These provisions are fully dealt with in section 5.10.2.

Similarly, Sec. 22B, which contains provisions aimed at limiting the utilisation of losses by limited partners in limited partnerships, is also concerned primarily with leasing arrangements. These provisions are discussed fully in section 4.5.15.5.

The specific anti-avoidance provisions of Sec. 15A, which deem certain lump sums for the sale of the right to receive income to be trading receipts, were introduced to counter schemes developed to exploit a court decision in Australia which held such sums to be of a non-taxable capital nature. Ironically, however, the Australian decision was reversed on appeal and, therefore, Sec. 15A is, in fact, now unnecessary (see *FC of T v Myer Emporium Limited* (87 ATC 4363)). Sec. 15A is discussed in detail under point (12) in section 4.5.4.

One other important specific anti-avoidance provision is Sec. 61B, which was introduced to curb trafficking in loss companies. Because of the complexities of this provision, it is discussed separately in the following section.

10.4.2 Sale of loss companies

Prior to the introduction of Sec. 61B, it was possible for the shareholders of a company with accumulated losses for Profits Tax purposes, to dispose of the company to a new owner who could put profitable business, on which he would otherwise be subject to Profits Tax, into the company to take advantage of the losses. There was no requirement that the business injected should in any way be similar to the business which gave rise to the losses.

Sec. 61B provides, however, that a loss brought forward in a company cannot be set off against profits if the Commissioner decides that:—

(1)   there has been any change in the shareholding of a company, as a

direct or indirect result of which, profits have arisen to the corporation; and

(2)   the sole or dominant purpose of the change in shareholding was for the purposes of using the losses to avoid a tax liability of the company or any other person (not necessarily a company).

This very simplistic wording should be contrasted with similar provisions in the UK, for example, where very lengthy and detailed clauses were enacted. The result is that the potential impact in Hong Kong is much wider than is probably intended and, in recognition of this, the Commissioner saw fit, when the provisions were introduced in 1986, to introduce a procedure for advance clearance of transactions which are likely to be potentially caught by Sec. 61B (see paragraphs 50 to 54 of *Departmental Interpretation & Practice Notes No. 15*, which is reproduced as Appendix 10).

Until 1 April 1998 any such rulings were arguably not binding on taxpayers or the Commissioner, as there was no legislative basis for granting advance rulings. From 1 April 1998, however, a formal advance ruling system was introduced (see section 10.5 below) and any rulings given must be in accordance with the relevant statutory provisions.

It should be noted that, although it is probably intended to pursue only situations where there is a change in control of a company (and the IRD in paragraph 54 of *Departmental Interpretation & Practice Notes No. 15* state that the provision is not intended to create unnecessary inhibitions in the case of genuine commercial company acquisitions or group reconstructions), the provisions in fact refer to any change in shareholding, including a change in a minority holding. In order to apply the provision, however, it is necessary for the Commissioner to show that the change in shareholding was the cause of the receipt of profits, which is obviously only likely to be the case where there is a change in control. There is only reference to a change in shareholding which does not seem to address the position where shares are registered in the name of a trustee (who might be merely a nominee) and a change occurs in the beneficiary which is, of course, not registerable in the register of shareholders. However, in considering possible loopholes in the wording of Sec. 61B, there must be entertained the possibility that the general anti-avoidance provisions in Sec. 61A (see subsequent sections) could be used against the arrangements subject to the possible legal argument that the provisions of Sec. 61B should be exhaustive in relation to the matters identified and the arrangements should not, therefore, be subject to further scrutiny under general anti-avoidance provisions.

Secondly, it should be noted that the sole or dominant purpose for the change of shareholding must be for the use of the losses to avoid tax. The Commissioner's view as to the meaning of dominant in this context is that the tax motive must outweigh all other motives put together. This is probably correct, although a view less favourable to the taxpayer would be a motive outweighing any of the other motives taken individually. The difficulty, however, either way, is in proving motives and weighing them against each other which is inevitably subjective and this is the essence of many disputes. It is, of course, not arguable that it should be the company (in which there has been a change of shareholding) that must be proved to have avoided tax because, as a matter of common sense, it will be some other person, possibly even an individual, which willingly transfers profitable business to the company, who achieves the tax saving.

In the case of group reconstructions where there is a change in direct ownership, notwithstanding no change in ultimate ownership, Sec. 61B will potentially apply if a company with losses has other group profitable business consolidated into it. Whether or not the provision can be successfully applied in this situation will depend upon proof of commercial reasons for the reorganisation other than tax avoidance. The IRD in *Departmental Interpretation & Practice Notes No. 15* state that Sec. 61B is not intended to create unnecessary inhibitions in the case of group reconstructions, although what this exactly means is not clear. Given that that comment can logically only relate to situations where there is potential for the provision to otherwise apply, the statement suggests that there will be situations where there is a change of ownership of a loss company within a group as a result of which profits are transferred to that company which the IRD will accept as not attracting the application of the provision. Nonetheless, in practice the IRD appear to rarely accept the transfer of profitable business to a loss company and will seek to challenge such an arrangement under either Sec. 61B or Sec. 61A (which is discussed below).

10.4.3 General anti-avoidance provisions

A general anti-avoidance provision sets out to permit the tax administration to ignore or modify, as appropriate, any transaction which has been designed or executed wholly or substantially for the purposes of avoidance of tax by legal means; for example, by relying upon loopholes in, or advantageous interpretations of, the law. Inevitably, such provisions are broad-based and have a potentially wider impact than the administration may intend to apply.

When considering general anti-avoidance provisions, it is useful to also examine some aspects of the rules of interpretation of tax statutes which have been developed over the years by the courts. This is because general anti-avoidance rules have to some extent developed as a response to the manner in which courts have interpreted tax statutes. Additionally, however, as discussed later there is uncertainty as to the application of the rules of interpretation developed by the courts to statutes which contain general anti-avoidance provisions.

As noted in section 1.1, tax statutes have traditionally been interpreted very narrowly because of their nature as a means of extracting money from the public. As a result, the courts have tended to adopt the view that the statutes are to be interpreted rather literally, with little room for the courts to read into the statute what might have been intended by the legislature. Over the years, this has led in other jurisdictions which have a British based legal system to the emergence of a principle based upon the decision in *IRC v Duke of Westminster* (19 TC 490), and many other cases like it, that every person is entitled to arrange his affairs in such a way so as to minimise the tax liability thereon. More specifically, those cases adopted the view that the form in which a transaction was carried through was not to be ignored for tax purposes by virtue of the substance or underlying intent of the transaction.

Decisions in the UK since the early 1980s, however, have served to somewhat erode this principle by introducing what was originally often referred to as the doctrine of "fiscal nullity", a term coined to refer to situations were a transaction or part of a transaction is, for fiscal (i.e. tax) purposes, effectively ignored. As discussed below, however, this term is now used less frequently by the courts, due to the fact that more recent cases have rejected the idea that a new doctrine was established by the relevant cases, but rather that the cases merely developed more modern approaches to existing rules. Accordingly, in this book, as is the case in many court decisions, the term "*Ramsay* principle" is used, being a reference to the first case which introduced the new rules, rather than "fiscal nullity". Because the *Ramsay* principle is a court developed concept, it has, and is likely to continue to, evolve over time as more cases are decided. Accordingly, in considering how the principle may be applied in a particular situation it is important to be aware of current judicial views rather than relying solely on older cases.

The *Ramsay* principle emerged from the case of *W T. Ramsay Limited v IRC* [1982] (AC 300) and brought about two changes to the way tax statutes were interpreted. First, the decision rejected the literal interpretation which had traditionally been applied to tax statutes and instead held that the normal rules of statutory interpretation should be applied. Second, the decision rejected the previously common practice of looking at and analysing the tax consequences of each step as a series of transactions separately. Instead, the court in *Ramsay* held that it was permissible to look at the effect of a series of transactions and apply the statute to that overall result. This aspect of the *Ramsay* decision was arguably further extended by *Furniss v Dawson* (55 TC 324), which appeared to suggest that where a transaction consisted of a chain of steps, any steps in that chain which had been inserted with no commercial motive other than the avoidance of tax were to be disregarded for tax purposes and the tax position was to be determined only in relation to the overall end result. In the *Furniss v Dawson* case, an individual had negotiated an arm's length sale of a family company. As a straight sale of the shares would have given rise to a liability to Capital Gains Tax, he arranged that a company be formed in the Isle of Man to take over his company on a share for share exchange and then for the Isle of Man company to make the sale. The share for share exchange was exempt from Capital Gains Tax and there was no tax in the Isle of Man on the ultimate sale; therefore, Capital Gains Tax would have been avoided, or at least deferred, if the transaction had achieved its intended result. It was held that the participation of the Isle of Man company in the chain of events was for UK tax purposes only and that, therefore, the strict legal form of the transactions should be ignored and, instead, the individual should be assessed to Capital Gains Tax as if he had made the sale direct as planned.

Nonetheless, the apparently wide ambit of the *Ramsay* principle as applied in *Furniss v Dawson* (supra) has, perhaps, been narrowed in a number of more recent decisions. In particular, in *Craven v White* (62 TC 1) the House of Lords held that the principle that the Revenue could disregard intermediate steps in a series of transactions applied only where that series of transactions was pre-ordained and there was no practical likelihood that the pre-planned steps would not take place in the order ordained; in other words, the House of Lords suggested that intermediate steps could only be ignored where it was never contemplated that they would have an independent life. Further, in *Countess Fitzwilliam & Others v CIR* [1993] (1 WLR 1189) the House of Lords went further and noted that even the existence of a series of transactions which formed part of a pre-planned tax avoidance scheme was not sufficient, in itself, to deny the benefit of a specific statutory provision, unless the series of transactions was *"capable of being construed in a manner inconsistent with the application"* of such statutory provision.

An arguably even more restrictive interpretation of the principle was applied by the House of Lords in *Macniven v Westmoreland Investments Limited* (2001) (UKHL 6), where it was suggested that the correct approach was to ascertain the concept that the legislature had in mind when drafting the relevant provisions and then decide whether the transaction in question was within that concept. Lord Hoffman went on in that case to suggest that the concept that the legislature had in mind might be a purely legal one, where a strict legal analysis of the provision would be required or, alternatively, a commercial concept where it may be appropriate to look at the commercial effect of the overall transaction and ignore the legal effect of its individual elements.

The later case of *Barclays Mercantile Business Finance Limited v Mawson* [2004] (UKHL 51) provides an excellent overview of the previous cases and makes a number of succinct points. First, it rejects the notion that the *Ramsay* principle introduced a new doctrine of statutory interpretation applicable to taxing statutes, but was merely a more modern approach to interpreting statutory construction where more emphasis was placed on ascertaining the purpose of the provisions. This had been, at least implicitly, recognised in many of the cases since the early 1990s where, *inter alia*, the term "fiscal nullity doctrine" became less frequently used and the term "purposive interpretation" started appearing. Second, the court considered that a "purposive" interpretation of the relevant statutory provision was required to determine what was intended by that provision and then the transaction needed to be examined to decide whether it came within that purpose. Whilst this largely reflected the view of the court in the *Macniven* case (supra), the court rejected the distinction between commercial and legal concepts referred to in that case by Lord Hoffman. Third, the court explicitly rejected the notion, often understood to have been endorsed in the *Furniss v Dawson* case (supra), that any steps in, or elements of, a transaction which had no commercial purpose were to be disregarded for tax purposes. Indeed, the court suggested that provided the transaction in question was within what was intended by the tax statute, the fact that it was circular or pre-ordained was not a relevant consideration when applying the statute to the transaction. As a result of these findings, it will be appreciated that the current judicial views are less onerous than was generally understood to be the case following the decision in *Furniss v Dawson*.

Notwithstanding the foregoing developments in the interpretation of tax statutes over more than two decades, until recently there remained doubt as to the applicability of those principles to the IRO. For example, it was held *in D 52/86* that the *Ramsay* principle (in particular, as expressed in *Furniss v Dawson* (supra)) could not be applied in Hong Kong to taxes imposed by the IRO in view of the general anti-avoidance provisions in Secs. 61 and 61A (see subsequent sections). This view was in accordance with various decisions of the Australian courts (see, for example, *Lau v FC of T* (84 ATC 4618), and cases in New Zealand and Canada, which suggested that the doctrine could not apply were there was a statutory anti-avoidance provision. Those cases adopted the principle that a court should not interpret the law any more onerously than a statutory provision which is intended to be exhaustive on the matter.

The correctness of this view, however, began to be called into doubt by the decision of the House of Lords in *IRC v McGuckian* [1997] (STC 908) where Lord Cooke, in applying the principles established in *Furniss v Dawson* held that in interpreting taxing statutes a "purposive" approach was to be adopted and that such an approach was not appropriate only in the absence of statutory anti-avoidance provisions, but rather was to be seen as "antecedent to or collateral with" such provisions. This view is understandable, indeed arguably inevitable, given the trend of the courts to reject the idea that *Ramsay* introduced a new doctrine and instead to treat it as simply a modern approach to interpretation of tax statutes. Indeed, in *D 94/04* the Board of Review held that the *Ramsay* principle applied when interpreting the IRO, and in particular Secs. 16(1)(a) and 17(1)(b); they reached this conclusion specifically by following the dicta of Riberio PJ in the Court of Final Appeal decision of *Collector of Stamp Revenue v Arrowtown Assets Limited* [2004] (1 HKRC 90-129) where he reiterated that the *Ramsay* principle was "… *a general rule of statutory construction and an unblinkered approach to the analysis of the facts*." Further, this approach was adopted by the Court of First Instance in *CIR v Tai Hing Cotton Mill (Development) Limited* [2005] (1 HKRC 90-150), although on appeal (see CACV 343/2005) Rogers VP questioned whether this was a correct application of the *Ramsay* principle. Accordingly, there is now authority to suggest that, despite earlier cases to the contrary, the *Ramsay* principle applies when interpreting the IRO. Certainly the IRD adopts this view as evidenced by the comments in paragraphs 55 to 57 of *Departmental Interpretation & Practice Notes No. 15* and the fact that they have successfully sought to apply the principle in a number of cases. Nonetheless, in most circumstances this is likely to be of little more than academic interest as the general anti-avoidance provisions of the IRO will usually be a more effective means for the IRD to combat tax avoidance. This could theoretically change if the courts were, as a result of decisions in favour of taxpayers, to render the general anti-avoidance provisions less effective, although at present this seems unlikely.

Although it was previously uncertain whether the *Ramsay* principle applied when interpreting the IRO, the position was always clear in relation to Stamp Duty and Estate Duty as neither the SDO nor the EDO contain a general anti-avoidance provision. Moreover, it was implicitly accepted by the Court of Final Appeal that it could apply in relation to Estate Duty (see *Shiu Wing Limited & Ors. v CED* [2000] (1 HKRC 90-106), although the principle was not actually applied in that case. The Court of Final Appeal did, however, apply the principle to counter a transaction intended to avoid Stamp Duty in *Collector of Stamp Revenue v Arrowtown Assets Limited* [2004] (1 HKRC 90-129), which is discussed in section 11.10.4.

The Hong Kong law contains two general anti-avoidance provisions, Secs. 61 and 61A, which are discussed in the following sections. Sec. 61A was enacted much later than Sec. 61 and was considered necessary because of the relative ineffectiveness of Sec. 61. Sec. 61A is modelled on an Australian provision (although its drafting is less comprehensive than the Australian equivalent), and aims to counter the tax benefits arising from transactions undertaken for the sole or dominant purposes of obtaining such tax benefits. It is perhaps somewhat surprising that Sec. 61 was not repealed upon the introduction of Sec. 61A.

10.4.4 Section 61

Sec. 61 has been in the IRO from the very beginning and has its origins in the UK Commonwealth tax package introduced to many countries in the Commonwealth. It states that if an assessor is of the opinion that any transaction which either reduces, or would reduce, the amount of tax payable by any person is either artificial, or fictitious, or is a disposition not given effect to, the assessor may disregard any such transaction or disposition and raise an assessment accordingly.

The difficult area of interpretation is, of course, as to what is meant by artificial or fictitious and this has been examined in a number of cases both in and outside Hong Kong as a result of which the application of the provisions is a lot more limited than might at first be expected. Earlier decisions, however, tended to give Sec. 61 a wide application. In *CIR v Rico Internationale Ltd.* (HKTC 229), certain payments were regarded as artificial because they were motivated by non-commercial reasons, not documented or evidenced, and fixed in retrospect. However, part of the payments were allowed, representing the part which had been properly incurred for the purposes of earning assessable profits. In effect, therefore, Sec. 61 was used as a substitute for Sec. 20, although the judge observed that, strictly, if the assessor had regarded the transaction as artificial, Sec. 61 gave him authority to disregard the whole of the transaction.

In the later case of *Kum Hing Land Investment Co. Ltd. v CIR* (HKTC 301), a payment to another company was actually made and properly evidenced but it was held that payment is only a part of a transaction and that all surrounding circumstances, particularly the motives, must be considered and as the payment was not one which a businessman could reasonably be expected to make in the circumstances it was held to be both artificial and fictitious.

The comment in the *Kum Hing* case that the transaction was fictitious as well as artificial is somewhat surprising in that a transaction cannot be fictitious if it actually takes place and, as that case would have gone against the taxpayer in any event on the grounds that the transaction was artificial, it is doubtful whether any weight can be put on the point. In fact, in the much later case of *CIR v Douglas Henry Howe* (HKTC 936) a careful distinction was drawn between artificial and fictitious based on the authority of a decision of the Privy Council on an anti-avoidance provision in Jamaican tax law which is almost identical to Sec. 61, the case being *Seramco Ltd. Superannuation Fund Trustees v Income Tax Commissioner* [1977] (AC 287). As this established that a fictitious transaction is one which "the parties to it never intended should be carried out", the *Howe* case was pursued by the Commissioner before the Court only on the grounds that the transaction was artificial. Furthermore, the Court in the *Howe* case held that the transaction was not artificial because a transfer of a business by an individual to a company wholly owned by him, albeit for tax reasons, was not an unreasonable or unrealistic thing to do.

The *Howe* case, therefore, substantially cut down the application of Sec. 61 and certainly prevented its application solely on the basis that a transaction was motivated by tax reasons.

Around the same time, the *Ramsay* principle (commonly referred to at the time as the fiscal nullity doctrine) emerged in the UK and was seen as a court made general anti-avoidance provision; however, it was generally believed that this could not apply in relation to the IRO because of the existence of Sec. 61, even though the application of that provision was limited by court decisions. Accordingly, a more comprehensive general anti-avoidance provision, Sec. 61A, was enacted. Nonetheless, Sec. 61 has not been entirely forgotten. In *D 41/91* and *D 47/91* the Board of Review used its existence to limit the application of the principle developed by the UK courts in *Sharkey v Wernher* (36 TC 275) and similar cases (see section 4.5.11), although those Board of Review decisions involved transactions which took place before Sec. 61A became effective. It is also interesting to note that the Board of Review in *D 44/92* (as in a number of subsequent decisions), in finding for the Commissioner in a case involving the application of general anti-avoidance provisions, found that both Secs. 61 and 61A applied to the transaction.

10.4.5 Section 61A

Sec. 61A is a broad anti-avoidance provision which applies where a "tax benefit" has been derived by a person as a result of that person entering into a "transaction" and it would be concluded, having regard to a series of specified factors, that the person's sole or dominant purpose for entering into the transaction was to obtain the resulting tax benefit. Where the provision applies, an assistant commissioner is given discretionary powers to assess the relevant person in a manner which counters the tax benefit. Sec. 61A is fashioned very closely on a similar, although more comprehensively drafted, provision in the Australian tax law. As a consequence, Australian case law is particularly relevant in the interpretation of Sec. 61A although, as always, care should be taken in considering such case law as it is not strictly binding in Hong Kong and there are differences between the Australian and Hong Kong provisions.

There are clearly a number of important elements in the statutory provision, and these are considered below, together with a discussion of some of the case law applicable to the provision.

10.4.5.1 Meaning of transaction

A "transaction" is defined in Sec. 61A(3) to include an operation or a scheme (which could possibly be a multiplicity of interrelated transactions), whether or not enforceable or intended to be enforceable by legal proceedings. A transaction may, therefore, be viewed for the purpose of Sec. 61A either broadly (for example, as an overall scheme or arrangement which involves a series of individual steps) or narrowly (for example, as a single step in a broad scheme or arrangement). This distinction is important because a scheme or arrangement may have an overall commercial purpose, but one or more individual steps may be primarily designed to provide a tax benefit. In such circumstances, the taxpayer will undoubtedly seek to have the overall scheme treated as the transaction for the purpose of Sec. 61A, while the IRD will likely focus on the individual step or steps which are considered to give rise to a tax benefit.

One of the difficulties facing taxpayers is that where there is any tax driven element to an overall arrangement, if there is no limit on how narrowly a transaction can be defined it will always be possible to define the transaction as that tax driven element. This was recognised in one of the earlier Australian cases on the equivalent provision, *FCT v Peabody* (94 ATC 4663). In this regard, it should be noted that in Australia the equivalent legislation uses the term "scheme" rather than "transaction", although as "transaction" is defined in Hong Kong to include a "scheme", the Australian case law is still relevant and persuasive with regard to the meaning of "transaction" for the purpose of Sec. 61A. In the *Peabody* case the High Court noted that a scheme was not defined to include part of a scheme (just as in Hong Kong a transaction is not defined as including a part of a transaction) and it is possible that a set of circumstances may describe only part of a scheme and not a scheme itself. This would occur, the court said "... *where the circumstances are incapable of standing on their own without being robbed of all practical meaning*". This was generally interpreted as meaning that a scheme for the purpose of the provision must have a degree of completeness or coherence and, therefore, that there was a limit to how narrowly it could be defined. Doubt was cast on this view, however, in the later High Court decision of *Commissioner of Taxation v Hart* [2004] (HCA 26) where the court rejected the contention that having no limits on how narrowly a scheme can be defined will necessarily mean that it will always be possible to identify a tax driven transaction, but said that if that was the case the solution lay not in introducing tests which were not supported by the legislative wording but by looking to other aspects of the provision, most notably the sole or dominant purpose test.

The approach in the *Peabody* case was rejected by the Board of Review in *D 67/95* which involved an arrangement comprised of five steps. The Board held that the transaction for the purpose of Sec. 61A "... *constituted a single composite operation, wherein the whole was greater than the sum of its parts ... [and that those] ... parts ... were pre-ordained with little expectation that they would not materialize*".

Such an interpretation was, not surprisingly, contrary to what the Commissioner's representative had sought to argue. In reaching its conclusion that it was the wider transaction which it was appropriate to look to, the Board said:

> *"On this subject we are a little surprised that the Revenue is unwilling to concede the validity of the wider interpretation since it is particularly common in the interpretation of facts having tax implications for account to be taken of all the surrounding circumstances: ... We infer from the evidence and find as a matter of fact that the Scheme constituted a single composite operation, wherein the whole was greater than the sum of its parts...."*

That decision should also be contrasted with later decisions in Australia which tend to permit a narrow definition of scheme, rather than looking to a broader transaction. See, for example, the decision of the High Court of Australia in *FCT v Consolidated Press Holdings Limited* (2001 ATC 4343) where it was held that the general anti-avoidance provision could be invoked against particular elements of an overall transaction which give rise to tax advantages, even though the overall transaction may be predominantly commercial. This decision is considered further in section 10.4.5.3 below.

A slightly different approach was taken by the High Court of Australia in *Commissioner of Taxation v Hart* [2004] (HCA 26). In their decision, the court played down the significance of whether the "wider" scheme or the "narrower" scheme was to be considered for the purpose of the legislation and held that under either definition the anti-avoidance provision could apply. This conclusion appeared to be reached by rejecting the suggestion that if a commercial purpose was evident in the wider scheme that this would prevent a finding that the dominant purpose for entering into the transaction was to obtain a tax benefit. In particular, the court endorsed comments in earlier High Court decision of *FCT v Spotless Services Limited* (96 ATC 5201) where the court noted:

> *"A particular course of action may be both tax driven, and bear the character of a rational commercial decision. The presence of the latter characteristic does not determine in favour of the taxpayer whether, within the meaning of [the general anti-avoidance provision], a person entered into or carried out a 'scheme' for the dominant purpose of enabling a taxpayer to obtain a tax benefit."*

In other words, although the above passage was more directly concerned with the sole or dominant purpose test, it suggests that it is misconceived to focus on whether a transaction should be defined narrowly (to emphasise the tax aspects) or broadly (to emphasise the commercial aspects) as the existence of rational commercial grounds for entering into a transaction will not automatically preclude the application of the general anti-avoidance provision. On this basis, it seems that establishing the existence of a broad commercially driven transaction will not prevent the application of the provision if some aspect of that transaction was undertaken in a manner designed to confer a tax benefit on the taxpayer.

Another interesting case concerning the definition of a transaction was *D 109/03*. That case concerned a company which purchased two properties from its parent company which had owned and used them in its industrial business for many years. The terms of the sale and purchase agreements provided that the consideration included a portion of any profits derived by the company from the redevelopment and sale of the properties. The effect of this term was that a portion of the development profits became deductible to the company but were treated as a non-taxable capital profit in the hands of the parent company. The Board of Review held that when considering

Sec. 61A it was necessary for the IRD to identify with precision the transaction being impugned or challenged. (That is, the Board appeared to consider that it was not its role to determine from the evidence whether a transaction for the purpose of the provision was present and, if so, to define that transaction.) At the hearing, counsel for the IRD insisted that the entire sale and purchase agreement was challenged under Sec. 61A, rather than just the terms of the consideration. On this basis, the Board of Review held that as the sale and purchase agreement, by itself, could not give rise to any profit, there could be no tax benefit conferred upon the company by that agreement and, as such, Sec. 61A could have no application. Moreover, they concluded that the sale and purchase agreement could not be ignored as without it there would have been no redevelopment and no profit. One can only speculate whether the Board would have reached a different conclusion had counsel for the IRD argued that the terms of the consideration for the sale was a transaction which, by giving rise to deductions arguably greater than would have been the case in an outright sale, resulted in a tax benefit. Such a conclusion would, however, have required a finding that a term in a contract can be a "transaction" in its own right and capable of giving rise to a tax benefit.

The decision in *D 109/03* was overturned by the Court of First Instance in *CIR v Tai Hing Cotton Mill (Development) Limited* [2005] (1 HKRC 90-150) but reinstated by the Court of Appeal (see CACV 343/2005), although the meaning of "transaction" and the role of the Board of Review and courts in identifying a transaction was not explored further by either court as they merely accepted the relevant transaction as that originally impugned by the Commissioner; rather, the decisions revolved around other aspects of Sec. 61A. Nonetheless, in the subsequent decision of *HIT Finance Limited v CIR; Hongkong International Terminals Limited v CIR* (Inland Revenue Appeal Nos. 14 and 15 of 2005) Rogers VP again concluded that the onus was on the Commissioner to identify the impugned transaction and only minor alterations to the defined transaction should be permitted by the courts. This approach, which of course was consistent with that of the Board of Review in *D 109/03*, is in contrast to recent judicial authority in Australia. For example the High Court in *FCT v Peabody* (94 ATC 4663) held that the "scheme" as defined by the Commissioner was not critical and that if the Commissioner initially identified a wider scheme, he was not precluded from subsequently relying on a narrower scheme or transaction within that wider scheme, unless it resulted in procedural unfairness or prejudice for the taxpayer. In doing so, the High Court effectively over-ruled the Full Federal Court which had suggested that the Commissioner should be held to the scheme as originally identified. This view was effectively also adopted in the later High Court decision in *Commissioner of Taxation v Hart* [2004] (HCA 26), where the court went on to emphasise that the erroneous identification of the scheme by the Commissioner will not by itself result in the wrongful application of the provision unless the tax benefit to be cancelled is not a tax benefit within the meaning of the legislation. The court noted that this was clear from the legislation where the exercise of the Commissioner's powers under the legislation does not result from the formation of an opinion by him, but from supposedly objective facts. In other words, where the objective facts and circumstances specified in the legislation exist, the legislation is to be applied and the Commissioner's only discretion is with regard to which course of action is adopted to counter the tax benefit. Accordingly, making a mistake in identifying the scheme will not prevent the application of the provision if there is nonetheless a scheme which generates a tax benefit and the requisite sole or dominant purpose is present.

Note also that a transaction does not need to involve multiple parties. In *CIR v Yick Fung Estates Limited; Yick Fung Estates Limited v CIR* [1999] (1 HKRC 90-096) and *Yick Fung Estates Limited v CIR* [2001] (1 HKRC 90-112) both the Court of First Instance and the Court of Appeal rejected the suggestion that a "transaction", for the purpose of Sec. 61A, necessarily involved another person and held that the unilateral act of a company changing its accounting date could be a transaction for the purpose of the provision.

10.4.5.2 Tax benefit

A "tax benefit" is defined in Sec. 61A (3) as the avoidance, postponement or reduction of the liability to pay tax. The word "tax" is defined in Sec. 2 and is restricted to tax imposed under the IRO. Accordingly, although Sec. 61A can apply to arrangements intended to avoid salaries tax, profits tax or property tax, it could not apply to an arrangement (albeit unusual) where, for example, the dominant purpose was to avoid foreign tax, but which also resulted in an incidental Hong Kong tax advantage.

It is also important to note from the definition that a tax benefit is not limited to the permanent avoidance of a tax liability, but applies equally to the deferral of a liability. Accordingly, a transaction which has the effect of moving a liability to a later year is just as challengeable under Sec. 61A as a transaction which seeks to completely avoid a liability.

Nonetheless, the definition, by referring to the avoidance or postponement of the liability to pay tax, seems to implicitly assume that there already exists a liability to pay tax (which, presumably, may be an existing liability or a liability which is expected to arise as a result of other transactions). To determine the tax benefit by comparing the tax payable to the position had the transaction not been entered into seems in keeping with the purpose of the legislation, although certain difficulties could arise in practice. For example, the tax avoided through the implementation of a transaction intended to generate a loss to be offset against other profits may be readily ascertained. On the other hand, in the case of a commercially motivated transaction which could be implemented in a number of different ways but is, in fact, implemented in a particularly tax efficient manner, the tax benefit may be more difficult to measure as it would require an assumption to be made as to how the transaction would otherwise have been implemented.

Nonetheless, the argument that for a tax benefit to exist there must be some pre-existing tax liability was firmly rejected by the Court of Appeal in *Cheung Wah Keung v CIR* [2003] (I HKRC 90-124), although the reasoning for this was not explained apart from the observation that no reference to "pre-existing" liability appeared in Sec. 61A(3) or any other provision of the IRO. Nonetheless, this case was followed, and arguably extended, by the Court of First Instance in *CIR v Tai Hing Cotton Mill (Development) Limited* [2005] (1 HKRC 90-150). In that decision, the court pointed out that unlike the more comprehensively drafted Australian provision, there was no requirement for the IRD to identify a pre-existing liability which was reduced by the transaction. As a consequence, the court suggested that any reduction in tax could be considered to be a tax benefit; indeed, in the case before them the court found that the payment of an otherwise deductible amount was a tax benefit for the purpose of the provision even though the Board of Review had found as a fact that the amount was commercially realistic.

On appeal, however, the majority of the Court of Appeal (see *CIR v Tai Hing Cotton Mill (Development) Limited* (CACV 343/2005)) adopted a less onerous view of the meaning of "tax benefit". In particular, Rogers VP read down the comments in the *Cheung Wah Keung* case and explained that they were a reference to the specific words in the legislation and did not address the conceptual point which is to be derived from an overall examination of the whole of Sec. 61A. He concluded that the deduction of an amount incurred for the acquisition of stock-in-trade could not be a tax benefit within the meaning of Sec. 61A unless that amount was inflated or otherwise not genuine. Moreover, Rogers VP noted that incurring such an expense could not amount to the avoidance of a tax liability since such expenses ultimately give rise to a tax liability (as the purchasing of stock-in-trade leads to the derivation of profits through the employment of that stock-in-trade in the taxpayer's business). Le Pichon JA shared similar views to Rogers VP although she noted that there was nothing to prevent the deduction of an amount from falling within the definition of a tax benefit, but that not every deduction was a tax benefit. In the case before them, Le Pichon JA concluded that the amount in question was not a tax benefit. Tang VP, on the other hand, adopted a broad view of the definition of "tax benefit" and concluded that the deduction of any amount, including amounts for the purchase of stock-in-trade, would be within the meaning of the term. In reaching this conclusion he noted that Sec. 16 and Sec. 61A serve different purposes, with Sec. 61A intended to strike down arrangements aimed at avoiding tax. Since such arrangements may rely on the deduction of amounts pursuant to Sec. 16, such deductions cannot be rendered outside the scope of Sec. 61A without reducing the effectiveness of that provision. Note that although adopting a broad definition of "tax benefit", Tang VP still found for the taxpayer on the basis of other aspects of Sec. 61A.

Interestingly, shortly after the Court of Appeal heard the *Tai Hing Cotton Mill* case, the same judges heard the case of *HIT Finance Limited v CIR; Hongkong International Terminals Limited v CIR* (Inland Revenue Appeal Nos. 14 and 15 of 2005) which also involved Sec. 61A and the meaning of "tax benefit". Not surprisingly, the judges echoed their views expressed in the earlier decision. In particular, Le Pichon JA reiterated her comments in the earlier decision and Tang VP again concluded that the deduction of any amount fell within the definition of "tax benefit". The reasoning of Rogers VP in the earlier decision focused on the particular situation of the deduction of the cost of stock-in-trade. In the *HIT Finance Limited* case, however, the issue concerned the deduction of interest and Rogers VP reluctantly concluded that this meant the same reasoning could not apply and the deduction of such amounts could amount to a tax benefit in certain circumstances. Nonetheless, he considered that where a company borrowed and on-lent funds at a higher rate of interest it would be difficult to see how the claiming of a deduction for interest could be considered a tax benefit. More specifically, in the case before him he concluded that the deduction of the interest would not amount to a tax benefit unless there were other grounds for impugning the transaction.

Clearly, there are still disparate views amongst the judges of the Court of Appeal as to the meaning of "tax benefit". It is likely that the resulting uncertainty will remain until the matter is dealt with by the Court of Final Appeal.

10.4.5.3 Sole or dominant purpose

Once it has been ascertained that a person has entered into a transaction and that transaction would, but for Sec. 61A, result in the derivation of a "tax benefit", it is necessary to ascertain whether "it would be concluded that" the sole or dominant purpose for entering into the transaction was to obtain that tax benefit, as it is only if this is the case that the powers of the assistant commissioner as laid down in Sec. 61A can be exercised.

Given that current judicial attitudes are such that it is relatively easy for the IRD to establish that a "transaction" and a "tax benefit" for the purpose of Sec. 61A are present, the sole or dominant purpose test becomes particularly critical in analysing the provision. This is, however, not surprising as it is probably intended to be the crux of the provision. Indeed, this was noted by Callinan J in the High Court decision of *Commissioner of Taxation v Hart* [2004] (HCA 26) where, when considering the sole or dominant purpose test, he said:

> *"This will, in my view, in most cases be the critical question. The answer to it, both as a matter of statutory interpretation and as the Explanatory Memorandum indicates, was intended to be the fulcrum upon which most Pt IVA cases will turn, because the definition of a scheme, being as wide as it is, will relatively easily be satisfied, and the presence or absence of a tax advantage will also usually be readily apparent."*

Note that the sole or dominant purpose test is not applied only in respect of the person obtaining the tax benefit. It is possible for the provision to apply where it is established that Party A entered into the transaction in order to permit Party B to obtain the tax benefit. This may occur where a person gratuitously enters into a transaction to permit another person to obtain a tax benefit. More commonly, however, it would apply where a person enters into a transaction in order to permit another person to obtain a tax benefit, with the recipient of that tax benefit compensating the first party for participating in the transaction.

An Australian case where this was considered is *Vincent v FCT* (2002 ATC 4490). In that case, the dominant purpose of the person who derived the tax benefit in entering into the transaction was held not to be the derivation of that benefit. The scheme, however, involved companies owned and controlled by the promoter of the scheme and it was considered that the dominant purpose of those companies in entering into the scheme was to enable the taxpayer to derive the tax benefits and, therefore, the Australian equivalent of Sec. 61A was applied.

Another interesting aspect in determining intention is whether the purposes of persons other than the person deriving the tax benefit, but who are not parties to the transaction, may be relevant. See, for example, the *Consolidated Press Holdings Limited* case where advice provided by an external accountant was considered relevant in ascertaining the purpose of the relevant person in entering into the transaction. That is, if a transaction is promoted by an adviser as a means of avoiding tax, that motive may be imported to the person acting on that advice. This view was followed by the Board of Review in Hong Kong in *D 94/04,* where after having examined correspondence from a bank and a firm of professional advisers (which demonstrated that the arrangement was marketed as a tax avoidance scheme) the Board noted:

> *"We also accept that attributing the sole or dominant purpose of tax avoidance by a professional adviser ... to a "relevant person" such as [the taxpayer] within the meaning of Sec. 61A is both acceptable and appropriate"*

In determining a person's sole or dominant purpose, Sec. 61A(1) requires that regard be had to seven specified matters. It is not clear why the legislation was drafted this way, rather than having a simple sole or dominant purpose test to be determined on a totality of factors approach. It may have been that the seven factors were meant to provide guidance as to what was considered a relevant matter to take into account, but in doing so it raises the question of whether the actual intention of the parties to the transaction is relevant, or whether a judgement is to be reached as to what would be concluded from an examination only of the seven factors. A related issue which also arises is what happens if a factor outside of the seven tests provides strong or conclusive evidence as to the intention of a party in entering into a transaction? A strict interpretation, however, probably requires the ascertainment of what a reasonable person would conclude was the sole or dominant purpose for entering into the transaction by looking only at the specified factors, irrespective of the actual subjective intention. Further, drafting the law in this way attempts to make the test more objective than a test which requires the determination of actual intention, and it is probably no accident that the seven matters cover most of the matters one would look at to ascertain purpose, other than the actual intention.

Nonetheless, the role of actual intention in determining the sole or dominant purpose with regard to the specified factors has not always been ignored. For example, the Full Federal Court of Australia in *FCT* v *Consolidated Press Holdings Limited* (99 ATC 4945) appeared to suggest that what was required by the provision was a determination of the sole or dominant purpose, and although this needed to be made with reference to the statutory factors, it could be done as part of a "global assessment" of purpose. More specifically, the court said:

"The section requires the decision-maker, be it the Commissioner or the court, to have regard to each of these matters. It does not require that they be unbundled from a global consideration of purpose and slavishly ticked off. The relevant dominant purpose may be so apparent on the evidence taken as a whole that consideration of the statutory factors can be collapsed into a global assessment of purpose."

This approach was interesting because it was contrary to the apparent requirement of the legislation to look only to the specified factors and disregard the actual subjective intention of the parties. In other words, the legislation suggests that a person's actual intention may not, as a matter of fact, have been to derive the tax benefit, but if a consideration of the statutory factors would lead to the conclusion that the derivation of the tax benefit was the dominant purpose, the provision will apply. By looking to a "global assessment of purpose", however, and then applying this when considering the specific factors, it is less likely that the actual intention would be different from the intention found under Sec. 61A.

Nonetheless, this approach appears similar to the (earlier) decision of the Board of Review in *D 44/97* where it was suggested that a Board of Review was not limited to considering the seven tests but was permitted to consider a person's subjective intention in appropriate circumstances. The Board went on to note that statements of subjective intention which were relevant to one of the seven tests could be considered. This appears to suggest that a subjective intention in isolation would not be relevant to determining a person's sole or dominant purpose, but may be relevant when interpreting one of the seven factors. On appeal, (see the *Yick Fung* case) the Court of Appeal held that if the Board of Review had been endorsing a consideration of subjective purpose then it was wrong, but noted that a determination of objective purpose could not be made in a vacuum and subjective intention could be considered if it helped ascertain objective facts.

In summary, the above decisions seemed to move away from examining the statutory tests in isolation and in doing so appear to be accepting that actual intention has at least some relevance, rather than looking to an intention determined solely on the basis of the examination of a prescribed set of factors. The High Court of Australia in the *Hart* case, however, appears to have reverted to a stricter interpretation of the legislation. In particular, the judgement of Gummow and Haynes JJ states that the provision:

"... requires the drawing of a conclusion about purpose from the eight identified objective matters; it does not require, or even permit, any inquiry into the subjective motives of the relevant taxpayers or others who entered into or carried out the scheme or any part of it."

Accordingly, at the very least it seems necessary for the IRD, the Board of Review and courts to properly examine and consider the seven specified factors, although in doing so there is some Hong Kong authority for taking into account the subjective intention of the taxpayer.

The seven specified factors set out in Sec. 61A(1) are:

(1) The manner in which the transaction was entered into or carried out (Sec. 61A(1)(a)). In other words if, for example, a number of alternative approaches were possible, the one actually selected may be indicative of the motive. However, it is inevitable that a businessman would select the most tax efficient alternative; indeed, it would be strange if he did not, whatever his motives for entering into the transaction in the first instance.

(2) The form and substance of the transaction (Sec. 61A(1)(b)). Clearly, if the end result could have been achieved without the addition of steps which achieve the tax benefit, this will weigh against the taxpayer in evaluating motive. Likewise, if a transaction adopts a particular form which is not reflective of the substance of the transaction this may indicate a particular motive.

(3) The effect from a Hong Kong tax point of view that the transaction achieves (Sec. 61A(1)(c)). In other words, if the transaction had not been entered into, would more tax have been payable? However, this must clearly be viewed in the light of other considerations because, for example, a simple purchase of an asset will reduce tax liability by virtue of depreciation allowances. It is, therefore, also necessary to ask why the asset was purchased.

(4) The change in financial position of the person obtaining the tax benefit that either has resulted or will or may result from the transaction (Sec. 61A(1)(d)). This, to some extent is the necessary additional consideration to (3) above. Obviously if there is no change in the person's financial position apart from tax saving, this will weigh against him in determining motive.

(5) Any change in the financial position of a person connected, from a business, family or other point of view, with the person obtaining the tax benefit, which has resulted or may result from the transaction (Sec. 61A(1)(e)). This is essentially an extension of (4) above.

(6) Whether the transaction has created rights or obligations between the parties that would not normally be expected to be found between persons dealing at arm's length in similar circumstances (Sec. 61A (1)(f)). This is perhaps the test to be applied in conjunction with (1) above. An unusual relationship may well indicate the motive for choosing a particular alternative although again, care would be required in order not to jump to the wrong conclusion.

(7) The participation in the transaction of a company which is resident outside or carrying on business outside Hong Kong (Sec. 61A (1)(g)). In this context, "resident" probably means the place where it is centrally managed and controlled (see section 10.1.2). Of itself, this consideration is meaningless. In connection with (1), (2) and (3), however, the inclusion of an offshore company, particularly in relation to (2), may indicate a motive to divert profits outside Hong Kong with no other motive than the avoidance of tax. Obviously the place where the company is resident and incorporated will be a relevant consideration.

It is interesting that the above factors specify the matters to be examined, but generally do not provide any further guidance as to what aspects of those factors are to be treated as indicative of a tax or non-tax motive. This is understandable as the evaluation of motive is not intended to be entirely prescriptive but requires a common sense evaluation of the particular circumstances surrounding the specified factors. This is necessary because something which evidences a tax motive in one particular case may not indicate such a motive in another case. For a case where the Board of Review analysed the application of the seven factors particularly thoroughly, see *D 86/02*.

None of the foregoing considerations, however, can be taken in isolation; all must be considered and balanced in reaching a conclusion as to the sole or dominant motive although, as noted in *CIR v Yick Fung Estates Limited*; *Yick Fung Estates Limited v CIR* [1999] (1 HKRC 90-096) and effectively upheld on appeal (see *Yick Fung Estates Limited v CIR* [2001] (1 HKRC 90-112)), not all of the factors may have a bearing on the question of the sole or dominant purpose of a transaction. This cannot be other than a matter of opinion in the final analysis and, except in the most blatant cases, is likely to be contentious, particularly if applied too widely by the Commissioner. When there are tax motives (as will often be the case in many genuine commercial transactions which are properly planned) and also other non-tax motives, it is necessary to judge which dominates. The

Commissioner's view as to the meaning of dominant in this context is expressed in *Departmental Interpretation & Practice Notes No. 15* (which is reproduced as Appendix 10) and is that the tax motive must outweigh all other motives put together. This is probably correct, although a view less favourable to the taxpayer would be a motive outweighing any of the other motives taken individually. The difficulty, however, will be in weighing all the motives as they will not be equally balanced. The view is also expressed in *Departmental Interpretation & Practice Notes No. 15* that because the relevant words in relation to the motive test in Sec. 61A are "it would be concluded", rather than "could be concluded" or "might reasonably be concluded", that the provision will only apply where the sole or dominant tax motive is clearly evident. Again this view is probably correct, although it is still a matter of subjective judgement as to whether a tax motive is clearly evident.

Apart from the general difficulties in weighing up the seven factors, particular problems arise where a composite transaction clearly has the hallmarks of both a tax driven arrangement and a commercial transaction. This situation may arise where a tax driven arrangement is dressed up as, or justified on the basis that it is, a normal commercial transaction or where a commercial transaction is being undertaken but steps are inserted in the arrangement which generate tax benefits.

The importance of defining the transaction for the purpose of Sec. 61A was considered earlier where it was noted that if a wider commercial arrangement has tax driven elements, a conclusion that the sole or dominant purpose for entering into the transaction was to obtain those tax benefits may be easier to reach if the transaction is defined narrowly than if it is defined more broadly. There have been a number of cases where the courts have considered a wider commercial transaction within which there were steps which gave rise to a tax benefit and have approached the issue by looking at the broad arrangement and deciding whether it was predominantly commercial or predominantly tax driven. Examples of such cases include the Australian case of *FCT v Peabody* (94 ATC 4663), *D 44/92* and *D 67/95*.

This approach, however, began to find less favour following the decision of the High Court of Australia in *FCT v Spotless Services Limited* (96 ATC 5201). That case involved a company which had recently been floated and had a significant amount of cash from the IPO process. It wished to invest this cash in a suitable short term investment, but wanted the investment to be tax efficient. One option was to deposit the funds with a bank in Australia, but the interest would, in such circumstances, be subject to Australian tax. An alternative investment was proposed whereby, in essence, the money would be deposited in the Cook Islands at an interest rate about four percentage points less than the Australian rates and subject to a 5% withholding tax in the Cook Islands. As a result of the withholding tax borne, the interest was *prima facie* exempt from Australian tax and the after tax return became more attractive than depositing the funds at a higher interest rate in Australia.

The Full Federal Court held that the anti-avoidance provision did not apply because the dominant purpose of the taxpayer was to obtain the maximum return after payment of all applicable costs, including tax, and not to derive a tax benefit. In reaching this conclusion, the Full Federal Court had identified the scheme as the proposal to invest the money in the Cook Islands, to pay the withholding tax and to take all the necessary steps to implement the proposal. Earlier in the judgement, Cooper J said:

> *"[C]an it be objectively said that the dominant purpose of the taxpayers in making the investment was to obtain a tax benefit? In my view it cannot be said that such was their intention. In coming to this conclusion I accept that but for the operation of Sec. 23(q) the investment would not have been made because of a liability to pay Australian tax on the interest earned. However, a decision not to invest in the Cook Islands would be made, not for the reason that Australian tax would be payable, but rather because the interest rate offered on the investment in the Cook Islands would be insufficient to admit of a rational commercial decision to invest in the Cook Islands in preference to Australia.*

On appeal, the High Court was critical of the above passage and said that the references on the one hand to a "rational commercial decision" and on the other to the obtaining of a tax benefit as the dominant purpose of the taxpayers in making the investment suggested acceptance of a "false dichotomy". In other words, the court was saying that analysing the sole or dominant purpose as being either the pursuit of commercial objectives or the derivation of a tax benefit was wrong as these alternatives are not mutually exclusive and, therefore, the presence of a commercial motive does not necessarily preclude a finding that the sole or dominant purpose for entering into the transaction was to obtain a tax benefit. The court went on to accept that the taxpayer was seeking the best after tax return and that the scheme adopted achieved this objective. Noting that the interest earned under the scheme was four percentage points below the bank rates available in Australia, the court found that a reasonable person would conclude that the taxpayers, in entering into and carrying out the particular scheme, had as their dominant purpose the obtaining of the tax benefit in the statutory sense. They noted:

"The scheme was the particular means adopted by the taxpayers to obtain the maximum return on their money invested after payment of all applicable costs, including tax. The dominant purpose in the adoption of the particular scheme was the obtaining of the tax benefit."

The "false dichotomy" between a rational commercial decision and a tax driven transaction was also recognised in the *Consolidated Press Holdings Limited* case where the High Court of Australia held that the general anti-avoidance provision could be invoked against particular elements of an overall transaction which gave rise to a tax benefit, even though the overall transaction was predominantly commercial. The court specifically noted that it was permissible to look to the overall transaction to understand how the particular elements which gave rise to the tax benefits formed part of a wider commercial purpose, but this did not prevent the anti-avoidance provisions from being applied to those tax benefit generating steps. In that particular case, there was no doubt that the overall transaction was to participate in a takeover battle in the UK, nor was there any doubt that the structure employed to transfer funds to the UK was ancillary to that purpose and explicable by reference to that purpose, but the adoption of the structure in the form in which it appeared was found to be explicable only by reference to the dominant purpose of securing the tax advantage which the structure provided.

Two cases were heard together by the Full Federal Court in 2000 which at first glance appear to be contradictory to the decision in *Spotless*, and are more reminiscent of the reasoning in the *Peabody* case. These cases are *Eastern Nitrogen Limited v Commissioner of Taxation* (2001 ATC 4164) and *FCT v Metal Manufactures Limited* (2001 ATC 4152). Both cases involved sale and leaseback arrangements promoted by an investment bank. At the Federal Court level, the cases were decided differently. In *Eastern Nitrogen*, the court concluded that the tax benefit (the obtaining of a full deduction for the lease payments) was the dominant purpose for entering into the scheme and, therefore, applied the anti-avoidance provision. In *Metal Manufactures*, on the other hand, the court concluded that gaining access to long term finance to replace short term borrowings was the dominant purpose and decided that the anti-avoidance provision had no application.

On appeal, the Full Federal Court heard the cases together and, in both cases, decided that the anti-avoidance provision had no application. The reasons for this conclusion were spelt out more lucidly in the judgement in *Eastern Nitrogen* where the court said:

"To show that a business which depends on financiers to provide the recirculating

capital needed for the operation of the business, has obtained that finance at a net cost, after taking into account provisions of the [Act], that is less than the net cost of obtaining finance by another method, will not, in itself, show that the dominant, ruling or supervening purpose of the operator of the business is to obtain the tax benefit constituted by the extent to which the deductible outgoings incurred in respect of that borrowing will be greater than the deductible outgoings that would have been incurred under another method of obtaining finance. That is to say, something more must be shown than that the business has obtained finance at the best available net cost after-tax before it can be said that a tax benefit has arisen to which [the provision] applies."

The Court then went on to note:

"None of the matters referred to by his Honour suggests an objective conclusion that by obtaining finance at the best "after-tax cost", the appellant had a dominant purpose in entering the transaction for the provision of finance of obtaining a "tax benefit"."

It will be appreciated that this approach is in apparent contrast to the *Spotless* case where it was held that the manner in which a commercial transaction was entered into could point to a dominant purpose of obtaining a tax benefit and, therefore, that the anti-avoidance provision could apply. Reconciling the *Spotless* and *Eastern Nitrogen* cases is, therefore, somewhat difficult. One possible way is to look to whether a transaction has been "engineered" by contriving an arrangement or part of an arrangement, or whether the tax benefits flowed more directly as a result of a normal commercial arrangement. To illustrate this, the situation in *Spotless* can be considered a highly contrived arrangement to achieve a particular tax outcome, in that the complex series of steps involved did not resemble a normal arrangement for depositing money. Moreover, the arrangement was marketed heavily on the basis of its tax consequences. In *Eastern Nitrogen*, on the other hand, the arrangement was a more mainstream financing arrangement with no steps interposed solely or predominantly for tax purposes. This explanation also holds true for the *Consolidated Press Holdings* case where the court applied the provision to steps which were inserted not for any purpose necessary for the achievement of the overall commercial objective, but predominantly to generate tax benefits.

The *Hart* case is the latest decision of the High Court of Australia on the question of when the anti-avoidance provisions can apply to a commercial transaction. The case involved a financing product aimed at taxpayers who were financing their own residence and also wanted to acquire or refinance an income producing investment (generally property). One loan was advanced for both purposes, but separate accounts were maintained in respect of the portion applicable to the financing of the taxpayer's residence (in respect of which the interest was non-deductible) and the portion for investment purposes. Further, although the taxpayer was required to make regular payments of a pre-determined amount, they could choose to allocate this between accounts. If the whole payment was allocated to the interest and principal on the portion attributable to the financing of the taxpayer's residence, the interest and principal on the other portion increased; this had the ultimate effect of accelerating the repayment of the portion on which no interest deduction was allowable, and increasing the amount of deductible interest.

The High Court in *Hart* endorsed the statement in *Spotless* that a particular course of action may be both tax driven and bear the character of a rational commercial decision, and that the presence of the latter characteristic does not mean that the anti-avoidance provisions cannot be applied. In doing so, they overturned the decision of the Full Federal Court, which had decided in favour of the taxpayer on the basis that the dominant purpose for the taxpayers entering into the transaction was to raise finance and, therefore, the provisions could not apply. In other words, the High Court chose to follow the reasoning in *Spotless* and, in doing so, overturned the Full Federal Court decision which was decided more along the lines of *Peabody* and *Eastern Nitrogen*.

Interestingly, in *CIR v Tai Hing Cotton Mill (Development) Limited* [2005] (1 HKRC 90-150), the Court of First Instance noted the existence of the two different approaches of the Australian courts and appeared to attempt to reconcile them by looking to whether the original motivation for the transaction was tax or commercial purposes. It is, however, difficult to reconcile the authorities on such a basis as although the establishment of a dominant commercial purpose in *Eastern Nitrogen* and *Peabody* was accepted as preventing the application of the general anti-avoidance provision, in *Consolidated Press Holdings* there was also no doubt that the original motivation for the overall scheme was commercial but the court still applied the provision to elements of that scheme which generated tax benefits. Nonetheless, despite finding for the IRD, the Court of First Instance in *Tai Hing* clearly considered that the *Peabody* and *Eastern Nitrogen* cases remained good authority; this is good news for taxpayers as it provides a basis for automatically avoiding the application of Sec. 61A by demonstrating an overall commercial purpose, which would not necessarily be possible if the authority of those cases was rejected in favour of the approach adopted in *Spotless* and *Hart*.

The decision of the Court of First Instance was, however, overturned on appeal (see *CIR v Tai Hing Cotton Mill (Development) Limited* (CACV 343/2005)) and the decision of the Board of Review reinstated. Essentially, the Court of Appeal reasoned that the finding of the Board of Review as to the sole or dominant purpose for entering into the transaction was one of fact which could not be overturned by a court unless clearly erroneous or perverse and that there was nothing to suggest that this was the situation in the case before them. Accordingly, the court held that the judge in the lower court was not entitled to substitute his own view as to the sole or dominant purpose for that of the Board of Review. Because of the basis for the Court of Appeal's judgement, it was not necessary for them to consider the issue of whether an overall commercial purpose will prevent the application of Sec. 61A, although nothing in the judgement serves to disturb the comments or reasoning of the Court of First Instance in this regard.

The comments in the above case that the question of a person's sole or dominant purpose in entering into a transaction was a finding of fact for the Board of Review and that such a finding cannot be overturned by a court unless clearly erroneous or perverse were reiterated by the (identically constituted) Court of Appeal in the subsequent case of *HIT Finance Limited v CIR; Hongkong International Terminals Limited v CIR* (Inland Revenue Appeal Nos. 14 and 15 of 2005). Given that this aspect is usually the crux of Sec. 61A, it can be seen that the Board of Review plays a particularly important role in such cases. Accordingly, bearing in mind how broadly the terms "transaction" and "tax benefit" are interpreted, it seems that provided the Board of Review acts reasonably in determining the sole or dominant purpose there will be limited scope for the courts to overturn a decision of the Board in Sec. 61A cases.

10.4.5.4 Countering the tax benefit

If an assistant commissioner concludes that there has been a transaction and the sole or dominant purpose was the obtaining of a tax benefit, then he may raise an assessment upon the person or persons who he considers obtained a tax benefit, so as to counteract the advantage. He may do this by either:—

(1)   treating the transaction or any part of it, as if it had not been entered into or carried out (Sec. 61A(2)(a)). In other words, if it is a transaction or series of transactions solely to create a tax deduction or deferral or to divert profits offshore for example, he may treat the transaction as it would have been without any or all of the steps

involved and so disallow in whole or in part the deduction or deferral or assess the profits that would otherwise have been diverted. There are obviously many possibilities for the assistant commissioner to counteract the benefit under this method which substantially allows him to follow the substance rather than the form of the transaction (see section 10.4.1). In fact, reference to the facts in *Furniss v Dawson* as outlined in section 10.4.3 gives an illustration of the type of situation in which Sec. 61A might apply and as to how the benefit might be counteracted by ignoring the step that gave rise to the tax benefit and assessing based on the substance; or

(2)   in any other manner that he considers appropriate to counteract the benefit (Sec. 61A(2)(b)). Whereas the first method entitles him to make an assessment on the basis that no transaction had taken place, under this second option he will accept that the transaction has taken place but can modify the steps to admit an assessment that has the effect of imposing the tax that would have applied had the transaction been carried out in a normal commercial manner.

The two options are sufficiently wide to enable an assistant commissioner, having taken a view as to the extent of the benefit obtained, to take whatever action is necessary to ensure that the person is asked to pay the tax that he would have paid had the transaction not been created or modified. The provisions contain no power to assess any more than is necessary to counteract the benefit; they do not empower him to assess an offshore source of income unless it would have had an onshore source but for the tax-motivated arrangements. Assessments may, however, be made for more than one year if necessary.

Note, however, that Sec. 61A(2)(b) only limits the assessment on the person deriving the tax benefit and does not need to take into consideration any tax paid by another person. Nonetheless, it does not appear to be the intention of the IRD to use the provision to raise more tax than would have been payable had the relevant transaction not been entered into. For example, in paragraph 46 of *Departmental Interpretation & Practice Notes No. 15* (which is reproduced as Appendix 10) the IRD state that assessing the parties in a manner appropriate to counter the tax benefit may involve making corresponding adjustments to persons other than the person deriving the tax benefit, where such a person was assessed in respect of an amount which, pursuant to Sec. 61A is assessed to the recipient of the tax benefit. Another example is *D 44/92* which involved the sale and of intellectual property to an offshore company which then licensed it back to the original owner (a

Hong Kong company). The Board of Review held that the payments made by the Hong Kong company were non-deductible; however, an assessment under Sec. 15(1)(b) and Sec. 21A had been raised in respect of the offshore recipient of the license payments, but the IRD agreed in advance that such assessment would be cancelled if the license payments were found to be non-deductible, thereby avoiding effective double taxation.

10.4.5.5 Case law discussion

In the preceding sections, many of the landmark decisions concerning Sec 61A and the equivalent Australian provision were discussed. There are, however, many other decisions on the provisions which can provide useful guidance when considering situations involving similar facts. Examples of some of the arrangements to which Sec. 61A has been applied by the IRD are as follows:

- Assignment of rental income to a loss company — *D 20/92*.
- Sale of intellectual property to a related offshore company with a license back to a Hong Kong company — *D 44/92* and *D 67/95*.
- Sale of trademarks and claim of deduction under Sec. 16E — *D 52/96*.
- Change of accounting date — *D 44/97* and the subsequent appeal of *CIR v Yick Fung Estates Limited*.
- Provision of personal services through a company — *D 39/00* and the subsequent appeal of *Cheung Wah Keung v CIR*, *D 47/00*, *D 153/01*, *D 154/01*, *D 155/01*, *D 86/02*, *D 2/03*, and *D 96/04*.
- Arrangements concerning availability of deductions for interest payments pursuant to Secs. 16(1)(a) and 16(2) — *D 94/04*, *D 97/04* and *D 98/04*, and *HIT Finance Limited v CIR*; *Hong Kong International Terminals Limited v CIR* (Inland Revenue Appeals 14 & 15 of 2005)
- Property redevelopment within a group of companies – *D 109/03* and the subsequent appeals of *CIR v Tai Hing Cotton Mill (Development) Limited*.

Out of all of the above cases, the taxpayer was successful only in *D 67/ 95*, *D 52/96* and *D 109/03*, with the decision in the latter case being overturned then reinstated on appeal. Additionally, the taxpayer was successful in *HIT Finance Limited; Hongkong International Terminals Limited* case but the matter was remitted to the Board of Review for further consideration and the outcome was not known at the time of writing. Apart from these cases, however, there are numerous other instances where the IRD has challenged an arrangement by applying Sec. 61A, but either the taxpayer has not objected and appealed or the matter has been settled by means of a compromise with the IRD.

Apart from considering the basic elements of Sec. 61A, case law also raises and deals with other interesting aspects of the provision. For example, it is sometimes suggested that Sec. 61A cannot, or should not, be applied in a manner whereby it operates to override a specific provision in the IRO. For example, it might be argued that provided an interest expense meets the specific requirements of Secs. 16(1), 16(1)(a) and 16(2), the deduction should not be denied under Sec. 61A simply because it was part of a transaction designed to obtain that deduction. Although such an argument found favour with the courts in Australia on a number of occasions in the 1970's, and indeed was adopted by the Board of Review in *D 52/86*, later court decisions have tended to take a contrary view. For example, in *CIR v Challenge Corporation Limited* [1987] (1 AC 155) the majority of the Privy Council noted that tax avoidance schemes generally depend on the exploitation of specific statutory provisions and, therefore, general anti-avoidance provisions would be ineffective if they were made subordinate to specific statutory provisions. It should be noted, however, that in that decision, Lord Oliver, dissenting, expressed the view that an anti-avoidance provision should not override a provision which granted a particular right to a taxpayer; in essence, Lord Oliver appeared to be suggesting that the principle originally expounded in *IRC v Duke of Westminster* (see section 10.4.3) that a taxpayer is entitled to arrange his affairs in a manner so as to minimise his tax liability, still has a degree of validity. Nonetheless, when the issue came before the courts in Hong Kong in *CIR v Yick Fung Estates Limited*; *Yick Fung Estates Limited v CIR* [1999] (1 HKRC 90-096) and *Yick Fung Estates Limited v CIR* [2001] (1 HKRC 90-112), the matter was decided not by reference to the earlier cases, although these were considered, but on the basis of statutory construction. In particular, the court held that the words in Sec. 61A(1) "… *or would have had but for this section* …" in relation to the conferring of a tax benefit, meant that the provision was clearly intended to operate to override any specific provisions.

Although Sec. 61A is much broader than Sec. 61, and indeed was introduced because of the shortcomings of Sec. 61, it must be remembered that Sec. 61 still exists. This raises the issue of the relationship between the two provisions and, in particular, whether they can both apply to a single transaction. This issue was considered by the Court of First Instance in *Cheung Wah Keung v CIR* [2002] (1 HKRC 90-116) where, on appeal from the Board of Review, the taxpayer contended, *inter alia*, that the Board had simultaneously applied both Sec. 61 and Sec. 61A to the transaction. The taxpayer argued that this was wrong in law because if Sec. 61 is applied to a transaction, that transaction must be ignored, in which case there would be no transaction to which to apply Sec. 61A. The court, although rejecting the taxpayer's argument and finding that the Board of Review had in fact considered Sec. 61 and Sec. 61A separately, noted that the correct approach was to consider the application of Sec. 61 first, and that Sec. 61A could only then be applied if Sec. 61 was found to be inapplicable. In the case before it, the court noted that the Board of Review had considered the provisions as alternatives and found that both were capable of applying to the transaction, but that Sec. 61 alone was sufficient to deal with the original appeal. The decision of the Court of First Instance was upheld on appeal by the Court of Appeal (see [2003] (1 HKRC 90-124)). The effect of these decisions is that the Commissioner is not prevented from arguing the two provisions as alternatives in any particular case and that it is possible to find that a transaction could potentially be struck down under either; nonetheless, it is not possible to actually apply Sec. 61A after having decided that Sec. 61 applies.

The stated policy of the IRD, as contained in *Departmental Interpretation & Practice Notes No. 15* (see Appendix 10), is that the Sec. 61A should "... *strike down blatant or contrived tax avoidance arrangements but should not cast unnecessary inhibitions on normal commercial transactions by which taxpayers legitimately take advantage of opportunities available for the arrangement of their affairs.*" Whilst this policy is undoubtedly intended to give comfort to taxpayers that Sec. 61A will only be applied sparingly, unfortunately the terms used are vague and will inevitably be interpreted differently by different people. Nonetheless, it is interesting to note that in *D 52/96* the Board of Review, in finding for the taxpayer, referred to the above comments and considered that as there was no evidence that the transaction was a blatant or contrived exploitation of the terms of the IRO and, therefore, declined to apply the provision.

Further information concerning the IRD's views as to the application of Sec. 61A can be found in *Departmental Interpretation & Practice Notes No. 15* (which is reproduced as Appendix 10). That document also contains information to be provided in connection with an advance ruling application (see discussion below) in connection with the provision.

10.5 Advance Rulings

From 1 April, 1998, the IRO has contained provisions, in Sec. 88A and Sch. 10, which allow advance rulings to be obtained on the interpretation of statutory provisions in certain circumstances. The purpose of the advance ruling system has been stated by the IRD to be to provide an increased level of certainty to taxpayers, to promote consistency in the application of the IRO and to minimise disputes between the IRD and taxpayers.

As is discussed more fully below, rulings are granted to the taxpayers named in the ruling, in respect of the interpretation of a specified provision of the IRO in relation to a particular transaction or arrangements. Accordingly, a ruling is binding only in relation to the person to whom it is granted and in respect of the transaction or arrangement identified. Nonetheless, in *Departmental Interpretation & Practice Notes No. 31*, the IRD have stated that they may (and, in fact, they do) publish selected rulings (edited to ensure that the parties cannot be identified) where those rulings are considered to be of general interest. The IRD cautions, however, that the published rulings are for reference only and cannot be relied upon unless the facts are identical to those in the original ruling application and there have been no changes in the relevant statutory provisions or case law interpretation of those provisions. Moreover, the IRD warns that it may not follow an administrative practice set out in a ruling if it turns out that such practice is used as a tax avoidance device.

Sec. 88A provides the statutory mechanism for the granting by the IRD of advance rulings and provides for the payment of prescribed fees by applicants (Sec. 88A(3)), although the Commissioner is given a discretion to waive such fees in exceptional circumstances (Sec. 88A(5)). Sec. 88A(4) provides that any fees paid by an applicant are to be refunded if the Commissioner does not make a ruling pursuant to the relevant application. This would apply where, for example, the IRD was not required pursuant to Sch. 10 to rule on a particular issue (see further below), but not where the IRD made a ruling but such ruling was different to that sought in the application.

Sec. 88A(8) exempts the Government, the Commissioner as well as any other public officer from any liability in respect of the *bona fide* exercise of any power or the performance of any duties in connection with Sch. 10. This is clearly intended to prevent any legal action being taken against the Commissioner or IRD staff in respect of losses sustained as a result of the giving of an unfavourable ruling or not giving a ruling at all. It seems unlikely, however, that the *bona fide* performance of duties under this provision would, in any event, very often give rise to legal liabilities for the Commissioner or IRD staff, as rulings merely express the IRD's interpretation of the law. Moreover, rulings are not binding on the applicant as tax returns can be filed on a basis inconsistent with the ruling (although such inconsistency must be noted in the return) and the matter pursued, if necessary, through the normal appeal channels.

Details of the operation of the advance ruling system are contained in Sch. 10, which is itself comprised of two Parts. The contents of each of these Parts are discussed separately below.

10.5.1 Sch. 10, Part I

Part I of Sch. 10 contains detailed rules governing the format of applications for rulings, the circumstances in which the Commissioner can decline to make a ruling or indeed is not permitted to make a ruling and the matters which are required to be set out in a ruling. More particularly, Sec. 1 provides that the Commissioner may, upon application, make a ruling upon how any provision of the IRO applies to the applicant or to an arrangement described in the application. Although the clause states that the Commissioner may make a ruling, because there are further rules which specify when the Commissioner may, or is required, to decline to issue a ruling, there appears to be little scope for the Commissioner to arbitrarily refuse to give a ruling; accordingly, a ruling can be expected to be granted in all cases except where the Commissioner has specific grounds, pursuant to Sch. 10, to refuse the request. Nonetheless, Sec. 1 specifies a number of matters in respect of which a ruling application cannot be made. These are the imposition or remission of penalties, the correctness of a return or information supplied by a person, the prosecution of a person or the recovery of a debt owing by a person.

Even if a ruling application is made in respect of a permitted issue, Sec. 2 provides that the Commissioner may decline to make a ruling if:

(1)   the application requires the Commissioner to determine or establish a question of fact. This would allow the Commissioner to decline to rule, for example, on a question of when a business commenced. Additionally, in paragraph 7(a) of *Departmental Interpretation & Practice Notes No. 31*, the IRD suggests that under this provision they will refuse to give a ruling on whether or not a gain on disposal of property is taxable (i.e. is of a revenue or capital nature);

(2)   the Commissioner considers that the ruling would require assumptions to be made on any matter. It should be noted that the need to make assumptions does not preclude the issue of a ruling, it merely gives the Commissioner the right to refuse the request. Indeed, Sec. 10 specifically permits the making of an assumption by the Commissioner for the making of a ruling, although Sec. 11 limits the power to make such assumptions by providing that an assumption cannot be made in respect of any information which the applicant can

provide. Moreover, Sec. 12(c) requires the ruling to state any material assumptions which the Commissioner has made in issuing a ruling;

(3) the matter upon which the ruling is sought is subject to an objection or appeal, whether by the applicant or another person. This prevents the Commissioner from having to rule on a matter which is already the subject of a dispute and may become the subject of litigation; or

(4) the matter on which the ruling is sought is the subject of a tax return pursuant to the IRO which has already been lodged, or is due for lodgement.

See also paragraph 9 of *Departmental Interpretation & Practice Notes No. 31*, where the IRD sets out a list of additional circumstances in which they will generally decline to give a ruling. Included in this list are statements that they will not provide rulings concerning the interpretation of generally accepted accounting principles or commercial practices, or on issues involving the interpretation of foreign law; it was not, however, necessary to include such statements in the document, however, as Sch. 10 quite clearly only permits a ruling to be given on the interpretation of a statutory provision of the IRO.

Further, under Sec. 3 the Commissioner is not permitted to issue a ruling if:

(1) he considers the arrangement which is the subject of the application is not seriously contemplated. Note that this requires a subjective exercise of judgement by the Commissioner;

(2) the application is frivolous or vexatious;

(3) the IRD is undertaking an audit of the applicant or an arrangement which is similar to the arrangement which is the subject of the ruling, for any period for which the proposed ruling would apply;

(4) the Commissioner considers that the applicant has not provided sufficient information in relation to the application; or

(5) the Commissioner considers that it would be unreasonable to make a ruling in view of the resources at his disposal.

If, pursuant to either Secs. 2 or 3 the Commissioner does not make a ruling, he is required by Sec. 4 to notify the applicant in writing of his decision and the reasons therefore.

If, however, the Commissioner does make a ruling in relation to an arrangement, the Commissioner is bound by Sec. 5 to apply that ruling in relation to the period for which the ruling was given, provided that the existence of the ruling was disclosed in the relevant return. However, it is important to note that a ruling given in respect of an arrangement applies only in respect of a particular provision of the IRO if that provision is specifically referred to in the ruling (Sec. 6). For example, a ruling may be issued in relation to an arrangement which states that a particular amount falls for deduction pursuant to Sec. 16(1) IRO. While, subject to the issues discussed above, such a ruling would be binding on the Commissioner in relation to Sec. 16(1) IRO, the Commissioner would not be prevented from denying the deduction pursuant to Sec. 17(1)(c) IRO if the amount was of a capital nature.

Since rulings will generally be given in advance of the implementation of an arrangement, their validity will, of course, be subject to the arrangement having been implemented in accordance with the facts as set out in the relevant ruling application. This is formally provided for in Sec. 7 which renders a ruling inapplicable in relation to an arrangement where the arrangement is materially different to the arrangement identified in the ruling, there was a material omission or misrepresentation in the associated ruling application or an assumption made by the Commissioner in making the ruling proves to be incorrect.

There are very specific rules as to the contents of an application and these are contained in Sec. 8. In particular, every ruling application must:

(1)   identify the applicant. Although this seems obvious, it must be remembered that an arrangement will involve more than one party and, therefore, it becomes important to identify the particular party to which a ruling is to relate;

(2)   disclose all relevant facts and documents in connection with the arrangement to which the application relates. The requirement to disclose facts is probably superfluous given that Sec. 7 renders a ruling inapplicable where there was a material omission or misrepresentation in the relevant application. However, the requirement to disclose all documents should not be overlooked;

(3)   state the provision of the IRO upon which a ruling is sought;

(4)   state the proposition of law which is relevant to the issues raised in the ruling;

(5)   provide any other information which the IRD may specify in writing for the purposes of the ruling application. Sec. 9 provides the Commissioner with the power to make such a request for further information; and

(6)   be accompanied by a draft ruling. In other words, the taxpayer is required to provide a first draft of the ruling sought.

See also Part F and the appendices of *Departmental Interpretation & Practice Notes No. 31* which sets out the information and documentation generally required by the IRD before considering a ruling application, as well as additional lists of information required in relation to ruling requests on specific issues. It should also be noted that the IRD has developed a standard form on which it requires ruling applications to be made.

Sec. 12 provides that a ruling must state:

(1) the name of the person to whom the ruling applies. This seems obvious, but it is nonetheless important since a ruling only applies to the person to whom it is made and not necessarily to any other parties to the same transaction;

(2) the provision of the IRO to which the ruling applies. Again, this is important since, as discussed above, a ruling only applies in relation to a provision expressly mentioned in the ruling (Sec. 6);

(3) the arrangement to which it applies. Again, this is important as Sec. 5 provides that a ruling applies only, *inter alia*, to an arrangement and, therefore, it is important that the arrangement be identified;

(4) the period to which the ruling applies. In *Departmental Interpretation & Practice Notes No. 31*, the IRD states that a ruling in respect of a particular arrangement will be valid for the period to which that arrangement relates. The same *Practice Note* suggests that where, however, a ruling is in respect of an arrangement that is intended to apply to similar arrangements capable of application over an extended period of time, rulings will be given for a period of no more than two years of assessment from the date of issue; and

(5) any material assumptions made by the Commissioner in relation to the ruling.

Once given, a ruling can be withdrawn by the Commissioner at any time by notice in writing stating the reasons for the withdrawal (Sec. 13). Nonetheless, if the arrangement in question has been implemented prior to the withdrawal, it will continue to apply for the remainder of the period for which it was granted provided that the person to whom the ruling was granted has complied with Sec. 15 (see discussion below) in submitting any relevant returns (Sec. 14(b)(i)). If, however, the arrangement has not been implemented at the time of withdrawal of the ruling, or the person to whom the ruling was granted failed to comply with Sec. 15 in submitting any relevant returns, the ruling ceases to apply from the date of the withdrawal.

Where a ruling has been granted in relation to a provision of the IRO and that provision is repealed, in full or in part, or amended during the period of application of the ruling, the ruling ceases to apply, to the extent of the repeal or amendment, from the effective date of the repeal or amendment (Sec. 16). In paragraph 28 of *Departmental Interpretation & Practice Notes No. 31*, the IRD states that where the provision of the IRO upon which the ruling is given is the subject of a decision of the courts and such decision applies an interpretation to the provision which is contrary to that adopted in the ruling, the ruling shall cease to apply from the date of that decision. This view, however, has no support in the legislation and, accordingly, would seem to be incorrect as well as inconsistent with the purpose of the legislative provisions.

10.5.2 Sch. 10, Part II

Part II of Sch. 10 deals with fees for ruling applications.

Sec. 1(a) provides that where a ruling is sought on whether profits are to be treated as taxable under Sec. 14 of IRO as arising in or derived from Hong Kong (i.e. as having a Hong Kong source), the application fee is, subject to the discussion below, $30,000. For a ruling on any other matter, the application fee is, again subject to the discussion below, $10,000.

Where the time spent by the IRD in considering an application exceeds an amount as specified in Sec. 3, additional fees calculated on the basis of the number of excess hours spent on the application are to be charged at the rates set out in Sec. 1(b). Additionally, Sec. 2 provides that an applicant for a ruling must also reimburse the IRD for any costs or reasonable disbursements, including costs incurred in obtaining external advice, in relation to the application.

For the avoidance of doubt, Sec. 4 specifies that the above fees and expenses are still payable where an applicant withdraws an application for a ruling, but only to the extent that those expenses are incurred before the Commissioner receives notice of withdrawal of the application.

10.6 Other Miscellaneous Matters

10.6.1 Board of Inland Revenue

The constitution of the Board of Inland Revenue under the IRO has been dealt with in Chapter 1. One of the prime functions of the Board is its power under Sec. 85(1) to make the Inland Revenue Rules. It can make any such rules for carrying out the provisions of the IRO and for the ascertainment and determination of any income or profits assessable under the IRO. It is not, however, a unilateral power because all such rules must be submitted to the Chief Executive and are subject to the approval of the Legislative Council (Sec. 85(4)).

Apart from the general purposes for which the rules may be made by the Board of Inland Revenue, Secs. 85(2) and 85(3) lay down some specific purposes which are:

(1) to set out the procedures to be followed on application for refunds and relief;
(2) to provide for any matter which the IRO requires to be prescribed;
(3) to prescribe what is to be included in the definitions of "Plant or Machinery" and "Implement, Utensil or Article";
(4) to prescribe any procedure to be followed in relation to an appeal to the Board of Review; and
(5) to prescribe fines on summary conviction not exceeding a Level 1 penalty in each case.

Once any rule has been made and approved by the Legislative Council it becomes, in effect, a part of the IRO and is enforceable as such.

The Board of Inland Revenue is also granted the power to determine the specifications and form of any IRD form necessary for the administration of the IRO (Sec. 86(1)). It is also required to specify the system, templates and particulars required to be provided under the electronic filing system (Sec. 51AA(2)) and the particulars required to be provided under the telefiling system (Sec. 51AA(3)). In order to fulfil these duties, the Board usually meets at least once a year, although this generally takes place through the circulation of papers. Where the Board has fixed the specification of a form of application or return, such application or return is invalid unless made strictly in the prescribed form (see *CIR v Mayland Woven Labels Factory* (HKTC 627)). It is specifically provided in Sec. 86(2) that where a form is purported to have been specified by the Board, this is to be taken as so until the contrary is proved.

10.6.2 Tax Reserve Certificates

These are a means by which a taxpayer can provide for future payment of income taxes and at the same time earn interest thereon.

The certificates can be purchased direct from the Inland Revenue Department or through a number of banks in Hong Kong and are sold in multiples of $50. The interest, which varies in rate with market conditions but is relatively low, is only credited where the certificate is used in payment of tax and not when it is encashed; such interest is, however, exempt from Profits Tax (Sec. 26A(1)(a)). The interest is computed from the date of issue of the certificate up to the due date of payment of the tax, even if presented in advance of that due date.

Where certificates presented in payment of tax, exceed (together with accumulated interest) the tax due, the IRD will issue a balance certificate or refund in cash, as required. Where only part of a certificate is required to pay tax, the IRD is required by Rule 7(1)(b) of the *Tax Reserve Certificates (4th Series) Rules* to compute interest on an amount of principal equal to the nearest $50 in excess of the tax due, (i.e. if tax of $2,775 is payable and a certificate for $5,000 is tendered, interest will be computed on $2,800) and the balance is refunded as appropriate.

In connection with the holdover of tax in dispute (see section 8.4), the Commissioner may order that a holdover will only be given on condition that a Tax Reserve Certificate is purchased to cover the amount of tax in dispute. Such a Tax Reserve Certificate issued in these circumstances, whilst carrying the same rate of interest, is much different in its application to the certificates voluntarily purchased to cover future tax liabilities and they are specially marked to avoid misapplication (Sec. 71(7)(b)). These specially marked certificates cannot be used for any purpose other than in settlement of the tax in dispute if ultimately held to be due (Sec. 71 (7)(e)) and when used in such manner they, quite logically, carry no interest (Sec. 71(7)(c)) because they are merely replacing the payment which should have been made at the original due date. Where, however, the tax in dispute is wholly or partly ultimately held not to be due, the certificate or part of certificate not used to pay tax may be applied in the following manner:

(1)   If the certificate is not more than three years old, the taxpayer may request a new certificate for the amount not used, carrying the same date and rate of interest as the original, which may be used to pay other tax liabilities in the usual way. Alternatively the taxpayer may ask for repayment of the principal amount and, by the same logic as previously mentioned, interest from the date of issue of the certificate to the date of determination of the dispute (Sec. 71(7)(d) (i)).

(2)   If the certificate is more than three years old, only the option of repayment with interest, as in (1), is available (Sec. 71(7)(d)(ii)).

10.6.3 Trusts, trustees and deceased estates

The IRO does not separately and comprehensively deal with the tax position of a trustee or of an executor of a deceased estate and it is necessary therefore to look to the law as it stands to see whether and how they are chargeable. There are, however, a number of provisions in the IRO affecting the powers and liabilities of executors, for example:

(1) An executor can be assessed in respect of income or profits arising to the deceased but no assessment (other than an assessment to additional tax under Sec. 82A) can be raised on him more than one year after the date of death or one year after the date of filing the Estate Duty Affidavit if later (Sec. 54). Note that *D 3/79* held that a penalty assessment under Sec. 82A cannot be raised against an estate because it is not a person. An assessment under Sec. 82A can however be raised against the personal representative personally if he has committed an offence. Note that if the *Revenue (Abolition of Estate Duty) Bill 2005*, which was before the Legislative Council at the time of writing, is passed in its present form, Sec. 54 will be amended. Under the proposed amendment, Sec. 54 will operate as at present in respect of a person who dies before the date of abolition of Estate Duty. In respect of a person who dies on or after the date of abolition of Estate Duty, no affidavit will, of course, be required for Estate Duty, and the time limit for raising an assessment (other than an assessment for additional tax under Sec. 82A) will be three years after the end of the year of assessment in which the person died.

(2) An executor cannot claim Personal Assessment in respect of income arising to the estate after the date of death except that a share of partnership profits arising to an individual after his death can be related back to a Personal Assessment for the year of death and the executor can make the election (Secs. 41(2) and 41(2A)).

(3) An executor can claim repayment of tax due to a deceased (Sec. 79 (2)).

(4) An executor is included in the definition of an "owner" in Sec. 2 and is therefore chargeable to Property Tax if rental income is received.

The question of assessment of a trustee to Profits Tax is more difficult and is covered in section 4.3.1.

10.6.4 Notice of no objection to deregister a private company

From 11 November, 1999, Sec. 291AA of the *Companies Ordinance* came into effect, thereby permitting a defunct private company to be deregistered, in certain circumstances, without the need for a formal liquidation. One condition for this provision to apply, however, is that the application for such deregistration must be accompanied by a written notice from the Commissioner stating that the Commissioner has no objection to the company being deregistered (Sec. 291AA(3)(b) of the *Companies Ordinance*). This is intended, presumably, to ensure that the Registrar of Companies does not deregister a company which owes taxes, thereby preventing the Commissioner from taking recovery action against that company.

To permit the Commissioner to issue such a notice, however, the IRO required amendment and, therefore Sec. 88B and Schedule 11 were introduced. Sec. 88B merely authorises the Commissioner to issue, on application, the notice envisaged by the *Companies Ordinance* on payment of the fee specified in Schedule 11. That fee is currently $350, but can be changed by order of the Secretary for the Treasury.

Chapter 11 ■

International Aspects of Hong Kong Taxation

11.1 Introduction

This book is predominantly concerned with the law and practice regarding taxes imposed by the laws of Hong Kong. Hong Kong is not, however, isolated from the rest of the world in terms of foreign trade and investment. Accordingly, this chapter examines some international aspects of taxation to highlight various issues faced by overseas enterprises investing in Hong Kong and Hong Kong enterprises investing abroad.

In particular, this chapter looks at some common features of tax systems around the world and how these may give rise to double taxation in relation to cross border transactions and the means by which such double taxation may be avoided or mitigated. But cross border transactions or foreign investment can present tax planning opportunities and this chapter also discusses some anti-avoidance provisions commonly found in domestic tax legislation which aim to counter such tax planning opportunities. Having looked at these issues in general terms, the chapter then considers some of the common tax issues which arise in the context of investment into, and out of, Hong Kong.

The material covered in this chapter is often loosely referred to as "international tax". It is important to remember, however, that taxation is fundamentally a domestic issue as it is imposed by jurisdictions on the basis of their sovereign right to tax residents of, or economic activity occurring within, the jurisdiction. In other words, there are no true "international" taxes, notwithstanding the existence of double taxation agreements between countries and moves to harmonise the tax systems of certain regions, most notably the European Union. As such, the term "international tax" really only refers to how a domestic tax system impacts on a transaction which has international elements. Nonetheless, the lack of consistency between domestic jurisdictions can bring about potentially onerous consequences for certain businesses or transactions and the role of a tax adviser in relation to such transactions is to understand why such consequences arise and advise on the means by which such consequences may be avoided or mitigated.

Except where specifically noted, the discussions in this chapter focus on corporate tax issues as this is the area of Hong Kong tax where international transactions have the greatest impact. The international aspects of Salaries Tax are, however, largely covered in chapter 3. Property Tax, being a tax on income from land or buildings in Hong Kong has limited international aspects although, as with the other taxes, where it is incurred by a non-resident a credit for the tax may be granted in a foreign jurisdiction (see section 11.2.3).

Finally, this chapter should be seen as no more than an introduction to a complex topic which is worthy of a book in its own right. The space devoted to the material here is very limited and hence the discussions touch only very briefly on some of the main aspects of the topic.

11.2 General Principles of International Taxation

Although each jurisdiction's taxation system is unique, many share common features and elements and approach various matters in similar ways. Accordingly, when studying the taxation of international transactions it is important to have a broad appreciation of these common features. The paragraphs below look to some such features, the problems they can give rise to and the issues which they seek to address.

11.2.1 Residence and source as a basis for taxation

The imposition of taxes is generally seen as the sovereign right of a country or territory. In other words, each jurisdiction's right to impose and enforce tax laws, although potentially limited by its own constitution, is generally respected by other countries even if those tax laws are different to those imposed in other jurisdictions.

Nonetheless, traditionally one jurisdiction has not assisted another jurisdiction to enforce their tax laws. This has meant that in order to be effective and enforceable most jurisdictions have limited the basis of their tax laws to:

- persons (either individual or corporate) who are either nationals of, or resident in, the jurisdiction;
- economic activity occurring in the jurisdiction; and
- income or profits from property located in the jurisdiction.

This has led to the common position where jurisdictions seek to impose tax on a residence basis and / or a source basis.

A residence basis of taxation is where tax is imposed on the income or profits of a resident irrespective of from where such income or profits are derived (i.e. where they have their source). A resident for this purpose is as defined in the relevant legislation, but for an individual it is usually determined by the person's particular facts and circumstances focusing on physical presence, maintenance of a home, family and social ties, income and financial activities and, occasionally, citizenship. More specifically, the tests usually look at where the person's home and family are located or where the person's centre of social and financial interests lay, but overlaying that may be a test of physical presence to deem a person to be a resident where they spend a significant amount of time in a jurisdiction notwithstanding that under the general tests they may be considered resident elsewhere.

For a company, residence is usually determined in the first instance by the place of incorporation. Because, however, such a test is easy to avoid without restricting a company's right to carry on business in the jurisdiction, corporate residence may also be determined on the basis of the place of central management and control, or sometimes the place of effective management, of a company. Typically, a jurisdiction will deem as a resident any corporation incorporated in the jurisdiction, or incorporated elsewhere but centrally managed and controlled (or effectively managed) in the jurisdiction.

A source based system of taxation on the other hand is where a jurisdiction seeks to tax income or profits from a source in the jurisdiction, which would typically include amounts derived from a business carried on in the jurisdiction and amounts derived from property (including, but not necessarily limited to, real property, financial assets and intellectual property) located in the jurisdiction.

The combined effect of these two bases of taxation is that jurisdictions commonly seek to tax residents on their worldwide income (i.e. income derived from any jurisdiction) and non-residents on their income arising within the jurisdiction. There are, of course, many exceptions to this common basis of taxation. For example, Hong Kong essentially imposes tax only on a source basis and many jurisdictions which adopt a residence basis of taxation grant extensive exemptions in respect of income or profits which arise outside of the jurisdiction. Nonetheless, it is the prevalence of these bases of taxation which set the stage for double taxation to arise in international transactions.

11.2.2 Double taxation

One of the main issues in the taxation of international transactions is the potential for an amount of income or profit to fall to be taxed in two or more jurisdictions; this is known as international (or juridical) double taxation. As was discussed above, jurisdictions commonly tax residents on their worldwide income and non-residents on their income arising within the jurisdiction. This immediately gives rise to a risk of double taxation as one jurisdiction may seek to tax an amount on the basis that it is derived by a resident of the jurisdiction and another may seek to tax the same amount on the basis that it has a source in the jurisdiction. Competing claims of this type can be referred to as residence-source conflicts and are the most common scenario under which international double taxation potentially arises.

International double taxation can, however, also potentially arise under other circumstances. For example, differences in the legislation determining the residence status of a person may mean that two jurisdictions each treat the same person as a resident; we will refer to this situation as a residence-residence conflict. Further, differences in rules governing the source of income or profits may mean that two or more jurisdictions each treat the same amount as having a source in their jurisdiction; we will refer to this as a source-source conflict.

It is also important to be aware that just as conflicts between domestic tax systems can give rise to double taxation, they can also give rise to the position where an amount of income or profit falls outside the charge to tax in any jurisdiction. Although this situation is undoubtedly less common, it nonetheless occurs and advisers need to be aware of the planning opportunities that such situations offer.

International double taxation is to be distinguished from economic double taxation which is the situation where the same profits are effectively taxed in the hands of two separate persons. This can arise where a company is taxed on its operating profits, but those profits are effectively taxed again in the hands of shareholders when the profits are distributed by way of a dividend. To avoid this, many jurisdictions exempt dividends from tax or operate dividend imputation systems where credits for corporate tax paid are attached to dividends. Economic double taxation can also occur where, for example, a transfer pricing adjustment (see section 11.2.7.1) is made in one jurisdiction but there is no corresponding adjustment in the other jurisdiction. It is important to note that economic double taxation can arise within a jurisdiction or across international borders and this presents difficulties in dealing with it on an international basis.

11.2.3 Relief from double taxation

Although the potential for double taxation in international investments or transactions is common, most jurisdictions accept that it should be mitigated or avoided as it potentially leads to distortions in investment decisions; this can in turn result in economic inefficiencies by diverting resources from where they would otherwise be most profitably employed. Consequently, most jurisdictions make provision for some form of relief from double taxation. This relief can be granted on a unilateral basis through incorporation into domestic law, or a bilateral basis through entering into double taxation agreements with other jurisdictions. Quite commonly, unilateral and bilateral relief in fact co-exist.

It is normal for unilateral double taxation relief to be granted by jurisdictions which tax their residents on worldwide income. International custom generally provides that this takes the form of the home jurisdiction (i.e. the jurisdiction of residence of the taxpayer) giving up, or modifying, its right to tax residents on income which has been subject to foreign tax in the source (or host) jurisdiction. There are a number of forms which this relief from double taxation can take, although the most common forms are the credit method and the exemption method. Under the credit method, the home jurisdiction grants a credit for tax suffered in the host jurisdiction, while under the exemption method foreign income which has suffered tax in the host jurisdiction is exempted from tax in the home jurisdiction. Nonetheless, there are other less common methods such as the deduction method under which host jurisdiction tax paid is allowed as a deduction in the home jurisdiction and the reduction method where foreign income which has suffered tax in the host jurisdiction is taxed at a reduced rate in the home jurisdiction.

As noted, under the credit method, a credit for the source (or host) jurisdiction tax is granted in the residence (or home) jurisdiction; in other words, the residence jurisdiction tax payable is reduced by the amount of the foreign tax suffered. The precise terms under which the tax credit is granted may vary between jurisdictions, although generally the amount of the credit is limited to the amount of tax payable in the residence jurisdiction on the relevant income. Although this concept is straightforward, issues can arise if the amount of foreign income is calculated differently in the source jurisdiction and residence jurisdiction. Typically such differences arise due to different approaches between the jurisdictions in determining the income attributed, and the expenses allocated, to the source jurisdiction. Similar issues can arise under the exemption method; that is, although it is accepted that foreign income subject to tax in the source jurisdiction is exempt in the residence jurisdiction, differences in the means of allocating income and expenses can mean that the amount of net foreign income for the purposes of the exemption in the residence jurisdiction may be different from the amount subject to tax in the source jurisdiction.

Whether a jurisdiction chooses to adopt the credit or the exemption method (or indeed any other method) of double taxation relief is a matter of policy in the jurisdiction. Most jurisdictions to some extent adopt as an ideal the concept that the tax system should not distort investment decisions, although such a concept can be interpreted in different ways. Some jurisdictions adhere to a concept known as capital-export neutrality which suggests that a resident should face no difference from a tax perspective between investing in their home jurisdiction and abroad. Such a view tends to favour the adoption of the credit method in order that the home jurisdiction tax rate is suffered on all income (unless the host country tax rate is higher).

On the other hand, some jurisdictions favour the concept of capital-import neutrality which suggests that a resident investing abroad should not be disadvantaged by being subject to home jurisdiction tax on foreign earnings as this would put the resident in a less competitive position than a resident of the host jurisdiction. Adopting this view tends to lead to the adoption of the exemption method.

Although common, unilateral double taxation relief can only effectively address double taxation arising under residence-source conflicts, albeit such conflicts are the most common reason for potential international double taxation. Because residence-residence and source-source conflicts arise as a result of differing domestic provisions, they are difficult to resolve on a unilateral basis as they would require one jurisdiction to ignore its domestic law provisions. Instead, such conflicts can generally only be dealt with on a bilateral basis (i.e. through the entering into of double taxation agreements), although it is important to note that such double taxation agreements also address residence-source conflicts.

Economic double taxation, being an issue which can arise in an international context as well as a purely domestic context can also be dealt with on a unilateral basis. This is usually done by exempting dividends from tax or adopting a dividend imputation system. A dividend imputation system involves giving a credit to shareholders for corporate tax suffered, although this usually applies only in a domestic scenario (i.e. where the company and the shareholder are resident in the same jurisdiction). Nonetheless, some jurisdictions unilaterally allow credits for underlying foreign tax (i.e. foreign corporate tax suffered by a company resident abroad but paying dividends to a resident of the jurisdiction) in certain circumstances, although this tends to be more restricted than a domestic dividend imputation system. As discussed in section 11.2.6.9 below, however, such relief for underlying foreign tax is generally not dealt with on a bilateral basis.

11.2.4 Double taxation agreements — general

Double taxation agreements (DTAs) are bilateral agreements entered into between countries primarily to deal with the issue of double taxation. More than 2,000 such agreements are currently in existence. Although DTAs are individually negotiated, they are typically based on one of a number of model agreements, the most common of which is that promulgated by the Organisation for Economic Co-operation and Development (OECD). This is commonly referred to as the OECD Model Treaty. The OECD Model Treaty was first published in 1963, but has undergone significant revisions over the intervening years. It is now published in loose-leaf form so that any terms can be revised, with the unanimous agreement of OECD member states, without the need to publish a whole new version of the agreement. Although the OECD Model Treaty as well as the various other model agreements, contain standard provisions, those provisions are intended only as a guide and when a DTA is negotiated, it is usual that variations to the standard terms are included.

The OECD Model Treaty is often considered to be quite restrictive regarding the rights of the source jurisdiction to tax amounts and, as a consequence, not favourable for developing countries which tend to be importers of capital and intellectual property. For this reason, the United Nations (UN) developed another model DTA which is intended to offer more benefits to developing economies by giving the source jurisdiction greater rights to tax amounts. Nonetheless, unless otherwise stated, in the remainder of this chapter discussions will centre on the OECD Model Treaty.

As noted, the principal purpose of a DTA is to avoid double taxation and this is achieved by modifying the rights of the respective jurisdictions to impose tax on specified types of income. In other words, they prevent a jurisdiction from taxing an amount, or permit it to tax the amount to a limited extent only.

As DTAs are international treaties between jurisdictions, and because they are essentially intended to modify the contracting states' rights regarding taxation, they generally over-ride domestic law. Care should, however, be taken in assuming that DTAs will always over-ride domestic law as a DTA is usually incorporated into a contracting state's domestic law through particular legislative provisions and such legislation can sometimes govern the interpretation of a particular term or clause in a DTA. Moreover, occasionally a contracting state will, subsequent to the implementation of a DTA, pass a domestic law which will affect the interpretation of existing DTAs.

DTAs are not subject to interpretation by international courts. As a result, there is no jurisprudence governing the interpretation of the terms of DTAs which can be applied in all jurisdictions. Rather, the parties to a DTA are generally required to work together to interpret a DTA in accordance with the customary international law as set out in the *Vienna Convention on the Law of Treaties*. Essentially, this requires that disputes be resolved in accordance with the mutual intentions of the parties when entering into the DTA. To assist in this process, the OECD publishes "commentaries" on the OECD Model Treaty. These commentaries, which are agreed by OECD member states, discuss the terms of the model agreement in some depth and contain examples of how the terms should be applied in various situations. The commentaries also, however, permit member states to express observations, or note reservations, about particular terms or interpretations of a provision of the model agreement. That is, a state may observe that it disagrees with a particular interpretation contained in a commentary, or may reserve its position on a term. By noting such observations, a state is putting existing and future DTA partners on notice that it will not agree to a particular interpretation. Similarly, by noting a reservation a state is putting future DTA partners on notice that it does not wish to include a particular term in its DTAs in the form contained in the model agreement.

Even where countries provide for unilateral double taxation relief, DTAs offer a number of benefits. This is because, as discussed above, not all instances of double taxation can be resolved on a unilateral basis. In particular, double taxation resulting from residence-residence and source-source conflicts cannot readily be addressed on a unilateral basis. Moreover, double taxation agreements ensure a degree of consistency in rules between jurisdictions and also contain other terms governing taxation between the contracting states.

11.2.5 Structure of double taxation agreements

As noted above, every DTA is individually negotiated although they are generally based on a model and, therefore, have many features in common. Generally they are comprised of chapters, within which there are various articles. By way of example, the structure of the OECD Model Treaty is shown in Figure 11.1 below.

As can be seen, the OECD Model Treaty begins by defining the scope of the agreement. This essentially involves defining the persons covered, which are residents of one or both of the contracting states, and the taxes covered which are generally existing taxes and future taxes of a similar nature.

The next chapter of the OECD Model Treaty deals with definitions. The relevant articles deal with a limited number of specific terms, most notably the terms "resident" and "permanent establishment". Some terms are, however, defined elsewhere in the DTA (i.e. in the article where the term is

Figure 11.1 Structure of OECD Model Agreement

Chapter	Articles	Topic	Examples
1	1, 2	Scope	Persons covered Taxes covered
2	3–5	Definitions	General definitions Residence Permanent establishment
3, 4	6–22	Taxation of income and capital	Dividends, interest, employment, capital gains, business profits, etc.
5	23	Double tax relief	Credit method, exemption method
6	24–29	Special provisions	Non-discrimination Mutual agreement procedure Exchange of information
7	30–31	Final provisions	Entry into force Termination

used), or may be clarified in the commentaries on the relevant article. The article containing general definitions also provides that where a term is not defined in the DTA, it is to be interpreted in accordance with the domestic law of the jurisdiction of the tax to which the DTA is being applied, although only where the context does not require otherwise. Accordingly, where a term is not defined in a DTA and the context is such that referring to the domestic law definition is inappropriate, it may be appropriate to look to definitions or jurisprudence of another jurisdiction.

Chapters 3 and 4 of the OECD Model Treaty contain the more important operative provisions under which the contracting states' rights to tax amounts, and the extent to which they may be taxed, are set out. This is followed by Chapter 5, which comprises the provision under which relief for double taxation is to be provided.

The remainder of the document deals with special provisions including mutual agreement procedures, which are essentially the means of resolving disputes, exchange of information, non-discrimination and administrative provisions regarding entry into force and termination.

11.2.6 Overview of key provisions of double taxation agreements

In the following paragraphs, some of the more important provisions of DTAs are identified and briefly discussed. These discussions, unless otherwise specified, relate to the terms of the current version of the OECD Model

Treaty and the article numbers quoted refer to the articles of that agreement. Again, however, it must be emphasised that every DTA is separately negotiated and almost invariably contains variations from the model on which it is based; accordingly, the contents of any DTA and the numbering of the articles will not necessarily follow those of the OECD Model Treaty.

11.2.6.1 Resolving residence-residence conflicts

As discussed earlier, one situation in which international double taxation can occur is where two jurisdictions each treat the same person as resident in their jurisdiction and subject to tax in that jurisdiction on the person's worldwide income. This usually arises due to differences between the domestic law definitions of residence in the relevant jurisdictions, although it can occur even where the definitions are the same. For example, it is not unusual for a jurisdiction to define residence in the first instance on the basis of where the person has the closest family and business connections, but to also include a provision to deem a person who is present in the jurisdiction for a specified amount of time to be a resident. Accordingly, a person may be resident in one jurisdiction under the general test while at the same time being deemed resident in another jurisdiction on the basis of their physical presence in that jurisdiction.

The resolution of residence-residence conflicts is important in terms of a DTA because in order to avoid double taxation it is necessary to allocate the primary right to tax to one of the jurisdictions. As we shall see, DTAs allocate the primary right to tax an amount to either the residence or the source jurisdiction; accordingly, it is critical to be able to establish the jurisdiction of residence of a person for the purpose of a DTA, and also avoid the position where the person is considered to be resident in both jurisdictions.

DTAs address this issue through the application of a tie-breaker clause. More specifically, in the first instance a resident of a jurisdiction for the purpose of a DTA is defined in Article 4(1) as a person who, under the laws of that jurisdiction, is liable to tax *"... by reason of his domicile, residence, place of management or any other criterion of a similar nature......"*. Articles 4(2) and 4(3), however, then prescribe rules for determining in which jurisdiction a person will be treated as resident for the purpose of the DTA if they are a resident of both jurisdictions under the domestic law of those jurisdictions. For an individual, these rules involve applying a hierarchy of tests which start with looking to where the person has a permanent home available to him, then look to the centre of his vital interests (or where his personal and economic relations are closer), the place of habitual abode and, finally, citizenship. If after applying these tests it is still not possible to identify the jurisdiction of which the individual should be a resident for the purpose of the DTA, the matter is to be dealt with by the relevant tax authorities under the mutual agreement procedure (see section 11.2.6.11).

For a person other than an individual, the tie-breaker provisions operate by deeming a person who is resident under the domestic laws of both jurisdictions to be a resident only in the jurisdiction where the place of effective management is situated. For example, many jurisdictions will deem as resident a corporation incorporated in the jurisdiction together with a corporation which is incorporated elsewhere but which is centrally managed and controlled, or effectively managed, in the jurisdiction. If a corporation was incorporated in one of the jurisdictions which was a party to a DTA, but effectively managed in the other jurisdiction, for the purpose of the DTA it would be deemed a resident only of the latter jurisdiction.

It is important to appreciate that the tie-breaker provisions of Article 4 apply only for the purpose of the DTA; in other words, the provisions apply only to determine which jurisdiction has the primary right to tax a particular amount of income and which jurisdiction is required to grant double tax relief. The provision does not deem the person to not be a resident of one of the jurisdictions under the domestic law of that jurisdiction. That is, for the purpose of the domestic law of the jurisdictions the person will generally continue to be a resident of both, but the existence of a DTA under which the person is deemed a resident of only one of the jurisdictions will mean that most double taxation is eliminated through the allocation of taxing rights and the granting of double tax relief. Double taxation may, however, still arise in respect of income not dealt with under the DTA or income arising in a third country.

11.2.6.2 Resolving source-source conflicts

It was noted earlier that double taxation can also arise where two jurisdictions each treat the same item of income or profit of a particular taxpayer as having a source in their jurisdiction. This can arise where a resident of a third jurisdiction earns income or profit which each of the two jurisdictions asserts a right to tax or, more commonly, where one jurisdiction treats the recipient of the income or profit in question as a resident, but refuses to recognise the amount as having a source in the other jurisdiction as a result of which it refuses to grant double tax relief in respect of that amount.

DTAs deal with this type of conflict by defining the source of various types of income, or at least by defining which jurisdiction has the primary taxing right and which is required to grant double taxation relief. This is not, however, dealt with in a single article. In some cases, the issue is addressed in the article dealing with the particular type of income. For example, in respect of business profits, Article 7 which is discussed below sets out the rights of a country to tax such amounts, and the requirement to give double tax relief, which effectively eliminates most source-source conflicts in respect of such income. (Note that the business profits article deals mainly with residence-source conflicts, but by determining which jurisdiction has the primary right to tax it also deals with the position where two jurisdictions cannot agree on the source of an item of such income.) Similarly, the dividend and interest articles (Articles 10 and 11 respectively) give limited taxing rights to the source country, with the source being effectively defined in those articles. For types of income or profit not dealt with by a specific article, Article 21 will apply and again by allocating primary taxing rights will generally deal with source-source conflicts.

11.2.6.3 Permanent establishments

A particularly important element of a DTA is the provision regarding the taxation of business profits. As noted earlier, jurisdictions tend to tax residents on a worldwide basis and non-residents on income from a source within the jurisdiction. With regard to the latter, most tax systems contain provisions defining the circumstances in which a non-resident is liable to tax in the jurisdiction. Commonly, for business profits, jurisdictions do not attempt to tax business profits of a non-resident unless a specified threshold of activity exists in the jurisdiction; this threshold is commonly referred to as a "permanent establishment" (PE). In other words, if the activity in the jurisdiction does not constitute a PE as defined in the domestic legislation, no liability to tax in respect of business profits will arise in that jurisdiction.

The domestic law definition of a PE varies between jurisdictions which, *inter alia*, is one reason why source-source conflicts may arise. For example, the foreign jurisdiction may consider a PE exists and, therefore, that they have a right to tax, whilst the residence jurisdiction may take the view that there is no PE in the other jurisdiction and, therefore, the source of the business profits remains in the residence jurisdiction. In this regard, it will be noted that the existence of a PE is used as a basis, or at least a proxy, for determining the source of business profits.

DTAs contain a definition of PE in Article 5, which serves to ensure consistency between jurisdictions when determining the rights of a host country to tax business profits and the requirement for the residence jurisdiction to grant relief from double taxation. The DTA definition has several aspects to it. First, it provides a general definition, then goes on to deem various inclusions and exclusions and, finally, contains an alternative test for certain situations where a PE would not otherwise exist.

The general definition in Article 5 refers to a *"…..fixed place of business through which the business of an enterprise is wholly or partly carried on."* This is extended to specifically include a place of management, a branch, an office, a factory a workshop, a mine, oil or gas well or quarry and a building or construction site or installation project lasting more than twelve months. Even if an activity constitutes a PE under these tests, however, it is deemed not to be a PE if the activities are limited to those listed in Article 5(4), which are essentially activities of a preparatory or auxiliary nature including the storage of goods, the purchasing of goods and the collection of information.

An alternative PE test is contained in Article 5(5) and provides that notwithstanding the other tests, an enterprise will be deemed to have a PE in a jurisdiction where they have an agent, other than an agent who is legally and economically independent of the person, who acts on behalf of the enterprise and has and habitually exercises in the jurisdiction an authority to conclude contracts in the name of the enterprise. It is important to note that this provision operates only to deem a person to have a PE; it does not operate to deem a PE to not exist. That is, if a person has a PE in a jurisdiction under the general tests, this will remain the case even if they do not have an agent who habitually exercises a general authority to conclude contracts in the jurisdiction on behalf of the person.

The existence of a PE in a jurisdiction has implications under several articles of a DTA. Perhaps most importantly, Article 7 renders any profits attributable to that PE to be taxable in the jurisdiction of the PE. Article 7 provides further guidance on how to determine the assessable profits of PE for this purpose and requires the adoption of transfer pricing principles in relation to any related party transactions including transactions recognised between the PE and the head office. This article also requires that in calculating the profits of a PE, all expenses attributable to the PE shall be deducted even if those expenses are incurred in another jurisdiction. For example, if the head office incurs expenses, including executive and general administrative expenses, which are attributable to the profits of the PE, these are to be deducted against the profits of the PE.

In addition to Article 7, the existence of a PE is relevant to Article 13 (capital gains), Article 21 (other income) and Article 22 (capital). Moreover, the existence of a PE is relevant to Article 10 (dividends), Article 11 (interest) and Article 12 (royalties) where the restriction of the rights of the source jurisdiction to tax the amounts does not apply where the amounts are derived through a PE.

11.2.6.4 Dividends

Article 10 deals with dividends and the basic intention of the provision is to allow the source jurisdiction, or more correctly the jurisdiction in which the company paying the dividend is a resident, only limited taxing rights. In particular, the article specifies a maximum tax rate which a source jurisdiction can apply to a dividend earned from the jurisdiction by a resident of the other jurisdiction. This is generally collected by way of a withholding tax.

It is important to remember that a DTA does not impose tax but only modifies a jurisdiction's right to tax and, therefore, even if the DTA grants the source country the right to tax a dividend, that right can only be exercised where domestic law already taxes such amounts. For example, although the Hong Kong — Thailand DTA permits Hong Kong to impose up to 10% tax on a dividend paid by a Hong Kong resident company to a Thai shareholder, no tax is actually imposed because Hong Kong does not tax dividends.

The limitation of the source jurisdiction's right to tax a dividend does not, however, apply where the owner of the shares in question carries on business in that jurisdiction through a PE and the shareholding is effectively connected with that PE. In such circumstances, the dividend is to be dealt with in accordance with Article 7 (business profits) and the source jurisdiction retains the right to tax the dividend fully in accordance with its domestic law.

The rate at which the source country is permitted to tax dividends is subject to negotiation by the contracting states. The OECD Model Agreement recommends a rate of 5% if the beneficial owner is a company which holds at least 25% of the capital of the company paying the dividends and 15% in all other cases. Nonetheless, this is one area of DTAs where there is a wide range of variations as a result of individual negotiations.

11.2.6.5 Interest

Article 11 deals with interest and, as in the case of dividends, provides that the source jurisdiction generally has only limited rights to tax interest. The OECD Model Treaty suggests a rate of 10%, although again this is subject to negotiation between the relevant jurisdictions. As with dividends, the liability to tax in the source jurisdiction is typically collected by means of a withholding tax, and can only be imposed where such a liability exists under domestic law.

A number of exceptions to the general rules regarding the source jurisdiction's taxing rights over interest apply. As is the case with dividends, the rights to tax are not limited where the recipient of the interest carries on business in the source jurisdiction through a PE and the interest is effectively connected with that PE. In such circumstances, the provisions of Article 7 are deemed to apply and the source jurisdiction retains the right to tax the amount fully in accordance with its domestic law.

Article 11(6) also provides that where the payer and recipient of interest are associated and the amount of the interest is excessive, the general provisions of Article 11 are to apply only to that part of the total interest which is not excessive. Accordingly, any excessive portion of such interest may be taxed in accordance with normal domestic law in the source jurisdiction; this may mean, for example, that a higher rate of withholding tax is applied or normal income tax rates are applied to the amount.

11.2.6.6 Royalties

Article 12 deals with royalties and provides that such amounts shall be taxable only in the residence jurisdiction, unless the recipient carries on business in the source jurisdiction through a PE and the royalties are effectively connected with that PE. In such circumstances, the provisions of Article 7 are to apply and the amounts become subject to tax in the source jurisdiction in accordance with its domestic law.

Although the elimination of a source jurisdiction's right to impose tax on royalties paid to a resident of a DTA partner is provided for in the OECD Model Treaty, it is not universally accepted or adopted. Indeed, in the commentary on Article 12, fourteen OECD member states reserve their right to seek to impose withholding tax on such royalties; additionally, 25 non-member states of the OECD have expressed their disagreement with the article and their desire to impose such withholding tax. This is reflected in the fact that many DTAs, including those based on the OECD Model Treaty, in fact grant limited taxing rights to the source jurisdiction in respect of royalties.

11.2.6.7 Employment income

Article 15 deals with employment income and generally provides that such income is taxable only in the jurisdiction of residence of the employee, unless the employment is exercised in the other jurisdiction. Nonetheless, the jurisdiction in which the employment is exercised is not permitted to impose tax on the relevant income if the employee is present in the jurisdiction for periods in aggregate of less than 183 days in any twelve month period commencing or ending in the fiscal year concerned, the remuneration is paid by or on behalf of an employer resident outside the jurisdiction and the remuneration is not borne by a PE in the jurisdiction.

Special provisions apply, however, in respect of income from employment exercised aboard a ship or aircraft operated in international traffic (Article 15(3)), directors' fees (Article 16), income of artistes and sportsmen (Article 17), pensions (Article 18) and income from government service (Article 19).

11.2.6.8 Associated enterprises

Article 9 is concerned with transfer pricing, which is discussed in section 11.2.7.1 below, and provides that where there are enterprises in each of the contracting states which are associated and are not dealing with each other on an arm's-length basis, the parties may be assessed on the basis of the profits which would have been earned had the parties in fact been dealing on an arm's-length basis. As we shall see later, transfer pricing provisions in domestic law typically authorise similar adjustments, and one effect of Article 9 is to ensure that the domestic transfer pricing provisions are not rendered ineffective by a DTA.

Additionally, however, Article 9(2) provides that where one jurisdiction has made a transfer pricing adjustment to increase the amount of assessable income in the jurisdiction, the other jurisdiction shall make an appropriate adjustment to the assessable income of the other enterprise. This is generally referred to as a corresponding adjustment. It is important to note that it is not automatic that a corresponding adjustment be made or that the amount of any such adjustment is the same as the adjustment made by the other jurisdiction. The requirement is only that an appropriate adjustment be made and the commentary to the provision envisages that a corresponding adjustment will be made only where the jurisdiction is satisfied that the adjustment made in the other jurisdiction is justified in both principle and amount. Accordingly, where a jurisdiction is not so satisfied, some level of double taxation may arise. Clearly there is scope for such double taxation where the two jurisdictions cannot agree on the transfer pricing methodology to be adopted or the comparable data to be used in ascertaining an arm's-length price for a transaction, although the commentary suggests that such disputes should be dealt with through the mutual agreement procedure thereby minimising the instances of double taxation.

11.2.6.9 Double tax relief

Double tax relief is provided for in Article 23 of the OECD Model Treaty which contains as alternatives Articles 23A, prescribing the exemption method, and Article 23B providing for the credit method.

Under the exemption method, any income which is subject to tax in the source jurisdiction in accordance with the DTA is to be exempt in the residence jurisdiction. The article goes on, however, to provide that the exemption method should not be adopted in respect of dividends and interest which have been subject to only limited tax in the source jurisdiction; rather, the credit method should be adopted in respect of such income. Additionally, the article specifically provides that where an amount is exempt from tax in the source jurisdiction pursuant to the DTA (rather than the domestic legislation), the exemption method should not be applied in respect of that income in the residence jurisdiction.

Although Article 23A generally provides that income subject to tax in the source jurisdiction shall be exempt in the residence jurisdiction, Article 23A(3) permits the residence jurisdiction to take that exempt income into account when calculating the tax rate to be applied to income which is not so exempt. That is, where progressive tax rates are adopted in the residence jurisdiction, it is permissible to add in the exempt income when ascertaining which tax rate should apply. This is commonly referred to as exemption with progression.

The alternative Article 23B deals with the credit method under which the residence jurisdiction is required to grant a tax credit in respect of tax payable in the source jurisdiction in accordance with the DTA. In other words, the tax payable in the source jurisdiction is to be deducted from the tax payable on the same income in the residence jurisdiction. The tax credit available, however, is limited to the amount of tax payable on that income in the residence jurisdiction.

It is important to note that DTAs generally deal only with international double taxation and not economic double taxation (except perhaps with regard to providing for corresponding adjustments in transfer pricing cases, as discussed in section 11.2.6.8 above). In particular, the OECD Model Treaty does not mandate the granting of credits for underlying corporate tax on dividends received by a resident of one jurisdiction from a company resident in the other jurisdiction. This is not, however, because such relief is not considered appropriate; but as a result of differences in opinion between states as to exactly how this issue should be addressed. Indeed, the commentary on Article 23A of the OECD Model Treaty suggests that the problem of economic double taxation should be addressed but, noting the practical difficulties of obtaining widespread agreement between member states on the issues, recommends that the issue be addressed in bilateral negotiations between states.

11.2.6.10 Non-discrimination

One aim of DTAs is to encourage investment between jurisdictions and in order to facilitate this DTAs attempt to eliminate any discrimination in the manner in which a jurisdiction taxes enterprises of the other jurisdiction. This is addressed by Article 24 which provides that:

- a national of one contracting state cannot be subject to tax or any taxation requirement in the other contracting state on a more burdensome basis than that faced by nationals of that other state in the same circumstances.
- Stateless persons who are resident in one of the contracting states shall not be taxed on a more burdensome basis than what residents of either of the contracting states face in the same circumstances.
- The taxation of a PE of a resident of one contracting state located in the other contracting state shall not be taxed on a less favourable basis than an enterprise of that state carrying on the same activities.
- Interest, royalties and other disbursements paid by an enterprise of one state to a resident of the other state shall generally be deductible under the same conditions as if they had been paid to a resident of the first contracting state.
- Enterprises of a contracting state which are owned by residents of the other contracting state shall not be subjected to any tax or tax requirement in the first mentioned state which is more burdensome than that to which enterprises of the first state are subjected.

11.2.6.11 Mutual agreement procedure

The mutual agreement procedure is prescribed in Article 25 and is in the first instance a process for the resolution of disputes over the interpretation and application of the DTA. More specifically, where a person believes that the action of one or both of the contracting states gives rise to a tax outcome which is not in accordance with the DTA, the person may invoke the mutual agreement procedure. This involves the person applying to the competent authority of the contracting state of which he is a resident (even if it is the other state which the person believes is acting contrary to the DTA). The term "competent authority" is defined in the DTA and is usually the taxation authority of the relevant contracting state.

On receiving such an application, if the competent authority is satisfied that the complaint is justified it can take appropriate action on its own to arrive at a satisfactory solution or, if it cannot deal with the matter itself it can seek to reach an agreement with the competent authority of the other contracting state. It should be noted that where the mutual agreement procedure does involve consultation or negotiation between the relevant competent authorities, although the taxpayer effectively initiates the process they take no part in the actual consultation or negotiation process.

More generally, Article 25(3) requires the competent authorities to resolve by mutual agreement any difficulties or doubts regarding the interpretation and application of the DTA and also to consult together for the elimination of double taxation in cases not specifically dealt with under the DTA.

11.2.6.12 Exchange of information

Article 26 comprises provisions under which the contracting states may exchange information relevant to the application of the DTA or their own domestic tax laws. To ensure privacy, the article requires any information passed from one contracting state to the other to be kept secret in the same manner as any other tax information obtained by the relevant tax authority. Essentially this means that the information can only be used for the assessment or collection of taxes, or in the course of court proceedings in relation to a tax dispute.

It is provided in Article 26(2) that a contracting state will not be obligated to provide information if doing so would require the carrying out of administrative measures in contravention of the laws or administrative practices of either of the contracting states, to supply information which is not normally obtainable under the laws of either of the contracting states or to supply information which would disclose any trade or business secrets. Nonetheless, Article 26(4) makes it clear that subject to the foregoing limitations, a contracting state cannot refuse to provide information requested simply because it is of no interest or relevance to that state. Finally, article 26(5) expressly provides that a contracting state may not refuse to provide information solely because the information is held by a bank or other financial institution or other person acting in an agency or a fiduciary capacity.

As with most articles, Article 26 has undergone many changes over the years and has tended to become more comprehensive over time. As such, not all DTAs have the same, or the current version, of the exchange of information article. Indeed, although Hong Kong's DTAs have all been negotiated in recent years, they contain an earlier, slightly less comprehensive version of the article.

11.2.6.13 Mutual assistance in collection of taxes

As a general rule, most jurisdictions do not normally permit the enforcement or collection through the courts of a debt due to the tax authority of another jurisdiction. This has opened the way for tax evasion through maintaining assets outside of a jurisdiction which is seeking to tax a person. In order to prevent such evasion, Article 27 was introduced into the OECD Model Agreement. This article is intended to permit one contracting state to apply its laws applicable to the collection of its own taxes to amounts due to the other contracting state. In other words, the article generally permits tax due to one contracting state to be enforced against assets of the debtor in the other contracting state. Nonetheless, to preserve the sovereign right of a jurisdiction to impose taxes, a dispute as to the validity of a particular assessment of one contracting state cannot be raised in the courts or administrative tribunals of the other contracting state even though the assessment is permitted to be enforced in that state.

Because this article contravenes the general policy of most jurisdictions, domestic law will often need to be amended to permit this article to be adopted. In recognition of this the OECD accepts that the article should not be adopted unless the contracting states are satisfied that it is in accordance with domestic law and policy. For this reason, many DTAs, even recently negotiated DTAs, do not include this article. For example, none of Hong Kong's DTAs adopt this article.

11.2.6.14 Other articles

Apart from the matters discussed above, there are various other articles in the OECD Model Treaty. These include:

- Income from immoveable property (Article 6)
- Shipping, inland waterways transport and air transport (Article 8)
- Capital gains (Article 13)
- Directors' fees (Article 16)
- Artistes and sportsmen (Article 17)
- Pensions (Article 18)
- Government service (Article 19)
- Students (Article 20)
- Capital (Article 22)

11.2.7 Anti-avoidance in an international context

This section examines some common anti-avoidance provisions which are enacted to counter tax planning in an international context. In each case, the planning strategy is identified together with the means by which jurisdictions seek to counter such strategies.

11.2.7.1 Transfer pricing

Transfer pricing is probably one of the earliest means of international tax planning and involves the shifting of profits between jurisdictions through intra-group transactions as a means of reducing the overall burden. This is potentially attractive because different jurisdictions have different tax rates and different bases of determining assessable income or profit. Accordingly, in the simplest scenario, if a group manufactures a product in a company resident in a low tax jurisdiction and sells it through a retailing subsidiary in a high tax jurisdiction, the total group profit will be apportioned between the two jurisdictions on a basis determined by the price at which the product is transferred from the manufacturing company to the retailing company. By setting this price high, more profit is derived in the low tax jurisdiction of the manufacturing company and less profit is derived in the high tax jurisdiction of the retailing company.

A more complex variation of this is to establish another subsidiary, in a low tax country such as a traditional tax haven, which is interposed in the transaction between the manufacturing and retailing companies. That is, the new interposed subsidiary purchases the product from the manufacturing company and sells it to the retailing company, thereby shifting a portion of the profits which would otherwise be taxable in one of those jurisdictions to the tax haven subsidiary.

These strategies may be countered in a number of ways, including (but not limited to) specific transfer pricing provisions, general anti-avoidance rules or double taxation agreements. Typically, however, jurisdictions enact specific transfer pricing rules to ensure that they have the legislative power to make transfer pricing adjustments where appropriate; that is, to increase income or reduce expenses for tax purposes where they believe related parties are not dealing on an arm's-length basis. Such adjustments may comprise both primary adjustments and secondary adjustments.

A primary adjustment is simply where income is increased or expenses are reduced, thereby increasing the net assessable income. A secondary adjustment occurs, for example, where the party which has had its profits increased is deemed to have paid a dividend out of those additional profits and a withholding tax liability is assessed, or the party is deemed to have made a contribution to the capital of the related party and a capital duty liability is imposed. Additionally, it should be noted that any excessive payments of interest or royalties may lose the benefit of reduced rates of tax under a DTA.

In addition to primary and secondary adjustments, an adjustment to a transfer price may result in interest on the additional tax as well as penalties and may also result in increased scrutiny of other transactions. Moreover, an adjustment may result in double taxation due to the fact that there may not be a corresponding reduction in assessable income in the other jurisdiction, or not in respect of the full amount of the adjustment in the other jurisdiction. In particular, although as discussed in section 11.2.6.8 above, Article 9(2) of the OECD Model Treaty provides for such corresponding adjustments, it requires both jurisdictions to agree on the methodology and comparable data for determining an arm's-length price and a failure to agree will likely result in some level of double taxation.

A key element of transfer pricing provisions is the establishment of arm's-length prices, or the allocation of overall profits of a group of related parties on an arm's-length basis. There are various means by which such arm's-length prices or allocations can be made, although no single method can be applied or is applicable in every situation. Most jurisdictions therefore permit the adoption of various different methods depending on the circumstances.

Because transfer pricing is generally seen as a global issue for tax authorities and in any particular case has application across two or more jurisdictions, the OECD has taken an interest in the issue. In particular, OECD has published, on the basis of its work, various reports and guidelines for dealing with transfer pricing. The latest comprehensive report is *Transfer Pricing Guidelines for Multinational Enterprises and Tax Administrations* which was published in July 1995, although a number of revisions and additions have subsequently been made. This report, *inter alia*, sets out the various methods which the OECD considers acceptable for determining arm's-length prices or profit allocations. Although a full discussion is beyond the scope of this book, these methods are divided into "traditional transaction methods" and "transactional profit methods". The traditional transaction methods are preferred and comprise the comparable uncontrolled price, resale price and cost plus methods, all of which aim to identify an arm's-length price for particular transactions. The transactional profit methods, which comprise the profit split method and the transactional net margin method, in broad terms attempt to allocate overall profits between the related parties, rather than determining transfer prices for individual transactions.

Nonetheless, the OECD is of the view that transactional profit methods should be used only as a last resort where traditional transaction methods are inappropriate or cannot be applied. This is often the case where valuable intellectual property is included in the goods or services being transferred.

The OECD report contains extensive discussions of the various methods for determining transfer prices or allocating profits and the issues relevant to particular types of transactions, but also deals with many other aspects of transfer pricing. For example, it discusses appropriate procedures to be adopted by tax administrations in avoiding and dealing with transfer pricing disputes both between taxpayers and a tax administration and between tax administrations, particularly where adjustments are made pursuant to Article 9 of the OECD Model Treaty.

Additionally, through a chapter added in 1998, the OECD report considers the concept of cost-contribution agreements. In essence, these are agreements whereby different members of a group jointly develop intellectual property. By doing this, each member obtains the rights to the intellectual property and no transfer of those rights between members is required; this reduces the risk of transfer pricing adjustments. Nonetheless, such agreements could still theoretically be used to obtain favourable tax outcomes and the OECD report sets guidelines to determine whether a particular cost contribution agreement should be considered consistent with the general arm's-length requirement for intra-group transactions.

Furthermore, the OECD report also discusses the issue of documentation and provides guidance to tax administrations and taxpayers with regard to what documentation is relevant or appropriate to establish arm's-length prices for transactions in order to avoid or resolve disputes. The report favours an approach of requiring taxpayers to prepare contemporaneous documentation in support of their transfer pricing policies. Such a requirement has been adopted by many tax jurisdictions and typically requires a group to undertake a full transfer pricing study to support the transfer pricing policies adopted. Such a study would generally identify and describe:

- the transaction together with its specific terms and conditions;
- the relationship between the parties, the functions performed, the assets used and the risks assumed by each party;
- the transfer pricing methodology adopted and the comparable data used (together with an assessment of the comparability of that data and any adjustments required to enhance that comparability); and
- any assumptions, strategies and policies affecting the transfer price.

Although such studies are often a statutory requirement, even where they are not they can remain a very valuable exercise for taxpayers as they may protect the taxpayer from penalties if a transfer pricing adjustment is made. Moreover, they may reduce the time taken to deal with a transfer pricing dispute and possibly shift the onus of proof to the tax authority to demonstrate that a transfer price adopted is incorrect.

Although a contemporaneous transfer pricing study has many advantages, it will not generally guarantee that a tax authority will not seek to make an adjustment. A higher level of certainty can, however, be obtained by entering into an advance pricing agreement (APA). An APA is an agreement between a taxpayer group and a tax authority as to the determination of transfer prices in relation to a specified group of transactions. An APA may be entered into with only a single tax administration, in which case it is referred to as unilateral, or with two or more tax authorities (i.e. it may be bilateral or multilateral). Which is appropriate depends in any particular case on the taxpayer group's operations, transactions and whether relevant DTAs exist. Often only a unilateral APA will be appropriate where, for example, there is manufacturing in a low tax jurisdiction with the product all being sold to a related party in a higher tax jurisdiction. A bilateral or multilateral APA on the other hand may be appropriate if a manufacturing company in a low tax jurisdiction is selling to related parties in a number of high tax jurisdictions, or in the case of global trading of financial instruments by a financial institution, being a situation which can give rise to difficulties regarding the allocation of the overall profit between jurisdictions.

APAs are intended to be binding agreements, although they are generally prospective rather than retrospective and also are typically valid only for a specified period. The existence of an APA, however, does not guarantee that a transfer pricing audit will not be undertaken by the tax authority, although the purpose of such an audit would generally be to ensure compliance with the APA. Also, although intended to be binding, a tax authority will generally retain the power to cancel an APA if it found that it is not being correctly implemented, or that there were instances of fraud or misrepresentation during the negotiation process.

11.2.7.2 Controlled Foreign Corporation (CFC) Rules

As noted earlier, it is common for jurisdictions to tax residents on their worldwide income, while allowing some form of relief for foreign taxes suffered in order to eliminate or mitigate double taxation. The liability to tax on foreign income, however, can in the absence of countering legislation be avoided, or at least deferred, by arranging for it to be derived through a non-resident subsidiary. That is, if a resident of a particular jurisdiction (country A) expects to derive income from a lower tax jurisdiction (country B), rather than deriving it directly they may choose to establish a subsidiary which is resident in country B (or indeed another low tax jurisdiction) through which the relevant income would be derived. In general terms, the profits of a subsidiary in country B would not be taxable in country A until remitted by way of a dividend. Accordingly, the adoption of such a structure may permit the deferral, possibly for an indefinite period, of country A tax in respect of the profits of the subsidiary in country B. Such structures can be particularly effective and straightforward to establish and operate for the purpose of holding passive assets, such as bank deposits, shares and intellectual property.

In order to prevent such deferral, many jurisdictions have enacted controlled foreign corporation (CFC) rules. The intention of these rules is to impose tax on the shareholders of certain non-resident companies in respect of that shareholder's interest in the undistributed profits of such non-resident. Note that the rules do not aim to impose tax on the non-resident company, as to do so would arguably mean that a country was trying to impose an extra-territorial tax; rather, the rules seek to tax the underlying owner(s) of the non-resident company on their share of the undistributed profits. Such rules are usually quite complex as most jurisdictions recognise that they need to strike a balance between preventing the deferral but without rendering foreign subsidiaries of their residents uncompetitive by subjecting them to higher rates of tax than other companies doing business in the same market. Accordingly, the rules tend to be more concerned with arrangements under which income from passive assets is derived through such offshore companies.

CFC rules, being domestic law provisions designed to achieve a particular outcome in the context of the domestic tax system, vary significantly between jurisdictions. Nonetheless, there are a number of basic features of such provisions which can be examined in order to appreciate the differences between those systems.

The starting point with CFC rules is to define the companies or other entities to which the provisions apply. As the name suggests, the provisions are generally concerned with non-resident companies "controlled" by residents of the jurisdiction imposing the rules. The relevance of the control requirement is that in the absence of control the ability of the owners to prevent distributions in order to obtain the deferral benefit is limited. Control can be defined in various ways but typically it involves setting a threshold of ownership of the shares of the company. That is, control by residents of a jurisdiction may be defined as being where more than 50% of the share capital is beneficially owned by residents of the jurisdiction. But also relevant to the question of control is the number of residents of the jurisdiction in whose hands control lies. For example, if the shares of the company are held by a large number of unrelated residents of the jurisdiction, it is possible that no single shareholder or group of shareholders could be said to control the company. Accordingly, the control definition may look to whether the 50% of share ownership is in the hands of a limited number of shareholders or groups of related shareholders. That is, the test may be refined to be, for example, whether five or fewer residents, together with their associates, own at least 50% of the share capital of the company. Additionally, the rules need also to be able to deal with the issues of different classes of shares including non-participating or non-voting shares, direct and indirect ownership and ownership through nominee or trust arrangements.

Having identified whether a company is a CFC, the next step is to identify the shareholders which are to be assessed in respect of that company's profits. This could be all resident shareholders who have an interest in the company, it may be only corporate shareholders or it may be shareholders who have a minimum ownership interest. With regard to the latter, it might be that the interests of all resident shareholders are taken into account when determining whether a company is a CFC, but only shareholders with, say, a 10% or greater shareholding are assessed in respect of a portion of the CFC's profits. The rules also need to be able to deal with the position where there is ownership for only part of the fiscal year and in particular whether an apportionment of the attributable profits should be made or whether only shareholders at the end of the fiscal year are assessed.

The next aspect of CFC rules to be considered is what profits of the CFC are to be attributed to the attributable shareholders. As noted earlier, in enacting CFC rules, a jurisdiction will generally recognise a need to balance the countering of a possible tax deferral with the need to ensure genuine businesses do not become uncompetitive. Consequently, profits from active (as opposed to passive) business activities may be exempt from the attribution, although sometimes only to the extent that the profits are derived from transactions with non-related parties. That is, although income from active business such as a trading transaction may be exempt from the provisions, a profit from a trading transaction where either the buyer or seller is related may not enjoy that exemption. Moreover, when income of a CFC is assessed to an attributable shareholder, a credit for any foreign tax suffered by the CFC is normally granted. Accordingly, there may be exemptions for CFCs resident in jurisdictions where the tax rate is similar to or greater than that of the jurisdiction imposing the CFC regime.

Apart from excluding from attribution income from particular jurisdictions or activities, exemptions from CFC rules may be granted for other reasons. For example, the UK grants an exemption where a certain percentage of the CFCs profits are distributed each year by way of dividend as in such circumstances the tax deferral is limited. The UK also grants an exemption where the shareholder of the CFC is a publicly listed company, although it is not clear why such an exemption is considered justified. Exemptions may also be given where it can be established that the intention of setting up the CFC was other than to obtain a deferral, given the difficulty of objectively establishing a taxpayer's intention, however, such an approach appears to risk significantly undermining the CFC rules. On the other hand, in practical terms it allows the relevant tax authority a broad discretion to exempt a taxpayer from the provisions where the tax authority considers it appropriate. Finally, some countries provide a *de minimus* exemption; that is an exemption where the shareholding or the attributable income is below a specified level. This is justified on the basis that the compliance costs of a CFC regime can be significant and it is inequitable for taxpayers to be required to bear such costs when their attributable income is minimal.

CFC rules also need to be able to deal with subsequent distributions of profits which have been attributable to shareholders. As the intention of CFC provisions is to prevent tax deferrals, rather than to impose double taxation, it is important that subsequent distributions of income previously attributed to shareholders are not taxed again. Although this is straightforward in theory, practical difficulties can arise because distributions may comprise both attributed and non-attributed income; additionally, the profits of some years may have been attributed but not others as the company may not have been a CFC in some years and the relevant shareholder may not have been an attributable shareholder in some years because of varying levels of shareholding.

11.2.7.3 Thin capitalisation rules

When an enterprise is considering making an investment in a foreign jurisdiction, particularly where the investment is in the form of a subsidiary company, one of the issues to be considered is whether the investment should be funded with debt or with equity. This funding decision is in many cases driven by commercial considerations; however, the tax consequences of the decision may be very significant. In particular, if an investment is financed by way of equity, the return to the investor is in the form of dividends. The payment of a dividend is generally not a deductible expense, but may attract significant rates of withholding tax and may be assessable to the recipient without any credit for underlying corporate tax paid (depending on the tax system in the jurisdiction of residence of the shareholder). The non-deductibility of a dividend paid combined with the assessability of the dividend to the shareholder means that economic double taxation arises.

Where an investment is financed with debt advanced by the investor, on the other hand, the return to the investor is in the form of interest. Such interest is generally deductible and subject to lower rates of withholding tax than dividends. Although the interest may be assessable to the investor, economic double taxation is generally avoided. Moreover, sometimes structures can be put in place which result in a deferral or avoidance of an assessment to tax on the interest paid by, for example, deriving the amount through an associate subject to no or low rates of tax or through the use of a hybrid instrument or entity.

As a result of the differences between the tax consequences of debt and equity funding, there is often a preference for funding an investment in a foreign jurisdiction in the form of debt rather than equity. As most corporate groups are, however, funded with a mixture of debt and equity many jurisdictions consider that funding investments in their jurisdiction with excessive amounts of debt unfairly erodes their ability to collect tax from the economic activity taking place in that jurisdiction. Such arrangements can be countered by administrative rulings, general anti-avoidance provisions or specific legislative provisions.

Specific provisions targeting excessive debt financing are known as thin capitalisation provisions, because they address the use of inappropriately low amounts of equity to finance operations. Essentially, they operate to limit the amount of debt in respect of which the interest is deductible to an amount considered appropriate. Traditionally, the determination of whether the amount of debt finance is excessive has been determined by the application of simple debt : equity ratio. For example, a jurisdiction may adopt a 2 :1 ratio of debt : equity which means that interest on debt to the extent that the amount of that debt exceeds twice the equity of the company will be disallowed. Such an approach is, however, arbitrary and takes no account of the different levels of debt funding in a group. In other words, it imposes a debt : equity ratio on a particular member of the group which may be much lower than the debt : equity ratio of the overall group. Accordingly, a more modern approach, and one which is endorsed by the OECD Committee on Fiscal Affairs, is to look to all of the facts and circumstances of a group in determining whether the amount of debt funding is excessive. Although more complex, such an approach is likely to be fairer because it will take into account the overall funding of a group in deciding whether one particular member of the group is financed excessively by way of debt.

Another means of determining whether debt funding is excessive is the approach adopted by the United States with its "earnings-stripping" rules. These rules provide that interest paid by a company to certain shareholders will not be deductible where it exceeds 50% of the company's income. Interestingly, however, the rules contain a "safe harbor" provision under which the rules are not applied where the company has a debt : equity ratio of less than 1.5:1.

Another aspect of thin capitalisation rules which varies between jurisdictions is whether all debt, or just related party debt, is to be subject to restrictions. Traditionally, many jurisdictions looked only to related party debt, but because of the potential to circumvent the rules through back-to-back loans, as well as the fact that groups can achieve the same results by using external debt (particularly where that debt is simply moved from another part of the group), some jurisdictions have concluded that logically all debt should be subject to the provisions.

Finally, thin capitalisation rules will sometimes contain provisions dealing with the treatment of any disallowed interest expenses. For example, sometimes such amounts, being considered a return on disguised equity, are deemed to be a dividend and subject to dividend withholding tax.

11.2.7.4 Treaty shopping

We saw earlier that DTAs offer significant benefits, although perhaps the most notable in terms of tax planning is the reduction in withholding tax rates on dividends, interest and royalties. This has led for many years to the interposing in structures or transaction of an entity resident in a jurisdiction which has concluded an attractive DTA with a particular country. The jurisdiction of residence of such an entity typically would also have favourable domestic tax rules which allow the various types of income to pass through with minimal tax exposure. This process of interposing entities solely to obtain DTA benefits has become known as "treaty shopping".

Treaty shopping, although widespread, has not always been welcomed by tax authorities as some consider it to be an abuse in that the benefits of a DTA are obtained by persons who were not the intended beneficiaries. It is, however, difficult for a tax authority to unilaterally act to prevent such perceived abuse as it occurs pursuant to an international agreement between two separate jurisdictions. Nonetheless, attempts to prevent it have been made and are continuing to be made by various countries, although most notably the United States.

In particular, many years ago the United States was successful on a number of occasions in convincing the courts to disregard an interposed company (resident in a jurisdiction which had a favourable DTA with the United States) in a structure on the basis that it was merely a conduit with no commercial rationale or substance and that it should, therefore, be ignored for tax purposes. Having ignored the interposed company, the transaction was taxed on the basis that the benefits of the favourable DTA were not available. Nevertheless, not all such cases were successful and, indeed, success came mostly in the most blatant of cases.

Later, the United States enacted legislation which specifically permitted certain conduit companies to be disregarded and, in particular, those involved in specified financing and licensing arrangements. These provisions were somewhat controversial as they could unilaterally operate to ignore the effect of a DTA. In this regard, although DTAs are normally expected to over-ride domestic provisions, under United States law a domestic provision and an international treaty essentially have equal weight, but where there the two are inconsistent precedence is given to the later enacted provision. Accordingly, these provisions were effective in over-riding a DTA existing at the time of enactment of the provisions, but they would not over-ride a later DTA.

A more modern approach to perceived abuse of DTAs, of which the United States is again at the forefront, is the incorporation of limitation of benefits (LOB) clauses into DTAs. An LOB clause may be quite complex but the intention is to restrict the benefits under the DTA to persons who are genuinely residents of the relevant jurisdictions. In other words, the LOB clause is intended to prevent a resident from a third jurisdiction establishing an entity in one of the jurisdictions of the DTA to act as a conduit and obtain treatment or benefits under the DTA which would not otherwise be available. The first DTA to contain a comprehensive LOB clause was the revised US — Netherlands DTA of 1994, and they have now become a feature of many new DTAs entered into by the United States. More generally, however, LOB clauses are still not common in DTAs and it is interesting to note that the current OECD Model Treaty still does not contain a LOB article.

11.3 International Tax Aspects of Inbound Investment

Some basic principles of international tax were discussed above. In this section, we examine the situation of inbound investment to Hong Kong (i.e. where a non-resident makes an investment in Hong Kong, either by way of a branch or a subsidiary) and, in particular, identify the key tax issues of such investment.

11.3.1 Carrying on business and permanent establishments

As we saw in chapter 4, for a liability to Profits Tax to arise, a person must carry on a trade, profession or business in Hong Kong and derive profits from such trade, profession or business which arise in or are derived from Hong Kong (i.e. profits which have a source in Hong Kong). Accordingly one of the first issues to be considered when an investment is made in Hong Kong by a non-resident person is whether that investment amounts to the carrying on of a business in Hong Kong.

We also noted in chapter 4 that there is no comprehensive statutory definition of what is meant by carrying on business in Hong Kong; similarly, the limited case law on the topic makes it difficult to formulate clear rules on the issue. In particular, there is no single test or factor which can be used to determine whether an activity exceeds this basic threshold for a liability to potentially arise. Nonetheless, the Hong Kong case law on the issue does suggest that little needs to be done in Hong Kong for a person to be considered to be carrying on business there. It is also clear that the definition of "permanent establishment" (PE) contained in IRR 5 is not intended to set a threshold for chargeability as that Rule is concerned only with quantification of assessable profits where such a PE exists and does not appear to be currently interpreted as meaning that no liability can arise in the absence of a PE.

If, however, an investment is made in Hong Kong by a resident of a jurisdiction with which Hong Kong has concluded a DTA, the domestic law position will be over-ridden and a liability to Hong Kong tax can arise only if a PE, as defined in the relevant DTA, exists. In other words, a DTA offers some protection from the uncertainties of the position under domestic law by imposing a test that requires a PE (as defined) to exist before a liability can arise. Because PE is extensively defined in Hong Kong's DTAs and discussed in the commentaries, there is far less uncertainty as to the meaning of the term than in the case of the more general test for liability as contained in the IRO.

Theoretically, it is possible that a PE as defined in the DTA may exist but the activity may not amount to the carrying on of a business in Hong Kong under domestic law; in such circumstances, a liability to Hong Kong tax would still not arise as a DTA cannot impose a liability where one does not exist under domestic law.

11.3.2 Determination of assessable profits

Again, the determination of assessable profits for Profits Tax purposes was discussed in chapter 4. Essentially, the assessable profits of an enterprise are those which are attributable to the trade, profession or business carried on in Hong Kong and which have a Hong Kong source. Where an investment is made by a resident of a jurisdiction with which Hong Kong has concluded a DTA, however, the assessable profits of a PE are to be determined in accordance with Article 7, which is discussed above. Article 7 provides that all profits attributable to a PE in Hong Kong may be subject to Hong Kong tax; however, domestic law provides only that Hong Kong source profits are taxable and this principle should not be over-ridden by the DTA. For example, a PE in Hong Kong may place cash on deposit with a bank outside Hong Kong. The interest from that deposit, being attributable to the PE, could theoretically be assessed in accordance with Article 7; however, the interest would have a non-Hong Kong source under current law and practice and, therefore, no Hong Kong tax could be imposed on the amount.

Article 7 also provides that the profits of a PE are to be ascertained by applying transfer pricing principles; that is, by determining the profits which would have been derived by the PE if it were dealing with its head office or other branches of the same entity on arm's-length terms. This may require the overall profit from a transaction to be allocated between the different parts of an entity on the basis of respective contributions, activities, assets used, risks assumed, etc. Under the domestic provisions, however, assessable profits are not generally ascertained on this basis; rather, the whole of an amount of profit may be attributed to only a limited range of the activities giving rise to it. This is most evident in the cases where it has been accepted that profits arise in two or more jurisdictions (as a result of activities taking place in each of those jurisdictions) but there has been no apportionment of the profits between those jurisdictions for Profits Tax purposes. Accordingly, the profits determined under domestic provisions could theoretically be greater or smaller than those ascertained under Article 7 of a DTA. In such a case, the assessable profits should actually be the smaller of the two alternatives; this is again because although the DTA can operate to limit the otherwise assessable profits, if the domestic provisions seek to tax only a smaller amount the DTA cannot operate to increase that amount.

11.3.3 Double tax relief

Where a non-resident who is taxed in their jurisdiction of residence on a worldwide basis makes an investment in Hong Kong which gives rise to a Hong Kong tax liability, the potential for double taxation arises. As noted in section 11.2.3, relief from such double taxation may be available on a unilateral or bilateral basis, but in either case international custom is that the jurisdiction imposing tax on a residence basis is required to give relief for tax imposed on a source basis in another jurisdiction. As Hong Kong generally imposes tax only on income or profit which has a source in Hong Kong, it will normally be a matter for the residence jurisdiction to provide double tax relief. This will be granted in accordance with the domestic laws of that jurisdiction (unilateral relief) or pursuant to the terms of a DTA with Hong Kong (bilateral relief). Table 11.1 below summarises the existing agreements which Hong Kong has with other jurisdictions which deal with double taxation.

11.3.4 Financing an investment in Hong Kong

Hong Kong imposes no thin capitalisation provisions. As such, adherence to a particular debt : equity ratio when financing a company investing in Hong Kong is not, *prima facie*, required. Nonetheless, the normal advantages of financing a foreign investment excessively through debt are not generally available due to the severe restrictions on interest deductibility contained in Sec. 16(2) IRO, which is discussed in chapter 4.

To recap, as a general principle interest expenses are not deductible unless the recipient is subject to tax on the receipt of the interest. Although there are various exceptions to this general rule, these are subject to stringent requirements to prevent circumvention of the rules. In short, where a non-resident person makes a loan to an associated company, the interest will generally not be deductible for Hong Kong tax purposes. Interest on genuine borrowings from a financial institution is, on the other hand, generally deductible although again there are various legislative provisions designed to prevent the deduction of interest on bank loans which are ultimately funded by an associate.

As is the case in most jurisdictions, where a Hong Kong investment is financed by way of equity the dividends paid on that equity investment are non-deductible. Nonetheless, as interest paid to a foreign parent is generally non-deductible, financing a Hong Kong investment by equity may (from a Hong Kong tax perspective) be no less tax efficient than debt financing. Also, as Hong Kong imposes no withholding tax on dividends there is no additional tax leakage from financing by this means. Moreover, because dividends are taxed on a concessional basis in many jurisdictions, financing by way of equity may, in fact, be more tax efficient than debt financing, particularly where the parent is in a higher tax jurisdiction. That is, from a Hong Kong perspective there may be no difference between debt and equity financing, but from the investor's perspective it may be preferable to receive a concessionally taxed (or exempt) dividend than interest which is taxable.

11.3.5 Branch vs subsidiary

When making an investment into Hong Kong, another important question to be considered is whether to make the investment through a branch of an existing foreign company or through a newly established subsidiary. Because residents and non-residents (i.e. branches and subsidiaries) are taxed on the same basis and at the same rates, there is theoretically little from a Hong Kong tax perspective to favour one over the other.

When a branch is used, however, there can sometimes be practical difficulties with the determination of assessable profits. This is because although a Hong Kong branch may keep its own accounts, the IRD may not always be satisfied that these correctly reflect all relevant income and expenses. That is, the IRD may consider that income booked in another branch has a Hong Kong source and is attributable to the Hong Kong branch operation, or may consider that expenses booked in the Hong Kong branch are attributable to the derivation of profits of an overseas branch. Where the IRD is not satisfied that the Hong Kong branch's accounts truly reflect the profits assessable in Hong Kong, they are empowered under the Inland Revenue Rules to assess the profits on a basis different to those accounts. The IRD's powers under the Inland Revenue Rules are discussed in chapter 4.

These difficulties are much less likely to be an issue with a subsidiary, however, as any dealings with other parts of the group should reflect the fact that two legally independent entities are dealing with each other and there is less scope for the income and expenses of one to be recorded in the books of the other. Moreover, for Hong Kong tax purposes a subsidiary would normally be required by statute to be independently audited and this makes it much harder in practice for the IRD to challenge the correctness of the accounts.

Another practical difference in the tax treatment of a branch and a subsidiary relates to the deductibility of expenses incurred by the head office or parent company abroad. Where a subsidiary is established, any management charges levied by the foreign parent would normally be deductible subject to the usual requirements; in essence, this means that provided the charges are properly documented so as to establish that they are incurred by the subsidiary and the amounts are commercially reasonable, they would generally be deductible. This is the case even where the parent company incorporates a mark-up into the management charges levied.

Where, on the other hand, the Hong Kong investment is made through a branch, any charges levied by the head office on the branch are non-deductible on the basis that a head office and branch are simply parts of the same entity and cannot contract with each other; accordingly, any such charges cannot be considered incurred in a legal sense and therefore fail to meet the basic conditions for deductibility. Nonetheless, any expenses incurred directly by the head office which relate to the derivation of the assessable profits of the branch are technically deductible; however, as a practical matter, the IRD generally resists the deduction of such amounts on the basis of difficulties in establishing the quantum of the amount and the extent of the nexus to the assessable profits of the Hong Kong branch. Moreover, even where such expenses are allowed as a deduction, the amount is limited to the actual expenses incurred with no mark-up being permitted.

In summary, although a branch and subsidiary are theoretically taxed on the same basis, as a matter of practice the use of a subsidiary generally offers a lower risk of the assessable profits being queried or adjusted by the IRD as income and expenses are captured in such an entity with more certainty.

11.3.6 Transfer pricing

As noted in chapter 4, Hong Kong has no comprehensive transfer pricing provisions of the type found in other developed jurisdictions and the limited provision which does exist is difficult to apply in practice. Moreover, although Hong Kong's DTAs contain an associated enterprises article (see section 11.2.6.8 above), it seems unlikely that this could be invoked to increase the profits of a Hong Kong enterprise when this is not permitted under Hong Kong domestic law as generally a DTA should not be interpreted as imposing a liability which does not exist under domestic law.

Although the absence of a comprehensive provision may facilitate tax planning, difficulties can arise when transfer pricing adjustments are made in another jurisdiction but in respect of transactions involving a Hong Kong business. For example, suppose that a Hong Kong business sells goods to a related party in country A. Further suppose that in country A the tax authorities establish that the price at which the sales take place is too high and increase the assessable profits of the associate by reducing the cost of sales. In Hong Kong, because there is no general requirement that related party transactions be undertaken on arm's-length terms, there are no provisions by which a corresponding adjustment of the assessable profits downwards can be made. Consequently, double taxation can effectively occur in such situations.

The position is, however, different where a DTA exists as all of Hong Kong's DTAs contain an associated enterprise clause under which corresponding adjustments are required in a jurisdiction where the other jurisdiction makes a transfer pricing adjustment in relation to transactions between the relevant jurisdictions (see section 11.2.6.8 above). Although such adjustments are neither permitted nor required by domestic provisions, the DTA will clearly over-ride domestic law in this regard.

11.4 International Tax Aspects of Outbound Investment

In the following sections, various tax aspects arising from the investment abroad by a Hong Kong enterprise are considered.

11.4.1 Assessability of foreign profits

Generally, when a Hong Kong business invests abroad it will be expected that the profits from that investment will be accepted as being related to a business carried on abroad and will likely have a source outside Hong Kong. As such, they should not normally be subject to Hong Kong Profits Tax.

Nonetheless, care needs to be taken in assuming that no Hong Kong tax liability will exist, particularly where the transactions of the foreign business are closely linked to activities undertaken in Hong Kong. For example, a Hong Kong business providing services may establish a foreign branch which obtains new engagements from businesses in the foreign jurisdiction but some part of the services rendered under those engagements take place in Hong Kong. Another example is where a manufacturer sets up an operation in a foreign jurisdiction which undertakes assembly of products, but with some related activities continuing to take place in Hong Kong. In such situations, the business may be considered to be carried on in both jurisdictions; moreover, the profits may be considered as having a source in both jurisdictions with the result that an apportionment of profits may be appropriate with some portion being liable to Hong Kong tax. Indeed, even though the business is carried on in two jurisdictions, the profit may be considered to arise wholly in one of the jurisdictions and if this was Hong Kong, then the whole of the profit would be liable to Profits Tax. A more complete discussion as to the source and apportionment of profits can be found in chapter 4.

The situation where a portion of the profits of a foreign operation are considered to have a Hong Kong source and attributable to a Hong Kong business is in practice more likely to arise where the foreign operation is established as a branch. Where the operation is established as a subsidiary of the Hong Kong enterprise, the situation is less likely to arise because the Hong Kong business and the foreign subsidiary need to deal with each other as separate entities. That is, any services provided by one to the other, or any transfers of goods between them, should be carried out pursuant to agreements, preferably documented. Transfer pricing considerations aside, the profits derived by each entity would then be determined in accordance with their accounts which would reflect those intercompany agreements.

Nonetheless, even where a subsidiary is employed, the issue may still arise. This is because activities of a foreign subsidiary may still be undertaken by an associate (i.e. the parent company) in Hong Kong on behalf of the subsidiary and this may lead to a finding that the subsidiary is carrying on business in Hong Kong, through the activities of the associate, and that Hong Kong source profits are derived from such business. In an extreme example, this may occur where a group sets up a tax haven company to undertake certain transactions and then operates that company through associated persons or companies in Hong Kong. The problem can also arise in less extreme situations; see, for example, the cases of *CIR v Orion Caribbean Limited* [1997] (1 HKRC 90-089) and *Lam Soon Trademark Limited v CIR* [2004] (1 HKRC 90-137) which are discussed in chapter 4.

Notwithstanding the possibility that a foreign subsidiary may still be subject to Hong Kong tax in certain circumstances, any dividends paid by that subsidiary will be exempt from Hong Kong Profits Tax in the hands of the Hong Kong owner, irrespective of the tax position of the subsidiary itself. Moreover, Hong Kong has not enacted any CFC rules so there is generally no attribution of profits of a foreign entity to its Hong Kong owners. A limited exception to this applies, however, in relation to certain non-resident entities which are considered to be carrying on business in Hong Kong but benefit from the exemption under Sec. 20AC IRO; as discussed under point (17) in section 4.5.3, a portion of the profits of such entities may in certain circumstances be assessed to a resident who owns an interest in the entity.

Where profits are subject to Hong Kong Profits Tax as well as foreign tax, only limited double tax relief is generally available under Hong Kong domestic law. Indeed, in most cases there is no relief available for taxes imposed on net income or profits in the foreign jurisdiction other than in the very limited cases of interest income and gains from the redemption, sale or maturity of certain financial instruments. A greater degree of relief will, however, generally be available where a DTA exists with the jurisdiction in which the foreign tax is payable. These issues are discussed more fully below.

11.4.2 Unilateral double tax relief

In section 11.2.3 the concepts of double taxation and double taxation relief were discussed. As noted, international custom usually requires a jurisdiction seeking to tax an amount on a residence basis to modify its basis of taxation where the income is also subject to tax in another jurisdiction on the basis of its source.

Because under Hong Kong law only income and profits arising in or derived from Hong Kong (i.e. having a Hong Kong source) are generally subject to tax, there is not normally any necessity for Hong Kong to provide any relief from double taxation. For example, if a Hong Kong company has a branch in the UK or the USA, the profits of that branch may be subject to UK or USA tax but generally not Hong Kong tax. If, however, a foreign company has a branch in Hong Kong the profits of which are subject to Hong Kong Profits Tax as well as tax in the jurisdiction of residence of the company, under international custom it is up to the jurisdiction of residence to grant relief for the double taxation which may otherwise arise.

Nonetheless, double taxation can also potentially occur when Hong Kong source rules conflict with those of another jurisdiction as well as in those circumstances where offshore sources of income are deemed to be taxable in Hong Kong. In either of these situations, however, the amount of relief available in Hong Kong is limited.

Until limited relief by means of allowing a deduction for foreign tax was introduced, the only relief for foreign tax was under the Commonwealth income tax relief provisions, which were repealed in 1998. Some relief by way of a deduction for foreign tax was introduced in conjunction with an extension of the Profits Tax charge to certain offshore interest income, first in the case of financial institutions and later, for a limited period, in relation to all corporations and other persons carrying on a trade, profession or business in Hong Kong. Because interest income in these cases may have suffered tax elsewhere (either by direct assessment or withholding), taxing it in Hong Kong without recognition of this in some way would be unreasonable; therefore, Sec. 16(1)(c) IRO was introduced to allow the foreign tax suffered to be deducted as an expense against the taxable income. Although the provisions relating to the taxation of non-Hong Kong source interest income derived by persons other than financial institutions have since been repealed, the provisions for relief have been left in place so that even though such persons pay tax only on Hong Kong source interest income (although note that most bank interest is effectively exempt under the *Exemption from Profits Tax (Interest Income) Order* of 1998), they are still able to claim relief by way of deduction in the unlikely event that foreign tax is payable on the same interest income. Note that statutory relief is not available for foreign tax generally, but only for taxes suffered on interest income and certain profits from the disposal or redemption of certificates of deposit and bills of exchange which are subject to Profits Tax. Also, a deduction is not available if relief under Part VIII of the IRO, which is discussed below, applies. For a further discussion of Sec. 16(1)(c), see section 4.5.8.

The foregoing discussion concentrates on the statutory provision governing the deductibility of foreign taxes. In *D 43/91*, however, a shipping company was allowed a deduction for foreign taxes levied on the company's gross receipts earned in various countries. The Board of Review's reasoning in that case revolved around the fact that the taxes were imposed on turnover, irrespective of whether profits resulted, and the payment was essential if the company was to continue to derive income from the countries in question. Accordingly, the Board concluded, the taxes were expenses incurred in the course of the generation of the company's profits chargeable to Profits Tax and, therefore, qualified for the deduction under the general deduction provision. Although the taxpayer in that case was a shipping company whose assessable profits were computed in accordance with the former Sec. 23B, the Board of Review nonetheless made it clear that the taxes met the conditions for deductibility under Sec. 16(1). Indeed, it was as a consequence of this decision that Sec. 16(1)(c) was amended to extend its application to all corporations (and not just those managed and controlled in Hong Kong) and the IRD issued *Departmental Interpretation & Practice Notes No. 28* to explain the circumstances in which they were prepared to allow a deduction for foreign taxes not otherwise deductible pursuant to Sec. 16(1)(c).

11.4.3 Bilateral double tax relief

Double tax relief may also be given pursuant to Sec. 49 which grants the Chief Executive in Council full power to enter into comprehensive double

Table 11.1 Hong Kong's current agreements concerning double taxation

Comprehensive DTAs	
Belgium	Thailand
Mainland of China	
Agreements Dealing with Shipping Income Only	
United States of America	United Kingdom
The Netherlands	Germany
Norway	Denmark
Agreements Dealing with Airline Income Only	
Republic of Korea	New Zealand
Canada	Mainland of China
The Netherlands	Germany
United Kingdom	Israel
Mauritius	Denmark
Norway	Sweden
Iceland	Bangladesh
Croatia	Kenya
Kuwait	Switzerland
Estonia*	Macau SAR*
Finland*	Russia*
Jordan*	
(* — not yet in force at time of writing)	
Agreements Dealing with Both Shipping and Airline Income	
Sri Lanka	Singapore

taxation agreements. This provision has existed for many years, although the first comprehensive double taxation agreement, being with Belgium, was not concluded until 2003. Nonetheless, it is also under the authority of Sec. 49 that agreements related to shipping and airline income have been entered into. A summary of the jurisdictions which currently have agreements with Hong Kong dealing with double taxation is contained in Table 11.1.

Sec. 50 contains detailed provisions for the granting of credits for foreign tax where such credit is required under the terms of a double tax agreement which has been the subject of an order of the Chief Executive in Council pursuant to Sec. 49. This provision has existed for many years, but had no effect until 1998 when a limited double tax agreement with the Mainland of China was concluded. The section now applies, however, to the double taxation agreements concluded with Belgium, Thailand and the Mainland of China and is likely to have increasing application as the Government continues to enter into comprehensive double taxation agreements. (At the time of writing negotiations for further such agreements had commenced with seven other countries.) It is interesting to note that as a domestic provision, Sec. 50 could be over-ridden by the terms of a DTA; however, all of Hong Kong's existing DTAs provide for the granting of credits in Hong Kong for foreign tax (i.e. tax paid in the country with which the relevant DTA was concluded) and specifically state that such credits are subject to the terms of Hong Kong tax law governing tax credits, thereby ensuring the applicability of Sec. 50.

As noted, Sec. 50(1) provides that tax credits are only available where tax is payable in another jurisdiction in respect of which the Chief Executive in Council has made an order pursuant to Sec. 49 to give effect to a double taxation agreement which has been concluded with that jurisdiction, and that order requires such foreign tax to be credited against tax payable in Hong Kong. Sec. 50(2) further provides that a credit is only available to a person who is resident in Hong Kong in the relevant year.

The IRO contains no definition of "resident" for this purpose, although see the discussion in section 6.3 concerning the interpretation of the term in relation to individuals by the courts in other jurisdictions. Nonetheless, Hong Kong's DTAs contain a definition which is likely to be considered relevant for the purpose of Sec. 50. For a discussion of such definition and the IRD's interpretation of it, see *Departmental Interpretation and Practice Notes No. 44*. This document specifically refers to the DTA with the Mainland of China but as the definition of resident in that agreement is the same as in Hong Kong's other DTAs (although in relation to the DTA with Belgium the definition is contained in a protocol), the same considerations should apply to those other DTAs.

The amount of any credit allowable under this provision is limited to the Hong Kong tax payable on the relevant income, with the rate of Hong Kong tax payable on the income being determined by dividing the total Hong Kong tax chargeable on the person for the year by the person's total income for the year (Sec. 50(3)). In calculating amount of income for this purpose, Sec. 50(5) provides that:

(a)   no deduction shall be allowed for any foreign tax;

(b)   where the amount of Hong Kong tax chargeable depends on the amount received in Hong Kong, the amount is to be increased by the foreign tax levied on that income. As no income is taxed on a remittance basis in Hong Kong, this provision can have no application; and

(c)   where the income includes a dividend and pursuant to the relevant order under Sec. 49 foreign tax not levied directly or by deduction is to be taken into account in determining the credit to be allowed, the amount of income is to be increased by the amount of such foreign tax. As dividend income is not currently subject to tax in Hong Kong, no credit could ever be available in respect of foreign tax on a dividend, irrespective of how such foreign tax was calculated and, accordingly, this provision can presently have no application.

Notwithstanding the above provisions, however, a deduction is allowed for any amount by which the foreign tax on the relevant income exceeds the credit available for such foreign tax.

Total income for the purposes of Sec. 50(3) is to be calculated without deduction of any foreign tax (Sec. 50(6)). Sec. 50(4) further provides that without prejudice to Sec. 50(3), the total tax credits available to a person for a year cannot exceed the total Hong Kong tax payable for the year.

Any claim for a credit in respect of foreign tax must be made within two years after the end of the relevant year of assessment, and in the event of any dispute as to the amount of credit allowable, the claim is subject to objection or appeal in the same manner as an assessment to tax (Sec. 50 (9)). Interestingly, Sec. 50(8) allows a taxpayer to elect not to take advantage of the credits which may otherwise be allowable; if such an election is made, it would appear that pursuant to Sec. 50(5), the whole amount of the foreign tax would be allowable as a deduction for Hong Kong tax purposes.

Notwithstanding any restrictions which would otherwise apply, where a tax credit is granted under this provision and the Hong Kong tax payable is subsequently adjusted such that the credit given is found to have been excessive or insufficient, there is a time limit of two years from the time when all necessary assessments, adjustments or determinations are made, either in Hong Kong or elsewhere, as are material in determining the allowable credit, in which a taxpayer may make a claim for further credit or the IRD can raise an additional assessment to reduce the credit previously given (Sec. 50(10)).

Although Sec. 4 normally imposes stringent secrecy provisions on IRD staff, where an arrangement concerning double taxation has been entered into with another country, it is inevitably necessary for the respective revenue authorities to exchange information from time to time in order to administer that agreement. Accordingly, Sec. 49(5) permits the disclosure to an authorized officer of a government with which an agreement has been made which is the subject of an order under Sec. 49, of any information required to be disclosed under such agreement. Of course, such agreements contain provisions under which such exchange of information is permitted, but Sec. 49(5) makes it clear that these will not contravene Sec. 4.

For some practical examples of the calculation of credits under Sec. 50, see paragraphs 131 to 134 of *Departmental Interpretation & Practice Notes No. 44.*

11.4.4 Withholding taxes

When making an investment abroad, a Hong Kong enterprise may be exposing itself to withholding taxes on dividends, interest and royalties. Because dividends are exempt from tax in Hong Kong, no double tax relief for dividend withholding taxes is available. As such, any dividend withholding tax is a direct expense against profit. Further, as dividend withholding taxes can be imposed at significant rates there is usually an incentive to put in place structures to minimise such withholding taxes. Typically this will involve treaty shopping; that is interposing a suitable holding company between the Hong Kong enterprise and the foreign investment in order to mitigate the leakage of tax as a result of withholding taxes.

At present, Hong Kong's DTA with Belgium offers much scope for treaty shopping as a means of minimising dividend withholding tax. This is due to the fact that Belgium generally imposes no withholding tax on dividends paid by a Belgian resident company to Hong Kong and dividends received by a Belgian company can be largely exempt from tax if certain conditions are satisfied. Nonetheless, it should not be readily assumed that all the necessary conditions can be easily satisfied and up to date advice from an appropriate adviser in Belgium should always be obtained before implementing any structures involving a Belgian resident entity.

An effective treaty shopping structure does not, however, actually need to involve a jurisdiction with which Hong Kong has a DTA. The necessary features of the interposed company are that it must be resident in a jurisdiction which has DTAs with the jurisdictions in which the investments are ultimately made, it must impose little or no income tax on dividends received and it must be able to pay out a dividend with minimal withholding tax. While the latter requirement may be achieved pursuant to a DTA, there are in fact many jurisdictions which have entered into numerous DTAs (although not with Hong Kong) but which do not impose any dividend withholding tax under domestic law. Moreover, many such jurisdictions do not subject dividends received to tax in the jurisdiction. Accordingly, such jurisdictions can offer a very effective means for mitigating dividend withholding taxes in respect of investments ultimately held by a Hong Kong enterprise and, indeed, such structures were widely employed before Hong Kong had entered into any comprehensive DTAs.

As noted, investments by a Hong Kong enterprise abroad may also give rise to withholding tax on interest and royalty payments. Interest payments from a non-resident may still be assessable in Hong Kong as a result of the rules governing the source of interest for Hong Kong tax purposes (see chapter 4), although in such cases a deduction for any withholding tax suffered should be available under Sec. 16(1)(c), as discussed in section 11.4.2. Where a high rate of interest withholding tax is suffered, it may be possible to interpose an entity to reduce the overall tax burden in a similar manner to that discussed in relation to dividends.

Similarly, royalties derived from non-residents and subject to withholding tax may still be assessable in Hong Kong as a result of the case law in relation to the source of royalty income (see *HK-TVB International Limited v CIR* [1992] (1 HKRC 90-064) and *Lam Soon Trademark Limited v CIR* [2004] (1 HKRC 90-137), both of which are discussed in chapter 4). Unlike in the case of interest, even where the royalty is assessable to Profits Tax, any withholding tax will not be deductible under the specific provision of Sec. 16(1)(c). Nonetheless, the IRD has confirmed in *Departmental Interpretation & Practice Notes No. 28* that provided the withholding tax is levied on gross royalties rather than the net profit from those royalties, the withholding tax would normally be deductible under the general deduction provision of Sec. 16(1).

11.4.5 Financing a foreign investment

When deciding how a Hong Kong enterprise is to fund a foreign operation, there are a number of considerations. From a Hong Kong perspective, the principal issue to be considered is the deductibility of interest expenses in relation to a foreign investment. In particular, if the foreign operation is in the form of a subsidiary, any interest expenses incurred to acquire the shares in that subsidiary will be non-deductible on the basis that they will not be incurred in generating assessable profits as the dividends from that investment will be statutorily exempt from Hong Kong tax.

Where a subsidiary is used, however, finance can also be advanced to that subsidiary by way of a loan from the Hong Kong parent. The loan can be arranged so as to give the interest earned by the Hong Kong parent a source outside Hong Kong. Under these circumstances, the interest will not be assessable in Hong Kong, although any related financing costs would not be deductible. Although not assessable in Hong Kong, the interest may remain deductible in the foreign jurisdiction and, subject to the amount of any withholding tax, this may permit a tax efficient means of repatriating profits from the foreign subsidiary. The benefits of such a structure could be enhanced by having the Hong Kong enterprise charge a mark-up on the interest (which may be justifiable under transfer pricing principles), which would result in greater deductions in the foreign jurisdiction and the earning of a non-taxable margin in Hong Kong. Nonetheless, care needs to be taken to ensure that the deductibility of the interest in the foreign jurisdiction is not adversely impacted by failure to comply with any thin capitalisation requirements in that jurisdiction.

If the Hong Kong enterprise needs to borrow from a bank to finance its advance to the foreign subsidiary, there may be advantages in arranging for the subsidiary to instead borrow the amount directly. Such advantages include the possibility of being able to avoid withholding tax on the interest by arranging the borrowing through a bank in the foreign jurisdiction, and also external borrowings may not be taken into account for the purpose of any thin capitalisation rules.

Where the foreign investment is in the form of a branch of a Hong Kong company, any interest expense attributable to that operation will also be non-deductible to the extent that the profits of the branch are not subject to Hong Kong tax, which will generally be the case. Any such interest expenses may, however, be deductible in the foreign jurisdiction under the domestic law of that jurisdiction or under Article 7 of a DTA (see section 11.2.6.3 above).

11.4.6 Hong Kong expenses relating to foreign investment

When a Hong Kong enterprise makes an investment abroad, it is common that expenses will be incurred in Hong Kong on an ongoing basis in relation to that investment. If, however, the profits from the foreign investment are not taxable in Hong Kong, those expenses will be non-deductible. This situation exists irrespective of whether the foreign operation is in the form of a branch or a subsidiary.

Where a subsidiary is used as the vehicle for the foreign investment, a disallowance of the expenses can be avoided by passing the expenses on to the subsidiary by way of a management fee or charge. Although such a fee or charge will usually be assessable in Hong Kong, a deduction will normally be available for the related expenses and the management fee may be deductible in the foreign jurisdiction; if it is so deductible and the foreign tax rate is higher than the Hong Kong tax rate and no withholding tax is imposed, this may represent a tax efficient means of repatriating profits from the foreign subsidiary.

For completeness, it should be noted that the above discussion is concerned predominantly with expenses which can be identified as directly related to the foreign investment. It will be recalled from chapter 4 that where a company holds investments in subsidiaries, Inland Revenue Rule 2C may require an automatic disallowance of expenses based on the cost of the investments.

The position is different where the foreign operation is organised as a branch of a Hong Kong company. In these circumstances, the expenses will remain non-deductible in Hong Kong (to the extent the foreign branch profits are not subject to Hong Kong tax) and imposing a management fee or charge on the foreign branch would be ignored for Hong Kong tax purposes as transactions between branches of the same entity, or between a head office and a branch, are generally ignored for Hong Kong tax purposes. Nonetheless, those expenses may be deductible in the foreign jurisdiction as being expenses related to the derivation of income or profit assessable in that jurisdiction and, indeed, where a DTA exists between Hong Kong and the foreign jurisdiction such a deduction would generally be required under the Article 7 (see section 11.2.6.3 above).

11.4.7 Transfer pricing

A foreign jurisdiction into which a Hong Kong enterprise invests may have more comprehensive and sophisticated transfer pricing provisions that currently exist in Hong Kong. As a consequence, any transactions between related parties may be subject to adjustment in the foreign jurisdiction pursuant to transfer pricing provisions.

As discussed in section 11.3.6, there are no provisions under Hong Kong domestic law pursuant to which a corresponding adjustment may be made in Hong Kong if profits are increased in a foreign jurisdiction in relation to transactions with a Hong Kong associated party; accordingly, there is a risk of double taxation arising in such circumstances and care needs to be taken to ensure any related party transactions are conducted on arm's-length terms and conditions. Nonetheless, such corresponding adjustments are authorised where a DTA exists between Hong Kong and the foreign jurisdiction, although as discussed in section 11.2.6.8 such adjustments are not automatic but require the relevant jurisdiction to agree the principle and quantum of the original adjustment.

Chapter 12 ■
Stamp Duty

12.1 Legislation

Stamp Duty is an important source of revenue for the Hong Kong Government. Nonetheless, because its yield is closely linked to activity in the Hong Kong property and stock markets, total collections are somewhat volatile. This is demonstrated by the fact that in the year ended 31 March 1998, Stamp Duty collections were $29.1 billion, or 21.1% of all revenue collected by the IRD. As a result of the depressed property and stock markets in subsequent years, however, collections in the year to 31 March 2003 had declined to $7.5 billion, or only 8% of total tax collected by the IRD; subsequently, stamp duty revenue has increased with increased activity in the property market.

The law governing the charge and collection of Stamp Duty is contained in the *Stamp Duty Ordinance* (SDO). The SDO is made up of nine Parts with Sections from 1 to 66, and four Schedules. In this chapter, all references to Parts, Sections or Schedules are references to the SDO unless otherwise stated. The SDO is administered by the Stamp Office which is a part of the IRD. The officer in charge of the Stamp Office, and therefore responsible for the administration of the SDO, is the Collector of Stamp Revenue who is also the Commissioner of Inland Revenue.

12.2 Scope of the Charge

A fundamental rule of Stamp Duty is that it is a tax levied on instruments evidencing transactions, not on the transactions themselves. An "instrument" is defined in Sec. 2 as including "every written document". If there is no instrument evidencing a transaction there can be no Stamp Duty, although the SDO and the *Conveyancing and Property Ordinance* require the bringing into existence of documents as evidence of certain transactions. Accordingly, if a transaction is effected orally, as is possible in the case of most leases of immovable property for a period less than three years, then the transaction cannot be chargeable with Stamp Duty. Nonetheless, if a lease which could be effected orally is actually reduced to writing, that document is a chargeable instrument.

It is interesting to note that under Part IIIA of the SDO, certain unwritten agreements for the sale of immovable residential property are effectively made subject to Stamp Duty. This is not, however, a departure from the general rule that an instrument must exist before a liability to Stamp Duty arises. Rather, it is achieved by defining (in Sec. 29A(1)(f)) notes, memoranda or other evidence of an unwritten agreement for the sale of immovable residential property to themselves be an agreement for such a sale. As such, there is still an instrument to be stamped, even though that instrument is not, in normal terms, an agreement for sale.

12.2.1 The four Heads of Charge

The instruments chargeable with Stamp Duty are as set out in the four Heads of the First Schedule to the SDO. The Heads of Charge are as follows:

Head 1   Immovable property in Hong Kong
Head 2   Hong Kong stock
Head 3   Hong Kong bearer instruments
Head 4   Duplicates and counterparts of instruments chargeable under Heads 1, 2 and 3

Full details of the instruments covered by each Head are discussed in various sections below.

12.2.2 Territorial nature of charge

As with other taxes in Hong Kong, Stamp Duty is territorial in scope. The concept of territoriality is, however, reflected in the nature of the property which is the subject of the relevant transaction, as opposed to the place where the instrument is executed.

As is discussed more fully in this chapter, Stamp Duty is chargeable on certain instruments effecting, amongst other things, the transfer or lease of immovable property situated in Hong Kong, and the transfer of Hong Kong stock. Moreover, Sec. 4(1) explicitly provides that if the execution takes place outside Hong Kong, the instrument is still chargeable with Hong Kong Stamp Duty. The period allowed for stamping the instrument of transfer of Hong Kong stock is, however, longer if the execution takes place outside Hong Kong.

12.3 Immovable Property in Hong Kong

Head 1 of the First Schedule to the SDO provides the basic rules and amount of Stamp Duty payable in respect of certain instruments dealing with immovable property situated in Hong Kong and is subdivided into Heads 1(1), 1(1A) and 1(2). The first two of these are concerned with conveyances on sale and certain other agreements for the sale, and transfers of, immovable property in Hong Kong. Head 1(2) deals with leases of immovable property in Hong Kong.

Immovable property is defined in the *Interpretation and General Clauses Ordinance* and essentially means land, any estate, right, interest in or easement over land as well as things attached to the land (i.e. buildings).

There are normally three instruments involved in the sale of immovable property, namely a temporary (provisional) sale and purchase agreement, a formal sale and purchase agreement and a conveyance on sale (which is more commonly referred to as an "assignment"). Head 1(1) is concerned only with the last of these steps and imposes Stamp Duty on every conveyance on sale (as defined).

Traditionally, neither a temporary sale and purchase agreement nor a formal sale and purchase agreement were liable to Stamp Duty, as such agreements do not generally fall within the definition of a conveyance on sale. As a measure to discourage residential property speculation, however, and in particular the practice of speculating in properties still under development, Head 1(1A) was introduced in 1992 to render agreements for the sale of residential property chargeable to Stamp Duty at the same rates as a conveyance on sale. To avoid double duty arising, however, a conveyance on sale made following such a chargeable agreement for sale (and in accordance with that agreement) attracts only a nominal amount of Stamp Duty.

A more detailed discussion of each of the sub-heads under Head 1 is contained below.

12.3.1 Conveyance on sale

Sec. 2 defines "conveyance" to mean every instrument (including a surrender) and every decree or order of any court whereby any immovable property is transferred to or vested in any person.

"Conveyance on sale" is also defined in Sec. 2 and means every conveyance whereby any immovable property, upon the sale thereof, is transferred to or vested in a purchaser or any other person on his behalf or by his direction, and includes a foreclosure order.

Accordingly, not every conveyance is a conveyance on sale and a conveyance not within the meaning of a "conveyance on sale" is not chargeable to Stamp Duty. For example, a mortgage document or other legal charge over property, although possibly constituting a conveyance, would not be a conveyance on sale. Nonetheless, because of the broad definitions of both conveyance and conveyance on sale, a wide range of instruments are made subject to duty under this head. In addition to formal conveyances, for example, a declaration of trust over immovable property will be dutiable under this head. Further, as discussed in section 12.3.2 below, a deed of gift is deemed a conveyance on sale at market value as is a conveyance on sale for consideration less than market value.

In addition, Sec. 26(1) provides that any agreement for the sale of an equitable estate or interest in any immovable property shall be chargeable with Stamp Duty as if it were a conveyance on sale. An agreement in the normal form for a sale and purchase of immovable property in Hong Kong is not, however, generally dutiable under this provision as such an agreement deals with only a legal estate and provides for completion at a later date through execution of a legal assignment (see *Lee On Construction Co. Ltd. v Collector of Stamp Revenue* (1 HKTC 792)). Further, pursuant to Sec. 29E, the provision has no application in the case of an agreement for the sale and purchase of residential property which is generally rendered chargeable to Stamp Duty under Part IIIA, which is further discussed in section 12.3.3 below.

Subject to various exceptions, which are discussed throughout this chapter, every actual or deemed conveyance on sale of immovable property in Hong Kong attracts Stamp Duty at the *ad valorem* rates prescribed in Head 1(1). The applicable rate is based upon the consideration given for the conveyance and the current rates are set out in Table 12.1 below. One important exception applies where a conveyance on sale is pursuant to, and in conformity with, a sale and purchase agreement which is itself chargeable to Stamp Duty at the *ad valorem* rates specified in Head 1(1A) and has, in fact, been properly stamped; such a conveyance on sale is chargeable with only a fixed rate of Stamp Duty of $100. Section 12.3.3 below discusses the

Table 12.1 Stamp Duty payable on immovable property under Heads 1 (1) and (1A) (Rates applicable from 28 February 2007)

Consideration or Market Value	Duty Payable
$1–$2,000,000	$100
$2,000,001–$2,351,760	$100 + [10% of (consideration less $2,000,000)]
$2,351,761–$3,000,000	1.5% of consideration
$3,000,001–$3,290,320	$45,000 + [10% of (consideration less $3,000,000)]
$3,290,321–$4,000,000	2.25% of consideration
$4,000,001–$4,428,570	$90,000 + [10% of (consideration less $4,000,000)]
$4,428,571–$6,000,000	3% of consideration
$6,000,001–$6,720,000	$180,000 + [10% of (consideration less $6,000,000)]
Above $6,720,000	3.75% of consideration

circumstances under which a sale and purchase agreement is chargeable to Stamp Duty.

Where the consideration given for a conveyance on sale of immovable property consists, in whole or in part, of stock (i.e. shares), such consideration (or part thereof) is to be treated for the purpose of ascertaining the amount of Stamp Duty payable as being the value of that stock at the date of conveyance (Sec. 22(1)). Similarly, Sec. 22(2) provides that to the extent the consideration is securities other than stock, the consideration is to be taken as the principal plus interest due on the security.

In the absence of specific provisions, it would be possible to reduce the quantum of the Stamp Duty payable by breaking down one conveyance chargeable at the maximum rate of 3.75% into several conveyances with the consideration for each being below $6,720,000. In this way, the application of the top rate of Stamp Duty of 3.75% would be avoided. In order to stop such practices, however, Sec. 29 provides that if a dutypayer wishes to enjoy the progressive rates of Stamp Duty rather than the maximum rate of 3.75%, he or she must include in the instrument a statement certifying that the transaction does not form part of a larger transaction or series of transactions in respect of which the consideration or value, or aggregate consideration or value, exceeds that amount. If no such statement is included in the instrument, the top rate of 3.75% is charged on the instrument even though the consideration or value of the instrument does not exceed $6,720,000. The insertion of a certificate in accordance with Sec. 29 does not, however, necessarily mean that the transaction will, in practice, enjoy the benefit of a lower Stamp Duty rate. The Collector may still examine the circumstances of the sale to determine whether there are related transactions entered into by the same purchasers and the same sellers.

In determining whether two or more transactions are part of a larger transaction for this purpose, the Stamp Office have stated in a leaflet that they are guided by whether there is "co-ordination or interdependence between the transactions". As an example, the Stamp Office states that where a purchaser is at liberty to purchase a flat with or without the car parking space, it may be accepted that the purchase of the flat and the car parking space under separate agreements are not to be treated as part of a larger transaction even where there is a pre-condition that the purchaser of the car parking space should be a purchaser or owner of a flat in the complex at the time of such purchase. On the other hand, where there is a pre-condition that the flat and the car parking space must be sold together, the execution of separate agreements for the purchase of the flat and the car parking space will be treated as part of a larger transaction for the purpose of this provision.

A practical example of the application of these rules is illustrated in Example 12.1.

■ Example 12.1

Mr. Chan purchased a residential flat and a car parking space in the same building in North Point from Mr. Wong. The purchase prices of the flat and the car parking space were $3,500,000 and $400,000 respectively. Under the deed of mutual covenant covering the building, there was a requirement that the car parking space should only be sold to a purchaser or owner of a flat in the building. Mr. Chan asked Mr. Wong to prepare two separate purchase and sale agreements (i.e. one for the flat and one for the car parking space).

With the insertion of the Sec. 29 certificate, the Stamp Duty on these two sale and purchase agreements will be separately computed according to their own stated consideration. The total Stamp Duty payable is calculated as follows:

Stamp Duty on the flat ($3,500,000 × 2.25%)	$78,750
Stamp Duty on the car park (below $2,000,000)	100
Total Stamp Duty payable	$78,850

However, even with the insertion of the Sec. 29 certificate, the Collector is likely to look into the circumstances to see whether they are genuinely separate transactions not forming part of a series of transactions. In this case, because Mr. Chan could have purchased the flat without the car parking space, the Stamp Office may accept that the two agreements are not part of a single larger transaction and agree to the calculation of the Stamp Duty as set out above. If, on the other hand, the deed of mutual covenant had required that the flat and the car parking space be sold together, the Stamp Office would treat the two transactions as a single transaction executed with two separate agreements. In such circumstances, the transactions would be aggregated and the Stamp Duty calculated on the basis of the combined value of the property. The Stamp Duty payable would, therefore, be $87,750 [which is equal to 2.25% × ($3,500,000 + $400,000)].

The Stamp Duty chargeable under this head is payable within 30 days after the execution of the relevant document (except in the case of a vesting order consequential upon an order for sale or partition or a foreclosure order, where Note 2 to Head 1(1) provides that the Stamp Duty must be paid before the relevant order is signed by the Registrar).

12.3.2 Gifts and transfers at less than full value

In the case of a conveyance of immovable property without any valuable consideration, the only instrument effecting the transfer is the deed of gift (also referred to as the assignment or conveyance). In such circumstances, there is, of course, no conveyance on sale and, therefore, Stamp Duty would not, *prima facie*, be chargeable. However, such a deed of gift is deemed chargeable with Stamp Duty pursuant to Sec. 27(1) which reads as follows:

> "Any conveyance of immovable property operating as a voluntary disposition *inter vivos* shall be chargeable with stamp duty as a conveyance on sale, with the substitution of the value of the property conveyed for the amount or value of the consideration for the sale."

In other words, a deed of gift is deemed a conveyance on sale and is chargeable with *ad valorem* Stamp Duty under Head 1(1), with the amount of Stamp Duty payable being based on the value of the property.

Additionally, Sec. 27(4) effectively deems a transfer at less than full value to be a voluntary disposition *inter vivos* to which Sec. 27(1) applies. Again, the effect is to calculate the Stamp Duty payable on the basis of the market value rather than the amount specified in the relevant document.

There are, however, a number of exemptions from the operation Sec. 27 (4). Most of these are contained in Sec. 27(5), and the more important are:

- a conveyance for nominal consideration to secure the repayment of an advance or loan;
- a conveyance to effect the appointment of a new trustee;
- a conveyance under which no beneficial interest in the property passes; and
- a conveyance to a beneficiary by a trustee.

For a discussion of the ascertainment of the value of property to which Sec. 27 applies, see section 12.7 below.

12.3.3 Agreements for the sale of residential property

As noted earlier, Head 1(1A) was introduced in 1992 as a measure aimed at discouraging speculation in respect of residential property. This Head is governed by Part IIIA (Secs. 29A to 29H) and operates to render all "agreements for sale" in respect of such property chargeable with Stamp Duty at *ad valorem* rates, rather than only the formal assignment as is generally the case with non-residential property. The Stamp Duty rates applicable to such agreements are separately specified in Head 1(1A), but are in fact the same as the rates applicable to conveyances on sale as summarised in Table 12.1 above.

Where any Stamp Duty is payable under this provision, the time for stamping is set out in Head 1(1A), including the notes thereto. Generally, the relevant instrument is stampable within 30 days after execution; however, from 1 April, 1999, the rules were relaxed and Sec. 29C(11) now provides that the time for stamping can be extended in prescribed circumstances and upon application to the Collector within 30 days after execution of the agreement, for up to three years or until 30 days after the conveyance on sale of the property, whichever comes first. As an anti-avoidance provision, however, payment becomes due earlier if another agreement is made for the sub-sale of the property, there is another agreement made whereby the first purchaser transfers his interest or permits a conveyance of the property to another person or another agreement for sale is made by the original vendor to a person introduced by the first purchaser or otherwise at the direction of the first purchaser. The conditions for extending the time for stamping under Sec. 29C(11) are contained in Sec. 29C(12) and essentially require the Collector to be satisfied that the vendor under the agreement is registered in the Land Registry as the owner of the property or that all of the instruments through which the vendor acquired his rights in the property have, if they are stampable, been duly stamped. Alternatively, if the Collector is not so satisfied, the extension of time for stamping can still be obtained if satisfactory security for payment of the duty is provided to the Collector.

As with conveyances on sale, Part IIIA contains an anti-avoidance provision (Sec. 29G), which operates to prevent dutypayers from dividing a single transaction into a series of transactions in order to benefit from lower rates of duty applicable to smaller transactions. This provision operates to require the relevant instrument to be certified as not forming part of a larger transaction if the dutypayer wishes to benefit from a Stamp Duty rate less than the maximum of 3.75%.

Additionally, an agreement for sale at less than market value will generally be deemed by Sec. 29F (which has a similar effect to Sec. 27(4), which is discussed in section 12.3.3 above) to be a voluntary disposition *inter vivos* and the value for the purposes of calculating the duty taken as the market value rather than the consideration specified. An exemption from this provision applies, however, to an agreement for sale made for nominal consideration for the purposes of securing repayment of a loan or advance.

Sec. 29A provides an extensive definition of the term "agreement for sale" which is sufficiently broad to include all temporary and formal sale and purchase agreements in respect of immovable property, but also extends to a range of other agreements which grant rights (including pre-emption rights) or options over immovable property. The definition also encompasses any notes, memoranda or other instrument which evidence an unwritten agreement for the sale of immovable property. Nonetheless, an unwritten sale agreement is required by Sec. 29B(1) to be reduced to writing within 30 days.

Sec. 29A(5), however, provides that Head 1(1A) has no application to an "agreement for sale" of non-residential property. Accordingly, it is important to understand the difference between "residential property" and "non-residential property" and these terms are defined in Sec. 29A(1) as follows:

- "residential property" means immovable property other than non-residential property;
- "non-residential property" means immovable property which, under the existing conditions of:
  - (i)   a Government lease or an agreement for a Government lease;
  - (ii) a deed of mutual covenant, within the meaning of Sec. 2 of the *Building Management Ordinance*;
  - (iii) an occupation permit issued under Sec. 21 of the *Building Ordinance*; or
  - (iv) any other instrument which the Collector is satisfied effectively restricts the permitted user of the property,

  may not be used, at any time during the term of the Government lease in respect of the property or during the term of the Government lease that has been agreed for in respect of the property (as is appropriate), wholly or partly for residential purposes.

In other words, the categorisation of a property as residential or non-residential is governed by the permitted use, rather than the actual use.

As noted, the practical effect of Head 1(1A) and Part IIIA is to impose Stamp Duty on the execution of temporary sale and purchase agreements at the same rates as would generally apply to a conveyance on sale. The subsequent formal sale and purchase agreement and conveyance on sale executed in conformity with the terms of the temporary sale and purchase agreement is subject to only a fixed Stamp Duty of $100 as provided under Note 3 to Head 1(1A) and Sec. 29D(2)(a) respectively. Note, however, that pursuant to Sec. 29D(6)(c) a conveyance on sale is not considered executed in conformity with an agreement for sale unless such conveyance is in favour of the person or all of the persons named in the agreement for sale. Additionally, Sec. 29A(3) provides that an agreement will only be considered to be made between the same persons as a previous agreement where, *inter alia*, if there is more than one purchaser, the interest to be acquired by each purchaser is the same as under the previous agreement. If the parties are not the same, or there is more than one purchaser and the interest acquired by each purchaser is not the same as under the previous agreement, the conveyance on sale attracts Stamp Duty at normal rates, in addition to the Stamp Duty payable on the temporary sale and purchase agreement; an exception to this provision applies, however, where the conveyance on sale is in favour of a parent, spouse or child of the person named in the agreement for sale. Where a conveyance on sale is in favour of only some of the persons named in the agreement for sale, such conveyance is chargeable with Stamp Duty at normal rates, less a portion representing the proportion of the property which was conveyed to a person or persons named in the agreement for sale (Sec. 29D(5)).

If no temporary sale and purchase agreement is executed in respect of a particular transaction, then the formal sale and purchase agreement is liable to Stamp Duty at the rates specified in Head 1(1A).

If an agreement for sale is not stamped, the conveyance on sale is chargeable with Stamp Duty under Head 1(1), and the agreement for sale is chargeable with a fixed Stamp Duty of $100. The stamping period of the conveyance on sale is not counted from the date of execution of such conveyance on sale but from the date of execution of the agreement for sale. If the conveyance on sale is not stamped within the relevant period (being 30 days from the execution of the agreement for sale), penalties for late stamping may be imposed in accordance with Sec. 9(1), which is discussed in section 12.13 below.

If a formal sale and purchase agreement is executed within 14 days after the execution of a temporary sale and purchase agreement, and the terms of both agreements are the same, then only the formal sale and purchase agreement is chargeable with Stamp Duty at the rates applicable to a conveyance on sale. The temporary sale and purchase agreement is exempt from Stamp Duty in such circumstances as provided for in Note 2 to Head 1 (1A).

Generally, however, if a change of owner takes place in respect of all or a part of the property before the execution of the assignment, the sub-sale and purchase agreement is also chargeable with Stamp Duty at the rates prescribed in Head 1(1) on the proportion of the property which changed hands, pursuant to Sec. 29C(5) in conjunction with Secs. 29D(4) and 29D (5). Similarly, Secs. 29D(4) and (5) provide that where the formal assignment is to the original purchaser plus another party, or to only some of the original purchasers, Stamp Duty in accordance with Head 1(1) is chargeable on the proportion of the property which was not assigned in accordance with the original agreement. If, however, the change in ownership is to the spouse, a parent or child of the original purchaser, these provisions will operate to only impose Stamp Duty on the sub-sale or assignment at a flat rate of $100 pursuant to Notes 4 and 5 to Head 1(1A).

Further information concerning the stamping of agreements for the sale and purchase of residential property can be found in *Stamp Office Inter-pretation and Practice Notes No. 1.*

12.3.4 Leases

An agreement for the lease of immovable property in Hong Kong is chargeable with Stamp Duty in accordance with Head 1(2) of the First Schedule. In accordance with the general principle that Stamp Duty is imposed only upon instruments, a lease which has not been reduced to writing (e.g. an oral lease or an agreement pursuant to a written offer and verbal acceptance) will not attract Stamp Duty as there is no chargeable instrument. This is an important point in practice as under the *Conveyancing and Property Ordinance*, certain leases for periods not exceeding three years do not need to be in writing.

The consideration under a lease may comprise a premium (i.e. a lump sum payment) and/or rent (a periodic payment). To the extent that the consideration under the lease is premium, Stamp Duty is chargeable on the same scale as a conveyance on sale (i.e. as under Head 1(1)). To the extent the consideration under the lease is rent, Stamp Duty is chargeable in accordance with Table 12.2 below. In other words, where consideration under a lease comprises both a premium and rent, the different elements of the consideration will attract Stamp Duty calculated in different ways.

A lease is required to be stamped within 30 days after the date of execution. Head 1(2) provides that all parties to the lease, as well as other persons executing the document, are liable for payment of the Stamp Duty, although in practice the amount is normally shared equally between the lessor and lessee.

Sec. 16(2) provides that an agreement for a lease is chargeable with Stamp Duty as though it was itself a lease for the term and consideration mentioned in the agreement. The stamping period is also 30 days from the date of execution of the agreement. If a lease is subsequently drawn up in pursuance

Table 12.2 Rate of Stamp Duty on lease under Head 1(2)

Lease Period	Rate of Stamp Duty
Lease period is uncertain	0.25% of the average yearly rent
One year or less	0.25% of the total rent of the lease
More than one year but not more than 3 years	0.5% of the average yearly rent
More than three years	1% of the average yearly rent

of a duly stamped agreement for lease, the Stamp Duty payable on that lease is a fixed amount of $3, and the stamping period is also 30 days after execution.

Sec. 17 provides that an instrument which serves to increase the rent reserved on a lease chargeable with Stamp Duty, shall itself be dutiable as a lease, but only in respect of the additional rent charged.

12.4 Hong Kong Stock

Head 2 of the First Schedule deals with the calculation and collection of Stamp Duty in respect of the transfer of "Hong Kong stock". "Stock" is defined in Sec. 2 as:

(a) any shares, stocks, debentures, loan stocks, funds, bonds, or notes of or issued by any body, whether corporate or unincorporate, or any government or local government authority, or any other similar investment of any description;

(b) any units under a unit trust scheme; and

(c) any right, option or interest in or in respect of any stock referred to in paragraph (a) or (b), other than any such right, option or interest under an employees' share purchase or share option scheme.

However, except for the purposes of Sec. 22 (see below), "stock" does not include any:

- loan capital;
- bill of exchange or promissory note,
- certificate of deposit within the meaning of Sec. 2 of the *Inland Revenue Ordinance* (see Chapter 4);
- Exchange Fund debt instrument or Hong Kong dollar denominated multilateral agency debt instrument within the meaning of the *Inland Revenue Ordinance* (see Chapter 4);
- bond issued under the *Loans Ordinance*; or
- debentures, loan stocks, funds, bonds or notes denominated otherwise than in the currency of Hong Kong except to the extent that the same shall be redeemable, or may at the option of any person be redeemed, in the currency of Hong Kong.

"Hong Kong stock" is also defined in Sec. 2 and means stock, the transfer of which is required to be registered in Hong Kong. Accordingly, Hong Kong stock will only ever comprise certain securities, the ownership of which is recorded on a register maintained in Hong Kong. In practice, this means that it is usually only shares in companies which keep their register of members in Hong Kong (mainly Hong Kong incorporated companies or companies listed on the Stock Exchange of Hong Kong) which are within the definition of Hong Kong stock.

12.4.1 Sale and purchase

When a person purchases or sells Hong Kong stock, as either principal or agent, he or she is required by Sec. 19(1):

(a)   to execute a contract note (usually referred to as a bought note or a sold note), which is liable to Stamp Duty at the rate of 0.1% on the consideration or the value of the shares bought and sold. As each of the purchaser and seller must execute a contract note, the total Stamp Duty on a transaction is 0.2%;

(b)   to execute an instrument of transfer, which is subject to a fixed amount of Stamp Duty of $5;

(c)   to cause an endorsement on the instrument of transfer or, in the case of electronic stamping (see section 12.15.6), to cause a stamp certificate to be issued in respect of the instrument, to the effect that *ad valorem* Stamp Duty has been paid on the contract notes; and

(d)   if he is an agent, to transmit the stamped contract note to his principal.

The time permitted for stamping contract notes and instruments of transfer is set out in Table 12.3.

Table 12.3 Stamping period for contract notes and instruments of transfer

	Executed in Hong Kong	Executed outside Hong Kong
Contract note	within 2 days after execution	within 30 days after execution
Instrument of transfer	before execution	within 30 days after execution

12.4.2 Exemptions

Exemptions from Sec. 19(1) apply to stock borrowing and stock return transactions, provided certain conditions are met (Sec. 19(11)). This is discussed further in section 12.4.4 below. Additionally, Sec. 19(1C) provides an exemption for sales or purchases under a "market contract". A market contract is defined in Sec. 19(16) and takes the meaning given to the term by Sec. 2 of the *Securities and Future (Clearing Houses) Ordinance*, and essentially means a transaction between a broker and a clearing house.

    A further exemption from the requirements of Sec. 19 applies to any sale or purchase of Hong Kong stock which is specified in the Fourth Schedule as an exempted transaction (Sec. 19(1D)(a)). This effectively exempts such transactions from Stamp Duty under Head 2(1); additionally, however, Sec. 19(1D)(b) specifically provides that those transactions are not chargeable under Head 2(4) which applies to transfers not caught by any other provision of Head 2. The transactions exempted under the Fourth Schedule are the sale or purchase of any "specified derivative", which is broadly defined as an option (but not a futures contract) over approved regional stocks or an approved basket of stocks, or a bond or note which is convertible at the holder's option into approved regional stocks or an approved basket of stocks, where that option, bond or note is, if effected in Hong Kong, subject to the rules of the Stock Exchange of Hong Kong. An "approved regional stock" is a stock listed on a regional stock exchange approved for the purpose of the provision by the Stock Exchange of Hong Kong. An approved basket of stocks is a basket made up of stocks listed on either the Stock Exchange of Hong Kong or an approved regional stock exchange, provided that no more than 40% of the value of the basket comprises stocks listed on the Stock Exchange of Hong Kong.

Sec. 47A contains a broad exemption in respect of any instrument of transfer in connection with certain transfers of units in unit trust schemes (which, as discussed in section 12.4.6 below, may be dutiable as transfers of Hong Kong stock) where the scheme is a "registered scheme" or an "approved pooled investment fund" as defined in the *Mandatory Provident Fund Schemes Ordinance*. The exemption does not apply to all transfers in MPF schemes, but only to transfers:

(1) in the case of a unit in a constituent fund of a registered scheme, from the manager of the scheme to a person who is a member of the scheme or intends to become a member of the scheme, provided that the manager's power to effect the transfer does not arise from a previous transfer to him of that or another unit (Sec. 47A(1)); or

(2) in the case of a unit in a unit in an approved pooled investment fund, from the manager of that fund to the trustee or manager of a constituent fund of a registered scheme, provided that the power of the manager to transfer that unit does not arise from a previous transfer to him of that or another unit (Sec. 47A(2));

Additionally, under Sec. 30(4), where the holder of a unit in a unit trust scheme redeems that unit (i.e. gives up his interest therein without selling it to another person), that person is deemed to have sold the unit to the manager of the unit trust scheme (who may then either extinguish the unit or sell it to another person); as such, a liability to stamp duty would, *prima facie*, arise if the unit is within the definition of Hong Kong stock. Nonetheless, Secs. 47A(3) and 47A(4) grant an exemption from stamp duty in respect of the instrument of transfer in circumstances where Sec. 30(4) applies but the unit trust scheme is a constituent fund of a registered scheme or an approved pooled investment fund, and the transfer is effected by extinguishing the unit.

12.4.3 Gifts and transfers at less than full value

In the case of transfer of Hong Kong stock other than by way of sale, the only instrument brought into existence in connection with the transfer is generally the instrument of transfer itself as there is no bought note or sold note involved. In these circumstances, Head 2(3), which applies to voluntary dispositions *inter vivos*, provides that the instrument of transfer is chargeable with *ad valorem* Stamp Duty at the rate of 0.2% of consideration or value of the shares transferred plus a fixed Stamp Duty of $5. The Stamp Duty is payable within 7 days after the execution of the instrument of transfer if it is executed in Hong Kong or 30 days after the execution if it is executed outside Hong Kong.

Additionally, Sec. 27(4) operates to treat a transfer at less than full value to also be a voluntary disposition *inter vivos*, with the effect that the Stamp Duty is calculated with respect to the market value of the stock transferred, rather than the stated consideration. For a further discussion of Sec. 27(4), see section 12.3.2 above and section 12.7 below.

12.4.4 Transfers of beneficial interest other than by way of sale

Sec. 19(1E) was introduced as a measure to avoid a potential loss of Stamp Duty revenue which it was perceived may have occurred following the introduction of the Central Clearing and Settlement System for transactions conducted through the Stock Exchange of Hong Kong. In particular, under that system, most stock of listed companies is held in a central depository and registered in the names of nominees. As such, an instrument of transfer is no longer required to transfer stock other than by way of a sale and purchase.

The provision applies where there is a passing of beneficial interest in Hong Kong stock other than on sale and purchase and the transaction is:

(a)   effectuated other than by means of an instrument of transfer; and

(b) effectuated under or through a recognized clearing house (the meaning of which is as defined in Sec. 2 of the *Securities and Futures (Clearing Houses) Ordinance*) or any other person or organisation.

In these circumstances, Sec. 19(1E)(a) provides that the transaction is deemed to be a sale and purchase of Hong Kong stock; accordingly, the requirements of Sec. 19(1) apply to the parties to the transaction. For the purpose of determining who, in these circumstances, incurs obligations under Sec. 19(1), it is provided in Sec. 19(1E)(b) that the person disposing of the stock is deemed to be the person effecting the sale, the person acquiring the stock is deemed to be the person effecting the purchase and the person maintaining the record of the transaction, shall (if they are not also a principal in the transaction or a recognized clearing house) be deemed to be the agent effecting the sale and purchase. Moreover, the same provision deems the consideration for the deemed sale and purchase to be the value of the stock which is the subject of the transaction.

Notwithstanding the fact that a transaction to which these provisions apply is deemed to be a sale and purchase, Sec. 19(1E)(c) provides that the transaction will still be exempt from Stamp Duty where the exemption under Sec. 27(5) (see section 12.10.5) would have applied had the transaction been effected as a voluntary disposition *inter vivos*.

For a further discussion as to the practical application of Sec. 19(1E), see *Stamp Office Interpretation & Practice Notes No. 4.*

12.4.5 Stock borrowing and lending

A sale or purchase of stock is defined in broad terms in Sec. 19(16) as including any disposal or acquisition (other than an allotment) for valuable consideration. Accordingly, the lending and borrowing of Hong Kong stock would, but for the specific exemptions discussed below, be chargeable to Stamp Duty as if it was a sale and purchase of stock. As with any other sale and purchase of Hong Kong stock, the Stamp Duty rate on a stock borrowing transaction would, *prima facie*, be 0.2% of the higher of the consideration or the value of the stock being borrowed and lent. When the stock is returned, it would be treated as another sale and purchase of stock and Stamp Duty would, *prima facie*, again be payable at the rate of 0.2%.

Sec. 19(11), however, provides that a borrowing of stock, and a return of stock under a stock borrowing transaction, are generally exempt from the provisions of Sec. 19(1) and, therefore, from the Stamp Duty which would otherwise be payable. For this purpose, a "stock borrowing" is a borrowing in respect of stock the sale and purchase of which in Hong Kong is subject to the rules and practices of the Hong Kong Stock Exchange, irrespective of whether the stock is obtained directly from the lender or indirectly through a recognized clearing house. The exemption in Sec. 19(11) is, however, subject to various provisions, the more important of which are set out in Sec. 19(12). In particular, Sec. 19(12) provides that a stock borrowing is deemed to be a sale and purchase of the borrowed stock (and therefore subject to Stamp Duty) if:

(a)   the borrower ceases to be required to make a stock return under the stock borrowing and lending agreement (Sec. 19(12)(a)). For the definition of "stock return", see Sec. 19(16);

(b)   the purpose of the borrowing was not a "specified purpose" (Sec. 19(12)(b)); or

(c)   the borrower fails to comply with a valid demand by the lender under the relevant stock borrowing and lending agreement for the return of the stock (Sec. 19(12)(c)).

For the purpose of the above tests, references to stock borrowed or lent extend to part of such stock or the reasonable equivalent to such stock. With regard to the last point, this ensures, for example, that it is not necessary for exactly the same stock to be returned to the lender for the exemption to apply, but that the return of equivalent stock will be sufficient. Moreover, the term "reasonable equivalent" is defined in Sec. 19(16) to include monies which the Collector is satisfied reasonably and fairly represent the value of the stock in question.

The specified purposes in relation to Sec. 19(12)(b) are defined in Sec. 19(16) as follows:

(i)   the settling of a sale of Hong Kong stock, wherever effected, whether by a borrower himself or another person;

(ii)   the settling of a future sale of Hong Kong stock, whether agreed or not when such stock borrowing is effected and whether by a borrower himself or another person;

(iii) the replacement, in whole or in part, of Hong Kong stock obtained by a borrower under another stock borrowing;

(iv)   the on-lending of the borrowed stock to another borrower who effects a stock borrowing in respect of such stock on-lent; or

(v)   such other purpose as the Collector may, in writing, allow either generally or in any particular case.

The most common purpose, in practice, under which a stock borrowing qualifies as being for a specified purpose is where the borrowing is used to settle a sale of Hong Kong stock effected on the floor of the Stock Exchange of Hong Kong.

Although a stock borrowing transaction may otherwise be exempt from Stamp Duty, Sec. 19(12A) provides that the exemption will be lost unless, within 30 days after the stock borrowing is effected, the relevant agreement is presented to the Collector, along with such other information and documentation which the Collector may request and a fee, the amount of which is as specified by the Financial Secretary in the *Gazette*. The current fee is $270.

The stock borrower must keep proper records of the stock borrowed and returned, and produce them for the inspection of the Collector upon request (Sec. 19(13)).

Further information on the exemption applicable to stock borrowing and lending can be found in *Stamp Office Interpretation and Practice Notes No. 2*.

12.4.6 Unit trusts

A unit in a unit trust is included in the definition of stock contained in Sec. 2. Accordingly, if the transfer of a unit in a unit trust is required to be registered in Hong Kong, it is treated as Hong Kong stock and such a transfer is chargeable with Stamp Duty. The rules governing the charge to Stamp Duty on transfers of units in unit trusts are, however, more complicated than those concerning transfers of other types of Hong Kong stock, and are dealt with separately in Part IV of the SDO, although certain elements of Sec. 19 are also of direct relevance.

Part IV effectively deems as a transfer by way of sale, the following:

(1) the requirement or authorisation by a person that the manager or trustee of a unit trust scheme treat that person as no longer interested in a unit but not to treat another person as interested in the unit (Sec. 30(4)). This would occur when a person wished to redeem his unit; or

(2) the requirement or authorisation by the manager of a unit trust that the trustee of that unit trust treat a person as entitled to a unit and their power to do so arises from the previous transfer to the manager or trustee of that or another unit (Sec. 30(5)). This would occur when a person acquires a unit which had previously been redeemed by another person but was not cancelled.

By deeming the above to be transfers by way of sale, the parties are required to prepare, execute and stamp contract notes in accordance with Sec. 19(1); this gives rise to a liability to stamp duty at *ad valorem* rates. Moreover, any instrument by which the person gives the requirement or authorisation is deemed to be a transfer by way of sale falling within Head 2(4) and, therefore, subject to a flat rate of stamp duty of $5.

Additionally, where a person authorises or requires the manager or trustee of a unit trust to treat that person as no longer interested in a unit but to treat another person as having an entitlement to that unit (i.e. the person has either sold or given away his unit), that person is deemed by Sec. 30(3) to have transferred that unit. Furthermore, Sec. 30(3) deems any instrument under which the person notifies the manager or trustee of the requirement or authorisation to be a transfer operating as a voluntary disposition *inter vivos* or a transfer falling within Head 2(4), depending on the exact nature of the transaction. The effect of this is that where the transfer is by way of sale, Sec. 19(1) would require contract notes to be prepared, executed and stamped with stamp duty at *ad valorem* rates under Head 2(1) based on the consideration paid, and the notice of requirement or authorisation issued by the person would be subject to a flat rate of stamp duty of $5 under Head 2(4). On the other hand, if the transfer was by way of a voluntary disposition *inter vivos*, the instrument under which the person notifies the manager or trustee of the relevant requirement or authorisation would be dutiable under Head 2(3) at *ad valorem* rates plus a flat amount of $5.

Nonetheless, Sec. 19(1A) provides an exemption from Sec. 19(1), and therefore Stamp Duty at *ad valorem* rates under Head 2(1) (or Head 2(3)), to an otherwise stampable sale or purchase of a unit in a unit trust where such sale or purchase is effected by:

(a)   extinguishing a unit; or
(b)   the managers of the unit trust under a power which arises:
  - from the transfer to them of that unit or some other unit within the previous two months; or
  - otherwise than from a previous transfer to them of that or any other unit.

This provision reflects the practical reality that transfers of units in unit trusts are usually effected by selling the units back to the managers, who then either extinguish the units or resell them to another person. The provision therefore operates to provide that no *ad valorem* Stamp Duty under Head 2 (1) is payable in respect of transfers to the managers, unless the managers hold the units for more than two months after acquisition, in which case *ad valorem* Stamp Duty is payable on both the purchase and sale by the managers. Although *ad valorem* Stamp Duty is not payable on the transfers referred to above, nominal Stamp Duty of $5 is payable under Head 2(4) on every such transfer.

In circumstances where *ad valorem* Stamp Duty is paid on an acquisition of units by the managers of a unit trust scheme, but within two months of such acquisition the units are extinguished, the managers may apply under Sec. 19A for a refund of the Stamp Duty paid. Note, however, that the application for refund must be made within the relevant two-month period.

In addition to the exemption from the *ad valorem* Stamp Duty referred to above, an exemption is also available from the Stamp Duty imposed at the flat rate of $5 under Head 2(4) on certain transfers of units in a unit trust. In particular, from 14 November 2003, Sec. 47B operates to exempt from Stamp Duty under Head 2(4) any instrument deemed to be a transfer under Secs. 30(3), 30(4) or 30(5), where the transaction is also exempt from *ad valorem* rates of Stamp Duty pursuant to Sec. 19(1A).

12.5 Bearer Instruments

A bearer instrument is defined in Sec. 2 as:

> *"any instrument to bearer by delivery of which any stock can be transferred, but does not include an instrument relating to stock which consists of a loan expressed in terms other than in the currency of Hong Kong except to the extent that the loan is repayable, or may at the option of any person be repaid, in the currency of Hong Kong."*

"Hong Kong bearer instrument" is also defined in Sec. 2 as:

> *"a bearer instrument issued:*
>
> *(a) in Hong Kong; or*
>
> *(b) elsewhere by or on behalf of a body corporate formed, or an unincorporated body of persons established, in Hong Kong;"*

Head 3 of the First Schedule provides that a Hong Kong bearer instrument is stampable before issue, and that the Stamp Duty is payable at the rate of 3% of the value of the bearer instrument at the time of issue. An exemption applies, however, in respect of any units in a unit trust scheme where the terms of the scheme restrict the fund to investing in loan capital.

12.6 Duplicates and Counterparts

Head 4 of the First Schedule provides that duplicates and counterparts of instruments chargeable under Heads 1, 2 and 3 are chargeable with Stamp Duty at a fixed rate of $5. If the Stamp Duty payable in respect of the original instrument is less than $5, however, the Stamp Duty chargeable on the duplicate or counterpart is the same as that charged on the original instrument. The stamping period is seven days from the date of execution, or such longer period as is allowed for the original instrument.

12.7 Determination of Stamping Value

As discussed in previous sections, the value upon which Stamp Duty is calculated is effectively the higher of the consideration stated in the relevant instrument or the value of the immovable property or stock which is the subject of that instrument. As a matter of practice, the Collector initially charges Stamp Duty based on the stated consideration. If, however, it is considered at a later date that the value of the immovable property or stock transferred is more than the stated consideration, the Collector will raise a further assessment demanding additional Stamp Duty based on the excess of such value over the stated consideration.

The stamping value of a transfer of immovable property is based on the market value of the property free from any encumbrance. The market value is usually supplied by the Commissioner of Rating and Valuation. The date for determining the valuation of a non-residential property is the date of the assignment. However, the Collector, as a concession, normally accepts the valuation of the property at the date of the sale and purchase agreement as the value for stamping and payment of Stamp Duty (see *Zung Fu Co. Ltd. v Collector of Stamp Revenue* (1 HKTC 853)).

The value for Stamp Duty purposes of a transfer of stock is based upon the net asset value of the stock being transferred. In determining this value the Collector usually, as a matter of practice, takes the latest accounts of the company whose shares are the subject of the transfer and revalues the assets of that company to their market value at the time of the transfer.

12.8 What Constitutes Consideration

It is, of course, important to know what is included as consideration for the purpose of determining the value upon which Stamp Duty is calculated. In this regard, it is clear that consideration extends beyond cash and includes benefits or money's worth, debts assigned or waived, securities, commodity or services performed. Some of these issues are considered further below.

12.8.1 Debts waived and assigned

In addition to general principles, Sec. 24(1) provides that consideration for Stamp Duty purposes includes debts waived or assigned, and that debts include contingent liabilities. For example, if a borrower assigns to the lender his immovable property of a value of $2,000,000 as a full settlement of a debt in the amount of $2,500,000, the value taken for stamping the conveyance is $2,500,000 (i.e. the whole of the amount of the debt repaid). In such circumstances, however, the person liable for the duty may apply pursuant to Sec. 24(2) to have the Stamp Duty payable on the conveyance based on the value of the property (i.e. $2,000,000). If the Stamp Duty is calculated under that provision, the dutiable instrument must be adjudicated in accordance with the provisions of Sec. 13, which is discussed below.

Further, Sec. 24(3) effectively provides that where there is a transfer of shares in a body corporate and the transferee assumes a liability of that body corporate, the amount of the liability so assumed is to be taken as consideration for the transfer when calculating the Stamp Duty payable.

For a further discussion of Sec. 24 and examples as to its practical application, see *Stamp Office Interpretation and Practice Notes No. 3.*

12.8.2 Methods of calculation of monetary consideration

Sec. 23 sets out rules for dealing with consideration payable in instalments and provides that where consideration consists of periodic payments not exceeding 20 years, the value for Stamp Duty purposes is the total amount payable (Sec. 23(1)). If, however, the consideration consists of periodic payments over a period exceeding 20 years, the value for stamping is the total amount payable within the first 20 years after the date of execution of the relevant instrument (Sec. 23(2)). Where the consideration consists of periodic payments for a life or lives, the value for stamping is the total amount payable within 12 years after the date of execution of the relevant instrument (Sec. 23(3)).

12.8.3 Consideration less than market value

Sec. 27(4) has been referred to earlier and provides that if the stated consideration is below the market value of the property or stock transferred, the transfer is deemed to be a voluntary disposition *inter vivos* (except where the consideration is marriage) and that the market value is to be used as a basis for the computation of Stamp Duty. It is important to note that this applies even where the parties have acted at arm's length (see *Lap Shun Textiles Industrial Co. Ltd. v Collector of Stamp Revenue* (1 HKTC 880)).

12.8.4 Exchange and partition of property

Sec. 25(7) provides that if two immovable properties are exchanged, and a deed of exchange is prepared (rather than two separate sale and purchase agreements or two separate assignments), the computation of Stamp Duty will not be based on the total value of the two properties, but only on any equality money payable. Equality money is the higher of the amount payable by one owner to the other owner or the difference in the value of the two properties. Sec. 25(7) also provides that if there is a partition of immovable property, the Stamp Duty is also charged only on any equality money paid.

Similar provision is made in Sec. 29C(10) in respect of an exchange involving residential property or the partition of a residential property. That is, Stamp Duty on such an exchange or partition is calculated only on the basis of any equality money. Note that in the case of an exchange, Sec. 29C (10) applies irrespective of whether only one or both of the properties are residential properties. Previously, the Collector was of the view that the provision applied only where both properties were residential properties and that if only one residential property was involved, the agreement should be stampable as if it were a chargeable agreement for the sale of that property. In the current version of *Stamp Office Interpretation and Practice Notes No.1*, however, the Collector accepts that the provision is applicable where a residential property is exchanged for a non-residential property.

12.8.5 Contingency principle

Stamp Duty is generally assessed on the basis of the circumstances existing at the date of execution of the relevant instrument and cannot be altered or otherwise affected by subsequent events. If, however, the consideration is determined based on a future event, the consideration will only be ascertained after that event has occurred. In such circumstances, the consideration is unascertainable at the date of the execution of the instrument and no duty can be assessed.

Where, however, a maximum amount of consideration is provided for in the instrument, the Stamp Duty will be computed on such amount payable, even though the final amount may be lower than the maximum amount. There is no provision under which a dutypayer can, in such circumstances, obtain a refund at a later date when the future event has occurred and the final consideration is ascertained. Conversely, if only a minimum amount of consideration is provided in the instrument, the Stamp Duty will be computed on the minimum amount even though the final amount is higher than such minimum amount. The Collector cannot raise an additional assessment to Stamp Duty at a later date when the future event has occurred and the consideration is ascertained.

If neither a maximum nor minimum consideration is specified in the instrument, the Collector may invoke Sec. 27(4) to treat the transaction as a voluntary disposition *inter vivos* if the effect is to confer a substantial benefit on the transferee; in such circumstances, Sec. 27(1) would operate to assess the instrument to Stamp Duty on the basis of the market value of the property passing (see further, sections 12.3.2, 12.4.2, 12.7 and 12.9.1).

■ Example 12.2

A landlord lets a shop for two years to a tenant who uses it as a supermarket. The agreed rental is 10 per cent of the turnover of the supermarket for the period of the lease. The turnover is based on the figure reported in audited accounts. No maximum or minimum amount is stated in the lease agreement. As the rental depends on a future event, and cannot be ascertained at the date of the execution of the lease agreement, the Stamp Duty payable is the minimum provided in Head 1(2), i.e. 50 cents per $100 thereof. The Stamp Duty payable on the lease is, therefore, 50 cents.

Notes:
(a) If a maximum rent of $400,000 per month and a minimum rent of $300,000 per month is put in the lease agreement, the Stamp Duty payable is $24,000 ($400,000 × 12 × 0.5%). The Stamp Duty is payable within 30 days after the execution of the lease agreement.
(b) If only a minimum rent of $300,000 per month is put in the lease agreement, the Stamp Duty payable is $18,000 ($300,000 × 12 × 0.5%). The Stamp Duty is again payable within 30 days after the execution of the lease agreement.

12.9 Adjudication

Adjudication is a procedure governed by Sec. 13 under which the Collector adjudicates (i.e. determines) whether an instrument is chargeable to Stamp Duty and, if it is chargeable, what amount of Stamp Duty is payable. Adjudication is normally optional and elected by either the Collector or the dutypayer, although there are a number of circumstances where it is mandatory (see discussion below). It can be a very useful procedure where there is any doubt as to the amount of duty payable as, once adjudicated, the instrument is final and conclusive for the purposes of the SDO (unless an appeal is lodged). Accordingly, in cases of uncertainty as to, for example, the value of property being transferred, the risk of the Stamp Duty being increased some time after the transaction has occurred is removed.

12.9.1 Voluntary disposition *inter vivos*

As Stamp Duty is a charge on an instrument, the value upon which Stamp Duty is to be calculated can usually be ascertained at the time of stamping by reference to that instrument. In the case of a voluntary disposition *inter vivos* (i.e. a gift in a person's lifetime), however, there is no consideration stated on the instrument. In order to proceed with the registration of the instrument with either the land registry (in the case of immovable property) or the company's registrar (in the case of stock), the dutypayer may request the Collector to adjudicate the instrument. In such circumstances the Collector endorses the instrument to the effect that the instrument is pending adjudication, and the dutypayer can register the instrument with either the land registry or the company's registrar. When the value has been ascertained, the Collector issues a Stamp Duty assessment for the collection of Stamp Duty. After the payment of the Stamp Duty, the Collector endorses the instrument to note that it has been adjudicated.

12.9.2 The importance of adjudication

Adjudication is important in the administration of the SDO for the following reasons:

(a)   it is part of the process of appeal as explained in section 12.14 below;

(b)   once an instrument is endorsed as "adjudicated", no further Stamp Duty can be charged on the instrument because the instrument is final and conclusive for all purposes of the SDO unless an appeal is lodged within one month of the assessment (Sec. 13(8));

(c)   it is compulsory in the following situations:

  (i)   in the case of a voluntary disposition *inter vivos* (Sec. 27(3)); and

  (ii)   in the case of transfer in consideration of debts (Sec. 24(2)); and

(d)   it is compulsory in respect of certain other exempt instruments, such as in respect of a transfer in consideration marriage (Sec. 27(4)), a gift to an exempted institution (Sec. 44) and a transfer within a corporate group (Sec. 45).

12.9.3 Fee for adjudication

Prior to 2000, Sec. 13(1) provided that a flat fee of $20 was payable in respect of each and every adjudicated instrument. With effect from 1 June, 2000, however, the SDO was amended and the adjudication fee is now determined in accordance with Secs. 13(1), (1A), (1B), (1C) and the Fifth Schedule. Under the new rules, the adjudication fee is generally $50. However, most (but not all) adjudications which are mandatory under the SDO are exempt from the fee. More specifically, Sec. 13(1B) provides that the adjudication fee shall not be payable where the adjudication is required by:

- Sec. 24(2) (transfers in consideration of debts);
- Sec. 27(3) (voluntary dispositions *inter vivos* generally);
- Sec. 29F(2) (voluntary dispositions *inter vivos* under Part IIIA);
- Sec. 29H(3) (exemption from Part IIIA provisions for intra-group transfers);
- Sec. 44(3) (gifts to exempted institutions);
- Sec. 45(3) (transfers within a corporate group);
- Note 4 to head(1) of First Schedule (foreclosure order in respect of immovable property); or
- Note 3 to head 2(3) of First Schedule (foreclosure order in respect of Hong Kong stock).

12.10 Exemptions and Reliefs

There are a number of provisions in the SDO which provide exemption or relief in the case of what would otherwise be a dutiable transaction. The more important of these are discussed in the following paragraphs.

12.10.1 Transactions with the Government, leases of consular premises, etc.

Sec. 39 provides an exemption from Stamp Duty for, *inter alia*, conveyances on sale to the Government, Government leases, and certain instruments executed by the Housing Authority. Moreover, Sec. 41 grants a general exemption to the Government in respect of any other instruments which would otherwise be chargeable with Stamp Duty.

Further, Sec. 42 provides that the Government, the Central People's Government, any person acting on behalf of the Government or the Central People's Government, or an incorporated public officer shall be exempt from Stamp Duty in respect of any lease agreement. Additionally, Sec. 43 provides an exemption from Stamp Duty in respect of leases and conveyances on sale by "exempted persons" in respect of "exempted premises"; essentially, this applies to certain diplomatic staff in respect of certain consular premises. In either case, however, the other party to any such lease or conveyance is deemed liable for 50% of the Stamp Duty which would otherwise be payable on the instrument, unless that other person is the Central People's Government, the Government, an incorporated public officer or an "exempted person."

12.10.2 Gifts in consideration of marriage

Although a gift of immovable property in Hong Kong or Hong Kong stock is normally dutiable as a gift *inter vivos*, Sec. 27(4) provides an exemption from Stamp Duty if the instrument effecting the transfer of property or stock is executed in consideration of marriage. Such an instrument is, however, required to be adjudicated under Sec. 13, which is discussed above.

12.10.3 Gifts to charitable institutions

Sec. 44 provides that if immovable property in Hong Kong or Hong Kong stock is transferred to an exempted institution as a gift, the transfer is exempt from Stamp Duty. In order to satisfy the requirement of being duly stamped, the instrument is required to be adjudicated under Sec. 13. In order to obtain the exemption, the transfer must be an absolute gift in that the donor must not receive or retain any benefit from the transfer. If the transfer is not an absolute gift, such transfer will be treated as a voluntary disposition *inter vivos* under Sec. 27(1), and subject to Stamp Duty on the market value of the property or stock, as the case may be. An exempted institution is defined in Sec. 38 of the SDO as a charitable institution or trust of a public character which is exempt from tax under Sec. 88 of the IRO.

12.10.4 Transfers within a corporate group

Sec. 45 provides an exemption from Stamp Duty in relation to certain transfers of stock and conveyances of immovable property within a corporate group. The provision applies where the transferor and transferee are associated corporations as defined in Sec. 45(2), which provides that two corporations are associated where one is beneficial owner of not less than 90 per cent of the issued share capital of the other, or a third corporation is beneficial owner of not less than 90 per cent of the issued share capital of each of them. It is important to note that there is no requirement for any of the companies to be Hong Kong companies in order to qualify as associated for the purpose of this provision.

It is also important to note that this test looks only at the ownership of nominal share capital, with no regard to different rights attaching to different classes of shares. In recognition of this, there have been occasions where the ownership of a company under this test has been arranged to remain with one company through the issue of a different class of shares, while the economic value of the company is transferred. A typical example would be if a company (Company A) owned a piece of real property which an unrelated party (Company B) wished to purchase. If the real property was sold from Company A to Company B, it would attract Stamp Duty of up to 3.75%. If, however, Company A formed a subsidiary (Company C) and transferred the real property to that company, an exemption from Stamp Duty would, *prima facie*, be available under Sec. 45. As discussed below, however, that exemption would likely be lost if Company C was then sold to Company B as the relationship between Companies A and C, which was a requirement to qualify for the exemption, would be broken. To avoid this, Company C would issue deferred shares (i.e. shares with no voting rights, and with only such limited rights to participate in dividends or proceeds on liquidation that they were effectively worthless) to Company A. Sufficient deferred shares would be issued to comprise at least 90% of the total issued share capital. The ordinary shares would then be sold to Company B, with the consideration attracting Stamp Duty at the rate of only 0.2%, and the deferred shares would remain with Company A. Under such an arrangement, because 90% of the issued share capital of Company C would remain with Company A, the exemption from Stamp Duty on transfer of the real property would purportedly be preserved, but the full economic ownership of Company C would in effect pass to Company B.

An arrangement of the above type was the subject of litigation in *Arrowtown Assets Limited v Collector of Stamp Revenue* [2002] (1 HKRC 90-114) and [2003] (1 HKRC 90-126) and *Collector of Stamp Revenue v Arrowtown Assets Limited* [2004] (1 HKRC 90-129). The Collector of Stamp Revenue sought to challenge the transaction on a number of grounds, some of which are discussed below. One particular ground on which a challenge was mounted, however, was that the principle established in *W.T. Ramsay Limited v IRC* [1982] (AC 300) (see discussion in section 10.4.3) applied to permit the issue of deferred shares to be disregarded when considering whether the ownership requirement for the exemption was met. Interestingly, both the District Court and the Court of Appeal rejected such an argument and held that the *Ramsay* principle could not render such deferred share arrangements ineffective. On appeal, however, the Court of Final Appeal held that the *Ramsay* principle authorised the court to take a purposive interpretation of the legislative provisions and that as it could not have been the intention of the legislature to grant the exemption where full economic ownership of a company was held by a person unrelated to the person holding the majority of the issued share capital, the principle operated to strike down the arrangement.

In addition to the 90% ownership test, for the Sec. 45 exemption to apply other conditions must also be fulfilled. In particular, Sec. 45(4) provides that the exemption is only available where the transfer or conveyance is not part of an arrangement whereby:

(a)   the consideration or any part thereof is provided by a party other than another corporation which is associated, within the meaning of Sec. 45(2) as discussed above, with either the transferor or transferee (Sec. 45(4)(a));

(b)   the relevant interest in the Hong Kong stock or immovable property was previously conveyed, transferred, purchased or sold directly or indirectly by a person who is not an associated person in terms of Sec. 45(2) (Sec. 45(4)(b)); or

(c)   the transferor and transferee were to cease to be associated within the meaning of Sec. 45(2) by reason of a change in the percentage of the issued share capital of the transferee held by the transferor or a third corporation (Sec. 45(4)(c)).

On a strict interpretation, Sec. 45(4)(a) would mean that the exemption was not available where the transferee borrowed the funds from an unrelated party to finance the acquisition. According to the *Law Society of Hong Kong Circular to Members No. 1/83* dated 31 January 1983, however, the Collector has advised that the provision will not be treated as operating to deny the exemption where the consideration for the transfer is borrowed by the transferee from a bank, provided that the loan is on normal terms and in the ordinary course of the bank's business, and the bank does not obtain any rights over the property other than as security.

See, however, the *Arrowtown Assets* case (supra) for a case where this provision was subject to litigation. The facts of the case were quite complex but essentially involved a transfer of land within a corporate group from the original owner to one of its indirect subsidiaries, but with the transfer being part of a broader arrangement under which the land was to be redeveloped in conjunction with two unrelated property developers. Under the terms of the broader agreement, the original owner of the land, being the company which transferred that land to its indirect subsidiary, was to receive deferred consideration representing a portion of the surplus on the redevelopment; additionally, the property developer companies were to acquire an interest in the shares of an intermediate holding company of the company to which the land had been transferred. The District Court held that the deferred consideration was received from an unrelated party (being the developers) and as such Sec. 45(4)(a) was breached. In finding this, the court rejected the argument that the deferred consideration was in fact consideration for entering into the agreement under which the development was to occur, rather than consideration for the transfer of the land between the original owner and its subsidiary. On appeal, however, this finding was overturned by the Court of Appeal which noted that although the deferred consideration was payable under an agreement to which the unrelated company was a party, that consideration was still only payable between related parties (i.e. the original owner and its subsidiary). This finding was essentially upheld on appeal by the Court of Final Appeal.

The denial of Stamp Duty relief under Sec. 45(4)(a) is effectively expanded by Sec. 45(5) which provides that the consideration will be treated as having been provided by, or received by, a non-associated party if the purchaser is enabled to pay the consideration, or the vendor parts with the consideration, through participation in a transaction with a non-associate involving a payment or other disposition. In the *Arrowtown Assets* case, (supra), the District Court held that this condition was also breached because the consideration received by the original owner of the land, which was in the form of a loan note, was assigned (albeit to an associate) as part of a broader arrangement under which significant payments were made to the group which originally owned the land by a non-associated party (being a company owned by the developers); that transaction was in connection with the sale of shares in an intermediate holding company of the company to which the land had been assigned. Again, however, this finding was overturned by the Court of Appeal which held that Sec. 45(5) is a subsidiary provision which serves to explain Sec. 45(4)(a) but does not create a liability to Stamp Duty where one does not exist under Sec. 45(4)(a). Further, the Court of Appeal considered that Sec. 45(5) was concerned only with a "parting" of consideration to a non-associate and in the present case the parting of the consideration by the original owner was to an associate and, therefore, Sec. 45(5) could not apply. Although this was the ultimate basis of their decision, the Court of Appeal also considered that the parting with the consideration was not in consequence of the transaction under which the shares were sold to a non-associate.

On appeal, the Court of Final Appeal agreed that Sec. 45(5) had no application, although their reasoning was somewhat different. In particular, the Court of Final Appeal read Sec. 45(5) as amounting to an additional restriction on the relief otherwise available, although where it overlapped with Sec. 45(4)(a) it could not narrow the scope of that provision. They also rejected the suggestion of the Court of Appeal that Sec. 45(5) was concerned only with parting of consideration to a non-associate, considering that any parting with consideration was potentially caught. As with the Court of Appeal, however, the Court of Final Appeal held that in the case before them the consideration was not parted with as a consequence of the transaction under which shares were sold to a non-associate, rather, they held that the parting with the consideration was a condition precedent to that share sale and, therefore, was not caught by the provision.

It is also interesting to note that the cessation of association referred to in (c) is only in relation to the transferee. That is, in cases where the exemption is obtained because the transferor and transferee effectively have a common parent, the provision does not require the transferor to remain in the same corporate group as the transferee.

In addition to the above conditions, Sec. 45(5A) provides that even if the transfer was not part of an arrangement whereby the transferor and transferee were to cease to be associated in the manner described in (c) above, if for any reason they do actually so cease to be associated within two years the Stamp Duty exemption will be lost and the normal Stamp Duty will become payable in respect of the transaction within 30 days. Payment of the Stamp Duty after this 30-day period can result in late payment penalties being applied under Sec. 9 (see section 12.13 below). Sec. 45(5A)(a) requires the parties to notify the Collector of the fact that they have ceased to be associated within 30 days of such cessation and Sec. 45(7) imposes a penalty at level 2 (currently $5,000) in respect of a failure to comply with such notification requirement.

12.10.5 No change of beneficial interest

Sec. 27(5) provides that if there is no beneficial interest effected by a conveyance or transfer of stock, the instrument is exempt from Stamp Duty. This situation usually applies to an instrument effecting an appointment of a trustee holding the property or stock on behalf of the owner, or effecting the return of the property or stock from a trustee to a beneficiary. An important requirement to obtain this exemption, however, is that the circumstances giving rise to the exemption are set out in the conveyance or transfer. For a case where a claim for exemption under this provision failed because, *inter alia*, the assignments did not contain information on the circumstances of the transfer which was consistent with the claim for exemption, see *Chan Li Chai Medical Factory (Hong Kong) Limited v Collector of Stamp Duty* [2001] (1 HKRC 90-111).

12.11 Assessment and Payment of Stamp Duty

Stamp Duty, essentially being a tax levied on instruments, has traditionally been denoted on the face of the instrument when it is presented to the Stamp Office for stamping and payment of the requisite amount of duty. Nonetheless, as discussed further in section 12.15.6 below, Sec. 18E came into effect on 2 August 2004 and permits the issue of a stamp certificate (either in paper form or as an electronic record) in certain circumstances. Moreover, Sec. 18B permits the effective stamping of copies of documents in prescribed limited circumstances. As such, the Collector is usually not required to issue any Stamp Duty assessment if the Stamp Duty is based on the consideration stated in the instrument.

An assessment is, however, issued in certain circumstances. In particular, when the value of the immovable property or stock being transferred cannot be ascertained at the time of submission of the instrument for stamping, the Collector subsequently issues a Stamp Duty assessment informing the dutypayer of the amount of Stamp Duty payable. Such procedure applies in cases of voluntary disposition *inter vivos* (i.e. gifts) and when the value of the property or stock transferred exceeds the stated consideration. If the dutypayer disagrees with the Stamp Duty assessment raised, he may lodge an appeal against the assessment to the District Court (see section 12.14 below).

In the case of a gift *inter vivos*, if the party assessed fails to pay the Stamp Duty as demanded within one month from the date of assessment, penalties as provided for in Sec. 9(1) (see section 12.13 below) may be imposed. Further, the relevant instrument will not be treated as duly stamped until both the penalty and the Stamp Duty charged have been paid.

If, in cases where the value of the property transferred exceeds the stated consideration, the dutypayer fails to pay the Stamp Duty attributable to such excess as demanded within one month from the date of assessment, Additional Stamp Duty (in the nature of interest) is payable at the rate of 4 cents per $100 or part thereof per day until the amount demanded has been paid (Sec. 13(10)).

Sec. 13(8) provides that after the expiration of a period of one month from the date of a Stamp Duty assessment, the assessment becomes final and conclusive for all purposes unless an appeal is made against the assessment in accordance with Sec. 14 (see section 12.14 below).

12.12 Recovery of Stamp Duty

Sec. 4(3) provides that if Stamp Duty is not paid in accordance with the due date as imposed in the Stamp Duty assessment, the parties to the execution of the instrument are jointly and severally liable for the payment of the Stamp Duty and the Collector may take civil action to recover the unpaid Stamp Duty together with any penalties imposed.

In the case of conveyances of immovable property, all the parties executing the sale and purchase agreement, assignment, or other relevant instrument are jointly and severally liable for the payment of the Stamp Duty. Nonetheless, the Collector will usually, in the first instance, issue the assessment to the purchaser or donee, as the case may be. In the case of purchase or sale of stock, each party is liable for its own share of Stamp Duty (i.e. 0.1% on each side of the transaction). In the case of the transfer of stock as a gift, both parties are jointly and severally liable to the payment of Stamp Duty because they both sign the instrument of transfer.

12.13 Late Stamping

Any instrument which is required to be stamped must be stamped within the time limit specified in the relevant Head of the First Schedule. If an instrument is not stamped within the time limit, it may be subject to a penalty for late stamping under Sec. 9(1). Table 12.4 sets out the scale of late stamping penalties.

The Collector has a discretion under Sec. 9(2), however, to waive in whole or in part, any late stamping penalty. In considering the exercise of such discretion, the Collector will normally take into account any reasons offered by the dutypayer for the failure to stamp the instrument within the statutory deadline.

Table 12.4 Penalty charged on late stamping

Period Late	Penalty
Less than 1 month	2 times the duty payable
More than 1 month but less than 2 months	4 times the duty payable
More than 2 months	10 times the duty payable

12.14 Appeals

If a dutypayer is dissatisfied with a Stamp Duty assessment, Sec. 14(1) provides that he may lodge an appeal against the assessment to the District Court within one month from the date of the assessment. Sec. 14(5B), however, provides that the period for lodging an appeal can be extended if the dutypayer is prevented by illness, absence from Hong Kong or other reasonable cause from lodging the appeal within the one-month period. The dutypayer must, however, generally pay the Stamp Duty before lodging an appeal, although Secs. 14(1A) and (1B) allow the Collector or court to postpone payment of the duty, wholly or in part, upon provision of satisfactory security for payment thereof. For a case concerning the exercise of the discretion under Secs. 14(1A) and 14(1B) by a court, see *Wan Wah Shing v Collector of Stamp Revenue* [2005] (1 HKRC 90-152). Where, pursuant to either the exercise of the Collector's discretion or an order of the court, the payment of all or a portion of the Stamp Duty is postponed (but any amount required to be paid has been paid), the Collector is required by Sec. 14(1C) to endorse the instrument to that effect.

When a person files an appeal pursuant to Sec. 14(1), they can require the Collector or state and sign a case setting forth the question upon which his opinion was required and the assessment was made by him. In essence, this is a procedure by which the Collector can be made to explain the process by which he reached the opinions or conclusions upon which the disputed assessment was made. Where a case is so required of the Collector by the appellant, the Collector must comply with the requirement, following which the matter can be set down for hearing (Sec. 14(2)). Upon hearing the case, the court will decide the question submitted and, if the relevant instrument is found to be dutiable, the court must assess the amount of Stamp Duty due (Sec. 14(3)). This appears to prevent the court remitting the matter back to the Collector for further consideration as to the quantum of the liability.

If the amount of Stamp Duty assessed by the court is less than the amount originally assessed by the Collector, Sec. 14(4) provides that the excess is to be refunded along with any excess penalty paid under Sec. 9 in respect thereof. Conversely, Sec. 14(5) provides that if the court decides that the amount of Stamp Duty assessed by the Collector is not excessive, the court is to issue an order confirming the assessment. Interestingly, the combined effect of Secs. 14(4) and 14(5) appears to be that the court has no power to increase an assessment, which they might otherwise be inclined to do if, for example, the dispute concerned valuation and they concluded that the value the Collector adopted in assessing the amount of Stamp Duty was too low.

12.15 Other Issues

12.15.1 Substance over form

When considering whether an instrument is chargeable with Stamp Duty, the Collector does not look at the name of the instrument, but rather looks into the nature of the agreement to see whether it is subject to Stamp Duty. In other words, a principle of "substance over form" is applied in determining whether an instrument is chargeable with Stamp Duty.

On occasions, a dutypayer may seek to avoid the payment of Stamp Duty by labelling a stampable instrument as an unstampable instrument. An example would be presenting a lease with the label of a licence agreement. A lease is chargeable with Stamp Duty while a licence agreement does not fall within one of the four chargeable heads. The distinction between a lease and a licence is that a lease provides the tenant an exclusive right of possession, making it more difficult for the landlord to evict the tenant. A licence agreement, on the other hand, provides the licensee a right of occupation only, and such right may be revoked at will by the licensor. In order to attempt to avoid a liability, a dutypayer may present a licence agreement with a clause having the effect of granting an exclusive right of possession. In such circumstances, however, the Collector would likely ignore the label of the agreement as a licence and charge the agreement with Stamp Duty as a lease.

12.15.2 Non-admissibility of unstamped instruments

Under Sec. 15(1), if a stampable instrument is not stamped in accordance with the provisions of the SDO, such instrument is not admissible as evidence in any proceedings except in criminal proceedings or civil proceedings taken by the Collector to recover any Stamp Duty and/or penalties. Exceptions to this rule apply, however, in respect of civil proceedings before a court where the court orders, upon the personal undertaking of a solicitor, to cause such instrument to be stamped and any penalty payable under Sec. 9 in respect thereof to be paid, or where the instrument has been endorsed by the Collector under Sec. 14(1C) (see section 12.14). Sec. 15(2) also provides that, other than in limited cases described in Sec. 15(3), an unstamped instrument (which is required to be stamped) cannot be acted upon, filed or registered by any public officer (including land registrars in the case of sale or purchase or transfer of immovable property) or body corporate (including the company's registrar in the case of a transfer of stock).

12.15.3 Remission of Stamp Duty by the Chief Executive

The Collector is empowered to waive the whole or part of any penalty under Sec. 9(2), but he does not have the power to remit the Stamp Duty chargeable on a stampable instrument. The power of remission of Stamp Duty is vested in the Chief Executive under Sec. 52.

12.15.4 Failure to disclose facts and circumstances affecting Stamp Duty

Stamp Duty is a tax levied on an instrument, and the value for stamping must, subject to certain exceptions discussed above, be ascertained at the time of execution of the instrument. Sec. 11(1) provides that all the facts and circumstances which affect the liability of an instrument to Stamp Duty, or affect the amount of Stamp Duty chargeable on the instrument, are to be disclosed in that instrument. Sec. 11(2) provides further that any person who, with intent to defraud the Government executes an instrument in which all relevant facts and circumstances are not set out, or who is employed or otherwise involved in the preparation of such an instrument and neglects to set out all relevant facts and circumstances, commits an offence. Sec. 60 provides that the penalty for such an offence is a fine at level 6 (currently $100,000), and imprisonment for one year.

Sec. 11(3), however, gives the Collector the power to compound any such offence, although that power can only be exercised prior to the commencement of criminal proceedings in relation to the offence.

Where any facts or circumstances affecting the liability to Stamp Duty are not set out in the relevant instrument as required by Sec. 11(1), the Collector is empowered by Sec. 11(4) to either refuse to stamp the instrument or to stamp it subject to whatever conditions he thinks fit.

12.15.5 Copies of instruments

Although Stamp Duty is fundamentally a tax on instruments and is generally denoted on the face of such instrument, since 1 April, 1999 provisions have existed (Sec. 18B) whereby a copy of the relevant instrument can, in prescribed circumstances, be presented for stamping in lieu of the original. It is, however, important to note that these provisions have only limited application. For example, Sec. 18B(1) provides that it is only where the

Collector is satisfied that it would be impracticable in the circumstances for the original instrument to be presented, or be required to be presented, that a copy is acceptable. Moreover, the Collector is required by Sec. 18B(4) to be satisfied that the copy presented is a true copy of the original.

Nonetheless, when a copy is permitted to be presented to the Collector, the Collector does not stamp that copy but is required by Sec. 18B(2) to stamp a certificate issued by him (assuming all other conditions are met which would permit the original instrument to be duly stamped). Once the certificate is stamped, the original instrument is deemed to have been stamped for all purposes of the SDO.

The method by which copies are stamped changed slightly with effect from 2 August 2004. From that date, Part IIA came into effect. Part IIA is discussed in more detail in section 12.15.6 below, but essentially facilitates a system of electronic stamping of documents. Concurrent with this, Sec. 18B was amended to permit the stamping of a copy of an instrument by the issue of a stamp certificate under the electronic stamping system.

12.15.6 Electronic stamping

As noted elsewhere in this chapter, the stamping of instruments generally takes place by denoting on the face of the instrument the amount of Stamp Duty charged and paid. This manual process of stamping instruments is, however, in many ways outdated and fails to take advantage of efficiencies offered by modern technology. As a consequence, the Stamp Office has developed a system of electronic stamping of instruments. To facilitate such a system, significant changes to the legislative framework were required and these came into effect on 2 August 2004.

The principal amendments to facilitate electronic stamping were the introduction of Part IIA (Secs. 18C to 18J) which contains the basic legal provisions governing the alternative means of stamping documents. This essentially provides that as an alternative to presenting an instrument for stamping, the Collector may, upon application, issue a stamp certificate. The stamp certificate can be issued either in paper form or as an electronic record.

Sec. 18D provides that electronic stamping is available in respect of instruments chargeable under Heads 1, 2 or 4 of the First Schedule. Sec. 18F, however, provides that only instruments specified by the Collector can be dealt with under the new system. This reflects the fact that electronic stamping will be introduced progressively for different types of instruments. Indeed, at the time of writing the Collector had specified that electronic stamping was generally available only in respect of property transactions (in particular, agreements for sale chargeable under Head 1(1A), conveyances on sale chargeable under Head 1(1) and tenancy agreements chargeable under Head 1(2)(b)) which are stamped within the normal time limits, although late stamping and payment of penalties in respect of instruments which are not more than four years late and which do not involve a request for remission of penalty can also be undertaken through the electronic stamping system. Adjudication cases cannot, however, be dealt with through the new system, nor can cases involving an application for exemption or relief under Part V or through the exercise of the Chief Executive's discretion pursuant to Sec. 52. Note also that at the present time, stock transactions cannot be dealt with under the electronic stamping system.

Under the electronic stamping system, an application can be made either through submission of a paper form or electronically. The stamp certificate is then issued either in paper form or as an electronic record via the internet, depending on the method of submission of the application. Payment of the stamp duty can be made either on-line or through existing payment channels.

Appendices ■
Practice Notes
Issued by the Inland
Revenue Department

The following selection of Practice Notes issued by the IRD are reproduced in the following pages. Practice Notes not reproduced here can be obtained through the IRD website (www.info.gov.hk/ird). For a full list of current Practice Notes, see Table 1.1 in Chapter 1.

APPENDIX 1

Departmental Interpretation & Practice Notes
No. 1 (Revised)

Profits Tax

Part A : Valuation of Stock-in-Trade and Work-in-Progress

Part B : Ascertainment of Profits and the Valuation of Work-in-Progress

(A) Building and Engineering Contracts

(B) Property Development and Property Investment

These notes are issued for the information of taxpayers and their tax representatives They contain the Department's interpretation and practices in relation to the laws as it stood at the date of publication. Taxpayers are reminded that their right of objection against the assessment and their right of appeal to the Commissioner, the Board of Review or the Court are not affected by the application of these notes.

These notes replace those issued in October 1998.

LAU MAK Yee-ming, Alice
Commissioner of Inland Revenue

July 2006

Our web site : www.ird.gov.hk

CONTENT

PART A
Valuation of Stock-in-Trade and Work-in-Progress

It is essential for the proper computation of taxable profits for a given period that opening and closing stock-in-trade be correctly valued. The argument sometimes encountered that the matter corrects itself if the stock is correctly valued in subsequent years cannot be accepted.

2. These Departmental Interpretation and Practice Notes ("DIPN"), which do not cover professional work-in-progress, are intended to explain the bases of valuation that are acceptable for taxation purposes as such valuations may not always be the same as those used by auditors for the purpose of commercial accounting.

3. As there are no specific provisions relating to stock valuation for taxation purposes in the Inland Revenue Ordinance ("the Ordinance"), other than section 15C which relates to cessation of business, ordinary commercial principles and practice have first to be looked at. In this regard, the recommendations contained in *HKAS 2 (Inventories)*, issued by the Hong Kong Institute of Certified Public Accountants ("HKICPA") are broadly acceptable to the Department. Reservations the Department has in respect of certain recommendations are referred to in later paragraphs. Further guidance can be found in decided cases.

4. The objective of *HKAS 2* is to "*prescribe the accounting treatment for inventories*". It applies to all inventories, except:

(a) work in progress arising under construction contracts, including directly related service contracts;

(b) financial instruments;

(c) biological assets related to agricultural activity and agricultural produce at the point of harvest;

(d) inventories of agricultural and forest products, agricultural produce after harvest, and minerals and mineral products, to the extent that they are measured at net realisable value in accordance with well-established practices in those industries; and

(e) inventories held by commodity broker-traders who measure their inventories at fair value less costs to sell.

For the purposes of these DIPN, the term "stock" or "stock-in-trade" generally has the same meaning as the term "inventories" in *HKAS 2*.

The Basic Rule

5. The basic rule, whether for accounting or taxation purposes, is that stock should be valued at the lower of cost or market value *(Whimster v. C.I.R., 12 TC 813)*. Nowadays, the term "net realisable value" (see below) is used rather than market value.

Meaning of "Cost" or "Net Realisable Value"

6. The Departmental view is basically that the "cost" of stock means the actual or historical cost. As set out in paragraphs 10 to 17 of *HKAS 2*, this includes all costs incurred directly on the purchase, conversion and bringing the stock to its existing location and condition. Also included is any overhead expenditure which can appropriately be allocated to the cost of stock and carried forward in the circumstances of the business, instead of being recognised as a revenue expense in the period in which it was incurred. In limited circumstances, borrowing costs are included in the cost of stock [see paragraphs 11 and 12 of *HKAS 23 (Borrowing Costs)*].

7. For "net realisable value", the Department accepts that the term has the meaning stated in paragraph 6 of *HKAS 2*, i.e. "*the estimated selling price* in the ordinary course of business less the estimated costs of completion and *the estimated costs necessary to make the sale*". See also paragraph 10 below.

Court Decisions

8. The Courts have ruled on certain methods of valuation:

(a)   In the case of *Ahmedabad New Cotton Mills Ltd. v. Bombay Commissioners of Income Tax, 8 ATC 575,* it was held that where opening and closing stocks have been undervalued, the true profits can only be established by raising both valuations.

(b)   *C.I.R. v. Cock* Russell & *Co. Ltd., 29 TC 387,* established the right to apply cost or lower market value to individual items of stock.

(c)   In *Minister of* National *Revenue v. Anaconda American Brass Ltd., 34 ATC 330,* the L.I.F.O. method of determining cost was rejected by the Privy Council.

(d)   In *Patrick v. Broadstone, 35 TC 44,* the base stock method was rejected, even though it was accepted as sound commercial practice in the cotton spinning trade.

(e)   In *Duple Motor Bodies Ltd. v. Ostime, 39 TC 537,* consistency in the basis of valuation of stock and work-in-progress was stressed. The Courts, however, in refusing to decide between the rival claims of direct cost and oncost methods of valuation as a broad principle, found that the direct cost method, which had been consistently applied in the past, was one of the methods recognised as sound accountancy practice and saw no reason, in the circumstances of that case, to compel a change to the oncost basis.

(f)   In *Freeman,* Hardy & *Willis v. Ridgeway, 47 TC 519,* it was held that for tax purposes replacement value is not acceptable.

(g)   In *Pearce v. Woodall*-Duckham *Ltd., 51 TC 271,* it was held that the estimated accrued profits resulting from the change in valuation method of work in progress in that case should be treated as a taxable receipt for the year in which the amount was first revealed and brought into account.

Standard Cost and Retail Method

9. Use of the standard cost method or retail method for measuring the cost of stock in justifiable circumstances, as explained in paragraphs 21 and 22 of *HKAS 2,* is acceptable for taxation purposes, provided that the method is regularly reviewed, revised and applied on a consistent basis.

Net Realisable Value

10. To arrive at a valuation acceptable for taxation purposes based on net realisable value, the expression "the estimated costs to be incurred to make the sale" mentioned in paragraph 6 of *HKAS 2* would not include general selling costs. In practice, specific identifiable items of expenditure directly related to the stock in question, including provision for commission and brokerage which would have been incurred on sale, would be allowed.

Replacement Cost

11. The "replacement cost" (sometimes referred to as "replacement value") of stock is the estimated amount for which, in the ordinary course of business, the stock could be acquired or produced. As was pointed out in paragraph 8(f) above, replacement cost is not acceptable for taxation purposes, as, where the replacement cost is less than the net realisable value, the effect would be to take account of a loss greater than that which is expected to be incurred. Replacement cost is not recommended in *HKAS 2*, except in the circumstances mentioned in paragraph 32 of the Standard. In the circumstances mentioned in that paragraph, the replacement cost of materials may be the best available measure of their net realisable value, and it will also accordingly be acceptable for taxation purposes.

Basis of Valuation Used

12. Since more than one interpretation can be placed on such expressions as "net realisable value" or "cost", the Assessor should be made aware as to exactly what basis of valuation has been used. In addition, where the basis adopted for the valuation of stock and work-in-progress is one that is clearly not acceptable for tax purposes, the adjustment that is considered necessary should be made in the figure of profit returned for assessment. The basis on which the adjustment is made should be brought to the notice of the Assessor.

13. Once a satisfactory basis of valuation has been agreed, the Department will normally only require information concerning any subsequent change to be given in the taxpayer's annual return.

Shares and Securities Held as Trading Stock

14. Shares and securities are financial instruments and thus outside the scope of *HKAS 2*. The accounting treatment of these financial assets is, however, covered by *HKAS 39*. According to *HKAS 39*, financial assets that are acquired or held for the purpose of trading are classified as "financial assets at fair value through profit or loss". They are measured at fair value with all resulting gains and losses recognised in the profit and loss account as and when they arise.

15. For taxation purposes, the Department will follow the accounting treatment stipulated in the *HKAS 39* in the recognition of profits or losses in respect of these financial assets. Accordingly, the change in fair value is assessed or allowed when the change is taken to the profit and loss account.

16. *HKAS 39* defines "fair value" to be the amount for which an asset could be exchanged, or a liability settled, between knowledgeable, willing parties in an arm's length transaction. Valuation methods previously permitted for financial instruments prior to the time when *HKAS 39 became effective*, such as the lower of cost or net realisable value basis, will not be accepted for both accounting and taxation purposes.

17. An exception to this is for small and medium-sized entity ("SME") which qualifies for reporting under the SME Financial Reporting Standard ("SME FRS"). The SME FRS adopts historical cost method as the principal basis of preparation and requires shares and securities to be valued at the lower of cost and net realisable value. This valuation basis will also, accordingly, be acceptable for taxation purposes.

Work-in-Progress

18. *HKAS 2* recommends that work-in-progress should include direct costs and a systematic allocation of fixed and variable production overheads incurred in converting materials into finished goods. It is already general practice for overheads to be so included, but the Department also accepts as valid a valuation, if consistently adopted, based on direct cost only, i.e. cost of material plus wages. This is in accordance with the decision in *Duple Motor Bodies* [referred to at paragraph 8(e) above].

Keeping Stock Records

19. Section 51C of the Ordinance requires a person carrying on business in Hong Kong to keep sufficient records, in English or Chinese, of his income and expenditure to enable his assessable profits to be readily ascertained. The required records include statements (including quantities and values) of trading stock held by the person at the end of each accounting period. All records of stocktakings from which any statement of trading stock has been prepared should be retained. Such records should include:

(a) a list describing each article of stock on hand (including raw materials and work in progress), together with the value of each;
(b) who did the stock-taking;
(c) how the stock-taking was done;
(d) the date of the stock-taking; and
(e) the basis of the valuation.

It is an offence not to keep sufficient business records, with conviction carrying a maximum penalty of $100,000.

Undervaluations

20. From time to time, a clear undervaluation of stock for taxation purposes is revealed in accounts submitted or discovered in the course of a Field Audit examination by the Department. An undervaluation giving rise to an understatement of profits for a year may result from:

(a) a change from one valid basis of valuation to another;
(b) the use of a non-valid basis of valuation for both opening and closing stock;
(c) a change from a non-valid basis of valuation to a valid basis;
(d) a change from a valid basis of valuation to a non-valid basis; or
(e) an omission of stock or an incorrect estimation of quantity or value.

Quantification of Understatements of Profits

21. In quantifying understatements of the kinds referred to in paragraph 20(a) to (e) above, the Department would in general adopt the following approaches:

(a) *Change from one valid basis to another*
     The opening stock figure in the year of change should remain the same as the closing stock figure for the preceding year. Consequently, the Department will not allow a tax free uplift where the change would result in a higher opening figure, or seek to tax the business where the change would result in a lower opening figure, in response to any contention that the opening and closing figures are normally valued on the same basis.
(b) *Non-valid basis of valuation for both opening and closing stock*
     (i)   Both opening stock and closing stock must be valued on a valid basis which is appropriate for the stock in question;
     (ii) Depending on the facts of the case, the Department will review liabilities for earlier years;
(c) *Change from a non-valid basis to a valid basis*
     (i)   The opening stock must be revalued on the same basis as the closing stock;
     (ii) The liabilities for earlier years will be reviewed if it is considered appropriate;

   (iii) In a case where there is no question of fraudulent or negligent conduct, the total tax sought to be recovered for past years would not exceed the "tax saving" resulting from the uplift of the opening valuation for the year of change.

  (d) *A change* from *a valid basis to a non-valid basis*
   (i) The closing stock is to be revalued on the same valid basis as the opening stock;
   (ii) The valid basis must be followed for future years.

  (e) *Omission of stock or incorrect estimation*
   For cases where a valid basis is used, but there has been omission of stock or incorrect estimation, the auditor will ascertain the amount of understatement by a method which is appropriate in the circumstances. Various matters may be taken into account, e.g. the production process and the average stock-holding period.

22. The Department will consider the question of penalty action where an understatement of profits results from an incorrect valuation of stock, such as an omission or incorrect estimation as mentioned in paragraph 20(e) above.

PART B
Ascertainment of Profits and the Valuation of Work-in-Progress

(A) Building and Engineering Contracts
(B) Property Development and Property Investment

These notes deal with the above subjects as one, because there are aspects which are interrelated, although at the same time there are special features of each.

2. Normally, infrastructure and property development projects take more than one year to complete. As such, the application of proper principles in relation to revenue recognition and valuation of work-in-progress can have an appreciable bearing on the annual tax position. For this reason, it is desirable that the relevant principles on the above subject be stated, together with the Department's policy and practice.

General View of the Inland Revenue Department

3. In so far as revenue recognition and valuation of work in progress are concerned, the Department generally accepts the principles promulgated by the HKICPA in relevant accounting standards, including *HKAS 11* (Construction Contracts), HKAS 18 (Revenue), HKAS 23 (Borrowing Costs) and HK Interpretation 3 (Revenue — Pre-completion Contracts for the Sale of Development Properties) ("HK-Int 3").

BUILDING AND ENGINEERING CONTRACTS

Ascertainment of Assessable Profits

4. In the absence of any express or implied statutory rule in the Inland Revenue Ordinance ("the Ordinance") specifying how profits from long-term contracts should be ascertained, established accounting principles also apply for profits tax purposes. This position is reflected in the judgment of Sir Thomas Bingham, M.R., in *Gallagher v. Jones [1993] STC 537*, where he said at page 555:

> *"Subject to any express or implied statutory rule, of which there is none here, the ordinary way to ascertain the profits or losses of a business is to apply accepted principles of commercial accountancy. That is the very purpose which such principles are formulated ... so long as such principles remain current and generally accepted they provide the surest answer to the question which the legislation requires to be answered."*

5. This view is also supported by the Court of Final Appeal judgment in *CIR v. Secan Limited and Ranon Limited, 5 HKTC 266*, where Lord Millett said:

> *"Both profits and losses therefore must be ascertained in accordance with the ordinary principles of commercial accounting as modified to conform with the Ordinance. Where the taxpayer's financial statements are correctly drawn in accordance with the ordinary principles of commercial accounting and in conformity with the Ordinance, no further modifications are required or permitted."*

6. *HKAS 11* lays down that when the outcome of a construction contract can be estimated reliably, contract revenue (including any money retained under the contract) and contract costs associated with the construction contract should be recognised as revenue and expenses respectively by reference to the stage of completion of the contract activity at the balance sheet date (paragraph 22 of *HKAS 11*). This Standard does not adopt the realisation or completion of contract method which recognises profits only when a contract is completed. Profits recognised in the financial statements of an accounting year under the percentage of completion method should also be adopted for tax purposes for that year. If financial statements are prepared using this method, profits must not be excluded from assessment by way of a computational adjustment on the ground that the profits are not assessable until the entire contract is completed.

7. Paragraphs 22, 32 and 36 of *HKAS 11* provide that any expected excess of total contract costs over total contract revenue for a contract should be recognised as an expense immediately. In other words, a loss on the contract as a whole should be recognised in the accounts as soon as it is foreseen.

8. The Department's position in relation to the treatment of such an overall loss has recently been reviewed. The *Secan* case establishes the principle that the tax treatment should follow the accounting treatment. The Department's view is that the principle should generally apply to all types of income and expense, except as otherwise provided for in the Ordinance. As the making of provisions for foreseen losses is required by generally accepted accounting principles, and is not inconsistent with the provisions of the Ordinance, following *Secan*, the Department agrees that a full deduction should be allowed in the year the provisions are recognised in the accounts, provided that they are (a) made in accordance with the requirements of *HKAS 11*; and (b) estimated with sufficient accuracy.

9. An assessment for a year raised in accordance with paragraph 6 above cannot be reopened if a loss on the same contract is subsequently incurred. It is considered that section 70A cannot have application in such circumstances as the earlier estimation of profits would have been an exercise of judgement. The loss incurred would have to be set off against other assessable profits of the same year or carried forward to future years. However, where a contract is the only one undertaken by a taxpayer and the taxpayer has ceased business after the completion of the contract, the Department, as a concession, is prepared to re-open earlier years where profits were assessed, if an overall loss situation has eventuated on completion of the contract.

10. A contract is regarded as having been completed when a final certificate is issued by the supervising architect or consulting engineers.

11. Assessments already finalised on the completion basis in the fiscal year 1997/98 will not be reopened, but the following practice will apply to any assessment which remains open in that fiscal year and all future years:

(a) the "percentage of completion" basis of assessment will apply to contracts that commenced in that open year of assessment and all subsequent years until their completion;

(b) the "realisation" or "completion" basis of assessment previously accepted by assessors for profits tax purposes for unfinished contracts that commenced in a year of assessment prior to that open year of assessment will continue to apply to those contracts in every year from commencement until their completion.

Change in Basis of Valuation

12. Where there is a change in the basis of valuation of long-term contracts from one valid basis to another, the opening figure in the year of change must, for taxation purposes, be the same as the closing figure for the preceding year. [This is in line with the decision in *Pearce v. Woodall-Duckham Ltd.* referred to in paragraph 8(g) of Part A].

13. The Department will not accept a claim for a tax-free uplift based on the grounds that the opening and closing figures in the year of change must be on the same basis. However, the Department will accept the continuance of the existing basis for long term contracts current at the beginning of the year of change, with the new basis being applied only to contracts entered into during or after the year of change.

PROPERTY DEVELOPMENT

14. For the purposes of these DIPN, the term "property development" refers to development for profit by sale, whereas "property investment" refers to development for letting or some other long-term use in a trade, profession or business.

Date of Commencement

15. Where a person first enters into a property development project, he is regarded as having commenced business for the purposes of section 18C of the Ordinance when he takes the first clear step towards that end. This may be the date of acquisition of the site, or if the land has been held for some time, when some definite move is made towards development.

When is Profit Brought In

16. It is common practice for agreements for sale of flats or units in a development to be entered into before or during construction. These normally provide for payment of a deposit and instalments to the developer, with a provision that failure to meet any payments due under the agreement will result in the forfeiture of all payments made.

17. Notwithstanding that agreements for sale are entered into and part payments are received prior to the completion of the building, the profit on sale is regarded normally as arising when the contract is capable of completion by performance and the purchaser can be given possession. The sale is therefore regarded as taking place when the Occupation Permit in respect of the relevant unit is issued by the Building Authority.

18. This view is consistent with *HK-Int 3* issued by the HKICPA in May 2005 (this Interpretation was first issued in March 2005 as *SSAP-Int 24*). *HK-Int 3* concludes that pre-completion contracts for the sale of development properties do not meet the definition of construction contracts set out in *HKAS 11* if the contracts in question are not specifically negotiated for the construction of the properties. As a result, the stage of completion method shall not be used to recognise revenue arising from such contracts. Property developers need to apply *HKAS 18* in recognising revenue arising from pre-completion contracts for the sale of development properties. In broad terms, this Standard requires property developers to recognise profits at the time when the risks and rewards of ownership of properties have been transferred. In other words, profits are only recognised upon completion of a building.

19. In respect of pre-completion contracts entered into prior to the effective date of the *HK-Int 3* and with profits already recognised under the stage of completion method, there are two ways to deal with the contracts. The developers could continue to account for these contracts using the percentage of completion method or by restating the prior year profits through equity accounts.

20. The first method will not have any taxation consequence. Regarding the second method, the following assessing practice will apply:

(a) Profits derecognised will not be allowed for deduction as expenses in the current year (profits derecognised are not expenses);

(b) Profits derecognition does not arise from a change of valuation of trading stock (the valuation remains the lower of cost or net realisable value);

(c) Back year assessments will not be reopened under section 70A because back year returns did not contain any error or omission; and

(d) Profits assessed under the stage of completion method but derecognised on the adoption of *HK-Int 3* will not be assessed again in subsequent years (presumption against double taxation).

21. The most common practice nowadays is for property developers to team up with financial institutions to provide loan facilities to the initial buyers of their newly developed properties. Normally, a buyer has to make a down payment with the balance financed by a mortgage loan. Upon receipt of the entire consideration, the property developer assigns the legal title of the property to the buyer who, in turn, executes a mortgage deed in favour of the financial institution as mortgagee. Under such circumstances, the profit should be brought in according to the practice described in paragraph 17 above.

22. Sales may also take place on instalment terms. *HKAS 18* provides that there are two methods of recognising revenue for the sale of properties under instalment terms. The developers may either recognise sales in full at the time when the risks and rewards associated with the ownership of the properties have been transferred ("the full accrual method") or only to the extent of cash received ("the instalment method"). A relevant factor distinguishing the adoption of these two methods is whether there is evidence on the buyer's commitment to complete payment with reference to the buyer's initial and continuing payments.

23. The choice of the appropriate accounting method depends on the taxpayer's circumstances and the management should be in the best position to make judgement on this. In the absence of specific provisions governing the timing of assessment in the Ordinance, the Department's position is that the accounting treatment made in accordance with accepted accounting principles should be followed for tax purposes. Any excess of total payments over the cash price is treated as interest and is assessable when paid or credited.

24. In *C.I.R. v. Montana Lands Ltd., 1 HKTC 334,* the contracts for sale provided for payment by instalments over a period of 100 months, with assignment of the property deferred until payment of the final instalment. The taxpayer adopted the instalment method to account for the revenue. The Court held that the company's method of bringing in only the portion of the profit that was represented by the instalments received was in accordance with established accountancy principles, and should be followed for taxation purposes. The Department considers that this method can be adopted for taxation purposes in similar circumstances.

25. However, in *D103/99*, the taxpayer adopted the full accrual method in the recognition of profits for the units sold under instalment terms. The taxpayer also declared and paid an interim dividend for that financial year. For tax return purposes, the taxpayer made an adjustment to exclude the profits attributable to the outstanding instalments in respect of the instalment sales. The Board held that the *Montana Lands* case is not applicable. In *Montana Lands* case, the directors adopted the cash receipts accounting method, while in the present case, they chose the full accrual method and even paid a dividend. Therefore, the Board held that the profits in respect of future instalments receivable were correctly assessed to profits tax.

Overhead Expenditure

26. In many cases, the period covered by a development project will extend over two or more years of assessment. The same considerations will apply as to when and if so, to what extent, overhead expenditure should be included for tax purposes in the cost of work-in-progress, as in the case of building contractors. Here again it may not be the general practice to carry forward any of the overhead expenses in the developer's accounts or to treat only some as in the nature of oncost. This may be accepted when there is relatively little effect on the overall tax position, but the Department must reserve the right to examine the position more closely where circumstances so require.

27. Borrowing costs that are directly attributable to the acquisition of land, old buildings or the construction of units in a development project should be included as part of the cost of these assets until substantially all the activities necessary to prepare the development for sale are completed. This is in agreement with *HKAS 23*.

PROPERTY INVESTMENT

28. Where a person incurs expenditure on the acquisition and construction of a property which is to be used for the purposes of his trade or business, or for the production of income by way of letting, it is of primary importance that all capital expenditure is correctly treated for taxation purposes; it is always necessary that there be a strict application of proper principles in distinguishing between revenue and capital expenditure.

29. Where the person is carrying on business and there is already an established organisation, it is necessary to see that all overhead expenditure, including administration expenses, correctly attributable to the acquisition of the site and the construction of the property, are properly capitalised. These will include finance expenses up to the date when the property is capable of being used for the production of profits (*HKAS 23* and the Privy Council judgment in *Wharf Properties Ltd. v. C.I.R. [1997] STC 351* refer). This will usually be the date of the Occupation Permit or the date from which rent is first receivable. After that date, interest is correctly a revenue charge.

30. The remuneration of employees and staff directly engaged on the planning, construction and fitting up of the property should also be included in the expenses charged to the cost of the property.

CONCLUSION

31. The practice of the Department is not to insist upon a strict application of the full requirements and principles in small cases, or where the tax deferral effect is insignificant.

32. However, where the method of accounting in use results in a distortion of the true and fair profits for taxation purposes, it is expected that necessary adjustments will be made in returns and computations. Where detailed costing records are not available and the cost of work-in-progress is based solely on direct costs, a reasonable estimate should be made of the indirect expenses and general overhead properly attributable to the cost of production and work-in-progress.

APPENDIX 2

Departmental Interpretation & Practice Notes
No. 2 (Revised)

PROFITS TAX

Part A: Industrial Buildings Allowances

Part B: Commercial Buildings Allowances

These notes are issued for information and guidance of taxpayers and their authorised representatives. They have no binding force and do not affect a person's right of objection or appeal to the Commissioner, the Board of Review or the Courts.

These notes replace those issued on 20 July 1983.

Wong Ho-sang
Commissioner of Inland Revenue

April 1999

CONTENTS

<h1 align="center">INTRODUCTION</h1>

1. Whereas expenditure of a capital nature is generally not deductible, Section 18F of the Inland Revenue Ordinance (the Ordinance) provides for the assessable profits of a person for any year of assessment to be decreased by the amount of any allowances made to the person under Part VI of the Ordinance, and to be increased by the amount of any balancing charge directed to be made on the person under the same Part. The relevant allowances and charges apply in respect of certain (a) industrial buildings and structures; (b) commercial buildings and structures; and (c) machinery and plant.

2. This Departmental Interpretation & Practice Note (DIPN) is concerned with the provisions of Part VI relating to (A) industrial buildings and structures, and (B) commercial buildings and structures. The provisions concerning machinery and plant are discussed in DIPN No. 7 (Revised).

<h1 align="center">PART A
INDUSTRIAL BUILDINGS ALLOWANCES</h1>

Trades Which Qualify

3. The term "industrial building or structure" is defined, for the purposes of Part VI, in Section 40(1) of the Ordinance and commences with the following enumeration —

"industrial building or structure" means any building or structure or part of any building or structure used —
- (a) for the purposes of a trade carried on in a mill, factory or other similar premises; or
- (b) for the purposes of a transport, tunnel, dock, water, gas or electricity undertaking or a public telephonic or public telegraphic service; or
- (c) for the purposes of a trade which consists of the manufacture of goods or materials or the subjection of goods or materials to any process; or
- (d) for the purposes of a trade which consists in the storage –
  - (i) of goods or materials which are to be used in the manufacture of other goods or materials; or
  - (ii) of goods or materials which are to be subjected in the course of a trade to any process; or
  - (iii) of goods or materials on their arrival into Hong Kong; or
- (e) for the purposes of the business of farming; or
- (f) for the purposes of scientific research in relation to any trade, profession or business, …" ["profession" has been included with effect from the year of assessment 1998/99.]

4. It should be noted that for a building or structure (or part of a building or structure) to qualify, it must be used for the purposes of a trade, undertaking, service, business or profession as specified in paragraphs (a) to (f) of the definition, and not be excluded under the proviso to the definition. In this regard it is pertinent that except for paragraphs (b), (e) and (f), only trades qualify. It should not be thought that a building or structure can only qualify under (c) if it is used for the purposes of a trade which involves a manufacturing process; allowances may also be granted if the trade consists of the subjection of goods or materials to any process.

5. Guidance in relation to the question of whether a trade consists of the subjection of goods or materials to any process can be obtained from the High Court decision in the case of *CIR v Aberdeen Restaurant Enterprises Ltd* [1988] (2 HKTC 330). One of the issues considered in the case was whether a floating restaurant qualified as an industrial structure. The main thrust of the argument for the taxpayer was that cooking of food amounted to the subjection of goods or material to a process or processes. In considering the issue, Jones J. referred to the Judgement of the Court of Appeal in *Vibroplant Ltd. v Holland* [1982] (54 TC 658) where it was accepted, in relation to the equivalent provision in the United Kingdom's legislation, that "'process' connotes a substantial measure of uniformity of treatment or system of treatment". Jones J. went on to hold that the restaurant boat did not qualify for the allowances. In doing so he said, at pages 351 and 352, —

> "However, does the preparation and cooking of food come within the definition of the subjection of goods to any process. "Process" is defined in the shorter Oxford Dictionary inter alia as "a continuous and regular action or succession of actions, taking place or carried on in a definite manner; a continuous (natural or artificial) operation or series of operations. A particular method of operation in any manufacture."
>
> From the authorities, it is clear that in order to determine whether a building is an industrial building or structure, it is necessary to look at the legislation to ascertain its meaning. The words of the section show that the legislature intended allowances to be claimed by those engaged in the manufacture of goods or in the subjection of goods to a process. A restaurant has been described in the *Rael-Brook case* [1967] (2 Q.B. 65) as a service industry, but it is plain that it is not a manufacturing industry. Nor, as was submitted by Mr Feenstra, is it akin to a factory or mill but rather to a retail shop. Again, I am unable to agree that the cooking of food results in a uniformity of treatment as urged upon me by Mrs Clough. Each individual dish is prepared separately depending on the order placed by the customer. I can see no distinction between the cooking of food and the carrying out of the repairs in the *Vibroplant case* [1982] (42 TC 658). Repairs have no uniformity and are different in the same way as the cooking of food. It is again far removed from the *Kilmarnock case* [1966] (42 TC 675) which encompassed a definite process and a trade of manufacturing....
>
> I do not consider that the legislation was ever intended to extend to the business of a

restaurant. The trade of the restaurant has nothing to do with manufacturing or processing. Accordingly, I am satisfied that the restaurant boat and kitchen boat, three bridges or gangways do not qualify for the allowances for they are not industrial buildings or structures."

6. The following are examples regarded as satisfying the test of "subjection of goods or materials to any process" –
- an explosives shed used in the trade of quarrying and mining;
- buildings used in the trade of motion picture procedures;
- buildings used for the purposes of the trade of fumigation and extermination (i.e. pest control which might be performed outside of the premises) — see Hong Kong Inland Revenue Board of Review decisions *D 3/87* and *D 4/87*, Volume 2, page 329; and
- buildings used to screen and pack coal for sale — *Kilmarnock Equitable Co-operative Society Ltd. v CIR* (42 TC 675).

7. The following are examples of buildings which would not satisfy the test in question —
- buildings used for wage packeting, as notes and coins held as currency are not goods for processing — *Buckingham v Securties Properties Ltd.* (53 TC 292); and
- buildings used by banks for processing cheques and other documents, as these are not regarded as "goods or materials" — *Girobank plc v Clarke* (1998 STC 182).

Storage

8. In order to come within paragraph (d) of the definition, the trade itself must be one of storage. Godowns or warehouses for the storage of goods or materials which are to be sold by the storer or are for use or consumption within the trade of the storer would not rank for industrial building allowances under this paragraph.

Part of a Trade

9. There is no provision in the Ordinance for making an allowance where only part of a trade qualifies. In a case heard by the Supreme Court of Hong Kong, *Tai On Machinery Works Ltd. v CIR* (HKTC 411), allowances were refused to a retail distributor of goods who claimed to have subjected the goods to a process, it being held that the alleged processing was, at best, part of the trade and not the trade itself.

Buildings Which Qualify

10. The allowances can apply to all buildings and structures *used in qualifying trades*, other than categories specifically excluded by the second proviso to the definition of "industrial building or structure" (see paragraph 15 below).

11. The words "building" and "structure", which are not defined in the Ordinance, are construed as having their ordinary meanings. In practice the term "structure" is interpreted as covering artificial works that are not commonly regarded as buildings, such as walls, bridges, dams, roads, bore holes and wells, sewers, water mains, tunnel linings and wharves. In addition, the practice is to regard boundary walls, railway sidings and other works forming part of the premises as qualifying for the allowances.

12. Any buildings or structures provided for and in use for the welfare of workers, or for the housing of manual workers, employed in a specified trade, undertaking or business will also rank for allowances.

Part of a Building or Structure

13. The definition of "industrial building or structure" includes part of a building or structure. Where a building or structure is used only partly for the purposes of a qualifying trade, only the relevant proportion of the capital expenditure will generally qualify for allowances. However, proviso (i) to the definition stipulates that where the capital expenditure on the part of the building or structure which is not an industrial building or structure does not exceed one-tenth of the total capital expenditure, the whole building shall be treated as an industrial building or structure.

14. When additions are made to an existing building, the expenditure incurred ranks for separate allowances.

Buildings Excluded

15. The second proviso to the definition of "industrial building or structure" excludes from the meaning of the term any building or structure, or part of any building or structure, used as a —
    (i)   dwelling house (other than as a dwelling house for the housing of manual workers),
    (ii) retail shop,
    (iii) showroom,
    (iv) hotel, or
    (v) office.
It should, however, be kept in mind that even if part of a building is excluded by virtue of this proviso, the remainder of the building, or some part of it, may still qualify (see paragraph 13 above).

Capital Expenditure Incurred on Construction

16. The allowances (which are granted under Sections 34 and 35) are based on the capital expenditure incurred on the construction of the building (or structure). Such expenditure does not include the cost of the site or that of the preparation and levelling of the land. However, it can include expenditure on ordinary work done preparatory to laying foundations, and on laying drains, sewers and water-mains to serve the building or structure.

17. The allowable expenditure does not include anything that is reimbursed by any grant, subsidy, or similar financial assistance, or any expenditure which is deductible under Part IV of the Ordinance (e.g. expenditure on building refurbishment under Section 16F). On the other hand, it includes interest paid and any commitment fee incurred in respect of a loan obtained for the purpose of providing an industrial building.

Persons Entitled to the Allowances

18. Allowances are granted to any person who is entitled to an interest in an industrial building, where that interest is the relevant interest (see paragraph 21 below) in relation to the capital expenditure incurred on the construction of that building.

19. It is not necessary for the building to be used for a qualifying purpose by the owner himself. Accordingly, where a building is leased and used by the occupant for a qualifying purpose, the landlord, being the person having the relevant interest in the capital expenditure incurred on construction, is entitled to the allowances.

20. No allowances are due to a lessee who merely pays rent and/or a premium for the lease of a building and who has not himself incurred capital expenditure on construction or acquired the relevant interest of a person who did incur such expenditure. However, a tenant who incurs expenditure on a building which he occupies for the purposes of a qualifying trade, profession or business will have a relevant interest for the purposes of the allowances.

Relevant Interest

21. "Relevant Interest" is determined at the time when the capital expenditure is incurred. It is defined in Section 40(1) in the following terms –

> " "relevant interest" means, in relation to any expenditure incurred on the construction of a building or structure the interest in that building or structure to which the person who incurred the expenditure was entitled when he incurred it;"

22. A relevant interest can be acquired where the person who incurred the expenditure sells the whole of his interest in (i) the building, or (ii) part of the building. For example, A holds a lease of land from the HKSAR Government for 99 years. He gives B a lease for 50 years and B erects an industrial building thereon at a cost of $10M. After some time B assigns the balance of his lease to C, who acquires the relevant interest which B had in the capital expenditure incurred on the construction of the building. C is entitled to annual allowances calculated under Section 34(2)(b), and also to balancing allowances at the expiration of the lease under Section 35(1)(b). If, however, B merely sub-let the premises to C for a term of years (i.e. the sub-lease expires before the end of B's lease from A), the relevant interest would not pass and C would not be entitled to any industrial building allowance. B, however, having retained the relevant interest would continue to be entitled to the allowances, provided C is carrying on a qualifying trade, profession or business.

Buildings and Structures Bought Unused

23. Where capital expenditure is incurred on the construction of a building and before it is used, the relevant interest therein is sold, Section 35B provides that —

    (a) no allowances may be claimed in respect of that expenditure by the seller and any initial allowances already made under Section 34 shall be withdrawn, with additional assessments raised if necessary;

    (b) the person who buys that interest is deemed to have incurred, on the date on which the purchase price is payable, capital expenditure on construction of an amount equal to —

        (i) the net price paid by the purchaser for that interest if the interest is sold by a builder or developer in the course of his trade; and

        (ii) in any other case, the lesser of the net price paid by the purchaser for that interest or the actual cost of construction.

24. Should there be more than one sale before the building is used, (b) above applies only in relation to the last sale so that the final purchaser who uses the building is entitled to the allowances. In the case of (b)(i), the final purchaser would get allowances based on the lesser of the net price of the first sale or the net price paid by him (see the proviso to Section 35B). For example, in 1996 D constructs a building at a cost of $10M and sells it to E for a net price of $15M. E then sells it to F for a net price of $14M. F uses the building in his qualifying trade. Then, F would be the person entitled to the allowances calculated on an amount depending on whether D carries on a building trade and has sold the building in the ordinary course of his trade. If so, the allowances will be granted on $14M, the lesser of the net price paid by F and the net price of the first sale. In any other case, F would only be entitled to allowances based on $10M, being the actual cost of construction which is less than the net price of $14M paid by him.

25. The "net price" referred to in the two previous paragraphs excludes, of course, the price of the land on which the building stands.

Initial Allowance

26. Since the 1965/66 year of assessment, Section 34(1) has provided for an initial allowance of one-fifth of the capital expenditure incurred on the construction of an industrial building to be made to the person who incurred the expenditure. The allowance is made for the year of assessment in the basis period for which the expenditure was incurred.

27. Initial allowance is granted as expenditure is incurred, and there is no requirement that the building must be in use. However, proviso (b) to Section 34(1) stipulates that any initial allowance made under the section before a building is used shall be disallowed (and appropriate additional assessments made) if the building is not an industrial building when it first comes to be used.

28. Where the cost of construction is paid in instalments, initial allowance is made by reference to the instalments due for payment in the basis period of the year of assessment under consideration.

Annual Allowance

29. Since the 1965/66 year of assessment, annual allowances have been computed in accordance with paragraphs (a) and (b) of Section 34(2). Where the person claiming the allowance incurred the capital expenditure on the construction of the building, the annual allowance is 4% of the capital expenditure. However, if the person acquired the building after the capital expenditure on construction had been incurred (i.e. it was sold as an existing industrial building), the calculation of the allowance for the purchaser depends on when the building was first used as an industrial building, —

    (a) if first used *before* the commencement of the basis period for the year of assessment commencing on 1 April 1965, the allowance is calculated by reference to the "residue of expenditure" (see paragraph 31 below) immediately after the sale. The allowance is arrived at by multiplying the residue of expenditure by two and dividing the resulting figure by the number of years of assessment comprised in the period which begins with the first year of assessment for which the buyer is entitled to an annual allowance (or would be so entitled if the building had at all material times continued to be an industrial building), and ends with the fiftieth year after the year in which the building was first used; or

    (b) if first used *on or after* the commencement basis period for the year of assessment commencing on 1 April 1965, the allowance is arrived at by dividing the residue of expenditure by the number of years of assessment comprised in the period which begins with the first year of assessment for which the buyer is entitled to an annual allowance (or would be so entitled if the building had at all material times continued to be an industrial building), and ends with the twenty-fifth year after the year of assessment in which the building was first used.

30. Two conditions must be satisfied before a person becomes entitled to annual allowance in respect of an industrial building for any year of assessment —

(a) the building must be in use as an industrial building at the end of the person's basis period for the year of assessment; and

(b) the person must be entitled to an interest in the building at the end of the basis period for the year of assessment (and that interest must be the relevant interest in relation to the capital expenditure for which the allowance is claimed).

Residue of Expenditure

31. The term "residue of expenditure" is defined in Section 40(1) as meaning in relation to an industrial building, in effect, the amount of the capital expenditure incurred on the construction of the building, reduced by the amount of any initial, annual or balancing allowance made, and increased by any balancing charge made. The definition of the term also requires that in computing the residue of expenditure in relation to a building, there shall also be deducted in respect of any year in which no initial or annual allowance fell to be made (e.g. due to the building not being used as an industrial building), an amount equal to 2% of the capital expenditure for each such year prior to the year of assessment commencing on 1 April 1965, and 4% of the capital expenditure for that year or any subsequent year of assessment.

Balancing Allowances and Charges

32. Under Section 35(1), when any of the following events occurs to an industrial building —

(a) the relevant interest in the building is sold; or

(b) that interest, being a leasehold interest, comes to an end otherwise than on the person entitled thereto acquiring the interest which is reversionary thereon; or

(c) the building is demolished, destroyed or, without being demolished or destroyed, ceases altogether to be used,

a balance is struck between the residue of expenditure immediately before the event and the sale price, insurance, salvage or compensation moneys (if any). If the residue exceeds the sale price or other moneys, the difference is allowed as a balancing allowance. If the difference is the other way, it forms a balancing charge. A balancing charge is not to exceed the total of initial and annual allowances previously made to the person.

33. No charge or allowance falls to be made unless the building was an industrial building at the time of the event. Further, no balancing allowance is given where the building is demolished for purposes unconnected with the trade, profession or business for which the building was used. Thus, for example, where the land is ripe for re-development, and the building is demolished to enable the land to be sold unencumbered, no balancing allowance is given, even though the building was in use as an industrial building immediately prior to demolition.

Termination of a Leasehold Interest

34. If a lessee has incurred capital expenditure on a building, a balancing allowance or charge does not arise when the lease comes to an end if the lessee remains in possession with the consent of the lessor without a new lease being granted. His leasehold interest is treated as continuing (Section 35A(a)). If a new lease is granted to the lessee, or if the old lease is extended by reason of an option available to the lessee, the second lease is treated as a continuation of the first lease (Section 35A(b)). If the lessee buys the property from the lessor during the currency of the lease, the lessee's interest in any capital expenditure incurred is deemed to continue unaltered, and accordingly no balancing allowance is applicable.

Examples

35. Examples 1 to 4 of the Appendix illustrate the calculation of allowances and charges in respect of industrial buildings.

PART B
ALLOWANCES — COMMERCIAL BUILDINGS

Buildings Which Qualify

36. For the purposes of Part VI of the Ordinance, a commercial building or structure is defined in Section 40(1) to mean —

> "any building or structure or part of any building or structure used by the person entitled to the relevant interest for the purposes of his trade, profession or business other than an industrial building or structure".

Provided that it is used for an appropriate purpose, part of a building may qualify as a commercial building (i.e. it is not necessary for the whole building to be used for a qualifying purpose).

Expenditure Which Qualifies

37. As with industrial buildings, the allowances granted in respect of commercial buildings (and structures), under Sections 33A, 33B and 36, are based on the capital expenditure incurred on construction. In this regard, the comments made in paragraphs 16 and 17 of Part A above, under the heading "Capital Expenditure Incurred on Construction", are also pertinent to commercial buildings. However, it should be noted that Section 35B, which is concerned with buildings bought unused (see paragraph 23), does not have any application in relation to a commercial building.

Persons Entitled to the Allowances

38. An allowance in respect of a commercial building or structure is granted to a person where at the end of a basis period for a year of assessment the person is entitled to an interest in the building, provided that the interest is the "relevant interest" in relation to the capital expenditure incurred on the construction of the building. The meaning of the term "relevant interest" in relation to commercial buildings is the same as for industrial buildings (see paragraph 21 above). Prior to the year of assessment 1969/70, an allowance in respect of a commercial building could only be made to the owner of the building. From 1969/70, however, a tenant has been able to claim in respect of capital expenditure he has incurred on additions to a building, or for which he has thus acquired the relevant interest.

Rebuilding Allowance — Years of Assessment Prior to 1998/99

39. Section 36 provides for an allowance, known as "rebuilding allowance", to be granted where at the end of the basis period for a year of assessment prior to 1998/99 a person was entitled to an interest in a commercial building and that interest was the relevant interest in relation to capital expenditure incurred on the construction of the building. For each year of assessment from 1990/91 to 1997/98, the rebuilding allowance is 2% of the capital expenditure incurred on the construction of the building. For years of assessment prior to 1990/91, the rebuilding allowance rate is 0.75%.

40. Section 36(2) provides that that no rebuilding allowance may be made to a person in respect of any year of assessment after 1997/98 (i.e. where "the basis period for that year of assessment is subsequent to the basis period for the year of assessment commencing on 1 April 1997").

41. It should be noted that for assessments in respect of the 1997/98 and earlier years of assessment, the Ordinance does not provide for any balancing allowance or charge to be made where a person sold or otherwise ceased to use a commercial building.

Allowances for 1998/99 and Subsequent Years of Assessment

42. With effect from the year of assessment 1998/99, rebuilding allowance ceased to be applicable, and was replaced by a regime which is more closely aligned with that for industrial buildings — it likewise provides for "annual allowances", "balancing allowances" and "balancing charges". The amendments made to the Ordinance to implement the new regime did not affect the meaning of key terms such as "commercial building or structure", and "relevant interest". However, the definition of "residue of expenditure", which previously was only relevant to industrial buildings (see paragraph 31 above), was amended to also have a similar meaning in relation to commercial buildings. In particular, the expression is defined in Section 40(1) in the following terms —

"residue of expenditure" —

(a) in relation to a commercial building or structure, means the amount of the capital expenditure, incurred on the construction of the building or structure reduced by —

(i)   the amount of any annual allowance made under Section 33A;

(ii) the amount of any balancing allowance made under Section 33B, and increased by any balancing charges made under Section 33B:

Provided that in computing the residue of expenditure there shall be written off, in respect of any year in which no annual allowance fell to be made under Section 33A, an amount of one-twenty-fifth of the capital expenditure, and for the purposes of this proviso "year" means the period which would have comprised a year of assessment commencing on 1 April 1998 or any subsequent year of assessment in respect of which an annual allowance would have fallen to be made under Section 33A if the building or structure had been in use as a commercial building or structure;"

Annual Allowance

43. Section 33A(1) provides for an allowance, known as "annual allowance", to be made to a person where at the end of the basis period for the year of assessment the person "is entitled to an interest in a building or structure which is a commercial building or structure and where that interest is the relevant interest in relation to the capital expenditure incurred on the construction of that building or structure".

The Most Straightforward Situation

44. The annual allowance made to a person is computed in accordance with the terms of Section 33A. The most straightforward situation is where the capital expenditure on construction was incurred by the person on or after the commencement of the basis period for the year of assessment 1998/99 and the relevant interest has not been sold by the person. For such a case, Section 33A (1) provides for an annual allowance equal to one-twenty-fifth (i.e. 4%) of the capital expenditure incurred on the construction of the building. On this basis, and having regard to Section 33A(3) (which provides, in essence, that the annual allowance granted for any year of assessment cannot exceed the residue of expenditure prior to the making of the allowance), the allowance can be claimed for a maximum of 25 years.

45. Section 33A(2) and (4) cater for circumstances which vary from the situation described in paragraph 44 above, i.e. they respectively have application where the relevant interest has been sold and where the capital expenditure was incurred prior to the commencement of the year of assessment 1998/99.

*Where the Commercial Building or Structure Was Constructed Prior to
1998/99*

46. Where the expenditure was incurred prior to the commencement of the
basis period for the year of assessment 1998/99, Section 33A(4) has application.
In this situation, for the purpose of calculating annual allowances under Section
33A (i.e. for 1998/99 and subsequent years of assessment), the actual capital
expenditure incurred on construction is deemed to have been reduced. In essence,
the figure used is the actual capital expenditure reduced by the aggregate of the
rebuilding allowances which would have been made under Section 36 to the
person in respect of the building in all years of assessment prior to 1998/99 if at
all times during the period of the person's entitlement to the relevant interest
the building was used for the purposes of producing chargeable profits.

47. The balance of the capital expenditure thus arrived at (which will generally
be the capital expenditure incurred on construction less the aggregate of
rebuilding allowances previously granted) is used to ascertain the annual
allowance made under Section 33A(1) (i.e. 4% of the balance). The annual
allowance in respect of such transitional cases can be claimed for a period of 25
years, commencing with the year of assessment 1998/99. This follows from
Section 33A(4)(b) which provides that for such a building or structure, the year
of assessment commencing 1 April 1998 shall be deemed to be the year of
assessment in which the building was first used.

48. It should be noted that the application of Section 33A(4) is not restricted to
cases where a building was a commercial building or structure immediately
prior to the commencement of the 1998/99 year of assessment. The provisions
of the subsection also apply to cases where a building was put to some other use
(e.g. as private accommodation unrelated to any trade, profession or business),
or was vacant, as at the end of the 1997/98 year of assessment, and only
subsequently came to be used as a commercial building.

Where the Relevant Interest Has Been Sold

49. Section 33A(2) provides that where the relevant interest in a commercial
building is sold, the annual allowance is subsequently calculated by reference
to the residue of expenditure immediately after the sale (rather than as 4% of
the capital expenditure). The subsection specifies two methods of ascertaining
the proportion of the residue of expenditure immediately after the sale to be
claimed as an annual allowance.

50. The first method has application where the building was constructed prior
to the commencement of the year of assessment 1998/99 (i.e. it is a building to
which subsection (4) applies). For such a case, subsection (2) prescribes, in
effect, that the annual allowance is the amount arrived at by dividing the residue
of expenditure immediately after the sale by the number of years of assessment

comprised in the period which begins with the year of assessment in which the sale occurred, and ends with the year of assessment 2023/24 (i.e. "the 25th year of assessment after the year of assessment in which this section commences").

51. The <u>second method</u> prescribed in subsection (2) applies in any other case (i.e. where subsection (4) does not apply to the building because it was constructed after the commencement of the year of assessment 1998/99). For such a case, subsection (2) provides that where the relevant interest is sold, the annual allowance is the amount arrived at by dividing the residue of expenditure immediately after the sale by the number of years of assessment comprised in the period which begins with the year of assessment in which the sale occurred and ends with the year of assessment which is the 25th year after the year of assessment in which the building was first used.

Balancing Allowances and Charges

52. Reflecting to a large extent the provisions of Section 35 concerning industrial buildings, Section 33B(1) provides for a balancing allowance or balancing charge to be made where any of the following events occurs to a building, while the building is a commercial building –

"(a) the relevant interest in the building or structure is sold;

(b) the relevant interest in the building or structure, being a leasehold interest, comes to an end otherwise than on the person entitled thereto acquiring the interest which is reversionary thereon; or

(c) the building or structure is demolished or destroyed or, without being demolished or destroyed, ceases altogether to be used."

The allowance or charge is made for the year of assessment in the basis period for which the event occurs.

Balancing Allowances

53. Section 33B(2)(a) provides that where the residue of expenditure immediately before the occurrence of an event referred to in subsection (1)(a) to (c) exceeds the sale, insurance, salvage or compensation moneys (if any) arising from the event, a balancing allowance shall be made. If the residue of expenditure immediately before the event is nil, a balancing charge is made on the amount of the sale or other moneys. Where the amount of such moneys exceeds the amount of the residue, a balancing charge is made in respect of the excess.

54. It should be noted, however, that Section 33B(2)(b) stipulates that no balancing allowance is to be made where the building in question is demolished for purposes unconnected with or not in the ordinary course of conduct of the trade, profession or business of the person in relation to which the building was used to qualify for an annual allowance under Section 33A. Thus, for example, if a commercial building were to be demolished to enable land to be sold unencumbered, no balancing allowance would be made.

Balancing Charges

55. Where the sale, insurance, salvage or compensation moneys arising from the event exceed the residue of expenditure (if any) immediately before the occurrence of an event referred to in subsection (1)(a) to (c), Section 33B(3)(a) provides that a balancing charge shall be made in respect of the excess. However, by virtue of Section 33B(3)(b) the amount of a balancing charge is limited to the amount of the annual allowances, if any, made to the person under Section 33A.

Termination of a Leasehold Interest

56. Section 33B(1)(b) covers the normal case where a leasehold interest ends on expiry of a lease. Thus if A agrees to lease a commercial building to B for a particular period, and B becomes entitled to a relevant interest in relation to capital expenditure incurred on further construction, B will generally become entitled to a balancing allowance where his leasehold interest terminates at the end of the lease period. This will also be the case if A and B agree to early termination of the lease, although a balancing charge could arise if compensation is paid by A to B.

57. However, a balancing allowance (or charge) will not be made where a lessee does not vacate a commercial building at the expiration of his leasehold interest. Section 33B(1)(b) excludes the case where the person acquires the reversionary interest (e.g. where the lessee purchases the property from the lessor). Where acquisition does not take place, but the lessee remains in possession of the building with the consent of the lessor without a new lease being granted, Section 35A(a) provides that leasehold interest shall be deemed to continue (and accordingly a balancing allowance cannot be granted under Section 33B(1)(b)). With the same result, Section 35A(b) provides that where a new lease is granted to the lessee, the second lease is treated as a continuation of the first lease.

Examples

58. Examples 5 to 9 of the Appendix illustrate the calculation of rebuilding allowances, annual allowances, balancing allowances and balancing charges in respect of commercial buildings.

APPENDIX

ALLOWANCES FOR INDUSTRIAL BUILDINGS
AND STRUCTURES

■ Example 1

X constructed a factory at a cost (excluding the value of the site) of $500,000. The amount was due when the factory was first used, in February 1992. X carries on a qualifying trade, and makes up accounts to 31st December each year.

The factory was sold on 31 October 1996 for $420,000 (excluding the value of the site), to Y who started a similar trade on 10 November 1996, and makes up accounts to 31 March. X continues to trade.

	$	$
X: 1992/93		
Cost		500,000
Initial Allowance @ 20%	100,000	
Annual Allowance @ 4%	20,000	120,000
		380,000
1993/94 to 1995/96		
Annual Allowance 3 years @ 4%		60,000
Residue before sale		320,000
1996/97		
Sale price		420,000
Balancing Charge		100,000
Y: 1996/97		
Residue before sale		320,000
Add Balancing Charge made on X		100,000
Residue after sale		420,000
Annual Allowance*		20,000

* Calculation of Annual Allowance for Y
  - Year of first use 1991/92 (Note that this is not necessarily the year for which Allowances were first given)
  - 25th year after year of first use 2016/17
  - Y is entitled to Annual Allowance from 1996/97 onwards
  - Number of years from 1996/97 to 2016/17 = 21
  - Amount of Annual Allowance to Y: 1/21 × $420,000 = $20,000

[Note that only Y gets an allowance for 1996/97.]

■ Example 2

A constructed a factory at a cost (excluding the value of the site) of $2,000,000. It was completed and brought into use in July 1992. The building contract provided that instalments should be paid monthly and $500,000 was due and paid before 31 March 1992. The balance was paid during the year ended 31 March 1993.

A has carried on a qualifying trade since 1985, and makes up accounts to 31 March each year.

The factory was sold to B, who had been carrying on a qualifying trade for some years, on 31 October 1995 for $5 million (including the value of the site). B makes up accounts to 30 June each year. The site value is estimated at $2.5M. A continues to trade.

		$	$
A:	1991/92		
	Cost		2,000,000
	Initial Allowance @ 20% of $500,000		
	(No Annual Allowance as Building not in use at 31.3.1992)		100,000
			1,900,000
	1992/93		
	Initial Allowance @ 20% of $1,500,000	300,000	
	Annual Allowance @ 4% of $2,000,000	80,000	380,000
			1,520,000
	1993/94 & 1994/95		
	2 Years' Annual Allowance		160,000
	Residue before sale		1,360,000
	1995/96		
	Sale price ($5M less 2.5M)		2,500,000
	Excess		1,140,000
	Balancing Charge, limited to allowances given		640,000
B:	1996/97		
	Residue before sale		1,360,000
	Add Balancing Charge made on X		640,000
	Residue after sale		2,000,000
	Annual Allowance*		90,910

* Calculation of Annual Allowance for B
  - Year of first use 1992/93
  - 25th year after year of first use 2017/18
  - B is entitled to Annual Allowance from 1996/97 onwards
  - Number of years from 1996/97 to 2017/18 = 22
  - Amount of Annual Allowance to B: 1/22 × $2,000,000 = $90,910
  - Final year of allowance 2017/18 (Annual Allowance $90,890)

[Note that neither A nor B receives Annual Allowance in respect of 1995/96. There is, however, no Notional Allowance written off, as the building was an Industrial Building throughout.]

■ Example 3

C erected a building at a cost of $800,000 in September 1990 and straightaway used it as a workshop in his existing manufacturing trade. He makes up accounts to 31 December each year.

In January 1993 he sold the building for $700,000 to D, who used it for a time as a showroom in his existing manufacturing business. In May 1994 D re-converted it to a workshop. D makes up accounts to the 31 March each year. C continues to trade. [Site values are excluded throughout.]

		$	$
C:	1990/91		
	Cost		800,000
	Initial Allowance @ 20% of $800,000	160,000	
	Annual Allowance @ 4% of $800,000	32,000	192,000
			608,000
	1991/92 & 1992/93		
	Annual Allowance — 2 years @ 4%		64,000
	Residue before sale		544,000
	1993/94		
	Sale price		700,000
	Balancing Charge		156,000
D:	1993/94		
	Residue before sale		544,000
	Balancing Charge made on C		156,000
	Residue after sale		700,000
	Notional Allowance*		32,000
			668,000
	1994/95 onwards		
	Annual Allowance**		29,167

*   D did not qualify for Annual Allowance until 1994/95. However, a Notional Allowance has to be written off for 1993/94 (not 1992/93, as C received Annual Allowance that year). The amount of the Notional Allowance is 4% of the capital expenditure, NOT the amount of the Annual Allowance which would otherwise have been given.

** Calculation of Annual Allowance
  - Year of first use 1990/91
  - 25th year after year of *first* use 2015/16
    If D had used the building for a qualifying purpose throughout, his first year of allowance would have been 1992/93.
  - From 1992/93 to 2015/16 inclusive is 24 years
  - The amount of Annual Allowance to D: 1/24 × $700,000 = $29,167
  - Final year of allowance 2016/17 (Annual Allowance $26,326)

[Note that D would get Commercial Building Allowance for 1992/93 and 1993/94 equal to 2% of the $800,000 cost of the building (i.e. $16,000 each year). This would have no effect on the Industrial Building Allowance.]

■ Example 4

Following Example 3, D instead used the building as a showroom and then, in May 1994, sold it to E for $750,000 (i.e. without converting it back to a workshop). E used the building for a qualifying trade and makes up accounts to 31 March each year.

		$
		$
D:	1993/94	
	Residue after the previous sale by C to D in 1992/93 while in use as industrial building	700,000
	Notional Allowance for 1993/94*	32,000
		668,000

* D did not qualify for Annual Allowance for 1993/94, and thus a Notional Allowance has to be written off. The amount of Notional Allowance is 4% of the capital expenditure, NOT the amount of the Annual Allowance which would otherwise have been given.

E: 1994/95

Residue of expenditure (Section 40(1))	668,000
Annual Allowance**	29,167

** Calculation of Annual Allowance for Company E
- Year of first use 1990/91
- 25th year after year of first use 2015/16
- If D had used the building for a qualifying purpose, his first year of allowance would have been 1992/93
- From 1992/93 to 2015/16 inclusive is 24 years
- The amount of Annual Allowance to E: $1/24 \times \$700,000 = \$29,167$
- Final year of allowance 2016/17 (Annual Allowance $26,326)

[Note that if neither C nor D had used the building prior to its sale to E, E would be entitled to Initial and Annual Allowances. If C carried on a building construction trade and sold the building in the ordinary course of his trade the allowances would be based on capital expenditure of $700,000 (i.e. the lesser of the net price paid by E and the net price on the first sale — s.35B(b)(ii)(a)).

If C did not carry on a building construction trade, E would be entitled to allowances based on capital expenditure of $750,000 (i.e. the lesser of the net price paid by E and the original cost of construction of $800,000 (s.35B(b)(ii)(b)).]

ALLOWANCES FOR COMMERCIAL BUILDINGS AND STRUCTURES

■ Example 5

Computation of Annual Allowances in respect of a Commercial Building acquired before 1 April 1998 where ownership is retained by the same person during the 1998/99 year of assessment.

Company F purchased *Shop 1* from a developer at a price of $2,000,000 on 1 November 1988. *Shop 2* was purchased for $6,000,000 on 1 October 1994. The costs of construction of *Shop 1* and *Shop 2* are ascertained to be $1,000,000 and $2,000,000 respectively. Company F makes up its accounts to 31 March each year.

	$	$
Company F		
Shop 1: 1988/89 to 1997/98		
Cost of construction		
Rebuilding Allowance		1,000,000
• 1988/89 to 1989/90 — 2 years @ 3/4% of $1M	15,000	
• 1990/91 to 1997/98 — 8 years @ 2% of $1M	160,000	175,000
Residue under s.33A(4)		825,000
1998/99 onwards		
Annual Allowance* @ 4% of $825,000		33,000

* Final year of allowance 2022/23

Company F
Shop 2: 1994/95 to 1997/98

Cost of construction	2,000,000
Rebuilding Allowance — 4 years @ 2% of $2,000,000	160,000
Residue under s.33A(4)	1,840,000
1998/99 onwards	
Annual Allowance* @ 4% of $1,840,000	73,600

* Final year of allowance 2022/23

■ Example 6

Computation of Balancing Allowance, Balancing Charge and Annual Allowances in respect of an "old" Commercial Building (i.e. one constructed prior to 1998/99) sold in 1998/99.

Scenario 1
Following Example 5, assume Company F sold Shop 1 to Company G for $750,000 (excluding site) on 28 February 1999. Company G makes up its accounts to 31 March each year.

	$
Company F	
Shop 1: 1998/99	
Residue under s.33A(4) — see Example 5	825,000
Annual Allowance	NIL
Residue before sale	825,000
Sale price	750,000
Balancing Allowance	75,000
Company G	
Shop 1: 1998/99	
Residue before sale	825,000
Balancing Allowance made to Company F	75,000
Residue after sale	750,000
Annual Allowance*	28,847

* Calculation of Annual Allowance for Company G
  - First year of Annual Allowance to Company G 1998/99
  - 25th year after 1998/99 is 2023/24
  - Number of years from 1998/99 to 2023/24 is 26
  - Annual Allowance, 1998/99 onwards: 1/26 × $750,000 = $28,847
  - Final year of allowance for Company G 2023/24 (Annual Allowance $28,825)

Scenario 2
Following Example 5, assume Company F sold *Shop 1* to Company G for $2,000,000 (excluding the value of site) on 28 February 1999. Company G makes up its accounts to 31 March each year.

	$
Company F	
Shop 1: 1998/99	
Residue under s.33A(4) — see Example 5	825,000
Annual Allowance	NIL
Residue before sale	825,000
Sale price	2,000,000
Balancing Charge*	NIL

* Note that under s.33B(3)(b), no Balancing Charge made on Company F since it was
  not entitled to any Annual Allowance in the year of assessment 1998/99.

Company G
Shop 1: 1998/99

Residue before sale	825,000
Balancing Charge on Company F	NIL
Residue after sale	825,000
Annual Allowance 1998/99 onwards** —	
1/26 × $825,000 = $31,731	31,731

** Calculation of Annual Allowance for Company G
  • First year of Annual Allowance to Company G 1998/99
  • 25th year after 1998/99 is 2023/24
  • Number of years from 1998/99 to 2023/24 is 26
  • Annual Allowance, 1998/99 onwards: 1/26 × $825,000 = $31,731
  • Final year of allowance for Company G 2023/24 (Annual Allowance $31,725)

■ Example 7

Computation of Balancing Allowance, Balancing Charge and Annual Allowances in respect
of an old Commercial Building sold after 1998/99.

Scenario 1
Following Example 5, assume Company F sold *Shop 2* to Company H for $1,600,000
(excluding the value of the site) on 15 March 2000. Company H makes up its accounts to
31 March each year.

Company F
Shop 2: 1998/99

Residue under s.33A(4) — see Example 5	1,840,000
Annual Allowance	73,600
	1,766,400
1999/2000	
Residue before sale	1,766,400
Sale price	1,600,000
Balancing Allowance	166,400

Company H
Shop 2: 1999/2000

Residue before sale	1,766,400
Balancing Allowance made to Company F	166,400
Residue after sale	1,600,000
Annual Allowance 1999/2000 onwards*	64,000

* Calculation of Annual Allowance for Company H
  • First year of Annual Allowance to Company H 1999/2000
  • 25th year after 1998/99 is 2023/24
  • Number of years from 1999/2000 to 2023/24 is 25
  • Annual Allowance, 1999/2000 onwards: 1/25 × $1,600,000 = $64,000
  • Final year of allowance for Company H 2023/24 (Annual Allowance $64,000)

Scenario 2
Following Example 5, assume Company F sold *Shop 2* to Company H for $4,000,000

(excluding the value of the site) on 15 March 2000. Company H makes up its accounts to 31 March each year.

		$
Company F		
Shop 2:	1998/99	
	Residue under s.33A(4) — see Example 5	1,840,000
	Annual Allowance	73,600
	Residue before sale	1,766,400
	1999/2000	
	Residue before sale	1,766,400
	Sale price	4,000,000
	Excess	2,233,600
	Balancing Charge*	73,600

* Balancing Charge made on Company F is restricted to Annual Allowance claimed. In this year of assessment 1998/99

		$
Company H		
Shop 2:	1999/2000	
	Residue before sale	1,766,400
	Balancing Charge made on Company F	73,600
	Residue after sale	1,840,000
	Annual Allowance**, 1999/2000 onwards:	
	$1/25 \times \$1,840,000 = \$73,600$	73,600

** Final year of allowance for Company H 2023/24 (Annual Allowance $73,600)

■ Example 8

Computation of Annual Allowances for Newly Completed Commercial Buildings acquired on or after 1 April 1998.

Company J acquired *Office 3* from a developer on 1 May 1999 at a price of $20M (including the value of the site). The cost of construction is ascertained to be $6,250,000. Company J makes up its accounts to 31 December each year.

		$
Company J		
Office 3:	1999/2000 onwards	
	Cost of construction	6,250,000
	Annual Allowance @ 4% of $6,250,000	250,000

■ Example 9

Computation of Balancing Allowance, Balancing Charge and Annual Allowances for New Commercial Building Disposed/Acquired after 1998/99.

Scenario 1

Following Example 8, assume Company J sold *Office 3* to Company K for $4,000,000 (excluding the value of the site) on 2 January 2005. Company K makes up its accounts to 31 January each year.

$

Company J
Office 3: 1999/2000 to 2003/04
        Cost of construction   6,250,000
        Annual Allowance — 5 years @ 4% of $6,250,000   1,250,000
                                                  5,000,000

        2004/2005
        Residue before sale   5,000,000
        Sale price   4,000,000
        Balancing Allowance   1,000,000

Company K
Office 3: 2004/2005
        Residue before sale   5,000,000
        Balancing Allowance made to Company J   1,000,000
        Residue after sale   4,000,000
        Annual Allowance 2004/2005 onwards*   190,477

* Calculation of Annual Allowance for Company K
- First year of Annual Allowance to Company K is 2004/05
- 25th year after 1999/2000 is 2024/25
- Number of years from 2004/05 to 2024/25 is 21
- Annual Allowance, 2004/05 onwards: 1/21 × 4,000,000 = $190,477
- Final year of allowance for Company K 2024/25 (Annual Allowance $190,460)

Scenario 2
Following Example 8, assume Company J sold *Office 3* to Company K for $8,000,000
(excluding the value of the site) on 2 January 2005. Company K makes up its accounts to
31 January each year.

$

Company J
Office 3: 1999/2000 to 2003/04
        Cost of construction   6,250,000
        Annual Allowance — 5 years @ 4% of 6,250,000   1,250,000
                                                  5,000,000

        2004/2005
        Residue before sale   5,000,000
        Sale price   8,000,000
        Excess   3,000,000
        Balancing Charge*   1,250,000

* Balancing Charge made on Company J restricted to Annual Allowances allowed in the
years of assessment 1999/2000 to 2003/04)

Company K
Office 3: 2004/2005
        Residue before sale   5,000,000
        Balancing Charge made on Company J   1,250,000
        Residue after sale   6,250,000
        Annual Allowance 2004/05 onwards**:
            1/21 × $6,250,000 = $297,620   297,620

** Final year of allowance for Company K 2024/25 (Annual Allowance $297,600)

APPENDIX 3

Departmental Interpretation & Practice Notes
No. 4 (Revised)

**LEASE PREMIUMS / NON-RETURNABLE DEPOSITS / KEY OR
TEA MONEY / CONSTRUCTION FEES ETC.**

These notes are issued for the information of taxpayers and their tax representatives. They contain the Department's interpretation and practices in relation to the law as it stood at the date of publication. Taxpayers are reminded that their right of objection against the assessment and their right of appeal to the Commissioner, the Board of Review or the Court are not affected by the application of these notes.

These notes replace those issued in July 2005.

LAU MAK Yee-ming, Alice
Commissioner of Inland Revenue

February 2006

Our web site: http://www.ird.gov.hk

CONTENT

ASSESSABILITY OF LEASE PREMIUMS

Premiums on leases are frequently referred to as non-returnable deposits, key or tea money, construction fees, tenancy rights or other terms. Sometimes, taxpayers or their representatives are inclined to assume that receipts of lease premiums or of moneys of a similar nature are capital receipts, and consequently fail to show them separately in their accounts or computations. Such an assumption should not be made, because these receipts, by virtue of the nature of the trade or business carried on by the recipient, can often be, and more frequently are, revenue receipts. Moreover, the fact that premium under a lease or tenancy agreement is being regarded as capital expenditure by the payer does not necessarily turn it into a capital receipt in the hands of the recipient.

2. By the definition of "business" in section 2 of the Inland Revenue Ordinance (the Ordinance), corporations letting property are carrying on a business, and so are other persons sub-letting property held by them under a lease other than from the Government. Persons dealing in property are carrying on a trade. It is therefore important that all persons carrying on a property letting or dealing business should give full information concerning such receipts in their accounts supporting the tax returns filed with the Department.

3. Taxpayers or their representatives, if they claim the captioned receipts to be capital receipts, have to ascertain and report the precise facts and the exact legal relationship between the parties occasioned by any agreement to receive or pay such items.

4. In a property letting or dealing business, a lease premium is part of a payment for the use of the property and therefore is an income of a revenue nature. This view is supported by the Court of Appeal decision in the *East African Tax Case No. 37 — A.L. et al v. The Commissioner of Income Tax [E.A.T.C. Vol. 2 at page 148]* which held that the premiums in that case were received for the use of a capital asset and not for its realization and that they were therefore income receipts and taxable.

5. The editors of Halsbury's Laws of Hong Kong, at paragraph 370.174 of Vol. 24, expressed a similar view —

> "Where a person dealing in land may be considered carrying on a business (and therefore subject to profits tax), the receipt of rent, lease premiums, construction fees and other miscellaneous sums arising from dealings with land should also be included as trading receipts irrespective of the possible capital nature from the viewpoint of the payee."

6. Generally accepted accounting practice[1] requires that premium receipts be

---

[1] Hong Kong Accounting Standard 17 — Leases, issued by the Hong Kong Institute of Certified Public Accountants.

spread over the term of the lease for the purpose of recognizing them as income. If the accounts are prepared on such basis, the premium receipts will be assessed to profits tax accordingly.

INTERACTION WITH PROPERTY TAX

7. Under section 5B(4) of the Ordinance, a lease premium is deemed for property tax purposes to be payable in equal monthly instalments during the period of the right of use of the property subject to a maximum period of 3 years. Accordingly, property tax may be charged on such a basis. Nevertheless, any property tax so paid is available for set off against the profits tax payable by the owner of the property under section 25 of the Ordinance. Any excess property tax paid will be refunded. Furthermore, where the owner is a corporation, the exemption from property tax provided under section 5(2)(a) may also be available.

EXAMPLES

8. The following examples illustrate the operation of paragraphs 6 and 7 above.

Example 1

Company H carries on a property letting business. While retaining substantially all the risks and rewards incidental to its ownership, it leases one of its properties for a term of 2 years at a premium of $1,200,000. Assume that it closes its accounts on 31 March each year.

According to Hong Kong Accounting Standard 17 (paragraphs 4 and 8), the lease will be an operating lease and hence the lease premium "shall be recognised in income on a straight line basis over the lease term" (paragraph 50), i.e. over the 2-year period. Therefore, half of the premium will be assessed to profits tax in Year 1 and half in Year 2.

Property tax assessments may be issued to Company H. Pursuant to section 5B (4), half of the premium will be charged to property tax in Year 1 and half in Year 2. Company H is entitled to set off the property taxes paid against its profits taxes payable on the premium for these 2 years and have the balance refunded, if any (section 25).

Alternatively, Company H can apply for property tax exemption under section 5(2)(a) of the Ordinance, leaving the premium to be assessed to profits tax.

Example 2

Same scenario as in Example 1 except that the lease is for a term of 6 years.

According to Hong Kong Accounting Standard 17 (paragraph 50), the lease premium will be recognised in income on a straight line basis over the 6-year period. Therefore, 1/6 of the premium (or $200,000) will be assessed to profits tax in each of the years from Year 1 to Year 6.

Property tax assessments may be issued to Company H. Pursuant to section 5B (4), the premium will be deemed to be payable and hence assessed over a maximum period of 3 years. Hence, 1/3 of the premium (or $400,000) will be charged to property tax in each of the Years 1, 2 and 3. Company H is entitled to set off the property taxes paid against its profits taxes payable for these 3 years respectively and have the balance refunded, if any (section 25). No question of set-off/refund will arise starting from Year 4.

The computation of taxes payable for the 6 years is as follows —

Year 1 (2005–06)	Property Tax paid: $400,000 × 80% × 16% = $51,200	Profits Tax assessment*: $200,000 × 17.5% = Less: Property tax paid Tax refund	$35,000 $51,200 ($16,200)
Year 2 (2006–07)	Property Tax paid: $400,000 × 80% × 16% = $51,200	Profits Tax assessment*: $200,000 × 17.5% = Less: Property tax paid Tax refund	$35,000 $51,200 ($16,200)
Year 3 (2007–08)	Property Tax paid: $400,000 × 80% × 16% = $51,200	Profits Tax assessment*: $200,000 × 17.5% = Less: Property tax paid Tax refund	$35,000 $51,200 ($16,200)
Year 4 (2008–09)	Property Tax paid: NIL = $51,200	Profits Tax assessment*: $200,000 × 17.5% = Less: Property tax paid Tax refund	$35,000 Nil $35,000
Year 5 (2009–10)	Property Tax paid: NIL = $51,200	Profits Tax assessment*: $200,000 × 17.5% = Less: Property tax paid Tax refund	$35,000 Nil $35,000
Year 6 (2010–11)	Property Tax paid: NIL = $51,200	Profits Tax assessment*: $200,000 × 17.5% = Less: Property tax paid Tax refund	$35,000 Nil $35,000
Total tax paid	Property Tax paid: $153,600	Net Profits Tax paid:	$56,400

Grand Total of Tax Paid:	$210,000 (or 17.5% on premium, representing the total Profits Tax charged)

NB: * Assuming no other income chargeable to profits tax and no expenses claim.

Similarly, Company H can also apply for property tax exemption under section 5(2)(a) of the Ordinance.

APPENDIX 4

Departmental Interpretation & Practice Notes
No. 5 (Revised)

PROFITS TAX
Deductions for Expenditure on —
(A) Scientific Research
(B) Technical Education
(C) Patent Rights, etc.
(D) Building Refurbishment
(E) Prescribed Fixed Assets

These notes are issued for the information and guidance of taxpayers and their authorised representatives. They have no binding force and do not affect a person's right of objection and appeal to the Commissioner, the Board of Review or the Courts.

These notes replace those issued on 29 December 1989.

LAU MAK Yee-ming, Alice
Commissioner of Inland Revenue

October 2003

Our web site: http://www.ird.gov.hk

CONTENT

Paragraph

Appendix

INTRODUCTION

It is a canon of taxation that capital expenditure is not normally an allowable deduction in ascertaining the assessable profit of any trade, profession or business. The introduction in 1965 of section 16B and section 16C respectively relating to scientific research and technical education marked an important change from the normal principle of allowing tax deductions. This was followed successively by the enactments in 1983 of section 16E (relating to patent rights), in 1996 of section 16F (relating to hotel refurbishment), which, in 1998, was extended to all non-domestic buildings, and in 1998 of section 16G (relating to prescribed fixed assets).

(A) SCIENTIFIC RESEARCH — SECTION 16B

2. Section 16B was enacted in 1965 to allow expenditure incurred by a person carrying on a trade or business for scientific research related to that trade or business as a deduction. The deduction allowable included capital expenditure on plant or machinery but excluded capital expenditure on land or buildings. In 1998, the section was extended to a person in a profession. At the same time the definition of scientific research was expanded to include feasibility studies and market research.

3. Expenditure on scientific research may be in the form of a payment to an approved research institute, or expenditure on in-house scientific research undertaken by a person, or expenditure incurred by a person to acquire technology in relation to his trade, profession or business.

Meaning of scientific research

4. For the years of assessment from 1965/66 to 1997/98, the term "scientific research" was defined to mean "any activities in the fields of natural or applied science for the extension of knowledge" [section 16B(4)(a)]. Scientific research is generally regarded as embracing the application of new scientific principles in an existing area of research, or the application of existing principles in a new area of research. This covers research work to develop new products, new lines and also the improvement of existing products.

5. With effect from the year of assessment 1998/99, the definition of "scientific research" was expanded to cover any systematic, investigative or experimental activities carried on for the purposes of any feasibility study or in relation to any market, business or management research [section 16B(4)(a), definition as amended in 1998].

Scientific research related to that trade, profession or business

6. Scientific research is to be treated as related to a trade, profession or business if it may lead to or facilitate an extension, or an improvement in the technical efficiency, of that trade, profession or business [section 16B(5)(b)(i)], or is medical research which has a special relation to the welfare of workers employed in that trade or class of trade [section 16B(5)(b)(ii)].

7. Thus scientific research undertaken by a trader with the object of branching out into a new line of business or of improving the technical efficiency of his existing business will be treated as related to the trade; also expenditure by a trader for research into an occupational disease peculiar to his industry would be treated as related to his trade. "Scientific research" can therefore be described as working for tomorrow to develop new products, new lines and improvements to present production. It does not, however, cover "quality control" which is better described as working for today and today's production to ensure that what has been produced is up to standard [see *Australian Board of Review Decision in 12 CTBR (NS) Case 5*].

Payments to approved research institutes

8. Payments to approved research institutes are allowable if the payments are for specific scientific research related to that person's trade, profession or business, or for general research if the object of the institute is the undertaking of scientific research related to the class of trade, profession or business to which that person belongs.

9. An approved research institute is defined in section 16B(4)(a) as "any university, college, institute, association or organization which is approved in writing for the purposes of this section by the Commissioner as an institute, association or organization for undertaking scientific research which is or may prove to be of value to Hong Kong". Prior to 1 April 1996, the Director of Education was responsible for granting the approval. An approval operates from a date, whether before or after the date of approval, specified in the instrument of approval, and can be withdrawn at any time. A list of approved institutes is provided in the **Appendix**.

10. The deduction is allowed irrespective of the actual usage of the funds by the approved institute for either capital or revenue purposes. Thus, payments for establishing or extending an approved research institute, payments towards the administration of the approved research institute and payments for the actual carrying out of the scientific research are allowable as long as the object of the approved institute is the undertaking of scientific research related to the class of trade, profession or business to which that person belongs.

Capital expenditure on plant and machinery

11. Capital expenditure on plant or machinery purchased by a taxpayer for scientific research related to his trade, profession or business is allowable in full as a deduction for the basis period during which it was incurred. If the expenditure

is incurred before the trade commences, it should be treated as incurred in the first basis period.

12. When such plant or machinery ceases to be used for scientific research and is then sold, the sales proceeds, to the extent of the amount of deduction previously allowed, are treated as a trading receipt accruing at the time of the sale or the date immediately preceding the cessation of business if the sale occurs on or after the date of cessation. The time of sale is the time of completion of the sale or the time when possession is given, whichever is the earlier.

13. Plant or machinery destroyed shall be treated as if it had been sold immediately before the destruction. Any insurance money, compensation money or money received shall be treated as if it were the proceeds of sale and be assessed as a trading receipt. The amount assessable shall not exceed the deduction previously allowed.

Capital expenditure on land or buildings

14. No deduction is allowable under section 16B in respect of any capital expenditure incurred by a taxpayer on land or buildings or on alterations, additions or extensions to buildings. When such expenditure results in a relevant interest in a building, then Industrial Building Allowances under section 34 are granted on the capital expenditure on a building used for scientific research purposes, irrespective of the nature of trade carried on [see section 40].

Capital expenditure in acquiring rights in, or arising out of, scientific research

15. It is specifically provided in section 16B(5)(a) that no deduction is allowed for any expenditure incurred in acquiring rights in, or arising out of, scientific research. Effective from the year of assessment 1998/99, a reference to rights includes a reference to a share or interest in such rights. However, if the rights acquired are patented rights, the expenditure can amount to an allowable deduction under section 16E.

Expenditure outside Hong Kong

16. Where any payment or expenditure which qualifies for deduction under section 16B is made or incurred outside Hong Kong, it is necessary to consider whether it is allowable in full. If the trade, profession or business is carried on solely in Hong Kong, then the full amount of the expenditure is allowable as a deduction in arriving at the chargeable profits.

17. Where the trade, profession or business is carried on partly in and partly out of Hong Kong, it is necessary to consider the whole of the activities of the trade, profession or business to arrive at a reasonable proportion of such expenditure which relates to the production of chargeable profits. This is a question of fact to be determined in the light of the circumstances of each case.

Subsidies and grants received

18. Where a person incurs expenditure on scientific research and part of such expenditure is, or is to be, met directly or indirectly by the Government of Hong Kong, or by any government or public or local authority, or by any other person, only the net amount qualifies for deduction under section16B.

Sale of rights in or arising out of scientific research

19. With effect from the year of assessment 1998/99, where any rights in, or arising out of, scientific research, the expenditure on which has been allowed as a deduction under section 16B, are sold, the sale proceeds shall be treated as trading receipts. The amount assessable shall not exceed the amount of deduction previously allowed.

20. The sale proceeds accrue as income at the time of sale, which is the time of completion of the sale of the rights. If, however, the sale occurs on or after the date of cessation of the trade, profession or business, the sale proceeds accrue as income immediately before the cessation.

(B) TECHNICAL EDUCATION — SECTION 16C

21. Section 16C was introduced as from the year of assessment 1965/66 to allow payments made by a person carrying on a trade or business for technical education. Effective from the year of assessment 1998/99, the section was extended to a person carrying on a profession.

22. Under section 16C, a person carrying on a trade, profession or business in Hong Kong is allowed a tax deduction for any payment to be used for the purposes of technical education related to that trade, profession or business at any university, university college, technical college or other similar institution which is approved by the Commissioner. The recognition of the institution for this purpose shall start from whatever date is specified in the approval. This may be before or after the date of approval [section 16C(3)(a)]. Prior to 1 April 1996, the approval was given by the Director of Education. The approval given can be withdrawn at any time. A list of approved institutions is provided in the **Appendix**.

Deductible payments

23. For the purposes of section 16C, technical education is deemed to be related to a trade, profession or business if and only if it is of a kind specially requisite for persons employed in that class of trade, profession or business.

24. The deduction applies to any payment to an approved institution to be used for the purposes of technical education related to a particular trade, profession or business. It does not have to be directly for the education of any person or persons actually employed in the particular business at the time of payment. The deduction extends to a payment to establish a unit or for the general maintenance of a unit at an approved institution so as to provide technical education of a kind specially suited or requisite to a particular class of trade, profession or business. However, contributions in response to appeals made for funds to be used on purchase of capital equipment would not be allowable.

25. Where payments are made for the technical education of particular persons, the payment may be made to either the students or the approved institution.

26. The intention of section 16C is to broaden and not to restrict what would ordinarily be allowable deductions. So expenditure by an employer on the technical training or education of any of his employees may be allowed under section 16(1) even if the institution is not an approved institution.

(C) PURCHASE AND SALE OF PATENT RIGHTS, RIGHTS TO KNOW-HOW — SECTION 16E

27. Section 16E was introduced to provide an incentive to promote technological progress in local industry by allowing as a deduction the capital cost of acquiring patent rights, trademarks or designs. The deduction is effective from the year of assessment 1982/83 and onwards. This deduction is additional to that for the royalty or recurrent payment in connection with the use of the patent right, trademark or design. Such expenditure will continue to be allowable under section 16(1).

28. As a measure to prevent exploitation,

was amended on 12 March 1992 by the Inland Revenue (Amendment) Ordinance 1992. One amendment was to substitute the term "trade mark or design" by "know-how" so as to restrict the deduction to expenditure on industrial information and techniques on manufacturing of goods. Another amendment was to deny a deduction for transactions between associated parties. The amendments apply to contracts entered into on or after 18 April 1991.

Meaning of patent rights, know-how

29. The terms "patent rights" and "know-how" are defined in section 16E. "Patent rights" means "the right to do or authorize the doing of anything which would, but for that right, be an infringement of a patent". "Know-how" means "any industrial information or techniques likely to assist in the manufacture or processing of goods or materials".

Allowable deduction

30. Under section 16E, any expenditure incurred by a person on the purchase of patent rights or rights to any know-how is deductible if –

- the rights are for use in Hong Kong in the trade, profession or business carried on by the person,
- they are incurred in the production of that person's chargeable profits, and
- the rights are not purchased wholly or partly from an associate.

31. A deduction is allowed when the expenditure is incurred. There is no requirement that the patent or know-how, once acquired, must be used in the production of profits chargeable in the year of purchase. It is sufficient if the person claiming the deduction can show that at the time of purchase the purpose of acquiring the right was for use solely in Hong Kong. However, adjustment of the deduction may have to be considered if the subsequent facts prove otherwise.

For use in Hong Kong

32. The phrase "for use in Hong Kong" is not defined in section 16E. According to the Shorter Oxford English Dictionary, the word "use" means "the act of using the thing for any purpose, the fact, state or condition of being so used; utilization or employment for or with some aim or purpose; application or conversion to some end".

Apportionment of the expenditure

33. If the patent right or the right to the know-how is purchased for use partly in and partly outside Hong Kong, the expenditure shall be allowable to the extent of the use in Hong Kong on a basis reasonable and appropriate in the circumstances of the case. Such basis is clearly one of fact, to be determined on all the relevant facts including the terms of the agreement relating to the rights acquired, the manner and the use to which the patent is immediately put, the range and scope of the activities both within and outside Hong Kong and whether the whole of the profit is subject to tax.

Purchase of rights from associate

34. No deduction is allowable under section 16E(2A) if the patent rights, etc. are purchased wholly or partly from an associate, irrespective of whether or not the price was at an arms-length. The meaning of "associate" is widely defined in subsection 4 of section 16E. It covers natural persons, partners in a partnership, or corporations under common control and trusts.

35. In the case of a trust, and for the purpose of section 16E(2A) the purchase or sale of a patent right etc. by the trustee of the trust or a corporation controlled by the trustee would be regarded as the purchase or sale, as the case may be, by each trustee, the corporation and the beneficiary under the trust [section 16E (2B)].

Subsequent disposal

36. If the whole or part of the cost of the patent rights or rights to know-how has been allowed as a deduction from the assessable profits, then the proceeds on the subsequent disposal of such rights are to be treated as a trading receipt. Any surplus arising from such sale, although capital in nature, is thus subject to

37. Where only part of the patent cost has been allowed, only that part of the proceeds as are attributable to the relevant cost of the patent shall be assessed as a trading receipt. The basis of apportionment of the sale price will again have to depend on the facts of each case.

38. The sale proceeds shall be treated as a trading receipt accruing at the time of sale, or immediately before the discontinuance if the sale occurs after the business has been permanently discontinued.

39. The 1992 Amendment Ordinance referred to in paragraph 28 provides that the provisions of section 16E, in force immediately before the commencement of that Ordinance, continue to apply to patent rights etc. purchased under contracts entered into before 18 April 1991 and also to proceeds received from the disposal of such rights whether before or after 18 April 1991, as if the amendments had not been enacted.

(D) CAPITAL EXPENDITURE ON HOTEL / BUILDING REFURBISHMENT — SECTION 16F

40. Section 16F was introduced as from the year of assessment 1996/97. For the years of assessment 1996/97 and 1997/98, a deduction is allowed on capital expenditure on the renovation or refurbishment of a hotel. With effect from the year of assessment 1998/99, the deduction was extended to the renovation or refurbishment of buildings other than domestic buildings. Any expenditure allowed under this section will not qualify for depreciation allowances under Part VI of this Ordinance.

41. The term "domestic building or structure" is defined in section 16F. It means any building or structure used for habitation, but does not include any building or structure used as a hotel or guesthouse. It is the actual use or intended use of the building, not the type of the building, that counts. "Hotel" and "guesthouse" have the same meaning as in the Hotel and Guesthouse Accommodation Ordinance (Cap. 349). Thus, the deduction does not apply to buildings used for letting for residential purposes or as directors' or staff quarters.

When allowable

42. Capital expenditure meeting the requirements under section 16F is allowed as a deduction by five equal instalments, the first of which is allowed in the basis period during which the expenditure was incurred and the remaining four instalments in the basis periods of the four succeeding years of assessment. If the relevant property is sold before the instalments are fully granted, the person entitled to the instalments is still granted the instalments as if the property had not yet been sold.

Qualifying expenditure

43. To qualify for deduction, the expenditure incurred must be a renovation or refurbishment in nature. The words "renovation" and "refurbishment" are not defined in the Ordinance.

44. According to the Shorter Oxford English Dictionary, "renovation" means renewal or restoration, and "refurbishment" is renovation. Renovation or refurbishment expenditure can be either capital or revenue in nature, depending on whether the expenditure results in improving or repairing the building or structure concerned. Renovation expenditure of a capital nature is deductible in the manner specified under section 16F while renovation expenditure of a revenue nature is deductible under section 16(1)(e).

45. The Shorter Oxford English Dictionary defines "repair" as "Restoration of some material thing or structure by the renewal of decayed or worn out parts by refixing what has become loose or detached". It should be noted that in the *Privy Council case of Auckland Gas Co. Ltd. v CIR in 2000, (STC 527)*, Lord Nicholls of Birkenhead stated that "the solution is not to be found by any rigid test or description. The answer depends upon a consideration of all the circumstances. They may not all point in the same direction. Then it may be temptingly easy to say the answer is a question of fact and impression. That would be a mistaken approach…. The distinction between repair and replacement is not so unascertainable that it must be placed in the category of an unformulated question of fact." Thus the question of improvement or repairs to a building or structure is one of fact and degree and close examination of the facts of the particular case is required. The commonly used test for this purpose is the "entirety" test. If the entirety of a building or structure is replaced, it is improvement; and if part of the entirety is replaced, it is repair.

Non-qualifying expenditure

46. The deduction under section 16F does not apply to capital expenditure incurred –
  * for a building which is used or intended to be used as a domestic building;
  * to enable the building to be first used substantially by the person for the production of chargeable profits;
  * to enable the building to be used for a purpose different from that for which it was used immediately before the capital expenditure was incurred.

47. Thus, capital expenditure incurred on the initial construction, decoration or fitting out of a commercial building or structure, and expenditure on alteration of a building to enable a different usage do not qualify for the deduction under section 16F but they may qualify for commercial building allowance under section 33A.

(E) EXPENDITURE ON THE PROVISION OF PRESCRIBED FIXED ASSET — SECTION 16G

48. Section 16G was effective from the year of assessment 1998/99 and onwards to allow a deduction for specified capital expenditure incurred by a person for the provision of a prescribed fixed asset. The section also offered, for the year of assessment 1998/99, a one off, irrevocable option to elect the write-off of the reduced value of prescribed assets already owned and in use prior to 1998/99.

Specified capital expenditure

49. The term "specified capital expenditure" is defined in section 16G(6). It means any capital expenditure incurred by a person on the provision of a "prescribed fixed asset", but does not include –
   (a)   capital expenditure that may be deducted under any other section;
   (b)   capital expenditure incurred under a hire-purchase agreement.

Prescribed fixed asset

50. "Prescribed fixed asset" in turn is defined in section 16G(6) to mean:
   (a)   the following items of machinery or plant specified in the First Part of the Table annexed to Rule 2 of the Inland Revenue Rules as is used specifically and directly for any manufacturing process:

Item	Nature of the assets
16	Type and blocks
20	Bleaching and finishing machinery and plant
24	Electronics manufacturing machinery and plant
26	Plastic manufacturing machinery and plant including moulds
28	Silk manufacturing machinery and plant
29	Sulphuric and nitric acid plant
31	Textile and clothing manufacturing machinery and plant
33	Weaving, spinning, knitting and sewing machinery
35	Any other machinery or plant, not specified in items 1 to 34

   (b)   computer hardware, other than that which is an integral part of any machinery or plant;
   (c)   computer software and computer systems; but does not include an "excluded fixed asset".

51. "Excluded fixed asset" means a fixed asset in which any person holds the rights as a lessee under a lease [section 16G(6)].

Manufacturing process

52. To qualify for a deduction under section 16G, the machinery or plant must be used specifically and directly for any manufacturing process. As the term "manufacturing process" is not defined in the Ordinance, we have to refer to its ordinary meaning. According to the Shorter Oxford Dictionary, it means a series of activities or operations, usually carried out inside a factory or any other similar premises, for the creation of any new product.

53. Though the term "manufacturing process" is capable of a wide interpretation, it does not include construction. In fact, bulldozers and graders commonly used in construction works are not included in the definition of prescribed fixed asset in section 16G(6).

Computer hardware

54. Prescribed fixed asset includes computer hardware which is not an integral part of any machinery or plant. In other words, stand-alone computer hardware qualifies for deduction but computer hardware forming an integral part of an item of machinery or plant will not be granted the section 16G deduction unless the machinery or plant containing the computer hardware happens to be a prescribed fixed asset.

Computer software & computer system

55. Capital expenditure incurred on computer software and a computer system used in the production of chargeable profits is deductible under section 16G. This includes the relevant consultancy fees and associated costs. Prescribed fixed asset used partly in the production of chargeable profits

56. Where a prescribed fixed asset is used partly in the production of chargeable profits, the deduction under section 16G shall be such part of the specified capital expenditure as is proportionate to the extent of the use of the asset in the production of the chargeable profits. On sale of such a prescribed fixed asset, the proportionate amount of sale proceeds attributable to the portion used in the production of chargeable profits, limited to the amount of deduction previously allowed under section 16G, shall be treated as a trading receipt.

Sale of the prescribed fixed asset

57. Where the prescribed fixed asset in respect of which a deduction has been allowed under section 16G is sold, the sale proceeds not exceeding the amount of deduction previously allowed shall be treated as a trading receipt.

58. The relevant trading receipt shall accrue and be assessable at the time of sale, or the date immediately before the discontinuance of business if the sale occurs on or after the date on which the trade, profession or business is permanently discontinued.

59. The time of sale shall be construed as a reference to the time of completion of the sale, or the time which possession of the asset is given, whichever is the earlier.

Controlled sale

60. Where the prescribed fixed asset is sold, the seller has control over the buyer, or vice versa, or both are under the common control of some other person, or the buyer and seller are husband and wife, the Commissioner may determine the true market value of the asset if he is of the opinion that the sale price does not represent its true market value.

Destruction of the prescribed fixed asset

61. Where a prescribed fixed asset is destroyed, the asset shall be treated as if it had been sold immediately before the destruction. Any insurance moneys or other compensation of any description received and any money received in respect of the remains of the asset shall be treated as if it were the sale proceeds.

Prescribed fixed asset already owned and in use prior to 1998/99

62. For the year of assessment 1998/99 only, where a person owned and had in use any prescribed fixed asset prior to the year of assessment 1998/99, he may elect to claim as a deduction the reduced value of such asset as at the beginning of the basis period for 1998/99.

63. The reduced value of the prescribed fixed asset as at the beginning of the basis period for 1998/99 shall be the amount of capital expenditure incurred on the provision of that asset as reduced by the depreciation allowances granted on that asset in accordance with Part VI of the Ordinance in all years of assessment prior to 1998/99.

64. The election shall be in writing and shall be lodged before the expiration of one month after the date of the notice of assessment for the year of assessment 1998/99. Such an election, once made, is irrevocable.

APPENDIX

Approved Institutes Under Sections 16B and 16C of the Inland Revenue Ordinance

Approved Research Institutes under Section 16B(4)(a)

Sir Sik-nin Chau Foundation for Industrial Development
The Chinese Language Press Institute Ltd.
Federation of Hong Kong Industries (Testing Centre)
Hong Kong Plastics Technology Centre Co. Ltd.

Approved Institutes under Section 16C(1)

A. University and Technical Institutes

The Hong Kong Polytechnic University
Hong Kong Institute of Vocational Education (Morrison Hill)
   (formerly known as Morrison Hill Technical Institute)
Hong Kong Institute of Vocational Education (Kwun Tong)
   (formerly known as Kwun Tong Technical Institute)
Hong Kong Institute of Vocational Education (Lee Wai Lee)
   (formerly known as Lee Wai Lee Technical Institute)
Hong Kong Institute of Vocational Education (Haking Wong)
   (formerly known as Haking Wong Technical Institute)
Hong Kong Institute of Vocational Education (Kwai Chung)
   (formerly known as Kwai Chung Technical Institute)

B. Training Centres

Automobile Industry Training Centre
Electrical Industry Training Centre
Electronics Industry Training Centre
Textile Industry Training Centre
Plastics Industry Training Centre
Printing Industry Training Centre
Machine Shop and Metal Working Industry Training Centre
Welding Training Centre
Hospitality Industry Training & Development Centre
   (formerly known as Hotel Industry Training Centre)
Seamen's Training Centre
The Management Development Centre of Hong Kong

Note – Please check the web site of the Inland Revenue Department (at http://
www.info.gov.hk/ird) for the latest update of the lists.

APPENDIX 5

**Departmental Interpretation & Practice Notes
No. 7 (Revised)**

MACHINERY AND PLANT —
DEPRECIATION ALLOWANCES

These notes are issued for the information and guidance of taxpayers and their authorized representatives. They have no binding force and do not affect a person's right of objection or appeal to the Commissioner, the Board of Review or the Courts.

These notes replace those issued on 5 March 1981.

LAU MAK Yee-ming, Alice
Commissioner of Inland Revenue

August 2002

Our web site : http://www.info.gov.hk/ird

INDEX

APPENDIX A(i)
Rates of Depreciation, as prescribed by the Board of
Inland Revenue

APPENDIX A(ii)
Items included in the expression "any implement, utensil
or article", as prescribed by the Board of Inland Revenue

APPENDIX B
Items which qualify as machinery or plant

APPENDIX C
Items which do not qualify as machinery or plant

Part I — INTRODUCTION

1. Sections 12(1)(b) and 12(5) of the Inland Revenue Ordinance (the Ordinance) provide for depreciation allowances and charges calculated in accordance with Part VI of the Ordinance to be taken into account in ascertaining the net assessable income of a person subject to Salaries Tax. Similarly, section 18F of the Ordinance provides for depreciation allowances and charges made under Part VI to be taken into account in ascertaining the assessable profits of a person subject to Profits Tax.

2. For years of assessment prior to 1980/81, the relevant provisions of Part VI are contained within sections 37, 37A, 38 and 39 (referred to in this Practice Note as "the old scheme"). A revised scheme, known as "the pooling system", was introduced with effect from the 1980/81 year of assessment by the Inland Revenue (Amendment) (No. 4) Ordinance 1980. The calculation of depreciation allowances under the pooling system is basically provided by sections 39B, 39C and 39D. In certain circumstances, provisions of the old scheme, rather than of the pooling system, may apply in respect of a year of assessment subsequent to 1979/80.

Persons entitled to the allowances

3. Depreciation allowances in respect of machinery and plant are not restricted to persons carrying on particular kinds of trades, professions or businesses. Rather, the allowances under sections 37 and 39B are available to every person carrying on a trade, profession or business in respect of which the person is chargeable to Profits Tax under Part IV of the Ordinance. Similarly, by virtue of section 12(1)(b), all employees are entitled to depreciation allowances where the use of plant or machinery is essential to the production of assessable income.

Expenditure which qualifies

4. Depreciation allowances are made in respect of "capital expenditure" incurred on the provision of machinery or plant. The term "capital expenditure" is defined in section 40(1), for the purposes of Part VI of the Ordinance, to include interest and commitment fees incurred in respect of a loan made for the purpose of financing the provision of machinery or plant. On the other hand, the definition excludes expenditure which is reimbursed by way of or is attributable to any grant, subsidy or similar financial assistance. It also excludes, in relation to the person incurring the expenditure, any expenditure which is allowed to be deducted in ascertaining for the purpose of Part IV of the Ordinance the profits of a trade, profession or business carried on by that person. It follows that depreciation allowances cannot be claimed in relation to expenditure which qualifies for deduction under, for example, section 16B (in respect of scientific research), 16F (on building refurbishment) or 16G (on the provision of a prescribed fixed asset).

5. It should be noted that section 16G, which came into effect on 1 April 1998, provides for the situation where a qualifying item of machinery or plant was acquired in an earlier year of assessment and has accordingly been the subject of depreciation allowances. In such a case, if an appropriate election is made, a deduction is allowed under the section in respect of the 1998/99 year of assessment for the capital expenditure incurred on the provision of the item, reduced by the aggregate of initial and annual allowances made to the person concerned in prior years of assessment. The relevant amount ceases to qualify for depreciation allowances and must accordingly be excluded in relation to their computation for the 1998/99 and subsequent years of assessment.

6. Sections 37 and 39B refer to "capital expenditure on the provision of machinery or plant", and subsection (2) of section 37 refers to "the cost of the asset". Both phrases are construed as meaning the net cost of acquisition of the asset to the owner for the time being who is claiming the allowances. In this regard, the net cost of acquisition represents the supplier's price for the item, plus any charges relating to freight, insurance, delivery, import duties etc., and less any discounts, rebates, subsidies etc. accorded to the purchaser. The decision in *C.I.R. v. Hong Kong Bottlers Ltd. (H.K.T.C. 497)* was to the effect that cost is to be taken as meaning the same as capital expenditure incurred by the person claiming the allowance (but see paragraph 31 below as to machinery and plant which is acquired other than by purchase).

7. Hire purchase interest charges do not form part of the qualifying expenditure (see paragraphs 37 and 38 below).

Meaning of "machinery or plant"

8. The Ordinance does not provide an exhaustive definition of "machinery or plant". However, section 40 of the Ordinance and Rule 2 of the Inland Revenue Rules provide assistance in determining what constitutes "machinery or plant" for the purposes of making depreciation allowances. The following points are pertinent in this regard.

- Section 40(1) provides, *inter alia*, that " "capital expenditure on the provision of machinery or plant" includes capital expenditure on alterations to an existing building incidental to the installation of that machinery or plant for the purposes of the trade, profession or business".

- Rule 2 provides that items specified in the second column of the First Part of a table annexed to the rule are deemed to be included the expression "machinery or plant" (see Appendix A(i)). On the other hand, the rule also provides that items specified in the second column of the Second part of that Table (Appendix A(ii)) are deemed *not* to be included in that expression (accordingly depreciation allowances cannot be made), but instead are deemed for the purposes of the Ordinance to be included in the expression "any implement, utensil and article". The latter grouping includes such items as loose tools, crockery and linen which are normally dealt with under the "replacement" basis specified in section 16(1)(f). Finally, Rule 2 provides that wharves shall not be or be deemed to be "plant or machinery".

9. Nevertheless, as has been stated above, the term "machinery or plant" is not exhaustively defined, and for the purposes of depreciation allowances, the Table annexed to Rule 2 per Appendix A(i) lists as the last of the items "machinery or plant not specified in items 1-32". Accordingly, where depreciation allowances are claimed in respect of expenditure on an item not specifically listed, it is necessary to consider whether the item falls within the general description of "machinery or plant".

10. The meaning of the phrase "machinery or plant" has been considered in a number of cases by the courts in Hong Kong and other common law jurisdictions. On the basis of the principles established, the Department has taken positions in relation to a number of items which are not specifically listed in Appendix A (i) or (ii). In this regard, Appendix B enumerates items which are recognized as machinery or plant, and Appendix C enumerates items which are not so recognized.

Capital expenditure incurred prior to commencement of business

11. Where a person carries on a trade and incurs capital expenditure on the provision of assets for a *new* trade about to be commenced, the Ordinance does not provide for deductions or allowances to be granted in respect of the expenditure against the profits of the *existing* trade. However, section 40(2) provides, for the purposes of Part VI, that in such a situation the expenditure is treated as if it were incurred on the day that the new trade commences. Accordingly, if the expenditure is incurred on the provision of machinery or plant, allowances can be granted against the profits of the new trade, once it has commenced.

12. Where a person ceases to carry on a particular trade and transfers machinery or plant previously used in it to another trade which he carries on, it is not considered that the person is entitled to claim more than one annual allowance in respect of that machinery or plant for any one year of assessment. This is because the allowance is granted to the "person" and not to the "trade".

Basis Period

13. The basis period for the purpose of calculating depreciation allowances is generally the same as that used by the taxpayer concerned for the purpose of computing assessable profits. The term "basis period" is defined in section 40 (1) so that for the purposes of Part VI, apart from where either of two specified exceptions is applicable, it has the same meaning as that assigned to it by section 2 of the Ordinance (i.e. " "basis period" for any year of assessment is the period on the income or the profits of which tax for that year ultimately falls to be computed"). The two exceptions, so far as is relevant, are –

    (a) where two basis periods overlap, the period common to both is deemed to fall into the first period only; and

    (b) where there is an interval between the end of the basis period for one year of assessment and the beginning of the basis period for the next succeeding year of assessment, the interval is deemed to fall into the second basis period.

14. The meaning assigned to the term "basis period" in Part VI ensures that on a change of accounting date by a taxpayer, initial allowance is only granted once in respect of expenditure incurred in a period which is common to two basis periods, and also that the allowance is not lost where expenditure is incurred during an interval between two basis periods.

Part II — THE "POOLING SYSTEM" — 1980/81 Onwards

Background

15. As was mentioned earlier, the "pooling system" for making depreciation allowances was introduced by the Inland Revenue (amendment) (No. 4) Ordinance 1980 and has been in effect since the year of assessment 1980/81. The pooling system was not introduced with the intention of fundamentally changing the depreciation allowances or charges made under the old scheme. Rather, the intention was merely to save time and expense by modifying the old scheme to reduce the need to maintain detailed depreciation records in respect of individual items of machinery and plant. The pooling system seeks to achieve this objective by, in essence, creating a single "pool" of expenditure in respect of all items of machinery or plant which qualify for a particular rate of annual allowance.

The Allowances

Initial Allowance

16. Section 39B(1) provides for an initial allowance to be made where "a person carrying on a trade, profession or business incurs capital expenditure on the provision of machinery or plant" for the purposes of producing profits chargeable to Profits Tax. As with the corresponding provision under the old scheme (section 37(1)), section 39B(1) provides that the initial allowance is made to the person for the year of assessment in the basis period for which the expenditure is incurred. There is no requirement that the asset must be in use in the basis period, but the allowance is subject to the asset eventually being acquired and used in the trade carried on.

17. As initial allowance is made in respect of capital expenditure "incurred", it is not limited to sums actually paid. Where a contractual obligation exists, the due date for payment of deposits, instalments, etc. will be regarded as the date when the expenditure is incurred, even if actual payment occurs at a later date. It should be noted, however, that no allowance can be made in respect of what is merely a contingent liability. It follows that a deposit or advance payment is not recognised as expenditure incurred on the provision of machinery or plant unless it has been paid on a nonrefundable basis in respect of a binding purchase contract. In the absence of a written contract, the date of delivery of the asset is normally taken to be the date on which the expenditure is incurred.

18. The rate of initial allowance for any year of assessment commencing on or after 1 April 1989 is 60% (section 39B(1A)(a) and, where the old scheme is applicable, section 36A(3)(c)).

Annual Allowance

19. Section 39B(2) provides for an annual allowance to be given for each year of assessment. This is calculated at the appropriate rate on the reducing value of each class or *pool* of machinery or plant. A class of machinery or plant is made up of all such items eligible for the same rate of annual allowance (see paragraph 21). Unlike the position in respect of annual allowances under the old system (see section 37(2)), there is no requirement under the pooling system to the effect that the asset must be owned and in use at the end of the basis period.

20. Section 39B(2) provides, in effect, for annual allowance to be made to a person where he has at some time (not necessarily during the basis period for the current year of assessment) owned and had "in use" any machinery or plant for the purpose of producing profits chargeable to Profits Tax. It is the Department's view that the words "in use" should not be strictly construed. Thus where a machine is temporarily idle during the last few days of a basis period, e.g. awaiting commencement of a new production run, the machine is considered to be "in use" for the purposes of the allowance. In regard to spare parts, e.g. reserve engines for taxis, the Department's position is that where these are "on the bench" ready for installation and use, they qualify for the allowance. However, where spares are held in store for issue or are held crated as received from the supplier, they are not considered to be "in use" for the purposes of the allowance.

Annual Allowance rates

21. Section 39B(3) provides that the annual allowance shall be calculated at the rates of depreciation prescribed by the Board of Inland Revenue and shall be computed on the reducing value of each class of machinery or plant. The rates prescribed by the Board are set out in the third column of the First part of the Table annexed to Rule 2 of the Inland Revenue Rules. The Table (see Appendix A(i)) specifies the rates of depreciation for certain classifications of machinery and plant and, for those not specifically itemized, lays down a general rate of 20%. [The same rates apply in respect of annual allowances made under the old scheme (section 37(2)).]

Calculation of the allowances

22. Apart from its role in relation to the rates of depreciation, section 39B(3) also provides that the annual allowance "shall be computed on the reducing value of each class of machinery or plant.". Section 39B(4), (5), (6) and (7) detail what is meant by the reducing value of a class of machinery or plant. In essence, the "reducing value" of a class of machinery or plant (i.e. the figure which is multiplied by the prescribed rate of depreciation to calculate the annual allowance to be made in respect of the class concerned for the year of assessment under consideration) is arrived at by *aggregating* (as applicable) –

(a) the reducing value of the class (i.e. the "pool") brought forward from the end of the previous year of assessment;

(b) the amount of qualifying capital expenditure incurred on the provision of machinery and plant of the same class during the basis period for the current year, less any initial allowance given in respect of that expenditure. [Expenditure does not qualify if incurred in respect of machinery or plant which is either under hire-purchase (section 39C(1)(a)) or only partly used for the purpose of producing chargeable profits (section 39C(1)(b)). These categories are further discussed in Part II below];

(c) the reducing value (i.e. capital expenditure incurred less any initial or annual allowances made), as at the end of the previous year of assessment, of each item of machinery or plant acquired under hirepurchase which passed into the ownership of the person during the previous year of assessment (see section 39C(2) and paragraphs 37 and 38 below);

(d) in respect of each item of machinery or plant owned and used by the person for any period immediately before using it to produce chargeable profits in the particular year of assessment, the actual cost of the item less the notional annual allowances which would have been made under section 37 if the owner had used the item since acquisition for the purpose of producing chargeable profits (see section 39B(6) and paragraphs 25–27 below);

(e) the reducing value taken over (as a result of succession during the year of assessment to a trade, profession or business) of machinery or plant acquired without being purchased (see section 39B(7) and paragraph 31 below);

and *deducting* (as applicable) –

(f) the aggregate of any sale, insurance, salvage or compensation money received in respect of any item of machinery or plant belonging to that class disposed of during the basis period (see section 39B(4)(e) and paragraphs 28, 49 and 50 below); and

(g) the reducing value (determined by the Commissioner) of any machinery or plant previously used wholly and exclusively in the production of profits which ceased to be so used during the basis period (see section 39C(3) and paragraph 30 below).

23. The following examples illustrate the operation of the pooling system. [In considering the examples in this Practice Note, it should be assumed, unless information to the contrary is provided, that the taxpayer concerned is carrying on a trade, profession or business in Hong Kong and that the machinery or plant is used therein by the taxpayer for the purpose of producing profits chargeable to Profits Tax.]

■ Example 1

24. A taxpayer commenced business on 2 February 1994. The accounts of the business are made up to 31 December each year. During the first year of trading, the following items of machinery and plant were purchased:

1 motor car	$150,000	(30% annual allowance rate)
3 electric cookers	$50,000	(30% annual allowance rate)
1 set of office furniture	$20,000	(20% annual allowance rate)
2 room air-conditioning units	$28,000	(20% annual allowance rate)

Machinery and plant depreciable at the same annual allowance rate is "pooled" together for the purpose of calculating the depreciation allowances. For the year of assessment 1994/95, the company is entitled to depreciation allowances totalling $176,640, computed as follows:

	30% Pool $	20% Pool $	Allowance $
Cost	200,000	48,000	
Less: I. A. (60%)	120,000	28,800	148,800
	80,000	19,200	
Less: A. A.	24,000	3,840	27,840
Reducing value c/f	56,000	15,360	
		Total	176,640

During the year ended 31 December 1995, the motor car was damaged beyond repair in an accident. The insurance company paid $30,000 and the taxpayer also obtained $1,000 from a scrap dealer for the wreck. During the same year, a new van was purchased for $180,000, an electric cooker was disposed of for $3,000, and a room air-conditioning unit was sold for $2,000, replaced with a new one purchased for $8,000.

For the year of assessment 1995/96, the taxpayer would be entitled to depreciation allowances totalling $144,312, computed as follows:

	30% Pool	20% Pool	Allowance
	$	$	$
Reducing value b/f	56,000	15,360	
Add: New assets	180,000	8,000	
	236,000	23,360	
Less: I. A.	108,000	4,800	112,800
	128,000	18,560	
Less: Sale proceeds	34,000 *	2,000	
	94,000	16,560	
Less: A. A.	28,200	3,312	31,512
Reducing value c/f	65,800	13,248	
		Total	144,312

* Sale proceeds: $34,000 = $30,000 + $1,000 + $3,000

Assets brought into the business after non-business use

25. Under both the old scheme and the pooling system (see sections 37(2A) and 39B(6)), notional allowances have to be computed if an item of machinery or plant is owned and used by a person before he uses it for the purpose of producing profits chargeable to tax. In such a case, for the purpose of calculating the annual allowance in respect of the item (i.e. the amount to be included in the pool where the pooling system is applicable), the capital expenditure incurred on the provision of the item is computed by deducting from its actual cost the notional amount of the annual allowance that would have been made under section 37 to the owner if since acquiring the machinery or plant he had used it for the purpose of producing profits chargeable to tax. There is no provision for deducting a notional initial allowance from the actual cost.

26. No entitlement to initial allowance arises in such circumstances. This is because entitlement only arises under the respective Profits Tax and Salaries Tax provisions where it can be said of the relevant capital expenditure that it was incurred on the provision of *machinery or plant for the purpose of producing profits chargeable to tax under Part VI*, or in the case of employment, *machinery or plant the use of which is essential to the production of the assessable income*. It follows that where the expenditure is incurred for some other purpose, irrespective of how the machinery or plant is subsequently used, the requirement for entitlement is not satisfied.

■ Example 2

27. A taxpayer, who had been trading for some years, purchased a car for private use on 10 May 1994 at a cost of $160,000. The car was transferred to business use on 12 August 1996. The taxpayer's accounts are made up to 31 March each year.

	30% Pool
	$
Actual Cost	160,000
Less: **1994/95** Notional annual allowance	
$160,000 × 30%	48,000
	112,000
Less: **1995/96** Notional annual allowance	
$112,000 × 30%	33,600
Notional cost of asset	78,400

Note: For the purposes of the 30% pool in the 1996/97 and subsequent years of assessment, the car would be treated as if it had been purchased on 12 August 1996 for $78,400.

Proceeds of machinery or plant disposed of

28. The Ordinance makes it clear that any sale, insurance, salvage or compensation moneys received in respect of machinery or plant which has been included in a pool is to be deducted in ascertaining the reducing value of the pool (section 39B(4)(e)) and, where cessation is involved, in calculating any balancing charge required to be made under section 39D(2)(b) (see paragraph 32 below). Thus, if machinery or plant is destroyed, the sum to be taken into account is generally the total of any insurance, salvage or compensation received. However, section 39D(6) provides that the total amount taken into account is *not to exceed* the capital expenditure incurred on the provision of the particular item. Where the asset was introduced into the business after non-business use, the relevant figure is the capital expenditure computed in accordance with section 39B(6) (i.e. the actual cost of the asset less notional annual allowances for the years of non-business use).

■ Example 3

29. The reducing value of a taxpayer's 30% pool after 1995/96 allowances was $36,000. During the year ended 30 June 1996, a van which had cost $138,000 was sold for $140,000. A car, which had been purchased in July 1993 for $320,000, was introduced into the business on 1 September 1995. The accounts of the taxpayer are made up to 30 June each year.

Year of Assessment 1996/97

	30% Pool
	$
Reducing value b/f	36,000
Add: Notional cost of car introduced *	156,800
	192,800
Less: Disposal value (restricted to actual cost)	138,000

		54,800
Less: A.A.		16,440
Reducing value c/f		38,360

* Computation of the notional cost of the car for the purpose of its introduction into the business (see paragraphs 25 and 26 above):

		$
Actual cost of the car		320,000
Less: Notional annual allowances for years of non-business use (two complete years) –		
• **1994/95** notional annual allowance $320,000 × 30%	96,000	
• **1995/96** notional annual allowance $224,000 × 30%	67,200	163,200
Notional cost for business under section 39B(6)		156,800

Note: (i) No initial allowance is due on the car introduced as no capital expenditure was incurred during the basis period.

(ii) Any new expenditure has to be added to the pool before disposal proceeds are deducted. Even though the van was sold for $2,000 more than its purchase price, a balancing charge is not made. This is because section 39D(1) provides that a balancing charge can arise only where at the end of the basis period for a year of assessment the aggregate reductions made under section 39B(4) exceed aggregate capital expenditure on the class of machinery or plant, i.e. including purchases made during the basis period (see paragraph 32 below).

Assets removed from pool for non-business use

30. Where an item of machinery or plant which has been used wholly and exclusively in the production of chargeable profits ceases to be so used (e.g. when it becomes used wholly or partly for private purposes), its reducing value must be deducted from that of the pool for the year of assessment during the basis period for which the change occurred. The reducing value of the machinery or plant is deemed, under section 39C(3), to be the amount which the Commissioner considers the item in question would have realised if sold in the open market at the time it ceased to be wholly and exclusively used in the production of chargeable profits. Depreciation allowances are separately calculated for the year of change, and for subsequent years for so long as the item continues to be used (partly or wholly) in the production of chargeable profits (see paragraphs 43 and 44 below).

Succession to a trade, etc.

31. The provisions of section 39B(7) cater for the situation where a person succeeds to a trade, profession or business and are broadly similar to those of section 37(4), relating to the old scheme. Thus, if on succession to a trade,

ownership of machinery or plant passes to the successor without it being sold to him, the reducing value of each pool of expenditure unallowed to the old proprietor is taken over by the new proprietor. The successor is entitled to annual allowance under section 39B(2) once the machinery or plant is used to produce chargeable profits in his trade. The successor is not, however, entitled to any initial allowance in respect of such machinery or plant (section 39B(8)). For the purpose of calculating any subsequent reduction from the pool or balancing charge on disposal, the cost of the asset acquired by the successor in this way will be deemed to be equal to the reducing value of the pool taken over.
Balancing Allowances and Balancing Charges

32. Section 39D(2) provides that where a person ceases to trade and the sale etc., moneys received for the machinery or plant are less than the reducing value in the pool, a balancing allowance equal to the difference is to be made. This is the *only situation* in which a balancing allowance can be given — any sum received on the disposal of an asset at any other time is simply deducted from the value of the pool. A balancing charge can, however, arise whenever disposal proceeds exceed the reducing value of the pool (i.e. not only on the disposal of a class of machinery or plant on the cessation of trading). However, it should be noted that by virtue of section 39D(3), no balancing charge or balancing allowance can arise where on cessation machinery or plant passes to a successor to whom the reducing value of the machinery or plant is transferred under section 39B(7).

■ Example 4

33. A taxpayer owned three motor vehicles as at 30 June 1994. During the year ended 30 June 1995 he sold one for $130,000 without replacing it, and during the following year another for $60,000, again without replacing it. In each case the vehicle was sold for less than its original cost. The accounts of the business are made up to 30 June each year.

The reducing value carried forward after the 1994/95 allowances was $125,000 for the 30% pool. As a result of the disposals, balancing charges, computed as follows, would be made:

Year of Assessment 1995/96

	30% Pool
	$
Reducing value b/f	125,000
Less: Disposal value	130,000
Balancing charge [s.39D(1)(a)]	5,000
Reducing value c/f [s.39D(1)(b)]	nil

Year of Assessment 1996/97

	30% Pool $
Reducing value b/f	nil
Less: Sale proceeds	60,000
Balancing charge [s. 39D(1)(a)]	60,000

■ Example 5

34. A taxpayer commenced trading in 1976. His accounts were made up to 30 September each year. On 15 May 1996 he ceased trading. During the final year he purchased machinery costing $20,000, which qualified for the 20% annual allowance rate.

The reducing values of the 20% and 30% pools after the 1995/96 allowances were $13,000 and $21,000 respectively. On cessation, the machinery and plant were sold for $15,000 and $28,000, for the 20% and 30% pools respectively. The resulting balancing allowance and balancing charge for the cessation year would be computed as follows –

Year of Assessment 1996/97

	30% Pool $	20% Pool $
Reducing value b/f	21,000	13,000
Add: New asset		20,000
		33,000
Less: I. A.		12,000
		21,000
Less: Sale proceeds	28,000	15,000
Balancing allowance [s. 39D(2)]		6,000
Balancing charge [s. 39D(2)]	7,000	

Note: As a matter of practice, no annual allowance is computed for the year of cessation, but initial allowance is due on capital expenditure incurred during the final basis period.

Assets put out of use upon cessation of a trade, etc.

35. Section 38(4) and section 39D(4) and (5) contain similar rules to the effect that where machinery or plant is put out of use by reason of a person ceasing to carry on a trade, the person is deemed to have received immediately prior to the cessation sale proceeds for the machinery or plant of such amount as the Commissioner may consider it would have realised if sold in the open market. However, if within twelve months of the date of cessation the taxpayer sells the asset, he may claim the adjustment of any balancing allowance or balancing charge which may have been made to or on him as if the actual sale had taken place immediately prior to the date of cessation. The sections provide for such an adjustment to be made, notwithstanding that the assessment may otherwise have become final and conclusive under the provisions of section 70. These sections are not considered to apply where following the cessation of a trade any machinery or plant previously used therein is transferred to another trade carried on by the same person, whether or not there is an intervening period between the cessation and the transfer.

■ Example 6

36. On 15 February 1995 a taxpayer ceased to carry on a business. The accounts of the business had been made up to 31 March each year. The items of machinery and plant included in the 30% pool, which originally cost $75,000 and had a reducing value of $21,000 after the 1993/94 allowances, were sold shortly after cessation of the business for $80,000.

Items (consisting of office furniture) in the 20% pool, which originally cost $20,000 and had a reducing value of $6,400 after the 1993/94 allowances, had not been sold when the accounts for the final period of trading were submitted to the Inland Revenue Department. In accordance with section 39D(4), the Commissioner placed an open market value of $7,200 on the furniture.

On 7 June 1995, a Notice of Assessment was issued to the taxpayer advising the assessable profits under section 18D for the final year of assessment of the business, i.e. 1994/95. No objection was lodged in respect of the assessment. However, on 11 November 1995, the taxpayer advised the Department that the office furniture had been sold for $5,000, and claimed adjustment to the assessment in accordance with section 39D(5). Balancing charges, computed as follows, would have been included in the original assessment:

	30% Pool	20% Pool	
	$	$	
Reducing value b/f	21,000	6,400	
Less: Sale price	80,000	7,200	[s. 39D(4)]
Balancing charge*	59,000	800	

* The balancing charge for the 30% pool would be restricted, in effect, under section 39D(6) to $54,000, being the total of the allowances previously granted to the taxpayer, i.e. $75,000 – $21,000.

The total balancing charge would be $54,800 i.e. $54,000 + $800.

Upon receipt of the claim under section 39D(5), a revised assessment would be issued to reflect the following adjustment to the balancing charge previously made in respect of the 20% pool:

	20% Pool
	$
Reducing value b/f	6,400
Less: Actual sale proceeds	5,000
Balancing allowance	1,400
Add: Previous balancing charge now withdrawn	800
Reduction in assessment	2,200

Part III — SITUATIONS WHERE THE POOLING SYSTEM DOES NOT APPLY

Assets acquired under hire purchase agreements

37. Section 39C(1)(a) provides that the pooling system does not apply in respect of machinery or plant being acquired under hire purchase (i.e. machinery or plant in respect of which section 37A applies). The initial and annual allowances due in respect of expenditure incurred on the provision of such machinery or plant must be calculated separately, as per Example 7 below. In effect, the legislation provides that for each year of assessment in the basis period for which the taxpayer has made an instalment payment, an initial allowance is made in respect of the capital element of the instalment payments made during the basis period. However, when the instalment payments are completed and no further initial allowance is due, the reducing value of the asset is added to the appropriate pool, i.e. in the year of assessment following the year of assessment during the basis period for which the machinery or plant passes into the ownership of the taxpayer (section 39C(2)).

■ Example 7

38. A taxpayer acquired a suite of office furniture at a hire purchase price $220,000 in January 1995. The cash price was $160,000. A deposit of $10,000 was paid in January 1995. The first of 24 monthly instalments was paid in February 1995. The taxpayer closes his accounts on 31 March annually. Depreciation allowances would be made to the taxpayer as follows:

	20% HP	Allowance	Y/A
	$	$	
Cost	160,000		
Less: I. A. ($10,000+150,000 × 2/24) × 60%	13,500	13,500	
	146,500		
Less: A. A.	29,300	29,300	
	117,200		
		42,800	1994/95

Less: I. A. ($150,000 × 12/24 × 60%)	45,000	45,000	
	72,200		
Less: A. A.	14,440	14,440	
	57,760		
		59,440	1995/96
Less: I. A. ($150,000 × 10/24 × 60%)	37,500	37,500	
	20,260		
Less: A. A.	4,052	4,052	
Reducing value c/f*	16,208		
		41,552	1996/97

* The reducing value figure of $16,208 would be transferred to the 20% pool in the year of assessment 1997/98

Total depreciation allowances not to exceed total capital expenditure

39. It should be appreciated that initial and annual allowances are provided under the Ordinance as a process of allocation of capital expenditure. It therefore follows that where an item of machinery or plant is acquired under a hire purchase agreement, the total amount of depreciation allowances made to a taxpayer should not exceed the amount of capital expenditure incurred on the item. The following example provides an illustration of a situation where the limitation would be applied.

■ Example 8

40. A taxpayer entered into a hire purchase agreement in July 1993 to acquire a tractor, at a hire purchase price of $250,000. A deposit $30,000 was paid. The hire purchase price included interest of $40,000. The first of 36 monthly instalments was paid in August 1993. The taxpayer makes up accounts to 31 December each year. The following depreciation allowances would be made to the taxpayer.

	30% HP		Allowance	Y/A
	$		$	$
Cost	210,000			
Less: I. A.*[1]	33,000	33,000		
	177,000			
Less: A. A.	53,100	53,100	86,100	1993/94
	123,900			
Less: I. A.*[2]	36,000	36,000		
	87,900			
Less: A. A.	26,370	26,370	62,370	1994/95
	61,530			
Less: I. A. *[2]	36,000	36,000		
	25,530			

Less: A. A.	7,659	7,659	43,659	1995/96
	17,871			
Less: I.A. *3	17,871	17,871	17,871	1996/97
Accumulated deprecation allowances			210,000	

*1 ($30,000 + $180,000 × 5/36) × 60%
*2 $180,000 × 12/36 × 60%
*3 The amount of depreciation allowance made to the taxpayer in the year of assessment
1996/97 would be $17,871, notwithstanding the payment of capital expenditure of
$35,000 (i.e. $180,000 × 7/36).

Balancing Allowance concession

41. It is recognised that in some cases where machinery or plant under a hire
purchase agreement is repossessed by, or voluntarily returned to, the vendor,
the taxpayer's total capital expenditure may exceed the sum of the depreciation
allowances made prior to the disposal and whatever amount, if any, is received
from the vendor upon the latter's disposal of the repossessed or returned asset.
In such a situation (i.e. where the machinery or plant is under hire purchase),
the Ordinance does not provide for any balancing allowance to be made to the
taxpayer in respect of the excess. The Department does, however, by way of an
extra-statutory concession, grant such an allowance.

■ Example 9

42. In June 1995 a taxpayer entered into a hire purchase agreement to acquire
office furniture. The hire purchase price of the furniture was $120,000, including
an interest element of $20,000. A deposit $10,000 was paid in June 1995, and
the first of the 24 monthly instalments covering the balance was paid in July
1995. The taxpayer ceased paying instalments in April 1996 (i.e. after 9
instalments had been paid), shortly after which the furniture was repossessed
(the taxpayer did not receive any payment from the vendor after the repossession).
The taxpayer continued to carry on the business. The accounts of the business
are made up to 31 December each year.

Whereas the total amount of capital expenditure paid by the taxpayer was
$43,750 (i.e. $10,000 + $90,000 × 9/24), the total of the depreciation allowances
which could be made to the taxpayer under section 37A would be, as can be
seen below, $42,350 (i.e. $19,500 + $16,100 + $6,750). In the circumstances, a
concessional allowance in respect of the difference of $1,400 (i.e. $43,750 –
$42,350) would be made to the taxpayer.

	20% HP	Allowance	Y/A
	$		
Cost	100,000		
Less: I.A.	19,500	19,500 *1	

	80,500			
Less: A.A.	16,100	16,100	35,600	1995/96
	64,400			
Less: I.A.	6,750	6,750 *2		
Reducing value	57,650 *3			
Concessional allowance*4			1,400	8,150	1996/97
Total allowances				43,750

*1 ($10,000 + $90,000 × 6/24) × 60%
*2 ($90,000 × 3/24) × 60%
*3 Reducing value of $57,650 will be eliminated for the purpose of calculating depreciation
    allowances for future assessments.
*4 Excess of capital expenditure incurred over initial and annual allowances $1,400 (i.e.
    $43,750 – $42,350)

Machinery or plant used partly for the purposes of the trade, etc.

43. Section 39C(1)(b) provides, in effect, that the pooling system does not apply to assets which are used only partially for producing chargeable profits. The allowances due in respect of any such asset need to be separately calculated in accordance with the old scheme so that the appropriate apportionment for non-business usage can be made (under section 12(2), 18F(1) or 19E(1)). Any such reduction does not affect the calculation of subsequent allowances which are computed in the first place as if the full amount had been granted, and then apportioned as appropriate in relation to the extent to which the asset is or has been used (a) in the production of the chargeable profits and (b) for other purposes (section 39A).

44. Even if partial non-business use ceases, and the asset is then used wholly for business purposes, separate calculations must continue. This is because any balancing charge on subsequent disposal of the asset has to be apportioned to take into account the earlier non-business usage.

45. The following example illustrates the method of calculating the allowances and balancing charge where the proportion of non-business use has not been constant –

■ Example 10

46. A taxpayer commenced to carry on a business on 1 June 1991, on which date he purchased a motor vehicle for $280,000. This vehicle was used wholly for business purposes until 31 March 1992. As from 1 April 1992 (after the taxpayer had sold his private car), the vehicle was used partly for private purposes, with the estimated private use being 50% of the total annual mileage. Twelve months later, the private use portion had declined to 25%. In June 1994 the vehicle was sold for $60,000. The taxpayer's accounts are made up to 31 March each year.

	30%	Allowances made against business profits	Adjustment in respect of private use	Y/A
	$	$	$	
Cost *1	280,000			
Less: I. A.	168,000	168,000 (100%)		
	112,000			
Less: A. A.	33,600	33,600 (100%)		
		201,600		1991/92
Reducing value	78,400			
Less: A. A.	23,520	11,760 (50%)	11,760	1992/93
Reducing value	54,880			
Less: A. A.	16,464	12,348 (75%)	4,116	1993/94
		225,708	15,876	
Reducing value	38,416			
Sale proceeds	60,000			
Excess over Reducing value	21,584			
Balancing Charge	20,165*2		1,419	1994/95

*1 For the 1991/92 year of assessment, the cost would have been included as part of the 30% pool. The reducing value of the car at the end of that year (i.e. $78,400) would have been excluded from the pool for the separate calculation of depreciation allowances in 1992/93 (i.e. the year in which the car ceased to be used wholly for business purposes).

*2 For the 1994/95 year of assessment, a balancing charge, calculated as follows, would be made –

$21,584 × $225,708 / ($225,708 + $15,876) = $20,165

Part IV — MISCELLANEOUS PROVISIONS

Commissioner's discretion — rate of Annual Allowance

47. Both proviso (b) to section 37(2) and section 39(B)(11) empower the Commissioner in his discretion to allow a higher rate for annual allowance than that prescribed by the Board of Inland Revenue. An application for an increased rate of allowance should include the following details –

(a) the estimated working life of the asset;

(b) the anticipated disposal/scrap value of the asset at end of its working life; and

(c) where excessive wear and tear is claimed in respect of the use of an asset on a specific project, the possibility of it being restored/repaired for further use in the business on completion of the project.

48. At the present time, the rates of initial and annual allowances are such that the Commissioner considers it is unlikely that any claim for a higher annual allowance could be justified.

Assets sold together

49. Particularly where cessation occurs, it is not uncommon to find that assets are sold together for one price, without the consideration in respect of each asset being separately specified. Where this occurs the Commissioner is empowered, by virtue of the provisions of section 38A, to allocate a price to each individual asset.

Transactions between related parties

50. Section 38B provides for the situation where the Commissioner is of the opinion that the sale price of an asset, which qualifies for initial or annual allowances, does not represent its true market value, and any of the following circumstances are applicable –

    (a)   the buyer is a person over whom the seller has control; or

    (b)   the seller is a person over whom the buyer has control; or

    (c)   both the seller and the buyer are persons over both of whom some other person has control; or

    (d)   the sale is between a husband and wife, not being a wife living apart from her husband.

In such a case, the section provides that the Commissioner may determine the true market value at the time of the sale, and that value is deemed to be the sale price of the asset for the purpose of calculating the allowances and charges under part VI of the Ordinance.

Commissioner's power to direct that the "old scheme" should apply

51. Section 36A(2) gives the Commissioner power to direct the extent and the duration for which the provisions of the old scheme shall continue to apply for any year of assessment from 1980/81 onwards, whenever he is satisfied that the application of any of the provisions of the pooling system to particular machinery or plant would be impracticable or inequitable.

APPENDIX A(i)

**RATES OF DEPRECIATION, AS
PRESCRIBED BY THE BOARD OF INLAND REVENUE**
[From Rule 2 of the Inland Revenue Rules]

TABLE

FIRST PART

Item	*Rate of Depreciation*
1. Air-conditioning plant excluding room air-conditioning units	10%
2. Bank safe deposit boxes, doors and grills	10%
3. Broadcasting transmitters	10%
4. Cables (electric)	10%
5. Lamp standards (street) — gas or electric	10%
6. Lifts and escalators (electric)	10%
7. Mains (gas or water)	10%
8. Oil tanks	10%
9. Shipping —	
Ships, junks and sampans	10%
Lighters	10%
Tugs	10%
10. Sprinklers	10%
11. Domestic appliances	20%
12. Furniture (excluding soft furnishings)	20%
13. Room air-conditioning units	20%
14. Shipping —	
Launches and ferry vessels	20%
Hydrofoils	20%
15. Taxi meters	20%
16. Type and blocks (if not dealt with on renewals basis)	20%
17. Aircraft (including engines)	30%
18. Bar syphon apparatus	30%
19. Bicycles	30%
20. Bleaching and finishing machinery and plant	30%
21. Concrete pipe moulds	30%
22. Electric cookers and kettles	30%
23. Electronic data processing equipment	30%
24. Electronics manufacturing machinery and plant	30%
25. Motor vehicles	30%
26. Plastic manufacturing machinery and plant including moulds	30%

27. Shipping —
   Outboard motors 30%
28. Silk manufacturing machinery and plant 30%
29. Sulphuric and nitric acid plant 30%
30. Tank lorries 30%
31. Textile and clothing manufacturing machinery and plant 30%
32. Tractors — bull dozers and graders 30%
33. Weaving, spinning, knitting and sewing machinery 30%
34. Machinery or plant, not specified in items 1 to 33, and used
   for the purposes of a transport, tunnel, dock, water, gas or
   electricity undertaking or a public telephone or public
   telegraphic service 10%
35. Any other machinery or plant, not specified in items 1 to
   34 .... 20%

APPENDIX A(ii)

"IMPLEMENTS, UTENSILS AND ARTICLES", AS PRESCRIBED BY THE BOARD OF INLAND REVENUE
[From Rule 2 of the Inland Revenue Rules]

TABLE

SECOND PART

Item

1. Belting.
2. Crockery and cutlery.
3. Kitchen utensils.
4. Linen.
5. Loose tools.
6. Soft furnishings (including curtains and carpets).
7. Surgical and dental instruments.
8. Tubes for X-ray and infra-red machines.

APPENDIX B

ITEMS WHICH QUALIFY AS MACHINERY OR PLANT

In addition to the items specified in the First Part of the Table annexed to Rule 2 of the Inland Revenue Rules, the following items are recognized as "machinery or plant" for the purposes of the depreciation allowances:–

Item

(i)   Design and process plans (for the construction of a machine to be used in the production of the saleable product of the taxpayer).

(ii)   Display platforms.

(iii)   First Registration Tax (paid on acquisition of a new motor vehicle).

(iv)   Iron gates (where not an integral part of a building or structure).

(v)   Office partitioning (where not an integral part of a building or structure).

(vi)   Poster-boards (advertisement hoardings).

(vii)   Signboards.

(viii) Dry docks.

(ix)   Lighting and décor items installed to provide atmosphere or ambience in, but not forming an integral part of, licensed premises such as hotels and restaurants whose trade includes the provision of "atmosphere" or "ambience".

(x)   Barrister's books.

APPENDIX C

ITEMS WHICH DO NOT QUALIFY AS MACHINERY OR PLANT

Item

(i)   Acoustic tile ceilings (installed as an integral part of a building).

(ii)   Ceiling lighting points.

(iii) Cocklofts.

(iv) Fish ponds and fish storage barge.

(v)   Shop fronts, fixed wall and floor coverings, suspended ceilings, raised floors, balustrades and stairs.

(vi) Telephone cable and wiring (installed as an integral part of a building).

(vii) Wiring and electrical fixtures and fittings (installed as an integral part of a building).

(viii) Car parks and piers.

(ix) Canopies over petrol-filling stations

(x)   Car-wash halls (i.e buildings housing washing and control equipment).

---

* [Challengeable; being built into the building does not of itself disqualify the expenditure, it depends upon what it is used for. — Author]

APPENDIX 6

**Departmental Interpretation & Practice Notes
No. 9 (Revised)**

MAJOR DEDUCTIBLE ITEMS UNDER SALARIES TAX

These notes are issued for the information of taxpayers and their tax representatives. They contain the Department's interpretation and practices in relation to the laws as it stood at the date of publication. Taxpayers are reminded that their right of objection against the assessment and their right of appeal to the Commissioner, the Board of Review or the Court are not affected by the application of these notes.

These notes replace those issued in September 2002.

LAU MAK Yee-ming, Alice
Commissioner of Inland Revenue

September 2006

Our Web site: http://www.info.gov.hk/ird

CONTENT

MAJOR CATEGORIES OF ALLOWABLE DEDUCTIONS

A taxpayer may claim, among other things, the following allowable deductions
for the purpose of computing his salaries tax liability –

(a) all outgoings and expenses incurred in the production of his assessable
income;

(b) self-education expenses paid;

(c) allowances calculated in accordance with Part VI of the Inland Revenue
Ordinance (the Ordinance) in respect of capital expenditure on machinery
or plant the use of which is essential to the production of his assessable
income; and

(d) approved charitable donations made.

HOW DEDUCTIONS ARE TO BE CLAIMED

2. The Tax Return-Individuals [B.I.R. 60] provides for entries to be made for
claiming various deductions. Receipts need not be submitted with the completed
return although they should be retained for eventual verification, if required by
the Department. Since the onus of proving the validity of the deduction claim is
on the taxpayer, it is in his own interest to keep full and contemporaneous records
for all his claims.

OUTGOINGS AND EXPENSES

3. Section 12(1)(a) of the Ordinance provides that deductions may be claimed
for –

> *"all outgoings and expenses, other than expenses of a domestic or private
> nature and capital expenditure, wholly, exclusively and necessarily incurred
> in the production of the assessable income".*

4. In order to be qualified for deduction, therefore, the expenditure must satisfy
each of the following tests in addition to not being expenditure of a domestic or
private nature or of a capital nature, e.g. expenditure to acquire an asset –

(a) it must have been "incurred";

(b) it must have arisen "wholly and exclusively" in the production of the
income; and

(c) it must have been "necessary" in the production of the income.

"INCURRED"

5. The word "incurred" has been judicially considered on a number of occasions
and the authorities are generally agreed that for an expenditure to have been
incurred it must be an established liability or a definite commitment which
arose in the year of assessment in which it is sought to be claimed as a deduction.
Actual payment during the year in question is not necessary, but where payment
has not been made before the end of that year, no deduction can be allowed

unless there existed on the last day of that year an actual and known liability or obligation of *ascertainable amount*. A mere rough estimate, a contingent liability or an anticipated future outgoing will not therefore generally rank for deduction.

"WHOLLY" AND "EXCLUSIVELY"

6. These words are not to be considered too narrowly. Where expenditure is incurred for more than one purpose (e.g. running expenses of a car used partly for private purposes), such expenditure should be apportioned (usually on a mileage basis), and the part attributable to the employment would be allowed, provided the other tests are satisfied.

"NECESSARILY"

7. The word "necessarily" is to be construed as meaning essential to the conduct of the employment. It is not sufficient that the expenditure is related to the production of the income and possibly facilitates and aids the production of income. The basic test is whether the expenditure is vital to the employment to the extent that it would not be possible for the taxpayer to produce the income from the employment without incurring that expenditure. If the duties imposed by the employer require the expenditure to be incurred, one would expect that the employer will pay for such expenditure. Hence, it is hard for an employee to claim that he has paid for expenditure that his duties require him to incur, unless in the contract of employment the employee is required to bear the necessary expenses. However, it does not follow that because the employer has required the expenditure to be incurred by the employee that such expenditure is necessarily admissible: the test is "not whether the employer imposes the expense but whether the duties do, in the sense that, irrespective of what the employer may prescribe, the duties cannot be performed without incurring that particular outlay". *[Brown v. Bullock 40 TC 1.]*

"IN THE PRODUCTION OF THE ASSESSABLE INCOME"

8. The meaning of this phrase had been discussed in the Supreme Court case of *Commissioner of Inland Revenue v. Humphrey, HKTC 451* together with the wording in similar provisions in the United Kingdom Income Tax Acts ["in the performance of the duties"] and the Australian Income Tax Assessment Act ["in gaining or producing the assessable income"]. The judgment in the Supreme Court was made on the basis that as far as the appeal in that case was concerned (a claim for travelling expenses from home to office) the difference in phraseology between the Taxing Acts, the Hong Kong provision having a certain affinity to the wording of the Australian Taxing Act, was immaterial.

9. Expenses are not incurred "in the performance of the duties" if they are incurred only to *enable* the duties to be performed e.g. travelling expenses between the taxpayer's home and his place of employment; expenditures to acquire an employment or appointment; or the costs of memberships to social or sports clubs whether or not required by the employer. It is noteworthy that certain of the items mentioned also fail to qualify as allowable deductions under the other tests referred to in the preceding paragraphs.

10. Similarly, a distinction must be drawn between an expense incurred *in* gaining income and one incurred necessarily *for* the purpose of gaining it. This point was considered in the court case of *Commissioner of Inland Revenue v. Robert P. Burns, 1 HKTC 1181*, in which the Court rejected the claim for legal expenses incurred by a horse trainer in an appeal against disqualification: such expenses were merely incurred for the purpose of seeing that the claimant was not precluded from earning his assessable income and were therefore not incurred in the production of it.

11. Neither would sums paid upon termination of the employment contract by an employee, e.g. payment in lieu of notice, be admissible: they are not incurred in the production of income but are made in order to have the contract terminated and/or to avoid possible action for damages by the employer. *[See Board of Review Case No. BR 9/78.]*

EXPENSE ALLOWANCES FROM EMPLOYER

12. Allowances which are reasonable in amount and do no more than covering the employee's travelling, accommodation and related expenses incurred when he is working away from his usual base or place of residence as required by his employer would not be brought into charge as assessable income. However, any claim for expenses in excess of the employer's reimbursement would be expected to fail the test of "necessarily" incurred and would not be allowed. Moreover, a reimbursement from an employer for disallowable expenses incurred by an employee would be assessable.

SPECIFIC ITEMS OF EXPENDITURE

Clothing

13. The cost, if borne by the employee, of the replacement of special clothes required by the nature of the employment would be allowable (e.g. overalls). Otherwise, the test "wholly and exclusively" would not be expected to be complied with.

Commission-payment for services

14. Employees who are commission earners may need to pay commission to others in order to earn that income. Provided the conditions under section 12(1)(a) are satisfied, such payments are allowable deductions. It is important though that full information about the nature of the payment and the recipients should be provided to the Department.

Entertainment expenses

15. The claimant is expected to be able to show that any expenditure claimed was necessarily incurred and that it would not have been possible to have produced the income from the employment without incurring such expenditure. Mere social entertaining would be debarred as not being "wholly and exclusively incurred". Any entertaining must be shown to have been necessarily incurred directly as part of business negotiations and records kept should not only give details of the cost and the names of the persons entertained but the nature of the business in question. It goes without saying that the excess of any round sum entertainment allowance over admissible entertainment expenses incurred is assessable as income from an office or employment.

Payments to assistants

16. In general, such expenses would not be "necessarily" incurred. However, in case, for example, an employee is remunerated on a commission basis, a claim for such payments would be admitted provided that the necessity can clearly be shown for the need of assistance in the light of the volume of business transacted and the amounts paid can also be regarded as reasonable for the work done.

Subscriptions to professional societies etc.

17. Although it is considered that subscriptions to professional societies etc. are in general not allowable under a strict interpretation of the wording of the Ordinance, in practice an allowance is admitted where the holding of a professional qualification is a prerequisite of employment and where the retention of membership and the keeping abreast of current developments in the particular profession are of regular use and benefit in the performance of the duties. Any such allowance is to be restricted to the subscription to one professional association. *[See Board of Review Case No. BR 19/73.]*

Subscriptions and fees paid to Trade Unions would not qualify.

Travelling expenses

18. Reasonable expenses of travel from one place of employment to another would be admitted, while expenses of travel from home to office are not. Allowable expenses are restricted to those necessarily incurred in the performance of duties. If for example motor car expenses are claimed, regard would be had as to whether the amount claimed is reasonable having regard to the availability of public transport and taxis.

19. If the nature of the employment is such that the use of a car is necessary to the carrying out of the duties, the claim should include information as to the basis on which the employer reimburses expenditure incurred, and the extent to which the car is used for purposes other than for the employment. The cost of repairs and running expenses would be apportioned as between private use and use for the employment.

ALLOWANCES FOR CAPITAL EXPENDITURE

20. Under section 12(1)(b) of the Ordinance, "allowances calculated in accordance with Part VI in respect of capital expenditure on machinery or plant the use of which is essential to the production of the assessable income" are deductible. Information as to the calculation of allowances under this provision is contained in Departmental Interpretation and Practice Notes No. 7 (Revised).

21. Claims under this provision would not arise other than in an employment in which the employer does not reimburse the employee for the use of the machinery or plant (the most common example would be a motor car) and where the employee can show that the use of the plant or machinery is essential to the performance of the duties giving rise to the assessable income.

SELF-EDUCATION EXPENSES

22. Commencing from 1 April 1996, a taxpayer can claim under section 12(1) (e) of the Ordinance for a deduction of self-education expenses he paid. From year of assessment 2000/01 onwards, expenses of self-education are defined to include fees, including tuition and examination fees, in connection with a prescribed course of education, fees of examination set by an education provider, or trade, professional or business association.

23. A prescribed course of education is one undertaken at specified education providers. Specified education providers include universities, technical colleges, schools registered under the Education Ordinance, and any other institutions approved by the Commissioner. For details of the approved institutions, please visit the Department's homepage at *www.ird.gov.hk*. A prescribed course of education also includes a training or development course provided by a trade, professional or business association. From the year of assessment 2004/05 onwards, the term also includes a training or development course accredited or recognized by certain professional bodies, institutions, associations that are specified in Schedule 13 of the Ordinance.

24. The course of education or the examination undertaken must be for gaining or maintaining qualifications for use in any employment. General interest classes, for example, a Tai Chi course, will not qualify as an employment-related course unless say, a Tai chi instructor employment is contemplated.

25. Fees that have been reimbursed or are reimbursable by an employer or any other person are not allowable. The deduction is allowed in the year of assessment in which the expenses were paid; the period covered by the courses is irrelevant.

The total amount of self-education expenses that may be deducted in any year of assessment shall not exceed the amount specified in relation to that year in Schedule 3A of the Ordinance. From year of assessment 2001/02 onwards, the maximum amount that can be claimed is $40,000.

CONCESSIONARY DEDUCTIONS UNDER PART IVA

26. Section 12B(1)(a) provides that in ascertaining the net chargeable income of a person, the deductions under Part IVA comprising approved charitable donations, elderly residential care expenses, home loan interest and contributions to recognized retirement schemes shall be allowed whenever appropriate.

Approved Charitable Donations

27. Section 26C(1) of the Ordinance provides that where a person or his/her spouse, not being a spouse living apart from the person, makes any approved charitable donations during any year of assessment, a deduction in respect of the aggregate amount of the approved charitable donations shall be allowable to the person for that year of assessment provided that the aggregated amount is not less than $100.

28. If the person is chargeable to salaries tax, no deduction shall be allowable to him/her in respect of –

(a) any sum which is allowable under profits tax; and

(b) any sum by which the aggregated amount of the approved charitable donations is in excess of 25%[1] of his/her assessable income for that year as reduced by the deductions provided under section 12(1)(a) and (b) for that year of assessment. If the person and his/her spouse have elected joint-assessment under section 10(2) of the Ordinance, then the deduction limit is set at 25%[1] of the aggregate of assessable income as reduced by deductions under section 12(1)(a) and (b).

29. Where a person has made an election for personal assessment under section 41 in any year of assessment, no deduction shall be allowable to that person for that year of assessment in respect of any approved charitable donation –

(a) which is allowable as deduction under profits tax;

(b) which has been allowed as a deduction to his/her spouse against the total income of that spouse that is required to be aggregated under section 42A(1);

(c) which, when aggregated with any sum that is allowable as a deduction

---

[1] 25% is for any year of assessment commencing on or after 1 April 2003. For any year of assessment up to and including the year of assessment commencing 1 April 2002, the percentage is 10%.

under section 16D for that year of assessment, is in excess of 25%[1] of the total amount of –
(i)   the total income of that person for that year of assessment;
(ii) approved charitable donations which is allowable as a deduction under section 16D; and
(iii) self-education expenses which is allowable as a deduction under section 12(1)(e).

30. Where there are more than one claimants for the same donation, unless agreement is reached amongst themselves, no allowance for the contentious donation will be granted.

31. Fuller details on the deduction for approved charitable donations are set out in the Departmental Interpretation and Practice Notes No. 37.

Elderly Residential Care Expenses

32. With effect from the year of assessment 1998/99, a person may claim a deduction for elderly residential care expenses paid by the person or his/her spouse to a residential care home in respect of his/her or his/her spouse's parent or grandparent under salaries tax and personal assessment. A person chargeable to tax at standard rate is also entitled to the deduction.

33. The following conditions must be satisfied before the deduction is granted –
(a)   the parent/grandparent is aged 60 or above at any time in the year of assessment, or under 60 but entitled to claim an allowance under the Government's Disability Allowance Scheme; and
(b)   the residential care home is licensed or exempted from licensing under the Residential Care Homes (Elderly Persons) Ordinance, or is a nursing home registered under the Hospitals, Nursing Homes and Maternity Homes Registration Ordinance.

34. The deduction is allowed for the expenses actually paid to a residential care home in respect of residential care received, subject to a maximum of $60,000 for a year of assessment for each parent or grandparent.

35. The deduction is allowed in respect of a parent/grandparent to only one claimant for a year of assessment. Should the deduction be allowed to a person, he or any other person is not entitled to claim dependent parent/grandparent allowance and additional parent/grandparent allowance for the same parent/grandparent for the same year of assessment.

36. For the purpose of processing the claim, the Assessor may ask the claimant to produce the following information and documents –
(a)   particulars of the parent/grandparent, i.e. name, Hong Kong identity card number, date of birth and if aged under 60, reference number under the Government's Disability Allowance Scheme;

    (b) the name and address of the residential care home; and

    (c) the amount paid and receipt(s) issued by the residential care home or other documentary evidence for the payment.

37. Fuller details on the deduction for elderly residential care expenses are set out in the Departmental Interpretation and Practice Notes No. 36.

Home Loan Interest

38. With effect from the year of assessment 1998/99, home loan interest paid is deductible under section 26E of the Ordinance from a person's assessable income under salaries tax or from a person's total income under personal assessment. A person chargeable to tax at standard rate is also entitled to the deduction.

39. For the purposes of processing the claim, the Assessor may ask the claimant to produce the following documents –

    (a) proof of ownership of the dwelling;

    (b) proof of dwelling being used as his place of residence;

    (c) loan agreement or mortgage deed; and

    (d) receipts for repayment of loan.

40. Fuller details on the deduction for home loan interest are set out in the Departmental Interpretation and Practice Notes No. 35.

Contribution to Recognized Retirement Schemes

Mandatory Provident Fund Scheme (MPFS)

41. With effect from 1 December 2000, employees (full-time or part-time) and self-employed persons, except the exempt persons under the MPFS Ordinance, are required to participate in a MPFS. For employees or self-employed persons earning over $4,000 per month, the mandatory contribution is 5% of the person's income. The maximum contribution is $1,000 per month or $12,000 per year. Insofar as salaries tax is concerned, section 26G(3)(b) provides for deduction of the amount of mandatory contributions paid by a person as an employee during a year of assessment, to the extent of the amount specified in Schedule 3B.

Recognized Occupational Retirement Schemes (RORS)

42. Where a person, as an employee, opts to participate in a MPF-exempted RORS instead of joining a MPFS, the amount of deduction allowable under section 26G(3)(a) is the lesser of –

    (i) the amount of the contributions paid by the person to the RORS; and

    (ii) the amount of the mandatory contributions that the person would have been required to pay had that scheme been a MPFS.

The amount of the deduction cannot exceed the amount specified in Schedule 3B.

FALSE CLAIMS

43. The wilful submission of an incorrect return or the making of a false statement in connection with a claim for any deduction or allowance by a person, renders the person (or any person who has assisted the person to evade tax) liable to a fine on summary conviction at level 3 (i.e. $10,000 at current level) and a further fine of treble the amount of tax which has been undercharged in consequence of the offence or which would have been undercharged if the offence had not been detected, and to imprisonment for six months, and on indictment to a fine at level 5 (i.e. $50,000 at current level) and a further fine of treble the amount of tax so undercharged or which would have been so undercharged and to imprisonment for three years

APPENDIX 7

Departmental Interpretation & Practice Notes
No. 10 (Revised)

THE CHARGE TO SALARIES TAX

These notes are issued for the information of taxpayers and their tax representatives. They contain the Department's interpretation and practices in relation to the law as it stood at the date of publication. Taxpayers are reminded that their right of objection against the assessment and their right of appeal to the Commissioner, the Board of Review or the Court are not affected by the application of these notes.

These notes replace those issued in December 1987.

LAU MAK Yee-ming, Alice
Commissioner of Inland Revenue

June 2007

Our Web site: http://www.info.gov.hk/ird

CONTENT

(A) BASIC CHARGE — EMPLOYMENTS

Introduction

The basic charge to Salaries Tax is imposed by section 8(1) of the Inland Revenue Ordinance ("the Ordinance") on income "arising in or derived from Hong Kong" from any office or employment of profit. No general rules are given in the Ordinance for determining whether income "arises in or is derived from Hong Kong". However, in deciding this question in connection with employment, it has long been accepted that it is necessary to establish the place where the employment, the source of income, is located.

2. This Departmental Interpretation & Practice Notes No. 10 ("DIPN 10") was first issued in January 1982 and revised in December 1987 after the High Court decision in *Commissioner of Inland Revenue v. George Andrew Goepfert, 2 HKTC 210*. In the 1987 version of DIPN 10, the Department has accepted that in the great majority of cases, the question of Hong Kong or non-Hong Kong employment can be resolved by considering the three factors, namely, (a) contract of employment, (b) residence of the employer, and (c) place of payment of remuneration.

3. Since the issue of the 1987 revision of DIPN 10, the Board of Review had heard over 30 cases on the source of employment. While most Boards had taken into account the above-mentioned three factors in their decision, some Boards had expressed the view that the 1987 revision was inaccurate and misleading and the three-factor test promulgated in the Notes was contrary to the "totality of facts" test set out by MacDougall, J. in the *Goepfert* decision[1]. There is indeed a need to bring the 1987 version up-to-date.

4. In this present revision, the Department does not seek to introduce a new approach in determining the source of employment. The Department still holds the view that the above-mentioned factors are the major factors in determining source of employment. This revision intends to set out in clearer terms the Department's practices in determining the source of employment.

The Goepfert decision

5. The question of where the employment or the source of income was located was decided by the High Court in 1987 in the *Goepfert* case. After referring to a number of UK cases and decisions of the Board of Review, MacDougall, J., made the following comments on the approach to resolve the issue:

---

[1] Particularly strong criticism of the three-factor test promulgated in the 1987 version of the Notes can be found in Case No. D40/90, 5 IRBRD 306, at p.314, Case No. D87/00, 15 IRBRD 750, at p.764, Case No. D125/02, 18 IRBRD 179, at p.185.

(a) "It follows that the place where the services are rendered is not relevant to the enquiry under section 8(1) as to whether income arises in or is derived from Hong Kong from any employment. It should therefore be completely ignored." (page 236)

(b) "Specifically, it is necessary to look for the place where the income really comes to the employee, that is to say, where the source of income, the employment, is located. As Sir Wilfred Greene said, regard must first be had to the contract of employment.

This does not mean that the Commissioner may not look behind the appearances to discover the reality. The Commissioner is not bound to accept as conclusive, any claim made by an employee in this connexion. He is entitled to scrutinise all evidence, documentary or otherwise, that is relevant to this matter." (page 237)

(c) "If any authority be needed for this basic proposition one needs only to refer to the words of Lord Normand at page 155 of *Bray v. Colenbrander*[2]: 'My Lords, in each of these appeals the Respondent entered into a contract of employment with an employer resident abroad. The contract was in each case entered into in the country of the employer's residence and it provided for payment of the employee's remuneration in that country. Parenthetically it should be said that there is no suggestion that the payment was nominal or pretended, or that the real or genuine place of payment was not the place specified in the contract. Nothing, therefore of what follows in this opinion in any way touches a case where the designated place of payment is challenged as nominal or pretended and unreal.'" (page 237)

(d) "There can be no doubt therefore that in deciding the crucial issue, the Commissioner may need to look further than the external or superficial features of the employment. Appearance may be deceptive. He may need to examine other factors that point to the real locus of the source of income, the employment. It occurs to me that sometimes when reference is made to the so called 'totality of facts' test it may be that what is meant is this very process. If that is what it means then it is not an enquiry of a nature different from that to which the English cases refer, but is descriptive of the process adopted to ascertain the true answer to the question that arises under section 8(1)." (page 237)

(e) "Having stated what I consider to be the proper test to be applied in determining for the purpose of sec. 8(1) whether income arises in or is derived from Hong Kong from employment, the position may, in my view, be summarised as follows.

If during a year of assessment, a person's income falls within the basic charge to salaries tax under section 8(1), his entire salary is subject

---

[2] Reported in 34 TC 138

to salaries tax wherever his services may have been rendered, subject only to the so called '60 days rule' that operates when the taxpayer can claim relief by way of exemption under section 8(1A)(b) as read with section 8(1B). Thus, once income is caught by section 8(1) there is no provision for apportionment.

I hasten to add, however, that the '60 days rule' does not apply to the income derived from services rendered by those persons who, by the operation of section 8(1A)(b)(i) are excluded from enjoying the benefit conferred by section 8(1A)(b)(ii) as read with section 8(1B)." (page 238)

(f)   "On the other hand, if a person, whose income does not fall within the basic charge to salaries tax under section 8(1), derives income from employment in respect of which he rendered services in Hong Kong, only that income derived from the services he actually rendered in Hong Kong is chargeable to salaries tax. Again, this is subject to the '60 days rule'." (page 238)

6. The Department accepts the learned judge's view and would follow the above approach. No doubt, the contract of employment is the key factor in ascertaining the location of the employment. In the course of examination, the Department may need to look further than the external or superficial features of the employment. In determining where the source of income, the employment, is located, the Department will take into account all of the relevant facts, with particular emphasis on:

(a)   where the contract of employment was negotiated and entered into, and is enforceable, whether in Hong Kong or outside Hong Kong;

(b)   where the employer is resident, whether in Hong Kong or outside Hong Kong; and

(c)   where the employee's remuneration is paid to him, whether in Hong Kong or outside Hong Kong.

Source is a practical hard matter of fact. The Department's practice is set out below.

Contract of employment

Written contract

7. The contract to be considered is that which is currently in force and which is the basis for the relationship of master and servant existing between the employer and employee. The fact that the contract may have been entered into many years earlier will not diminish its relevance in considering this factor.

However, if certain terms in the agreement have been varied subsequently, alterations and additions to the initial agreement should also be taken into account in so far as they may affect the determination of where the source of employment is located.

8. The Department expects to be provided with a copy of the employment contract properly executed by the employer and employee. In the past, there were taxpayers claiming they had employment with entities outside Hong Kong but their employment contracts were not in writing. Having regard to the present day standard regarding parties' rights and obligations and the fact that they can sue or be sued, the Department would have difficulty in accepting that no written contract exists to record what the parties have agreed. For this reason, the Department would expect that a written contract be provided. If, as a matter of fact, a written contract does not exist, the taxpayer is nevertheless required to provide a document from his employer certifying the terms of his appointment, the effective date of the appointment, etc. The document should be signed by the parties.

Parties to the contract

9. While the Department would generally accept the parties named in the contract as the relevant parties, the Department would take steps to verify the genuineness of the relationship between the parties if warranted by circumstances. For example, if a company in its capacity as an employer, sponsors an individual to gain entry into Hong Kong to take up employment and has represented to other Government departments to that effect, this will be a factor for the Department to take into account together with other relevant facts in determining whether an employer-employee relationship exists between the sponsor and the individual.

10. In testing whether a true employer-employee relationship exists between the parties, the Department would also consider who has the legal liability to pay or control over the employee, the capacity in which the employee represents himself to third parties, whether the employee is part of the organisation of the employer, etc.

Contract negotiated and concluded

11. It would be up to the taxpayer to provide the full facts as to where and when the negotiation took place, the persons taking part in the negotiation, the matters discussed, the terms agreed, etc. If a written contract was subsequently executed, a copy of the contract needs to be provided.

12. If the employer is resident in Hong Kong, it is unlikely that a claim for non-Hong Kong employment will be accepted even if it is shown that negotiation takes place outside Hong Kong or a contract of employment is signed outside Hong Kong. The following Board of Review Decision serves to illustrate the point:

Case No. D8/92, 7 IRBRD 107

The taxpayer was resident in the USA when he received a written offer of employment from a company in Hong Kong. The taxpayer accepted the employment contract by signing and returning to Hong Kong the offer which he had received. The employer was a member of a multi-national group and the taxpayer's duties included responsibility not only for the Hong Kong company which employed him but also other companies within the Group in the Far East. The Board of Review decided at page 110 that:

> "He was not employed by any company in the United States and he was not subject to any master and servant relation with any United States company. His master and servant relation was clearly with the company in Hong Kong with whom he entered into an employment contract. In the circumstances of this case the fact that he was physically in the United States when he received the employment contract is not material."

The Department will adopt the same approach as set out in the above case.

Enforceability of contract

13. In a contract of employment, the parties are free to choose the governing law so far as it is bona fide, legal, not against public policy, and unambiguous. Where there is no express choice of law, the choice of law can be inferred from the terms of the contract and the general circumstances of the case. Where there is no express or implied choice of law, the contract is governed by the system of law with which the contract has its closest and most real connection (*Bank of India v. Gobindram Naraindas Sadhwant, [1988] 2 HKLR 262*).

14. From the above guideline, in determining where an employment contract is enforceable, it is necessary in certain circumstances to ascertain where the employee habitually performs his work, the business that engaged him and where that business is located. It may also be necessary to consider the place where the parties would take legal action in enforcing terms of the contract from a practical perspective, see for example, Board of Review Decisions, Case No. *D20/97, 12 IRBRD 161*, at page 172 and Case No. *D59/03, 18 IRBRD 626*, at page 651.

Residence of employer

15. The employer for this purpose is the person who, in the relationship of master and servant, is the true employer of the employee.

Central management and control

16. In determining the residence of a corporation, the Department will take into account where the corporation's central management and control is located. The "central management and control" test is a well-established common law principle widely adopted in many jurisdictions for determining residence of companies. Under this principle, a company resides where its real business is carried on, and the real business is carried on where the central management and control actually abides. The classic exposition is by Lord Loreburn, L.C. in *De Beers Consolidated Mines Ltd. v. Howe, [1906] 5 TC 198* at pages 212 and 213,

> "In applying the conception of residence to a Company, we ought, I think to proceed as nearly as we can upon the analogy of an individual. A Company cannot eat or sleep, but it can keep house and do business. We ought, therefore, to see where it really keeps house and does business. An individual may be of foreign nationality, and yet reside in the United Kingdom. So may a Company. Otherwise it might have its chief seat of management and its centre of trading in England under the protection of English law, and yet escape the appropriate taxation by the simple expedient of being registered abroad and distributing its dividends abroad. The decision of Chief Baron Kelly, and Baron Huddleston in the *Calcutta Jute Mills v. Nicholson* and the *Cesena Sulphur Company v. Nicholson*, now thirty years ago, involved the principle that a Company resides for purposes of Income Tax where its real business is carried on. Those decisions have been acted upon ever since. I regard that as the true rule; and the real business is carried on where the central management and control actually abides."

17. In *Charter View Holdings (BVI) Ltd. v. Corona Investments Ltd. & Another, [1998] 1 HKLRD 469*[3], the issue of whether the plaintiff was ordinarily resident in Hong Kong was before Keith J, who made the following comments at page 471:

> "In *Insurance Co. of the State of Pennsylvania v. Grand Union Insurance Co. Ltd. [1988] 2 HKLR 541*, the Court of Appeal held that, for the purpose of O.23 r.1(1)(a)[4], the ordinary residence of a limited company is to be decided by reference to where its central management and control is. However, the application of that test is not straightforward. It was considered in *Re Little Olympian Each Ways Ltd. [1995] 1 WLR 560*. Three propositions can be derived from the judgment of Lindsay J:
>
> (i)   The mere assertion of where the company's central management and control is unsatisfactory. What are needed are the primary facts on which that assertion is based.
>
> (ii) All the circumstances in which the company carries on its business should be taken into account, though the weight to be applied to each factor will obviously differ from case to case. Those factors include the

---

[3] This case was referred to in Jade Harbour Ltd. v. Eltones Profits Ltd. & Another, [2005] 3 HKLRD 158.

[4] The Rules of the High Court (Cap. 4, Sub. Leg.), Order No. 23.

provisions of the company's objects clause, the place of incorporation, the place where the company's real trade and business is carried on, the place where the company's books are kept, the place where the company's administration is carried out, the place where the directors with power to disapprove of local steps or to require different ones to be taken themselves meet or are resident, the place where its chief office is or where the company secretary is to be found, and the place where most significant assets are.

(iii) In applying the test to a non-trading company, it may be more important than would otherwise be the case to have regard to the nature of the company's corporate activities."

18. The issue of whether a company was centrally managed and controlled outside Hong Kong or in Hong Kong was critically examined in Board of Review Decision Case No. *D123/02, 18 IRBRD 150.* The Department will follow the above guiding principles in ascertaining where a limited company resides. In general, importance is attached to the place where the directors hold board meetings. In many cases, the directors meet in the country where the business operations take place, and central management and control is clearly located in that place. In other cases, the directors may exercise central management and control in one jurisdiction, while the actual business operations may take place in another. The place of board meetings, however, is significant only in so far as those meetings constitute the medium through which central management and control is exercised. The location where central management and control is exercised is a question of fact and each case must be decided on its own facts. When reaching a conclusion in accordance with case law principles, only factors which exist for genuine commercial reasons will be accepted.

Parent and subsidiary

19. In applying the "central management and control" test in the situation of a subsidiary company and its parent operating in another territory, the Department would normally regard the subsidiary and its parent as separate legal entities, each being managed and controlled by its own board of directors. While it is normal for a parent company to exert influence and exercise power over the subsidiary company, it is not always the case that the subsidiary is resident in the same territory as the parent. Regard will be given to the degree of autonomy with which the board of directors in the subsidiary deals with such matters as to investment, production, marketing and procurement without reference to the parent. In this regard, the Department is mindful of the comments by the Board of Review in Case No. *D59/03, 18 IRBRD 626,* at page 653:

"Even if Company A's final and supreme authority were to come from its parent company, Company D in the United States of America, we do not accept the Representative's assertion that Company A was centrally managed and controlled by its parent company in the United States of America. In arriving at this stance we are mindful of the *Union Corporation* case[5] where it was held the formula 'where the central power and authority abides' does not demand that the court should look, and look only, to the place where the final and supreme authority is found, and also the decision in *De Beers* case[6] that what was required was 'a scrutiny of the course of business and trading'. Thus, we find Company A was resident in Hong Kong for the purpose of this tax assessment."

Establishing employer's residence

20. In support of claims that the employer is centrally managed and controlled outside Hong Kong, the Department would require information of the identities and capacities of the persons (in the employer's organisation) who are responsible for the central management and control, the specific tasks undertaken by these persons and where they are located while exercising management and control, etc. Documentary proof may be required. The Department will generally accept certified copies of directors' reports and minutes of meetings for the purpose.

Place of payment of remuneration

21. In Board of Review Decision Case No. *D20/97, 12 IRBRD 161*, the Board had the following observation at page 173:
> "... it would seem to be absurdly simple and inappropriate in this age of electronic banking to reach our decision on the basis that the place of payment determined the source of employment income in this case. Surely source of employment, which should be determined as a 'hard practical matter of fact', should not depend in the final analysis upon the place from where an employee is actually paid. Accordingly, we decided to look more broadly, from a practical perspective, at where the Taxpayer's employment was located."

22. The significance of the place of payment for the present purpose was considered by Deputy High Court Judge To in *Lee Hung Kwong v. Commissioner of Inland Revenue, 6 HKTC 543*. The learned judge pointed out that:
> "In *Bray and Colenbrander; Harvey and Breyfogle*[7], after reviewing the earlier authorities, Lord Normand concluded ...: 'The House of Lords ... in *Foulsham v Pickles*[8] have definitely decided that in the case of an employment the locality of the source of income is not the place where the activities of the employee are exercised but the place either where the

---

[5] Union Corporation Ltd. v. CIR, [1953] 34 TC 207
[6] De Beers Consolidated Mines Limited v. Howe, [1906] 5 TC 198
[7] Reported in 34 TC 138
[8] Reported in 9 TC 261

> contract for payment is deemed to have a locality or where the payments
> for the employment are made, which may mean the same thing."

Thus, where the source of income is from an employment, the locality of the source of income is the place where the contract for payment is deemed to have a locality. By "contract for payment", Lord Normand must mean the contract of employment based on which the employee earned his payment and not necessarily the place where the payments are made. The place of payment is of course an important indicator of the locality of the contract and is prima facie the locality of the contract. But it is not conclusive: see for example *Bennett v Marshall*[9]. If an employee enters into a contract of employment in Hong Kong with an employer resident in Hong Kong but had his salary paid into his Swiss bank account, it can hardly be doubted that the locality of his contract is in Hong Kong. His income is from a Hong Kong source. In most cases, the place of payment is the locality of the contract. That must be why Lord Normand said that the two **may** mean the same thing, but not that the two mean the same thing." (paragraph 24)

23. The Department will readily follow the above approach. Payment of the remuneration made outside Hong Kong, when viewed on its own, should not be a determinative factor in ascertaining the source of employment. Other facts have to be considered as well. Remuneration here is not restricted to the monthly salary but includes all perquisites and benefits in kind which are included in the definition of income. In support of claims that salaries are paid outside Hong Kong, the Department would require the taxpayer to provide details of bank accounts and documentary proof of such payments.

Look further than the external or superficial features

24. If a person claims that his employment with an employer resident in Hong Kong has been changed to a related company of the employer, which is resident outside Hong Kong, and there is little apparent change in the terms of employment, the Department will look deeper than the external or superficial features of the employment. Similarly, attention will be given to cases where locally-engaged employees claim that they hold offshore contracts of employment. These examples are not meant to be exhaustive.

Summing up

25. In summary, if the source of employment is located in Hong Kong, any income derived from that employment falls within the basic charge to Salaries Tax under section 8(1), irrespective of where the employee renders his services (subject to the exclusion referred to in (C) below). Thus, once income is caught by section 8(1) there can be no claim for the so-called time apportionment.

---

[9] Reported in 22 TC 73

However, if a non-Hong Kong employment exists then any income derived from that employment falls outside the basic charge and liability to Salaries Tax can only arise under section 8(1A), which brings to charge income derived from services actually rendered in Hong Kong. In the latter cases, it will be necessary to apportion the total income, usually on a time-in time-out basis.

(B) EXTENSION OF CHARGE – EMPLOYMENT

26. In general, the Department would accept that a non-Hong Kong employment exists if the contract of employment was negotiated, entered into and enforceable outside Hong Kong with an employer who is resident outside Hong Kong and the employee's remuneration is paid to him outside Hong Kong. Typically, the taxpayer holds an employment in his home country and is assigned by his employer to take up duties outside his home country. The taxpayer is required by his employer to be based in Hong Kong and to travel outside Hong Kong to perform some of the duties. During the period of his assignment outside his home country, the employer-employee relationship with his home country employer still subsists so that at the end of the assignment, the taxpayer will be re-located to his home country and continue to work for his home-country employer.

27. General statements made by taxpayers or their representatives that they hold overseas employments with an overseas entity will not normally be accepted at their face value. The information required in support of claims will be the same as that set out in the foregoing paragraphs under (A) BASIC CHARGE – EMPLOYMENT. A non-Hong Kong employment accepted by the Department is subject to review periodically. The Appendix provides some examples of Hong Kong and non-Hong Kong employments.

28. Where a non-Hong Kong employment exists, consideration will be given to the liability arising under the extension to the basic charge contained in section 8(1A). Subsection (a) of section 8(1A) extends the charge by specifically including as income arising in or derived from Hong Kong, all income derived from services rendered in Hong Kong, including leave pay attributable to such services. This subsection relates only to employments; it does not apply to office of profit (see (D) below).

29. For the purposes of quantifying the amount of income derived from services rendered in Hong Kong, the Department will usually look at the number of days an employee spent in Hong Kong and apportion his remuneration including leave pay on a time-in time-out basis. In exceptional circumstances where the application of this basis would be inappropriate a different approach may be adopted. For instance, if an employee can establish that the rate of remuneration for the services he renders outside Hong Kong is substantially greater than the rate he receives in Hong Kong, the apportionment can be made on the basis of the actual remuneration attributable to the services rendered in Hong Kong.

30. In order to arrive at the amount of income derived from services rendered in Hong Kong, an employee should include in his Salaries Tax Return, apart from remuneration received locally, all other remuneration related to his employment, for example, receipts from his overseas parent company or head office.

(C) EXCLUSION FROM CHARGE–EMPLOYMENT

31. Subsection (b) of section 8(1A) excludes from the charge to Salaries Tax income from services rendered by persons (other than Government employees and ship and air crew) who in the basis period of a year of assessment render all their services outside Hong Kong. For the purposes of this exclusion, services rendered during visits to Hong Kong not exceeding a total of 60 days in the basis period of a year of assessment are to be ignored [section 8(1B)]. In other words, a person who renders services in Hong Kong during visits for not more than a total of 60 days in the basis period of a year of assessment will have no liability to Salaries Tax.

32. Thus, an employee deriving income from a Hong Kong employment, who is posted to, say, Singapore or Tokyo to represent his firm and in the basis period of a year of assessment renders all his services there, will be wholly exempt from Salaries Tax. However, if he visits Hong Kong for 61 days or more and, during the visits, renders some services here he will be liable on the whole of his income derived in a year. Similarly, an employee deriving income from a non-Hong Kong employment will not be liable if he is here to carry out short assignments during visits to Hong Kong which do not exceed a total of 60 days in the basis period of a year of assessment. On the other hand, if his visits exceed 60 days he will be liable under the extended charge of section 8(1A)(a) on that part of his income which is derived from services rendered in Hong Kong including leave pay attributable to such services.

33. The exclusion under section 8(1A)(b) only refers to visits, e.g. a person may be chargeable even though he spent 60 days or less in the basis period of a year of assessment in Hong Kong if this is the start or finish of a long period of residence in Hong Kong or his presence does not constitute a "visit".

(D) DIRECTORS' FEES

34. Fees paid to persons who hold the office of director of a corporation whose central management and control are exercised in Hong Kong, are income arising in or derived from Hong Kong and chargeable to Salaries Tax under the basic charge of section 8(1) irrespective of where the person resides. This is because the office of director of a corporation is located in a place where the central management and control of the corporation is exercised (see *McMillan v. Guest, 24 TC 190*). Thus, if an office is located in Hong Kong, any fees derived from the office can be said to arise in Hong Kong. Neither the extension to the basic charge under section 8(1A), nor the exclusion under section 8(1A)(b) or (c), has any application to directors' fees. They apply only to income from employment. This issue was before the Board of Review in Case No. *D123/02, 18 IRBRD 150* in which the Board found that the office of director held by the taxpayer was located in Hong Kong. In this case, the Board found that part of the superior and directing authority of the company was exercised in Hong Kong.

(E) SHIP AND AIRCRAFT PERSONNEL

35. The liability of ship and aircraft personnel is determined under section 8(1) and section 8(1A)(a) in the same way as other employees. However, there are important exemptions to be considered under subsection 8(2)(j) which excludes from charge income derived from services rendered by persons of this category who were present in Hong Kong on not more than 60 days in the basis period and a total of 120 days falling partly in each of the basis periods for two consecutive years of assessment, one of which is the year of assessment being considered. The broad effect of this exclusion is to exempt from charge members of the crew of a ship or an aircraft other than those who spend a substantial portion of their time in Hong Kong (including territorial waters).

(F) EXCLUSION – TAX PAID OUTSIDE HONG KONG

36. Following the introduction of section 8(1A)(c) with effect from 1 April 1987, income derived by a person from services rendered outside Hong Kong is excluded from the charge to Salaries Tax if, in the territory where the services are rendered, the person is chargeable to and has paid tax of substantially the same nature as Salaries Tax in respect of that income. For example, if a person holding a Hong Kong employment derives income from rendering services in the Mainland on 100 consecutive days in a year and pays Individual Income Tax to a Mainland authority on that income, section 8(1A)(c) will operate to exclude that income from the charge to Salaries Tax in Hong Kong.

37. Whether a particular foreign tax is of substantially the same nature as Salaries Tax is a question of fact to be considered in each case. Whilst the Department would generally accept as sufficiently similar any tax on employment income levied on the employee by the government of the territory in which the services were rendered, the Department would not accept a tax or levy charged otherwise than by reference to the amount of employment income derived as coming within the scope of section 8(1A)(c). Neither the rate of tax levied in the foreign territory nor the assessment method under which the amount of tax paid was determined by the taxing authorities is relevant to the issue. In order to qualify under section 8(1A)(c) all that is required is chargeability to and actual payment of the foreign tax. For example, if an American citizen holding a Hong Kong employment renders services in the US on 50 days and is assessed to US income tax on his world income, including the income derived from those services, then provided he has paid some US income tax, the Department will accept that tax has been paid on the 50 days' income and section 8(1A)(c) will apply to exclude that income from the charge to tax here. On the other hand, if the level of his total world income is such that no US income tax is payable, section 8(1A)(c) cannot apply.

38. On a practical point, cases may arise where the basis period for assessment to Hong Kong Salaries Tax, the year ended 31 March, may differ from that of the foreign territory in which services are rendered. For instance, at the time the assessment to Hong Kong tax is made, the foreign tax, although chargeable, may not actually have been assessed and paid. In this situation, the taxpayer should lodge an objection against the assessment to Hong Kong tax on the foreign income on the grounds that foreign tax will in due course be paid. Upon receipt of the objection the assessor will, where justified, order that the tax in dispute be held over unconditionally. Once the foreign tax has been paid and proof thereof submitted by the taxpayer, the objection will be allowed and the Hong Kong tax will be discharged. Similarly, the likelihood that foreign tax is to be paid will be accepted as a valid reason for holding over Provisional Salaries Tax where the taxpayer can show that once foreign tax is paid his assessable income (after excluding that part subject to the foreign tax) will be less than 90% of that for the previous year.

39. There may also be a situation in which the taxpayer is not aware that he or she has a liability to foreign tax when the Hong Kong Salaries Tax assessment is received. Thus, an objection would not be raised as mentioned in the paragraph above. If the taxpayer has to pay foreign tax after the objection period has expired, he or she can still rely on section 70A to file a claim for relief under section 8 (1A)(c) within 6 years after the end of the assessment or within 6 months after the date of the notice of assessment if later, for the omission in the return.

40. It should be noted that as a matter of practice section 8(1A)(c) has application to Hong Kong employments only. This is because persons holding non-Hong Kong employments will be chargeable to tax in Hong Kong only on income derived from services rendered here. Such persons are, of course, not chargeable to tax on income derived from services rendered outside Hong Kong.

APPENDIX

Examples on Source of Employment

■ **Example 1   Assignment to Hong Kong**

The taxpayer was initially employed by Company A. He worked in the US. Due to a change of his roles and responsibilities, he entered into a new employment contract with Company B. The negotiation and conclusion processes for both employment contracts took place in the US. Company B deposited his remuneration into his bank account in the US.

Company B immediately assigned the taxpayer to Hong Kong to oversee the Asia Pacific operations of Group X. The Hong Kong subsidiary of Company B acted as the sponsor of the taxpayer's Hong Kong work visa. The taxpayer remained an employee of Company B throughout his Hong Kong assignment. Companies A and B were both US resident companies of substance. They were affiliated companies of Group X, a US-based conglomerate with business operations all over the world.

On being satisfied with the above facts, the assessor accepted that the taxpayer had a non-Hong Kong employment. The taxpayer provided to the assessor a copy of his employment contract with Company B, information and documents to show that Company B was a company of substance with its management and control in the US and his remuneration was paid by Company B into his bank account in the US.

■ **Example 2   Transfer of employment to Hong Kong and reporting lines**

The taxpayer was an employee of C Inc. and he worked in the US. C Inc. was a US resident company. The taxpayer was offered an appointment with the subsidiary of C Inc. in Hong Kong. By an agreement dated 1 March 2005 signed with C (Hong Kong) Ltd, he agreed to work in the subsidiary as Marketing Director from 1 April 2005. The negotiation of the contract terms took place in the US with the human resources director of C Inc. C (Hong Kong) Ltd was a company incorporated in Hong Kong and its operations were managed by a board of directors resident in Hong Kong. The taxpayer's employment contract dated 1 March 2005 was with C (Hong Kong) Ltd, which sponsored the taxpayer's entry into Hong Kong to take up employment.

As part of his job, the taxpayer had to travel frequently around Asia Pacific to meet with clients. The taxpayer carried a business card describing himself as Marketing Director of C (Hong Kong) Ltd, bearing a Hong Kong correspondence address and telephone number. As Marketing Director, the taxpayer had to report to the board of directors of C Inc. in the US.

On being satisfied with the above facts, the assessor was of the view that the taxpayer had a Hong Kong employment. As the taxpayer had entered into a contract of employment with C (Hong Kong) Ltd., a company resident in Hong

Kong, the source of his employment was Hong Kong. As part of his duties, a taxpayer might be required to report to persons outside Hong Kong but this should not be a decisive factor.

■ **Example 3   Salary and benefit paid in Hong Kong**

The Taxpayer was an employee of E Ltd, a company resident in Italy. E Ltd sent the taxpayer to its Hong Kong buying office to take charge of the sourcing operations. The taxpayer had to travel to the Mainland and neighbouring countries in the performance of his duties. The employment agreement with E Ltd was negotiated and concluded in Italy prior to the taxpayer's arrival into Hong Kong.

The taxpayer agreed with E Ltd that he would not be tax equalised to Italy because the tax rate in Hong Kong was lower than that in Italy. The taxpayer received his salary and benefits in Hong Kong dollars. He joined the Hong Kong Mandatory Provident Fund and was covered under the Hong Kong medical scheme.

On being satisfied with the above facts, the assessor accepted that the taxpayer had a non-Hong Kong employment. Documentary proof similar to those mentioned in Example 1 was provided to the assessor.

■ **Example 4   Place of payment and location where payment is borne**

The taxpayer was residing in the UK. He was offered employment as Regional Controller of F Asia Pacific Ltd. F Asia Pacific Ltd was incorporated in the Cayman Islands. The taxpayer's employment contract was initially negotiated in the UK through a recruitment agency appointed by F Asia Pacific Ltd. The offer letter was sent to the taxpayer in the UK. The taxpayer accepted the offer and signed the contract while he was in the UK.

F Asia Pacific Ltd was the regional headquarter of a group of companies in Asia. Its office was in Hong Kong. It was managed by a board of directors in Hong Kong. The taxpayer had to travel around Asia for business. His salary was partly paid into his bank accounts in Hong Kong and the UK. F Asia Pacific Ltd recovered the taxpayer's salary cost from its subsidiaries and associates in the Asia Pacific.

On being satisfied with the above facts, the assessor was of the view that the taxpayer had a Hong Kong employment. As the taxpayer had entered into a contract of employment with F Asia Pacific Ltd., a company resident in Hong Kong, the source of his employment is Hong Kong. The assessor did not consider recovering the costs by the employer from companies outside Hong Kong was a relevant factor to be taken into account in the circumstances.

**Departmental Interpretation & Practice Notes
No. 13A**

**PROFITS TAX
DEDUCTIBILITY OF INTEREST EXPENSE**

These notes are issued for the information and guidance of taxpayers and their authorised representatives. They have no binding force and do not affect a person's right of objection and appeal to the Commissioner, the Board of Review or the Courts.

LAU MAK Yee-ming, Alice
Commissioner of Inland Revenue

December 2004

Our web site : www.ird.gov.hk

CONTENT

INTRODUCTION

Interest expense, insofar as it is incurred in the production of the chargeable profits of a person, is deductible from the assessable profits of the person. With the gradual removal of interest tax in the 1980's and the limitation in taxing offshore interest income earned by a person carrying on business in Hong Kong, the taxation scheme on interest receipts and interest payments have become asymmetrical, in that interest income is not taxable while interest expenses are tax deductible. Recognising the risk of revenue loss that might be caused by tax avoidance schemes that would take advantage of the lack of symmetry in tax treatment on interest, specific rules were introduced in 1984 and 1986 to restrict the deduction of interest under certain circumstances. The interest deduction scheme has been revamped substantially by the recent amendments introduced by the Inland Revenue (Amendment) Ordinance 2004 (the 2004 Amendment Ordinance), with a view to bolstering up the interest deduction rules. This Interpretation and Practice Note sets out the Department's views and practices on the interest deduction scheme that applies before and after the commencement of the 2004 Amendment Ordinance, which came into operation on 25 June 2004. *[The practices of the interest deduction scheme that applied before the commencement of 2004 Amendment Ordinance were previously included in the DIPN No. 13.]*

INTEREST DEDUCTION SCHEME BEFORE THE COMMENCEMENT OF THE 2004 AMENDMENT ORDINANCE

2. Following the abolition of interest tax, anti-avoidance measures were enacted in relation to interest deductions under profits tax to protect the profits tax yield. In addition to the interest being incurred in the production of chargeable profits, specific conditions must also be satisfied before interest expenses could be allowed as deductions in computing assessable profits. In practice, these measures required all claims for deductions in respect of interest payable on moneys borrowed for the purpose of producing assessable profits to be supported by sufficient details and/or documentary evidence to satisfy at least one of the six prescribed conditions in section 16(2)(a) to (f). *[Sections of the Main Ordinance referred to in paragraphs 2–9 are those provisions that were in force before the commencement of the 2004 Amendment Ordinance.]*

Conditions for Deduction

3. Conditions (a) and (b) were largely self-explanatory and referred to borrower taxpayers who were financial institutions or public utilities. All borrowings by a financial institution satisfied condition (a), while any borrowings by public utilities at a rate of interest not exceeding a specified rate satisfied condition (b).

4. Condition (c) applied to borrowings from persons other than financial institutions or overseas financial institutions. It would be satisfied by the borrower establishing that any interest payable on the loan was chargeable to profits tax under the Inland Revenue Ordinance (IRO). Where the money borrowed had been made available to the borrower in Hong Kong, it would generally be clear that any interest paid on the loan would be chargeable to profits tax in the hands of the lender who was carrying on a trade or business in Hong Kong, as the interest income was sourced in Hong Kong. In such cases, to demonstrate that condition (c) was satisfied, it would be sufficient to disclose the identity of the lender, the place of his business, and the place where the money borrowed was made available to the borrower, so as to establish that the interest paid was chargeable to profits tax. On the other hand, where the loan was made available to the borrower outside of Hong Kong as an offshore loan, there would be a prima facie presumption that any interest payable was not chargeable to profits tax (for being incurred outside Hong Kong)) and that condition (c) was not satisfied. This presumption could, of course, be rebutted by the borrower demonstrating that notwithstanding the loan being offshore, the lender nevertheless carried on business in Hong Kong and was chargeable to profits tax on the interest received.

5. Condition (d) referred to moneys borrowed from financial institutions or overseas financial institutions. Its practical application was best explained by distinguishing such borrowings into those that satisfied the condition and those that did not. A loan from a financial institution (whether local or overseas) would satisfy condition (d) if –

- The loan was not secured or guaranteed by any deposit made with that or another financial institution; or
- The loan was secured or guaranteed against a deposit with that or another financial institution, by –
  - the borrower or on his behalf, or,
  - a person who was closely associated with the borrower (an associate as defined in section 16(3)),
  and the interest received on the deposit was subject to profits tax.

Where a loan from a financial institution was secured or guaranteed against a deposit with that or another financial institution and the interest received on the deposit was not chargeable to tax in Hong Kong, condition (d) would not be satisfied.

The following examples illustrate the above situations —

Example 1

Mr A carried on business as a plastics manufacturer. In order to obtain additional working capital, he borrowed from a local bank. This borrowing was secured by a mortgage over the factory premises owned by Mr A.

Because the loan was not secured by a deposit, the borrowing clearly satisfied condition (d).

Example 2

Mr B carried on an export/import business in Hong Kong. In order to obtain additional working capital, he borrowed from a local bank. The borrowing was secured by a fixed deposit with that same bank registered in the name of Mr B's wife, who carried on no business in Hong Kong.

The interest received by Mrs B was not chargeable to tax in Hong Kong and as the relationship between Mr and Mrs B (as husband and wife) was one within the class of "associates" prescribed in section 16(3), the borrowing by Mr B did not satisfy condition (d).

Example 3

C Limited carried on business in Hong Kong as an electronics manufacturer. For the purpose of acquiring new factory premises, C Limited borrowed from a local bank. This borrowing was partly secured by a fixed deposit with the same bank registered in the name of D Limited, a wholly owned subsidiary of C Limited. D Ltd carried on business in Hong Kong.

Although the borrowing was secured against a deposit owned by an "associated corporation", condition (d) was satisfied because the interest on the deposit was chargeable to profits tax in the hands of D Limited.

Example 4

E Limited carried on business in Hong Kong as consultants. Mr E, who was the major shareholder and managing director of E Limited, received dividends and a salary from the company. For the purposes of expanding its business, E Limited borrowed from a local bank. This borrowing was secured by a fixed deposit in the name of Mr E with a Cayman Islands financial institution.

Being both a shareholder and a director of E Limited, Mr E was related to E Limited as an associate within the terms of section 16(3). As Hong Kong tax was not chargeable on interest received by Mr E from the Cayman Islands deposit, the borrowing by E Limited did not satisfy condition (d).

6. In practice, the most appropriate way of establishing that condition (d) was satisfied was for the taxpayer to submit a statement with his return setting out details of both the borrowing and the security or guarantee provided for the loan. Where the security or guarantee took the form of a deposit owned by a person other than the borrower, the relationship between that person and the borrower and whether that person carried on a business in Hong Kong should be clearly explained. Further, if the borrowing was from a financial institution which did not carry on business in Hong Kong, then sufficient details of that institution should be provided so as to enable the Commissioner to determine whether it was an overseas financial institution which could be recognized for the purposes of section 16(2), (3) and (4). To qualify as an overseas financial institution, the institution in question must be adequately supervised by a supervisory authority.

7. **Condition (e)** would be satisfied by the borrower establishing that –
- the money had been borrowed wholly and exclusively to finance capital expenditure on machinery and plant, or for the purchase of trading stock, for the purpose of producing chargeable profits; and
- the lender was not an associate of the borrower in terms of section 16 (3).

8. Finally, **condition (f)** related to corporate borrowings by way of debentures or other "marketable instruments". As regards the interest payable on debentures, the condition would be satisfied where such debentures were listed on a stock exchange in Hong Kong or any other stock exchange recognized by the Commissioner. Insofar as "marketable instruments" were concerned, the condition would be satisfied if the instruments were issued –
- bona fide and in the course of carrying on business and was marketable in Hong Kong or any other major financial centre approved by the Commissioner; or
- pursuant to the authorisation of the Securities and Futures Commission under section 105 of the Securities and Futures Ordinance *[under section 4(2)(g) of the Protection of Investors Ordinance before 1 April 2003.]*.

9. Condition (f) would also be satisfied where the borrowing was from an associated corporation and the moneys borrowed in the hands of the associated corporation arose entirely from the proceeds of an issue of debentures or marketable instruments as described above. As for borrowings from associated corporations, the deduction for interest paid by the borrowing corporation was restricted to the amount of interest paid by the associated corporation to the holders of its debentures or instruments.

INTEREST DEDUCTION SCHEME AFTER THE COMMENCEMENT OF THE 2004 AMENDMENT ORDINANCE

10. The 2004 Amendment Ordinance has introduced substantial amendments to the interest deduction scheme. The conditions for interest deduction under section 16(2)(a) to (f) as regards the types of loans remain, in broad terms, the same as before. However, the condition under section 16(2)(d) on the loan not being secured or guaranteed by a deposit that can generate tax free interest has been removed to a new provision [section 16(2A)] which has a broader application. New provisions have also been added to restrict the deduction of interest despite the satisfaction of the respective conditions under section 16(2).

The new scheme of interest deduction after the 2004 Amendment Ordinance is discussed below.

Conditions for Deduction

Conditions (a) and (b) — borrowings by financial institutions and public utilities

11. No amendment has been made to these two conditions. All borrowings by a financial institution and any borrowings by public utilities at a rate of interest not exceeding a specified rate will continue to satisfy conditions (a) and (b) respectively.

Condition (c) — borrowings from persons other than financial institution

12. The main part of this subsection remains unchanged. The comments in paragraph 4 above continue to apply. In addition, interest deduction on a loan satisfying this condition is also subject to the new restrictions under section 16 (2A) and (2B).

Condition (d) — borrowings from financial institutions or overseas financial institutions

13. This condition will be satisfied if the loan is borrowed from a financial institution or an overseas financial institution. The requirement that the loan is not being secured by a deposit of the borrower or his associate that can generate tax free interest is removed from this condition, but a similar test is added as a criterion for restricting interest deduction under section 16(2A). On top of that, deduction of interest payable on this type of loan is further subject to the new restrictions under section (2B).

Condition (e) — borrowings for specified purposes

14. As before, this condition will be satisfied by the borrower establishing that —
  * the money has been borrowed wholly and exclusively to finance capital expenditure on machinery and plant, or for the purchase of trading stock, for the purpose of producing chargeable profits; and
  * the lender is not an associate of the borrower in terms of section 16(3).
Deduction of interest under this type of loan is subject to the new restrictions under section 16(2A) and (2B).

Condition (f) — interest on debentures and debt instruments

15. This condition continues to relate to corporate borrowings by way of debentures or other marketable debt instruments. For the interest payable on debentures, the condition will be satisfied where such debentures are listed on a stock exchange in Hong Kong or any other stock exchange recognized by the Commissioner. Insofar as debt instruments are concerned, the condition will be satisfied if the instruments are issued –

    (A) bona fide and in the course of carrying on business and is marketed in Hong Kong or any other major financial centre recognized by the Commissioner; or

    (B) pursuant to any agreement or arrangements, where the issue of an advertisement, invitation or document in respect of the agreement or arrangements to the public has been authorized by the Securities and Futures Commission under section 105 of the Securities and Futures Ordinance.

Marketed

16. The two conditions relating to the interest deduction on debt instruments resemble closely the corresponding provisions that prevailed immediately before the 2004 Amendment Ordinance. The only major difference is that debt instruments (other than those issued under an agreement or arrangement with the approval of the Securities and Futures Commission) that qualify for interest deduction have to be actually marketed in Hong Kong or in a major financial centre recognized by the Commissioner. This means that to satisfy the condition, not only should the instrument be marketable, there should also be some actual marketing activities conducted when, or shortly after, the instrument is issued.

17. Whether an instrument has been marketed is a matter of fact to be determined by reference to the common market practices. The followings are some of the conditions the existence of which may indicate that the instrument has been marketed –

    (i)   road-shows or meetings with potential investors are conducted before the issue of the instrument;

    (ii)   research reports on the issuer are published by major market participants;

    (iii) the instrument is rated by reputable credit rating agencies, e.g. Standard and Poor's, Moody's, Fitch IBCA, etc.;

    (iv) the instrument is cleared through one of the recognized clearing systems, e.g. the CMU (Central Moneymarkets Unit) of the Hong Kong Monetary Authority, Euroclear, Clearstream, etc.;

    (v)   the description of the instrument is displayed on major real-time financial information networks, e.g. Reuters, Bloomberg, Telerate, etc.;

    (vi) one or more market participants agree to quote bid prices on the instrument under normal market conditions;

    (vii) evidence that shows the existence of trading of the instrument in the secondary markets, e.g. transaction records in the clearing systems.

Issue of debentures or instruments through associated corporation

18. As before, condition (f) will also be satisfied where the borrowing is from an associated corporation and the moneys borrowed in the hands of the associated corporation arose entirely from the proceeds of an issue of debentures or instruments as described above. As for borrowings from associated corporations, the deduction of interest paid by the borrowing corporation is restricted to the amount of interest paid by the associated corporation to the holders of its debentures or instruments.

19. Deduction of interest under this condition is subject to the ne restriction under section 16(2C).

Limitation of Deduction of Interest

20. The 2004 Amendment Ordinance lays down restrictions on interest deduction under certain circumstances. Deduction of interest on loans borrowed from non-financial institutions (condition (c) loans), borrowed from financial institutions (condition (d) loans) or borrowed for specified purposes (condition (e) loans) will all be subject to two additional tests under section 16(2A) and (2B) –

Section 16(2A)

(i) the loan is not secured by a deposit or loan made by the borrower or a person associated with the borrower with or to the lender, a financial institution, an overseas financial institution or an associate of any of these parties, where the interest generated by such deposit or loan is not taxable (i.e. the secured-loan test); and

Section 16(2B)

(ii) there is no arrangement in place such that the interest payment is ultimately paid back to the borrower or to a person connected with the borrower (i.e. the interest flow-back test).

21. As regards the deduction of interest on debentures or debt instruments, it will be subject to the same interest flow-back test (section 16(2C) as that mentioned in paragraph 20(ii) above). Nevertheless, failure to comply with these tests does not necessarily disqualify the interest expense in its entirety from a deduction claim. In the case of a partial failure, the restriction on interest deduction will only be confined to the portion of the interest relating to the portion of loan, debenture or debt instruments that failed the tests and the time in which the failure persisted.

22. Bankers may have the right to utilise balances in deposit accounts of a customer to set off the outstanding loan and interest payable by that customer in the case of default in repayment of the loan. Despite such right of the bankers, the balances in deposit accounts of a customer who also borrows money from the bank would not be taken as a security of the loan if the custome's right to withdraw the deposit is not restricted at any time before he defaults in repayment of the loan. Such deposit, which the depositor has unrestricted right to operate before the bank exercises the right of set-off, does not appear to be, by nature, a security for the loan.

Restriction under section 16(2A) [The secured-loan test]

23. Restriction of deduction under section 16(2A) applies to interest deduction claims on loans satisfying the conditions under section 16(2)(c), (d) or (e). The provision is triggered when the following situation exists at any time during the basis period of the borrower in respect of which interest deduction is claimed –
  (i)   the payment of any interest or the repayment of any principal of the loan in question is secured or guaranteed by a deposit (or a loan);
  (ii) the said deposit (or loan) is made by the borrower or an associate of his with (or to) a specified person;
  (iii) the specified person is either –
        a. the lender or an associate of the lender;
        b. a financial institution or an associate of a financial institution; or
        c. an overseas financial institution or an associate of an overseas financial institution; and
  (iv) the deposit or loan generates interest income that is not chargeable to tax in Hong Kong.
The term "associate" has the same meaning before and after the 2004 Amendment Ordinance, as defined in section 16(3).

24. This section, when applicable, will reduce the interest deduction by an amount calculated on a basis as is most reasonable and appropriate in the circumstances of the case, having regard to the amount of interest income arising from deposit or loan in question. The following examples illustrate the Department's practice.

Example 5

Taxpayer F borrowed $1M from Bank G at 5% interest rate p.a. The loan was secured by a fixed deposit of $1M earning tax-free interest of 4% p.a. There was no other security. In the year of assessment, F earned interest of $40,000 from the deposit and paid interest of $50,000 on the loan.

The amount of interest expenses allowable for deduction will be reduced by $40,000, being the tax-free interest earned. In other words, the allowable interest is $10,000.

Example 6

The $1M loan in Example 5 was secured by a deposit of $500,000 and some *shares which were also worth $500,000. The deposit generated tax-free interest of $20,000.*

The amount of interest expenses allowable for deduction will be reduced by the amount of tax-free interest ($20,000) generated from the deposit. In other words, the allowable interest is $30,000.

Example 7

The $1M loan in Example 5 was secured by a deposit of $2M that generated tax-free interest of $80,000. There was no other security.

The amount of interest expenses allowable for deduction will be reduced by $40,000, which is calculated as follows —

$$\$80,000 \times \frac{\$1M \ (loan)}{\$2M \ (deposit)} = \$40,000$$

Example 8

The $1M loan in Example 5 was secured by a deposit of $1M (which generated tax-free deposit interest of $40,000) and some shares valued at $500,000.

The amount of interest expenses allowable for deduction will be reduced by $26,667, which is calculated as follows –

$$\$40,000 \times \frac{\$1M \ (deposit)}{\$1.5M \ (deposit \ + \ shares)} = \$26,667$$

The value of shares used as security may vary from time to time. For the purposes of this calculation, a reasonable basis of averaging, such as by reference to month end balances, will be accepted.

Example 9

A deposit of $2M (generating tax-free interest of $80,000) was used to secure a loan of $1M used for financing onshore business activities and another loan of $1.5M used for financing offshore businesses. Interest incurred on the onshore business loan was $50,000 and that on the offshore business loan was $80,000.

In this example, the deposit was used to secure two loans. The amount of interest expenses allowable for deduction will be reduced by $32,000, which is calculated as follows –

$$\$80,000 \times \frac{\$1M \ (onshore \ loan)}{\$2.5M \ (onshore \ loan \ + \ offshore \ loan)} = \$32,000$$

Example 10

The two loans in Example 9 were secured by a deposit of $4M, which generated tax-free interest of $160,000. There was no other security.

In this example, the portion of deposit that was used to secure the two loans is $2.5M / $4M; and out of this portion, the part attributable to the onshore loan is $1M / $2.5M. The amount of interest expenses allowable for deduction will be reduced by $40,000, which is calculated as follows –

$$\$160,000 \times \frac{\$2.5M}{\$4M} \times \frac{\$1M}{\$2.5M} = \$40,000$$

Trusts

25. In considering the relation between the borrower and the holder of the deposit or loan used as security, if a deposit or loan is made by a trustee of a trust or a corporation controlled by such a trustee, the deposit or loan shall be deemed to have been made by each of the trustee, the corporation and the beneficiary under the trust [section 16(2D)]. Section 16(3) contains a definition of "beneficiary under the trust".

Restriction under section 16(2B) [The interest flow-back test]

26. Deduction of interest on loans that satisfy the conditions under section 16(2)(c), (d) or (e) will be restricted if there is an arrangement under which the interest payable will be paid, directly or through an interposed person, back to the borrower or to a person connected with the borrower who is not an "excepted person" within the meaning of section 16(2E)(c). The provision applies where the said arrangement exists at any time during the basis period of the borrower for the year of assessment in respect of which deduction is claimed for the interest on the respective loan. Any payment of interest to a trustee or a corporation controlled by the trustee is deemed to be a payment to each of the trustee, the corporation and the beneficiary under the trust [section 16(2E)(b)].

27. The term "arrangement" is defined in section 2. It includes –
  (a) any agreement, arrangement, understanding, promise or undertaking, whether expressed or implied, and whether or not enforceable or intended to be enforceable, by legal proceedings; and
  (b) any scheme, plan, proposal, action or course of action or course of conduct.

The provision for restricting interest deduction will be invoked whenever arrangements are in place, irrespective of whether the passing of interest has actually occurred.

28. In this section, the reference to "any sum payable by way of interest on the loan borrowed" is expanded by section 16(2E)(a) to cover the payment of interest or principal in respect of any other loan, the repayment of which is secured by the payment of interest or repayment of principal of the loan in question (e.g. the second loan is advanced by way of sub-participating in the first loan borrowed by the borrower).

Example 11

Company H borrowed a loan of $100M from Bank J. Bank J entered into a loan sub-participation arrangement with Company K, which is an associated company of Company H. Under the arrangement, Company K advanced a loan of $100M to Bank J on the condition that the repayment of principal and interest of this loan by Bank J to Company K would only be made on the condition of the repayment of principal and interest of the bank loan by Company H to Bank J. In practical terms, Bank J is risk free.

In this situation, the interest paid by Bank J to Company K is treated as if it were the interest on the loan borrowed by Company H from Bank J when the restriction of section 16(2B) is considered. As the interest was paid to an associated company of the borrower (Company H) of the loan, the interest deduction claim would be denied.

Interest Apportionment

29. Triggering the application of section 16(2B) does not necessarily mean that the whole amount of interest incurred on a loan will be disqualified for deduction. Indeed the section allows for apportionment of interest expenses in two ways –

- The provision applies to arrangements that cover interest payable on a part of a loan, and this allows apportionment of interest in the case where only part of the loan in question is subject to an arrangement under which the interest payable will be reverted back to the borrower or his connected person.
- Where the arrangement is in place for only part of the basis period during which the loan interest is incurred, the interest expenses can be apportioned on a time basis. This means that only the portion of interest attributable to the period of time during which the arrangement is in place will be disallowed from deduction.

Example 12

Company L borrowed a loan of $10M from Bank M at the interes rate of 10% p.a. At its inception, $7M of the loan was sub-participated by Company N, an associate company of Company L. The repayment by Bank M to Company N of the principal and interest of the $7M loan was made conditional to or secured by the repayment of principal and interest of the $10M loan made by Company L to Bank M. In a year of assessment Company

L paid interest of $1M to Bank M, and correspondingly Bank M paid interest in the amount attributable to the $7M loan to Company N.

In this example only $7M of the total loan was sub-participated by a person connected with the borrower (Company L). Thus only the interest attributable to the sub-participated portion, that is the amount of $700,000 ($1M × 7/10), is subject to the adjustment under section 16(2B). As this part of the loan was participated for the whole period during which interest was incurred, the full amount of the $700,000 interest would be disallowed by section 16(2B). However, the interest on the remaining part of loan which was not sub-participated by the borrower or a person connected to him (in this case interest of $300,000) would be allowable for deduction.

Example 13

If in Example 12, the loan of $7M (C) was sub-participated by Company N for only 6 months (A) during the basis period of the year of assessment (B) concerned, the operation of section 16(2B) will be as follows –

	($M)
Interest payable on the portion of loan which was sub-participated to Company N	0.7
Deduct: by the amount (A/B × C) (183days / 365 days × $0.7M)	0.35
Interest on sub-participated loan deductible	0.35
Add: Interest on the portion of the loan that is not sub-participated ($3M/$10M × $1M)	0.3
Total interest deduction	0.65

Note that the amount of interest paid on the sub-participated loan (the loan advanced by Company N to Bank M), even if of different amount, is not relevant in the computation.

Restriction under section 16(2C) [Interest flow-back test on debt instruments]

30. Like interest on ordinary loans, deduction of interest on debentures or debt instruments that satisfy the conditions under section 16(2)(f) will be restricted if there is an arrangement under which the interest payable will be paid, directly or through an interposed person, back to the borrower (the issuer) or to a person connected with the borrower who is not an "excepted person" within the meaning of section 16(2F)(c). The provision applies when the said arrangement exists at any time during the basis period of the borrower for the year of assessment in respect of which deduction is claimed for the interest on the respective loan. Any payment of interest to a trustee or a corporation controlled by the trustee is deemed to be a payment to each of the trustee, the corporation and the beneficiary under the trust [section 16(2F)(b)].

31. Again, the term "arrangement" has a wide coverage as defined in section 2 (see paragraph 27 above). The provision for restricting interest deduction will be invoked whenever arrangements are in place, irrespective of whether the passing of interest has actually occurred. Peculiar to the nature of debentures and debt instruments, the term includes the holding of debentures or debt instruments either directly or beneficially (i.e. holding any interest in debentures or debt instruments).

32. In this section, the reference to "any sum payable by way of interest on the debentures or instruments concerned" is expanded by section 16(2F)(a) to cover the payment of interest or principal in respect of any other loan the repayment of which is secured by the payment of interest or repayment of principal of the debentures or instruments concerned (see Example 11 above).

Interest Apportionment

33. Section 16(2C) allows for apportionment of interest expenses in three ways –

- The provision applies to arrangements in relation to interest expenses payable on any debentures or instruments within an issue. This allows for apportionment of interest expenses when only some of the debentures or instruments issued are held by the borrower or a connected person of the borrower.
- The provision also applies to arrangements that cover interest expenses payable in the interest on any debentures or instrument concerned. This allows apportionment of interest expenses in the case where the beneficial interest in a debenture or an instrument is shared among a number of persons, and only some of such persons are connected with the issuer.
- Where the arrangement is in place for only part of the basis period of the issuer during which the loan interest claimed for deduction was incurred, the interest expenses can be apportioned on a time basis. This means that only the portion of interest expenses attributable to the period of time during which the arrangement was in place will be disallowed from deduction.

Example 14

Corporation P issued debentures in amount of $100M in a recognized overseas stock market. Out of the issue, an associated company of Corporation P subscribed $80M and acquired the remaining $20M debentures from the market in the middle of the year of assessment. During the year of assessment concerned total interest in the amount of $10M was paid. Corporation P *adopts a basis period that corresponds to a year of assessment (i.e. for year ended 31 March).*

The interest deduction calculation will be as follows –

	($M)
Interest on $80M debentures subscribed by the associated company	8
Reduced by the amount attributable to the holding of the associated company	8
Balance deductible	0
Interest on the $20M debentures acquired by the associated company in the middle of the year	2
Reduced by the amount attributable to the holding of the associated company (183 / 365 × $2M)	1
Interest on this portion of debenture deductible	1
Total interest deduction ($0M + $1M)	1

Persons Connected with the Borrower [Section 16(3B)]

34. This is a new concept under the interest flow-back test. A person is regarded as being connected with the borrower if the person is –
    (a) an associated corporation of the borrower; or
    (b) a person (other than a corporation) –
        (i)   who controls the borrower;
        (ii) who is controlled by the borrower; or
        (iii) who is under the control of the same person as is the borrower.

35. The term "associated corporation" is defined in section 16(3). This definition has not been changed by the 2004 Amendment Ordinance. The meaning of the term "control" [which is formerly defined in section 16(3)] is now provided under section 16(3A). So far as a corporation is concerned, the meaning of control has not been changed by the 2004 Amendment Ordinance. However, it has been expanded to cover the situation of controlling a person who is not a corporation.

Excepted Persons

36. This is another new concept under the interest flow-back test. Interest restriction under the test does not apply where under the arrangement concerned, the interest flows to a connected person who is an "excepted person". The definitions of excepted person under sections 16(2E)(c) and 16(2F)(c) are the same and cover the following categories –
    •   a person who is charged to tax in respect of the interest in question;
    •   a person acting as a bare trustee;

- a beneficiary of a unit trust to which section 26A(1A)(a)(i) or (ii) applies, where the interest payment is in respect of a specified investment scheme;
- a member of a recognized retirement scheme, or a similar scheme established outside Hong Kong accepted by the Commissioner;
- a public body (which is defined under section 3 of the Interpretation and General Clauses Ordinance, Cap 1, as including the Executive Council, the Legislative Council, and District Council, any other urban, rural or municipal council, any department of the Government, and any undertaking by or of the Government);
- a body corporate of which the Government owns more than half in nominal value of the issued share capital; or
- a financial institution or an overseas financial institution.

Exemption for Market Makers of Debt Instruments

37. Section 16(2G) provides for an exemption from the interest deduction restriction under section 16(2C) in respect of debentures or debt instruments. The restriction does not apply where under an arrangement interest on debentures or debt instruments is payable to a market maker who holds such debentures or instruments in the ordinary course of conduct of his trade, profession or business in respect of market making, notwithstanding that the market maker is a person connected with the issuer.

38. The purpose of holding the debentures or debt instruments must be for providing liquidity for such securities. Under normal circumstances, long-term or substantial holdings of the securities will not be considered as consistent with market making activities. For this purpose, a holding of over 5% of an issue for a period of over 3 months will not be taken as a holding of the securities in the ordinary course of conduct of market making activities, unless the Commissioner is satisfied that there are reasonable explanations for doing so.

39. To qualify for the exemption, the market maker must be a person who –
- is a licensed or registered dealer of securities under the Securities and Futures Ordinance (Cap. 571), or in a major financial centre outside Hong Kong recognized by the Commissioner;
- in the ordinary course of conduct of the market making business, holds himself out as being willing to buy and sell securities for his own account and on a regular basis; and
- is actively involved in market making in securities issued by a wide range of unrelated institutions.

APPLICATION OF THE GENERAL ANTI-AVOIDANCE PROVISION (SECTION 61A)

40. While the conditions and restrictions on interest expenses deduction under section 16 lay down specific rules governing the interest deduction scheme, compliance with such rules and conditions does not preclude the application of the general anti-avoidance provision under section 61A in cases that satisfy the conditions specified in section 61A. Support for this proposition can be found in the Privy Council decision of *CIR v. Challenge Corporation Limited, [1986] STC 548*, and the Court of Appeal decision of *Yick Fung Estates Ltd. v. CIR, 5 HKTC 52*.

GRANDFATHERING PROVISIONS

41. The application of the new interest deduction provisions of the 2004 Amendment Ordinance is set out in section 16(5A). As a general rule, the new scheme will apply to interests incurred after the commencement of the 2004 Amendment Ordinance, that is, on or after 25 June 2004.

42. Nevertheless, interest incurred under a transaction which was the subject of an advance clearance, or under an arrangement which was the subject of an advance ruling given under section 88A, can be grandfathered from the application of the new scheme. To qualify for grandfathering, the advance clearance or the advance ruling must have been given by the Commissioner, before 25 June 2004, on the issue that the transaction or the arrangement, as the case may be, would not fall within the terms of section 61A. Deductions of interest expenses arising from these transactions or arrangements (incurred after 25 June 2004) are governed by the provisions that were in force before the amendments made by the 2004 Amendment Ordinance are effected [see paragraphs 2–9 above], as if the amendments of the 2004 Amendment Ordinance to section 16 had not taken effect.

DUTY OF THE TAXPAYER TO DISCLOSE DETAILS OF INTEREST DEDUCTION CLAIMS

43. It is the duty of the taxpayer who makes a claim for interest deduction to disclose the full details of the facts that may affect the deductibility of the interest concerned. It is therefore necessary for him to ascertain and to disclose in the tax return whether there is any arrangement in place that may trigger the interest deduction restriction provisions under section 16(2A), (2B) or (2C).

APPENDIX 9

**Departmental Interpretation & Practice Notes
No. 14 (Revised)**

PROPERTY TAX

These notes are issued for the information and guidance of taxpayers and their authorised representatives. They have no binding force and do not affect a person's right of objection and appeal to the Commissioner, the Board of Review or the Courts.

These notes replace those titled (A) Property tax from 1983–84 onwards (B) Provisional property tax issued on 7 December 1983.

LAU MAK Yee-ming, Alice
Commissioner of Inland Revenue

February 2005

Our web site: http://www.info.gov.hk/ird

**DEPARTMENTAL INTERPRETATION AND PRACTICE NOTES
No. 14 (REVISED)**

CONTENT

CHARGE OF PROPERTY TAX

Meanings of "Owners"

1. Property Tax is imposed under section 5(1) of the Inland Revenue Ordinance (the Ordinance). It is charged on the owner of any land or/and buildings wherever situated in Hong Kong and shall be computed at the standard rate on the net assessable value of such land or/and buildings for each year.

2. "Owner" in respect of any land or/and buildings is defined in section 2 of the Ordinance as including –
   (a) a person holding the land or/and buildings directly from the Government. Under normal circumstances, "owner" is primarily taken as the person(s) whose name(s) is registered in the Land Registry;
   (b) a beneficial owner;
   (c) a tenant for life;
   (d) a mortgagor;
   (e) a mortgagee in possession;
   (f) a person with adverse title to land receiving rent from buildings or other structures erected on that land;
   (g) a person who is making payments to a co-operative society registered under the Co-operative Societies Ordinance for the purpose of the purchase of the land or/and buildings;
   (h) a person who holds land or/and buildings subject to a ground rent or other annual charge; and
   (i) an executor of the estate of an owner.

3. The definition of "owner" in this section is an inclusive one and is by no means restrictive on the ordinary meaning of the word. Incorporated Owners formed by the owners of a building under the Buildings Ordinance has been ruled as the owner of the common parts of the building and is chargeable to Property Tax where the rights, powers, privileges and duties of the owners in relation to the common parts of the building would be exercised and performed by, and the liabilities of the owners in relation to the common parts of the building would be enforceable against the Incorporated Owners to the exclusion of the owners [see *BOR Case D27/98*].

Meanings of "Land or/and Buildings"

4. "Land or/and buildings" is normally given its ordinary meaning. Section 7A of the Ordinance extends its meaning to include "piers, wharves and other structures". Some examples of structures are: walls, dams, advertising signs, light box, oil station, etc.. They also include that part of the common area within a building not specifically assigned to any one owner but intended to be used for the benefit of all the owners of the building.

5. Except for the purpose of considering tax exemption under section 5(2) [see paragraph 21], "buildings" should include any part of a building.

Change of Ownership

6. As Property Tax is charged on the owner of a property, it is pertinent to identify the date of change of ownership in the property so as to ascertain the Property Tax liability of both the old and new owners in the case of a property transfer.

7. Most property transactions start with the entering into an agreement for sale and purchase of property between the vendor and the purchaser. The possession and the title to the property will be transferred to the purchaser at a later date by an assignment or other conveyance instrument upon completion of the sale and purchase. Technically speaking, during the period from the date of executing the agreement for sale and purchase to the completion of the transaction, a duality of ownership exists. Whilst the vendor remains the legal owner of the property, the purchaser, upon entering into the agreement for sale and purchase and on payment of part of the purchase price as a deposit, has become the equitable owner of the property. The date for switching the entitlement of the rental income arising from the property from the vendor to the purchaser would normally be determined in the terms of the agreement for sale. For Property Tax purposes, the party who entitles to receiving the rent will be charged to Property Tax.

Computation of Property Tax

8. Property Tax is charged at the standard rate on the net assessable value of the land or/and buildings. The net assessable value is computed as follows –

Relevant Provisions under the Ordinance		$
s.5B(2)	Consideration receivable in respect of the right of use of the property	A
s.7C(2)	Add: Rent recovered	B
		C
s.7C(1) & (3)	Less: Irrecoverable rent	(D)
	Assessable Value	E
s.5(1A)(b)(i)	Less: Rates paid by owner*	(F)
		G
s.5(1A)(b)(ii)	Less: 20% on 'G' as standard allowance for repairs and outgoings	(H)
	Net Assessable Value	I

* excluding Government rent (see paragraph 17).

THE ASCERTAINMENT OF ASSESSABLE VALUE

Meaning of Assessable Value

9. Section 5B(2) provides that the assessable value of a property for each year of assessment shall be the consideration, in money or money's worth, payable in that year to, to the order of or for the benefit of, the owner in respect of the right of use of that land or buildings or land and buildings. Examples of sums received or receivable to be included in the assessable value are –
(a) rent;
(b) payments for the right of use of premises under licence;
(c) lump sum premium;
(d) service charges, management fee etc. paid to the owner; and
(e) owner's expenditure e.g. repairs, borne by the tenant.

10. A lump sum premium paid in respect of a lease exceeding one year will be spread, on an equal monthly basis, over the period of the lease or over a 3-year period from the commencing date of the lease, whichever is the shorter.

11. For example –

A premium of $60,000 was received on 31 March 1999 from a lease of 5 years commencing on 1 June 1999 and ending on 31 May 2004.

The premium is to be spread over the 3-year period from 1 June 1999 to 31 May 2002 and assessed under Property Tax as follows –

Year of Assessment		**Assessable Value**
1999/2000	$60,000 × 10/36 =	$16,667
2000/01	$60,000 × 12/36 =	$20,000
2001/02	$60,000 × 12/36 =	$20,000
2002/03	$60,000 × 2/36 =	$ 3,333
		$60,000

12. Section 5B(6) specifically includes as consideration any sum payable in respect of the provision of any services or benefits connected with or related to the right to use the property. Hence, the management fee paid by a tenant to a landlord who rents out the whole block of building to different tenants and provides management service to all the tenants in the building should be included in ascertaining the assessable value of the respective property.

13. Nevertheless, if it is provided in the tenancy agreement that the tenant is responsible for the payment of the management fee, the fee so paid should not be included as consideration payable in respect of the right of use of the relevant property even though it is paid through the landlord. In such an event the landlord merely acts as agent for the tenant.

14. Where the tenancy agreement is silent as regards the party who shoulders the responsibility of paying the management fee, but the **established fact** shows that the landlord is accustomed to pay the management fee to the management service provider out of the lump sum he receives monthly from the tenant and that he has no right to claim for a repayment from the tenant, only the net sum received by the landlord (as reduced by the management fee paid by him) should be included as consideration payable in respect of the right of use of the relevant property. In this situation, it is assumed that the contractual obligation of the parties is the same as in paragraph 13 above.

Irrecoverable Consideration

15. Section 7C(1) provides that in ascertaining the assessable value, if any consideration payable on or after 1 April 1983 in respect of the property is proved to the satisfaction of the Assessor to be irrecoverable in any year of assessment, the irrecoverable amount shall be allowable as a deduction in that particular year of assessment. If the assessable value for that year is insufficient to cover the irrecoverable amount, the balance shall be deducted, under section 7C(3), in the latest year of assessment in which the assessable value is sufficient for the deduction. Any claims made for the deduction of irrecoverable consideration should be supported by documentary evidence.

Rent Recovered

16. Recovery of amounts previously deducted as irrecoverable should be included as assessable value in the year of recovery.

DEDUCTIONS FROM THE ASSESSABLE VALUE

Rates

17. Where the owner agrees to pay the rates in respect of the property, the rates paid by the owner can be deducted from the assessable value [section 5(1A)].

However, the Government rent payable in respect some properties after 1 July 1997 is not deductible.

Allowance for Repairs and Outgoings

18. A special allowance for repairs and outgoings can be deducted from the assessable value in ascertaining the net assessable value. The amount of the allowance is 20% of the assessable value of the property,

(a) including rent recovered, if any, as set out in paragraph 16; and

(b) after deduction of irrecoverable considerations and rates, if any,

as set out in the paragraphs 15 and 17) .

19. This allowance is given irrespective of the actual amount of expenditure incurred by the owner. The percentage may be amended by resolution of the Legislative Council [section 5(1B)].

RELIEF AND EXEMPTIONS

Tax set-off under section 25

20. Where the property is owned and used by a person carrying on a trade, profession or business in Hong Kong, the Property Tax payable for any year of assessment can be used to offset against the Profits Tax payable for the same year, provided that –

(a) the profits derived from the property are part of the profits of the trade, profession or business; or

(b) the property is occupied or used by the owner for the purposes of producing profits assessable to Profits Tax.

Exemption for Corporations under section 5(2)(a)

21. Section 5(2)(a) provides for exemption from Property Tax in respect of any property owned by a corporation provided that the corporation would be entitled under section 25 to a set-off of the Property Tax which, if exemption were not granted under section 5(2)(a), would be paid by the corporation.

Exemption under sections 87 and 88

22. By virtue of section 87 of the Ordinance, the Chief Executive in Council may exempt any person, office or institution from payment of the whole or portion of the Property Tax that is chargeable. The approved charitable institutions or trusts of a public character are exempt from Property Tax under section 88.

PROPERTY LETTING AMOUNTING TO A BUSINESS

23. By definition, letting and sub-letting by a corporation and sub-letting by any person other than a corporation amount to a business [section 2]. As such, the rental income so arising is chargeable to Profits Tax.

24. For other cases, whether the property letting amounts to a business is to be considered within the ordinary meaning and concept of the term "business". While it is a question of fact to be determined in each case, it is the view of the Department that there is strong indication of business in the following circumstances –

(a) the number of properties let is substantial and the owner has engaged some staff to handle tenancies and to deal with the tenants;

(b) the properties are of a special class such as ballrooms, cinemas or restaurants, and that additional services are provided by the landlord such as the landlord being the licencee of the ballroom, cinema or restaurant (see *Louis Kwan-nang KWONG & Carlos Kowk-nang KWONG v. CIR, 2 HKTC 541*);

(c) letting by a property dealer: the rents are regarded as income of the property dealing business; or

(d) the letting is incidental to and is therefore part of the trade or business as would be the situation of a trader who owns a property which he uses partly for his trade and letting that part which is surplus to his immediate requirements.

PROVISIONAL PROPERTY TAX

25. Provisional Property Tax is payable by every person who is chargeable to Property Tax, i.e. the owner of any land and/or buildings. The provisional tax for any year of assessment is payable at the standard rate on the net assessable value of the preceding year and will be applied against the final Property Tax for that year when ascertained. Any excess is then applied against the provisional tax liability for the succeeding year and the amount not so applied will be refunded to the taxpayer.

26. Subsections (2) and (3) of section 63M allow for estimated Provisional Property Tax charges to be raised where the assessable value of the preceding year was calculated in respect of a period of less than 1 year, or for the year in which a person first becomes chargeable to Property Tax and for the succeeding year thereof.

27. The demand for provisional tax may be issued separately to the person liable or included in a notice of assessment to Property Tax with such specified due date for payment as may be fixed by the Commissioner.

28. A claim may be made in writing for holding over the whole or part of the provisional tax payable on any of the grounds listed in paragraph 29 below. The claim must be received by the Commissioner not later than the later of –

(a) 28 days before the due date of payment of the provisional tax; or

(b) 14 days after the date of the notice for payment of provisional tax.

29. The grounds for holding over include –
   (a) the assessable value for that year of assessment is, or is likely to be, less than 90% of the assessable value for the year preceding the year of assessment or of the estimated sum on which the charge has been made;
   (b) the person charged has ceased, or will before the end of the year of assessment cease, to be an owner of land and/or buildings and that the assessable value for the year of assessment is, or is likely to be, less than the sum on which the charge has been made;
   (c) the person charged has elected personal assessment for that year of assessment and such personal assessment is likely to reduce his liability to tax; or
   (d) a valid objection has been lodged against the assessment to Property Tax for the year preceding the year of assessment.

PROPERTY TAX RETURNS AND ASSESSMENT

30. Prior to the year of assessment 1993/94, separate Property Tax returns and assessments were issued for each individual property unit irrespective of the nature of ownership.

31. From 1 April 1993 onwards, the Inland Revenue Department introduced a composite tax return system for individual taxpayers. Since then the property income, depending on the types of property ownership, are to be declared as follows:
   (a) Properties **solely** owned by an individual –
       (i) Details of all such properties should be declared in the Tax Return – Individuals (Form B.I.R.60) issued to the sole owner under the personal tax file of the individual owner.
       (ii) One consolidated Property Tax assessment would be raised on the individual owner in respect of all his solely owned properties.
   (b) Properties **not solely** owned by an individual –
       (i) Details of each property should be declared on the respective Property Tax Return (Form B.I.R.57 or B.I.R.58) issued to the owners under the corresponding Property Tax file for that property.
       (ii) Separate Property Tax assessments would be raised on the owner or co-owners [the joint owners and owners in common] in respect of each property.

32. For some properties jointly owned or co-owned by individuals, a simple Advice Letter instead of a Property Tax Return will be issued to the owners to review their tax liability and to remind them of the obligation to notify chargeability [see paragraph 34]. No reply to the Letter is required if the property is not let. If the property has been let out, the owners are only required to state the commencement date of the lease at the lower portion ("Letting Notification") of the Letter and return it to the Department. Then Property Tax returns for the relevant years in which the property was let will be sent for their completion.

OBLIGATIONS OF PROPERTY OWNERS

Filing of Returns – section 51(1)

33. Property owners are obliged to complete the tax returns issued to them and return them to the Inland Revenue Department within the time limit stipulated in the tax returns (which is normally one month from the date of issuing the return). The return should still be completed for official updating purposes even if the relevant property is occupied by the owner or any other person without consideration.

Notification of Chargeability to Tax – section 51(2)

34. Every person who is chargeable to Property Tax for any year of assessment but has not received a return form is required to notify the Commissioner of Inland Revenue in writing that he is so chargeable within four months after the end of that year of assessment (e.g. on or before 31 July 2005 for the year of assessment 2004/05).

Notification of Cessation of Ownership – section 51(6)

35. Where the ownership of a property has changed as a result of a sale or transfer, the vendor or the transferor must notify the Department of the change in writing within one month after the sale or transfer is effected.

Notification of Change of Address – section 51(8)

36. A person chargeable to Property Tax who changes his address should, within one month, inform the Commissioner of Inland Revenue in writing of the particulars of the change.

Keeping of Sufficient Rental Records – section 51D

37. Owners of properties must keep sufficient records of rent received, such as lease agreements and duplicates of rent receipts, to enable their tax liability to be readily ascertained. Such records should be retained for a period of not less than 7 years.

Notification of Change in Exemption Status – section 5(2)(c)

38. Where the owner is a corporation exempted from Property Tax under section 5(2)(a), the owner should notify the Commissioner in writing within 30 days of any change in the ownership or use of the property or any other circumstances affecting the exemption previously granted.

Responsibility of Joint Owners or Co-owners – section 56A

39. Where two or more persons are joint owners or owners in common of any property, each and every owner will have full responsibility for doing all such acts required to be done under the Ordinance as if he is the sole owner, including the filing of tax returns and paying the tax [section 56A(1)]. Furthermore, this obligation does not relieve or affect any right or obligation of the joint owners or owners in common as between themselves [section 56A(2)].

40. If any person has paid Property Tax for which he would not have been liable except for the provisions of section 56A(1), he may recover such tax from the person who is liable [section 56A(3)].

Letting of Common Areas of a Building

41. Normally, the common areas of a building such as side shop, car-park, external wall, roof top, etc. are collectively owned by the individual owners of the building. If any part of the common areas is let out, the rental income derived is chargeable to Property Tax. The owners are responsible for reporting the rental income and paying the tax. If the owners have not received the Property Tax return relating to the common areas let, they are required to notify the Commissioner in writing.

42. In *Board of Review Case No. D80/02*, it was held that an individual owner of a residential unit in a building complex was a co-owner of the car-parking spaces in the building and therefore section 56A would be applicable to him. The Board did not accept the contention that for section 56A to apply, there must be an instrument naming all persons who are or were co-owners of the car-parking spaces in question. Furthermore, the Board considered that the purported hardship of the captioned ruling on the individual owner concerned would not have any relevance and could not affect the construction of section 56A.

43. However, when an owners' corporation is formed, section 16 of the Building Management Ordinance (Cap. 344) provides that the rights and duties of the owners relating to the common parts of the building shall be exercised and performed by the incorporated owners of the building. Therefore, the incorporated owner is required, on behalf of all the owners of the building, to report the income and pay the tax.

APPENDIX 10

Departmental Interpretation & Practice Notes
No. 15 (Revised)

(A) LIMITATION OF LOSS RELIEF (SECTION 22B)
(B) LEASING ARRANGEMENTS (SECTION 39E)
(C) GENERAL ANTI-AVOIDANCE PROVISION (SECTION 61)
(D) GENERAL ANTI-AVOIDANCE PROVISION (SECTION 61A)
(E) LOSS COMPANIES (SECTION 61B)
(F) RAMSAY PRINCIPLE
(G) PENALTY ON TAX AVOIDANCE CASES
(H) GUIDELINES ON LEASE FINANCING
(I) ADVANCE RULINGS

These notes are issued for the information of taxpayers and their tax representatives. They contain the Department's interpretation and practices in relation to the law as it stood at the date of publication. Taxpayers are reminded that their right of objection against the assessment and their right of appeal to the Commissioner, the Board of Review or the Court are not affected by the application of these notes.

These notes replace those issued on 1 May 1986, on 15 November 1990 and in September 1992.

LAU MAK Yee-ming, Alice
Commissioner of Inland Revenue

January 2006

Our web site : www.ird.gov.hk

CONTENT

INTRODUCTION

An important attribute of an equitable tax system is that taxpayers are not able to avoid the imposition of taxation through the use of fictitious, artificial or contrived arrangements. The Government of the Hong Kong Special Administrative Region attempts to secure this attribute by enacting both specific and general anti-avoidance provisions in the Inland Revenue Ordinance ("the Ordinance"). These notes lay down broad statements on the interpretation and practices to be adopted by the Department in respect of a number of specific and general anti-avoidance provisions, namely sections 22B, 39E, 61, 61A and 61B. They also specify the information and documents that are required to be provided in relation to applications for advance ruling concerning leveraged lease transactions, general anti-avoidance provision (section 61A) and changes in shareholding. In addition, these notes set out the Department's minimum required standards in respect of leveraged lease transactions if they are to be acceptable under the Ordinance.

PART A —
LIMITATION OF LOSS RELIEF (SECTION 22B)

Limitation of loss relief

2. Section 22B generally applies in respect of a share of a loss incurred under a transaction entered into on or after 15 November 1990. The section limits the amount of loss which a limited partner can set off against his other assessable profits in a year of assessment.

3. Three categories of persons are within the definition of a limited partner. First, a person who is a limited partner in a partnership registered under the Limited Partnerships Ordinance (Cap. 37). Second, a person who, albeit a general partner, is not entitled to or does not take part in the management of the partnership and whose liability (or liability beyond a certain limit) for debts or obligations incurred by the partnership may be met by another person. Third, a person who under the laws of a foreign territory is not entitled to or does not take part in the management of the partnership and who is not liable beyond a certain limit for debts or obligations incurred by the partnership.

4. A limited partner cannot claim a loss set-off in excess of the "relevant sum", which is the amount of his contribution to the partnership as at the end of the relevant year of assessment in which the loss is sustained. If the person ceased to be a partner in the partnership during that year of assessment the appropriate time is the time when he so ceased.

5. The loss set-off of a limited partner is restricted to the lesser of:
    (a) his share of the partnership loss; or
    (b) the relevant sum.

6. Any loss not set off is carried forward in the partnership and set off against future assessable profits of the partnership. They are not available for set-off against other assessable profits which the limited partner may have in subsequent years.

7. In applying the provisions it is necessary to ascertain the amount of the limited partner's contribution to the partnership. This is the aggregate of the amounts of capital contributed to the partnership and not withdrawn, whether directly or indirectly, or otherwise received back, and any profits or gains which have not been withdrawn from the partnership, whether in money or money's worth. Anything which the limited partner is, or may be, entitled to draw out, receive back, or be reimbursed from another person at any time whilst the partnership carries on the trade, profession or business must be deducted.

PART B —
LEASING ARRANGEMENTS (SECTION 39E)

The position in general

8. Section 39E was enacted to limit the opportunities for tax deferral or avoidance through sale and leaseback, offshore equipment leasing and leveraged leasing arrangements. In broad terms section 39E operates to deny to a lessor (owner) initial and annual allowances ("depreciation allowances") in respect of any machinery or plant owned by him where a person holds rights as lessee under a lease of the machinery or plant and:

    (a) the machinery or plant was previously owned and used by the lessee or his associate (i.e. a sale and leaseback arrangement), or

    (b) the machinery or plant, other than a ship or aircraft or any part thereof, is while the lease is in force:

        (i) used wholly or principally outside Hong Kong by a person other than the lessor; or

        (ii) the whole or a predominant part of its cost of acquisition or construction was financed directly or indirectly by a non-recourse debt (i.e. a leveraged lease arrangement); or

    (c) the machinery or plant is a ship or aircraft or any part thereof and:

        (i) the lessee is not an operator of a Hong Kong ship or aircraft; or

        (ii) the whole or a predominant part of its cost of acquisition or construction or the part thereof was financed directly or indirectly by a non-recourse debt.

The lease

9. Under section 2 of the Ordinance, lease in relation to any machinery or plant includes:

    (a) any arrangement under which a right to use it is granted by the owner to another person; and

(b) any arrangement under which a right to use it, being a right derived directly or indirectly from a right referred to in paragraph (a), is granted by a person to another person, but does not include a hire-purchase agreement or a conditional sale agreement unless the Commissioner considers that the right under the agreement to purchase or obtain the property in the goods would reasonably be expected not to be exercised.

Party identification

10. In general the reference to "taxpayer" in section 39E connotes the lessor (owner) who has incurred capital expenditure on the provision of the machinery or plant being leased. The party which ultimately uses the machinery or plant is described as the "end-user", who is either:

(a) the lessee, either alone or with others, or

(b) an "associate" of the lessee.

For this purpose the term "associat" has been defined widely in section 39E (5) in order to prevent circumvention of the provision by the interposition of third parties.

Sale and leaseback

11. Denial of depreciation allowances in section 39E(1)(a) is intended to prevent an overall tax benefit being obtained through the sale and leaseback of machinery or plant.

12. Section 39E(1)(a) refers to leased machinery or plant which at any time prior to its acquisition by the lessor was owned and used by the end-user. "Owned" is not defined but is a word of common usage and in practice will be given its ordinary meaning. "Used" is defined to include "held for use" meaning installed ready for use or held in reserve. The term "ready" denotes a condition of functional operability.

13. Section 39E(2) provides an exception to the general rule that no initial or annual allowances will be granted in respect of machinery or plant acquired under a sale and leaseback arrangement. This exception applies in the situation where:

(a) a lessor purchases machinery or plant from an end-user at a price not greater than the price paid to the supplier (being a supplier who is not an end-user) by the end-user; and

(b) no initial or annual allowances have been made to the end-user in respect of that machinery or plant prior to its acquisition by the lessor.

Example 1

Company L is a leasing company whereas Company A is a manufacturing company. Both companies are carrying on business in Hong Kong. Under a sale and leaseback arrangement, Company A after revaluing its old machinery and plant sold them to Company L.

Company L in turn leased the machinery and plant back to Company A for rental. Before the arrangement, depreciation allowances on the machinery and plant were made to Company A. Company L would be denied depreciation allowances in respect of the machinery and plant under section 39E(1)(a) because they were owned and used by Company A prior to acquisition. The exception in section 39E(2) did not apply because depreciation allowances were previously granted to Company A.

Example 2

Company B purchased machinery of $100 million. Before putting them into use and claiming any depreciation allowances, Company B sold to and leased back from Company L the machinery. Under the sale and leaseback arrangement, Company B obtained cash proceeds of $100 million which was the price he paid the supplier and was required to pay a rental of $11 million for a consecutive period of ten years. Assuming each instalment contained an effective finance charge of $1 million whereas the market interest should have been $2 million, Company B in effect transferred the depreciation allowances to Company L in return for a lower rate of interest. Company B after receiving the cash of $100 million applied the money for other commercial transactions to produce chargeable profits.

The conditions in section 39E(2) are satisfied. Company L would not be denied depreciation allowances. Company B in effect made use of the sale and leaseback arrangement to obtain cheaper finance for its business use. Company L, the lessor, had in effect committed capital into the machinery, incurring genuine commercial risk. The whole arrangement is a normal commercial transaction.

14. Because entitlement to these allowances is mandatory upon acquisition of machinery or plant, in order for the exception in paragraph 13 to apply it will be necessary for the end-user to submit a disclaimer to the Commissioner in writing within 3 months of the date on which the machinery or plant was acquired, or within such further period as the Commissioner may permit. Generally, the Department will not entertain requests for an extension of the 3 months disclaimer period. A notice of disclaimer should be accompanied by the following information:

    (a) a description of the relevant asset;
    (b) the name and address of the supplier;
    (c) the date of purchase from and price paid to the supplier;
    (d) the date of sale to and price paid by the lessor; and
    (e) the name and address of the lessor.

The above information must be supported by copies of purchase and sale agreements or invoices and the lease agreement.

15. After submitting notice of a disclaimer, the end-user might decide to retain the right to claim depreciation allowances and seek to cancel the sale and leaseback arrangement. As a concession, the Department is prepared to allow the withdrawal of a disclaimer, provided that the relevant assessment has not yet become final and conclusive.

Used wholly or principally outside Hong Kong

16. The "used wholly or principally outside Hong Kong" condition in section 39E(1)(b)(i) aims to encourage the generation of economic benefits in Hong Kong by the use of the machinery or plant in Hong Kong.

17. The question whether a particular item of machinery or plant is used "wholly or principally" outside Hong Kong is a question of fact to be decided having regard to the circumstances of the case. The following matters are, however, likely to be relevant in determining the issue:
  (a) the place where the asset is physically located and put to use or held for use;
  (b) the nature of the asset;
  (c) the nature of the end-user's business;
  (d) the locality in which the asset is, under the terms of the lease, designated for use throughout the period of the lease.

Example 3

Company L is a leasing company carrying on business in Hong Kong. Company C is an enterprise carrying on business in Mainland China. Company L leased its machinery to Company C for rental.

Company L would be denied depreciation allowances in respect of the machinery under section 39E(1)(b)(i) because the machinery was used wholly outside Hong Kong. It should be noted that no deduction would be given under section 16G because the machinery under a lease is an "excluded fixed asset" as defined in section 16G(6). As a practice, the rental income accrued to Company L from leasing the machinery would be regarded as non-taxable.

18. No doubt cases will arise where leased machinery or plant will be used, either in one year, or, over a period of years, both within and outside Hong Kong. In these cases the Department will look at each leased asset and each year of assessment separately. If in a particular year the machinery or plant is used wholly or principally in Hong Kong then the prescribed depreciation allowances will be granted. On the other hand, if in a particular year the machinery or plant is not used wholly or principally in Hong Kong then no allowances will be granted. For the purposes of determining the written down value of the item to be carried forward, the notional amount of allowances which would have been granted had the item been used in Hong Kong will be deducted from the written down value brought forward. Any balancing adjustments on the sale of the item will be calculated on a pro-rata basis.

19. Under a contract processing arrangement with a Mainland Chinese enterprise, a Hong Kong company is often required to provide machinery or plant for the use of the Mainland Chinese enterprise. Such arrangement is a lease as defined in section 2 (see paragraph 9) and therefore section 39E needs to be considered. Even though the machinery or plant is not used wholly or principally in Hong Kong, the Department as a concession is prepared to allow 50 per cent of the depreciation allowances on the leased machinery or plant on the condition that the profits from manufacturing activities of the Hong Kong company are assessed on a 50:50 basis. The concession however will not apply where the Hong Kong company has ceased to be owner of the machinery or plant. For example, the Hong Kong company will be denied depreciation allowances on the machinery or plant which are injected as its share of equity of a "foreign investment enterprise" ("FIE") in the Mainland, as such machinery or plant is owned by the FIE.

Example 4

Company D is carrying on a manufacturing business in Hong Kong. Under a contract processing arrangement with a Mainland Chinese enterprise, Company D is required to provide machinery and plant to the Mainland Chinese enterprise for the latter's processing work. Company D did not charge the Mainland Chinese enterprise any rental for the use of the machinery and plant. Although no rental is charged, the arrangement is still a lease as defined in section 2. As the machinery or plant is under a lease, it is an "excluded fixed asset" under section 16G(6) and falls outside the purview of section 16G. Hence, no deduction under that section would be given. Strictly, Company D should be denied depreciation allowances in respect of the machinery and plant leased to the Mainland Chinese enterprise under section 39E(1)(b)(i). However, if the profits from the manufacturing activities of Company D are assessed on a 50:50 basis, the Department would be prepared to grant 50 per cent of the depreciation allowances as a concession.

Example 5

Company G is carrying on business in Hong Kong and is the holding company of Company H. Company H is a wholly owned foreign enterprise set up as a separate legal person in the Mainland. Company G purchased machinery and plant and injected them into Company H as its capital contribution in specie. As a result of the capital contribution, Company G has ceased to be owner of the machinery and plant. In effect, Company G has sold the machinery and plant in return for its equity interest in Company H. The question of a lease does not arise. Thus Company G would not be entitled to any depreciation allowances.

Ships or aircraft

20. Where the asset is a leased ship or aircraft the law prescribes a different test for deciding whether initial or annual allowances shall be granted to the taxpayer (lessor) — see section 39E(1)(c). In such cases the question is not whether the ship or aircraft is used wholly or principally outside Hong Kong but whether the person holding rights as lessee (the end-user) is an operator of a Hong Kong ship or aircraft. An operator of a Hong Kong ship or aircraft is a person who carries on business as an operator of ships or aircraft being a business controlled and managed in Hong Kong and:

   (a) in the case of an aircraft, holds an air operator's certificate issued under the Air Navigation (Hong Kong) Order 1995 (Cap. 448 sub. leg. C); or

   (b) in the case of a ship, is responsible for meeting all, or a substantial portion of the operating expenses of the ship and the ship operates mainly in the waters of Hong Kong or between the waters of Hong Kong and waters within the river trade limits.

Leveraged leases

21. A leveraged lease arrangement, as it has become known to this Department, is typically one in which a partnership of companies acquires machinery or plant (generally ships or aircraft) which it leases for a term of years to a lessee and where, by reason of the "leverage" obtained from the borrowing of a substantial non-recourse loan, the members of the partnership are effectively at risk for no more than a relatively small part of the funds used to acquire the asset. The lenders' security for the substantial amounts lent to acquire the asset is limited to the asset itself and/or by way of a charge over the lease and the related lease payments.

22. So far as it relates to leveraged leases, section 39E denies initial and annual allowances to a taxpayer (lessor) where the whole or a predominant part of the cost of machinery or plant was financed directly or indirectly by a non-recourse debt.

23. The term "non-recourse debt" is defined extensively in section 39E(5) but in broad terms means, as mentioned above, a method of financing where the borrower has no absolute liability in respect of the borrowing and in the event of default in repayment the rights of the lender are restricted to the asset itself or the income generated by it. For the purposes of this provision the Department will generally accept that where a taxpayer (lessor) actually contributes or is fully at risk for at least 51 per cent of the cost of the asset then the financing is not predominantly by a non-recourse debt and in such cases section 39E(1) will have no application.

**PART C —
GENERAL ANTI-AVOIDANCE PROVISION
(SECTION 61)**

The position in general

24. Section 61 empowers the Assessor to disregard certain transactions or dispositions and assess the taxpayer accordingly. This section is not a charging section, but serves to protect the liability for tax established under other sections of the Ordinance. This proposition is consistent with the dicta of Richardson J in *Challenge Corporation Limited [1986] 8 NZTC 5,001 [CA]* on the status of New Zealand's general anti-avoidance provision (at page 5,019):

> "Section [the relevant general anti-avoidance provision] is not an independent charging provision. It does not itself create a liability for income tax; its function is to protect the liability for income tax established under other provisions of the legislation."

25. The essential factors for section 61 to apply are:
  (a) there must be a transaction;
  (b) the transaction has the effect of reducing the tax payable by the taxpayer concerned; and
  (c) the transaction is artificial or fictitious, or that any disposition is not in fact given effect to.

The "transaction"

26. The scope of section 61 was considered in the Hong Kong tax cases *Rico Internationale Limited v. CIR [1965] 1 HKTC 229* and *Kum Hing Land Investment Company Limited v. CIR [1967] 1 HKTC 301*. Both cases concerned payment of commissions which were held to be artificial and fictitious as no real service was rendered. In the Kum Hing case, the Court held that the word "transaction" in section 61 must include the whole of any particular transaction, and not merely part of it. Therefore, "transaction" in that case was not merely the payment and receipt of the commission but included the whole transaction from the inception of the idea to pay commission to the final completion of the deal. The significance of this ruling is that although a part of the transaction (i.e. payment and receipt of commission) may be real, the transaction as a whole may be held as both artificial and fictitious. When the Assessor is considering whether or not a transaction as a whole is artificial or fictitious, he would take into consideration all the surrounding circumstances to form an opinion.

The meaning of artificial or fictitious

27. The words "artificial" and "fictitious" though not defined in the Ordinance have been considered in *CIR v. Douglas Henry Howe, 1 HKTC 936*. In the decision, Cons J followed the Privy Council decision in *Seramco Limited Superannuation Fund Trustee v. ITC [1977] AC 287* and adopted the following interpretations:

(a) "artificial" is an adjective in general use in the English language, capable of bearing a variety of meanings according to the context; and

(b) a "fictitious" transaction is one which those who are ostensibly the parties to it never intended should be carried out.

28. In *Cheung Wah Keung v. CIR, 5 HKTC 698*, Woo JA at the Court of Appeal held that whether a transaction which is commercially unrealistic must necessarily be regarded as being "artificial" depends on the circumstances of each particular case and that commercial realism can be one of the considerations for deciding artificiality. To ascertain whether a transaction is artificial, it is thus necessary to scrutinise the terms of the particular transaction to be impugned and the circumstances in which it was made and carried out.

29. When the transaction is disregarded pursuant to section 61, the Assessor must look at the reality of the payment and the relationship of parties to the transaction and then proceed to raise an assessment on the person concerned.

<h2 style="text-align:center">PART D —
GENERAL ANTI-AVOIDANCE PROVISION (SECTION 61A)</h2>

The position in general

30. The general anti-avoidance provision, section 61A, was introduced in 1986 to strike down blatant tax avoidance arrangements. While section 61A gives the Department a degree of discretion to disregard or reconstruct a transaction, it, like section 61 (see paragraph 24), is not a charging section; and a balance will be struck between the interests of the Department and taxpayers. The practice to be followed by this Department in applying section 61A will be in line with the stated policy which laid behind the introduction of this provision, namely, that it should strike down blatant or contrived tax avoidance arrangements but should not cast unnecessary inhibitions on normal commercial transactions by which taxpayers legitimately take advantage of opportunities available for the arrangement of their affairs.

31. In brief, the general anti-avoidance provision, section 61A, applies to any transaction entered into for the sole or dominant purpose of enabling a person to obtain a tax benefit. Where it applies section 61A provides for an assessment to be made as if the transaction or any part thereof had not been entered into or carried out or in such other manner as is considered necessary to counteract the tax benefit which would otherwise be obtained.

32. Section 61A is modelled on the Australian general anti-avoidance provision

(Part IVA of ITAA 1936). The Australian authorities on this topic are highly pertinent to the interpretation of this section.

Section 61A — the basic questions

33. In order that section 61A may apply to a taxpayer there are three prerequisites:
   (a)   there must be a transaction as defined;
   (b)   the taxpayer must obtain a tax benefit as defined; and
   (c)   having regard to seven specific matters, the transaction must be entered into or carried out for the sole or dominant purpose of enabling the taxpayer to obtain a tax benefit.

If the three prerequisites are satisfied, section 61A applies and the Assistant Commissioner shall cancel the tax benefit.

Existence of a "transaction"

34. "Transactio" is defined to include a transaction, operation or scheme whether or not such transaction, operation or scheme is or is intended to be enforceable by legal proceedings. The term will therefore cover situations involving single, multiple or composite transactions. In *Yick Fung Estates Limited v. CIR, 5 HKTC 52*, Rogers JA at the Court of Appeal ruled that a transaction can be carried out by a person alone and need not for two parties to be involved. In other words, a transaction can be carried out by a sole protagonist and includes a unilateral scheme, plan etc.

35. For section 61A to apply, the identified transaction, operation or scheme must fall within the broad definition of "transaction". In *FCT v. Spotless Services Limited, 32 ATR 309*, Cooper J at the Australian Federal Court said (at page 338):

> *"the parties to the scheme, insofar as they are known, must be identified and the terms or content of any agreement, arrangement, understanding, promise or undertaking and the steps or stages of any course of action or proposal, insofar as they are relevant, be identified. It is not sufficient to identify a scheme by reference to a hoped for fiscal outcome."*

36. In *FCT v. Peabody, 28 ATR 344*, the Australian High Court ruled that if a wider scheme has been identified, the Commissioner may also rely on a narrow scheme (sub-scheme) as meeting Part IVA. In other words, if part of a wider transaction may be identified as a transaction in itself, the Commissioner is not precluded from relying upon it for the purposes of section 61A.

Was a tax benefit obtained

37. "Tax benefit" is defined in section 61A(3) to mean "the avoidance or postponement of the liability to pay tax or the reduction in the amount thereof".

The Departmental view is that the definition contemplates the following situations:
(a) The avoidance of liability by getting out of the way of or escaping from or preventing an anticipated liability to tax in respect of income which has "accrued" to the taxpayer.
(b) The postponing of liability for tax by shifting the incidence of tax on an amount or stream of income to a later year or years.
(c) The reduction in the amount of tax by altering the quantum of assessable income to a level lower than it would have been or might reasonably be expected to have been but for the transaction.

38. In *Cheung Wah Keung v. CIR*, Woo JA rejected the argument that section 61A(3) requires some pre-existing liability to tax which is being avoided, or some pre-existing circumstances which would give rise to, or might be expected to give rise to, a liability to pay tax.

What was the sole or dominant purpose

39. Section 61A provides that in deciding the sole or dominant purpose of the person who entered into or carried out the transaction only seven specified matters are to be taken into account. These matters are:
(a) *The manner in which the transaction was entered into or carried out*
In considering the manner, the relevant factors to take into account include:
(i)   the way in which the particular transaction was structured;
(ii) the background of the transaction, the time at which the transaction was entered into and the alternative purposes which could objectively be attributed to the taxpayer in entering into the transaction;
(iii) whether the transaction which the taxpayer entered into was promoted by a professional adviser; and
(iv) the way in which the taxpayer operated before and after the transaction and the relevant commercial practices.

(b) *The form and substance of the transaction*
Form refers to the legal rights and obligations created by a transaction; it is the legal effect of the transaction. Substance on the other hand means the practical or commercial end result of a transaction as opposed to its legal effect. In considering this matter it is necessary to compare the legal effect of the transaction with its commercial end result.

(c) *The result in relation to the operation of this Ordinance that, but for this section, would have been achieved by the transaction*
The relevant result is that which would arise out of the normal operation of the provisions within the Ordinance excluding the possible application of section 61A. Equally relevant is the result which would have arisen had the transaction not been entered into. It involves a comparison

between the two results.

(d) *Any change in the financial position of the relevant person that has resulted, will result, or may reasonably be expected to result, from the transaction*
This matter compares the financial position of the relevant person after the transaction has been entered into with that which would have existed had the transaction not been entered into.

(e) *Any change in the financial position of any person who has, or has had, any connection (whether of a business, family or other nature) with the relevant person, being a change that has resulted, will result or may reasonably be expected to result from the transaction*
This matter focuses on the change in the financial position of any person connected with the transaction, irrespective of whether the person has any family or business connection with the taxpayer.

(f) *Whether the transaction has created rights and obligations which would not normally be created between persons dealing with each other at arm's length under a transaction of the kind in question*
This test looks at the rights or obligations created by the transaction in contrast to (a) above which looks at the method or manner in which it was entered into or carried out. The actual rights and obligations created are to be compared with those that would normally be created under a similar transaction carried out at arm's length. In making this comparison due regard must, of course, be given to the surrounding circumstances. The presence of unusual features arising from the transaction need to be carefully considered.

(g) *The participation in the transaction of a corporation resident or carrying on business outside Hong Kong*
This test requires, in particular, an examination of a special purpose vehicle to the transaction that was incorporated outside Hong Kong.

40. It is necessary for the Assistant Commissioner to consider each of the seven matters referred to in paragraphs (a) to (g) of section 61A(1). However, not all of the matters will be equally relevant in every case. Before a conclusion on purpose can be reached, the Assistant Commissioner must weigh carefully the seven matters and have regard to all the relevant evidence. Regard must be had to all the matters and not merely (c) which is the tax consequence criterion. The matters listed are of varying kinds and obviously do not have equal weight, for example, because there are seven matters it does not mean that a 14 per cent mark can be attached to each of them. In this regard, (a) and (b), the manner in which the transaction was entered into and form and substance are in the nature of items that form a background picture to the transaction and help to set the scene. The next three matters, (c) to (e), involve monetary questions: the tax saving for the taxpayer, how much he is otherwise in or out of pocket, and the same for connected persons. In other words, these three matters direct attention to the tax and non-tax economic realities of the transaction in question and call for a contrast between them. Finally there are matters (f) and (g) which, where they are present, can be relevant as indicators of a purpose of obtaining a tax benefit; they are not, however, conclusive.

41. Section 61A requires that having regard to the seven listed matters a decision must be made as to whether it would be concluded that the transaction was entered into for the sole or dominant purpose of obtaining the tax benefit in question. In arriving at the decision, the strength or otherwise of the various resulting conclusions in respect of the seven matters must be looked at globally. The conclusion in section 61A(1) is an objective one which a reasonable person would draw on the basis of the seven matters viewed in their proper context. It is also the Departmental view that because the words of section 61A are "would be concluded", and not "could be concluded" or "might reasonably be concluded", the provision will only be applied in cases where the sole or dominant tax purpose is clearly evident.

42. The presence of a commercial objective in a particular transaction does not mean that section 61A will necessarily have no application to that transaction. In *FCT v. Spotless Services Limited, 34 ATR 183*, the Australian High Court observed that a person may enter into or carry out a transaction for the dominant purpose of enabling the relevant person to obtain a tax benefit where that dominant purpose is consistent with the pursuit of commercial gain in the course of carrying on a business.

43. Although the conclusion under section 61A(1) is an objective one, it does not mean that the intention of the person or their advisers can never be relevant. In *FCT v. Consolidated Press Holdings Ltd, 47 ATR 229*, the Australian High Court ruled that there can be situations whereby attributing the purpose of a professional adviser to one or more persons to the transaction is both possible and appropriate. It is clear that subjective purpose is not one of the seven listed matters. However, evidence of the subjective purpose, in some cases, may be relevant to one or more of the seven matters.

44. Obviously no problems will arise in cases where the sole purpose of a transaction was to obtain a tax benefit or even where there were only two purposes. However, in cases where there are more than two purposes it may be more difficult to determine whether the "dominant" purpose was the obtaining of a tax benefit. At the same time, the words "dominant purpose" are well known in the field of taxation law and their interpretation should pose few problems. In *FCT v. Spotless Services Limited*, the Australian High Court observed that, in its ordinary meaning, "dominant" indicates that purpose which was the "ruling, prevailing, or most influential purpose". In other words, it is not a case of comparing individual purposes but of dividing those purposes into "tax purposes" on the one hand and "non-tax purposes" on the other. Before section 61A can apply those tax purposes must outweigh the non-tax purposes.

The mechanics of an assessment

45. Where the three prerequisites mentioned in paragraph 33 are satisfied, then section 61A(2) applies to enable an assessment to be made by an Assistant Commissioner by either of the following methods:
  (a) "as if the transaction or any part thereof had not been entered into or carried out" — this means that the assessment is made on the basis that the transaction or part of it did not take place and the tax liability of the taxpayer is arrived at by disregarding all the consequences of the transaction or part thereof.
  (b) "in such manner as the assistant commissioner considers appropriate to counteract the tax benefit which would otherwise be obtained" — here the Assistant Commissioner will form an opinion as to what the situation would have been had the transaction been carried out at "arm's lengt" or in a normal manner. In other words, he will make an assessment on the basis that the transaction did take place but was entered into or carried out in the manner normally employed in carrying out such a transaction by parties at arm's length.

46. Section 61A has an overriding effect and the Assistant Commissioner is entitled to counteract the tax benefit in an appropriate manner. In applying section 61A(2) the Assistant Commissioner will adopt the following broad principles:
  (a) The ultimate assessment to be made must be within the scope of the Ordinance. For example, an amount of income on which it is sought to charge the taxpayer must be an amount of income received or accrued (albeit by a person other than the taxpayer now to be charged) and properly chargeable on general principles.
  (b) Where a taxpayer could have achieved a particular financial result in two different ways, one of which would have attracted tax and the other not, there being no abnormal features in either event, the Assistant Commissioner will not contend that an assessment should be made on the basis that the taxpayer followed a method which would have attracted tax. In other words, the Department accepts that a taxpayer is not obliged to maximise his tax liability.
  (c) A manner appropriate to counteract a tax benefit may involve:
       (i) Making adjustments to assessments for years subsequent to the year of assessment in which the transaction was entered into where the tax benefit would otherwise have been obtained in those subsequent years;
       (ii) Making corresponding adjustments to assessments of other persons affected by the transaction. For example, if a particular amount of income received by one person is to be assessed to another person

pursuant to section 61A then that income will be deleted from the assessment of the original recipient.

47. Where the situation demands, the Assistant Commissioner will seek to assess, and to issue assessments to, more than one person in respect of the same tax benefit. In *Nina T. H. Wang v. CIR, 3 HKTC 483*, Mayo J recognised at the Court of Appeal that there was no inherent objection to the Commissioner entertaining alternative assessments. Although it is possible for multiple concurrent assessments in respect of the same benefit to co-exist, the Assistant Commissioner will exercise the power under section 61A(2) to ensure that tax will ultimately be collected from the relevant person truly liable.

Application of the two general anti-avoidance provisions

48. Sections 61 and 61A give similar powers to disregard the transaction in question. In *Cheung Wah Keung v. CIR*, the Court of Appeal held that the application of the two sections, both aiming at tax-avoidance transactions, is not mutually exclusive. The decision of the Court of Appeal in the Yick Fung case also makes it clear that the "choice principle" has no application in relation to section 61A, namely a taxpayer is not entitled to "choose" to enter into a transaction which has a sole or dominant purpose of enabling him to obtain a tax benefit.

49. Where a tax avoidance arrangement has been made to exploit a specific relief or exemption afforded by a particular section of the Ordinance in such a way that is not intended by the legislature, the general anti-avoidance provisions of sections 61 and 61A can be applied to deny the favourable tax consequences even if the taxpayer has complied literally with the requirements of the particular section. The case in point is *CIR v. Challenge Corporation Limited [1986] STC 548*, which has decided that a general anti-avoidance provision is of general application and can apply to specific relief/exemption provisions. The Challenge case has also decided that a general anti-avoidance provision can apply notwithstanding the existence of specific anti-avoidance provisions. It is relevant to note that in *Yick Fung*, Rogers JA said (at page 119) "the wording of section 61A " ... that transaction has, or would have had but for this section, the effect ... "makes quite clear that section 61A has an overriding effect".

PART E —
LOSS COMPANIES (SECTION 61B)

The position in general

50. The Ordinance has always contained provisions which enable companies, which in a year of assessment have sustained a loss in any trade, profession or business, to carry forward the amount of that loss for set-off against profits in subsequent years of assessment. The Inland Revenue (Amendment) Ordinance

1986 introduced provisions which seek to give effect to a policy of restricting the trafficking in loss companies for the purpose of tax avoidance. In general terms, section 61B is aimed at the situation where companies with accumulated tax losses are sold for their losses to the proprietors of businesses which are trading profitably. Once ownership of the loss company has changed hands the profitable business is introduced into the company and the losses brought forward are set off against profits derived. Section 61B will restrict this avoidance practice by allowing the Commissioner to refuse to set off losses brought forward where he is satisfied that the sole or dominant purpose of a change in shareholding was the utilisation of those losses to obtain a tax benefit.

Matters for consideration

51. For the purpose of section 61B the Department would consider a change of shareholding as having been effected whenever shares are transferred from one person to another person. In other words, a change of shareholding takes place when shares are transferred to a person who was not previously a shareholder and also when shares are transferred from one existing shareholder, who may or may not continue to be a shareholder, to another existing shareholder.

52. The second element to the application of section 61B is the Commissioner's satisfaction that as a direct or indirect result of the change in shareholding, "profits" have been received by or accrued to the company during any year of assessment. In order to decide whether profits have been received as a result of the change of shareholding the flow of profits before and after the change will be examined, having particular regard to matters such as:
    (a)   the nature and conduct of the company's business,
    (b)   income and expenditure patterns,
    (c)   management and control,
    (d)   the background of the party to whom shares were transferred.

53. It should also be noted that section 61B refers to profits received during "any" year of assessment. Consequently, section 61B may apply even where profits are introduced in any year subsequent to the change of shareholding.

54. The final matter which must be considered is whether the sole or dominant purpose of the change in shareholding was the utilisation of the losses to avoid or reduce the tax liability of the company or any other person. In other tax jurisdictions comparable legislation uses as indicators of purpose factors such as, continuity of business and level of ownership and major changes in the nature and conduct of business. These matters will obviously have some relevance in Hong Kong. At the same time it is recognised that because of the more dynamic economic environment existing in Hong Kong other factors may constitute more important indicators of purpose. Furthermore it has never been the intention that section 61B should create unnecessary inhibitions in the case of genuine commercial company acquisitions or group reconstruction which involve changes in shareholding. It is therefore not likely that the Department would attempt to apply section 61B in these situations. Finally, in applying section 61B the Department will regard the phrase "dominant purpose" as having the same meaning as that explained in paragraph 44 in relation to section 61A. In other words the dominant purpose is the purpose which outweighs all other purposes combined.

PART F — RAMSAY PRINCIPLE

55. The Ramsay principle was developed by the courts in the United Kingdom to strike out intermediate steps in a series of transactions or a composite transaction, which were entered into for no commercial purpose, so as to subject the end result of the transaction to scrutiny for tax purposes.

56. This principle is regarded as an approach in statutory interpretation, a purposive interpretation, in a number of English and Hong Kong cases such as *Collector of Stamp Revenue v. Arrowtown Assets Ltd 6 HKTC 273*. The principle as explained by Ribeiro PJ in Arrowtown was adopted by the House of Lords in *Barclays Mercantile Business Finance Limited v. Mawson [2005] STC 1* (at page 13):

> "[T]he driving principle in the *Ramsay* line of cases continues to involve a general rule of statutory construction and an unblinkered approach to the analysis of the facts. The ultimate question is whether the relevant statutory provisions, construed purposively, were intended to apply to the transaction, viewed realistically."

57. In applying the provisions laid down in the Ordinance, the Commissioner is entitled to adopt this purposive interpretation of the statutory provisions to the facts viewed realistically. Being an interpretation approach, the Ramsay principle can co-exist and operate alongside the general anti-avoidance provisions. As was stated by *Lord Cooke* (at page 920) in *IRC v. McGuckian [1997] STC 908*, the Ramsay approach to the interpretation of taxing Acts did not depend on general anti-avoidance provisions such as were found in Australasia; rather, it was antecedent to or collateral with them. Under this principle, the Commissioner in appropriate cases is thus entitled to look at the substance of the transactions and not just their legal forms. Sir Anthony Mason also expounded the Ramsay principle in *Shiu Wing Ltd. v. CED 5 HKTC 338* (at page 411). He said the principle was both a rule of statutory construction applicable to revenue statutes and an approach to the analysis of facts. Where there was a single pre-ordained, composite transaction intended to be carried out in its entirety, the Commissioner would not ignore the composite character and apply the legislation to the individual constituent steps separately. If the purpose of intermediate steps in the composite transaction was fiscal, the Commissioner would disregard them and bring the composite transaction within a charging provision.

PART G — PENALTY ON TAX AVOIDANCE CASES

58. Penalties are provided in the Ordinance to ensure compliance by taxpayers with the various statutory requirements. In the present context, non-compliance includes, among other things, the submission of incorrect returns and giving incorrect statement or information. Any wrongdoing in these respects committed "wilfully with intent to evade or to assist any person to evade tax" (section 82) or "without reasonable excuse" (sections 80 and 82A) may attract penalty by way of prosecution or imposition of pecuniary penalty.

59. Penalty action is therefore not confined to evasion cases, but may also apply to tax avoidance cases to which the general anti-avoidance provisions have been successfully applied, provided that the conditions laid down in the relevant penalty provision have been satisfied. Thus, the mere labeling of a scheme as a tax avoidance scheme may not exonerate the taxpayer from penalty.

60. Generally speaking, tax evasion attracts heavier penalty than tax avoidance. However, the dividing line between the two is very thin. As a simple practical test to distinguish the two: if a scheme whose possibility of success is entirely dependent upon the Department never finding out the true facts (i.e. facts have not been disclosed in the return, accounts or any statement submitted to the Department), it is likely to be a scheme of tax evasion rather than tax avoidance.

61. On the penalty aspect of tax avoidance cases, the Department takes the following views:
   (a) Whether a certain tax avoidance scheme may be regarded as a tax evasion arrangement and be penalised as such depends on the availability of evidence to prove that the tax avoidance scheme was a sham set up for the purposes of tax evasion. No single factor may conclusively lead to such a conclusion. The wrongdoer would be penalised if there is sufficient admissible evidence to prove that the taxpayer and/or his tax advisor has committed an offence under section 80(2) or section 82 of the Ordinance;
   (b) The provisions in section 61/61A and section 80(2)/82A are not mutually exclusive. As such, penalty actions can be invoked under section 80(2) or section 82A against the taxpayer concerned regardless of whether section 61 or section 61A has been applied to bring the profits/income in question into the tax net.

62. In considering whether any penalty action should be invoked, the facts and the circumstances of the particular case will be carefully examined. In general, the Department will impose penalty on the taxpayers if there were elements of dishonesty or fraudulence involving the use of artificial or fictitious devices, or where the transactions (e.g. expenditure claims) were false or unsubstantiated.

**PART H —
GUIDELINES ON LEASE FINANCING**

Leases in general

63. Following the enactment of section 39E with its application to sale and leaseback and certain leveraged lease situations it is considered appropriate to lay down what the Department considers are basic requirements for all leases. In this regard in recent years it has become clear that some so-called leases are in fact purchase agreements. The position has now been reached where it will be necessary for Assessors to carefully consider whether payments made by a "lessee" are lease rentals or whether they are, in substance, consideration for the sale of the goods purported to be leased. In the latter case, of course, the payments would be outgoings of a capital nature which are not deductible for profits tax purposes although they may qualify for initial and annual allowances.

64. In line with tax administrations in other parts of the world, factors to be examined by this Department to determine the question will include:
  (a) the existence of any agreement, express or implied, and whether in the lease agreement or in subsidiary documents or correspondence, under which the property in the goods would pass from the lessor to the lessee, and
  (b) the degree of relativity between the "residual value", by which the amount of monthly lease rentals is usually determined, and the reasonable commercial value of the goods at the expiry date of the lease.

65. So far as factor (a) is concerned, an agreement will generally be regarded as a purchase agreement if the lessee has a right or option to purchase the goods. If in the opinion of the Commissioner, such right or option would reasonably be expected not to be exercised, then such an agreement, notwithstanding its form, is a lease as defined. An agreement will be accepted as a lease, as distinct from a purchase agreement, if the lessee does not, either during the term of the lease or at its end, have an obligation, right or option to purchase the goods. It will correspondingly be unacceptable if the lessor has a right or option to require the lessee to purchase. An agreement is unlikely to be accepted as a lease if an associate of the lessee is given an obligation, right or option to purchase or the lessor has a right or option to require an associate of the lessee to purchase on the basis that such an arrangement is made to circumvent the law. Any right in the lessee to nominate a third party purchaser will be examined to ensure that it does not amount to an arrangement for purchase. An agreement for the lessee to have obligations, rights or options to lease the goods for extended further periods, and the terms of any such extension will also be examined to determine whether the entire arrangement really amounts to a purchase.

66. As to residual values, it is the usual commercial practice for the amount of rent to be calculated, in so far as it is designed to cover the cost of the goods, on the basis of the difference between the cost of the goods and their assessed residual value at the end of the lease. Accordingly, the larger the residual value, the smaller would be the lease rentals. The residual value should represent a fair estimate of the market value of the goods at expiration of the lease.

Leveraged leases

67. In situations where the tax deferral benefits to a leveraged lessor represent a substantial part of the lessor's effective return on its own (non-leveraged) investment there may be a question whether section 61A would apply, i.e. whether it would be concluded that a lessor's participation had attaching to it a sole or dominant purpose of obtaining a tax benefit. It is therefore considered appropriate to set out the Department's views on the minimum standards with which leveraged lease transactions must comply if they are to be acceptable under the Ordinance. In this regard it is expected that future leveraged lease transactions should observe the following requirements.

Period of the lease

68. Generally, the lease period should not exceed 10 years. In appropriate cases the Department will consider longer periods where it can be established that the leased machinery or plant has an economic life greater than 10 years.

Rental rebate

69. Lease transactions which provide for a rental rebate to be paid to the lessee upon expiry or termination of the lease will not be acceptable.

Number of partners

70. Transactions involving more than 3 partners or where any partner's share in the profits/losses of the partnership is less than 30% will not be acceptable.

Partnership accounting period

71. Where partners in a leveraged lease partnership have common accounting periods, the return of income of the partnership should be furnished for the same accounting period. Where the partners do not share common accounting periods the Department will, as a general proposition, accept a partnership accounting period which corresponds to that of the majority partner(s).

Losses

72. The transaction should result in assessable profits to the partnership, before the set-off of losses, after the first three years' operation of the lease. The Department requires a profit of at least 1% of the cost of machinery or plant in the fourth year of assessment.

Rental structure

73. The total rental payable under the lease should be payable in equal amounts over the term of the lease — pro-rata in the first year where that year is less than a full year of income. Where rentals are payable in arrears it is expected that the partnership will return as assessable profits for a year the amount of rent that has been earned during the year; ie the assessable profits for a year will include rentals accrued at the end of the year.

Ships and aircraft

74. The lessee/ultimate end user must be a Hong Kong operator (see paragraph 20). Transactions involving ships will not generally be given a clearance.

Advances by lessee

75. The lease should not involve any arrangement for the lodging by the lessee with the lessor of security deposits or for the lessee to make any kind of advance to the lessor. In relation to partners' capital contributions, this requirement would extend to any indirect arrangements having much the same practical effect as an advance by the lessee to the lessor. No objection will be taken, however, where the lessee enters into back-to-back loan arrangements with the lessor on identical terms and conditions that apply to an existing loan between the lessee and a third party lender where that loan had been raised originally by the lessee to purchase the machinery or plant.

Premature termination of lease

76. If the lessee has a right to terminate the lease on payment of an amount to the lessor — for example, once the tax-loss phase of the partnership's life has passed — the amount so paid will be treated as assessable profits of the partnership. Similarly, amounts received by partners for an assignment of partnership interests will be regarded as assessable profits of the recipient.

Interest

77. Interest on moneys borrowed to produce assessable profits is incurred, and thus is allowable as a deduction, when it becomes due and payable. However, transactions under which more than what would normally be a year's interest is sought to be deducted in one year — or more than an appropriate portion where the first income year is not a complete year — will not be acceptable. Transactions which will not be acceptable will include those where the whole of the interest applicable to a loan is payable by instalments before any repayments of principal are to be made, and those where interest is capitalised back into a loan in any year because, inter alia, rental is insufficient to meet commitments under the loan.

Non-recourse debt

78. Financing on a recourse basis should be for at least 51% of the cost of the machinery or plant throughout the term of the lease.

Equity

79. In cases which do not involve a limited partnership it is expected that lessors themselves contribute capital for at least 35% of the cost of the machinery or plant. Interest free and interest bearing loans, even with recourse, will not be accepted. The minimum capital contribution should be maintained throughout the term of the lease. The partners must be fully at risk in relation to their capital contributions to the partnership. Arrangements, direct or indirect but having the same practical effect, which would result in reducing the capital at risk by the partners below 35% of the cost of the machinery or plant are not acceptable. The Department will not accept lease transactions where the partners use borrowed funds to specifically finance their capital contributions to the lease partnership. Such capital contributions will be required to be financed from the general pool of funds out of which the partner funds assets in the normal course of business.

Profit Motive

80. The lessors (which generally should be financial institutions) must demonstrate a profit motive, aside from gaining tax benefits, for the transaction. This will generally be regarded by the Department as being satisfied where the aggregate taxable income of the lessors (or investors) over the term of the lease, after the set-off of losses, is not less than 1% of the cost of the machinery or plant.

General

81. Leveraged lease transactions that do not comply with these requirements may lead the Department to conclude that the arrangement has a sole or dominant purpose of obtaining a tax benefit. On the other hand it should not be assumed that because a transaction does comply it will thereby not be considered in the context of section 61A. There are other aspects of lease arrangements which do not lend themselves to specific guidelines but which, if encountered in practice, may lead to a conclusion that the arrangement has a dominant purpose of obtaining a tax benefit.

82. Finally, the requirements set out above will be reviewed from time to time and amended as necessary in the light of actual experience.

PART I — ADVANCE RULINGS

Information to be supplied

83. The Department requires maximum disclosure in connection with requests for advance rulings. A request for an advance ruling must contain the information and documents as listed in paragraph 15 of Departmental Interpretation and Practice Notes No. 31 ("Advance Rulings"). The specific information required to be provided in respect of rulings on leveraged lease transactions, general anti-avoidance provision (section 61A) and changes in shareholding are set out below:

1. Leveraged lease transactions

(a) Lessee
  (i)   Full name and Profits Tax file number.
  (ii) Place of incorporation and residence.
  (iii) Place of operations at which the lessee proposes to use the equipment to be leased.
  (iv) If the arrangements are to be a sale and lease back, advise the date on which the equipment was first used or is proposed to be first used by the lessee and/or by any associate of the lessee.
  (v)   Where a headlease or loan financing is involved, details of the arrangement, cash collaterals, cash flows, interest and other deductions should be provided.

(b) Equipment to be leased
  (i)   Sequence of events, including dates, relating to the ordering, delivery and construction, if any, of the equipment.
  (ii) A schedule of the equipment showing for each item, its cost, its depreciation rates and the amount of its cost qualifying for initial and annual depreciation allowances.
  (iii) A break-up of costs will be necessary where costs exceed amounts payable to suppliers and construction contractors.
  (iv) The proposed residual value and how it has been determined.
  (v)   Advise whether any item of the equipment has previously been subject to advance clearance/advance ruling applied for by the lessee or any other person and if so, give the details.

(c) Lessor partnership
  (i)   Full name of the partnership.
  (ii) Full names of the partners, their book balance dates and the amount of equity to be contributed by each.
  (iii) Advise nature of each partner's normal business operations.
  (iv) Profits Tax file number of each partner.
  (v)   The amount of debt, equity and the debt equity ratio.

(vi) A statement of the forecast annual partnership losses and profits over the term of the lease, including details of rental, depreciation, interest and other deductions.

(vii) A statement setting out details of all cash flows, with dates, forming part of or associated with the leasing arrangements, supported by explanations of any cash flows that do not enter into the calculation of the partnership losses or profits.

(viii) A statement showing in the event of an early termination of the lease details of the termination sums payable to the lessor and how the lessor's aggregate taxable income of not less than 1% of the cost of machinery or plant (see paragraph 80) can be achieved.

(ix) A statement showing the return on investment in the leveraged lease partnership to be derived by each partner and how it is calculated.

(d) Borrowings

(i) A schedule of borrowings including dates and the amount of each draw down.

(ii) A schedule of proposed repayments of principal and payments of interest, including dates.

(iii) Rates of interest.

(iv) Where a lessee to lessor loan is involved details as in (i), (ii) and (iii) above should be provided in respect of the reciprocal loan between the lessee and lender.

(v) Where the borrowings are secured by deposit or loan, or sub-participation arrangement is in place, give details as in (i), (ii) and (iii) above.

(e) Documents and information

(i) A set of all documentation involved should be provided.

(ii) Expected date of execution.

(iii) The period of the lease.

(iv) Draw attention to any provisions in the documents that may have a bearing on tax considerations, eg options or rights in the lessee or an associate to purchase.

II. General anti-avoidance provision — section 61A

(a) The transaction

Full details of each stage of the proposed transaction, operation or scheme including:

(i) its proposed date of execution; and,

(ii) its purpose.

(b) The parties

The following particulars in respect of all parties to the transaction:

(i) full name and address;

(ii) in the case of corporations, place of incorporation;

    (iii) Hong Kong business registration number and Profits Tax file number, if any; and,

    (iv) any relevant connection between the parties, for example, whether individuals are family relatives, whether corporations are in any way associated, whether individuals have shareholdings in corporations, etc.

(c) The details

All the details which are necessary to form a conclusion as to the purpose of the transaction having regard to the seven matters prescribed in section 61A (1) — in this regard refer to paragraph 39 of the notes.

III. Loss companies

(a) The loss company itself
    (i)   Full name and address.
    (ii) Business registration number and Profits Tax file number.
    (iii) Details of proposed changes in shareholding including full names and addresses of both vendor and purchaser together with the number of shares to change hand.
    (iv) Likely changes in management to be made after change in shareholding.

(b) Business of loss company
    (i)   Details of business carried on by the loss company before the proposed change in shareholding, including its profitability.
    (ii) Proposed changes to (i) to be made after change in shareholding.
    (iii) Details of business presently engaged by persons who are to acquire shares in the loss company.

(c) Acquisition
    (i)   The manner in which vendor and purchaser were introduced to each other.
    (ii) Any prior connections between vendor and purchaser.
    (iii) The reasons for the sale and acquisition.

84. In relation to advance rulings on leveraged lease transactions, the Department should be advised of the name of the lessor partnership and its business registration number as soon as they are available. When the initial Profits Tax return is submitted a copy of all relevant documentation to the transaction should be forwarded. In the case where aircraft is involved, this should include a copy of the Certificate of Acceptance.

Time for the lodgement of ruling requests on proposed leveraged lease transactions

85. Requests for advance rulings on proposed leveraged lease transactions must be filed at least 8 weeks from the anticipated implementation date of the contemplated arrangement. The Department will not accept applications where the anticipated implementation date for the transaction is more than 5 months after the date of application. Failure to supply any required information may lead to the Department's refusal of the application. A minimum period of 8 weeks will generally be required to process applications. However, the Department will not be bound by such period if the application does not contain all material information required for its processing.

86. The Department will not entertain applications for holdover of provisional tax lodged by the partners in the leveraged lease partnership if the request for an advance ruling has not been filed at least 8 weeks before the due date for payment of the provisional tax.

APPENDIX 11

Departmental Interpretation & Practice Notes
No. 16 (Revised)

SALARIES TAX
TAXATION OF FRINGE BENEFITS

These notes are issued for the information and guidance of taxpayers and their authorised representatives. They have no binding force and do not affect a person's right of objection or appeal to the Commissioner, the Board of Review or the Courts.

These notes replace those issued on 29 January 1991.

LAU MAK Yee-ming, Alice
Commissioner of Inland Revenue

October 2003

Our web site: http://www.info.gov.hk/ird

DEPARTMENTAL INTERPRETATION AND PRACTICE NOTES
No. 16 (REVISED)

CONTENT

Notes

INTRODUCTION

Following the enactment of the Inland Revenue (Amendment) Ordinance 1991 ("the 1991 Amendment"), it is considered necessary to explain why the Ordinance has been amended and lay down broad statements on the practice to be adopted by the Inland Revenue Department in relation to the taxation of fringe benefits received by employees and office holders. In the latter regard, this Practice Note is concerned with fringe benefits other than direct monetary payments to employees and benefits in respect of accommodation and gains from shares and stock.

BACKGROUND TO THE 1991 AMENDMENT

2. The case of *David Hardy Glynn v The Commissioner of Inland Revenue 3 HKTC 245* had significant implications in relation to the taxation of fringe benefits and ultimately led to the introduction of the 1991 Amendment under consideration. Before turning to the significance of the decision, it is relevant to outline the assessing practice followed by the Department in respect of fringe benefits before the case arose.

Pre-*Glynn* Assessing Practice

3. Section 8(1) of the Ordinance lays the charge to Salaries Tax on "every person in respect of his income arising in or derived from Hong Kong" from any office or employment of profit and any pension. There is no exhaustive definition of "income from any office or employment". However, some of the more common kinds of income are enumerated in section 9(1) and the word "perquisite", albeit undefined, has been included since the introduction of the Ordinance.

4. Prior to the *Glynn* case, it was accepted by the Department and practitioners generally that principles derived from UK case law determined whether perquisites, or fringe benefits, were taxable. The Department's assessing practice was based on the understanding that UK decisions had established that benefits received in a form other than money, unless covered by specific provisions in the Ordinance, could only be treated as chargeable income if they took the form of "money's worth". A benefit was regarded as constituting money's worth if it was capable of being converted into money (by sale or some other means) by the recipient or involved the discharge of a personal liability of the employee. On the other hand, if the Department recognized that the employee was not liable for the relevant expense and the benefit was inconvertible, it was generally accepted that the benefit was not chargeable.

5. With regard to education benefits, however, the Department consistently took the view that any payment made by an employer in respect of education expenses of an employee's child represented a chargeable benefit to the employee. This position was based on the understanding that it was not possible for an employee as a parent to transfer the liability for the education of his children to a third party. Any payment made by the employer was treated as discharging the employee's liability and accordingly regarded as "money's worth".

The *Glynn* Case — the Court of Appeal decision

6. In the *Glynn* case, school fees in respect of Mr. Glynn's daughter were paid direct to the school by his employer. The issue, in broad terms, was whether the payments constituted chargeable income of Mr. Glynn or escaped chargeability by virtue of the arrangements used to make the payments.

7. The majority of the Court of Appeal held that the payments in question had been correctly treated by the Department as being chargeable to Salaries Tax. The decision (reported in *2 HKTC 383*) was significant in at least two respects. Firstly, because all three members of the Court agreed that it had wrongly been assumed that UK authorities were directly relevant and applicable in Hong Kong and, secondly, because a majority found that the word "perquisite" in the Ordinance should be given its wide ordinary meaning. A strict application of the decision would have required the taxation of all benefits derived by an employee from his employment.

The Administration's response to the Court of Appeal decision

8. In view of the implications of the decision, particularly in relation to the identification and valuation of benefits, the Administration decided that the Ordinance should be amended to accord with the practice followed by the Department before the *Glynn* case arose. This decision was announced by the Department in a public statement issued in March 1989. It was also announced that the Department would continue to apply its pre-Glynn practice pending the introduction of the legislation. Shortly afterwards, drafting work commenced on the proposed legislation but finalization was held in abeyance pending the outcome of Mr. Glynn's appeal to the Privy Council.

Outcome of the Privy Council Appeal

9. In contrast to the Court of Appeal's decision, the Privy Council held that UK authorities on the meaning of expressions in UK tax legislation are of assistance in construing identical expressions in the Ordinance concerning the same subject matter. It was also held that "perquisite" has the same meaning in the Ordinance as it has in the UK legislation.

10. The decision (reported in *3 HKTC 245*) reflected the Department's pre-Glynn understanding of what constituted a chargeable perquisite to the extent that it recognized that the term includes:

(a) money which can be obtained from property which is capable of being converted into money; and

(b) money which is paid in discharge of a debt of the employee.

However, the Judicial Committee went further when it held that there is no difference between a debt of the taxpayer discharged by an employer pursuant to the contract of service and money paid for the benefit of an employee by his employer pursuant to the contract of service. The Privy Council was of the view that money paid at the request of an employee is equivalent to money paid to the employee. In this regard it was stated that an identifiable sum required to be expended by an employer pursuant to a contract of service for the benefit of the employee, is money paid at the request of the employee and is taxable as either part of the employee's salary or as a monetary perquisite.

11. The decision did not, however, encompass all benefits derived by an employee from his employment. Inconvertible benefits not involving the expenditure of money or expenditure not attributable wholly or proportionately to one employee were recognized as not being chargeable[1]. As an example, the Privy Council mentioned a nursery school provided by an employer for the children of all its employees. It also accepted that benefits resulting from expenditure by an employer for a non-contractual reason — for example on compassionate grounds — escaped chargeability if lacking the elements of expectation and continuity. The Privy Council's position concerning such benefits reflected the Department's pre-Glynn practice.

12. On the other hand, the decision represented a departure from the Department's pre-Glynn practice in that it was not consistent with the view that an inconvertible benefit escaped chargeability to Salaries Tax if the employer rather that the employee was the party liable for the payment of the relevant expense.

13. As the Privy Council's decision in the *Glynn* case confirmed that not all employment benefits come within the charge to Salaries Tax, it mitigated to a certain extent the effects of the Court of Appeals decision. Nevertheless, the decision, and in particular its effective rejection of the "liability test" as a determinant of chargeability, made it clear that the scope of the then legislation was wider than the Department had understood it to be pre-Glynn.

DETAILS OF THE 1991 AMENDMENT

14. As foreshadowed in the announcement after the Court of Appeal decision, the Ordinance was amended to accord with the Department's pre-Glynn assessing practice in respect of fringe benefits. A "liability test", contained in subparagraph (iv) to section 9(1)(a), was introduced to exclude from chargeability any benefit where the relevant payment is one for which the employer has the sole liability. The exclusion does not apply to any payment made by an employer to discharge a liability of an employee and, as previously, such a payment would normally be chargeable to Salaries Tax as a perquisite.

15. The exclusion provided by section 9(1)(a)(iv) is subject to section 9(2A)[2], which ensures that convertible benefits and education benefits remain chargeable to Salaries Tax, even if it can be argued that the employer has the liability for the relevant payment.

16. Two definitions were added to section 9(6)[3] of the Ordinance. A definition of "child of an employee", along the lines used in Part V of the Ordinance, has been inserted for the purposes of the provision concerning the taxation of education benefits. The second definition is of "employee" and this has been defined to include a holder of an office. This latter definition has been included to make it clear that the exclusion of benefits from chargeable income by section 9(1)(a)(iv) applies to an employee and an office holder. Further, the definition ensures that accommodation benefits provided to office holders are chargeable to the same extent as those provided to employees.

17. Section 8(2)(g) of the Ordinance has been amended to confirm that the exemption from Salaries Tax in respect of amounts arising from educational endowments applies only for the benefit of the person receiving the relevant education. This is to preclude any argument that an education benefit, provided by an employer in respect of a child of an employee, is not chargeable income of the employee by virtue of section 8(2)(g).

TREATMENT OF PARTICULAR BENEFITS

18. Set out below are details of how the Department views the taxation position of various categories of non-cash fringe benefits derived by employees and office holders from their employers or others. As the particular arrangements under which fringe benefits are provided can have a bearing on the taxation consequences, the examples provided are in broad terms only. It must be stressed that whilst the Department recognizes and accepts that employment packages may legitimately be structured in a variety of ways, action will be taken in respect of blatant or contrived tax avoidance arrangements. In the latter regard, it is relevant that section 61A of the Ordinance provides that, in broad terms, where it is concluded that a transaction has been entered into for the sole or dominant purpose of obtaining a tax benefit, an assessment may be made in a manner appropriate to counter the tax benefit. Furthermore, section 61 of the Ordinance provides for artificial or fictitious transactions and dispositions to be disregarded. However, in relation to the examples below it has been assumed that the benefits are provided under circumstances which would not warrant the application of the anti-avoidance provisions.

Liability of Employee discharged by Employer

19. The Privy Council confirmed in the *Glynn* case that perquisite includes money which is paid in discharge of a debt of the employee. This position has not been affected by the 1991 Amendment discussed above. Accordingly, where such a payment is made by an employer, the amount of the payment is regarded by the Department as chargeable income of the employee.

Convertible Benefits

20. The Privy Council also confirmed that perquisite includes money which can be obtained from property which is capable of being converted into money. The introduction of the "liability test" in section 9(1)(a)(iv) has not affected the position. Section 9(2A)[2] provides that the test shall not operate to exclude from income "any benefit capable of being converted into money by the recipient"[4].

21. Where a benefit takes the form of an asset which can be converted into money by sale, the Department's basic approach will be to take as the amount assessable the sum which the asset might reasonably be expected to fetch if sold in the open market at the time of receipt of the benefit; i.e. the "second-hand" value[5].

22. Benefits[6] which are not convertible into money by sale are sometimes convertible by other means. For example, an employee might be provided by his employer with the free use (but not ownership) of a car under an arrangement which would allow the employee to "surrender" the car and take additional wages instead. Such a benefit would be viewed by the Department as being convertible into money and accordingly chargeable (see *Heaton v Bell 46 TC 211*). It is not possible to lay down hard and fast valuation rules to cover benefits which come within this category. The approach taken will depend on the nature of the benefit and the circumstances under which it is provided. In general terms, however, the aim will be to ascertain, as objectively as possible, the amount of money the employee could obtain if he chose to ìconvertî the benefit. For the example given, the Department would treat as assessable income each year the amount of additional wages the employee would have received if he had chosen to forego the benefit.

Education Benefits

23. Amounts "paid by an employer in connection with the education of a child of an employee" are by virtue of section 9(2A) not subject to the "liability test" in section 9(1)(a)(iv). Accordingly, where such a payment is made pursuant to the employee's contract of employment, then irrespective of whether the employee or the employer is the party liable for the relevant expense, the amount paid will be treated as chargeable income of the employee.

24. The Department will interpret the expression "paid by an employer in connection with the education of a child" as covering not only payments for tuition expenses, but also payments for incidental education expenses such as boarding fees and the cost of school outings. Amounts paid before 1 April 2003 in respect of passages in connection with education are not chargeable by virtue of the terms of sections 9(1)(a)(i) and (ii) of the Ordinance. However, with the repeal of sections 9(1)(a)(i) and (ii) by Revenue (No. 2) Ordinance 2003, these payments will be chargeable with effect from 1 April 2003.

25. In accordance with the decision in an English case, *Barclays Bank v Naylor 39 TC 256*, the Department recognizes that an employee does not receive a chargeable benefit where a payment is made in respect of education expenses of his or her child using income of the child which has been provided by a genuine discretionary trust funded by the employer.

Car (or Boat) made available by an Employer for the Private Use of an Employee

26. Where an employee is allowed to use for private purposes a car owned by his employer, the Department accepts that the benefit is not chargeable, provided that the employee is not in any way able to convert the benefit into money [compare the position outlined at para. 22 above].

27. If ownership of the car is transferred to the employee, the benefit is chargeable to Salaries Tax at its convertible value at the time of receipt [see para. 21 above].

28. A chargeable benefit will also arise if the employer discharges an expense relating to private use for which the employee is liable. The assessable amount will be the sum paid by the employer to discharge the expense [see para. 19 above].

Recreational Facilities/Holiday Homes provides for the Use of Employees

29. Such benefits are not chargeable to Salaries Tax, provided that the employee is not in any way able to convert the benefit into money.

Payment of Utilities by the Employer

30. Where an employer is the only party liable to pay the cost of utilities provided to an employee's residence, payments made by the employer come within the scope of the new exclusion from income [section 9(1)(a)(iv)]. Since utilities provided cannot be converted by the employee into money, the exception to the exclusion in respect of convertible benefits [section 9(2A)(a)] does not apply. As a matter of practice, if the account rendered by the utility company is in the name of the employer only, the Department will accept that no chargeable benefit arises.

31. Other benefits supplied in respect of an employee's residence — such as furniture and domestic servants — will also not be chargeable to tax if they are provided under circumstances where the employer is the only party liable for the relevant expense and the employee cannot convert the benefit into money.

Loans provided to Employees at less than Market Interest Rates

32. The Department accepts that interest-free and low interest loans provided by employers to employees are not chargeable benefits where the cost involved in providing the benefit is the sole liability of the employer. This acceptance is based on the understanding that the benefit received by the employee (i.e. paying less that market rates) is not of itself convertible into money.

Credit Cards

33. Credit cards are sometimes provided by employers to employees under arrangements where expenses charged using the card are billed to and paid for the employer. Where such a card is used for private purposes by an employee, the Department considers that the benefit obtained is chargeable to Salaries Tax. This is because in ordinary usage the holder of the card (i.e. the employee) has a liability to pay for the goods or services received which is effectively discharged by the employer when the card is used. As discussed in para. 19 above, the amount of the liability so discharged represents a chargeable benefit.

Club Benefits

34. It is accepted that no chargeable benefit arises in respect of the cost of acquisition of corporate membership of a club. The Department recognizes that as entitlement to corporate membership benefits may be transferred from one employee to another it is not possible to attribute such expenditure to a particular employee. On the other hand, where an employer makes a payment in respect of an individual membership fee or other club expense for which an employee is personally liable, the payment will constitute chargeable income of the employee.

Holiday Journey Benefits

35. Prior to 1 April 2003, the value of any holiday warrant or passage granted by an employer to an employee was exempt from salaries tax, as long as the benefit had been used for travel. Similarly, allowance for the purchase of holiday warrant or passage and allowance for the transportation of the employee's personal effects in connection with the holiday warrant or passage were exempt, in so far as they had been used for the purpose. Following the enactment of Revenue (No. 2) Ordinance 2003 which came into effect on 1 April 2003, the exemption from tax of such benefits has been removed.

36. In addition, section 9(2A) was amended to the effect that all payments by an employer in connection with a holiday journey for the benefit of the employee, irrespective of whether it is convertible into cash and whether the primary liability for the benefit is the employee's own, the actual amounts paid by the employer will be assessable to tax with effect from 1 April 2003. For details, please refer to Departmental Interpretation & Practice Notes No. 41.

Note

1. In contrast, a different approach is adopted by the Department on holiday journey benefits accruing from 1 April 2003, see Departmental Interpretation & Practice Notes No. 41, para. 18.
2. Section 9(2A) was further amended by Revenue (No. 2) Ordinance 2003 to provide for the taxation of holiday journey benefits with effect from 1 April 2003.
3. The definition of "holiday journey" was further added by Revenue (No. 2) Ordinance 2003.
4. The relevant phrase was changed to "any benefit that is capable of being converted into money by the recipient" by the Revenue (No. 2) Ordinance 2003.
5. This approach is not applicable to holiday journey benefits accruing from 1 April 2003. For details, see Departmental Interpretation & Practice Notes No. 41.
6. Holiday journey benefits accruing from 1 April 2003 are excluded. For taxation of holiday journey benefits, see Departmental Interpretation & Practice Notes No. 41.

APPENDIX 12

Departmental Interpretation & Practice Notes
No. 18 (Revised)

**ASSESSMENT OF INDIVIDUALS UNDER SALARIES TAX AND
PERSONAL ASSESSMENT**

These notes are issued for the information and guidance of taxpayers and their authorised representatives. They have no binding force and do not affect a person's right of objection and appeal to the Commissioner, the Board of Review or the Courts.

These notes replace those issued in September 1989.

LAU MAK Yee-ming, Alice
Commissioner of Inland Revenue

January 2005

Our web site: http://www.ird.gov.hk

**DEPARTMENTAL INTERPRETATION AND PRACTICE NOTES
No. 18 (REVISED)**

CONTENT

Appendices

PART I – INTRODUCTION

The Inland Revenue (Amendment) (No. 3) Ordinance 1989, which came into effect on 1 April 1990, introduced changes in the basis of assessing Salaries Tax on husbands and wives and the election procedure for Personal Assessment. The previous Salaries Tax regime whereby the incomes of married couples were aggregated was replaced with a new system of separate taxation. For all final assessments issued on or after 1 April 1990, husbands and wives are treated as separate individuals for tax purposes, unless a joint assessment is elected in the prescribed circumstances. Married women are also entitled to elect Personal Assessment on the same basis as their husbands.

Marriage

2. A definition of "marriage" is in section 2 of Inland Revenue Ordinance ("the Ordinance") and the validity of a marriage is determined by the law of the place where it was celebrated. Marriages solemnized in Hong Kong are recognized under paragraph (a) of the definition when they have been celebrated in accordance with the Marriage Ordinance. Recognition also extends to customary marriages celebrated in accordance with Chinese law and custom prior to 7 October 1971, which have been declared to be valid by the Marriage Reform Ordinance.

3. There is no legislation in Hong Kong that specifically validates foreign marriages whose validity is governed by private international law. Paragraph (b) of the definition recognizes foreign marriages if they have been contracted in accordance with the law of the place where the marriage took place between persons having the capacity to do so. However, in cases where foreign law permits polygamous marriages, this recognition extends to marriages that are only potentially polygamous because the husband has not married more than one wife. In any circumstance where a marriage is both potentially and actually polygamous through the husband having more than one wife, only the marriage between the husband and the principal wife is recognized — any other forms of marriage existing concurrently are not accepted for the purposes of the Ordinance.

4. In line with the definition of "marriage", the words "husband" and "wife" are defined respectively as married man and woman whose marriages are valid marriages within the terms of that definition.

Same-Sex Marriages

5. A same-sex marriage is not regarded as a valid marriage for purposes of the Ordinance. Although the definition of "marriage" in section 2(1) does not expressly oust one between persons of the same sex, it does make reference to a marriage between a "man" and any "wife". Under section 2, "husband" means a married man and "wife" means a married woman. "Spouse" is defined under the same section as a husband or wife. Marriage in the context of the Ordinance is thus intended to refer to a heterosexual marriage between a man and a woman. Parties in a same-sex marriage cannot be "husband/wife" and they would be incapable of having a "spouse".

Husbands and Wives Living Apart

6. Section 2(3) prescribes the situations in which a husband and wife shall be deemed to be living apart from each other in the following three situations:–
  (a) under a decree or order of a competent court in or outside of Hong Kong;
  (b) under a duly executed deed of separation or any instrument of similar effect; or
  (c) in such circumstances that the Commissioner is of the opinion that the separation is likely to be permanent.

7. Where a husband and wife are living apart from each other pursuant to paragraphs (a) or (b), the production of copies of the legal documentation specified will be sufficient evidence of separation. When formal legal proceedings for separation have not been instituted or are not finalized, the couple will be required to demonstrate that their separation is likely to be permanent. While the circumstances surrounding each situation will vary, each case will be reviewed on its own merits and evidence of separation proceedings in progress will generally be accepted. In the absence of any form of legal proceedings, a letter from each spouse confirming the date of separation and that it is likely to be permanent will likewise, in general, be acceptable.

PART II – SALARIES TAX

Separate Taxation

8. Under separate taxation, each spouse will be individually responsible for all aspects of his or her personal taxation affairs including lodgment of returns, claiming his or her entitlement to allowances, raising objections to assessments and settlement of the tax payable. Section 10(1) provides that a husband and wife, unless jointly elect to be assessed on their aggregated incomes under section 10(2), will be separately assessed on their respective incomes on the same basis as unmarried taxpayers.

9. As with all other taxpayers, married women known to be in receipt of salary income will be issued with returns and any married woman deriving a chargeable income for any year of assessment must notify the Commissioner of her liability to assessment within the 4-month period immediately following the end of the relevant year of assessment if she has not been issued with a tax return for individuals.

Joint Assessment

10. Under separate taxation it is possible, in certain circumstances, for married couples to pay more tax in total under separate taxation than they would have paid under the former aggregation system. The two situations where this may occur are:–

    (a) one spouse has an entitlement to allowances under Part V that exceeds his or her net assessable income (referred to as an "unabsorbed allowance") while the other spouse continues to remain chargeable to tax; and

    (b) the levels of income of the spouses, while being chargeable to tax, are such that the total tax payable by them under separate taxation is greater than the tax otherwise payable if their incomes are aggregated (this arises because prior to the year of assessment 1990/91, Married Person's Allowance, which was $2,000 more than the sum of two Basic Allowances, provided the couple with a greater tax relief than separate taxation).

An example to illustrate the situation in (a) is shown in Appendix A.

11. To provide relief to married couples adversely affected by the above situations, a system of joint assessment is available to permit a husband and wife to jointly elect to have their incomes and allowance entitlements aggregated in any year of assessment. In essence, the procedural aspects of the calculation of their combined net chargeable income when joint assessment is elected mirror the procedures for calculating the aggregated net chargeable income of a husband and wife under the previous aggregation system of taxation.

12. Where joint assessment is elected under section 10(2)(a) because one spouse has unabsorbed allowances, the spouse who was liable to tax prior to the election will continue to be liable to pay the tax charged under joint assessment. In contrast to this, where an election is made under section 10(2)(b) by a husband and wife who are both individually chargeable, they must nominate which of them will become liable for the tax payable on their aggregated net chargeable income. The nomination of the chargeable spouse is an integral part of the election process and any variation in the nomination will constitute a withdrawal of the election.

13. An election for joint assessment must be made by the husband and wife by jointly signing the tax return for individuals or prescribed form which will be issued by this Department once it has been determined that an entitlement to make an election exists. It may be made at any time during the year of assessment concerned or the following year of assessment, or before the expiration of one month after the date on which the assessment becomes final and conclusive, whichever is the later. In addition, the Commissioner may allow a further extension of time to make an election in circumstances as he considers to be reasonable, including, for instance, when either spouse has been absent from Hong Kong for an extended time or a spouse only has an unabsorbed allowance agreed after the expiration of the election period.

14. For joint assessment purposes, marriages which occur during a year of assessment are deemed to have taken place at the commencement of that year. Therefore, the total incomes which accrued to the husband and the wife in the year of marriage (both before and after marriage) will be combined into a single net chargeable income. In the case of the death of a spouse, an executor has the same rights of election for joint assessment as the deceased would have had.

15. Any withdrawal of an election must be in writing and jointly signed by the husband and wife. The time limits for withdrawing an election are the same as those specified for making an election. If a joint assessment election is withdrawn, the assessment position of each spouse will be restored to a pre-election basis. Once withdrawn, an election cannot be made again for that same year. A withdrawal of an election is only considered to have occurred when a husband and wife give a signed written notification to that effect. Where a husband and wife no longer qualify to elect joint assessment as a result of reassessment, any prior valid election which has not been formally withdrawn will be treated as having lapsed. If, as a consequence of a further assessment, the couple again qualify for joint assessment the lapsed election will be reactivated.

Objections in respect of Joint Assessments

16. The objection provisions of section 64 of the Ordinance remain basically unchanged. However, a right of objection is provided under section 64(9) to a taxpayer with an unabsorbed allowance electing to be jointly assessed with his or her spouse under section 10(3)(a). This right is limited to matters relating to the quantification of the unabsorbed allowance only and cannot serve to reopen the taxable spouse's assessment in connection with issues unrelated to the joint assessment itself.

17. Once an objection has been made against a joint assessment by a spouse with unabsorbed allowances, the procedures provided by section 64(10), which are similar to the established procedures for settlement or determination of ordinary objections, will apply. Where a settlement cannot be agreed, the couple will jointly and severally have the right to appeal to the Board of Review.

Deductions from Assessable Income

18. Deductions of expenses, including expenses of self-education, and depreciation allowances remain personal to the individual who incurred them. In any year of assessment in which allowable deductions exceed the individual's assessable income, the loss will be carried forward in his or her name. However, where a husband and a wife elect to be jointly assessed, their net assessable incomes will in the first instance be computed individually but prior to either of them becoming entitled to carry forward their loss to the subsequent year of assessment, any excess of expenses and depreciation allowances must be set off as far as is possible against the net assessable income of his or her spouse.

Losses

19. Losses will be carried forward in the name of the individual who incurred them and set off against his or her future net assessable income. However, in any year of assessment in which joint assessment is elected the loss will firstly be set off against the individual's assessable income and then that of his or her spouse before the residue of the loss not set off is carried forward to the subsequent year of assessment. In the subsequent year of assessment, if joint assessment is again elected, inter-spouse set off of losses will take place for that year.

Calculation of Net Chargeable Income

20. A person's net chargeable income is computed by deducting from his or her net assessable income the appropriate concessionary deductions and allowances to which the person is entitled as specified under Part IVA and Part V of the Ordinance respectively. The concessionary deductions under Part IVA include:–

(a) Approved charitable donations,
(b) Elderly residential care expenses (from year of assessment 1998/99 onwards),
(c) Home loan interest (from year of assessment 1998/99 onwards),
(d) Mandatory contributions to Mandatory Provident Fund Scheme or

Recognized Occupational Retirement Scheme (from year of assessment 2000/01 onwards).

21. When joint assessment has been elected the net assessable incomes of the husband and wife are aggregated into a single sum from which are deducted those concessionary deductions and permitted allowances to arrive at an aggregated net chargeable income.

Charitable Donations

22. Married couples, irrespective of whether they are single income or two income family, are permitted to deduct approved charitable donations made by their spouses. While the aggregate of the donations must not be less than $100 and neither spouse can deduct donations that exceed 25% (10% for years prior to year of assessment 2003/04) of his or her assessable income as reduced by expenses and depreciation allowance, no restriction is imposed on the transfer of unutilized donations between spouse provided that there is no duplication of claims. In the case of joint assessment, the maximum deduction that may be allowed for charitable donations cannot exceed 25% (10% for years prior to year of assessment 2003/04) of the aggregate of their assessable incomes as reduced by expenses and depreciation allowance.

23. Where a deduction for the same charitable donations is claimed by, or has been allowed to, more than one person then the parties must agree amongst themselves which of them will be entitled to claim the deduction. The necessary reassessments will be made once the parties have reached an agreement. If the claimants are unable to agree amongst themselves as to which of them will claim the donation, the Commissioner is authorized to allow the deduction on such basis as appears to be just in the circumstances, having regard to the information in his possession at that time.

Calculation of Salaries Tax

24. Salaries Tax is charged at rates specified in the Second Schedule on the net chargeable income (see paragraph 20) and is not to exceed the tax payable at the standard rate specified in the First Schedule on the taxpayer's net assessable income (see paragraph 18) as reduced by such concessionary deductions under Part IVA (see paragraph 20) allowable to the person. When joint assessment is elected, the tax charged is not to exceed the tax payable at the standard rate on the aggregate of the net assessable incomes of the husband and wife as reduced by such concessionary deductions allowable to them.

Provisional Salaries Tax

25. Any taxpayer chargeable to Salaries Tax in respect of any year of assessment is liable to pay Provisional Salaries Tax for that year. Under separate taxation, unless joint assessment is elected, each spouse will be individually charged provisional tax in respect of his or her own income. When joint assessment is elected, the following year's provisional tax will be charged on a joint assessment basis in the name of the spouse chargeable under section 10(3).

PART III – ALLOWANCES

26. The allowance provisions contained in Part V of the Ordinance are as follows:–

    Section 28 -   Basic Allowance
    Section 29 -   Married Person's Allowance
    Section 30 -   Dependent Parent Allowance
    Section 30A - Dependent Grandparent Allowance (with effect from 1994/95)
    Section 30B - Dependent Brother or Dependent Sister Allowance (with effect from 1996/97)
    Section 31 -   Child Allowance
    Section 31A - Disabled Dependant Allowance (with effect from 1995/96)
    Section 32 -   Single Parent Allowance

The rates at which allowances are granted and maximum entitlement to Child Allowance are specified in the Fourth Schedule of the Ordinance.

Basic Allowance

27. All taxpayers chargeable to tax under Salaries Tax or Personal Assessment (Part III or Part VII of the Ordinance) are entitled to Basic Allowance unless he/she is:–

    (a) assessable at the standard rate according to the provisions in section 13 or 43 as the case may be; or
    (b) married and his/her spouse did not have any income chargeable to Salaries Tax.
    (c) married and has elected Personal Assessment with his/her spouse who is not living apart from him/her.

When a taxpayer is married and his/her spouse did not derive any income assessable to Salaries Tax under Part III of the Ordinance, the taxpayer is to be granted Married Person's Allowance instead of Basic Allowance. Section 28(2) precludes a taxpayer to be granted both the Basic Allowance and the Married Person's Allowance in the same year of assessment.

Married Person's Allowance

28. Married Person's Allowance will be granted to a taxpayer who was married at any time during the year of assessment and:-

    (a) his or her spouse did not have any income chargeable to Salaries Tax;
    (b) the taxpayer and his or her spouse have elected to be jointly assessed; or

(c)   the taxpayer has elected to be personally assessed under Part VII with his/her spouse who is not living apart from him/her.

29. The full amount of the Married Person's Allowance may be granted in any year of marriage, separation, divorce or death, irrespective of the actual date in the year on which the event occurred.

30. Where a husband and wife are living apart from each other, a Married Person's Allowance can only be granted if the claimant is maintaining or supporting the other spouse. When an allowance is granted in these circumstances then, for the purposes of Personal Assessment, the husband and wife shall not be treated as living apart from each other and they are required to jointly elect to be personally assessed. A claim for maintaining and supporting a spouse may, however, be revoked at any time during the year of assessment to which it applies or within the next six years.

31. In the case of *Sit Kwok Keung v. CIR, 5 HKTC 647*, the Court of Appeal ruled that the taxpayer was not entitled to Married Person's Allowance in respect of payments made towards the support of a former spouse in years subsequent to the year of assessment in which the divorce became absolute. When a marriage is dissolved, the relationship of husband and wife no longer exists from the date on which a divorce order becomes absolute.

Dependent Parent Allowance

32. Dependent Parent Allowance may be granted where a parent of a taxpayer or his or her spouse, being a spouse not living apart, at any time during that year of assessment, was:–
   (a)   ordinarily resident in Hong Kong; and
   (b)   aged 60 or more or, if aged under 60, was eligible to claim an allowance under the Government's Disability Allowance Scheme; and
   (c)   maintained by the taxpayer or the spouse by either residing with the taxpayer and/or his/her spouse, otherwise than for full valuable consideration, for a continuous period of 6 months, or the taxpayer and/ or his/her spouse has contributed not less than $12,000 in the year of assessment ($1,200 for years before 1998/99) in money towards the parent's maintenance.

33. The term "parent" includes a natural, adoptive and step father or mother of the taxpayer or his/her living or deceased spouse.

34. To qualify as a dependent parent, the parent must be ordinarily resident in Hong Kong. In substance, the term "ordinarily resident in Hong Kong" means that the parent must have his or her normal and usual place of residence in Hong Kong. A taxpayer cannot be granted an allowance in respect of a dependent parent who is ordinarily resident outside of Hong Kong solely by virtue of that parent holding a Hong Kong Permanent Identity Card. For the purpose of the

Dependent Parent Allowance, it is not relevant that the dependent parent also received income during the year of assessment in respect of which the claim was made.

35. The amount of the allowance is set out at Item 3 of the Fourth Schedule. The allowance has two components — the standard allowance and the additional allowance. While the standard allowance will be granted for each qualifying dependent parent, an additional allowance will be granted when the parent resided, otherwise than for the full valuable consideration, with the taxpayer and his or her spouse continuously throughout the year of assessment. Dependent Parent Allowance shall not be granted (either claimed by the same taxpayer or by any other person) if the elderly residential care expenses deduction is granted in respect of the same dependent parent.

Dependent Grandparent Allowance

36. From year of assessment 1994/95 onwards, Dependent Grandparent Allowance may be granted, in accordance with Item 4 of the Fourth Schedule, to a taxpayer who, during the year of assessment, maintained his/her grandparents or that of the spouse, being a spouse not living apart. The conditions to be fulfilled as well as the allowance granted are the same as that relating to Dependent Parent Allowance set out in paragraphs 32 to 35 above.

37. The term "grandparent" includes a natural, adoptive and step grandfather or grandmother of the taxpayer or his/her living or deceased spouse. In respect of the same dependent grandparent, only one individual will be granted an allowance for tax purposes. The allowance is mutually exclusive with Dependent Parent Allowance in respect of the same dependant who may be in a dual capacity. Similar to Dependent Parent Allowance, no Dependent Grandparent Allowance is granted if the elderly residential care expenses deduction is granted in respect of the same dependant.

Dependent Brother or Dependent Sister Allowance

38. From year of assessment 1996/97 onwards, a taxpayer may be granted Dependent Brother or Dependent Sister Allowance if a taxpayer or the spouse, being a spouse not living apart, has maintained in the year of assessment an unmarried brother or sister of whom the taxpayer or the spouse has the sole or predominant care. The term "brother or sister" means a natural, adoptive and step brother or sister of the taxpayer or his/her living or deceased spouse.

39. Age restrictions, similar to those on Child Allowance, are imposed on the dependants. At any time in the year of assessment the dependent person maintained by the taxpayer must fulfill one of the following three conditions:–
    (a) under the age of 18;
    (b) of or over the age of 18 but under the age of 25 and was receiving full

time education at a university, college, school or other similar educational establishment; or

(c) of or over the age of 18 and was, by reason of physical or mental disability, incapacitated for work.

40. The allowance, at the rate set out at Item 5 of the Fourth Schedule, is mutually exclusive with Child Allowance in respect of the same dependant who may be in a dual capacity.

Child Allowance

41. Taxpayers are entitled to claim Child Allowance in respect of any unmarried child that the taxpayer was maintaining at any time during the year of assessment. The term "child" is defined in section 27 to include any child of a person or his or her spouse or former spouse, whether or not born in wedlock, and to include the adopted or step child of either or both of them. The intention of the legislation is that any taxpayer providing care and support to a child to whom he has lawful custody should be entitled to an allowance, subject to apportionment where there is more than one person claiming the allowance.

42. The term "adopted" applies with equal validity to a child for the purposes of Child Allowance and Single Parent Allowance as it does to the parent-child relationship specified for Dependent Parent Allowance. With effect from 1 January 1973, i.e. the implementation date of the Adoption Ordinance (Cap. 290), an adoption order validating the adoption must be made under that ordinance while adoptions made under Chinese law and custom prior to the implementation date of the ordinance are also recognized. For an overseas adoption, it is recognized in Hong Kong if it is legally valid according to the law of the place where it took place and the adoptive parents have a superior right in respect of the custody of the child to that of the natural parents.

43. For the purposes of Child Allowance, the child must be:–

(a) under the age of 18;

(b) of or over 18 but under 25 and was receiving full-time education at a school, college, university or other similar educational institution, or

(c) of or over 18 and was by reason of physical or mental disability, incapacitated for work.

44. Apart from a husband and wife not living apart from each other, where more than one person is entitled to claim an allowance in respect of the same child for the same year of assessment the allowance is to be apportioned by the Commissioner having regard to the contributions made by each individual to the maintenance and education of the child during that year. In the case of a husband and wife not living apart from each other, their **total** entitlement to Child Allowance may only be claimed en bloc by the spouse as the couple may nominate. The nomination of the spouse to claim the Child Allowance may not be revoked without the consent of the Commissioner whose decision on the matter is final and not subject to objection or appeal. In general, consent to vary a nomination will not be unreasonably withheld where a change of nomination will result in a reduction in the overall tax liability of the husband and wife.

Disabled Dependant Allowance

45. From year of assessment 1995/96 onwards, Disabled Dependant Allowance may be granted in respect of a disabled family member of whom a taxpayer is entitled to claim Married Person's Allowance, Child Allowance, Dependent Brother or Sister Allowance, Dependent Parent Allowance, Dependent Grandparent Allowance or to an expense deduction of elderly residential care expenses. The disabled dependant must be eligible to claim an allowance under the Government's Disability Allowance Scheme.

46. The amount of allowance is prescribed in Item 7 of the Fourth Schedule. If Disabled Dependant Allowance is granted in respect of a disabled dependent child of whom the respective Child Allowance was apportionable for a year of assessment, the Disabled Dependant Allowance for that year of assessment should be also apportioned on the same basis.

Single Parent Allowance

47. Single Parent Allowance may be claimed if, any time during the year of assessment, a taxpayer had the sole or predominant care of a dependent child in respect of whom he or she was entitled to claim a Child Allowance. The allowance is of a single amount and does not increase with the number of children concerned. The term "sole or predominant care" relates to custodial responsibility for the child i.e. the actual day-to-day care, supervision, well-being and control of the child and the onus of proof vested upon the taxpayer making the claim (see *Sit Kwok Keung v. CIR, 5 HKTC 647*).

48. The allowance cannot be granted, however, if the person, at any time during that year of assessment, was married and not living apart from his or her spouse or has only made contributions to the maintenance and education of the child during the year of assessment. Where custody of a child changes at some point during the year the allowance will normally be apportioned on a time basis.

Claims by More Than One Person

49. Except when a Child Allowance and the corresponding Disabled Dependant Allowance are apportioned respectively under section 31(2) and section 31A (2), allowances for any individual dependent parent, grandparent, brother, sister, child or disabled dependant will not be given in respect of the same dependent person to more than one person in the same year of assessment.

50. When it is detected that, save as permitted by sections 31(2) and 31A(2), two or more persons are eligible and have claimed an allowance in respect of the same parent, grandparent, brother, sister, child or disabled dependant for the same year of assessment, the claimants will be required to agree amongst themselves who will claim the allowance. As a practical measure, the Department will accept a written withdrawal of the claim from one of the claimants in favour of the other as sufficient evidence that the parties have reached agreement.

51. Except as permitted by sections 31(2) and 31A(2), where allowance in respect of the dependent person has been granted:–

    (a)   to two or more persons; or

    (b)   to a husband and wife not living apart from each other; or

    (c)   to a taxpayer and, within 6 months of its being granted, another person appears to be entitled to the allowance,

the claimants will then be invited to agree which of them will have the allowance. When the claimants are unable to reach agreement within a reasonable time, additional assessments will be raised under section 60 in a manner which, on the basis of the information available at the time when they are raised, appears to be just.

PART IV – PERSONAL ASSESSMENT

Election for Personal Assessment

52. Any individual who is 18 years of age or over may elect to be personally assessed if he or she is a permanent or temporary resident of Hong Kong. A "permanent resident" is an individual who ordinarily resides in Hong Kong, and a "temporary resident" is an individual who stays in Hong Kong, whether continuously or otherwise, for more than 180 days in the year of assessment to which the election relates or 300 days in two consecutive years of assessment, one of which must be the year to which the election relates.

53. When the individual is married and not living apart from his or her spouse and if that spouse also has income assessable under the Ordinance, then the individual cannot elect to be personally assessed unless the spouse also does so. A married person who does not satisfy the residential conditions may make an election if his or her spouse falls within those requirements. An individual whose spouse is not entitled to elect Personal Assessment may however does so in respect of his or her own income. Where Married Person's Allowance is granted in respect of a husband and wife living apart, they are to be treated as not living apart from each other for the purpose of Personal Assessment and joint election is required.

54. Election for Personal Assessment must be made within two years after the end of the year of assessment in respect of which the election is made or within two months after the issue of a notice of assessment or a notice of additional assessment in respect of which the election is made, whichever is the later.

Calculation of Total Income

55. Under Personal Assessment, income chargeable to Salaries Tax, Profits Tax and Property Tax of an individual taxpayer are aggregated before interest payable on money borrowed for the acquisition of property let is deducted to arrive at the total income. The total income may further be reduced by:–

(a) Such deductions as allowable to the individual under Part IVA (see paragraph 20),

(b) Business losses incurred in the year of assessment.

56. For a husband and wife who have elected to be personally assessed, their reduced total incomes are in the first instance computed individually before being aggregated. For the purposes of computing the couple's joint income, a husband and wife who marry during the year of assessment are **deemed** to have married each other at the commencement of that year of assessment.

Losses

57. Where the aggregate amount of the concessionary deductions under Part IVA of the Ordinance and the business loss of a taxpayer under Part IV exceeds his or her total income, only that part of the excess representing business loss under Part IV will be carried forward to set off the total income of the taxpayer for future years of assessment. In general, prior years' losses brought forward under Personal Assessment will only be set off against the total income of the taxpayer when Personal Assessment is elected. Where Personal Assessment is not elected, incomes of the taxpayer will be assessed under the respective primary charge and the loss will be carried forward for set off in the next year when an election is made.

58. Losses incurred by married taxpayers will be computed individually. However, in any year of assessment where Personal Assessment is elected, the loss will be set off against the total income of both the individual to whom the loss belongs and his or her spouse before any unused residue can be carried forward. In any year of assessment in which a spouse with a loss brought forward does not elect to be personally assessed because he or she has no income, and his or her spouse does so individually, the loss will still be set off against the chargeable income of the electing spouse for that year of assessment, and only the balance of the loss will be carried forward to the subsequent year of assessment in the name of the spouse who incurred it. An example illustrating the operation of section 42(6) is at Appendix B.

Lodgment of Returns and Assessment to Tax

59. Taxpayers electing Personal Assessment are only required to complete the relevant parts of the tax returns issued for individuals and have the returns jointly signed by the taxpayers and their spouses in the event the couple elect Personal Assessment.

60. The reduced total income of the taxpayer after deduction of allowances under Part V of the Ordinance is charged at rates specified in the Second Schedule and is not to exceed the tax payable at the standard rate specified in the First Schedule on the taxpayer's total income or the joint income of the couple after being reduced by any allowable concessionary deductions under Part IVA and business losses but before the deduction of the allowances under Part V.

61. Married couples electing to be personally assessed will receive separate notices of assessment for the apportioned tax attributable to their respective incomes, computed by reference to the ratio that their respective reduced total income bears to their reduced joint total income.

Appendix A

EXAMPLE OF WHERE JOINT ASSESSMENT MAY BE ELECTED

Unabsorbed allowance situation (Year of Assessment 2003/04)

	Mr. A	Mrs. A
	$	$
Income from employment	200,000	70,000
Less: employment related expenses	(1,000)	-
Net Assessable Income	199,000	70,000
Less: Charitable donations	(500)	-
Basic Allowance	(104,000)	(104,000)
Dependent Parent Allowance	(30,000)	
Child Allowance (1 child)	(30,000)	
Net Chargeable Income	34,500	NIL
Unabsorbed allowance	NIL	(34,000)
Tax Payable	850	NIL

Joint assessment reducing overall taxation liability

	Joint assessment Mr. & Mrs. A
	$
Net Assessable Income	269,000
Less : Deductions and Allowance	(268,500)
Net Chargeable Income	500
Tax Payable	10

Appendix B

ILLUSTRATION OF THE APPLICATION OF SECTION 42(6)
TO THE TRANSFER OF LOSSES BETWEEN SPOUSES IN
PERSONAL ASSESSMENT

Year 1 (Husband and wife jointly elect personal assessment)

	Mr. A	Mrs. A
	$	$
Salary income	230,000	
Property income	50,000	
Business loss		(40,000)
	280,000	(40,000)
Inter-spouse loss set off (section 42(5))	(40,000)	(40,000)
Total income after loss set-off	240,000	NIL

Net Assessable Income	240,000
Less: Married Person's Allowance (Year 2003/04)	208,000
Net Chargeable Income	32,000

Year 2 (Husband and wife jointly elect personal assessment)

	Mr. A	Mrs. A
	$	$
Salary income	100,000	
Property income	50,000	
Business loss (business ceased on 31 March)		(350,000)
	150,000	(350,000)
Inter-spouse loss set off (section 42(5))	(150,000)	(150,000)
Total income after loss set-off	NIL	(200,000)
Loss carried forward		(200,000)

Year 3 (Only husband elects personal assessment – wife has no income)

	Mr A	Mrs A
	$	$
Salary income	100,000	
Property income	50,000	
	150,000	0
Inter-spouse loss set off [section 42(6)]	(150,000)	
Total income after loss set-off	NIL	NIL

Statement of loss

Loss brought forward		(200,000)
Loss set off under section 42(6)		150,000
Loss carried forward		(50,000)

APPENDIX 13

Inland Revenue Department Hong Kong
DEPARTMENTAL INTERPRETATION & PRACTICE NOTES
No. 21 (REVISED 1998)

LOCALITY OF PROFITS

These notes are issued for the information and guidance of taxpayers and their authorised representatives. They have no binding force and do not affect a person's right of objection or appeal to the Commissioner, the Board of Review or the Courts.

These notes replace those issued in April 1996 entitled "Locality of profits".

WONG Ho-sang
Commissioner of Inland Revenue

March 1998

LOCALITY OF PROFITS

Introduction

The territorial concept has always been fundamental to the taxation of profits in Hong Kong. Only those profits which arise in or are derived from Hong Kong are liable to tax here. However, while the territorial concept is clear, its application in particular cases at times remains a contentious issue between the Department and practitioners with numerous disputes being referred to the Board of Review and the Courts. The decisions of the Privy Council in *CIR v Hang Seng Bank* (3 HKTC 351) and *HK-TVB International v CIR* (3 HKTC 468), established guidelines to assist in locating the source of profits. More recently, the decision of the privy Council in *CIR v Orion Caribbean Limited* reaffirmed the principles and guidelines laid down in the *Hang Seng* and *HK-TVBI* cases and confirmed the appropriateness of the "operations test". The guiding principle is that "One looks to see what the taxpayer has done to earn the profits in question and where he has done it."

2. The *Hang Seng Bank, HK-TVBI* and *Orion Caribbean* decisions do not set out rules to cover all cases where the locality of profits is in issue, rather they clarify the general principles to be followed in determining the locality of profits.

The purpose of this note is to state what the Department considers are the general principles laid down by the Privy Council and then give specific examples applying those principles. At the same time, it must be emphasised that each case will be determined on is own facts. As commented on in *Orion Caribbean*, Hang Seng did not, when speaking of "profits earned 'by the exploitation of property assets by letting property, lending money or dealing in commodities or securities' lay down a rule of law. Rather, the case affirmed that "No simple legal test can be employed." This was illustrated in *Magna Industrial Company Limited v CIR*, a case falling within the so-called "rare case dictum" of *HK-TVBI* (see also paragraph 29).

3. It should also be noted that the Department will look closely at any particular circumstances where there is an apparent artificial attempt to turn profits which arise in or are derived from Hong Kong (Hong Kong profits) into profits which arise in or are derived from outside Hong Kong (offshore profits). It would be of considerable help to the Department if taxpayers and their representatives could anticipate requests from Assessors for the information needed to verify claims that profits arise in or are derived from outside Hong Kong. An initial claim for offshore profits should alway be supported with reasons which can be substantiated with evidence.

Basic tests for liability to Profits Tax

4. In order for a person to be chargeable to profits tax, three conditioins must be satisfied —
  (a) The person must carry on a trade, profession or business in Hong Kong;
  (b) The profits to be charged must be from such trade, profession or business carried on by the person in Hong Kong; and
  (c) The profits must be profits arising in or derived from Hong Kong.

Principles on which locality of profits is determined

5. Assuming the first two conditions stated above are satisfied, liability to profits tax will only arise if a person's profits arise in or are derived from Hong Kong. The basic principles for determining the locality of profits can be summarised as follows —
  (a) The question of locality of profits is a hard, practical matter of fact. No universal rule will cover every case. Whether profits arise in or are derived from Hong Kong depends on the nature of the profits and the transactions giving rise to them.
  (b) The broad guiding principle is that one looks to see what the taxpayer has done to earn the profits in question and where he has done it. In other words, the proper approach is to ascertain what were the operations which produced the relevant profits and where those operations took place.

    (c) The distinction between Hong Kong profits and offshore profits is made by reference to gross profits arising from individual transactions.

    (d) In certain situations, where gross profits from an individual transaction arise in different places, they can be apportioned as arising partly in and partly outside Hong Kong.

    (e) The place where day to day investment decisions are taken does not generally determine the locality of profits.

    (f) The absence of an overseas permanent establishment of a Hong Kong business does not, of itself, mean that all of the profits of that business arise in or are derived from Hong Kong. However, as stated in *HK-TVBI* "it can only be in rare cases that a taxpayer with a principal place of business in Hong Kong can earn profits which are not chargeable to profits tax."

Trading Profits

6. The question of the locality of profits derived from trading in commodities or goods has produced the most controversy. This issue is important and needs to be clarfied. Generally the determining factor, as indicated in the Privy Council decisions, is the place where the contracts for purchase and sale are effected. However, as the Court of Appeal noted in *Magna*, the totality of facts must be looked at in determining what the taxpayer did to earn the profit: "… the question where the goods were bought and sold is important. But there are other questions. For example: How were the goods procured and stored? How were the sales solicited? How were the orders processed? How were the goods shipped? How was the financing arranged? How was payment effected?" This reflected the statement by the High Court that "More often than not, it would not be the quantity of activities but the nature and quality of them that matters more. The cause and effect of such activities on the profits is the determining factor. It is what role such activities played and the relative importance of them in the making of profits that would usually tilt the scale and not the number of activities carried out at a particular place." The headnote to Case No. *D 9/89*, quoted by the Court of Appeal in *Magna*, is also worthy of note: "Generally, the employment of staff and the maintenance of an office in Hong Kong, with all necessary services and facilities including telephone and telex, are the essence of a trading company's activities. Where these are all in Hong Kong, it could be concluded that the resultant profits have a Hong Kong source. The fact that goods are located and delivered outside Hong Kong is not material for this purpose."

7. The Department considers that because the locality of profits is a hard, practical matter of fact, "effected" cannot merely mean legally executed (as this would depend on formal legal rules of offer and acceptance) and thus must contemplate the actual steps leading to the existence of the contracts including the negotiation and, in substance, conclusion and execution of the contracts.

8. On the basis of the opinions expressed in paragraphs 6 and 7 and in the light of the various court decisions, the Department's views which are reflected in its assessing practice on the locality of profits derived from trading in commodities or goods by a business carried on in Hong Kong can be summarised as follows —

   (a)   Where both the contract of purchase and contract of sale are effected in Hong Kong, the profits are fully taxable.

   (b)   Where both the contract of purchase and contract of sale are effected outside Hong Kong, no part of the profits are taxable.

   (c)   Where either the contract of purchase or contract of sale is effected in in Hong Kong, the initial presumption will be that the profits are fully taxable. Matters, such as those mentioned in paragraph 6 above, will be examined to determine the issue.

   (d)   Where the sale is made to a Hong Kong customer, the sale contract will usually be taken as having been effected in Hong Kong.

   (e)   Where the commodities or goods are purchased from either a Hong Kong supplier or manufacturer, the purchase contract will usually be taken as having been effected in Hong Kong.

   (f)   Where the effecting of the purchase and sale contracts does not require travel outside Hong Kong but is carried out in Hong Kong by telephone, fax etc., the contracts will be considered as having been effected in Hong Kong.

   (g)   The purchase and sale contracts are important factors but the totality of facts must be looked at to determine the locality of the profits.

9. There may be cases where the activities of a Hong Kong trading business are limited to the following –

   (a)   issuing or accepting an invoice (not order) to or from an ex-Hong Kong customer or supplier (whether related or not) on the basis of contracts of sale or purchase already effected by an ex-Hong Kong associate;

   (b)   arranging letters of credit;

   (c)   operating a bank account, making and receiving payments; and

   (d)   maintaining accounting records.

This situation commonly arises when a Hong Kong business, as a member of a group and pursuant to group directives, carries out the above activities and "books" the profits in Hong Kong. Provided the activities of the Hong Kong business do not include the acceptance or issue of sale or purchase orders in or from Hong Kong, the profits would not be taxable. In other words, the Department considers that where the Hong Kong business accepts or issues sale or purchase orders in Hong Kong, the guidelines in paragraph 8 apply.

10. A trading company, carrying on business outside Hong Kong, may set up a branch in Hong Kong to act as a buying office. The activities of the branch are confined to the purchase of goods in Hong Kong and it is not involved in their sale, either in Hong Kong or elsewhere. In such a situation, a liability to Hong Kong profits tax would not arise. The function of a buying office may also be carried out by a subsidiary company or by an accredited agent (either related or unrelated). However, as for a branch, the subsidiary company or accredited agent must not be involved in the sale of the goods. On the other hand, any commission or other remuneration earned by the subsidiary company or accredited agent for performing its services in Hong Kong will be fully taxable.

11. Having regard to the points expressed above, it will be apparent that, in the Department's view, the question of apportionment does not arise in relation to trading profits. Trading profits will be either wholly taxable or wholly non-taxable.

12. Cases may arise where it is claimed that contracts of purchase and of sale have been effected outside Hong Kong by employees of the Hong Kong business travelling abroad or by fully accredited overseas agents. In this context, an agent is regarded as fully accredited if it has, and habitually exercises, a general authority to negotiate and conclude contracts on behalf of his principal. Normally the activities of a fully accredited agent and an employee are accorded the same weight if it can be shown that the employee has full authority to conclude contracts without reference to the business in Hong Kong. In considering claims that contracts have been effected outside Hong Kong by employees, Assessors will require details of travelling, hotel and subsistence expenses in respect of each individual transaction. Where it is claimed that contracts are effected by overseas agents it will be necessary to provide agency agreements or other documentary evidence to support the claim.

Manufacturing Profits

13. The Department considers that, where goods are manufactured in Hong Kong, the profits arising from the sale of such goods will be fully taxable because the profit making activity is considered to be the manufacturing operation carried out in Hong Kong.

14. In the situation where a Hong Kong company manufactures goods partly in Hong Kong and partly outsided Hong Kong, say in the Mainland, then that part of the profits which relates to the manufacture of the goods in the Mainland will not be regarded as arising in Hong Kong.

15. A Hong Kong manufacturing business, which does not have a licence to carry on a business in the Mainland, may enter into a processing or assembly arrangement with a Mainland entity. Under these arrangements, the Mainland entity is responsible for processing, manufacturing or assembling the goods that are required to be exported to places outside the Mainland. The Mainland entity provides the factory premises, the land and labour. For this, it charges a processing fee and exports the completed goods to the Hong Kong manufacturing business. The Hong Kong manufacturing business normally provides the raw materials. It may also provide technical know-how, management, production skills, design, skilled labour, training and supervision for the locally recruited labour and the manufacturing plant and machinery. The design and technical know-how development are usually carried out in Hong Kong.

16. In law, the Mainland processing unit is a sub-contractor separate and distinct from the Hong Kong manufacturing business and the question of apportionment strictly does not arise. However, recognising that the Hong Kong manufacturing business is involved in the manufacturing activities in the Mainland (in particular in the supply of raw materials, training and supervision of the local labour) the Department is prepared to concede, in cases of this nature, that the profits on the sale of the goods in question can be apportioned. In line with paragraphs 21–22 below, this apportionment will generally be on a 50:50 basis.

17. If, however, the manufacturing in the Mainland has been contracted to a sub-contractor (whether a related party or not) and paid for on an arm's length basis, with minimal involvement of the Hong Kong business, the question of apportionment will not arise. For the Hong Kong business, this will not be a case of manufacturing profits but rather a case of trading profits. Profits of the Hong Kong business will be calculated by deducting from its sales the cost of goods sold, including any subcontracting charges paid to the sub-contractor in the Mainland. The taxation of such trading profits will be determined on the same basis as for a commodities or goods trading business.

18. The following examples further illustrate the Department's views on this subject –

Example 1
A Hong Kong company manufactures goods in Hong Kong and sells them to overseas customers. The fact that the company has sales staff based overseas does not give a part of the profits an overseas source. This is not a case for apportionment. The whole of the profits are liable to profits tax.

Example 2
A Hong Kong garment manufacturer has a factory in the Mainland where sweater panels are knitted. These panels are then transported to the manufacturer's factory in Hong Kong where they are sewn together into finished garments for sale. This would be a case where the manufacturing profit could be apportioned.

19. As a corollary to example 1, where a company manufactures goods outside Hong Kong and sells them to Hong Kong customers, the manufacturing profits are not liable to profits tax. However, in the exceptional case where the sale activities in Hong Kong are so substantial as to constitute a retailing business, the profits attributable to the retailing activities are fully taxable.

Other Profits

20. The Department regards the locality of the following types of profits to be as follows –

Income or Profits	*Locality*
(a) Rental income from real property.	Location of the property.
(b) Profits from the sale of real estate.	Location of the property.
(c) Profits from the purchase and sale of listed shares.	Location of the stock exchange where the shares in question are traded.
(d) Profits from the sale of securities issued outside Hong Kong and not listed on an exchange.	Place where the contracts of purchase and sale are effected (except financial institutions in instances where Section 15(1)(l) applies).
(e) Service fee income.	Place where the services are performed which give rise to the fees. It should be noted that in the case of an investment adviser that where the adviser's organisation and operations are located only in Hong Kong, profits derived in respect of the management of the clients' funds are considered to have a Hong Kong source. Included in chargeable sums are not only management fees and performance fees but also rebates, commissions and discounts received by the adviser from brokers located in Hong Kong or elsewhere in respect of securities transactions executed on behalf of clients.
(f) Interest earned by persons other than financial institutions.	Determined on the basis set out in DIPN No. 13 (Revised).
(g) Royalties other than those deemed chargeable under Section 15 (1) (a) or (b).	Determined on the same basis as trading profits (see paras 6 8 above).
(h) Cross-border land transportation in come.	Normally the place of uplift of the passengers or goods. However, where the contract of carriage does not distinguish between outward and inward transportation apportionment will not be permitted.

In addition, in cases where Section 39E(1)(b)(i) of the Inland Revenue Ordinance operates to disallow depreciation allowances in respect of leased machinery or plant, the income from leasing such machinery or plant will generally be regarded as nontaxable.

Apportionment of Profits

21. The Department accepts that, notwithstanding the absence of a specific provision for apportionment of profits in the *Inland Revenue Ordinance*, there are certain situations in which an apportionment of the chargeable profits is appropriate. The example of manufacturing profits has already been stated above. A further example is service fee income where the services are perfromed partly in Hong Kong and partly outside.

22. Although the Department accepts that apportionment is permissible under the Inland Revenue Ordinance, it does not consider it will have a wide application. The Department believes that where apportionment is appropriate it will, in the vast majority of cases, be on a 50:50 basis. Further, it will be necessary to scale down claims for general expenses of the business which contribute indirectly to earning both the Hong Kong and offshore profits. This should be done in the ratio that offshore profits bear to total profits. General expenses in this context refer to all indirect expenses. Requests to re-open previous year assessments to permit apportionment will not be entertained (Section 70A — prevailing practice).

Sale or Purchase Commission

23. This refers to situations where commission income is earned both by securing buyers for a manufacturer's products and by securing manufacturers to make products required by customers. Typically the comission income is a percentage of the invoiced value of the goods. In such cases the Department considers that the activity which gives rise to the commission income is the arrangement of the business to be transacted between principals. The source of the income is the place where the activities of the commission agent are performed. The place where the principals are located, how they are identified by the commission agent and the place where incidental activities are performed prior to or subsequent to the earning of the commission are not generally relevant.

24. Commission income may also arise where a business is carried on in Hong Kong but the activities which give rise to the commission are not in Hong Kong. In such cases, the commission is not taxable. Typical of these situations are the following examples-

Example 3 — Sales or purchase agencies

A Hong Kong business holds the "Fast Area" sales or purchasing representation for a product or group of products sold into the area or sourced in the area by principals who are associated concerns, the Hong Kong business and the associates being members of a group under the control of a common parent organisation. The Hong Kong business is appointed agent for the area, either by formally executed agreements or by a directive from the parent organisation and is remunerated by a "commission" on all sales and/or purchases in its area. The Hong Kong business may either –

(a)   actively solicit orders ex-Hong Kong, on behalf of its principals by sending employee representatives overseas for the purpose or by employing sub-agents overseas; or

(b)   factually do nothing whatsoever, either itself or through subagents.

Example 4 — Passive commission

A similar organisational set-up to the agencies above, but in this case the Hong Kong business is given sales or purchase responsibility for group products in the "Far East Area" as a principal. Factually, the Hong Kong business is unable to handle all or any of the group range of products and sales into or purchases from the area are therefore entirely made by associated concerns. It is never intended that the Hong Kong business will perform any purchasing or sales function. The Hong Kong business receives an "infringement commission" for which it does nothing (except possibly the rendering of some "sales service" ex-Hong Kong).

Alternatively, it may be the case that the Hong Kong business sells or buys group products in Hong Kong (profits thereon are, of course, subject to Hong Kong profits tax) and in addition receives "commissions" on sales or purchases by associated concerns in the "Far East Area". These commissions are paid in pursuance of a parent organisation directive. These commissions are paid in pursuance of a parent organisation directive. The Hong Kong business has no formal function or contractual position in relation to the associates' transactions in the "Far East Area", i.e. it has no "area responsibility" either as princpal, agent or sales representative and renders no service in respect of the commission it receives.

Group Service Companies

25. This refers to cases where a Hong Kong company, usually a member of a multinational group, renders support services, such as marketing and training, to group members located throughout the Asia/Pacific region. The services are rendered substantially in Hong Kong. Inter-group charges are made at an agreed mark-up of cost (typically 5% or 10%) and represent a reward for the services provided plus a recoupment of 100% of the costs incurred by the Hong Kong company.

26. The profits, being the mark-up, derived by the Hong Kong company for its services are regarded by the Department as wholly assessable. However, in some cases the inter-group charges have been grossed up to reflect the imposition of a withholding tax on the service charges by the country in which the group entity receiving the services is resident. In these cases the Department will allow the Hong Kong company to deduct, from the service fee charged, the foreign withholding tax paid. The effect is to assess the Hong Kong on the net (of withholding tax) service fee received. This reflects the principle set out in DIPN No. 28, issued in July 1997, concerning the deductibility of foreign taxes that are charged on earnings, regardless of whether or not a profit is mased.

Financial Institutions

27. In 1986 the Department reached agreement with practitioners and their financial institution clients on the taxation treatment of certain interest and related fee income. This recognised the practical difficulties associated with determining the assessable profits of such institutions and provided them with added certainty in their taxation affairs. The agreement reduced the large number of disputes which had arisen following the 1978 amendment to Section 15 (1)(i) of the *Ordinance*.

28. Following the decision in the *Hang Seng Bank* case questions have been raised about certain aspects of this practice. However, in the interest of maintaining certainty the Department is prepared to continue with this treatment. The opportunity is now taken to set out details of that treatment.

Types of Income	*Tax Treatment*
1. Interest from loans	100% Non taxable
(a) Offshore loans initiated, negotiated, approved and documented by an associated party outside Hong Kong and funded outside Hong Kong, i.e. funds raised and loaned direct to the borrower by a non-resident, e.g. head office, branch, or subsidiary etc. albeit through or in the name of the Hong Kong institution.	100% Taxable
(b) Offshore loans initiated, etc. by the Hong Kong institution and funded by it in/from Hong Kong.	50% Taxable
(c) Offshore loans initiated, etc. by an associated party outside Hong Kong but funded by the Hong Kong institution.	50% Taxable
(d) Offshore loans initiated, etc. by a Hong Kong institution but funded by offshore associates. It is considered that this category only applies to start-up positions where the Hong Kong institution has yet to establish a market presence.	

Note on "Funding"

For claims concerning loans funded by offshore associates, two essential requirements will have to be satisfied, namely —

(i) that the Hong Kong institution does not have the authority to seek its own source of funds in respect of the loans; and

(ii) there must be documentary evidence to show that funds have been directly provided by an offshore associate even though such funds may have been routed through another vehicle in Hong Kong. In other words, arbitrary funding by another group vehicle in Hong Kong will not satisfy this requirement.

Note on "Initiation"

"Initiation" refers to the efforts exerted in obtaining the particular business including solicitation, negotiation and structuring of the loans. The financial institution must be able to substantiate that the mandate or invitation to participate was secured as a direct result of the activities of an associated party outside Hong Kong for an offshore claim to succeed.

2. Interest on Certificates of Deposit (Cds)

Acquisition of CDs will be treated in a similar fashion to deposit placements. This treatment is predicated on the fact that the Hong Kong institution operates within previously approved parameters as to credit limits and prime banks with whom it may operate. In other words, there is an obvious distinction to be drawn between CDs and loans.

100% Taxable

3. Interest from securities other than CDs

A similar approach to be adopted as for interest from loans (see 1 above). If there is to be any attribution of interest to offshore intervention, the role of the Hong Kong institution must be that of a mere intermediary in the purchase and sale of securities with no discretion in the matter. It is unlikely any claim for exemption will be entertained in instances where the Hong Kong institution possesses its own security dealing capability and is active in this capacity.

See (1) above

4. Participation, Commitment etc. fees
   To follow the tax treatment accorded to related loans.   See (1) above

5. Active fee
   To be determined by reference to the "Activity Test",   Depends on the
   i.e. services performed to earn the fee.   particular facts of
                                                               the case

6. Guarantee/underwriting fees
   A principal consideration of source is related to whether   Depends on the
   or not the risk under the guarantee or underwriting   particular facts of
   commitment is evaluated and is to be borne by the Hong   the case
   Kong institution. In instances where the Hong Kong
   institution has no discretion on the acceptance or
   rejection of offshore instructions, and undertakes no
   risk, such fees will be accepted as merely "booked"
   and not assessable.

"Booked" Profits

29. As previously indicated, the existence of a business carried on in Hong Kong is not decisive of a source of profits subject to profits tax. However, it will "only be in rare cases that a taxpayer with a principal place of business in Hong Kong can earn profits which are not chargeable to profits tax under s. 14" (*TVBI*). The performance in Hong Kong of activities which do not of themselves give rise to the profits, such as the rental of office premises, recruitment of general staff, etc., also do not, in themselves, determine the locality of profits. Where, however, commissions, fees, profits on sales, etc., relate to sales to, or services rendered to, Hong Kong customers, the resultant profits will generally continue to be liable to profits tax. The Department takes a serious view of schemes and devices which seek to "book" Hong Kong profits offshore. It will not hesitate to apply the general anti-avoidance provisions in such instances and, where appropriate, impose penalties in blatant cases involving the non-disclosure of relevant facts. The opportunity is taken to remind taxpayers and their authorised representatives of the need to accurately complete the return concerning transactions for or with non-residents.

Advance Rulings

30. To provide certainty in this area the Department will, commencing 1 April 1998, provide advance rulings on the locality of profits to businesses. This service is subject to the payment of a fee. Further details are contained in *Departmental Interpretation & Practice Notes No. 31*.

Conclusion

31. The reaction to the DIPN issued in November 1992 and the April 1996 revision on this subject has been generally favourable. However, with the experience gained since their issue, combined with the decisions in *Magna* and *Orion Caribbean*, it is considered that an update of the position, particularly as regards trading profits, might be helpful. I hope that this revised DIPN will further reduce the possibility of and the areas of dispute between taxpayers and the Department.

32. Finally, I should reiterate that the examples outlined in this DIPN represent simple, and straightforward situations and should be viewed accordingly. As stated at the outset, each case needs to be considered in the light of its own particular circumstances and facts. There is no simple legal test that can be employed.

APPENDIX 14

**Inland Revenue Department
Hong Kong
DEPARTMENTAL INTERPRETATION & PRACTICE NOTES
No. 38 (Revised)**

**SALARIES TAX
EMPLOYEE SHARE OPTION BENEFITS**

These notes are issued for the information and guidance of taxpayers and their authorised representatives. They have no binding force and do not affect a person's right of objection and appeal to the Commissioner, the Board of Review or the Courts.

These notes replace those issued in February 2001.

LAU MAK Yee-ming
Commissioner of Inland Revenue

March 2005

Our web site : http://www.ird.gov.hk

CONTENT

INTRODUCTION

The purpose of this Practice Note is to outline the assessing practice followed by the Inland Revenue Department (the Department) in relation to benefits obtained from share option schemes by employees and office holders. Typically, an employee receives a right to acquire shares at a nominated price some time in the future. Usually the shares are in the employer company itself or in a related company (e.g. the parent company of the employer or another company in the same group). The employee is not obliged to make any purchase until he "exercises" the option. Accordingly, there is an incentive for such an employee to work towards making the company concerned more profitable or valuable, which would increase his or her likelihood of being able to make a gain through exercising the right and acquiring the shares.

Taxation treatment prior to the introduction of specific provisions

2. The Inland Revenue Ordinance (the Ordinance) has since 1971 contained specific provisions relating to the taxation of benefits received from employee share option schemes. Prior to their introduction, a share option benefit would be charged to Salaries Tax if it could be regarded as a "perquisite" and hence, by virtue of section 9(1)(a) of the Ordinance, fall within the inclusive definition of income from an office or employment of profit. In the absence of any decision from the courts in Hong Kong concerning share option benefits, guidance on the issue of what constituted a chargeable perquisite was obtained from United Kingdom cases.

3. In 1961 the House of Lords handed down a decision in *Abbott v. Philbin 39 TC 82*, which had considerable impact on the taxation of benefits associated with share option schemes. The decision was important not only in that it provided guidance as to what should be regarded as a perquisite, but also in that it led to the introduction of specific share option provisions in the United Kingdom and Hong Kong.

4. The taxpayer concerned in *Abbott v. Philbin* was the secretary of a company that had decided to grant options over certain shares to executives of the company and its subsidiaries. The taxpayer was offered the opportunity to acquire at a cost of £1 for every 100 shares a non-transferable option, valid for ten years, to purchase 2,000 shares at the market price ruling at the date of the offer. The taxpayer accepted the offer in October 1954. The following year the taxpayer exercised his right under the option and applied for and was allotted 250 shares at the specified option price.

5. In accordance with what was then the normal practice of the Revenue, a sum equal to the difference between the current market price and the amount paid for the shares (plus a proportionate part of the cost of the option) was included in the taxpayer's assessment for the year in which the option was exercised.

However, the House of Lords held that the benefit of the option contract could be converted into money, even though it was nonassignable (the employee could have obtained money from a third party by agreeing to exercise the option when instructed and thereupon transfer the shares), and that as such it was a perquisite which was taxable on its value at the time of grant and not on the value when exercised.

6. The law relating to share options was subsequently amended in the United Kingdom to, in effect, over-rule the decision in *Abbott v. Philbin*. In essence, the legislation gave statutory support to what had been the Revenue's earlier practice in respect of binding option rights.

Amendments in Hong Kong

7. The UK amendments were considered locally in the course of the deliberations of the Second Inland Revenue Ordinance Review Committee, which delivered its final Report to the Government in 1968. The following excerpt from the Report is pertinent —

> "169. The Commissioner asked us to consider the introduction of a provision for determining the value of income derived by an employee from the exercise of an option to take up shares in the corporation which employs him. We noted that it has been found necessary in the U.K. to lay down the basis for determining the value to be treated as income. The principle which the Commissioner wished to establish is that the value to be brought to charge as income should be calculated, and should be deemed to arise, at the time the option is exercised. The income to be charged should be the difference between —
>
> (a) the open market value of the shares at the date of exercise of the option (or in the case of an assignment or release, the consideration received for the assignment or release); and
> (b) the cost of acquiring the shares including any consideration (apart from services in his office or employment) which the employee gave for the option.
>
> 170. WE RECOMMEND that there should be included, as an additional paragraph to Section 9(1), 'any gain made by a director or employee of a corporation from the exercise of a right, obtained from the corporation, to acquire shares therein' and that the principle which the Commissioner wished to establish should also be incorporated in the enabling provisions."

8. The Ordinance was subsequently amended by Inland Revenue (Amendment) Ordinance 1971 to introduce, amongst other provisions, section 9(1)(d), 9(4) and 9(5). The Explanatory Memorandum of the Bill for the Amendment Ordinance contained the following —

> "The principal purpose of this Bill is to implement recommendations contained in Part II of the Report of the Inland Revenue Ordinance Review Committee.
>
> ...

6. Clause 6 (which follows section 25 of the U.K. Finance Act 1966) amends section 9 by adding new subsections (4) and (5) to provide for the charge to tax of any share options acquired by a person as a result of his employment. The manner of valuation of such options for tax purposes is also provided for." [at C646]

9. The amendments were agreed as proposed by the Legislative Council without comment.

SCHEME OF THE LEGISLATION

10. Briefly, the legislation has the following three main elements —

- The first, section 9(1)(d), in effect provides that income from an office or employment includes any gain realized by the exercise, assignment or release of a share option obtained by a person as an employee or office holder of a company.
- The second, section 9(4), specifies the basis of calculation of any realized gain that comes within the scope of section 9(1)(d).
- The third, section 9(5), provides that where a gain may be taxable by virtue of section 9(1)(d) in respect of the exercise of a right, the receipt of the right cannot be charged to tax under any other provision of the Ordinance.

The three elements are further discussed below, together with related matters.

Section 9(1)(d)

"any gain realized by the exercise of, or by the assignment or release of, a right to acquire shares or stock ..."

11. Section 9(1)(d) only has application where an employee (or office holder) has exercised, assigned or released a "right" to acquire shares. In this regard it is accepted that the term "right" refers to a legally enforceable right; not a "mere expectation", such as where a person is invited to apply for shares in circumstances where the invitation may be withdrawn at any time. It should be noted, however, that in the latter situation a taxable perquisite would generally be received if an application were to be accepted and shares allotted. Such a perquisite, if meeting the other requirements for chargeability, would be taxable to the extent of the difference between the price for which the shares could be sold and the price paid for them: *Weight v. Salmon 19 TC 174.*

12. The taxpayer in that case was the managing director of a company. In addition to a fixed salary, he was given the privilege each year of applying for unissued shares at their par value, which was less than the market value. The taxpayer accordingly applied for shares and they were issued to him. He was assessed to tax on the difference between the par and market values at the date the shares were allotted. The case eventually came before the House of Lords where the assessment was upheld. The decision was considered in *Abbott v. Philbin* where Lord Reid, at page 123, emphasised that that case could be distinguished as a binding option had not been involved —

> "The case of Weight v. Salmon seems to me to be entirely different. There the servant had no enforceable right at all until he got his shares. He got his shares because the company chose to give him something then, to give him a perquisite when the shares were issued. But, in this case, the Appellant getting his shares did not flow from any voluntary act of the company when the shares were issued. It flowed from the company's voluntary act in the previous year, when they gave him an option by which they were thereafter bound. It would, I think, require some peculiar circumstances to make a mere expectation capable of being turned to pecuniary account."

13. The respective meanings of the terms "exercise", "assignment" and "release", within the context of these provisions, are discussed in paragraphs 16 to 32 below, in relation to section 9(4).

"… shares or stock in a corporation obtained by a person as the holder of an office in or an employee of that or any other corporation"

14. The words in section 9(1)(d) quoted above dictate that the following points should be kept in mind when considering the application of the share option provisions —

- The provisions can only apply where an option (i.e. a right to acquire shares or stock in a corporation) is obtained by an employee of a company or by the holder of an office in a company. Where such an option is obtained by a person who is employed other than by a company (e.g. by a partnership), chargeability generally depends on whether the option itself can be regarded as a perquisite, under section 9(1)(a), derived from Hong Kong (see paragraphs 2–5 above).
- For the provisions to apply, the shares (or stock) to which the option relates need not be in the company in which the person concerned is an employee or office holder. For example, the option could be granted in respect of shares in the overseas parent company of the local company employing the taxpayer.

Section 9(4)

15. As has been indicated above, section 9(4) must be applied to ascertain the quantum of any gain that comes within the scope of section 9(1)(d). In this regard —

- section 9(4)(a) details what is taken to be "the gain realized" where a right of a kind referred to in section 9(1)(d) is exercised; and
- section 9(4)(b) similarly provides for cases where the gain is realized by assignment or release of such a right.

Section 9(4)(a)

"… by the exercise"

16. The Ordinance does not define what is meant by the word "exercise" in the context of section 9(1)(d). Nor is it possible, given the great variety of terms and conditions which can govern the operation of share option schemes, to state exhaustively how the word is construed in practice. Generally, however, a taxpayer is considered to have exercised an option when he has taken whatever steps are necessary to convert the offer contained in the option agreement into a contract to purchase the relevant shares. Depending on the terms of the option agreement, this may require no more than the employee providing the party concerned with written confirmation of acceptance of the offer. On the other hand, an agreement may contain provisions that deem an option to be validly exercised only when particular requirements are satisfied (e.g. that payment for the shares be made in a certain manner or that the "exercise" of the option be approved by the board of directors of the company). Provided that they are genuine and have not been inserted with a view to facilitating tax avoidance, such requirements will be recognised by the Department in ascertaining the time of exercise of an option.

The critical time

17. It is important to ascertain the point in time at which an option is exercised. This is because section 9(4)(a) provides, briefly put, that the gain realized by "the exercise at any time" of a share option is based on the amount which could be obtained for the shares acquired in the open market "at that time". In other words, the gain is required to be calculated by reference to the open market value on the day of exercise and it will generally not be relevant to consider value at any later date. However, following the decision of the Board of Review in case *D 43/99, IRBRD, vol. 14, 448*, if a taxpayer can establish that because of circumstances beyond his control he did not acquire the relevant shares (in the sense that the shares had been issued to him) until a date subsequent to the date of exercise, the Department will accept the adoption of that later date for the purposes of the provisions. It should be pointed out, however, that in case *D 120/02, IRBRD, vol. 18, 125*, the Board drew a distinction between "a share certificate" and "a share". The Board held that a share could be regarded as a bundle of rights, the non-availability of the share certificate did not prevent the vesting of the rights and thus the Appellant in that case acquired the shares when her name was entered in the Register of Shareholders and became entitled to dividends and voting rights.

A notional gain must be computed

18. The gain that has to be calculated is a notional one; the question of chargeability does not depend on whether or not the employee sells the shares acquired as a result of exercising the option. Even if no sale takes place, such as where the shares are held as an investment, the employee will nonetheless be chargeable (assuming that the income has a Hong Kong source) in respect of any notional profit arrived at as a result of the application of section 9(4)(a) to the circumstances at the time of the exercise of the option. Any subsequent gain derived from the actual sale of the shares would not be subject to Salaries Tax.

Computation method

19. Section 9(4)(a) provides, broadly put, that for the purposes of section 9(1)(d) the gain realized by the exercise at any time of an option shall be taken to be the difference between (a) the amount which a person might reasonably expect to obtain from a sale in the open market, at the time of exercise of the option, of the shares acquired and (b) the amount or value of the consideration given for the shares and the grant of the option.

20. Section 9(4) also provides that the entire consideration shall be apportioned if it is for something beside the shares covered by the option. A proviso to the subsection makes it clear that the consideration cannot include any amount in respect of the performance of the duties of the office or employment, and that the amount or value of the consideration given for the grant of the option cannot be deducted more than once.

Open market value

Restrictions on sale

21. Share options are sometimes granted on the condition that restrictions will apply in relation to the disposal of any shares acquired under the scheme (e.g. as to when or to whom the shares can be sold). The restriction on disposal of the shares are relevant in determining the amount "which a person might reasonably expect to obtain from a sale in the open market". This is a valuation exercise to be undertaken in the light of the facts of each particular case, see for example, *D 120/02, IRBRD vol. 18, 125*, where a 25% discount was allowed to reflect the five year restriction period against alienation of the shares.

Quoted shares

22. Where the shares are listed on a stock exchange, the open market value of the shares acquired can be taken as the closing quotation value for shares of the same kind on the date the option is exercised. In practice, the Department will consider a request for downward adjustment of the quoted value if there is evidence to suggest that, because of the number involved, a sale of the shares obtained from exercising the option would only be possible at a reduced price, i.e. a "slump effect" would be induced if the shares in question were to be made available for sale. This practice reflects the decision of the Board of Review in case *D 46/95, IRBRD, vol. 10, 308*. If the shares are listed in Hong Kong and overseas at the same time, it is normal practice for the Department to adopt the price quoted on the Hong Kong Stock Exchange. If the shares are listed on two non-Hong Kong exchanges, the taxpayer may select the more favourable price.

23. Once the open market value of the shares is ascertained, the gain for the purposes of section 9(1) (i.e. the amount to be treated as income from an office or employment) is arrived at by deducting from this figure the consideration given for the grant of the option and the consideration given for the shares in question. It is accepted that the latter amount can include any brokerage, stamp duty or other charges that would have been levied if the notional sale had actually taken place.

Unquoted shares

24. Where the option exercised is in respect of shares in a private company (i.e. one which is not quoted on a recognised stock exchange at the date of exercise), it will generally not be possible to look to an actual sale of shares of the same kind to arrive at a valuation. And, because of the variations in circumstances that may be involved, it is not possible to say that for all such companies there is a single valuation method (e.g. reference to "dividend yield", "earnings yield" or "asset backing") which could appropriately be used to determine the open market value. It is also pertinent that the application of section 9(4)(a) in relation to such cases has not been considered by any court in Hong Kong.

25. Nevertheless, it is considered that guidance as to the correct approach to be used can be drawn from estate duty case-law concerning the open market value of private company shares. [See, for example: *Commissioners of Inland Revenue v. Crossman (1937) AC 26; In re Lynall (DECD.) (1971) 47 TC 375; and In re Harry Charrington (DECD.) (1975) HKLR 81.*] In this regard, the Department considers that the correct objective is to ascertain what price a hypothetical willing, but not anxious, purchaser would need to pay a hypothetical willing, but not anxious, seller in the open market to acquire the subject shares on the date of exercise of the option. Furthermore, in undertaking this exercise it should be assumed that —
  - the shares are offered for sale to the world at large so that all potential purchasers have an equal opportunity to make an offer as a result of it being openly known what is offered for sale (*Lynall* p. 411);
  - the hypothetical purchaser would not rely only on information published by the company, but would also consider its prospects having regard to matters of public knowledge, at the date of exercise, concerning the

company, its directors and management and relevant business trends and developments (*Lynall* p. 411);

- the seller would give as much information as he was entitled to give. If not a director, he would provide the information he could get as a shareholder. If he was a director with confidential information, it should not be assumed that it would be disclosed to the public without the consent of the board of directors of the company (*Lynall* p. 406 & p. 413);
- the sale price paid would not be exceptional i.e. it should not be increased over what could be regarded as an ordinary market price to reflect a premium a particular buyer might pay because of special reasons unique to that party (*Crossman* p. 44);
- any conditions requiring satisfaction under the articles of association of the company to enable an open market sale to take place would be satisfied (e.g. the directors of the company would not exercise any discretion to refuse to register the transfer of the shares, and any existing shareholder's right of pre-emption would be waived); and
- following acquisition of the shares, the hypothetical purchaser would be subject to (and hence this would be reflected in the valuation) any restrictions imposed by the provisions of the articles of association relevant to the shares in question (e.g. relating to the alienation and transfer of shares in the company).

26. Where an option has been exercised over shares in a private company, it will sometimes be useful for officers of the Department to meet representatives of the company (subject to the appropriate authority being given by the employees concerned) with a view to agreeing the valuation on exercise. Negotiations can begin as soon as the exercise has taken place and there is no need to wait until the end of the tax year. In the first instance, a request for a meeting should be sent to the Commissioner. The request should be accompanied by details of the basis of valuation proposed, together with relevant supporting documents.

Section 9(4)(b)

27. Section 9(4)(b) provides for cases where a right to acquire shares is assigned or released. The gain is taken to be the difference between the amount or value of the consideration for the assignment or release and the amount or value of the consideration for the grant of the right (i.e. the amount paid for the option).

Assignment

28. In the context of section 9(4)(b), it is considered that the term "assignment" refers to the situation where an employee (or office holder) transfers the whole of his interest in rights acquired under an option agreement to a third party. In order to ascertain whether a purported assignment was for tax avoidance purposes, the Department will generally require copies of all agreements and other documentation relating to the grant of the option and the assignment to be submitted for consideration. If it is not otherwise apparent, the employee (assignor) will also be required to advise —

- whether the option agreement prohibited any assignment and if so whether the prohibition was subsequently waived;
- whether the employer was notified of the assignment;
- whether the assignor retained any interest in the option right and if so the nature of that interest;
- whether the party to whom the right was assigned (i.e. the assignee) could, as a result of the assignment, formally exercise the option;
- whether any vesting period under the option agreement had been completed prior to the assignment;
- the nature of the relationship, if any, of the assignor to the assignee;
- the amount of and terms of payment of the consideration for the assignment; and
- the basis used to decide upon the consideration in respect of the assignment.

Release

29. Within the context of section 9(4)(b), the term "release" refers to the situation where an employee, without exercising his right to acquire shares under a share option scheme, agrees to the discharge of that right either for valuable consideration or under seal (i.e. release by deed).

30. To simply allow an option right to lapse by not exercising it within the option period would not amount to a "release" within the context of section 9(4)(b). Likewise, if an employer were empowered under a share option agreement to unilaterally cancel an option right in certain circumstances and did so, this would not constitute a release.

31. It should be noted, however, that if an employee were to receive compensation because he had suffered a loss as a result of having to delay the exercise of an option, the compensation would be regarded as a perquisite chargeable to Salaries Tax (if derived from Hong Kong) by virtue of sections 8(1) and 9(1)(a) of the Ordinance: see the decision of the Board of Review in case *D 4/91, IRBRD, vol. 5, 542*. By parity of reasoning, the same would apply in respect of any compensation received by an employee for agreeing to let an option expire without exercising it (as distinct from agreeing to the legal discharge of the option).

Exchange of rights

32. Cases sometimes arise where a right to acquire shares of a particular type is exchanged for a right to acquire shares of another type, e.g. as a result of a take-over or restructuring of a company. In such a case (i.e. where a straight exchange is involved, without the employee also receiving monetary consideration), the Department will generally accept that the exchange does not constitute an assignment or release for the purposes of section 9(1)(d). Accordingly, no Salaries Tax liability arises as a result of the exchange itself. Instead, the relevant provisions are applied in relation to the right received in exchange, when it is subsequently exercised, assigned or released (taking into account any consideration given for the grant of the original right). The Department should be consulted regarding the appropriate basis of assessment, by writing to the Commissioner, in any case where the consideration received in exchange includes both a new right and a monetary payment.

Section 9(5)

33. As has been indicated in paragraph 5 above, prior to the introduction of the specific provisions in the Ordinance dealing with share options, if an employee or office holder acquired an enforceable right to obtain shares in a company, the person concerned was assessable on the value of the right at the time of its grant, less any sum paid for it. The specific provisions, on the other hand, impose liability in respect of the subsequent exercise, assignment or release of the right. The role of section 9(5) is to ensure that a person who acquires a right is not subject to double taxation i.e. in respect of the receipt of the right (as a perquisite) and under the specific share option provisions. In essence, the subsection looks ahead and provides that where a person may become chargeable by virtue of section 9(1)(d) in respect of any gain which may be realized by the exercise of a right, the person cannot be charged to Salaries Tax under any other provision in respect of the receipt of the right (i.e. on the basis that a perquisite falling within section 9(1)(a) has been received).

34. Section 9(5) would not prevent the receipt of a right being charged to Salaries Tax as a perquisite if it were to become apparent in a particular case that no amount would be chargeable by virtue of section 9(1)(d). In practice, however, if at the time a right is obtained there is a possibility that an amount may eventually be chargeable by virtue of section 9(1)(d), the Department will not in any event (i.e. irrespective of the ultimate outcome) seek to charge an amount under any other provision.

APPLYING THE PROVISIONS

General principles

35. Apart from valuation issues, questions concerning the application of the share option provisions most frequently arise in relation to situations where employment circumstances change between the time of grant of the right to acquire the shares and the time of exercise of the right, and cases involving employees who have non-Hong Kong employments. In considering the various circumstances, it may be useful to keep the following points in mind —

(i)   When a person is granted a right to acquire shares by virtue of his employment, he derives income in the form of a perquisite. Normally, if derived from Hong Kong, the perquisite would be chargeable to Salaries Tax in the year of assessment in which the person obtains it. However, by virtue of the specific provisions under section 9(1)(d) and 9(5), the person is not necessarily charged to tax in the year in which the perquisite is derived, but on a notional basis in the year of assessment in which the right is subsequently exercised, assigned or released.

(ii) Section 9(1)(d) provides that any gain realized by the exercise, assignment or release of the rights constitutes "income from employment".

(iii) The gain in respect of the exercise etc. of the right is calculated on a notional basis in accordance with section 9(4), and is assessable to the extent that it is derived from Hong Kong. The gain is taken to accrue to the taxpayer in the year of assessment in which the right is exercised etc. and, by virtue of section 11B, falls for assessment in that year of assessment (rather than the year in which the benefit of the right was derived).

(iv) Section 9(1)(d) and associated provisions provide for the calculation and timing of any charge to Salaries Tax in respect of a share right benefit. They do not, however, have any bearing on the question of when the benefit is actually derived, which is determined by the time of grant of the relevant right.

(v)   While some options are allowed to be exercised without any conditions, some may require certain conditions to be fulfilled before the option can be exercised. The concept of "vesting" is common in share options. An option will generally be considered to have vested when all conditions for its exercise have been satisfied and the employee is free to exercise without restriction. Among the typical conditions, it is frequently required that the employee continues to work for the employer for a certain period of time. For the present purposes, an option will be regarded as vested when such period has expired. Therefore, "vesting period" here normally means the period from the date of grant of option, or such date as mentioned in the terms of the grant, to the first available date that an employee is entitled to exercise the option.

Hong Kong employment

36. Although section 9(1)(d) provides that any gain realized (calculated in accordance with section 9(4)), by the exercise, assignment or release of the rights constitutes "income from employment", the gain is only chargeable to Salaries Tax if it comes within the scope of section 8(1)(a), i.e. if it can correctly be described as "income arising in or derived from Hong Kong". In other words, one has to consider whether the income had a source in Hong Kong.

37. The source of the income mentioned in paragraph 36 above is the right to acquire shares obtained by the person as an employee. As such, if the person had a Hong Kong employment at the time of the grant of the right, the income is also regarded as having been derived from Hong Kong. Any gain realized by the subsequent exercise etc. of the right will be chargeable to Salaries Tax unless the gain is excluded by virtue of section 8(1A)(b), i.e. where the person renders outside Hong Kong all the services in connection with his employment. In the latter regard, if a right is granted to an employee on an unconditional basis during a year of assessment in which the person renders all services in respect of his employment outside Hong Kong, any gain subsequently realized, even if realized whilst the person is working in Hong Kong will not be charged to Salaries Tax. Although the gain is considered to accrue to the person in the year of assessment in which the right is exercised, it is recognised as having been derived from the services rendered outside Hong Kong.

Example 1

The taxpayer had a Hong Kong employment. He was granted an unconditional right to subscribe for shares. He ceased employment and exercised his option after cessation of employment.

38. Cessation of employment does not prevent the application of the share option provisions. As the taxpayer concerned had a Hong Kong employment at the time of grant of the right, the relevant income was derived from Hong Kong and accordingly is chargeable to Salaries Tax in the year of assessment in which the right is exercised. It should be noted that as the application of section 9(1)(d) is concerned with notional income, rather than any payment made to an employee, section 11D cannot apply in relation to the income — i.e. it cannot act to deem the amount to have been received by the employee on the last day of his employment. Instead, the income simply falls to be assessed in respect of the year of assessment in which it accrued to the employee i.e. the year of assessment in which the right was exercised.

Example 2

The taxpayer had a Hong Kong employment. All services were rendered in Hong Kong prior to and during the year the unconditional grant of the right was granted to him. During the year of assessment in which the right was exercised, the taxpayer rendered all services outside Hong Kong in connection with the same employment.

39. As the taxpayer had a Hong Kong employment, the gain would be treated as having been derived from Hong Kong. The gain would only be excluded from the charge to Salaries Tax by virtue of section 8(1A)(b)(ii), taking into account section 8(1B), if all services were rendered outside Hong Kong in the year of grant of the right. The gain, calculated in accordance with section 9(4), would fall for assessment in the year of assessment in which the right was exercised. The fact that the taxpayer did not render any services in Hong Kong during the year of exercise would not in itself have any bearing on whether the gain would be chargeable to Salaries Tax, see *D 4/02, IRBRD, vol. 17, 400.*

Example 3

The taxpayer had a Hong Kong employment. All services were rendered outside Hong Kong in the year of assessment in which the right was unconditionally granted, but rendered inside Hong Kong during the year of assessment in which the right was exercised.

40. As the taxpayer rendered all services outside Hong Kong during the year of assessment in which the right was granted, and as it was granted on an unconditional basis which did not involve services being rendered in Hong Kong, it would be accepted that the gain on realization should qualify for exemption by virtue of section 8(1A)(b)(ii), taking into account section 8(1B), notwithstanding the fact that the taxpayer was rendering services in Hong Kong during the year in which the right was actually exercised.

Example 4

The taxpayer had a Hong Kong employment. The right was conditionally granted, subject to the completion of a vesting period of 2 years from 1 April 2000. The position during the vesting period was as follows:

Year ended
31.3.2001   More than 60 days in Hong Kong rendering services
31.3.2002   No services rendered in Hong Kong

He exercised the option on 1 July 2002. During the year ended 31 March 2003, he did not render service in Hong Kong.

41. The chargeability of any gain on exercise would not hinge on where (or if) the taxpayer was rendering services in the year of assessment in which the right was exercised. Unlike the situation with a non-Hong Kong employment where the primary purpose is to ascertain the income derived from services rendered in Hong Kong, for a Hong Kong employment case, income can only be excluded from the charge to Salaries Tax if the taxpayer renders outside Hong Kong all the services in connection with his employment (taking into account the 60 days allowance provided under section 8(1B)).

42. Accordingly, having regard to the latter point in the previous paragraph, if during any year of assessment included in the vesting period, the taxpayer rendered services in Hong Kong during visits exceeding 60 days, all of the gain from the exercise of the option would be chargeable to Salaries Tax. On the other hand, if during each such year the taxpayer's visits did not exceed a total of 60 days, no part of the gain would be treated as chargeable (section 8(1A)(b)(ii) and (1B) would apply).

Non-Hong Kong employment

43. Where a person has a non-Hong Kong employment at the time of grant, the gain will have a non-Hong Kong source and will not be chargeable to Salaries Tax unless it comes within the scope of section 8(1A)(a) i.e. if it is derived from services rendered in Hong Kong. In this regard, the Department will generally accept that no liability to Salaries Tax arises where a right is granted on an unconditional basis (or on completion of a vesting period of a conditional grant) prior to a person rendering any services in Hong Kong, notwithstanding that the right may be exercised after the person commences to render such services.

44. The more complex situation is the one where a person with a non-Hong Kong employment is granted the right subject to a vesting period during which services are rendered both in and outside Hong Kong. In such a situation, it is considered that the gain on the subsequent exercise etc. of the right should not be fully assessable in Hong Kong as it can partly be attributed to services rendered outside Hong Kong. On the other hand, because the gain can be partly attributed to services in Hong Kong, the benefit should to some extent be chargeable to Salaries Tax.

45. In considering the appropriate proportion, if any, of the gain to be treated as derived from services rendered in Hong Kong, regard must, of course, be had to the terms of the contract governing the grant of the right and to any other relevant facts. In the case of a non-Hong Kong employment, however, the Department will generally accept that it is equitable to have regard to the number of days in Hong Kong plus leave days attributable to services in Hong Kong during the period from the date of conditional grant to the date the employee became unconditionally entitled to exercise the right (i.e., the vesting period) to the total number of days in the period, notwithstanding that it may only be exercised after a further period. In other words, the assessable amount of the gain can generally be arrived at by applying the following formula —

$$\frac{\text{Days in Hong Kong plus attributable leave during vesting period}}{\text{Total number of days in the vesting period}} \times \frac{\text{Gain calculated in accordance with sections } 9(1)(d) \text{ and } 9(4)}{1}$$

46. For example, if the vesting period was two years (i.e. 730 days) and the person's days in Hong Kong plus leave days attributable to service in Hong Kong were 292 days during the period, 40% of the gain would be assessable in the year of exercise of the right (i.e. 292 / 730 = 40%). For the purpose of counting the number of days in Hong Kong, only one day is generally counted in respect of the days of arrival and departure (the so-called "midnight rule"). This is consistent with the assessing practice usually applied in relation to time apportionment claims under section 8(1A)(a) and (c).

47. The provisions of section 8(1A)(b)(ii), as read with section 8(1B), may be relevant in relation to the calculation of the proportion referred to above. By virtue of section 8(1A)(b)(ii), chargeable income does not include income derived from services rendered by a person who renders outside Hong Kong all the services in connection with his employment. In this regard, section 8(1B) provides that in determining whether or not all services are rendered outside Hong Kong, services rendered during visits not exceeding a total of 60 days in the basis period for the year of assessment are not to be taken into account. Accordingly, if services are rendered by the taxpayer in Hong Kong during visits of less than 60 days during any year of assessment that falls within the vesting period, the days concerned are not taken into account in computing the proportion of the gain attributable to services rendered in Hong Kong. To illustrate, if in the example used in paragraph 46 the vesting period had covered the period 1 January 2001 to 31 December 2002, and the taxpayer had only rendered services in Hong Kong for a total of 40 days during the 2000/01 year of assessment (with the remaining 252 "Hong Kong days", of the total of 292 days, falling in 2001/02), the chargeable proportion of the gain for year 2001/ 02 would be taken to be 34%, i.e. 252/730.

48. It should be noted that for the purpose of determining whether section 8 (1B) is applicable (i.e. in ascertaining whether or not services were rendered in Hong Kong during visits exceeding a total of 60 days), the basis of counting days differs slightly from the "midnight rule" referred to above. More particularly, the decision of the Board of Review in case *D 29/89*, IRBRD, vol. 4, 340, is applied, where it was held that "any part of a day counts as a 'day' for the purpose of section 8(1B)". This decision was also followed in case *D 12/94, IRBRD, vol. 9, 131*.

49. The chargeable portion of a gain of the kind referred to under the previous point is calculated separately from other chargeable income. Although the chargeable portion will fall for assessment in the year of assessment in which the gain is realized, it is calculated by reference to the "days in" and "days out" during the vesting period, which may have taken place in earlier years of assessment. The person's other assessable income, if any, is calculated separately (and may involve a different time apportionment calculation in respect of remuneration for services rendered during that year).

50. The Ordinance does not require that the person be currently employed at the time of exercise etc. for section 9(1)(d) to be applied. Liability, if any, to assessment to Salaries Tax arises at the time the right is granted and cannot be extinguished by deferring exercise etc. until after cessation of employment. Where a right is exercised after cessation, the gain is treated as assessable income for the year of assessment in which the exercise takes place (section 11D cannot apply to treat the gain as having accrued to the person on the last date of his employment as the exercise of a right does not involve any payment by the employer to the person).

Example 5

The taxpayer had a non-Hong Kong employment. All services were rendered outside Hong Kong in the year of assessment in which the right was unconditionally granted, but rendered inside Hong Kong during the year of assessment in which the right was exercised.

51. As the taxpayer rendered all services outside Hong Kong during the year of assessment in which the right was granted, and as it was granted on an unconditional basis that did not involve services being rendered in Hong Kong, the right would accordingly be recognised as having been derived from services rendered outside Hong Kong. As such, the gain on exercise of the right would not be chargeable to Salaries Tax.

Example 6

The taxpayer had a non-Hong Kong employment. All services were rendered in Hong Kong during the year of assessment in which the right was unconditionally granted, but during the year of assessment in which the right was exercised, the taxpayer rendered all services in connection with the employment outside Hong Kong.

52. As the taxpayer rendered all services in connection with the employment in Hong Kong during the year of assessment in which the right was granted, and as it was granted on an unconditional basis which did not involve services being rendered outside Hong Kong, the gain on exercise would be fully chargeable to Salaries Tax by virtue of section 8(1A)(a) (i.e. the gain would fall within the words "income derived from services rendered in Hong Kong"). The timing of the exercise of the right would determine the year of assessment in respect of which the gain is chargeable, but would not otherwise be relevant. The chargeability of the gain depends on where the person rendered the services from which the benefit, i.e. the right, was derived; not on where the taxpayer was rendering services at the time of the subsequent exercise of the right. Likewise, if the taxpayer had ceased the employment prior to exercising the right, it would not have any bearing on the issue of chargeability.

Example 7

The taxpayer had a non-Hong Kong employment. Services were rendered inside and outside Hong Kong during the year of assessment in which the right was unconditionally granted and during the year in which it was exercised.

53. If the right was unconditionally granted to the taxpayer before he commenced to render any services for the employer concerned in Hong Kong, it would be accepted that the right was not derived from services rendered in Hong Kong, and accordingly no part of the gain calculated under section 9(4) in respect of the exercise of the right would be chargeable to Salaries Tax.

54. If, however, the right was unconditionally granted to the taxpayer after he had commenced to render services in Hong Kong, part of the gain would be regarded as having been derived from services rendered in Hong Kong. In practice, in such a case, the right would be treated as having been derived from the services rendered during the course of the year of assessment in which it was granted. Accordingly, the assessable portion would be calculated using the same "time basis" ratio applied in relation to the other income derived by the person in the year of assessment of the grant. The actual assessable amount would, of course, also depend on the amount of the gain calculated in accordance with section 9(4), and would be assessable in the year of assessment in which the right was exercised. The fact that the taxpayer rendered some services in Hong Kong during the year of assessment in which the right was exercised would not in itself have any bearing on whether the gain on exercise would be chargeable to Salaries Tax.

Example 8

The taxpayer had a non-Hong Kong employment. The right was conditionally granted subject to the completion of a vesting period during which services were rendered partly inside and partly outside Hong Kong.

55. In a case involving a non-Hong Kong employment, because of the terms of section 8(1A)(a), it is necessary to ascertain the extent to which the income (i.e. the gain on exercise) was derived from services rendered in Hong Kong. The approach to use in such a case is explained in paragraphs 44 to 48 above. The assessable portion, if any, would be chargeable to Salaries Tax in respect of the year of assessment in which the right was exercised.

Changes from Hong Kong to Non-Hong Kong employment or vice versa during vesting period

56. The option may be granted at the time when the taxpayer holds a Hong Kong employment or non-Hong Kong employment, subject to the completion of a vesting period. During the vesting period, the taxpayer's source of employment changes from a Hong Kong to a non-Hong Kong employment, or vice versa. Given that the taxpayer holds both a Hong Kong and non-Hong Kong employment during the vesting period, the assessable gain of the option is apportioned between the periods covered by the two employments.

Example 9

The taxpayer had a non-Hong Kong employment at the time when the option was conditionally granted subject to the completion of a vesting period during which the taxpayer's employment was changed to a Hong Kong employment within the same group of companies.

57. As the option was derived by the taxpayer from both the non-Hong Kong employment and the Hong Kong employment, it is necessary to apportion the share option gain, which can be done by simple time apportionment, to ascertain the amount of the gain attributable to each employment. The portion attributable to the Hong Kong employment would be fully assessed or fully exempt in accordance with the principles and examples set out in paragraphs 36 to 42 above. On the other hand, the portion of the gain attributable to the non-Hong Kong employment would be fully exempt or further apportioned to arrive at the amount attributable to services rendered in Hong Kong pursuant to the principles and examples set out in paragraphs 43 to 55 above.

PERSONS DEPARTING PERMANENTLY FROM HONG KONG

58. It will be appreciated from what is said above that a gain realized from the exercise, assignment or release of a share option after permanent departure from Hong Kong might nonetheless be chargeable to Salaries Tax. However, with a view to finalising the Salaries Tax liabilities of such persons prior to departure, the Department will, as a concession, allow a person to elect to have the liability ascertained on the basis of a notional exercise of the option. More particularly, the Department will accept that the liability, if any, can be finalized on the basis of the gain (calculated in accordance with section 9(4)(a)) that would have been realized if the option had been exercised on a day within 7 days before the date of submission of the person's tax return for the final assessment applicable to the year of assessment in which he or she permanently departs from Hong Kong. It should be noted that if the person concerned has a non-Hong Kong employment and the option in question is a conditional one in respect of which the vesting period has not expired on the date of the notional exercise, the gain should nonetheless be calculated on the basis that the vesting period would be deemed to end on that date.

59. If a person wishes to make such an election, an election form cum computation of gain statement per the Appendix should be attached to the return to the effect that the gain is offered for assessment on the understanding that no further liability will arise when the option is actually exercised, assigned or released (i.e. after departure from Hong Kong). The election should be made in respect of all grants received but not exercised prior to cessation of employment for Hong Kong salaries tax purposes and / or departure from Hong Kong. Election relating to some of the grants or only part of a grant is not accepted.

60. As a further concession, the Department is prepared to accept an election made within 3 months from the date of permanent departure from Hong Kong if it has not been made before departure. In this kind of situation, the date of departure will be taken as the date of the notional exercise for purposes of calculating the gain.

61. An election once made cannot be withdrawn before the actual exercise, assignment or release, except (i) within the objection period of the assessment in which the gain of the notional exercise is included, or (ii) total forfeiture of the options with no replacement or compensation before the actual exercise. On the other hand, if it transpires that the gain in respect of the actual exercise, assignment or release is less than the amount assessed in respect of the notional exercise, the Department will favourably consider any application for appropriate amendment and re-assessment.

REPORTING REQUIREMENTS

Employees

62. Where, by virtue of section 9(1)(d) and the related provisions referred to above, a person is chargeable to Salaries Tax in respect of a gain realized by the exercise, assignment or release of a right to acquire shares or stock in a corporation, the person is obliged to inform the Department of the fact. Just as chargeability does not depend on the person being employed at the time of exercise, or on the right being in respect of shares in any particular company, these factors have no bearing on the person's obligation to inform the Department. The only exception is where a person has elected for a notional exercise of the options as set out in paragraphs 58 to 61 above. If all tax liability has been settled through a notional exercise, the person is not required to inform the Department at the time of actual exercise.

63. The requirement to inform the Department can generally be satisfied when the person submits his or her "Tax Return — Individuals" (B.I.R.60) for the year of assessment in which the right is exercised etc. Details of the necessary particulars are listed in the completion guide issued with each such return.

64. The obligation to inform the Department does not, however, depend on a tax return being issued to the person. Section 51(2) of the Ordinance provides, in effect, that where a person chargeable to Salaries Tax has not been required by an Assessor to furnish a return, he is nonetheless required to inform the Commissioner that he is so chargeable not later than 4 months after the end of the basis period for the year of assessment concerned.

65. As with any other income that is chargeable to tax, serious consequences may follow if a person fails to meet his obligations under the Ordinance in respect of any chargeable gain arising from the exercise, assignment or release of a right to acquire shares or stock. In this regard it is worth noting that the penalty provisions of the Ordinance may apply where a person fails to notify the Commissioner that he is chargeable to tax, fails to comply with a notice to submit a return, or makes an incorrect return by omitting or understating anything. In such cases, depending on the nature of the shortcoming, prosecution action may be taken or additional tax imposed (see sections 80, 82 and 82A of the Ordinance). The Ordinance also provides for various recovery measures to be adopted, depending on the circumstances, where a person has failed to pay tax which is due and payable or if it appears likely that this will happen —

- section 75 provides for recovery action in the District Court where a person defaults in the payment of tax;
- section 76 for recovery from debtors of the taxpayer and certain other parties where tax payable is in default, or the person concerned has left Hong Kong or in the opinion of the Commissioner is likely to leave Hong Kong without paying the tax; and
- section 77 for the Commissioner to seek a Departure Prevention Order from a District Court Judge where a person has not paid all the tax assessed and there are reasonable grounds for believing that the person intends to depart, or has departed, from Hong Kong to reside elsewhere.

Employers

66. Employers are also required to provide information in respect of share option benefits received by employees. Section 52(4) provides that where an employer commences to employ in Hong Kong an individual who is or is likely to be chargeable to Salaries Tax, the employer must within three months of the date of commencement of such employment notify the Commissioner in writing of, amongst other things, the individual's terms of employment. Accordingly, if the terms of employment provide for participation in a share option scheme, full details of how the scheme operates should be supplied to the Commissioner. Details should also be provided if an employee has been granted a share option prior to commencing to be employed in Hong Kong but not yet exercised by him. The option may be not fully vested and may only become vested and exercisable after rendering services in Hong Kong, or the option may be fully vested but granted as an inducement to take up employment in Hong Kong. In both of these situations, the subsequent gains realized by the exercise, assignment or release of the options are income from office or employment under section 9 (1)(d). Details thus need to be provided. Particulars should include the number and type of shares covered by the option, the consideration (if any) paid for the grant of the option, the consideration required to exercise the option and the period within which the option must be exercised. The information may, if the employer wishes, be provided in either case as an attachment to a form I.R.56E (the standard form available from the Department which an employer may use to comply with notification requirements under section 52(4)).

67. It is also relevant that employers are generally issued with a notice each year, under section 52(2) of the Ordinance, which requires the submission of returns detailing the remuneration of employees (i.e. forms B.I.R.56A and I.R.56B). The notes accompanying the forms set out the nature of the information required in respect of rights to acquire shares that have been granted, exercised, assigned or released. Employers should be aware when completing these forms that, in effect, the information is called for where a gain calculated in accordance with section 9(4) of the Ordinance has been realized during the year of assessment covered by the return in respect of a right granted "at any time". In other words, the information should be supplied if such a gain was realized during the year, irrespective of whether the person concerned was a current or former employee at the time of exercise. However, in the case of a former employee, no information need be provided to the Commissioner where the gain realized was less than the basic allowance for the relevant year and it is known that during the relevant year the person concerned did not derive any other income chargeable to Salaries Tax (e.g. where the person was employed by another company in the same group and worked wholly outside Hong Kong throughout the year).

68. Particulars of gains realized under share option schemes are also requested on forms I.R.56F and I.R.56G which, respectively, may be completed by an employer to comply with requirements under section 52(5), to notify the Commissioner where an employee is about to cease to be employed, and section 52(6), to notify the Commissioner when an employee is about to depart from Hong Kong.

69. Where an employer is required to report details in respect of a gain realized by the exercise etc. of a share option, the gain should be calculated in accordance with section 9(4) of the Ordinance and reported accordingly. The employer should not make an apportionment of the gain for reporting in the employer's return even if the employee (or former employee) might be entitled to time-basis apportionment of his / her income by virtue of section 8(1A)(a). Details of the calculation of any such apportionment should only be included in the tax return of the individual concerned.

APPLICATION

70. The Department will generally act in accordance with the Practice Note in relation to assessments raised after its issue and objections concerning relevant gains that are subsequently finalized. Exceptionally, a different basis of assessment may be used in any particular case if it is considered that section 61 or section 61A of the Ordinance should be applied. In such circumstances, the assessment may be made either on the basis that the relevant share option scheme or any part of it had not been entered into, or in such other manner as is considered appropriate to counteract the tax benefit that would otherwise be obtained. It should also be noted that where an assessment made prior to the issue of this Practice Note was regarded as final and conclusive in terms of section 70 of the Ordinance, it will not be reopened for the purpose of making an adjustment to reflect any change of practice detailed in the Practice Note.

SHARE OR STOCK AWARDS

71. This Practice Note deals only with the taxation of share options. Other than being granted share options, taxpayers may also receive share awards at the outset without having to exercise an option to acquire shares. The grant of such share or stock awards constitutes taxable perquisites. The timing of derivation of the benefit and of valuation of the benefit for tax purposes will generally be determined by terms governing the awards and circumstances under which the awards are granted. The Department will deal with the tax treatment of share or stock awards in a separate Practice Note.

APPENDIX

File No. : _______________________

To : Commissioner of Inland Revenue

Salaries Tax
Departing Permanently from Hong Kong
Election for Notional Exercise of Share Option

Year of Assessment: _______________________

I hereby elect to ascertain the salaries tax liability relating to the share option granted to me by my employer(s) but not yet exercised, assigned or released (as listed below) on the basis of a notional exercise of the option. The notional gain of $_______________________ as shown in the attached computation is offered for assessment to salaries tax on the understanding that no further tax liability will arise when the same share option is actually exercised, assigned or released after my departure from Hong Kong.

Name of corporation, the shares of which are subject of the grant	Total number of shares covered by the grant	Date of Grant if applicable	Date of Vesting,	Final Date for exercise of the option granted

(Please attach additional sheets if the space above is insufficient)

Signature : _______________________

Name : _______________________

Hong Kong Identity Card / Passport No. : _______________________

Date : _______________________

File No. : ______________________

Computation of Gain on Notional Exercise of Share Option[1]

Year of assessment:______________________________

Notional Exercise Date[2]: ______________________________

Date of departure from Hong Kong: ______________________

	[A]	[B]	[C]	[D]	[E]
Date of grant[3]	Total no. of shares covered by the grant	Market Price[4] per share at Notional Exercise Date	Consideration paid for the grant, if any	Consideration required for exercising the option granted[5]	Gain on Notional Exercise[6] $E = [(A \times B) - C - D]$
$	$	$	$	$	$
Total Gain on Notional Exercise of all Options Granted					

(Please attach additional sheets if the space above is insufficient.)

1 Election should be made in respect of all shares in all of the grants received prior to cessation of employment for Hong Kong salaries tax purposes (Paragraph 59, DIPN No. 38).
2 Notional Exercise Date can be (i) any one day within seven days before the date of submission of the return for the final assessment of the year of assessment the person permanently departs from Hong Kong if election is made before departure, and (ii) the date of permanent departure from Hong Kong if election is made after departure (Paragraphs 58 and 60, DIPN No. 38).
3 Please attach documents / correspondence from employer in support of the grant.
4 Market Price refers to the closing quotation value on Notional Exercise Date (Paragraph 22 of DIPN No. 38).
5 Consideration required may include sums payable on exercise, brokerage, stamp duty, etc. associated with exercise (Paragraph 23, DIPN No. 38).
6 Gross amount of gain should be reported. If you are entitled to time-basis apportionment of income, please provide details of the calculation in accordance with paragraphs 44–48 of DIPN No. 38 in a separate computation.

APPENDIX 15

Inland Revenue Department
Hong Kong
DEPARTMENTAL INTERPRETATION & PRACTICE NOTES
No. 42

PROFITS TAX
PART A : TAXATION OF FINANCIAL INSTRUMENTS
PART B : TAXATION OF FOREIGN EXCHANGE DIFFERENCES

These notes are issued for the information of taxpayers and their tax representatives. They contain the Department's interpretation and practices in relation to the law as it stood at the date of publication. Taxpayers are reminded that their right of objection against the assessment and their right of appeal to the Commissioner, the Board of Review or the Court are not affected by the application of these notes.

LAU MAK Yee-ming
Commissioner of Inland Revenue

November 2005

Our web site: http://www.ird.gov.hk

CONTENT

INTRODUCTION

Hong Kong is a major financial centre in the Asia Pacific region. Financial instruments are widely used by companies in Hong Kong to achieve investment, trading or hedging objectives. In May 2004, the Hong Kong Institute of Certified Public Accountants issued two new accounting standards dealing with financial instruments. The first one, HKAS 32, contains the requirements for the presentation of financial instruments and identifies the information that should be disclosed. The second one, HKAS 39, establishes the principles for the recognition and measurement of financial instruments.

2. The scope of, and accounting treatments prescribed by, HKAS 32 and HKAS 39 differ significantly from the existing accounting standard (i.e. SSAP 24) that governs the accounting and disclosure requirements of debt and equity securities. HKAS 32 and HKAS 39 superseded SSAP 24 when they came into effect on 1 January 2005. Part A of this Practice Note sets out the views of the Department regarding the tax treatment of gains or losses in respect of various financial instruments to which HKAS 32 and HKAS 39 apply.

3. In Hong Kong, business is often transacted in foreign currencies. Gains or losses will result from such transactions due to the fluctuation in the rates of exchange of the foreign currencies. In March 2004, the Hong Kong Institute of Certified Public Accountants issued HKAS 21 which deals with the effects of changes in foreign exchange rates. In the light of the development in case law and accounting, the Department has reviewed the tax treatment of foreign exchange differences. Part B of this Practice Note explains the current practice and the reasons for changing it.

PART A: TAXATION OF FINANCIAL INSTRUMENTS

BACKGROUND

Relevance of accounting standards for taxation purposes

4. Profits tax is charged on every person carrying on a trade, profession or business in Hong Kong in respect of his assessable profits arising in or derived from Hong Kong. The Inland Revenue Ordinance (the Ordinance) itself does not contain a comprehensive definition of the term "assessable profits". However, the Court of Final Appeal, in *CIR v. Secan Ltd & Ranon Ltd, 5 HKTC 266*, established the principle that the assessable profits or losses of a taxpayer must be ascertained in accordance with the ordinary principles of commercial accounting, as modified to conform with the Ordinance. Delivering the unanimous decision of the Court, Lord Millett NPJ said at page 330:—

> "Both profits and losses therefore must be ascertained in accordance with the ordinary principles of commercial accounting as modified to conform with the Ordinance.

Where the taxpayer's financial statements are correctly drawn in accordance with the ordinary principles of commercial accounting and in conformity with the Ordinance, no further modifications are required or permitted. Where the taxpayer may properly draw its financial statements on either of two alternative bases, the Commissioner is both entitled and bound to ascertain the assessable profits on whichever basis the taxpayer has chosen to adopt."

5. The English authorities are also relevant. In *Gallagher v Jones, [1993] STC 537*, one of the authorities cited in Secan, Sir Thomas Bingham MR, having considered various authorities, concluded at pages 555–556:—

"The object is to determine, as accurately as possible, the profits or losses of the taxpayers' businesses for the accounting periods in question. Subject to any express or implied statutory rule, of which there is none here, the ordinary way to ascertain the profits or losses of a business is to apply accepted principles of commercial accountancy. That is the very purpose for which such principles are formulated. As has often been pointed out, such principles are not static: they may be modified, refined and elaborated over time as circumstances change and accounting insights sharpen. But so long as such principles remain current and generally accepted they provide the surest answer to the question which the legislation requires to be answered

…

The authorities do not persuade me that there is any rule of law such as that for which the taxpayers contend and the judge found. Indeed, given the plain language of the legislation, I find it hard to understand how any judge-made rule could override the application of a generally accepted rule of commercial accountancy which (a) applied to the situation in question, (b) was not one of two or more rules applicable to the situation in question and (c) was not shown to be inconsistent with the true facts or otherwise inapt to determine the true profits or losses of the business."

6. The decision by the Court of Final Appeal in Secan has reaffirmed the general principle that, subject to statutory modifications, in the measurement of profits or the timing of income the ordinary principles of commercial accounting should be followed. Thus, in deciding when and how the profit or loss derived from a financial instrument is to be recognised or measured, the accounting treatments under HKAS 39 are relevant, except where there is a specific express statutory provision or where the accounting classification and the legal classification of a financial instrument differ.

Overview of HKAS 32 and HKAS 39

7. The term "financial instrument" is defined in HKAS 32 as "any contract that gives rise to a financial asset of one entity and a financial liability or equity instrument of another entity". HKAS 32 also contains definitions of the terms "financial asset", "financial liability" and "equity instrument". It is not proposed to list out all the relevant definitions here. HKAS 32 should be consulted for the detailed definitions that are also applicable to HKAS 39.

8. Broadly speaking, HKAS 39 divides financial assets and financial liabilities into four categories, each with a different accounting treatment. A very brief summary is as follows:—

    (a) "Financial assets or financial liabilities at fair value through profit or loss" are :—

        (i) financial assets acquired and financial liabilities incurred for the purpose of trading and all derivatives that are not hedges; or

        (ii) those financial assets or financial liabilities designated by the entity as at fair value through profit or loss upon initial recognition. They are measured at fair value with all resulting gains and losses recognised in the profit and loss account as and when they arise.

    (b) "Held-to-maturity investments" are non-derivative financial assets with fixed or determinable payments and fixed maturity that an entity has the positive intention and ability to hold to maturity. They are accounted for at amortised cost. Profits or losses are recognised upon impairment, derecognition or through amortisation.

    (c) "Loans and receivables" are non-derivative financial assets with fixed or determinable payments that are not quoted in an active market. They are accounted for at amortised cost. Profits or losses are recognised upon impairment, derecognition or through amortisation.

    (d) "Available-for-sale financial assets" are those non-derivative financial assets that are designated as available for sale or are not classified as above. They are measured at fair value with all resulting gains and losses taken to the equity account instead of the profit and loss account. On disposal, gains or losses previously taken to the equity account are recycled or transferred to the profit and loss account.

9. It should be pointed out that the above accounting classifications do not necessarily determine whether the financial assets or financial liabilities are capital or revenue in nature.

ASSESSING PRACTICE

The issues

10. Pursuant to section 14(1), only profits arising in or derived from Hong Kong are chargeable to profits tax and profits arising from the sale of capital assets are not taxable. In the context of financial instruments, the following issues need to be examined:—

    (a) Timing of assessment

    (b) Legal form and economic substance

    (c) Capital v revenue nature of the income

    (d) Deduction of expenses

    (e) Locality of profits

    (f) Hedge accounting

    (g) Embedded derivatives

(h) Transitional adjustments

Timing of assessment

11. Under HKAS 39, when a financial asset or financial liability is recognised initially, an entity shall measure it at its fair value. In the case of a financial asset or financial liability not at fair value through profit or loss, transaction costs that are directly attributable to the acquisition or issue of the financial asset or financial liability should be added to the fair value. The "fair value" is the amount for which an asset could be exchanged, or a liability settled, between knowledgeable, willing parties in an arm's length transaction.

12. After initial recognition, HKAS 39 requires an entity to measure:—
  (a) "Financial assets at fair value through profit or loss", including derivatives that are assets, and "available-for-sale financial assets" at their fair values without any deduction for transaction costs it may incur on sale or other disposal;
  (b) "Loans and receivables" at amortised cost using the effective interest method;
  (c) "Held-to-maturity investments" at amortised cost using the effective interest method; and
  (d) "Financial liabilities" at amortised cost, except for financial liabilities at fair value through profit or loss which are measured at fair value.
Financial assets designated as hedged items are subject to measurement under the hedge accounting requirements (see paragraphs 34 to 40 below).

13. On the whole, the Department will follow the accounting treatment stipulated in HKAS 39 in the recognition of profits or losses in respect of financial assets of revenue nature (see paragraphs 23 to 26). Accordingly, for financial assets or financial liabilities at fair value through profit or loss, the change in fair value is assessed or allowed when the change is taken to the profit and loss account. For available-for-sale financial assets, the change in fair value that is taken to the equity account is not taxable or deductible until the assets are disposed of. The cumulative change in fair value is assessed or deducted when it is recognised in the profit and loss account in the year of disposal. For loans and receivables and held-to-maturity investments, the gain or loss is taxable or deductible when the financial asset is derecognised or impaired and through the amortisation process. Valuation methods previously permitted for financial instruments, such as the lower of cost or net realisable value basis, will not be accepted.

Example 1

Company A is a securities trading company incorporated in Hong Kong. It closes its books on 31 December each year. At the beginning of 2005, it purchased by way of subscription a medium term note due 2008 issued by the treasury arm of a listed company. The note has a face value of $100,000 and an interest of 8 per cent per annum payable at year end. Assuming at the end of 2005, the fair value of the note is $110,000 indicating that the market interest rate has fallen. On 31 December 2005, in accordance with HKAS 39, the following journal entries should be made:—

Account	Debit	Credit
	$	$
Investment — medium term note	10,000	
Profit & loss — increase in fair value		10,000
Interest receivable	8,000	
Profit & loss — interest income		8,000

The interest of $8,000 and the increase of $10,000 in fair value recognised in the profit and loss account are accrued profits under HKAS 1. Furthermore, they would be realised profits under section 79A(3) of the Companies Ordinance available for distribution as dividends. For profits tax purposes, the increase in fair value would be an assessable profit of the year of assessment 2005/06 even though Company A has not sold or disposed of the note in that year of assessment.

If Company A sells the note in the following year at $130,000, the gain of $20,000 will be assessed in the year of assessment 2006/07.

14. Under HKAS 39, the amortised cost of a financial asset or financial liability should be measured using the "effective interest method". Under HKAS 18, interest income is also required to be recognised using the effective interest method. The effective interest rate is the rate that exactly discounts the estimated future cash payments or receipts through the expected life of the financial instrument. The practical effect is that interest expenses, costs of issue and income (including interest, premium and discount) are spread over the term of the financial instrument, which may cover more than one accounting period. Thus a discount expense and other costs of issue should not be fully deductible in the year in which a financial instrument is issued. Equally, a discount income cannot be deferred for assessment until the financial instrument is redeemed.

15. The Department does not accept the argument that when the financial instruments are marked to market, the profits recognised in the profit and loss account are unrealised profits and therefore not taxable until realised in later periods. Such argument is essentially based on the decision in *Willingale v. International Commercial Bank Ltd, [1978] STC 75*.

16. The rationale of the decision in Willingale had been considered in the Gallagher case. When commenting on the decision in Willingale, Sir Thomas Bingham MR said at page 555:—

> "This was therefore a case in which there was evidence of two accounting treatments, both of them accepted by the responsible professional opinion. The bank succeeded because a majority held that the discounts were not, like interest, earned from day to

day, but were earned when realised. To account for them earlier was, in the view of the majority, to violate the 'overriding principle of tax law' (as Sir John Pennycuick called it in the Court of Appeal (see *[1977] STC 183 at 196*) that profits must not be anticipated. The speech of Lord Keith (*[1978] STC 75 at 86–87*) does, however, show that in appropriate circumstances the accounting practice of accrual may be acceptable."

17. In respect of the timing of assessment, the Department would agree with the approach taken by the United Kingdom's Inland Revenue. The following extract from its Business Income Manual 31095 is relevant:—

> "Over the years the Courts have been concerned with the time at which profits are to be brought into charge to tax under Case I and II of Schedule D, and a number of judge made principles have emerged. But in recent years the Courts have become increasingly reluctant to discern judge made tax principles which override generally accepted commercial accounting practice.

> What is, or is not, commercially acceptable accounting treatment is a question of fact not law. Furthermore the Courts have recognised that accounting practice evolves over time. In principle, therefore, it is possible for a modern Court to come to a different decision from one taken in the past on the sole ground that the accounting treatment has changed. This is because two cases can be distinguished on the basis of their accountancy facts, even though the other facts may be identical. The Courts therefore have proceeded to ensure that the law does not become tied to outdated accountancy practice and to decisions taken where judges were forced to take a view of commercial practice in the absence of any accountancy evidence at all."

18. Notwithstanding that a taxpayer may hitherto claim on the basis of *Willingale* that the taxation of profits recognised in the profit and loss account in relation to financial instruments being marked to market should be deferred to a later period when they are "realised", there is now no longer any legal basis to make a similar claim. In essence, what HKAS 39 advocates is, in relation to profits on financial instruments, to recognise those profits by including them in the profit and loss account as profits, so as to reflect the changes of circumstances over time and the sharpening of accounting insights on the way the profits on financial instruments are presented and recognised. With the introduction of HKAS 39, the taxpayer can no longer rely on *Willingale* in support of its claim. This is not because *Willingale* which holds that profits should not be anticipated is no longer good law. The crucial reason is that unlike *Willingale* where the taxpayer could, at the material time, adduce professional opinion that the alternative accounting treatment was also made in accordance with accepted accounting principle, the taxpayer in the present case would not now be in a position to adduce such evidence in the light of HKAS 39.

Legal form and economic substance

19. Pursuant to HKAS 32, the issuer of a financial instrument shall classify the instrument, or its component parts, on initial recognition as a financial liability, a financial asset or an equity instrument in accordance with the economic substance of the arrangement.

20. In analysing a financial instrument, the Department takes the view that the starting point is to decide its nature according to its legal form rather than the accounting treatment or the underlying economic characteristics. Determining the legal form of a financial instrument will involve an examination of the legal rights and obligations created by the instrument. If the purported legal form of a financial instrument is not consistent with such rights and obligations, then it is necessary to look beyond the label given to the financial instrument.

21. The labels of "liability" and "equity" may not reflect the legal nature of the financial instrument. In these circumstances, it is necessary to take into account other factors which include the character of the return (e.g. whether fixed rate return or profit participation), the nature of the holder's interest in the issuer company (e.g. voting rights and rights on winding-up), the existence of a debtor and creditor relationship and the characterisation of the instrument by general law.

Example 2

Company B, a company registered under the Companies Ordinance, issued preference shares with a par value of $100 million and a dividend of 10 per cent per annum. Puttable options attached to the preference shares permit the redemption of the instruments for cash. The holders have rights to attend members meetings, to receive notices of general meetings and to approve resolutions. The directors can omit the dividend without throwing the company into bankruptcy.

Though the preference shares are accounted for as financial liabilities and the dividends declared are charged as interest expenses to the profit and loss account under HKAS 32, the preference shares will be treated for tax purposes as share capital because the relationship between the holders and the company is not a debtor and creditor relationship. Dividends declared will not be allowed for deduction as interest expenses and will not be assessed as interest income.

22. HKAS 32 requires the issuer of a compound financial instrument to split the instrument into a liability component and an equity component and present them separately in the balance sheet. The Department, while recognising that the accounting treatment might reflect the economic substance, will adhere to the legal form of the compound financial instrument and treat the compound financial instrument for tax purposes as a whole.

Example 3

Company C issued 2,000 convertible bonds each having a face value of

$1,000,000 with a five-year term and an annual interest rate of 10 per cent. At any time up to maturity, each bond can be converted into 250,000 ordinary shares. The terms of issue provide for a monetary settlement of bonds that have not been converted into ordinary shares.

Though in the accounts of Company C, the convertible bonds are split in accordance with HKAS 32 into equity components and debt components, they will be treated as debts because the company stands in the position of debtor of a money debt and the subordinate right to convert need not be exercised. Interest payments will be allowed for deduction if the conditions in section 16 are satisfied.

Capital / Revenue nature of the income

23. Profits arising from the sale of capital assets are excluded from the charge of profits tax. Capital profits or losses, if any, recognised in the profit and loss account will be excluded from the computation of assessable profits. The accounting treatment, by itself, cannot operate to change the character of an asset from investment to trading and vice versa. Whether the asset is of capital or revenue nature is a question of fact and degree and all the surrounding circumstances, including the accounting treatment, have to be considered. Well-established tax-principles like the "badges of trade" will continue to be applicable. In deciding whether a financial instrument is a capital or trading asset, the intention at the time of acquisition of the financial instrument is always relevant.

24. By definition, a financial asset or financial liability at fair value through profit or loss includes a financial asset or financial liability that is held for trading. It is classified as trading if it is acquired or incurred principally for the purpose of selling or repurchasing; or there is a pattern of short-term profit-taking. Typically, unless it is a designated and effective hedging instrument, a derivative will be classified as held for trading. Thus, the change in fair value and the gain or loss on disposal, recognised in the profit and loss account, are prima facie taxable or deductible as the case may be.

25. Normally, loans and receivables, held-to-maturity investments and available-for-sale financial assets are trading assets where the taxpayer is a financial institution or it carries on an insurance, money lending, securities dealing or finance business because financial assets are often acquired in the course of the business with a view to resale at a profit. In *CIR v. Sincere Insurance & Investment Co Ltd, 1 HKTC 602*, the disposal of leasehold properties was held to be part of the normal business of an insurance company.

26. It should be noted there are specific provisions that apply to particular types of financial instruments. Section 14A provides that interest from and gains or profits from the sale, disposal or redemption on maturity or presentment of "qualifying debt instruments" will be assessed at half rate. Section 15(1)(j), (k) and (l) deem as chargeable receipts gains or profits from the sale, disposal or redemption on maturity or presentment of "certificates of deposit" and "bills of exchange". Section 26A excludes interest and profits derived from certain financial instruments from profits tax. The taxability of the sums stipulated in aforesaid legislative provisions should not be affected by the accounting practice under HKAS 39.

Deduction of expenses

27. For the purpose of ascertaining profits in respect of which a person is chargeable to profits tax, section 17(1)(c) provides that no deduction shall be allowed in respect of any expenditure of a capital nature or any loss or withdrawal of capital. HKAS 39 in this respect does not prescribe any rules for distinguishing capital and revenue expenditures. Whether the expenditure is capital or revenue in nature is a question of law. The accounting treatment will not determine the nature of the expenditure.

28. In deciding the nature of an expenditure, capital or revenue, it is necessary to examine the facts and the circumstances. Where the expenditure is a one-off payment that brings into existence an asset or advantage for the enduring benefit of the trade, it is likely to be a capital expenditure. In *Sun Newspaper Ltd v. FCT, [1938] 1 AITR 403*, Dixon J observed at page 410 that expenditure was of a capital nature if its purpose was to establish, replace, or enlarge the capital structure of the taxpayer's business. In contrast, recurrent expenses connected with the process of operating it are generally considered to be revenue in nature.

29. In *CIR v. Tai On Machinery Works Ltd, 1 HKTC 411*, McMullin J, after referring to the textbook Spicer and Pegler, held that interest payments on a loan to finance the construction of a building which was a capital asset were non-deductible payments of a capital nature to the extent that the payments were made before the building could be used to produce profits. In *Wharf Properties Ltd v. CIR, 4 HKTC 310*, Lord Hoffmann at the Privy Council said whether interest payment was of a capital or revenue nature depended on the purpose for which the money was required during the relevant period. In *FCT v. Energy Resources of Australia, 29 ATR 553*, the Australian Federal Court observed that in some circumstances a discount expense incurred by the issuer of a discount note may be loss of a capital nature.

Example 4

Company D is an importer and exporter of household wares. It has made a forward purchase £1,000,000 that relates to the future payment of the purchase price of machinery acquired for use in its business. The currency forward contract is clearly for the purpose of hedging against the foreign currency risk arising from the purchase of the machinery and Company D consistently adopts a basis adjustment.

The nature of the gain or loss arising from the currency forward contract depends on the nature of the underlying asset. Thus the gain or loss from the currency forward contract will be capital in nature. It will be taken into account in determining the capital expenditure incurred on the provision of the machinery for depreciation allowances purposes. Such gain or loss will similarly be taken into account for depreciation allowances purposes if the company does not "basis adjust" (i.e. it is simply debited or credited to the profit and loss account).

Example 5

Company E is a retailer. It has entered into forward contracts to hedge against foreign exchange risks in relation to goods purchased from various overseas suppliers, thus reducing fluctuations in the costs of its inventory.

Profits and losses from the forward contracts will be taken into account as part of the profits and losses of the trade because they relate closely to the purchase of the inventory.

Example 6

Company F has borrowed money at a floating rate of interest for purchase of trading stock and enters into an interest rate futures contract with a view to protecting itself against rises in interest rates.

Profits and losses relating to the interest rate futures contract will be taken into account as trading income or expenditure because the interest rate futures contract closely relates to money borrowed on revenue account for the purchase of trading stock.

30. HKAS 39 contains rules governing the determination of impairment losses. In short, all financial assets must be evaluated for impairment except for those measured at fair value through profit or loss. As a result, the carrying amount of loans and receivables should have reflected the bad debts and estimated doubtful debts. However, since section 16(1)(d) lays down specific provisions for the deduction of bad debts and estimated doubtful debts, the statutory tests for deduction of bad debts and estimated doubtful debts will apply. Impairment losses on other financial assets (e.g. bonds acquired by a trader) will be considered for deduction in the normal way.

31. It should be noted that under a pass-through arrangement whereby an obligation to transfer the cash flows from the financial asset is assumed and the financial asset has been derecognised, it does not necessarily follow that the interest payments included in the cash outflows have fulfilled the conditions in section 16(2).

Example 7

Company G and Company H are carrying on business in Hong Kong. They are not connected. Company H advanced an interest bearing loan of $100 million to Company G. Company H funded its advances to Company G with a non-recourse loan from Company I, which is a company operating outside Hong Kong. Company H does not earn an interest spread and is only required to make payments of interest and repayments of principal out of the cash flows it receives from Company G. There is no assignment of the loan or of the cash flows by Company H. Under the above arrangement, Company H has neither any risk nor reward. Thus under HKAS 39 Company H has derecognised from its accounts the advance to Company G and the non-recourse loan from Company I.

Though Company H has derecognised the loan in its accounts, the interest payments made by Company H to Company I will be denied deduction under section 16(2)(c) because Company I is not chargeable to profits tax in respect of the interest income it receives. The interest received by Company H from Company G remains chargeable to tax under section 14 alone or in conjunction with section 15(1)(f) depending on the facts of the case. In law, Company H remains entitled to collect interest from Company G.

Example 8

Same facts as in Example 7. Assume Company G and Company I are connected.

The interest payments made by Company G to Company H will be denied deduction under section 16(2B).

Locality of profits

32. The ascertainment of the source of an income is a practical, hard matter of fact. No simple, single, legal test can be employed. However, there is a substantial body of case law on the determination of the locality of profits. The broad guiding principle is to look at what the taxpayer has done to earn the profit in question and where he has done it. The Department has set out its views on the locality of profits in Departmental Interpretation & Practice Notes No. 21 (Revised 1998). The general principle of law in this area is not affected by the accounting practice under HKAS 39.

33. It should be noted that section 15(1)(l) deems as chargeable profits gains or profits from the sale, disposal or redemption of certificates of deposit or bills of exchange through or from the business of a financial institution notwithstanding the moneys for the acquisition were made outside Hong Kong or the sale, disposal or redemption is effected outside Hong Kong.

Hedge accounting

34. Hedge accounting is an exception to the usual rules used for accounting of financial instruments. Application of hedge accounting is permitted under HKAS 39 if strict criteria (see paragraph 36) are met. Hedge accounting means designating a hedging instrument, normally a derivative, as an offset to changes in the fair value or cash flows of the hedged item which can be an asset, liability, firm commitment or forecasted future transaction exposed to a risk of change in value or changes in future cash flows. Hedge accounting matches the offsetting effects of the fair value changes in the hedged item and the hedging instrument. If the hedging relationship comes to an end, hedge accounting must be discontinued prospectively.

35. Hedging relationships are of three types:—
    (a) "Fair value hedge" is a hedge of the exposure to changes in fair value of a recognised asset or liability or an unrecognised firm commitment, or an identified portion of such an asset, liability or firm commitment, that is attributable to a particular risk and could affect profit or loss.
    (b) "Cash flow hedge" is a hedge of the exposure to variability in cash flows that is attributable to a particular risk associated with a recognised asset or liability or a highly probable forecast transaction and could affect profit or loss.
    (c) "Hedge of a net investment" in a foreign operation is a hedge of the interest in the net assets of that operation.

36. As a result of HKAS 39, a hedging relationship qualifies for hedge accounting if, and only if, all of the following conditions are met:—
    (a) At the inception there is formal designation and documentation of the hedging relationship and the entity's risk management objective and strategy.
    (b) The hedge is expected to be highly effective in achieving offsetting changes in fair value or cash flows attributable to the hedged risk.
    (c) For cash flow hedges, a forecast transaction that is the subject of the hedge must be highly probable and must present an exposure to variations in cash flows that could ultimately affect profit or loss.
    (d) The effectiveness of the hedge can be reliably measured.
    (e) The hedge is assessed on an ongoing basis and determined actually to have been highly effective.

37. In a fair value hedge, the profit or loss from remeasuring the hedging instrument is recognised immediately in the profit and loss account. At the same time, the carrying amount of the hedged item is adjusted and the change is also recognised immediately in the profit and loss account. In a cash flow hedge, the portion of the profit or loss on the hedging instrument that is an effective hedge is recognised directly in equity and is recycled to the profit and loss account when the hedged cash flows affect the profit. In other words, in these types of hedges, only the net result is shown in the profit and loss account. Any hedge ineffectiveness, even if the hedge continues to be effective overall, is recognised in the profit and loss account of the current period. As a practice, the Department considers that the tax treatment should follow the above accounting treatment of the hedging relationship.

38. If the hedging relationship qualifies for hedge accounting under HKAS 39 and is accounted for as such, the Department considers that the hedged item and the hedging instrument should not be considered separately because hedging is an attempt to mitigate the impact of economic risks of the hedged items. A distinct locality should not be imputed on to the hedging instrument and the locality of the hedging instrument should follow that of the hedged item. Regarding the nature of the profit or loss, capital or revenue, arising from the hedging instrument, the Department accepts that it depends on the nature of the hedged item.

39. Hedge accounting will not occur in any one of the following situations even though a hedge exists:—

    (a) the hedge relationship fails to satisfy the conditions in paragraph 36 above;

    (b) the hedge relationship satisfies the conditions in paragraph 36 above but hedge accounting is not adopted; or

    (c) hedge accounting is discontinued because the hedge becomes ineffective.

In the absence of hedge accounting, the hedging instrument and the hedged item are accounted for separately in the accounts. It follows that the changes in their values are not set off against each other. The tax treatments for the hedging instrument and the hedged item are therefore considered separately unless the hedging instrument is as a matter of fact a hedge against the hedged item even though hedge accounting is not or cannot be adopted. That may occur for example in the case of a small business where documentation is not properly done. In such situations, the tax treatment of the hedging instrument and the hedged item may not necessarily be considered separately even though they are accounted for separately in the accounts. The facts and circumstances of each individual case have to be examined to determine whether the hedging instrument is really a hedge against the hedged item and should be treated together with the hedged item as a whole.

40. Enterprises sometimes control their group financial activities through a central treasury unit that trades with external third parties. This avoids a subsidiary having to go directly to the market to find a hedge. The usual practice is for the central treasury unit to execute a hedge with an external third party and that the terms and conditions of that hedge are passed on to the subsidiary through an internal hedge. An internal hedge will normally not be accepted unless there is a corresponding external hedge because an internal hedge will be eliminated on consolidation and will not achieve any commercial results for the group as a whole. It is recognised and accepted that the netting of exposures within a group on an arm's length basis by the treasury unit is possible. However, the taking of any net exposure would require a factual basis and would suggest that the central treasury unit is trading in derivatives. Often a group treasury company would not be taking any position of significance. In short, the Department holds the view that hedge accounting should normally be available to those internal or centralised hedging activities with "matched external transactions" that are entered into on a one for one basis.

Example 9

Company J is buying and selling commodities (e.g. metals). The commodities are purchased from suppliers located in Australia and sold to enterprises located in the Mainland. The profits from the commodity trade are fully assessable to profits tax. To guarantee the sales prices of the commodities, Company J is to short futures contracts on the commodities with appropriate settlement dates on an overseas exchange. The futures contracts qualify for hedge accounting and are accounted for as such.

The locality and nature of the commodity futures follow those of the underlying onshore trading transactions. The commodity futures are ancillary to the trading transactions and the intention is not to speculate in commodity futures.

Example 10

Company K whose base currency is the Hong Kong dollar, carrying on a garment trading business in Hong Kong, held as investment yen-denominated shares listed on the Tokyo Stock Exchange and in order to eliminate the perceived risk of a fall in their value, entered into a forward contract with a local financial institution to sell for Hong Kong dollars an amount of yen equivalent to the yen value of the shares. The forward contract qualifies for hedge accounting and is accounted for as such.

The forward contract and the shares will be given similar tax treatment because the forward contract is regarded as ancillary to the offshore capital transaction in shares. The forward contract in essence was part and parcel of an offshore investment.

Embedded derivatives

41. An embedded derivative is a component of a hybrid instrument that contains a non-derivative host contract. Embedded derivatives can be found in a number of financial instruments, including put options in bonds, callable bonds, put options on preference shares etc. In legal form, a hybrid instrument is one single instrument. Accordingly, for accounting purposes, the embedded derivative and the host contract are not separated. This was the situation before HKAS 39. However, under HKAS 39, an embedded derivative is now required to be separated from the host contract if:—

(a) the hybrid instrument is not recorded at fair value with profits or losses taken to profit and loss account;

(b) a separate instrument with the same terms as the embedded derivative would meet the definition of a derivative; and

(c) the economic characteristics and risks of the embedded derivative are not closely related to the economic characteristics and risks of the host contract.

42. For tax purposes, the nature (i.e. capital or revenue) and locality of profit and loss of the hybrid instrument are determined on the basis that it is one single instrument. In other words, the nature and locality of profit and loss arising from the embedded derivative and the host contract should always be the same. Under HKAS 39, the embedded derivative and the host contract are required to be separated under certain circumstances. However, notwithstanding such change in accounting requirement, the same tax treatment will be applied because in its legal form the hybrid instrument is still one single instrument.

43. Where the embedded derivative has been separated from the host contract and the accounting treatments of changes in the carrying amounts of the embedded derivative and the host contract differ, the Department so far as timing of assessment is concerned is prepared to accept the accounting treatment under HKAS 39 as the tax treatment. The Department does not accept that the entire gain will only be taxed in the year the hybrid instrument is sold.

Transitional adjustments

44. HKAS 39 itself prescribes the transitional adjustments for trading financial assets or liabilities when a taxpayer first adopts HKAS 39. According to HKAS 39, the cumulative change in fair value of the trading financial assets or liabilities in the periods prior to the adoption of HKAS 39 should be accounted for by adjusting the opening balance of retained earnings, i.e. a prior period adjustment.

45. The Department considers that a prior period adjustment for the trading financial asset or liability should be treated as a taxable receipt for an increase in retained profits or a deductible expense for a decrease in retained profits in the year of assessment in which the prior period adjustment is recognised in the retained earning. This view is supported by the case of *Pearse v. Woodall-Duckhall Ltd, [1978] 51 TC 271*. In that case, a taxpayer changed the basis of valuing its work-in-progress in 1969 and included the surplus on revaluation in the profit and loss appropriation account. Templeman J held that the "anticipated profit for work carried out prior to 1969 falls to be taxed in the year 1969 when it is first revealed and first brought into account".

Example 11

Company L is a money lender. Prior to 1 January 2005, it did not record its currency swap agreements and interest rate swap agreements in its balance sheet. On 1 January 2005, Company L after ascertaining the fair value of the unexpired agreements recognised a profit of $500,000 which it credited to its retained profits as a prior period adjustment.

The prior period adjustment of $500,000 relates to trading financial assets and should be treated as a taxable receipt in the year of assessment in which the prior period adjustment is recognised, i.e. year of assessment 2005/06.

46. In the case of available-for-sale financial assets, according to HKAS 39, on its first adoption, all cumulative changes in fair value of such assets in the prior periods should be recognised in the equity account. On subsequent disposal, the cumulative gain or loss previously taken to the equity account is transferred to the profit or loss account. The Department would accept that the cumulative change in fair value is taxable or deductible, as the case may be, in the year in which it is eventually transferred to the profit and loss account, i.e. not in the year of first adoption of HKAS 39. This practice would apply only if the assets are of a revenue nature.

ANTI-AVOIDANCE

47. It has to be emphasised that when tackling transactions to avoid tax, the Assistant Commissioner is prepared to invoke the powers in section 61A to recharacterise a financial transaction, including reclassification of the nature of the financial instrument and the nature of the income or expense, so as to counteract tax benefits obtained by the relevant person or persons who entered into or carried out the financial transaction for the sole or dominant purpose of obtaining such tax benefits.

EFFECTIVE DATE

48. HKAS 32 and HKAS 39 are applicable for annual periods beginning on or after 1 January 2005. The aforementioned assessing practices will apply starting from the year of assessment 2005/06.

PART B: TAXATION OF FOREIGN EXCHANGE DIFFERENCES

BACKGROUND

Accounting practice

49. Business concerns may carry out transactions as a result of which they receive or make payments in foreign currency. The circumstances may vary considerably; foreign currencies received may be converted into Hong Kong dollars immediately or after a lapse of time; or the concern's accounts may be kept in foreign currency. At the same time, they may carry out transactions or hold assets or liabilities denominated in foreign currencies. In preparing the annual accounts, translation of the foreign currency transactions are necessary. HKAS 21 deals with the effects of changes in foreign exchange rates and has replaced SSAP 11 with effect from 1 January 2005.

50. Under HKAS 21, a foreign currency transaction is to be recorded on initial recognition in the functional currency, by applying to the foreign currency amount the spot exchange rate between the functional currency and the foreign currency at the date of the transaction. At each balance sheet date, foreign currency monetary items shall be translated using the closing rate; non-monetary items that are measured in terms of historical cost in a foreign currency shall be translated using the exchange rate at the date of the transaction; and non-monetary items that are measured at fair value in a foreign currency shall be translated using the exchange rates at the date when the fair value was determined.

51. Exchange differences arising on the settlement of monetary items or on translating monetary items at rates different from those at which they were translated on initial recognition during the period or in previous financial statements will normally be recognised in profit or loss in the period in which they arise.

Overview of the case law

52. While HKAS 21 has laid down the factors for determining the functional currency of an entity, the Department accepts that a foreign company may maintain its Hong Kong Branch accounts in its home country currency. For tax purposes, however, its assessable profits or losses for each year must be expressed in Hong Kong dollar terms (*CIR v. Malaysian Airline System Berhad, 3 HKTC 775*).

53. Exchange gains or losses are neither taxable nor allowable if they are of a capital nature. In *CIR v. General Garment Manufactory (Hong Kong) Ltd, 4 HKTC 532*, the exchange loss was found deductible because, notwithstanding the Board's limited analysis, the intention at the time of acquisition of the foreign currency was to dispose of it quickly for profit, not to acquire a permanent investment. In *CIR v. Li & Fung, 1 HKTC 1193*, Garcia J held in the High Court that although the sums in question originated as trading income the exchange loss was not deductible because their nature was altered to that of capital investment when accumulated and placed on deposits over time.

54. Whether a borrowing is on capital account or revenue account is a question of law to be determined on the facts of each particular case. A gain or loss of fixed capital is an item on capital account, while a gain or loss of circulating capital is an item on revenue account. In *Avco Financial Services Ltd v. FCT,*

[1982] 13 ATR 63, it was held that exchange losses incurred in respect of funds borrowed by a person who carried on business of borrowing and lending money or dealing in foreign exchange were inherently on revenue account unless the funds were used to strengthen that person's profit-making capital base. In the case of an ordinary trading company, loans are on revenue account if they are temporarily fluctuating and incurred in meeting the ordinary running expenses of the business. In *CIR v. Chinachem Finance Co Ltd, 3 HKTC 529*, it was held at the High Court that in deciding whether a loss arising from borrowing was made on capital or revenue account, regard must be made to the length and other terms of borrowing and to the nature of the person's trade.

55. Exchange gains or losses arising in or derived outside Hong Kong are neither taxable nor allowable. Normally, exchange differences arising from capital investment in a "foreign operation" as defined in HKAS 21 should not have any effect on the assessable profits.

ASSESSING PRACTICE

Existing practice

56. In the case of financial institutions, the assessing practice is that the exchange gains or losses recognised in the profit and loss accounts in accordance with accounting practice are assessed or allowed for deduction. There has been no argument on the question of taxing unrealised exchange gain or allowing unrealised losses.

57. However, other taxpayers recognise the gains or losses in the profit and loss account but exclude them in the tax computation due to unrealisation. It has long been the Department's practice to accept the taxpayer's tax computation provided that the treatment is followed consistently and that subsequent adjustment is made upon realisation.

Reasons for change

58. Following the general principle laid down by the Court of Final Appeal in the *Secan* case that assessable profits must be ascertained in accordance with the ordinary principles of commercial accounting, the Department has reviewed the existing practice in paragraph 57 above and decided to cease this practice. In other words, all taxpayers including financial institutions should treat exchange gains or losses recognised in the profit and loss account, whether realised or not, as taxable receipts or deductible expenses. An adjustment in the tax computation on the ground that an exchange difference has not yet realised will not be accepted.

59. As noted above, the Secan case requires the tax treatment to follow the accounting treatment. This principle applies to financial instruments. There is no reason why it should not be applied to exchange gains or losses as well. The Department considers that the change of practice brings about a tax treatment of exchange gains and losses that is consistent with the treatment of other types of income and expenses.

Example 12

Company M is carrying on an import and export business in Hong Kong. It makes up its accounts to 31 December each year. On 31 October 2005, it sold goods at a price of €10,000 to a customer in Germany. The exchange rate at the time of sale was €1 = $9. A receivable of $90,000 shows up in the accounts. Assuming that as at 31 December 2005, the exchange rate is €1 = $10, the journal entries at year end will be:—

Account	Debit	Credit
	$	$
Receivable	10,000	
Profit & loss — exchange gain		10,000

The exchange gain of $10,000 will be assessable profit of the year of assessment 2005/06.

60. The new practice is similar to the approach of the UK Revenue of taxing or allowing unrealised exchange differences. The following is an extract from its Business Income Manual BIM 39510 on this topic:

"(Finance Act 1998) requires Case I profits to be computed in accordance with generally accepted accounting practice, subject to any over-riding rule of law. So in general a business must bring into its Case I computation all exchange gains and losses shown in its accounts, whether realised or unrealised, provided that they conform to the general principles (of taxability and deductibility)." (Emphasis added.)

EFFECTIVE DATE

61. The revised practice will be applied by the Department to any foreign exchange differences for the year of assessment 2005/06 and subsequent years. Accordingly, taxpayers and their representatives should adopt the revised practice in the preparation of profits tax returns for these years of assessment. Where an unrealised exchange difference has been excluded from the tax computation in an earlier year of assessment, it should be adjusted in the tax computation for the year 2005/06.

Index

References after the entries are to section numbers; those in parentheses represent point and paragraph numbers which are preceded by "#" and "P" respectively.